T0189568

Lecture Notes in Computer Science 13534

More information about this series at https://link.springer.com/bookseries/558

Shiqi Yu · Zhaoxiang Zhang · Pong C. Yuen ·
Junwei Han · Tieniu Tan · Yike Guo ·
Jianhuang Lai · Jianguo Zhang (Eds.)

Pattern Recognition and Computer Vision

5th Chinese Conference, PRCV 2022
Shenzhen, China, November 4–7, 2022
Proceedings, Part I

Springer

Editors

Shiqi Yu [ID]
Southern University of Science
and Technology
Shenzhen, China

Pong C. Yuen [ID]
Hong Kong Baptist University
Hong Kong, China

Tieniu Tan
Institute of Automation
Chinese Academy of Sciences
Beijing, China

Jianhuang Lai
Sun Yat-sen University
Guangzhou, China

Zhaoxiang Zhang
Institute of Automation
Chinese Academy of Sciences
Beijing, China

Junwei Han
Northwestern Polytechnical University
Xi'an, China

Yike Guo
Hong Kong Baptist University
Hong Kong, China

Jianguo Zhang [ID]
Southern University of Science
and Technology
Shenzhen, China

ISSN 0302-9743   ISSN 1611-3349 (electronic)
Lecture Notes in Computer Science
ISBN 978-3-031-18906-7   ISBN 978-3-031-18907-4 (eBook)
https://doi.org/10.1007/978-3-031-18907-4

This Springer imprint is published by the registered company Springer Nature Switzerland AG
The registered company address is: Gewerbestrasse 11, 6330 Cham, Switzerland

Preface

Welcome to the proceedings of the 5th Chinese Conference on Pattern Recognition and Computer Vision (PRCV 2022) held in Shenzhen, China!

PRCV was established to further boost the impact of the Chinese community in pattern recognition and computer vision, which are two core areas of artificial intelligence, and further improve the quality of academic communication. Accordingly, PRCV is co-sponsored by four major academic societies of China: the China Society of Image and Graphics (CSIG), the Chinese Association for Artificial Intelligence (CAAI), the China Computer Federation (CCF), and the Chinese Association of Automation (CAA).

PRCV aims at providing an interactive communication platform for researchers from academia and from industry. It promotes not only academic exchange but also communication between academia and industry. In order to keep track of the frontier of academic trends and share the latest research achievements, innovative ideas, and scientific methods, international and local leading experts and professors are invited to deliver keynote speeches, introducing the latest advances in theories and methods in the fields of pattern recognition and computer vision.

PRCV 2022 was hosted by the Southern University of Science and Technology and Shenzhen Polytechnic. We received 564 full submissions. Each submission was reviewed by at least three reviewers selected from the Program Committee and other qualified researchers. Based on the reviewers' reports, 233 papers were finally accepted for presentation at the conference, comprising 40 oral presentations and 193 posters. The acceptance rate was 41%. The conference took place during November 4–7, 2022, and the proceedings are published in this volume in Springer's Lecture Notes in Computer Science (LNCS) series.

We are grateful to the keynote speakers, Alan Yuille from Johns Hopkins University, USA, Kyoung Mu Lee from the Korea National Open University, South Korea, Zhengyou Zhang from the Tencent AI Lab, China, Yaonan Wang from Hunan University, China, Wen Gao from the Pengcheng Laboratory and Peking University, China, Hong Qiao from the Institute of Automation, Chinese Academy of Sciences, China, and Muming Poo from the Institute of Neuroscience, Chinese Academy of Sciences, China.

We give sincere thanks to the authors of all submitted papers, the Program Committee members and the reviewers, and the Organizing Committee. Without their contributions, this conference would not have been possible. Special thanks also go to all of the sponsors.

October 2022

Tieniu Tan
Yike Guo
Jianhuang Lai
Jianguo Zhang
Shiqi Yu
Zhaoxiang Zhang
Pong C. Yuen
Junwei Han

Organization

Steering Committee Chair

Tieniu Tan — Institute of Automation, Chinese Academy of Sciences, China

Steering Committee

Xilin Chen — Institute of Computing Technology, Chinese Academy of Sciences, China

Chenglin Liu — Institute of Automation, Chinese Academy of Sciences, China

Yong Rui — Lenovo, China

Hongbing Zha — Peking University, China

Nanning Zheng — Xi'an Jiaotong University, China

Jie Zhou — Tsinghua University, China

Steering Committee Secretariat

Liang Wang — Institute of Automation, Chinese Academy of Sciences, China

General Chairs

Tieniu Tan — Institute of Automation, Chinese Academy of Sciences, China

Yike Guo — Hong Kong Baptist University, Hong Kong, China

Jianhuang Lai — Sun Yat-sen University, China

Jianguo Zhang — Southern University of Science and Technology, China

Program Chairs

Shiqi Yu — Southern University of Science and Technology, China

Zhaoxiang Zhang — Institute of Automation, Chinese Academy of Sciences, China

Pong C. Yuen — Hong Kong Baptist University, Hong Kong, China

Junwei Han — Northwest Polytechnic University, China

Organizing Committee Chairs

Jinfeng Yang | Shenzhen Polytechnic, China
Guangming Lu | Harbin Institute of Technology, Shenzhen, China
Baoyuan Wu | The Chinese University of Hong Kong, Shenzhen, China
Feng Zheng | Northwest Polytechnic University, China

Sponsorship Chairs

Liqiang Nie | Harbin Institute of Technology, Shenzhen, China
Yu Qiao | Shenzhen Institute of Advanced Technology, Chinese Academy of Sciences, China
Zhenan Sun | Institute of Automation, Chinese Academy of Sciences, China
Xiaochun Cao | Sun Yat-sen University, China

Publicity Chairs

Weishi Zheng | Sun Yat-sen University, China
Wei Jia | Hefei University of Technology, China
Lifang Wu | Beijing University of Technology, China
Junping Zhang | Fudan University, China

Local Arrangement Chairs

Yujiu Yang | Tsinghua Shenzhen International Graduate School, China
Yanjie Wei | Shenzhen Institute of Advanced Technology, Chinese Academy of Sciences, China

International Liaison Chairs

Jingyi Yu | ShanghaiTech University, China
Qifeng Liu | Shenzhen Polytechnic, China
Song Guo | Hong Kong Polytechnic University, Hong Kong, China

Competition Chairs

Wangmeng Zuo | Harbin Institute of Technology, China
Di Huang | Beihang University, China
Bin Fan | University of Science and Technology Beijing, China

Tutorial Chairs

Jiwen Lu   Tsinghua University, China
Ran He   Institute of Automation, Chinese Academy of
           Sciences, China
Xi Li   Zhejiang University, China
Jiaying Liu   Peking University, China

Special Session Chairs

Jing Dong   Institute of Automation, Chinese Academy of
           Sciences, China
Zhouchen Lin   Peking University, China
Xin Geng   Southeast University, China
Yong Xia   Northwest Polytechnic University, China

Doctoral Forum Chairs

Tianzhu Zhang   University of Science and Technology of China,
           China
Shanshan Zhang   Nanjing University of Science and Technology,
           China
Changdong Wang   Sun Yat-sen University, China

Publication Chairs

Kui Jia   South China University of Technology, China
Yang Cong   Institute of Automation, Chinese Academy of
           Sciences, China
Cewu Lu   Shanghai Jiao Tong University, China

Registration Chairs

Weihong Deng   Beijing University of Posts and
           Telecommunications, China
Wenxiong Kang   South China University of Technology, China
Xiaohu Yan   Shenzhen Polytechnic, China

Exhibition Chairs

Hongmin Liu   University of Science and Technology Beijing,
           China
Rui Huang   The Chinese University of Hong Kong, Shenzhen,
           China

Kai Lei   Peking University Shenzhen Graduate School,
                                China
Zechao Li   Nanjing University of Science and Technology,
                                China

Finance Chairs

Xu Wang   Shenzhen Polytechnic, China
Li Liu   Southern University of Science and Technology,
                                China

Website Chairs

Zhaofeng He   Beijing University of Posts and
                                Telecommunications, China
Mengyuan Liu   Sun Yat-sen University, China
Hanyang Peng   Pengcheng Laboratory, China

Program Committee

Yuntao Chen   TuSimple, China
Gong Cheng   Northwest Polytechnic University, China
Runmin Cong   Beijing Jiaotong University, China
Bin Fan   University of Science and Technology Beijing,
                                China
Chen Gong   Nanjing University of Science and Technology,
                                China
Fuyuan Hu   Suzhou University of Science and Technology,
                                China
Huaibo Huang   Institute of Automation, Chinese Academy of
                                Sciences, China
Sheng Huang   Chongqing University, China
Du Huynh   University of Western Australia, Australia
Sen Jia   Shenzhen University, China
Baiying Lei   Shenzhen University, China
Changsheng Li   Beijing Institute of Technology, China
Haibo Liu   Harbin Engineering University, China
Chao Ma   Shanghai Jiao Tong University, China
Vishal M. Patel   Johns Hopkins University, USA
Hanyang Peng   Pengcheng Laboratory, China
Manivannan Siyamalan   University of Jaffna, Sri Lanka
Anwaar Ulhaq   Charles Sturt University, Australia
Changdong Wang   Sun Yat-sen University, China

Dong Wang	Dalian University of Technology, China
Jinjia Wang	Yanshan University, China
Xiwen Yao	Northwest Polytechnic University, China
Mang Ye	Wuhan University, China
Dingwen Zhang	Northwest Polytechnic University, China
Ke Zhang	North China Electric Power University, China
Man Zhang	Beijing University of Posts and Telecommunications, China
Qieshi Zhang	Shenzhen Institute of Advanced Technology, Chinese Academy of Sciences, China
Xuyao Zhang	Institute of Automation, Chinese Academy of Sciences, China
Bineng Zhong	Guangxi Normal University, China
Quan Zhou	Nanjing University of Posts and Telecommunications, China

Contents – Part I

Machine Learning, Multimedia and Multimodal

Optimization and Neural Network and Deep Learning

Theories and Feature Extraction

Architecture Colorization
via Self-supervised Learning and Instance Segmentation

Sen Liu⑩, Hang Chen⑩, and Li Li⁽✉⁾⑩

School of Computer and Artificial Intelligence, Wuhan Textile University,
Wuhan, China
{1904240301,1904240302}@mail.wtu.edu.cn, lli@wtu.edu.cn

Abstract. In recent years, building coloring has become one of the hot
spots in computer vision. In this paper, we design an instance segmentation module consisting of a region proposal network (RPN) and a backbone network, which can effectively avoid the effect of coloring between
multiple objects. At the same time, we combine the feature map and the
weights of the separated parts for fusion to avoid the coloring position
error caused by segmentation. Meanwhile, we propose a self-supervised
architectural coloring model that can construct positive and negative
samples to achieve contrast constraints to solve the problem of unlabeled
datasets. The model filters out unnecessary image noise based on architectural features and improves the effectiveness of the loss function by
obtaining more accurate structural details. We provide a dataset and perform segmentation to help train the coloring weights for all seasons. We
conducted extensive ablation experiments with multiple datasets. The
experimental results visually demonstrate the excellent performance of
our model.

Keywords: Self-supervised learning · Architecture colorization ·
GANs · Instance segmentation

1 Introduction

Converting architectural grayscale images into color photographs is an act full
of art. This technique can stimulate the artistic creativity of designers and evoke
fond memories. Initially, people used dots, lines to prompt computer coloring
[12,14,22]. Later, example images were used to guide the computer coloring
[6,24,25]. But both require human intervention, and these models are inefficient
for generating a large number of images to inspire. With the development of
neural networks, the pursuit of automatic computer generation of colored images
has been pursued. Such cross-domain image-to-image translation can usually
have better results with training on paired data sets. But in reality, it is difficult
to label every image, and we aim to get a satisfactory result after training with

© The Author(s), under exclusive license to Springer Nature Switzerland AG 2022
S. Yu et al. (Eds.): PRCV 2022, LNCS 13534, pp. 3–16, 2022.
https://doi.org/10.1007/978-3-031-18907-4_1

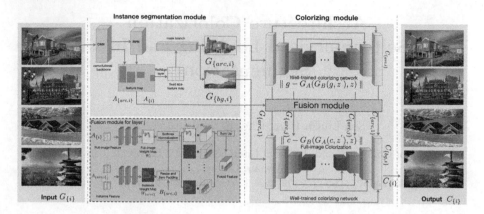

Fig. 1. Overall flowchart of our model

unlabeled image datasets. So we introduced unsupervised learning. In the past, the coloring of unsupervised GAN usually resulted in color spreading.

In this paper, we propose a new framework for the colorizing problem in unsupervised image-to-image translation. First, we adopt a segmentation module that separates the input grayscale image for building and background using instance segmentation. The color leakage arising from coloring between different objects is avoided by coloring them separately. Secondly, we used a fusion module to keep the consistency of the image coloring by the information of the feature map for the separated part, encoding the information that should be kept in the translation process. For the coloring module, we invoked a line sensitivity self-supervised GAN to train the shader according to the characteristics of the architecture. Architects want to be able to observe the four seasons and the display of day and night when coloring a building. We provide a Building Facade dataset, which can compensate for the lack of public building datasets. At the same time, we implement the changing seasons and the coloring of day and night. Our framework is able to enhance the distinction between buildings and backgrounds, compensating for the coloring leakage of unsupervised models. Our model can be extended to similar photo coloring and can be applied to the color restoration of buildings, inspiring the design of future buildings and coloring buildings in virtual worlds.

Three main contributions of our work are as follows:

- We propose a self-supervised GAN network model. The loss function is modified according to the characteristics of architectural images, and positive and
  negative samples are constructed to achieve contrast constraints. It can get
  rid of the dependence on dataset annotation. The trained coloring network
  has a similar effect to the supervised model.
- We propose an instance segmentation-fusion module. To avoid mutual color
  interference between multiple objects in self-supervised learning, we train a
  segmentation module. The image is segmented as well as the feature maps

and weights of each part are obtained. The fusion module fuses the colored pictures based on the information. There is basically no color leakage between objects, and the color contrast between objects is strong and harmonious.
- We provide a high-definition building dataset (Building facade). The buildings in the dataset are categorized in detail by season, style, morning, and evening. Compared with the existing dataset, our collection of buildings is more comprehensive and specific, and more suitable for training related to architectural design.

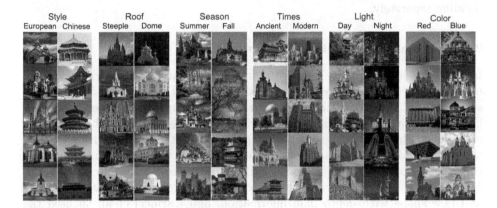

Fig. 2. Classification of the Building Facade dataset and partial image presentation

2 Related Work

Here, we review the related work in the coloring of architectural black and white pictures, the coloring method based on the depth map, and the coloring method of converting related gray-scale pictures into color pictures in the past.

2.1 Architecture Colorization Method

In the initial work on architectural colorization, the colorization results tended to focus on color coverage. Liron et al. [14] took user strokes to help color the buildings. Good coloring results were obtained. Since strokes are propagated using low-level similarity measures, a lot of researchers' editing is usually required to obtain realistic results. In order to reduce the workload of researchers, the later methods focus on designing better automatic colorization method [5]. Maximilian bachl et al. [2] colored architectural objects by adjusting the restriction information in CGAN. The lack of restrictions on the line structure led to distortion in the generated images. Stanislas Chaillou et al. [4] enhanced the positioning information in the line structure and small object placement to make the colorized images more reasonable. Wang et al. [18] performed colorization for sketches, which is playable but the colorization results still need to be manually selected. I. Anokhin et al. [1] averaged the coloring by information of each pixel, the boundary effect is reasonable but the boundary has obvious pixelation. Qian et al. [17] directly analyzed the line art of the building line drawing directly. The above model starts to focus on the special structure of the building's own lines, but there is no consideration for the coloring contrast between the building and the background. The designers often want to know whether the building and the background are in harmony when they refer to the design. Our model takes this into account and can reasonably color the background and the building separately.

2.2   Natural Image Colorizing Methods

In order to automatically generate more accurate and realistic color images, many other techniques have been utilized to assist with colorizing. Su et al. [16] stained the objects by cutting and separating them from each other. Zhu et al. [27] proposed a new semantic segmentation model to better reduce the generation of artifacts. Zheng et al. [26] added artistic shadows to the base colorizing to make the generated images William et al. [19] obtained object information by reversing the depth map, K. Lai et al. [8] added artificial interference to obtain information, M. Schwarz et al. [15] separated the object and background to maintain the pose and flow shape with depth map information, and Carlucci et al. [3] used the residual paradigm to make the RGB-D map to color pictures, with the effect of reflecting more feature information than manual interference and having stronger classification ability. There are also artificially assisted graffiti coloring [13,14,22] and reference example pictures to copy colors for coloring [5,10,21]. In this paper we have combined their ideas for a more precise treatment between buildings and objects, highlighting the beauty of the lines of the buildings.

2.3   Nature Image Generation Methods

The most popular example of image synthesis techniques nowadays are mainly classified into convolutional neural network-based methods and generative adversarial network-based methods. Convolutional neural networks propose semantic and multimodal In order to model semantics, Iizuka et al. [6] and Zhao et al. [25] proposed a two-branch architecture that jointly learns and fuses local image features and global priors. Zhang et al. [24] used a cross-channel encoding scheme to provide semantic interpretability, which was also implemented by Larsson et al. Among the existing coloring methods, a large number of GAN-based approaches have also been generated. Pix2pix model proposed by Isola et al. [7] uses image pairs for training to achieve convincing results for photo-to-map, photo-to-sketch, and photo-to-label transformations. Zhu et al. [28] proposed an extension of multimodal translation, and tao et al.'s ArchGANs were able to achieve architectural line coloring. However, these methods are too crude and give little consideration to the structural aspects of the building. Satisfactory results were not achieved for the treatment of the different faces, lines, and corners of the building. Our model will outperform the staining results of past unsupervised learning models.

3   Methods

As shown in Fig. 1, the grayscale image G_i is passed through the instance segmentation module to obtain the grayscale image $G_{arc,i}$ of the building body, the background grayscale image $G_{bg,i}$, the corresponding building feature image $A_{arc,i}$, the feature image A_i of the complete image and the corresponding bounding box $B_{arc,i}$ of the building body. $g_{arc,i}$, $G_{bg,i}$ are simultaneously and separately colored by the trained $A_{arc,i}$, $A_{bg,i}$, A_i enter the fusion module. During the coloring process, each layer of the network structure is integrated with the feature maps to maintain the consistency of the separate coloring. Finally the complete color image C_i is output by the coloring network of the background.

Fig. 3. For each parts of our model for ablation experiment comparison, the effect is shown in the figure. The third row only uses the baseline dyeing effect, the fourth row adds a segmentation module to the previous row, and the fifth row adds a fusion module to the previous row.

3.1   Datasets

We contributed Building Facade, a medium-sized dataset of building fronts, to the community. Building Facade has several attractive features. First, it is now a publicly available dataset of larger building fronts. Second, some of the images are labeled with information about the main body of the building, doors, and windows, which can be used to train the segmentation model. Thirdly, it is also divided by building function and color, which makes it easier for others to find the labeled building images they need when using it. The initial display of the data set is as Fig. 2.

Web images are a common source for constructing datasets. We downloaded the keywords through crawler software on three major image search sites, Baidu, Google, and Bing. This includes images involved in forums as well as blogs, and a total of 18,983 images were collected. We filtered and screened them. Finally, we got 10121 architectural pictures of high quality. We classified them according to function and color. Our dataset fills the gap of such a dataset.

Fig. 4. The dividing effect of the dividing module for the basic shape of the building is shown.

3.2   Instance Segmentation Predictive Networks

We adopt the Mask-RCNN framework to build our instance segmentation module. The main purpose of the segmentation module is to help us separate the main body of the building, doors, windows, and backgrounds. First, we train the model on the COCO dataset to get the basic parameters. Second, we annotated some of the images in our dataset for transfer learning of basic parameters. This allows us to obtain better separation results on smaller training sets.

The input images are pre-processed as 512×512 into a pre-trained neural network to obtain the building body $A_{arc,i}$ and the corresponding feature maps A_i of each object. After that, ROI align and classification operations are performed on the remaining ROI. The FCN operation is performed in each ROI by BB regression and generating MASK. During training, we define the multitasking loss for each sample ROI as $L = L_{cls} + L_{box} + L_{mask}$ while using the average binary cross-entropy loss. This loss does not lead to the competition when segmenting windows, doors, and building bodies relative to pixel-free softmax and multi-metric cross-entropy loss. The input grayscale map $H_{[i]}$ can eventually be segmented to obtain the background grayscale map $H_{ground[i]}$, the door and window grayscale map $H_{win[i]}$, and the building body grayscale map $H_{ari[i]}$.

3.3 Colorizing Module

Unmarked and unpaired images were sampled by C and H domains. The aim of the model is to train a generator $H_A: C \to H$ to map an image $c \in C$ to another image $h \in H$. Training by using two GANs to implement unsupervised learning. The color gan learns the generator G_A and the discriminator D_A to distinguish between the false input of G_A and the real generation of G domain. The same is true for the learning generator G_B and discriminator D_B for grayscale gan. The images $c \in C$ are translated into the domain G using G_A. The $G_A(c, z)$ is evaluated by D_A, and z is the random noise. $G_A(c, z)$ as input to G_B. Translate to $G_B(G_A(c, z), z')$ output, z_0 is random noise. Two gan are trained with mutual input and output. The training is performed with the sample in the domain as a positive sample and the output of the other gan as a counterexample. The ultimate goal is for the generator G_A to be able to fool the discriminator D_A with a fake output. Minimize reconstruction losses: $||G_A(G_B(g, z'), z) - g||$. The G_A after training is completed as the basic coloring network. In order to enhance the training effect of the model, we add the contrast learning of discriminator to G_A, G_B respectively to determine the positive and negative, so that both have the characteristics of Contrastive Self-Supervised Learning (1):

$$L_{con}(f; \tau, M) \triangleq \underset{\substack{(c,g) \sim G_i \\ \{c_i^-\}_{i=1}^M \overset{i.i.d.}{\sim} G_i}}{E} [-log \frac{e^{f(c)^T f(g)/\tau}}{e^{f(c)^T f(g)/\tau} + \sum_i e^{f(c_i^-)^T f(g)/\tau}}] \qquad (1)$$

Where, as in traditional GAN, the goal of the discriminator is to compare the generated fake samples with the real ones. Nevertheless, here we use the loss format advocated by Wasserstein GAN-GP instead of the WGAN used in the original DualGAN. The weight clipping used in the past was able to independently restrict the range of values of each network parameter. The discriminator loss, in order to widen the difference in the scores of the samples, would produce a strategy of letting all parameters go to the extremes, either taking the maximum or the minimum value. This can easily lead to a situation where the gradient vanishes or the gradient explodes. Our restriction via Lipschitz is to require that the gradient of the discriminator does not exceed $\Delta_{|C-G|}$. One can try to set an additional loss term to reflect this (2).

$$loss = ReLU[|||\nabla_x G(x)||_p - \Delta_{|C-G|}] \qquad (2)$$

Similarly, the discriminator wants to open the gap between the scores of true and false samples, so it naturally wants the gradient to be better and the variation to be larger, so the gradient norm will be around $\Delta_{|C-G|}$ after the discriminator is fully trained. The new discriminator loss after weighted merging is (3):

$$L(G) = -E_{g_1 \sim P_t}[G(g)] + E_{g_2 \sim P_f}[G(g)] + \lambda E_{g \sim G}[|||\nabla_g G(g)||_p - 1]^2 \qquad (3)$$

Since it is not necessary to impose Lipschitz restrictions on the entire sample space, restrictions in the concentration region are sufficient. in the true sample

C_t, the false sample C_f, and a 0-1 random number Uniform $[0, 1]$. Sampling by random interpolation on the concatenation of c_t and c_f (4):

$$\hat{c} = \epsilon C_t + (1 - \epsilon)C_f \qquad (4)$$

The distribution satisfied by $\hat{x}$ obtained by sampling is noted as $P_{\hat{x}}$, and the final discriminant loss is obtained as (5):

$$L(X) = \lambda E_{x \sim P\hat{x}}[\|\nabla_x G(x)\|_p - 1]^2 - E_{x \sim P_t}[G(x)] + E_{x \sim P_g}[G(x)] \qquad (5)$$

Both generators G_A and G_B use the same loss function, and on past conditional image synthesis, it was found that the L_2 distance would be more prone to blurring than using the L_1 distance. Using we continue to keep the L_2 distance.

For the discriminator structure Markovian PatchGAN architecture is explored in [8], it assumes that the distance between pixels beyond a particular patch is independent only at the patch level rather than sizing and modeling the image at the patch level on the full image. Such a configuration is effective in capturing local high-frequency features such as texture and style, but not in modeling global distribution. It meets our needs well because recovery loss encourages the preservation of global and low-frequency information, and the discriminator is specified to capture local high-frequency information. The patch size discriminator operation is fixed at 70×70, and the image resolution is mostly 512×512. The overall loss function is (6):

$$\max_{G_1,G_2,E_1,E_2} \min_{D_1,D_2} L(G_1, G_2, E_1, E_2, D_1, D_2) = \lambda_c(L_c^{c_1} + L_c^{c_2}) + \lambda_g(L_g^{g_1} + L_g^{g_2})$$

$$+\lambda_x(L_x^{x_1} + L_x^{x_2}) + L_{GAN}^{x_1} + L_{GAN}^{x_2} \qquad (6)$$

3.4   Fusion Model

For the convenience of presentation, we only introduce the fusion module at layer j. The input to the fusion module at layer j is A_i, and the set $A_{arc,i}$, $B_{arc,i}$. Both are predicted by a small neural network with three convolutional layers to predict the full image weight map W_i and the weight map $W_{arc,i}$ of the building subject, respectively. In order to fuse the feature map $A_{arc,i}$ of each building to the full image feature map A_i. Enter the building body bounding box $B_{arc,i}$, who defines the size and position of the building. We adjust the building feature $A_{arc,i}$ and the corresponding weight map $W_{arc,i}$ to match the size of the full map, and zero padding is performed during the adjustment. The adjusted building feature $\hat{A}_{arc,i}$ and weight map $\hat{W}_{arc,i}$. After that, we stack all the weight maps, apply softmax on each pixel, and get the fused features by weighting and formula (7).

$$C_i = \sum(\prod G_{arc,i} A_{arc,i} W_{arc,i} + \prod G_i A_i W_i) \qquad (7)$$

4   Experiments

We describe in detail the qualitative and quantitative experiments of our system. In Sect. 4.1, we verify that our dataset yields better results for training building coloring. Then, we describe the effect of our trained instance segmentation model in Sect. 4.2. In Sect. 4.3, we show a qualitative example of basic coloring. In Sect. 4.4, we evaluate our complete coloring network.

Fig. 5. A comparison of the results of our model after training for different datasets. It can be clearly seen that our dataset has better experimental results.

Table 1. Our model is compared quantitatively with six models commonly used in the past using three different data sets. The compared metrics are LPIPS, PSNR, and SSIM.

Method	Imagenet ctest10k			COCOStuff validation split			Building facade		
	LPIPS ↓	PSNR ↑	SSIM ↑	LPIPS ↓	PSNR ↑	SSIM ↑	LPIPS ↓	PSNR ↑	SSIM ↑
Iizuka et al. [6]	0.203	23.718	0.915	0.187	23.869	0.923	0.147	25.583	0.951
Larsson et al. [9]	0.187	25.105	0.921	0.185	25.062	0.931	0.159	25.721	0.947
Zhang et al. [24]	0.239	21.795	0.885	0.232	21.837	0.892	0.203	22.561	0.941
Yi et al. [23]	0.164	25.176	0.912	0.156	25.875	0.907	0.167	24.928	0.936
Lei et al. [11]	0.205	24.542	0.917	0.193	24.584	0.922	0.169	25.073	0.943
Wu et al. [20]	0.137	26.993	0.924	0.137	27.534	0.936	0.125	27.677	0.956
Ours	**0.151**	**26.980**	**0.933**	**0.144**	**26.787**	**0.933**	**0.130**	**27.167**	**0.952**
Yi et al. [23]	0.153	26.142	0.927	0.149	26.551	0.915	0.144	26.825	0.943
Ours	**0.132**	**27.562**	**0.937**	**0.131**	**27.792**	**0.942**	**0.127**	**27.985**	**0.954**

4.1 Datasets

We randomly select one thousand high-definition architectural images from ImageNet, Massachusetts, and Building Facade respectively. We do not use any other model to learn style information supervision. For a fair comparison, all images are adjusted to 512 × 512 resolution for training. As shown in Fig. 5, our dataset is more suitable for coloring training in the building class. Our collection of architectural images is more suitable for orientation selection. Each image clearly shows the frontal view of the building.

Countries have different architectural styles, and they tend to be brightly colored and contrasting. The pictures after coloring should also basically match the architectural color characteristics. Many buildings are not just black, white, gray, and yellow. Simply coloring out this basic color is hardly an inspiration for the designer's color choice. The dataset we collected ensures that both the positive features of the building are clear and that the architectural color design is preserved. European, Chinese, and Japanese buildings are also divided to be able to ensure that the coloring model is applicable to all grayscale architectural images. The experimental results show that the coloring model trained by our dataset has more vivid coloring and stronger contrast. There is a higher artistic aesthetics.

4.2 Instance Semantic Segmentation

The instance segmentation module of our model is designed to solve the color leakage between objects. to refine the effect of coloring after self-supervised learning. We compare the effect graph by direct coloring without segmentation and with segmentation involved. From Fig. 6, it is clear that the segmentation module can effectively solve the color leakage situation. Also, we quantified the success rate of the segmentation model. The success rate is quantified as the ratio of the total number of buildings and pictures that the segmentation module can successfully predict. We coarsely classify and test the buildings: pagoda-shaped (47.2%), flat-topped (84.1%), dome-shaped (83.9%), odd-shaped (57.7%), and ancient (76.2%). Our success rate is not ideal for some buildings with more unusual shapes, but the correct rate for basic living buildings is satisfactory. It shows that the instance segmentation can effectively separate the buildings from the background and can provide relevant picture information of different buildings, which is beneficial to the later module coloring. For the segmentation module for the basic building has trained a better segmentation effect. As the Fig. 4.

4.3 Model Analysis

We used our dataset for training and testing, and for each module, an Ablation experiment was performed separately. The comparison effect of each model is shown in Fig. 4. For the LPIPS, PSNR, and SSIM metrics of the evaluation models, we compared the last 5 bits of the coloring models by comparing the data under different comparisons of the three datasets. The specific metrics are shown in Table 1. Our model is also capable of converting a grayscale map into the corresponding colors for the four seasons and for day and night. We compare the converted results with the previous model results, as shown in Fig. 7.

Fig. 6. The splitting model is able to solve the case of color leakage between different objects. Figures a and c are the shading effects without instance segmentation, and Figures e and g are the corresponding shading effects after using the instance segmentation module. It can be clearly seen that the instance segmentation module can effectively avoid color leakage.

Our model pre-sizes the input images to 512×512. Model data for pix2pix model development network for some migration. We train this network using the Adam optimizer and set the weight decay to 0.0005. The moderum and moderum2 used for the Adam optimizer are rationalized and set. For the learning rate, we took the cyclic learning rate (CLR). The initial learning rate was set to 0.001 and the upper bound was set to 0.006. The batch size was set to 1, and 1000 images were trained for each epoch. After the experiment, we found that it takes nearly 100 epochs to get better experimental results.

We use many metrics to evaluate the distance between the coloring result and the actual image, including L1 distance, Root Mean Squared Error (RMSE) and Peak Signal to Noise Ratio (PSNR). We also use the edge detection rate as a metric because we believe that a good coloring result may improve the edge detection result. We apply the Canny edge detector to find edge pigmentation and then calculate the ratio as the ratio of the number of edge pixels detected by the actual image to the number of edge pixels detected by the coloring result. If this ratio is close to 1, the edge detection result on the coloring result is closer to the real image. The average ratio is 0.942 after nearly 1000 tests.

Our model is also able to multimodal a grayscale image. A grayscale image can be converted into a color image for spring, summer, autumn, and winter. The ability to reflect the seasonal color scheme for different seasons is ideal for designers to optimize. We can also convert day and night to reflect the same building at different times of the day and night.

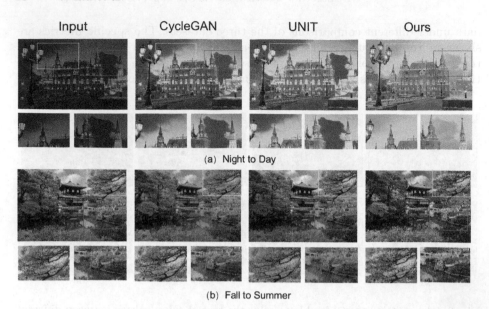

(a) Night to Day

(b) Fall to Summer

Fig. 7. Our model is compared with cycleGAN, UNIT model. Our model has the best presentation for the tasks of day and night transformation and seasonal color transformation for the input images.

4.4   Fusion Function

For the consideration of the fusion module, we consider it in conjunction with the separation module. The main role of the fusion module is to localize the objects of multiple classes separated by the segmentation module by using the weights and feature maps provided in the segmentation module. And the correct position of each part is fused. The correct and reasonable coloring image is obtained. Without the fusion module, direct coloring and stitching will produce uncomfortable residual shadows and affect the realism of the image. As in Fig. 3.

5   Limitations and Discussion

The performance of our segmentation model is not yet satisfactory for buildings with more peculiar shapes. This can lead to the presence of unpleasant vignettes in the subsequent shading and blending process. Incorrect separation can result in the unseparated parts of the building being colored as a background color and false-color leakage after fusion. This is an undertraining on the model, not a methodological error.

6   Conclusion and Future Work

We propose a coloring model to segment the input images by means of an instance segmentation module. The coloring of the segmented model can effectively avoid the effect of coloring between multiple objects. While segmenting, we are able to obtain feature maps and weight information of different objects. This information will help us to recover the complete picture of the fusion module. For the training of the coloring module, we use self-supervised learning for training, which can greatly reduce the dependency on the dataset. For the existing dataset, we found that a large dataset of building facades is missing, and we contributed the building facade dataset to be able to supplement a part of it for the study. For the final coloring results, we perform a comprehensive evaluation by various metrics. The experimental results show that our model outperforms other methods from both quantitative and qualitative perspectives. For future research, we would like to improve the accuracy of the segmentation module to perfect the coloring effect for buildings with special shapes.

References

1. Anokhin, I., Demochkin, K., Khakhulin, T., Sterkin, G., Lempitsky, V., Korzhenkov, D.: Image generators with conditionally-independent pixel synthesis. CoRR, pp. 14278–14287 (2020)
2. Bachl, M., Ferreira, D.C.: City-GAN: learning architectural styles using a custom conditional GAN architecture. CoRR (2019)
3. Carlucci, F.M., Russo, P., Caputo, B.: (de)^{2}co: deep depth colorization. IEEE Robot. Autom. Lett. **3**, 2386–2393 (2018)
4. Chaillou, S.: ArchiGAN: artificial intelligence x architecture. In: Yuan, P.F., Xie, M., Leach, N., Yao, J., Wang, X. (eds.) Architectural Intelligence, pp. 117–127. Springer, Singapore (2020). https://doi.org/10.1007/978-981-15-6568-7_8
5. He, M., Chen, D., Liao, J., Sander, P.V., Yuan, L.: Deep exemplar-based colorization, pp. 1–16 (2018)
6. Iizuka, S., Simo-Serra, E., Ishikawa, H.: Let there be color!: joint end-to-end learning of global and local image priors for automatic image colorization with simultaneous classification. ACM Trans. Graph. (Proc. of SIGGRAPH 2016) **35**, 110:1–110:11 (2016)
7. Isola, P., Zhu, J.Y., Zhou, T., Efros, A.A.: Image-to-image translation with conditional adversarial networks. In: 2017 IEEE Conference on Computer Vision and Pattern Recognition (CVPR), pp. 5967–5976 (2017)
8. Lai, K., Bo, L., Ren, X., Fox, D.: A large-scale hierarchical multi-view RGB-D object dataset. In: 2011 IEEE International Conference on Robotics and Automation, pp. 1817–1824 (2011)
9. Larsson, G., Maire, M., Shakhnarovich, G.: Learning representations for automatic colorization. In: Leibe, B., Matas, J., Sebe, N., Welling, M. (eds.) ECCV 2016. LNCS, vol. 9908, pp. 577–593. Springer, Cham (2016). https://doi.org/10.1007/978-3-319-46493-0_35
10. Lee, J., Kim, E., Lee, Y., Kim, D., Chang, J., Choo, J.: Reference-based sketch image colorization using augmented-self reference and dense semantic correspondence, pp. 5800–5809 (2020)
11. Lei, C., Chen, Q.: Fully automatic video colorization with self-regularization and diversity. In: 2019 IEEE/CVF Conference on Computer Vision and Pattern Recognition (CVPR), pp. 3748–3756 (2019)
12. Levin, A., Lischinski, D., Weiss, Y.: Colorization using optimization. In: ACM SIGGRAPH 2004 Papers, pp. 689–694. Association for Computing Machinery, New York (2004)

13. Luan, Q., Wen, F., Cohen-Or, D., Liang, L., Xu, Y.Q., Shum, H.Y.: Natural image colorization. In: Proceedings of the 18th Eurographics Conference on Rendering Techniques, pp. 309–320 (2007)
14. Qu, Y., Wong, T.T., Heng, P.A.: Manga colorization. In: ACM SIGGRAPH 2006 Papers, pp. 1214–1220. Association for Computing Machinery (2006)
15. Schwarz, M., Schulz, H., Behnke, S.: RGB-D object recognition and pose estimation based on pre-trained convolutional neural network features. In: 2015 IEEE International Conference on Robotics and Automation (ICRA), pp. 1329–1335 (2015)
16. Su, J.W., Chu, H.K., Huang, J.B.: Instance-aware image colorization. In: 2020 IEEE/CVF Conference on Computer Vision and Pattern Recognition (CVPR), pp. 7965–7974 (2020)
17. Sun, Q., et al.: A GAN-based approach toward architectural line drawing colorization prototyping. Vis. Comput. **38**, 1–18 (2021)
18. Wang, S.Y., Bau, D., Zhu, J.Y.: Sketch your own GAN. CoRR, pp. 14050–14060 (2021)
19. Williem, Raskar, R., Park, I.K.: Depth map estimation and colorization of anaglyph images using local color prior and reverse intensity distribution. In: 2015 IEEE International Conference on Computer Vision (ICCV), pp. 3460–3468 (2015)
20. Wu, Y., Wang, X., Li, Y., Zhang, H., Zhao, X., Shan, Y.: Towards vivid and diverse image colorization with generative color prior. In: Proceedings of the IEEE/CVF International Conference on Computer Vision (ICCV), pp. 14377–14386, October 2021
21. Xu, Z., Wang, T., Fang, F., Sheng, Y., Zhang, G.: Stylization-based architecture for fast deep exemplar colorization, pp. 9360–9369 (2020)
22. Yatziv, L., Sapiro, G.: Fast image and video colorization using chrominance blending. IEEE Trans. Image Process. **15**, 1120–1129 (2006)
23. Yi, Z., Zhang, H., Tan, P., Gong, M.: DualGAN: unsupervised dual learning for image-to-image translation. CoRR, pp. 2868–2876 (2017)
24. Zhang, R., Isola, P., Efros, A.A.: Colorful image colorization. CoRR, pp. 649–666 (2016)
25. Zhao, J., Liu, L., Snoek, C.G.M., Han, J., Shao, L.: Pixel-level semantics guided image colorization. CoRR (2018)
26. Zheng, Q., Li, Z., Bargteil, A.: Learning to shadow hand-drawn sketches. In: The IEEE/CVF Conference on Computer Vision and Pattern Recognition (CVPR), pp. 7436–7445 (2020)
27. Zhu, F., Zhu, Y., Zhang, L., Wu, C., Fu, Y., Li, M.: A unified efficient pyramid transformer for semantic segmentation (2021)
28. Zhu, J.Y., Zhang, R., Pathak, D., Darrell, T., Efros: toward multimodal image-to-image translation. In: Advances in Neural Information Processing Systems, pp. 466–477 (2017)

Dual-Rank Attention Module for Fine-Grained Vehicle Model Recognition

Wen Cai[2], Wenjia Zhu[3], Bo Cheng[2], Longdao Xu[2], Ye Yu[1,2(✉)], Qiang Lu[1,2], and Wei Jia[1,2]

[1] Key Laboratory of Knowledge Engineering With Big Data, Ministry of Education, Hefei University of Technology, Hefei 230009, China
[2] School of Computer Science and Information, Hefei University of Technology, Hefei 230009, China
yuye@hfut.edu.cn
[3] Anhui Baicheng-Huitong Co., Ltd., Hefei 230088, China

Abstract. Vehicle fine-grained recognition is an important task in the field of intelligent transportation. However, due to the subtle differences between different vehicle models, and the tremendous difference caused by the different pose of the same vehicle model, the effect of vehicle recognition is less successful and still require further research. In this paper, we propose a dual-rank attention module (DRAM), which can reduce visual interference caused by vehicle multi-pose. In addition, combined with the attention mechanism, our method can not only mine the discriminative features of the vehicle model but also increase the feature richness and improve the accuracy of vehicle model recognition. In this paper, in the initial stage of the network, the STN is used to transform the vehicle pose, meanwhile, the whole image is weighted by the global attention to mine the subtle discriminant features. At the high part of the network, after fusing multi-level feature maps top-down, we designed a fused channel attention module to enhance the feature response of the current category. It achieves 94.1% and 96.9% top-1 accuracy on the Stanford Cars and CompCars datasets, which is more than 2.1% higher than the original baseline network VGG19 but only adds a few parameters. Experimental results show that the DRAM can effectively improve the accuracy of vehicle fine-grained recognition.

Keywords: Vehicle model recognition · Dual-rank attention · Feature fusion in top-down · Vehicle pose transform

This work is partly supported by grants of the National Natural Science Foundation of China (No. 61906061 and No. 62076086) and Open Foundation of the Key lab (center) of Anhui Province Key Laboratory of Intelligent Building & Building Energy Saving (No. IBES2021KF05).

Supplementary Information The online version contains supplementary material available at https://doi.org/10.1007/978-3-031-18907-4_2.

1   Introduction

Vehicle Model Recognition (VMR) plays a strikingly important role in various Intelligent Transportation System (ITS) applications. For example, a vision-based VMR system can help police quickly and accurately search and identify suspicious vehicle information from a large number of vehicles in the collected surveillance video to find the target vehicle. In addition, vehicle models can be used to analyze and study traffic flow to make strategies for traffic control. Thus, VMR has attracted extensive interest and has substantial research value and application prospects [29, 30].

VMR is a typical fine-grained classification problem that faces great challenges for the following reasons: 1) vehicle appearance is easily influenced by the natural environment (e.g. environmental lighting or complex weather conditions); 2) Large amount of vehicle models exist and the differences between some models may be small; 3) the vehicle images may be captured from different angles resulting in great appearance differences of the same vehicle. Hence, the commonly accepted solution is to mine discriminative information as much as possible from local regions for the VMR tasks [31, 32].

In this paper, we propose a novel dual-rank attention module (DRAM), which can effectively strengthen the feature map to find more discriminative regions. The DRAM includes two parts, the low-rank transform residual attention module (LTRA) and high-rank fused channel attention module (HFCA), which can be inserted into some famous backbone networks (e.g. VGG or ResNet), and are proven to increase their fine-grained vehicle model recognition ability. In this paper, we mainly insert the DRAM module to VGG19 and then demonstrate the effectiveness of DRAM through experiments. Our main contributions can be summarized as follows: as follow:

1) We propose a dual-rank attention module for VMR, which includes two parts, i.e., the LTRA module and the HFCA module, which are applied to the lower part and higher part of the network respectively.
2) We utilize STN to optimize the input for the network, which can reduce the influence of multi-pose appearance differences of vehicles. To the best of our knowledge, this is the first time that STN is investigated for VMR.
3) We design a channel attention module that is applied on the fused feature maps, and the feature maps are fused through upsampling of multi-resolution feature maps and then fused through concatenation.

2   Related Works

2.1   Weakly-Supervised Method

Without using additional annotation information, weakly supervised recognition methods try to automatically learn important local regions. Yang et al. [1]

designed a Navigator-Teacher-Scrutinize network to realize the self-monitoring mechanism, which can effectively locate the key regions of the object without hand-generated parts annotations. To reduce the computation cost of multiple features extraction, Foo et al. [2] only detected the vehicle headlamp as the feature of vehicle models, although it achieved a good result on their generated dataset, the effect was still not satisfactory on the large dataset of CompCars [3]. Fu et al. [4] proposed a recurrent attention-based CNN model including an attention proposal subnetwork (APN), which iteratively generated attention regions from coarse to fine by taking previous predictions as a reference and proved effective on the Stanford Cars dataset [5]. Bai et al. [6] incorporated intra-class variance obtained by grouping into triplet embedding to improve the performance of fine-grained recognition. Weakly supervised recognition methods only need class labels to complete model training and can also achieve good results; thus, in this paper, we choose to solve VMR problem based on weakly-supervised methods.

2.2   Researches Related to Attention Mechanism

Attention mechanism has played an important role in deep learning to mimic human visual mechanisms. For CNN, usually, the attention mechanism is used to improve network performance, which mainly contains two methods, i.e., channel attention and spatial attention. Jie et al. [7] proposed a squeeze-excitation module to allocate the weight of each channel, so as to help the network learn important feature information. Lin et al. [8] proposed SPACE, which provides a unified probabilistic modeling framework that combines the spatial attention and scene-mixture approaches.

In the tasks of fine-grained image recognition, visual attention has been extended to many different methods, from single-stage attention to multi-stage attention, and good results have been achieved. In addition, they also have verified the effectiveness of fine-grained vehicle datasets. Zhu et al. [9] use a cascaded approach to reduce training difficulty and computational costs while removing irrelevant information. This approach is known as the hard attention mechanism. Zheng et al. [10] designed a multi-level attention CNN to locate regions and extract features in a mutually reinforced way. Zhao et al. [11] used multiple LSTMs to design diversity attention to extract discriminant features to the greatest extent. The diversity of attention structure greatly enhances the richness of discriminant features.

2.3   Researches Related to STN

The STN allows the spatial manipulation of input data within the network by the spatial transformer to maintain the spatial consistency of data. In the field of object recognition, STN-related networks have mainly been applied in face recognition and person re-identification (ReID). Zhong et al. [12] utilized a spatial transformer to warp the face image according to the predicted 2-D transformation parameters which are obtained by a localization network and then utilized a classification network to extract features of the warped image for face recognition. Luo et al. [13] introduced a STNReID for partial ReID, which uses STN to sample the most similar patch from the holistic to match the partial image. In sum, STN provides an end-to-end learning mechanism that can be seamlessly incorporated into a CNN to explicitly learn how to transform the input data to achieve spatial invariance. STN can act not only on the input image but also on the convolution feature map in the deep layer of the network.

Although STN has been applied to some object recognition tasks, it has not been used to solve VMR problem. What's more, the advantages of STN have not been fully utilized. Thus, in this paper, we try to study STN to make it more valuable by designing an attention mechanism based on STN.

3   Methodology

Our DRAM includes two parts, the LTRA module, and the HFCA module. Among them, the LTRA module is used at the lower part of the network flow, and its main purpose is to transform the input image and obtain the optimized input for the following network. HFCA module is used at the higher part of the network flow, and its main purpose is to improve the richness of the classification features and highlight the subtle discriminative features. The combination of LTRA and HFCA can well improve the classification accuracy of vehicle models.

In order to understand the structure of LTRA and HFCA easily, we inserted them into the VGG19 structure and formed the VGG19-DRAM network, which is illustrated in Fig. 1. In VGG19-DRAM, LTRA is inserted right after the input image, and HFCA is inserted at the high part of the network, which is near the fully connected layer.

In the next sections, we will detail the structure of the LTRA module and HFCA module.

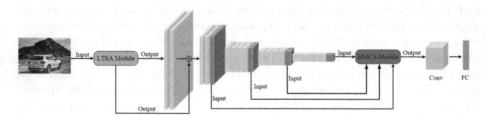

Fig. 1. The network structure of VGG19-DRAM.

3.1   The LTRA Module

The main structure of the LTRA module is illustrated in Fig. 2. In fine-grained VMR problems, usually the vehicles appear in different poses and sizes, which increases the difficulty of their recognition. In order to overcome the above-mentioned difficulty, a spatial transformer network (STN) is adopted here to transform the input image to obtain the optimized input for the following CNN.

Different from other face recognition or hyperspectral image recognition work which inserts STN directly into their network pipeline, we use STN to calculate the weights of attention maps. In this case, the network converges faster which makes the network easier to train, and the recognition accuracies are also improved.

By convention, our spatial transformer network includes three parts: localization network, grid generator, and sampler. The localization network learns the parameter of an affine transformation. The grid generator uses the predicted transformation parameter to construct a sampling grid, which gets the output of a group of pixel points after sampling and transformation. The Sampler is to fill the pixels to the new grid and form the original feature maps according to the sampling grid.

Specially, in this study, the localization network includes five convolutional layers with convolutional kernel size of 3, each followed by a BN and a ReLU layer, two maximum pooling layers, and three fully connected layers, and adopts 2D affine transformation as the transformation type. And we adopted the filling method of bilinear interpolation as described in the original STN [14].

First, the vehicle images with the size of $224 \times 224 \times 3$ are input to STN to obtain the transformed feature maps. Then, the attention weights are calculated through the sigmoid activation function. At last, the output feature maps are obtained through an element-wise product of the original input image and the attention weights. The output of LTRA has the same size as the input, only changing the pose and size of the vehicle in the input image.

The output of LTRA is passed forward through two branches. The first branch is passed directly forward to the start of VGG19. The second branch is passed to the location of conv1_2 in VGG19, forming the residual unit. The element-wise product with attention weights in LTRA range from zero to one will degrade the value of features in convolutional layers, thus, we short connect the feature maps from LTRA to the next convolution layers in order to enhance features.

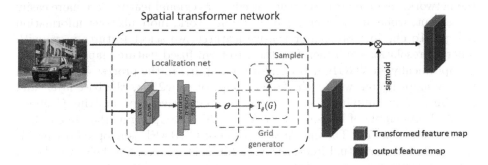

Fig. 2. Structure of LTRA module. (In the localization network of STN, blue blocks denote the convolutional layers and ReLU, and blue rectangles denote the fully connected layer respectively. In addition, $\otimes$ represents element-wise product.) (Color figure online)

3.2   The HFCA Module

Our HFCA module contains two parts, i.e., multi-level feature fusion and channel attention module. The detailed structure is shown in Fig. 1 and Fig. 3. In CNN, increasing the richness of features can improve classification performance. For features of different resolutions, different information will be kept or enhanced; thus, we collect features of different resolutions from the network and fuse them to form the fused feature maps. However, the combination of fused feature maps is complex and cannot highlight the key areas of the image. Therefore, we embed the channel attention module after the fused feature maps, which can not only weight the important information but also improve the feature response of the fused feature maps.

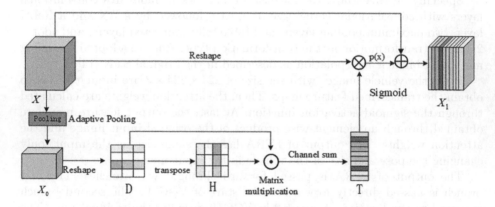

Fig. 3. The detail of channel attention algorithm.

Multi-level Feature Fusion. For feature maps of different resolutions, different information will be kept or enhanced. Usually, at the shallower part of the network, shape information such as edge or regional features are more easily to be kept, while at the deeper part of the network, more abstract information is kept. To obtain more comprehensive features, we select features maps with different resolutions and then fuse them to form fused feature maps.

Specifically, in VGG19 network, for upsampling in the process of multi-level feature maps fusion, we use the feature maps of conv2_2 as the base layer, and the times of up sampling is set to 2, 4, and 8 respectively for applying Content-Aware ReAssembly of Features (CARAFE) [15] upsampling method in conv3_3, conv4_3 and conv5_3. The upsample method of CARAFE is adopted because it can aggregate contextual information within a large receptive field, which can help our network to mine subtle discriminant features. After the process of up sampling operation, the size of feature maps of the four layers are $56 \times 56 \times 512$.

After the process of upsampling, multi-layer feature maps are fused at the channel-level by the fusion method of "concat". The fused feature maps contain not only the discriminative detailed features at the bottom parts, but also the global semantic features at the top parts, which effectively improves the feature richness and the recognition effect of vehicles.

Channel Attention Module. The above-fused feature maps come from different levels of the network Fig. 1; thus, they have complex characteristics. If they are directly used as the final representation, it cannot highlight important features because of redundant features in them. In addition, each channel feature map at the high level of a network can be regarded as a class-specific response, different channel responses are associated with each other, and we could emphasize interdependent feature maps to improve the feature representation of the specific class. Inspired by the Dual Attention Network (DANet) [16], we design a channel attention module to enhance the feature representation of the current class. The input of the channel attention module is the fusion feature maps $X \in R^{W*H*C}$.

In order to reduce the amount of calculation, before calculating the channel weights, the fused feature maps are down-sampled twice through the adaptive average pool (AP) [17] layer. After the AP layer, fused feature maps are converted to $X_0 \in R^{W_0*H_0*C_0}$, and the number of channels remains the same. Our channel attention function can be formulated as:

$$M_c(X) = X \oplus (\sigma(\omega(H \odot D)) \otimes X) \tag{1}$$

$$\omega(x_i) = \sum_{p=1}^{c} x_i \tag{2}$$

where X represents the fused feature maps, c is the channel numbers, $\odot$ represents the matrix multiplication, σ is the Sigmoid function. In addition, and x_i represents the ith channel feature maps of X. The $M_c(X)$ is the output of our channel attention module, which has the same size of X.

The detailed process of the channel attention module is described in the Fig. 3. Firstly, X_0 is reshaped into $D \in R^{Z*C}$, and the $H \in R^{C*Z}$ is the transpose of R^{Z*C}. Then, the similarity map of $T' \in R^{C*C}$ is obtained by matrix multiplication of D and H, which learns the interdependencies among channel maps by calculating the similarity between 2D maps. The second step is to sum each pixel of the channel to get the channel weight matrix $T \in R^{C*1}$, and then we use the Sigmoid function to activate the channel weight matrix, which converts the weight value into 0 and 1. The third step is to weigh the X with channel weight matrix by element-wise product and get the output of the channel attention module $p(x)$.

After channel-wise attention weighting, the feature response of the current class can be enhanced and the feature response of other classes can be suppressed. It should be noted that the Sigmoid function transforms the elements into the range of 0–1. If we use the weighted channel as the final classification representation, it will weaken the feature representation of the corresponding channel. Therefore, after the channel-wise weighting, we apply element-wise add to $p(x)$ and X to get the output of fused channel attention X_1, which not only imposes the feature response but also increases the amount of feature information, thus improving the vehicle recognition effect.

Compared with the attention module proposed in DANet [16], which also calculates 2D similarity maps to get attention weights, our work is an improvement of their channel attention module. Our channel attention has two advantages. Firstly, we adopt an Adaptive-average-pooling layer to process the input feature maps, which can greatly reduce the calculation amount of similarity maps. Secondly, we sum the similarity maps in the channel level, which can weigh important channels with a larger value.

4   Experimental Results and Analysis

In this section, we firstly show the processes and the results of the experiments with different vehicle datasets, then we compare the performance of the proposed method with other methods. Ablation experiments are shown in the appendix.

4.1   Datasets and Experimental Environments

We conduct experiments on two representative fine-grained vehicle model datasets Stanford Cars and web-nature CompCars, respectively.

The Stanford Cars Datasets: it contains 16,185 images of 196 classes. This dataset is split into 8144 training and 8041 testing images. Unless otherwise specified, our experiments are carried out without bounding boxes for the Stanford Cars datasets.

The Web-Nature CompCars Datasets: it contains 431 car models with a total of 52083 multi-view vehicle images, and 70% of the data are used for training, while the other 30% are used for testing.

Experimental Hardware Environments: CPU: Intel Core i7-6700; Memory: 16 GB; Graphics Cards: NVIDIA GeForce RTX 1080Ti; Video Memory: 8 GB.

4.2   Implementation Details

Some hyperparameters and tricks in our experiments are as follows. Our experiments' optimization strategy is stochastic gradient descent, for which the initial learning rate is 0.01, and the batch size is set to 32. In addition, we adopt cosine learning decay. The data augmentation strategy is that we first random flip with a probability of 0.5, and resize all samples to 256×256, then crop five images of 224×224 from the center and four corners of the image. We perform a mirroring operation on the five images. Thus, for each sample, ten training images are obtained. Finally, we subtract the mean of the entire dataset for all input images.

4.3   Experimental Results and Analysis

Evaluation on Stanford Cars Datasets. To demonstrate the effectiveness of our method, we compare the classification accuracy of VGG19+DRAM with some state-of-the-art methods on the Stanford Cars datasets. The experimental results are shown in Table 1.

Table 1. Comparison with some methods for VMR on the Stanford Cars datasets.

Model	Backbone	Size	Anno	Top-1 Acc
Sina et al.	ResNet-34	224	✓	87.8%
FCAN	ResNet-50	512	✓	91.3%
OPAM	VGG-16	–	✗	92.5%
Ji et al.	VGG-16	–	✗	92.9%
MAMC	ResNet-101	448	✗	93.0%
MaxEnt	DenseNet-161	–	✗	93.0%
CAM	ResNet-50	224	✗	93.1%
HBPASM	ResNet-34	500	✗	93.8%
Liu et al.	M-Net+VGG16	224	✗	93.4%
Bamboo [34]	ViT-B/16	224	✗	93.9%
ACNet	ResNet-50	448	✗	**94.6%**
VGG19	VGG-19	448	✗	92.1%
AS-DNN	VGG-19	448	✗	94.0%
MaskCov	ResNet-50	384	✗	94.1%
Ours	VGG-19	224	✗	94.1%
Ours	VGG-19	448	✗	**94.8%**

According to the results in Table 1, on the Stanford Cars datasets, previous methods using part-level annotations (i.e., Sina et al. [18] and FCAN [19]) only achieved less than 92.0% top-1 accuracy. In the recent weakly supervised methods, many of them apply attention mechanisms to improve recognition accuracy, our method achieved the best 94.8% top-1 accuracy. ACNet [20] combines binary tree structure with CNN to capture the feature representation of image learning from coarse to fine, and embedded attention structure to learn discriminant features, and achieved Top-1 accuracy of 94.6%, a little lower than that of our method. In addition, Liu et al. [21] and CAM [22] introduced a long-short term memory (LSTM) network to learn attention information via the long-range dependency on all features. CAM generated global attention information by LSTM to capture subtle differences and achieved 93.1% top-1 accuracy, and Liu et al. encoded inputted features to spatially representations by spatial LSTM and achieved 93.4% top-1 accuracy. However, CAM used more LSTM units, and

Liu et al. introduced two CNN streams, added more model parameters, which is not as efficient as our DRAM module.

Other weakly supervised methods adopted a specific algorithm to improve recognition accuracy, such as MaxEnt [23] provide a training routine that maximizes the entropy of the output probability distribution by using Maximum-Entropy, and HBPASM [24] proposed the hierarchical bilinear pooling to learning discriminative regions, which also achieved good results but still lower than ours.

Evaluation on CompCars Web-Nature Dataset. The vehicle images provided by CompCars web-nature dataset vary greatly in pose and size too. In addition, the ComCars dataset contains more vehicle model types and a larger number of vehicle images than the Stanford Cars dataset. Thus, the Comp-Cars dataset is more challenging. To verify the effectiveness of our method, we carried out experiments on the CompCars dataset too and compared the results with those of some state-of-the-art methods. The experimental results are shown in Table 2. Some methods use multi-stream CNN to better extract features. AV-CNN [25] uses VGG19 and AlexNet to fuse a dual branch CNN, which only achieves the lower Top-1 accuracy of 91.3%. Similarly, Cao et al. [26] deploys the baseline network with the following sub-CNNs, which combined vehicle viewpoint recognition and vehicle model recognition to form an end-to-end view-aware vehicle classification framework, and improved the Top-1 accuracy to 93.7%. Other methods think the key local features of vehicles were very important for fine-grained vehicle recognition, such as COOC [27] and ID-CNN [28]. COOC utilizes the learned high-rank features in deep networks with co-occurrence layer to obtain unsupervised part information, and achieved 95.6% of Top-1 accuracy, while ID-CNN proposed a selective multi-convolution region

Table 2. Comparison with some methods for VMR on the CompCars datasets.

Model	Backbone	Size	Top-1
AV-CNN	VGG16+AlexNet	224	91.3%
Gao et al.	ResNet-50	–	93.7%
Hu et al.	AlexNet	400	94.3%
CAM	ResNet50	224	95.3%
A^3M	ResNet50	448	95.4%
COOC	ResNet50	–	95.6%
DRATS [33]	NAS-based	–	95.9%
ID-CNN	VGG19	224	96.2%
VGG19	VGG19	224	93.9%
Ours	VGG-19	224	**96.9%**
Ours	VGG-19	448	**97.7%**

feature extraction network, which achieves the better 96.2% Top-1 accuracy. It is noted that our DRAM with the backbone of VGG19 achieved the 96.9% of Top-1 accuracy, higher than all methods listed in Table 2. Because our dual-rank attention fusion structure can fully mine the discriminative features of vehicle models and increase the richness of feature information without using any part annotation.

5 Conclusion

In the paper, we proposed a novel attention module DRAM for fine-grained VMR task, which includes two parts, LTRA and HFCA modules, inserted at the lower and higher level of the network, respectively. We embedded DRAM with VGG19, and demonstrate the effectiveness of our method. Experiments are carried out based both on CompCars and Stanford dataset. The experimental results demonstrate that our proposed method can achieve higher recognition accuracy than some state-of-the-art fine-grained VMR methods.

References

1. Yang, Z., et al.: Learning to navigate for fine-grained classification. In: ECCV, pp. 420–435 (2018)
2. Soon, F.C., et al.: PCANet-based convolutional neural network architecture for a vehicle model recognition system. IEEE Trans. Intell. Transp. Syst. **20**(2), 749–759 (2019)
3. Yang, L., et al.: A large-scale car dataset for fine-grained categorization and verification. In: CVPR (2015). https://doi.org/10.1109/CVPR.2015.7299023
4. Fu, J., et al.: Look closer to see better: recurrent attention convolutional neural network for fine-grained image recognition. In: CVPR (2017). https://doi.org/10.1109/CVPR.2017.476
5. Jonathan, K., et al.: 3D object representations for fine-grained categorization. In: 3DRR (2013)
6. Em, Y., et al.: Incorporating intra-class variance to fine-grained visual recognition. In: IEEE International Conference on Multimedia and Expo (ICME), vol. 1, pp. 1452–1457 (2017). https://doi.org/10.1109/ICME.2017.8019371
7. Hu, J., et al.: Squeeze-and-excitation networks. In: CVPR (2018)
8. Lin, Z., et al.: Space: unsupervised object-oriented scene representation via spatial attention and decomposition. arXiv preprint arXiv:2001.02407 (2020)
9. Yousong, Z., et al.: Attention CoupleNet: fully convolutional attention coupling network for object detection. IEEE Trans. Image Process. **28**(1), 113–126 (2018)
10. Heliang, Z., et al.: Learning multi-attention convolutional neural network for fine-grained image recognition. In: 2017 IEEE International Conference on Computer Vision (ICCV), pp. 5209–5217 (2017)
11. Bo, Z., et al.: Diversified visual attention networks for fine-grained object classification. IEEE Trans. Multimedia **19**(6), 1245–1256 (2017)
12. Yuanyi, Z., et al.: Toward end-to-end face recognition through alignment learning. IEEE Signal Process. Lett. **24**(8), 1213–1217 (2017)

13. Hao, L., et al.: STNReID: deep convolutional networks with pairwise spatial transformer networks for partial person re-identification. IEEE Trans. Multimedia **22**(11), 2905–2913 (2020)
14. Max, J., et al.: Spatial transformer networks. In: Advances in Neural Information Processing Systems, vol. 28, pp. 2017–2025 (2015)
15. Jiaqi, W., et al.: CARAFE: Content-Aware ReAssembly of FEatures. In: ICCV, pp. 3007–3016 (2019)
16. Jun, F., et al.: Dual attention network for scene segmentation. In: Proceedings of the IEEE/CVF Conference on Computer Vision and Pattern Recognition, pp. 3146–3154 (2020)
17. Lin, M., et al.: Network in network. arXiv preprint arXiv:1312.4400 (2013)
18. Ghassemi, S., et al.: Fine-grained vehicle classification using deep residual networks with multiscale attention windows. In: IEEE International Workshop on Multimedia Signal Processing, pp. 1–6 (2017)
19. Liu, X., et al.: Fully convolutional attention localization networks: efficient attention localization for fine-grained recognition. arXiv preprint arXiv:1603.06765, vol. 1, no. 2 (2016)
20. Ruyi, J., et al.: Attention convolutional binary neural tree for fine-grained visual categorization. In: CVPR, pp. 10468–10477 (2020)
21. Lin, W., et al.: Deep attention-based spatially recursive networks for fine-grained visual recognition. IEEE Trans. Cybern. **49**(5), 1791–1802 (2018)
22. Ye, Y., et al.: CAM: a fine-grained vehicle model recognition method based on visual attention model. Image Vis. Comput. **104**, 104027 (2020)
23. Dubey, A., et al.: Maximum-entropy fine grained classification. In: Advances in Neural Information Processing Systems, vol. 31, pp. 635–645 (2018)
24. Min, T., et al.: Fine-grained classification via hierarchical bilinear pooling with aggregated slack mask. IEEE Access **7**, 117944–117953 (2019)
25. Shijin, L.I., et al.: Research on fine-grain model recognition based on branch feedback convolution neural network. In: ICCSE, pp. 47–51 (2019)
26. Cao, J., et al.: End-to-end view-aware vehicle classification via progressive CNN learning. In: CCF Chinese Conference on Computer Vision, pp. 729–737 (2017)
27. Elkerdawy, S., Ray, N., Zhang, H.: Fine-grained vehicle classification with unsupervised parts co-occurrence learning. In: Leal-Taixé, L., Roth, S. (eds.) ECCV 2018. LNCS, vol. 11132, pp. 664–670. Springer, Cham (2019). https://doi.org/10.1007/978-3-030-11018-5_54
28. Yanling, T., et al.: Selective multi-convolutional region feature extraction based iterative discrimination CNN for fine-grained vehicle model recognition. In: International Conference on Pattern Recognition (ICPR), pp. 3279–3284 (2018)
29. Ye, Y., et al.: Embedding pose information for multiview vehicle model recognition. IEEE Trans. Circuits Syst. Video Technol. (TCSVT) (2022)
30. Changdong, Y., et al.: A method of enhancing data based on AT-PGGAN for fine-grained recognition of vehicle models. J. Image Graph. **25**(3), 593–604 (2020)
31. Ye, Y., et al.: A multilayer pyramid network based on learning for vehicle logo recognition. IEEE Trans. Intell. Transp. Syst. **22**(5), 3123–3134 (2021)
32. Ye, Y., et al.: Vehicle logo recognition based on overlapping enhanced patterns of oriented edge magnitudes. Comput. Electr. Eng. **71**, 273–283 (2018)
33. Tanveer, M., et al.: Fine-tuning DARTS for image classification. In: 2020 25th International Conference on Pattern Recognition (ICPR), pp. 4789–4796 (2021)
34. Zhang, Y., et al.: Bamboo: Building Mega-Scale Vision Dataset Continually with Human-Machine Synergy (2022)

Multi-view Geometry Distillation for Cloth-Changing Person ReID

Hanlei Yu[1,2], Bin Liu[1,2(✉)], Yan Lu[1,2], Qi Chu[1,2], and Nenghai Yu[1,2]

[1] School of Information Science and Technology,
University of Science and Technology of China, Hefei, China
{hanleiyu,luyan17}@mail.ustc.edu.cn, {flowice,qchu,ynh}@ustc.edu.cn
[2] Key Laboratory of Electromagnetic Space Information,
Chinese Academy of Science, Beijing, China

Abstract. Most person re-identification (ReID) methods aim at retrieving people with unchanged clothes. Meanwhile, fewer studies work on the cloth-inconsistency problem, which is more challenging but useful in the real intelligent surveillance scenario. We propose a novel method, named Multi-View Geometry Distillation (MVGD), taking advantage of 3D priors to explore cloth-unrelated multi-view human information. Specifically, a 3D Grouping Geometry Graph Convolution Network ($3DG^3$) is proposed to extract ReID-specific geometry representation from the 3D reconstructed body mesh, which encodes shape, pose, and other geometry patterns from the 3D perspective. Then, we design a 3D-Guided Appearance Learning scheme to extract more accurate part features. Furthermore, we also adopt a Multi-View Interactive Learning module (MVIL) to fuse the different types of features together and extract high-level multi-view geometry representation. Finally, these discriminative features are treated as the teacher to guide the backbone by the distillation mechanism for better representations. Extensive experiments on three popular cloth-changing ReID datasets demonstrate the effectiveness of our method. The proposed method brings 9% and 7.5% gains in average in terms of rank-1 and mAP metrics against the baseline, respectively.

Keywords: Person re-identification · 3D priors

1 Introduction

Person ReID is a task that retrieves the specific person under different camera views. Although this task is studied extensively, the majority of existing methods assume that pedestrians do not change their clothes and relate clothes with persons' identities. These methods tend to depend on clothes color and style consequently [5, 24, 30], which can be an issue when different pedestrians wear similar clothes, or the same person appears in unseen clothes.

© The Author(s), under exclusive license to Springer Nature Switzerland AG 2022
S. Yu et al. (Eds.): PRCV 2022, LNCS 13534, pp. 29–41, 2022.
https://doi.org/10.1007/978-3-031-18907-4_3

To tackle this problem, researchers pay more and more attention to the cloth-changing ReID task and are dedicated to extracting clothes-invariant features. Most cloth-changing ReID methods [3,7,10,13,19,24,30,33] extracted features from the 2D image domain directly. Chen *et al.* [2] tried to introduce 3D priors to learn the pedestrian cloth-invariant features. They proposed to learn the 3D shape feature for texture-insensitive person ReID by adding 3D body reconstruction as an auxiliary task, which pushes the feature to do multi-task learning, including the ReID metric and 3D body reconstruction simultaneously. Although their method achieved state-of-the-art performance because of the cloth-independent 3D priors, it suffered from a large task gap. Under that pipeline, the learned feature is guided to carry the reconstruction-specific 3D geometry information, which can benefit the 3D reconstruction task but is not suitable for the person retrieval problem.

In this paper, we propose a novel 3D-based method named Multi-View Geometry Distillation (MVGD) to bridge the task gap between 3D reconstruction and ReID task from two different but complementary aspects, as shown in Fig. 1.

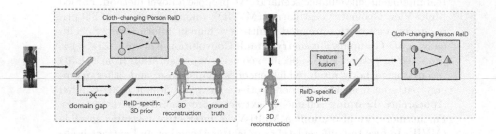

Fig. 1. Illustration of the difference between our algorithm and the existing cloth-invariant 3D shape feature learning methods. The existing method adopts multi-task learning, including ReID metric and 3D body reconstruction, which enforces the feature to carry the reconstruction-specific 3D priors, which is not suitable for the person retrieval problem, as depicted on the left. While our method focuses on filling the gap between 3D reconstruction and the ReID task to exploit ReID-specific 3D geometry information, as shown on the right.

We first try to narrow the task gap from the feature extraction view. The proposed method focuses on extracting features involved in the ReID-specific 3D representation. We utilize a pretrained body reconstructor to extract the 3D body mesh of person images. With the help of 3D body mesh, we propose a 3D Grouping Geometry Graph Convolution Network (3DG^3) to extract ReID-specific 3D geometry information encodes 3D patterns, *i.e.* shape, pose, and other geometry patterns in 3D space. Moreover, to align the 3D geometry information with 2D appearance features, we also project reconstruction mesh to 2D pixel coordinate to acquire both part locations and 2D pose information and develop a 3D-Guided Appearance Learning to extract fine-grained part appearance features. Every person is represented as a set of 3D ReID-specific part features and corresponding 2D fine-grained representations.

We further bridge the gap between the extracted 3D and 2D representations from the feature fusion view. A novel fusion module named Multi-View Interactive Learning (MVIL) is proposed to fuse the different types of features, including 2D appearance and 3D geometry feature, and extract high-level multi-view geometry representation for each person. Specifically, we first fuse the two types of features and construct a feature aggregation module based on the transformer methodology. It essentially propagates two kinds of information across different human body parts and fuses the 2D and 3D representations based on the high-level relationships between each body part. Finally, this powerful fused feature will propagate its richer and discriminative geometry and identity information back to the appearance stream, so we do not need to compute 3D information in the testing stage, reducing the inference cost and leading to solid representation.

In summary, our contributions are listed as follows: 1) We propose an end-to-end Multi-View Geometry Distillation framework (MVGD) to take advantage of 3D priors to solve cloth-changing person ReID task. 2) A 3D grouping geometry graph convolution network is presented to narrow the gap between the 3D reconstruction and the ReID task in the feature extraction aspect. Furthermore, we develop a 3D-guided method to learn fine-grained appearance features. 3) We introduce a multi-view interactive learning module to extract high-level multi-view geometry representation, which bridges the 3D gap in the feature fusion aspect. We evaluate our method on three widely-used cloth-changing ReID datasets, *i.e.* LTCC [24], VC-Clothes [30] and PRCC [33] and the experiment results demonstrate the effectiveness of our method.

2   Related Work

Cloth-Changing Person ReID. Many works studied the Person ReID problem [8,9,14,21,28,31,34], while few investigations have looked into the cloth-changing area so far. Among them, Gao *et al.* [7] used multi granular embedding to extract semantic information that is not sensitive to cloth change, Jin *et al.* [13] chose gait recognition as an auxiliary task to learn cloth-agnostic representation. Hong *et al.* [10] and Chen *et al.* [3] proposed a mutual learning framework and utilized contour feature learning as regularization to excavate shape-aware features.

3D Representation. Point Cloud is an essential geometric point set captured by 3D data acquisition devices, providing rich geometric, shape, and scale information. Current work in this subject can be classified into three categories [25], converting a point cloud to a regular grid [32], regarding a point cloud as a set [22,23], or treating it as a graph [25,26]. In this work, instead of treating the 3D reconstruction model as a point cloud, we regard it as the graph formulation. At the same time, every vertex is viewed as one node in the graph and uses graph convolution layers to compute the local feature (Fig. 2).

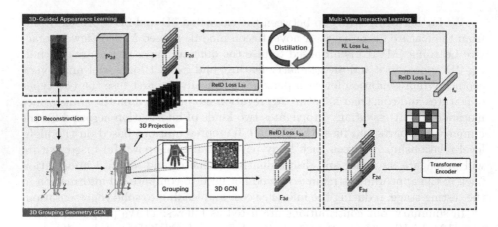

Fig. 2. Overview of our Multi-View Geometry Distillation Framework. Our network architecture takes images and the reconstructed 3D human mesh as input and outputs multi-view geometry representation.

3   Method

3.1   3D Grouping Geometry Graph Convolution Network

We choose the Skinned Multi-Person Linear model (SMPL) [20], a widely used parameterized model, to build the 3D human body. To achieve this goal, we use the SMPL oPtimization IN the loop (SPIN) [18] as our 3D reconstructor. We follow this work and pretrain this model on the large-scale 3D human pose estimation benchmark Human3.6M [12] to ensure high reconstruction quality.

The total SMPL mesh output, including 6890 vertices, is a graph structure by nature. It can be denoted as $\mathcal{M} = (\mathcal{V}, \mathcal{A})$, where $\mathcal{V}$ means the vertices and $\mathcal{A}$ is the adjacency matrix indicating the edge between each vertex. Although these dense vertices can provide more details, learning their features will lead to extreme computation cost requirements.

To tackle the accuracy-cost trade-off, we propose to extract part 3D features, which includes the shape and pose discriminative information but do not require a high computational cost. We first compute the joint coordinates[1] $\mathcal{J} = \{j_i\}_{i=1}^{13}$ by the SMPL regressor [20]. These joints provide us with skeleton positions and mark crucial human body parts. And then, each joint is combined with the fixed number of near-neighbor points to generate clusters by utilizing the ball query [23] method, which allocates points within a certain distance radius to each joint. After that, each joint is represented as $\mathcal{M}_i = (\mathcal{V}_i, \mathcal{A}_i)$, where i indicates the part index here. We then construct a group of part-specific feature extractors to compute the local 3D representations, respectively.

Each part-specific feature extractor aims to extract specific shapes and geometry structures of different parts. We view each point in one cluster as a graph

---

[1] Our 13 joints include head, shoulders, elbows, wrists, hips, knees, and ankles.

node and use a Graph Convolutional Network [17] to extract the relationships in each cluster and abstract the high-level multi-view geometry patterns for each joint. The n-th graph convolution layer in $3DG^3$ can be written as follows:

$$\mathcal{X}_i^{(n+1)} = \mathcal{D}_i^{\frac{1}{2}} \mathcal{A}_i \mathcal{D}_i^{\frac{1}{2}} \mathcal{X}_i^{(n)} \mathcal{W}_i^{(n)}, \tag{1}$$

where $\mathcal{D}_i$ is the i-th degree matrix computed on the part adjacency matrix $\mathcal{A}_i$. and $\mathcal{W}_i \in \mathbb{R}^{k \times l}$ is the weight matrix. $\mathcal{X}_i^{(n)}$ is input of the graph convolutional layer. Note that $\mathcal{X}_i^{(0)} = \mathcal{V}_i$. We define the final feature output as $F_{3d} = \{f_{3d}^i\}_{i=1}^{13}$. We concatenate all local 3D features as the 3D global feature f_{3d}^g and use classification and triplet losses [9] to form the 3D feature learning loss $\mathcal{L}_{3d}$:

$$\mathcal{L}_{3d} = \mathcal{L}_{cls}(f_{3d}^g) + \mathcal{L}_{tri}(f_{3d}^g).$$

$$\mathcal{L}_{cls}(f_{3d}^g) = -\sum_{i=1}^{N} g_j log p_j^{3d} \tag{2}$$

$$\mathcal{L}_{tri}(f_{3d}^g) = [d_{a,p} - d_{a,n} + \alpha]_+$$

For classification loss, p_j^{3d} is the probability of feature f_{3d}^g belonging to j-th class and g_j is the one-hot identity label. N is the class number. As for triplet loss, α is a margin, $d_{a,p}$ is the distance between a positive pair from the same identity, $d_{a,n}$ is the distance between a negative pair from a different identity.

After training, our 3D grouping geometry graph convolution network can learn to extract part features, including discriminative identity information.

3.2   3D-Guided Appearance Learning

This module aims to discover 2D part representation. For the given image, we first feed it into a typical image-based CNN to obtain feature maps m. We use a global average pooling operations to obtain the global appearance representation f_{2d}^g. Moreover, to get the local part appearance feature, we project 3D joint coordinates to 2D images and generate heatmaps h followed by a normal distribution with human pose prior. And then, we use that heatmap to mask out each part's features. The procedures is formulated in Eq. (3).

$$F_{2d} = \{f_{2d}^i\}_{i=1}^{13} = g(m \otimes h), \tag{3}$$

where $g(\cdot)$ is the average-pooling operation. This procedure can extract the fine-grained part features because of the accurate joint location. The fine-grained part can distinguish the human body from the background noise, leading to stronger robustness. To train those features well, we also use classification and triplet losses to form the appearance representation learning loss $\mathcal{L}_{2d}$:

$$\mathcal{L}_{2d} = \mathcal{L}_{cls}(f_{2d}^g) + \mathcal{L}_{tri}(f_{2d}^g). \tag{4}$$

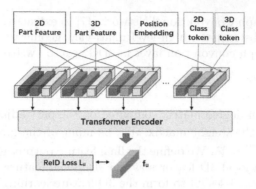

Fig. 3. The framework of feature level geometry interaction. Each input token is a feature set included the 2D part feature, the 3D part feature, and a learnable position encoding. A class token is prepended to the input tokens, and its final output is used as a global fused feature.

3.3 Multi-view Interactive Learning

Feature Level Interaction. We made several alters to adapt the transformer [29] to our task. Belonging to the transformer definition, we view each part as the input token of the transformer. For i-th token, we organize its feature as a feature set included the 2D part feature $f_{2d}^i \in R^{(d_{2d})}$ to provide richer pedestrian appearance information, the 3D part feature $f_{3d}^i \in R^{(d_{3d})}$ to introduce the geometry patterns and a learnable position encoding $p^i \in R^{(d_{2d}+d_{3d})}$ to indicate the part order. Given input tokens, we first compute the token feature vector by the following process:

$$r_i = \text{concat}(f_{2d}^i, f_{3d}^i) + p^i, \tag{5}$$

where $\text{concat}(\cdot, \cdot)$ means concatenate two input vectors in the channel-wise domain. The input token can be denoted as $\mathcal{R} = \{r_i\}_{i=0}^{13}$. Note that $i = 0$ represents the global token which is computed based on global features.

And except that, a class token is prepended to the input tokens to learn the fused feature. All these tokens are sent into a two-layer transformer module. We use multi-head attention [29] to further focus on more critical positions. The framework of one head interaction in our module is shown in Fig. 3. To train the fused representation f_u, We use classification and triplet losses to form the multi-view representation learning loss $\mathcal{L}_u$:

$$\mathcal{L}_u = \mathcal{L}_{cls}(f_u) + \mathcal{L}_{tri}(f_u). \tag{6}$$

Logit Level Interaction. As the multi-view feature f_u and the appearance feature f_{2d}^g for the same people should have similar prediction probabilities, we use Kullback Leibler (KL) Divergence to measure the similarity between the multi-view geometry representation and backbone classification distributions p_u and p_b. The p_b is based on the backbone features which is computed by $g(m)$, where $g(\cdot)$ and m are average-pooling and backbone feature maps respectively. The KL distance between p_x and p_y can be formulated as:

$$D_{KL}\left(p^x \parallel p^y\right) = \sum_{i=1}^{N} p_i^x log\frac{p_i^x}{p_i^y}, \tag{7}$$

To encourage 2D part representation learning more comprehensive knowledge from multi-view geometry representation, we minimize the knowledge distillation loss as:

$$\mathcal{L}_{kl} = D_{KL}\left(p^u \parallel p^b\right) + D_{KL}\left(p^b \parallel p^u\right). \tag{8}$$

3.4   Uncertainty-Aware Loss Function

The entire optimization process of our method can be treated as multi-task learning. The total loss function can be written as $\mathcal{L}_{ReID} = \sum_k w_k \cdot \mathcal{L}_k$. It is trivial to tune the loss weights for each task manually. So we propose to utilize the Uncertainty Multi-Task Learning [6,15] to adjust the weights dynamically. Specifically, it can control the balance of each task in each stage of the training. Our total loss function can be written as follow:

$$\begin{aligned}
\mathcal{L}_{ReID} = &\frac{1}{2\sigma_{3d}^2}\mathcal{L}_{3d} + \frac{1}{2\sigma_{2d}^2}\mathcal{L}_{2d} \\
&+ \frac{1}{2\sigma_u^2}\mathcal{L}_u + \frac{1}{2\sigma_{kl}^2}\mathcal{L}_{kl} + log\sigma_{3d} \\
&+ log\sigma_{2d} + log\sigma_u + log\sigma_{kl},
\end{aligned} \tag{9}$$

where σ denotes the model's observation noise parameter, which captures how much uncertainty we have in the outputs. Large scale value σ will decrease loss contribution, and the scale is regulated by the $log\sigma$ in case the extreme large σ.

4   Experiment

We evaluate our method on three banchmark cloth-changing ReID datasets: PRCC [33], LTCC [24], and VC-Clothes [30]. We adopt ResNet50 [8] pretrained on ImageNet [4] as backbone for our 2D appearance stream. The input images are resized to 256×128. The batch size is 64, with 16 identities and 4 samples for each person. The last spatial down-sampling operation in the backbone network is set to 1 followed [21,28]. Random horizontal flipping and random erasing [35] are used for data augmentation. The optimizer is Adam [16] with a warm-up strategy that linearly increases the learning rate from 3×10^{-5} to 3×10^{-4} in the first 10 epochs. We train for 120 epochs and decrease the learning rate by 10 at epoch 40 and 80.

Table 1. Performance on clothing change person ReID datasets. "R@k" denotes rank-k accuracy. "mAP" denotes mean average precision. "-" denotes unspecified. Performance is measured by (%).

Model	PRCC		LTCC		VC-Clothes	
	R@1	R@10	R@1	mAP	R@1	mAP
ResNet [8]	19.4	52.4	20.1	9.0	36.4	32.4
PCB [28]	22.9	61.2	23.5	10.0	62.0	62.2
SPT+SED [33]	34.4	77.3	-	-	-	-
SE+CEDS [24]	-	-	26.2	12.4	-	-
Part-aligned [30]	-	-	-	-	69.4	67.3
RCSANet [11]	48.6	50.2	-	-	-	-
MAC-DIM [3]	48.8	77.5	29.9	13	82.0	80.0
Chen *et al.* [2]	51.3	86.5	31.2	14.8	79.9	81.2
FSAM [10]	54.5	86.4	38.5	16.2	78.6	78.9
Baseline	45.6	76.0	27.1	11.1	73.4	70.8
Our Model	54.5	85.8	36.0	16.3	82.6	78.4

Table 2. Performance (%) comparison of combining different components in our method.

Methods	A	3DG^3	FLI	LLI	PRCC		LTCC		VC-Clothes	
					R@1	R@10	R@1	mAP	R@1	mAP
1	×	×	×	×	45.6	76.0	27.1	11.1	73.4	70.8
2	✓	×	×	×	47.5	79.2	29.4	14.1	75.6	74.0
3	✓	✓	×	×	50.0	77.6	33.7	15.3	78.4	74.6
4	✓	×	✓	×	50.6	79.7	30.9	14.5	77.8	75.2
5	✓	✓	✓	×	52.6	83.4	34.2	14.8	80.3	75.6
6	✓	✓	✓	✓	54.5	85.8	36.0	16.3	82.6	78.4

Table 3. Performance (%) comparison of the design of 2D part representation module.

Methods	PRCC		LTCC		VC-Clothes	
	R@1	R@10	R@1	mAP	R@1	mAP
A*	47.3	79.5	30.2	14.5	75.3	74.1
A	47.5	79.2	29.4	14.1	75.6	74.0
A* + 3DG^3 + MVIL	51.2	80.3	31.6	15.0	80.2	76.8
A + 3DG^3 + MVIL	54.5	85.8	36.0	16.3	82.6	78.4

Table 4. Performance (%) comparison of the design of 3D grouping geometry graph convolution network.

Methods	PRCC		LTCC		VC-Clothes	
	R@1	R@10	R@1	mAP	R@1	mAP
PointNet*	50.6	83.2	30.6	13.7	79.0	75.6
PointNet	51.3	84.5	33.4	15.5	80.1	76.0
GCN*	50.9	82.6	30.8	11.7	78.8	76.8
GCN	54.5	85.8	36.0	16.3	82.6	78.4

4.1 Comparison with State-of-the-Art

We compare our method with several competitors, including deep learning baselines, such as ResNet [8], state-of-the-art common ReID models, such as PCB [28], and state-of-the-art deep learning models on cloth-changing ReID. Our approach significantly exceeds [24,30,33], and surpasses all compared methods in rank-1 accuracy on VC-Clothes [30], and is comparable with FSAM [10] on PRCC [33] and LTCC [24] as shown in Table 1.

Note that our method outperforms the learning 3D shape method of Chen *et al.* [2] on all the three datasets in rank-1 accuracy by average 3.6% gains. Simultaneously, We get comparable even better results to FSAM [10] only distilling features at the final representation level, while FSAM is a more complex multi-scale distillation method, which proves our method's effectiveness. It inspired us that using multi-grained dense interactive may also improve our performance.

4.2 Comparison with Existing 3D Cloth-Changing ReID Method

Chen *et al.* [2] tried to introduce 3D priors by adding 3D body reconstruction as an auxiliary task. It pushes the feature to focus on the 3D reconstruction task rather than discriminative representation, which leads the feature to lose discriminative for accurate details reconstruction. While our Multi-View Geometry Distillation (MVGD) focuses on learning cloth-irrelevant 3D representation and fuses the 3D geometry features with the 2D corresponding information for better global features as illustrated in Fig. 1. Our method outperforms theirs on all the three datasets in rank-1 accuracy and to prove the negative influence of the task gap, we construct a 3D baseline following the original paper's Fig. 1(a). It extracts one single feature which can tackle identification and reconstruction tasks simultaneously. We use the same 3D body reconstructor to regress SMPL parameters as the training targets of the 3D reconstruction branch as the baseline for a fair comparison. The whole model achieves 43.9 rank-1 and 66.4 rank10 on PRCC. Note that this 3D baseline gets worse performance than only 2D features, proving the negative influence of the task gap. Our model reduces the task gap from the feature extraction and fusion aspects, focusing on extracting features involved in the ReID-specific 3D representation.

4.3 Ablation Study

We conduct a series of experiments to show the effectiveness of each component in our proposed MVGD, including the 3D-guided appearance learning (A), the 3D grouping geometry graph convolution network ($3DG^3$), and the multi-view geometry interaction (MVGI). We set ResNet50 and an average pooling as our baseline. As shown in Table 2, our proposed MVGD significantly outperforms the baseline model by 8.9%/8.9%/9.2% on PRCC [33]/LTCC [24]/VC-Clothes [30] in rank-1 accuracy respectively.

Effectiveness of the Appearance Stream. A denotes the 3D-guided appearance learning and 2nd row in Table 2 shows that A can improve performance by 1.9%/2.3%/2.2% on three datasets in rank-1 accuracy. Table 3 presents training results of two types of part features. A uses the method described in Sect. 3.2, and A* uses off-the-shelf human parsing model [1,27] to estimate keypoint heatmaps and get part joint features through an outer product and global average pooling operations on feature maps from Resnet50. We observe that although A achieves relatively low performance compared with A*, it improves integrating with $3DG^3$ and MVIL block, which shows that mapping 3D joint locations to 2D images can align 3D features with appearance features, compared with using estimated 2D heatmaps straightway. It also alleviates the computational cost of pose estimation.

Effectiveness of the 3D Grouping Geometry Graph Convolution Network. 3rd row in Table 2 represents the result of adding 3D grouping geometry graph convolution network with appearance stream, training ReID-specific 3D geometry feature described in Sect. 3.1. We also append a training loss on the concatenation of the 3D joint feature and corresponding image appearance to interact with the appearance feature. The backpropagation will influence both parts. Compared with 2nd row in Table 2, 3rd row achieves a 2.5%/4.3%/2.8% rank-1 improvement on three datasets. As for Table 4, PointNet* and GCN* stands for using only one single network to process all parts of human mesh, PointNet and GCN stands for using the individual network for each joint mesh. Both 1st & 2nd row and 3rd & 4th row confirms that multi-network outperforms single-network. As shown in 1st row and 3rd row, single PointNet, and GCN performed nearly, while multi-network can reveal the superiority of spreading information between points shown in 2nd row and 4th row.

Effectiveness of the Multi-view Geometry Interaction Block. 4th row in Table 2 feed the part appearance feature into transformer encoder layers and add training loss on the output global feature. It achieves a 3.1%/1.5%/2.2% rank-1 improvement on three datasets. By comparing 4th and 5th row, we can conclude that fuse 3D geometry feature with appearance feature and using transformer layers can propagate two kinds of information across different parts of the human body and fuse the 2D and 3D representations based on the high-level relationships between each body part, which achieves a 3.3% rank-1 improvement on LTCC [24]. The results of 5th and 6th row indicate that propagating the richer multi-view geometry and identity information back to the appearance network can help learn more accurate and discriminative features.

5   Conclusions

In this work, we have presented Multi-View Geometry Distillation (MVGD) to introduce 3D priors to explore ReID-specific human information for the cloth-changing ReID problem. The main technical contributions include introducing a 3D grouping geometry graph convolution network, 3D-guided appearance learning, and a multi-view interactive learning module (MVIL). The experimental results have demonstrated the effectiveness of our proposed method.

References

1. Cao, Z., Hidalgo, G., Simon, T., Wei, S.E., Sheikh, Y.: Openpose: realtime multi-person 2D pose estimation using part affinity fields. IEEE Trans. Pattern Anal. Mach. Intell. **43**(1), 172–186 (2019)
2. Chen, J., et al.: Learning 3D shape feature for texture-insensitive person re-identification. In: Proceedings of the IEEE/CVF Conference on Computer Vision and Pattern Recognition, pp. 8146–8155 (2021)
3. Chen, J., Zheng, W.S., Yang, Q., Meng, J., Hong, R., Tian, Q.: Deep shape-aware person re-identification for overcoming moderate clothing changes. IEEE Trans. Multimedia (2021)
4. Deng, J., Dong, W., Socher, R., Li, L.J., Li, K., Fei-Fei, L.: Imagenet: a large-scale hierarchical image database. In: 2009 IEEE Conference on Computer Vision and Pattern Recognition, pp. 248–255. IEEE (2009)
5. Fan, L., Li, T., Fang, R., Hristov, R., Yuan, Y., Katabi, D.: Learning longterm representations for person re-identification using radio signals. In: Proceedings of the IEEE/CVF Conference on Computer Vision and Pattern Recognition, pp. 10699–10709 (2020)
6. Gal, Y., Ghahramani, Z.: Dropout as a Bayesian approximation: representing model uncertainty in deep learning. In: International Conference on Machine Learning, pp. 1050–1059. PMLR (2016)
7. Gao, Z., Wei, H., Guan, W., Nie, W., Liu, M., Wang, M.: Multigranular visual-semantic embedding for cloth-changing person re-identification. arXiv preprint arXiv:2108.04527 (2021)
8. He, K., Zhang, X., Ren, S., Sun, J.: Deep residual learning for image recognition. In: Proceedings of the IEEE Conference on Computer Vision and Pattern Recognition, pp. 770–778 (2016)
9. Hermans, A., Beyer, L., Leibe, B.: In defense of the triplet loss for person re-identification. arXiv preprint arXiv:1703.07737 (2017)
10. Hong, P., Wu, T., Wu, A., Han, X., Zheng, W.S.: Fine-grained shape-appearance mutual learning for cloth-changing person re-identification. In: Proceedings of the IEEE/CVF Conference on Computer Vision and Pattern Recognition, pp. 10513–10522 (2021)
11. Huang, Y., Wu, Q., Xu, J., Zhong, Y., Zhang, Z.: Clothing status awareness for long-term person re-identification. In: Proceedings of the IEEE/CVF International Conference on Computer Vision (ICCV), pp. 11895–11904, October 2021

12. Ionescu, C., Papava, D., Olaru, V., Sminchisescu, C.: Human3.6M: large scale datasets and predictive methods for 3D human sensing in natural environments. IEEE Trans. Pattern Anal. Mach. Intell. **36**(7), 1325–1339 (2013)
13. Jin, X., et al.: Cloth-changing person re-identification from a single image with gait prediction and regularization. arXiv preprint arXiv:2103.15537 (2021)
14. Kalayeh, M.M., Basaran, E., Gökmen, M., Kamasak, M.E., Shah, M.: Human semantic parsing for person re-identification. In: Proceedings of the IEEE Conference on Computer Vision and Pattern Recognition, pp. 1062–1071 (2018)
15. Kendall, A., Gal, Y., Cipolla, R.: Multi-task learning using uncertainty to weigh losses for scene geometry and semantics. In: Proceedings of the IEEE Conference on Computer Vision and Pattern Recognition, pp. 7482–7491 (2018)
16. Kingma, D.P., Ba, J.: Adam: a method for stochastic optimization. arXiv preprint arXiv:1412.6980 (2014)
17. Kipf, T.N., Welling, M.: Semi-supervised classification with graph convolutional networks. arXiv preprint arXiv:1609.02907 (2016)
18. Kolotouros, N., Pavlakos, G., Black, M.J., Daniilidis, K.: Learning to reconstruct 3d human pose and shape via model-fitting in the loop. In: Proceedings of the IEEE/CVF International Conference on Computer Vision, pp. 2252–2261 (2019)
19. Li, Y.J., Weng, X., Kitani, K.M.: Learning shape representations for person re-identification under clothing change. In: Proceedings of the IEEE/CVF Winter Conference on Applications of Computer Vision, pp. 2432–2441 (2021)
20. Loper, M., Mahmood, N., Romero, J., Pons-Moll, G., Black, M.J.: SMPL: a skinned multi-person linear model. ACM Trans. Graph. (TOG) **34**(6), 1–16 (2015)
21. Luo, H., Gu, Y., Liao, X., Lai, S., Jiang, W.: Bag of tricks and a strong baseline for deep person re-identification. In: Proceedings of the IEEE/CVF Conference on Computer Vision and Pattern Recognition Workshops (2019)
22. Qi, C.R., Su, H., Mo, K., Guibas, L.J.: Pointnet: deep learning on point sets for 3D classification and segmentation. In: Proceedings of the IEEE Conference on Computer Vision and Pattern Recognition, pp. 652–660 (2017)
23. Qi, C.R., Yi, L., Su, H., Guibas, L.J.: Pointnet++: deep hierarchical feature learning on point sets in a metric space. arXiv preprint arXiv:1706.02413 (2017)
24. Qian, X., et al.: Long-term cloth-changing person re-identification. In: Proceedings of the Asian Conference on Computer Vision (2020)
25. Shi, W., Rajkumar, R.: Point-GNN: graph neural network for 3D object detection in a point cloud. In: Proceedings of the IEEE/CVF Conference on Computer Vision and Pattern Recognition, pp. 1711–1719 (2020)
26. Simonovsky, M., Komodakis, N.: Dynamic edge-conditioned filters in convolutional neural networks on graphs. In: Proceedings of the IEEE Conference on Computer Vision and Pattern Recognition, pp. 3693–3702 (2017)
27. Sun, K., Xiao, B., Liu, D., Wang, J.: Deep high-resolution representation learning for human pose estimation. In: Proceedings of the IEEE/CVF Conference on Computer Vision and Pattern Recognition, pp. 5693–5703 (2019)
28. Sun, Y., Zheng, L., Yang, Y., Tian, Q., Wang, S.: Beyond part models: person retrieval with refined part pooling (and a strong convolutional baseline). In: Proceedings of the European Conference on Computer Vision (ECCV), pp. 480–496 (2018)
29. Vaswani, A., et al.: Attention is all you need. In: Advances in Neural Information Processing Systems, pp. 5998–6008 (2017)
30. Wan, F., Wu, Y., Qian, X., Chen, Y., Fu, Y.: When person re-identification meets changing clothes. In: Proceedings of the IEEE/CVF Conference on Computer Vision and Pattern Recognition Workshops, pp. 830–831 (2020)

31. Wang, G., Yuan, Y., Chen, X., Li, J., Zhou, X.: Learning discriminative features with multiple granularities for person re-identification. In: Proceedings of the 26th ACM International Conference on Multimedia, pp. 274–282 (2018)
32. Yang, B., Luo, W., Urtasun, R.: Pixor: real-time 3D object detection from point clouds. In: Proceedings of the IEEE Conference on Computer Vision and Pattern Recognition, pp. 7652–7660 (2018)
33. Yang, Q., Wu, A., Zheng, W.S.: Person re-identification by contour sketch under moderate clothing change. IEEE Trans. Pattern Anal. Mach. Intell. **43**(6), 2029–2046 (2019)
34. Zheng, L., Huang, Y., Lu, H., Yang, Y.: Pose-invariant embedding for deep person re-identification. IEEE Trans. Image Process. **28**(9), 4500–4509 (2019)
35. Zhong, Z., Zheng, L., Kang, G., Li, S., Yang, Y.: Random erasing data augmentation. In: Proceedings of the AAAI Conference on Artificial Intelligence, vol. 34, pp. 13001–13008 (2020)

Triplet Ratio Loss for Robust Person Re-identification

Shuping Hu[1], Kan Wang[1,2], Jun Cheng[3], Huan Tan[1], and Jianxin Pang[1(✉)]

[1] UBTech Robotics Corp Ltd, Shenzhen, China
{shuping.hu,kan.wang,huan.tan,walton}@ubtrobot.com
[2] SIAT, Chinese Academy of Sciences, Beijing, China
[3] Institute for Infocomm Research, A*STAR, Singapore, Singapore
cheng_jun@i2r.a-star.edu.sg

Abstract. Triplet loss has been proven to be useful in the task of person re-identification (ReID). However, it has limitations due to the influence of large intra-pair variations and unreasonable gradients. In this paper, we propose a novel loss to reduce the influence of large intra-pair variations and improve optimization gradients via optimizing the ratio of intra-identity distance to inter-identity distance. As it also requires a triplet of pedestrian images, we call this new loss as triplet ratio loss. Experimental results on four widely used ReID benchmarks, i.e., Market-1501, DukeMTMC-ReID, CUHK03, and MSMT17, demonstrate that the triplet ratio loss outperforms the previous triplet loss.

Keywords: Person re-identification · Metric learning · Triplet ratio loss

1 Introduction

The goal of person re-identification (ReID) is to identify a person of interest using pedestrian images captured across disjoint camera views. Due to its widely deployment in real-world applications such as intelligent surveillance, ReID has become an important topic [6,12,14,32,33,37–39,42,48,52].

The key to robust ReID lies in high-quality pedestrian representations. However, due to the presence of detection errors, background occlusions and variations on poses, extracting discriminative pedestrian representations in ReID is still challenging [18,25,27,31,34]. Previous methods typically adopt two different strategies to improve the quality of pedestrian representations for ReID. The first strategy involves equipping the deep network with various modules to enhance the discriminative ability of extracted features [2,5,27,30,32]. In comparison, the second strategy leaves the network unchanged and designs loss function that directly optimizes the extracted features. Existing loss functions for ReID can be categorized into two groups: classification-based and distance-based loss functions [4,24,26,28,29], of which the triplet loss [24] is the most popular one. In brief, the triplet loss typically optimizes pedestrian features via maximizing the inter-identity distances and minimizing the intra-identity distances.

© The Author(s), under exclusive license to Springer Nature Switzerland AG 2022
S. Yu et al. (Eds.): PRCV 2022, LNCS 13534, pp. 42–54, 2022.
https://doi.org/10.1007/978-3-031-18907-4_4

(a)   (b)   (c)

Fig. 1. Illustration of intra-pair variations. The distance of the negative pair in (a) (b) (c) is moderate, small and large, respectively. The green boxes indicate the anchor and positive images while the red boxes denote the negative images. (Color figure online)

However, the triplet loss has two inherent problems. First, the quality of the pedestrian features optimized with triplet loss is heavily affected by intra-pair variations due to the fixed margin. More specifically, first, for the three triplets presented in Fig. 1, the distance of the negative pair is moderate, small and large, respectively. This means a reasonable margin for the triplet in Fig. 1(a) is inappropriate for triplets in both Fig. 1(b) and Fig. 1(c). This is because the triplet constraint becomes too tight or loose for the two triplets, respectively. Second, the distance of the negative pair is small for triplet in Fig. 1(b); therefore triplet loss might result in a collapsed ReID model when using an improper triplet sampling strategy. From the mathematical point of view [36], this is because the triplet loss only gives slight repelling gradient[1] for hard negative image while gives large attracting gradient (see footnote 1) for hard positive image. Therefore, the embeddings of all pedestrian images will shrink to the same point.

Given the above, it is induced that an effective loss function is needed to adjust the margin according to the respective triplet and provide more reasonable gradient during the training stage. Accordingly, in this paper, we propose a novel loss called, triple ratio loss.

First, different from the triplet loss which optimizes the "difference" between intra-identity distance and inter-identity distance, in brief, the proposed triplet ratio loss directly optimizes the "ratio" of the intra-identity distance to inter-identity distance. More specifically, for a triplet, the triplet ratio loss requires the "ratio" to be smaller than a pre-defined hyper-parameter. Based on the goals and the approach, we name it as "triplet ratio loss". Intuitively, as shown in Fig. 2(a), $\{A, P_0, N_0\}$ which denotes a triplet (A, P_0, N_0 represents the anchor, positive, negative image in the triplet, respectively) is active but hard to be optimized for triplet loss since the intra-identity distance is larger than the decision boundary (The left boundary of the red rectangle). Besides, $\{A, P_2, N_2\}$ has no contribution to triplet loss since the intra-identity distance is already smaller than the respective decision boundary. In comparison, as illustrated in Fig. 2(b), the proposed triplet ratio loss is able to relax the tight constraint for triplet $\{A, P_0, N_0\}$ and tighten the loose constraint for triplet $\{A, P_2, N_2\}$.

---

[1] Repelling gradient denotes the gradient that pushes the features away from each other, while attracting gradient indicates the gradient that pulls the features closer.

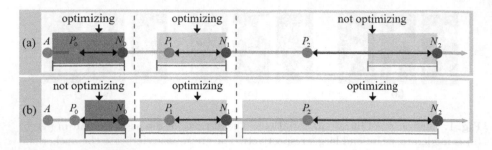

Fig. 2. During optimization, (a) For triplet loss, $\{A, P_0, N_0\}$ is active while $\{A, P_2, N_2\}$ has no contribution. (b) For triplet ratio loss, $\{A, P_2, N_2\}$ is adopted while $\{A, P_0, N_0\}$ is abandoned. The red/blue/green rectangle represents the region where positive samples need to be optimized with $N_0/N_1/N_2$. (Color figure online)

Second, the proposed triplet ratio loss improves the convergence of the ReID model. Compared with triplet loss, the triplet ratio loss drives the gradients of features in the same triplet to be adjusted adaptively in a more reasonable manner. More specifically, the triplet ratio loss adjusts the gradients for the anchor image, positive image and negative image considering both the inter-identity distance and intra-identity distance. Therefore, the triplet ratio loss gives larger repelling gradient for hard negative pair. Consequently, the proposed triplet ratio loss encourages the ReID model easier to converge and is able to prevent ReID models from shrinking to the same point [36].

The contributions of this work can be summarized as follows:

- We study the two problems that related to triplet loss for robust ReID: 1) intra-pair variations and 2) unreasonable gradients.
- We propose the triplet ratio loss to address aforementioned problems via optimizing the ratio of the intra-identity distance to inter-identity distance.
- Extensive experimental results on four widely used ReID benchmarks have demonstrated the effectiveness of the proposed triplet ratio loss.

2   Related Work

We divide existing deep learning-based ReID methods into two categories, i.e., deep feature learning or deep metric learning-based methods, according to the way adopted to improve pedestrian representations.

Deep Feature Learning-Based Methods. Methods within this category target on learning discriminative representations via designing powerful backbone. In particular, recent methods typically insert attention modules into the backbone model to enhance the representation power [2,5]. Besides, part-level representations that sequentially perform body part detection and part-level feature extraction have been proven to be effective for ReID, as the part features contain fine-grained information [27,30].

Deep Metric Learning-Based Methods. Methods within this category can be further categorized into two elemental learning paradigms, i.e., optimizing via class-level labels or pair-wise labels. Methods using class-level labels, e.g., the softmax loss [17,29,40], typically learn identity-relevant proxies to represent different identities of samples. In comparison, the methods based on pair-wise labels usually enhance the quality of pedestrian representations via explicitly optimizing the intra-identity and inter-identity distances [4,24,26,29]. As one of the most popular method that using pair-wise labels, the triplet loss [24] has been proven to be effective in enlarging the inter-identity distances and improving the intra-identity compactness.

However, triplet loss has three inherent limitations [10,24,36]. First, the performance of triplet loss is influenced by the triplet sampling strategy. Therefore, many attempts have been made to improve the triplet selection scheme [36,41], e.g., the distance-weighted sampling and correction. Second, the intra-identity features extracted by models are not sufficiently compact, which leads to the intra-pair variations. Accordingly, some methods [3,11] have been proposed to constraint the relative difference between the intra-identity distance and inter-identity distance, and push the negative pair away with a minimum distance. Third, the choice of the constant margin is also vital for the learning efficiency. More specifically, too large or too small value for the margin may lead to worse performance. To this end, subsequent methods was proposed to adjust the margin based on the property of each triplet [8,44]. However, these variants of triplet loss still methodically adopt the margin-based manner [3,8,11,44].

In comparison, the proposed triplet ratio loss introduce a novel ratio-based mechanism for optimization: optimizing the ratio of intra-identity distance to inter-identity distance. Therefore, the triplet ratio loss could adaptively adjust the margin according to respective triplet so as to weaken the influence of intra-pair variations. Besides, the optimization gradients are also improved to be more reasonable by the proposed triplet ratio loss; therefore the ReID model enjoys faster convergence and more compact convergence status.

3   Method

3.1   Triplet Loss

As one of the most popular loss function for ReID, the triplet loss [24] aims at improving the quality of pedestrian representations via maximizing the inter-identity distances and minimizing the intra-identity distances. More specifically, the triplet loss is formulated as follows:

$$\mathcal{L}_{\text{triplet}} = \sum_{a,p,n \in \mathcal{N}} \left[D\left(\mathbf{f}_i^a, \mathbf{f}_i^p\right) - D\left(\mathbf{f}_i^a, \mathbf{f}_i^n\right) + \alpha \right]_+. \tag{1}$$

Here α is the margin of the triplet constraint, and $\mathcal{N}$ indicates the set of sampled triplets. $\mathbf{f}_i^a$, $\mathbf{f}_i^p$, $\mathbf{f}_i^n$ represent the feature representations of the anchor image, positive image and negative image within a triplet, respectively. $D(\mathbf{x}, \mathbf{y}) = \parallel \mathbf{x} - \mathbf{y} \parallel_2^2$

represents the distance between embedding $\mathbf{x}$ and embedding $\mathbf{y}$. $[\cdot]_+ = \max(0, \cdot)$ denotes the hinge loss. During the optimization, the derivatives for each feature representations are computed as follows:

$$\frac{\partial \mathcal{L}_{\text{triplet}}}{\partial \mathbf{f}_i^a} = 2(\mathbf{f}_i^n - \mathbf{f}_i^p), \quad \frac{\partial \mathcal{L}_{\text{triplet}}}{\partial \mathbf{f}_i^p} = 2(\mathbf{f}_i^p - \mathbf{f}_i^a), \quad \frac{\partial \mathcal{L}_{\text{triplet}}}{\partial \mathbf{f}_i^n} = 2(\mathbf{f}_i^a - \mathbf{f}_i^n). \quad (2)$$

However, the triplet loss simply focuses on obtaining correct order for each sampled triplet, it therefore suffers from **large intra-pair variations** [26] and **unreasonable repelling gradient for $\mathbf{f}_i^n$** [36].

3.2 Triplet Ratio Loss

To address the aforementioned two drawbacks, we propose the triplet ratio loss which optimizes triplets from a novel perspective. In brief, the triplet ratio loss directly optimizes the "ratio" of the intra-identity distance to inter-identity distance. More specifically, the triplet ratio loss is formulated as:

$$\mathcal{L}_{\text{tri\_ratio}} = \sum_{a,p,n \in \mathcal{N}} \left[\frac{D\left(\mathbf{f}_i^a, \mathbf{f}_i^p\right)}{D\left(\mathbf{f}_i^a, \mathbf{f}_i^n\right)} - \beta \right]_+, \quad (3)$$

where $\beta \in (0, 1)$ is the hyper-parameter of the triplet ratio constraint.

During the optimization, the derivatives of the triplet ratio loss with respect to $\mathbf{f}_i^a$, $\mathbf{f}_i^p$, $\mathbf{f}_i^n$ are:

$$\frac{\partial \mathcal{L}_{\text{tri\_ratio}}}{\partial \mathbf{f}_i^a} = \frac{-2D\left(\mathbf{f}_i^a, \mathbf{f}_i^n\right) \cdot \left(\mathbf{f}_i^p - \mathbf{f}_i^a\right) - 2D\left(\mathbf{f}_i^a, \mathbf{f}_i^p\right) \cdot \left(\mathbf{f}_i^a - \mathbf{f}_i^n\right)}{\left[D\left(\mathbf{f}_i^a, \mathbf{f}_i^n\right)\right]^2},$$

$$\frac{\partial \mathcal{L}_{\text{tri\_ratio}}}{\partial \mathbf{f}_i^p} = \frac{2(\mathbf{f}_i^p - \mathbf{f}_i^a)}{D\left(\mathbf{f}_i^a, \mathbf{f}_i^n\right)}, \quad (4)$$

$$\frac{\partial \mathcal{L}_{\text{tri\_ratio}}}{\partial \mathbf{f}_i^n} = \frac{2D\left(\mathbf{f}_i^a, \mathbf{f}_i^p\right) \cdot \left(\mathbf{f}_i^a - \mathbf{f}_i^n\right)}{\left[D\left(\mathbf{f}_i^a, \mathbf{f}_i^n\right)\right]^2}.$$

- **Addressing the intra-pair variations.** Compared with triplet loss, the triplet ratio loss handles the intra-pair variations via adjusting the constraint for $\mathbf{f}_i^p$ according to $D\left(\mathbf{f}_i^a, \mathbf{f}_i^n\right)$. More specifically, first, the triplet ratio loss relatively relaxes the constraint on the intra-identity pair when $D\left(\mathbf{f}_i^a, \mathbf{f}_i^n\right)$ is small. Second, it encourages the constraint on the intra-identity pair to be tighter, when $D\left(\mathbf{f}_i^a, \mathbf{f}_i^n\right)$ is large. For example, when setting the value of α and β as 0.4[1], the constraint deployed on the intra-identity pair is adjustable for each triplet in triplet ratio loss, but rigid in triplet loss. More specifically, for the triplet in Fig. 1(b) where $D\left(\mathbf{f}_i^a, \mathbf{f}_i^n\right) = 0.5$, the triplet loss requires $D\left(\mathbf{f}_i^a, \mathbf{f}_i^p\right) \leq 0.1$; while the triplet ratio loss only requires $D\left(\mathbf{f}_i^a, \mathbf{f}_i^p\right) \leq 0.2$; therefore it **relaxes** the constraint on the intra-identity pair. Besides, for the triplet in Fig. 1(c) that $D\left(\mathbf{f}_i^a, \mathbf{f}_i^n\right) = 1$, the triplet ratio loss requires $D\left(\mathbf{f}_i^a, \mathbf{f}_i^p\right) \leq 0.4$. This constraint is **tightened** compared with that of triplet loss that requires $D\left(\mathbf{f}_i^a, \mathbf{f}_i^p\right) \leq 0.6$.

---

[1] 0.4 is an empirical value for both α [31] and β. Please refer to Sect. 4.2 for extensive evaluation on the value of β.

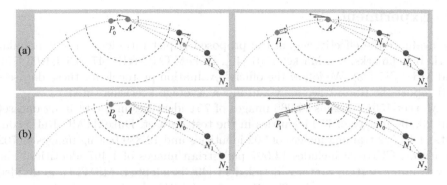

Fig. 3. Gradients for $\mathbf{f}_i^a$, $\mathbf{f}_i^p$, $\mathbf{f}_i^n$ when respectively using (a) Triplet loss and (b) Triplet ratio loss. The green/red dot denotes the positive/negative images. The red/blue/green dotted line denotes the decision boundary for positive sample with negative sample $N_0/N_1/N_2$. The red/blue/green arrows denote the gradients of $\mathbf{f}_i^a$, $\mathbf{f}_i^p$, $\mathbf{f}_i^n$ with negative sample $N_0/N_1/N_2$. (Color figure online)

- **Addressing the gradients issue.** During the training stage, the triplet ratio loss provides $\mathbf{f}_i^n$ a more reasonable repelling gradient. As illustrated in Eq. (4), the amplitude of repelling gradient for $\mathbf{f}_i^n$ is inversely related to $D\left(\mathbf{f}_i^a, \mathbf{f}_i^n\right)$. Therefore, as shown in Fig. 3, the amplitude of repelling gradient for $\mathbf{f}_i^n$ becomes reasonably significant when $D\left(\mathbf{f}_i^a, \mathbf{f}_i^n\right)$ is small, which is coherent to the intuition. In opposite, when $D\left(\mathbf{f}_i^a, \mathbf{f}_i^n\right)$ is large that has almost satisfied the optimization purpose, the repelling gradient for $\mathbf{f}_i^n$ becomes slight so that weak optimization is employed. This is intuitive since $\mathbf{f}_i^n$ does not need much optimization in this situation. However, the triplet loss assigns counter-intuitive repelling gradient for $\mathbf{f}_i^n$ as presented in Fig. 3.

Besides, the gradients for both $\mathbf{f}_i^n$ and $\mathbf{f}_i^p$ are also become more reasonable in triplet ratio loss. As illustrated in Eq. (4), gradient for $\mathbf{f}_i^n$ is determined by both $D\left(\mathbf{f}_i^a, \mathbf{f}_i^n\right)$ and $D\left(\mathbf{f}_i^a, \mathbf{f}_i^p\right)$, gradient for $\mathbf{f}_i^p$ is determined by $D\left(\mathbf{f}_i^a, \mathbf{f}_i^n\right)$. More specifically, first, the amplitude of gradient for $\mathbf{f}_i^n$ is proportional to $D\left(\mathbf{f}_i^a, \mathbf{f}_i^p\right)$. This means that the attention on $\mathbf{f}_i^n$ will not be significant if the intra-identity pedestrian images are similar to each other. Second, the amplitude of gradient for $\mathbf{f}_i^p$ is inversely proportional to $D\left(\mathbf{f}_i^a, \mathbf{f}_i^n\right)$. Therefore, a triplet where the pedestrian images in the inter-identity pair are obviously dissimilar will not put emphasis on optimizing $\mathbf{f}_i^p$.

During the training stage, the ReID model is optimized with both cross-entropy loss and triplet ratio loss, the overall objective function can be therefore written as follows:

$$\mathcal{L} = \mathcal{L}_{\text{CE}} + \lambda \mathcal{L}_{\text{tri\_ratio}}. \tag{5}$$

Here $\mathcal{L}_{\text{CE}}$ represents the cross-entropy loss, λ denotes the weight of triplet ratio loss and is empirically set to 1.

4 Experiment

We evaluate the effectiveness of the proposed triplet ratio loss on four popular ReID benchmarks, i.e., Market-1501 [45], DukeMTMC-reID [47], CUHK03 [16], and MSMT17 [35]. We follow the official evaluation protocols for these datasets and report the Rank-1 accuracy and mean Average Precision (mAP).

Market-1501 contains 12,936 images of 751 identities in the training dataset and 23,100 images of 750 identities in the test dataset. DukeMTMC-ReID consists of 16,522 training images of 702 identities and 19,889 testing images of 702 identities. CUHK03 includes 14,097 pedestrian images of 1,467 identities. The new training/testing protocol detailed in [49] is adopted. MSMT17 is divided into a training set containing 32,621 images of 1,041 identities, and a testing set comprising 93,820 images of 3,060 identities.

4.1 Implementation Details

Experiments are conducted using the PyTorch framework. During the training stage, both offline and online strategies are adopted for data augmentation [16]. The offline translation is adopted and each training set is enlarged by a factor of 5. Besides, the horizontal flipping and the random erasing [50] with a ratio of 0.5 are utilized. All images mentioned above are resized to 384×128.

ResNet50 [9] trained with only cross-entropy is used as the baseline. ImageNet is used for pretrain. In order to sample triplets for the triplet ratio loss, we set P to 6 and A to 8 to construct a batch (whose size is therefore 48). The value of β is set as 0.4 for CUHK03 and 0.7 for the other three datasets. The standard stochastic gradient descent (SGD) optimizer with a weight decay of 5×10^{-4} and momentum of 0.9 is utilized for model optimization. All the models are trained in an end-to-end fashion for 70 epochs. The learning rate is initially set to 0.01, then multiplied by 0.1 for every 20 epochs.

4.2 Impact of the Hyper-Parameter β

In this experiment, we evaluate the performance of triplet ratio loss with different value of β on Market-1501 and CUHK03-Label. The other experimental settings are consistently kept to facilitate the clean comparison.

From the experimental results illustrated in Fig. 4, we can make the following two observations. First, the performance of the triplet ratio loss tends to be better when the value of β increases; this is because a small value of β leads to too strict constraint on intra-identity distances. Second, the performance of the triplet ratio loss drops when the value of β further increase. This is because a large value of β brings loose constraints on intra-identity distances; therefore it harms the intra-identity compactness.

4.3 Triplet Ratio Loss vs. Triplet Loss

We show the superiority of the proposed triplet ratio loss over triplet loss by comparing them from both quantitative and qualitative perspectives.

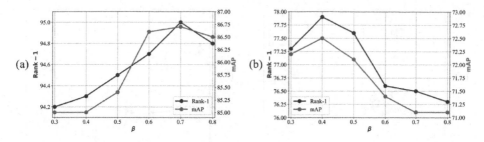

Fig. 4. The Rank-1 accuracy and mAP using different value of β on (a) Market-1501 dataset and (b) CUHK03-Label dataset.

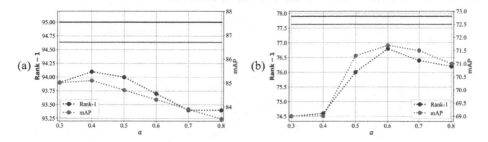

Fig. 5. The Rank-1 accuracy and mAP using different value of α on (a) Market-1501 dataset and (b) CUHK03-Label dataset. The blue and red solid lines denote the Rank-1 accuracy and mAP of using triplet ratio loss. (Color figure online)

Table 1. Evaluation of triplet ratio loss on ResNet50. R-1 in Table 1 and Table 2 denotes the Rank-1 accuracy.

Method	Market-1501		Duke		CUHK03-D		CUHK03-L		MSMT17	
	R-1	mAP	R-1	mAP	R-1	mAP	R-1	mAP	R-1	mAP
Baseline	91.6	81.1	84.6	71.2	63.2	59.1	67.9	63.0	68.3	41.4
w/ Triplet loss	94.1	85.1	86.8	73.5	74.1	68.3	76.8	71.7	75.4	51.4
w/ Triplet ratio loss	95.0	86.7	88.6	76.4	75.4	69.3	77.9	72.5	79.3	55.2

We compare the performance of triplet ratio loss with that of triplet loss under different value of α (the margin of triplet loss) in Fig. 5. It is concluded that the triplet ratio loss consistently outperforms triplet loss in both Rank-1 accuracy and mAP. For example, the triplet ratio loss beats the best performance of triplet loss by 0.9% in Rank-1 accuracy and 1.6% in mAP on Market-1501. The above experiments demonstrate the superiority of triplet ratio loss. Besides, the experimental results listed in Table 1 show that triplet ratio loss brings consistent performance improvement for the baseline: in particular, the Rank-1 accuracy is improved by 11.0% while mAP is also promoted by 13.8% on MSMT17. These experimental results verify the effectiveness of the proposed triplet ratio loss.

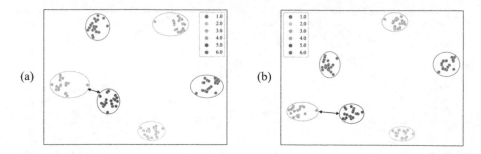

Fig. 6. Distribution of the pedestrian features extracted by ResNet-50 that trained respectively with (a) Triplet loss and (b) Triplet ratio loss.

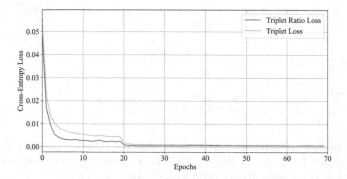

Fig. 7. The cross-entropy loss curves of the training process on Market-1501.

The conclusion is further supported by visualizing the features optimized by triplet ratio loss and triplet loss in Fig. 6, as well as the curves associated with the cross-entropy loss when adopting the two losses in Fig. 7. After assessing Fig. 6 and Fig. 7, we can make the following observations: first, the features optimized with triplet ratio loss are more compact than that learned using triplet loss; this indicates the triplet ratio loss is more effective on **addressing the intra-pair variations**. Second, the cross-entropy loss with triplet ratio loss converges faster than that with triplet loss. This is because triplet ratio loss improves optimization procedure via providing **more reasonable gradients**. The above analyses prove the superiority of triplet ratio loss.

4.4   Comparison with State-of-the-Art

We compare the proposed triplet ratio loss with state-of-the-art methods on Market-1501 [45], DukeMTMC-ReID [47], CUHK03 [16], and MSMT17 [35]. For fair comparison, we divide existing approaches into two categories, i.e., holistic feature-based (HF) methods and part feature-based (PF) methods.

Table 2. Performance comparisons on four popular benchmarks. "-" represents these results are not available.

Methods		Market-1501		Duke		CUHK03-D		CUHK03-L		MSMT17	
		R-1	mAP	R-1	mAP	R-1	mAP	R-1	mAP	R-1	mAP
PF	PCB+RPP [27]	93.8	81.6	83.3	69.2	63.7	57.5	-	-	78.2	52.5
	CASN (PCB) [46]	94.4	82.8	87.7	73.7	71.5	64.4	73.7	68.0	-	-
	Auto-ReID [22]	94.5	85.1	-	-	73.3	69.3	77.9	73.0	69.8	43.6
	MHN-6 (PCB) [1]	95.1	85.0	89.1	77.2	71.7	65.4	77.2	72.4	-	-
	BAT-net [7]	95.1	87.4	87.7	77.3	76.2	73.2	78.6	76.1	79.5	56.8
	MuDeep [21]	95.3	84.7	88.2	75.6	71.9	67.2	75.6	70.5	-	-
	MGN [30]	95.7	86.9	88.7	78.4	66.8	66.0	68.0	67.4	-	-
	DSA-reID [43]	95.7	87.6	86.2	74.3	78.2	73.1	78.9	75.2	-	-
HF	SFT [19]	93.4	82.7	86.9	73.2	-	-	68.2	62.4	73.6	47.6
	PGR [15]	93.9	77.2	83.6	66.0	-	-	-	-	66.0	37.9
	IANet [13]	94.4	83.1	87.1	73.4	-	-	-	-	75.5	46.8
	CAL [23]	94.5	87.0	87.2	76.4	-	-	-	-	79.5	56.2
	OSNet [51]	94.8	84.9	88.6	73.5	72.3	67.8	-	-	78.7	52.9
	3DSL [2]	95.0	87.3	88.2	76.1	-	-	-	-	-	-
	BDB-Cut [5]	95.3	86.7	89.0	76.0	76.4	73.5	79.4	76.7	-	-
	IDE*+AM-Softmax [29]	92.4	83.8	-	-	-	-	-	-	75.6	49.3
	IDE*+Soft‡+Tri† [20]	94.1	85.7	86.2	75.9	-	-	-	-	-	-
	IDE*+Circle loss [26]	94.2	84.9	-	-	-	-	-	-	76.3	50.2
	IDE*+Soft‡+Ratio	95.0	86.7	88.6	76.4	75.4	69.3	77.9	72.5	79.3	55.2
	IDE*+Soft‡+Ratio**	**95.8**	**93.6**	**91.6**	**88.7**	**83.7**	**83.9**	**85.8**	**85.6**	**83.5**	**71.3**

† Triplet loss   ‡ Softmax loss   * ResNet-50   ** Re-ranking [49]

After examining the results tabulated in Table 2, we can make the following observations. First, compared with the PF-based methods, equipping ResNet-50 with the proposed triplet ratio loss achieves comparative performance though PF-based methods extract fine-grained part-level representations. Second, equipping ResNet-50 with the proposed triplet ratio loss also achieves comparative performance when compared with the state-of-the-art HF-based methods. For example, the Rank-1 accuracy of our method is the same as that of 3DSL [2], a most recent method that requires additional 3D clues, with the mAP of our method is merely lower than that of 3DSL by 0.6% on Market-1501. Third, compared with works that explore loss functions for ReID, the proposed method achieves the best performance when using the same backbone for feature extraction. Specifically, the proposed triplet ratio loss outperforms Circle loss [26] by 3.0% and 5.0% in terms of the Rank-1 accuracy and mAP, respectively, on the MSMT17 benckmark. At last, the Re-ranking [49] further promotes the performance of triplet ratio loss: the triplet ratio loss finally achieve 95.8% and 93.6%, 91.6% and 88.7%, 83.7% and 83.9%, 85.8% and 85.6%, 83.5% and 71.3% in terms of the Rank-1 accuracy and mAP, respectively, on each dataset. The above comparisons justify the effectiveness of triplet ratio loss.

5 Conclusion

In this paper, we propose a novel triplet ratio loss to address two inherent problems: 1) heavily influenced by intra-pair variations and 2) unreasonable gradients, that associated with triplet loss. More specifically, first, the triplet ratio loss directly optimizes the ratio of intra-identity distance to inter-identity distance, therefore the margin between intra-identity distance and inter-identity distance could be adaptively adjusted according to respective triplet. Second, the triplet ratio loss adjusts the optimization gradients for embeddings considering both the inter-identity distances and intra-identity distances. The experimental results on four widely used ReID benchmarks have demonstrated the effectiveness and superiority of the proposed triplet ratio loss.

Acknowledgements. This work was supported in part by the National Natural Science Foundation of China under Grant U2013601, and the Program of Guangdong Provincial Key Laboratory of Robot Localization and Navigation Technology, under Grant 2020B121202011 and Key-Area Research and Development Program of Guangdong Province, China, under Grant 2019B010154003.

References

1. Chen, B., Deng, W., Hu, J.: Mixed high-order attention network for person re-identification. In: ICCV, pp. 371–381 (2019)
2. Chen, J., et al.: Learning 3D shape feature for texture-insensitive person re-identification. In: CVPR, pp. 8146–8155 (2021)
3. Cheng, D., Gong, Y., Zhou, S., Wang, J., Zheng, N.: Person re-identification by multi-channel parts-based CNN with improved triplet loss function. In: CVPR, pp. 1335–1344 (2016)
4. Chopra, S., Hadsell, R., LeCun, Y.: Learning a similarity metric discriminatively, with application to face verification. In: CVPR, pp. 539–546 (2005)
5. Dai, Z., Chen, M., Gu, X., Zhu, S., Tan, P.: Batch dropblock network for person re-identification and beyond. In: ICCV, pp. 3690–3700 (2019)
6. Ding, C., Wang, K., Wang, P., Tao, D.: Multi-task learning with coarse priors for robust part-aware person re-identification. TPAMI **44**(3), 1474–1488 (2022)
7. Fang, P., Zhou, J., Roy, S.K., Petersson, L., Harandi, M.: Bilinear attention networks for person retrieval. In: ICCV, pp. 8029–8038 (2019)
8. Ha, M.L., Blanz, V.: Deep ranking with adaptive margin triplet loss. arXiv preprint arXiv:2107.06187 (2021)
9. He, K., Zhang, X., Ren, S., Sun, J.: Deep residual learning for image recognition. In: CVPR, pp. 770–778 (2016)
10. Hermans, A., Beyer, L., Leibe, B.: In defense of the triplet loss for person re-identification. arXiv preprint arXiv:1703.07737 (2017)
11. Ho, K., Keuper, J., Pfreundt, F.J., Keuper, M.: Learning embeddings for image clustering: an empirical study of triplet loss approaches. In: ICPR, pp. 87–94 (2021)
12. Hou, R., Chang, H., Ma, B., Huang, R., Shan, S.: BiCnet-TKS: learning efficient spatial-temporal representation for video person re-identification. In: CVPR, pp. 2014–2023 (2021)

13. Hou, R., Ma, B., Chang, H., Gu, X., Shan, S., Chen, X.: Interaction-and-aggregation network for person re-identification. In: CVPR, pp. 9317–9326 (2019)
14. Huang, T., Qu, W., Zhang, J.: Continual representation learning via auto-weighted latent embeddings on person ReID. In: PRCV, pp. 593–605 (2021)
15. Li, J., Zhang, S., Tian, Q., Wang, M., Gao, W.: Pose-guided representation learning for person re-identification. TPAMI **44**(2), 622–635 (2022)
16. Li, W., Zhao, R., Xiao, T., Wang, X.: Deepreid: deep filter pairing neural network for person re-identification. In: CVPR, pp. 152–159 (2014)
17. Liu, W., Wen, Y., Yu, Z., Yang, M.: Large-margin softmax loss for convolutional neural networks. In: ICML, vol. 2, p. 7 (2016)
18. Liu, X., Yu, L., Lai, J.: Group re-identification based on single feature attention learning network (SFALN). In: PRCV, pp. 554–563 (2021)
19. Luo, C., Chen, Y., Wang, N., Zhang, Z.: Spectral feature transformation for person re-identification. In: ICCV, pp. 4975–4984 (2019)
20. Luo, H., Gu, Y., Liao, X., Lai, S., Jiang, W.: Bag of tricks and a strong baseline for deep person re-identification. In: CVPR W (2019)
21. Qian, X., Fu, Y., Xiang, T., Jiang, Y.G., Xue, X.: Leader-based multi-scale attention deep architecture for person re-identification. TPAMI **42**(2), 371–385 (2020)
22. Quan, R., Dong, X., Wu, Y., Zhu, L., Yang, Y.: Auto-ReID: searching for a part-aware convnet for person re-identification. In: ICCV, pp. 3749–3758 (2019)
23. Rao, Y., Chen, G., Lu, J., Zhou, J.: Counterfactual attention learning for fine-grained visual categorization and re-identification. In: ICCV, pp. 1025–1034 (2021)
24. Schroff, F., Kalenichenko, D., Philbin, J.: Facenet: a unified embedding for face recognition and clustering. In: CVPR, pp. 815–823 (2015)
25. Shu, X., Yuan, D., Liu, Q., Liu, J.: Adaptive weight part-based convolutional network for person re-identification. Multimedia Tools Appl. **79**, 23617–23632 (2020). https://doi.org/10.1007/s11042-020-09018-x
26. Sun, Y., et al.: Circle loss: a unified perspective of pair similarity optimization. In: CVPR, pp. 6398–6407 (2020)
27. Sun, Y., Zheng, L., Yang, Y., Tian, Q., Wang, S.: Beyond part models: person retrieval with refined part pooling (and a strong convolutional baseline). In: ECCV, pp. 480–496 (2018)
28. Tao, D., Guo, Y., Yu, B., Pang, J., Yu, Z.: Deep multi-view feature learning for person re-identification. TCSVT **28**(10), 2657–2666 (2017)
29. Wang, F., Xiang, X., Cheng, J., Yuille, A.L.: Normface: L2 hypersphere embedding for face verification. In: ACM MM, pp. 1041–1049 (2017)
30. Wang, G., Yuan, Y., Chen, X., Li, J., Zhou, X.: Learning discriminative features with multiple granularities for person re-identification. In: ACM MM, pp. 274–282 (2018)
31. Wang, K., Ding, C., Maybank, S.J., Tao, D.: CDPM: convolutional deformable part models for semantically aligned person re-identification. TIP **29**, 3416–3428 (2019)
32. Wang, K., Wang, P., Ding, C., Tao, D.: Batch coherence-driven network for part-aware person re-identification. TIP **30**, 3405–3418 (2021)
33. Wang, P., Ding, C., Shao, Z., Hong, Z., Zhang, S., Tao, D.: Quality-aware part models for occluded person re-identification. arXiv preprint arXiv:2201.00107 (2022)
34. Wang, W., Pei, W., Cao, Q., Liu, S., Lu, G., Tai, Y.W.: Push for center learning via orthogonalization and subspace masking for person re-identification. TIP **30**, 907–920 (2020)
35. Wei, L., Zhang, S., Gao, W., Tian, Q.: Person transfer GAN to bridge domain gap for person re-identification. In: CVPR, pp. 79–88 (2018)

36. Wu, C.Y., Manmatha, R., Smola, A.J., Krahenbuhl, P.: Sampling matters in deep embedding learning. In: ICCV, pp. 2840–2848 (2017)
37. Wu, Y., Lin, Y., Dong, X., Yan, Y., Ouyang, W., Yang, Y.: Exploit the unknown gradually: one-shot video-based person re-identification by stepwise learning. In: CVPR, pp. 5177–5186 (2018)
38. Ye, M., Lan, X., Leng, Q., Shen, J.: Cross-modality person re-identification via modality-aware collaborative ensemble learning. TIP **29**, 9387–9399 (2020)
39. Ye, M., Li, J., Ma, A.J., Zheng, L., Yuen, P.C.: Dynamic graph co-matching for unsupervised video-based person re-identification. TIP **28**(6), 2976–2990 (2019)
40. Yi, D., Lei, Z., Liao, S., Li, S.Z.: Learning face representation from scratch. arXiv preprint arXiv:1411.7923 (2014)
41. Yu, B., Liu, T., Gong, M., Ding, C., Tao, D.: Correcting the triplet selection bias for triplet loss. In: ECCV, pp. 71–87 (2018)
42. Yu, S., et al.: Multiple domain experts collaborative learning: multi-source domain generalization for person re-identification. arXiv preprint arXiv:2105.12355 (2021)
43. Zhang, Z., Lan, C., Zeng, W., Chen, Z.: Densely semantically aligned person re-identification. In: CVPR, pp. 667–676 (2019)
44. Zhao, X., Qi, H., Luo, R., Davis, L.: A weakly supervised adaptive triplet loss for deep metric learning. In: ICCV W (2019)
45. Zheng, L., Shen, L., Tian, L., Wang, S., Wang, J., Tian, Q.: Scalable person re-identification: a benchmark. In: ICCV, pp. 1116–1124 (2015)
46. Zheng, M., Karanam, S., Wu, Z., Radke, R.J.: Re-identification with consistent attentive siamese networks. In: CVPR, pp. 5735–5744 (2019)
47. Zheng, Z., Zheng, L., Yang, Y.: Unlabeled samples generated by GAN improve the person re-identification baseline in vitro. In: ICCV, pp. 3754–3762 (2017)
48. Zhong, Y., Wang, X., Zhang, S.: Robust partial matching for person search in the wild. In: CVPR, pp. 6827–6835 (2020)
49. Zhong, Z., Zheng, L., Cao, D., Li, S.: Re-ranking person re-identification with k-reciprocal encoding. In: CVPR, pp. 1318–1327 (2017)
50. Zhong, Z., Zheng, L., Kang, G., Li, S., Yang, Y.: Random erasing data augmentation. In: AAAI, pp. 13001–13008 (2020)
51. Zhou, K., Yang, Y., Cavallaro, A., Xiang, T.: Omni-scale feature learning for person re-identification. In: ICCV, pp. 3701–3711 (2019)
52. Zhou, Z., Li, Y., Gao, J., Xing, J., Li, L., Hu, W.: Anchor-free one-stage online multi-object tracking. In: PRCV, pp. 55–68 (2020)

TFAtrack: Temporal Feature Aggregation for UAV Tracking and a Unified Benchmark

Xiaowei Zhao🆔 and Youhua Zhang$^{(\boxtimes)}$🆔

Anhui Provincial Engineering Laboratory for Beidou Precision Agriculture Information, School of Information and Computer, Anhui Agricultural University, Hefei, China
zhangyh@ahau.edu.cn

Abstract. Research on object detection and tracking has achieved remarkable progress in recent years. Due to the superior viewing angle and maneuverability advantages of unmanned aerial vehicles (UAVs), the application of UAV-based tracking is also undergoing rapid development. But since the targets captured by UAVs are tiny and all have similarities and low recognition, this leads to the great challenge of multiple-object tracking (MOT). To solve the two problems mentioned above, We propose TFATracking, a comprehensive framework that fully exploits temporal context for UAV tracking. To further reflect the effectiveness of the algorithm and promote the development of UAV object tracking, we present a large-scale, high-diversity benchmark for short-term UAV multi-object tracking named T2UAV in this work. It contains 20 UAV-captured video sequences with a total number of frames over 12k and an average video length of over 600 frames. We conduct a comprehensive performance evaluation of 8 MOT algorithms on the dataset and present a detailed analysis. We will release the dataset for free academic use.

Keywords: UAV tracking · Benchmark datasets · Mutil-object tracking

1 Introduction

Multi-object tracking (MOT) is an indispensable long-term research direction of computer vision [1–3]. The primary purpose is to identify the object appearing in each video frame and mark the action trajectory. This task is widely use in security monitoring, action recognition, event video analysis, unmanned driving, and other fields. Due to the superiority of UAVs, the research on multi-object tracking based on UAV platforms has also attracted more and more attention, and bring great convenience to our life. There are two types of MOT algorithms, detection-based tracking [5,6] and trajectory prediction-based tracking [1,4]. Most tracking algorithms use tracking-by-detection. Use the object detection algorithm to detect the object of interest in each frame, obtain the corresponding position coordinates, classification, and confidence, and then associate the detection result with

S. Yu et al. (Eds.): PRCV 2022, LNCS 13534, pp. 55–66, 2022.
https://doi.org/10.1007/978-3-031-18907-4_5

the detection object in the previous frame to achieve object tracking. This kind of method improves the detection accuracy of the object. Still, it discards the temporal relationship between some adjacent frames in the process of object detection, making it difficult to achieve stable and reliable tracking results. Another problem is that in tracking tiny objects because the original reliable feature information of tiny objects is less, it is difficult for ordinary feature extraction backbone networks such as DLA to detect the position of the object accurately. In this work, we address the problem of multi-object UAV tracking and aim to answer the following two questions. How to design a suitable algorithm to enhance the feature representation of tiny objects and make full use of the video sequences for robust multi-object UAV tracking? How to create a video benchmark dataset to advance the research and development of multi-object UAV tracking?

We propose a new tracking method named TFAtrack to solve the first problem. The method is optimized based on the FairMOT algorithm. It replaces the original DLA backbone network with the YOLOv5 backbone network with the advantages of a multi-layer feature extraction network, multiple scale detection heads and inserts CBAM into it. And we fuse the image from the previous frame of the keyframe to solve the problem of insufficient available feature information for tiny objects and make full use of temporal feature information to achieve a more accurate tracking effect.

Second, most multi-object tracking datasets are video sequences shot from a horizontal perspective, leading to overlapping between objects and low viewing angles. These problems are more evident in tiny marks. The UAV can overcome these problems with its flexible maneuverability and superior extensive viewing angle range. So we collected 20 drone video sequences for multi-object tracking. The dataset contains most real-world challenges in multi-object UAV tracking tasks. More importantly, it contains multiple tiny objects in different real-world scenarios. The contributions of this paper are summarized as follows:

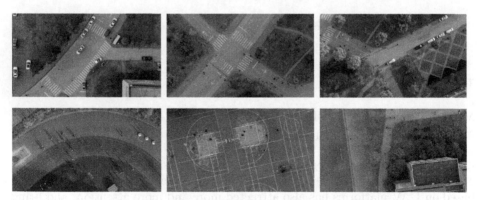

Fig. 1. Details of targets in different scenarios in our dataset.

- We propose a novel temporal feature aggregation tracking algorithm to deal with the problem of insufficient feature information caused by the tiny object in the process of image feature extraction.

- We integrate CBAM and YOLOv5 into our tracking algorithm, which can help the network to find the region of interest in images that have large region coverage.
- We create a unified benchmark dataset that contains most of the real-world challenges in multi-object UAV tracking.
- We carry out an extensive experiment to demonstrate the effectiveness of the proposed approaches.

2   Related Work

According to the relevance of our work, we review related works following three research areas, including tracking by detection,temporal-based tracking, and attention mechanism.

2.1   Tracking by Detection

With the rapid development of object detection [8–10] more and more tracking methods begin to use more powerful detectors to improve tracking performance. RetinaNet [11] is starting to be used by various tracking methods, such as [12]. Wang et al. [13] propose an MOT system that merges the appearance embedding model into a single detector so that the model can output detection results at the same time as the corresponding embedding. CornerNet [14] based on Anchor-free object detection algorithm, and CenterNet [9] removes inefficient and complex Anchors operations to enhance the detection effect of objects. CenterTrack is based on this to get a powerful tracking effect. JDE [13] learns the object detection and corresponding appearance embedding simultaneously from a shared backbone. The FairMOT [15] multi-object tracking algorithm proposed by Zhang et al. based on JDE solves the problem that the anchor generated by the Anchor-Based detector is not suitable for learning appropriate Re-ID information. And by applying the DLA-34 [16] backbone network to fuse multi-scale image features to combat the appearance change of the object due to motion, the tracking performance is better improved. At the same time, the extracted features are used for object detection and Re-ID pedestrian appearance feature extraction, which balances the detection branch and the Re-ID branch. And currently, since the backbone network of the YOLO series [8,10] has a good balance of accuracy and speed, it has also been widely used in the field of object tracking [13,17–19].

However, unlike object detection, when objects are tiny, and occlusion or motion blur occurs, the difficulty of concatenating object detection and matching each frame increases. They also cannot achieve global optimization. Therefore, combining the keyframes in the detection process with the object feature information of the previous frames is necessary.

2.2   Temporal-Based Tracking

In object tracking, the object needs to be continuously detected and tracked. Although this will bring various challenges, the persistence of time still brings us a lot of feature information before and after to ensure the object detection accuracy of the process, thus improving the tracking performance. Wang et al. propose [20], bridges individual video frames and explores the temporal context across them through a transformer architecture for robust object tracking. CTracker [21] enters the network through two frames and forms node pairs and then links each node pair into a complete trajectory according to the chain algorithm. FGFA [22] improves the motion blur, video out-of-focus, and other problems in the video and integrates the information of the front and rear frames to realize the object detection in the video. However, they give up applying Re-ID features while paying attention to the temporal context information to obtain a higher tracking speed, ignoring the tracking accuracy.

2.3 Attention Mechanism

Inspired by research on the direction of human vision and their ideas, the attention mechanism is proposed. In computer vision tasks, to let the network learn more concerning features, make the model pay attention to important information and the part of the information in the image to assist judgment and ignore irrelevant background information, etc., an attention mechanism is introduced. Its main categories are self-attention, soft attention, and intricate attention. After a lot of research, it has been proved that the attention mechanism is flexibly inserted into each part of the convolutional network. The calculation amount of the model is increased within a reasonable range so that the model can achieve better results. For example, the widely use SEnet [23] improves the representation ability of the model by enabling the network to dynamically modulate the weights of each channel, thereby recalibrating the features. The globally averaged pooled features are employed to compute channel-wise attention. The BAM [24] module passes two parallel channels of attention and spatial attention to produc the final 3D attention Force MAP. The CBAM [25] proposed by Woo et al. based on SEnet [23] concatenates channel attention and spatial attention along two independent dimensions and uses global average pooling and max pooling to obtain the attention map, Line-adaptive feature refinement. It is a lightweight generic module.

3   Overview

The proposed model is performed on FairMOT [26], an MOT tracker recently proposed by Zhang et al. is a variant of the end-to-end tracking algorithm. In this section, we first describe the inference process of FairMOT and then elaborate on the details of our proposed model.

3.1   Baseline Tracker

FairMOT adopts the idea of joint detection and tracking and further optimizes the problems existing in the JDE algorithm. For example, the anchors-based

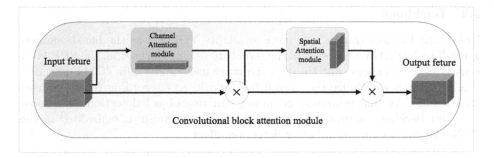

Fig. 2. The overview of CBAM module. Two sequential submodules are used to refine the feature map that goes through CBAM, residual paths are also used.

method is not friendly regarding Re-ID, and the anchor-free algorithm should be used. Multi-layer feature fusion can detect the object more accurately. Low-dimensional feature vectors should be used for the one-shot method when performing Re-ID. The CenterNet is used in the detection part, and Deepsort is use for tracking, but the two tasks are trained end-to-end. It also adds Deep Layer Aggregation (DLA) [16] through ResNet-34 [7] as the backbone network for object feature extraction and perform non-maximum suppression (NMS) according to the heatmap score to extract the most significant key points. It keeps the locations of key points with heatmap scores greater than a threshold (Fig. 3).

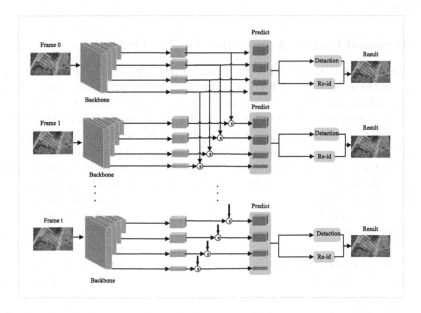

Fig. 3. Shows the overview of our Network structure. ⊗ represents the concatenate operation of the feature element.

3.2 Backbone

Unlike the baseline tracker, our method adopts YOLOv5 as the backbone network. The YOLOv5 series adopts the structure of CSPDarknet53, the SPP layer is used as the backbone, and the neck structure uses PANet and YOLO detection head. To further optimize the overall framework, and according to the characteristics of UAV images and its advantages in tiny object detection, we choose it as our backbone network. And the attention mechanism is embedded in the PANet of the neck to get a better detection effect.

3.3 Convolutional Block Attention Module

CBAM [25] is a simple but effective attention module. The structure is shown in Fig. 2. It has received extensive attention since it can be easily plugged into well-known CNN architectures with negligible overhead, and it can be trained in an end-to-end manner with better results. Given a feature map, CBAM derives an attention map along both channel and space dimensions and then multiplies the attention map with the input feature map for adaptive feature refinement. Large coverage areas often contain confusing geographic elements on images captured by drones. Utilizing CBAM can extract attention regions, which helps the YOLOv5 backbone resist confusing information and focus attention on useful objects. According to the experiments in this paper, after integrating CBAM into the PANet of the neck in the YOLOv5 backbone, the performance of the tracking method is greatly improved which proves the effectiveness of this attention module.

3.4 Temporal Feature Aggregation for Tracking

In this section, the detailed structure of our framework is shown in Fig. 4. We propose to further improve the detection and tracking performance of tiny objects by fusing the additional feature information of the temporal context while retaining the Re-ID operation on the fused features. We simultaneously send the image of the previous frame when we detect the keyframe. Same as the Siamese network [27], we use the same backbone network for feature extraction. Different from algorithms that utilize temporal context information for tracking, we fuse these temporal information before making predictions on the resulting features. This increases the effectiveness of tiny target features. Since the video content is presented in the form of frames, the difference of the same object in adjacent frames is insignificant. So we first extract feature information of different scales in the current and previous frames through the YOLOv5 backbone. We then use the concatenate operation to fuse the same scale features between the two frames. And then send them to the detection head of the YOLOv5 network for prediction. At the same time, the Re-ID method of FairMOT is retained, the fused feature information is used for feature Re-ID, and finally, the tracking result is obtained. This method solves the problem of insufficient feature information caused by tiny objects and realizes the optimization of identification between different object ids. It ensures that the temporal context information of the video frame is fully utilized. When the initial frame is detected, since it does not have the information of the previous frame, we fuse it with its features for prediction.

4 T2UAV Benchmark

Large-scale datasets are essential for tiny object tracking because they can be used to train trackers and evaluate different tracking algorithms. Based on this, we provide a large-scale tiny object UAV tracking benchmark called T2UAV. In this section, we will analyze it in detail.

4.1 Large-Scale Data Collection

Multi-object tracking video datasets collected by UAV are scarce in object tracking. This paper presents our T2UAV benchmark. Our dataset is used to take shots from the perspective of a UAV. The aim is to provide a large-scale and highly diverse multi-object tracking benchmark for real-world scenarios and challenges. To this end, we use drones to capture video data in a wide range of different scenes and complex object backgrounds. We have carefully selected environmental conditions to simulate practical applications, such as drone video surveillance, drones for traffic control, and other applications. Figure 1 shows a typical example of the T2UAV dataset where we can see the tracking of objects in different scenarios. We collected 20 video sequences using drones. The total number of video frames is 10912 frames, and the average video length is over 600 frames. We divided the dataset into a training set and a test set. Details are shown in Table 1.

Table 1. The details of our T2UAV benchmark.

Benchmark	Video	Min frames	Mean frames	Max frames	Total frames
T2UAV(train)	15	435	727	1619	10912
T2UAV(test)	5	126	386	712	1928

4.2 High-Quality Annotation

We use the smallest bounding box to represent the state of the object, including position and scale. Also, for labels with low visibility, missing and inaccurate labels may appear. We also had a professional inspector check the frame to ensure that the labels for each object accurately frame these tiny objects. For the convenience of training the dataset, the format of the annotation file is the same as MOT16 [28].

5   Experiments

The experiments are run on the computer with Intel(R) Xeon(R) Silver 4210 CPU (32G RAM), GeForce RTX 3090 GPU.

5.1   Evaluated Algorithms

We evaluate the most representative trackers on our benchmark. These trackers cover mainstream tracking algorithms, and they are DeepSort [1], JDE [13], MOTR [29], SORT [4], CenterTrack [5], Siam-MOT [27], FairMOT [26], and CTrack [30].

5.2   Evaluation Metrics

We employ widely used tracking evaluation metrics, including MOTA, MOTP, TP, FP, FN, Rcll, Fra, Pcn, for evaluating the performance of different trackers. Where FP (false positive) is the target error detection. FN (False Negatives) is the target of missed detection, while TP (true positive) indicates the correct target detected. Rcll (recall) is a measure The performance of the detector divided by the total number of correct targets detected in the detector. While Frag represents the total number of fragments in the video.

MOTA (Multiple Object Tracking Accuracy) is calculated according to FP and FN, representing the tracking accuracy and negatively correlated with the number of FN, FP, and ID, which is calculated as follows:

$$MOTA = 1 - \frac{\Sigma_t \left(FN_t + FP_t + IDSW_t \right)}{\Sigma_t GT_t} \tag{1}$$

where t is the index of each frame in the video, and GT is the number of ground truth objects we annotated in each frame. In our benchmark, the range of MOTA is expressed as a percentage $(-\infty, 100]$ of course, when the number of trackers exceeds the number of all objects, MOTA will also be negative.

MOTP (Multiple Object Tracking Precision) is the average dissimilarity between all true positives and their corresponding ground-truth objects, which is computed as:

$$MOTP = \frac{\Sigma_{t,i} d_{t,i}}{\Sigma_t c_t} \tag{2}$$

d is the average metric distance between the detected object and the annotated ground truth in all frames. The overlapping ratio of the bounding box is used to measure where the larger the MOTP is, and c is the number of successful matches in the current frame.

5.3   Overall Performance

We use some representative trackers to test the dataset to demonstrate the effectiveness of our training dataset and obtained the test results shown in Table 2. All the results are directly obtained from the official MOT Challenge evaluation server [31]. We can see that the tracking effect of the FairMOT algorithm is the best, with MOTA and MOTP reaching 58.891 and 66.949, respectively.

Table 2. Overview of T2UAV dataset training performance on different trackers. The best results are shown in bold.

Method	MOTA↑	MOTP↑	Rcll↑	Prcn↑	Frag↓	TP↑	FN↓	FP↓
SORT [4]	45.43	62.425	56.902	84.569	368	8051	6098	1469
MOTR [29]	46.576	62.755	49.565	85.156	477	7013	7136	**357**
Deep sort [1]	51.346	62.215	59.835	82.263	374	8466	5683	1128
Ctrack [30]	55.516	65.123	69.185	83.738	181	9789	6360	1901
Siam-MOT [27]	56.66	64.924	70.33	83.975	198	9951	4198	1099
JDE [13]	56.965	61.815	68.323	85.929	**124**	9667	4482	1583
Center track [5]	57.714	65.038	69.906	85.363	200	9891	4258	1696
FairMOT [26]	**58.891**	**66.949**	**76.041**	**88.819**	199	**10759**	**3390**	2232

Ablation Study. For the choice of the backbone network, we have tried many types, such as Resnet, DLA, and YOLOv5. We list the experimental results in Table 3. We can see that when we replace the backbone network with YOLOv5, the effect is significantly improved. MOTA and MOTP are 61.086 and 65.128, respectively. As is shown in Table 4, compared with the previous result, after we added CBAM modules to the detector heads in the YOLOv5 backbone network, MOTA and MOTP are improved by 62.216 and 66.56, the effect was significantly enhanced. And we also conducted ablation experiments on the method of Temporal Feature Aggregation (TFA), we can see that after adding the TFA, the MOTA and MOTP are increased to 63.644 and 67.412, respectively. These results prove the effectiveness of our proposed method.

Table 3. Evaluate different backbone networks on the dataset. The best results are shown in bold.

Backbone	MOTA↑	MOTP↑	Rcll↑	Prcn↑	Frag↓	TP↑	FN↓	FP↓
Resdcn_34	56.753	61.856	68.217	**85.796**	120	9652	4497	1598
DLA_34	58.891	**66.949**	76.041	82.819	199	**10759**	3390	2232
YOLOX	60.464	62.455	**87.997**	85.076	**88**	9055	5094	**469**
YOLOV5	**61.086**	65.128	75.723	84.256	208	10714	**3435**	2002

Table 4. Evaluating the effectiveness of the TFA method and the CBAM module. The best results are shown in bold.

Method	MOTA↑	MOTP↑	Rcll↑	Prcn↑	Frag↓	TP↑	FN↓	FP↓
YOLOV5+TFA	62.867	61.667	**75.659**	85.722	124	**10705**	3444	1783
YOLOV5+CBAM	62.216	66.56	77.221	84.104	188	10926	3223	2065
YOLOV5+TFA+CBAM	**63.644**	**67.412**	71.673	**86.142**	108	10141	**408**	1109

Visual Analysis. In order to further demonstrate our tracking performance, we show some visual inspection effects in Fig. 4. We can see that our method can still track accurately with smaller and denser objects.

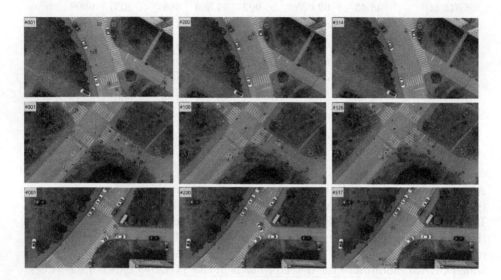

Fig. 4. Some visualization of detection results on test set of T2UAV.

6   Conclusion

We provide a high-quality bounding box annotation multi-object UAV tracking benchmark. And according to the characteristics of the object in the dataset, based on the FairMOT we also propose a simple and effective TFAtracking algorithm, which can significantly improve the tracking performance of the tracker on this dataset. Our large number of experiments on the dataset also proved the effectiveness of this method. And through the release of this dataset, I believe it will help the research of multi-object UAV tracking.

References

1. Wojke, N., et al.: Simple online and realtime tracking with a deep association metric. In: 2017 IEEE International Conference on Image Processing (ICIP), pp. 3645–3649 (2017)
2. Yu, F., et al.: POI: Multiple Object Tracking with High Performance Detection and Appearance Feature (2016)
3. Dicle, C., et al.: The way they move: tracking multiple targets with similar appearance. In: Proceedings of the IEEE International Conference on Computer Vision, pp. 2304–2311 (2013)
4. Bewley, A., et al.: Simple online and realtime tracking. In: 2016 IEEE International Conference on Image Processing (ICIP), pp. 3464–3468 (2016)

5. Zhou, X., Koltun, V., Krähenbühl, P.: Tracking objects as points. In: Vedaldi, A., Bischof, H., Brox, T., Frahm, J.-M. (eds.) ECCV 2020. LNCS, vol. 12349, pp. 474–490. Springer, Cham (2020). https://doi.org/10.1007/978-3-030-58548-8_28
6. Ha, Q., et al.: MFNet: towards real-time semantic segmentation for autonomous vehicles with multi-spectral scenes. In: International Conference on Intelligent Robots and Systems (IROS), pp. 5108–5115 (2017)
7. He, K., et al.: Deep residual learning for image recognition. In: Proceedings of the IEEE Conference on Computer Vision and Pattern Recognition, pp. 770–778 (2016)
8. Ge, Z., et al.: Yolox: exceeding yolo series in 2021. arXiv preprint arXiv:2107.08430pp (2021)
9. Duan, K., et al.: Centernet: keypoint triplets for object detection. In: Proceedings of the IEEE/CVF International Conference on Computer Vision (2019)
10. Redmon, J., et al.: Yolov3: an incremental improvement. arXiv preprint arXiv:1804.02767 (2018)
11. Lin, T.-Y., et al.: Focal loss for dense object detection. In: Proceedings of the IEEE International Conference on Computer Vision, pp. 2980–2988 (2017)
12. Lu, Z., et al.: Retinatrack: online single stage joint detection and tracking. In: Proceedings of the IEEE/CVF Conference on Computer Vision and Pattern Recognition, pp. 14668–14678 (2020)
13. Wang, Z., Zheng, L., Liu, Y., Li, Y., Wang, S.: Towards real-time multi-object tracking. In: Vedaldi, A., Bischof, H., Brox, T., Frahm, J.-M. (eds.) ECCV 2020. LNCS, vol. 12356, pp. 107–122. Springer, Cham (2020). https://doi.org/10.1007/978-3-030-58621-8_7
14. Law, H., et al.: Cornernet: detecting objects as paired keypoints. In: Proceedings of the European Conference on Computer Vision (ECCV), pp. 734–750 (2018)
15. Woo, S., et al.: Fairmot: on the fairness of detection and re-identification in multiple object tracking. Int. J. Comput. Vis. 1–19 (2021)
16. Yu, F., et al.: Deep layer aggregation. In: Proceedings of the IEEE Conference on Computer Vision and Pattern Recognition, pp. 2403–2412 (2018)
17. Liang, C., et al.: One More Check: Making "Fake Background" Be Tracked Again. arXiv preprint arXiv:2104.09441 (2021)
18. Chen, L., et al.: Real-time multiple people tracking with deeply learned candidate selection and person re-identification. In: 2018 IEEE International Conference on Multimedia and Expo (ICME), pp. 1–6 (2018)
19. Chu, P., et al.: Transmot: spatial-temporal graph transformer for multiple object tracking. arXiv preprint arXiv:2104.00194 (2021)
20. Wang, N., et al.: Transformer meets tracker: exploiting temporal context for robust visual tracking. In: Proceedings of the IEEE/CVF Conference on Computer Vision and Pattern Recognition, pp. 1571–1580 (2021)
21. Peng, J., et al.: Chained-tracker: chaining paired attentive regression results for end-to-end joint multiple-object detection and tracking. In: Vedaldi, A., Bischof, H., Brox, T., Frahm, J.-M. (eds.) ECCV 2020. LNCS, vol. 12349, pp. 145–161. Springer, Cham (2020). https://doi.org/10.1007/978-3-030-58548-8_9
22. Zhu, X., et al.: Flow-guided feature aggregation for video object detection. In: Proceedings of the IEEE International Conference on Computer Vision, pp. 408–417 (2017)
23. Hu, J., et al.: Squeeze-and-excitation networks. In: Proceedings of the IEEE Conference on Computer Vision and Pattern Recognition, pp. 7132–7141 (2018)
24. Park, J., et al.: Bam: bottleneck attention module. arXiv preprint arXiv:1807.06514 (2018)

25. Woo, S., et al.: Cbam: convolutional block attention module. In: Proceedings of the European Conference on Computer Vision (ECCV), pp. 3–19 (2018)
26. Zhang, Y., et al.: A simple baseline for multi-object tracking. arXiv preprint arXiv:2004.01888 (2020)
27. Shuai, B., et al.: SiamMOT: siamese multi-object tracking. In: Proceedings of the European Conference on Computer Vision (ECCV), pp. 12372–12382 (2021)
28. Milan, A., et al.: MOT16: A Benchmark for Multi-Object Tracking (2016)
29. Zeng, F., et al.: MOTR: End-to-End Multiple-Object Tracking with TRansformer. arXiv preprint arXiv:2105.03247 (2021)
30. Liang, C., et al.: Rethinking the competition between detection and ReID in multi-object tracking. arXiv preprint arXiv:2010.12138 (2020)
31. Bernardin, K.: Evaluating multiple object tracking performance: the clear mot metrics. EURASIP J. Image Video Process. 1–10 (2008)

Correlated Matching and Structure Learning for Unsupervised Domain Adaptation

Xingping Luo[1], Yuwu Lu[2(✉)], Jiajun Wen[1], and Zhihui Lai[1]

[1] College of Computer Science and Software Engineer, Shenzhen 518055, GD, China
[2] School of Software, South China Normal University, Guangzhou 510631, GD, China
luyuwu2008@163.com

Abstract. For cross-domain tasks in real-world, a source domain and a target domain often have different marginal probability distribution and conditional probability distribution. To leverage the distribution difference between the source and target domain, domain adaptation has been applied in many fields. Unfortunately, as most of the existing domain adaptation methods only focus on eliminating the distribution discrepancy between the two domains, they do not make full use of the correlation information and data distribution structure between the two domains. In this paper, we put forward a novel domain adaptation method named correlated matching and structure learning (CMSL), which considers the association information between source and target domains, and extracts the feature representation and thus can learn the maximization correlation features between the two domains. Simultaneously, the class centroids of the source data are used to cluster the target data, and a local manifold self-learning strategy is introduced to the target domain to preserve the underlying structure of the data. Experimental results on six data benchmarks show that our proposed method achieves good classification performance and outperforms several state-of-the-art unsupervised domain adaptation methods.

Keywords: Domain adaptation · Cross-domain learning · Correlated matching · Structure learning

1 Introduction

Most of traditional machine learning methods often need many labeled data to train an effective model and demand that both the training and test data satisfy the independent identically distribution. However, in real application scenarios, this assumption is usually not established. That is, the training and test data often have different feature distributions. Compared with the training data, the test data lack a lot of effective annotation information. Thus, to achieve high accuracy on the learning model, it needs to pay generous time cost and expensive labor cost. Therefore, people choose another strategy, namely transfer learning [1–6], to transfer useful knowledge from the source domain for solving the target tasks. Transfer learning makes full use of cross-domain information between the source and target domains to transfer knowledge effectively.

S. Yu et al. (Eds.): PRCV 2022, LNCS 13534, pp. 67–80, 2022.
https://doi.org/10.1007/978-3-031-18907-4_6

As an important branch of transfer learning, domain adaptation has attracted widely attention in recent years [7–11]. The main problem of domain adaptation is how to reduce the distribution discrepancy between the source and target domains. Recent research works [12–14] have focused on finding a shared latent space, where the difference of feature distribution can be minimized and the data structure information can be maintained as much as possible. For example, transfer component analysis (TCA) [7] is proposed to reduce the marginal distribution of the source and target domains by minimizing the maximum mean discrepancy (MMD) distance. Joint distribution adaptation (JDA) [8] takes into consideration of the fact that the conditional distribution between the source and target domains is distinct in the real scenarios and applies the conditional distribution based on the marginal distribution, and resorts the sufficient statistics of class-conditional distribution to replace the posterior conditional probability which is hard to obtain. On the basis of JDA, balanced distribution adaptation (BDA) [9] introduces different weight coefficients to the marginal distribution and conditional distribution for considering their different levels of importance. Furthermore, joint geometrical and statistical alignment (JGSA) [10] aims to reduce the distributional and geometrical divergence between the source and target domains by learning a pair of adaption matrices, respectively. Global-label-consistent classifier (GLCC) [11] takes the correlation and complementary information of multiple features into consideration when learning a common model.

In domain adaptation, it is equally important to maintain the intra structure of high dimensional data from the original feature space to the low dimensional feature space and to explore the maximum correlation between the source and target data. Making full use of the correlation information between the source and target domains for knowledge transfer would greatly benefit to domain adaptation. If the correlation information between the two domains can be effectively used for feature extraction, the learned feature representation would greatly improve the classification performance of the target data. Since canonical correlation analysis (CCA) [15] is an advanced and mature technology in multivariate data analysis, we expect to achieve better results if taking the advantage of this technology by extracting the maximum correlated features between the source and target domains. Thus, Wang et al. [16] proposed a canonical correlation discriminative learning (CCDL) method to make full use of the correlation information between two domains data. However, these domain adaptation methods cannot ensure to jointly obtain the maximum correlation in the shared latent feature space and preserve the structure information within the two domains.

In this paper, to jointly utilize the correlation information and data distribution structure of the data for unsupervised domain adaptation, we put forward a novel domain adaptation method named correlated matching and structure learning (CMSL), which combines local manifold structure, class discriminant information, and correlation learning together. Specifically, the most correlated features between the two domains are extracted to ensure that the useful features are transferred for the target tasks. Simultaneously, we preserve the structure information both in the source and target domains and match the class centroids between them to encode discriminant information of the data. Extensive experiments have been conducted on four data benchmarks. The results demonstrate the superior performance of CMSL.

The main contributions of the paper can be summarized as follows:

(1) A novel correlated matching and structure learning (CMSL) method is proposed for unsupervised domain adaptation, which considers the correlation information, local manifold information, and data structure distribution simultaneously.

(2) By utilizing a novel designed CCA regularization term, feature representations with the maximum correlation between the source and target domains are obtained. Besides, two specific Laplacian matrices in the source and target domains are designed to preserve the structure information in both domains as much as possible.

2 Method

The source domain data is $X_s \in R^{m \times n_s}$, which have the label $Y_s \in R^{n_s}$, the source data is sampled from marginal distribution $P(X_s)$, and we define the source domain as $\{x_{si}, y_{si}\}_{i=1}^{n_s}$. The target data $X_t \in R^{m \times n_t}$ is sampled from marginal distribution $P(X_t)$. We define the target domain as $\{x_{tj}\}_{j=1}^{n_t}$, where m is the feature dimension, n_s and n_t are the number of data samples from the source and target domains, respectively. Under normal circumstances, we assume that neither the source domain nor target domain has the same marginal probability distribution and conditional probability distribution. That is, $P(X_s) \neq P(X_t)$ and $Q(Y_s|X_s) \neq Q(Y_t|X_t)$. Specifically, this paper focuses on homogeneous unsupervised domain adaptation which means that the target data is without labels.

2.1 Formulation

Correlated matching and structure learning (CMSL) aims to learn the maximization correlated features from the source and target domains and reduce the domain discrepancies by preserving the structure information and matching the cluster centroids between them. The overall objective problem can be formulated as follows:

$$\min_{P, F, G_t, S} \Upsilon(P) + \alpha \Theta(P, F, G_t) + \Omega(P, F) + \gamma \Psi(P, S) + \beta \Phi(P). \tag{1}$$

The first term $\Upsilon(P)$ is proposed to obtain the maximization correlated features from the two domains. The second term $\Theta(P, F, G_t)$ aims to generate the class centroids in the target domain. The third term $\Omega(P, F)$ is used to match the class centroids between the source and target domains. $\Psi(P, S)$ is devoted to preserving the structure information in the domains. The last term $\Phi(P)$ is used to avoid trivial solutions. α, β, and γ are three hyper-parameters to balance each term in our method. We will introduce each term of the objective problem as follows.

It is proverbial that CCA is a powerful technique for finding the correlation between two sets of multidimensional variables. It makes use of two sets of the samples and projects them onto a lower-dimensional space in which the most correlated features are obtained. We apply the regularization term of CCA to maximize the correlation between the source domain and the target domain. And two constraints derived from CCA aims to improve the capability of generalization. Thus, we obtain the following formula:

$$\Upsilon(P) = ||P^T X_s - P^T X_t||_F^2,$$
$$\text{s.t. } P^T X_s X_s^T P = I_d, P^T X_t X_t^T P = I_d. \tag{2}$$

However, the numbers of the training samples from the source and target domains used in (2) must be the same, which limits the performance of domain adaptation. To overcome this limitation, we rewrite (2) as follows:

$$\Upsilon(P) = ||P^T X_s K_1 - P^T X_t K_2||_F^2,$$
$$\text{s.t. } P^T X_s X_s^T P = I_d, P^T X_t X_t^T P = I_d, \tag{3}$$

where $K_1 = [I_{n_s}, 0_{n_s \times n_t}], K_2 = [I_{n_t}, 0_{n_t \times n_s}], I_{n_s}$ and I_{n_t} are identity matrices.

We apply a simple but effective algorithm, K-means algorithm [17], to obtain the target cluster centroids of different classes. Then, we initialize the target data with the pseudo labels learned by the SVM classifier, which is trained in the source domain and then applied to the target domain to get the indicator matrix G. The core idea of K-means algorithm is trying to make the intra samples of different classes to be as close as possible after each iteration, which can be formulated as follows:

$$\Theta(P, F, G_t) = ||P^T X_t - F G_t^T||_F^2, \tag{4}$$

where $F \in R^{d \times C}$ is the class centroids matrix of the target data and $G_t \in R^{n_t \times C}$ is the indicator matrix, $G_{ij} = 1$ if the label of the sample is j, otherwise $G_{ij} = 0$.

To match the cluster centroids of the same class between the source and target domains in the common latent space and to obtain the class centroids of the source domain, we calculate the mean value of the samples with the same label in the source domain to represent each class centroid. We try to make the cluster centroids of the source and target data to be as close as possible by minimizing the Euclidean distance between them. This can be mathematically expressed as:

$$\Omega(P, F) = ||P^T X_s E_s - F||_F^2, \tag{5}$$

where $E_s \in R^{n_s \times C}$. The element of matrix E_s is defined as $(E_s)_{ij} = 1/n_s^j$ if the label of this sample is j, and n_s^j is the number of samples labeled j in the source domain.

Since local manifold self-learning is a promising technique to enhance the capability of the cluster centroids by exploiting the local manifold structure of data. Thus, we apply the adjacency matrix S of the low-dimensional space to capture the intrinsic local manifold structure of the target data, which can be formulated as follows:

$$\Psi_t(P, S) = \sum_{i,j=1}^{n_t} \left\| P^T x_{ti} - P^T x_{tj} \right\|_2^2 S_{ij} + \delta S_{ij}^2 = 2tr(P^T X_t L_t X_t^T P) + \delta ||S||_F^2,$$
$$\text{s.t. } S1_{n_t} = 1_{n_t}, 0 \leq S_{ij} \leq 1, \tag{6}$$

where S is the adjacency matrix and L_t is the Laplacian matrix in the target domain, which can be defined as $L_t = D - S$, and $D_{ii} = \sum_{j \neq i} S_{ij}$, otherwise, $D_{ij} = 0$.

We preserve the structure information in the source domain by minimizing the distance between each pair of samples in the common latent space and apply different weight coefficients in each class to balance the weight of different classes of samples. Thus, we have the following formula:

$$\Psi_s(P) = \sum_{i,j=1}^{n_s} \left\| P^T x_{si} - P^T x_{sj} \right\|_2^2 W_{ij} = 2tr(P^T X_s L_s X_s^T P), \tag{7}$$

where W_{ij} is the element of W, which is defined as $W_{ij} = \begin{cases} 1/n_s^c, & y_{si} = y_{sj} = c \\ 0, & \text{otherwise} \end{cases}$, and L_s is defined as:

$$(L_s)_{ij} = \begin{cases} 1 - 1/n_s^c, & \text{if } i = j \\ -1/n_s^c, & \text{if } i \neq j, y_{si} = y_{sj} = c \\ 0, & \text{otherwise} \end{cases} \tag{8}$$

By combining (6) and (7), we can obtain the following simplified formulation which aims to preserve the structure information in the source and target domains:

$$\Psi(P, S) = 2tr(P^T X_s L_s X_s^T P) + 2tr(P^T X_t L_t X_t^T P) + \delta \|S\|_F^2 = tr(P^T X L X^T P) + \delta \|S\|_F^2, \tag{9}$$
$$\text{s.t. } S1_{n_t} = 1_{n_t}, 0 \leq S_{ij} \leq 1,$$

where $X = [X_s, X_t] \in R^{m \times n}$, $n = n_s + n_t$, and $L = diag(2L_s, 2L_t)$. Then, we introduce the following regularization term of P to control the complexity of the model:

$$\Phi(P) = \|P\|_F^2. \tag{10}$$

By combining (3), (4), (5), (9) and (10), we obtain our objective function as

$$\min_{P,F,G_t,S} \left\| P^T X_s K_1 - P^T X_t K_2 \right\|_F^2 + \left\| P^T X_s E_s - F \right\|_F^2$$
$$+ \alpha \left\| P^T X_t - F G_t^T \right\|_F^2 + \beta \|P\|_F^2 + \gamma (tr(P^T X L X^T P) + \delta \|S\|_F^2), \tag{11}$$

s.t. $P^T X H X^T P = I_d, P^T X_s X_s^T P = I_d, P^T X_t X_t^T P = I_d, G_t \in \{0,1\}^{n_t \times C}, S1_{n_t} = 1_{n_t}, 0 \leq S_{ij} \leq 1$ where I_d is an identity matrix with dimension d. H is a centering matrix, which is calculated as $H = I_n - \frac{1}{n} 1_{n \times n}$. The first constraint in (11) is derived from principal component analysis (PCA). The second and the third constraints are inspired by CCA, which aims to make our model be more generalized and robust. We reformulate the objective function in a brief mathematical expression as follows:

$$\min_{P,F,G,S} \left\| P^T X_s K_1 - P^T X_t K_2 \right\|_F^2 + \left\| P^T X E - F \right\|_F^2$$
$$+ \alpha \left\| P^T X V - F G^T \right\|_F^2 + \beta \|P\|_F^2 + \gamma (tr(P^T X L X^T P) + \delta \|S\|_F^2), \tag{12}$$

s.t. $P^T X H X^T P = I_d, P^T X_s X_s^T P = I_d, P^T X_t X_t^T P = I_d, G \in \{0,1\}^{n \times C}, S1_{n_t} = 1_{n_t}, 0 \leq S_{ij} \leq 1$, where $V = diag(0_{n_s \times n_s}, I_{n_t})$, $E = [E_s; 0_{n_t \times C}]$, $G = [0_{n_s \times C}; G_t]$, and $L = diag(L_s, L_t)$.

2.2 Optimization

There are total four variables F, P, G, and S in our objective function. The objective function is convex in each variable while holding the other three variables fixed, but not convex simultaneously. For this reason, we iteratively optimize the objective function by alternatingly optimize each variable while holding the remaining variables fixed.

The objective function can be split into the following sub-problems:

(1) Update F: We fix P, G, and S in the objective function and obtain the following equation related to F:

$$\min_F \left\| P^T XE - F \right\|_F^2 + \alpha \left\| P^T XV - FG^T \right\|_F^2. \tag{13}$$

Taking the derivation of F and make it to be zero, we can obtain the following expression:

$$F = (P^T XE + \alpha P^T XVG)(\alpha G^T G + I_C)^{-1}. \tag{14}$$

(2) Update P: With F, G, and S fixed and substitute (14) into (12) to replace F, the sub-problem can be reformulated briefly as below equation:

$$\min_P tr(P^T (X_s X_s^T - X_s K_1 K_2^T X_t^T - X_t K_2 K_1^T X_s^T + X_t X_t^T + XRX^T + \gamma XLX^T + \beta I_m)P),$$
$$\text{s.t. } P^T XHX^T P = I_d, P^T X_s X_s^T P = I_d, P^T X_t X_t^T P = I_d, \tag{15}$$

where

$$R = EE^T - E(\alpha G^T G + I_C)^{-1}(E + \alpha VG)^T + \alpha VV^T - \alpha VG(\alpha GG^T + I_C)^{-1}(E + \alpha VG)^T.$$

However, we cannot choose any classical linear strategies to solve the sub-problem (15) for the reason is that (15) is a nonlinear optimization problem. Then we apply Lagrangian multiplier method and (15) can be reformulated as follows:

$$tr(P^T (X_s K_1 K_1^T X_s^T - X_s K_1 K_2^T X_t^T - X_t K_2 K_1^T X_s^T$$
$$+X_t K_2 K_2^T X_t^T + XRX^T + \gamma XLX^T + \beta I_m)P) \tag{16}$$
$$+tr((I_d - P^T X_s X_s^T P + I_d - P^T X_t X_t^T P + I_d - P^T XHX^T P)\Pi),$$

where $\Pi = diag(\Pi_1, \Pi_2, ..., \Pi_d) \in R^{d \times d}$ is the Lagrange multiplier. By setting the derivative of (16) with respect to P as zero, we have:

$$(X_s K_1 K_1^T X_s^T - X_s K_1 K_2^T X_t^T - X_t K_2 K_1^T X_s^T + X_t K_2 K_2^T X_t^T + XRX^T + \gamma XLX^T + \beta I_m)P$$
$$= (X_s X_s^T + X_t X_t^T + XHX^T)P\Pi. \tag{17}$$

Then the adaptation matrix P can be obtained by calculating the above equation, and P is consisted of d-smallest eigenvectors of (17).

(3) Update G: When we fixed F, P, and S, the optimization of G-sub-problem can be transformed to optimize G_t. As we obtain the cluster centroids of the target data F, we update the label of each sample in the target domain by calculating the Euclidean distance between samples projected in the latent space and then the nearest class cluster centroid will be selected. This can be expressed in the following mathematical form:

$$(G_t)_{ik} = \begin{cases} 1, k = \arg\min_j \left\| P^T x_{ti} - F(:, j) \right\|_2^2 \\ 0, otherwise \end{cases}. \tag{18}$$

(4) Update S: According to [18], the optimization problem regard to S can be split into n_t sub-problems with fixed F, P, and G. Then the optimization problem can be defined as follows:

$$\min_{S_{i,:}1_{n_t}=1,0\leq S_{ij}\leq 1} \sum_{j=1}^{n_t} \left\| P^T x_{ti} - P^T x_{tj} \right\|_2^2 S_{ij} + \delta S_{ij}^2. \tag{19}$$

(19) can be rewritten as follows:

$$\min_{S_{i,:}1_{n_t}=1,0\leq S_{ij}\leq 1} \left\| S_{i,:} + \frac{A_{i,:}}{2\delta} \right\|_2^2, \tag{20}$$

where $A_{i,:}$ is the i-th row of A, $A_{ij} = \left\| P^T x_{ti} - P^T x_{tj} \right\|_2^2$, $S_{i,:}$ is the i-th row of S, and δ is a hyper-parameter.

We apply the Lagrange multiplier method to solve the nonlinear Eq. (20). And we have:

$$\min_{S_{i,:}} \left\| S_{i,:} + \frac{A_{i,:}}{2\delta} \right\|_2^2 - \mu(S_{i,:}1_{n_t} - 1) - S_{i,:}\eta^T, \tag{21}$$

where μ is a Lagrange scale coefficient and 1_{n_t} is a column vector with all elements are 1. We can obtain S_{ij} in a closed form as follows:

$$S_{ij} = \max(z - \frac{A_{ij}}{2\delta}, 0), z = \frac{1}{k} + \frac{1}{2k\delta} \sum_{j=1}^{k} \tilde{A}_{ij}. \tag{22}$$

$\tilde{A}$ is obtained by sorting the elements of each row of A in a form small to large. $\tilde{A}_{ij}$ is the element of $\tilde{A}$. According to [19], δ can be obtained by calculating the following equation.

$$\delta = \frac{1}{n_t} \sum_{i=1}^{n_t} (\frac{k}{2} \tilde{B}_{i,k+1} - \frac{1}{2} \sum_{j=1}^{k} \tilde{B}_{ij}), \tag{23}$$

where $\tilde{B}_{ij}$ is the entry of $\tilde{B}$, which is obtained by sorting the elements of each row of B. B is obtained by calculating the distance between the samples in the original space. That is, $B_{ij} = \left\| x_{ti} - x_{tj} \right\|_2^2$. The complete CMSL procedure is presented in Algorithm 1.

3 Experimental Results

To verify the performance of our method, we selected several state-of-the-art approaches for comparison, including nearest neighbor (NN), TCA [7], JDA [8], BDA [9], JGSA [10], geodesic flow kernel (GFK) [20], domain invariant and class discriminative (DICD) [21], centroid matching and local manifold self-learning (CMMS) [18], easy transfer learning (EasyTL) [22].

Algorithm 1 CMSL

Input: Source data $\{X_s, Y_s\}$; target data $\{X_t\}$; initialize the target label matrix G_t with a linear SVM classifier and the initial adjacency matrix S is obtained by solving (27); hyper-parameters α, β, γ; subspace dimensionality d; neighborhood size k; iterations T.

Output: Target label matrix G_t

1 t=1
2 **While** $t \leq T$ do
3 Obtain matrix P by solving the generalized eigenvalue problem and get d smallest eigenvectors in (17)
4 Obtain F by calculating eq. (14)
5 Obtain G_t by eq. (18)
6 Obtain each row of S by solving eq. (22)
7 t=t+1
End
Return Target label matrix G_t

3.1 Datasets and Parameter Setting

Office31 [23] consists of three subsets, which are Amazon (A), DSLR (D), and Webcam (W). These three subsets have 2,817, 498, and 795 samples, respectively. The feature dimensions of each sample is 4,096. There are 31 common classes in total. In our experiment, we construct six cross-domain classification tasks, i.e., "A → D", "A → W", ..., and "W → D".

Office-Caltech10 [12] contains 2,531 images in total with four domains: Amazon (A), Caltech (C), DSLR (D), and Webcam (W). There are 958 image samples in Amazon subset, 1,123 samples in Caltech, 157 samples in DSLR, and 295 samples in Webcam. These four subsets share 10 common classes. We conducted our experiment on the Office-Caltech10 dataset with 800 dimensional features. Thus, twelve cross-domain tasks are constructed as follows: "A → C", "A → D", ..., and "W → D".

Amazon Review [24] is a sentiment analysis dataset consisting of four categories: Kitchen appliance (K), DVDs (D), Electronics (E), and Books (B). Each category contains the consumers' reviews about the products collected from the Amazon website and the corresponding positive or negative evaluations. Thus, 12 cross-domain emotion classification tasks are obtained, i.e., "B → D", "B → E", ..., and "K → E".

COIL20[1] is a dataset containing 1,440 grayscale images and each image pixel size is 32 × 32. There are 20 different objects and each object has 72 pictures as each object rotates 360° horizontally. In our experiment, we follow the setting in [10] and split the dataset into two subsets: COIL1 and COIL2. COIL1 contains the images at the directions of [0°, 85°] ∪ [180°, 265°] and COIL2 contains the images at the directions of [90°, 175°] ∪ [270°, 355°]. Therefore, two cross-domain tasks are obtained, i.e., "C1 → C2" and "C2 → C1".

The data we obtained are labeled source data and unlabeled target data and thus the cross-validation method cannot be performed on our experiments to find the optimal parameters. The experimental results in comparing methods are cited from the original papers or run the codes are implemented provided by the authors. For TCA, GFK, JDA, BDA, DICD, JGSA, CMMS, we search for $d = \{10, 20, ..., 100\}$ to find their optimal dimension of their common subspace. The best value of regularization parameter for projection is searched in the range of $\{0.01, 0.02, 0.05, 0.1, 0.2, 0.5, 1.0\}$. For the other methods, we adopt the default parameters used in their public codes or follow the procedures for tuning parameters according to the corresponding original papers. In our method, we fixed $d = 100$, $k = 10$, and leaving α, β, and γ tunable. The regularization parameter β is searched in the range of $[0.1, 0.5, 0.6, 1, 100, 1000, 10000]$, and the parameters α and γ are searched in the range of $[0.001, 0.002, 0.01, 0.1, 0.5, 10, 100]$ and $[10, 100, 1000, 10000, 100000, 900000][10, 100, 1000, 10000, 100000, 900000]$, respectively.

3.2 Results

The classification accuracy on the Amazon review and COIL20 datasets is shown in Table 1 and we marked the highest accuracy in bold. The average classification accuracy of CMSL on the Amazon Review dataset is 83.1%, which is 3.6% higher than the second best strategy EasyTL. In particular, all of the 12 cross-domain tasks achieve the best performance compared with the other 9 methods. Moreover, the classification accuracy of CMSL on the COIL20 dataset is 100% both in "C1 → C2" and "C2 → C1" tasks, which means that the classifier trained in the source domain can classify the target samples exactly, and confirms that our approach can transfer the most related information for domain adaptation.

The classification accuracy on the Office-Caltech10 is shown on Table 2. It is worth noting that our method achieves the best average accuracy with a 2.7% improvement over the second best method CMMS. And the classification accuracy of CMSL has been significantly improved compared with GFK, JDA, and DICD. 6 out of all 12 tasks achieve the best performance, while the second best method CMMS only obtains the best performance on two tasks: "C → A" and "D → A". Specifically, CMSL achieves 68.5% on the task "C → W" with a 6.8% improvement over the second best method CMMS.

---

[1] https://github.com/jindongwang/transferlearning.

Table 1. Accuracy (%) on Amazon Review and COIL20 datasets

Task	1NN	TCA	GFK	JDA	BDA	DICD	JGSA	EasyTL	CMMS	CMSL
B → D	49.6	63.6	66.4	63.8	64.2	63.2	66.6	79.8	79.6	**82.3**
B → E	49.8	60.9	65.5	64.4	62.1	64.1	75.0	79.7	79.9	**83.3**
B → K	50.3	64.2	69.2	66.1	65.4	65.2	72.1	80.9	82.4	**85.2**
D → B	53.3	63.3	66.3	65.0	62.4	66.2	55.5	79.9	76.3	**82.0**
D → E	51.0	64.2	63.7	63.0	66.3	62.4	67.3	80.8	81.3	**83.6**
D → K	53.1	69.1	67.7	64.3	68.9	63.1	65.6	82.0	82.1	**84.5**
E → B	50.8	59.5	62.4	60.8	59.2	60.6	51.6	75.0	76.6	**80.8**
E → D	50.9	62.1	63.4	61.9	61.6	61.7	50.8	75.3	78.2	**80.8**
E → K	51.2	74.8	73.8	65.7	74.7	66.9	55.0	84.9	82.1	**87.4**
K → B	52.2	64.1	65.5	63.0	62.7	64.1	58.3	76.5	75.1	**81.1**
K → D	51.2	65.4	65.0	58.9	64.3	59.6	56.4	76.3	75.8	**81.1**
K → E	52.3	74.5	73.0	69.3	74.0	68.0	51.7	82.5	82.0	**85.6**
AVG	51.3	65.5	66.8	63.9	65.5	63.8	60.5	79.5	79.3	**83.1**
Task	1NN	TCA	GFK	JDA	BDA	DICD	JGSA	EasyTL	CMMS	CMSL
C1 → C2	83.6	88.5	72.5	89.3	97.2	95.7	91.3	80.7	86.1	**100**
C2 → C1	82.8	85.8	74.2	88.5	96.8	93.3	91.3	78.6	88.2	**100**
AVG	83.2	87.2	73.4	88.9	97.0	94.5	91.3	79.7	87.2	**100**

Table 2. Accuracy (%) on Office-Caltech10 dataset

Task	1NN	TCA	GFK	JDA	BDA	DICD	JGSA	EasyTL	CMMS	CMSL
A → C	26.0	40.8	41.0	39.4	40.8	42.4	41.5	**42.3**	39.4	38.7
A → D	25.5	31.9	40.7	39.5	43.3	38.9	47.1	48.4	53.5	**55.4**
A → W	29.8	37.6	41.4	38.0	39.3	45.1	45.8	43.1	56.3	**60.7**
C → A	23.7	44.9	40.2	44.8	44.9	47.3	51.5	52.6	**61.0**	60.0
C → D	25.5	45.9	40.0	45.2	47.8	49.7	45.9	50.6	51.0	**62.4**
C → W	25.8	36.6	36.3	41.7	38.6	46.4	45.4	53.9	61.7	**68.5**
D → A	28.5	31.5	30.7	33.1	33.1	34.5	38.0	38.3	**46.7**	46.1
D → C	26.3	32.5	31.8	31.5	32.5	34.6	29.9	**36.1**	31.9	33.0
D → W	63.4	87.1	87.9	89.5	91.9	91.2	**91.9**	86.1	86.1	88.5
W → A	23.0	30.7	30.1	32.8	33.0	34.1	39.9	38.2	40.1	**43.1**
W → C	19.9	27.2	32.0	31.2	28.9	33.6	33.2	35.4	35.8	**38.6**
W → D	59.2	90.5	84.4	89.2	91.7	89.8	**90.5**	79.6	89.2	89.8
AVG	31.4	44.8	44.7	46.3	47.2	49.0	50.0	50.5	54.4	**57.1**

These experimental results demonstrate that CMSL learns the maximization correlated features between the source and target domains in the lower latent space and maintains data structure information as much as possible in the original space when projecting them into the lower spaces jointly, while some of the conventional unsupervised domain adaptation methods only focus on minimizing the distribution discrepancies between the source and target domains and thus leads to the ignorance of correlation between the two domains.

Table 3. Accuracy (%) on Office31 dataset

Task	1NN	TCA	GFK	JDA	BDA	DICD	JGSA	EasyTL	CMMS	CMSL
A → D	59.8	61.9	61.8	65.5	59.0	66.5	69.5	65.3	72.9	**74.3**
A → W	56.4	57.6	58.9	70.6	54.0	73.3	70.4	66.0	74.7	**76.7**
D → A	38.1	46.3	45.7	53.7	44.5	56.3	56.6	50.5	**60.7**	60.2
D → W	94.7	93.8	96.4	98.2	90.2	96.9	**98.2**	93.3	97.6	97.4
W → A	39.8	43.3	45.5	52.1	45.4	55.9	54.2	50.6	60.3	**60.5**
W → D	98.4	98.6	**99.6**	99.2	97.2	99.4	99.2	97.2	**99.6**	**99.6**
AVG	64.5	66.9	68.0	73.4	65.1	74.7	74.7	70.5	77.6	**78.1**

The results on the Office31 dataset is shown in Table 3. As seen from the Table 3, CMSL obtains the optimal average classification accuracy, which is 78.1%. It has 0.5% improvement compared with CMMS.

3.3 Parameters Sensitivity and Convergence Analysis

In our experiments, we fixed the feature dimension and made the hyperparameters tunable. We conducted parameters sensitivity and iterations convergence experiments on tasks "C → W (SURF)", "C1 → C2", "A → W", and "E → K". We also fixed two of three parameters on their optimal values and adapt the remainder parameter in each task. The results are shown in Fig. 1(a)–(c). For the parameter α, we explore the optimal value in a range of [0.001, 100]. We can see that the optimal values of α are different on the four tasks. On the task "C1 → C2", we can obtain the optimal value in the range of [0.001, 0.01]. While on the task "A → W", significant improvement of fault type on the classification performance can be obtained when the value exceeds 0.1 and achieves the highest accuracy at 0.5. The classification performance fluctuates steadily in a wide range from 0.001 to 100 on the task "E → K". For the parameter β, we conducted the sensitivity experiment ranging from 0.1 to 100000, and the classification accuracy curve graph is given in Fig. 1(b). The parameter β has a great influence on the classification performance on the task "A → W", which achieves the optimal performance when the value is 0.6. We also observe that when we increase the parameter value of β over 1, the classification accuracy on the task "C1 → C2" apparently drops and reaches its lowest accuracy at 100000. On the contrast, the classification performance achieves apparent

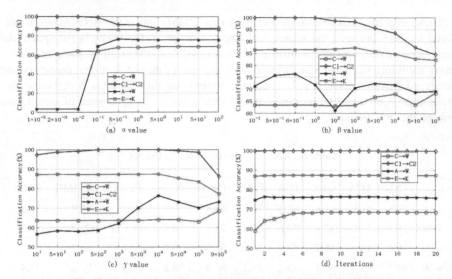

Fig. 1. Parameter sensitivity and convergence analysis of CMSL.

improvement when we increase the value from 100 to 10000 on the task "C → W (SURF)". Moreover, the accuracy is not sensitive to β in the range of [0.1, 1000] on the task "E → K".

We also explored the influence of different values of parameter γ on the classification accuracy ranging from 10 to 900000. The classification accuracy curve graph is shown in Fig. 1(c). We can obtain the highest accuracy when the value ranges from 1000 to 10000 on the task "C1 → C2". The first-best accuracy on the task "A → W" is around 10000 when we fixed the other two parameters as their optimal values. Furthermore, we carried out extensive experiments on the four tasks for the iteration convergence and the result is given in Fig. 1(d). We conducted the experiments for 20 iterations and all of the four tasks can reach their best performance after 10 iterations.

We also utilize the $t-SNE$ visualization tool to present the projected features of the target data on the task "C1 → C2" using different methods in Fig. 2. From Fig. 2, we can see that some of the projected features cannot be separated effectively by using CMMS method and part of data from various categories are mixed together in the Fig. 2(a), which leads to the decline of classification performance. The projected target features of different categories are compacted tightly by using CMSL method (Fig. 2(b)).

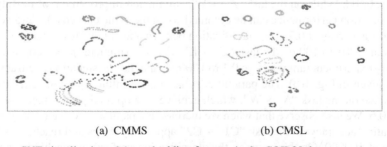

(a) CMMS   (b) CMSL

Fig. 2. $t-SNE$ visualization of the embedding features in the COIL20 dataset on the task C1 → C2. (a) CMMS embedding features, (b) CMSL embedding features

4   Conclusion

In this paper, we propose a correlated matching and structure learning (CMSL) approach for unsupervised domain adaptation. In CMSL, the maximization correlated features are extracted from the source and target domains. The pseudo labels of the target data are assigned by structure matching learning. The local manifold self-learning strategy of the target data is also introduced in CMSL to preserve the inherent local connection of the target samples. At the same time, the projected target features in the common latent space can preserve the structure information in the original space. Furthermore, the cluster centroids of the source and target domains with the same category are as closely as possible. Extensive experiments on five visual datasets and one sentiment analysis dataset verify that CMSL outperforms several state-of-the-art domain adaptation methods.

Acknowledgements. This work was supported by the National Natural Science Foundation of China (Grant Nos. 62176162, 61976145, and 62076129), the Guangdong Basic and Applied Basic Research Foundation (2019A1515011493, 2021A1515011318), the China University Industry-University-Research Innovation Fund (2020HYA02013), the Shenzhen Municipal Science and Technology Innovation Council (JCYJ20190808113411274), and the Major Project of the New Generation of Artificial Intelligence of China (2018AAA0102900).

References

1. Zhang, L., Wang, S., Huang, G., Zuo, W., Yang, J., Zhang, D.: Manifold criterion guided transfer learning via intermediate domain generation. IEEE Trans. Neural Netw. Learn. Syst. **30**(12), 3759–3773 (2019)
2. Yan, C., Li, L., Zhang, C., Liu, B., Zhang, Y., Dai, Q.: Cross-modality bridging and knowledge transferring for image understanding. IEEE Trans. Multimedia **21**(10), 2675–2685 (2019)
3. Xiao, N., Zhang, L.: Dynamic weighted learning for unsupervised domain adaptation. In: CVPR, pp. 15237–15246 (2021)
4. Wei, G., Lan, C., Zeng, W., Chen, Z.: MetaAlign: coordinating domain alignment and classification for unsupervised domain adaptation. In: CVPR, pp. 16638–16648 (2021)
5. Wang, S., Zhang, L., Zuo, W., Zhang, B.: Class-specific reconstruction transfer learning for visual recognition across domains. IEEE Trans. Image Process. **29**, 2424–2438 (2020)
6. Zhang, L., Zuo, W., Zhang, D.: LSDT: latent sparse domain transfer learning for visual adaptation. IEEE Trans. Image Process. **25**(3), 1177–1191 (2016)
7. Pan, S.J., Tsang, I.W., Kwok, J.T., Yang, Q.: Domain adaptation via transfer component analysis. IEEE Trans. Neural Netw. **22**(2), 199–210 (2011)
8. Long, M., Wang, J., Ding, G., Sun, J., Yu, P.S.: Transfer feature learning with joint distribution adaptation. In: CVPR, pp. 2200–2207 (2013)
9. Wang, J., Chen, Y., Hao, S.: Balanced distribution adaptation for transfer learning. In: ICDM, pp. 1129–1134 (2017)
10. Zhang, J., Li, W., Ogunbona, P.: Joint geometrical and statistical alignment for visual domain adaptation. In: CVPR, pp. 1859–1867 (2017)
11. Zhang, L., Zhang, D.: Visual understanding via multi-feature shared learning with global consistency. IEEE Trans. Multimedia **18**(2), 247–259 (2016)

12. Yan, H., Li, Z., Wang, Q., Li, P., Xu, Y., Zuo, W.: Weighted and class-specific maximum mean discrepancy for unsupervised domain adaptation. IEEE Trans. Multimedia **22**(9), 2420–2433 (2020)
13. Li, L., Zhang, Z.: Semi-supervised domain adaptation by covariance matching. IEEE Trans. Pattern Anal. Mach. Intell. **41**(11), 2724–2739 (2019)
14. Zhang, L., Fu, J., Wang, S., Zhang, D., Dong, Z., Chen, C.P.: Guide subspace learning for unsupervised domain adaptation. IEEE Trans. Neural Netw. Learn. Syst. **31**(9), 3374–3388 (2020)
15. Hotelling, H.: Relations between Two Sets of Variates. Biometrika (1936)
16. Wang, W., Lu, Y., Lai, Z.: Canonical correlation discriminative learning for domain adaptation. In: Bäck, T., et al. (eds.) PPSN 2020. LNCS, vol. 12269, pp. 567–580. Springer, Cham (2020). https://doi.org/10.1007/978-3-030-58112-1_39
17. Hua, M., Lau, M., Pei, J., Wu, K.: Continuous K-means monitoring with low reporting cost in sensor networks. IEEE Trans. Knowl. Data Eng. **21**(12), 1679–1691 (2009)
18. Tian, L., Tang, Y., Hu, L., Ren, Z., Zhang, W.: Domain Adaptation by class centroid matching and local manifold self-learning. IEEE Trans. Image Process. **29**(10), 9703–9718 (2020)
19. Nie, F., Wang, X., Huang, H.: Clustering and projected clustering with adaptive neighbors. In: KDD, pp. 977–986 (2014)
20. Gong, B., Shi, Y., Sha, F., Grauman, K.: Geodesic flow kernel for unsupervised domain adaptation. In: CVPR, pp. 2066–2073 (2012)
21. Li, S., Song, S., Huang, G., Ding, Z.: Domain invariant and class discriminative feature learning for visual domain adaptation. IEEE Trans. Image Process. **27**(9), 4260–4273 (2018)
22. Wang, J., Chen, Y., Yu, H., Huang, M., Yang, Q.: Easy transfer learning by exploiting intra-domain structures. In: Proceedings of IEEE International Conference on Multimedia Expo, pp. 1210–1215, July 2019
23. Saenko, K., Kulis, B., Fritz, M., Darrell, T.: Adapting visual category models to new domains. In: Daniilidis, K., Maragos, P., Paragios, N. (eds.) ECCV 2010. LNCS, vol. 6314, pp. 213–226. Springer, Heidelberg (2010). https://doi.org/10.1007/978-3-642-15561-1_16
24. McAuley, J., Targett, C., Shi, Q., Hengel, A.: Image-based recommendations on styles and substitutes. In: Proceedings of the 38th International ACM SIGIR Conference on Research and Development in Information Retrieval, pp. 43–52 (2015)

Rider Re-identification Based on Pyramid Attention

Jiaze Li[1,2] and Bin Liu[1,2(✉)]

[1] University of Science and Technology of China, Hefei, China
flowice@ustc.edu.cn
[2] Key Laboratory of Electromagnetic Space Information, Chinese Academy of
Sciences, Hefei, China

Abstract. In recent years, object re-identification (ReID) based on deep
learning has made great progress, and research in this field mainly focuses
on person and vehicle. However, the researchers ignore an important target: riders. Electric bikes are an essential part of modern transportation
scenarios, so identifying riders and monitoring their behavior on a large
scale is critical to public safety management. To bridge the research gap
of rider ReID, this paper proposes a pyramid attention network (PANet),
which utilizes the pyramid structure to capture multi-scale clues and discovers key regional features from fine to coarse. PANet first learns fine-
grained attention in local small regions, then gradually aggregates local
regions to expand the scope of attention exploration, and finally conducts global coarse-grained attention learning. We implement two different dimensional attention computations in the pyramid attention network: spatial attention and channel attention. Experiments on BPReID
and MoRe datasets demonstrate the effectiveness of this network design,
which can achieve better performance with limited computational overhead.

Keywords: Rider re-identification · Pyramid attention · Deep learning

1 Introduction

The purpose of object re-identification is to match related objects in different
images or video sequences. We have witnessed the rapid development of ReID
systems in recent years, mainly focusing on person re-identification [1,10] and
vehicle re-identification [5,8]. The importance of these targets is related to the
growing needs for public safety and traffic control. In this case, the researchers
overlook an important target: riders. This paper refers to person riding electric
bikes as rider, where electric bike is the general name of electric bicycle and
electric motorcycle.

In the context of green travel and urban traffic congestion, electric bikes have
gradually become an important part of the traffic scene. Due to the large number,
electric vehicles affect urban traffic safety and are often associated with crimes.

© The Author(s), under exclusive license to Springer Nature Switzerland AG 2022
S. Yu et al. (Eds.): PRCV 2022, LNCS 13534, pp. 81–93, 2022.
https://doi.org/10.1007/978-3-031-18907-4_7

For example, riders driving illegally resulting in serious traffic accidents [4]. Therefore, rider re-identification is crucial for electric bike riding management.

Person and rider re-identification both focus on person's clothes, accessories and carrying items when extracting features. The difference is that there are more features available for rider re-identification, such as the color and model of the electric bike. But the methods of person re-identification always ignore these features and treat electric bike as a kind of occlusion obstacle. Therefore, the person re-identification methods cannot be directly applied to the task of rider re-identification. Meanwhile, the problem of rider re-identification is more prominent: (1) Since the speed of electric bike is higher than the walking speed of person, the image is prone to motion blur; (2) The consistency of image features of electric bike is low under the change of viewpoints, which leads to more serious pose changes; (3) Electric bike can carry people, and some images have multiple recognition objects. Specifically as shown in Fig. 1. In conclusion, rider re-identification is more challenging than person re-identification. Despite its importance, rider re-identification is rarely mentioned in the literature. To the best of our knowledge, the relevant studies are BikePerson Re-identification [15] and Motorcycle Re-identification [6]. It is imperative to explore the method for rider re-identification.

motion blur   pose change   multiple objects

Fig. 1. Challenges for rider ReID.

In order to solve the above problems, this paper proposes a pyramid attention network (PANet) referring to the ideas in [2] to better capture the features of rider. Different from the traditional feature pyramid method that extracts features at different scales and aggregates them, PANet utilizes the attention model to learn multi-scale features and merge them. As shown in Fig. 2, the pyramid attention module (PAM) in our network first learns fine-grained attention in small local regions, then gradually aggregates local regions, expands the scope of attention exploration, and finally conducts global coarse-grained attention learning, which can better discover discontinuous key region features.

Many existing ReID works add attention mechanism to guide feature aggregation, but most of these methods have some problems: (1) Many methods exploit attention in a supervised manner, requiring some external semantic clues; (2) Other unsupervised or weakly supervised methods require the use of stacks of convolution of different sizes to capture attention, which expands the network size and increases training difficulty. The proposed pyramid attention network only utilizes identity labels as supervision to generate attention and can achieve better performance with limited computational overhead compared to other attention models. And the pyramid attention module, as a lightweight module, can be inserted into CNN networks of any architecture in a plug-and-play manner.

In summary, the main contributions of this paper are as follows:

- To better capture the discriminative features contained in the rider image, this paper introduces a pyramid attention network to explore key regions in the image in a fine-to-coarse multi-scale attention learning manner.
- We apply the pyramid attention network to the spatial and channel dimensions and demonstrate that the network can effectively explore salient clues in rider ReID.
- Extensive experiments demonstrate that our method can achieve better performance with limited computational overhead compared to other attention models.

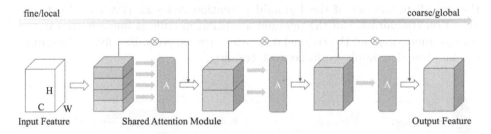

Fig. 2. Architecture of the pyramid attention module (PAM).

2   Related Work

2.1   Rider Re-identification

As far as we know, there are few existing studies on rider re-identification. Yuan et al. [15] focus on the bike-person re-identification problem for the first time, propose a large-scale bike-person re-identification dataset named BPReid, and develop a new automatic segmentation method that can remove noise in images. In fact, the challenges faced by the campus environment and realistic urban surveillance systems are not the same, so Figueiredo et al. [6] propose the first large-scale motorcycle re-identification dataset (MoRe) and evaluate the training tricks in the deep learning model, providing a strong baseline for the motorcycle re-identification. In order to better capture the salient information of rider images, we choose to use the attention mechanism to focus on the salient regions to learn robust features.

2.2   Attention Model

The purpose of attention is to focus on important features and suppress irrelevant features, which is very compatible with the goal of object re-identification. Chen et al. [3] solve the occlusion problem in ReID by using the attention mechanism to guide the model to mask the occlusion and accurately capture body parts. AANet [13] integrates individual attributes and attribute attention into a unified classification framework, where attribute labels are used to guide attention learning. Zhang et al. [16] propose an efficient relation-aware global attention (RGA) module which learns the attention of each feature node from the global perspective of the relationship between features. However, the above methods are costly in the process of data processing and model training. Compared with other attention models, the PANet proposed in this paper is able to achieve better performance with limited computational overhead.

3   Proposed Method

In this section, we first adopt ResNet50 as the backbone network to introduce the overall framework of the Pyramid Attention Network (PANet). Next, the attention computation in the pyramid attention module is implemented in the spatial dimension and the channel dimension, respectively. Finally, we introduce the loss function employed in network training.

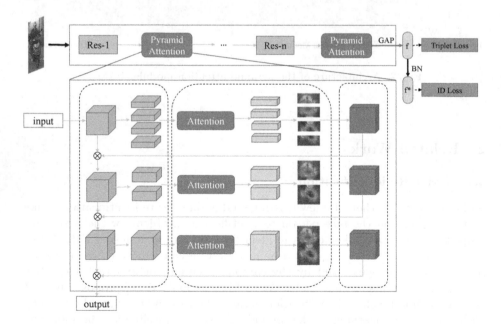

Fig. 3. Architecture of pyramid attention network.

3.1 Pyramid Attention Network

Rider re-identification has more discriminative features and more prominent challenges than person re-identification, and compared with person images, the continuity of key regions in rider images is worse. Therefore, we propose a multi-scale network based on pyramid attention, which exploits the pyramid structure to capture attention at multiple scales. PANet gradually guides the network to focus on key regions by applying the pyramid attention module after multiple convolutional stages of the backbone network.

The structure of Pyramid Attention Network (PANet) is shown in Fig. 3. Given a rider image I to be retrieved, the corresponding intermediate feature tensor $X \in \mathbb{R}^{C \times H \times W}$ is obtained after multiple convolution stages of the backbone network ResNet50, where H is height, W is width, and C is the number of channels. X is then fed into the pyramid attention module to capture multi-scale clues.

PAM contains different levels of attention models $\mathcal{P} = \{\mathcal{P}_i\}$, where $\mathcal{P}_i$ represents the i-th level pyramid. The network learns key region features at different scales in different pyramid levels. Figure 3 shows the attention model structure of the three-level pyramid. In PAM, the segmentation operation is first performed on X_i, where X_i is the feature tensor of the i-th level, and s segmentation feature tensors $X_{i,j}, j = 1, 2, \cdots, s$ are obtained. The number of feature segmentation is based on an exponential decline of 2. For example, if the pyramid is at level i and the total number of levels is p, then $s = 2^{p-i}$. With the increase of pyramid level, the scope of attention exploration gradually increases and the number of segmentation features decreases, shifting from learning fine-grained attention to learning coarse-grained attention. In the spatial dimension, the segmentation is performed along the height to obtain $X_{i,j} \in \mathbb{R}^{C \times \frac{H}{s} \times W}$; In the channel dimension, the segmentation is performed along the channel to obtain $X_{i,j} \in \mathbb{R}^{\frac{C}{s} \times H \times W}$.

In order to reduce model parameters and achieve lightweight computation, we learn a shared attention model $\mathcal{A}_i$ in each level of the pyramid to capture the salient clues of each segmentation feature tensor. Then, for the learned sub-attention map $A_{i,j}$, they are combined into the global attention feature map A_i of the same size as X_i. The specific calculation formula is as follows:

$$A_i = [\mathcal{A}_i (X_{i,j})]_{j=1}^s \tag{1}$$

where $[\cdot]_{j=1}^s$ represents the concatenation of s sub-attention maps. Aggregated attention A_i is the overall attention feature map learned by the i-th pyramid.

The pyramid attention module guides the network to start from scattered local fine-grained clues by exploring from fine to coarse, and gradually pay attention to the key regions of the overall image of the rider, which can better discover discontinuous salient clues. After obtaining the overall attention feature map A_i, the network find more discriminative features:

$$X_{i+1} = \sigma (A_i) * X_i \tag{2}$$

where σ represents the sigmoid function. The feature X_i is re-weighted by the normalized attention and fed into the next level of the pyramid to explore a larger range of attention learning. If $i = p$, then X_{p+1} is input to the next convolution layer of the backbone network as the output of the pyramid attention module. Finally, the network outputs the feature map after the attention is focused for loss calculation.

3.2 Attention Model

There are two different dimensions of attention computation in the proposed pyramid attention network—spatial attention and channel attention.

Spatial attention focuses on the most discriminative regions in the input feature map, ignoring irrelevant regions. This paper borrows ideas from [14] for spatial attention computation. Specifically, given the intermediate feature tensor $X \in \mathbb{R}^{C \times H \times W}$, the spatial attention model will learn a spatial attention feature map of size $H \times W$. As shown in Fig. 4a, in order to calculate spatial attention, the model first conducts average pooling and maximum pooling operations on X along the channel direction, and aggregates channel information to obtain $X_{avg}^S \in \mathbb{R}^{1 \times H \times W}$ and $X_{max}^S \in \mathbb{R}^{1 \times H \times W}$, which represent average pooling and maximum pooling characteristics of channels respectively, and then the two are concatenated to obtain a two-layer feature descriptor. Then a 3×3 convolutional layer is applied to generate the spatial attention map $A^S \in \mathbb{R}^{H \times W}$. The spatial attention map is calculated as:

$$A^S = \sigma \left(conv \left([X_{avg}^S, X_{max}^S] \right) \right) \tag{3}$$

where $conv$ represents a 3×3 convolution operation.

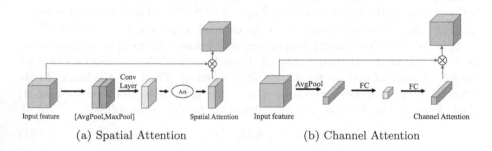

(a) Spatial Attention   (b) Channel Attention

Fig. 4. Diagram of spatial attention and channel attention

Channel attention assigns greater weight to channels that display higher responses, helping the model focus on more salient features. In this paper, the squeezed excitation block (SE) [7] is adopted as the channel attention model. Specifically, given the intermediate feature tensor $X \in \mathbb{R}^{C \times H \times W}$, the channel attention model will learn a channel attention feature map of size C. As shown in Fig. 4b, the channel attention model consists of a global average pooling layer and two fully connected layers. First, the model performs global average pooling on X to obtain $X_{avg}^C \in \mathbb{R}^{C \times 1 \times 1}$ to achieve low-dimensional embedding. At this time, the feature has only the channel dimension and no spatial dimension. Then input X_{avg}^C into the fully connected layer to compress the channel to reduce the amount of computation, and next restore the number of channels after the second full connection, and complete the mapping transformation to obtain the channel attention map $A^C \in \mathbb{R}^C$. The channel attention map is calculated as:

$$A^C = \sigma \left(FC \left(FC \left(X_{avg}^C \right) \right) \right) \tag{4}$$

where FC indicates the fully connected layer. In the specific application, X is replaced by the segmentation feature tensor $X_{i,j}$ to learn the sub-attention maps, and then merge them.

3.3   Loss Function

This paper uses triplet loss and ID loss to train the network. For image pairs in the embedding space, the ID loss mainly optimizes the cosine distance, and the triplet loss mainly optimizes the Euclidean distance. Using triplet loss and ID loss during training process can easily cause one loss to decrease while the other oscillates or even increases.

To overcome the above problems, we introduce the BNNeck structure [9]. As shown in Fig. 3, BNNeck performs batch normalization on feature f to obtain f^*, then f and f^* are used to calculate triplet loss and ID loss respectively. The normalization balances each dimension of f^*, makes it more suitable for computation in cosine space, and makes it easier for the ID loss to converge. BNNeck effectively alleviates the conflict between the ID loss and the triplet loss minimization process. The triple loss calculation formula is:

$$L_{Tri} = [d_p - d_n + \alpha]_+ \tag{5}$$

where $[\cdot]_+ = max\,(\cdot,\,0)$, d_p and d_n are the feature distances of positive and negative pairs respectively. α is the interval hyperparameter, which is set to 3 in this paper. The triplet loss is learned with Euclidean distance as the distance metric.

Given a rider image, y represents the real ID label, p_i represents the predicted logarithm of the presumed image ID of i, and the ID loss is calculated as follows:

$$L_{ID} = \sum_{i=1}^{N} -q_i \log{(p_i)} \begin{cases} q_i = 0, & y \neq i \\ q_i = 1, & y = i \end{cases} \tag{6}$$

In order to prevent overfitting, we apply Label Smoothing [12] on ID loss. The final loss in the training is the sum of triplet loss and ID loss.

4   Experiments

4.1   Datasets and Implementation Details

Most of the existing datasets are for person ReID and vehicle ReID, and the rider ReID-related datasets we collected are BPReID [15] and MoRe [6]. The

BPReID dataset is collected on campus and contains three vehicle types: bicycles, electric motorcycles, and electric bicycles. The MoRe dataset is the first large-scale motorcycle ReID database captured by urban traffic cameras.

Considering that the utilization rate of electric bikes is far higher than that of bicycles in real traffic scene, and for the purpose of unifying the image content of the two datasets, this paper uses the electric motorcycles and electric bicycles in the BPReID dataset and the entire MoRe dataset. The specific information is shown in Table 1.

In this paper, mean Average Precision (mAP) and Cumulative match characteristic (CMC) are used to evaluate the performance of rider re-identification methods on datasets.

Table 1. Rider Re-ID datasets

Dataset	Release time	Number of cameras	Number of ID	Number of images
BPReID [15]	2018	6	1257	25103
MoRe [6]	2021	10	3827	14141

We choose the ResNet50 as the baseline model. During training, ResNet50 trained on ImageNet task is used as a pre-trained model, and all images are resized to 256×128. In addition, we adopt the data augmentation technique Random Erasing Augmentation [17], as well as random horizontal flipping, random cropping, etc. During the training process, batch size is selected as 64, the last stride is set to 1, Adam optimizer is employed to iteratively train 120 epochs for all models by using warmup method.

4.2 Ablation Study

To explore the effectiveness of each component in PANet, this section first conducts ablation experiments on both spatial and channel PANet. As shown in Table 2, we compare the differences between spatial pyramid attention network (PANet_S) and channel pyramid attention network (PANet_C) at different pyramid levels. PANet_C3 represents an attention network with a three-level channel pyramid.

PANet vs. Baseline. Table 2 shows the comparison of PANet_C, PANet_S related models with baseline. We can observe that the performance of both PANet_S and PANet_C is greatly improved compared to the baseline. PANet_C2 achieves +9.3%/+9.1% performance improvement on mAP and R-1 on the BPReID dataset, and achieves +4.2%/+4.5% performance improvement on the MoRe dataset. It proves the effectiveness of the pyramid attention network proposed in this paper.

Channel Attention vs. Spatial Attention. Overall, the method employing channel attention outperforms spatial attention in both datasets. For channel

Table 2. Comparative results with baseline model

Model	BPReID				MoRe			
	mAP	R-1	R-5	R-10	mAP	R-1	R-5	R-10
Baseline	49.9%	47.0%	61.4%	73.6%	86.7%	84.6%	94.6%	96.6%
PANet_S1	57.4%	54.5%	67.3%	79.6%	90.6%	88.7%	96.5%	98.1%
PANet_S2	57.8%	**56.8%**	**68.6%**	80.0%	89.5%	87.2%	95.7%	98.1%
PANet_S3	56.6%	55.4%	68.0%	78.0%	88.3%	86.4%	95.7%	97.3%
PANet_C1	56.0%	53.9%	66.6%	78.6%	89.7%	88.2%	96.1%	97.8%
PANet_C2	**59.2%**	56.1%	67.9%	**80.4%**	**90.9%**	**89.1%**	**97.3%**	**98.4%**
PANet_C3	56.9%	53.7%	67.8%	78.9%	89.9%	88.4%	96.5%	98.2%
PANet_SC	58.0%	54.7%	67.4%	78.7%	90.4%	88.7%	96.2%	98.2%

attention, on the MoRe dataset, mAP and R-1 are 1.4%/1.9% and 1.6%/1.2% higher than spatial attention PANet at level = 2 and 3 respectively. In the low-level pyramid, the performance of spatial attention is similar to or even better than channel attention. It suggests that localizing regions of interest is easier than exploring discriminative features without adding fine-grained attention. Therefore, the addition of fine-grained attention exploration makes it easier for the network to discover discriminative features, and exploring discriminative features has a greater impact on model performance. PANet_SC refers to feature calculation by combining spatial attention and channel attention, and it can be seen that the performance of the combined attention is not improved. As shown in Table 3, the performance of the RGA_SC combined with spatial attention and channel attention is also not improved, so we speculate that the two attention mechanisms are not complementary in this task.

Influence of Pyramid Levels. In order to explore Influence of pyramid levels on the model performance, the experiments compare the performance of PANet with different levels on the rider re-identification. In PANet_C/Si, i indicates that PAM is an i-level pyramid structure with i attention modules. It can be observed from Table 2 that the addition of fine-grained attention exploration leads to a significant improvement in model performance. In addition, it can be found that as the number of pyramid levels increases, the performance improvement slows down. This is because the image resolution is limited, and increasing the number of pyramid levels under saturation cannot discover deeper salient semantic clues. We also conducts experiments shown in Fig. 5 on the BPReID dataset to explore the appropriate level. It can be seen that when pyramid level = 2, the network performs better in channel and spatial. Considering the model performance and computational cost, this paper chooses a 2-level pyramid attention network for subsequent experiments.

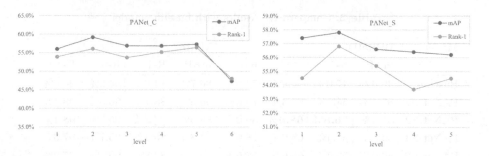

Fig. 5. The mAP and Rank-1 accuracy with different level for PANet_C and PANet_S on BPReID dataset.

4.3   Comparison with the State-of-the-Art

Due to the lack of existing researches on the rider re-identification, this paper selects the RGA model [16] that performs well in the person re-identification for comparative analysis, which also utilizes spatial attention and channel attention. We retrain the RGA and SENet [7] models under the same experimental setting, where SENet is a ResNet50 network using channel attention. Because [15] adopts non-deep learning methods and the data ranges in experiment is distinct, so no comparison is made with it. The experimental results are shown in Table 3.

Table 3. Comparative results with the State-of-the-Art

Model	BPReID				MoRe			
	mAP	R-1	R-5	R-10	mAP	R-1	R-5	R-10
MoRe [6]	-	-	-	-	86.4%	83.4%	-	-
SENet	56.4%	53.5%	67.1%	77.9%	88.8%	87.0%	95.7%	97.7%
RGA_S	56.3%	54.8%	67.4%	78.1%	87.2%	84.7%	94.3%	97.1%
RGA_C	57.2%	55.7%	68.0%	79.4%	87.8%	85.5%	95.2%	97.9%
RGA_SC	55.0%	52.9%	66.0%	77.5%	88.6%	86.4%	95.4%	97.8%
PANet_S2	**57.8%**	**56.8%**	**68.6%**	**80.0%**	**89.5%**	**87.2%**	**95.7%**	**98.1%**
PANet_C2	**59.2%**	**56.1%**	**67.9%**	**80.4%**	**90.9%**	**89.1%**	**97.3%**	**98.4%**

PANet achieves +4.5%/+5.7% performance improvement on mAP and R-1 compared to the current state-of-the-art research [6] on the MoRe dataset. Compared with the retrained SENet, PANet achieves better performance on both datasets. On the BPReID dataset, PANet achieves a performance improvement of +2.8%/+2.6% on mAP and R-1. Compared with the RGA model, PANet outperforms RGA in terms of spatial attention and channel attention. This strongly demonstrates the effectiveness of the proposed PANet model.

Table 4. Computational overhead and number of parameters for different models

Model	Computation (GFLOPS)	Parameters (M)
Baseline	4.07	23.51
SENet	4.07	26.04
PANet_S2	4.07	23.51
PANet_C2	4.08	27.77
RGA_S	6.62	26.73
RGA_C	7.02	26.60

One of the core advantages of proposed PANet is that the model can achieve better performance with less computational overhead compared to other models. To evaluate the efficiency of our method, this paper compares the computational overhead and number of parameters of PANet, baseline, SENet and GRA models. As shown in Table 4, PANet is similar to baseline and SENet in computational overhead, but the model performance of PANet is better than both the baseline and SENet. The RGA model has a much higher computational cost than PANet in the two attention calculation methods, and the model performance is also lower than PANet. Taking channel attention as an example, the efficiency of PANet_C is improved by 41.88% compared with RGA_C. In terms of the number of parameters, PANet_S has similar number of parameters to baseline, and fewer parameters than other model parameters, and the performance is also better than the baseline, SENet and RGA models. The model parameters of PANet_C are increased by 4.26M compared to the baseline, but the model performance achieves +9.3%/+9.1% improvement on mAP and R-1. Compared with the RGA, they have similar number of parameters, but PANet_C model has better computational overhead and performance. To sum up, it is proved that our pyramid attention network has more efficient computation and superior performance.

4.4 Attention Visualization

This section applies Grad-CAM [11] to the baseline and PANet for qualitative analysis. Grad-CAM generates a heatmap of class activations on input images to identify discriminative regions. As shown in Fig. 6, PANet covers the rider's region better than the baseline, ignoring background noise. The increase of pyramid attention makes the network focus on the discriminative regions of rider images. Compared with the baseline, PANet pays more attention to the features of the rider's vehicle. Therefore, the pyramid attention network proposed in this paper is more suitable for rider re-identification.

Compared with PANet_C1, PANet_C2 focuses more on salient features of riders and vehicles, such as logos on clothes, lights, trunks, etc., when the pyramid levels are further deepened. Furthermore, we find that heads are often ignored in

Baseline

PANet_C1

PANet_C2

PANet_S2

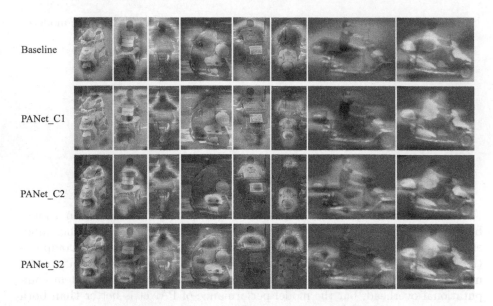

Fig. 6. Grad-CAM visualization on different models.

PANet because faces are usually of low resolution and cannot be discriminated reliably.

5   Conclusion

To bridge the research gap of rider re-identification, this paper proposes a pyramid attention network. This network employs a fine-to-coarse method which captures salient clues in local regions from fine-grained attention learning, and then combines local regions for larger-scale attention learning, gradually guiding the network to discover salient clues, and can better discover discontinuous key region features in images. We also apply PANet to the spatial and channel dimensions respectively. Extensive ablation studies demonstrate the high efficiency and superior performance of our design on rider ReID.

References

1. Ahmad, S., Scarpellini, G., Morerio, P., Del Bue, A.: Event-driven re-id: a new benchmark and method towards privacy-preserving person re-identification. In: Proceedings of the IEEE/CVF Winter Conference on Applications of Computer Vision, pp. 459–468 (2022)
2. Chen, G., Gu, T., Lu, J., Bao, J.A., Zhou, J.: Person re-identification via attention pyramid. IEEE Trans. Image Process. **30**, 7663–7676 (2021)
3. Chen, P., et al.: Occlude them all: occlusion-aware attention network for occluded person re-id. In: Proceedings of the IEEE/CVF International Conference on Computer Vision, pp. 11833–11842 (2021)

4. Dischinger, P.C., Ryb, G.E., Ho, S.M., Braver, E.R.: Injury patterns and severity among hospitalized motorcyclists: a comparison of younger and older riders. In: Annual Proceedings/Association for the Advancement of Automotive Medicine, vol. 50, p. 237. Association for the Advancement of Automotive Medicine (2006)

5. Fernandez, M., Moral, P., Garcia-Martin, A., Martinez, J.M.: Vehicle re-identification based on ensembling deep learning features including a synthetic training dataset, orientation and background features, and camera verification. In: Proceedings of the IEEE/CVF Conference on Computer Vision and Pattern Recognition, pp. 4068–4076 (2021)

6. Figueiredo, A., Brayan, J., Reis, R.O., Prates, R., Schwartz, W.R.: More: a large-scale motorcycle re-identification dataset. In: Proceedings of the IEEE/CVF Winter Conference on Applications of Computer Vision, pp. 4034–4043 (2021)

7. Hu, J., Shen, L., Sun, G.: Squeeze-and-excitation networks. In: Proceedings of the IEEE Conference on Computer Vision and Pattern Recognition, pp. 7132–7141 (2018)

8. Luo, H., et al.: An empirical study of vehicle re-identification on the AI city challenge. In: Proceedings of the IEEE/CVF Conference on Computer Vision and Pattern Recognition, pp. 4095–4102 (2021)

9. Luo, H., Gu, Y., Liao, X., Lai, S., Jiang, W.: Bag of tricks and a strong baseline for deep person re-identification. In: Proceedings of the IEEE/CVF Conference on Computer Vision and Pattern Recognition Workshops (2019)

10. Qi, F., Yan, B., Cao, L., Wang, H.: Stronger baseline for person re-identification. arXiv preprint arXiv:2112.01059 (2021)

11. Selvaraju, R.R., Cogswell, M., Das, A., Vedantam, R., Parikh, D., Batra, D.: Grad-cam: visual explanations from deep networks via gradient-based localization. In: Proceedings of the IEEE International Conference on Computer Vision, pp. 618–626 (2017)

12. Szegedy, C., Vanhoucke, V., Ioffe, S., Shlens, J., Wojna, Z.: Rethinking the inception architecture for computer vision. In: Proceedings of the IEEE Conference on Computer Vision and Pattern Recognition, pp. 2818–2826 (2016)

13. Tay, C.P., Roy, S., Yap, K.H.: Aanet: attribute attention network for person re-identifications. In: Proceedings of the IEEE/CVF Conference on Computer Vision and Pattern Recognition, pp. 7134–7143 (2019)

14. Woo, S., Park, J., Lee, J.Y., Kweon, I.S.: CBAM: convolutional block attention module. In: Proceedings of the European Conference on Computer Vision (ECCV), pp. 3–19 (2018)

15. Yuan, Y., Zhang, J., Wang, Q.: Bike-person re-identification: a benchmark and a comprehensive evaluation. IEEE Access 6, 56059–56068 (2018)

16. Zhang, Z., Lan, C., Zeng, W., Jin, X., Chen, Z.: Relation-aware global attention for person re-identification. In: Proceedings of the IEEE/CVF Conference on Computer Vision and Pattern Recognition, pp. 3186–3195 (2020)

17. Zhong, Z., Zheng, L., Kang, G., Li, S., Yang, Y.: Random erasing data augmentation. In: Proceedings of the AAAI Conference on Artificial Intelligence, vol. 34, pp. 13001–13008 (2020)

Temporal Correlation-Diversity Representations for Video-Based Person Re-Identification

Litong Gong[1,4], Ruize Zhang[1,2], Sheng Tang[1,3](✉), and Juan Cao[1]

[1] Key Laboratory of Intelligent Information Processing, Institute of Computing Technology, Chinese Academy of Sciences, Beijing, China
{gonglitong19s,zhangruize21b,ts,caojuan}@ict.ac.cn
[2] University of Chinese Academy of Sciences, Beijing, China
[3] Research Institute of Intelligent Computing, Zhejiang Lab, Hangzhou, Zhejiang, China
[4] Hangzhou Zhongke Ruijian Technology Co., Ltd., Hangzhou, China

Abstract. Video-based person re-identification is a challenging task due to illuminations, occlusions, viewpoint changes, and pedestrian misalignment. Most previous works focus more on temporal correlation features, which leads to a lack of detailed information. In this paper, we emphasize the importance of keeping both correlation and diversity of multi-frame features simultaneously. Thus, we propose a Temporal Correlation-Diversity Representation (TCDR) network to enhance the representation of frame-level pedestrian features and the temporal feature aggregation abilities. Specifically, in order to capture correlated but diverse temporal features, we propose a Temporal-Guided Frame Feature Enhancement (TGFE) module, which explores the temporal correlation with a global perspective and enhances frame-level features to achieve the temporal diversity. Furthermore, we propose a Temporal Feature Integration (TFI) module to aggregate multi-frame features. Finally, we propose a novel progressive smooth loss to alleviate the influence of noisy frames. Extensive experiments show that our method achieves the state-of-the-art performance on MARS, DukeMTMC-VideoReID and LS-VID datasets.

Keywords: Person re-identification · Feature enhancement · Deep learning

1 Introduction

Person Re-Identification (Re-ID) has been widely used in video surveillance, which aims to match specific pedestrians from a large amount of image and video data. In recent years, although video-based Re-ID technology [7,12,18] has developed rapidly, it still faces challenges due to illuminations, occlusions, viewpoint changes, and pedestrian misalignment.

Recently, the research of video-based Re-ID focuses on temporal information modeling. A typical pipeline is to first extract multi-frame features independently

© The Author(s), under exclusive license to Springer Nature Switzerland AG 2022
S. Yu et al. (Eds.): PRCV 2022, LNCS 13534, pp. 94–105, 2022.
https://doi.org/10.1007/978-3-031-18907-4_8

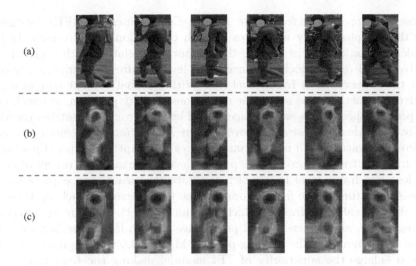

(a)

(b)

(c)

Fig. 1. Visualization of attention maps. (a) Original images. (b) Attention maps of temporal correlation feature across frames. (c) Attention maps of temporal correlation and diversity feature across frames. Temporal correlation tends to focus on temporal shared parts, such as T-shirts and shorts, while temporal diversity is inclined to cover non-shared parts, such as left shoe and right shoe. Intuitively, temporal correlated but diverse features can combine the complementary attributes of the non-shared and shared parts, which is more beneficial to reduce overfitting caused by very similar shared parts.

without any temporal cues, and only in the final stage, perform temporal feature aggregation, such as through temporal attention mechanisms [12,18] or recurrent neural networks [18,23]. In addition, the non-local block [15] is widely used for modeling long-term temporal information [8,10], which extracts attentive features across frames by multi-stage temporal feature aggregation. Besides, 3D convolution can directly model temporal information, which is verified by the works [11] on the video-based Re-ID. The above approaches achieve the expected performance on video-based Re-ID.

Although an increasing number of approaches are focusing on temporal cues modeling, these methods focus too much on the correlation between multi-frame features but ignore the diversity of consecutive frames. As shown in Fig. 1, the excessive correlation between multiple frames only focuses on the shared salient parts of the temporal sequence, which makes it difficult to distinguish similar identities in appearance. Obviously, components varying in pedestrian motion between consecutive frames tend to contain richer diverse features, and these diversified details of non-shared parts are more discriminative, which is a strong complement to the temporal correlation information.

In this paper, to address the above problem, we propose a *Temporal Correlation-Diversity Representation* (TCDR) framework to explore sufficient correlated but diverse representations between multiple frames. Specifically, we propose a *Temporal-Guided Frame Feature Enhancement* (TGFE) module to mine the complementary attributes of both correlation and diversity. In this module, correlation blocks explore the temporal correlation with a global perspective, and diversity blocks enhance frame-level features for temporal diversity under the supervision of frame-level loss. With a global context temporal perspective, our method also solves the ambiguous identity problem, in which multiple people appear in the same image caused by the error in pedestrian tracking. Finally, we further propose a *Temporal Feature Integration* (TFI) module to yield a video-level feature from multi-frame features by adaptive temporal pooling.

During the training process, we propose a co-optimization strategy of video-level loss and frame-level loss, which facilitates the learner to explore diverse frame-level features more freely. However, due to the error of tracking, there are inevitably several noisy frames, which introduces uncertainty during supervised training. Thus, we propose a novel progressive smooth loss to weaken the influence of noisy frames in the training process. Meanwhile, the progressive smooth loss can enlarge the superiority of TFI module, making the temporal feature aggregation more effective than temporal average pooling.

In summary, the main contributions of our work are three-fold: (1) We emphasize the importance of temporal correlation and diversity and propose a novel TCDR framework to explore the complementary attributes of both correlation and diversity. (2) We further propose a progressive smooth loss to handle the ambiguous identity problem and reinforce the effect of the temporal feature integration module. (3) Extensive experiments show that our proposed method outperforms existing state-of-the-art methods on several widely-used video-based Re-ID datasets.

2 Related Work

Video-Based Person Re-ID. Most video person re-identification methods focus on temporal information modeling. Many works [18,23] make full use of RNN to extract temporal features in consecutive frames. However, Zhang et al. [20] point out that the RNN is not optimal to learn temporal dependencies and propose an efficient orderless ensemble strategy. 3D convolution [13,14] directly model spatio-temporal clues, which are widely used in video-based Re-ID tasks [3,11]. However, a large number of 3D convolutional structures need to be stacked to improve the temporal receptive field, resulting in huge parameters, which is difficult for network optimization. Temporal feature aggregation makes full use of temporal cues of video frames. Recent works [8,10] utilize the non-local block [15] to perform continuous temporal feature aggregation, which aims to explore the long-term temporal clues effectively. However, the premature integration of temporal features can reduce the ability to exploit discriminative details. Thus, most of the existed methods tend to focus on the shared salient parts to learn temporal correlation but ignore the diversity of features across frames, which leads to the redundancy of features.

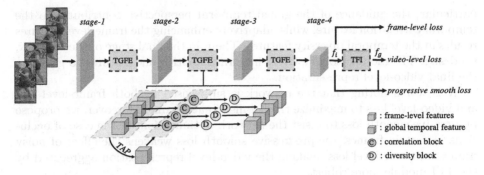

Fig. 2. Illustration of the whole framework of TCDR. The input sequence is fed into a CNN backbone. TGFE is our proposed temporal-guided frame feature enhancement module which can be inserted into any stage of the backbone. TFI is a temporal feature integration module which aggregates frame-level features f_i into the video-level feature f_g. The whole training process is supervised by video-level loss, frame-level loss, and progressive smooth loss.

Attention Methods. The attention module has become a necessary part of CNN. CBNet [16] and SENet [9] perform attention operations from spatial and channel dimensions, respectively, to enhance the representation of image-level features. Besides, the Non-Local [15] module is proposed for the first time to solve the long-term dependency and learn self-attentive features from spatio-temporal dimension. Besides, ABDNet [1] first captures spatial diversity features within a single image with the assistance of attention operations and orthogonality in image-based Re-ID tasks, while our approach, is to increase the diversity between features in the *temporal dimension*, focusing on capturing the diversity of features between multiple frames in video-based Re-ID tasks. Recently, BiCNet [6] utilizes divergence loss to guide *spatial attention mask* generation to enhance the diversity of visual representations in consecutive frames. Different from BiCNet, on one hand, our TCDR network simply decouples features from the temporal dimension and exploits comprehensive features from *both spatial and channel dimensions* under the supervision of frame-level loss. On the other hand, we also propose progressive smoothing loss to combine frame-level loss with video-level loss to supervise the model to yield more discriminative appearance features of pedestrians.

3 The Proposed Method

3.1 Overall Architecture

Our proposed TCDR network is shown in Fig. 2. Given a video clip, we sample T frames, denoted as $\mathbf{V} = \{\mathbf{I}_1, \mathbf{I}_2, ..., \mathbf{I}_T\}$. To model temporal cues, the temporal-guided frame feature enhancement module is designed to guide the learning of frame-level features with global temporal information across all frames. In particular, the guidance of the global temporal perspective contributes to the temporal correlation feature, while adaptively enhancing the frame-level features results in the temporal diversity features. Then, in the final stage of the network, we design TFI module to adaptively integrate multi-frame features to generate the final video-level representation.

It is worth noting that the network is supervised by both frame-level loss and video-level loss to maximize the details of each frame. Moreover, we propose progressive smooth loss to assist the network optimization. In the case of occlusions in certain frames, the progressive smooth loss weakens the effect of noisy frames on frame-level loss, making the video-level representation aggregated by the TFI module more robust.

3.2   Temporal-Guided Frame Feature Enhancement

The temporal-guided frame feature enhancement module is designed to capture the correlated but diverse frame-level features. Unlike the non-local based approaches, our method does not perform multi-frame feature aggregation. We explore the features of each frame independently while considering the global context temporal cues. The TGFE module performs feature enhancement in both channel dimension and spatial dimension, with TGFE-C module and TGFE-S module, respectively, as shown in Fig. 3. TGFE sequentially performs correlation and diversity feature mining.

TGFE-C Module: The input is the output feature of the previous stage $\mathbf{X} \in \mathbb{R}^{N \times T \times C \times H \times W}$, where N is the batch size. T and C denote temporal dimension and feature channels, respectively. H and W correspond to the height and width of the feature map. Performing temporal average pooling (TAP) on $\mathbf{X}$, we obtain the global temporal feature $\mathbf{X}_g \in \mathbb{R}^{N \times 1 \times C \times H \times W}$. Then we input $\mathbf{X}$ and $\mathbf{X}_g$ into the correlation block to obtain the correlation mask guided by global temporal cues. Specifically, after two independent 1×1 convolutional layers, $\mathbf{X}$ and $\mathbf{X}_g$ are dimensioned down to obtain $\mathbf{X}'$ and $\mathbf{X}'_g$, and the reduction factor is r. Next, we perform global mean pooling (GAP) on $\mathbf{X}'_g$ to obtain global temporal representation $\mathbf{G}_c \in \mathbb{R}^{N \times 1 \times C/r}$. Then, guided by the global channel information $\mathbf{G}_c$, we generate the spatial attention ϕ_c of each frame over the global temporal perspective. The whole computation is formulated as:

$$\phi_c = \zeta(\mathbf{X}' \cdot GAP(\mathbf{X}'_g)), \phi_c \in \mathbb{R}^{N \times T \times 1 \times HW}, \tag{1}$$

where $\zeta(\cdot)$ denotes the softmax operation.

After that, we input the original $\mathbf{X}$ with the temporal correlation mask ϕ_c into the diversity block to further explore the diverse features of the non-shared regions in $\mathbf{X}$. In detail, we perform the following operations:

$$\mathbf{A}_c = \sigma(\mathbf{W}_c(\mathbf{X} \cdot \phi_c)) \odot \mathbf{X}. \tag{2}$$

Here W_c is the learnable parameters of 1×1 convolution (Update-C), $\odot$ indicates the channel-wise multiplication, σ indicates the sigmoid function, and $\mathbf{A}_c \in \mathbb{R}^{N \times T \times C \times 1 \times 1}$ denotes the frame-level correlated but diverse features.

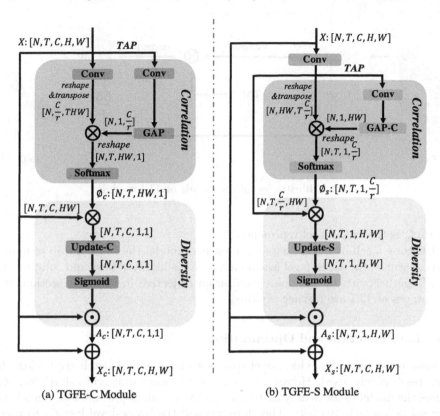

Fig. 3. Illustration of the details of TGFE module. (a) and (b) are the structures for feature enhancement at the channel and spatial positions, respectively.

Finally, $\mathbf{A}_c$ is connected $\mathbf{X}$ by the residual block, and we can obtain the output feature $\mathbf{X}_c = \mathbf{X} + \mathbf{A}_c$. The whole calculation process is shown in Fig. 3(a).

TGFE-S Module: Similar to the TGFE-C module, the TGFE-S module is designed to enhance frame-level features by spatial position. As shown in Fig. 3(b), TGFE-S also performs temporal correlation and diversity mining respectively.

3.3   Temporal Feature Integration

The temporal feature integration module is designed to adaptively aggregate the frame-level features in the final stage to yield the entire video-level representation. Based on self-attention, TFI performs adaptive attention pooling to fully explore the contribution of each frame to the temporal representation.

As shown in Fig. 4, after obtaining the temporal attention mask $\mathbf{W}$, we can then integrate the multi-frame features to yield the overall representation, calculated as follows:

$$\boldsymbol{f}_g = \mathbf{W} \cdot \mathbf{F}, \tag{3}$$

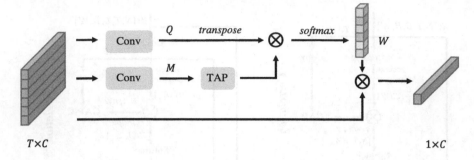

Fig. 4. Illustration of the details of TFI module

where $\boldsymbol{f}_g$ is the video-level representation.

Utilizing a self-attention-based approach to model the relationship of multi-frame features, the video-level feature after TFI is highly robust and comprehensive. Together with the unique optimization objective in the next section, the advantages of TFI are further explored.

3.4 Loss Function and Optimization

In most previous works, video-level cross-entropy loss and batch triplet loss [5] have been widely used. However, we find that using only video-level loss $\mathcal{L}_v$ causes the model to focus only on temporal shared salient parts, which makes the representation lack diversity. Therefore, we add the frame-level loss $\mathcal{L}_f$ to mine each frame for detailed cues as many as possible and yield more discriminative features.

Nevertheless, the frame-level loss faces the ambiguous identity problem due to occlusions and background clutter of individual frames, as shown in Fig. 5(a). Therefore, we design a progressive smooth loss to alleviate the effect of noisy frames and to further enhance the aggregation of TFI module. The formula is described as:

$$\mathcal{L}_{ps} = \frac{1}{N} \sum_{i=1}^{N} |p(\frac{1}{T} \sum_{k=1}^{T} \boldsymbol{f}_{ik}) - p(\boldsymbol{f}_i) + m|_+, \tag{4}$$

where $p(\cdot)$ denotes the predicted probability of a label in the ground truth and m is a predefined margin. $|\cdot|_+$ is similar to the *ReLU* function.

As shown in Fig. 5, by setting the margin between the prediction probability of global features and frame-level features, the network does not optimize down in the wrong direction under the ambiguity identity problem. Supervision with progressive smooth loss greatly improves the robustness of temporal features.

Finally, the overall loss is as follows:

$$\mathcal{L}_{all} = \mathcal{L}_v + \lambda \mathcal{L}_f + \gamma \mathcal{L}_{ps}, \tag{5}$$

where λ and γ are weighting factors.

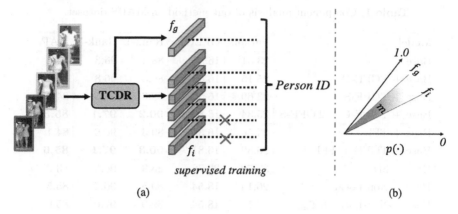

(a)   (b)

Fig. 5. (a) Illustration of the ambiguous identity problem. The images in the red box contain two pedestrians due to occlusions, which introduce uncertainty (such as the ambiguous labels as shown by the red crosses) during supervised training. (b) Illustration of the progressive smooth loss, which indicates adding a margin between the global feature f_g and frame-level features f_i to predict the identity probability.

4   Experiments

4.1   Datasets and Evaluation Protocol

Datasets We evaluate our approach in three publicly available datasets, including MARS [21], DukeMTMC-VideoReID [17] and LS-VID [10].

Evaluation Protocol. We use standard evaluation metrics, including Cumulative Matching Characteristics (CMC) and Mean average precision (mAP).

4.2   Implementation Details

We employ ResNet-50 [4] as our backbone, in which the stride of the last layer is set to 1. In the training phase, we only randomly sample $T = 4$ frames in the stride of 8 for each sequence as input. The input images are resized to 256×128. We apply the commonly used random horizontal flipping and random erasing [22] data augmentation strategies. To train with hard mining triplet loss [5], we randomly sample 8 identities in each batch, each identity with 4 sequences. The Adam optimizer is used to train a total of 150 epochs, in which the initial learning rate is set to 0.0003 with a decay factor of 0.1 per 40 epochs. We simply use $\lambda = \gamma = 1$ and do not adjust them carefully. Moreover, we perform TGFE-C before TGFE-S brings better benefits, which is the arrangement we finally choose.

4.3   Ablation Study

In this section, our baseline is built on ResNet-50 [4] with temporal average pooling, using only $\mathcal{L}_v$ as the optimization objective.

Table 1. Component analysis of our method on MARS dataset.

Model	Params	GFLOPs	Rank-1	Rank-5	mAP
Base	23.51	16.38	88.6	96.3	83.4
Base + TGFE-C	25.15	16.65	89.5	96.8	84.7
Base + TGFE-S	23.69	16.53	89.6	96.5	84.4
Base + TGFE-C + TGFE-S	25.34	16.80	**90.2**	**97.1**	**85.3**
Base + TFI	24.56	16.38	89.3	96.6	84.1
Base + TGFE + TFI	26.39	16.81	**90.3**	**97.1**	**85.6**
Base + 3D	33.70	22.76	88.9	96.3	83.9
Base + Non-Local	26.14	18.54	89.5	96.8	85.5
Base + Non-Local + $\mathcal{L}_{all}$	26.14	18.54	89.9	97.0	85.6
Base + TGFE + TFI + $\mathcal{L}_{all}$	26.39	16.81	**90.6**	**97.3**	**87.0**

Table 2. The results on MARS dataset using different loss functions.

Model	$\mathcal{L}_f$	$\mathcal{L}_{ps}$	Rank-1	Rank-5	mAP
Base	✗	✗	88.6	96.3	83.4
	✓	✗	89.2	96.7	84.6
	✗	✓	88.8	96.3	84.1
	✓	✓	**89.6**	**97.0**	**85.4**
TCDR	✓	✓	**90.6**	**97.3**	**87.0**

Effectiveness of TGFE and TFI. As shown in Table 1, we add TGFE-C and TGFE-S modules to stages 2 and 3 of the backbone, respectively, both of which improve accuracy over the baseline. Using both, our model improves by 1.6% in Rank-1 and 1.9% in mAP. The results indicate that TGFE captures correlated but diverse details, which can enhance discrimination in cases where the shared parts are too similar. Moreover, replacing the temporal average pooling (TAP) with TFI can further improve the feature aggregation ability. The joint use of TGFE and TFI achieves further boosts, which shows the effectiveness of TGFE and TFI.

Impact of Loss Functions. Table 2 shows the detailed ablations of different loss functions. We find that using the frame-level loss $\mathcal{L}_f$ gains a 1.2% boost on mAP, perhaps because using frame-level loss can facilitate the exploration of diversified details. Also, adding $\mathcal{L}_{ps}$ alone has limited improvement, but in conjunction with $\mathcal{L}_f$, it achieves further boost. We conclude that $\mathcal{L}_{ps}$ alleviates the influence of noisy frames and brings better benefits when using frame-level loss.

Comparisons with Other Temporal Modeling Methods. As shown in Table 1, our proposed TCDR is superior in terms of both the complexity and performance compared to Base + 3D, and we argue that the fixed convolution

Table 3. Comparison with the state-of-the-art method on MARS and DukeMTMC-VideoReID datasets. The best results are shown in bold.

Method	MARS		DukeMTMC		LS-VID	
	mAP	Rank-1	mAP	Rank-1	mAP	Rank-1
EUG [17]	42.5	62.7	63.2	72.8	-	-
QAN [12]	51.7	73.7	-	-	-	-
M3D [11]	74.1	84.4	-	-	40.1	57.7
VRSTC [8]	82.3	88.5	93.5	95.0	-	-
GLTR [10]	78.5	87.0	93.7	96.3	44.3	63.1
MGH [19]	85.8	90.0	-	-	-	-
TCLNet [7]	85.1	89.8	96.2	96.9	70.3	81.5
AP3D [3]	85.1	90.1	95.6	96.3	73.2	84.5
BiCNet [6]	86.0	90.2	96.1	96.3	75.1	84.6
STMN [2]	84.5	90.5	95.9	97.0	69.2	82.1
TCDR(Ours)	**87.0**	**90.6**	**96.5**	**97.3**	**77.9**	**86.0**

kernel in 3D convolution limits the diversity between multiple frames. For Base + Non-Local, our method achieves similar performance, but with fewer flops. Moreover, Non-Local + $\mathcal{L}_{all}$ does not bring more favorable results, indicating that non-local blocks aggregate temporal information earlier, making it unable to decouple frame-level features to explore temporal diversity. The above experimental results show that TCDR mines the correlation-diversity representations across frames with less computational complexity.

4.4   Comparison with State-of-the-Art Methods

We summarize the results of recent works on the MARS dataset in Table 3. Our proposed TCDR achieves 90.6% in Rank-1 and 87.0% in mAP with sampling only 4 frames per clip for training. More remarkably, the significant improvement in mAP demonstrates the excellent performance in the ranking of retrieval results. Besides, our method achieves 86.0% and 77.9% on Rank-1 and mAP on LS-VID datasets, which surpasses the state-of-the-art method by a large margin(2.8% for mAP and 1.4% for Rank-1). As discussed above, benefitted by multi-frame diversity and correlation representations, our approach shows strong robustness and competitiveness across the three benchmarks.

4.5   Visualization Analysis

As shown in Fig. 6(a), we find that the baseline only focuses on the shared salient parts between multiple frames, e.g. bags and clothes, but ignores the diversity within individual frames, such as shoes. In contrast, our method captures more comprehensive features and achieves a combination of correlation and diversity between multiple frames. Besides, Fig. 6(b) demonstrates the robustness of our

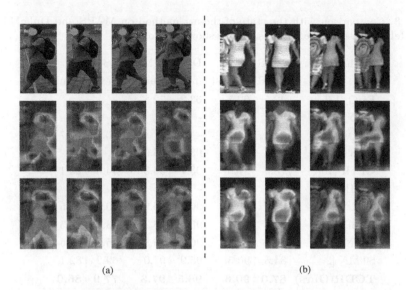

(a)   (b)

Fig. 6. Visualization of attention maps on different frames of our method. (a) Visualization across different frames. (b) Visualization under the ambiguous identity problem. The first row is the original frame image, the second row is the visualization of the baseline, and the third row is the visualization of our method.

method to noisy frames. The ambiguous identity problem arises when multiple pedestrians appear in the same frame. Our approach extracts more robust frame-level features guided by the global temporal information, which solves the ambiguous identity problem well.

5 Conclusions

In this paper, we propose a novel Temporal Correlation-Diversity Representation network for video-based Re-ID. Our proposed TGFE module explores the temporal correlation with a global perspective and enhances frame-level features to achieve temporal diversity. TFI yields a more robust pedestrian representation by temporal self-attention modeling. Combined with our proposed progressive smooth loss, our proposed TCDR captures both the temporal correlation and explores the diversity of multi-frame features with the co-optimization strategy. The state-of-the-art performance in widely-used datasets demonstrates the superiority of TCDR.

Acknowledgment. The research work is supported by the National Key Research and Development Program of China (2021AAA0140203), the Zhejiang Provincial Key Research and Development Program of China (No. 2021C01164), the Project of Chinese Academy of Sciences (E141020). Juan Cao thanks the Nanjing Government Affairs and Public Opinion Research Institute for the support of "CaoJuan Studio" and thank Chi Peng, Jingjing Jiang, Qiang Liu, and Yu Dai for their help.

References

1. Chen, T., et al.: ABD-Net: attentive but diverse person re-identification. In: ICCV (2019)
2. Eom, C., Lee, G., Lee, J., Ham, B.: Video-based person re-identification with spatial and temporal memory networks. In: ICCV (2021)
3. Gu, X., Chang, H., Ma, B., Zhang, H., Chen, X.: Appearance-preserving 3D convolution for video-based person re-identification. In: ECCV (2020)
4. He, K., Zhang, X., Ren, S., Sun, J.: Deep residual learning for image recognition. In: CVPR (2016)
5. Hermans, A., Beyer, L., Leibe, B.: In defense of the triplet loss for person re-identification. arXiv preprint arXiv:1703.07737 (2017)
6. Hou, R., Chang, H., Ma, B., Huang, R., Shan, S.: BiCnet-TKS: learning efficient spatial-temporal representation for video person re-identification. In: CVPR (2021)
7. Hou, R., Chang, H., Ma, B., Shan, S., Chen, X.: Temporal complementary learning for video person re-identification. In: ECCV (2020)
8. Hou, R., Ma, B., Chang, H., Gu, X., Shan, S., Chen, X.: VRSTC: occlusion-free video person re-identification. In: CVPR (2019)
9. Hu, J., Shen, L., Sun, G.: Squeeze-and-excitation networks. In: CVPR (2018)
10. Li, J., Wang, J., Tian, Q., Gao, W., Zhang, S.: Global-local temporal representations for video person re-identification. In: ICCV (2019)
11. Li, J., Zhang, S., Huang, T.: Multi-scale 3D convolution network for video based person re-identification. In: AAAI (2019)
12. Liu, Y., Yan, J., Ouyang, W.: Quality aware network for set to set recognition. In: CVPR (2017)
13. Qiu, Z., Yao, T., Mei, T.: Learning spatio-temporal representation with pseudo-3D residual networks. In: ICCV (2017)
14. Tran, D., Bourdev, L., Fergus, R., Torresani, L., Paluri, M.: Learning spatiotemporal features with 3D convolutional networks. In: ICCV (2015)
15. Wang, X., Girshick, R., Gupta, A., He, K.: Non-local neural networks. In: CVPR (2018)
16. Woo, S., Park, J., Lee, J.Y., Kweon, I.S.: CBAM: convolutional block attention module. In: ECCV (2018)
17. Wu, Y., Lin, Y., Dong, X., Yan, Y., Ouyang, W., Yang, Y.: Exploit the unknown gradually: one-shot video-based person re-identification by stepwise learning. In: CVPR (2018)
18. Xu, S., Cheng, Y., Gu, K., Yang, Y., Chang, S., Zhou, P.: Jointly attentive spatial-temporal pooling networks for video-based person re-identification. In: ICCV (2017)
19. Yan, Y., et al.: Learning multi-granular hypergraphs for video-based person re-identification. In: CVPR (2020)
20. Zhang, L., et al.: Ordered or orderless: a revisit for video based person re-identification. Trans. Pattern Aanal. Mach. Intell. **43**, 1460–1466 (2020)
21. Zheng, L., et al.: Mars: a video benchmark for large-scale person re-identification. In: ECCV (2016)
22. Zhong, Z., Zheng, L., Kang, G., Li, S., Yang, Y.: Random erasing data augmentation. In: AAAI (2020)
23. Zhou, Z., Huang, Y., Wang, W., Wang, L., Tan, T.: See the forest for the trees: Joint spatial and temporal recurrent neural networks for video-based person re-identification. In: CVPR (2017)

FIMF Score-CAM: Score-CAM Based Visual Explanations via Fast Integrating Multiple Features of Local Space for Deep Networks

Jing Li[1,2] and Dongbo Zhang[1,2(✉)]

[1] College of Automation and Electronic Information, Xiangtan University, Xiangtan, China
zhadonbo@163.com
[2] National Engineering Laboratory of Robot Visual Perception and Control, Xiangtan
University, Xiangtan, China

Abstract. The interpretability of deep networks is a hot issue in the field of computer vision. This paper proposes a FIMF Score-CAM model that fast integrates multiple features of local space. The model only needs to perform a forward convolution calculation on the image once to extract the feature maps, and then the feature selection template is introduced to integrate the features of different channels in local space to improve the ability of model interpretation. The FIMF Score-CAM model is superior to the existing mainstream models in interpreting the visual performance and fairness indicators of the decision-making, having more complete explanation of the target class and the advantage of fast calculation speed. Meanwhile, in some network models requiring larger convolution calculation, the operation time is reduced by more than 90% compared to Score-CAM.

Keywords: Class activation mapping · Model interpretation · Deep network

1 Introduction

In recent years, CNN has achieved great success in various visual tasks such as image classification [1], object detection [2], and semantic segmentation [3]. However, the lack of in-depth understanding of the intrinsic principle of convolution network, which makes it difficult to give sufficient trust to its decision-making results. In order to clarify the decision-making mechanism of the CNN network to explain the reasoning basis of the convolutional network, the research on the interpretability of the CNN model has become a hot issue in the field of computer vision.

The visualization of the CNN network is an important way to study its interpretability. At present, the visualization research methods of CNN are mainly divided into three categories including gradient back-propagation methods [4, 5], mask-based methods [6, 7] and CAM-based methods (class activation mapping) [8–11]. ① The gradient is a kind of local information, which intuitively reflects the influence of changes in local information on the output of decision-making. But this type of method is susceptible to

Noise disturbance and difficult to understand. ② The mask-based method mainly modifies the local region of the input image through mask operation, so as to find the

S. Yu et al. (Eds.): PRCV 2022, LNCS 13534, pp. 106–117, 2022.
https://doi.org/10.1007/978-3-031-18907-4_9

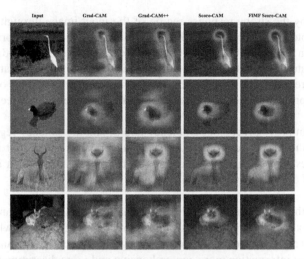

Fig. 1. Examples of class discriminative saliency maps. Column 1 is the original image, and column 2–5 shows the class saliency maps generated by Grad-CAM, Grad-CAM+, Score-CAM, and our model respectively. The saliency maps generated by gradient-free Score-CAM and our model have less background noise. At the same time, compared with Score-CAM, the target class saliency maps generated by our model have better completeness.

discriminative region that plays an important role in the specific decision output. This type of method often requires a large number of mask processing and calculation, and the speed is very slow. ③ CAM-based methods locate the salient region of the target class in the image by linearly weighting the feature maps output by the convolutional layer, having attracted the attention of researchers because of their simple calculation and high accuracy. Grad-CAM [9] uses the gradient value of backward propagation as the weight estimation. Grad-CAM++ [10] accurately calculates the gradient of each pixel of the feature map when weighting. But the gradient is unstable, and gradient mismatch may occur. Score-CAM [11] abandons the gradient calculation and then greatly improves the discriminative performance of the region to become a SOTA work in this field. However, because Score-CAM needs to upsample each feature map and multiply it by the original image, and then perform feature extraction again through forward propagation, it leads to a lot of redundant calculation. Meanwhile, the heatmap produced by Score-CAM often cannot cover the complete target class.

Since the sliding filter is used in the convolution layer, the output and input of CNN have the same length-width ratio. That means a certain region of the feature image can be considered as the feature region of the corresponding region of the original image after the convolution operation. In addition, the semantic information of the feature image is sparse and it makes strong responses only in local regions. Wang's [11] purpose of adding interference to the input image is also to highlight the strong response regions of the input image. Therefore, when calculating the weight of the feature image of the target channel to the target category, we can approximately regard it to be the weight of the original image corresponding to the strong response region of the feature image to the target category. Based on the above analysis, the corresponding feature region, which was generated by the strong response region of the input image through CNN, can be directly intercepted from each feature channel. It is not necessary to perform convolution calculation again like Score-CAM to extract features. Moreover, we introduce the feature selection template to integrate the local activation information of each feature channel to obtain the feature map of all channels in the corresponding region of the original image, and output the probability of the target category through the full connection layer and Softmax layer.

In order to improve processing efficiency and obtain the saliency region of objects with higher faithfulness, we propose a visual interpretable model that fast integrates multiple features of local space. Some visualization results are shown in Fig. 1. The contributions of our work are as follows:

(1) In this method, the feature selection templates with elements 0 and 1 are introduced to extract multiple semantic information in local space, which can fully retain the feature information of the active regions of each feature map, making the interpretable information more comprehensive and more discriminative.
(2) Our model only needs to perform forward propagation once, which avoids making forward convolution calculation on multiple perturbing input images multiple times like Score-CAM, so as to achieve higher computational efficiency.
(3) Compared with similar methods, the model in this paper can obtain a more complete class saliency map, which has good application prospects and practical value.

2 Related Works

CAM: CAM [8] considers that the feature maps output by the last layer of the convolution layer contains clear semantic information, and after the semantic features of each channel are combined by linear weighting, a visualization heatmap containing class discriminative positioning information can be obtained. In order to obtain the weight, firstly, a global average pooling layer needs to be added after the feature map, and be connected with the output layer at the same time. The trained connection weight is used as the weight of the corresponding feature map. Since we only focus on the features that have a positive effect on target class, the *ReLU* function is introduced to process the linearly weighted visualization heatmap to retain the positive information for better visualization explanation.

Grad-CAM and Grad-CAM++: The weight estimation of feature map in CAM is realized after adding a global average pooling layer to compress the features to one dimension. Because not all models have a global average pooling layer, so the CAM has great limitations in specific applications. Therefore, in order to enhance the applicability of the CAM model, Grad-CAM [9] uses the local gradient of the convolution layer as the weight of the feature map, which can be calculated by the gradient backpropagation output by the target class.

Because Grad-CAM only averages the gradient matrix when calculating the weight of feature map, Grad-CAM cannot provide an accurate explanation when there are multiple similar targets in the image. In order to solve this problem, Grad-CAM++ [10] fully considered the importance of each positioning element in the gradient matrix to the output, and it calculated the weight of each element in the gradient matrix through the high-order derivative.

Score-CAM: Because the gradient is unstable and easy to be disturbed by noise, the gradient will disappear or explode in the process of gradient propagation, which may cause that the contribution of some feature maps with a large weight to the output may be very low, while some feature maps with low weight make a greater contribution to the output. In order to solve this problem, Wang [11] proposed a gradient-free method Score-CAM. Score-CAM combines the idea of mask and CAM, adds perturbation to the original input image through the feature map, and estimates the importance of the corresponding feature map by using the change of output class score. The visualization heatmap generated by this method has strong class discrimination.

$$H_l^k = s\left(Up\left(A_l^k\right)\right) \tag{1}$$

$$C\left(A_l^k\right) = f\left(X \bigcirc H_l^k\right) - f(X_b) \tag{2}$$

$$L_{Score-CAM}^c = ReLU\left(\sum_k a_k^c A_l^k\right) \tag{3}$$

$$a_k^c = C\left(A_l^k\right) \tag{4}$$

where $C\left(A_l^k\right)$ represents the contribution of feature map A_l^k to class c relative to the baseline image; A_l^k is the k-th feature map of the l-th layer; $\bigcirc$ represents Hadamard product; X represents the input image; $Up(.)$ is the upsampling function; $s(.)$ is the function of normalizing the feature map to the [0, 1]; $f(.)$ represents forward propagation function; H_l^k is the mask image that A_l^k is upsampled to the input size and normalized; $X \bigcirc H_l^k$ is the disturbance map obtained after H_l^k is point-wise multiplied on the input image and X_b is the baseline image. X_b in Score-CAM is a pure black image, that is, an image with all elements being 0.

3   Our Method

Processing flow diagram of Score-CAM includes Phase 1: extracting original image features; Phase 2: masking the input image using the feature map after upsampling, re-extracting features through CNN forward propagation (*e.g.* The network is resnet50, and 2048 feature maps will be generated for the last convolution layer, so the forward propagation process needs to be repeated 2048 times), and then estimating the contri-bution of the feature map. It can be seen from formula (2) and above analysis that the Score-CAM needs to re-extract features through the common convolution network CNN after perturbing the input image with each feature map. Because the convolution calcu-lation is time-consuming, the calculation amount of Score-CAM is far more than other mainstream CAM models. Since the feature map represents specific semantic features, its actual role in perturbing the input is to highlight the regions associated with specific semantic features in the original image and suppress uncorrelated regions. In fact, the features of these regions that need to be highlighted have been extracted through the

CNN network in Phase 1. It can be directly extracted from the feature map of Phase 1, and there is no need to re-calculate the feature extraction through the CNN network. Based on the above consideration and analysis, we can completely avoid the unnecessary time-consuming CNN feature extraction processing in Phase 2. At the same time, considering the contribution of specific regions to the output, we propose a FIMF Score-CAM to directly process at the feature map level to calculate the weight of each feature map. The processing framework of this method is shown in Fig. 2.

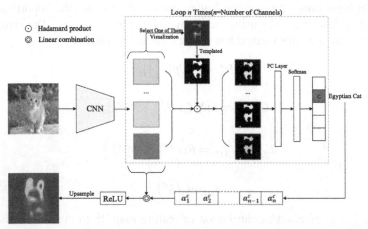

Fig. 2. Schematic diagram of FIMF Score-CAM. For each channel feature map, extract its strong response local region template then intercept the features of other channel feature maps in the local region, and obtain n new feature maps containing only local features. Finally, we calculate their contribution to the target class through the full connection layer and Softmax layer.

In order to integrate the feature information of a specific region, it is necessary to extract the information of all feature channels in the relevant region. We define A as the feature map of the target convolution layer $A = \{A^1, A^2 ..., A^n\}$ and firstly select the k-th feature map A^k of the target convolution layer (The selection order can be selected randomly or sequentially. As long as the k-th feature map corresponds to the k-th weight, the results will not be inconsistent), and then set the elements greater than 0 in A^k to 1 and the elements less than or equal to 0 to 0 to obtain the template T^k:

$$T_{ij}^k = \begin{cases} 1, A_{ij}^k > 0 \\ 0, A_{ij}^k \leq 0 \end{cases} \tag{5}$$

The feature selection template with elements 0 and 1 helps to fully extract the weak feature information of the active region of the feature map, and completely retain the feature information of the active region of each feature map, so as to highlight the valuable information and make the interpretable region generated by the model more complete.

Then, the template T^k and each feature map are used for point-wise multiplication to extract the specific region feature map B^m of n channels. B^m retains the original feature information at the active position of A^k in each channel feature map, and the inactive position of A^k is set to 0:

$$B^m = T^k \bigcirc A^m m \in \{1, \ldots, n\} \tag{6}$$

The operation after defining the target convolution layer to be displayed in the model is $Y = f(A)$ (*e.g.* suppose that the network contains *three convolution layers + averagepool + FC + Softmax*, and we choose to visualize the features extracted by the third convolution layer for the target class, then $f(.)$ is the *averagepool + FC + Softmax*), where Y is the output of Softmax layer. We define $B = \{B^1, B^2 \ldots, B^n\}$. Recording the k-th channel of the feature map A of the l-th convolution layer as A_l^k, and the baseline is defined as X_b (in this method, X_b is n feature maps with element 0), so the contribution of the feature response map A_l^k of channel k is:

$$C\left(A_l^k\right) = f(B) - f(X_b) \tag{7}$$

For a given target class c, the final visualization heatmap is calculated by the following formula:

$$L_{FIMFScore-CAM}^c = ReLU\left(\sum_k a_k^c A_l^k\right) \tag{8}$$

$$a_k^c = C\left(A_l^k\right) \tag{9}$$

4 Experiments

In order to verify the superiority of our model, we have carried out comparative experiments with the classic work of CAM series, Grad-CAM, Grad-CAM++, Score-CAM, including completeness of class saliency maps and model performance evaluation, perturbation analysis, localization evaluation and processing efficiency. The data set used in the experiment is the ILSVRC 2012 [12], and the models used are from the pre-training model provided by the Pytoch model zoo.

5 Completeness of Class Saliency Maps and Model Performance Evaluation

If the class saliency map can better cover the complete target region, it indicates that the saliency map output by the model can observe the object more comprehensively and has better interpretability for the target class. In order to measure the completeness of the class saliency maps output by different models to the target class interpretation, it can be on the premise of ensuring precision and at the same time having a large recall index. The precision and recall formulas are as follows:

$$Precision = \frac{Num(boundingbox \cap heatmap)}{Num(heatmap)} \tag{10}$$

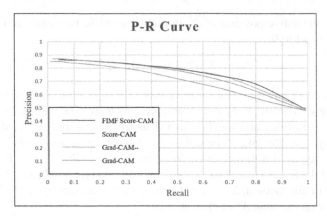

Fig. 3. P-R curves corresponding to different model methods.

$$Recall = \frac{Num(boundingbox \cap heatmap)}{Num(boundingbox)} \qquad (11)$$

the numerator represents the number of pixels of the saliency map falling in the target class bounding box; the denominator of precision formula represents the total number of effective pixels in the generated saliency map, and the denominator of the recall formula represents the number of pixels in the bounding box.

In order to better evaluate the comprehensive performance of different models, we randomly select 500 images with a single bounding box in the ILSVRC 2012 validation set, and draw the P-R curves of mainstream work of CAM series and the method in this paper concerning the evaluation method in [13]. Since the pixel value of the saliency map generated by the model ranges from 0 to 1, we select 10 thresholds at an interval of 0.1, calculate the precision and recall indicators corresponding to the saliency map in 10 cases, and finally draw the P-R curve as shown in Fig. 3. As can be seen from Fig. 3, Grad-CAM++, Score-CAM and FIMF Score-CAM are all ahead of Grad-CAM. Because the strong response regions generated by the three models are basically the same, the effects of the three models are basically the same when the recall is lower than 0.4. When the recall is higher than 0.4, the gradient-free method is comprehensively ahead of the gradient-based method. When the recall is lower than 0.7, the performance of our model is basically similar to that of Score-CAM. When the recall is higher than 0.7, the performance of the comprehensive index of our model has been greatly improved. At this time, the performance of FIMF Score-CAM is much better than that of existing classical models.

6   Perturbation Analysis

Interpretability model faithfulness index is usually used to evaluate the object recognition ability of the model. The faithfulness of CAM-based methods is evaluated by adding perturbation to the input image [10, 11]. The basic assumption is that adding perturbation to the relevant region of the target class in the input image will reduce the class confidence. Referring to Grad-CAM++ and combining it with the masking idea

Table 1. Faithfulness evaluation of object recognition by different models (%)

Method	Grad-CAM	Grad-CAM++	Score-CAM	FIMF Score-CAM
Average drop (Higher is better)	42.35	40.79	42.27	**43.66**
Average increase (Lower is better)	10.20	14.20	11.80	**8.80**

Fig. 4. The visualization of Class discriminative results and multiple occurrences of the same class

[6], we add a perturbation to the original image by masking the saliency region generated by the model, and measure the faithfulness of the model by using the decrease rate of image recognition confidence after adding the perturbation. The formula is expressed as:

$$Y = I \bigcirc (1 - L^c) \tag{12}$$

where L^c is the generated saliency map; Y is the image after adding perturbation to the original image I, and $\bigcirc$ represents *Hadamard product*. Because the background noise of the saliency map generated by the gradient-based method is large, and the saliency map generated by the gradient-free method is relatively "clean". So, we select the top 50% of the pixels as the effective pixels according to [11] and set other pixels to 0 for testing.

We use two quantitative indicators to evaluate the importance of the saliency map generated by the model of the target class.

1) We calculate the confidence drop degree of each image about the same class. The greater the drop, the greater the contribution of the saliency region generated by the model to the target class. The formula of the average drop rate is as follows:

$$Average \ Drop = \frac{1}{N} \sum_{i=1}^{N} \frac{\max(0, O_i^c - Y_i^c)}{O_i^c} \times 100 \tag{13}$$

where Y_i^c is the confidence of class c in the i-th image output by the model after adding perturbation to the original image; O_i^c is the confidence of the i-th image output by the model about class c, and N is the number of images.

2) Generally, adding perturbation information will reduce the confidence of the model. If the confidence of the model increases after adding perturbation information, it indicates that the saliency map generated by the model has poor explanatory ability for the target class. We measure this index by calculating the proportion of the number

of images with increased confidence in all images:

$$Average\ Increase = \sum_{i=1}^{N} \frac{Sign(Y_i^c > O_i^c)}{N} \times 100 \tag{14}$$

the *Sign(bool)* function indicates that if the input bool type is true, 1 will be output, and if false, 0 will be output, and the meaning of other parameters is same as formula (13).

We randomly selected 500 images in ILSVRC 2012 validation set for the above index test, and the results are shown in Table 1. It can be seen that the average drop index and average increase index of our model are greatly improved compared with the previous mainstream models, reaching 43.66%, 8.8%. It shows that the interpretable region generated by our model has a good ability to identify target classes and plays a better role in object recognition. Our model can distinguish different classes and locate multiple same class objects as shown in Fig. 4.

Table 2. Performance evaluation results based on target localization

Method	Grad-CAM	Grad-CAM++	Score-CAM	FIMF Score-CAM
$Loc_I^c(\delta = 0)$ (Higher is better)	0.61	0.62	**0.74**	0.71
$Loc_I^c(\delta = 0.5)$ (Higher is better)	0.81	0.82	**0.84**	**0.84**

7   Localization Evaluation

In this section, we evaluate the target localization capability of our model. We evaluate the target localization ability by combining the threshold selection strategy proposed by Grad-CAM++ and the energy-based pointing game proposed by Score-CAM. Specifically, we first give a threshold, and the elements below this threshold in the saliency map are set to 0. Then, we binarize the input image with the bounding box of the target class, the inside region is assigned to 1 and the outside region is assigned to 0. Then, we point-wise multiply it with generated saliency map, and sum over to gain how much energy in target bounding box. This method is called threshold energy pointing game, and its calculation formula is:

$$Loc_I^c(\delta) = \frac{\sum L_{(i,j)\in bbox}^c}{\sum L_{(i,j)\in bbox}^c + \sum L_{(i,j)\notin bbox}^c} \tag{15}$$

where $L_{(i,j)}^c$ represents the value of the saliency map of the target class at coordinates (i, j); c represents the target class; I is the input image and δ represents the set threshold. Its value ranges from 0 to 1. We randomly select 500 images with only one bounding box in the ILSVRC 2012 validation set, and then test them when the thresholds are 0 and 0.5 respectively. The results are shown in Table 2.

In terms of target localization ability, FIMF Score-CAM lags behind Score-CAM slightly, which indicates that FIMF Score-CAM also brings some background noise when the localization completeness is better than Score-CAM. And with the increase of threshold, this gap is gradually decreasing, which shows that our model is basically consistent with the high corresponding region of Score-CAM. Meanwhile, our model and Score-CAM are significantly ahead of gradient-based Grad-CAM and Grad-

Table 3. Model test speed on CPU

CPU	VGG16	VGG19	ResNet50	ResNet101	ResNet152	GoogLeNet	Inception_v3
Score-CAM (s)	37.2	47.3	214	359	508	68.2	146
FIMF Score-CAM (s)	9.3	9.6	13.7	13.3	13.6	3.5	10.6
Decrease (%)	75.0	79.7	93.6	96.3	97.3	94.9	92.7

Table 4. Model test speed on GPU

GPU	VGG16	VGG19	ResNet50	ResNet101	ResNet152	GoogLeNet	Inception_v3
Score-CAM (s)	2.1	2.9	23.7	51.6	65.1	14.8	42.5
FIMF Score-CAM (s)	1.9	1.9	13.6	14.4	14.2	4.2	14.5
Decrease (%)	9.5	34.5	42.6	72.1	78.2	71.6	65.7

CAM++. It is also verified that the saliency map generated by the gradient-free method has less background noise, concentrated saliency regions and better interpretability. Figure 4 shows the image test results of multiple same target classes. Obviously, for multiple targets, FIMF Score-CAM also shows good localization ability.

8 Comparison of Model Calculation Efficiency

Because each image is preprocessed, the image size of the input model is (224 × 224 × 3). Therefore, the processing speed of the model for each image is basically the same. We use different CNN networks for a single image in the CPU and GPU environment to test the calculation time of Score-CAM and FIMF Score-CAM. The CPU is Intel E5 2678v3 and the GPU is Geforce RTX 3090. The models used are respectively the pre-train models VGG16, VGG19 [14], ResNet50, ResNet101, ResNet152 [15], GoogLeNet [16], Inception_v3 [17] in the Pytorch model zoo. We use the speed decrease rate to describe the speed increase of FIMF Score-CAM compared to Score-CAM. We define the speed decrease rate formula as follow:

$$Decrease = 1 - \frac{T_{FIMFScore-CAM}}{T_{Score-CAM}} \tag{16}$$

where T represents the time required for the corresponding model to process a single image.

As shown in Tables 3 and 4 under the same hardware environment, the running speed of the FIMF Score-CAM model on CPU and GPU is significantly improved compared with Score-CAM. When running the ResNet152 on the CPU, FIMF Score-CAM only takes 3% of the time consumed by Score-CAM to complete the image processing. On the model with rather more convolution layers, FIMF Score-CAM speeds up by more than 90%, greatly improving the operation speed. When running ResNet152 on GPU, the time consumed by our model is reduced by about 78.2% compared with Score-CAM. On other models, our running speed is also significantly improved. Because the convolution calculation speed of GPU is much higher than that of CPU, the speed improvement of running small networks on GPU is less than that of other large-scale networks. The above practical test results show that the model in this paper has significantly faster computational efficiency than Score-CAM.

9   Conclusion

Based on the Score-CAM model, we propose the FIMF Score-CAM model which can fast integrate multiple features of local space. It is superior to all existing mainstream models in terms of interpretability index. The interpretation of target classes is more complete and our model has the advantage of fast calculation speed. We have verified the advantages of FIMF Score-CAM in a variety of experiments. The model has good application prospect, and can explain the CNN model quickly and accurately.

Acknowledgment. This work was supported in part by the Joint Fund for Regional Innovation and Development of NSFC (U19A2083), Key Project of Guangdong Provincial Basic and Applied Basic Research Fund Joint Fund (2020B1515120050), Hunan Provincial Natural Science Foundation (2020JJ4090).

References

1. Krizhevsky, A., Sutskever, I., Hinton, G.E.: ImageNet classification with deep convolutional neural networks. In: NIPS, pp. 1097–1105 (2012)
2. Liu, W., et al.: SSD: single shot multiBox detector. In: Leibe, B., Matas, J., Sebe, N., Welling, M. (eds.) ECCV 2016. LNCS, vol. 9905, pp. 21–37. Springer, Cham (2016). https://doi.org/10.1007/978-3-319-46448-0_2
3. Chen, L.-C., Zhu, Y., Papandreou, G., Schroff, F., Adam, H.: Encoder-decoder with atrous separable convolution for semantic image segmentation. In: Ferrari, V., Hebert, M., Sminchisescu, C., Weiss, Y. (eds.) ECCV 2018. LNCS, vol. 11211, pp. 833–851. Springer, Cham (2018). https://doi.org/10.1007/978-3-030-01234-2_49

4. Springenberg, J.T., Dosovitskiy, A., Brox, T., Riedmiller, M.: Striving for simplicity: the all convolutional net. *arXiv preprint* arXiv:1412.6806 (2014)
5. Simonyan, K., Vedaldi, A., Zisserman, A.: Deep inside convolutional networks: visualising image classification models and saliency maps. *arXiv preprint* arXiv:1312.6034 (2013)
6. Fong, R.C., Vedaldi, A.: Interpretable explanations of black boxes by meaningful perturbation. In: ICCV, pp. 3429–3437 (2017)
7. Wagner, J., Kohler, J.M., Gindele, T., Hetzel, L., Wiedemer, J.T., Behnke, S.: Interpretable and fine-grained visual explanations for convolutional neural networks. In: CVPR, pp. 9097–9107 (2019)
8. Zhou, A., Khosla, A., Lapedriza, A.O., Torralba, A.: Learning deep features for discriminative localization. In: CVPR, pp. 2921–2929 (2016)
9. Selvaraju, R., Cogswell, M., Das, A., Vedantam, R., Parikh, D., Batra, D.: Grad-CAM: visual explanations from deep networks via gradient-based localization. In: ICCV, pp. 618–626 (2017)
10. Chattopadhay, A., Sarkar, A., Howlader, P., Balasubramanian, V.N.: Grad-CAM++: generalized gradient-based visual explanations for deep convolutional networks. In: WACV, pp. 839–847 (2018)
11. Wang, H., et al.: Score-CAM: score-weighted visual explanations for convolutional neural networks. In: CVPRW, pp. 24–25 (2020)
12. Russakovsky, O., et al.: ImageNet large scale visual recognition challenge. Int. J. Comput. Vis. **115**(3), 211–252 (2015)
13. Borji, M -M. Cheng, H.J., Li, J.: Salient object detection: a benchmark. IEEE Trans. Image Process. **24**(12), 5706–5722 (2015)
14. Simonyan, K., Zisserman, A.: Very Deep Convolutional Networks for Large-Scale Image Recognition, pp. 1–14. Computational and Biological Learning Society (2015)
15. He, K., Zhang, X., Ren, S., Sun, J.: Deep residual learning for image recognition. In: CVPR, pp. 770–778 (2016)
16. Szegedy, W., et al.: Going deeper with convolutions. In: CVPR, pp. 1–9 (2015)
17. Szegedy, V., Vanhoucke, S., Ioffe, J.S., Wojna, Z.: Rethinking the inception architecture for computer vision. In: CVPR, pp. 2818–2826 (2016)

Learning Adaptive Progressive Representation for Group Re-identification

Kuoyu Deng[1], Zhanxiang Feng[1], and Jian-Huang Lai[1,2,3]($\boxtimes$)

[1] School of Computer Science and Engineering, Sun Yat-sen University, Guangzhou, China
dengky8@mail2.sysu.edu.cn, {fengzhx7,stsljh}@mail.sysu.edu.cn
[2] Guangdong Province Key Laboratory of Information Security Technology, Guangzhou, China
[3] Key Laboratory of Video and Image Intelligent Analysis and Application Technology,
Ministry of Public Security, Guangzhou, People's Republic of China

Abstract. Group re-identification (re-id) aims to retrieve a group of people across different surveillance cameras. Due to the change of group layout and membership, group re-id is much more difficult than person re-id. How to address these problems for group re-id is under-explored. In this paper, we propose the Adaptive Progressive group representation Learning Network (APLN) which consists of three innovations: First, we propose a progressive group representation method which fuses individual features together with relation features. Second, we propose a member mask to ignore the impact of changes in the number of members. The member mask is beneficial to getting a more robust group representation from volatile group samples. Third, we propose to use group proxy node as the global representation of the group context graph to obtain precise group context graph information by focusing on more significant individuals. Experimental results demonstrate that our proposed method outperforms the state-of-the-art performance on several group re-id datasets. Compared with the previous methods, the parameters of our model are much fewer and the inference speed is faster.

Keywords: Group re-identification · Person re-identification · Transformer

1 Introduction

Group re-identification (re-id) refers to retrieving a group of people from multiple cameras [1], which is attracting increasing research attention. Given an image containing multiple people as probe, the target is to retrieve group images with similar members from the gallery. People often walk in groups so that associating with other people in the same group can provide rich context information. Therefore, identifying a group is more robust than identifying an individual. However, the variations of group layout and membership number make the task more difficult. The existing person re-id methods can not solve these problems. How to represent a group has become an urgent problem to be solved.

© The Author(s), under exclusive license to Springer Nature Switzerland AG 2022
S. Yu et al. (Eds.): PRCV 2022, LNCS 13534, pp. 118–129, 2022.
https://doi.org/10.1007/978-3-031-18907-4_10

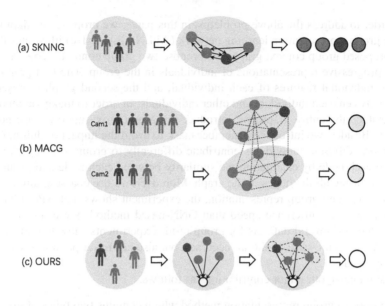

Fig. 1. Illustration of the existing group context graph structure. (a) represents the methods of SKNNG. (b) represents the methods of MACG. (c) represents our proposed group context graphs. The white node represents our proposed group proxy node. Our method can avoid the impact of dummy nodes and pay more attention to prominent individuals to adaptively represent different population groups.

The current popular method is to construct a group context graph. The existing group context graph is shown in Fig. 1. Zhu et al. [2] (as shown in Fig. 1(a)) search the closest two individuals in space as neighbors for each individual in a group, then fuse the features of individuals and their neighbors to search for the most similar group. Only two group members are related to each individual, so the group graph context information is incomplete. However, we believe that spatial information is helpful on a specific dataset. The position changes between groups of people are unpredictable in the real scene, so it doesn't work well in situations where the position changes a lot. Yan et al. [3] (as shown in Fig. 1(b)) divide the individual feature map into four parts. For intra-group attention, they learn attention information from different parts of the same individual and different parts of different individuals. For inter-group attention, they learn the attention between different individuals from two images in the same group. However, this method needs two group images for training at the same time. When the number of members of the group is limited, they will copy one of the individual features to fill in the missing graph nodes. This strategy may mislead the model understanding the entire group. When the number of members changes, the representation ability of the model will also be affected. Besides, the graph neural network (GNN) [4] refers to representing graphs with a large number of nodes, it is not suitable for group re-id tasks. In addition, the calculation speed of GNN is slow, which limits the development of this model in practical application scenarios.

In order to address the above problems, in this paper, we propose an adaptive progressive group representation learning network (APLN). Figure 1(c) illustrates the idea of our proposed group context graph. We propose two group context graphs representing two progressive representations of individuals in the group. The first graph represents the individual features of each individual, and the second graph represents the relation between each individual and other individuals. In order to make the model better understand the entire graph, we introduce the group proxy node to fuse nodes of the graph. Besides, we introduce a member mask to avoid the impact of dummy nodes. Furthermore, different individuals contribute differently to group saliency. We assign weight to each node by calculating the similarity between each node and group proxy node when fusing all the nodes in the graph. Moreover, we use coarse-grained individual feature learning group representation, the experiment shows that APLN has fewer parameters and less inference speed than GNN-based method. We evaluate our proposed method on several datasets for group re-id. Experiments show that our network not only achieves the state-of-the-art accuracy, but also has fewer parameters and faster inference speed.

We summarize our major contributions as follows.

- We propose a group representation method which contains two types of group context graphs to represent individual features and associated features respectively. Further, We design the adaptive progressive group representation learning network (APLN) structure.
- We introduce the group proxy node to obtain the representation of the entire graph and focus more on significant individuals in a group. Besides, we set the member mask to avoid the impact of dummy nodes.
- Experiments on three datasets indicate that our network outperforms other previous methods for group re-identification. Moreover, compared with the existing group representation network, our model has fewer parameters and faster inference speed.

2 Related Work

2.1 Person Re-identification

Person re-id aims to retrieve pedestrians across non-overlapping cameras. The methods based on deep learning have been studied deeply [5,6]. However, most existing methods are limited to learning individual features in the bounding box of a single person. So person re-id suffers from changing posture and perspective of the pedestrians. The surrounding pedestrians of an individual is rarely considered. Therefore, a large amount of contextual information has not been noticed.

2.2 Transformer

Transformer has made great progress in the task of NLP [7,8]. Recently, more and more visual tasks have introduced the transformer structure and have great effects. Recently, Vit [9] proposes a network composed of pure transformers and achieves the state-of-the-art on image recognition tasks. DETR [10] utilizes transformer in the detection

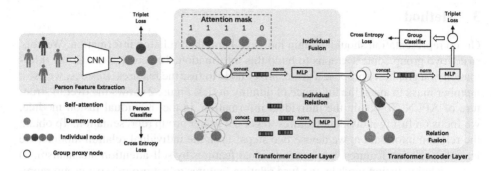

Fig. 2. Structure of the proposed adaptive progressive group representation learning network (APLN) for group re-id. We first apply CNN to extract the features of each person in the group. Then we employ two transformer encoder layers to learn group adaptive progressive representation. Specifically, in the first transformer layer, we fuse individual apparent features to obtain primary group representations and learn the associations between individual features. In the second transformer layer, we integrate this association and merge it with the primary group representation to obtain the progressive group representation.

head for object detection. Since then, more and more tasks have introduced transformers to improve performance such as Re-ID [11,12], etc. In this paper, we propose a transformer-based network for group re-identification and achieve the state-of-the-art.

2.3   Group Re-identification

Figure 2 shows the overall structure of APLN. Group re-id focuses on the global representation of the entire group. Existing methods fall into four categories. (1) Hand-craft feature type: Most early methods considered designing hand-craft features to represent a group, such as center rectangular ring and block-based ratio-occurrence descriptors [1], co-variance descriptor [13], sparse dictionary [14], weighted multi-grain representation [15]. However, hand-crafted features can not obtain robust representation from changing appearance. (2) Transfer learning type: Some work apply transfer learning to learn group features from person re-id datasets due to the lack of training samples. [16,17] employ the generated group samples to train the GNN and obtain group features. However, the distribution drift of different data sets will reduce the generalization ability of the model. (3) individuals match type: [18] used individual features to calculate the similarity between groups. [2] integrated neighbors information into individual features. However, the lack of group context information reduces the ability to represent group samples. (4) Multi-attention context type: [3] constructed a context graph to exploit dependencies among different people. However, this method failed to avoid the impact of the variable membership number.

Different from the above methods, we propose a novel group representation method, which introduces a group proxy node to learn the complete group context information and a member mask to avoid the impact of membership change on group representation.

3 Method

Group representation should contain individual and their relation information. We construct two group context graphs to build this information. To perceive the global information of a graph, we propose a group proxy node to fuse the features. Besides, we use a member mask to avoid the influence of dummy nodes. Figure 2 shows the overall structure of APLN. To obtain the individual information, in the individual fusion module, we focus on fusing individual features to get the junior group representation. To obtain the relation information, we devise two steps: 1) In the individual relation module, we learn the relation features between individual features by self-attention mechanism. 2) In the relation fusion module, we fuse relation features to get progressive group representation. We will introduce each module in detail below.

3.1 APLN

Member Mask Configuration. Given a group image, we obtain a series of person images denoted as $\{I_i | i = 1, 2, 3...n\}$, where n denotes the number of people in the group. We use ResNet-50 [19] as the backbone to extract individual features. Then the output of the pooling layer after the last convolutional layer (conv5_3) is extracted as the feature of individuals, which is denoted as $\{X_i | i = 1, 2, 3...n\} \in \mathcal{R}^{n \times r}$, where r denotes dimensions of individual features obtained by CNN. The n is uncertain, but the length of the feature sequence input to the model needs to be fixed. When the number of group members is small, we randomly select a member feature to supplement the sequence to a fixed length. When there are too many group members, we directly crop the feature sequence to a fixed length. The resulting individual feature sequence is expressed as

$$Z = \{X_1; X_2; ...; X_n; P_1; P_2; ...; P_{N-n}\} \in \mathcal{R}^{N \times r}, \tag{1}$$

where X represents the features of individuals, P represents the features to be supplemented when the personnel is insufficient, n represents the number of people in the group and N represents the length of the input feature sequence. Corresponding to Eq. 1, we set the member mask to mark which features are invalid. The member mask is denoted as

$$Mask = \{1_1; 1_2; ...; 1_n; 0_1; 0_2; ...; 0_{N-n}\} \in \mathcal{R}^{N \times 1}. \tag{2}$$

In addition, we set up a group proxy node to obtain the global representation of the entire group context graph whose shape is the same as that of individual features. The group proxy node is a learnable parameter, represented as $G \in \mathcal{R}^{1 \times r}$.

Individual Fusion. In this module, we fuse the individual representations to obtain primary group representations by self-attention mechanism. The input of self-attention is a triplet of query, key and value. We calculate the queries, keys, and values of the group proxy node and individual features, which can be expressed as

$$\begin{aligned} [G_q, Z_q] &= [G, Z] \cdot W_q, \\ [G_k, Z_k] &= [G, Z] \cdot W_k, \\ [G_v, Z_v] &= [G, Z] \cdot W_v, \end{aligned} \tag{3}$$

where $W_q \in \mathcal{R}^{r \times h}$, $W_k \in \mathcal{R}^{r \times h}$ and $W_v \in \mathcal{R}^{r \times h}$ are linear projections. Notably, the group proxy node and individual features share the same parameters. Then the group proxy node calculates the similarity with all individual features to mining specific information. To avoid the effects of invalid features, the similarity with the features of the dummy node will be calculated as $-\infty$. The formula is expressed as

$$
S^{ZG} = \begin{cases} -\infty, & Mask = 0, \\ \frac{[G_k, Z_k]G_q^T}{\sqrt{d_k}}, & Mask = 1, \end{cases}
\tag{4}
$$

where d_k represents the scaling factor equal to the dimension of the query, key, and value. Then we apply the softmax function to normalize the similarity to get the weight of each node, and then multiply each node by the weight. The formula is expressed as

$$
SA^{ZG} = Softmax(S^{ZG})[Z_v, G_v] + G.
\tag{5}
$$

We calculate SA^{ZG} separately for m times to fuse individual features of members in multiple subspaces, and then splice them into output shown as

$$
MSA([Z, G]) = [SA_1^{ZG}; SA_2^{ZG}; \ldots; SA_m^{ZG}]W_o,
\tag{6}
$$

where $W_o \in \mathcal{R}^{mc \times d}$ and c is typically set to d/m. Then the junior group representation (JGR) is obtained by MLP and the residual connection. According to the common usage of the transformer, layer norm is applied before $MSA(\cdot)$ and MLP blocks. The formula is as

$$
JGR = MSA([Z, G]) + MLP(MSA([Z, G])).
\tag{7}
$$

Individual Relation. In this module, we explore the relation information between individuals based on Eq. 3. We calculate the similarity between individual features by self-attention mechanism. The formula is expressed as

$$
S^{ZZ} = \begin{cases} -\infty, & Mask = 0, \\ \frac{Z_k Z_q^T}{\sqrt{d_k}}, & Mask = 1, \end{cases}
\tag{8}
$$

where d_k represents the dimension of query, key, and value. Then we apply the softmax function to normalize the similarity to get the weight of each node, and then multiply each node by the weight. The formula is expressed as

$$
SA^{ZZ} = Softmax(S^{ZZ})Z_v + Z.
\tag{9}
$$

We calculate SA^{ZZ} separately for m times to mine multiple potential association representations, and then splice them into output shown as

$$
MSA(Z) = [SA_1^{ZZ}; SA_2^{ZZ}; \ldots SA_m^{ZZ}]W_o,
\tag{10}
$$

where $W_o \in \mathcal{R}^{mc \times d}$ and c is typically set to d/m, and layer norm is applied before $MSA(\cdot)$ and MLP blocks. Then the individual relation representation (R) is obtained by MLP and the residual connection. The formula is as

$$
R = MSA(Z) + MLP(MSA(Z)).
\tag{11}
$$

Relation Fusion. In this module, we fuse individual relation features into the group proxy node to get our progressive group representation. We fuse the relation representation (R) obtained in the third module with junior group representation (JGR) by the self-attention mechanism. The query, key and value can be expressed by the formula as

$$JGR_q = JGR \cdot W_q,$$
$$[R_k, JGR_k] = [G, JGR] \cdot W_k, \tag{12}$$
$$JGR_v = JGR \cdot W_v,$$

where $W_q \in \mathcal{R}^{r \times h}$, $W_k \in \mathcal{R}^{r \times h}$ and $W_v \in \mathcal{R}^{r \times h}$ are linear projections. We use the group proxy node to fuse the relation information by calculating the similarity with all nodes. The similarity with the features of the dummy node will be calculated as $-\infty$. The formula is expressed as

$$S^{RG} = \begin{cases} -\infty, & Mask = 0, \\ \frac{[R_k, JGR_k] JGR_q^T}{\sqrt{d_k}}, & Mask = 1, \end{cases} \tag{13}$$

where d_k represents the scaling factor. Then we apply the softmax function to normalize the similarity to get the weight of each node, and then multiply each node by the weight. The formula is expressed as

$$SA^{RG} = Softmax(S^{RG})[R_v, JGR_v] + R. \tag{14}$$

Notably, we calculate SA^{RG} separately for m times, and then splice them into output shown as $MSA([R, JGR]) = [SA_1^{RG}, SA_2^{RG}, ..., SA_z^{RG}]W_o$, where $W_o \in \mathcal{R}^{mc \times d}$ and c is typically set to d/m. Then the progressive group representation (PGR) is obtained by MLP and the residual connection. The layer norm is applied before $MSA(\cdot)$ and MLP blocks. The formula is as

$$PGR = MSA([R, JGR]) + MLP([R, JGR]). \tag{15}$$

3.2 Loss Functions

To train our model, we employ the loss function on individual features and progressive group representation to minimize the deviation between predictions and ground truths. For the individual features Y_p from Eq. 1, we use triplet loss to increase the distance between samples between classes and reduce the distance of samples within classes. For the triples set of Y_p and its triplet set $\{Y_p^a, Y_p^p, Y_p^n\}$ where Y_p^p and Y_p^n are positive and negative samples of anchor sample Y_p^a. The triplet loss of person features L_p^t can be shown as

$$L_p^t = \left\| Y_p^a - Y_p^p \right\|_2^2 + \left\| Y_p^a - Y_p^n \right\|_2^2 + m, \tag{16}$$

where m denotes margin. Then after batch normalization processing of Y_p, we use the ID loss function to train the classifier. The ID loss is the cross-entropy loss without label smoothing. For the person ground truth label $\overline{Y_p}$, the classifier loss of person features L_p^{ID} can be shown as:

$$L_p^{ID} = -\sum_{i=1}^{n} \overline{Y_g^i} \log(Y_p^i). \tag{17}$$

Finally, we use triplet loss and ID loss to increase the distance between samples between classes and reduce the distance of samples within classes. For the group representation Y_g from Eq. 15 and its triplet set $\{Y_g^a, Y_g^p, Y_g^n\}$ where Y_g^p and Y_g^n are the representation of the same group and different group for anchor group sample Y_g^a respectively. Triplet loss Y_g^t can be expressed as

$$L_g^t = \left\| Y_g^a - Y_g^p \right\|_2^2 + \left\| Y_g^a - Y_g^n \right\|_2^2 + m. \tag{18}$$

As for ID loss of group features, we use the cross entropy function which can be expressed by

$$L_g^{ID} = -\sum_{i=1}^{n} \overline{Y_g^i} \log(Y_g^i). \tag{19}$$

Above all, we use these loss functions to jointly train our framework. the loss L used can be denoted as

$$L = \alpha_1 L_p^t + \beta_1 L_p^{ID} + \alpha_2 L_g^t + \beta_2 L_g^{ID}, \tag{20}$$

where α_1, β_1, α_2, and β_2 are the hyper-parameters.

4 Experiment

4.1 Datasets

To verify that APLN is effective on datasets of different scales, we evaluate the APLN on three different datasets. We chose the largest dataset (CSG [3]) and two small-scale datasets (Road Group [15,20] and DukeMTMC Group [15,20,21]). The CSG dataset has 3.8K images from 1.5K labeled groups. In contrast, the Road Group and DukeMTMC Group only have above 300 images from more than 100 labeled groups. And there are only two samples in each class. For deep learning methods, the small scale of the dataset is a challenge for the stability of the model.

4.2 Implementation Detail

We train our network using PyTorch framework and optimize the network on Adam optimizer [22] for 325 epochs. The initial learning rate is set to 0.0003 and is reduced to 0.00003 at the 200-th epochs. We utilize pre-trained ResNet50 [19] pre-trained to extract individual features. The person images are resized to 256×128 as inputs. The number of patches in the transformer is 5 and the number of the head in the multi-head self-attention is 4. We train the APLN on RTX 8000 GPU with a batch size of 16. For hyperparameters, the margin of triplet is set to 1.2. To make the model pay more attention to the group representation ability, we make the group representation loss weight slightly larger than the individual representation loss weight, so α_1, α_2, β_1 and β_2 are set to 1.2, 1.2, 1, 1 respectively. Same as MACG, we split CSG into fixed training and test sets, where 859 groups are utilized for training and 699 groups for testing. During testing, the images in the test set are sequentially selected as the probe, while the remaining images are regarded as the gallery setting. As for Duke Group and Road Group, we partition the datasets into training sets and test sets with equal sizes. We use the Cumulative Matching Characteristics (CMC) as the evaluation metric.

Table 1. Comparison with the state-of-the-art group re-id methods. R-k (k = 1, 5, 10, 20) denotes the Rank-k accuracy (%).r

Method	CSG				DukeMTMC group				Road group			
	R-1	R-5	R-10	R-20	R-1	R-5	R-10	R-20	R-1	R-5	R-10	R-20
CRRRO-BRO	10.4	25.8	37.5	51.2	9.9	26.1	40.2	64.9	17.8	34.6	48.1	62.2
Covariance	16.5	34.1	47.9	67.0	21.3	43.6	60.4	78.2	38.0	61.0	73.1	82.5
PREF	19.2	36.4	51.8	70.7	22.3	44.3	58.5	74.4	43.0	68.7	77.9	85.2
BSC+CM	24.6	38.5	55.1	73.8	23.1	44.3	56.4	70.4	58.6	80.6	87.4	92.1
MGR	57.8	71.6	76.5	82.3	48.4	75.2	89.9	94.4	80.2	93.8	96.3	97.5
DoT-GNN	–	–	–	–	53.4	72.7	80.7	88.6	74.1	90.1	92.6	98.8
GCGNN	–	–	–	–	53.6	77.0	**91.4**	**94.8**	81.7	94.3	96.5	97.8
MACG	63.2	75.4	79.7	84.4	57.4	79.0	90.3	94.3	84.5	95.0	96.9	98.1
Ours	**83.1**	**91.1**	**93.8**	**95.8**	**60.2**	**79.5**	87.5	92.0	**85.2**	**95.1**	**96.9**	**100.0**

4.3 Group Re-identification

We compare our model with other state-of-the-art methods for group re-id including CRRRO-BRO [1], Covariance [13], PREF [14], BSC+CM [23], MGR [20], Dot-GNN [16] GCGNN [2] and MACG [3]. As shown in Table 1, APLN achieves 83.1% rank-1 accuracy on the CSG dataset, which is almost 20% higher than MACG. In addition, APLN also outperforms the state-of-the-art methods on the Road Group dataset and DukeMTMC Group dataset. Due to the difficulty of training on small-scale datasets, the improvement in effect is not as significant as that of CSG dataset. On the DukeMTMC Group dataset, the R-1 accuracy of APLN reaches 60.2% which is 2.8% better than MACG. As for the Road Group, the R-1 accuracy of APLN reaches 85.2%, with a margin of 0.7% compared with MACG.

4.4 Ablation Study

To provide more views of the performance of the APLN, we conduct a lot of ablation experiments on the CSG dataset by isolating each key component, i.e., progressive group representation, member mask and group proxy node.

Effect of the Progressive Group Representation. To show the benefit of the progressive group representation (PGR), we conduct the ablation study by isolating the individual features (IF) and relation features (RF). The results are shown in the 3rd, 6th and 8th lines of Table 2. The effect of fusing two features is better than using one alone. We confirm that these two features are indispensable for the PGR.

Effect of the Member Mask. To show the benefit of the member mask, the 1st, 2nd, 4th and 5th lines in Table 2 indicate the experiment on isolating the member mask (denoted as M). When the member mask is applied in IF and RF, the effect can be improved by 9.1% and 11.1% respectively. We confirm that the member mask plays in a key role in APLN.

Table 2. Ablation study on the CSG dataset, where R-k denotes the Rank-k accuracy (%).

Methods	R-1	R-5	R-10	R-20
IF (w/o M, w/o P)	62.7	76.8	80.7	85.2
IF (w/ M, w/o P)	71.8	84.2	88.0	91.2
IF (w/ M, w/ P)	77.8	87.8	91.2	93.8
RF (w/o M, w/o P)	66.9	79.0	83.7	87.4
RF (w/ M, w/o P)	78.0	88.8	91.4	93.4
RF (w/ M, w/ P)	79.8	89.4	92.8	94.8
PGR	**83.1**	**91.1**	**93.8**	**95.8**

Effect of the Group Proxy Node. To show the benefit of the group proxy node, the 2nd, 3rd, 5th and 6th lines in Table 2 indicate the experiment on isolating the group proxy node (denoted as P). When we remove the group proxy node, we splice the features and then fuse the features through the MLP. When the group proxy node is applied in IF and RF, the effect can be improved by 6.0% and 1.8% respectively. We confirm that the group proxy node has an important role in APLN.

Table 3. Comparison of parameters and operating speed between our network and MACG.

Method	Params	CSG	DUKE	ROAD	Platform
MGR	–	–	18.9 min	11.5 min	i7-7700
GCGNN	–	–	2.0 s	1.7 s	GTX 1080
MACG	212M	6.7 min	10.3 s	9.2 s	GTX 2080ti
Ours	110M	47.9 s	1.5 s	1.5 s	GTX 2080ti

Parameters and Inference Speed. We compare the parameters and the running time of the entire matching process with the state-of-the-arts on several datasets. As shown in Table 3, APLN is competitive both in terms of parameters and inference speed. The data in the 1st and 2nd lines are from [2]. The data in the 3rd and 4th lines are the results of our experiment with NVIDIA GeForce GTX 2080ti GPU. Compared with MACG, our inference speed is much faster and the parameters are fewer. We believe that the coarse-grained individual features and concise attention information makes the amount of parameters and inference time less.

Loss Weight. Table 4 shows the experimental results for our method under different weights of loss functions. We achieve the best result when the weights of triplet loss and ID loss are 1.2 and 1 respectively.

Table 4. Ablation study of weights of two types of loss functions

Triplet:ID	R-1	R-5	R-10	R-20
0.8:1	80.4	89.6	92.5	94.5
1:1	81.9	91.0	92.7	94.8
1.2:1	**83.1**	**91.1**	**93.8**	**95.8**
1.5:1	81.6	90.9	92.7	95.2

Table 5. Abation study of the maximum length of input sequence.

Length	R-1	R-5	R-10	R-20
4	82.1	91.4	93.3	95.4
5	**83.1**	**91.1**	**93.8**	**95.8**
6	82.0	90.6	93.3	95.4

Feature Sequence Length. Table 5 shows the influence of the input feature sequence length. When the length is 5, the proposed method achieves the best performance.

5   Conclusion

In this paper, we propose the adaptive progressive group representation learning network (APLN). We introduce the group proxy node to obtain the representation of the entire graph and focus more on significant individuals in a group. We set the member mask to avoid the impact of dummy nodes. Experiments on three datasets indicate that our network outperforms other previous methods for group re-identification.

Acknowledgments. This project was supported by the NSFC (62076258, 61902444), and the Project of Natural Resources Department of Guangdong Province ([2021]34).

References

1. Zheng, W.S., Gong, S., Xiang, T.: Associating groups of people. In: British Machine Vision Conference (2009)
2. Zhu, J., Yang, H., Lin, W., Liu, N., Wang, J., Zhang, W.: Group re-identification with group context graph neural networks. IEEE Trans. Multimed. **23**, 2614–2626 (2020)
3. Yan, Y., et al.: Learning multi-attention context graph for group-based re-identification. IEEE Trans. Pattern Anal. Mach. Intell. (2020)
4. Kipf, T.N., Welling, M.: Semi-supervised classification with graph convolutional networks. arXiv preprint arXiv:1609.02907 (2016)
5. Wang, G., Lai, J., Huang, P., Xie, X.: Spatial-temporal person re-identification. In: Proceedings of the AAAI Conference on Artificial Intelligence, vol. 33, pp. 8933–8940 (2019)
6. Zhang, Q., Lai, J., Feng, Z., Xie, X.: Seeing like a human: asynchronous learning with dynamic progressive refinement for person re-identification. IEEE Trans. Image Process. **31**, 352–365 (2021)

7. Devlin, J., Chang, M.W., Lee, K., Toutanova, K.: BERT: pre-training of deep bidirectional transformers for language understanding. arXiv preprint arXiv:1810.04805 (2018)

8. Vaswani, A., et al.: Attention is all you need. In: Advances in Neural Information Processing Systems, pp. 5998–6008 (2017)

9. Dosovitskiy, A., et al.: An image is worth 16×16 words: transformers for image recognition at scale. arXiv preprint arXiv:2010.11929 (2020)

10. Zhu, X., Su, W., Lu, L., Li, B., Wang, X., Dai, J.: Deformable DETR: deformable transformers for end-to-end object detection. arXiv preprint arXiv:2010.04159 (2020)

11. He, S., Luo, H., Wang, P., Wang, F., Li, H., Jiang, W.: TransReID: transformer-based object re-identification. arXiv preprint arXiv:2102.04378 (2021)

12. Li, Y., He, J., Zhang, T., Liu, X., Zhang, Y., Wu, F.: Diverse part discovery: occluded person re-identification with part-aware transformer. In: Proceedings of the IEEE/CVF Conference on Computer Vision and Pattern Recognition, pp. 2898–2907 (2021)

13. Cai, Y., Takala, V., Pietikainen, M.: Matching groups of people by covariance descriptor. In: 2010 20th International Conference on Pattern Recognition, pp. 2744–2747. IEEE (2010)

14. Lisanti, G., Martinel, N., Bimbo, A.D., Foresti, G.L.: Group re-identification via unsupervised transfer of sparse features encoding. In: 2017 IEEE International Conference on Computer Vision (ICCV) (2017)

15. Xiao, H., et al.: Group re-identification: leveraging and integrating multi-grain information. In: Proceedings of the 26th ACM International Conference on Multimedia, pp. 192–200 (2018)

16. Huang, Z., Wang, Z., Hu, W., Lin, C.W., Satoh, S.: DoT-GNN: domain-transferred graph neural network for group re-identification. In: The 27th ACM International Conference (2019)

17. Huang, Z., Wang, Z., Tsai, C.C., Satoh, S., Lin, C.W.: DotSCN: group re-identification via domain-transferred single and couple representation learning. IEEE Trans. Circ. Syst. Video Technol. **31**(7), 2739–2750 (2020)

18. Mei, L., Lai, J., Feng, Z., Xie, X.: From pedestrian to group retrieval via siamese network and correlation. Neurocomputing **412**, 447–460 (2020). https://doi.org/10.1016/j.neucom.2020.06.055

19. He, K., Zhang, X., Ren, S., Sun, J.: Deep residual learning for image recognition. In: Proceedings of the IEEE Conference on Computer Vision and Pattern Recognition, pp. 770–778 (2016)

20. Lin, W., et al.: Group reidentification with multigrained matching and integration. IEEE Trans. Cybern. **51**(3), 1478–1492 (2019)

21. Ristani, E., Solera, F., Zou, R., Cucchiara, R., Tomasi, C.: Performance measures and a data set for multi-target, multi-camera tracking. In: Hua, G., Jégou, H. (eds.) ECCV 2016. LNCS, vol. 9914, pp. 17–35. Springer, Cham (2016). https://doi.org/10.1007/978-3-319-48881-3_2

22. Kingma, D.P., Ba, J.: Adam: a method for stochastic optimization (2014)

23. Zhu, F., Chu, Q., Yu, N.: Consistent matching based on boosted salience channels for group re-identification, pp. 4279–4283, September 2016. https://doi.org/10.1109/ICIP.2016.7533167

General High-Pass Convolution: A Novel Convolutional Layer for Image Manipulation Detection

Zecheng Tang[iD] and Yang Liu[✉][iD]

School of Digital Media and Design Arts, Beijing University of Posts and Telecommunications, Beijing, China
yang.liu@bupt.edu.cn

Abstract. Image Manipulation Detection is different from most computer vision tasks, such as Image Classification. The latter pays more attention to image content, while the former focuses more on manipulation trace. However, plain convolutional layer tends to learn features that represent image content rather than features that represent manipulation trace, which degrades the performance of traditional CNNs on Image Manipulation Detection. Inspired by constrained convolutional layer proposed by Bayar et al., we propose General High-Pass Convolution, a new form of convolutional layer which is capable of motivating CNNs to learn manipulation trace features. General High-Pass Convolution is designed to simulate a set of learnable high-pass filters to suppress the image content, thus motivating the CNNs to learn manipulation trace features which are mainly present in the high-frequency components of the image. We conduct comprehensive experiments to evaluate the effectiveness of General High-Pass Convolution. The experimental results show that General High-Pass Convolution achieves better performance than Bayar et al.'s constrained convolutional layer, and can be combined with CNN backbone networks to improve their performance on Image Manipulation Detection, such as VGG and ResNet.

Keywords: Image manipulation detection · CNN · Learnable high-pass filter

1 Introduction

With the increasing development of image processing techniques and user-friendly image editing software, image processing techniques are becoming more accessible and easier to use. However, some people use image processing techniques for image forgery.

So far, image forgery has been widespread and has caused inestimable damage to many fields, such as academia [1,5], journalism and judicial forensics [34]. Bik et al. [5] found that at least 1.9% of 20,621 biomedical papers published in 40

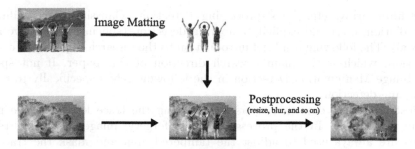

Fig. 1. The general process of image forgery

scientific journals from 1995 to 2004 exhibited signs of deliberate manipulation, and Stern et al. [31] estimated that each of the retracted papers could result in an average of \$392,582 in direct costs, implying a much higher indirect cost from misguided research and validation of academic misconduct. These figures are just the tip of the iceberg, from which the importance of Image Manipulation Detection can be seen. The general process of image forgery is shown in Fig. 1.

Over the past few decades, researchers have proposed various methods for Image Manipulation Detection. In general, these methods are aimed at detecting the following three types of information [34]: capture parameters (camera model, color filter array, etc.), post-processing trace (Gaussian filtering, bilinear interpolation, etc.) and explicit tampering trace (splicing, copy-move and removal). Among them, post-processing trace refers to the trace left by some image processing techniques. In the process of image forgery, explicit tampering is always accompanied by some image processing techniques, such as interpolation algorithms for resizing and rotating the tampered area, blurring and image noise for masking the trace of explicit tampering, etc.

Much of the previous work on post-processing detection has focused on detecting the trace left by a specific type of image processing technique. While these targeted methods have achieved many good results, there are some deficiencies. Since these methods are designed to detect a specific type of image processing technique, and image forgers have multiple image processing techniques to choose from, it is necessary to select a corresponding method for each possible image processing techniques. In addition, when a new image processing technique is developed, it is necessary to go back to the design of new detection method, which is time-consuming and labor-intensive. Therefore, there has been great interest in how to design a general post-processing detection method that can detect the trace of many different image processing techniques [3,4,9,11,14,26].

2   Related Works

2.1   Research History

Until now, the research on Image Manipulation Detection has gradually developed in three different directions: capture parameter detection (camera model, color filter array, etc.), post-processing detection (Gaussian filter, bilinear interpolation, etc.) and explicit tampering detection (splicing, copy-move and removal). The following is a brief introduction to the research of post-processing detection, which is the main research direction of this paper. If not specified, Image Manipulation Detection in the following refers specifically to post-processing detection.

Post-processing detection refers to detecting the trace left by image processing techniques. In the process of image forgery, image processing techniques are always used to adjust the tampered area and mask the trace of explicit tampering to create convincing image forgery. As described in Sect. 1, much of the previous work on post-processing detection has focused on detecting the trace left by a specific type of image processing techniques, such as median filter [2,6,7,17,28,35], Gaussian filter [16] and interpolation algorithms [13,18,23,25]. J. Chen et al. [7] found that the traditional form of CNN doesn't perform very well on Image Manipulation Detection, so they add a Median Filter Residual layer before the first layer of their CNN architecture, and improved the accuracy by 6%–7%. Inspired by the SPAM features [24] introduced two median filtering feature sets, a global probability feature set (GPF) based on the empirical cumulative distribution function of k-order ($k = 1, 2, \ldots$) difference and a local correlation feature set (LCF) based on the correlation between neighboring difference pairs in the difference domain, and then used a C-SVM with RBF kernel to classify these features to perform Image Manipulation Detection. Although these methods work well, they are designed for only one type of image processing technique, and cannot be reused to detect new image processing techniques. Therefore, there has been great interest in how to design a general Image Manipulation Detection method that can detect the trace of many different image processing techniques [3,4,9,11,14,26].

Most of the previous work on general Image Manipulation Detection method is inspired by research on Steganalysis, such as SRM [12], LBM [29] and SPAM [24]. Qiu et al. [26] analyzed the similarity between Steganography and image manipulation, and proposed a forensic strategy for Image Manipulation Detection by borrowing some powerful features from Steganalysis. Goljan et al. [14] introduced a color rich model (CRM) based on color filter array (CFA) for the Steganalysis of color images, which can also perform general Image Manipulation Detection, since most image processing techniques break the constraint introduced by CFA. While these methods show great promise, they each learn manipulation trace features with the help of pre-selected handcrafted features, except Bayar et al.'s constrained convolutional layer [3,4].

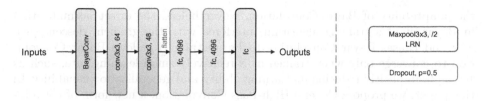

Fig. 2. Illustration of Bayar et al.'s CNN architecture.

2.2 Bayar Convolution

Bayar et al. [3] proposed a general CNN-based Image Manipulation Detection method without relying on any pre-selected features. They designed a CNN architecture (see Fig. 2), in which the first convolutional layer is used to model a set of filters, with the following constraint placed on this layer:

$$\begin{cases} w(\frac{H}{2}, \frac{W}{2}) = -1 \\ \sum_{i \neq \frac{H}{2}, j \neq \frac{W}{2}} w(i,j) = 1 \end{cases} \tag{1}$$

where $w(i,j)$ means the filter weight at the (i,j) position, and $w(\frac{H}{2}, \frac{W}{2})$ means the filter weight at the center of the filter window. We refer to this constrained convolutional layer as Bayar Convolution. Actually, the above constraint is a special form of the high-pass filter constraint showed as follows:

$$\sum_{i=0, j=0}^{H-1, W-1} w(i,j) = 0 \tag{2}$$

where H, W are the height and width of the filter window, respectively.

Bayar et al. described the role of Bayar Convolution as "Predict each pixel value on the basis of its neighbors according to a fixed rule, calculate the prediction error, create a lower dimensional feature vector or test statistic from these prediction errors, then make a decision on the basis of this feature vector or test statistic" [3]. Many methods for Image Manipulation Detection or Steganalysis can be seen as specific instances of Bayar Convolution, such as SRM [12] and SPAM [24]. In other words, Bayar Convolution can be seen as *generalization* of these methods. However, the gradient descent algorithm used by CNN for parameter optimization cannot solve such conditional extremum problem. Therefore, Bayar et al. proposed a training algorithm that normalizes the sum of the weights of the non-central positions of Bayar Convolution after each backward propagation to satisfy the constraint.

These filters in Bayar Convolution play the role of pre-selected features used in other general Image Manipulation Detection methods. However, unlike them, the weights of these filters are learnt from the training data, which indicates the adaptability of Bayar Convolution. Nevertheless, the direct normalization in Bayar et al.'s training algorithm interferes with the gradient descent process and causes Bayar Convolution to be unstable. It allows Bayar Convolution to converge only when trained at a relatively small learning rate, such as $1e-6$ [3], implicitly reducing its learning ability and generalization capability. In this paper, we propose General High-Pass Convolution, a new form of convolutional layer which is inspired by Bayar Convolution, and is capable of leveraging the gradient descent process to satisfy the constraint.

3   Proposed Method

3.1   High-Pass Filter

As is known, the human eye is sensitive to low-frequency signals and insensitive to high-frequency signals. This visual perceptual property of the human eye determines the frequency domain property of image processing techniques used in image forgery. It's evident that these image processing techniques should not be easily perceived by the human eye. Since the human eye is sensitive to low-frequency signals but not to high-frequency signals, the impact of these image processing techniques should be concentrated in the high-frequency components of the image, so as to make it less perceivable to the human eye. To prove our inference, we test the frequency domain property of various image processing techniques used in image forgery (see Fig. 3).

It can be seen intuitively that the image is almost visually unchanged after processed by these image processing techniques, while in the frequency domain, the changes are mainly concentrated outside the central region which represents the low-frequency components. The test results show that the low-frequency component of the image contains most of the visual information, i.e., the image content, while the trace left by image processing techniques, i.e., the manipulation trace, is mainly concentrated on the high-frequency component of the image. Therefore, we can get an *inductive bias*: the high-frequency component of the image is far more important than the low-frequency component in Image Manipulation Detection. However, according to the *spectral bias* proposed by Rahaman et al. [27] and the *F-principle* proposed by Xu et al. [33], CNNs focus more on low-frequency components than on high-frequency components during training (see Fig. 4), which has a adverse effect on Image Manipulation Detection. To alleviate this problem, we propose General High-Pass Convolution, a set of learnable high-pass filters to suppress the low-frequency components that contain little manipulation trace, thus prompting CNNs to learn manipulation features from the high-frequency components of the image.

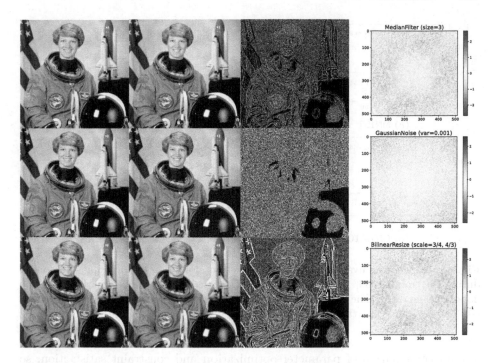

Fig. 3. The test results of three image processing techniques commonly used in image forgery. Columns from left to right are: the original image, the processed image, the difference between the original image and the processed image, and the spectrum of difference. A two-dimensional Hanning window is applied to the image before Discrete Fourier Transformation to avoid spectral leakage, and the zero-frequency component is shifted to the center of the spectrum.

3.2 General High-Pass Convolution

Inspired by Bayar Convolution [3], we propose General High-Pass Convolution[1] (GHP Convolution), a new convolutional layer which satisfies the high-pass filter constraint in Eq. (2). GHP Convolution is aimed to simulate a set of learnable high-pass filters to suppress the low-frequency components of the image, i.e., roughly the image content, while passing through those useful high-frequency components that contain most of the manipulation trace. GHP Convolution can be seen as a further *generalization* of Bayar Convolution, and there are two main differences between Bayar Convolution and GHP Convolution. The first difference is the constraint. GHP Convolution discards the non-essential constraint that the center weight of the convolution kernel must be -1, and retains only the fundamental constraint that the sum of the convolution kernel weights must be 0. The second difference is the training method. Towards the goal of making it robust and stable, we propose a gradient-based training method, which provides

---

[1] The code is available at https://github.com/newcomertzc/GHP-Convolution.

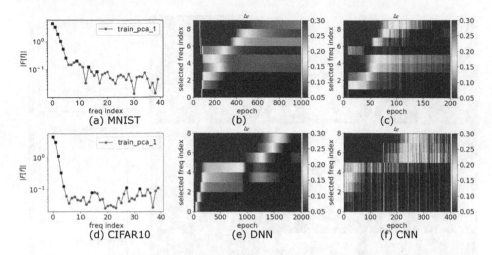

Fig. 4. Frequency analysis of DNN output function along the first principle component during the training [33]. The selected frequencies used in analysis are marked by black dots in (a) and (d). The differences (Δ_F) between predictions and labels are shown in (b), (c), (e) and (f) as the number of epochs changes.

a good combination of parameter optimization and constraint satisfaction, so that constraint satisfaction does not interfere with parameter optimization. The following is a brief description of the theoretical basis for our training method.

First, for any linear filter F, its weights can be expressed as a linear combination of the weights of the high-pass filter H and the weights of the low-pass filter L (see Eq. 3):

$$
F = \begin{bmatrix} w_{11} & w_{12} & \cdots & w_{1n} \\ w_{21} & w_{22} & \cdots & w_{2n} \\ \vdots & \vdots & \ddots & \vdots \\ w_{m1} & w_{m2} & \cdots & w_{mn} \end{bmatrix} = H + \alpha \cdot mn \cdot L \tag{3}
$$

$$
H = \begin{bmatrix} w_{11} - a & w_{12} - a & \cdots & w_{1n} - a \\ w_{21} - a & w_{22} - a & \cdots & w_{2n} - a \\ \vdots & \vdots & \ddots & \vdots \\ w_{m1} - a & w_{m2} - a & \cdots & w_{mn} - a \end{bmatrix} \tag{4}
$$

$$
L = \begin{bmatrix} 1/mn & 1/mn & \cdots & 1/mn \\ 1/mn & 1/mn & \cdots & 1/mn \\ \vdots & \vdots & \ddots & \vdots \\ 1/mn & 1/mn & \cdots & 1/mn \end{bmatrix} \tag{5}
$$

where m and n are the height and width of the filter kernel respectively, and a is the average of the weights of F. Hence, we can decompose any linear filter into two parts, i.e., the high-pass part and the low-pass part. This equation leads to the following inference: for any linear filter, its response to the low-frequency component is determined by the sum of its weights. The smaller the absolute value of the sum of its weights, the smaller its response to the low-frequency components, i.e., the stronger its suppression of the low frequency components. Therefore, satisfying the constraint in Eq. (2) can be approximated as an unconditional optimization problem as follows:

$$minimize \left| \sum_{i=0,j=0}^{H-1,W-1} w(i,j) \right| \tag{6}$$

It is not difficult to find that the target of this optimization problem is actually somewhat similar to that of L1 regularization and L2 regularization: the target of L1 regularization and L2 regularization is to make the absolute value of the weights as small as possible, whereas the target of this optimization problem is to make the absolute value of the sum of the weights as small as possible. Inspired by L1 regularization and L2 regularization, we finally adopt a *filter-wise* regularization approach to solve this optimization problem. For GHP Convolution with weights of size (Out, C, H, W), the regularization loss function and the total loss function are defined as follows:

$$L_{reg} = \sum_{n=0,k=0}^{Out,C} \left| \sum_{i=0,j=0}^{H,W} w(n,k,i,j) \right| \quad \text{(L1 reg)} \tag{7}$$

$$L_{reg} = \sum_{n=0,k=0}^{Out,C} (\sum_{i=0,j=0}^{H,W} w(n,k,i,j))^2 \quad \text{(L2 reg)} \tag{8}$$

$$L = L_{clf} + \alpha \cdot L_{reg} \tag{9}$$

Equation (7) is the regularization loss function adopting L1 regularization, and Eq. (8) is the regularization loss function adopting L2 regularization. Equation (9) gives the calculation of the total loss function, where L_{clf} denotes the classification loss, L_{reg} denotes the regularization loss function, and is the penalty factor of the regularization loss. This approach allows GHP Convolution to gradually satisfy the constraint without causing much interference in parameter optimization. We refer to this regularization constraint method as soft-constraint training method, which corresponds to the hard-constraint training method proposed by Bayar et al. [3].

4   Experiments and Evaluation

4.1   Automatic Dataset Generation

Inspired by the work of Zhou et al. [36] and Wu et al. [32], we adopt a self-supervised learning style approach to train the networks. We use images from ImageNet-1k [10] and COCO [19] as base images which play the same role as

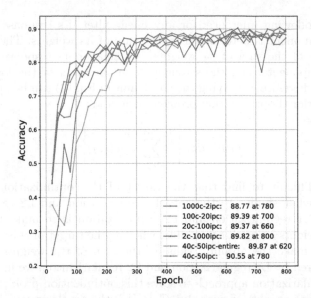

Fig. 5. The experimental results of training the same network with different subsets of ImageNet-1k. Each subset contains 2000 images. 40c-50ipc means 40 classes are randomly selected from the 1000 classes of ImageNet-1k, and then 50 images are selected from each selected class. 40c-50ipc-entire means that the subset will be re-selected in each epoch, which is equivalent to use the entire dataset. The best accuracy and corresponding number of epochs are given in the legend.

unlabeled data in self-supervised learning to generate manipulated images, i.e., images that be processed by image processing techniques. We use ImageNet-1k to generate dataset for Image Manipulation Classification, and use COCO to generate dataset for Image Manipulation Segmentation.

Classification Dataset Generation. We use images from ImageNet-1k as base images to generate the classification dataset because of its enormous amount and diverse content. In the experiment, however, we find that better results are obtained using a subset of ImageNet-1k compared to using the entire dataset (see Fig. 5). According to this experimental results, we choose the ImageNet-1k subset consisting of 40 classes with 50 images per class as the base images in the following experiments.

At the beginning of each epoch, all base images are randomly manipulated and labeled in one of the following ways:

– **Original:** Remain unchanged.
– **Nearest Resampling:** Resize or rotate the image using nearest neighbor interpolation. The scaling factor for resizing can be any value between 0.5 and 2, and the rotation angle can be any angle.

- **Bilinear Resampling:** Resize or rotate the image using bilinear interpolation. The scaling factor for resizing can be any value between 0.5 and 2, and the rotation angle can be any angle.
- **Bicubic Resampling:** Resize or rotate the image using bicubic interpolation. The scaling factor for resizing can be any value between 0.5 and 2, and the rotation angle can be any angle.
- **Median Filter:** Apply a median filter to the image. The kernel size of this median filter is 3, 5 or 7.
- **Box Filter:** Apply a box filter (also known as mean filter) to the image. The kernel size of this box filter is 3, 5 or 7.
- **Gaussian Filter:** Apply a Gaussian filter to the image. The kernel size of this Gaussian filter is 3, 5 or 7, corresponding to a Gaussian kernel standard deviation of 0.8, 1.1, 1.4, respectively.
- **AWGN:** Add additive white Gaussian noise to the image. The standard deviation of Gaussian noise can be any value between 0.03 and 0.1.
- **Poisson Noise:** Add Poisson noise to the image. The expectation of Poisson noise is deter-mined according to the pixel value of the image.
- **Impulse Noise:** Add impulse noise (also known as salt and pepper noise) to the image. The ratio of impulse noise to the entire image can be any value between 0.01 and 0.05, and the ratio of salt noise to pepper noise can be any value between 0 and 1.

Afterwards, JPEG compression is applied to all images except those unchanged images with the label "**Original**". The reasons for using JPEG compression are discussed in detail in Sect. 4.2. Then, cut each image into 4 patches of size 224×224, for a total of up to 8000 patches. No padding or resizing are used during the cutting process.

The validation dataset is generated with images of the validation set of ImageNet-1k. For a fair comparison, the validation dataset is fixed, i.e., it doesn't change at the beginning of each epoch.

Segmentation Dataset Generation. We use images from COCO as base images to generate the segmentation dataset, as these images are labeled with pixel-level instance annotations. The generation process of the segmentation dataset is similar to that of the classification dataset, with the following two differences:

1. The manipulated images in the segmentation dataset are generated by randomly selecting an instance from the image, randomly manipulate it, and then splice this manipulated instance onto another randomly selected image.
2. The image patches in the segmentation dataset are filtered so that only patches with a ratio of the manipulated area to the entire image between 0.03 and 0.6 are kept. There is no limit to the number of image patches cut out from one image.

4.2 JPEG Compression

Why do we need JPEG compression when generating dataset for Image Manipulation Detection? To answer this question, we should start with the blocking effect of JPEG images. In the process of JPEG compression, each channel of the image is split into image blocks of size 8×8. Since each image block is independently transformed and quantized in the JPEG compression process, there is a certain discontinuity between the edges of these image blocks, which is called the blocking effect of JPEG images.

All the images in ImageNet-1k are JPEG images. For Image Manipulation Detection, it calls for careful consideration. Most image processing techniques used in image forgery are neighborhood operations that destroy the blocking effect of JPEG images. Therefore, without JPEG compression of these manipulated images, an unrealistic situation arises in the generate dataset: all images without JPEG blocking effect are manipulated images, whereas all images with JPEG blocking effect are original images. This unrealistic situation can greatly mislead the networks.

Additionally, JPEG is the most commonly used image format. Therefore, in practice, many manipulated images are stored in JPEG format. Therefore, the networks trained with JPEG compressed images will be more accurate and robust.

For the above reasons, JPEG compression is necessary and beneficial when generating dataset for Image Manipulation Detection. In our experiments, the ratios of different JPEG compression qualities and different chroma subsampling of the generated manipulated images are consistent with that of the original images in ImageNet-1k.

4.3 Experimental Results

To comprehensively evaluate the performance of our proposed GHP Convolution on Image Manipulation Detection, we conduct the following two experiments. In the experiments, we train the networks from scratch using RAdam optimizer [20] with a batch size of 32. The learning rate is set to 1e−4, and other hyperparameters are set to default values. For simplicity, only the green channel of the image is used to train the networks, which follows the practice in Bayar et al.'s work [3].

Comparison Between GHP Convolution and Bayar Convolution. To demonstrate that GHP Convolution outperforms Bayar Convolution, we re-implement the CNN architecture proposed by Bayar et al. [3] (see Fig. 2), and refer to it as BayarCNN. We replace the first convolutional layer in BayarCNN, i.e., Bayar Convolution layer, with GHP Convolution layer, and refer to this modified variant as BayarCNN-GHP. Furthermore, we carefully initialize the weights of Bayar Convolution (the weights of Bayar Convolution are randomly initialized) using the weights calculated by subtracting the normalized box filter (mean filter) weights from the all-pass filter weights, and refer to this modified

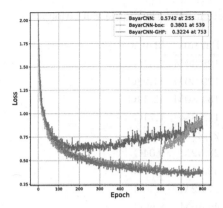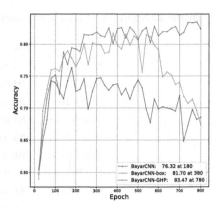

Fig. 6. Training loss and validation accuracy of these networks on the classification dataset. The orange line represents BayarCNN, the blue line represents BayarCNN-box, and the green line represents BayarCNN-GHP. The lowest loss, best accuracy and corresponding number of epochs are given in the legend. (Color figure online)

variant as BayarCNN-box. We train the above three networks with the generated classification dataset, and the results are shown in Fig. 6.

The experimental results show that BayarCNN-GHP achieves the best performance, which proves that GHP Convolution outperforms Bayar Convolution. In addition, both BayarCNN and BayarCNN-box fall into overfitting, while BayarCNN-GHP converges well, which proves that GHP Convolution is more stable than Bayar Convolution.

Experiment of the Generalization Capability of GHP Convolution. For simplicity, we combine GHP Convolution and backbone networks by adding a GHP Convolution layer directly before the backbone network, which is similar to BayarCNN [3]. First, we explore which regularization function (L1 regularization or L2 regularization) should be adopted in GHP Convolution and whether a batch normalization (BN) layer should be added between the GHP Convolution layer and the backbone network. The experimental results show that adopting L1 regularization without adding a batch normalization layer is the best choice. Afterwards, to demonstrate the generalization capability of GHP convolution, we combine it with three CNN backbone networks, VGG [30], ResNet [15], and ConvNeXt [21]. For each backbone network, We first test its variants with different depth, such as ResNet-50 and ResNet-101, to determine the optimal depth, and then combine it with GHP Convolution layer. To do ablation study, we also test adding a plain convolutional layer directly before the backbone network. The experimental results are shown in Table 1 and Table 2.

To our surprise, adding a plain convolutional layer also improves the performance of the backbone networks. However, when adopting ResNet or ConvNeXt as the backbone network, GHP Convolution outperforms plain convolutional layer, and when adopting VGG as the backbone network, there is little

Table 1. Accuracy of backbone classification networks on the validation set.

Model	Acc	Params	MACs
VGG-11	85.16	128.80M	7.57G
VGG-13	**91.64**	129.00M	11.28G
VGG-16	90.14	134.30M	15.44G
ResNet-18	84.90	11.18M	1.74G
ResNet-34	85.51	21.28M	3.60G
ResNet-50	**86.67**	23.52M	4.04G
ResNet-101	85.98	42.51M	7.77G
ConvNeXt-T	**86.40**	27.82M	4.46G
ConvNeXt-S	85.72	49.46M	8.69G

Table 2. Accuracy of combined classification networks on the validation set.

Model	Acc	Params	MACs
VGG-13	91.64	129.00M	11.28G
Conv-VGG-13	**92.08**	129.00M	11.61G
GHPConv-VGG-13	92.00	129.00M	11.61G
ResNet-50	86.67	23.52M	4.04G
Conv-ResNet-50	90.60	23.56M	4.49G
GHPConv-ResNet-50	**91.01**	23.56M	4.49G
ConvNeXt-T	86.40	27.82M	4.46G
Conv-ConvNeXt-T	87.58	27.84M	4.53G
GHPConv-ConvNeXt-T	**88.40**	27.84M	4.53G

difference (0.08%) between the performance of GHP Convolution and that of plain convolutional layer.

Then, we conduct further experiments. We select variant classification networks of VGG, ResNet and extend these networks to FCN network [22] or DeepLabV3 network [8] for Image Manipulation Segmentation. We use their original weights as pretrained weights, and train these segmentation networks on the segmentation dataset. The experimental results (see Table 3) show that although GHP Convolution sometimes performs close to plain convolutional layer on Image Manipulation Classification, it clearly outperforms plain convolutional layer on downstream tasks, i.e., Image Manipulation Segmentation. In addition, the DeepLabV3 network based on GHPConv-ResNet-50 achieves the best performance on the segmentation dataset, which shows that DeepLabv3 network outperforms FCN network on Image Manipulation Segmentation (consistent with the situation on Semantic Segmentation).

Table 3. Global accuracy and mean IoU of segmentation networks on the validation set.

Model	Mean IoU	Global Acc	Params	MACs
Conv-FCN-VGG-16-8s	55.67	89.54	129.01M	46.15G
GHPConv-FCN-VGG-16-8s	**56.85**	**89.89**	129.01M	46.15G
Conv-FCN-ResNet-50-8s	48.46	87.26	32.98M	26.92G
GHPConv-FCN-ResNet-50-8s	**49.19**	**87.59**	32.98M	26.92G
Conv-DeepLabV3-ResNet-50-8s	58.89	91.11	39.66M	31.76G
GHPConv-DeepLabV3-ResNet-50-8s	**59.63**	**91.35**	39.66M	31.76G

5 Conclusions

In this paper, we propose a novel convolutional layer named General High-Pass Convolution for Image Manipulation Detection, which outperforms constrained convolutional layer proposed by Bayar et al. [3]. Furthermore, this convolutional layer can be combined with CNN backbone networks, such as VGG, ResNet and ConvNeXt, to improve their performance on Image Manipulation Detection, while its computational cost is small. Finally, the philosophy behind our work that the high-frequency components of image contribute most to Image Manipulation Detection, can also be applied to other works in this field.

In the experiments, we find that newer backbone networks [15,21] abnormally do not achieve higher performance. Our future research will explore the reasons behind it and the ways to further improve their performance on Image Manipulation Detection.

References

1. Acuna, D.E., Brookes, P.S., Kording, K.P.: Bioscience-scale automated detection of figure element reuse, p. 269415. BioRxiv (2018)
2. Anumala, U., Okade, M.: Forensic detection of median filtering in images using local tetra patterns and J-divergence. In: 2020 National Conference on Communications (NCC), pp. 1–6. IEEE (2020)
3. Bayar, B., Stamm, M.C.: A deep learning approach to universal image manipulation detection using a new convolutional layer. In: Proceedings of the 4th ACM Workshop on Information Hiding and Multimedia Security, pp. 5–10 (2016)
4. Bayar, B., Stamm, M.C.: Constrained convolutional neural networks: a new approach towards general purpose image manipulation detection. IEEE Trans. Inf. Forensics Secur. **13**(11), 2691–2706 (2018)
5. Bik, E.M., Casadevall, A., Fang, F.C.: The prevalence of inappropriate image duplication in biomedical research publications. MBio **7**(3), e00809–16 (2016)
6. Chen, C., Ni, J., Huang, R., Huang, J.: Blind median filtering detection using statistics in difference domain. In: Kirchner, M., Ghosal, D. (eds.) IH 2012. LNCS, vol. 7692, pp. 1–15. Springer, Heidelberg (2013). https://doi.org/10.1007/978-3-642-36373-3_1

7. Chen, J., Kang, X., Liu, Y., Wang, Z.J.: Median filtering forensics based on convolutional neural networks. IEEE Sig. Process. Lett. **22**(11), 1849–1853 (2015)
8. Chen, L.C., Papandreou, G., Schroff, F., Adam, H.: Rethinking atrous convolution for semantic image segmentation. arXiv preprint arXiv:1706.05587 (2017)
9. Cozzolino, D., Poggi, G., Verdoliva, L.: Recasting residual-based local descriptors as convolutional neural networks: an application to image forgery detection. In: Proceedings of the 5th ACM Workshop on Information Hiding and Multimedia Security, pp. 159–164 (2017)
10. Deng, J., Dong, W., Socher, R., Li, L.J., Li, K., Fei-Fei, L.: ImageNet: a large-scale hierarchical image database. In: 2009 IEEE Conference on Computer Vision and Pattern Recognition, pp. 248–255. IEEE (2009)
11. Fan, W., Wang, K., Cayre, F.: General-purpose image forensics using patch likelihood under image statistical models. In: 2015 IEEE International Workshop on Information Forensics and Security (WIFS), pp. 1–6. IEEE (2015)
12. Fridrich, J., Kodovsky, J.: Rich models for steganalysis of digital images. IEEE Trans. Inf. Forensics Secur. **7**(3), 868–882 (2012)
13. Gallagher, A.C.: Detection of linear and cubic interpolation in JPEG compressed images. In: The 2nd Canadian Conference on Computer and Robot Vision (CRV 2005), pp. 65–72. IEEE (2005)
14. Goljan, M., Fridrich, J.: CFA-aware features for steganalysis of color images. In: Media Watermarking, Security, and Forensics 2015, vol. 9409, pp. 279–291. SPIE (2015)
15. He, K., Zhang, X., Ren, S., Sun, J.: Deep residual learning for image recognition. In: Proceedings of the IEEE Conference on Computer Vision and Pattern Recognition, pp. 770–778 (2016)
16. Hwang, J.J., Rhee, K.H.: Gaussian filtering detection based on features of residuals in image forensics. In: 2016 IEEE RIVF International Conference on Computing & Communication Technologies, Research, Innovation, and Vision for the Future (RIVF), pp. 153–157. IEEE (2016)
17. Kang, X., Stamm, M.C., Peng, A., Liu, K.R.: Robust median filtering forensics using an autoregressive model. IEEE Trans. Inf. Forensics Secur. **8**(9), 1456–1468 (2013)
18. Kirchner, M.: Fast and reliable resampling detection by spectral analysis of fixed linear predictor residue. In: Proceedings of the 10th ACM Workshop on Multimedia and Security, pp. 11–20 (2008)
19. Lin, T.-Y., et al.: Microsoft COCO: common objects in context. In: Fleet, D., Pajdla, T., Schiele, B., Tuytelaars, T. (eds.) ECCV 2014. LNCS, vol. 8693, pp. 740–755. Springer, Cham (2014). https://doi.org/10.1007/978-3-319-10602-1_48
20. Liu, L., et al.: On the variance of the adaptive learning rate and beyond. arXiv preprint arXiv:1908.03265 (2019)
21. Liu, Z., Mao, H., Wu, C.Y., Feichtenhofer, C., Darrell, T., Xie, S.: A convnet for the 2020s. In: Proceedings of the IEEE/CVF Conference on Computer Vision and Pattern Recognition, pp. 11976–11986 (2022)
22. Long, J., Shelhamer, E., Darrell, T.: Fully convolutional networks for semantic segmentation. In: Proceedings of the IEEE Conference on Computer Vision and Pattern Recognition, pp. 3431–3440 (2015)
23. Mahdian, B., Saic, S.: Blind authentication using periodic properties of interpolation. IEEE Trans. Inf. Forensics Secur. **3**(3), 529–538 (2008)
24. Pevny, T., Bas, P., Fridrich, J.: Steganalysis by subtractive pixel adjacency matrix. IEEE Trans. Inf. Forensics Secur. **5**(2), 215–224 (2010)

25. Popescu, A.C., Farid, H.: Exposing digital forgeries by detecting traces of resampling. IEEE Trans. Sig. Process. **53**(2), 758–767 (2005)

26. Qiu, X., Li, H., Luo, W., Huang, J.: A universal image forensic strategy based on steganalytic model. In: Proceedings of the 2nd ACM Workshop on Information Hiding and Multimedia Security, pp. 165–170 (2014)

27. Rahaman, N., et al.: On the spectral bias of neural networks. In: International Conference on Machine Learning, pp. 5301–5310. PMLR (2019)

28. Rhee, K.H., Chung, I.: Improved feature vector of median filtering residual for image forensics. In: 2018 IEEE 5th International Conference on Engineering Technologies and Applied Sciences (ICETAS), pp. 1–4. IEEE (2018)

29. Shi, Y.Q., Sutthiwan, P., Chen, L.: Textural features for steganalysis. In: Kirchner, M., Ghosal, D. (eds.) IH 2012. LNCS, vol. 7692, pp. 63–77. Springer, Heidelberg (2013). https://doi.org/10.1007/978-3-642-36373-3_5

30. Simonyan, K., Zisserman, A.: Very deep convolutional networks for large-scale image recognition. arXiv preprint arXiv:1409.1556 (2014)

31. Stern, A.M., Casadevall, A., Steen, R.G., Fang, F.C.: Financial costs and personal consequences of research misconduct resulting in retracted publications. Elife **3**, e02956 (2014)

32. Wu, Y., AbdAlmageed, W., Natarajan, P.: ManTra-Net: manipulation tracing network for detection and localization of image forgeries with anomalous features. In: Proceedings of the IEEE/CVF Conference on Computer Vision and Pattern Recognition, pp. 9543–9552 (2019)

33. Xu, Z.-Q.J., Zhang, Y., Xiao, Y.: Training behavior of deep neural network in frequency domain. In: Gedeon, T., Wong, K.W., Lee, M. (eds.) ICONIP 2019. LNCS, vol. 11953, pp. 264–274. Springer, Cham (2019). https://doi.org/10.1007/978-3-030-36708-4_22

34. Zampoglou, M., Papadopoulos, S., Kompatsiaris, Y.: Large-scale evaluation of splicing localization algorithms for web images. Multimed. Tools Appl. **76**(4), 4801–4834 (2016). https://doi.org/10.1007/s11042-016-3795-2

35. Zhang, Y., Li, S., Wang, S., Shi, Y.Q.: Revealing the traces of median filtering using high-order local ternary patterns. IEEE Sig. Process. Lett. **21**(3), 275–279 (2014)

36. Zhou, P., Han, X., Morariu, V.I., Davis, L.S.: Learning rich features for image manipulation detection. In: Proceedings of the IEEE Conference on Computer Vision and Pattern Recognition, pp. 1053–1061 (2018)

Machine Learning, Multimedia
and Multimodal

Thangka Mural Line Drawing Based on Dense and Dual-Residual Architecture

Nianyi Wang[1](✉)⬤, Weilan Wang[2]⬤, and Wenjin Hu[1]⬤

[1] School of Mathematics and Computer Science, Northwest Minzu University, Lanzhou, Gansu, China
livingsailor@gmail.com
[2] Key Laboratory of China's Ethnic Languages and Information Technology of Ministry of Education, Northwest Minzu University, Lanzhou, Gansu, China

Abstract. Thangka murals are precious cultural heritage for Tibetan history, literature, and art. Digital line drawing of Thangka murals plays a vital role as a fundamental digital resource for Thangka protection. Digital Thangka line drawing can be categorized as image edge detection to extract visually salient edges from images. Although existing edge detection methods have progressed, they failed to generate semantically plausible edges, especially in-object edges. We propose a novel deep supervised edge detection solution to generate line drawings of Thangka mural images. Compared to existing studies, firstly a new Dense and Dual-Residual architecture (DDR) is proposed to propagate correct edge features effectively in CNN layers by using both short-range and long-range feature memory; Secondly, a new 2-phase loss function strategy is designed to focus on in-object edge detection. Experiments on different datasets (BIPED and Thangka) show that the proposed method is able to produce more richer edge maps comparing to the existing methods.

Keywords: Edge detection · Line drawings · Thangka mural

1 Introduction

Thangka murals have become important cultural heritage to study Tibetan history, literature, and art [29]. Digital line drawing of Thangka murals plays a vital role not only as an abstracted expression of Thangka for art appreciation but also as a fundamental digital resource for Thangka protection.

Digital Thangka line drawing can be classified as image edge detection, aims to extract visually salient edges and object boundaries from images. Although edge detection methods have progressed, there exist obvious limitations. 1) Traditional non-learning methods tend to either generate fake edges or lack important edges (Fig. 1(b)). This is because the traditional methods usually extract low-level local cues of brightness, colors, gradients, and textures. However, it is difficult to use these local low-level cues to produce object-level line information and image semantics [17]. 2) Learning-based methods face serious problems too although they have outperformed the non-learning methods in recent years [17, 24, 31]. The most common problems for learning-based methods such as lacking of in-object edges also inevitably lead to unsatisfactory edge detection results.

Deep supervised learning has been used in existing learning-based edge detection methods such as HED [31], RCF [17], BDCN [9]. However, the existing deep learning based methods also fail to generate satisfactory edge maps because the lack of effective network architecture to propagate edge information properly in Convolutional Neural Network (CNN) layers. As a result, only parts of lines appear in the final result while some vital edge details disappear (for example, in Fig. 1(c), the inner details of the green ribbon disappear).

In this paper, we propose a better edge detection method for generating line drawings of Thangka mural images. The proposed method consists of two parts: 1) a novel Dense and Dual-Residual architecture (DDR, Fig. 2(a)) is proposed to propagate edge features effectively from shallow layers to deep layers of CNN. DDR consists of a Global Residual connection (GR) and staked Dense & Local Residual connection blocks (DLR, Fig. 2(b)). DDR stabilizes the training of deeper networks and propagates edge features correctly with both long and short range feature memory. 2) a new 2-phase loss function strategy is designed to focus on in-object edge detection. We utilizes the Weighted Cross Entropy loss (WCE) [31] for pretrain stage and a new Pixel-level FocalLoss (PFL) (inspired by [16]) for finetune stage. Our 2-phase loss function strategy enables training accurate edge detectors by preventing the missing of true edges.

Experiments show that our method provides a satisfactory edge detector for generating accurate line drawings for Thangka murals. In summary, the main contributions of this work are:

1. A novel deep CNN leaning framework Dense and Dual-Residual architecture (DDR) for edge detection is proposed to produce line drawings of Thangka murals.
2. A new 2-phase loss function strategy based on Weighted Cross Entropy loss and Pixel-level FocalLoss is designed to train accurate edge detectors.
3. The proposed method produces more plausible and richer edge maps for Thangka murals compared to the existing methods.

(a)   (b)   (c)   (d)

Fig. 1. The proposed method produces richer edge details (Fig. 1(d)). The existing learning-based methods failed to generate vital edge details (e.g.: no details in the green ribbon in Fig. 1(c)) while traditional non-learning method such as Canny tends to generate discontinuous edge fragments because of the absence of high-level image semantics (Fig. 1(b)). Figure 1(a)) is a Thangka mural.

2   Related Work

There have emerged a large number of works on edge detection. For a detailed review see [7]. Broadly speaking, most edge detection methods can be categorized into three groups: 1) traditional edge detectors; 2) classic learning based methods; and 3) recent deep learning methods.

2.1   Traditional Non-learning Edge Detectors

Early non-learning methods mainly focused on the utilization of texture, intensity, and color gradients. Sobel detector computes the gradient map and then generates edges by thresholding the gradient map [13]. The widely adopted Canny detector [3] uses Gaussian smoothing as a preprocessing step and then adopts a bi-threshold to produce edges [19]. Among the early edge detectors, the Canny operator is still very popular because of its notable efficiency. Besides these early pioneering methods, mammal vision systems were associated with the processing of edge and contour [8]. However, these methods have poor accuracy.

For the traditional non-learning methods, the absence of high-level image semantics is the biggest issue, which inevitably leads to either generating fake edges or lacking real edges.

2.2   Classic Learning-Based Edge Detection Methods

Konishi et al. [14] proposed the first data-driven methods. [21] formulated changes in brightness, color, and texture as Pb features, and trained a classifier to combine the information from these features. Arbelaez et al. developed Pb into gPb [1]. In [15], Sketch token was proposed to represent mid-level information for contour detection. StructuredEdges [5] employed random decision forests to represent the structure of image patches and to produce edges by inputting color and gradient as features. Other methods such as BEL [4], Multi-scale [25], sparse representation [18], and dictionary learning [30], obtained acceptable results in most of the cases as well.

However, all these classic learning-based methods still have limitations in challenging scenarios since they tended to rely on hand-crafted features and had to employ sophisticated learning paradigms.

2.3   Deep Learning Methods

In recent years, deep convolutional neural networks (CNN) based methods achieved state-of-the-art performance for edge detection, such as N4-Fields [6], Deep-Contour [26], DeepEdge [2], and CSCNN [12]. Some newest methods have demonstrated promising F-score performance improvements. Xie et al. [31] proposed an efficient and accurate edge detector, HED, by connecting side output layers with a holistically-nested architecture. Using the same architecture of HED, Liu et al. proposed an improved architecture RCF [17], to learn richer

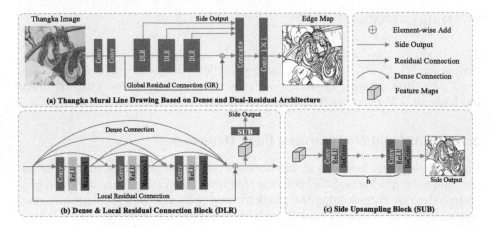

Fig. 2. Thangka mural line drawing framework based on Dense and Dual-Residual architecture (DDR) (Fig. 2(a)). DDR consists of a Global Residual connection (GR) and staked Dense & Local Residual connection blocks (DLR) (Fig. 2(b)). DDR not only allows dense and local residual connections in each DLR block (short-range feature fusion) but also allows direct global residual connection between shallow and deep DLR blocks (long-range feature fusion). Each DLR block adopts a Side Upsampling Block (SUB) (Fig. 3(c)) to generate side output (side edge map). The proposed 2-phase loss function strategy is adopted during pretrain and finetune stages to supervise the side output of each DLR block.

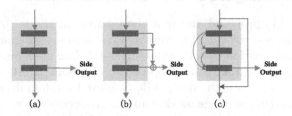

Fig. 3. The proposed Dense & Local Residual connection block (DLR) improves the existing learning methods by adopting Dense Connection (green lines in Fig. 3(c)) and Local Residual Connection (red line) in each block. HED [31] only utilizes CNN features from the last layer of each Conv block (Fig. 3(a)); RCF [17] improves HED by utilizing CNN features from all layers of each Conv block (Fig. 3(b)). Nevertheless, both of them have no global or local skip connections between blocks, which weakens the propagation ability of edge features. (Color figure online)

deep representations by extracting features from all convolutional layers. [9] proposed Bi-Directional Cascade Network (BDCN) structure, where each layer is supervised at its specific scale, rather than directly applying the same supervision to all CNN outputs. Inspired by both HED and Xception, [24] proposed a new method DexiNed to generate thin edge maps.

Although these methods have advanced the state-of-the-art, all of them still inevitably generate fake edges or miss true edges since they fail to propagate rich edge details correctly. Besides this, they paid no attention to hard pixel distinguishment, which leads to inaccurate edge maps as well.

3   Methodology

The proposed edge detection method consists of two parts: 1) a novel Dense and Dual-Residual architecture (DDR) to propagate edge features effectively from shallow layers to deep layers of CNN; and 2) a new 2-phase loss function strategy to focus on in-object edge detection.

3.1   Dense and Dual-Residual Architecture (DDR)

Although the existing deep learning methods such as HED [31], RCF [17], have achieved the state of art results for edge detection, they still fail to propagate abundant edge details correctly through deep networks, which inevitably leads to inaccurate edge maps. Figure 2(a) shows the proposed DDR architecture. The DDR network produces side edge map by a Side Upsampling Block (SUB, see Figs. 2(b) and 2(c)) at each DLR block (see Fig. 2(b)). All side edge maps from the SUBs are concatenated together to output a fused edge map.

There are two different kinds of skip connections in DDR: 1) Global and Local Residual Connection (red lines in Fig. 2), and 2) Dense Connection (green curves in Fig. 2), which are inspired by ResNet [10] and DenseNet [11], respectively. As inter-block connections, the Global and Local Residual Connections are responsible for residual feature propagation between different DLR blocks while Dense Connection propagates local features across sub-blocks in each DLR block. There are 3 sub-blocks in each DLR block and each sub-block contains one 3×3 convolution layer, one ReLU activation layer and one max-pooling layer. Since our DDR is a multi-scale learning, it is necessary to restore each side output to the scale of ground truth image by Side Upsampling Block (SUB). Inspired by HED [31] and DexiNed [24], we adopt a deconvolution strategy in SUB (see Fig. 2(c)).

Summary of Advantages: Figure 3 illustrates the differences and improvements of our DDR to some existing representative deep learning methods. Powered by both Dense Connection (green curves in Fig. 3(c)) and Local Residual Connection (red line), our DDR not only stabilizes the training of deeper networks, but also propagates richer edge details correctly with both short-range and long-range feature memory.

3.2   2-Phase Loss Function Strategy

Our 2-phase loss function strategy utilizes two different loss functions for two training stages respectively: 1) for pretrain stage, the Weighted Cross Entropy loss (WCE) [31] is adopted to obtain rough edge map features; and 2) for finetune stage, inspired by FocalLoss [16] and [28], we adopt a Pixel-level FocalLoss (PFL) to more focus on hard pixels and less focus on easy pixels.

Weighted Cross Entropy Loss (WCE) for Pretrain Stage. Let (i, j) be a pixel in an image I, $y(i, j)$ be ground truth pixel, $y'(i, j)$ be prediction $P(y = 1|x)$. For simplicity, we use y for $y(i, j)$, y' for $y'(i, j)$. For a single image, we use the Weighted Cross Entropy loss [31] to supervise our model, which is tackled as:

$$L_{WCE} = \sum_{i,j}(-\alpha \, y \, log(y')$$
$$- (1 - \alpha) \, (1 - y) \, log(1 - y')) \tag{1}$$

where α is an adaptive parameter that can be configurated automatically for each image. α is defined as:

$$\alpha = Y_- \, / \, (Y_+ + Y_-) \tag{2}$$

where Y_+ and Y_- denote the edge and non-edge ground truth label sets of an image, respectively. As for a typical image, the distribution of edge/non-edge pixels is heavily biased: 90% of the ground truth is non-edge, like in HED [31], α is a class-balancing weight for each image which can easily offset the imbalance between edge and non-edge pixels.

Pixel-Level FocalLoss (PFL) for Finetune Stage. After the first stage training converges, a new Pixel-level FocalLoss PFL is designed for finetune stage:

$$L_{PFL} = \sum_{i,j}(-\alpha \, y \, (1 - y')^\gamma \, log(y')$$
$$- (1 - \alpha) \, (1 - y) \, (y')^\gamma \, log(1 - y')) \tag{3}$$

where the hyperparameter γ is a value greater than 0 that set manually, the role of $(1 - y')^\gamma$ is to reduce the focus on easy positive pixels. Because the value of $(1 - y')^\gamma$ has less impact to easy positive pixels ($y' > 0.5$) than to hard positive pixels ($y' < 0.5$). Similarly, the role of $(y')^\gamma$ is to reduce the focus on easy negative pixels.

Although the loss structure of our PFL is similar to FocalLoss [16], there are still key differences:

1. The proposed PFL is to focus on hard pixels of an image (pixel-level balancing) while FocalLoss is to focus on hard samples of an image dataset (sample-level balancing).
2. The parameter α is an adaptive parameter that can be automatically set in our PFL while it is a hyperparameter that needs to be set manually in FocalLoss.

Summary of Advantages: The proposed 2-phase loss function strategy puts more focuses on hard pixels, and is capable of learning richer edge details and training accurate edge detectors by avoiding the generation of false edges.

4   Experimental Results and Analysis

4.1   Dataset and Experiment Setup

Although there are some popular datasets such as BSDS [20], NYUD [27], PAS-CAL [23], CID (contains only 40 contour images) [8], all of them are for training and evaluation of contour or boundary detection (here the words contour and boundary mean the edges between objects), but not for detailed edge detection (both in-object and inter-object edges). BIPED [24] is a new and better dataset for edge detection. To the best of our knowledge, There are only two publicly available datasets intended for edge detection MDBD [22], BIPED [24]. However, edges in MDBD dataset have not been cross validated and contain wrong annotations in some cases [24]. Hence, edge detector algorithms trained by these incorrectly annotated edges would be misguided.

In this work, we adopt BIPED as a training dataset since there is no edge map ground truth for Thangka murals. The dataset was randomly split into a training set (65%), a validation set (15%), and a testset (20%). Like HED, data augmentation process has been performed on the training set and validation set by random splitting, rotation, cropping, and flipping. For testing, we use both the above-mentioned BIPED testset and our Thangka images.

We trained our model on NVIDIA P100 GPU. In order to validate and compare the performance of our proposed edge detector, two state-of-the-art methods HED [31] and RCF [17] were also trained with the BIPED dataset; in addition, the classic non-learning detector CANNY [3] was also evaluated.

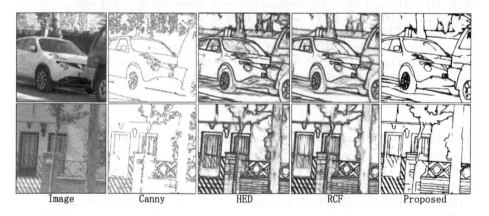

| Image | Canny | HED | RCF | Proposed |

Fig. 4. The proposed method is capable of generating visually clear thinner edge maps comparing to the classic non-learning method Canny and the existing representative learning methods. Canny detector either produces fake edges or lacks real edges; what's more, it contains no high-level image semantics. Although HED [31] and RCF [17] can generate better edge maps than Canny, their results still generate fake edges.

4.2   Performance on BIPED Testset

Table 1. Quantitative evaluation shows that our method outperformed the traditional method Canny and 2 classic learning-based methods HED and RCF.

Method	ODS	OIS	AP
Canny [3]	0.717	0.722	0.514
HED [31]	0.809	0.817	**0.764**
RCF [17]	0.823	0.826	0.754
Proposed	**0.830**	**0.841**	0.759

Thangka Images   Canny   HED   RCF   Proposed

Fig. 5. Our method achieved the best edge maps on Thangka testset. Canny detector inevitably either produces fake meaningless edges or lacks semantically important edges. HED [31] and RCF [17] failed to generate important in-object edges. For the edge results of HED and RCF, nearly all lines in the red area are totally missing in the first row of Fig. 5; in the second row, edge details of the Buddha's breast and the instrument are missing in HED and RCF while the edge details of lines of halo disappear in all 3 methods. On the contrary, our method is capable of generating nearly every important edge and represents the edge semantics of the original mural images well.

Quantitative Evaluation. We adopt the BIPED testset to evaluate edge detection accuracy using three standard measures: Average Precision (AP), F-score at both Optimal Dataset Scale (ODS) and Optimal Image Scale (OIS), where $F = \frac{2 \times Precision \times Recall}{Presicion + Recall}$. Like previous works [9,17,24,31], a standard non-maximal suppression (NMS) [5] is adopted to obtain the final edge maps.

The quantitative evaluation results are shown in Table 1. In Table 1, our method achieved the best results on both ODS and OIS measures. Although the AP score of our method is not as high as HED, it still outperformed the remaining non-learning and learning-based methods. This validated the effectiveness of our methods.

Qualitative Evaluation. Figure 4 shows some visual comparisons on the BIPED testset. We can easily find the visual differences between different edge detection methods. The proposed method is capable of generating visually clear thinner edge maps compared to the classic non-learning method Canny and the existing representative learning methods. Canny detector either produces fake edges or lacks real edges; what's more, it contains no high-level image semantics. Although HED [31] and RCF [17] can generate better edge maps than Canny, their results still not only contain plenty of unnecessary shadow areas around edges but also generate fake edges.

4.3 Performance on Thangka Testset

Figure 5 shows the visual comparison on the Thangka testset. Our method achieved the best edge maps with clear edges of both in-objects and inter-objects. Canny detector inevitably either produces fake meaningless edges or lacks semantically important edges because of its inherent characteristics we mentioned before. HED [31] and RCF [17] failed to generate some important edges (especially those in-object edges). For the edge results of HED and RCF, nearly all lines in the red area are totally missing in the first row of Fig. 5; in the second row, edge details of both the Buddha's breast and the instrument are missing in HED and RCF while the edge details of lines of halos disappear in all 3 methods. On the contrary, our method is capable of generating nearly every important edge and represents the edge semantics of the original mural images well.

From the above test results we can find that although HED and RCF are all trained with the same dataset BIPED like our method, they still cannot achieve satisfactory edge maps. By combining our DDR architecture and 2-phase loss function strategy, the edge detection performance of our method outperformed the other non-learning and learning methods. Figure 6 shows more edge maps of Thangka murals generated by our method.

We performed a user study on the Thangka test set to further evaluate the art performance of Thangka line drawings and the subjective feeling of Thangka artists. 50 professional evaluators (experts and students of Thangka art) and 150 general evaluators are invited to evaluate Thangka line drawings generated by the above 4 methods. We set up 2 criteria for subjective evaluation: 1) line correctness and 2) artistic quality. We randomly chose 10 mural images from the Thangka testset for the invited participants to evaluate. Figure 7 shows the results. In Fig. 7, the numbers are the averaged percentages of the votes on the edge maps that are regarded to be the best ones. In our user study, 58% of the 150 general evaluators believed that our results have the best visual performance while 47% of the 50 professional evaluators chose our edge maps as the best ones. The user study shown that our method outperformed the other methods and achieved the best performance.

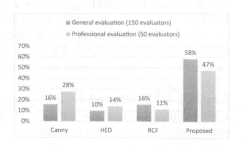

Fig. 7. The user study shown that our method outperformed the other methods and achieved the best performance. 50 professional evaluators (experts and students of Thangka art) and 150 general evaluators are invited to evaluate Thangka line drawings generated by the 4 methods. The numbers in the figure are the averaged percentages of the votes on the edge maps that are regarded to be the best ones. 58% of the 150 general evaluators believed that our results have the best visual performance while 47% of the 50 professional evaluators chose our edge maps as the best ones.

Fig. 6. More edge examples of Thangka murals generated by our method. The proposed method achieved state-of-art edge detection performance by generating visually satisfactory and semantically plausible edge maps for Thangka mural images.

5   Conclusion

We proposed a novel edge detection method for generating accurate line drawings of Thangka murals. Our method consists of two parts: 1) a novel Dense and Dual-Residual architecture (DDR) to stabilize the training of deeper networks and propagate correct edge features using both short-range and long-range feature memory; 2) a new 2-phase loss function strategy to focus on in-object edge detection. The line drawings of the Thangka mural images are successfully produced by our method. Experiments on different datasets show that our method is able to produce more visually plausible and richer thin edge maps. Both objective and subjective evaluations validated the performance of our method.

Acknowledgment. This work is jointly supported by NSFC (Grant No. 61862057, No. 62061042), the Fundamental Research Funds for the Central Universities (Grant No. 31920210140), and Program for Innovative Research Team of SEAC ([2018]98).

References

1. Arbelaez, P., Maire, M., Fowlkes, C., Malik, J.: Contour detection and hierarchical image segmentation. IEEE Trans. Pattern Anal. Mach. Intell. **33**(5), 898–916 (2010). https://doi.org/10.1109/TPAMI.2010.161
2. Bertasius, G., Shi, J., Torresani, L.: Deepedge: a multi-scale bifurcated deep network for top-down contour detection. In: Proceedings of the IEEE Conference on Computer Vision and Pattern Recognition, pp. 4380–4389 (2015). https://doi.org/10.1109/cvpr.2015.7299067
3. Canny, J.: A computational approach to edge detection. IEEE Trans. Pattern Anal. Mach. Intell. **6**, 679–698 (1986). https://doi.org/10.1109/tpami.1986.4767851
4. Dollar, P., Tu, Z., Belongie, S.: Supervised learning of edges and object boundaries. In: 2006 IEEE Computer Society Conference on Computer Vision and Pattern Recognition (CVPR 2006), vol. 2, pp. 1964–1971. IEEE (2006). https://doi.org/10.1109/CVPR.2006.298
5. Dollár, P., Zitnick, C.L.: Fast edge detection using structured forests. IEEE Trans. Pattern Anal. Mach. Intell. **37**(8), 1558–1570 (2014). https://doi.org/10.1109/TPAMI.2014.2377715
6. Ganin, Y., Lempitsky, V.: N^4-fields: neural network nearest neighbor fields for image transforms. In: Cremers, D., Reid, I., Saito, H., Yang, M.-H. (eds.) ACCV 2014. LNCS, vol. 9004, pp. 536–551. Springer, Cham (2015). https://doi.org/10.1007/978-3-319-16808-1_36
7. Gong, X.-Y., Su, H., Xu, D., Zhang, Z.-T., Shen, F., Yang, H.-B.: An overview of contour detection approaches. Int. J. Autom. Comput. **15**(6), 656–672 (2018). https://doi.org/10.1007/s11633-018-1117-z
8. Grigorescu, C., Petkov, N., Westenberg, M.A.: Contour detection based on nonclassical receptive field inhibition. IEEE Trans. Image Process. **12**(7), 729–739 (2003). https://doi.org/10.1109/tip.2003.814250
9. He, J., Zhang, S., Yang, M., Shan, Y., Huang, T.: Bi-directional cascade network for perceptual edge detection. In: Proceedings of the IEEE Conference on Computer Vision and Pattern Recognition, pp. 3828–3837 (2019). https://doi.org/10.1109/cvpr.2019.00395
10. He, K., Zhang, X., Ren, S., Sun, J.: Deep residual learning for image recognition. In: Proceedings of the IEEE Conference on Computer Vision and Pattern Recognition, pp. 770–778 (2016). https://doi.org/10.1109/cvpr.2016.90
11. Huang, G., Liu, Z., Van Der Maaten, L., Weinberger, K.Q.: Densely connected convolutional networks. In: Proceedings of the IEEE Conference on Computer Vision and Pattern Recognition, pp. 4700–4708 (2017). https://doi.org/10.1109/cvpr.2017.243
12. Hwang, J.J., Liu, T.L.: Pixel-wise deep learning for contour detection. arXiv preprint arXiv:1504.01989 (2015)
13. Kittler, J.: On the accuracy of the Sobel edge detector. Image Vis. Comput. **1**(1), 37–42 (1983). https://doi.org/10.1016/0262-8856(83)90006-9
14. Konishi, S., Yuille, A.L., Coughlan, J.M., Zhu, S.C.: Statistical edge detection: learning and evaluating edge cues. IEEE Trans. Pattern Anal. Mach. Intell. **25**(1), 57–74 (2003). https://doi.org/10.1109/TPAMI.2003.1159946
15. Lim, J.J., Zitnick, C.L., Dollár, P.: Sketch tokens: a learned mid-level representation for contour and object detection. In: Proceedings of the IEEE Conference on Computer Vision and Pattern Recognition. pp. 3158–3165 (2013). https://doi.org/10.1109/cvpr.2013.406

16. Lin, T.Y., Goyal, P., Girshick, R., He, K., Dollár, P.: Focal loss for dense object detection. In: Proceedings of the IEEE International Conference on Computer Vision, pp. 2980–2988 (2017). https://doi.org/10.1109/iccv.2017.324
17. Liu, Y., et al.: Richer convolutional features for edge detection. IEEE Trans. Pattern Anal. Mach. Intell. **41**(8), 1939–1946 (2019). https://doi.org/10.1109/tpami.2018.2878849
18. Mairal, J., Leordeanu, M., Bach, F., Hebert, M., Ponce, J.: Discriminative sparse image models for class-specific edge detection and image interpretation. In: Forsyth, D., Torr, P., Zisserman, A. (eds.) ECCV 2008. LNCS, vol. 5304, pp. 43–56. Springer, Heidelberg (2008). https://doi.org/10.1007/978-3-540-88690-7_4
19. Marr, D., Hildreth, E.: Theory of edge detection. Proc. R. Soc. London. Ser. B. Biol. Sci. **207**(1167), 187–217 (1980). https://doi.org/10.1098/rspb.1980.0020
20. Martin, D., Fowlkes, C., Tal, D., Malik, J.: A database of human segmented natural images and its application to evaluating segmentation algorithms and measuring ecological statistics. In: Proceedings Eighth IEEE International Conference on Computer Vision, ICCV 2001, vol. 2, pp. 416–423. IEEE (2001). https://doi.org/10.1109/ICCV.2001.937655
21. Martin, D.R., Fowlkes, C.C., Malik, J.: Learning to detect natural image boundaries using local brightness, color, and texture cues. IEEE Trans. Pattern Anal. Mach. Intell. **26**(5), 530–549 (2004). https://doi.org/10.1109/TPAMI.2004.1273918
22. Mély, D.A., Kim, J., McGill, M., Guo, Y., Serre, T.: A systematic comparison between visual cues for boundary detection. Vision. Res. **120**, 93–107 (2016). https://doi.org/10.1016/j.visres.2015.11.007
23. Mottaghi, R., et al.: The role of context for object detection and semantic segmentation in the wild. In: Proceedings of the IEEE Conference on Computer Vision and Pattern Recognition, pp. 891–898 (2014). https://doi.org/10.1109/CVPR.2014.119
24. Poma, X.S., Riba, E., Sappa, A.: Dense extreme inception network: towards a robust cnn model for edge detection. In: The IEEE Winter Conference on Applications of Computer Vision, pp. 1923–1932 (2020). https://doi.org/10.1109/wacv45572.2020.9093290
25. Ren, X.: Multi-scale improves boundary detection in natural images. In: Forsyth, D., Torr, P., Zisserman, A. (eds.) ECCV 2008. LNCS, vol. 5304, pp. 533–545. Springer, Heidelberg (2008). https://doi.org/10.1007/978-3-540-88690-7_40
26. Shen, W., Wang, X., Wang, Y., Bai, X., Zhang, Z.: DeepContour: a deep convolutional feature learned by positive-sharing loss for contour detection. In: Proceedings of the IEEE Conference on Computer Vision and Pattern Recognition, pp. 3982–3991 (2015). https://doi.org/10.1109/cvpr.2015.7299024
27. Silberman, N., Hoiem, D., Kohli, P., Fergus, R.: Indoor segmentation and support inference from RGBD images. In: Fitzgibbon, A., Lazebnik, S., Perona, P., Sato, Y., Schmid, C. (eds.) ECCV 2012. LNCS, vol. 7576, pp. 746–760. Springer, Heidelberg (2012). https://doi.org/10.1007/978-3-642-33715-4_54
28. Wang, N., Wang, W., Hu, W.: Thangka mural line drawing based on cross dense residual architecture and hard pixel balancing. IEEE Access. **99**, 1 (2021)
29. Wang, W., Qian, J., Lu, X.: Research outline and progress of digital protection on thangka. In: Advanced Topics in Multimedia Research, p. 67 (2012)
30. Xiaofeng, R., Bo, L.: Discriminatively trained sparse code gradients for contour detection. In: Advances in Neural Information Processing Systems, pp. 584–592 (2012)
31. Xie, S., Tu, Z.: Holistically-nested edge detection. In: Proceedings of the IEEE International Conference on Computer Vision, pp. 1395–1403 (2015). https://doi.org/10.1109/iccv.2015.164

Self-supervised Adaptive Kernel Nonnegative Matrix Factorization

Furong Deng[1,3], Yang Zhao[2(✉)], Jihong Pei[1,3], and Xuan Yang[2]

[1] ATR Key Laboratory, Shenzhen University, Shenzhen 518060, China
[2] College of Computer Science and Software Engineering, Shenzhen University,
Shenzhen 518160, China
zhaoyang1990@szu.edu.cn
[3] Guangdong Key Laboratory of Intelligent Information Processing,
Shenzhen University, Shenzhen 518060, China

Abstract. The kernel function to imply nonlinear mapping is crucial for kernel nonnegative matrix factorizations (KNMF), which determines whether the model can properly represent the data. However, the analysis and adaptive learning of parameters in the kernel function are lacking in existing methods. The kernel parameters of most methods are randomly selected, and the purpose and motivation of kernel function construction is weak. To address this problem, a self-supervised adaptive kernel non-negative matrix factorization (SAKNMF) is proposed to handle image recognition tasks. Kernel methods are used to achieve non-linearization. Firstly, the data is devided into multiple clusters by fuzzy clustering as self-supervised information. Then, according to the self-supervision information, the discriminative constraints that can adaptively learn the kernel parameters are constructed in the objective function. Based on the new objective function, the Gaussian kernel function parameters, basis matrix and coefficient matrix are jointly optimized. The kernel function constructed by the learned parameters enables the nonlinear mapped basis images to cover the mapped samples in the same cluster and distinguish other different clusters. So that the model can finally learn features that reflect the sample difference and have good generalization. Experiments show that our method can learn appropriate kernel width in different datasets, and the recognition accuracy is better than the state-of-the-art methods.

Keywords: Nonnegative matrix factorization · Kernel method · Self-supervised learning · Adaptive Gaussian kernel

This work was supported in part by the National Natural Science Foundation of China under Grant (62071303, 61871269), Guangdong Basic and Applied Basic Research Foundation (2019A1515011861), Shenzhen Science and Technology Projection (JCYJ 20190808151615540), China Postdoctoral Science Foundation (2021M702275).

Supplementary Information The online version contains supplementary material available at https://doi.org/10.1007/978-3-031-18907-4_13.

1   Introduction

Nonnegative matrix factorization (NMF), as a classical representation learning method, was first proposed by D. Lee [1,2]. It realized the intuitive expression of "parts constitute the whole". Compared with other representation methods such as PCA [3] and DLDA [4], NMF contains more semantic information in processing non-negative physical signals. However, the NMF tends to retain all the details of the data, including the features that are not conducive for classification. Some researchers focused on the discriminant features and proposed a series of NMF with supervised learning [5,6]. Using the label information, they maximized the differentiation between classes. However, when no label information is provided, these methods cannot explicitly construct discriminant properties. Some methods adopted manifold preserving [7] or image enhancement [8] to learn distinguishing features. The above linear discriminant NMF methods use the linear projection of the basis to represent the data. However, there is a problem in dealing with nonlinear data: the linear projection cannot maintain the nonlinear manifold well. When the data distribution is complex, the linear method is prone to errors in classification [9].

To deal with nonlinear data better, a series of kernel nonnegative matrix factorizations are proposed. Zhang et al. expanded the original NMF to kernel NMF and found its superiority in processing complex data [10]. Buciu et al. used a polynomial kernel to approximate the inner product in feature space, and the basis images learned by the model are closer to human faces [11]. Chen et al. proposed radial basis function kernel non-negative matrix factorization (KNMF-RBF), which achieved good performance in face recognition [12]. In their follow-up work, they considered label information to learn discriminant representation [13]. In recent studies, Chen et al. proposed a general kernel-based non-negative matrix factorization (GKBNNMF), and simplifies the learning process of the basis matrix, making this method widely applicable to different kernels [14]. Qian et al. constructed a new Mercer kernel function, called cosine kernel function, which has the advantage of robustness to noise. Taking advantage of this kernel, they further proposed a cosine kernel-based NMF (CKNMF) method [15].

An appropriate kernel parameter is crucial for KNMF. It determines the learning quality of the model. The selection of parameter is also affected by the distribution of the dataset and the number of basis. Taking the Gaussian kernel as an example, kernel width is an important parameter, which controls the coverage of the basis. When the kernel width is too large, the basis covers all samples. At this time, the responses of all samples on a certain basis tend to be the same. When the kernel width is too small, the learned basis only covers a small range of samples, and the model is prone to fall into the local minimum. At present, there are few studies on adaptive learning of kernel parameters. In addition, most of the existing unsupervised nonnegative matrix factorizations learn by minimizing reconstruction errors. They focused on all the details from data, which is not conducive to learning discriminant features. In this paper, a discriminant adaptive Gaussian kernel nonnegative matrix factorization is proposed to solve the above problems. Firstly, fuzzy clustering is used to divide the samples into several clusters. Then the discriminant constraint is introduced to make the basis cover the same cluster samples as much as possible and distinguish the different cluster samples. Based on this criterion, the algorithm jointly optimizes the kernel width, basis matrix, and coefficient matrix, so that the model can finally learn the characteristics that reflect the sample difference and have good generalization. The main contributions can be summarized as follows:

1) A self-supervised adaptive kernel non-negative matrix factorization is proposed. According to the self-supervised information provided by fuzzy clustering, we construct a new objective function that can adaptively learn the parameters of the Gaussian kernel function and the factorization results of nonlinear NMF. For unsupervised data, maximize the consistency of features in the embedding space for data with intrinsic similarity. The features extracted by the learned basis images are more suitable for recognition tasks.

2) A discriminative adaptive parameter learning method for Gaussian kernel function is proposed. A discriminant term based on the fisher ratio value is constructed in the objective function to learn the kernel parameters. When the data is projected through the nonlinear mapping implicit in the kernel function, the mapped basis covers more data with the same clustering characteristics under the self-supervised information, reducing the response to different clustering samples. The adaptability of the kernel function in different datasets is enhanced.

2 RBF Kernel Nonnegative Matrix Factorization

To better process the data of nonlinear manifolds, Chen et al. proposed RBF kernel nonnegative matrix factorization (KNMF-RBF) [12]. The sample x_i represents a column vector with m dimensions, the matrix $X = [x_1, x_2, \cdots, x_n] \in R^{m \times n}$ denotes a dataset with n samples, $W = [w_1, w_2, \cdots, w_r] \in R^{m \times r}$ represents the basis matrix, where each column w_i is called the basis image, $H = [h_1, h_2, \cdots, h_n] \in R^{r \times n}$ represents the embedding of data.

This method uses the Gaussian kernel function to map data to feature space and represent data as $\varphi(x_i) = \Sigma_{j=1}^r \varphi(w_j) h_{ji}$, where $\varphi(\cdot)$ represents a nonlinear mapping. The inner product in feature space is given by the Gaussian kernel function $k(a, b) = \varphi(a)^T \varphi(b) = \exp(-\gamma \| a - b \|^2)$, where γ is kernel width. The optimization problem is defined as

$$\min_{W, H} \| \varphi(X) - \varphi(W)H \|_F^2, \quad s.t. W \geq 0, H \geq 0. \tag{1}$$

KNMF-RBF has a good effect on nonlinear data processing, but it is sensitive to kernel width. When the kernel width is too large, the difference between the responses of the sample is reduced. When the kernel width is too small, the model will easily fall into the local minimum. This method lacks the analysis of kernel width, and its adaptability to different datasets is not ideal.

3   The Proposed Method

As the calculation of feature space inner product, there is a nonlinear mapping behind different kernel functions, which maps samples to the feature space of higher dimension. For Gaussian kernel, it calculates the inner product of two Gaussian function. Thus, it corresponds to a nonlinear mapping of a sample x_i to a Gaussian function $\varphi(x_i)$. The peak of $\varphi(x_i)$ is located at x_i, and the kernel width affects the coverage of the function. Kernel width plays a key role in model learning, so a kernel width adaptive learning method is necessary. Discriminant adaptive Gaussian kernel nonnegative matrix factorization learns kernel width from separability. Similar samples are relatively close in space, and they tend to be in the same cluster. When each basis function can precisely cover each cluster, the model has better discriminative properties for the representation. However, when the kernel width is too small, the basis only covers a few samples. When the kernel width is too large, the basis covers all the data. The responses of samples on the basis are high, which loses the discriminant characteristics between samples. As shown in Fig. 1, to adaptively adjust the kernel width, we maximize the sample consistency within the cluster so that the kernel width covers samples in the same cluster as much as possible. Meanwhile, the difference of samples between clusters is maximized so that the kernel width would not be too large, leading to the loss of discriminant features. Based on this idea, self-supervised adaptive kernel nonnegative matrix factorization (SAKNMF) is proposed in this paper.

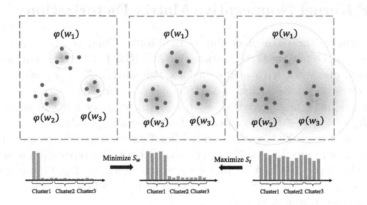

Fig. 1. Adaptive learning of kernel width by maximizing the cluster consistency

3.1   Self-supervised Adaptive Kernel Nonnegative Matrix Factorization

The purpose of the SAKNMF is to decompose the nonlinear mapped samples into $\varphi(X) = \varphi(W)H$. Self-supervised information is used to enhance the discriminative ability of the kernel function and decomposition results. Our method uses fuzzy clustering to divide the samples into several clusters. Then the discriminant constraint is constructed according to pseudo-labels and added into the objective function. Finally, it jointly optimizes the kernel width, basis matrix and coefficient matrix, so that the model can learn a kernel width and representation that is conducive to classification.

We measure the similarity between samples $X = [x_1, x_2, \cdots, x_n] \in R^{m \times n}$ and classify the samples with high similarity as the same cluster. By solving the following optimization problem, all samples can be divided into several clusters.

$$\min_{V} \|X - XV^TV\|_F^2, \quad s.t. \ V \geq 0. \tag{2}$$

$V \in R^{r \times n}$ is a indicator matrix of self-supervised learning, which indicates the probability of each sample belonging to different clusters after normalization. We define the similarity matrix $\tilde{L} = V^TV$, and normalize it by $L = D^{-\frac{1}{2}}\tilde{L}D^{-\frac{1}{2}}$. Matrix L provides self-supervised information that specifies the probability that which samples are in the same cluster, so that the variance of each cluster can be obtained. Matrix D is a diagonal matrix. Each diagonal element of matrix D equals the sum of the corresponding column of the matrix $\tilde{L}$. According to the self-supervised information, the objective function of SAKNMF is set as

$$J_{full}(W, H, \gamma) = J_{err}(W, H) + J_{ss}(\gamma), \tag{3}$$

where $J_{err}(W, H) = \|\varphi(X) - \varphi(W)H\|_F^2$ is the error term for factorization, and $J_{ss}(\gamma) = \alpha \frac{tr(S_w)}{tr(S_t)}$ is the self-supervised constraint term used to learn the kernel width γ. S_w is the within-cluster divergence matrix of samples' features. S_t is the total divergence matrix. The samples' features are represented as $K_{WX} = \varphi(W)^T\varphi(X)$ for the reason that K_{WX} is more directly related to classification features than H in discriminant constraint [16]. Thus S_w and S_t are

$$S_w = \sum_{j=1}^{n}([K_{WX}]_{\cdot j} - \sum_{i=1}^{n} L_{ji}[K_{WX}]_{\cdot i})([K_{WX}]_{\cdot j} - \sum_{i=1}^{n} L_{ji}[K_{WX}]_{\cdot i})^T, \tag{4}$$

$$S_t = \sum_{j=1}^{n}([K_{WX}]_{\cdot j} - \frac{1}{n}\sum_{i=1}^{n}[K_{WX}]_{\cdot i})([K_{WX}]_{\cdot j} - \frac{1}{n}\sum_{i=1}^{n}[K_{WX}]_{\cdot i})^T, \tag{5}$$

where the elements in the matrix K_{WX} are obtained by the kernel function calculation, $[K_{WX}]_{ij} = k(w_i, x_j) = \exp(-\gamma\|w_i - x_j\|^2)$. L_{ij} is denoted as the element in the ith row and jth column of matrix L. S_w and S_t can be written in matrix form, $S_w = K_{WX}GK_{WX}^T$, $S_t = K_{WX}MK_{WX}^T$. The matrix G is defined as $G = (I - L)(I - L)^T$, matrix M is defined as $M = (I - \frac{1}{n}1_{n \times n})(I - \frac{1}{n}1_{n \times n})^T$. $1_{n \times n}$ is a matrix with all elements 1. It is worth mentioning that $\sum_{i=1}^{n} L_{ji}K_{WX_i}$ is the center of the cluster where the sample j is located. S_w calculates the difference between each sample and the cluster to which it belongs, and then constructs the total variance within the cluster. The trace of S_w donates as $tr(S_w)$, which measures the consistency of the expression of similar samples, while $tr(S_t)$ measures the differentiation of data.

When optimizing W and H, we not only consider the reconstruction error of the model but also consider the consistency of similar data and the difference of data of dissimilar data. The weight is controlled by α. When we optimize γ, we only consider the influence of kernel width on data separability. Finally, the basis matrix W, coefficient matrix H, and kernel width γ are obtained by solving the following optimization problem

$$\min_{W,H,\gamma} \{J_{err}(W,H) + J_{ss}(\gamma)\} \quad s.t. \ W \geq 0, H \geq 0, \gamma > 0.$$

We used the projected gradient method to get the updating formulas,

$$W^{(t+1)} = P\left[W^{(t)} - \alpha_t \frac{\partial J_{full}(W^{(t)}, H, \gamma)}{\partial W^{(t)}}\right], \tag{6}$$

$$H^{(t+1)} = P\left[H^{(t)} - \beta_t \frac{\partial J_{full}(W, H^{(t)}, \gamma)}{\partial H^{(t)}}\right], \tag{7}$$

$$\gamma^{(t+1)} = \hat{P}\left[\gamma^{(t)} - \theta_t \frac{\partial J_{full}(W, H, \gamma^{(t)})}{\partial \gamma^{(t)}}\right], \tag{8}$$

where α_t donates update step, $P[\cdot] = \max[\cdot]$ is a projected function that guarantees the nonnegative of $W^{(t+1)}, H^{(t+1)}$. Operation $\hat{P}[\cdot] = \max[\cdot, \gamma^{(t)}/10]$ guarantees that $\gamma^{(t+1)}$ is positive. The derivatives of optimization variables are

$$\begin{aligned}
\frac{\partial J_{full}}{\partial W^{(t)}} = & - 4\gamma\rho_1 W^{(t)} diag(K_{WX}^{(t)} G K_{WX}^{(t)^T}) + 4\gamma\rho_1 X(K_{WX}^{(t)^T} * (G K_{WX}^{(t)^T})) \\
& + 4\gamma\rho_2 W^{(t)} diag(K_{WX}^{(t)} M K_{WX}^{(t)^T}) - 4\gamma\rho_2 X(K_{WX}^{(t)^T} * (M K_{WX}^{(t)^T})) \\
& - 2\gamma X(K_{WX}^{(t)^T} * H^T) - 2\gamma W^{(t)} diag(H K_{WX}^{(t)} H H^T) \\
& + 2\gamma W^{(t)}(K_{WW}^{(t)} * H H^T) + 2\gamma W^{(t)} diag(H K_{WX}^{(t)^T}),
\end{aligned} \tag{9}$$

$$\frac{\partial J_{full}}{\partial H^{(t)}} = - 2K_{WX} + 2K_{WW} H^{(t)^T} H^{(t)}, \tag{10}$$

$$\frac{\partial J_{full}}{\partial \gamma^{(t)}} = \rho_1 tr((B * K_{WX}^{(t)}) G K_{WX}^{(t)^T}) - \rho_2 tr((B * K_{WX}^{(t)}) G K_{WX}^{(t)^T}), \tag{11}$$

where $\rho_1 = \frac{1}{tr(S_t)}$, $\rho_2 = \frac{tr(S_w)}{tr(S_t)^2}$, each element of matrix B is defined as $b_{ij} = \|w_i - x_j\|^2$. To ensure convergence, the update step α_t is searched based on the Armijo-Goldstein criterion

$$J_{full}(W^{(t+1)}, H, \gamma) - J_{full}(W^{(t)}, H, \gamma) \leq \sigma \langle \frac{\partial J_{full}(W^{(t)}, H, \gamma)}{\partial W^{(t)}}, W^{(t+1)} - W^{(t)} \rangle, \tag{12}$$

where σ is a constant from 0 to 1, which controls the maximum update step range. $\langle \cdot, \cdot \rangle$ represents the inner product between two matrices. There are similar constraints on the search range for steps β_t and θ_t. The idea of the criterion is to find an update step that makes the objective function value decreases sufficiently.

The steps α_t, β_t and θ_t are finally selected as the first value that satisfies the Armijo-Goldstein criterion. When the following condition is met, the model is considered to have converged

$$abs\left(\frac{J_{full}(\boldsymbol{W}^{(t+1)}, \boldsymbol{H}, \gamma) - J_{full}(\boldsymbol{W}^{(t)}, \boldsymbol{H}), \gamma}{J_{full}(\boldsymbol{W}^{(t+1)}, \boldsymbol{H}, \gamma)}\right) \leq \epsilon, \tag{13}$$

where ϵ is a convergence threshold, $abs(\cdot)$ is used to calculate absolute value. Experimental results on the convergence of the proposed method are given in the Supplementary Material. The process of the method is given in Algorithm 1.

Algorithm 1. SAKNMF

Require:
    training data $\boldsymbol{X}$, number of basis images r, kernel width γ, weight α, convergence threshold ϵ, update step parameters β and σ;
Ensure:
    basis matrix $\boldsymbol{W}$, coefficient matrix $\boldsymbol{H}$, kernel width γ;
    Initialize $\boldsymbol{W}$ and $\boldsymbol{H}$
    while γ does not converge **do**
        while $\boldsymbol{W}$ and $\boldsymbol{H}$ do not converge **do**
            Compute $\boldsymbol{S}_w$ and $\boldsymbol{S}_t$
            Search update step α_t
            Update $\boldsymbol{H}$ with Eq. (7)
            Search update step β_t
            Update $\boldsymbol{W}$ with Eq. (6)
        end while
        Search update step θ_t
        Update γ with Eq. (8)
    end while

3.2   Image Recognition

Given a training samples matrix $\boldsymbol{X}$, the model learns the basis matrix $\boldsymbol{W}$, the coefficient matrix $\boldsymbol{H}$, and the kernel width γ. The features of the training dataset used for classification are obtained from

$$H = K_{WW}^+ K_{WX}, \tag{14}$$

where, K_{WW}^+ is the pseudo inverse of the kernel matrix K_{WW}, and K_{WX} is the responses of the training samples on the basis matrix. For a new sample $\boldsymbol{y}$, we use the following formula to extract features

$$h_y = K_{WW}^+ K_{Wy}, \tag{15}$$

where $\boldsymbol{K}_{Wy}$ is the responses of the new sample on the basis matrix, and $\boldsymbol{h}_y$ is the embedding of the new sample. Considering the scale equivalence of the image, $\boldsymbol{H}$ and $\boldsymbol{h}_y$ are normalized to the hypersphere. Using the nearest neighbor rule, the image is classified into the category that is closest to $\boldsymbol{h}_y$.

4   Experimental Results and Analyses

In this chapter, we test the performance of algorithms on different datasets. The first section introduces the datasets we use and the parameter setting of each comparison algorithm. The second section evaluates the recognition accuracy in different numbers of training samples. In the third section, the adaptive kernel width robustness of the method is evaluated.

4.1   Datasets and Parameters Setting

We use several open-source face datasets, including FERET, CMU, and Yale. The FERET dataset contains 720 images with a resolution of 92×112 containing different lighting conditions and expressions. The subjects include different ages, skin tones, and genders. The CMU dataset provides a total of 3808 face images of 56 people, including different lighting conditions, different orientations, and other changing factors. The resolution of each sample is 92×112. The Yale dataset provides a total of 165 face images of 15 individuals, including different expressions, different wearable devices, and other changes, with a resolution of 65×75 for each sample. In the data preprocessing, the wavelet transform and histogram equalization are used to resize the resolution of 28×23 and adjust the image gray scale.

The linear methods NMF [1,2], GNMF [17] and kernel-based methods KPCA [18], PNMF [11], RBF-KNMF [12], GKBNNMF [14] are selected for comparison in the experiment. KPCA retained components with eigenvalues greater than 0.001. KPCA adopts the Gaussian kernel. The r of NMF, GNMF, PNMF, RBF-KNMF, GKBNNMF, and SAKNMF is set to 200; In GNMF, the graph is constructed by K nearest neighbors, and the weight of the edge is defined as the inner product of two samples. In PNMF, the exponential of the polynomial kernel is set to 4. In KNMF-RBF, kernel width γ of Gaussian kernel is selected in the range of $[1e-7, 1e-2]$. In GKBNNMF, the rank of the symmetric NMF used to approximate the kernel matrix is set to 200. In SAKNMF, α is set to 0.01, β is set to 0.8, σ is set to 0.2, and the convergence threshold is set to $1e-5$.

4.2   Experiment on Images Classification

We tested the face recognition accuracy of different algorithms on FERET, Yale, and CMU data sets. Firstly, we determine the training number (TN) of every class. Then we randomly selected TN samples for each category as the training dataset and the rest as the testing dataset. The final result is a mean accuracy of five times recognition. In FERET, Yale, and CMU datasets, the accuracy of

Table 1. Mean accuracy (%) versus TN on the FERET and CMU datasets.

TN	FERET				CMU				
	2	3	4	5	5	15	25	35	45
KPCA [18]	73.92	81.16	87.33	89.50	65.14	65.63	70.55	74.63	78.96
	(3.22)	(2.06)	(1.57)	(1.62)	(1.16)	(0.60)	(2.07)	(1.48)	(2.43)
NMF [1]	72.87	82.27	82.17	87.33	64.38	76.82	80.86	80.84	80.00
	(0.82)	(0.76)	(1.96)	(1.80)	(0.33)	(0.58)	(0.55)	(0.48)	(0.85)
GNMF [17]	69.04	78.22	81.08	85.50	57.33	73.79	79.54	80.64	80.83
	(1.18)	(0.69)	(0.86)	(0.95)	(0.40)	(0.60)	(0.98)	(0.52)	(0.91)
PNMF [11]	75.00	81.05	80.25	86.83	66.70	77.33	80.23	80.60	80.13
	(0.90)	(1.06)	(1.12)	(2.31)	(1.03)	(0.72)	(0.38)	(0.67)	(0.87)
KNMF-RBF [12]	73.01	80.03	84.82	89.82	62.62	77.07	79.79	81.19	80.89
	(2.01)	(1.50)	(1.44)	(2.07)	(0.52)	(0.47)	(0.34)	(1.39)	(0.88)
GKBNNMF [14]	62.00	69.05	75.75	82.33	56.62	75.65	79.62	80.53	80.98
	(3.22)	(2.69)	(2.97)	(3.19)	(0.72)	(0.63)	(1.32)	(0.51)	(0.80)
SAKNMF	**79.84**	**86.75**	**90.74**	**91.72**	**71.30**	**80.19**	**81.62**	**81.31**	**81.34**
	(1.10)	(1.36)	(1.68)	(2.40)	(1.6)	(0.75)	(0.90)	(0.56)	(0.90)

Table 2. Mean accuracy (%) versus TN on the Yale datasets.

TN	Yale				
	4	5	6	7	8
KPCA [18]	58.28	65.11	61.87	70.56	72.33
	(2.40)	(4.75)	(4.10)	(3.23)	(4.09)
NMF [1]	68.38	71.55	70.66	68.67	69.78
	(2.27)	(1.68)	(5.07)	(3.20)	(1.98)
GNMF [17]	69.52	73.11	71.20	70.67	67.56
	(0.67)	(0.92)	(1.78)	(2.23)	(1.98)
PNMF [11]	62.47	65.11	61.07	63.67	60.89
	(2.65)	(4.08)	(2.73)	(5.19)	(4.86)
KNMF-RBF [12]	65.62	67.10	70.7	72.37	78.05
	(3.06)	(3.33)	(2.31)	(1.94)	(1.28)
GKBNNMF [14]	61.14	62.00	68.27	68.00	68.89
	(2.72)	(3.95)	(4.15)	(4.87)	(3.49)
SAKNMF	**71.28**	**73.03**	**74.42**	**78.33**	**81.48**
	(3.27)	(4.20)	(2.77)	(2.54)	(1.65)

each algorithm in the different number of training samples is shown in Tables 1 and 2. From the table, we can draw the following conclusions:

1) Linear methods perform better in the dataset with high consistency within the class, while nonlinear methods have higher accuracy in datasets with large diversity within the class. In FERET, samples are affected by different lighting conditions and different wearables. The in-class difference is large. Linear methods PCA, NMF, and GNMF do not represent these complex data well, while nonlinear methods have a better fitting ability for these data.

However, in the Yale dataset with high in-class consistency, linear methods are higher in the case of fewer training samples, while nonlinear methods KNMF-RBF and PNMF require more training samples for fitting.

2) Compared with other kernel NMF methods, our method has higher accuracy in different datasets. KNMF-RBF is susceptible to the influence of kernel width. GKBNNMF uses a combination of nonlinear mapped samples to represent a nonlinear mapped basis. It is influenced greatly by data distribution characteristics and is easy to produce over-fitting. SAKNMF learns the kernel width and basis from the perspective of maximum cluster differentiation and achieves high accuracy in different data sets, which is more stable and robust than other methods.

Our method can maintain high accuracy in different training samples. Especially when the number of training samples is small, the accuracy of our method is significantly higher than other algorithms.

4.3   Experiment of Kernel Width Robustness

To further verify the robustness of kernel width, we set different initial values of the kernel width to evaluate the final learned kernel width and its accuracy. Figure 2 shows the relationship between accuracy and different initial values of kernel width. The kernel width finally learned by SAKNMF is given in the Supplementary Material. We can draw the following conclusions:

1) Compared with KNMF-RBF, SAKNMF shows robustness and accurate and stable recognition in different initial kernel widths. As can be seen from the green curve, KNMF-RBF is greatly affected by the kernel width. Taking FERET dataset as an example, the optimal kernel width can make the model accuracy reach 85%, while the poor kernel width can reduce the model

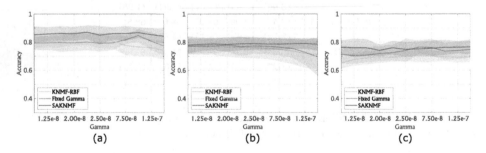

Fig. 2. Relationship between accuracy and different initial values of kernel widths on FERET(a), CMU(b) and Yale(C) databases. The abscissa represents the ratio of the initial kernel width to the variance of the database and the ordinate represents the accuracy. The blue curve represents the accuracy of SAKNMF, the red curve represents the accuracy of SAKNMF without adjusting the kernel width, and the green curve represents the accuracy of KNMF-RBF. (Color figure online)

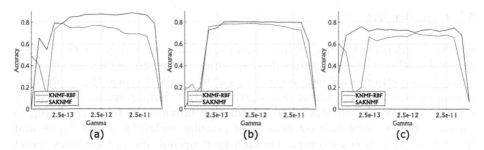

Fig. 3. The accuracy versus the initial kernel width with a larger range of values on FERET(a), CMU(b), Yale(c) databases. The abscissa represents the ratio of the initial kernel width to the variance of the dataset and the ordinate represents the accuracy.

accuracy to 78%. The accuracy curve in blue represents the accuracy of our method. The blue curve is generally at the top, which indicates that the accuracy of our method is higher than KNMF-RBF at different initial kernel widths. When the adaptive learning of kernel width is considered, the model can learn better kernel width and the accuracy of the model is more stable.

2) Constructing the discriminant constraints by fuzzy clustering helps discriminant learning of the algorithm to a certain extent. The red curve represents the accuracy of our method without adjusting the kernel width. It can be seen that with the influence of discriminant constraints, the accuracy of the model is higher than KNMF-RBF in a small range. This shows that the accuracy of the model can be improved to a certain extent by maximizing the consistency of similar samples, but its performance is still sensitive to the kernel width.

3) In different datasets, SAKNMF can always find a kernel width that enhances the differences between samples. We test it in different TN. The results show that the kernel width of SAKNMF converges adaptively to a small interval. Meanwhile, it can be seen that the optimal kernel width is not related to the number of training samples, but to the dataset itself.

We extend the testing range of the initial kernel width to [2.50E−13, 2.50E−04] to evaluate the effective range of kernel width for KNMF-RBF and SAKNMF. Figure 3 shows the change of accuracy. It can be seen that when the kernel width is set to extremely large, the accuracy of KNMF-RBF and SAKNMF drops below 0.1. This is because the extremely large kernel width tends to project the samples uniform, thus losing the distinction of the samples. When the kernel width is set to extremely small, the accuracy of KNMF-RBF and SAKNMF wobble obviously. The extremely small kernel width will reduce the coverage range of the basis, thus causing the model to fall into the local minimum. In general, SAKNMF and KNMF-RBF have similar effective kernel width range, but SAKNMF performs more accurately and stably than KNMF-RBF at different initial values.

5   Conclusion

Parameter adaptive learning method is an important way to improve the robustness of kernel nonnegative matrix decomposition. However, there is no clear criterion for selecting kernel parameters in most methods. To solve this problem, a self-supervised adaptive kernel nonnegative matrix decomposition (SAKNMF) is proposed. We use self-supervised information provided by fuzzy clustering to enhance the representation consistency of samples within the same cluster and the differences between clusters. Through joint optimization of gaussian kernel parameters, basis matrix and coefficient matrix, the model can finally learn a kernel width and representation that is beneficial to distinguish samples. Experiments show that our method can learn appropriate kernel parameters in different databases, and the recognition accuracy is better than NMF, GNMF, KPCA, PNMF, RBF-KNMF, and GKBNNMF methods.

References

1. Lee, D.D., Seung, H.S.: Learning the parts of objects by non-negative matrix factorization. Nature **401**(6755), 788–791 (1999)
2. Lee, D.D., Seung, H.S.: Algorithms for non-negative matrix factorization. In: Advances in Neural Information Processing Systems, pp. 556–562 (2001)
3. Turk, M., Pentland, A.: Eigenfaces for recognition. J. Cogn. Neurosci. **3**(1), 71–86 (1991)
4. Yu, H., Yang, J.: A direct LDA algorithm for high-dimensional data with application to face recognition. Pattern Recogn. **34**(10), 2067–2070 (2001)
5. Zhang, Y., Li, X., Jia, M.: Adaptive graph-based discriminative nonnegative matrix factorization for image clustering. Signal Process. Image Commun. **95**, 116253 (2021)
6. Ma, J., Zhang, Y., Zhang, L.: Discriminative subspace matrix factorization for multiview data clustering. Pattern Recogn. **111**, 107676 (2021)
7. Wang, W., Chen, F., Ge, Y., Huang, S., Zhang, X., Yang, D.: Discriminative deep semi-nonnegative matrix factorization network with similarity maximization for unsupervised feature learning. Pattern Recogn. Lett. **149**, 157–163 (2021)
8. He, K., Fan, H., Wu, Y., Xie, S., Girshick, R.: Momentum contrast for unsupervised visual representation learning. In: Proceedings of the IEEE/CVF Conference on Computer Vision and Pattern Recognition, pp. 9729–9738 (2020)
9. Li, Y., Hu, P., Liu, Z., Peng, D., Zhou, J.T., Peng, X.: Contrastive clustering. In: Proceedings of the AAAI Conference on Artificial Intelligence, vol. 35, pp. 8547–8555 (2021)
10. Zhang, D., Zhou, Z.-H., Chen, S.: Non-negative matrix factorization on kernels. In: Yang, Q., Webb, G. (eds.) PRICAI 2006. LNCS (LNAI), vol. 4099, pp. 404–412. Springer, Heidelberg (2006). https://doi.org/10.1007/978-3-540-36668-3_44
11. Buciu, I., Nikolaidis, N., Pitas, I.: Nonnegative matrix factorization in polynomial feature space. IEEE Trans. Neural Netw. **19**(6), 1090–1100 (2008)
12. Chen, W.S., Huang, X.K., Fan, B., Wang, Q., Wang, B.: Kernel nonnegative matrix factorization with RBF kernel function for face recognition. In: 2017 International Conference on Machine Learning and Cybernetics (ICMLC), vol. 1, pp. 285–289. IEEE (2017)

13. Chen, W.S., Liu, J., Pan, B., Chen, B.: Face recognition using nonnegative matrix factorization with fractional power inner product kernel. Neurocomputing **348**, 40–53 (2019)
14. Chen, W.S., Ge, X., Pan, B.: A novel general kernel-based non-negative matrix factorisation approach for face recognition. Connect. Sci. **34**(1), 785–810 (2022)
15. Qian, H., Chen, W.S., Pan, B., Chen, B.: Kernel non-negative matrix factorization using self-constructed cosine kernel. In: 2020 16th International Conference on Computational Intelligence and Security (CIS), pp. 186–190. IEEE (2020)
16. Kotsia, I., Zafeiriou, S., Pitas, I.: A novel discriminant non-negative matrix factorization algorithm with applications to facial image characterization problems. IEEE Trans. Inf. Forensics Secur. **2**(3), 588–595 (2007)
17. Cai, D., He, X., Han, J., Huang, T.S.: Graph regularized nonnegative matrix factorization for data representation. IEEE Trans. Pattern Anal. Mach. Intell. **33**(8), 1548–1560 (2010)
18. Schölkopf, B., Smola, A., Müller, K.R.: Nonlinear component analysis as a kernel eigenvalue problem. Neural Comput. **10**(5), 1299–1319 (1998)

Driver Behavior Decision Making Based on Multi-Action Deep Q Network in Dynamic Traffic Scenes

Kai Zhao[1], Yaochen Li[1(✉)], Yuan Gao[1], Hujun Liu[2], Anna Li[1], Jiaxin Guo[1], and Yuehu Liu[3]

[1] School of Software Engineering, Xi'an Jiaotong University, Xi'an, China
yaochenli@mail.xjtu.edu.cn
[2] School of Computer Science and Technology, Xi'an Jiaotong University, Xi'an, China
[3] Institute of Artificial Intelligence and Robotics, Xi'an Jiaotong University, Xi'an, China

Abstract. Driving behavior decision-making takes an essential part in autonomous driving. The training process of recent deep reinforcement learning methods is slow when faced with large state spaces of dynamic traffic scenes. In this paper, a driving behavior decision-making framework based on Multi-Action deep Q network (Multi-Action DQN) is proposed. The Multi-Action DQN can optimize the value of multiple actions in each training step and learn the relativity between actions, to achieve better convergence speed and stability. Besides, an improved vehicle training method is designed to construct a series of road environments with increasing complexity, so that the trained vehicle can imitate the human learning process from easy to difficult, and gradually learn stronger abilities. In order to alleviate blind exploration, the curiosity exploration strategy is applied to motivate vehicle exploration the state with a higher curiosity reward. The proposed Multi-Action DQN is evaluated in the Atari game environment of OpenAI GYM. The experiments on Carla simulation platform demonstrate the effectiveness of the proposed driving behavior decision-making framework.

Keywords: Driving behavior decision-making · Deep reinforcement learning · Temporal difference · Multi-Action deep Q network

1 Introduction

Studies have shown that autonomous driving technology will bring disruptive changes in enhancing road safety and reducing urban traffic congestion [1]. In terms of functional structure, autonomous driving systems can be divided into three modules: environment perception, driving behavior decision, and transmission control. Among them, the performance of the driving behavior decision module are the core indicator to measure the level of autonomous driving [2]. Driving behavior decision methods are mainly divided into rule-based and deep

S. Yu et al. (Eds.): PRCV 2022, LNCS 13534, pp. 174–186, 2022.
https://doi.org/10.1007/978-3-031-18907-4_14

reinforcement learning algorithm-based decision making methods. Rule-based decision making mosels are suitable for simple closed traffic environments and cannot cope well with dynamic traffic scenarios [3, 4].

Deep reinforcement learning models are end-to-end decision making methods, mapping environmental information from sensors directly to driving behavior. Deep reinforcement learning uses the deep neural network to simulate policy, and trains the neural network through the agent's continuous interaction with the environment, which makes the neural network infinitely close to the optimal policy. Deep reinforcement learning has good solutions for high-dimensional state space tasks, therefore considered as an important direction to achieve intermediate and high-level autonomous driving.

Due to the extremely large state space in dynamic traffic scenarios, the autonomous driving vehicle training process is very slow and even appears to explore the environment blindly [5]. In addition, temporal difference method can only optimize a single action value at each training step and cannot learn an effective policy quickly. Therefore, we propose Multi-Action DQN as the core of the multi-action temporal difference to speed up the action value optimization process. Then, we propose a new driving behavior decision framework based on Multi-Action DQN, as shown in Fig. 1. The framework is trained to approximate the optimal driving behavior policy by Multi-Action DQN, and it is trained in a series of road environments with increasing difficulty. Besides, the trained vehicle uses the curiosity strategy [6] to explore the environment. We conducted sufficient experiments in CARLA simulator, and the results show that the proposed framework can effectively handle the task of driving behavior decision in dynamic traffic scenarios; meanwhile, we tested the performance of Multi-Action DQN based on OpenAI GYM, and the results show that our method has significantly improved convergence speed and stability.

The contributions can be summarized as following:

- The Multi-Action DQN is proposed. The Multi-Action DQN is able to optimize all action values in each training step, and it is able to learn the relativity between individual actions, which enables to achieve better convergence speed and stability.
- An improved training method for autonomous vehicles is proposed. The method is that the trained vehicle gradually learns the driving behavior decision experience and applies the experience learned in simple environments to more difficult environments, and eventually cope with complex dynamic traffic scenarios.
- The Curious Explor1aion Strategy is applied. The curiosity exploration strategy can effectively alleviate the problem of blind exploration in the high-dimensional state space.

2   Related Work

The learning process of reinforcement learning is similar to the human learning process, in which the intelligence learns during the interaction with the

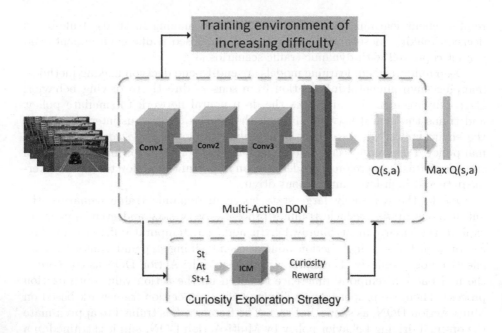

Fig. 1. Overall structure of the framework.

environment. To simplify the modeling problem of reinforcement learning, a Markov decision process is established. Its modeling process for autonomous vehicle driving [7,8] is as follows: The autonomous driving task contains a road environment and a trained vehicle, while the environment generates states and rewards, the trained vehicle performs actions according to a policy, and gets a reward and updates the policy. The vehicle makes a decision to select an action in the current state, and after executing the action, the environment generates a new state and gives a reward value back to the vehicle. Then the vehicle makes another decision to select an action in the new state, and again after executing the action, the environment generates a new state and gives a reward value back. Above is the interaction process between the intelligence and the environment.

The methods to solve reinforcement learning problems are mainly three kinds: dynamic programming, Monte Carlo and temporal difference [9]. The temporal difference method requires only two consecutive states with corresponding rewards for each iteration. It is more flexible and has a faster training rate, therefore is currently the mainstream method to solve reinforcement learning problems. In this paper, a new idea of temporal differencing is proposed in Multi-Action DQN. Practical training often uses the n-step temporal difference method [10]. And as n gets larger, it actually tends to use the complete state sequence, and the n-step temporal difference is equivalent to the Monte Carlo method.

With the development of deep learning, DeepMind team [12] proposed DQN algorithm, which used experience pool playback to reduce the correlation between samples; soon after that, the DeepMind team [13] proposed the target network,which improved the stability and generalization ability of the algorithm; Van Hasselt et al. [14] proposed the Double DQN algorithm, which decoupled action selection and value estimation by constructing two Q networks to suppress the overestimation problem; Wang et al. [15] proposed the Dueling DQN based on the competing network structure algorithm, which decomposes Q values into state values and dominance functions to improve the convergence efficiency of the algorithm; Hessel et al. [16] proposed the RainBow DQN algorithm by fusing previous improvements together; Ye et al. [17] used deep Q networks to train the following behavior and lane changing behavior of self-driving vehicles; Pin Wang et al. [18] designed a deep Q network with a closed greedy strategy for lane changing strategy learning.

The above studies improved the algorithm accuracy and convergence speed by modifying the structure and form of deep Q networks, deep reinforcement learning still suffers from long training and blind environmental exploration problems. Those problems are pronounced in dynamic traffic scenes, with complex state spaces and sparse rewards.

3   A Multi-Action Deep Q-Network Based Decision Framework for Driving Behavior

For blind exploration of trained vehicles in dynamic traffic scenarios and long training process, this paper proposes a new self-driving behavior decision framework, including three parts.

3.1   Multi-Action Deep Q-Network

The temporal difference method requires only two consecutive states with corresponding rewards for each iterative update. The Bellman equation is the basis of the temporal difference method, which can be used to express the sum of discounts for all future rewards.

$$G(t) = R_{t+1} + \gamma Q \left(S_{t+1}, A_{t+1} \right) \tag{1}$$

Equation(1) is called the temporal difference target (TD Target), based on this, the temporal difference error (TD Error) can be further deduced.

$$\begin{aligned} \text{TD Error} &= \text{TD Target} - Q \left(S_t, A_t \right) \\ &= R_{t+1} + \gamma Q \left(S_{t+1}, A_{t+1} \right) - Q \left(S_t, A_t \right) \end{aligned} \tag{2}$$

The temporal difference method has a distinctive feature: it uses only a single action value, i.e., the value of the action being performed, when calculating TD Target and TD Error. This feature makes the temporal difference method only optimize a single action value in each training step, which limits the learning efficiency of the neural network. Therefore, we propose a multi-action temporal difference method, which uses all action values in the action space instead of a single action value in each training step. We convert all action values into probability distributions, and let the probability distribution of the current moment fit

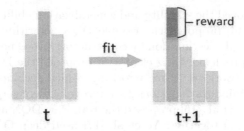

Fig. 2. Multi-Action Temporal-Difference Learning.

the probability distribution of the next moment. The structure of this method is shown in Fig. 2. At the next moment, we calculate the sum of all action values and rewards, and the multi-action temporal difference target is probability distribution of the sum. The multi-action temporal difference error is the KL scatter error of the probability distribution at the current moment and the next moment.

Based on the multi-action temporal difference method, we propose the Multi-Action Deep Q Network (Multi-Action DQN), our method optimizes multiple action values in each training step, enabling the network to make full use of the action value information, and can learn the relativity between each action to achieve better convergence speed and stability.

$$\text{TD Target } = \rho_{t+1}\left(Q_{t+1}\left(s_{t+1}, A, \theta_t\right), r_{t+1}\right) \tag{3}$$

$$\rho_t = \rho_t\left(Q_t\left(s_t, A, \theta_t\right)\right) \tag{4}$$

In Eq. (3), ρ_{t+1} denotes the probability distribution of the sum of action value and reward at the next moment. In Eq. (4), ρ_t denotes the probability distribution of action value at the current moment. θ_t denotes the network parameters. The corresponding loss equation is expressed as follows.

$$\text{TD Error } = \sum \rho_{t+1} \log \frac{\rho_{t+1}}{\rho_t} \tag{5}$$

$$\text{Loss}\left(\theta_t\right) = \mathbb{E}_{s,a\sim\rho(\cdot)}\left[\sum \rho_{t+1} \log \frac{\rho_{t+1}}{\rho_t}\right] \tag{6}$$

In Eq. (6), $\rho(\mathbf{s}, \mathbf{a})$ is a probability distribution over states and actions. The parameter θ_t from the previous update is kept constant when optimizing the loss function. The temporal difference target is dependent on θ_t, since the target value in supervised learning is usually determined before the training starts.

Based on the Multi-Action DQN, in order to better cope with the problem of large dimensionality of state space and action space, this paper further introduces the idea of hierarchical reinforcement learning, which can decompose the dynamic traffic scenario driving behavior decision task into high and low level subtasks. Specially, the goal of the high level subtask is to make macroscopic vehicle behavior decisions based on the environment perception information and global navigation path, including going straight, overtaking, turning

---

Algorithm 1. Multi-Action DQN

0: **Intput:** D-empty replay buffer; θ-initial network parameters; θ^--copy of θ;
0: **Output:** Well-trained parameters θ;
1: **for** *episode* $= 1$ to N **do**
2:     Initialize state S;
3:     **for** $t = 1 : T$ **do**
4:         Select an action a_t by ϵ-greedy policy;
5:         Execute action a_t and observe reward r_t and state s_{t+1};
6:         Store transition (s_t, a_t, r_t, s_{t+1}) in D;
7:         Sample random minibatch of transitions (s_t, a_t, r_t, s_{t+1}) from D;

$$\text{TD Target } = \begin{cases} \rho(r_t) & \text{for terminal } s_{t+1} \\ \rho(Q_{t+1}(s_{t+1}, a'; \theta), r_t) & \text{for non - terminal } s_{t+1} \end{cases}$$

8:         Compute KL divergence error as TD error between the two distributions

$$\text{TD Error } = \sum \rho_{t+1} \log \frac{\rho_{t+1}}{\rho_t}$$

9:         Preform a gradient descent step on the above error for parameter θ
10:     **end for**
11: **end for**

---

left and right, and stopping. The goal of the low-level subtask is to decide the micro-vehicle behavior based on the environment-aware information and macro-vehicle behavior, including throttle amplitude, steering wheel rotation angle, and handbrake control. By delaminating the driving behavior decision task into two subtasks, the problem of exploding spatial dimensions of state actions can be effectively solved.

3.2   Improved Training Methods for Autonomous Vehicles

Inspired by the idea of Curriculum Learning [11], we propose a new training method for autonomous vehicles - Vehicles Curriculum Learning (VCL). The method controls the difficulty of the training environment based on two factors: the amount of vehicles and pedestrians in the environment, and the length of the path from the start to the end. By gradually increasing the values of these two factors in a stepwise manner, a series of simulated training environments with incremental difficulties are constructed, and the entropy of the training environment and training samples increases gradually in this process.

In essence, VCL is to change the distribution of the difficulty of the training samples. Depending on the difficulty of the training samples, the easy samples are initially given higher weights, which have a higher probability of being selected, then the difficult samples are given higher weights. After several iterations, the samples are finally weighted uniformly. In reinforcement learning, the training samples are environment-dependent, which means the complexity of the environment determines the difficulty of the training samples. The curriculum training method redistributes the sample distribution at the k-th training, and the formula is expressed as follows.

$$D_k(z) \propto W_k(z)P(z) \quad \forall z \tag{7}$$

These samples are called a course, if the entropy of the sample distribution at training and the weights used to redistribute the distribution are increasing, i.e., the following two conditions are satisfied.

$$H(D_k) < H(D_{k+\epsilon}) \quad \forall \epsilon > 0$$
$$W_{k+\epsilon}(z) \geq W_k(z) \quad \forall z, \forall \epsilon > 0 \tag{8}$$

3.3   Curiosity-Driven Exploration Strategies

In vehicle autonomous driving tasks, vehicles may need to sacrifice current benefits to choose non-optimal actions in expectation of greater long-term payoffs [19]. Therefore, this paper introduces a curiosity exploration strategy to control the trained vehicle to explore environmental states with higher curiosity incentives, and maximize long-term payoffs. An intrinsic curiosity module (ICM) is constructed in the driving behavior decision framework as shown in Fig. 3. The encoder in this paper needs to extract features from the states that are key elements of the road scene (features that can influence the actions of the intelligence, such as other vehicles, pedestrians, and road conditions) while removing

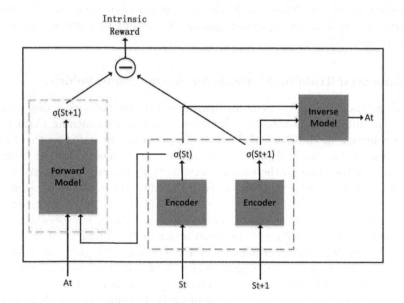

Fig. 3. The structure of intrinsic curiosity module.

irrelevant features from the road scene, such as the sky, trees, etc. The curiosity module uses a self-supervised approach to train the encoder, where the Inverse Model predicts the action in the state transfer based on two adjacent states and then uses the prediction error to train the encoder. The Forward Model predicts the feature vector of the next state based on the feature vector of the current state and the action, and uses the prediction difference as the intrinsic curiosity incentive. The following points need to be noted.

(a) The prediction error of Forward Model is only used for training Forward Model, not for training encoder.
(b) The inverse prediction error of the Inverse Model is used to train both the Inverse model and the encoder.
(c) The prediction error of Forward Model is also curiosity motivated to train our vehicle.

4 Experiments

This section consists of two parts, first a comparative evaluation of the proposed Multi-Action DQN based on the generic reinforcement learning algorithm, a test platform called OpenAI GYM, and then a comparative evaluation of the proposed driving behavior decision framework simulated on the Carla simulation platform.

4.1 OpenAI GYM

We build Atari game environments on the OpenAI GYM platform by selecting six classic Atari games: Crazy Climber, Road Runner, MS.Pac-Man, Time Pilot, Wizard of Wor, Asterix, to verify the performance of Multi-Action DQN. Dueling DQN and Double DQN were selected for comparison, with default use of preferred experience replay and competitive network structure in all algorithms. In the experiments, the three algorithms are trained in each game environment for 1e6 steps, the learning rate is set to 0.0001, the discount rate is set to 0.99, and the experience pool capacity is set to 1e4. The initial 1e4 steps are dedicated to collecting state transfer experience, after which the formal training starts.

Since the score values of the six games vary widely, we perform a normalization operation on the game scores as Eq. (9). $score_{MultiAction}$ denotes the score of the Multi-Action DQN algorithm.

$$score_{normalized} = \frac{score}{score_{MultiAction}} \tag{9}$$

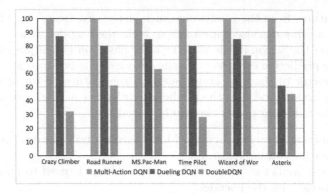

Fig. 4. Normalized scores on Atari games.

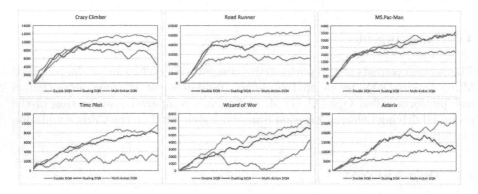

Fig. 5. Learning curves (in raw score) on Atari games.

Figure 4 shows the normalized score comparison, which indicates that Multi-Action DQN has the highest score in all games, at least 10% more than Dueling DQN, especially in Asterix, Road Runner, and Time Pilot, which is more than twice of Double DQN. The Multi-Action DQN algorithm is proved to have faster learning efficiency and convergence rate. The learning curves in the six games are shown in Fig. 5. Multi-Action DQN presents obvious advantages in the late training period, and the learning curve of the algorithm is more stable compared with Double DQN and Dueling DQN, and that indicates that Multi-Action DQN can indeed speed up the action value optimization and learn the relativity between actions to ensure the algorithm's convergence process more stable.

4.2 CARLA Simulation Platform

CARLA autonomous driving simulation platform is a set of open source software dedicated to vehicle autonomous driving research, jointly developed by Intel Labs, Toyota Research Institute, and Barcelona Computer Vision Center.

CARLA is able to support flexible configuration of sensing suites and environmental conditions for end-to-end imitation learning and reinforcement learning during training.

Three dynamic traffic simulation scenarios of increasing difficulty are set up according to the amount of surrounding vehicles and pedestrians as well as the complexity of the path, as detailed in Table 1.

Table 1. Dynamic traffic simulation scenario related settings

Difficulty level	Path length	Number of vehicles	Number of pedestrians	Number of turns	Number of traffic lights
Simple	5 km	20	10	3	3
Moderate	5 km	50	20	6	6
Difficulties	5 km	100	50	10	9

We have conducted full comparison experiments using four algorithms, Multi-Action DQN and DQN, DoubleDQN, and DuelingDQN, respectively. Prioritized experience replay is used by default in all algorithms and hierarchical training is performed using hierarchical reinforcement learning methods. The experiments were conducted in dynamic traffic simulation scenarios of simple, medium, and complex difficulty, and the performance of different reinforcement learning algorithms were measured by the 100-round average reward and training loss as evaluation metrics.

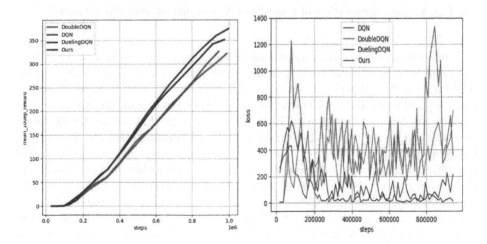

Fig. 6. Convergence effect of reward and loss in simple difficulty scenario.

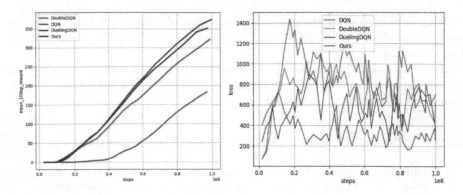

Fig. 7. Convergence effect of reward and loss in medium difficulty scenario.

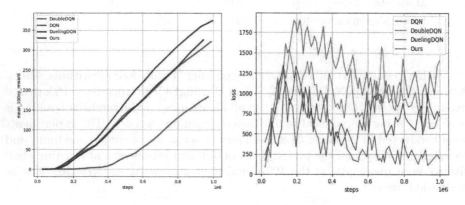

Fig. 8. Convergence effect of reward and loss in difficult difficulty scenarios.

The reward and loss convergence effects are shown in Figs. 6, 7 and 8. From the intuitive experimental results, it can be seen that the driving behavior decision framework in this paper obtains the most rewards and the losses converge more rapidly in the dynamic traffic scenarios of moderate and difficult difficulty, which has obvious advantages. The analysis suggests that Multi-Action DQN optimizes all action values simultaneously in each training step, and learns rich information about the relative relationship between each action, which makes the optimization process of action values faster and smoother, and avoids drastic changes in action values that lead to unstable loss convergence. In addition, the improved training method allows the vehicle to gradually accumulate decision experience, which enhances the stability of the training process. In the simple difficult traffic scenario, the driving behavior decision framework still converges faster, which indicates that the Multi-Action DQN-based driving behavior decision framework has good performance in a variety of scenarios and has certain generalization and versatility. Figure 9 reveals the continuous sequence of recorded images of vehicle driving in CARLA simulation platform.

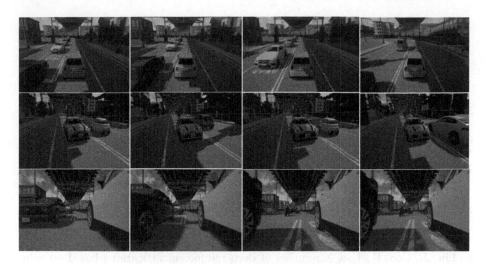

Fig. 9. CARLA visualization training interface.

5 Conclusions

This paper analyzes the shortcomings of the temporal difference method. It optimizes only a single action value in each step and learns slowly when dealing with high-dimensional state space tasks. Therefore, we propose the multi-action temporal difference method to speed up the action value optimization process. Furthermore, Multi-Action DQN is proposed, which can optimize multiple action values in each step and allows the network learning process to be more stable and reliable. Based on Multi-Action DQN, we propose a new driving behavior decision framework to solve the driving behavior decision task in dynamic traffic scenarios in an end-to-end manner, which also contains two key methods, namely an improved curriculum training method and a curiosity exploration strategy. Finally, in the experimental part, a comparative evaluation of Multi-Action DQN based on the OpenAI GYM, the driving behavior decision framework proposed on the Carla simulation platform is performed, respectively.

Acknowledgement. This research was supported in part by the Key R&D Plan of Shaanxi Province under grant number 2022GY-080, and the Postdoctoral Science Foundation of China under grant number 2021T140542.

References

1. Yang, G., et al.: Cooperative same-direction automated lane-changing based on vehicle-to-vehicle communication. J. Highway Transp. Res. Dev. **34**(1), 120–129 (2017)
2. Rong-Hui, Z., et al.: Lane change merging control method for unmanned vehicle under V2V cooperative environment. China J. Highway Transp. **31**(4), 180 (2018)

3. Baker, C.R., Dolan, J.M.: Traffic interaction in the urban challenge: putting boss on its best behavior. In: IEEE/RSJ International Conference on Intelligence Robots and Systems 2008, pp. 1752–1758 (2008)
4. Gindele, T., et al.: Design of the planner of Team AnnieWAY's autonomous vehicle used in the DARPA urban challenge 2007. In: IEEE Intelligent Vehicles Symposium 2008, pp. 1131–1136 (2008)
5. Zhang, X., Xie, L., Chu, X.: An overview of path following control methods for unmanned surface vehicles. J. Transp. Inf. Saf. **38**(1), 20–26 (2020)
6. Pathak, D., et al.: Curiosity-driven exploration by self-supervised prediction. In: International Conference on Machine Learning 2017, pp. 2778–2787 (2007)
7. Wei, J., et al.: A point-based MDP for robust single-lane autonomous driving behavior under uncertainties. In: IEEE International Conference on Robotics and Automation 2011, pp. 2586–2592 (2011)
8. Ulbrich S, Maurer M.: Probabilistic online POMDP decision making for lane changes in fully automated driving. In: 16th International IEEE Conference on Intelligent Transportation Systems (ITSC 2013), pp. 2063–2067 (2013)
9. Liu, J., Gao, F., Luo, X.: Survey of deep reinforcement learning based on value function and policy gradient. Chinese J. Comput. **42**(6), 1406–1438 (2019)
10. Hernandez-Garcia, J.F., Sutton, R.S.: Understanding multi-step deep reinforcement learning: a systematic study of the DQN target. arXiv preprint arXiv:1901.07510 (2019)
11. Florensa, C., et al.: Reverse curriculum generation for reinforcement learning. In: Conference on Robot Learning 2017, pp. 482–495 (2017)
12. Mnih, V., et al.: Playing Atari with deep reinforcement learning. arXiv preprint arXiv:1312.5602 (2013)
13. Mnih, V., et al.: Human-level control through deep reinforcement learning. Nature **518**(7540), 529–533 (2015)
14. Van Hasselt, H., Guez, A., Silver, D.: Deep reinforcement learning with double q-learning. In: Proceedings of the AAAI Conference on Artificial Intelligence (2016)
15. Wang, Z., et al.: Dueling network architectures for deep reinforcement learning. In: International Conference on Machine Learning, pp. 1995–2003 (2016)
16. Hessel, M., et al.: Rainbow: combining improvements in deep reinforcement learning. In: Thirty-Second AAAI Conference on Artificial Intelligence (2018)
17. Ye, Y., Zhang, X., Sun, J.: Automated vehicle's behavior decision making using deep reinforcement learning and high-fidelity simulation environment[J]. Transp. Res. Part C. Emerg. Technol. **107**, 155–170 (2019)
18. Wang, P., Chan, C.-Y., De La Fortelle, A.: A reinforcement learning based approach for automated lane change maneuvers. In: IEEE Intelligent Vehicles Symposium (IV) 2018, pp. 1379–1384 (2018)
19. Yang, T., et al.: Exploration in deep reinforcement learning: a comprehensive survey. arXiv preprint arXiv:2109.06668 (2021)

Federated Twin Support Vector Machine

Zhou Yang[iD] and Xiaoyun Chen[(✉)][iD]

School of Mathematics and Statistics, Fuzhou University, Fuzhou 350108, China
c_xiaoyun@fzu.edu.cn

Abstract. TSVM is designed to solve binary classification problems
with less computational overhead by finding two hyperplanes and has
been widely used to solve real-world problems. However, in real scenarios, the data used for learning is always scattered in different institutions
or users. At the same time, people pay more attention to the issue of
personal privacy leakage. Due to the complex privacy protection issues,
simply collecting all the data for model training is no longer acceptable. Federated learning has recently been proposed to solve this problem. It completes model training by sharing model parameter updates in
the form of data that remains local. But there is still no algorithm for
twin support vector machines under the framework of federated learning. Combining the characteristics of twin support vector machine and
federated learning, this paper proposes a federated twin support vector machine algorithm (FTSVM) and extends the twin support vector
machine based on stochastic gradient descent into a federated support
vector machine. We propose a unique initialization algorithm and integration algorithm to ensure the accuracy of the algorithm and the effectiveness of privacy protection. Accuracy experiments are carried out on
five datasets, and the accuracy is basically the same as that of the TSVM
based on gradient descent. Ablation experiments show that as the number of participants increases, the accuracy of the FTSVM is significantly
higher than the average accuracy of the Stand-alone TSVM. Time experiments show that the time overhead of FTSVM increases linearly with
the number of participants. These experiments demonstrate the accuracy, effectiveness, and possibility of application in real-world scenarios
of our proposed FTSVM.

Keywords: Twin Support Vector Machine · Federated learning ·
Stochastic gradient descent

1 Introduction

Many application scenarios in real life require the use of classification algorithms.
For example, in the bank lending business, it is necessary to determine whether
the lender meets the lending conditions and predict whether it will default in
repayment before deciding whether to issue a loan. In the face of a large number
of borrowers, manual review alone will increase the workload on the one hand,

S. Yu et al. (Eds.): PRCV 2022, LNCS 13534, pp. 187–204, 2022.
https://doi.org/10.1007/978-3-031-18907-4_15

and on the other hand, there will inevitably be the risk of human error. Therefore, it is necessary to use classification algorithms to predict user credit risks. In the medical field, classification models and algorithms can also be used for disease diagnosis, such as the diagnosis of COVID-9. The use of classification and recognition algorithms for abnormal detection of medical images can not only reduce the workload of doctors to read images, and improve the efficiency of diagnosis and treatment, but also provide technical support for online medical assistance systems.

Among all classification algorithms, the support vector machine (SVM) is one of the most classic algorithms. Since SVM was proposed by Cortes and Vapnik [3] in 1995, it has been widely used in regression classification problems. Although the performance of SVM is excellent, due to its high time overhead, Jayadeva et al. proposed a twin support vector machine (TSVM) [5,6] to find two non-parallel hyperplanes by solving two small QPPs. At present, there are many improved variants of TSVM. To reduce the training time of TSVM, Kumar and Gopal [9] proposed the least-squares TSVM (LS-TSVM) algorithm. Chen et al. [2] proposed a projected TSVM (P-TSVM) based on the principle of minimizing variance, which is computationally more complex than TSVM but has higher accuracy than TSVM and LS-TSVM. Besides the above two TSVM variants, inspired by TSVM and Par-v-SVM [4], Peng et al. also proposed two-parameter marginal SVM (TPMSVM) [11]. Xu et al. proposed a new TPMSVM based on pinball loss (Pin-TPMSVM) [15] with excellent noise handling capability.

However, with the progress of the times, the application of classification algorithms in real scenarios also began to have problems. When we try to apply classification algorithms to distributed environments such as wireless networks, privacy leakage caused by data sharing has become a fatal flaw. In modern society, people are paying more and more attention to the protection of personal privacy, and algorithms that will leak privacy are even more unacceptable. In response to this problem, the current mainstream privacy protection methods are differential privacy, cryptography-based encryption technology, and federated learning [7,8,10,16], of which federated learning is a new method that has recently emerged. It can complete the training of the model while the data is kept locally. Compared with the first two methods, federated learning no longer pays attention to the data itself, but starts with the algorithm process to obtain better performance and privacy protection.

At present, there has been a study combining basic SVM with federated learning to solve energy-saving computing tasks in wireless networks [13], but the proposed SVM-based federated learning is used to solve optimization problems rather than classification problems. This paper aims to propose a classification federated learning algorithm, considering that compared with SVM, its improved algorithm, Twin Support Vector Machine (TSVM), has the advantages of fast learning speed and is suitable for large-scale data. Since real distributed scenarios are often high-dimensional and large sample data, to be more suitable for federated learning classification applications in real scenarios, this paper transforms TSVM into a Federated Twin Support Vector Machine (FTSVM).

The rest of this paper will be organized in the following structure: In Sect. 2, the paper will elaborate on the basic principles of Twin Support Vector Machines, Stochastic Gradient Twin Support Vector Machines (SGTSVM), and the basic concepts of federated learning, giving several important mathematical formulae. In the third chapter, this paper proposes the basic framework of the federated twin support vector machine, gives the tasks of each role in the federated context in detail and gives the framework of the federated support vector machine. The experimental results will be given in Sect. 4, we present five datasets used for the experiments on which the accuracy, time, ablation experiments, and the comparison experiment of FTSVM and FSVM are performed. At the end of this paper, we give the conclusion.

2   Related Work

2.1   Twin Support Vector Machines

Consider a binary classification problem in the n-dimensional real space R_n. The training sample set is represented by $X \in R_{n \times m}$, where $X \in R_n$ are the samples labeled $y \in +1, -1$. We further organize m_1 samples of class $+1$ into a matrix $X_1 \in R_{n \times m_1}$, and m_2 samples of class -1 into a matrix $X_2 \in R_{n \times m_2}$.

TSVM [6] finds a pair of non-parallel hyperplanes in R_n, which can be expressed as

$$w_1^T x + b_1 = 0 \quad and \quad w_2^T x + b_2 = 0 \tag{1}$$

Make each hyperplane close to the samples of one class and some distance from the other class. To find the pair of nonparallel hyperplanes, one needs to get the solution to the original problem:

$$\begin{aligned} min_{w_1, b_1} \ &\tfrac{1}{2}(\|w_1\|^2 + b_1^2) + \tfrac{c_1}{2m_1}\|X_1^T w_1 + b_1\|^2 + \tfrac{c_2}{m_2}e^T \xi_1 \\ s.t. \quad &X_2^T w_1 + b_1 - \xi_1 \le -e, \xi_1 \ge 0 \end{aligned} \tag{2}$$

and

$$\begin{aligned} min_{w_2, b_2} \ &\tfrac{1}{2}(\|w_2\|^2 + b_2^2) + \tfrac{c_3}{2m_2}\|X_2^T w_2 + b_2\|^2 + \tfrac{c_4}{m_1}e^T \xi_2 \\ s.t. \quad &X_1^T w_2 + b_2 - \xi_2 \le -e, \xi_2 \ge 0 \end{aligned} \tag{3}$$

where c_1, c_2, c_3 and c_4 are positive parameters, $\xi_1 \in R_{m_2}$ and $\xi_2 \in R_{m_1}$ are slack variables. Their geometric meaning is clear. For example, for (2), its objective function makes the samples of class $+1$ approach the hyperplane $w_1^T x + b_1 = 0$ together with the regularization term, and the constraint makes each sample of the -1 class farther away than $1/\|w_1\|$ away from the hyperplane $w_1^T x + b_1 = -1$.

Once the solutions w_1, b_1 and w_2, b_2 for problems (2) and (3) are obtained, respectively, a new point $x \in R_n$ can then be assigned to a class based on the distance to the two hyperplanes in (1).

$$y = argmin_i \frac{|w_i^T x + b_i|}{\|w_i\|} \tag{4}$$

$|\cdot|$ Indicates absolute value.

2.2   Stochastic Gradient Twin Support Vector Machines

According to [14], we can find that compared with SVM, the sampling of TSVM is more stable and does not strongly depend on some special samples, such as support vector (SV), which indicates that SGD is more suitable for TSVM. Stochastic Gradient Twin Support Vector Machine (SGTSVM) constructs a pair of non-parallel hyperplanes by randomly selecting two samples from different classes in each iteration. Following the previous notation, we restate QPP (2) and (3) in TSVM as unconstrained problems:

$$min_{w_1,b_1} \frac{1}{2}(\|w_1\|^2 + b_1^2) + \frac{c_1}{2\,m_1}\|X_1^T w_1 + b_1\|^2 + \frac{c_2}{m_2}e^T(e + X_2^T w_1 + b_1)_+ \quad (5)$$

and

$$min_{w_2,b_2} \frac{1}{2}(\|w_2\|^2 + b_2^2) + \frac{c_3}{2\,m_2}\|X_2^T w_2 + b_2\|^2 + \frac{c_4}{m_1}e^T(e + X_1^T w_2 + b_2)_+ \quad (6)$$

where $(\cdot)+$ replaces the negative components of the vector with zeros.

To solve the above two problems, we construct a series of strictly convex functions $f_{1,t}(w_1, b_1)$ and $f_{2,t}(w_2, b_2)$, where $t \geqslant 1$:

$$f_{1,t} = \frac{1}{2}(\|w_1\|^2 + b_1^2) + \frac{c_1}{2}\|w_1^T x_t + b_1\|^2 + c_2(1 + w_1^T \hat{x}_t + b_1)_+ \quad (7)$$

and

$$f_{2,t} = \frac{1}{2}(\|w_2\|^2 + b_2^2) + \frac{c_3}{2}\|w_2^T x_t + b_2\|^2 + c_4(1 + w_2^T \hat{x}_t + b_2)_+ \quad (8)$$

where x_t and $\hat{x}_t$ are randomly selected from X_1 and X_2, respectively.

The sub-gradients of the above functions at $w_{1,t}, b_{1,t}$ and $w_{2,t}, b_{2,t}$ can be obtained as

$$\begin{aligned} \nabla_{w_{1,t}} f_{1,t} &= w_{1,t} + c_1(w_{1,t}^T x_t + b_{1,t})x_t + c_2\hat{x}_t sign(1 + w_{1,t}^T \hat{x}_t + b_{1,t})_+ \\ \nabla_{b_{1,t}} f_{1,t} &= b_{1,t} + c_1(w_{1,t}^T x_t + b_{1,t}) + c_2 sign(1 + w_{1,t}^T \hat{x}_t + b_{1,t})_+ \end{aligned} \quad (9)$$

and

$$\begin{aligned} \nabla_{w_{2,t}} f_{2,t} &= w_{2,t} + c_3(w_{2,t}^T x_t + b_{2,t})x_t + c_4\hat{x}_t sign(1 + w_{2,t}^T \hat{x}_t + b_{2,t})_+ \\ \nabla_{b_{2,t}} f_{2,t} &= b_{2,t} + c_3(w_{2,t}^T x_t + b_{2,t}) + c_4 sign(1 + w_{2,t}^T \hat{x}_t + b_{2,t})_+ \end{aligned} \quad (10)$$

SGTSVM starts with initial $w_{1,1}, b_{1,1}$ and $w_{2,1}, b_{2,1}$. Then, for $t \geqslant 1$, the update is given by

$$\begin{aligned} w_{1,t+1} &= w_{1,t} - \eta_t \nabla_{w_{1,t}} f_{1,t} \\ b_{1,t+1} &= b_{1,t} - \eta_t \nabla_{b_{1,t}} f_{1,t} \\ w_{2,t+1} &= w_{2,t} - \eta_t \nabla_{w_{2,t}} f_{2,t} \\ b_{2,t+1} &= b_{2,t} - \eta_t \nabla_{b_{2,t}} f_{2,t} \end{aligned} \quad (11)$$

where η_t is the learning rate, usually set to $1/t$. If the termination condition is satisfied, assign $w_{1,t}, b_{1,t}$ to w_1, b_1 and assign $w_{2,t}, b_{2,t}$ to w_2, b_2. Then, a new sample $x \in R_n$ can be predicted by (4).

2.3   Federated Learning

The primary task of federated learning is to complete the collaboration of different data owners without leaking information. The simplified federated learning model consists of participants and a coordinator. Participants refer to the data owners, and their needs are to obtain a global model without exchanging their data with others. The coordinator is an organization that coordinates all participants to complete the model training. It plays the role of synchronizing and processing intermediate data. Generally, it completes its tasks by collecting the information sent by the participants, sending synchronization signals, and updating information. Figure 1 briefly shows the basic process of federated learning. First, the n participants send the original data to the local server, where the data is initialized and trained. After the parameter update is obtained, the parameter update is sent to the coordinator for integration. The local server receives the integrated new parameters and performs a new round of iterations based on the new parameters. Finally, the model is obtained, and the samples are predicted and sent to the participants. Note that to protect privacy, the data, parameters, and integration parameters marked in the figure will not be exposed to other participants during the transmission process.

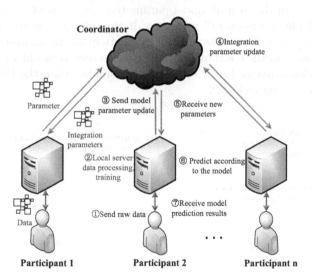

Fig. 1. Schematic diagram of federated learning

3   Federated Twin Support Vector Machines

3.1   Model Frame

Federated learning has been used in many classification models and data mining algorithms, such as neural network algorithms, graph community discovery algorithms, etc., and has achieved good results in medical and health care, bank lending and other fields. However, the field of federalization of twin support vector machines is still blank. As mentioned above, twin support vector machines have strong generalization ability and low computational cost and are more practical than other algorithms. Therefore, this paper proposes federated twin support vector machines, making twin support vector machines better applied to distributed scenarios such as wireless networks.

The Federated Twin Support Vector Machine (FTSVM) designed in this paper firstly runs the initialization algorithm jointly by each participant and the coordinator to obtain the overall dataset size. After the coordinator obtains the overall dataset size, the participants run the Stochastic Gradient Twin Support Vector Machine (SGTSVM) for several rounds in parallel locally to obtain model parameters (or gradients), which are sent to the coordinator after processing. After the coordinator receives the data of all participants, it runs the integration algorithm to obtain the overall model parameters (or gradients) update for this round and calculates the overall tolerance. If the tolerance is still greater than the threshold, the update is sent to each participant to continue to iterate. Each participant and the coordinator repeat the above steps until the maximum number of cycles is reached or the tolerance is smaller than the threshold. The rough process is given in Fig. 2.

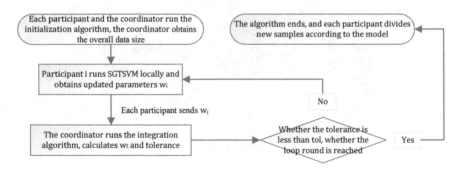

Fig. 2. FTSVM flow chart

Subsequent subsections will give the specific tasks and implementation details of the participants and the coordinator. The algorithm for solving the Federated Twin Support Vector Machine (FTSVM) model is given in Algorithm 1 at the end of this section.

3.2 Participants

The participants defined in this paper each have different data of samples. If they are used alone, only a partial model can be obtained, and the data of each participant cannot be effectively used. Federated learning connects each participant through the update of each round of model parameters, and finally obtains the global model.

Therefore, the task of each participant is to perform part of the process of the stochastic gradient twin support vector machine (SGTSVM), give the model update parameters, pass them to the coordinator, and then perform a new round of updates according to the parameters returned by the coordinator until the coordinator sends the signal to stop the iterative update. But in fact, the participants still have some detailed work to do. This is because in real scenarios, the data scale of each participant cannot be the same size. The specific reasons and details will be explained in detail in Sect. 3.3.

3.3 Coordinator

Initialization Algorithm. In the actual federation scenario, due to statistical heterogeneity, the data provided by each participant does not necessarily satisfy the independent and identical distribution, and considering that the number of samples involved in the training of each participant is different, if the coordinator simply averages the model parameters sent by each participant like FedSGD, it will inevitably deviate from the true value. Let us consider an extreme example. Suppose two participants, one only provides 10 samples, and the other participant provides 10,000 samples. The parameters learned by the latter must be closer to the real ones learned by 10010 samples, simple averaging will make the integration result deviate from the true value.

We naturally think of calculating the number of overall data samples, and each participant determines the importance of the local model parameters in the overall parameter update according to the proportion of the number of samples. Simply sending the number of samples of each participant to the coordinator and then adding and sending them back is unacceptable, because the number of samples of each participant is also privacy that needs to be strictly protected in the sense of federated learning. To achieve this effect, we must abide by several principles: 1. Participants cannot guess the dataset size of other participants based on the data transmitted between themselves and the coordinator. 2. The coordinator cannot infer the dataset size of the participant based on the information sent by the participant.

Constrained by this principle, we propose an initialization algorithm to help the coordinator obtain the overall dataset size and use it in subsequent integration algorithms. For the participants $H = H_1, ..., H_n$ and the corresponding dataset size $S = S_1, ..., S_n$, First participant randomly generate a sequence of lengths n $R = R_1, ..., R_n$, Among them, $R_{tol} = R_1 + R_2 + ... + R_n$ is a parameter known to the coordinator. The sequence R is passed between the participants, after each participant randomly selects a number from the sequence R without replacing it, adds R_j and S_i and sends it to the coordinator. At this time, the coordinator cannot infer the dataset size of a participant from the information sent by the participant. The coordinator adds up the data sent by all the participants to get $R_1 + R_2 + ... + R_n + S_1 + S_2 + ... + S_n$. After subtracting R_{tol} from this formula, the overall dataset size S_{tol} can be obtained.

Integration Algorithm. Note that at this point we have satisfied the second principle. In order to satisfy the first principle, we stipulate that the coordinator cannot send S_{tol} back to each participant. Consider the extreme case of only two participants. If the coordinator sends S_{tol} back to the two participants, the participants only need to differentiate to obtain the dataset size of the other participant. This paper modifies FedAvg as an integration algorithm to deal with the situation we encountered. The reason why FedAvg is chosen instead of FedSGD is that FedAvg transmits parameter updates, which is more thorough in protecting privacy than FedSGD's direct gradient transmission, and FedAvg allows participants to flexibly set local update rounds, which can reduce communication overhead.

The specific steps of the integration algorithm are: the participant H_i runs the SGTSVM to obtain the gradient g_i. For a given local update round $k \leqslant epoch$, the local parameter update formula is

$$w_{k+1}^i \leftarrow w_k^i - \eta_k g_i \qquad (12)$$

Since only the coordinator knows the size of the overall dataset, the participants need to send $w_{k+1}^i * S_i$ to the coordinator. For a given number of iterations $t \leqslant T$, the coordinator calculates the overall model parameters after collecting the model parameters of all participants

$$w_{t+1} \leftarrow \sum_{i=1}^{n} w_{k+1}^i * S_i / S_{tol} \qquad (13)$$

The coordinator sends w_{t+1} back to the participants as the w_0^i of each participant for the next iteration.

It should be noted that for the parameter transfer in Fig. 1, there may be privacy leakage, especially in the case of two participants. In the algorithm that uses a simple average to obtain integration parameters (such as FedSGD), the parameters of another participant can be obtained by simply calculating the sending and receiving parameters. In the weighted integration algorithm, you also need to know your own weight. But after taking the initialization and integration algorithm of this paper, this problem will no longer exist. Because the overall number of samples is only known by the coordinator, the participants cannot calculate the proportion of their own samples to obtain the weight, so there is no way to calculate the parameters of the other participant.

Iteration Terminate Condition. Federated Twin Support Vector Machine (FTSVM) aims to find two hyperplanes, in which the parameters that are updated iteratively are w_1, b_1, w_2, b_2. For the preset tolerance tol, we need to consider w, b at the same time, and the update of the two hyperplanes can be asynchronous, that is to say, after the update of hyperplane 1 is completed, the update of hyperplane 2 can still continue. We need to separate the iterative stopping judgments for the two hyperplanes.

Every time the coordinator calculates the new model parameters, it needs to compare them with the previous one to calculate whether the difference is less than the tolerance tol:

$$\|w_{1,t+1} - w_{1,t}\| + |b_{1,t+1} - b_{1,t}| < tol$$
$$\|w_{2,t+1} - w_{2,t}\| + |b_{2,t+1} - b_{2,t}| < tol \tag{14}$$

The two formulas respectively judge whether the iteration of the two hyperplanes is terminated. If the tolerance of a hyperplane is less than tol, the coordinator sends an iteration stop signal to each participant, and the hyperplane stops iterating, but the other hyperplane will continue to iterate until both hyperplanes stop iterating, and the algorithm ends.

The solution algorithm of the FTSVM model is given in Algorithm 1.

Algorithm 1: Federated Twin Support Vector Machine (FTSVM)

Input: participants $H_1, ..., H_n$, corresponding training dataset $X_{1,1}, ..., X_{1,n}$
positive class, $X_{2,1}, ..., X_{2,n}$ negative class, parameters c_1, c_2, c_3, c_4,
tolerance tol, Maximum iteration round T, local update maximum $epoch$

Output: w_1, b_1, w_2, b_2

1 Generate a random sequence $R = R_1, ..., R_n$ // initialization algorithm
2 **for** $i = 1, 2, ..., n$ **do**
3   Participant H_i send $S_i + R_j$ to coordinator
4   The coordinator calculates S_{tol}

5 Set $w_{1,1}, b_{1,1}, w_{2,1}, b_{2,1}$ to 0 // integration algorithm
6 **for** $t = 1, 2, ..., T$ **do**
7   **for** $i = 1, 2, ..., n$ **do**
8   **for** $k = 1, 2, ..., epoch$ **do**
9   Participant H_i randomly selects a pair of samples x_t and $\hat{x}_t$ from $X_{1,i}$ and $X_{2,i}$ respectively
10   Calculate the kth gradient g_k of H_i and update the model parameters
11             $w^i_{(1,2),k+1} \leftarrow w^i_{(1,2),k} - \eta_k g_k, b^i_{(1,2),k+1} \leftarrow b^i_{(1,2),k} - \eta_k g_k$
12   Send $(w^i_{1,t}, b^i_{1,t}, w^i_{2,t}, b^i_{2,t}) * S_i$ to coodinator
13   Coordinator updates $w_{1,t}, b_{1,t}, w_{2,t}, b_{2,t}$ according to (13) and returns the update to each participant
14   Coordinator judges if $\|w_{1,t+1} - w_{1,t}\| + |b_{1,t+1} - b_{1,t}| < tol$, stop update $w_{1,t+1}, b_{1,t+1}$, set $w_1 = w_{1,t+1}, b_1 = b_{1,t+1}$
15   Coordinator judges if $\|w_{2,t+1} - w_{2,t}\| + |b_{2,t+1} - b_{2,t}| < tol$, stop update $w_{2,t+1}, b_{2,t+1}$, set $w_2 = w_{2,t+1}, b_2 = b_{2,t+1}$

3.4 Federated Support Vector Machine

The federated learning based on SVM proposed in Federated Learning for Wireless Network Energy-Saving Task Computation [13] is only used to solve optimization problems. To be able to compare the performance of SVM with the Federated Twin Support Vector Machine (FTSVM) proposed in this paper, we transform Stochastic Gradient Support Vector Machine (PEGASOS) [12] into Federated Support Vector Machine (FSVM). The idea is similar to the Federated Twin Support Vector Machine (FTSVM). This section mainly introduces the Stochastic Gradient Support Vector Machine (PEGASOS) and the federated support vector machine algorithm, and finally gives the solution algorithm of the federated support vector machine model.

Stochastic Gradient Support Vector Machines. The Stochastic Gradient Descent Algorithm of SVM (PEGASOS) [12] describes the strongly convex problem by the following equation

$$
\begin{aligned}
&min_w \quad \tfrac{1}{2}\|w\|^2 + \tfrac{c}{m}e^T\xi \\
&s.t. \quad DX^Tw \geq e - \xi, \xi \geq 0
\end{aligned}
\tag{15}
$$

Rephrasing the above question as

$$
min_w \frac{1}{2}\|w\|^2 + \frac{c}{m}e^T(e - DX^Tw)_+
\tag{16}
$$

In the tth iteration $(t \geq 1)$, PEGASOS constructs a temporary function defined by a random sample $x_t \in X$

$$
g_t(w) = \frac{1}{2}\|w\|^2 + c(1 - y_tw^Tx_t)_+
\tag{17}
$$

Then, starting from the initial w_1, for $t \geq 1$, PEGASOS iteratively updates $w_{t+1} = w_t - \eta_t\nabla_{w_t}g_t(w)$, where $\eta_t = 1/t$ is the step size, $\nabla_{w_t}g_t(w)$ is the subgradient of $g_t(w)$ at w_t

$$
\nabla_{w_t}g_t(w) = w_t - cy_tx_t * sign(1 - y_tw_t^Tx_t)_+
\tag{18}
$$

When the termination condition is satisfied, the last w_t output is w. A new sample x can be predicted as

$$
y = sign(w^Tx)
\tag{19}
$$

Federated Support Vector Machine Algorithm. The federated support vector machine (FSVM) process designed in this paper is basically the same as the federated twin support vector machine. It also needs to run the initialization algorithm and the integration algorithm. The specific process is as follows:

i) Each participant and the coordinator run the initialization algorithm together, and the coordinator obtains the overall dataset size.

ii) After the coordinator knows the size of the overall dataset, the participants run the stochastic gradient support vector machine (PEGASOS) locally for several rounds in parallel to obtain model parameters (or gradients), which are sent to the coordinator after processing. After the coordinator receives the data of all participants, it runs the integration algorithm to obtain the overall model update parameters (or gradients) for this round and calculates the overall tolerance. If the tolerance is still greater than the set threshold, the update is sent to each participant for subsequent iterations.

iii) Each participant and the coordinator cycle through the above steps until the maximum number of cycles is reached or the tolerance is less than the threshold.

Algorithm 2: Federated Support Vector Machine (FSVM)

Input: participants $H_1, ..., H_n$, corresponding training dataset $X_1, ..., X_n$, parameters C, tolerance tol, Maximum iteration round T, local update maximum $epoch$

Output: w, b

1 Generate a random sequence $R = R_1, ..., R_n$ // initialization algorithm
2 **for** $i = 1, 2, ..., n$ **do**
3   Participant H_i send $S_i + R_j$ to coordinator
4   The coordinator calculates S_{tol}

5 Set w_1, b_1 to 0 // integration algorithm
6 **for** $t = 1, 2, ..., T$ **do**
7   **for** $i = 1, 2, ..., n$ **do**
8   **for** $k = 1, 2, ..., epoch$ **do**
9   Participant H_i randomly selects a samples x_t from X_i
10   Calculate the kth gradient g_k of H_i and update the model parameters
11             $w^i_{k+1} \leftarrow w^i_k - \eta_k g_k, b^i_{k+1} \leftarrow b^i_k - \eta_k g_k$
12   Send $(w^i_t, b^i_t) * S_i$ to coodinator
13   Coordinator updates w_t, b_t according to (13) and returns the update to each participant
14   Coordinator judges if $\|w_{t+1} - w_t\| + |b_{t+1} - b_t| < tol$, stop update
        $w_{1,t+1}, b_{1,t+1}$, set $w_1 = w_{1,t+1}, b_1 = b_{1,t+1}$

It should be pointed out that due to the difference between the SVM algorithm and the TSVM algorithm itself, the former divides the samples by finding a hyperplane, and the latter determines the sample category by finding two hyperplanes, so compared with the federated twin support vector machine, two hyperplane needs four positive parameters c_1, c_2, c_3, c_4 and solves two pairs of hyperplane parameters w_1, b_1, w_2, b_2 the federated support vector machine only needs one parameter C and solves a pair of hyperplane parameters w, b. The corresponding iterative termination condition only needs to become

$\|w_{t+1} - w_t\| + |b_{t+1} - b_t| < tol$. Also, the training dataset does not need to distinguish between positive and negative classes.

In Algorithm 2, we presents the solution algorithm of the FSVM model.

4   Experiments

4.1   Dataset and Experiment Setup

Due to the generally large amount of data in federal scenarios, this paper selects UCI [1] datasets with a large number of samples: Bank Market, Online Shopper, Skin, Credit and Bankruptcy on kaggal, these datasets come from banks, online shopping, facial recognition, credit loans and other common federal applications. Table 1 gives detailed descriptions of the five datasets.

Table 1. Description of artificial datasets

Name	No. of samples	Dimension	Ratio
Bank market	45211	17	0.117
Online shopper	12330	18	0.155
Skin	245057	4	0.208
Credit	30000	24	0.221
Bankruptcy	6819	96	0.032

Since none of the above datasets can be directly used for federated twin support vector machine (FTSVM), to verify the performance of the federated twin support vector machine model proposed in this paper under federated distribution conditions, this paper uses the dataset partitioning tool provided by Fedlab [17] to divide the 10% of the samples in each experimental dataset into the test set, and the remaining 90% of the samples are divided into n = 2, 4, 6, 8, and 10 subsets as the training set, where n represents the number of participants in the corresponding subset.

The Evaluation indicator used in this paper is the accuracy, that is, the proportion of the number of correctly predicted samples to all the test samples.

We first conducted an accuracy experiment to compare the effect of different numbers of participants on the accuracy, and compared the accuracy of FTSVM with that of a stand-alone Stochastic Gradient Twin Support Vector Machine (SGTSVM) to verify the correctness of our proposed FTSVM. Secondly, we conducted a time experiment to explore the change of time with the increase in the number of participants and compared the time overhead of FTSVM and SGTSVM. We also conduct ablation experiments aimed at verifying the effectiveness of FTSVM. Finally, we compare the accuracy and time overhead on FTSVM and Federated Support Vector Machine (FSVM).

4.2   Accuracy Experiment

The accuracy experiment aims to compare FTSVM and SGTSVM, and study the effect of the different number of participants on the accuracy. We conduct experiments on the accuracy of each dataset under the two algorithms, which are divided into 2, 4, 6, 8, and 10 participants under the FTSVM algorithm. From Fig. 3, we can see that the accuracy of each dataset under the SGTSVM and FTSVM algorithms is basically the same, only slightly different in the Shopper and Skin datasets, the FTSVM accuracy on Shopper is about 0.01 higher, FTSVM accuracy is about 0.01 lower on Skin. In theory, the accuracy of FTSVM should be less than or equal to SGTSVM. For the exception that the Shopper dataset is about 0.01 higher in the experiment, we guess it is due to the problem of dataset division, because the divided dataset will also get higher accuracy on SGTSVM. The reason lies in the division of support vectors. Under the FTSVM algorithm, the accuracy remains the same regardless of the number of participants in the experiment. This experimental result fully proves that FTSVM is a correct federal extension of TSVM, so FTSVM can maintain the same accuracy as SGTSVM, and the accuracy does not decrease with the increase in the number of participants.

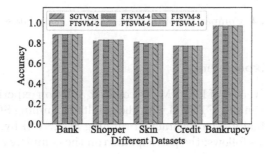

Fig. 3. Comparison of accuracy on each dataset

4.3   Runtime Experiments

To investigate the utility of FTSVM in large-scale participant scenarios, we conduct time experiments. We compare the running times of different algorithms and FTSVM for different numbers of participants on each dataset. Figure 4(a) shows the total running time of FTSVM for different participants, and we can see that it increases linearly. Since we are simulating the distributed computing process on a computer, the local operation of the algorithm by n participants is implemented through n cycles, but in fact, there is no sequential relationship between the n participants. They run the FTSVM algorithm in parallel, so Fig. 4(a) cannot accurately reflect the time overhead of each participant under the FTSVM. Therefore, we do some processing on the experimental results. Since the communication overhead between the participants and the coordinator is basically negligible under FTSVM, we divide the original time overhead by the number of participants as the time overhead for each participant to run FTSVM in parallel, and the results show in Fig. 4(b).

From Fig. 4(b), we can see that only the time overhead of 2-participants and 4-participants changes a little. After the number of participants exceeds 4, the time overhead becomes stable. We can foresee that as the number of participants continues to increase, the time overhead of each participant will remain basically unchanged, and according to Sect. 4.2, the accuracy will also remain unchanged, which shows that FTSVM is very suitable for applications in large-scale participant scenarios.

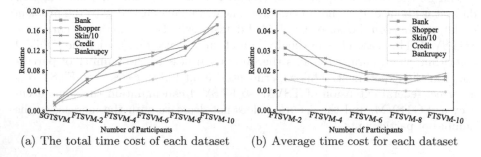

(a) The total time cost of each dataset   (b) Average time cost for each dataset

Fig. 4. Comparison of time overhead on each dataset

4.4   Ablation Experiment

To verify the effectiveness of FTSVM, we conduct ablation experiments. We compare the results of running FTSVM with the results of running SGTSVM by each participant individually. The accuracy of running SGTSVM by the participants alone is calculated as follows: the participants run the complete SGTSVM locally to obtain the corresponding accuracy, and the average of the accuracy of all participants is the SGTSVM accuracy of the corresponding number of participants. Denoted as SGTSVM-n in Fig. 5(a).

From Fig. 5(a), we can find that with the increase in the number of participants, the accuracy of SGTSVM generally shows a downward trend of fluctuation, which shows that SGTSVM without federal transformation cannot be used in the learning of multiple participants. For the two datasets Bank and Bankruptcy, we found that their accuracy did not fluctuate greatly with the number of participants. We analyzed that this is due to the very low proportion of positive samples in these two datasets, even in the case of multiple participants, the models trained by each participant can easily give prediction results that are all negative samples, resulting in no significant drop in accuracy. However, there are not many such situations in real application scenarios, so it is still very necessary to use FTSVM. At the same time, we found that the fluctuation of the Credit dataset with the highest proportion of positive samples in the five datasets is relatively stable, so we choose the Credit dataset for experiments, and compare the accuracy of the Credit dataset with SGTSVM and FTSVM under different numbers of participants.

We further illustrate the effectiveness of FTSVM in Fig. 5(b). From Fig. 5(b), we can find that as the number of participants increases from 2 to 100, the accuracy of FTSVM remains unchanged, which is the same as that of the stand-alone version of SGTSVM. But looking at the SGTSVM with multiple participants, with the increase of participants, the accuracy has been fluctuating and decreasing, and finally fluctuated around 0.5, which is easy to understand, because in the worst binary classification algorithm, each sample is randomly divided into positive and negative classes, the accuracy of 0.5 can be achieved when the number of samples is large enough. Combined with Fig. 5(a), we can fully illustrate the effectiveness of FTSVM. Compared with SGTSVM, FTSVM can keep the accuracy unchanged with the increase of participants, and it is consistent with the stand-alone version.

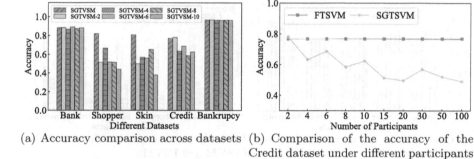

(a) Accuracy comparison across datasets

(b) Comparison of the accuracy of the Credit dataset under different participants

Fig. 5. Ablation experiment results

4.5   Performance of FTSVM and FSVM

The implementation of the federated support vector machine (FSVM) is obviously simpler than the implementation of the federated twin support vector machine (FTSVM), and the parameters passed are less, but we still choose to use the federated twin support vector machine. The reason is as stated in Sect. 2.1, the TSVM reduces the computational cost to a quarter of the SVM by solving two smaller QPP problems. However, the computational cost mentioned above refers to the computational cost of solving the QPP problem according to the KKT condition. Our FTSVM uses the gradient descent algorithm to solve it. Can the accuracy and computational cost still maintain advantages compared with FSVM?

The experimental results in Sect. 4.2 have demonstrated that the accuracy of FTSVM remains consistent regardless of the number of participants involved, so in Fig. 6(a), we use only one accuracy result to represent FTSVM. In Fig. 6(a), we can see that the accuracy of FTSVM and FSVM are exactly the same, and as far as FSVM is concerned, as the number of participants increases, the accuracy remains unchanged. In terms of accuracy, FTSVM for solving two small QPP problems is no lower than FSVM. This result is very satisfactory. After all, the goal of TSVM is to reduce time overhead rather than improve accuracy.

Figure 6(b) shows the time overhead of FTSVM and FSVM on each dataset. We selected four algorithms, SGTSVM, PEGASOS, FTSVM-10, and FSVM-10, to compare the time overhead. We can clearly see that the time overhead of the twin support vector machine and its federation algorithm represented by SGTSVM and FTSVM-10 is significantly smaller than that of PEGASOS and FSVM-10, which represent support vector machines. The time overhead of solving the QPP problem with the twin support vector machine mentioned above is one-quarter of that of the support vector machine. The experimental results here show that the time overhead of FTSVM is also between one-third and one-fourth that of FSVM when solved using the gradient descent algorithm.

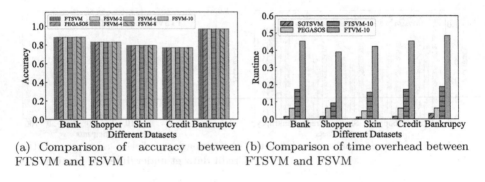

(a) Comparison of accuracy between FTSVM and FSVM

(b) Comparison of time overhead between FTSVM and FSVM

Fig. 6. Comparison of performance between FTSVM and FSVM

It can be seen from the above two comparative experiments that the accuracy of FTSVM and FSVM are consistent. The advantage of FTSVM is that its time overhead is smaller than that of FSVM, and it is more suitable for application in real scenarios.

5   Conclusion

This paper mainly focuses on the research of federated learning and twin support vector machines. For the first time, the federated twin support vector machine algorithm is proposed for the binary classification problem in the federated context. Combining the characteristics of federated learning and twin support vector machines, this paper proposes a unique initialization algorithm and integration algorithm, which ensures the accuracy of the algorithm and protects the privacy of the participants. Accuracy experiments on five datasets demonstrate the correctness of FTSVM. Time experiments demonstrate that FTSVM can be used in scenarios with large-scale participants. Ablation experiments demonstrate the effectiveness of FTSVM. The performance comparison experiment of FTSVM and FSVM shows the superiority of FTSVM. The FTSVM proposed in this paper fills the gap of federated learning in the field of TSVM algorithms. In the future, we can transform the least squares twin support vector machine or the projection twin support vector machine into a federated version, which will greatly improve the accuracy or efficiency. In addition, there are many multi-classification problems and nonlinear classification situations in real-world scenarios, which cannot be handled by FTSVM, and are also the direction of our future research.

References

1. Blake, C.: UCI repository of machine learning databases (1998). http://www.ics. uci.edu/~mlearn/MLRepository.html
2. Chen, X., Yang, J., Ye, Q., Liang, J.: Recursive projection twin support vector machine via within-class variance minimization. Pattern Recogn. **44**(10–11), 2643–2655 (2011)
3. Cortes, C., Vapnik, V.: Support-vector networks. Mach. Learn. **20**(3), 273–297 (1995)
4. Hao, P.Y.: New support vector algorithms with parametric insensitive/margin model. Neural Netw. **23**(1), 60–73 (2010)
5. Jajadeva, D., Khemchandani, R., Chandra, S.: Twin Support Vector Machines: Models, Extensions and Applications. Springer, Cham (2017). https://doi.org/10. 1007/978-3-319-46186-1
6. Khemchandani, R., Chandra, S., et al.: Twin support vector machines for pattern classification. IEEE Trans. Pattern Anal. Mach. Intell. **29**(5), 905–910 (2007)
7. Konečný, J., McMahan, H.B., Ramage, D., Richtárik, P.: Federated optimization: distributed machine learning for on-device intelligence. arXiv preprint arXiv:1610.02527 (2016)
8. Konečný, J., McMahan, H.B., Yu, F.X., Richtárik, P., Suresh, A.T., Bacon, D.: Federated learning: strategies for improving communication efficiency. arXiv preprint arXiv:1610.05492 (2016)
9. Kumar, M.A., Gopal, M.: Least squares twin support vector machines for pattern classification. Expert Syst. Appl. **36**(4), 7535–7543 (2009)
10. McMahan, B., Moore, E., Ramage, D., Hampson, S., Arcas, B.A.: Communication-efficient learning of deep networks from decentralized data. In: Artificial Intelligence and Statistics, pp. 1273–1282. PMLR (2017)
11. Peng, X.: TPMSVM: a novel twin parametric-margin support vector machine for pattern recognition. Pattern Recogn. **44**(10–11), 2678–2692 (2011)
12. Shalev-Shwartz, S., Singer, Y., Srebro, N., Cotter, A.: Pegasos: primal estimated sub-gradient solver for SVM. Math. Program. **127**(1), 3–30 (2011)
13. Wang, S., Chen, M., Saad, W., Yin, C.: Federated learning for energy-efficient task computing in wireless networks. In: ICC 2020–2020 IEEE International Conference on Communications (ICC), pp. 1–6. IEEE (2020)
14. Wang, Z., Shao, Y.H., Bai, L., Li, C.N., Liu, L.M., Deng, N.Y.: Insensitive stochastic gradient twin support vector machines for large scale problems. Inf. Sci. **462**, 114–131 (2018)

15. Xu, Y., Yang, Z., Pan, X.: A novel twin support-vector machine with pinball loss. IEEE Trans. Neural Netw. Learn. Syst. **28**(2), 359–370 (2016)
16. Yang, Q., Liu, Y., Chen, T., Tong, Y.: Federated machine learning: concept and applications. ACM Trans. Intell. Syst. Technol. (TIST) **10**(2), 1–19 (2019)
17. Zeng, D., Liang, S., Hu, X., Xu, Z.: FedLAB: a flexible federated learning framework. arXiv preprint arXiv:2107.11621 (2021)

Adversarial VAE with Normalizing Flows for Multi-Dimensional Classification

Wenbo Zhang[1] , Yunhao Gou[2,3] , Yuepeng Jiang[4] , and Yu Zhang[2,5(✉)]

[1] University of California Irvine, Irvine, USA
wenbz13@uci.edu
[2] Southern University of Science and Technology, Shenzhen, China
ygou@connect.ust.hk
[3] Hong Kong University of Science and Technology, Hong Kong, China
[4] City University of Hong Kong, Hong Kong, China
yuepjiang3-c@my.cityu.edu.hk
[5] Peng Cheng Laboratory, Shenzhen, China
yu.zhang.ust@gmail.com

Abstract. Exploiting correlations among class variables and using them to facilitate the learning process are a key challenge of Multi-Dimensional Classification (MDC) problems. Label embedding is an efficient strategy towards MDC problems. However, previous methods for MDC only use this technique as a way of feature augmentation and train a separate model for each class variable in MDC problems. Such two-stage approaches may cause unstable results and achieve suboptimal performance. In this paper, we propose an end-to-end model called Adversarial Variational AutoEncoder with Normalizing Flow (ADVAE-Flow), which encodes both features and class variables to probabilistic latent spaces. Specifically, considering the heterogeneity of class spaces, we introduce a normalizing flows module to increase the capacity of probabilistic latent spaces. Then adversarial training is adopted to help align transformed latent spaces obtained by normalizing flows. Extensive experiments on eight MDC datasets demonstrate the superiority of the proposed ADVAE-Flow model over state-of-the-art MDC models.

Keywords: Multi-Dimensional Classification · VAE · Normalizing flows

1 Introduction

Multi-Dimensional Classification (MDC) aims to solve the setting that each instance is associated with multiple class variables [7,8,16,17]. Each class variable represents an individual class space which possesses the semantics of an instance

---

W. Zhang—Work done while the author was at Southern University of Science and Technology.

Supplementary Information The online version contains supplementary material available at https://doi.org/10.1007/978-3-031-18907-4_16.

S. Yu et al. (Eds.): PRCV 2022, LNCS 13534, pp. 205–219, 2022.
https://doi.org/10.1007/978-3-031-18907-4_16

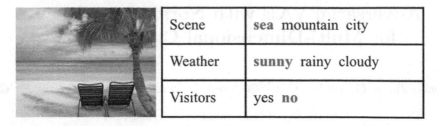

Scene	**sea** mountain city
Weather	**sunny** rainy cloudy
Visitors	yes **no**

Fig. 1. An example of multi-dimensional classification. The image is manually annotated by 3 class variables and the ground truth labels are in red. (Color figure online)

along one dimension. Under the MDC setting, there are wide real-world applications. For example, a document can be characterized by various dimensions such as topic and mood. HIV is associated with different sets of drugs. Figure 1 shows a typical example under the multi-dimensional image classification scenario. It is easy to see that MDC is a generalization of multi-label classification [26] since MDC reduces to multi-label classification if each class space corresponding to a class variable in MDC contains only two classes.

To solve MDC problems, one popular strategy is the Binary Relevance (BR) [26] which decomposes the MDC into a set of multi-class classification problems and builds a number of independent classifiers, one per class space. However, through this strategy, dependencies among class variables are ignored, which would degrade the classification performance. Therefore, recent MDC models focus on modeling class dependencies in different ways.

One common strategy is to utilize feature augmentation which models label dependencies in a manipulated feature space. For example, the Classifier Chains (CC) method [18] feeds the augmented instances to train a multi-class classifier based on the BR model. However, the CC model is sensitive to the order of labels and several techniques [14,25] are proposed to address this problem. By adapting a multi-label classification (MLC) technique with label embedding [1,2, 24,27] to the MDC setting, the LEFA method [23] seamlessly integrates the label embedding and feature augmentation to learn label correlations based on neural networks. Furthermore, by considering the heterogeneity of class spaces, the SLEM method [9] works in an encoder-decoder framework by utilizing the sparse property of the transformed label space. Based on margin-based techniques, the M^3MDC method [8] maximizes the classification margin on individual class variables and regularizes model relationships across class variables.

Label embedding techniques are effective for MDC problems and VAE has shown promising performance to learn label embeddings for MLC problems [1,27]. However, the embedded label space in MDC is usually highly sparse and correlated [23] by considering the heterogeneity of class spaces, which violates some assumptions in VAE. Specifically, there are two main issues for existing VAE-based label embedding methods when they are used to solve MDC problems. Firstly, the latent space in VAE is usually assumed to follow (diagonal) Gaussian distributions. This restriction does not meet the sparse and correlated requirements of the embedded space and has a significant impact on the quality of inference. Secondly, most approaches only utilize KL divergence to align the latent distribution of two branches. However, training with KL divergence only may not ensure that two complex non-Gaussian distributions are matched well. To solve those two issues, we propose a flow-based approach called ADversarial VAE with normalizing Flow (ADVAE-Flow). To address the first issue, after learning initial probabilistic latent spaces following Gaussian distributions, normalizing flows [3,12,19] are adopted to increase the flexibility of the learned probability distribution. It is expected that the transformed latent spaces are more expressive than Gaussian distributions. To address the second issue, except using KL divergence, adversarial learning [4,13,22] is included by adding a discriminator to distinguish the outputs of two branches in the decoder, which can better align the two transformed latent spaces.

The main contributions of this paper are summarized as follows: (i) an end-to-end ADVAE-Flow model is proposed with domain-specific encoders, flows and a shared decoder, which embeds correlated class variables into complex probabilistic latent spaces rather than multivariate Gaussian distributions; (ii) Adversarial learning is combined with the VAE model and it can provide better alignment for transformed latent spaces; (iii) Comprehensive experiments over eight MDC datasets demonstrate that the proposed ADVAE-Flow model outperforms state-of-the-art MDC methods.

2 Background

2.1 Variational Autoencoders

The VAE [11] is a likelihood-based generative model which consists of an encoder and a decoder. The encoder $q_\phi(z|x)$, also called the inference network, encodes a data sample x to a latent variable z, which is normally sampled from a multivariate Gaussian distribution with a lower dimension than the raw data space. The decoder $p_\theta(x|z)$ decodes the latent representation z back to the data space to reconstruct x. VAE aims to maximize the evidence lower bound (ELBO), which is formulated as

$$\mathbb{E}_{z \sim q_\phi} \left[\log p_\theta(x|z) \right] - \mathcal{KL} \left[q_\phi(z|x) \| P(z) \right],$$

where $\mathcal{KL}$ denotes the Kullback-Leibler (KL) divergence and $P(z)$, the prior of the latent variable, is usually assumed to be the standard Gaussian distribution. The decoder of VAE can also be used to predict the label y instead of reconstructing x. In this case, the objective function to be maximized can be formulated as

$$\mathbb{E}_{z \sim q_\phi} \left[\log p_\theta(y|z) \right] - \mathcal{KL} \left[q_\phi(z|x) \| P(z) \right].$$

2.2 Normalizing Flows

Normalizing flows [19] are likelihood-based generative models which construct flexible posteriors by transforming a simple base distribution with a series of

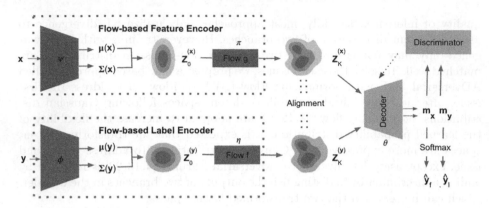

Fig. 2. The overall network architecture of ADVAE-Flow. In the flow-based feature encoder, the network parametrized by ϕ firstly maps a data point $\mathbf{x}$ into an initial Gaussian latent space and then the flow module $\mathbf{g}$ parametrized by π transform it into a complex latent space. Similarly, in the flow-based label encoder, the network parametrized by ψ and the flow module $\mathbf{f}$ parametrized by η map the corresponding label $\mathbf{y}$ to another latent space. Then, latent variables $\mathbf{z}_K^{(\mathbf{x})}$ and $\mathbf{z}_K^{(\mathbf{y})}$ are fed into a shared decoder separately to get their individual scores $\mathbf{m}_\mathbf{X}$ and $\mathbf{m}_\mathbf{Y}$. The two scores are fed into a discriminator to help the training and alignment. Finally, softmax functions are used to transform scores to probabilities for predictions $\hat{\mathbf{y}}_\mathbf{f}$ and $\hat{\mathbf{y}}_\mathbf{l}$. During the testing process, only $\hat{\mathbf{y}}_\mathbf{f}$ is used to make predictions for test instances.

invertible transformations and easily computable Jacobians. Given a variable $\mathbf{z}$ following an initial distribution $q_0(\mathbf{z})$ and an invertible transformation f, the density function for the transformed variable is computed as

$$p_1(\mathbf{z}') = p_0(\mathbf{z}) \left| \det\left(\frac{\partial f(\mathbf{z})}{\partial \mathbf{z}} \right) \right|^{-1},$$

where $\det(\cdot)$ denotes the determinant of a matrix and $\frac{\partial f(\mathbf{z})}{\partial \mathbf{z}}$ denotes the derivative of $f(\mathbf{z})$ with respect to $\mathbf{z}$. As a variant of normalizing flows, continuous normalizing flows (CNF) define mappings via a neural ordinary differential equation (ODE) [3,6], which uses continuous-time transformations instead of discrete flow layers. Specifically, we first sample from a base distribution as $\mathbf{z}_0 \sim p_{z_0}(\mathbf{z}_0)$, and then we solve an ordinary differential equation as $\mathbf{z}(t_0) = \mathbf{z}_0$, $\frac{\partial z(t)}{\partial t} = f(\mathbf{z}(t), t; \theta)$ to obtain $\mathbf{z}(t_1)$, where t_1 is the end time. The instantaneous change of variable formula can be used to obtain the change in the log-density under this transformation as

$$\frac{\partial \log q_t(\mathbf{z}(t))}{\partial t} = -\operatorname{tr}\left(\frac{\partial f}{\partial \mathbf{z}(t)} \right),$$

where $\operatorname{tr}(\cdot)$ denotes the trace of a matrix.

2.3　Adversarial Learning

In domain adaptation, to learn a model that can generalize well from a source domain to a target domain, a typical approach is to minimize the discrepancy of learned feature representations for the two domains [4, 22]. To achieve this, a domain classifier is utilized to discriminate between the source and target domains, and as a result, domain-invariant features can be learned. This idea is closely related to generative adversarial networks (GAN) [5].

3   ADVAE-Flow

Suppose there are L class spaces and the jth class space C_j $(1 \leq j \leq L)$ consists of K_j possible class labels. Given a pair of a data point and categorical labels denoted by $(\mathbf{x}, \mathbf{y}')$, we change the representation of $\mathbf{y}'$ to a stacked binary vector $\mathbf{y} = (\mathbf{y}_1, \mathbf{y}_2 \ldots \mathbf{y}_L)^\top$, where $\mathbf{y}_j \in \{0, 1\}^{K_j}$ denotes the one-hot representation for the label in the jth class space.

As shown in Fig. 2, the ADVAE-Flow model consists of 3 main components, including a two-branch flow-based encoder, a shared decoder and a discriminator. At the training stage, as two branches in the flow-based encoder, the flow-based feature encoder and label encoder first map a data instance and the corresponding label into a pair of Gaussian latent spaces, respectively. Then samples from the two latent spaces are fed to two flow-based transformations to obtain more complex distributions. In this component, we also need to match the two transformed latent spaces. Then a discriminator is used to distinguish the outputs from two branches and align the distributions of them, and a shared decoder can be used to make predictions based on transformed samples. During the testing process, only the data are fed into the flow-based feature encoder to make predictions.

3.1   Flow-Based Encoder

As illustrated in Fig. 2, the flow-based encoder consists of a flow-based feature encoder and a flow-based label encoder. They firstly transform data instances and the corresponding labels into two d-dimensional Gaussian distributions $q_\phi(\mathbf{z}_0^{(\mathbf{y})} \mid \mathbf{y}) = \mathcal{N}\left(\mu^\phi(\mathbf{y}), \Sigma^\phi(\mathbf{y})\right)$ and $q_\psi(\mathbf{z}_0^{(\mathbf{x})} \mid \mathbf{x}) = \mathcal{N}\left(\mu^\psi(\mathbf{x}), \Sigma^\psi(\mathbf{x})\right)$ through two encoder networks parametrized by ϕ and ψ respectively, where $\mathbf{z}_0$ represents initial latent variables, $\mu^\phi(\mathbf{y}), \mu^\psi(\mathbf{x}) \in \mathbb{R}^d$, $\Sigma^\phi(\mathbf{y}), \Sigma^\psi(\mathbf{x}) \in \mathbb{R}_+^{d \times d}$, and $\mathbb{R}_+^{d \times d}$ denotes the set of $n \times n$ positive semi-definite matrices.

Gaussian latent spaces are recently adopted for MLC problems [1, 27] and those studies assume a homogeneous class space which characterizes the relevance of specific concepts along one dimension. However, under the MDC scenario, the class spaces are usually heterogeneous to characterize semantics of data along different dimensions, which means the distributions of the latent spaces are complex than Gaussian distributions. To address this problem, we aim to increase the capacity of the latent distributions through normalizing flows.

We denote by $\mathbf{z}_0^{(\mathbf{x})}$ and $\mathbf{z}_0^{(\mathbf{y})}$ initial multivariate Gaussian latent variables encoded in the feature and label branch, respectively. They are fed into two flow models, respectively, to get more complex probability distributions. There are two types of flow layers we can use, including the finite flow and the continuous flow, and we introduce them in the following. Two branches of flows for data and labels are parametrized by π and η, respectively.

Finite Flows. We utilize two sets of invertible mappings $\mathbf{f}$ and $\mathbf{g}$ with K layers to transform the initial variable as

$$\mathbf{z}_K^{(y)} = f_K \circ \ldots \circ f_2 \circ f_1 \left(\mathbf{z}_0^{(y)} \right) \quad \mathbf{z}_0^{(y)} \sim q_\phi(\mathbf{z}_0^{(y)} | \mathbf{y})$$

$$\mathbf{z}_K^{(x)} = g_K \circ \ldots \circ g_2 \circ g_1 \left(\mathbf{z}_0^{(x)} \right) \quad \mathbf{z}_0^{(x)} \sim q_\psi(\mathbf{z}_0^{(x)} | \mathbf{x}),$$

where f_i and g_i $(i = 1, \ldots, K)$ denote a set of flow layers for label branch and feature branch, respectively, and $\circ$ denotes function composition.

We can compute the log density of transformed variables as

$$\ln q_\eta \left(\mathbf{z}_K^{(y)} | \mathbf{y} \right) = \ln q_\phi \left(\mathbf{z}_0^{(y)} | \mathbf{y} \right) - \sum_{k=1}^{K} \ln \left| \det \left(\frac{\partial f_k}{\partial \mathbf{z}_{k-1}^{(y)}} \right) \right|$$

$$\ln q_\pi \left(\mathbf{z}_K^{(x)} | \mathbf{x} \right) = \ln q_\psi \left(\mathbf{z}_0^{(x)} | \mathbf{x} \right) - \sum_{k=1}^{K} \ln \left| \det \left(\frac{\partial g_k}{\partial \mathbf{z}_{k-1}^{(x)}} \right) \right|. \tag{1}$$

Continuous Flows. The sequence of transformations shown in the finite flows can be regarded as an Euler discretization of a continuous transformation [3, 6]. For a continuous flow, given the initial time 0, the end time T, and two initial conditions $\mathbf{z}_0^{(y)}$ and $\mathbf{z}_0^{(x)}$, we can parametrize the transformations of the latent state via two ordinary differential equations (ODE) specified by two neural networks for the data and label branches, respectively, as

$$\frac{\partial \mathbf{z}_t^{(y)}}{\partial t} = f(\mathbf{z}_t^{(y)}, t), \quad \frac{\partial \mathbf{z}_t^{(x)}}{\partial t} = g(\mathbf{z}_t^{(x)}, t).$$

Using the instantaneous change of variables, we can obtain the change in the log-density, leading to the formulation of the log-density as

$$\log q_\eta(\mathbf{z}_T^{(y)} | \mathbf{y}) = \log q_\phi \left(\mathbf{z}_0^{(y)} | \mathbf{y} \right) - \int_0^T \text{tr} \left(\frac{\partial f}{\partial \mathbf{z}_t^{(y)}} dt \right)$$

$$\log q_\pi(\mathbf{z}_T^{(x)} | \mathbf{x}) = \log q_\psi \left(\mathbf{z}_0^{(x)} | \mathbf{x} \right) - \int_0^T \text{tr} \left(\frac{\partial f}{\partial \mathbf{z}_t^{(x)}} dt \right), \tag{2}$$

where T can be any continuous value larger than 0.

Aligning Latent Spaces. To make the encoders contain both the feature and class information, we align the latent spaces encoded by flow-based feature encoder and label encoder. Monte Carlo estimation of the KL divergence is used because close-form solutions are not available in this case. Here we will only show the KL divergence for finite flows because it is easy to generalize for continuous flows by replacing the sum of log-determinants with integrals. Specifically, to measure the divergence of the latent spaces, the KL divergence can be computed as

$$
\mathcal{L}_{\mathrm{KL}} = \mathcal{KL}\left[q_\eta(\mathbf{z}_K^{(y)} \mid \mathbf{y}) \| q_\pi(\mathbf{z}_K^{(x)} \mid \mathbf{x})\right]
$$

$$
= \mathbb{E}_{q_\eta(\mathbf{z}_K^{(y)} \mid \mathbf{y})}\left[\ln q_\eta(\mathbf{z}_K^{(y)} \mid \mathbf{y}) - \ln q_\pi(\mathbf{z}_K^{(x)} \mid \mathbf{x})\right]
$$

$$
= \mathbb{E}_{q_\phi(\mathbf{z}_0^{(y)} \mid \mathbf{y})}\left[\ln q_\phi(\mathbf{z}_0^{(y)} \mid \mathbf{y}) - \sum_{k=1}^{K} \ln \left|\det \frac{\partial f_k}{\partial \mathbf{z}_{k-1}^{(y)}}\right| - q_\psi(\mathbf{z}_0^{(x)} \mid \mathbf{x}) + \sum_{k=1}^{K} \ln \left|\det \frac{\partial g_k}{\partial \mathbf{z}_{k-1}^{(x)}}\right|\right]
$$

$$
\approx \frac{1}{M}\sum_{m=1}^{M}\left[\ln q_\phi(\mathbf{z}_{0,m}^{(y)} \mid \mathbf{y}) - \sum_{k=1}^{K} \ln \left|\det \frac{\partial f_k}{\partial \mathbf{z}_{k-1}^{(y)}}\right| - q_\psi(\mathbf{z}_{0,m}^{(y)} \mid \mathbf{x}) + \sum_{k=1}^{K} \ln \left|\det \frac{\partial g_k}{\partial \mathbf{z}_{k-1}^{(y)}}\right|\right],
$$

where $\mathbb{E}[\cdot]$ denotes the expectation, and $\mathbf{z}_{0,m}^{(y)}$ are sampled from $q_\phi(\mathbf{z}_0^{(y)} \mid \mathbf{y})$ to approximate the expectation via the Monte Carlo method.

3.2   Decoder

The shared decoder parametrized by θ firstly reads the samples $\mathbf{z}_K^{(x)}$ and $\mathbf{z}_K^{(y)}$ outputted by the flow-based encoder, and then outputs prediction scores $\mathbf{m_x} = (\mathbf{m}_{\mathbf{x},1}, \ldots, \mathbf{m}_{\mathbf{x},L})^\top$ and $\mathbf{m_y} = (\mathbf{m}_{\mathbf{y},1}, \ldots, \mathbf{m}_{\mathbf{y},L})^\top$, respectively, where $\mathbf{m}_{\mathbf{x},i}$, $\mathbf{m}_{\mathbf{y},i} \in \mathbb{R}^{K_i}$. Recall that L is the number of class spaces and K_i is the number of classes for the ith class space. The prediction scores can be transformed to probability through the softmax function. The loss function for the decoder is formulated as

$$
\mathbb{E}_{q_\eta}\left[\log p_\theta(\mathbf{y} \mid \mathbf{z}_K^{(y)})\right] + \mathbb{E}_{q_\pi}\left[\log p_\theta(\mathbf{y} \mid \mathbf{z}_K^{(x)})\right].
$$

3.3   Discriminator

Motivated by [13], where VAE is combined with GAN to create a stronger generative model, we introduce a discriminator network to distinguish which branch (i.e., the feature branch or the label branch) a prediction score (i.e., $\mathbf{m_x}$ and $\mathbf{m_y}$) outputted by the decoder comes from. Since in many cases the prediction in the label branch is better than the feature branch, the discriminator can enforce the outputs of the two branches to become as close as possible. The loss function of discriminator adopts the binary cross-entropy loss, which is formulated as

$$
\mathcal{L}_{\mathrm{ADV}} = \sum_{\mathbf{x},\mathbf{y}}\left(\log(\mathrm{Dis}(\mathbf{m_y})) + \log(1 - \mathrm{Dis}(\mathbf{m_x}))\right),
$$

where $\mathrm{Dis}(\cdot)$ denotes the discriminator.

3.4 Loss Function

The overall loss function consists of 3 parts. We denote the true label vector by $\mathbf{y}$. The reconstruction losses $\mathbb{E}_{q_\eta}\left[\log p_\theta(\mathbf{y} \mid \mathbf{z}_K^{(\mathbf{y})})\right]$ and $\mathbb{E}_{q_\pi}\left[\log p_\theta(\mathbf{y} \mid \mathbf{z}_K^{(\mathbf{x})})\right]$ can be approximated by the cross-entropy loss since they become the cross-entropy loss when the expectation is approximated by the finite sum. Let $\hat{\mathbf{y}}_f$ and $\hat{\mathbf{y}}_l$ denote the prediction probability of the feature and label branches, respectively. Then we compute the cross-entropy loss over all class spaces as

$$\mathcal{L}_{\mathrm{CE}} = \mathrm{CE}\left(\mathbf{y}, \hat{\mathbf{y}}_f\right) + \mathrm{CE}\left(\mathbf{y}, \hat{\mathbf{y}}_l\right),$$

where the cross-entropy loss $\mathrm{CE}(\cdot, \cdot)$ is defined as

$$\mathrm{CE}(\mathbf{y}, \hat{\mathbf{y}}) = \frac{1}{L}\sum_{i=1}^{L}\sum_{j=1}^{K_i} -y_{ij}\log\left(\hat{y}_{ij}\right),$$

where for ith classification task and its associated jth class, y_{ij} equals 1 if it is the true label and otherwise 0, and $\hat{y}_{ij}$ is the corresponding predicted probability.

Finally, including the KL divergence and adversarial loss, the overall loss function is formulated as

$$\mathcal{L} = \mathcal{L}_{\mathrm{CE}} - \lambda\mathcal{L}_{\mathrm{ADV}} + \beta\mathcal{L}_{\mathrm{KL}} \tag{3}$$

where λ and β are used to control the weighting of two terms. β governs the information bottleneck in β-VAE.

As shown in Algorithm 1, ADVAE-Flow model can be trained end-to-end using gradient-based techniques such as Adam [10]. Here we don't adopt usual min-max training objective in GAN. One problem with min-max formulation is instability during training hence models are very difficult to train reliably. Hence We follow the way of training procedure as the VAE-GAN in [13] where VAE-GAN are trained simultaneously. This is possible because we do not update all the network parameters with respect to the combined loss. In algorithm, we update the encoder with loss $\mathcal{L}_{\mathrm{CE}}$, $\mathcal{L}_{\mathrm{ADV}}$ and $\mathcal{L}_{\mathrm{KL}}$ and we use parameters to weight the ability to reconstruct vs fooling the discriminator. Then we update the discriminator only with $\mathcal{L}_{\mathrm{ADV}}$ to gain a better discrimination ability. In practice we observe that through our optimization procedure two embedding vectors are not pushed away.

Table 1. Statistics of MDC datasets. Here the suffixes n and x in the last column denote numeric and nominal features, respectively.

Dataset	Inst	Dim	Class/Dim	Feat
Oes10	359	16	3	298n
Voice	3136	2	4,2	19n
Rf1	8987	8	4,4,3,4,4,3,4,3	64n
SCM1d	9803	16	4	280n
COIL2000	9822	5	6,10,10,4,2	81x
Flickr	12198	5	3,4,3,4,4	1536n
Disfa.	13095	12	5,5,6,3,4,4,5,4,4,4,6,4	136n
Adult	18419	4	7,7,5,2	5n,5x

Algorithm 1. Training Algorithm

1: Initialize parameters: $\boldsymbol{\theta}_{\mathrm{ED}} = (\phi, \psi, \eta, \pi, \theta), \boldsymbol{\theta}_{\mathrm{Dis}}$
2: **while** iterations<maximum **do**
3: $\quad \mathbf{z}_0^{(\mathbf{x})}, \mathbf{z}_0^{(\mathbf{y})} \leftarrow \mathrm{Encoder}(\mathbf{x}, \mathbf{y})$
4: $\quad \mathbf{z}_K^{(\mathbf{x})}, \mathbf{z}_K^{(\mathbf{y})} \leftarrow \mathrm{Flow}(\mathbf{z}_0^{(\mathbf{x})}, \mathbf{z}_0^{(\mathbf{y})})$
5: $\quad$ Calculate $\mathcal{L}_{\mathrm{KL}}$
6: $\quad \mathbf{m_x}, \mathbf{m_y} \leftarrow \mathrm{Decoder}(\mathbf{z}_K^{(\mathbf{x})}, \mathbf{z}_K^{(\mathbf{y})})$
7: $\quad$ Calculate $\mathcal{L}_{\mathrm{ADV}}$
8: $\quad \hat{\mathbf{y}}_f, \hat{\mathbf{y}}_l \leftarrow \mathrm{Softmax}(\mathbf{m_x}, \mathbf{m_y})$
9: $\quad$ Calculate $\mathcal{L}_{\mathrm{CE}}$
10: $\quad \boldsymbol{\theta}_{\mathrm{ED}} \xleftarrow{+} -\nabla_{\boldsymbol{\theta}_{\mathrm{ED}}}(\mathcal{L}_{\mathrm{CE}} - \lambda\mathcal{L}_{\mathrm{ADV}} + \beta\mathcal{L}_{\mathrm{KL}})$
11: $\quad \boldsymbol{\theta}_{\mathrm{Dis}} \xleftarrow{+} -\nabla_{\boldsymbol{\theta}_{\mathrm{Dis}}}\mathcal{L}_{\mathrm{ADV}}$
12: **end while**

---

4   Experiments

In this section, we empirically evaluate the proposed ADVAE-Flow model.

4.1   Experimental Setup

We test the proposed method on 8 benchmark datasets. The datasets are collected and pre-processed in [9]. Their detailed characteristics are summarized in Table 1, including the number of instances (denoted by Inst), the number of dimensions (denoted by Dim), the number of class labels per dimension (denoted by Class/Dim) and the number of features (denoted by Feat). Here the number of class labels per dimension is recorded in turn and we only record unique numbers and remove repetitions by following [9]. In the same way as [9], We split each dataset into 10 folds, each of which contains a training set, a validation set, and a test set.

Table 2. The performance (in terms of mean ± std) of different models on 8 MDC datasets. The best result among all the models is shown in boldface. All the results of baseline models are based on the reported performance in [9].

Dataset	Hamming score							
	ADVAE-Flow		SLEM	BR	CP	BCC	ESC	gMML
	NF	CNF						
Oes10	0.799 ± 0.014	$\mathbf{0.803 \pm 0.014}$	0.763 ± 0.014	0.664 ± 0.019	0.179 ± 0.041	0.674 ± 0.028	0.633 ± 0.020	0.775 ± 0.017
Voice	0.960 ± 0.002	$\mathbf{0.961 \pm 0.010}$	0.944 ± 0.010	0.940 ± 0.010	0.916 ± 0.010	0.938 ± 0.010	0.931 ± 0.009	0.842 ± 0.009
Rf1	0.968 ± 0.002	$\mathbf{0.969 \pm 0.001}$	0.927 ± 0.002	0.852 ± 0.005	0.813 ± 0.010	0.855 ± 0.004	0.794 ± 0.007	0.730 ± 0.007
Scm1d	0.869 ± 0.003	0.869 ± 0.002	$\mathbf{0.884 \pm 0.003}$	0.725 ± 0.007	N/A	0.691 ± 0.007	N/A	0.697 ± 0.007
CoIL2000	$\mathbf{0.949 \pm 0.003}$	0.927 ± 0.004	0.899 ± 0.005	0.874 ± 0.005	0.738 ± 0.006	0.875 ± 0.005	0.851 ± 0.008	0.894 ± 0.004
Flickr	$\mathbf{0.800 \pm 0.004}$	0.796 ± 0.005	0.737 ± 0.018	0.715 ± 0.006	0.658 ± 0.008	0.715 ± 0.006	0.651 ± 0.007	0.779 ± 0.004
Disfa	0.931 ± 0.002	0.932 ± 0.003	$\mathbf{0.935 \pm 0.002}$	0.885 ± 0.003	N/A	0.883 ± 0.003	0.878 ± 0.003	0.884 ± 0.003
Adult	$\mathbf{0.723 \pm 0.003}$	0.718 ± 0.005	0.696 ± 0.006	0.701 ± 0.004	0.682 ± 0.005	0.680 ± 0.006	0.675 ± 0.006	0.705 ± 0.004

Dataset	Exact match							
	ADVAE-Flow		SLEM	BR	CP	BCC	ESC	gMML
Oes10	$\mathbf{0.097 \pm 0.039}$	0.096 ± 0.042	0.054 ± 0.036	0.064 ± 0.035	0.077 ± 0.041	0.079 ± 0.045	0.067 ± 0.037	0.079 ± 0.040
Voice	0.921 ± 0.019	$\mathbf{0.923 \pm 0.019}$	0.907 ± 0.012	0.884 ± 0.017	0.841 ± 0.016	0.881 ± 0.017	0.867 ± 0.016	0.699 ± 0.017
Rf1	0.765 ± 0.010	$\mathbf{0.767 \pm 0.020}$	0.581 ± 0.008	0.322 ± 0.011	0.319 ± 0.025	0.336 ± 0.010	0.275 ± 0.012	0.138 ± 0.011
Scm1d	0.231 ± 0.016	0.236 ± 0.013	$\mathbf{0.278 \pm 0.015}$	0.115 ± 0.010	N/A	0.123 ± 0.013	N/A	0.102 ± 0.009
CoIL2000	$\mathbf{0.791 \pm 0.013}$	0.703 ± 0.016	0.608 ± 0.016	0.515 ± 0.012	0.273 ± 0.012	0.520 ± 0.010	0.468 ± 0.019	0.576 ± 0.015
Flickr	$\mathbf{0.334 \pm 0.016}$	0.320 ± 0.012	0.248 ± 0.017	0.187 ± 0.011	0.125 ± 0.016	0.187 ± 0.011	0.114 ± 0.014	0.287 ± 0.009
Disfa	0.515 ± 0.013	0.520 ± 0.012	$\mathbf{0.539 \pm 0.015}$	0.378 ± 0.011	N/A	$0.377 \pm 0.011t$	0.374 ± 0.011	0.379 ± 0.011
Adult	0.287 ± 0.006	0.272 ± 0.009	$\mathbf{0.288 \pm 0.011}$	0.228 ± 0.006	0.282 ± 0.012	0.272 ± 0.007	0.269 ± 0.011	0.230 ± 0.009

Dataset	Sub-Exact match							
	ADVAE-Flow		SLEM	BR	CP	BCC	ESC	gMML
	NF	CNF						
Oes10	$\mathbf{0.216 \pm 0.071}$	0.213 ± 0.054	0.144 ± 0.051	0.119 ± 0.059	0.107 ± 0.044	0.142 ± 0.055	0.117 ± 0.048	0.176 ± 0.038
Voice	0.997 ± 0.001	$\mathbf{0.998 \pm 0.001}$	0.981 ± 0.011	0.996 ± 0.005	0.991 ± 0.005	0.996 ± 0.005	0.995 ± 0.005	0.985 ± 0.011
Rf1	0.980 ± 0.005	$\mathbf{0.983 \pm 0.004}$	0.877 ± 0.011	0.655 ± 0.017	0.580 ± 0.022	0.669 ± 0.015	0.542 ± 0.014	0.375 ± 0.014
Scm1d	0.456 ± 0.016	0.456 ± 0.018	$\mathbf{0.523 \pm 0.012}$	0.223 ± 0.016	N/A	0.206 ± 0.012	N/A	0.198 ± 0.015
CoIL2000	$\mathbf{0.956 \pm 0.006}$	0.938 ± 0.007	0.902 ± 0.013	0.873 ± 0.016	0.76 ± 0.016	0.875 ± 0.014	0.820 ± 0.017	0.903 ± 0.010
Flickr	$\mathbf{0.734 \pm 0.011}$	0.725 ± 0.010	0.611 ± 0.035	0.543 ± 0.015	0.426 ± 0.018	0.544 ± 0.017	0.414 ± 0.017	0.689 ± 0.016
Disfa	0.788 ± 0.007	0.789 ± 0.008	$\mathbf{0.791 \pm 0.008}$	0.596 ± 0.011	N/A	0.588 ± 0.009	0.575 ± 0.010	0.590 ± 0.009
Adult	0.685 ± 0.006	$\mathbf{0.679 \pm 0.010}$	0.624 ± 0.014	0.657 ± 0.010	0.599 ± 0.008	0.597 ± 0.012	0.586 ± 0.011	0.669 ± 0.008

Evaluation Metrics. Three widely-used metrics are used, including the Hamming Accuracy (HA), Exact Match (EM) and Sub-Exact Match (SEM). Let the test dataset be denoted by $\mathcal{S} = \{(\boldsymbol{x}_i, \boldsymbol{y}_i) \mid 1 \leq i \leq p\}$, where $\boldsymbol{y}_i = [y_{i1}, y_{i2}, \ldots, y_{iL}]^\top$ is the ground truth label vector of $\mathbf{x}_i$. Here L is the number of class spaces. Let $\hat{\boldsymbol{y}}_i = [\hat{y}_{i1}, \hat{y}_{i2}, \ldots, \hat{y}_{iL}]^\top$ be the predicted labels of $\mathbf{x}_i$. Then let $r^{(i)} = \sum_{j=1}^{L} \mathbf{1}_{[y_{ij}=\hat{y}_{ij}]}$ denote the number of classes predicted correctly of x_i, where $\mathbf{1}_{[\cdot]}$ is the indicator function. The three metrics are formally defined as

$$\text{HA} = \frac{1}{pL} \sum_{i=1}^{p} r^{(i)}$$

$$\text{EM} = \frac{1}{p} \sum_{i=1}^{p} \mathbf{1}_{[r^{(i)}=L]}$$

$$\text{SEM} = \frac{1}{p} \sum_{i=1}^{p} \mathbf{1}_{[r^{(i)} \geq L-1]}.$$

Baseline Models. We compare the proposed ADVAE-Flow model with six state-of-the-art MDC baselines, including Binary Relevance (BR) [26], Class Powerset (CP) [21], Ensembles of Super Class classifiers (ESC) [17], Bayesian chain classifiers (BCC) [25], gMML [15], and Sparse Label Encoding Methods (SLEM) [9]. BR solves MDC problems by training a number of independent multi-class classifiers for each class space. BCC, CP, and ESC model dependencies among different class spaces by ordering class spaces as a chain, conducting powerset transformation, and grouping class variables into super-classes, respectively. gMML decomposes the class spaces into a binary-valued label space via the one-vs-rest strategy and solves the resulting problem via a metric approach. SLEM follows the encoding-training-decoding framework combined with a multi-output regression model and orthogonal matching pursuit algorithm for prediction.

Implementation Details. For the proposed method, the latent dimension is empirically set as $\frac{1}{10}$ of the feature dimension plus the label dimension. We perform grid search on hyper-parameters, where λ, β, and the learning rate are chosen from $\{0.1, 1, 5, 10\}$, $\{1, 1.1, 2, 5, 10\}$, and $\{5e\text{-}3, 5e\text{-}4, 5e\text{-}5\}$, respectively.

The feature and label encoder and the shared decoder are three-layer fully connected neural networks and the discriminator is a four-layer fully connected neural network. Those neural networks adopt the ReLU as the activation function.

There are two variants of the proposed method based on the types of flow layers. The first variant (called ADVAE-Flow-NF) is based on a type of finite flows, called planar flow [19], and the second one (called ADVAE-Flow-CNF) is using continuous normalizing flow based on Neural ODE [3]. We use the same hidden units for both flow modules as [3]. Furthermore, as in the conditional VAE [20], our implementation concatenates each of labels and two initial latent variables with features. We perform all the computations on four NVIDIA TITAN RTX GPU with 96GB memory in total.

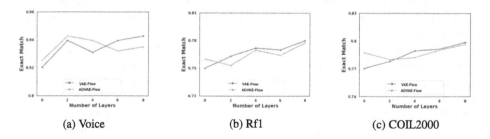

(a) Voice   (b) Rf1   (c) COIL2000

Fig. 3. The change of the EM scores for the Voice, Rf1 and COIL2000 datasets when the number of flow layers increases from 0 to 8 with and without the discriminator.

4.2   Analysis on Results

According to experimental results shown in Table 2, we have the following observations.

- ADVAE-Flow-NF and ADVAE-Flow-CNF outperforms all the baseline approaches on 6 datasets except the Scm1D and Disfa datasets. In those 6 datasets, the proposed methods achieve significantly better performance than state-of-the-art baseline methods, which demonstrate the superiority of the proposed methods. Taking the Rf1 dataset as an example, in terms of 3 metrics, ADVAE-Flow-NF yields 4.1%, 18,4%, and 10.3% improvements, respectively, over the best baseline (i.e., SLEM) on average. On the Scm1D and Disfa datasets, the performance of ADVAE-Flow-NF and ADVAE-Flow-CNF are comparable to the best baseline (i.e., SLEM).
- The BCC and ESC models construct the class dependencies in the original label space via the chain structure and super-class partition, respectively. The proposed models achieve superior performance against BCC and ESC on all datasets, which indicates the advantage of learning from encoded label space.
- The SLEM model utilizes the sparse property of the transformed label space to build an encoding-training-decoding framework, which is similar to label embedding because it also incorporate label into the model. Through the results, it seems that the proposed models, which learn latent spaces in an end-to-end manner, are generally more beneficial than such multi-stage methods.
- Two variants of the proposed ADVAE-Flow model (i.e., ADVAE-Flow-NF and ADVAE-Flow-CNF) have comparable performance in most cases, which implies that the finite flow and continuous flow have comparable capacity in ADVAE-Flow model.

4.3   Sensitivity Analysis and Ablation Study

We investigate how the discriminator and the flow layers affect the classification performance. Since the performance of utilizing finite and continuous flow layers is comparable and the training speed of the former is much faster, here we utilize finite flow layers.

We postulate that for datasets with more complex feature spaces and label spaces, increasing the number of layers would be particularly beneficial for improving the performance because flow layers would increase the capacity and flexibility of latent spaces. To verify this hypothesis, we train the proposed model with different numbers of flow layers with and without the discriminator on the Voice, Rf1, and COIL2000 datasets to see how the EM metric varies under these settings, where the variant without using the discriminator is called VAE-Flow. When the number of flows are 0 and there is no discriminator, the proposed model becomes the aligned VAE [1]. In Fig. 3, we show the EM score for these datasets with the number of layers being 2, 4, 6, 8 and 10. For the Rf1 and COIL2000 datasets where the number of features and labels are more than those of the Voice dataset, a larger number of layers has more positive impacts on the

EM score, which verifies the postulation. Moreover, it is possible that increasing layers beyond some threshold will negatively affect the performance due to the overfitting and unstable training.

According to Fig. 3, we can see that in VAE-Flow and ADVAE-Flow, using finite flows with an appropriate number of layers can improve the performance when compared with no flow corresponding to the case that the number of layers is 0. Moreover, we notice that sometimes VAE-Flow performs slightly better than ADVAE-Flow, especially when the feature and label dimensions are small (i.e., Voice dataset). One possible reason is that when the inputs of both branches are low-dimensional, the alignment of latent spaces is relatively easy and there is no need to use a discriminator which may lead to degenerated performance. Hence the discriminator does not always positively improve the performance. It mostly has a significant impact when the number of flow layers is small, especially for small datasets such as Voice.

5   Conclusion

In this paper, we propose an ADVAE-Flow model for both multi-dimensional classification. To improve the simple Gaussian assumption for latent spaces in previous studies, ADVAE-Flow utilizes normalizing flows to learn non-Gaussian latent distributions, which improve its expressive power. To better align the latent spaces, we build a discriminator to distinguish outputs from two branches in the spirit of adversarial learning. Through experiments, we show that ADVAE-Flow outperforms the state-of-the-art models for multi-dimensional classification. In our future studies, we will apply the ADVAE-Flow model to other learning problems.

Acknowledgements. This work is supported by NSFC general grant 62076118 and Shenzhen fundamental research program JCYJ20210324105000003.

References

1. Bai, J., Kong, S., Gomes, C.: Disentangled variational autoencoder based multi-label classification with covariance-aware multivariate probit model. arXiv preprint arXiv:2007.06126 (2020)
2. Chen, C., Wang, H., Liu, W., Zhao, X., Hu, T., Chen, G.: Two-stage label embedding via neural factorization machine for multi-label classification. In: Proceedings of the AAAI Conference on Artificial Intelligence, pp. 3304–3311 (2019)
3. Chen, R.T.Q., Rubanova, Y., Bettencourt, J., Duvenaud, D.K.: Neural ordinary differential equations. In: Bengio, S., Wallach, H., Larochelle, H., Grauman, K., Cesa-Bianchi, N., Garnett, R. (eds.) Advances in Neural Information Processing Systems, vol. 31. Curran Associates, Inc. (2018). https://proceedings.neurips.cc/paper/2018/file/69386f6bb1dfed68692a24c8686939b9-Paper.pdf
4. Ganin, Y., et al.: Domain-adversarial training of neural networks. J. Mach. Learn. Res. **17**(1), 2096–2130 (2016)

5. Goodfellow, I., et al.: Generative adversarial nets. Adv. Neural Inf. Process. Syst. **27**, 1–9 (2014)
6. Grathwohl, W., Chen, R.T.Q., Bettencourt, J., Sutskever, I., Duvenaud, D.: Ffjord: Free-form continuous dynamics for scalable reversible generative models. In: International Conference on Learning Representations (2019)
7. Jia, B.B., Zhang, M.L.: Multi-dimensional classification via KNN feature augmentation. Pattern Recogn. **106**, 107423 (2020)
8. Jia, B.B., Zhang, M.L.: Maximum margin multi-dimensional classification. IEEE Trans. Neural Netw. Learn. Syst. (2021)
9. Jia, B.B., Zhang, M.L.: Multi-dimensional classification via sparse label encoding. In: International Conference on Machine Learning, pp. 4917–4926. PMLR (2021)
10. Kingma, D.P., Ba, J.: Adam: a method for stochastic optimization. In: International Conference on Learning Representations (2014)
11. Kingma, D.P., Welling, M.: Auto-encoding variational Bayes. In: Bengio, Y., LeCun, Y. (eds.) 2nd International Conference on Learning Representations, ICLR 2014, Banff, AB, Canada, 14–16 April 2014, Conference Track Proceedings (2014). http://arxiv.org/abs/1312.6114
12. Kingma, D.P., Salimans, T., Jozefowicz, R., Chen, X., Sutskever, I., Welling, M.: Improved variational inference with inverse autoregressive flow. Adv. Neural. Inf. Process. Syst. **29**, 4743–4751 (2016)
13. Larsen, A.B.L., Sønderby, S.K., Larochelle, H., Winther, O.: Autoencoding beyond pixels using a learned similarity metric. In: International Conference on Machine Learning, pp. 1558–1566. PMLR (2016)
14. Liu, W., Tsang, I.W.: On the optimality of classifier chain for multi-label classification. Adv. Neural Inf. Process. Syst. **28**, 1–9 (2015)
15. Ma, Z., Chen, S.: Multi-dimensional classification via a metric approach. Neurocomputing **275**, 1121–1131 (2018)
16. Ma, Z., Chen, S.: A convex formulation for multiple ordinal output classification. Pattern Recogn. **86**, 73–84 (2019)
17. Read, J., Martino, L., Luengo, D.: Efficient Monte Carlo methods for multidimensional learning with classifier chains. Pattern Recogn. **47**(3), 1535–1546 (2014)
18. Read, J., Pfahringer, B., Holmes, G., Frank, E.: Classifier chains for multi-label classification. Mach. Learn. **85**(3), 333–359 (2011)
19. Rezende, D., Mohamed, S.: Variational inference with normalizing flows. In: International Conference on Machine Learning, pp. 1530–1538. PMLR (2015)
20. Sohn, K., Lee, H., Yan, X.: Learning structured output representation using deep conditional generative models. Adv. Neural. Inf. Process. Syst. **28**, 3483–3491 (2015)
21. Tsoumakas, G., Katakis, I., Vlahavas, I.: Random k-labelsets for multilabel classification. IEEE Trans. Knowl. Data Eng. **23**(7), 1079–1089 (2010)
22. Tzeng, E., Hoffman, J., Saenko, K., Darrell, T.: Adversarial discriminative domain adaptation. In: Proceedings of the IEEE Conference on Computer Vision and Pattern Recognition, pp. 7167–7176 (2017)
23. Wang, H., Chen, C., Liu, W., Chen, K., Hu, T., Chen, G.: Incorporating label embedding and feature augmentation for multi-dimensional classification. In: Proceedings of the AAAI Conference on Artificial Intelligence, pp. 6178–6185 (2020)
24. Yeh, C.K., Wu, W.C., Ko, W.J., Wang, Y.C.F.: Learning deep latent space for multi-label classification. In: Thirty-First AAAI Conference on Artificial Intelligence (2017)

25. Zaragoza, J.C., Sucar, E., Morales, E., Bielza, C., Larranaga, P.: Bayesian chain classifiers for multidimensional classification. In: Twenty-Second International Joint Conference on Artificial Intelligence (2011)
26. Zhang, M.L., Zhou, Z.H.: A review on multi-label learning algorithms. IEEE Trans. Knowl. Data Eng. **26**(8), 1819–1837 (2013)
27. Zhao, W., Kong, S., Bai, J., Fink, D., Gomes, C.: Hot-VAE: learning high-order label correlation for multi-label classification via attention-based variational autoencoders. arXiv preprint arXiv:2103.06375 (2021)

Fuzzy Twin Bounded Large Margin Distribution Machines

Qiang Jin, Shuangyi Fan, Denghao Dong, and Libo Zhang$^{(\boxtimes)}$

School of Artificial Intelligence, Southwest University, Chongqing 400715, China
lbzhang@swu.edu.cn

Abstract. Twin bounded large distribution machine (TBLDM) considers structural risk and marginal distribution issues, obtaining good efficiency, robustness, and generalization performance. However, it ignores the influence of noise and uncertainty of the input data, which is inevitable in reality. Aiming at the problem, this paper introduces the idea of fuzzy set theory and proposes a novel fuzzy TBLDM (FTBLDM). The fuzzy membership function is set to be related to the distance of the sample to the class center, which describes its importance and credibility level. By incorporating the membership degree into the object function, FTBLDM reduces the influence of outliers and noise on the optimal hyperplane. The effectiveness of our method is validated by experiments on a synthetic dataset and UCI benchmark datasets. Besides, to verify the anti-noise performance of the model, we conduct experiments on UCI datasets with noise. The results show that FTBLDM is able to produce promising results compared to several benchmark and state-of-the-art algorithms.

Keywords: Fuzzy membership · Large margin distribution · Twin support vector machine · Classification

1 Introduction

Support vector machine (SVM) is a well-known supervised learning method that aims to minimize the structural risk [1,3,8]. Specifically, it maximizes the separation of two parallel planes by maximizing the minimum margin, i.e. the minimum distance of the samples (support vectors) to the classification boundary. However, it has been verified that the margin distribution is more important than the minimum margin in optimizing generalization performance [5,10]. As a variation of SVM, the large margin distribution machine (LDM) optimizes the

This work is supported by the National Nature Science Foundation of China (No. 62106205), Fundamental Research Funds for the Central Universities (No. SWU021002), Natural Science Foundation of Chongqing (Nos. cstc2021jcyj-msxmX0824 and cstc2021 jcyj-msxmX0565), the project of science and technology research program of Chongqing Education Commission of China (Nos. KJQN202100207 and KJZD-K202100203), and the Chongqing Municipal Training Program of Innovation and Entrepreneurship for Undergraduate (Nos. S202210635266, and X202210635352).

S. Yu et al. (Eds.): PRCV 2022, LNCS 13534, pp. 220–231, 2022.
https://doi.org/10.1007/978-3-031-18907-4_17

marginal distribution, i.e., the margin mean and margin variance are utilized to obtain the optimal hyperplanes [12,13]. By optimizing the overall distribution of samples, LDM reduces the sensitivity to support vectors and achieves better generalization performance. Therefore, LDM has induced a wide concern in many fields due to its theoretical advantages and excellent classification performance [7,9,14].

LDM considers the contributions of all sample points, which greatly increases the computational complexity. In order to speed up the learning speed, Xu et al. [11] proposed a twin bounded large distribution machine (TBLDM) based on the idea of twin bounded support vector machines (TBSVM). It constructs a pair of non-parallel hyperplanes to solve two smaller-scale quadratic programming problems (QPPs) instead of one large-scale QPP. Specifically, it minimizes the distance of each hyperplane to one of the two classes, while ensuring that the distance to the other class is maximized. Compared with TBSVM, TBLDM is beneficial to reduce the structural risk and improve the classification performance. Therefore, TBLDM is a fast and robust classification method, which achieves good generalization performance.

In real datasets, noise and outliers are ubiquitous and unavoidable due to narrow data sources, errors in data collection, and other factors [15]. Furthermore, some samples are easy to classify while some others are not. Therefore, they should have different degrees of importance to the formation of the hyperplane. However, traditional LDMs, including TBLDM, treat each input sample equally, and fail to obtain excellent classification performance in some practical applications. In 2017, Cheng et al. proposed a cost-sensitive large margin distribution (CS-LDM) model, which takes into account the different importance of samples [2]. However, CS-LDM only considers the effect of imbalanced datasets, and does not mitigate the effects of noise well. Fuzzy set theory, proposed by Zadeh, is based on fuzzy mathematics and studies phenomena related to inexactness by utilizing the fuzzy membership [16]. Fuzzy membership degree indicates the extent to which an element belongs to a set, which can be utilized to denote the confidence level of the input sample [4,6].

Inspired by the aforementioned works, we introduce the fuzzy set theory to TBLDM, and propose a novel fuzzy TBLDM (FTBLDM). In FTBLDM, a coordination-based method is utilized to obtain the fuzzy membership degree of each sample point. Based on the distribution of input samples, the cluster center of each category is calculated separately. The fuzzy membership degree of one sample point is computed according to the Euclidean distance to the corresponding class center. The membership degree reflects the credibility and importance of a single sample point, which is considered when finding the optimal decision hyperplane. Therefore, FTBLDM reduces the influence of noise and outliers in the dataset, and improves the classification performance. Finally, in the experiments, FTBLDM outperforms some existing models on the UCI datasets and datasets with noise.

The arrangement of this paper is as follows. Section 2 introduces the related knowledge of LDM and TBLDM. In Sect. 3, we introduce the selection of fuzzy membership functions, and the formula derivation and optimization process for FTBLDM. In Sect. 4, artificial and UCI datasets are used to demonstrate the superiority. In Sect. 5, we summarize and look forward to our work.

2   Background

Suppose $S = \{(x_i, y_i) \mid i = 1, 2, \cdots, m\}$ is a set of binary classification training samples where $x_i \in R^n$ and the class label $y_i = \{-1, +1\}$. Here, data points x_i with labels $y_i = 1$ and -1 are represented by matrices $A \in R^{n \times m_1}$ and $B \in R^{n \times m_2}$, respectively. Let $\phi(x_i)$ as the feature maping of x_i. Denote the whole set of input matrix $X = [x_1, \cdots, x_m]$, the sample label column vector $y = [y_1, \cdots, y_m]^T$, a diagonal matrix $Y \in R^{m \times m}$ with $y_1, \ldots, y_m$ as the diagonal elements and the high-dimensional samples matrix $\phi(X) = [\phi(x_1), \cdots, \phi(x_m)]$. Besides, we set the kernel matrix $K = \phi(X)^T \phi(X) \in R^{m \times m}$, $K_A = \phi(A)^T \phi(X) \in R^{m_1 \times m}$, $K_B = \phi(B)^T \phi(X) \in R^{m_2 \times m}$.

The marginal mean and marginal variance of positive and negative classes in TBLDM are as follows

$$
\begin{cases}
\bar{\gamma}^+ = \dfrac{1}{m_1} y_A^T \phi(A)^T w_-, \hat{\gamma}^+ = w_-^T \phi(A) Q_1 \phi(A)^T w_- \\
\bar{\gamma}^- = \dfrac{1}{m_2} y_B^T \phi(B)^T w_+, \hat{\gamma}^- = w_+^T \phi(B) Q_2 \phi(B)^T w_+
\end{cases}
\tag{1}
$$

where $Q_1 = \frac{m_1 I_{m_1} - y_A y_A^T}{m_1^2}$ and $Q_2 = \frac{l_2 I_{m_2} - y_B y_B^T}{m_2^2}$ are symmetric nonnegative definite matrixs. The original TBLDM model with soft margin is:

$$
\min_{w_+, \xi_2} \frac{c_1}{2} \|w_+\|^2 + \frac{1}{2} \|\phi(A)^T w_+\|^2 - \lambda_1 \bar{\gamma}^- + \lambda_2 \hat{\gamma}^- + c_3 e_2^T \xi_2
$$
$$
\text{s.t.} \quad -\phi(B)^T w_+ + \xi_2 \geq e_2, \xi_2 \geq 0
\tag{2}
$$

and

$$
\min_{w_-, \xi_1} \frac{c_2}{2} \|w_-\|^2 + \frac{1}{2} \|\phi(B)^T w_-\|^2 - \lambda_3 \bar{\gamma}^+ + \lambda_4 \hat{\gamma}^+ + c_4 e_1^T \xi_1
$$
$$
\text{s.t.} \quad \phi(A)^T w_- + \xi_1 \geq e_1, \xi_1 \geq 0
\tag{3}
$$

where $\lambda_1, \cdots, \lambda_4 > 0$ are the parameters for trading-off the margin variances, the margin means and the complexity of models. c_1 and c_2 are the regularization coefficients. c_3 and c_4 are parameters that weighs the total error. e_1 and e_2 are all-ones vectors of the appropriate dimension.

Similar to the derivation of LDM, we can let $w_+ = \phi(X)\beta_1$ and $w_- = \phi(X)\beta_2$, where $\beta_1, \beta_2 \in R^m$ are coefficient vectors.

From the KKT necessary and sufficient optimality conditions and matrix variation, we can get β_1 as follows:

$$
\beta_1 = G_1^{-1} \left(\frac{\lambda_1}{l_2} K_B^T y_B - K_B^T \alpha_1 \right),
\tag{4}
$$

where $G_1 = c_1 K + K_A^T K_A + 2\lambda_2 K_B^T Q_2 K_B \in R^{m \times m}$, and α_1 is the nonnegative Lagrangian multipliers vector.

According to the Lagrangian function, we obtain the dual form of the first set of equations in Eq. (2) as follows

$$\min_{\alpha_1} \frac{1}{2} \alpha_1^T H_1 \alpha_1 - \left(\frac{\lambda_1}{l_2} H_1 y_B + e_2 \right)^T \alpha_1 \tag{5}$$
$$\text{s.t.} \quad 0 \le \alpha_1 \le c_3 e_2$$

where $H_1 = K_B G_1^{-1} K_B^T$, and $y_B = \left(y_1^-, \cdots, y_{m_1}^- \right)^T$.

Similarly, we can get the parameter β_2 of another hyperplane.

$$\beta_2 = G_2^{-1} \left(\frac{\lambda_2}{l_1} K_A^T y_A + K_A^T \alpha_2 \right), \tag{6}$$

where $G_2 = c_2 K + K_B^T K_B + 2\lambda_4 K_A^T Q_1 K_A \in R^{m \times m}$, and α_2 is the nonnegative Lagrangian multipliers vector.

The dual form of another set of equations in Eq. (3) as follows

$$\min_{\alpha_2} \frac{1}{2} \alpha_2^T H_2 \alpha_2 + \left(\frac{\lambda_3}{l_1} H_2 y_A - e_1 \right)^T \alpha_2 \tag{7}$$
$$\text{s.t.} \quad 0 \le \alpha_2 \le c_4 e_1$$

where $H_2 = K_A G_2^{-1} K_A^T$, and $y_A = \left(y_1^+, \cdots, y_{m_2}^+ \right)^T$.

3   FTBLDM

In this section, we first introduce our fuzzy membership method and construct statistics describing the marginal distribution of the inputs. Then, the structure of our proposed FTBLDM model is discussed in detail. Finally, the dual problem and the optimal solutions are deduced.

3.1   Fuzzy Membership Assignment

Fuzzy membership plays a key role in the noise reduction aspect of classification learning. It assigns different fuzzy memberships to the sample points, by taking into account the different contributions of the sample points to the classification plane. Considering the location relationship of sample points, a fuzzy membership function based on Euclidean distance is constructed. The fuzzy memberships of positive and negative classes are designed separately.

The class centers of the positive and negative samples are calculated according to the distance as follows

$$\begin{cases} C_+ = \frac{1}{l_1} \sum_{i=1}^{l_1} \varphi(x_i), y_i = +1 \\ C_- = \frac{1}{l_2} \sum_{i=1}^{l_2} \varphi(x_i), y_i = -1, \end{cases} \tag{8}$$

where $\phi(\boldsymbol{x}_j)$ represents the high-dimensional transformation of any input data point. After getting the class center, the scattering hypersphere radii of the positive and negative class sample points are respectively expressed as follows

$$\begin{cases} r_{\varphi+} = \max \| \varphi(\boldsymbol{x}_i) - C_+ \|, y_i = +1 \\ r_{\varphi-} = \max \| \varphi(\boldsymbol{x}_i) - C_- \|, y_i = -1 \end{cases} \tag{9}$$

Through the above preparations, the fuzzy membership functions of positive and negative sample points can be established as

$$\boldsymbol{s}_{i+} = \begin{cases} \mu \left(1 - \sqrt{\| \varphi(\boldsymbol{x}_i) - C_+ \|^2 / \left(r_{\varphi+}^2 + \delta \right)} \right) \\ \quad \text{if } \| \varphi(\boldsymbol{x}_i) - C_+ \| \geq \| \varphi(\boldsymbol{x}_i) - C_- \| \\ (1 - \mu) \left(1 - \sqrt{\| \varphi(\boldsymbol{x}_i) - C_+ \|^2 / \left(r_{\varphi+}^2 + \delta \right)} \right) \\ \quad \text{if } \| \varphi(\boldsymbol{x}_i) - C_+ \| < \| \varphi(\boldsymbol{x}_i) - C_- \|, \end{cases} \tag{10}$$

and

$$\boldsymbol{s}_{i-} = \begin{cases} \mu \left(1 - \sqrt{\| \varphi(\boldsymbol{x}_i) - C_- \|^2 / \left(r_{\varphi-}^2 + \delta \right)} \right) \\ \quad \text{if } \| \varphi(\boldsymbol{x}_i) - C_- \| \geq \| \varphi(\boldsymbol{x}_i) - C_+ \| \\ (1 - \mu) \left(1 - \sqrt{\| \varphi(\boldsymbol{x}_i) - C_- \|^2 / \left(r_{\varphi-}^2 + \delta \right)} \right) \\ \quad \text{if } \| \varphi(\boldsymbol{x}_i) - C_- \| < \| \varphi(\boldsymbol{x}_i) - C_+ \|, \end{cases} \tag{11}$$

where $\delta > 0$ is defined as a small constant which avoids the vanishing of $\boldsymbol{s}_{i+}$ and $\boldsymbol{s}_{i-}$, and $0 < \mu < 1$ is a adjustable constant.

3.2   Model Construction of FTBLDM

The task of FTBLDM is to find a pair of nonparallel hyperplanes $f_1(x) = w_1^T \phi(x) = 0$ and $f_2(x) = w_2^T \phi(x) = 0$. In FTBLDM, the definition of single sample margin is similar to LDM, which is expressed as

$$\begin{cases} \mu_1^i = y_1^i f_2(x_1^i) = y_1^i w_2^T \phi(x_1^i), i = 1, \cdots, m_1 \\ \mu_2^i = y_2^i f_1(x_2^i) = y_2^i w_1^T \phi(x_2^i), i = 1, \cdots, m_2 \end{cases} \tag{12}$$

Further we consider all samples, we can get the marginal mean and variance.

$$\begin{cases} \bar{\mu}_{(1)} = \frac{1}{m_1} \sum_{i=1}^{m_1} \mu_{(1)}^i, \hat{\mu}_{(1)} = \frac{1}{m_1} \sum_{i=1}^{m_1} \left(\mu_{(1)}^i - \bar{\mu}_{(1)} \right)^2 \\ \bar{\mu}_{(2)} = \frac{1}{m_2} \sum_{i=1}^{m_2} \mu_{(2)}^i, \hat{\mu}_{(2)} = \frac{1}{m_2} \sum_{i=1}^{m_2} \left(\mu_{(2)}^i - \bar{\mu}_{(2)} \right)^2 \end{cases} \tag{13}$$

Bring Eq. (12) into Eq. (13) and convert it to matrix form.

$$\begin{cases} \bar{\mu}_{(1)} = \frac{1}{m_1} y_{(A)}^T \phi(A)^T w_{(2)}, \hat{\mu}_{(1)} = w_{(2)}^T \phi(A) Q_1 \phi(A)^T w_{(2)} \\ \bar{\mu}_{(2)} = \frac{1}{m_2} y_{(A)}^T \phi(B)^T w_{(1)}, \hat{\mu}_{(2)} = w_{(1)}^T \phi(B) Q_2 \phi(B)^T w_{(1)}, \end{cases} \tag{14}$$

where $Q_1 = \frac{m_1 I_{m_1} - y_A y_A^T}{m_1^2}$ and $Q_2 = \frac{m_2 I_{m_2} - y_B y_B^T}{m_2^2}$ is the symmetric matrices. I_{m_1} and I_{m_2} are the all-ones matrix of the appropriate size.

Soft margin is a more robust processing method. Specifically, the soft margin model allows some errors when classifying sample points. Therefore, this paper constructs a soft-margin FTBLDM. We first consider the case where the samples are linearly separable in the original space. The linear FTBLDMs model is

$$\min_{w_{(1)}, \xi_1} \frac{1}{2}\|A^T w_{(1)}\|^2 + \frac{c_1}{2}\|w_{(1)}\|^2 + \lambda_1 \hat{\mu}_{(2)} - \lambda_3 \bar{\mu}_{(2)} + c_3 s_-^T \xi_2 \tag{15}$$
$$\text{s.t.} \quad -B^T w_{(1)} + \xi_2 \geq e_2, \xi_2 \geq 0,$$

and

$$\min_{w_{(2)}, \xi_2} \frac{1}{2}\|B^T w_{(2)}\|^2 + \frac{c_2}{2}\|w_{(2)}\|^2 + \lambda_2 \hat{\mu}_{(1)} - \lambda_4 \bar{\mu}_{(1)} + c_4 s_+^T \xi_1 \tag{16}$$
$$\text{s.t.} \quad -A^T w_{(2)} + \xi_1 \geq e_1, \xi_1 \geq 0.$$

where $\lambda_1, \lambda_2, \lambda_3, \lambda_4$ are parameters that weigh the complexity of the model. c_1 and c_2 constrain the added regularization terms. c_3 and c_4 are parameters that weigh the total error.

In real-world scenarios, the data is not all linearly separable. To solve this kind of problem, we generalize the linear FTBLDM to the nonlinear model

$$\min_{w_{(1)}, \xi_1} \frac{1}{2}\|\phi(A)^T w_{(1)}\|^2 + \frac{c_1}{2}\|w_{(1)}\|^2 + \lambda_1 \hat{\mu}_{(2)} - \lambda_3 \bar{\mu}_{(2)} + c_3 s_2^T \xi_2 \tag{17}$$
$$\text{s.t.} \quad -\phi(B)^T w_{(1)} + \xi_2 \geq e_2, \xi_2 \geq 0,$$

and

$$\min_{w_{(2)}, \xi_2} \frac{1}{2}\|\phi(B)^T w_{(2)}\|^2 + \frac{c_2}{2}\|w_{(2)}\|^2 + \lambda_2 \hat{\mu}_{(1)} - \lambda_4 \bar{\mu}_{(1)} + c_4 s_1^T \xi_1 \tag{18}$$
$$\text{s.t.} \quad -\phi(A)^T w_{(2)} + \xi_1 \geq e_1, \xi_1 \geq 0.$$

Although the FTBLDM model has many hyperparameters, its time cost is still considerable thanks to the structural advantages of the twin support vector machine, which can be seen from the follow-up experiments.

3.3 The Optimization and Dual Problem

Since FTBLDM has perfect symmetry, we only need to derive one set of equations, and the derivation process for the other set of equations is similar. Bring Eq. (14) into Eq. (17), we can get the following:

$$\min_{w_+, \xi_2} \frac{1}{2}\|\phi(A)^T w_{(1)}\|^2 + \frac{c_1}{2}\|w_{(1)}\|^2 + \lambda_1 w_{(1)}^T \phi(B) Q_2 \phi(B)^T w_{(1)}$$
$$- \frac{\lambda_2}{m_2} y_B^T \phi(B)^T w_{(1)} + c_3 s_2^T \xi_2 \tag{19}$$
$$\text{s.t.} \quad -\phi(B)^T w_{(1)} + \xi_2 \geq e_2, \xi_2 \geq 0$$

Algorithm 1. FTBLDM

Input: training set X, test point x, parameters sets c_1, c_2, c_3, c_4, λ_1, λ_2, λ_3, λ_4 and kernel parameter σ
Output: Predict label for test point x
1: Calculate the membership s_-, s_+ using Eq. (10) and Eq. (11);
2: Calculate the marginal mean and variance $\bar{\mu}_{(1)}, \hat{\mu}_{(1)}, \bar{\mu}_{(2)}, \hat{\mu}_{(2)}$ of training set X;
3: **repeat**
4:    Compute $K = \exp\left(\frac{-\|x_i - x_j\|_2}{2\sigma^2}\right)$;
5:    Calculate β_1 and β_2 using Eq. (22) and Eq. (23);
6:    Predict the label of x using Eq. (24);
7: **until** iterate over all parameters.
8: Select the best combination of parameters by prediction accuracy.

Inspired by the LDM [12], the matrix form of Eq. (19) can be written as

$$\min_{\beta_1, \xi_2} \frac{1}{2}\beta_1^T G_1 \beta_1 - \frac{\lambda_1}{m_2} y_B^T K_B \beta_1 + c_3 e_2^T \xi_2 \tag{20}$$
$$\text{s.t. } - K_B \beta_1 + \xi_2 \geq s_2, \xi_2 \geq 0,$$

where $G_1 = c_1 K + K_A^T K_A + 2\lambda_2 K_B^T Q_2 K_B$, and G_1 is a symmetric nonnegative definite matrice. According to the Lagrangian function method and the Kuhn-Tucker conditions (KKT), we can get the dual problem of Eq. (20) as follows:

$$\min_{\alpha_1} \frac{1}{2}\alpha_1^T H_1 \alpha_1 - \left(\frac{\lambda_1}{m_2}H_1 y_B + e_2\right)^T \alpha_1 \tag{21}$$
$$\text{s.t. } 0 \leq \alpha_1 \leq c_3 s_2,$$

where α_1 is a nonnegative Lagrangian multipliers vector and $H_1 = K_B G_1^{-1} K_B^T$. Furthermore, it is not difficult to see that FTBLDM and its corresponding dual problem have good similarity convexity, which is inherited from SVM. Then the β_1 can be calculated by the following formula

$$\beta_1 = G_1^{-1}\left(\frac{\lambda_1}{l_2}K_B^T y_B - K_B^T \alpha_1\right). \tag{22}$$

Similarly, according to another set of equations for FBLDM, we get

$$\beta_2 = G_2^{-1}\left(\frac{\lambda_2}{l_1}K_A^T y_A + K_A^T \alpha_2\right). \tag{23}$$

Once β_1 and β_2 are obtained, the decision function is as follows

$$f(x) = \arg\min_{i=1,2} \frac{|K(x, X)\beta_i|}{\sqrt{\beta_i^T K \beta_i}}, \tag{24}$$

where the kernel matrix $K(x, X) = [k(x, x_1), \cdots, k(x, x_m)] \in R^{1 \times m}$, x is the new data point. The iterative steps for FTBLDM are shown in the Algorithm 1.

4   Experiments

In this section, artificial and UCI datasets are used to validate the performance of FTBLDM. Details of 13 UCI datasets are shown in Table 1. To demonstrate the anti-noise performance, we conduct experiments on the UCI dataset with different amounts of Gaussian white noise added. Gaussian kernel is considered. Similar to the experimental setup for TSVM-related variants, in FTBLDM and TBLDM, $c_1 = c_2, c_3 = c_4, \lambda_1 = \lambda_3, \lambda_2 = \lambda_4$. In TLDM $c_1 = c_2, \lambda_1 = \lambda_3, \lambda_2 = \lambda_4$. In TBSVM, $c_1 = c_2, c_3 = c_4$. The parameters $c_i(i = 1, 2, 3, 4)$ and $\lambda_i(i = 1, 2, 3, 4)$ are chosen from $\{2^i | i = -6, ..., 6\}$, and the selection range of σ is $\{2^i | i = -6, ..., 6\}$. To obtain optimal values for all hyperparameters, five-fold cross-validation and grid search were used. QP technique is used to solve all algorithmic optimization problems. All experiments are completed on a PC with $8 \times 4.00\,\mathrm{GHz}$ CPU and 32 GB memory using MATLAB R2018a.

Table 1. Datasets description.

Dataset	Example	Feature	Class
Monks-2	601	6	2
Prlx	282	12	2
Credit-a	653	15	2
Australian	690	14	2
Statlog	270	13	2
Votes	435	16	2
Wpbc	198	34	2
Hepatitis	155	19	2
Wdbc	569	29	2
Ripley-predict	1000	2	2
Ecoil	537	7	2
Fertility	150	9	2
Glass	214	10	2

Table 2. Parameter settings for synthetic datasets with white Gaussian noise.

Type	Parameter	Setting
Normal	Mean of Class 1	[0.4, 0.4]
	Mean of Class 2	[1.7, 1.7]
	Covariances of Class 1 or 2	[0.2, 0; 0, 0.3]
	Numbers of Class 1 or 2	100
Noise	Mean of Class 1 or 2	[1, 1]
	Covariances of Class 1 or 2	[0.15, −0.1; −0.1, 0.15]
	Numbers of Class 1 or 2	15

4.1   Experiments on Artificial Datasets

We manually constructed a 2D dataset with positive and negative samples satisfying different Gaussian distributions. The specific settings of artificial datasets are shown in Table 2. To demonstrate the effectiveness of fuzzy membership functions, fuzzy membership graphs with and without noise added are shown in Fig. 1. The fuzzy membership function can assign lower fuzzy membership to some sample points, because these sample points are farther from the class and more likely to be noise.

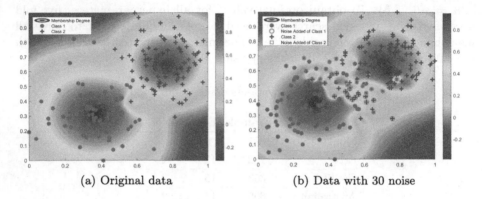

(a) Original data   (b) Data with 30 noise

Fig. 1. A schematic diagram of the fuzzy membership level.

4.2   Experiments on UCI Datasets

In this subsection, the performance of FTBLDM is evaluated utilizing the UCI benchmark datasets. The experimental results of FTBLDM are compared with the seven algorithms of SVM, LDM, CSLDM, TSVM, TLDM, TBSVM and TBLDM. The classification accuracy and running time of different algorithms on 13 datasets are shown in Table 3. Note that FTBLDM maintains the best classification accuracy on 10 of the 13 datasets, with an average classification accuracy of 90.59. And the remaining three datasets are second only to the first place. In addition, the ranking of different algorithms according to classification accuracy on each dataset is shown in Table 4. FTBLDM also has the highest average rank, which is 2.0. Specifically, compared with other algorithms, TBLDM has the best classification accuracy on the 4 datasets and ranks second on average, which indicates its good classification performance. However, compared to the TBLDM algorithm, our algorithm has better performance due to reducing the effect of noise and outliers. The performance of FTBLDM is significantly superior on 4 datasets, the performance is the same on 6 datasets, and the best accuracy relative to other algorithms. Therefore, compared to the three state-of-the-art algorithms (TBLDM, TLDM, TBSVM) and the four benchmark algorithms (LDM, TSVM, SVM, CSLDM), FTBLDM is the best algorithm.

Table 3. The comparative experimental results of 8 algorithms using Gaussian kernel.

Dataset	SVM	LDM	CSLDM	TSVM	TBSVM	TLDM	TBLDM	FTBLDM
	Acc	Acc	Acc	Acc	Acc	Acc	Acc	Acc
	Times(s)	Times(s)	Times(s)	Times(s)	Times(s)	Times(s)	Times(s)	Times(s)
Monks_2	87.73	87.27	82.41	88.89	87.73	90.97	88.89	**91.67**
	0.01438	0.01123	0.00260	0.03573	0.00622	0.45995	0.03017	0.01110
Plrx	69.51	65.85	71.43	67.07	70.73	74.39	70.73	**75.61**
	0.00309	0.00257	0.01470	0.04324	0.00436	0.01219	0.05240	0.02255
Credit-a	86.20	86.20	85.89	84.66	85.58	81.29	86.81	**87.42**
	0.03094	0.03222	0.03250	0.13608	0.01935	1.34868	0.19063	0.03018
Australian	87.50	86.63	82.85	79.94	84.30	88.08	86.92	**95.01**
	0.02471	0.07015	0.42560	0.10344	0.02791	0.32737	0.13476	0.01970
Heart-statlog	79.26	74.07	**84.44**	80.00	81.48	73.33	78.52	82.22
	0.00753	0.00426	0.03220	0.02847	0.00814	0.49944	0.02876	0.02697
Votes	94.89	95.32	55.76	94.89	**96.17**	**96.17**	95.74	**96.17**
	0.00546	0.00900	0.01350	0.01995	0.00663	0.17493	0.03364	0.03925
Wpbc	81.48	81.48	76.53	81.48	77.78	77.78	**84.26**	**84.26**
	0.00288	0.00339	0.01130	0.01920	0.01344	0.06251	0.03361	0.02669
Hepatitis	84.62	76.92	55.84	84.62	84.62	**87.18**	**87.18**	**87.18**
	0.00205	0.00248	0.00590	0.01117	0.00597	0.12440	0.02683	0.02496
Wdbc	97.63	100.00	95.77	97.04	76.92	98.22	100.00	100.00
	0.02480	0.04681	0.02560	0.04685	0.03299	0.16725	0.07766	0.08239
Ripley-predict	**92.00**	**92.00**	91.80	71.20	89.40	90.20	87.00	**92.00**
	0.05178	0.04738	0.05300	0.53428	0.01587	2.49893	0.48682	0.42791
Ecoli	96.06	96.06	**98.16**	96.06	97.64	97.64	97.64	97.64
	0.00556	0.00651	0.00780	0.02733	0.00665	0.32309	0.10256	0.10099
Fertility	94.00	94.00	72.00	94.00	**96.00**	**96.00**	**96.00**	**96.00**
	0.00252	0.00270	0.00540	0.01006	0.00364	0.24745	0.02223	0.00542
Glass	92.45	92.45	**94.34**	92.45	90.57	91.51	92.45	92.45
	0.00564	0.00639	0.01390	0.01626	0.00748	0.49980	0.03386	0.02737
Average Acc	87.95	86.79	80.56	85.56	86.07	87.90	88.63	**90.59**
Win/Tie/Loss	12/1/0	11/2/0	10/0/3	13/0/0	11/2/0	10/3/0	9/4/0	–

Table 4. The accuracy ranking of the 8 algorithms on the UCI datasets.

Dataset	SVM	LDM	CSLDM	TSVM	TBSVM	TLDM	TBLDM	FTBLDM
	Ranking	Ranking	Ranking	Ranking	Ranking	Ranking	Ranking	Ranking
Monks_2	5.5	7.0	8.0	3.5	5.5	2.0	3.5	1.0
Plrx	6.0	8.0	3.0	7.0	4.5	2.0	4.5	1.0
Credit-a	3.5	3.5	5.0	7.0	6.0	8.0	2.0	1.0
Australian	3.0	5.0	7.0	8.0	6.0	2.0	4.0	1.0
Heart-statlog	5.0	7.0	1.0	4.0	3.0	8.0	6.0	2.0
Votes	6.5	5.0	8.0	6.5	2.0	2.0	4.0	2.0
Wpbc	4.0	4.0	8.0	4.0	6.5	6.5	1.5	1.5
Hepatitis	5.0	7.0	8.0	5.0	5.0	2.0	2.0	2.0
Wdbc	5.0	2.0	7.0	6.0	8.0	4.0	2.0	2.0
Ripley_Predict	2.0	2.0	4.0	8.0	6.0	5.0	7.0	2.0
Ecoli	7.0	7.0	1.0	7.0	3.5	3.5	3.5	3.5
Fertility	6.0	6.0	8.0	6.0	2.5	2.5	2.5	2.5
Glass	4.0	4.0	1.0	4.0	8.0	7.0	4.0	4.0
Average	4.8	5.2	5.3	5.8	5.1	4.2	3.6	**2.0**

4.3   Experiments on Noisy Datasets

In order to verify the anti-noise performance of FTBLDM, experiments are carried out on some noisy datasets. Without loss of generality, two different scales of white Gaussian noise were used to process the dataset. The signal-to-noise ratio r of white Gaussian noise is set to 0.1 and 0.5, respectively. The experimental accuracies and rankings on the four noisy datasets are shown in Table 5. Note that the average rank of FTBLDM is 1.44, which is the highest. Furthermore, it exhibits the best accuracy on 6 datasets out of a total of 8. Therefore, the anti-noise performance of FTBLDM is better than the other 7 algorithms and is the best performing algorithm.

Table 5. Accuracy and ranking comparison on the UCI dataset with Gaussian noise.

Dataset	SVM	LDM	CSLDM	TSVM	TBSVM	TLDM	TBLDM	FTBLDM
	Acc	Acc	Acc	Acc	Acc	Acc	Acc	Acc
	Ranking	Ranking	Ranking	Ranking	Ranking	Ranking	Ranking	Ranking
monks-2 ($r = 0.1$)	67.13	67.13	63.89	63.89	67.36	68.06	68.75	**68.98**
	5.5	5.5	7.5	7.5	4	3	2	1
monks-2 ($r = 0.5$)	67.13	67.13	63.89	65.97	67.36	67.36	68.75	**68.98**
	5.5	5.5	8	7	3.5	3.5	2	1
ecoli ($r = 0.1$)	62.2	63.78	56.44	61.42	60.63	66.14	70.08	**72.44**
	5	4	8	6	7	3	2	1
ecoli ($r = 0.5$)	62.99	63.78	58.9	60.63	66.14	65.35	68.5	**69.29**
	6	5	8	7	3	4	2	1
votes ($r = 0.1$)	80.43	80.43	57.14	61.28	80.43	79.57	**86.38**	86.38
	4	4	8	7	4	6	1.5	1.5
votes ($r = 0.5$)	80.43	80.85	61.29	62.13	81.28	80.85	**87.66**	86.81
	6	5	8	7	3	4	1	2
wdbc ($r = 0.1$)	95.27	95.27	95.77	76.92	97.63	95.27	**98.22**	97.63
	6	6	4	8	2.5	6	1	2.5
wdbc ($r = 0.5$)	95.27	95.27	67.96	76.92	97.04	95.27	**97.63**	**97.63**
	4.5	4.5	8	7	3	6	1.5	1.5
Average Ranking	5.31	4.94	7.44	7.06	3.75	4.44	1.63	**1.44**
Win/Tie/Loss	8/0/0	8/0/0	8/0/0	8/0/0	7/1/0	8/0/0	4/2/2	–

5   Conclusion

Due to the uncertainty and inevitable noise in practical applications, samples always have different confidence levels. Based on the twin bounded large margin distribution machine (TBLDM), we introduce the fuzzy set theory and propose a novel fuzzy TBLDM (FTBLDM). Embedding fuzzy set theory into TBLDM enhances noise immunity and generalization performance. A coordinate-based fuzzy membership function is constructed, and the fuzzy membership is obtained to represent the confidence level. Moreover, FTBLDM describes the importance of each sample in the overall sample, improving the classification accuracy. A series of experiments on artificial datasets, UCI datasets, and noisy UCI datasets demonstrate the effectiveness and anti-noise performance of FTBLDM, which achieved better results than several benchmark and state-of-the-art algorithms. In the future, exploration on non-convex datasets, hyperparameter selection, and different forms of large-scale datasets will be some interesting work.

References

1. Burges, C.J.: A tutorial on support vector machines for pattern recognition. Data Min. Knowl. Disc. **2**(2), 121–167 (1998)
2. Cheng, F., Zhang, J., Wen, C.: Cost-sensitive large margin distribution machine for classification of imbalanced data. Pattern Recogn. Lett. **80**, 107–112 (2016)
3. Cristianini, N., Shawe-Taylor, J., et al.: An Introduction to Support Vector Machines and Other Kernel-Based Learning Methods. Cambridge University Press, Cambridge (2000)
4. Gao, B.B., Wang, J.J., Wang, Y., Yang, C.Y.: Coordinate descent fuzzy twin support vector machine for classification. In: 2015 IEEE 14th International Conference on Machine Learning nd Applications (ICMLA), pp. 7–12. IEEE (2015)
5. Gao, W., Zhou, Z.H.: On the doubt about margin explanation of boosting. Artif. Intell. **203**, 1–18 (2013)
6. Lin, C.F., Wang, S.D.: Fuzzy support vector machines. IEEE Trans. Neural Networks **13**(2), 464–471 (2002)
7. Liu, L., Chu, M., Gong, R., Peng, Y.: Nonparallel support vector machine with large margin distribution for pattern classification. Pattern Recogn. **106**, 107374 (2020)
8. Wang, H., Shao, Y., Zhou, S., Zhang, C., Xiu, N.: Support vector machine classifier via $l\_\{0/1\}$ soft-margin loss. IEEE Trans. Pattern Anal. Mach. Intell. (2021)
9. Wang, J., Geng, X., Xue, H.: Re-weighting large margin label distribution learning for classification. IEEE Trans. Pattern Anal. Mach. Intell. **44**(9), 5445–5459 (2021)
10. Wang, L., Sugiyama, M., Jing, Z., Yang, C., Zhou, Z.H., Feng, J.: A refined margin analysis for boosting algorithms via equilibrium margin. J. Mach. Learn. Res. **12**, 1835–1863 (2011)
11. Xu, H., McCane, B., Szymanski, L.: Twin bounded large margin distribution machine. In: Mitrovic, T., Xue, B., Li, X. (eds.) AI 2018. LNCS (LNAI), vol. 11320, pp. 718–729. Springer, Cham (2018). https://doi.org/10.1007/978-3-030-03991-2_64
12. Zhang, T., Zhou, Z.H.: Large margin distribution machine. In: Proceedings of the 20th ACM SIGKDD International Conference on Knowledge Discovery and Data Mining, pp. 313–322 (2014)
13. Zhang, T., Zhou, Z.H.: Optimal margin distribution machine. IEEE Trans. Knowl. Data Eng. **32**(6), 1143–1156 (2019)
14. Zhang, X., Wang, D., Zhou, Y., Chen, H., Cheng, F., Liu, M.: Kernel modified optimal margin distribution machine for imbalanced data classification. Pattern Recogn. Lett. **125**, 325–332 (2019)
15. Zhu, X., Wu, X.: Class noise vs attribute noise: a quantitative study. Artif. Intell. Rev. **22**(3), 177–210 (2004)
16. Zimmermann, H.J.: Fuzzy Set Theory-and Its Applications. Springer, New York (2011). https://doi.org/10.1007/978-94-010-0646-0

Harnessing Multi-Semantic Hypergraph for Few-Shot Learning

Hao Chen[1], Linyan Li[2], Zhenping Xia[1], Fan Lyu[3], Liuqing Zhao[1],
Kaizhu Huang[4], Wei Feng[3], and Fuyuan Hu[1(✉)]

[1] School of Electronic and Information Engineering, Suzhou University of Science
and Technology, Suzhou 215009, China
haochen@post.usts.edu.cn, {xzp,fuyuanhu}@mail.usts.edu.cn
[2] School of Information Technology, Suzhou Institute of Trade and Commerce,
Suzhou 215009, China
lilinyan@szjm.edu.cn
[3] College of Intelligence and Computing, Tianjin University, Tianjin 300192, China
{fanlyu,wfeng}@tju.edu.cn
[4] Electrical and Computer Engineering, Duke Kunshan University,
Kunshan 215316, China
kaizhu.huang@dukekunshan.edu.cn

Abstract. Recently, Graph-based Few Shot Learning (FSL) methods
exhibit good generalization by mining relations among the few examples
with Graph Neural Networks. However, most Graph-based FSL methods
consider only binary relations and ignore the multi-semantic information of the global context knowledge. We propose a framework of Multi-
Semantic Hypergraph for FSL (MSH-FSL) to explore complex latent
high-order multi-semantic relations among the few examples. Specifically,
we first build up a novel Multi-Semantic Hypergraph by identifying associated examples with various semantic features from different receptive
fields. With the constructed hypergraph, we then develop the Hyergraph
Neural Network along with a novel multi-generation hypergraph message passing so as to better leverage the complex latent semantic relations among examples. Finally, after a number of generations, the hyper-
node representations embedded in the learned hypergraph become more
accurate for obtaining few-shot predictions. In the 5-way 1-shot task
on miniImagenet dataset, the multi-semantic hypergraph outperforms
the single-semantic graph by 3.1%, and with the proposed semantic-
distribution message passing, the improvement can further reach 6.5%.

1   Introduction

Deep learning [3,8,19,20] usually requires big data to support its robustness.
In contrast, humans generalize well once having seen few examples. Few-Shot

This work was supported by the Natural Science Foundation of China (No. 61876121).

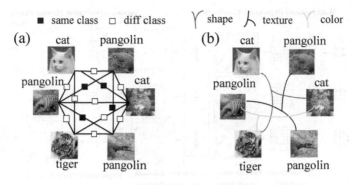

Fig. 1. (a) Graph-based FSL vs. (b) Multi-Semantic Hypergraph for FSL (ours). (Color figure online)

Learning (FSL), aiming at enabling machines to recognize unseen classes via learning from very few labeled data, has recently attracted much interest in various fields including computer vision, natural language processing, audio and speech recognition.

Early proposals exploit indiscriminate fine-tuning on the few training data. Such investigations tackle FSL like a usual data-sufficient task, which is unfortunately prone to overfitting. Recently, Meta Learning (ML) has been widely studied for FSL. ML-based methods introduce the concept of episode and construct a trainer that takes the few-shot training data and outputs a classifier. Among the ML-based FSL, Graph-based FSL methods are popular due to their capability to link the few number of examples with a topological graph structure. Then, with the Graph Neural Network (GNN), the relations among examples can be enhanced to help few-shot recognition. The graph, constructed to associate few examples in Graph-based FSL, leverages the binary and pair-wise relation only. That is, two examples will be linked if and only if they share the same label, as illustrated in Fig. 1(a).

Though Graph-based FSL achieves encouraging performance, in the real world, the binary and pair-wise relations can hardly reflect the latent semantic relations among examples. As shown in Fig. 1(b), the three images connected with yellow lines share the same semantic attribute "color" but different attributes "shape" and "texture". Despite different categories, they are semantically correlated. Failing to leverage such latent semantic information, Graph-based FSL is limited in obtaining a good FSL solution. In contrast to traditional graphs, hypergraph offers a more natural way to build complex latent semantic relations among examples. Specifically, a hyper-edge can connect two or more vertices with the same semantic attribute, which provides a possible semantic connection mode among few examples. Although only a few examples are available in FSL for training, multiple semantics are inherent among them.

Motivated by the desirable multi-semantic properties of hypergraphs, in this paper, we propose to construct Multi-Semantic Hypergraph for FSL (MSH-FSL). Our method is mainly divided into two parts: 1) constructing Multi-Semantic Hypergraph (MSH) and 2) learning Multi-Semantic Hypergraph Neural Network

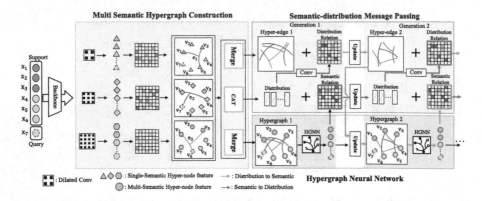

Fig. 2. Overall framework of our proposed Multi-Semantic Hypergraph for FSL (**MSH-FSL**). We take the 2-way 3-shot classification task as an example.

for FSL. First, in order to obtain complex latent semantic relations, we introduce three convolutional modules with different dilated kernels, which provides a variety of semantic features from different receptive fields. Then, for each example, some other examples with the most correlated semantic features are connected to it with an embedded hyper-edge, resulting in an MSH that captures rich latent semantic relations. After that, with the constructed Multi-Semantic Hypergraph, our MSH-FSL is learned to represent and leverage the complex latent semantic relations among examples, where the node and hyper-edge interact with each other in an iterative message passing manner to continuously optimize node and hyper-edge representations. Our main contributions are summarized as follows: 1) We propose the Hypergraph-based architecture to overcome the limitation of Graph-based FSL, $i.e.$, the binary and pairwise relations. 2) We propose the Multi-Semantic Hypergraph Neural Network for FSL (MSH-FSL) along with a novel hypergraph message passing to learn proper hyper-node representations with the constructed Multi-Semantic Hypergraph (MSH), which captures rich semantic embedded features and multiple semantic distribution features to guide few-shot recognition. 3) The experiments on three popular benchmark datasets show that the proposed method achieves the SOTA performance.

2   Related Work

GNN for Few-Shot Learning. Few-Shot Learning generally belongs to the meta-learning family, which consists of two popular learning methods, including gradient-based few-shot learning methods and metric-based few-shot learning methods. The gradient-based FSL methods learn to adapt to new classes by fine-tuning, and the metric-based FSL methods focus on extracting the knowledge that can be transferred between tasks. Unfortunately, both the families for FSL fail to learn the effective sample representations because they only consider each example independently. Recent research tries to leverage GNN to explore complex similarities among examples. For instance, DPGN [18] builds up a dual graph to model distribution-level relations of examples for FSL. ECKPN [2] proposes an end-to-end transductive GNN to explore the class-level knowledge. However, most Graph-based FSL methods ignore the various semantic information of an example as well as the multi-semantic relationship among different examples. Our method aims to construct hypergraph with high-order relationships and can mine multiple semantic information to perform inferences on FSL.

Hypergraph Learning. Hypergraph offers a natural way to model complex high-order relations. Recently, some researchers combine GNN and hypergraph to enhance representation learning. HGNN [4] and HyperGCN [17] propose to extend GNN to hypergraph on citation classification. [5] proposes a dynamic hypergraph neural network and [1] develops the line hypergraph convolutional networks. [16] designs a dual channel hypergraph convolutional network to improve Session-based recommendation. However, Hypergraph Neural Networks are only employed to tackle problems with massive examples such as person re-ID, stock prediction. Few researches have been found in engaging them for FSL. In this paper, we construct and harness feasible hypergraphs for mining complex latent semantic relations among few examples in FSL.

3   Method

3.1   Preliminary: Graph-Based FSL

An FSL framework contains a support and a query set sampled from a large dataset $\mathcal{D}$. At the training phase, the support set $\mathcal{S} = \{(x_i, y_i)\}_{i=1}^{N \times K} \subset \mathcal{D}_{\text{train}}$ has N classes with K samples in each (i.e., N-way K-shot), while the query set $\mathcal{Q} = \{(x_i, y_i)\}_{i=N \times K+1}^{N \times K+T} \subset \mathcal{D}_{\text{train}}$ has T samples from the N classes in total. $\mathcal{S}$ serves as the labeled training set, and the model is trained to minimize the loss over $\mathcal{Q}$. At the testing phase, the support and query set are sampled from the testing data $\mathcal{D}_{\text{test}}$. Here the label spaces of $\mathcal{D}_{\text{train}}$ and $\mathcal{D}_{\text{test}}$ are mutually exclusive. Due to the limited number of examples, traditional FSL methods are prone to overfitting. Some recent works explore constructing the graph relation amongst examples and leveraging GNN to enhance the FSL recognition. In contrast, we leverage hypergraph to construct such semantic relations (see Fig. 2).

3.2   Few-Shot Multi-Semantic Hypergraph

We define the Few-shot Multi-Semantic Hypergraph (MSH) as $\mathcal{H} = (\mathcal{V}, \mathcal{E})$. $\mathcal{V} = \{v_i\}_{i=1}^{|\mathcal{V}|}$ and $\mathcal{E} = \{e_i\}_{i=1}^{|\mathcal{E}|}$ denote the set of nodes and edges of the hypergraph respectively. Each hyper-node in $\mathcal{V}$ denotes an example in the union of support set $\mathcal{S}$ and query set $\mathcal{Q}$. $\mathcal{E}$ contains the hyper-edges connected these nodes. In MSH, a hyper-edge can link more than two hyper-nodes, which indicates the high-level semantic feature similarity. In the following, we illustrate how to construct such MSH in detail.

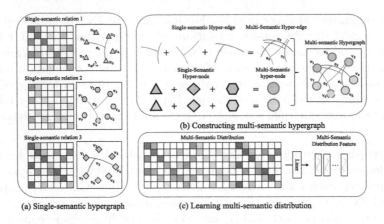

(a) Single-semantic hypergraph   (c) Learning multi-semantic distribution

Fig. 3. Multi-Semantic Hypergraph Construction. Given three different semantic features, we construct three subgraphs of semantic features by searching the most closely related nodes and merging the subgraphs to get the hypergraph.

Multi-semantic Node. The first step of constructing an MSH is how to obtain multi-semantic feature for a same example. In this paper, we choose a simple yet effective way that obtains multi-semantic features from different receptive fields via the dilated convolution [9]. For the whole training data $\mathbf{X}$, we have

$$\mathbf{U}^k = \text{DilatedConv}(\text{CNN}(\mathbf{X}), \gamma_k), \tag{1}$$

where $\mathbf{U}^k \in \mathbb{R}^{|\mathcal{V}| \times d}$ and d is the feature dimension. γ_k is the k-th dilation rate for convolutional kernel and $k \in \{1, \cdots, K\}$. Thus, with K different dilation rates, we obtain features with K different semantics. Then, we define the node multi-semantic representation $\mathbf{U} \in \mathbb{R}^{|\mathcal{V}| \times Kd}$ as the concatenation

$$\mathbf{U} = \left[\mathbf{U}^k, \quad \forall k \leq K \right], \tag{2}$$

where $[\cdot]$ denotes the concatenation operation. The core of multi-semantic hypernode is to make the feature with different semantic diverse as much as possible. Dilated convolution with different dilation rates has been proved effective for grabbing multi-semantic features, because different receptive fields yield enough attention on objects from small to large and from texture to whole.

Semantic-Level Hyper-edge. To construct a semantic-specific hyper-edge, we first compute the similarities between every two nodes. Specifically, for hypernodes in $\mathcal{V}$, we define their pair-wise symmetric relation matrix $\mathbf{A}^k \in \mathbb{R}^{|\mathcal{V}| \times |\mathcal{V}|}$ with the semantic type k as:

$$\mathbf{A}^k = f\left(\mathbf{U}^k; \mathbf{W}_k\right), \tag{3}$$

where $\mathbf{W}_k$ is the trainable parameter and the item

$$\mathbf{A}_{ij}^k = \sigma\left(\mathbf{W}_k^\top \left(\mathbf{U}_i^k - \mathbf{U}_j^k\right)^2\right). \tag{4}$$

σ is a sigmoid function. $\mathbf{A}_{ij}^k \in [0, 1]$ represents the strengths of the semantic similarity with semantic k between two connected hyper-nodes. Assuming there exist common features among similar nodes, for any hyper-node we pick up the top m $(m > 1)$ related to other ones, and the connection of them is the hyper-edge. For the semantic kind k, we connect hyper-nodes with hyper-edges $\mathcal{E}^k = \{e_i^k\}_i^{|\mathcal{E}^k|}$. In FSL, we set $|\mathcal{E}^k| = |\mathcal{V}|$ for achieving more informative hyper-edges. Then, the whole hyper-edges for multiple semantics can be obtained by the union $\mathcal{E} = \bigcup_k \mathcal{E}^k$, where $|\mathcal{E}| = K|\mathcal{V}|$.

The building process of MSH $\mathcal{H} = (\mathcal{V}, \mathcal{E})$ is shown in Fig. 3. First, for each dilation rate, we get single-semantic hyper-edges and connect the most closely related hyper-nodes with different semantics to build multi-semantic hyper-nodes $\mathcal{V}$. Second, the multi-semantic hyper-nodes $\mathcal{E}$ are obtained by ensembling every single semantic hyper-node feature, and the multi-semantic hyper-edges are the union of all single-semantic hyper-edges. Compared to the edge in the native graph, a hyper-edge in the constructed hypergraph can connect more than two nodes with similar semantic information w.r.t. the value of m. This leads to a more semantic-rich structured data form for FSL, and the next step is how to leverage the MSH to improve FSL.

3.3   Multi-Semantic Hypergraph Neural Network

Hypergraph Neural Network (HGNN) for MSH. After constructing the Multi-Semantic Hypergraph (MSH), we obtain significant information via updating the convolutional feature for each hyper-node. From the constructed hypergraph $\mathcal{H}$, a node-edge relation matrix $\mathbf{H} \in \mathbb{R}^{|\mathcal{V}| \times |\mathcal{E}|}$ is built with the entry

$$\mathbf{H}_{ij} = h(v_i, e_j) = \begin{cases} 1, & \text{if } v_i \in e_j, \\ 0, & \text{if } v_i \notin e_j. \end{cases} \tag{5}$$

Actually, $\mathbf{H}$ takes bridges among multiple semantics that hyper-nodes with different kinds of semantics will be highlighted. This is helpful for learning the relationship between different kinds of semantics.

Referring to the spectral hypergraph convolution proposed in [4], given hyper-node feature $\mathbf{U} \in \mathbb{R}^{|\mathcal{V}| \times Kd}$, we write Hypergraph Neural Network for MSH as:

$$\mathbf{U} = [\mathbf{U}, \mathbf{D}^{-1}\mathbf{B}\mathbf{D}\mathbf{B}^{-1}\mathbf{U}]\,\mathbf{W}, \tag{6}$$

where $[\ \cdot\ ]$ denotes the concatenation shortcut, and $\mathbf{W} \in \mathbb{R}^{2Kd \times Kd}$ is the learnable parameter. $\mathbf{B} \in \mathbb{R}^{|\mathcal{E}| \times |\mathcal{V}|}$ and $\mathbf{D} \in \mathbb{R}^{|\mathcal{V}| \times |\mathcal{E}|}$ represent the influence from each hyper-node to each hyper-edge and the opposite respectively. In this paper, we propose to construct $\mathbf{B}$ and $\mathbf{D}$ by the node-edge relation matrix $\mathbf{H}$ as

$$\mathbf{B} = \mathbf{H}^\top, \quad \mathbf{D} = \mathbf{H} \odot \mathbf{I}, \tag{7}$$

where $\mathbf{I} = [\mathbf{A}^k, \quad \forall k \leq K]$ and $\odot$ denotes the element-wise multiplication operation. By observing Eq. (6), the HGNN can obtain semantic information of hyper-nodes by aggregating hyper-node representations along with hyper-edges. Specifically, $\mathbf{D}^{-1}\mathbf{B}$ means that the hyper-nodes of the same hyper-edge are gathered with importance weights (node gathering). Then, $\mathbf{DB}^{-1}$ indicates that the hyper-edges associated with the same hyper-node are aggregated to learn the representation of this hyper-node (edge gathering).

Semantic-Distribution Message Passing. Although we associate hyper-nodes in a hypergraph via semantic-specific hyper-edges in the aforementioned section, the hypergraph may not be convincing enough because the edges we obtain are not perfectly reliable. This is because of the small number of examples in the FSL. Therefore, to further improve the rationality of hypergraph construction, we introduce multi-semantic distribution representation $\mathbf{V}$:

$$\mathbf{V} = \text{ReLU}\left(\mathbf{W}_{\mathrm{d}}^{\top}\mathbf{I} + \mathbf{b}_{\mathrm{d}}\right), \tag{8}$$

where $\mathbf{W}_{\mathrm{d}}$ and $\mathbf{b}_{\mathrm{d}}$ are learnable parameters. The distribution representation is equivalent to the relation similarity pack computed between any two hyper-nodes, which provides information that is not included in the visual content. Together with the hyper-node representation $\mathbf{U}$, $\mathbf{V}$ will be used to continuously optimize hypergraphs by iteratively updating with each other. Similar to Eq. (3), we can easily obtain the corresponding relation matrix $\mathbf{A}_{\mathrm{v}}$ and $\mathbf{A}_{\mathrm{u}}$ by

$$\mathbf{A}_{\mathrm{v}} = f\left(\mathbf{V}; \mathbf{W}_{\mathrm{v}}\right), \quad \mathbf{A}_{\mathrm{u}} = f\left(\mathbf{U}; \mathbf{W}_{\mathrm{u}}\right). \tag{9}$$

Also, the hyper-edge $\mathcal{E}_{\mathrm{v}}$ and $\mathcal{E}_{\mathrm{u}}$ w.r.t. distribution and multi-semantic representation can be obtained by pick up the top m items of $\mathbf{A}_{\mathrm{v}}$ and $\mathbf{A}_{\mathrm{u}}$. Then we update the hypergraph structure with the new hyperedge to update the two representations ($\mathbf{U}$ and $\mathbf{V}$) with an iterative message passing mechanism. In MSH-FSL, the semantic-distribution message passing continuously optimizes hypergraph structure and hyper-node feature representation through mutual learning between multi-semantic features and distribution features.

3.4   Objective

In this section, we introduce the objective used in our framework. First, the prediction for the node v_i in the query set can be computed a softmax after L generations of MHS-FSL, which is denoted as

$$\mathbf{p}_i = \text{softmax}(\sum_{j=1}^{NK} \mathbf{A}_{\mathrm{u}}^{(l)}(i, j) \cdot \mathbf{y}_j) \tag{10}$$

where $\mathbf{y}_j$ is the label of j-th example in the support set. $\mathbf{A}^{(l)}$ stands for the hyper-nodes relations in the constructed hypergraph after the final generation. The overall framework of the proposed MSH-FSL can be optimized in an end-to-end form by the following loss function:

$$\mathcal{L} = \sum_{i=1}^{|\mathcal{V}|} \sum_{l=1}^{(l)}(\lambda_1 \mathcal{L}_{\text{CE}}(\mathbf{p}_i, \mathbf{y}_i) + \lambda_2 \mathcal{L}_{\text{REL}}^{(l)}) \tag{11}$$

Table 1. Few-shot classification accuracies (%) on miniImageNet, tieredImageNet and CUB-200-2011. The backbone is all Resnet12 networks.

Methods	miniImageNet		tieredImageNet		CUB-200-2011	
	5way-1shot	5way-5shot	5way-1shot	5way-5shot	5way-1shot	5way-5shot
SNAIL [10]	55.71 ± 0.99	68.88 ± 0.92	–	–	–	–
TADAM [11]	58.50 ± 0.30	76.70 ± 0.30	–	–	–	–
Shot-Free [12]	59.04 ± 0.43	77.64 ± 0.39	66.87 ± 0.43	82.64 ± 0.39	–	–
MetaTrans [14]	61.20 ± 1.80	75.53 ± 0.80	65.62 ± 1.80	80.61 ± 0.90	–	–
TapNet [21]	61.65 ± 0.15	76.36 ± 0.10	63.08 ± 0.15	80.26 ± 0.12	–	–
Dense [7]	62.53 ± 0.19	78.95 ± 0.13	–	–	–	–
MetaOptNet [6]	62.64 ± 0.61	78.63 ± 0.46	65.81 ± 0.74	81.75 ± 0.53	–	–
DeepEMD [22]	65.91 ± 0.82	82.41 ± 0.56	71.16 ± 0.87	86.03 ± 0.58	75.65 ± 0.83	88.69 ± 0.50
IE-Distill [13]	67.28 ± 0.80	84.78 ± 0.52	72.21 ± 0.90	87.08 ± 0.58	–	–
DPGN [18]	67.77 ± 0.32	84.60 ± 0.43	72.45 ± 0.51	87.24 ± 0.39	75.71 ± 0.47	91.48 ± 0.33
MCGN [15]	67.32 ± 0.43	83.03 ± 0.54	71.21 ± 0.85	85.98 ± 0.98	76.45 ± 0.99	88.42 ± 0.23
ECKPN [2]	70.48 ± 0.38	85.42 ± 0.46	73.59 ± 0.45	88.13 ± 0.28	77.48 ± 0.54	92.21 ± 0.41
MSH-FSL (Ours)	**71.03 ± 0.49**	**87.06 ± 0.38**	**73.94 ± 0.44**	**89.45 ± 0.33**	**79.87 ± 0.41**	**92.39 ± 0.30**

where L is the generation number, where $\mathcal{L}_{\text{CE}}$ is the cross-entropy loss function. $\mathcal{L}_{\text{REL}}^{(l)}$ represents the relation loss of iteration l which can be computed by

$$\mathcal{L}_{\text{REL}}^{(l)} = \sum_{i}^{|\mathcal{V}|} \sum_{j}^{|\mathcal{V}|} (\alpha \mathcal{L}_{\text{BCE}}(\mathbf{A}_{\text{u}}^{(l)}(i,j), r_{ij}) + \beta \mathcal{L}_{\text{BCE}}(\mathbf{A}_{\text{v}}^{(l)}(i,j), r_{ij})) \qquad (12)$$

where $\mathcal{L}_{\text{BCE}}$ is the binary cross-entropy loss. r_{ij} is the ground truth relation. The hyper-parameters α and β are used to balance two loss functions. The relation loss plays a significant role in contributing to faster and better convergence.

4   Experiments

4.1   Datasets

miniImageNet contains 100 classes with 600 labeled instances for each category. We follow the standard protocol utilizing 64 classes as the training set, 16 classes as the validation set, and 20 classes as the testing set.

tieredImageNet has categories selected with a hierarchical structure to split training and testing datasets semantically. We use 351,97 and 160 classes for training, validation, and testing respectively. The average number of images in each class is 1,281.

CUB-200-2011-FS is initially designed for fine-grained classification, which contains 11,788 images from 200 classes. We split the 200 classes are divided into 100, 50, and 50 for training, validation, and testing.

4.2   Experimental Setup

Network Architecture and Training Details. We apply the same backbone ResNet12 to all our comparative experiments. To implement the FSL recognition, the output of the ResNet12 is reduced by a global average pooling and a fully-connected layer with batch normalization to obtain a 128-dimension instance embedding. In the 5-way 1-shot or 5-shot setting, we randomly sample 40 or 20 few-shot classification tasks to train one epoch. The Adam optimizer is used in all the experiments with the initial learning rate of 10^{-3}. We decay the learning rate by 0.1 per 15,000 iterations and set the weight decay to 10^{-5}.

Evaluation Protocols. We conduct experiments in 5-way 1-shot/5-shot settings on the three standard FSL datasets. We follow the evaluation process of previous approaches [18,22]. We randomly sample 10,000 tasks and report the mean accuracy (%).

4.3   Comparison Results

The main quantitative comparisons are reported in Table 1, where the average of each value and deviation is calculated on 10,000 test tasks. As observed, our method outperforms the current state-of-the-arts in both the 5-way 1-shot and 5-way 5-shot settings on the three datasets. We highlight two important observations as follows when examining our proposed model against the main competing methods, including DPGN, MCGN, ECKPN with ResNet12 backbone. 1). The proposed **MSH-FSL** achieves the state-of-the-art classification results compared with the recent methods on all three benchmarks in both the 5-shot and 1-shot settings. Especially in the 5-shot setting on the miniImageNet and tieredImageNet, our proposed method equipped with the ResNet12 achieves the accuracy improvement of 1% to 2% over the best of the other comapred models. 2). The proposed method tends to gain more improvements in the 5-shot setting than in the 1-shot setting. As the sample number in the 5-shot setting is larger than that in the 1-shot setting, more effective nodes can be associated in the hypergraph. Consequently, more effective semantic information can be aggregated, which is conducive to learning more accurate feature representation. Even with limited semantic information in the 1-shot setting, our MSH-FSL performs still superior to other latest methods on all three benchmarks.

4.4   Ablation Studies

In this part, we conduct more experiments to take a closer examination on the proposed method. We analyze how the hypergraph construction, the number of nodes in hyper-edge, and the iteration number of message passing would impact the performance of the proposed model.

Table 2. The impacts of the multi-semantic, hypergraph and message passing in the proposed MSH-FSL.

Method	5way-1shot	5way-5shot	Method	5way-1shot	5way-5shot
SS + G	61.61	75.83	+MP	67.63	84.78
MS + G	62.16	77.86	+MP	70.38	85.60
SS + H	62.02	77.39	+MP	68.26	84.42
MS + H	64.73	81.41	+MP	71.03	87.06

Impact of Constructing Hypergraph. We first conduct experiments to illustrate the advantages of multi-semantic against single-semantic information and hypergraph against graph. We list the experimental results in Table 2, in which SS represents single-semantic, MS represents multi-semantic, G represents the graph network structure, H represents the hypergraph network structure, and MP represents the message passing of semantic destruction. The results show that, in both 5-way 1-shot and 5-way 5-shot tasks, multi-semantic information and hypergraph structure can significantly improve the algorithm. In Fig. 4, we choose a 5-way 1-shot few-shot classification task from the miniImageNet test set and visualize it through the pre-trained DPGN [18] model and the MSH-FSL model we proposed. As shown in (a) and (b), the same sample of the same task has obtained different results through different semantic features describing the similarity of support-query. Such descriptions are not accurate, and different semantic features can be learned from a single sample. It also indicates that the single semantic relationship cannot distinguish well the similarity of support-query. Distinctively, by constructing a multi-semantic hypergraph structure as shown in (c), the prediction result has been significantly improved and exceeds the effect of the GNN structure. Multi-semantic fusion feature can better characterize the support-query similarities, which qualitatively illustrates the effectiveness of constructing multi-semantic hypergraph.

Impact of Node Number in Hyper-edge. As illustrated in Fig. 5(a), we set different node numbers from each semantic information for hypergraph construction on miniImagenet in the 5-way 5-shot setting. More nodes in the hyper-edge, more information will be obtained, and more complex the hypergraph could be. The experimental results show that as the number of nodes increases, the classification accuracy first increases then remains relatively stable, and finally decreases slowly. Particularly, when we increase the node number from 2 to 6, we observe a steady improvement of the classification accuracy, suggesting that building high-order complex association relationships between multiple samples can be beneficial to optimizing the representation characteristics of samples. On the other hand, when the number of nodes is too big, e.g. bigger than 7, it may introduce misleading or even negative semantic features as the target nodes; this would decrease the classification accuracy.

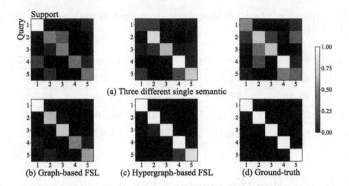

Fig. 4. Visualization of the support-query similarities in 5-way 5-shot setting. (a) represents support-query similarities updated by three different semantic features. (b) represents support-query similarities on the DPGN network. (c) indicates support-query similarities updated by the proposed MSH-FSL. (d) denotes the ground truth support-query similarities. The white denotes the high confidence and the black denotes the low confidence.

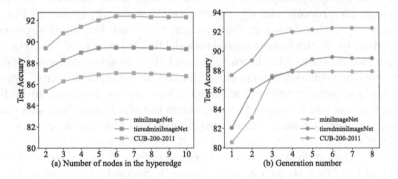

Fig. 5. The number of hyper-nodes and generations in 5-way 5-shot setting.

Impact of Message Passing. To study the effectiveness of the semantic-distribution message passing, we compare the experiments with and without message passing. As shown in Table 2, message passing brings further improvement to the performance for both graph and hypergraph-based FSL, which demonstrates the significance of the semantic-distribution message passing. We also conduct further experiments to obtain the trend of the test accuracy versus different generation numbers in MSH-FSL on the three datasets. In Fig. 5(b), with the generation number changing from 0 to 2, we observe significant accuracy gains. When the generation number changes from 2 to 10, the test accuracy increases by a small margin and the curve fluctuates in the last several generations. More generations need more iterations to converge, we choose generation number 6 as a trade-off between the test accuracy and the convergence time.

5   Conclusion

In this paper, we propose a Multi-Semantic Hypergraph for FSL (MSH-FSL) framework. In contrast to the binary and pairwise relations in Graph-based FSL, MSH-FSL can mine the deep latent semantic relations among a few examples. Motivated by this, we construct the Multi-Semantic Hypergraph via associating examples with different receptive fields. Then, with the constructed hypergraph, our MSH-FSL is built to leverage the complex latent semantic relations among examples via hypergraph message passing. The experimental results on three popular FSL datasets show the superiority of the proposed MSH-FSL.

References

1. Bandyopadhyay, S., Das, K., Murty, M.N.: Line hypergraph convolution network: applying graph convolution for hypergraphs (2020)
2. Chen, C., Yang, X., Xu, C., Huang, X., Ma, Z.: ECKPN: explicit class knowledge propagation network for transductive few-shot learning. In: Proceedings of the IEEE/CVF Conference on Computer Vision and Pattern Recognition, CVPR, pp. 6596–6605 (2021)
3. Du, K., et al.: AGCN: augmented graph convolutional network for lifelong multi-label image recognition. arXiv preprint arXiv:2203.05534 (2022)
4. Feng, Y., You, H., Zhang, Z., Ji, R., Gao, Y.: Hypergraph neural networks. In: Proceedings of the AAAI Conference on Artificial Intelligence, vol. 33, pp. 3558–3565 (2019)
5. Jiang, J., Wei, Y., Feng, Y., Cao, J., Gao, Y.: Dynamic hypergraph neural networks. In: IJCAI, pp. 2635–2641 (2019)
6. Lee, K., Maji, S., Ravichandran, A., Soatto, S.: Meta-learning with differentiable convex optimization. In: Proceedings of the IEEE/CVF Conference on Computer Vision and Pattern Recognition, CVPR, pp. 10657–10665 (2019)
7. Lifchitz, Y., Avrithis, Y., Picard, S., Bursuc, A.: Dense classification and implanting for few-shot learning. In: Proceedings of the IEEE/CVF Conference on Computer Vision and Pattern Recognition, CVPR, pp. 9258–9267 (2019)
8. Lyu, F., Wang, S., Feng, W., Ye, Z., Hu, F., Wang, S.: Multi-domain multi-task rehearsal for lifelong learning. In: Proceedings of the AAAI Conference on Artificial Intelligence, vol. 35, pp. 8819–8827 (2021)
9. Mehta, S., Rastegari, M., Caspi, A., Shapiro, L., Hajishirzi, H.: ESPNet: efficient spatial pyramid of dilated convolutions for semantic segmentation. In: Ferrari, V., Hebert, M., Sminchisescu, C., Weiss, Y. (eds.) ECCV 2018. LNCS, vol. 11214, pp. 561–580. Springer, Cham (2018). https://doi.org/10.1007/978-3-030-01249-6_34
10. Mishra, N., Rohaninejad, M., Chen, X., Abbeel, P.: A simple neural attentive meta-learner. In: International Conference on Learning Representations, ICLR (2018)
11. Oreshkin, B.N., Rodriguez, P., Lacoste, A.: TADAM: task dependent adaptive metric for improved few-shot learning. In: Proceedings of the 32nd International Conference on Neural Information Processing Systems, pp. 719–729 (2018)
12. Ravichandran, A., Bhotika, R., Soatto, S.: Few-shot learning with embedded class models and shot-free meta training. In: Proceedings of the IEEE/CVF Conference on Computer Vision and Pattern Recognition, CVPR, pp. 331–339 (2019)

13. Rizve, M.N., Khan, S., Khan, F.S., Shah, M.: Exploring complementary strengths of invariant and equivariant representations for few-shot learning. In: Proceedings of the IEEE/CVF Conference on Computer Vision and Pattern Recognition, CVPR, pp. 10836–10846 (2021)
14. Sun, Q., Liu, Y., Chua, T.S., Schiele, B.: Meta-transfer learning for few-shot learning. In: Proceedings of the IEEE/CVF Conference on Computer Vision and Pattern Recognition, CVPR, pp. 403–412 (2019)
15. Tang, S., Chen, D., Bai, L., Liu, K., Ge, Y., Ouyang, W.: Mutual CRF-GNN for few-shot learning. In: Proceedings of the IEEE/CVF Conference on Computer Vision and Pattern Recognition, CVPR, pp. 2329–2339 (2021)
16. Xia, X., Yin, H., Yu, J., Wang, Q., Cui, L., Zhang, X.: Self-supervised hypergraph convolutional networks for session-based recommendation. In: Proceedings of the AAAI Conference on Artificial Intelligence, vol. 35, pp. 4503–4511 (2021)
17. Yadati, N., Nimishakavi, M., Yadav, P., Nitin, V., Louis, A., Talukdar, P.: Hyper-GCN: a new method of training graph convolutional networks on hypergraphs. In: Proceedings of the 31st International Conference on Neural Information Processing Systems, NeurIPS, pp. 1511–1522 (2019)
18. Yang, L., Li, L., Zhang, Z., Zhou, X., Zhou, E., Liu, Y.: DPGN: distribution propagation graph network for few-shot learning. In: Proceedings of the IEEE/CVF Conference on Computer Vision and Pattern Recognition, CVPR, pp. 13390–13399 (2020)
19. Ye, Z., Hu, F., Lyu, F., Li, L., Huang, K.: Disentangling semantic-to-visual confusion for zero-shot learning. IEEE Trans. Multimedia (2021)
20. Ye, Z., Lyu, F., Li, L., Fu, Q., Ren, J., Hu, F.: SR-GAN: semantic rectifying generative adversarial network for zero-shot learning. In: 2019 IEEE International Conference on Multimedia and Expo (ICME), pp. 85–90. IEEE (2019)
21. Yoon, S.W., Seo, J., Moon, J.: TapNet: neural network augmented with task-adaptive projection for few-shot learning. In: International Conference on Machine Learning, ICML, pp. 7115–7123. PMLR (2019)
22. Zhang, C., Cai, Y., Lin, G., Shen, C.: DeepEMD: few-shot image classification with differentiable earth mover's distance and structured classifiers. In: Proceedings of the IEEE/CVF Conference on Computer Vision and Pattern Recognition, CVPR, pp. 12203–12213 (2020)

Deep Relevant Feature Focusing
for Out-of-Distribution Generalization

Fawu Wang, Kang Zhang, Zhengyu Liu, Xia Yuan$^{(\boxtimes)}$, and Chunxia Zhao

Nanjing University of Science and Technology, Nanjing 210094, China
{wfw,zhang_kang,yuanxia}@njust.edu.cn

Abstract. Convolution Neural Networks (CNNs) often fail to maintain their performance when they confront new test domains. Unlike human's strong ability of abstraction and connection, CNNs learn everything relevant and irrelevant from their training data while humans can understand its essential features and form. In this paper, we propose a method to improve the cross-domain object recognition ability from the model feature level: Our method masks the partial values of the feature maps to force models to focus on potentially important features. Multiple experiments on the PACS and VLCS confirm our intuition and show that this simple method outperforms previous domain generalization solutions.

Keywords: Domain generalization · Out-of-distribution generalization · Domain shifts · Feature focusing

1 Introduction

Despite the huge success of Convolutional Neural Networks (CNNs) when the testing and training data are independently sampled from the identical distribution, but can significantly fail otherwise. Their performance often degrades significantly when they encounter testing data from unseen environments. The testing distribution may incur uncontrolled and unknown shifts from the training distribution, which makes most machine learning models fail to make trustworthy predictions [2, 22]. To address this issue, out-of-distribution (OOD) generalization [23] is proposed to improve models' generalization ability under distribution shifts.

Essentially, the accuracy drop of trained models is mainly because of models learning too many background features that are irrelevant to the object in the training process [12, 17]. Because the distribution of training data is fixed, the better the training effect of the model, the better its fitting effect in this distribution, resulting in the model itself not only learning the features of the object but also learning irrelevant features in the case of distribution at the same time. It finally reduces the accuracy of models when distribution shifts. So how to reduce the bias of the model to these features is an important issue.

S. Yu et al. (Eds.): PRCV 2022, LNCS 13534, pp. 245–253, 2022.
https://doi.org/10.1007/978-3-031-18907-4_19

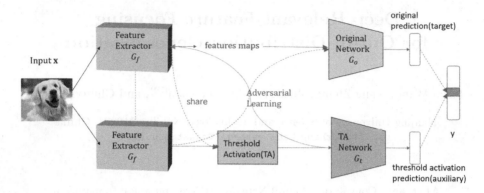

Fig. 1. Our NacNet consists of three parts: a feature extractor, a original Network and a threshold activation network that are jointly trained end-to-end. $\mathbf{G_f}$ is the feature extractor. $\mathbf{G_o}$ and $\mathbf{G_t}$ are classification networks. In the training phase, we train $\mathbf{G_f}+\mathbf{G_o}$ and $\mathbf{G_f} + \mathbf{G_t}$ successively in a batch. At test phase we use $\mathbf{G_f} + \mathbf{G_o}$ to predict results, where the TA module is only used in training phase.

In lasso [4] framework, it is proved theoretically that parameters can be constrained by adding regularization terms to improve the generalization ability of the model. And the basis of all of this is to reduce the feature bias by reducing the parameter values and finally achieve the purpose of generalization. In this paper, we start from the feature level and reverse control the model parameters by suppressing the feature values in the training process, so as to force the model to reduce the bias to the training data features in the training process to achieve the purpose of increasing the generalization ability of the model. The structure of our Neural activation Network (NacNet) is shown in Fig. 1. Our framework consists of original networks and Threshold Activation(TA) networks on the top of a feature extractor. In TA networks, we select the features whose activation range is within a certain range to force the network model to pay attention to the potential intrinsic correlation features in the data. In the training process, the TA module prevents the model from over-fitting the training data by suppressing the over-biased eigenvalues.

Through experiments, we found that CNNs would strongly associate too many irrelevant feature in the training process, resulting in the decline of generalization ability. At the same time, we demonstrate that NacNet is simple and We found that Nacnet can effectively suppress model bias across several cross-domain benchmarks such as PACS [13], and VLCS [25].

Our method is orthogonal to the majority of existing domain adaptation and generalization techniques that domain information for training (e.g. aligning the source and target domains [8,16,21]). In other words, NacNet only controls the intrinsic bias of CNNs without even requiring domain labels or multiple domains. Similar work can be called the OOD generalization method. The OOD generalization approach is more practical in real-world scenarios because it does not require domain labels. On the other hand, it can be quickly ported to a variety of new methods.

2   Related Work

2.1   Domain Generalization (DG)

The domain generalization method considers using multiple source domain data for training to improve the generalization ability of the model. A general idea is to extract domain invariant features from multiple source domains [27]. It believes that there is a unified expression in different domains [24], and many methods to extract unified features are made from this idea [1,15]. Some methods focus on exploiting the general learning strategy to promote the generalization capability [10,18]. Although the DG problem has many excellent experimental designs, it needs to actively divide different domains, which makes the DG method unable to be applied to practice.

2.2   Feature Decorrelation

Due to the interaction between features, the prediction performance of the model decreases feature decorrelation in the training process. Feature decorrelation mainly includes linear methods and nonlinear methods. The linear methods propose to decorrelate features by adding a regularize that imposes the highly correlated features not to be selected simultaneously [4,10]. The nonlinear methods use complex functions for feature remapping and weight selection for feature decorrelation [11,23,28].

3   Neural Activation Network (NacNet)

In normal training, CNNs tend to strongly associate environment, style, content, and other irrelevant features in data with objects, leading to the bias of the model towards data. Our NacNet contains three sections as shown in Fig. 1: a feature Extractor, an original Network, and a TA network. Threshold activation of some features by NacNet can reduce the model's bias to features in the training data, force the model to pay more attention to other features, and improve the generalization ability of the model.

3.1   Original Network

We first extract features and classification according to normal CNNs and let the network learn the features of the current training data domain.

Given an input training image $\mathbf{x}$, we first extract their feature maps $\mathbf{z} \in \mathbb{R}^{D \times H \times W}$ from the feature extractor $\mathbf{G_f}$, where $\mathbf{H}$ and $\mathbf{W}$ indicate spatial dimensions, and $\mathbf{D}$ is the number of channels. $\mathbf{G_o}$, $\mathbf{G_t}$ are classification network, where $\mathbf{G_o}$ is a original classification network, $\mathbf{G_t}$ is a classification network with TA module added. Loss L_o of $\mathbf{G_f} + \mathbf{G_o}$ acquisition formula is as follows:

$$\min_{\mathbf{G_f},\mathbf{G_o}} L_\mathbf{o} = -\mathbb{E}_{(\mathbf{x},\mathbf{y}) \in S} \sum_{k=1}^{K} \mathbf{y}_k \log \mathbf{G_o} \left(\mathbf{G_f}(\mathbf{x}) \right)_k \qquad (1)$$

where K is the number of class categories, $\mathbf{y} \in \{0,1\}^K$ is the one-hot label for input $\mathbf{x}$ and S is the training set.

3.2 Threshold Activation (TA) Network

After the normal learning and classification network, CNNs have a high degree of fit to the training data, which contains those irrelevant features. The work of our TA network is to selectively pass the feature maps $\mathbf{z}$ extracted from the feature extractor to suppress the transmission of high response features ans reduce the bias of the model to the features of the training data, so as to achieve the purpose of focusing attention on the potential important features of the target. For feature maps $\mathbf{z}$ extracted from $\mathbf{G_f}$, our TA activates feature maps $\mathbf{z}$ according to (2)

$$TA(z) = \sum_{h=1}^{H} \sum_{w=1}^{W} \begin{cases} z_{hw}, z_{hw} \leq \alpha \\ 0, z_{hw} > \alpha \end{cases} \tag{2}$$

where α is a random value within a certain range. Our TA module classifies data in combination with a new network $\mathbf{G_t}$. The loss L_t of $\mathbf{G_f} + \mathbf{G_t}$ is obtained by formula (3).

$$\min_{\mathbf{G_f}, \mathbf{G_t}} L_t = -\mathbb{E}_{(\mathbf{x}, \mathbf{y}) \in S} \sum_{k=1}^{K} \mathbf{y}_k \log \mathbf{G_t} \left(TA \left(\mathbf{G_f}(\mathbf{x}) \right) \right)_k \tag{3}$$

After the training and learning of Eqs. (1) and (3), the network attaches more importance to other potentially relevant features in normal feature recognition. Then the feature extractor $\mathbf{G_f}$ is trained to stabilize the prediction of $\mathbf{G_t}$ by minimizing the adverse loss $\mathbf{L_{adv}}$ calculated by the cross entropy between TA prediction and uniform distribution.

$$\min_{\mathbf{G_f}} L_{adv} = -\lambda_{adv} \mathbb{E}_{(\mathbf{x},) \in S} \sum_{k=1}^{K} \frac{1}{K} \log \mathbf{G_t} \left(TA \left(\mathbf{G_f}(\mathbf{x}) \right) \right)_k \tag{4}$$

where λ_{adv} is a weight coefficient. We refer to [20] for setting the value of λ_{adv}. Previous work [8] empirically found that matching with a uniform distribution provides more stable convergence than directly maximizing the entropy or using a gradient reversal layer. In our opinion, the loss reduction of Eq. (4) is in the same direction as that of our method. By calculating the average loss of the predicted values, the eigenvalues can be reduced, the model bias can be suppressed, and the model generalization performance can be improved.

3.3 Training Details

We train the network successively according to (1), (3), (4) in a batch of training. Firstly, Eq. (1) is trained to make the model learn the characteristics of the training data. Then, Eq. (3) is trained to restrain the model from over-bias to the training data. Finally, Eq. (4) is trained to further strengthen the inhibition effect. In this way, the model reduces the bias to the training data and focuses on the potentially important features. In the training, we follow the following steps:

1). Clear the gradient value.
2). Calculate the Loss.
3). Gradient descent minimizes losses.

We train in the order of (1), (3), (4) according to the above procedures.

Table 1. Results of the multi-source setting accuracy (%) on PACS. We reimplement the methods that require no domain labels on PACS with ResNet18 which is pre-trained on ImageNet [5] as the backbone network for all the methods. The reported results are average over three repetitions of each run. The title of each column indicates the name of the domain used as target. The best results of all methods are highlighted with the bold font.

	Art paint	Cartoon	Sketch	Photo	Avg.
D-SAM	77.33	72.43	77.83	95.30	80.72
JiGen	79.42	75.25	71.35	96.03	80.51
Epi-FCR	82.1	77.0	73.0	93.9	81.5
MASF	80.29	77.17	71.69	94.99	81.04
MMLD	81.28	77.16	72.29	**96.09**	81.82
SagNet	**83.58**	77.66	76.66	95.47	83.25
ResNet-18	78.12	75.10	68.43	95.37	79.26
NacNet	82.90	**80.37**	**78.35**	94.21	**83.96**

4   Experiments

4.1   Datasets

To evaluate the effect of NacNet, we conducted experiments on two data sets. **PACS** [13] contains seven target categories and four domains (Photo, Art Paintings, Cartoon, and Sketches). We follow the criteria of [13] for experiments. **VLCS** [25]aggregate data of four object classifications: PASCALVOC2007, LabelMe, Caltech, and Sun DataSets, which are also divided into four data domains. We randomly divide the data of each domain into training set (70%) and test set (30%) according to the criteria of [20].

4.2 Comparisons and Setting

DG problem is the task of training in one or more domains and finally testing on an unknown target domain. We also compared DG methods in recent years, including: D-SAM [6], JiGen [3], Epi-FCR [14], MASF [7], ADA [26], and MMLD [19]. We select Resnet-18 [9] as feature extractor and baseline model for NacNet. Our network use Adam as the learning optimizer, the batch size is 32, the initial weight is 0.0005, and the weight attenuation rate is 0. At the same time, the initial value of λ_{adv} is fixed to 0.1, and the parameter α is set to 0.5. The number of iterations is 5K. We use the following data augmentation for training: crops of random size and aspect, resizing to 224×224 pixels, random color jitter, random horizontal flips, normalization using the channel means and standard deviations, and grayscaling the image with 10% probability.

Table 2. Results of the multi-source setting accuracy (%) on VLCS. The reported results are average over three repetitions of each run.

	Caltech	Labelme	Pascal	Sun	Avg.
JiGen	96.17	62.06	70.93	71.40	75.14
ADA	74.33	48.38	45.31	33.82	50.46
MMLD	**97.01**	62.20	73.01	72.49	76.18
ResNet-18	91.86	61.81	67.48	68.77	72.48
NacNet	95.74	**68.29**	**73.59**	**73.58**	**77.80**

4.3 Multi-source Setting

We first experiment with multiple source domains to an unknown domain, training in multiple source domains and testing in a single target domain. We do not add domain labels in our experiment, and mix the data of multiple source domains in the experiment. The experimental results of other methods in the table are come from their papers. The experimental results are shown in the Tables 1 and 2. The results show that our method is superior to other methods on PACS (Table 1) and VLCS (Table 2). The experimental results on two data sets show that our average results are better than the comparison methods.

4.4 Ablation

We conduct two ablation experiments. On the one hand, we set the parameters α of our TA module. We first conduct experiments on the threshold parameters α of feature segmentation and proved that the generalization effect could be improved by making the feature zero with the eigenvalue greater than α. We then test the effect of different α. On the other hand, the Loss $\mathbf{L}_{adv}$ setting in

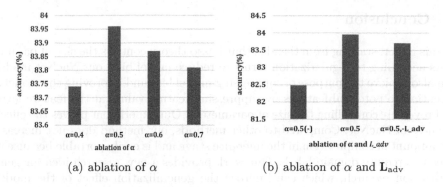

(a) ablation of α (b) ablation of α and $\mathbf{L}_{adv}$

Fig. 2. Multi-source domain generalization average accuracy (%) on PACS. α and $\mathbf{L}_{adv}$ ablation test results. $\alpha = *$ indicates the model effect when α takes different values; $\alpha = 0.5(-)$ means that when the eigenvalue is less than 0.5, it can be activated; otherwise, the eigenvalue is set to zero. $-\mathbf{L}_{adv}$ Indicates that no Loss $\mathbf{L}_{adv}$ is used.

the confrontation stage is compared with the influence of confrontation loss on the network. [20] shows that in a certain range $\lambda_{adv} = 0.1$ is helpful to improve the model generalization. The results are shown in Fig. 2.

As we can see from Fig. 2(a), α has the best effect when $\alpha = 0.5$. So we pick the value of α. According to the experiment in Fig. 2(b), it can be found that the lower part of the feature value can make the model better identify the out-of-distribution data.

Table 3. Results of the single-source setting accuracy (%) on PACS. The generalization effect of NacNac is much better than other methods in single-source setting. P, A, C, and S respectively represent the four domains of PACS data set (Photo, Art Paintings, Cartoon, and Sketches). A→C means to predict the results of C by using the data training of A data domain, and so on.

	A→C	A→S	A→P	C→A	C→S	C→P	S→A	S→C	S→P	P→A	P→C	P→S	Avg.
ResNet-18	62.3	49.0	95.2	65.7	60.7	83.6	28.0	54.5	35.6	64.1	23.6	29.1	54.3
JiGen	57.0	50.0	**96.1**	65.3	65.9	85.5	26.6	41.1	42.8	62.4	27.2	35.5	54.6
ADA	64.3	58.5	94.5	66.7	65.6	**83.6**	37.0	58.6	41.6	65.3	32.7	35.9	58.7
NacNet	**74.4**	**70.1**	94.6	**73.0**	**76.3**	83.1	**60.3**	**57.9**	**61.7**	**68.1**	**38.0**	**53.1**	**67.6**

4.5   Single-Source Setting

Our framework scales seamlessly to a single source with a single training domain because it does not require domain labels or multiple source domains. We trained NacNet on each of the PACS domains and evaluated them on the rest. As shown in Table 3, NacNet effectively improve generalization performance, while JiGen and ADA [26] are technically suitable for single-source DG, but our method is superior to them.

5 Conclusion

In this paper, starting from the idea that Lasso theory controls the size of parameters according to regularization terms to reduce model bias, our NacNet model can also achieve the purpose of suppressing model bias and improving the model's attention to potential features by suppressing feature values at the feature level and reversely controlling the size of parameters. Our experiment proves the effectiveness of NacNet. Compared to other methods, our method does not increase the amount of computation in the inference stage and is easily portable because it does not require domain labels. Our work provides a new research idea for generalization research, which can improve the generalization effect of the model from the feature level.

References

1. Ahuja, K., Shanmugam, K., Varshney, K., Dhurandhar, A.: Invariant risk minimization games. In: International Conference on Machine Learning, pp. 145–155. PMLR (2020)
2. Arjovsky, M., Bottou, L., Gulrajani, I., Lopez-Paz, D.: Invariant risk minimization. arXiv preprint arXiv:1907.02893 (2019)
3. Carlucci, F.M., D'Innocente, A., Bucci, S., Caputo, B., Tommasi, T.: Domain generalization by solving jigsaw puzzles. In: Proceedings of the IEEE/CVF Conference on Computer Vision and Pattern Recognition, pp. 2229–2238 (2019)
4. Chen, S.B., Ding, C., Luo, B., Xie, Y.: Uncorrelated lasso. In: Twenty-Seventh AAAI Conference on Artificial Intelligence (2013)
5. Deng, J.: A large-scale hierarchical image database. In: Proceedings of IEEE Computer Vision and Pattern Recognition (2009)
6. D'Innocente, A., Caputo, B.: Domain generalization with domain-specific aggregation modules. In: Brox, T., Bruhn, A., Fritz, M. (eds.) GCPR 2018. LNCS, vol. 11269, pp. 187–198. Springer, Cham (2019). https://doi.org/10.1007/978-3-030-12939-2_14
7. Donahue, J., Hoffman, J., Rodner, E., Saenko, K., Darrell, T.: Semi-supervised domain adaptation with instance constraints. In: Proceedings of the IEEE Conference on Computer Vision and Pattern Recognition, pp. 668–675 (2013)
8. Ganin, Y., et al.: Domain-adversarial training of neural networks. J. Mach. Learn. Res. **17**(1), 2030–2096 (2016)
9. He, K., Zhang, X., Ren, S., Sun, J.: Deep residual learning for image recognition. In: Proceedings of the IEEE Conference on Computer Vision and Pattern Recognition, pp. 770–778 (2016)
10. Huang, Z., Wang, H., Xing, E.P., Huang, D.: Self-challenging improves cross-domain generalization. In: Vedaldi, A., Bischof, H., Brox, T., Frahm, J.-M. (eds.) ECCV 2020. LNCS, vol. 12347, pp. 124–140. Springer, Cham (2020). https://doi.org/10.1007/978-3-030-58536-5_8
11. Kuang, K., Xiong, R., Cui, P., Athey, S., Li, B.: Stable prediction with model misspecification and agnostic distribution shift. In: Proceedings of the AAAI Conference on Artificial Intelligence, vol. 34, pp. 4485–4492 (2020)
12. Lake, B.M., Ullman, T.D., Tenenbaum, J.B., Gershman, S.J.: Building machines that learn and think like people. Behav. Brain Sci. **40** (2017)

13. Li, D., Yang, Y., Song, Y.Z., Hospedales, T.M.: Deeper, broader and artier domain generalization. In: Proceedings of the IEEE International Conference on Computer Vision, pp. 5542–5550 (2017)
14. Li, D., Zhang, J., Yang, Y., Liu, C., Song, Y.Z., Hospedales, T.M.: Episodic training for domain generalization. In: Proceedings of the IEEE/CVF International Conference on Computer Vision, pp. 1446–1455 (2019)
15. Li, Y., Gong, M., Tian, X., Liu, T., Tao, D.: Domain generalization via conditional invariant representations. In: Proceedings of the AAAI Conference on Artificial Intelligence, vol. 32 (2018)
16. Long, M., Cao, Z., Wang, J., Jordan, M.I.: Conditional adversarial domain adaptation. In: Advances in Neural Information Processing Systems, vol. 31 (2018)
17. Lopez-Paz, D., Nishihara, R., Chintala, S., Scholkopf, B., Bottou, L.: Discovering causal signals in images. In: Proceedings of the IEEE Conference on Computer Vision and Pattern Recognition, pp. 6979–6987 (2017)
18. Mancini, M., Bulo, S.R., Caputo, B., Ricci, E.: Best sources forward: domain generalization through source-specific nets. In: 2018 25th IEEE International Conference on Image Processing (ICIP), pp. 1353–1357. IEEE (2018)
19. Matsuura, T., Harada, T.: Domain generalization using a mixture of multiple latent domains. In: Proceedings of the AAAI Conference on Artificial Intelligence, vol. 34, pp. 11749–11756 (2020)
20. Nam, H., Lee, H., Park, J., Yoon, W., Yoo, D.: Reducing domain gap by reducing style bias. In: Proceedings of the IEEE/CVF Conference on Computer Vision and Pattern Recognition, pp. 8690–8699 (2021)
21. Saito, K., Kim, D., Sclaroff, S., Darrell, T., Saenko, K.: Semi-supervised domain adaptation via minimax entropy. In: Proceedings of the IEEE/CVF International Conference on Computer Vision, pp. 8050–8058 (2019)
22. Shen, Z., Cui, P., Zhang, T., Kunag, K.: Stable learning via sample reweighting. In: Proceedings of the AAAI Conference on Artificial Intelligence, vol. 34, pp. 5692–5699 (2020)
23. Sun, Y., Wang, X., Liu, Z., Miller, J., Efros, A.A., Hardt, M.: Test-time training for out-of-distribution generalization (2019)
24. Tobin, J., Fong, R., Ray, A., Schneider, J., Zaremba, W., Abbeel, P.: Domain randomization for transferring deep neural networks from simulation to the real world. In: 2017 IEEE/RSJ International Conference on Intelligent Robots and Systems (IROS), pp. 23–30. IEEE (2017)
25. Torralba, A., Efros, A.A.: Unbiased look at dataset bias. In: CVPR 2011, pp. 1521–1528. IEEE (2011)
26. Volpi, R., Namkoong, H., Sener, O., Duchi, J.C., Murino, V., Savarese, S.: Generalizing to unseen domains via adversarial data augmentation. In: Advances in Neural Information Processing Systems, vol. 31 (2018)
27. Wang, S., Yu, L., Li, C., Fu, C.-W., Heng, P.-A.: Learning from extrinsic and intrinsic supervisions for domain generalization. In: Vedaldi, A., Bischof, H., Brox, T., Frahm, J.-M. (eds.) ECCV 2020. LNCS, vol. 12354, pp. 159–176. Springer, Cham (2020). https://doi.org/10.1007/978-3-030-58545-7_10
28. Zhang, X., Cui, P., Xu, R., Zhou, L., He, Y., Shen, Z.: Deep stable learning for out-of-distribution generalization. In: Proceedings of the IEEE/CVF Conference on Computer Vision and Pattern Recognition, pp. 5372–5382 (2021)

Attributes Based Visible-Infrared Person Re-identification

Aihua Zheng[1,2,3], Mengya Feng[2,4], Peng Pan[2,4], Bo Jiang[1,2,4],
and Bin Luo[1,2,4(✉)]

[1] Information Materials and Intelligent Sensing Laboratory of Anhui Province,
Hefei, China
ahu_lb@163.com
[2] Anhui Provincial Key Laboratory of Multimodal Cognitive Computation,
Hefei, China
[3] School of Artificial Intelligence, Anhui University, Hefei, China
[4] School of Computer Science and Technology, Anhui University, Hefei, China

Abstract. Visible-infrared person re-identification (VI-ReID) is a challenging cross-modality pedestrian retrieval problem. Although there is a huge gap between visible and infrared modality, the attributes of person are usually not changed across modalities, such as person's gender. Therefore, this paper proposes to use attribute labels as an auxiliary information to increase cross-modality similarity. In particular, we design the identity-based attention module to filter attribute noise. Then we propose the attributes-guided attention module to drive the model to focus on identity-related regions. In addition, we re-weight the attribute predictions considering the correlations among the attributes. Finally, we use the attention-align mechanism to align the attribute branch with the identity branch to ensure identity consistency. Extensive experiments demonstrate that proposed method achieves competitive performance compared with the state-of-the-art methods under various settings.

Keywords: Person re-identification · Cross-modality · Attributes-based

1 Introduction

Cross-modality visible-infrared person re-identification (VI-ReID) [1] aims to match images of people captured by visible and infrared (including near-[1] and far-infrared (thermal) [2]) cameras. VI-ReID is challenging due to large visual differences between the two modalities and changing camera environments, leading to large intra- and cross-modality variations. To address the above challenges, a series of approaches have been proposed [3–6].

As auxiliary information, attributes have been proved as an effective information to boost the vision tasks [7]. Introducing attributes in VI-ReID has the following advantages: First, the attribute information is modality-invariant. That is, the attributes of pedestrians generally do not change due to modality changes.

ⓒ The Author(s), under exclusive license to Springer Nature Switzerland AG 2022
S. Yu et al. (Eds.): PRCV 2022, LNCS 13534, pp. 254–266, 2022.
https://doi.org/10.1007/978-3-031-18907-4_20

Therefore, with the help of attribute information, intra-class cross-modality similarity can be increased. Second, detailed attribute labels explicitly guide the network to learn the person representation by designated human characteristics. With only identity labels in datasets, it is hard for the VI-ReID networks to learn a robust semantic feature representation to infer the differences among pedestrians. With the attribute labels, the network is able to classify the pedestrians by explicitly focusing on some local semantic descriptions. Third, attributes can accelerate the retrieval process of VI-ReID by filtering out some gallery images without the same attributes as the query. Zhang *et al.* [8] propose a network to learn modality invariant and identity-specific local features with the joint supervision of attribute classification loss and identity classification loss. Simultaneously, they manually annotate attribute labels for SYSU-MM01 [1] dataset. However, they ignore the correlation between attribute and identity features, which will generate redundant information. Secondly, the correlations of attributes are not considered. Usually, a pedestrian presents multiple attributes at the same time, and correlations between attributes may help to re-weight the prediction of each attribute. For example "long hair" is highly correlated with gender being "female". In addition, they ignore the consistency of attribute and identity features. Two pedestrians with different identities may have the same attributes. At this time, pulling the distance between different identities through the loss function will impair the recognition ability of the network.

In order to solve the above problems and make full use of attribute information, we propose a novel attributes-based VI-ReID framework. It mainly consists of three key modules: identity-guided attention module (IA), attributes-guided attention module (AA) and attributes re-weighting module (RW). IA aims to obtain attention weights by computing the similarity between attribute features and identity features, and then weighting the attribute features to filter the attribute noise. AA uses attribute features and identity feature map to compute attention maps, with the aim of selecting regions of the feature map that are relevant to the intrinsic attributes, thus avoiding the network to focus on irrelevant information such as the background. Inspired by [9], an attributes re-weighting module (RW) is introduced to optimize attribute prediction by using the correlation between attributes. In addition, we propose an attention-align mechanism (ALG) to ensure identity consistency, which is achieved using attention alignment loss. Our main contributions are as follows:

- We propose an attributes-based VI-ReID, which improves the intra-class cross-modality similarity with attribute labels as auxiliary information.
- We propose an identity-guided attention module (IA), which aims to weight the attribute vectors using the correlation between attribute features and identity features.
- We propose an attributes-guided attention module (AA), which uses attention maps between attributes and identity feature map to drive the network more focused on attribute-related regions.
- We propose an attention-align mechanism (ALG), which uses attention alignment loss to ensure identity consistency.

2   Related Work

Visible-Infrared Person Re-ID. The visible-infrared cross-modality person re-identification (VI-ReID) [10] aims to match visible and infrared images of the same pedestrian under non-overlapping cameras. On the one hand, Wu *et al.* [1] first create the SYSU-MM01 dataset for the evaluation of VI-ReID. Ye *et al.* [3] propose to extract pedestrian features of different modalities using a two-stream network, and then further reduce the difference between the two modalities by constraining shared feature embedding. Subsequently, Ye *et al.* [11] solve the cross-modality discrepancy by a modality-aware collaborative learning approach. To make the shared features free of redundant information, Dai *et al.* [4] propose a GAN-based training method for shared feature learning.

All the above methods focus only on the learning of shared features and ignore the role of specific features. To address this problem, some methods based on modality-specific feature compensation have been proposed. Kniaz *et al.* [13] generate corresponding infrared images using visible images. Wang *et al.* [5] propose two-level difference reduction learning based on bidirectional loop generation to reduce the gap between different modalities. Lu *et al.* [6] use both shared and specific features for mutual transformation through a shared and specific feature transformation algorithm.

Attribute for Person Re-ID. Attributes, as an additional complimentary annotation, can provide higher-level semantic recognition information and have been introduced into pedestrian re-identification. Liu *et al.* [14] have annotated attributes for two datasets: Market-1501 and DukeMTMC-reID, and also designed a multi-task classification model using attribute labels to assist the person Re-ID task. Yang *et al.* [15] propose an HFE network based on cascaded feature embedding to explore the combination of attribute and ID information in attribute semantics for attribute recognition. Deep learning methods [16] use attributes to aid the supervision of joint training, thus improving the discrimination of identity features and enhancing the relevance of image pairs. To make full use of attribute information by dropping incorrectly labeled attributes, a feature aggregation strategy is proposed by Zhang *et al.* [17]. Tayet *et al.* [18] augment identity features with attribute attention graphs where class-sensitive activation regions for various attributes such as clothing color, hair, gender, etc. were highlighted.

The pedestrian attribute recognition task and the pedestrian re-identification task differ in their feature granularity approaches; the pedestrian re-identification task focuses on global features of pedestrian images, while the latter focuses on local features of pedestrian images. Most of the above approaches however ignore the differences between these two tasks.

3 Method

3.1 Architecture Overview

The overview of the proposed method is illustrated in Fig. 1. For the visible branch, it contains an attribute classification branch and an identity classification branch, which are used to extract attribute features and identity features, respectively. The infrared branch also follows this design. In identity classification branch, the input images including the visible images and infrared images are fed into the two-stream network to extra the image features. In attribute classification branch, we divide the feature map output from the fourth residual block of ResNet50 [20] into k overlapping horizontal sections (here $k = 8$) to learn the attribute features of pedestrians respectively.

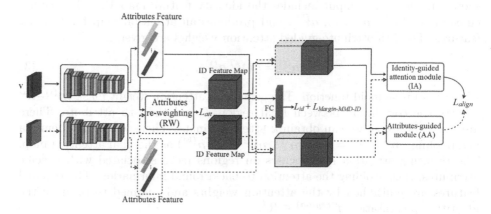

Fig. 1. Framework of attribute-based cross-modality person re-identification.

3.2 Attributes Re-Weighting Module (RW)

For a pedestrian, there is usually multiple attribute information at the same time, and there is a certain correlation between different attributes. For example, "gender" is related to "hair length", and "skirt" is related to "gender". The attributes re-weighting module aims to exploit the correlation between attributes to optimize attribute prediction. For image x, a set of attribute predictions $\{\widetilde{a}^{(1)}, \widetilde{a}^{(2)}, ..., \widetilde{a}^{(k)}\}$ can be obtained through the attribute classification branch, where $\widetilde{a}^{(j)} \in [0,1]$ is the j-th attribute prediction score. Following the same design as [9], we concatenate the prediction scores as vector $\widetilde{a} \in R^{1 \times k}$. Then the confidence score c for its prediction $\widetilde{a}$ is learned as,

$$\mathbf{c} = Sigmoid(\boldsymbol{w}\widetilde{\boldsymbol{a}}^T + \boldsymbol{b}), \tag{1}$$

where $w \in \mathbb{R}^{k \times k}$ and $b \in \mathbb{R}^{k \times 1}$ are trainable parameters. In this way, the attributes re-weighting module converts the original predicted label $\tilde{a}$ into a new prediction score as,

$$\mathbf{a} = c \cdot \tilde{a}^T . \tag{2}$$

For instance, when the prediction scores of "long hair" and "dress" are higher, the network may tend to increase the prediction score of "female".

3.3 Attributes-Guided Attention Module (AA)

Attribute features are usually associated with specific regions of an image. Therefore, we propose the attributes-guided attention module (AA) to select regions in identity feature map which are most relevant to intrinsic attributes. This can effectively avoid learning identity-independent features, such as background. As shown in Fig. 2. The input includes the identity feature map V and attribute embeddings $[a^{(1)}, a^{(2)}, ..., a^{(k)}]$, and produces an attention map for regional features. The i-th attribute-guided attention weights are given as,

$$m^{(i)} = \sigma(V^T a^{(i)}), \tag{3}$$

where $\sigma(x)$ is sigmoid function. The generated attention weight mask $m^{(i)} \in \mathbb{R}^L$ reflects the correlation between local region L and the i-th attribute. There are k attributes, so we can obtain k attention maps. Then, we merge them via maxpooling, $m^{(region)} = \max(m^{(1)}, m^{(2)}, ..., m^{(k)})$ as the final attention map. The resulting attention map focuses on regions more associated with specific attributes, thus avoiding the attention to background information. The regional features are multiplied by the attention weights and summed to produce the identity representation $f^{(region)} \in \mathbb{R}^d$,

$$f^{(region)} = \frac{1}{L} V m^{(region)} . \tag{4}$$

3.4 Identity-Guided Attention Module (IA)

IA aims to select attributes most related to identity as illustrated in Fig. 3. It takes the attribute embeddings $A = [a^{(1)}, a^{(2)}, ..., a^{(k)}]$ and the identity embedding $v^{(id)}$ as input. By calculating the similarity between attribute embeddings and identity embedding, the attention weights based on IA is obtained, and the calculation formula as,

$$s^{(attr)} = \sigma(A^T v^{(id)}). \tag{5}$$

The attribute features are fused via weighting. By this way, we can obtain attribute features $f^{(attr)}$, which is most relevant to pedestrian identity.

$$f^{(attr)} = \frac{1}{k} A s^{(attr)} . \tag{6}$$

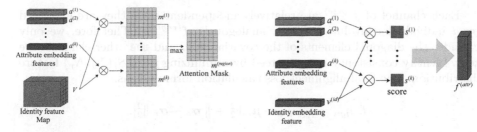

Fig. 2. Framework of attributes-guided attention module.

Fig. 3. Framework of identity-guided attention module.

3.5 Attention-Align Mechanism (ALG)

To ensure that the final features have identity consistency, we design an attention-align mechanism between identity-guided branch and the attribute-guided branch, which is implemented by attention alignment loss. Assuming that the features learned by the two branches belong to the same identity, the features of identity and attribute should follow the same distribution. Therefore, the two should have a high similarity. Both $f^{(attr)}$ and $f^{(region)}$ are 256-dim feature vectors. We regard each dimensional as a sample point in the 256-dim space and $f^{(attr)} \sim N_a(\boldsymbol{\mu}_a, \boldsymbol{\Sigma}_a)$, $f^{(region)} \sim N_r(\boldsymbol{\mu}_r, \boldsymbol{\Sigma}_r)$, where $\boldsymbol{\mu}$ is 256-dim mean vector and $\boldsymbol{\Sigma}$ is 256×256 covariance matrix. Inspired by [21], we adopt Jensen-Shannon (JS) divergence [22] to compute the similarity between N_a and N_r. The JS divergence between N_a and N_r as,

$$JS(N_a, N_r) = D_{KL}(N_a \parallel N) + D_{KL}(N_r \parallel N), \tag{7}$$

where N is the mixture $(N_a + N_r)/2$, and D_{KL} means the KullbackLeibler (KL) divergence. Since the $f^{(attr)}$ and $f^{(region)}$ are constrained by identity information, the feature space is compact and we can use $JS_1(N_a, N_r)$ to measure the similarity.

$$JS_1(N_a, N_r) = D_{KL}(N_a \parallel N_r) + D_{KL}(N_r \parallel N_a). \tag{8}$$

Given two distributions $N_0(\boldsymbol{\mu}_0, \boldsymbol{\Sigma}_0)$ and $N_1(\boldsymbol{\mu}_1, \boldsymbol{\Sigma}_1)$ with the same dimension d, the KL divergence is as,

$$D_{KL}(N_0 \parallel N_1) = \frac{1}{2}(tr(\sum_1^{-1} \boldsymbol{\Sigma}_0) + (\boldsymbol{\mu}_1 - \boldsymbol{\mu}_0)^T \sum_1^{-1} (\boldsymbol{\mu}_1 - \boldsymbol{\mu}_0) - d + \ln(\frac{det\boldsymbol{\Sigma}_1}{det\boldsymbol{\Sigma}_0})). \tag{9}$$

In this way, the similarity JS_1 can be rewritten as,

$$JS_1(N_a, N_r) = \frac{1}{2}(tr(\sum_1^{-1} \boldsymbol{\Sigma}_a) + (\boldsymbol{\mu}_r - \boldsymbol{\mu}_a)^T \sum_1^{-1} (\boldsymbol{\mu}_r - \boldsymbol{\mu}_a) - d + \ln(\frac{det\boldsymbol{\Sigma}_r}{det\boldsymbol{\Sigma}_a}))$$
$$+ \frac{1}{2}(tr(\sum_1^{-1} \boldsymbol{\Sigma}_r) + (\boldsymbol{\mu}_a - \boldsymbol{\mu}_r)^T \sum_1^{-1} (\boldsymbol{\mu}_a - \boldsymbol{\mu}_r) - d + \ln(\frac{det\boldsymbol{\Sigma}_a}{det\boldsymbol{\Sigma}_r})). \tag{10}$$

Each channel of $f^{(attr)}$ are relatively independent since they are extracted by d individual convolution filters, analogously $f^{(region)}$. Therefore, we only consider the diagonal elements of the covariance Σ and the other elements are zero. Identity consistency is guaranteed by minimizing the $JS_1(N_a, N_r)$ feature distribution. The final alignment loss calculation formula is as,

$$L_{align} = \frac{1}{2}[\| \boldsymbol{\mu}_a - \boldsymbol{\mu}_r \|_2^2 + \| \boldsymbol{\sigma}_a - \boldsymbol{\sigma}_r \|_2^2], \tag{11}$$

where $\boldsymbol{\mu}_a$ and $\boldsymbol{\mu}_r$ represent the mean vectors of $f^{(attr)}$ and $f^{(region)}$, respectively, and $\boldsymbol{\sigma}_a$, $\boldsymbol{\sigma}_r$ are vectors consisting of the diagonal elements of the covariance matrix.

3.6 Optimization

Attribute Classification Branch. In order to better learn attribute features, we set a classifier for each attribute to classify it through the constraints of attribute labels. In our model, the binary cross-entropy loss is used for optimization, we take the sum of all the suffered losses for k attribute predictions on the input image x_i as the loss for the i-th sample, and the loss calculation formula is as,

$$L_{att} = -\sum_{i=1}^{n}\sum_{j=1}^{k}[y_i \log(p_i) + (1 - y_i)\log(1 - p_i)], \tag{12}$$

where y_i represents the category of the i-th attribute, p_i the predicted value of the i-th attribute classifier, and k represents the number of attributes ($k = 8$).

Identity Classification Branch. For the identity classification branch, the identity loss is used for optimization, and the loss calculation formula is as,

$$L_{id} = -\sum_{i=1}^{n} \log \frac{e^{W_{y_i}^T x_i + b_{y_i}}}{\sum_{j=1}^{n} e^{W_j^T x_i + b_j}}, \tag{13}$$

where n represents the number of identitys, W_j represents the parameters for the j-th column, b represents the bias term, x_i denotes the features extracted by i-th sample belonging to the y_i class. Inspired by [23], we use MMD loss to minimize the intra-class distance. The overall objective function is,

$$L = L_{align} + L_{id} + \lambda_1 L_{att} + \lambda_2 L_{Margin-MMD-ID}. \tag{14}$$

4   Experiments

4.1   Datasets and Evaluation Metrics

SYSU-MM01 [1] is a large-scale dataset public by Wu et al. in 2017, which consists of visible and near-infrared images. The training set consists of 395 pedestrians, including 22,258 visible images and 11,909 infrared images. The test set consists of 96 pedestrians and contains 3,803 infrared images as a query set. It contains two different testing settings, all-search and indoor-search mode. Besides, we use the attribute labels marked by Zhang *et al.* [8], including eight attributes: gender (male, female), hair length (long, short), wearing glasses or not (yes, no), sleeve length (long, short), type of lower-body clothing (dress, pants), length of lower-body clothing (long, short), carrying backpack or not (yes, no), and carrying satchel or not (yes, no). For one certain attribute, the value of positive example is 1 and the value of negative example is 0.

RegBD [2] is collected by a dual-camera system, including 412 pedestrians and 8,240 images in total. Each identity has 10 different thermal images and 10 different visible images. Besides, we manually annotate the same eight attribute labels for this dataset according to the Zhang *et al.* [8].

All experimental settings follow the standard evaluation protocol of existing VI-ReID methods: the Cumulative Matching Characteristics (CMC) curve and the mean Average Precision (mAP). We adopt the CMC at rank-1, rank-10 and rank-20. Besides, all the experimental results are based on the average of 10 random trials.

4.2 Implementation Details

Following existing VI-ReID works, we adopt ResNet50 [20] as our backbone network for fair comparison. The last residual block is shared for each modality while the other blocks are specific. SGD optimizer is adopted for optimization, and the momentum parameter is set to 0.9. We set the initial learning rate to 0.1 with a warm-up strategy [24]. The learning rate decays by 0.1 at the 30th epoch and 0.01 at the 50th epoch, with a total of 80 training epochs. The hyperparameter λ_1 is set to 0.15, and the hyperparameter λ_2 is set to 0.25 following the setting in [23].

4.3 Comparison with State-of-the-Art Methods

Results on SYSU-MM01 Dataset. The results of SYSU-MM01 dataset are shown in Table 1. Our method significantly outperforms the existing methods under the challenging all-search mode. Although the rank-10 and rank-20 of our proposed method have a slight disadvantage in the indoor-search mode, but with significantly higher mAP as well as rank-1. The ATTR [8] first uses attributes however works modestly in VI-ReID. The main reason is that it simply embeds attribute information into the network without fully considering the relationship between attributes and identity features.

Results on RegDB Dataset. Table 2 shows the experimental results on the RegDB dataset. It can be seen that our proposed method has obvious advantages. In visible to thermal mode, our method improves 1.11% and 1.74% in rank-1 and mAP, respectively. Moreover, in thermal to visible mode, the our proposed method is close to the highest accuracy on rank-20, only 0.19% lower than it.

4.4 Ablation Study

Table 3 evaluates the effectiveness of four components including the attributes-based attention module (AA), the identity-based attention module (IA), the attributes re-weighting module (RW), and the attention-align mechanism (ALG) on the SYSU-MM01 dataset under all-search mode. Specifically, "B" indicates the baseline without the four components. By progressively introducing the four components, both rank-1 and mAP increase, which evidences the contribution of each component. Integrating all the four components reach the best performance, which verifies the mutual benefits of the components.

4.5 Other Analysis

Experiments on Different Networks. To further prove that our modules are plug-and-play, we experimented on three different networks. As shown in Table 4, our proposed method can significantly boost the performance by easily integrating into the existing networks.

Table 1. Comparison with the state-of-the-arts on SYSU-MM01 dataset on two different settings. Rank at r accuracy (%) and mAP (%) are reported. Herein, the best, second and third best results are indicated by red, green and blue fonts.

Settings		All search				Indoor search			
Method	Venue	$r = 1$	$r = 10$	$r = 20$	mAP	$r = 1$	$r = 10$	$r = 20$	mAP
Zero-Pad [1]	ICCV 17	14.80	54.12	71.33	15.95	20.58	68.38	85.79	26.92
TONE [3]	AAAI 18	12.52	50.72	68.60	14.42	20.82	68.86	84.46	26.38
HCML [3]	AAAI 18	14.32	53.16	69.17	16.16	24.52	73.25	86.73	30.08
cmGAN [4]	IJCAI 18	26.97	67.51	80.56	31.49	31.63	77.23	89.18	42.19
BDTR [25]	IJCAI 18	27.32	66.96	81.07	27.32	31.92	77.18	89.28	41.86
eBDTR [25]	TIFS 19	27.82	67.34	81.34	28.42	32.46	77.42	89.62	42.46
D^2RL [5]	CVPR 19	28.9	70.6	82.4	29.2	–	–	–	–
AlignGAN [10]	ICCV 19	42.40	85.00	93.70	40.70	45.90	87.60	94.40	54.30
AGW [26]	TPAMI 21	47.50	84.39	92.14	47.65	54.17	91.14	95.98	62.97
ATTR [8]	JEI 20	47.14	87.93	94.45	47.08	48.03	88.13	95.14	56.84
XIV-ReID [27]	AAAI 20	49.92	89.79	95.96	50.73	–	–	–	–
DDAG [28]	ECCV 20	54.75	90.39	95.81	53.02	61.02	94.06	98.41	67.98
cm-ssFT [6]	CVPR 20	61.60	89.20	93.90	63.20	70.50	94.90	97.70	72.60
NFS [29]	CVPR 21	56.91	91.34	96.52	55.45	62.79	96.53	99.07	69.79
CICL [30]	AAAI 21	57.20	94.30	98.40	59.30	66.60	98.80	99.70	74.70
HCT [31]	TMM 20	61.68	93.10	97.17	57.51	63.41	91.69	95.28	68.17
MID [33]	AAAI 22	60.27	92.90	–	59.40	64.86	96.12	–	70.12
GLMC [34]	TNNLS 21	64.37	93.90	97.53	63.43	67.35	98.10	99.77	74.02
SPOT [35]	TIP 22	65.34	92.73	97.04	62.25	69.42	96.22	99.12	74.63
MMD [23]	BMVC 21	66.75	94.16	97.38	62.25	71.64	97.75	99.52	75.95
AB-ReID	–	69.91	97.65	99.49	66.55	72.57	98.53	99.76	78.27

Table 2. Comparison with the state-of-the-arts on RegDB dataset on two different settings. Rank at r accuracy (%) and mAP (%) are reported. Herein, the best, second and third best results are indicated by red, green and blue fonts.

Settings		Visible to thermal				Thermal to visible			
Method	Venue	$r = 1$	$r = 10$	$r = 20$	mAP	$r = 1$	$r = 10$	$r = 20$	mAP
Zero-Pad [1]	ICCV 17	17.75	34.21	44.35	18.90	16.63	34.68	44.25	17.82
HCML [3]	AAAI 18	24.44	47.53	56.78	20.08	21.70	45.02	55.58	22.24
BDTR [25]	IJCAI 18	33.56	58.61	67.43	32.76	32.92	58.46	68.43	31.96
eBDTR [25]	TIFS 19	34.62	58.96	68.72	33.46	34.21	58.74	68.64	32.49
D^{2}RL [5]	CVPR 19	43.40	66.10	76.30	44.1	−	−	−	−
AlignGAN [10]	ICCV 19	57.90	−	−	53.60	56.30	−	−	53.40
XIV-ReID [27]	AAAI 20	62.21	83.13	91.72	60.18	−	−	−	−
DDAG [28]	ECCV 20	69.34	86.19	91.49	63.46	68.06	85.15	90.31	61.80
cm-ssFT [6]	CVPR 20	72.30	-	-	72.90	71.00	−	−	71.70
NFS [29]	CVPR 21	80.54	91.96	95.07	72.10	77.95	90.45	93.62	69.79
CICL [30]	AAAI 21	78.80	−	−	69.40	77.90	−	−	69.40
HCT [31]	TMM 20	91.05	97.16	98.57	83.28	89.30	96.41	98.16	81.46
HAT [32]	TIFS 20	55.29	92.14	97.36	53.89	62.10	95.75	99.20	69.37
MID [33]	AAAI 22	87.45	95.73	−	84.85	84.29	93.44	−	81.41
MMD [23]	BMVC 21	95.06	98.67	99.31	88.95	93.65	97.55	98.38	87.30
AB-ReID	−	96.17	98.79	99.84	90.69	94.83	98.07	99.01	89.42

Hyperparameters Analysis. We evaluate the effect of hyperparameter λ_1 on SYSU-MM01 dataset under the all-search and indoor-search modes, as shown in Fig. 4 and Fig. 5. Clearly, the highest recognition accuracy is achieved when λ_1 takes the value of 0.15 in both the all-search and indoor-search modes. Therefore, the value of the hyperparameter λ_1 in the Eq. (14) is set to 0.15.

Table 3. The effectiveness of modules we proposed. The rank-1 accuracy (%) and mAP (%) are reported.

Index	B	AA	IA	RW	ALG	rank-1	mAP
(1)	✓	✗	✗	✗	✗	60.74	55.97
(2)	✓	✓	✗	✗	✗	64.84	61.71
(3)	✓	✓	✓	✗	✗	66.58	64.89
(4)	✓	✓	✓	✓	✗	68.11	65.73
(5)	✓	✓	✓	✓	✓	**69.91**	**66.55**

Table 4. The effectiveness of modules we proposed. The rank-1 accuracy (%) and mAP (%) are reported.

Method	rank-1	mAP
AGW	47.50	47.65
AGW+Ours	59.47	58.94
(TSLFN+HC)	56.96	54.95
(TSLFN+HC+Ours)	63.38	61.73
(MMD)	66.75	62.25
(MMD+Ours)	69.05	65.50

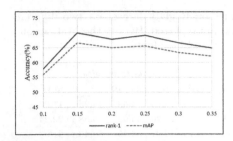 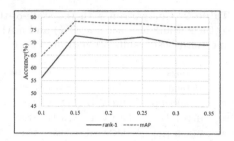

Fig. 4. Effect of hyperparameter λ_1 in all-search mode.   **Fig. 5.** Effect of hyperparameter λ_1 in indoor-search mode.

5   Conclusions

In this paper, we proposed attributes-based VI-ReID, which increases intra-class cross-modality similarity and mitigates heterogeneity with the help of auxiliary attribute labels. Specifically, attribute noise is filtered by the identity-based guided attention module. The model is prompted to focus on identity-related regions and filter irrelevant information such as background by the attributes-based guided attention module. At the same time, the attributes re-weighting module is designed to fully explore the correlation between attributes. Finally, we propose the attention-align mechanism to align the attribute branches and identity branches to ensure the consistency of pedestrian identity. Extensive experiments validate the effectiveness of our proposed approach.

References

1. Wu, A.C., Zheng, W.S., Yu, H.X., Gong, S., Lai, J.: RGB-infrared cross-modality person re-identification. In: Proceedings of the IEEE International Conference on Computer Vision, pp. 5380–5389 (2017)
2. Nguyen, D.T., Hong, H.G., Kim, K.W., Park, K.R.: Person recognition system based on a combination of body images from visible light and thermal cameras. Sensors **17**(3), 605 (2017)
3. Ye, M., Lan, X., Li, J., Yuen, P.: Hierarchical discriminative learning for visible thermal person re-identification. In: Proceedings of Thirty-Second AAAI Conference on Artificial Intelligence, pp. 7501–7508 (2018)
4. Dai, P., Ji, R., Wang, H., Wu, Q., Huang, Y.: Cross-modality person reidentification with generative adversarial training. In: Proceedings of International Joint Conference on Artificial Intelligence, pp. 677–683 (2018)
5. Wang, Z., Wang, Z., Zheng, Y., Chuang, Y.Y., Satoh, S.I.: Learning to reduce dual-level discrepancy for infrared-visible person re-identification. In: Proceedings of the IEEE Conference on Computer Vision and Pattern Recognition, pp. 618–626 (2019)
6. Lu, Y., et al.: Cross-modality person re-identification with shared-specific feature transfer. In: Proceedings of the IEEE Conference on Computer Vision and Pattern Recognition, pp. 13379–13389 (2020)

7. Cao, Y.-T., Wang, J., Tao, D.: Symbiotic adversarial learning for attribute-based person search. In: Vedaldi, A., Bischof, H., Brox, T., Frahm, J.-M. (eds.) ECCV 2020. LNCS, vol. 12359, pp. 230–247. Springer, Cham (2020). https://doi.org/10.1007/978-3-030-58568-6_14

8. Zhang, S., Chen, C., Song, W., Gan, Z.: Deep feature learning with attributes for cross-modality person re-identification. J. Electron. Imaging **29**(3), 033017 (2020)

9. Lin, Y., et al.: Improving person re-identification by attribute and identity learning. Pattern Recogn. **95**, 151–161 (2019)

10. Wang, G.A., Zhang, T., Cheng, J., Liu, S., Yang, Y., Hou, Z.: RGB-infrared cross-modality person re-identification via joint pixel and feature alignment. In: Proceedings of the IEEE/CVF International Conference on Computer Vision, pp. 3623–3632 (2019)

11. Ye, M., Lan, X., Leng, Q.: Modality-aware collaborative learning for visible thermal person re-identification. In: Proceedings of the 27th ACM International Conference on Multimedia, pp. 347–355 (2019)

12. Hao, Y., Wang, N., Li, J., Gao, X.: HSME: hypersphere manifold embedding for visible thermal person re-identification. In: Proceedings of the AAAI Conference on Artificial Intelligence, vol. 33, no. 1, pp. 8385–8392 (2019)

13. Kniaz, V.V., Knyaz, V.A., Hladůvka, J., Kropatsch, W.G., Mizginov, V.: Thermal-GAN: multimodal color-to-thermal image translation for person re-identification in multispectral dataset. In: Leal-Taixé, L., Roth, S. (eds.) ECCV 2018. LNCS, vol. 11134, pp. 606–624. Springer, Cham (2019). https://doi.org/10.1007/978-3-030-11024-6_46

14. Liu, X., et al.: HydraPlus-Net: attentive deep features for pedestrian analysis. In: Proceedings of the IEEE International Conference on Computer Vision, pp. 350–359 (2017)

15. Yang, J., et al.: Hierarchical feature embedding for attribute recognition. In: Proceedings of the IEEE/CVF Conference on Computer Vision and Pattern Recognition, pp. 13055–13064 (2020)

16. Li, H., Yan, S., Yu, Z., Tao, D.: Attribute-identity embedding and self-supervised learning for scalable person re-identification. IEEE Trans. Circ. Syst. Video Technol. **30**(10), 3472–3485 (2019)

17. Zhang, J., Niu, L., Zhang, L.: Person re-identification with reinforced attribute attention selection. IEEE Trans. Image Process. **30**, 603–616 (2020)

18. Tay, C.P., Roy, S., Yap, K.H.: AANET: attribute attention network for person re-identifications. In: Proceedings of the IEEE/CVF Conference on Computer Vision and Pattern Recognition, pp. 7134–7143 (2019)

19. Wang, Z., Jiang, J., Wu, Y., Ye, M., Bai, X., Satoh, S.I.: Learning sparse and identity-preserved hidden attributes for person re-identification. IEEE Trans. Image Process. **29**, 2013–2025 (2019)

20. He, K., Zhang, X., Ren, S., Sun, J.: Deep residual learning for image recognition. In: Proceedings of the IEEE Conference on Computer Vision and Pattern Recognition, pp. 770–778 (2016)

21. Goodfellow, I., et al.: Generative adversarial nets. In: Advances in Neural Information Processing Systems, vol. 27 (2014)

22. Kullback, S.: Information Theory and Statistics. Courier Corporation, New York (1997)

23. Jambigi, C., Rawal, R., Chakraborty, A.: MMD-ReID: a simple but effective solution for visible-thermal person ReID. arXiv preprint arXiv:2111.05059 (2021)

24. Luo, H., et al.: A strong baseline and batch normalization neck for deep person re-identification. arXiv preprint arXiv:1906.08332 (2019)

25. Ye, M., Lan, X., Wang, Z., Yuen, P.C.: Bi-directional center-constrained top-ranking for visible thermal person re-identification. IEEE Trans. Inf. Forensics Secur. **15**, 407–419 (2019)
26. Ye, M., Shen, J., Lin, G., Xiang, T., Shao, L., Hoi, S.C.: Deep learning for person re-identification: a survey and outlook. IEEE Trans. Pattern Anal. Mach. Intell. **44**, 2872–2893 (2020)
27. Li, D., Wei, X., Hong, X., Gong, Y.: Infrared-visible cross-modal person re-identification with an x modality. In: Proceedings of the AAAI Conference on Artificial Intelligence, vol. 34, no. 4, pp. 4610–4617 (2020)
28. Ye, M., Shen, J., J. Crandall, D., Shao, L., Luo, J.: Dynamic dual-attentive aggregation learning for visible-infrared person re-identification. In: Vedaldi, A., Bischof, H., Brox, T., Frahm, J.-M. (eds.) ECCV 2020. LNCS, vol. 12362, pp. 229–247. Springer, Cham (2020). https://doi.org/10.1007/978-3-030-58520-4_14
29. Chen, Y., Wan, L., Li, Z., Jing, Q., Sun, Z.: Neural feature search for RGB-infrared person re-identification. In: Proceedings of the IEEE/CVF Conference on Computer Vision and Pattern Recognition, pp. 587–597 (2021)
30. Zhao, Z., Liu, B., Chu, Q., Lu, Y., Yu, N.: Joint color-irrelevant consistency learning and identity-aware modality adaptation for visible-infrared cross modality person re-identification. In: Proceedings of the AAAI Conference on Artificial Intelligence, vol. 35, no. 4, pp. 3520–3528 (2021)
31. Liu, H., Tan, X., Zhou, X.: Parameter sharing exploration and hetero-center triplet loss for visible-thermal person re-identification. IEEE Trans. Multimedia, 4414–4425 (2020)
32. Ye, M., Shen, J., Shao, L.: Visible-infrared person re-identification via homogeneous augmented tri-modal learning. IEEE Trans. Inf. Forensics Secur. **16**, 728–739 (2020)
33. Huang, Z., Liu, J., Li, L., Zheng, K., Zha, Z.J.: Modality-adaptive mixup and invariant decomposition for RGB-infrared person re-identification. arXiv preprint arXiv:2203.01735 (2022)
34. Zhang, L., Du, G., Liu, F., Tu, H., Shu, X.: Global-local multiple granularity learning for cross-modality visible-infrared person reidentification. IEEE Trans. Neural Netw. Learn. Syst. (2021)
35. Chen, C., Ye, M., Qi, M., Wu, J., Jiang, J., Lin, C.W.: Structure-aware positional transformer for visible-infrared person re-identification. IEEE Trans. Image Process. **31**, 2352–2364 (2022)
36. Zhu, Y., Yang, Z., Wang, L., Zhao, S., Hu, X., Tao, D.: Hetero-center loss for cross-modality person re-identification. Neurocomputing **389**, 97–109 (2020)

A Real-Time Polyp Detection Framework for Colonoscopy Video

Conghui Ma[1], Huiqin Jiang[1(✉)], Ling Ma[2], and Yuan Chang[3]

[1] School of Electrical and Information Engineering, Zhengzhou University,
Zhengzhou, China
iehqjiang@zzu.edu.cn
[2] School of Computer and Artificial Intelligence, Zhengzhou University, Zhengzhou,
China
ielma@zzu.edu.cn
[3] The First Affiliated Hospital of Zhengzhou University, Zhengzhou, China

Abstract. Colorectal cancer is one of the most common malignant tumors in the world. Endoscopy is the best screening method for colorectal cancer, which uses a micro camera to enter the colorectal and check whether there are polyps on the internal mucosa. In order to assist doctors to work more accurately and efficiently, a real-time polyp detection framework for colonoscopy video is proposed in this paper. The swin transformer block is integrated into the CNN-based YOLOv5m network to enhance the local and global information of the feature map. Then, in order to reduce the influence of factors such as light changes and reflection, we use the ensemble prediction of time series to improve the temporal continuity of the detection results. The experimental results show that compared with the baseline network, the precision rate of our method is improved by 5.3% and the recall rate is improved by 3.5%. And compared with recent research, our method achieves a good trade-off between detection speed and accuracy.

Keywords: Polyp detection · Convolutional neural network · Transformer · Temporal information

1 Introduction

Colorectal cancer (CRC) is one of the most common malignant tumors in the world. Recent research indicates that the incidence of CRC will increase by 60% by 2023, with more than 1.1 million deaths [1]. Colonoscopy is the most important step in all CRC screening programs, which uses a micro camera to enter the colorectal and check whether there are polyps on the internal mucosa. Accurate and early polyp detection can improve the survival rate of patients. However, this examination is susceptible to human factors, such as the doctor's professional level and fatigue state. Therefore, the purpose of this study is to propose an efficient and accurate automatic polyp detection system to improve the efficiency and quality of doctors' work.

S. Yu et al. (Eds.): PRCV 2022, LNCS 13534, pp. 267–278, 2022.
https://doi.org/10.1007/978-3-031-18907-4_21

Polyp detector based on convolutional neural network (CNN) has been widely studied in recent years. The polyp detector for video data is usually based on a one-stage object detection algorithm, because the one-stage detection algorithm is fast and suitable for real-time detection tasks. Zhang et al. [2] propose a regression-based CNN framework for polyp detection. The framework uses the ResYOLO algorithm to detect polyps. Then, a tracker based on correlation filtering is used to filter and supplement the detection results of ResYOLO so as to incorporate the temporal information between video frames. Qadir et al. [3] propose an FP reduction unit to remove false positive samples and detect missed polyps in video frames, based on the consecutive detection outputs of the SSD [4] network. Zhang et al. [5] propose a detection framework to integrate spatial-temporal information. The framework sends the original image and optical flow diagram between neighboring frames into the SSD network to obtain two detection results. Then they combine the two results to generate the final result. Li et al. [6] applied the YOLOv3 [7] detection model on the video frame which has a great change compared with the previous frame, then the detection result of the mutation frame is used for other frames. And the YOLOv3 model is compressed. Therefore, this model has a high speed on CPU while ensuring accuracy. Tian et al. [8] propose a system to detect, localize and classify polyps from colonoscopy videos. The system uses a binary classifier to reject the useless frames in the colonoscopy video, such as frames with water jet sprays and feces, then use the method of few-shot anomaly detection to identify the frames containing polyps. Next, use the RetinaNet to locate and classify the polyps. Wu et al. [9] propose STFT (spatial-temporal feature transformation). Spatially, deformable convolution is used to align the features between adjacent frames, and the offset required by deformable convolution is obtained from the prediction result of the current frame. Then the attention value between features of adjacent frames is calculated, and the attention value is used to guide the feature fusion. Yu et al. [10] propose an end-to-end polyp detection model based on RetinaNet. They increase the number of anchor boxes in RetinaNet and use the dilated convolution to speed up. And attention gate module is used to suppress the useless information and enhance the useful information. Specifically, the module uses the semantic information in the deep feature to generate an attention map and then combines the attention map with the shallow feature.

Although the above polyp detection algorithms based on CNN have made great progress. However, to be applied to clinical diagnosis, there are still the following problems. One is the computational complexity, and the other is the low detection accuracy due to light changes and reflection during colonoscopy and the variable shape of polyps.

In order to achieve a good trade-off between detection speed and accuracy, a real-time polyp detection framework for colonoscopy video is proposed in this paper. The main work of this paper is as follows:

- In order to design a real-time algorithm, we compare the mainstream CNN based one-stage object detection methods on a polyp image dataset and choose the YOLOv5m network as the baseline network for this study.

- In order to extract the features of polyps with various shapes and improve the expression ability of feature map, the swin transformer block is integrated into the YOLOv5m network to enhance the local information and global information.
- To reduce the influence of factors such as light changes and reflection during colonoscopy, we design a temporal information fusion module that can compare and combine the detection results of previous frames and the current frame so as to improve the detection accuracy.

The experimental results show that compared with the baseline network, the precision rate of our method is improved by 5.3% and the recall rate is improved by 3.5%. According to the experimental results, our method achieves a good trade-off between detection speed and accuracy, and can assist doctors in detection to a certain extent.

2   Methods

The overview of our method is shown in Fig. 1, which includes the following steps: 1) For the input video sequence, the backbone network of YOLOv5m is used to extract the features of a single frame. 2) We design a feature aggregation network combined with swin transformer block to aggregate and optimize the extracted features so that the features can contain both local information and global information. 3) The YOLOv5m detection head is used to obtain the detection result of a single frame. 4) We design a temporal information fusion module to compare and combine the detection results of previous frames and the current frame and improve the temporal continuity of the detection results. In this section, we will introduce the specific structure of the feature aggregation network based on CNN and transformer, then introduce the algorithm of temporal information fusion module.

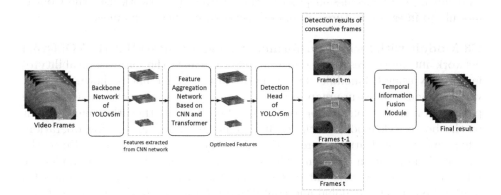

Fig. 1. Overview of our method.

2.1   Feature Aggregation Network Based on CNN and Transformer

The structure of the feature aggregation network based on CNN and transformer is shown in Fig. 2. We use the overall structure of the feature aggregation network of YOLOv5. Then, to further enhance the expression ability of features, we integrate the swin transformer block into C3 module to combine local and global information. In the following content, we will introduce the overall structure of the feature fusion network and the modified C3 module with swin transformer block.

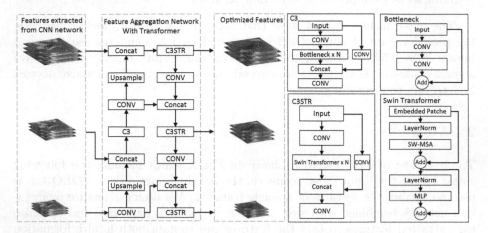

Fig. 2. Structure of feature aggregation network with transformer.

Feature Aggregation Network. Inspired by the PANet [11], the YOLOv5m network uses the top-down and bottom-up propagation path to aggregate features. Specifically, the feature is transmitted from top to bottom to enhance the feature with strong semantic information, and then the feature is transmitted from bottom to top to enhance the feature with strong location information. And during the transmission process, the YOLOv5m network uses the Concat module to integrate features of different scales by splicing channels.

C3 Module with Swin Transformer. Similar to CSPNet [12], the YOLOv5m network introduces residual connection and enhance the expression ability of features by using C3 module. The structure of the C3 module is shown in Fig. 2, which divides the feature map into two parts from the channel dimension. One part performs the convolution operation directly, and the other part is sent to the bottleneck module with residual structure after convolution operation, which makes the features spread through different network paths. Since the convolution operation of C3 module is a local operation, it can only model the relationship between adjacent pixels. Thus the small receptive field limits C3 module to extract the global and contextual information in the image, and this information is very useful for the network to detect the target.

The structure of transformer is mainly composed of self-attention module, fully connected neural network and residual connection. Through this structure, transformer can extract the dependencies between the elements of the input sequence, so as to obtain global information. By converting the image into a sequence and inputting the sequence into transformer, we can obtain the relationship between different regions of the image and capture abundant contextual information. Therefore, the combination of CNN and transformer can make the extracted features contain both local information and global information.

Specifically, we replace the bottleneck module in the original C3 module with the swin transformer (STR) block [13] to get C3STR module. The architecture of swin transformer block is shown in Fig. 2. Since the input of STR block is a sequence, the feature map $x \in \mathbb{R}^{H \times W \times C}$ is divided into N patches $x_p \in \mathbb{R}^{P \times P \times C}$, where (H, W) is the resolution of the feature map, C is the number of channels, (P, P) is the resolution of each patch, and $N = HW/P^2$ is the number of patches. Then, each patch is flattened and mapped to D dimensions, so the embedded patches is obtained. The function of the LayerNorm module is to make the input of each layer have the same distribution. The SW-MSA (shift window multi-head self-attention) module computes self-attention in each window (patch). The basic attention function is as follows:

$$\text{Attention}(Q, K, V) = \text{softmax}(\frac{QK^T}{\sqrt{d_k}} + B)V \tag{1}$$

where Q, K and V are the query, key and value matrices, B is a relative position bias matrix, and d_k is the dimension of vector key. STR block uses multi-head attention mechanism to extract information from different representation subspaces, which is expressed as follows:

$$\text{MultiHead}(I) = \text{Concat}(\text{head}_1, \cdots, \text{head}_h)W^O \tag{2}$$

$$\text{head}_i = \text{Attention}(IW_i^Q, IW_i^K, IW_i^V) \tag{3}$$

where I is the matrix obtained by flattening the feature map in the window, W_i^Q, W_i^K, W_i^V and W^O are parameter matrices. In order to introduce the dependency between different windows, STR block proposes shifted window approach, which changes the position of the window in consecutive STR blocks. Therefore, the shifted window approach introduces the connection between different windows and expands the receptive field. Then, the MLP (multilayer perceptron) is used to further extract features and transform the size of features. Considering the computational complexity of STR block, we only use C3STR module to replace the last three C3 modules in the feature aggregation network.

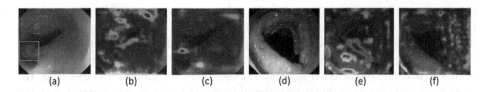

| (a) | (b) | (c) | (d) | (e) | (f) |

Fig. 3. (a) and (d) are original images with ground truth; (b) and (e) are heatmaps generated by the original YOLOv5m; (c) and (f) are heatmaps generated by our method.

The comparison of the feature map extracted before and after adding the C3STR module is shown in Fig. 3. According to this comparison and the experimental results, using our method to combine CNN and transformer can make the feature map contain both local and global information, and enhance the expression ability of the feature map, so as to improve the detection accuracy.

2.2 Temporal Information Fusion Module

The detection based on spatial features of a single frame in a colonoscopy video is easily affected by the subtle changes in the frame, such as light changes and reflections caused by camera jitter. Therefore, even if the detection network is used to detect frames that look very similar to human eyes, different results may be obtained. And this can lead to false positive and false negative samples as shown in Fig. 4. Therefore, we design a temporal information fusion module (TIFM), which uses the detection results of the previous frames to improve the temporal continuity of the detection results so as to improve the above problem.

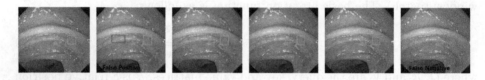

Fig. 4. A sequence of consecutive 6 frames in a colonoscopy video. The YOLOv5m network gives an error detection result in frame 2, and the polyp is missed in frame 6.

The detection result of the single frame detection network includes confidence score and bounding box. The confidence score is used to indicate the credibility of the detection and the bounding box is used to indicate the position of the polyp. The specific algorithm of the TIFM is shown in Algorithm 1. We calculate the average confidence (avg_conf) of the detection results of previous m frames, in our experiment we set m equal to 4. If the average confidence is greater than the threshold (avg_conf_thres), the current frame is considered to contain polyps. When the single frame detection network does not detect polyps in the current frame, the detection result of the previous frame (I_{C-1}) is extended as the detection result of the current frame (I_C). If the single frame detection network detects polyps in the current frame, we calculate the IOU value of each detection box in the current frame (I'_C) and the result of the previous frame. If there is at least one detection box that matches successfully, that is, the detection box of the current frame intersects the result of the previous frame, then the detection box with the maximum IOU value ($I_{C\_max\_iou}$) is taken as detection result of the current frame. If the matching is unsuccessful (including the case that no polyp is detected in the previous frame), the detection box with the highest confidence (I_{max_conf}) between detection boxes in the current frame and result of the previous frame is taken as result of the current frame. If the average confidence is less than the threshold, the current frame is considered to contain no polyps. According to the experimental results, TIFM can increase the precision rate and recall rate of detection result and the computational cost is small.

Algorithm 1. Algorithm of temporal information fusion module

Input: I'_C

1: $avg\_conf = \frac{1}{m} \sum_{i=1}^{m} conf_{t-i}$ ▷ calculate the average confidence
2: **if** $avg\_conf > avg\_conf\_thres$ **then**
3:    **if** $I'_C == None$ **then**
4:       $I_C = I_{C-1}$
5:    **else**
6:       $max\_iou, I_{C\_max\_iou} = F_1(I'_C, I_{C-1})$ ▷calculate the maximum IOU value
7:       **if** $max\_iou > 0$ **then**
8:          $I_C = I_{C\_max\_iou}$
9:       **else**
10:        $I_{max\_conf} = F_2(I'_C, I_{C-1})$ ▷ calculate the box with highest confidence
11:        $I_C = I_{max\_conf}$
12:       **end if**
13:    **end if**
14: **else**
15:    $I_C = None$
16: **end if**

Output: I_C

---

3 Experiments

Our model is implemented by Pytorch framework and trained on NVIDIA Tesla K80 GPU with a batch size of 16. And we use the SGD optimization method with 0.937 momentum, initial learning rate of 0.01 and 0.0005 weight decay. In order to test the inference speed of our method and compare it with recent research, we test the network on NVIDIA Tesla K80 GPU and NVIDIA GTX 1080 Ti GPU respectively.

3.1 Experimental Datasets

We use three public datasets for experiments. CVC-Clinic [14] contains 612 images with a resolution of 384×288. We increase the number of images in CVC-Clinic by data augmentation, each image in CVC-Clinic is rotated at different angles. In the end, we get 3750 images. ETIS-LARIB [15] contains 196 images with a resolution of 1225×966. CVC-ClinicVideo [16,17] consists of 18 different sequences and contains 11954 images in total with a resolution of 384×288 and each image contains one polyp or does not contain polyps.

For the comparative experiment of one-stage object detection algorithms, we use CVC-Clinic as our training set and evaluate each network on ETIS-Larib dataset. For the ablation experiment, we use CVC-Clinic as training set and evaluate each network on 5 videos (14, 15, 16, 17, 18) of CVC-ClinicVideo following [5] and [6]. For the comparative experiment with recent research, we use CVC-Clinic as training set and evaluate our network on 18 videos of CVC-ClinicVideo following [3]. Then we evaluate our network on 4 videos (2, 5, 10, 18) of CVC-ClinicVideo and use the rest 14 videos as training set following [9].

3.2 Evaluation Metrics

We use precision rate (P), recall rate (R), $F1$ score and frames per second (FPS) as indicators to evaluate the model. The frames per second refer to the number of images that the model can process per second. We define three kinds of samples to calculate the evaluation indicators. The true positive (TP) sample is a detection box with an IOU greater than 0.5 with the ground truth box. The false positive (FP) sample is a detection box with an IOU less than 0.5 with the ground truth box, and the false negative (FN) sample is a ground truth box with an IOU less than 0.5 with any detection box. The definitions of precision rate, recall rate and F1 score are as follows.

$$Precision = TP/(TP + FP) \tag{4}$$

$$Recall = TP/(TP + FN) \tag{5}$$

$$F1 = (2 \times Precision \times Recall)/(Precision + Recall) \tag{6}$$

3.3 Comparative Experiment of One-Stage Object Detection Algorithms

In order to select the baseline network of our detection framework, we use the mainstream one-stage object detection algorithms to conduct a comparative experiment. All these networks are trained on CVC-Clinic and evaluated on ETIS-Larib with NVIDIA Tesla K80 GPU. The experimental result is shown in Table 1. According to the result, the YOLOv5s model achieves the fastest detection speed, but the YOLOv5m model can achieve the best trade-off between speed and accuracy, so we choose the YOLOv5m model as our baseline network.

Table 1. Comparative experiment of one-stage object detection algorithms.

Network	P	R	F1	FPS
SSD	60.4	72.1	65.7	7.3
CenterNet [18]	75.9	56.0	64.4	8.9
YOLOv4 [19]	82.5	72.6	77.2	10.1
YOLOv5s	84.5	70.6	76.9	**46.7**
YOLOv5m	84.1	**73.6**	**78.5**	21.9
YOLOv5l	**87.1**	71.1	78.3	12.9

3.4 Ablation Experiment

We conduct an ablation experiment to analyze the effects of C3STR and TIFM on the YOLOv5m model. All these networks are trained on CVC-Clinic. And we evaluate each network on 5 videos (14, 15, 16, 17, 18) of CVC-ClinicVideo with NVIDIA Tesla K80 GPU and NVIDIA GTX 1080 Ti GPU respectively.

The experimental result is shown in Table 2. And the Precision-Recall curve before and after adding C3STR to YOLOv5m is show in Fig. 5. According to the experimental results, the effectiveness of the proposed method is verified. TIFM and C3STR both can improve the precision and recall of the network. Even though our method costs more computation than the original YOLOv5m network, it can still meet the requirements of real-time detection.

Table 2. Ablation experiment.

Network	P	R	F1	FPS (K80)	FPS (1080Ti)
YOLOv5m	78.3	69.6	73.7	**33**	**87**
YOLOv5m+TIFM	79.7	71.5	75.4	31	84
YOLOv5m+C3STR	82.5	72.5	77.2	29	67
YOLOv5m+C3STR+TIFM	**83.6**	**73.1**	**78.0**	27	66

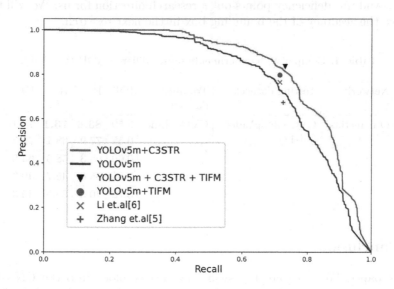

Fig. 5. Precision-Recall curve before and after adding C3STR to YOLOv5m. Recall and precision of our method and recent research.

3.5 Comparative Experiment with Recent Research

In order to further verify the effectiveness of our proposed method, we conduct a comparative experiment with recent research. The dataset setting and the experimental results are shown in Table 3. According to the results, our method outperforms methods [5] and [6] in both speed and accuracy. Compared with methods [3] and [9], our method has advantages in detection speed and meets the requirement of real-time detection.

Table 3. Comparative experiment with recent research.

Network	Testing dataset	Training dataset	P	R	F1	FPS	Device
Zhang et al. [5]	CVC-ClinicVideo (14–18)	CVC-Clinic	67.3	72.5	69.8	24	1080Ti
Li et al. [6]			76.5	71.5	73.9	35	CPU
Our method			**83.6**	**73.1**	**78.0**	**66**	1080Ti
Qadir et al. [3]	CVC-ClinicVideo (1–18)	CVC-Clinic	**96.6**	57.1	71.8	3	1080Ti
Our method			84.1	**75.1**	**79.4**	**66**	1080Ti
Wu et al. [9]	CVC-ClinicVideo (1,3,4,6–9,11–17)	CVC-ClinicVideo (2, 5, 10,18)	**95.0**	**88.0**	**91.4**	3	1080Ti
Our method			91.7	81.2	86.1	**66**	1080Ti

3.6   Comparative Experiments Under Different IOU Thresholds

In order to verify the performance of our method under different IOU thresholds, we further test our method when the IOU threshold is equal to 0.55, 0.6, 0.65 and 0.7 respectively. The experimental results are shown in Table 4. We find that when the IOU threshold is raised, the network performance will deteriorate. This result shows that the bounding box is not accurate enough to fit the position of polyps. And this deficiency points out a research direction for us. We will try to improve the accuracy of the bounding box in the next research.

Table 4. Comparative experiments under different IOU threshold.

Network	Testing dataset	Training dataset	IOU	P	R	F1
Our method	CVC-ClinicVideo (14-18)	CVC-Clinic	0.50	**83.6**	**73.1**	**78.0**
			0.55	77.9	68.1	72.7
			0.60	68.3	58.5	63.0
			0.65	55.0	45.7	49.9
			0.70	40.3	33.0	36.3

4   Conclusion

In this paper, We integrate the swin transformer block into the CNN-based YOLOv5m network to enhance the local and global information of the feature map so as to improve the detection accuracy. Then, in order to reduce the influence of factors such as light changes and reflection, we use the ensemble prediction of time series to improve the temporal continuity of the detection results. The experimental results show that compared with the baseline network, the precision rate of our method is improved by 5.3% and the recall rate is improved by 3.5%. And compared with recent research, our method achieves a good trade-off between detection speed and accuracy.

Acknowledgments. This work was supported by the Zhengzhou collaborative innovation major special project (20XTZX11020).

References

1. Arnold, M., Sierra, M.S., Laversanne, M., Soerjomataram, I., Jemal, A., Bray, F.: Global patterns and trends in colorectal cancer incidence and mortality. Gut **66**(4), 683–691 (2017)
2. Zhang, R., Zheng, Y., Poon, C., Shen, D., Lau, J.: Polyp detection during colonoscopy using a regression-based convolutional neural network with a tracker. Pattern Recogn. **83**, 209–219 (2018)
3. Qadir, H.A., Balasingham, I., Solhusvik, J., Bergsland, J., Aabakken, L., Shin, Y.: Improving automatic polyp detection using CNN by exploiting temporal dependency in colonoscopy video. IEEE J. Biomed. Health Inform. **24**(1), 180–193 (2019)
4. Liu, W., et al.: SSD: single shot multibox detector. In: Leibe, B., Matas, J., Sebe, N., Welling, M. (eds.) ECCV 2016. LNCS, vol. 9905, pp. 21–37. Springer, Cham (2016). https://doi.org/10.1007/978-3-319-46448-0_2
5. Zhang, P., Sun, X., Wang, D., Wang, X., Cao Y., Liu, B.: An efficient spatial-temporal polyp detection framework for colonoscopy video. In: IEEE 31st International Conference on Tools with Artificial Intelligence, pp. 1252–1259 (2019)
6. Li, X., Liu, R., Li, M., Liu, Y., Jiang L., Zhou, C.: Real-time polyp detection for colonoscopy video on CPU. In: 2020 IEEE 32nd International Conference on Tools with Artificial Intelligence, pp. 890–897 (2020)
7. Redmon, J., Farhadi, A.: Yolov3: an incremental improvement. arXiv e-prints https://arXiv.org/abs/1804.02767 (2018)
8. Tian, Y., et al.: Detecting, localising and classifying polyps from colonoscopy videos using deep learning (2021). https://arXiv.org/abs/2101.03285
9. Wu, L., Hu, Z., Ji, Y., Luo, P., Zhang, S.: Multi-frame collaboration for effective endoscopic video polyp detection via spatial-temporal feature transformation. In: 2021 Medical Image Computing and Computer Assisted Intervention, pp. 302–312 (2021)
10. Yu, J., Wang, H., Chen, M.: Colonoscopy polyp detection with massive endoscopic images (2022). https://arXiv.org/abs/2202.08730
11. Liu, S., Qi, L., Qin, H., Shi, J., Jia, J.: Path aggregation network for instance segmentation. In: 2018 IEEE/CVF Conference on Computer Vision and Pattern Recognition, pp. 8759–8768 (2018)
12. Wang, C.Y., Liao, H., Wu, Y.H., Chen, P.Y., Yeh, I.H.: CSPNet: a new backbone that can enhance learning capability of CNN. In: 2020 IEEE/CVF Conference on Computer Vision and Pattern Recognition Workshops, pp. 1571–1580 (2020)
13. Liu, Z., et al.: Swin transformer: hierarchical vision transformer using shifted windows (2021). https://arXiv.org/abs/2103.14030
14. Bernal, J., et al.: WM-DOVA maps for accurate polyp highlighting in colonoscopy: validation vs. saliency maps from physicians. Comput. Med. Imaging Graph. **43**, 99–111 (2015)
15. Silva, J., Histace, A., Romain, O., Dray, X., Granado, B.: Toward embedded detection of polyps in WCE images for early diagnosis of colorectal cancer. Int. J. Comput. Assist. Radiol. Surg. **9**(2), 283–293 (2013)
16. Angermann, Q., Bernal, J., Sánchez-Montes, C., Hammami, M., Histace, A.: Towards real-time polyp detection in colonoscopy videos: adapting still frame-based methodologies for video sequences analysis. In: International Workshop on Computer-assisted and Robotic Endoscopy Workshop on Clinical Image-based Procedures, pp. 1232–1243 (2017)

17. Bernal, J., et al.: Polyp detection benchmark in colonoscopy videos using GTCreator: a novel fully configurable tool for easy and fast annotation of image databases. Int. J. Comput. Assist. Radiol. Surg. **13**(1), 166–167 (2018)
18. Zhou, X., Wang, D., Krhenbühl, P.: Objects as points (2019). https://arXiv.org/abs/1904.07850
19. Bochkovskiy, A., Wang, C.Y., Liao, H.: Yolov4: optimal speed and accuracy of object detection. arXiv e-prints https://arXiv.org/abs/2004.10934 (2020)

Dunhuang Mural Line Drawing Based on Bi-Dexined Network and Adaptive Weight Learning

Baokai Liu[1], Shiqiang Du[1,2(✉)], Jiacheng Li[1], Jianhua Wang[1], and Wenjie Liu[1]

[1] Key Laboratory of China's Ethnic Languages and Information Technology of Ministry of Education, Chinese National Information Technology Research Institute, Northwest Minzu University, Lanzhou, China
[2] College of Mathematics and Computer Science, Northwest Minzu University, Lanzhou, China
shiqiangdu@hotmail.com

Abstract. Dunhuang murals are an excellent cultural heritage, a masterpiece of Chinese painting, and a treasure of Buddhist art. A large number of murals and sculptures have gone through thousands of years and are of high artistic value. Digital line drawings of the Dun- huang Murals can not only show the beauty of the line art of murals, but also guide the restoration of murals. It belongs to the direction of image edge detection in computer vision. The purpose of edge detection is to quickly and accurately locate and extract image edge feature information. Although some traditional detection algorithms and methods based on deep learning have made some progress, they have not achieved ideal results in generating mural datasets. Compared to existing methods, we propose a novel edge detection architecture Bi-Dexined network. Firstly, the adaptive weight in this method can well balance the weight influence of the fusion of different levels of feature maps on the final prediction result. Secondly, The upsampling path can extract deeper semantic information in the network. After testing on several different edge detection and mural datasets, our method can generate clearer and more reasonable edge maps than other methods.

Keywords: Edge detection · Bi-Dexined network · Adaptive weight learning · Dunhuang murals

1 Introduction

The Dunhuang murals are precious historical relics, which have extremely high research value in history, religion, archaeology and art. Dunhuang Mural line

---

The first author is a student.

S. Yu et al. (Eds.): PRCV 2022, LNCS 13534, pp. 279–292, 2022.
https://doi.org/10.1007/978-3-031-18907-4_22

drawing can not only show the artistic line beauty of murals, but also provide guidance for the restoration of the murals. Dunhuang Mural line drawing belongs to the task of image edge detection, which belongs to an important branch of computer vision and is of great significance to tasks such as image segmentation, object detection and feature description.

Many researchers have proposed many methods for edge detection research, which are mainly divided into traditional and based on deep learning methods. The traditional method mainly uses the low-level features such as color, brightness, texture, and gradient of the image to detect the edge of the image. Although great progress has been made, there are some limitations due to the lack of effective utilization of high-level semantic information. With the continuous improvement of computing power, convolutional neural network has been widely used for edge detection of objects due to its powerful semantic extraction ability. These edge detection methods are proposed [8,10,13,14,22] , such as HED, RCF, BDCN, RINDNet etc. However, as can be seen from the generated edge maps, these methods still have two shortcomings. i) The network structure does not consider the influence of the feature maps of different levels on the weight of the final prediction result, which makes the network not fully utilize the useful information in the feature maps of different levels. ii) The hard samples between edges and non-edges are ignored in the network, and the misclassification of these hard samples makes the network generate relatively thick edges. iii) There is no effective use of deep semantic information in the entire network structure, making the edge map not clear enough. For the above issues, we propose a new method to solve the above problems, and its main work includes the following aspects:

1) The proposed method allows the network to learn adaptive weights for feature fusion by assign- ing learnable weights to different feature maps, and effectively removes redundant information from different feature maps by fusing feature maps with different weight coefficients.
2) A hybrid loss function is used for our model to capture the structural information of the image and increases the weight of the hard sample in the loss function to improve the accuracy of the hard sample.
3) A novel Bi-Dexined network is proposed, which can obtain rich edge prediction feature maps more efficiently.

2   Related Works

People have been working on the task of edge detection for decades and have achieved a lot of results. Some of the classic algorithms have a very important impact on the research work of edge detection [7,11,15,16]. Generally speaking, the researchers divide these algorithms into two categories: i) Traditional approach; ii) Methods based on deep learning.

Traditional approach: these methods mainly identify and locate edge locations based on the parts of the image that have abrupt changes, such as Sobel, Prewitt, Laplacian and Canny [1]. However, these methods are not very accurate in practical applications. To this end, people have proposed edge detection algorithms based on artificial feature extraction, such as multi-scale feature detection algorithms and structured edge detection algorithms. Although these methods have achieved some remarkable results, the results of these methods are not ideal in some complex scenes.

Deep learning based algorithms: traditional edge detection techniques have made great progress, but still have great limitations. With the development of hardware devices, deep learning has made great progress in many vision tasks. In this case, people combine convolutional neural network with edge detection task, and propose a series of edge detection algorithms based on deep learning. Xie et al. [2] study a new edge detection algorithm, HED, which uses a fully convolutional neural network and a deep supervised network to automatically learn rich hierarchical representations, which greatly improves the detection speed. Liu et al. [3] further enrich the special diagnosis representation of each layer by efficiently using the features of each convolutional layer. Deng et al. [4] obtained clearer edges by introducing a new loss function and using hierarchical features to generate boundary masks. He et al. [5] propose Bi-Directional Cascaded Network. In this structure, a single layer is supervised by a specific scale of labels to generate richer multi-scale features. Although these edge detection methods based on multi-scale fusion have achieved good results, these algorithms ignore the influence of feature maps of different scales and the weights between different channels of each feature map, which will have an impact on the final prediction results.

3   Bi-Dexined Network for Edge Detection

This section will introduce architecture of our proposed edge detection model, named Bi-DexiNed, which consists of some botteneck structures, including a top-down and a bottom-up network structure. The entire network structure of our proposed edge detection is shown in Fig. 1. Top-down networks use dense blocks to obtain feature information at different scales. Bottom-up network extracts deeper semantic information and refine the generated edges. The feature information of the same size on the two paths is fused by deep supervision. Finally, the feature maps of these different levels are sent to the adaptive weight learning layer to obtain the final prediction result.

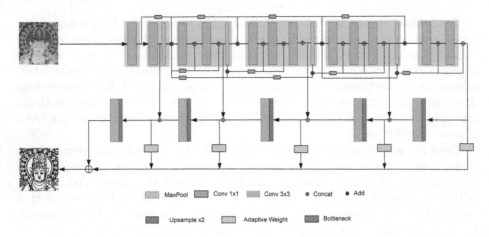

Fig. 1. Architecture of network

3.1 Network Architecture

Inspired by U-net [12,17,18] and DenseNet [9,19,20], we design the edge detection module as the bottom-up/top-down network because the structure can better capture useful information in different hierarchies. In the entire network structure, multiple feature maps at different stages are selected to obtain hierarchical features, and edge probability maps with richer semantic information will be generated by fusing features at different levels. We use the vgg-16 model as the backbone and stack bottleneck modules to extract feature information at different resolutions. In order to get richer edge information, we modified the module as follows to make it more suitable for edge detection: i) To capture high-level semantic information and refine the detection results of edges, we use bottleneck blocks and deconvolution modules to form the upsampling refinement path of the network. The bottleneck structure is mainly composed of three 1*1 convolutions and one 3*3 convolution. The two 1*1 convolutions are mainly to reduce the number of model parameters, so as to more effectively perform data training and feature extraction. Among them, C1 is the number of channels of the input feature map, and C2 is the number of channels corresponding to the output of different levels in the downsampling path. The use of two 3*3 convolutional layer residual modules significantly increases the parameters of the entire model, making the inference speed of the entire model slower. The structure of the two blocks is shown in Fig. 2. Then the output of each layer in the downsampling path is fused with the output of the corresponding layer of the refinement path to obtain the output results of different levels. ii) For the purpose of the feature information of different levels fully fused, the channel dimension fusion in the convolutional layer of each block is used, and the spatial dimension fusion is used between blocks. iii) We use deconvolution to upsample the feature maps of the top-down path.

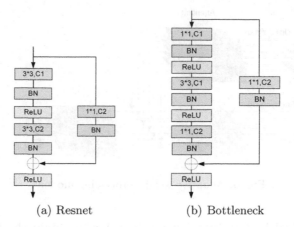

(a) Resnet   (b) Bottleneck

Fig. 2. Illustration of existing convolution blocks and bottleneck residual block.

3.2   Adaptive Weight Processing Module

Multi-scale feature fusion has an important impact on edge detection networks. The deep features have high-level semantic information and the receptive field is relatively large, while the shallow features have location information and the receptive field is relatively small. The fusion of the two features can achieve the purpose of enhancing the deep features and make the deep layers have more abundant edge information such as HED, RCF, BDCN, LPCB. However, these methods ignore the contribution value between different layer feature maps, and fuse the generated different feature map information with the same weight. In the DexiNed Network paper [10], the author assigns different weight values to different feature maps in the form of hyperparameters. Inspired by this, we add weight parameters to each output feature map of the network, so that the network can automatically learn the weight values of different feature maps. The structure is shown in the Fig. 3. This module mainly consists of two branches, one of which learns the importance of different channel features in each feature map by using the Squeeze-and-Excitation (SE) module [6,21], while the other branch learns the weight value of each pixel on the feature map. The specific steps are as follows:

For one of the branches above, we first initialize a weight map for each output feature map of different layers, and then upsample each weight map to the size of the output feature map. Finally, it is converted into a classification probability map using the softmax function as the final attention weight map. The following branch is to use the feature maps of different sizes obtained by the backbone network to first use the SeLayer module to obtain the attention weight values of different channels of each feature map, and then upsample the weighted feature maps to obtain weighted feature maps. Finally, the obtained weighted feature

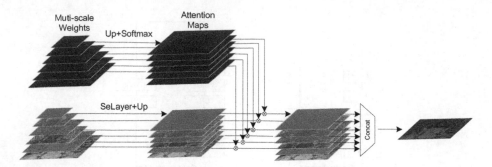

Fig. 3. Adaptive weight processing module.

map is multiplied by the attention weight value to obtain the final predicted feature map. The formula is expressed as:

$$\hat{P} = softmax_i(U(G_i(F_i))) \odot U(S_i(F_i)) \tag{1}$$

where $U(\cdot)$ denotes deconvolution to the same output feature map. F_i, G_i denote muti-scale weight maps and attention layers, which can all be implemented using 1*1 convolution. S_i denotes different SeLayers.

3.3 Loss Functions

Generally in edge detection network, people use balanced cross entropy loss function to solve the problem of imbalance between edge and non-edge samples. This loss function has a significant improvement effect on edge detection network [23–25]. However, it cannot solve the hard samples between edges and non-edges well, which makes the network generate a thicker edge map. To solve this problem, we propose a hybrid loss function, which can effectively solve hard samples and guarantee the consistency of the structure. We define the hybrid loss function as follows:

$$\mathcal{L} = \alpha_k \ell_{pfl} + \beta_k \ell_{ssim} \tag{2}$$

where ℓ_{pfl} is pixel-level focal loss(PFL), α and β are the weight values of each loss, respectively. We generally set α and β to 1 and 0.001, respectively. ℓ_{ssim} is Structural Similarity loss(SSIM). Our edge detection model is deeply supervised with six side outputs. These edge output feature maps are fused to obtain the final predicted feature map.

$$\ell_{pfl} = -\sum_{i,j}[\alpha(G(i,j)(1-P(i,j))^\gamma \log(P(i,j)) + (1-\alpha)(1-G(i,j))(P(i,j))^\gamma \log(1-P(i,j))]$$
$$\tag{3}$$

where $G(i,j) \in \{0,1\}$ is the groud truth label of the pixel(i,j) and P(i,j) is the predicted probability of edge. $\alpha = \frac{|Y^-|}{|Y^-|+|Y^+|}$ and $1 - \alpha = \frac{|Y^+|}{|Y^-|+|Y^+|}$ ($|Y^-|$ and $|Y^+|$ are the edge and non-edge, respectively.). γ is a hyper-parameters.

For an image, most of the pixels are non-edge, which leads to a very imbalance between edge and non-edge samples. α is a variable that achieves the balance between edge pixels and non-edge pixel samples. γ is a hyperparameter used to balance hard and easy samples, which needs to be set manually. For hard samples that are inaccurately classified, $(1 - P(i,j)) \rightarrow 1$, the loss value will not change. For samples with accurate classification, the loss value will decrease. By increasing the weight of hard samples in the loss function, the loss function is more inclined to the training of hard samples, which will help improve the classification accuracy of hard samples.

The SSIM is a metric used to measure the similarity between the reconstructed image and the original image. It can well capture the structural information of the image. Therefore, we add this loss into our loss function to capture the structural information of the edge detection label image. We take a patch of the same size from the predicted probability map and the binarized label map as the representation of x and y, respectively. where $x = \{x_i : i = 1, \dots, N^2\}$ and $y = \{y_i : i = 1, \dots, N^2\}$, The definition of SSIM is as follows:

$$\ell_{ssim} = 1 - \frac{(\mu_x^2 \mu_y^2 + C_1)(\sigma_x^2 + \sigma_y^2 + C_2)}{(2\mu_x \mu_y + C_1)(2\sigma_{xy} + C_2)} \tag{4}$$

where μ_x, μ_y and σ_x, σ_y represent the mean and variance of x and y, respectively. σ_{xy} is covariance. C_1 and C_2 are two very small values to avoid denominator of zero.

The SSIM loss assigns higher weight information to the edges of the image, which helps to focus the optimization on the edges. As network training progresses, edge and non-edge samples will be equally trained. This ensures that there are still enough gradients to drive the parameter optimization of the network.

4   Experimental Results and Analysis

4.1   Dataset Descriptions and Experiment Setup

There are many datasets for edge detection such as PASCAL, NYUD V2, BIPED, BSDS500. PASCAL-VOC dataset contains 21 categories with a total of 2913 images, 1464 in the training set and 1449 in the validation set. The NYUD V2 dataset consists of 1449 images of 640*480. It is composed of 795 training and 654 test images. BSDS500 is a dataset provided by the computer vision group of the University of Berkeley and is mainly used for image segmentation and object edge detection. There are 200, 100, and 100 images in the training set, validation set, and test set of the dataset, respectively. This dataset was manually annotated by 5 different people. That is, each image has 5 groundtruths. Generally, these annotation information can be used to increase data during network training. The BIPED dataset consists of 250 outdoor 1280*720 images, which are carefully annotated manually. Compared with several other datasets, the BIPED dataset has relatively rich edge texture annotation information. Therefore, we choose

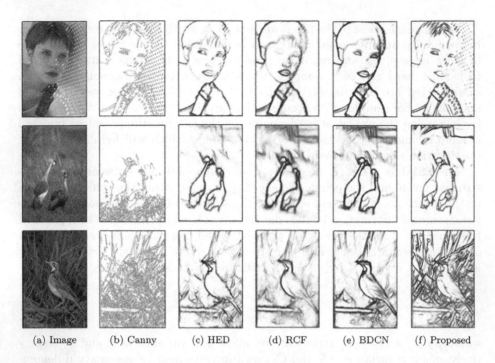

(a) Image   (b) Canny   (c) HED   (d) RCF   (e) BDCN   (f) Proposed

Fig. 4. BSDS500 dataset.

the BIPED dataset as the training dataset for our network. We randomly select 200 images from this dataset as training samples for the network. For testing, we selected some Dunhuang mural and BSDS500 dataset.

We use the pytorch platform to complete the construction of the entire model. The model converges after 30k iterations using the Adam optimizer with batch-size set to 8 and learning rate set to 1e-6. The model will be trained on two 2080Ti GPUs for about 15 days. The hyperparameters of the network include: batch size(8), learning rate(1e-6), weight-decay(1e-4), Image size(512*512). We use the adam optimizer to train our network. In addition to setting the above hyperparameters, the following strategies are used:

Data Augmentation: We perform data enhancement on 200 images in the BIPED dataset in terms of brightness, contrast, color, etc. We randomly set the color, contrast, and brightness values from 0.5 to 1.5, then we randomly rotate these images from 0 to 360, and finally crop these images to 512*512 to get an enhanced training dataset.

Feature Fusion: We use different feature enhancement methods for different feature layers. Two feature fusion methods, add and concat, are used between different blocks in the top-down path and within blocks respectively. The concat method increases the features of the image itself, while the information under each feature does not increase. However, the add method increases the amount

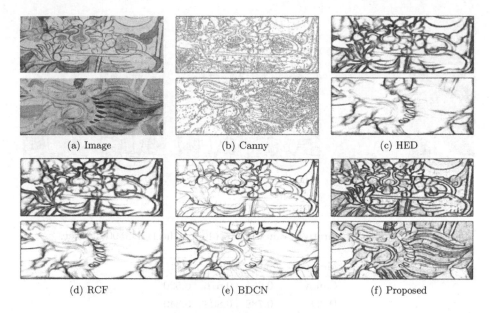

|(a) Image|(b) Canny|(c) HED|
|(d) RCF|(e) BDCN|(f) Proposed|

Fig. 5. Partial mural dataset.

of feature information of the image, but the dimension of the image itself does not increase. The combination of the two can make the network better extract the feature information of the image.

4.2   Performance on Public TestSet

We use the BSDS500 test dataset and the NYUD V2 dataset to evaluate the model on three standard evaluation metrics: Average Precision(AP), Optimal Dataset Scale(ODS) and Optimal Image Scale(OIS), In order to ensure the fairness of the comparison of various algorithms, we do not use non-maximal suppression for the final results obtained by all algorithms.

We compare our method with some state-of-the-art image edge detection methods on two public datasets, including HED, RCF, BDCN, DDS, etc. The evaluation results are shown in Fig. 7. Our method is not accurate when the recall rate is low in Fig. 7(a). The main reason is that the upsampling refinement module in the model captures the edge features of the image too much, resulting in some false positives in the prediction results. In general, our method achieves state-of-the-art results on most evaluation metrics, both in terms of BSDS500 and NYUD V2 dataset. We perform a quantitative comparison of the results in Table 1 and Table 2. On the BSDS500 dataset, the ODS and OIS F-measure of our method are 1.4% and 1.7% higher than DDS, respectively. For the NYUD V2 dataset, our method improves the ODS and OIS f-measure evaluation metrics by 1.4% and 2.6% compared with DDS, respectively.

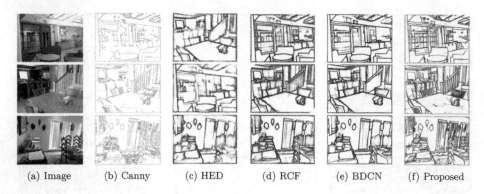

(a) Image   (b) Canny   (c) HED   (d) RCF   (e) BDCN   (f) Proposed

Fig. 6. NYUD dataset.

Table 1. The quantitative evaluation results on the BSDS500 dataset.

Method	ODS	OIS	AP
Canny	0.661	0.676	0.520
HED	0.788	0.808	0.840
RCF	0.811	0.830	0.846
BDCN	0.814	0.833	0.847
DexiNed-a	0.817	0.828	0.841
DDS	0.815	0.834	0.834
Ours	**0.829**	**0.851**	**0.857**

Figure 4 and Fig. 6 show some visualization results of different methods in the public dataset BSDS500 and NYUD V2 dataset, respectively. It can be seen from the different visual effects of different detection methods. Compared with several existing deep learning-based edge detection methods, The traditional Canny algorithm has a phenomenon of edge discontinuous and excessive segmentation. The reason for this phenomenon may be due to the lack of some high-level semantic information. Compared with the Canny algorithm, although HED, RCF, BDCN can generate a better edge map, they not only generate a relatively thick outline, but also lost a lot of detailed in- formation. From the experimental results, our method generates relatively clear edges and preserves more detailed information.

4.3   Performance on Mural TestSet

We use a variety of common algorithms to generate contour maps on the Dunhuang mural dataset, and the results are shown in Fig. 8. As can be seen from the actual visualization, our method can not only achieve the outline extraction of mural figures, but also obtain relatively clear edges for some areas with complex textures in the murals. We visualized the edge detection results of different edge

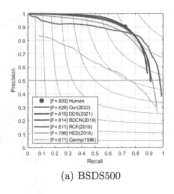 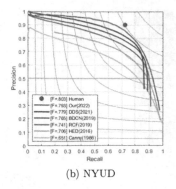

(a) BSDS500   (b) NYUD

Fig. 7. PR curves for different algorithms.

Table 2. The quantitative evaluation results on NYUD V2 dataset.

Method	ODS	OIS	AP
Canny	0.651	0.667	0.653
HED	0.706	0.734	0.549
RCF	0.741	0.757	0.749
BDCN	0.765	0.780	0.760
DexiNed-a	0.601	0.614	0.485
DDS	0.779	0.793	0.772
Ours	**0.793**	**0.819**	**0.849**

detection methods on the local pattern of the mural in Fig. 5. It can be seen that our method can obtain relatively clear edge contours, and other methods have some loss of details for the hands of mural characters and complex textured patterns. And for the line drawing extraction of the entire mural, the traditional Canny edge detector has a very serious over-segmentation effect on the detection of image edges. For the HED network, the texture details inside the mural task are lost, and the ideal detection effect cannot be achieved. However, the RCF and BDCN networks have produced relatively good results for the contour extraction of murals, but produced a relatively blurred segmentation effect at the edge of the image, and the loss of details in the murals is more serious.

From the above qualitative and quantitative results, our method gets satisfactory results on both the BSDS500 and NYUD V2 datasets. Moreover, our method also achieves relatively good visual effects on the mural dataset. The main reasons include the following three points: i) From the quantitative comparison of the above methods on public datasets, it can be seen that the adaptive weight strategy can more effectively balance the weight information of different levels of feature maps to obtain richer prediction feature maps. ii) Our proposed Bi-Dexined network can capture the details in the image edges more effectively. This is evidenced by visualizations from common datasets and mural datasets.

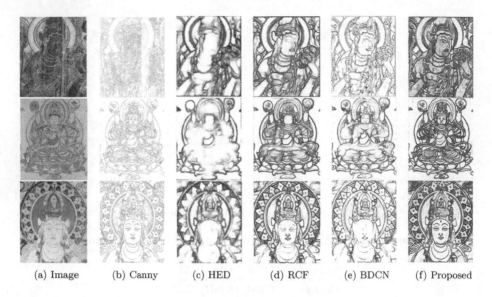

| (a) Image | (b) Canny | (c) HED | (d) RCF | (e) BDCN | (f) Proposed |

Fig. 8. Mural dataset.

iii) It can be seen from the portion edge contour map of the mural that the hybrid loss is used in the edge detection network, which can make the network generate relatively thin and continuous edges.

5   Conclusion

A network based on Bi-Dexined network and adaptive weight learning is proposed to generate clearer relatively clear line drawings of murals. It mainly consists of three parts: i) A novel network architecture can capture more detailed information in images through multiple cross-layer fusions. ii) A new hybrid loss function, on the one hand, can effectively solve the imbalance of positive and negative samples and the training problem of hard samples, on the other hand, it can effectively constrain the structural information of the generated edge map. iii) The adaptive weight learning strategy can dynamically balance the weight effects of different scale feature maps on the final prediction results. For the first time, we use a fully convolutional end-to-end network to generate edge contour maps of murals. The visualization results on public and mural datasets show that our proposed method can capture more edge details and generate sharper edge maps compared to existing methods. In the next work, we will combine edge detection and image inpainting networks to achieve occlusion and contour completion of damaged regions in images.

Acknowledgment. This work was supported in part by the National Natural Science Foundation of China (No. 61866033), the Outstanding Graduate "Innovation Star" of Gansu Province (No. 2022CXZX-202), the Introduction of Talent Research Project of

Northwest Minzu University (No. xbmuyjrc201904), and the Fundamental Research Funds for the Central Universities of Northwest Minzu University (No. 31920220019, 31920220130), and the Leading Talent of National Ethnic Affairs Commission (NEAC), the Young Talent of NEAC, and the Innovative Research Team of NEAC (2018) 98.

References

1. Canny, J.: A computational approach to edge detection. IEEE Trans. Pattern Anal. Mach. Intell. **6**, 679–698 (1986)
2. Xie, S., Tu, Z.: Holistically-nested edge detection. In: Proceedings of the IEEE International Conference on Computer Vision, pp. 1395–1403 (2015)
3. Liu, Y., et al.: Richer convolutional features for edge detection. In: Proceedings of the IEEE Conference on Computer Vision and Pattern Recognition, pp. 3000–3009 (2017)
4. Deng, R., et al.: Learning to predict crisp boundaries. In: Proceedings of the European Conference on Computer Vision (ECCV), pp. 562–578 (2018)
5. He, J., et al.: Bi-directional cascade network for perceptual edge detection. In: Proceedings of the IEEE/CVF Conference on Computer Vision and Pattern Recognition, pp. 3828–3837 (2019)
6. Hu, J., Shen, L., Sun, G.: Squeeze-and-excitation networks. In: Proceedings of the IEEE Conference on Computer Vision and Pattern Recognition, pp. 7132–7141 (2018)
7. Shen, W., et al.: Deepcontour: a deep convolutional feature learned by positive-sharing loss for contour detection. In: Proceedings of the IEEE Conference on Computer Vision and Pattern Recognition, pp. 3982–3991 (2015)
8. Pu, M., Huang, Y., Guan, Q., et al.: RINDNet: edge detection for discontinuity in reflectance, illumination, normal and depth. In: Proceedings of the IEEE/CVF International Conference on Computer Vision, pp. 6879–6888 (2021)
9. Iandola, F., Moskewicz, M., Karayev, S., et al.: DenseNet: implementing efficient convnet descriptor pyramids. arXiv preprint arXiv:1404.1869 (2014)
10. Poma, X.S., Riba, E., Sappa, A.: Dense extreme inception network: towards a robust CNN model for edge detection. In: Proceedings of the IEEE/CVF Winter Conference on Applications of Computer Vision, pp. 1923–1932 (2020)
11. Deng, R., Liu, S.: Deep structural contour detection. In: Proceedings of the 28th ACM International Conference on Multimedia, pp. 304–312 (2020)
12. Ronneberger, O., Fischer, P., Brox, T.: U-Net: convolutional networks for biomedical image segmentation. In: Navab, N., Hornegger, J., Wells, W.M., Frangi, A.F. (eds.) MICCAI 2015. LNCS, vol. 9351, pp. 234–241. Springer, Cham (2015). https://doi.org/10.1007/978-3-319-24574-4_28
13. Yu, Z., Feng, C., Liu, M.Y., et al.: CASENet: deep category-aware semantic edge detection. In: Proceedings of the IEEE Conference on Computer Vision and Pattern Recognition, pp. 5964–5973 (2017)
14. Wang, Y., Zhao, X., Huang, K.: Deep crisp boundaries. In: Proceedings of the IEEE Conference on Computer Vision and Pattern Recognition, pp. 3892–3900 (2017)
15. Lei, P., Li, F., Todorovic, S.: Boundary flow: a siamese network that predicts boundary motion without training on motion. In: Proceedings of the IEEE Conference on Computer Vision and Pattern Recognition, pp. 3282–3290 (2018)

16. Acuna, D., Kar, A., Fidler, S.: Devil is in the edges: learning semantic boundaries from noisy annotations. In: Proceedings of the IEEE/CVF Conference on Computer Vision and Pattern Recognition, pp. 11075–11083 (2019)
17. Fu, J., Liu, J., Tian, H., et al.: Dual attention network for scene segmentation. In: Proceedings of the IEEE/CVF Conference on Computer Vision and Pattern Recognition, pp. 3146–3154 (2019)
18. Yang, J., Price, B., Cohen, S., et al.: Object contour detection with a fully convolutional encoder-decoder network. In: Proceedings of the IEEE Conference on Computer Vision and Pattern Recognition, pp. 193–202 (2016)
19. Xue, N., Wu, T., Bai, S., et al.: Holistically-attracted wireframe parsing. In: Proceedings of the IEEE/CVF Conference on Computer Vision and Pattern Recognition, pp. 2788–2797 (2020)
20. Yu, Z., Liu, W., Zou, Y., et al.: Simultaneous edge alignment and learning. In: Proceedings of the European Conference on Computer Vision (ECCV), pp. 388–404 (2018)
21. Liu, Y., Lew, M.S.: Learning relaxed deep supervision for better edge detection. In: Proceedings of the IEEE Conference on Computer Vision and Pattern Recognition, pp. 231–240 (2016)
22. Khoreva, A., Benenson, R., Omran, M., et al.: Weakly supervised object boundaries. In: Proceedings of the IEEE Conference on Computer Vision and Pattern Recognition, pp. 183–192 (2016)
23. Zhang, Z., Xing, F., Shi, X., et al.: SemiContour: a semi-supervised learning approach for contour detection. In: Proceedings of the IEEE Conference on Computer Vision and Pattern Recognition, pp. 251–259 (2016)
24. Hu, Y., Chen, Y., Li, X., et al.: Dynamic feature fusion for semantic edge detection. arXiv preprint arXiv:1902.09104 (2019)
25. Xu, D., Ouyang, W., Alameda-Pineda, X., et al.: Learning deep structured multiscale features using attention-gated CRFs for contour prediction. Adv. Neural Inf. Process. Syst. **30** (2017)

Attention-Based Fusion of Directed Rotation Graphs for Skeleton-Based Dynamic Hand Gesture Recognition

Ningwei Xie$^{(\boxtimes)}$ (iD), Wei Yu, Lei Yang, Meng Guo, and Jie Li

China Mobile Research Institute, Beijing 100032, China
xieningwei@chinamobile.com

Abstract. Recent works on skeleton-based hand gesture recognition proposed graph-based representation of hand skeleton. In this paper, we propose a new attention-based directed rotation graph fusion method for skeleton-based hand gesture recognition. First, we present a novel double-stream directed rotation graph feature to jointly capture the spatiotemporal dynamics and hand structural information. We utilize the bone direction and rotation information to model the kinematic dependency and relative geometry in hand skeleton. The spatial stream employs a spatial directed rotation graph (SDRG) containing joint position and rotation information to model spatial dependencies between joints. The temporal stream employs a temporal directed rotation graph (TDRG), containing joint displacement and rotation between frames to model temporal dependencies. We design a new attention-based double-stream fusion framework ADF-DGNN, in which the two streams are fed into two directed graph neural networks (DGNNs), and the encoded graphs are concatenated and fused by a fusion module with multi-head attention to generate expressive and discriminative characteristics for identifying hand gesture. The experiments on DHG-14/28 dataset demonstrate the effectiveness of the components of the proposed method and its superiority compared with state-of-the-art methods.

Keywords: Dynamic hand gesture recognition · Directed rotation graphs · Multi-head attention · Directed neural networks · Double-stream fusion

1 Introduction

Dynamic hand gesture recognition is an active research area, attracts increasing interests due to its potential applications in various fields, e.g., human-computer interaction. Previous methods can be divided into two categories by the modality of inputs: image-based (RGB or RGB-D) [1] and skeleton-based methods. Compared to image data, skeleton-based data is more informative and robust against low-level issues in RGB imagery, e.g., light variation and occlusions. Therefore, we follow the research on skeleton-based method. Traditional methods [2–5] designed hand-crafted features to model dynamics of hand gestures. However, these features are inadequate to capture high-level semantics.

© The Author(s), under exclusive license to Springer Nature Switzerland AG 2022
S. Yu et al. (Eds.): PRCV 2022, LNCS 13534, pp. 293–304, 2022.
https://doi.org/10.1007/978-3-031-18907-4_23

Deep-learning-based methods [6–13] have significantly improved the recognition performance. They represent skeletal data by pseudo-images or sequential features, which are learned by neural networks to generate high-level features. However, these methods cannot explicitly model the hand structures.

Inspired by graph-learning based methods [14–16, 19, 22] in the action recognition field, recent works [17, 18] started to employ graph-based representation to jointly model structures and dynamics of hand skeleton. Li et al. [17] adapted the spatial-temporal graph convolutional network (ST-GCN) [14]. Chen et al. [18] applied multi-head attention (MHA) to automatically learn multiple graph structures with multi-head attention mechanism [23]. Unfortunately, these methods only consider joint information in graph construction, which causes loss of skeleton information. The bone information, including the bone direction and bone dynamics, and joint information can be complementary to each other and combined to form complete skeleton representation [19]. Besides, these methods lack of the analysis of rotation information underlying in hand skeleton, which better reflects subtle differences between similar gestures than position information. Employing the rotation information can further improve the recognition of the fine-grained hand gesture patterns with high intra-class variance and low inter-class variance [17]. Furthermore, the motion information in dynamic hand gesture is not explicitly analyzed.

To solve the problems, we propose an attention-based directed rotation graph fusion method for skeleton-based hand gesture recognition. First, we design a new double-stream directed rotation graph feature. We represent the joints and bones in each frame as the vertices and edges within a directed acyclic graph and define the bone direction to model the kinematic dependencies in hand skeleton. The spatial stream is composed of the spatial directed rotation graphs (SDRGs), each of which describes joint position and rotation between connected joints in a certain frame, to model the spatial dependencies. The temporal stream consists of the temporal directed rotation graphs (TDRGs), which employ joint displacement and temporal rotation between adjacent frames to model the temporal dependencies in hand gesture sequence.

DGNN is a network structure designed for directed acyclic graphs [16], which propagates and aggregates the attributes of vertices and edges, and updates the graph topology. Motivated by applications of DGNNs [25] and MHA [18], we design an attention-based double-stream fusion framework of DGNNs, namely ADF-DGNN, to perform joint spatiotemporal graph modelling and to adaptively fuse the encoded graph features utilizing multi-head attention mechanism. We employ two identical DGNN branches to model SDRGs and TDRGs. Then, the attention-based fusion module concatenates and fuses the two streams of encoded graph features. The spatial and temporal multi-head attention blocks learn multiple types of structural information, exchange and aggregate spatial and temporal information of nodes in concatenated graphs to generate expressive and discriminative characteristics for hand gesture recognition.

We conduct ablation studies and comparative experiments on standard dataset DHG-14/28 [4]. The results demonstrate the effectiveness of its each component and its superiority compared with the state-of-the-arts methods. Our main contributions are summarized as follows:

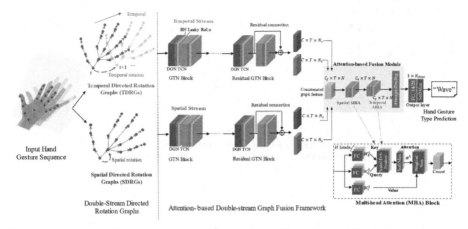

Fig. 1. Architecture of the attention-based fusion of double streams of directed rotation graphs for skeleton-based dynamic hand gesture recognition.

- Double-stream directed rotation graph feature, which employs bone direction and joint rotation to model kinematic dependency and relative geometry between joints, extracts motion information between frames to model temporal dependencies;
- ADF-DGNN framework, which adopts multi-head attention to fuse encoded directed rotation graph features and generates highly expressive and discriminative characteristics for accurate hand gesture recognition.

2 Method

The raw input data is a sequence of T frames, denoted by $\mathcal{S} = \{\mathcal{V}^1, ..., \mathcal{V}^T\}$, each of which contains a set of N_v joint coordinates denoted by $\mathcal{V} = \{\mathbf{v}_k = (x_k, y_k, z_k)\}_{k=1,...,N_v}$ in the 3D world space forming a full hand skeleton. The architecture of the proposed method, as shown in Fig. 1, consists of two major components, the double-stream directed rotation graph feature, and the attention-based double-stream graph fusion framework ADF-DGNN for hand gesture recognition.

2.1 Double-Stream Directed Rotation Graph Feature

In a human body part, there is a hierarchical relationship between the joints. The joints near the center of gravity physically control the more distant joints, e.g., the finger base drives movement of the tip. This kinematic dependency among joints has been proven to be useful for skeleton-based action recognition [16]. Conventional hand skeleton features cannot capture this modality. To address this, we construct a directed acyclic graph to represent hand skeleton and define the bone direction to model the kinematic dependency.

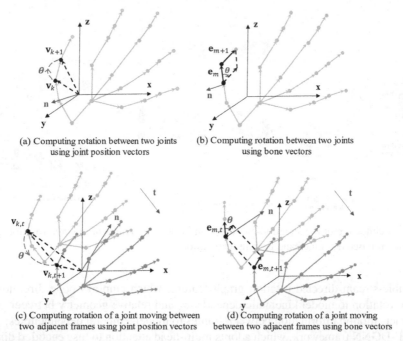

(a) Computing rotation between two joints using joint position vectors

(b) Computing rotation between two joints using bone vectors

(c) Computing rotation of a joint moving between two adjacent frames using joint position vectors

(d) Computing rotation of a joint moving between two adjacent frames using bone vectors

Fig. 2. Two different methods (a) and (b) to compute spatial rotation attributes for edges in spatial directed rotation graphs; two different methods (c) and (d) to compute temporal rotation attributes for edges in temporal directed rotation graphs.

A directed acyclic graph contains vertices and directed edges, which correspond to joints and bones in hand skeleton. The root vertex is defined by *Wrist* joint. Hence, the skeleton is formulated as a directed graph $\mathcal{G} = (\mathcal{V}, \mathcal{E})$, $\mathcal{V} = \{\mathbf{v}_k\}_{k=1,...,N_v}$ represents the vertex set, $\mathcal{E} = \{\mathbf{e}_m = \mathbf{v}_{m+1} - \mathbf{v}_m\}_{m=1,...,N_e}$ represents the set of N_e directed edges. The directed edges always point from vertices near the root (precursors) to vertices far from the root (successors). The initial graph topology is represented by an $N_v \times N_e$ incidence matrix $A = \{A_{k,m}\}_{k=1,...,N_v,m=1,...,N_e}$.

Then, we extract the spatial and temporal attributes for vertices and edges in the directed acyclic graph. The spatial stream $\mathcal{S}^{spatial} = \{\mathcal{G}^1, ..., \mathcal{G}^T\}$ consists of a series of SDRGs, in which each frame is a directed acyclic graph with topology represented by A. The attributes of SDRGs are denoted by $\mathbf{F}^{spatial} = (\mathbf{f}_v^{spatial}, \mathbf{f}_e^{spatial})$. The spatial vertex attribute $\mathbf{f}_v^{spatial}$ is a $C_{in} \times T \times N_v$ matrix of joint coordinates with channel number $C_{in} = 3$, describing the spatial position information of joints in each frame. Similarly, TDRGs forming the temporal stream $\mathcal{S}^{temporal} = \{\widehat{\mathcal{G}}^1, ..., \widehat{\mathcal{G}}^T\}$, share the same topology with the spatial graphs, the temporal attributes are denoted by $\mathbf{F}^{temporal} = (\mathbf{f}_v^{temporal}, \mathbf{f}_e^{temporal})$. The temporal vertex attribute $\mathbf{f}_v^{temporal}$ is the joint displacement matrix of size $C_{in} \times T \times N_v$. The joint displacement [16] is defined by the temporal difference of a joint's coordinate vectors in two adjacent frames, i.e., $\widehat{\mathbf{v}}_k^t = \mathbf{v}_k^{t+1} - \mathbf{v}_k^t$, where $\mathbf{v}_k^t$ and $\mathbf{v}_k^{t+1}$ are the coordinate vectors of vertex $\mathbf{v}_k$ at frame t and $t+1$ respectively.

Different from existing directed graph features employing the bone position vector and the bone displacement [16], we extract spatial and temporal rotation information from hand skeleton as the spatial and temporal edge attributes. It captures the relative geometry between connected joints and reflects subtle differences between similar gesture patterns. Besides, it remains insensitive to scale problems, e.g., difference of bone length of different individuals.

We set the spatial edge attribute $\mathbf{f}_e^{spatial}$ as a matrix of size $C_{in} \times T \times N_e$, composed of the Euler angles of joints relative to their successors in each frame. The temporal edge attribute $\mathbf{f}_e^{temporal}$ is a matrix of size $C_{in} \times T \times N_e$, composed of the Euler angles of each joint rotating between adjacent frames.

Formally, given two vectors $\mathbf{v}_1 = (x_1, y_1, z_1)$ and $\mathbf{v}_2 = (x_2, y_2, z_2)$ in the world coordinate system, the axis-angle representation of the rotation from $\mathbf{v}_1$ to $\mathbf{v}_2$ is formulated as:

$$\mathbf{n} = \mathbf{v}_1 \times \mathbf{v}_2, \quad \theta = \arccos(\frac{\mathbf{v}_1 \cdot \mathbf{v}_2}{|\mathbf{v}_1||\mathbf{v}_2|}). \tag{1}$$

The corresponding rotation matrix $\mathbf{R} \in \mathbb{R}^3 \times \mathbb{R}^3$ can be calculated using Rodrigues' rotation formula. Then, $\mathbf{R}$ is converted to the Euler angles using the method in [20].

There are two different ways to express the spatial rotation between connected joints, as shown in Fig. 2(a) and (b). One is to compute rotation from joint $\mathbf{v}_k$ to its successor $\mathbf{v}_{k+1}$ using their position vectors, the other [21] is to compute rotation from $\mathbf{e}_m$ to $\mathbf{e}_{m+1}$, which are the bone vectors starting from $\mathbf{v}_k$ and $\mathbf{v}_{k+1}$ respectively. Similarly, there are also two ways to express the joint temporal rotation, as shown in Fig. 2(c) and (d). One is using two position vectors of a joint rotating from a frame to the next frame, the other is using joint's out-coming bone vectors between the two frames.

In practice, we assume the incidence matrix is square, i.e., $N_v = N_e$, so we add a meaningless edge, whose attributes are all set to 0. The joint displacement and temporal rotation of the last time step are padded with 0.

2.2 Attention-Based Double-Stream Fusion Framework

Spatiotemporal Graph Learning by DGNNs. The basic graph-learning component of DGNNs is the directed graph network (DGN). Given the input vertex attribute matrix $\mathbf{f}_v$ and edge attribute matrix $\mathbf{f}_e$, the graph updating operation of DGN is formulated as:

$$\begin{aligned} \tilde{\mathbf{f}}_v &= \mathbf{H}_v([\mathbf{f}_v, \mathbf{f}_e \overline{A}^{s\top}, \mathbf{f}_e \overline{A}^{t\top}]), \\ \tilde{\mathbf{f}}_e &= \mathbf{H}_e([\mathbf{f}_e, \mathbf{f}_v \overline{A}^s, \mathbf{f}_v \overline{A}^t]). \end{aligned} \tag{2}$$

Here, $[\cdot, \cdot]$ denotes the concatenation operation, H denotes the fully-connected layer. A^s is the source incidence matrix, A^t is the target incidence matrix. The normalized version of A is defined as $\overline{A} = A\Lambda^{-1}$, $\Lambda_{i,i} = \sum_j A_{i,j} + \varepsilon$, where ε is a small number. In training procedure, incidence matrices can be learned as parameters. In this way, DGN is able to update the graph topology for better network optimization.

For temporal domain, the temporal convolutional network (TCN) [14, 16, 22] is adopted to add contextual information to graphs. We perform $k_t \times 1$ convolution on updated vertex attribute $\tilde{f}_v$ and the updated edge attribute $\tilde{f}_e$, and obtain convoluted results $\tilde{f}'_v$ and $\tilde{f}'_e$. k_t is the kernel size of temporal dimension. We combine the spatial graph learning with the temporal convolution into a basic spatiotemporal graph modelling module, indicated by GTN [16] in Fig. 1.

To increase the computing capability, we stack multiple GTN blocks in series and add residual connections to non-input GTN blocks. The residuals are defined as the vertex and edges attributes processed only by the TCN, indicated by $\mathbf{f}'_v, \mathbf{f}'_e$. The residuals are element-wisely added to original block outputs $\tilde{f}_v$ and $\tilde{f}_e$, respectively. Therefore, the outputs of residual GTN are formulated as $\mathbf{f}_v^{res} = \tilde{f}_v + \mathbf{f}'_v, \mathbf{f}_e^{res} = \tilde{f}_e + \mathbf{f}'_e$.

In the ADF-DGNN, we employ two identical DGNN branches to separately model the spatial and the temporal streams of directed rotation graph features. The spatial DGNN branch finally outputs the encoded vertex feature $\mathbf{f}_v^{spatial}$ of size $C \times T \times N_v$ and encoded edge feature $\mathbf{f}_e^{spatial}$ of size $C \times T \times N_e$, where C is the output channel number. Similarly, the temporal branch outputs encoded features $\mathbf{f}_v^{temporal}$ and $\mathbf{f}_e^{temporal}$.

Attention-Based Fusion Module. To combine the spatial and temporal streams for hand gesture recognition, we propose designing a fusion module, by which the two streams of information are fully exchanged and fused to participate in the end-to-end network optimization. We apply the multi-head attention (MHA) mechanism [23], as illustrated by the dotted box in Fig. 1.

For each frame, we concatenate the spatial and temporal graphs to form a single graph, in which each node contains all encoded spatial and temporal features of its corresponding vertex and edge. Therefore, the four encoded feature tensors $\mathbf{f}_v^{spatial}$, $\mathbf{f}_e^{spatial}$, $\mathbf{f}_v^{temporal}$, $\mathbf{f}_e^{temporal}$ are stacked along the channel dimension to obtain the $C_f \times T \times N$ feature tensor $\mathbf{f}$ of concatenated graphs, which is successively fused by the spatial and temporal MHA blocks [18].

Given the feature vector $\mathbf{f}_{t,i}$ of the node $\mathbf{v}_i^t$ in the concatenated graph at frame t, the h-th spatial attention head applies three fully-connected (FC) layers to map $\mathbf{f}_{t,i}$ into the key, query and value vectors, indicated by $\mathbf{K}_{t,i}^h, \mathbf{Q}_{t,i}^h, \mathbf{V}_{t,i}^h$. The spatial attention head computes the attention weight between nodes $\mathbf{v}_i^t$ and $\mathbf{v}_j^t$ as follows:

$$u_{(t,i)\to(t,j)}^h = \frac{\left\langle \mathbf{Q}_{t,i}^h, \mathbf{K}_{t,j}^h \right\rangle}{\sqrt{d}},$$

$$\alpha_{(t,i)\to(t,j)}^h = \frac{\exp(u_{(t,i)\to(t,j)}^h)}{\sum_{n=1}^N \exp(u_{(t,i)\to(t,n)}^h)}. \tag{3}$$

Here, d is the dimension of the key, query and value vectors, $u_{(t,i)\to(t,j)}^h$ is the scaled dot-product [23] of the query vector and the key vector of the two nodes within the same time step, then it is normalized by the SoftMax function. The attention weight measures the importance of information from $\mathbf{v}_i^t$ to $\mathbf{v}_j^t$, reflects the implicit association relationships between nodes learned by the attention head. To avoid the information passing in temporal domain, weights between nodes in different time steps are set to 0.

Then, each head calculates the weighted graph feature. In this procedure, information in nodes is transferred within same time step and aggregated based on the learned weights:

$$\mathbf{F}_{t,i}^h = \sum_{j=1}^{N} (\alpha_{(t,i) \to (t,j)}^h \cdot \mathbf{V}_{t,j}^h),\tag{4}$$

where $\mathbf{F}_{t,i}^h$ is the attention-weighted feature of the node $\mathbf{v}_i^t$ at frame t learned by the h-th head. The spatial MHA block finally concatenated the spatial attention features learned by all heads into $\mathbf{F}_{t,i}$. The obtained feature contains multiple types of structural information learned by different spatial attention heads.

Table 1. Ablation study on feature settings.

Features	Models	DHG-14	DHG-28
SDG	DGNN	92.91	89.12
TDG		90.89	86.95
SDRG-joint		93.27	89.9
SDRG-bone		91.53	87.03
TDRG-joint		92.05	87.72
TDRG-bone		89.79	85.44
SDG+TDG	**ADF-DGNN**	93.48	90.01
SDRG-joint+TDRG-joint		**94.46**	**91.61**
SDRG-bone+TDRG-bone		91.67	87.28

The temporal MHA block takes the output feature of spatial MHA block as its input and applies the above mechanism to the temporal domain. In this way, the result feature encodes the expressive and discriminative characteristics of hand gesture sequence in both spatial and temporal domains. We average-pool the result feature over node and temporal dimension, project it into a vector of size $1 \times N_{class}$ by a FC output layer. Finally, we employ the SoftMax function to make the prediction for the hand gesture label.

3 Experiments

In this section, we first describe the DHG-14/28 dataset and the implementation details of the proposed method. Then, we conduct ablation studies to evaluate the effectiveness of each component. Finally, we report the comparison results with the state-of-the-arts.

3.1 Experimental Setup

Dataset. The DHG-14/28 dataset [4] consists of 2800 video sequences covering 14 hand gesture types. Each gesture is performed 5 times by 20 performers in two configurations: using one finger and the whole hand. The sequences can be labeled with 14 or 28 classes depending on whether the performing configurations are distinguished. The length of the sequences ranges from 20 to 50 frames. Each frame contains the coordinates of 22 joints in the 3D world space forming a hand skeleton.

Implementation Details. We conduct preprocessing for raw input data. First, we uniformly sample all sequences to 20 frames. Then, we subtract every sequence by the Palm joint position of the first frame for alignment [5]. For fair comparison, we adopt the same data augmentation operations as the previous methods [5, 8, 18], including scaling, shifting, time interpolation and adding noise. We randomly select 70% sequences from every gesture for training and rest for validation. The performance criterion is defined by the average accuracy of 14 gestures or 28 gestures on the DHG-14/28 validation set.

Table 2. Ablation study on graph-learning modules

Graph-learning modules	Feature	DHG-14	DHG-28
ST-GCN [14]	SDRG-joint+TDRG-joint	92.97	88.8
Motif-ST-GCN [15]		94.02	90.59
GTN [16]		**94.46**	**91.61**

Table 3. Ablation study on fusion methods

Fusion methods	DHG-14	DHG-28
Score fusion [24]	93.74	90.13
FC-based fusion module [25]	94.07	91.5
Attention-based fusion module	**94.46**	**91.61**

In the ADF-DGNN, each DGNN branch consists of one input GTN and two residual GTN blocks. Both the DGN and the TCN are followed by a batch normalization (BN) layer and a Leaky ReLU layer. The output channel dimensions of the three blocks are set to 32, 64 and 64. The temporal convolution kernel sizes of the three blocks are 3, 5, 7, and the stride of the last GTN is set to 2. In the attention-based fusion module, both the spatial and the temporal MHA blocks are followed by a BN layer, a Leaky ReLU layer and a dropout layer. The output dimension of MHA blocks is set to 128. We train the ADF-DGNN to minimize the cross-entropy loss with stochastic gradient descent (SGD) for 200 epochs. We initialize the learning rate as 0.001, set the training batch to 32 and the dropout rate to 0.2.

3.2   Ablation Studies

Ablation Study on Feature Settings. We compare the method performance of different single-stream features, include: (1) spatial directed graph (SDG) [16], with the joint position vector as the vertex attribute, the bone vector as the edge attribute; (2) temporal directed graph (TDG) [16], with the joint displacement as the vertex attribute, the bone displacement as the edge attribute; (3) SDRG-joint, in which the spatial rotation is computed using joint position vectors; (4) SDRG-bone, in which the rotation information is computed using bone vectors; (5) TDRG-joint, in which the temporal rotation is computed using joint vectors in adjacent frames; (6) TDRG-bone, in which the temporal rotation is computed using bone vectors in adjacent frames. These features are modeled by a three-block DGNN followed by an average-pooling layer and the output layer. We also compare the performance of double-stream features modelled by the ADF-DGNN, include: (7) SDG+TDG, (8) SDRG-joint+TDRG-joint, and (9) SDRG-bone+TDRG-bone. The results are shown in Table 1. We observe that SDRG-joint and TDRG-joint perform better than SDG and TDG, respectively. Hence, the directed rotation graph features are demonstrated to be more robust and expressive on differences between similar gestures compared with the directed graph feature employing bone vectors. Besides, SDRG-joint, TDRG-joint, and their fused feature obtain higher accuracies than SDRG-bone, TDRG-bone and SDRG-bone+TDRG-bone, respectively. The rotation information extracted from two joint vectors is more intuitive and more suitable for the modelling by DGNNs. The double-stream features achieve better performance than any of their single streams. Therefore, the superiority of the double-stream fusion strategy, in which the spatial information and the contextual information in temporal domain are complementary to conduct better Laban gesture learning, is verified.

Table 4. Comparison with state-of-the-arts methods

Methods	Year	DHG-14	DHG-28
Motion Manifold [2]	2015	79.61	62.0
SoCJ+HoHD+HoWR [4]	2016	83.1	80.0
Motion Feature+RNN [6]	2017	84.68	80.32
NIUKF-LSTM [7]	2018	84.92	80.44
CNN+LSTM [8]	2018	85.6	81.1
DPTC [9]	2018	85.8	80.2
STA-Res-TCN [10]	2018	89.2	85.0
Parallel CNN [11]	2018	91.28	84.35
ST-GCN [14]	2018	91.2	81.7
HG-GCN [17]	2019	89.2	85.3
DG-STA [18]	2019	91.9	88.0
DGNN (single stream) [16]	2019	92.91	89.12
GREN [12]	2020	82.29	82.03
MLF LSTM (skeleton) [13]	2020	93.69	90.11
Ours		**94.46**	**91.61**

Ablation Study on Graph-Learning Modules. We experiment on different GCN variants ST-GCN [14] and Motif-ST-GCN [15] as the basic graph-learning module to compose the double-stream fusion framework. For fair comparison, we form the spatial stream for the two variants by concatenating the vertex and edge attributes of SDRG-joint along channel dimension. The temporal stream is similarly formed utilizing the vertex and edge attributes of TDRG-joint. The block number, the settings of the hyper-parameters and the attention-based fusion module are identically implemented. The results are shown in Table 2. DGN passes and aggregates the information of vertices and edges according to the bone directions represented by the source and target incidence matrices. Besides, DGN conducts flexible modelling of directed acyclic graphs, for it parameterizes and adaptively updates the graph topology encoded by the incidence matrices during network optimization. Therefore, GTN is more suitable for the skeleton-based hand gesture recognition task.

Ablation Study on Fusion Methods. We compare the performance of different double-stream fusion methods, as shown in Table 3. We experiment on the multiply-score fusion method [24], by which the SoftMax scores output by two pre-trained DGNN branches are multiplied in an element-wise way to generate the final score. We also experiment on a FC-based fusion module [25], in which the concatenated graph feature is only weighted by a single FC layer followed by an average-pooling layer and the output layer. The proposed attention-based fusion module achieves the best result.

Contrast with the score fusion which obtains sub-optimal result from separately trained branches, the proposed module enables the end-to-end training of entire framework to achieve the global optimization. Better than FC-based fusion module which only weights the concatenated graph feature by a single FC layer, the proposed module employs multi-head attention mechanism to generate discriminative spatiotemporal descriptions for hand gesture sequence. Therefore, the effectiveness of the proposed fusion method is verified.

3.3 Comparison with State-of-the-Arts Methods

To prove the superiority of the proposed method, we carry out a comparative survey of previous state-of-the-arts methods on the skeleton-based hand gesture recognition, as shown in Table 4. The compared state-of-the-art methods include traditional approaches using hand-crafted features [2, 4], deep-learning-based approaches [6–13] and graph-based approaches [14, 16–18]. All the above-mentioned methods extract skeleton-based features from hand gesture sequences as input. Our method extracts the double-stream directed rotation graph feature from skeleton-based hand gesture data and performs spatiotemporal graph modelling with the ADF-DGNN. It achieves outstanding performance on both DHG-14 and DHG-28, which demonstrates its superiority and generality for skeleton-based hand gesture recognition.

4   Conclusion

In this paper, we propose an attention-based directed rotation graph fusion method for skeleton-based hand gesture recognition. We extract the double-stream directed rotation graph feature to capture the spatiotemporal dynamics, and model the hand physical structure and kinematic dependency among joints. We design the ADF-DGNN, which employs the attention-based fusion module to fuse the two streams encoded by DGNNs, generates discriminative spatiotemporal descriptions of hand gestures, so that it achieves superior performance in skeleton-based hand gesture recognition.

The experiments on DHG-14/28 show that the attention-based fusion module effectively fuses spatial and temporal streams and achieves at least 1.71% accuracy improvement. The directed rotation graph feature is proven to conduct more robust and accurate description of hand gestures than existing directed graph features. The ablation study on different graph-learning modules verifies the effectiveness of the proposed framework structure. Overall, the proposed method outperforms the state-of-the-art methods with 0.77% accuracy improvement on DHG-14 and 1.5% on DHG-28.

The proposed method can be further modified and generalized to other sequential skeleton-based data, e.g., the skeleton-based action recognition. Our future work may focus on integrating diversity of features extracted from hand gesture videos, e.g., combining directed rotation graphs with RGB and depth information.

References

1. Rautaray, S.S., Agrawal, A.: Vision based hand gesture recognition for human computer interaction: a survey. Artif. Intell. Rev. **43**(1), 1–54 (2012). https://doi.org/10.1007/s10462-012-9356-9
2. Devanne, M., et al.: Human action recognition by shape analysis of motion trajectories on Riemannian manifold. IEEE Trans. Cybern. **45**(7), 1340–1352 (2014)
3. Ohn-Bar, E., Trivedi, M.: Joint angles similarities and HOG2 for action recognition. In: IEEE Conference on Computer Vision and Pattern Recognition Workshops, pp. 465–470. IEEE (2013)
4. De Smedt, Q., Wannous, H., Vandeborre, J.P.: Skeleton-based dynamic hand gesture recognition. In: IEEE Conference on Computer Vision and Pattern Recognition Workshops, pp. 1–9. IEEE (2016)
5. De Smedt, Q., Wannous, H., Vandeborre, J.P.: SHREC'17 track: 3D hand gesture recognition using a depth and skeletal dataset. In: Eurographics Workshop on 3D Object Retrieval (2017)
6. Chen, X., et al. Motion feature augmented recurrent neural network for skeleton-based dynamic hand gesture recognition. In: IEEE International Conference on Image Processing. IEEE (2017)
7. Ma, C., Wang, A., Chen, G., Xu, C.: Hand joints-based gesture recognition for noisy dataset using nested interval unscented Kalman filter with LSTM network. Vis. Comput. **34**(6–8), 1053–1063 (2018). https://doi.org/10.1007/s00371-018-1556-0
8. Nunez, J.C., et al.: Convolutional neural networks and long short-term memory for skeleton-based human activity and hand gesture recognition. Pattern Recogn. **76**, 80–94 (2018)
9. Weng, J., Liu, M., Jiang, X., Yuan, J.: Deformable pose traversal convolution for 3D action and gesture recognition. In: Ferrari, V., Hebert, M., Sminchisescu, C., Weiss, Y. (eds.) ECCV 2018. LNCS, vol. 11211, pp. 142–157. Springer, Cham (2018). https://doi.org/10.1007/978-3-030-01234-2_9
10. Hou, J., Wang, G., Chen, X., Xue, J.-H., Zhu, R., Yang, H.: Spatial-temporal attention res-TCN for skeleton-based dynamic hand gesture recognition. In: Leal-Taixé, L., Roth, S. (eds.) ECCV 2018. LNCS, vol. 11134, pp. 273–286. Springer, Cham (2019). https://doi.org/10.1007/978-3-030-11024-6_18

11. Devineau, G., et al.: Deep learning for hand gesture recognition on skeletal data. In: IEEE International Conference on Automatic Face and Gesture Recognition. IEEE (2018)
12. Ma, C., et al.: Skeleton-based dynamic hand gesture recognition using an enhanced network with one-shot learning. Appl. Sci. **10**(11), 3680 (2020)
13. Do, N.T., et al.: Robust hand shape features for dynamic hand gesture recognition using multi-level feature LSTM. Appl. Sci. **10**(18), 6293 (2020)
14. Yan, S., Xiong, Y., et al.: Spatial temporal graph convolutional networks for skeleton-based action recognition. In: 32th AAAI Conference on Artificial Intelligence (2018)
15. Wen, Y.H., et al.: Graph CNNs with motif and variable temporal block for skeleton-based action recognition. In: 33th AAAI Conference on Artificial Intelligence, vol. 33, pp. 8989–8996. Association for Computing Machinery, New York (2019)
16. Shi, L., et al.: Skeleton-based action recognition with directed graph neural networks. In: IEEE Conference on Computer Vision and Pattern Recognition, pp. 7912–7921. IEEE (2019)
17. Li, Y., et al.: Spatial temporal graph convolutional networks for skeleton-based dynamic hand gesture recognition. EURASIP J. Image Video Process. **1**, 1–7 (2019). https://doi.org/10.1186/s13640-019-0476-x
18. Chen, Y., et al.: Construct dynamic graphs for hand gesture recognition via spatial-temporal attention. arXiv, arXiv:1907.08871 (2019)
19. Shi, L., et al.: Nonlocal graph convolutional networks for skeleton-based action recognition. arXiv, arXiv:1805.07694 (2018)
20. Slabaugh, G.G.: Computing Euler angles from a rotation matrix, pp. 39–63 (1999). Accessed 6 Aug 2000
21. Vemulapalli, R., et al.: Rolling rotations for recognizing human actions from 3D skeletal data. In: IEEE Conference on Computer Vision and Pattern Recognition, pp. 4471–4479. IEEE (2016)
22. Shi, L., et al.: Two-stream adaptive graph convolutional networks for skeleton-based action recognition. In: IEEE Conference on Computer Vision and Pattern Recognition, pp. 12026–12035. IEEE (2019)
23. Vaswani, A., et al.: Attention is all you need. In: Advances in Neural Information Processing Systems 30 (2017)
24. Li, C., et al.: Skeleton-based action recognition using LSTM and CNN. In: IEEE International Conference on Multimedia and Expo Workshops, pp. 585–590. IEEE (2017)
25. Xie, N., et al.: Sequential gesture learning for continuous labanotation generation based on the fusion of graph neural networks. IEEE Trans. Circ. Syst. Video Technol. **32**, 3722–3734 (2021)

SteelyGAN: Semantic Unsupervised Symbolic Music Genre Transfer

Zhaoxu Ding[1], Xiang Liu[1,2], Guoqiang Zhong[1(✉)], and Dong Wang[1]

[1] College of Computer Science and Technology, Ocean University of China, Qingdao, China
gqzhong@ouc.edu.cn
[2] Innovation Center, Ocean University of China, Qingdao, China

Abstract. Recent progress in music genre transfer is greatly influenced by unpaired image-to-image transfer models. However, state-of-the-art unpaired music genre transfer models sometimes cannot keep the basic structure of the original song after genre transfer. In this paper, we propose SteelyGAN, a music genre transfer model that performs style transfer on both pixel-level (2D piano rolls) and latent-level (latent variables), by combining latent space classification loss and semantic consistency loss with cycle-connected generative adversarial networks. We also focus on music generation in individual bars of music with the novel Bar-Unit structure, in order to reduce coupling of music data within a 4-bar segment. We propose a new MIDI dataset, the Free MIDI Library, which features less data duplication and more comprehensive meta-data than other music genre transfer datasets. According to experiments and evaluations we perform separately on three pairs of music genres, namely Metal↔Country, Punk↔Classical and Rock↔Jazz, transferred and cycle-transferred music data generated by SteelyGAN have achieved higher classification accuracy, as well as better objective and subjective evaluation results than those generated by other state-of-the-art models.

Keywords: Symbolic music generation · Music genre transfer · Unpaired transfer

1 Introduction

With the development of deep learning and the expansion of its related fields, some art topics including music style transfer [2–4,14] and music generation [5,23,24] have been explored by many researchers.

Like various painting styles, there are many music genres that are distinguishable from one another, and each of these styles has its own rhythmic (syncopation in Funk, shuffle in Blues and swing in Jazz etc.), tonal (pentatonic

Supplementary Information The online version contains supplementary material available at https://doi.org/10.1007/978-3-031-18907-4_24.

scale and "blue note" in Blues, mixolydian mode in Rock and R&B music etc.) or harmonic features ("power chord" in Rock, dominant chord in Blues and Jazz etc.). Besides basic music genres, there are also many fusion styles that combine different genres of music, creating unique experiences for listeners. Besides fusing different styles of music, transferring pieces between two distinct genres is also an interesting topic, which could provide both novel experience for music listeners and valuable inspiration for musicians.

Musically, genre transfer aims to retain the chord progression and basic melody of the original music, while fusing it with harmonic, rhythm and tonal color of the target genre. For instance, in the case of transferring music from Rock to Jazz, genre transfer is achieved on three levels. Harmonically, we hope to change traids to accordant seventh chords with the same root notes. For example, major chords $(1-3-5)$ to major seventh $(1-3-5-7)$ or dominant seventh chords $(1-3-5-\flat7)$, and minor chords $(1-\flat3-5)$ to minor seventh chords$(1-\flat3-5-\flat7)$. Rhythmically, we hope to change the original 8th or 16th notes to triplets notes, in order to imitate the swing or shuffle rhythm in Jazz. Tonally, chromatic scales are often used in Jazz music, while major and minor scales are most common in Rock, so we hope to add more passing notes to transferred music in order to expand the diatonic scale.

As for music genre transfer task, Brunner et al. [2] design a symbolic music genre transfer model that achieve genre transfer between Jazz, Rock and Classical, by regarding music scores as 2D piano roll tensors like images and transferring them with a cycle-connected generative adversarial networks (GAN) model. However, it often fails to keep the basic structure of the original music, because it is only trained with pixel-level losses, which are classification loss and mean absolute error (MAE) between music data as 2D piano rolls. Considering the unique time-pitch structure of music data, models based on mere pixel-level losses are not enough for music-related tasks, and such models tend to fail when two domains are significantly different. Therefore, latent-level losses are important when it comes to abstract data like music, which include MAE and classification loss between encoded latent variables.

In this paper, we propose *SteelyGAN*, a new symbolic-domain approach to achieve music genre transfer. We name our network SteelyGAN as a tribute to Jazz-Rock band Steely Dan, which is a musical group famous for fusing various music genres including Jazz, Rock, Blues, Funk and Reggae. Architecture of our model is shown in Fig. 1. SteelyGAN adds more restrictions in the latent space on both consistency and distinctiveness between two genres, by considering *semantic consistency loss* and *latent space classification loss*. We also attach more importance to music generation in individual bars of music by implementing *Bar-Unit* structure in our network, which could temporarily decouple music segments into individual bars. We have constructed and used a new MIDI dataset for genre transfer experiment, namely *Free MIDI Library*, which features less data duplication, more available music genres and more easily accessible metadata than prominent MIDI dataset, the Lakh MIDI Dataset.

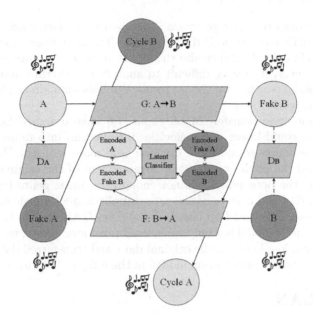

Fig. 1. Structure of the SteelyGAN genre transfer model.

2   Related Work

The idea of style transfer is first put forward by Gatys et al. [6]. With the development of deep convolutional networks [10,20], it is more feasible to extract stylish feature of one particular image, and at the same time, keep its original basic structure.

Since the basic concept of GAN is proposed by Goodfellow et al. [7], further studies including Conditional Generative Adversarial Network (CGAN) [15] and Deep Convolutional Generative Adversarial Network (DCGAN) [17] have introduced extra loss function and deeper CNN architectures into GAN. CycleGAN [27], DiscoGAN [9] and DualGAN [26] have enabled unpaired data translation, and have shown outstanding performance on image style transfer tasks without the need for paired data.

There are also some outstanding models that combine the architecture of Auto-encoder (AE) and Variational Auto-encoder (VAE) with GAN, such as Adversarial Auto-encoder [13] and VAE-GAN [11]. They outperform AE and VAE in latent-level learning, and can generate more realistic images than traditional GAN. Moreover, there are also some models that use both GAN and VAE/AE for unsupervised image-to-image transfer, such as Unsupervised Image-to-image Translation (UNIT) [12], Domain Transfer Network (DTN) [21] and XGAN [18].

With the development of waveform research and MIDI format parsing, advanced music generation systems are emerging, which can be divided into two main groups, audio-domain and symbolic-domain music generation. The former uses waveform data to generate music [1,16], while the latter uses sheet music data such as MIDI and MusicXML [5,8,19,24]. The advantage of audio-domain music generation is its flexibility and the ability to generate more unique timbre of sounds. However, it is very difficult to analyze the rhythm and tonic traits of generated audio, so that we choose to use symbolic-domain music generation methods in our work.

As for music style transfer, Malik et al. [14] have designed GenreNet and StyleNet which could inject note velocities information into music notes. This can make music scores sound more dynamic and more realistic. However, they haven't changed the pitch and duration arrangement of the original music, and simply altering the note velocity is not enough for music genre transfer tasks. Brunner et al. [2] build a state-of-the-art symbolic-domain music genre transfer model on Classic, Jazz and Pop based on the CycleGAN model. However, their music genre transfer model has only considered pixel-level losses, which are MAE and classification loss between the original data and transferred data, hence has neglected the semantic information hidden in the unique structure of music data.

3   SteelyGAN

In this section, we first introduce the architecture of SteelyGAN, then we propose the loss functions of SteelyGAN.

3.1   The Architecture of SteelyGAN

Our proposed SteelyGAN model, as shown in Fig. 1, consists of two generators, $G: A{\rightarrow}B$ and $F: B{\rightarrow}A$, two discriminators, D_A and D_B, as well as a binary classifier in the latent space. Generators $G: A{\rightarrow}B$ and $F: B{\rightarrow}A$ transfer music scores between genre A and B, while D_A and D_B discriminate transferred data from real samples in the dataset.

Bar-Unit. Bar-Unit is a two-layer convolutional structure, which is designed to detect detailed information in individual music bars within a single music segment and increase the novelty of each music bar by temporarily decoupling information of each bar within a 4-bar music segment. The structure of Bar-Unit is shown in Fig. 2.

There are four Bar-Unit modules in SteelyGAN generator, each corresponding to one bar of input segment. Upon entering Bar-Units structure, each input segment are divided into four parts in time dimension, note as x_1, x_2, x_3 and x_4, with each part containing information of one musical bar:

$$X \Longrightarrow [x_1, x_2, x_3, x_4], \tag{1}$$

Then each bar of music is sent separately into the accordant Bar-Unit structure. After passing through Bar-Units, outputs are merged with the original inputs by the ratio of $\mu : (1 - \mu)$, as shown in Eq. (2).

$$y_l = \mu BarUnit(x_l) + (1 - \mu)x_l, l = 1, 2, 3, 4. \tag{2}$$

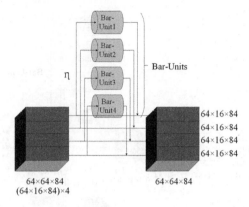

Fig. 2. Structure of the Bar-Unit module.

Equation (2) is inspired by dry/wet control knobs when mixing a song, thus it has a shortcut connection structure. We consider μ as the ratio of "wet" signal passing through Bar-Unit structure, and $(1 - \mu)$ as the ratio of "dry" signal before entering Bar-Unit structure, and each Bar-Unit shares the same μ.

After Eq. (2), y_1, y_2, y_3 and y_4 concatenate along the time dimension, so that each input data segment still contains information of 4 bars:

$$[y_1, y_2, y_3, y_4] \Longrightarrow Y, \tag{3}$$

Generator. SteelyGAN generator could be divided into seven parts, namely Conv I, Bar-Units, Conv II, ResNet-12, Conv III, ConvTranspose and Conv IV, as shown in Fig. 3. It uses convolutional layers Conv III to acquire latent space representation of input data.

Discriminator. SteelyGAN discriminator consists of seven convolutional layers, six of which have a (3×3) kernel, while the other one has a (7×7) kernel.

Genre Classifier. To test the performance of music genre transfer, and to analyze it by classification accuracy, we have trained a binary music genre classifier to distinguish samples between two genres in music genre transfer tasks.

3.2 Loss Functions

The loss functions of SteelyGAN include pixel-level losses (cycle-connected GAN loss, cycle-consistency loss and identity loss), semantic consistency loss and latent space classification loss.

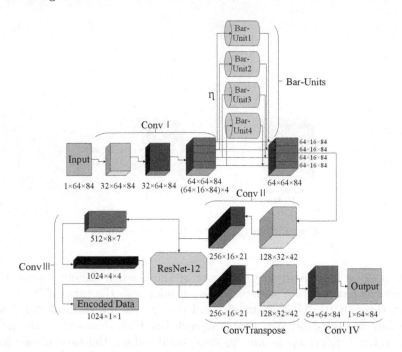

Fig. 3. Structure of the SteelyGAN generator.

Pixel-Level Losses. Pixel-level losses include cycle-connected GAN loss $L_{GAN}(G, D_B)$, $L_{GAN}(F, D_A)$, pixel-level cycle-consistency loss $L_{cyc}(G, F)$ and identity loss $L_{idt}(G, F)$:

$$L_{GAN}(G, D_B) = E_{b \sim p_{data(B)}}[||D_B(b)||_2] + E_{a \sim p_{data(A)}}[||(1 - D_B(G(a)))||_2], \quad (4)$$

$$L_{GAN}(F, D_A) = E_{a \sim p_{data(A)}}[||D_A(a)||_2] + E_{b \sim p_{data(B)}}[||(1 - D_A(F(b)))||_2], \quad (5)$$

$$L_{cyc}(G, F) = E_{a \sim p_{data(A)}}[||F(G(a)) - a||_1] + E_{b \sim p_{data(B)}}[||G(F(b)) - b||_1]. \quad (6)$$

$$L_{idt}(G, F) = E_{b \sim p_{data(B)}}[||G(b) - b||_1] + E_{a \sim p_{data(A)}}[||F(a) - a||_1]. \quad (7)$$

Semantic Consistency Loss. We consider the combination of Conv I, Bar-Units, Conv II and Conv III sub-modules in the generator to be an encoder structure that converts data from pixel-level tensors to latent-level variables. Therefore, we have encoders e_A and e_B that are essentially first several convolutional layers from generator G: $A \rightarrow B$ and F: $B \rightarrow A$. Here, $e_A(a)$ and $e_B(b)$ are latent representation of data samples from A and B. We acquire *encoded A* when A is passed through $G: A{\to}B$, and acquire *encoded fake B* when *fake B* is passed through $F: B{\to}A$.

We define semantic consistency loss $L_{sem_{con}}(e_A, e_B, G, F)$ as follows:

$$
\begin{aligned}
&L_{sem_{con}}(e_A, e_B, G, F) \\
&= E_{b\sim p_{data(B)}}[\||e_B(b) - e_A(G(b))\||_1] + E_{a\sim p_{data(A)}}[\||e_A(a) - e_B(F(a))\||_1].
\end{aligned}
\tag{8}
$$

Latent Space Classification Loss. We design a binary classifier in the latent space, noted as C_{lat}, and define latent space classification loss $L_{C_{lat}}(e_A, e_B, C_{lat})$ as follows:

$$
\begin{aligned}
&L_{C_{lat}}(e_A, e_B, C_{lat}) \\
&= E_{b\sim p_{data(B)}}[\||C_{lat}(e_B(b)), 1\||_2] + E_{a\sim p_{data(A)}}[\||C_{lat}(e_A(a)), 0\||_2].
\end{aligned}
\tag{9}
$$

Total Loss. The overall loss function of our model $L[G(e_A), F(e_B), D_A, D_B, C_{lat}]$ is a combination of 5 losses:

$$
\begin{aligned}
&L[G(e_A), F(e_B), D_A, D_B, C_{lat}] \\
&= L_{GAN}(G, D_B) + L_{GAN}(F, D_A) + \lambda_1 L_{cyc}(G, F) + \lambda_2 L_{idt}(G, F) \\
&\quad + \lambda_3 L_{sem_{con}}(e_A, e_B, G, F) + \lambda_4 L_{C_{lat}}(e_A, e_B, C_{lat}),
\end{aligned}
\tag{10}
$$

4 Experiments and Analysis

In this section, we first introduce our new MIDI dataset, Free MIDI Library. Then, we report our experiment and evaluation results on three music genres cases, namely Metal↔Country, Punk↔Classical and Rock↔Jazz.

4.1 Free MIDI Library Dataset

Due to the importance of genre tags in music genre transfer, we have constructed our own MIDI dataset, Free MIDI Library. The dataset contains 28,911 MIDI files on 17 music genres, and can be divided into 792,422 music segments.

Because the correspondence of each instrument in different genres is uncertain, and some instrumental parts may be empty at some parts of a song, we chose to merge all instrument (except for drums) sections into one piano channel. Each data sample from our dataset is in the shape of $(1, 64, 84)$, which contains information of 1 instrument track, 64 time steps and 84 pitches.

4.2 Genre Classification

The binary genre classifier was trained using Free MIDI Library Dataset. Because many music genres are very similar in style, such as sub-genres of rock music, classifier's performance on such similar genres is not promising. Besides, it is trivial to transfer between music genres that are already very similar. Through

Table 1. Classification accuracy of the genre classifier

Music genre	Accuracy
Metal↔Country	90.48%
Punk↔Classical	84.65%
Rock↔Jazz	70.14%

testing, we chose three pairs of music genres that have distinct features and have higher classification accuracy in comparison, as shown in Table 1.

As we can see from Table 1, classifier's accuracy on Metal↔Country and Punk↔Classical is higher than that of Rock↔Jazz, because there are more similarities between Rock and Jazz music.

4.3   Genre Transfer

We used the previously trained binary classifier to get classification accuracies on original data, transferred and cycle-transferred data. Because *Symbolic Music Genre Transfer* model proposed by Brunner et al. [2] (we use *SMGT* for short) was the only state-of-the-art model in unpaired symbolic music genre transfer, we had included it in the baselines and compared it with our SteelyGAN model. Ablation study was performed on latent space losses and Bar-Unit structure.

We chose 3 pairs of music genres displayed in Table 1 to train the genre transfer model. When calculating test accuracies, we classified the transferred data as their aimed genre, and cycle-transferred data as their original genre. In order to compare the overall performance of these music transfer models, we define an overall classification metric S_{total}^{D} as followed, where P is a previously trained binary classifier:

$$S_{total}^{D} = \frac{P(B|fake_B) + P(B|cycle_B)}{2} + \frac{P(A|fake_A) + P(A|cycle_A)}{2}, \qquad (11)$$

Therefore, higher S_{total}^{D} indicates better overall classification performance on both transferred music data and cycle-transferred music data. Results are shown in Table 2.

Table 2. Overall classification metric S_{total}^{D} of 3 genre transfer cases.

Model	Metal↔Country	Punk↔Classical	Rock↔Jazz
SMGT	77.65%	72.41%	66.01%
SteelyGAN w/o latent	73.53%	69.10%	62.34%
SteelyGAN w/o Bar-Unit	79.95%	79.71%	68.34%
SteelyGAN	**81.81%**	**82.85%**	**73.36%**

As we can see in Table 2, *SteelyGAN* model has higher S^D_{total} than *SteelyGAN without latent space losses, SteelyGAN without Bar-Unit Structure* and the state-of-the-art *SMGT* model in all genre transfer cases.

4.4   Objective Evaluation of Generated Music

In order to further evaluate the performance of our model in genre transfer task, we use 7 objective metrics for music evaluation, namely PC, NC, PR, PI, IOI [25], PP [5] and TD:

(1) *Pitch count (PC)*: Number of different pitches within a sample. This value ranges from 0 to 84.
(2) *Note count (NC)*: Number of notes within a sample.
(3) *Pitch range (PR)*: The subtraction of the highest and lowest pitch in semi-tones. This value ranges from 0 to 84.
(4) *Average pitch interval (PI)*: Average value of the interval between two con-secutive pitches in semitones.
(5) *Average inter-onset-interval (IOI)*: Average value of the time between two consecutive notes.
(6) *Polyphonicity (PP)*: Percentage of the number of time steps where more than two pitches are played to the total number of time steps.
(7) *Tonic distance (TD)*: Distance in semitones between the tonality of transferred, cycle-transferred and original music estimated by Krumhansl-Schmuckler algorithms [22]. This value ranges from 0 to 6.

For the first 6 metric, we compare the distance of value between the trans-ferred samples and samples of target genre, as well as distance between the cycle-transferred samples and samples of original genre. For the genre transfer of A↔B, we define Δ' and Δ'' as followed, where M is the chosen metric:

$$\Delta' = \left| \frac{M(fake_A) - M(A)}{2} \right| + \left| \frac{M(fake_B) - M(B)}{2} \right|, \tag{12}$$

$$\Delta'' = \left| \frac{M(cycle_A) - M(A)}{2} \right| + \left| \frac{M(cycle_B) - M(B)}{2} \right|. \tag{13}$$

Therefore, lower Δ' indicates that transferred samples are more similar to the target genre, and lower Δ'' indicates that cycle-transferred samples are more similar to the original genre.

For the TD metric, Δ' is defined as the average distance of the estimated tonality between the original and transferred samples in semitones, and Δ'' is the same distance between the original and cycle-transferred samples. Smaller value indicates that the generated music samples are closer to the original music samples in tonality.

We choose the case of Metal↔Country as the example of objective evaluation, and compare the Δ' and Δ'' of 100 original, transferred and cycle-transferred samples generated by 4 different models. Test results are shown in Table 3.

Table 3. Objective evaluation of Metal↔Country

Model		PC	NC	PR	PI	IOI	PP	TD
SMGT	Δ'	10.05	463.05	5.31	0.84	0.224	0.44	2.36
	Δ''	5.34	187.2	3.37	0.64	0.085	0.29	1.66
SteelyGAN w/o latent	Δ'	9.85	384.4	5.01	0.49	0.185	0.375	2.01
	Δ''	5.27	227.2	2.84	0.97	0.093	0.27	1.63
SteelyGAN w/o Bar-Unit	Δ'	**4.39**	**252.65**	2.29	0.35	**0.126**	0.3	2.36
	Δ''	**0.82**	**45.7**	1.02	0.4	**0.008**	0.07	0.81
SteelyGAN	Δ'	5.51	260.2	**1.43**	**0.24**	0.163	**0.28**	**1.95**
	Δ''	1.26	60.1	**0.48**	**0.3**	0.014	**0.06**	**0.71**

From the evaluation results of first 6 metrics, music samples transferred by *SteelyGAN* and *SteelyGAN without Bar-Unit Structure* are more similar to the target genre, and cycle-transferred data generated by these two models are also more similar to the original genre. Furthermore, from the result of TD metric, transferred and cycle-transferred models generated by *SteelyGAN* are closer to original music samples in tonality. This comprehensively demonstrates that latent level losses are effective in improving the performances of *SteelyGAN* on genre transfer.

4.5   Subjective Evaluation of Generated Music

In order to fully demonstrate SteelyGAN's performance in music transfer, we invited 30 people from internet with various musical backgrounds to rate 24 music clips transferred by *SMGT*, *SteelyGAN without latent space transfer*, *SteelyGAN without Bar-Unit Structure* and *SteelyGAN*. Rating items on music clips include *musicality* (good melody and rhythm, high aesthetic value), *naturalness* (close to human composition and performance), *creativeness* (not stale and dull) and *coherence* (notes are consecutive and smooth). The final score of each music sample is the average value of these four rating items. As shown in Fig. 4, music samples generated by SteelyGAN have the highest final scores on all 6 genre cases.

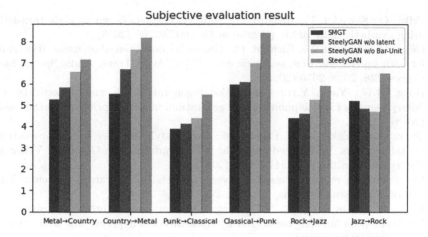

Fig. 4. User ratings of generated music samples.

5   Conclusion and Discussion

In this work, we have presented SteelyGAN, a semantic unsupervised music genre transfer model. SteelyGAN combine pixel-level and latent-level losses, and can inject stylish features of the aimed music genre to the input music sample while keeping its original tonality. We also present Bar-Unit structure that temporarily decouple input music segment into individual bars, which is proved to improve classification accuracies on transfer and cycle-transfer music samples. When conducting experiment, we use our constructed dataset Free MIDI Library Dataset and select three representative genre transfer cases, which are Metal↔Country, Punk↔Classical and Rock↔Jazz. Through the results of genre transfer experiments, SteelyGAN model have increased test accuracies on transferred and cycle-transferred data, and have achieved better results in both objective and subjective evaluations than state-of-the-art music genre transfer models.

Acknowledgment. This work was partially supported by the National Key Research and Development Program of China under Grant No. 2018AAA0100400, the Natural Science Foundation of Shandong Province under Grants No. ZR2020MF131 and No. ZR2021ZD19, and the Science and Technology Program of Qingdao under Grant No. 21-1-4-ny-19-nsh.

References

1. Van Den Broek, K.: Mp3net: coherent, minute-long music generation from raw audio with a simple convolutional GAN. arXiv e-prints pp. arXiv-2101 (2021)
2. Brunner, G., Wang, Y., Wattenhofer, R., Zhao, S.: Symbolic music genre transfer with CycleGAN. In: 2018 IEEE 30th International Conference on Tools with Artificial Intelligence (ICTAI), pp. 786–793 (2018)

3. Cífka, O., Şimşekli, U., Richard, G.: Supervised symbolic music style translation using synthetic data. arXiv preprint arXiv:1907.02265 (2019)
4. Cífka, O., Şimşekli, U., Richard, G.: Groove2Groove: one-shot music style transfer with supervision from synthetic data. IEEE/ACM Trans. Audio Speech Lang. Process. **28**, 2638–2650 (2020)
5. Dong, H.W., Yang, Y.H.: Convolutional generative adversarial networks with binary neurons for polyphonic music generation. arXiv preprint arXiv:1804.09399 (2018)
6. Gatys, L.A., Ecker, A.S., Bethge, M.: Image style transfer using convolutional neural networks. In: Proceedings of the IEEE Conference on Computer Vision and Pattern Recognition, pp. 2414–2423 (2016)
7. Goodfellow, I., et al.: Generative adversarial nets. In: Advances in Neural Information Processing Systems, pp. 2672–2680 (2014)
8. Hsiao, W.Y., Liu, J.Y., Yeh, Y.C., Yang, Y.H.: Compound word transformer: learning to compose full-song music over dynamic directed hypergraphs. arXiv preprint arXiv:2101.02402 (2021)
9. Kim, T., Cha, M., Kim, H., Lee, J.K., Kim, J.: Learning to discover cross-domain relations with generative adversarial networks. arXiv preprint arXiv:1703.05192 (2017)
10. Krizhevsky, A., Sutskever, I., Hinton, G.E.: ImageNet classification with deep convolutional neural networks. Adv. Neural. Inf. Process. Syst. **25**, 1097–1105 (2012)
11. Larsen, A.B.L., Sønderby, S.K., Larochelle, H., Winther, O.: Autoencoding beyond pixels using a learned similarity metric. In: International Conference on Machine Learning, pp. 1558–1566. PMLR (2016)
12. Liu, M.Y., Breuel, T., Kautz, J.: Unsupervised image-to-image translation networks. In: Advances in Neural Information Processing Systems, pp. 700–708 (2017)
13. Makhzani, A., Shlens, J., Jaitly, N., Goodfellow, I., Frey, B.: Adversarial autoencoders. arXiv preprint arXiv:1511.05644 (2015)
14. Malik, I., Ek, C.H.: Neural translation of musical style. arXiv preprint arXiv:1708.03535 (2017)
15. Mirza, M., Osindero, S.: Conditional generative adversarial nets. arXiv preprint arXiv:1411.1784 (2014)
16. Mor, N., Wolf, L., Polyak, A., Taigman, Y.: A universal music translation network. arXiv preprint arXiv:1805.07848 (2018)
17. Radford, A., Metz, L., Chintala, S.: Unsupervised representation learning with deep convolutional generative adversarial networks. arXiv preprint arXiv:1511.06434 (2015)
18. Royer, A., et al.: XGAN: unsupervised image-to-image translation for many-to-many mappings. In: Singh, R., Vatsa, M., Patel, V.M., Ratha, N. (eds.) Domain Adaptation for Visual Understanding, pp. 33–49. Springer, Cham (2020). https://doi.org/10.1007/978-3-030-30671-7_3
19. Shih, Y.J., Wu, S.L., Zalkow, F., Muller, M., Yang, Y.H.: Theme transformer: symbolic music generation with theme-conditioned transformer. IEEE Trans. Multimed. (2022)
20. Simonyan, K., Zisserman, A.: Very deep convolutional networks for large-scale image recognition. arXiv preprint arXiv:1409.1556 (2014)
21. Taigman, Y., Polyak, A., Wolf, L.: Unsupervised cross-domain image generation. arXiv preprint arXiv:1611.02200 (2016)
22. Temperley, D.: What's key for key? The krumhansl-schmuckler key-finding algorithm reconsidered. Music. Percept. **17**(1), 65–100 (1999)

23. Vasquez, S., Lewis, M.: MelNet: a generative model for audio in the frequency domain. arXiv preprint arXiv:1906.01083 (2019)
24. Wu, J., Hu, C., Wang, Y., Hu, X., Zhu, J.: A hierarchical recurrent neural network for symbolic melody generation. IEEE Trans. Cybern. **50**(6), 2749–2757 (2019)
25. Yang, L.-C., Lerch, A.: On the evaluation of generative models in music. Neural Comput. Appl. **32**(9), 4773–4784 (2018). https://doi.org/10.1007/s00521-018-3849-7
26. Yi, Z., Zhang, H., Tan, P., Gong, M.: DualGAN: unsupervised dual learning for image-to-image translation. In: Proceedings of the IEEE International Conference on Computer Vision, pp. 2849–2857 (2017)
27. Zhu, J.Y., Park, T., Isola, P., Efros, A.A.: Unpaired image-to-image translation using cycle-consistent adversarial networks. In: The IEEE International Conference on Computer Vision (ICCV), October 2017

Self-supervised Learning for Sketch-Based 3D Shape Retrieval

Zhixiang Chen[1,2], Haifeng Zhao[2,3]([✉]), Yan Zhang[1,2,4], Guozi Sun[1]([✉]),
and Tianjian Wu[2,4]

[1] School of Computer Science, Nanjing University of Posts and Telecommunications,
Nanjing 210023, China
`sun@njupt.edu.cn`
[2] School of Software Engineering, Jinling Institute of Technology,
Nanjing 211169, China
`zhf@jit.edu.cn`
[3] Jiangsu Hoperun Software Co. Ltd., Nanjing 210012, China
[4] School of Computer Science and Technology, Nanjing Normal University,
Nanjing 210023, China

Abstract. In recent years, sketch-based 3D shape retrieval (SB3DR) gets a lot of attentions in the computer vision community. The task is challenging due to the large domain gap between sketches and 3D shapes. Most of the existing methods solve the problem by the supervised learning to extract discriminative features in the common feature space. However, these methods rely on the good quality of training data annotations which is costly in practical scenarios. To address this problem, we propose a self-supervised learning approach for SB3DR. Motivated by the idea of instance discrimination, we regard the multiple views of a 3D shape as positive pairs, and model the relation of multi-views in a contrastive self-supervised learning framework which requires only positive samples to extract features. The proposed approach needs neither additional supervised dependencies nor ground-truth labels of 3D shapes, leading to a simpler training process. Moreover, we construct an enhanced triple loss to mitigate the gap between sketch and 3D shape domains. The experimental results on benchmark datasets show our approach can achieve the state-of-the-art performance at a comparable level.

Keywords: 3D shape · Sketch · Sketch based 3D shape retrieval · Self-supervised learning

1 Introduction

With the development of the Internet, there are many 3D shape models in the fields of computer-aided design, 3D printing and 3D animation, etc. It is tedious to find the target 3D shapes spreading in various 3D shape databases. Traditional text-based retrieval methods can only designate query by keywords, which is

© The Author(s), under exclusive license to Springer Nature Switzerland AG 2022
S. Yu et al. (Eds.): PRCV 2022, LNCS 13534, pp. 318–329, 2022.
https://doi.org/10.1007/978-3-031-18907-4_25

hard to describe structural details, thus can not capture the intent of the query. Compared with text keywords, sketches can better represent users' intuitive impressions on the 3D objects. Moreover, thanks to the current popularity of touch screens, sketches are easier to get, making 3D shape retrieval based on sketch becomes possible.

In a sketch-based 3D shape retrieval (SB3DR) task, sketches are used as the queries. The aim is to find the corresponding 3D shapes in the given 3D shape datasets. The main challenge of the SB3DR lies in the cross-domain gap between the sketch and 3D shape domains. In the past, content-based SB3DR methods [15] were used to bridge the gap between cross-domain data, but the retrieval has low performance with high cost. To address this problem, one of the popular approaches [22] is to project the 3D shapes onto a 2D plane from multiple perspectives so as to convert the cross-domain problem between sketches and 3D shapes into between sketches and 2D views, which can be solved by 2D-based methods [28]. In this way, sketches and 3D shapes are mapped to the common feature space. In retrieval, the k-Nearest Neighbors (kNN) method is used to rank the retrieved 3D shapes in a descending order based on the distance metric between sketches and 3D shapes, providing a paradigm for SB3DR solution.

In recent years, with the success of the convolutional neural networks (CNN) [9,16] on the ImageNet [4], deep learning has become a hot topic in the computer vision community. Existing works [22,26] proposed some CNN-based methods to solve SB3DR problems, extracting 3D shape features by average-pooling or max-pooling the multi-view features for the later retrieval. These deep learning approaches considered the multi-views as independent features of the 3D shapes, losing the related information between them, which consists of the common knowledge of the entire 3D shape feature space. Moreover, existing approaches highly depend on the quality of training data annotations. In the current era of data explosion, it requires plenty of time and effort for data annotation.

To address the above problems, we proposed a novel SB3DR approach using multi-view features under a self-supervised learning framework. The self-supervised learning [12] can provide supervised labels to the data by constructing "pretext" tasks, leveraging the cost of data annotations. In self-supervised learning, instance discrimination [2,8] learns features by mining relations and structural similarities between objects. Regarding multi-views as data augmentation of the 3D shapes, the generated multi-view features from a single 3D shape will be clustered in the feature space by instance discrimination. The benefit is that the multi-view features of the same 3D shape are as close as possible in the latent feature space, while features of different 3D shapes are as far away as possible, making different multi-view features of the same 3D shape being similar. This can reduce the information loss during the pooling process.

In summary, the main contributions of this paper are as follows:

Firstly, based on the idea that multi-views from the same 3D shape should have similar features, combining the instance discrimination, we first propose a self-supervised learning method to solve the problem of information loss caused by not considering the relation of each view when extracting the multi-view features of the 3D shape in the SB3DR task.

Secondly, we make the training process a pipeline of three branches. Our proposed model can improve the feature quality and information retention in the multi-view feature fusion of the 3D shape without any additional supervised dependencies, and build a multi-view model from data itself.

Thirdly, we constructed an enhanced triple loss to reduce the gap between the sketch domain and the 3D shape domain based on the original triple loss [25].

Finally, we conducted intensive experiment on benchmark datasets and compared with the state-of-the-art methods. The experimental results showed the effectiveness of the proposed method.

2   Related Work

2.1   Sketch Based 3D Shape Retrieval

Following the multi-view based 3D shape retrieval paradigm, there have been many previous works. The earlier works [13] are based on hand-crafted features, whereas recent works [3,26,27] are based on the multi-view CNNs [22]. Wang et al. [26] proposed Siamese which uses a set of joint networks to map sketches and 3D shapes into similar feature spaces. Thong et al. [24] proposed Open Search which projected cross-domain features onto a common hypersphere. Dai et al. [3] proposed DCML which uses correlation measure learning to reduce the domain gap between features of sketches. These methods considered multi-view in independent features in common feature space. Regarding to the relation between multi-views, Xie et al. [27] proposed LWBR which uses the Wasserstein center of gravity to fuse the multi-view features of the 3D shape and perform cross-domain matching. Qi et al. [20] proposed a fine-grained SB3DR approach using attention model.

The above supervised methods can achieve certain results, but the models are very complex, some of which rely on additional supervised dependencies such as semantics vectors of texts [30]. Existing methods focused on solving domain gap between cross-domain data by preliminary extracting multi-view features, which then were average-pooled or max-pooled as the features of the 3D shapes without considering the relation between multi-views. This makes the rich multi-view feature information lost in the process of pooling and impairs the representation ability of 3D shape features, which in turn affects the subsequent cross-domain data fusion process. In addition, the features obtained by supervised training are for a specific learning task and do not have a good generalization effect.

2.2   Self-supervised Learning

Self-supervised learning has been successfully applied in many fields. In computer vision, using pretext tasks [12], such as context prediction [5], jigsaw [17], deep cluster [1], rotation [7], contrastive predictive coding (CPC) [10], etc., can help the model learn features from unlabeled data, with the aim of performing well on downstream supervised learning tasks such as classification and retrieval. Previous works [11,18] have demonstrated the potential of self-supervised learning

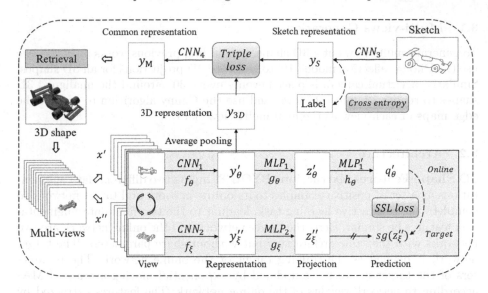

Fig. 1. Our proposed self-supervised learning architecture. sg means stop-gradient. Multi-views generation methods are introduced in Sect. 3.1. 3D shape features extraction branch, sketch features extraction branch and metric branch are introduced in detail in the rest of Sect. 3.2.

in solving cross-domain task in sketch-based image retrieval (SBIR) tasks [28]. Therefore, in SB3DR tasks, instead of relying on the supervision signal of external word vectors to help the SB3DR model achieve results in the process of supervised learning, it is better to directly use the pretext tasks constructed by self-supervised learning for training, which simplifies the model structure and makes training more efficient.

3   The Proposed Approach

Based on the idea of instance discrimination, Our proposed approach reduces the information loss of multi-view features during pooling, so as to extract 3D shape features with stronger representation. Our model consists of three branches, namely, the 3D shape feature extraction branch, sketch feature extraction branch and the metric branch, as shown in Fig. 1. Based on the BYOL [8] architecture, the 3D shape feature extraction branch extracts multi-view features, making the multi-view features from the same 3D shape be similar and reducing the information loss of multi-view features during later pooling. The sketch feature extraction branch uses CNN to extract the high-dimensional features of sketches. And the metric branch uses a linear function to project the features of the sketches and the 3D shapes onto a common feature space and retrieve them using the kNN algorithm.

3.1 Multi-views Generation

To generate multi-views of a 3D shape, resembling previous works [3,21,27], we use the Phong reflection model [19] to generate 2D projections for all 3D shapes. Similarly, a virtual camera is placed evenly every 30° around the unaligned 3D shapes to render 12 different views, and use the Canny algorithm to extract the edge maps of each view as the final multi-view data.

3.2 Architecture

3D Shape Features Extraction. BYOL [8] inputs two different data augmentations as a set of positive examples to its online network and target network to complete the contrastive learning task, leading to the two final data augmentation features be similar. Here, the target network and the online network are two networks with the same architecture but without share parameters. The target network is defined as the training target of the online network. The parameters of the target network are updated by exponential moving average (EMA) according to network weights of the online network. The features extracted by online network will be the last features.

Resembling to BYOL [8], we regard the 12 multi-views of the same 3D shape as "12 data enhancements of the 3D shape". Then we divide the first 6 views and the last 6 views into distinct groups according to the angles of the views. The benefit is that our model is encouraged to obtain similar multi-view features of the same 3D shape after training. The two groups of view data construct 6 pairs of "positive sample pair", which are used as the inputs of the online network and target network respectively.

Formally, we denote the total number of 3D shapes is N_{3D}, the 3D shape is $x_{3D} = \{x_{1,i}, x_{2,i}, ..., x_{N_{3D},i}\}, i = 1, 2, 3, ..., 12$, where i represents the perspective subscript. Divide the multi-views of each sample into two groups according to the generation order, as shown in Eq. 1:

$$\begin{cases} x' = x_{n,i}, i \leq 6 \\ x'' = x_{n,i}, i > 6 \end{cases} \quad n = 1, 2, 3 ..., N_{3D} \tag{1}$$

The two groups of inputs are fed into two CNNs f_θ and f_ξ that do not share parameters. Here, f_θ is used as the online network and the target network is f_ξ. Then we get the representation of two groups of the inputs in the feature spaces, i.e., $y'_\theta = f_\theta(x')$ and $y''_\xi = f_\xi(x'')$.

The original feature spaces are of low dimensional which doesn't contain enough discriminative information. To mine the high-dimensional information between multi-view features, we pass y'_θ and y''_ξ through two multilayer perceptron (MLP) layers that do not share parameters to obtain two high-dimensional nonlinear projections $z'_\theta = g_\theta(y'_\theta)$ and $z''_\xi = g_\xi(y''_\xi)$ in different latent spaces respectively.

Since these two groups of multi-views are regarded as "two kinds of data augmentation", their features should be similar and mutually predictable. That is, the projection of the target network can be obtained from the projection of the online network by a nonlinear transformation, and vice versa. z'_θ and z''_ξ are in different latent spaces, so we use another MLP layer h_θ to transform z'_θ to get $q'_\theta = h_\theta(z'_\theta)$, making q'_θ and z''_ξ be in the same latent space and can be mutually predictable. The training objective is to minimize the difference between q'_θ and z''_ξ, so the loss $\mathcal{L}_{SSL}(\theta, \xi)$ is defined as follows:

$$\mathcal{L}_{SSL}(\theta, \xi) \triangleq \left\| \overline{q'_\theta} - \overline{z''_\xi} \right\|_2^2 = 2 - 2 \cdot \frac{\left\langle q'_\theta, z''_\xi \right\rangle}{\left\| q'_\theta \right\|_2 \cdot \left\| z''_\xi \right\|_2} \tag{2}$$

where $\overline{q'_\theta} = \frac{q'_\theta}{\|q'_\theta\|}$, $\overline{z''_\xi} = \frac{z''_\xi}{\|z''_\xi\|}$, $\|\cdot\|_2$ denotes L2-norm. Equation 2 is the loss function of the prediction task for the online network. In order to improve the utilization of the multi-view data of the 3D shape, the two groups of data x' and x'' are exchanged and then input to f_θ and f_ξ respectively. The loss then is as follows:

$$\mathcal{L}_{SSL}(\xi, \theta) \triangleq \left\| \overline{q'_\xi} - \overline{z''_\theta} \right\|_2^2 = 2 - 2 \cdot \frac{\left\langle q'_\xi, z''_\theta \right\rangle}{\left\| q'_\xi \right\|_2 \cdot \| z''_\theta \|_2} \tag{3}$$

Therefore, the complete similarity loss is the average of two groups of multiple views before and after exchanging positions, as shown in Eq. 4:

$$\mathcal{L}_{3D}(\theta, \xi) = \frac{1}{2} \left(L_{SSL}(\theta, \xi) + L_{SSL}(\xi, \theta) \right) \tag{4}$$

Sketch Feature Extraction. We directly apply a CNN f_S to extract sketch features through a classification task. We denote the total number of sketches as N_S, the sketch domain as $x_S = \{x_1, x_2, ..., x_{N_S}\}$. The loss $\mathcal{L}_S$ is defined as the cross entropy between prediction labels and ground-truth labels, as follows:

$$\mathcal{L}_S = -\frac{1}{N_S} \sum_{n=1}^{N_S} \sum_{c=1}^{C} \log \frac{\exp\left(f_S\left(x_S\right)_C\right)}{\sum_{k=1}^{C} \exp\left(f_S\left(x_S\right)_k\right)} \tag{5}$$

Metric Branch. To retrieve cross-domain data by the kNN algorithm based on Euclidean distance, we firstly use the linear transformation f_m to map the high-dimensional sketch feature y_s and the 3D shape feature y_{3D} to a common feature space $y_M = \{f_m(y_s), f_m(y_{3D})\} \in \mathbb{R}^{256}$.

Then, in order to achieve better clustering for retrieval, we construct an enhanced triple loss based on the original triple loss. We firstly treat one domain data as anchors, and another domain data as their positive and negative samples, and then do in the same way by exchanging the domains. In this way, the cross-domain data will be pulled together in the common feature space. Moreover, the data in the same domain also need to be pulled closer along the same line.

The aim of the original triple loss is to make positive samples near to the anchors and negative samples far from anchors, which is defined as Eq. 6:

$$\mathcal{L}_T(a, p, n) = \max\{\|a - p\|_2 - \|a - n\|_2 + margin, 0\} \tag{6}$$

where a denotes anchor samples, p denotes positive samples of a, n denotes negative samples of a, $margin$ denotes the margin between different classes.

Finally, let $j = \{a, p, n\}$, S_j denotes sketches, V_j denotes 3D shapes. Based on Eq. 6, We denote the enhanced triple loss $\mathcal{L}_M$ shown as follows:

$$\mathcal{L}_M = \mathcal{L}_T(S_a, V_p, V_n) + \mathcal{L}_T(V_a, S_p, S_n) + \mathcal{L}_T(V_a, V_p, V_n) \tag{7}$$

where $\mathcal{L}_T(S_a, V_p, V_n)$ and $\mathcal{L}_T(V_a, S_p, S_n)$ achieve clustering the cross-domain data in the common feature space, $\mathcal{L}_T(V_a, V_p, V_n)$ achieves clustering the data of the 3D shape domain.

With these ingredients at hands, we train the three branches mentioned above respectively. The outputs of 3D shape features extraction branch and sketch features extraction branch are the inputs of the metric branch. As the result, we make the training process of the three branches a pipeline.

4   Experiments

In this section, we first introduce two benchmark datasets, i.e., SHREC14 [15] and PART-SHREC14 [21], and then introduce the implementation details of the model, and compare our proposed method with several SOTA supervised methods through a number of evaluation indicators. The experimental results show the comparable performance of our proposed method.

4.1   Datasets

SHREC14 contains 13680 sketches and 8987 3D shapes, with a total of 171 classes. There are 50 sketches per class in the training set and 30 sketches per class in the testing set. The 3D shape data are derived from several datasets. The number of 3D shapes in each class ranges from 10 to 300.

PART-SHREC14 is a part of SHREC14, and only 48 classes whose number of 3D shapes is greater than or equal to 50 are selected. It includes 3840 sketches and 7238 3D shapes. The splits of sketches follows the same rules of SHREC14, while 3D shapes are split into 5,812 for training and 1,426 for testing.

4.2   Implementation Details

The RestNet-50 [9] pre-trained on ImageNet was used as the backbone for all CNNs, and the input of fc at the last fully connected layer is taken as the feature of data, with a feature dimension of 2048. The momentum update parameter of

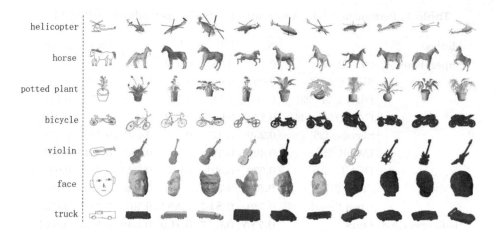

Fig. 2. Qualitative results of our method on PART-SHREC14 dataset. For each sketch query, we show the top-10 3D shape results. The green color represents the correct examples in the query results, and the red color represents the incorrect examples. The details are described in Sect. 4.4.

the EMA method of the target network is set to 0.996. The Stochastic Gradient Descent (SGD) optimizer was used for all trainings.

The sketch feature extraction branch was trained for 120 epochs, the initial learning rate was set to 0.01, and decayed by 0.5 every 20 epochs. The 3D shape feature extraction branch was trained for 120 epochs, the initial learning rate was set to 0.001, and decayed by 0.1 every 30 epochs. The metric branch consists of two fully connected layers 2048-1024-1024-256. The initial learning rate was 0.01, and decayed by 0.5 every 500 epochs, with a total of 4000 epochs of training.

4.3 Evaluation Metric

Following [14], we use six retrieval metrics for evaluation. Nearest Neighbor (NN) stands for Precision@1. First tier (FT) represents recall@K, where K represents the number of 3D shapes in the dataset that belong to the same class as the query sketch. Second tier (ST) stands for recall@2K. E-measure (E) represents the F1 score of the top 32 retrieval results. Discounted cumulative gain (DCG) is defined as the normalized weight value associated with the position of positive examples in the retrieval results. Mean average precision (mAP) is obtained by calculating the integral of the precision-recall curve.

4.4 Results

Performance Comparison. We compare our proposed method with the state of the art (SOTA) methods [3,6,13,21,23,26,27,29] both on the SHREC14 and PART-SHREC14 datasets under six evaluation metrics, as shown in Table 1

Table 1. Performance comparison with the SOTA methods on SHREC14.

Method		NN	FT	ST	E	DCG	mAP
Supervised	CDMR [6]	0.109	0.057	0.089	0.041	0.328	0.054
	SBR-VC [13]	0.095	0.050	0.081	0.037	0.319	0.050
	DB-VLAT [23]	0.160	0.115	0.170	0.079	0.376	0.131
	CAT-DTW [29]	0.137	0.068	0.102	0.050	0.338	0.060
	Siamese [26]	0.239	0.212	0.316	0.140	0.496	0.228
	LWBR [27]	0.403	0.378	0.455	0.236	0.581	0.401
	DCML [3]	0.578	0.591	0.647	**0.723**	0.351	0.615
	SEM [21]	**0.804**	0.749	0.813	0.395	0.870	0.780
	Open Search [24]	0.789	**0.814**	**0.854**	0.561	**0.886**	**0.830**
Self-supervised	**Ours**	**0.715**	**0.647**	**0.709**	**0.639**	**0.835**	**0.644**

Table 2. Performance comparison with the SOTA methods on PART-SHREC14.

Method		NN	FT	ST	E	DCG	mAP
Supervised	Siamese [26]	0.118	0.076	0.132	0.073	0.400	0.067
	SEM [21]	**0.840**	0.634	0.745	0.526	0.848	0.676
	Open Searh [24]	0.816	**0.799**	**0.891**	**0.685**	**0.910**	**0.831**
Self-supervised	**Ours**	**0.677**	**0.604**	**0.711**	**0.582**	**0.842**	**0.678**

and Table 2. We have the following observations: (1) Compared with the methods [3,6,13,23,26,29] which do not consider the relation between multi-views, our method beat all of above on the SHREC14 dataset and the PART-SHREC14 dataset. This implies that the relation of multi-views plays an important role in the discrimination of different 3D shape features, resulting in better retrieval performance. (2) Compared with LWBR [27] that considers multi-view relation, our method has better performance, as it benefits from the contrastive self-supervised learning method to extract robust features. (3) Meanwhile, the performance of our method gets surpassed by that of the supervised methods [21,24], especially on SHREC14 dataset, which has many classes with few samples. Whereas it still has better result on E-measure. It indicates that our proposed method can keep a good balance between precision and recall. As the self-supervised learning is highly dependent on large amount of data input during training process, the classes with fewer samples can hardly learned good features for the downstream tasks. Regarding to the PART-SHREC14 dataset, which has larger amount of samples, we can get not only a better E-measure, but also a better mAP.

Qualitative Results. Figure 2 shows partial retrieval top-10 results on PART-SHREC14. Our proposed method can retrieve correct classes with distinct structures, such as helicopters, horses, and potted plants. When the classes have high

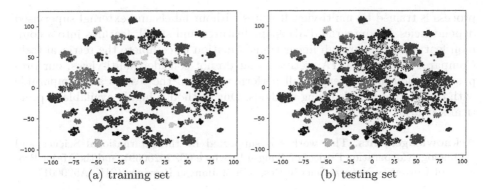

(a) training set   (b) testing set

Fig. 3. Visualization of the sketch and shape features on PART-SHREC14 dataset. The figures show the distribution of sketch and 3D shape features of all 48 classes in the fusion feature space. Figure 3(a) is the distribution on the training set, while Fig. 3(b) is on the testing set. The details are described in Sect. 4.4.

semantic similarity, the retrieval gets some wrong results, such as bicycles, violins, faces, and trucks. However, we can still get correct 3D shapes matching query sketches in the first few retrievals. As a matter of fact, due to the simple lines and abstract structure of the sketch itself, there are ambiguities in the described semantics. For example, the sketches of a truck and the sketches of a car, as shown in the last row of Fig. 2, are difficult to accurately distinguish the real semantics even for human beings. In many practical scenarios, it is necessary to consider some similar 3D shapes as query results of semantically ambiguous sketches. Therefore, our method is still highly available in practice although some false positive samples exist in the semantically similar classes.

Visualization. We visualized the feature distribution of the PART-SHREC14 dataset in the common feature space as shown in Fig. 3. We get good feature distributions of various classes in the common feature space on the training set. The distribution of testing set is basically consistent with that of the training set. It implies that the good generalization performance of our method.

5   Conclusion

This paper proposed a novel self-supervised learning approach for sketch based 3D shape retrieval. We used CNN to extract the features of sketches and 3D shapes respectively. In order to reduce the information loss of multi-view features after pooling and enhance the representation ability of extracted features, we constructed a self-supervised task based on the idea of instance discrimination, which enables different multi-views of the same 3D shape to predict each other in a high-dimensional feature space. In this way, the model is guided to keep the feature output of multi-views of the same 3D shape consistent. The process is trained by multi-view features without labels and external supervised dependencies. We integrated 3D shape features and sketch features into a common feature space through linear transformation to complete the retrieval task. Compared with the SOTA methods that do not consider multi-views, our proposed method has better overall performance, and the results are comparable with those supervised learning methods. Our method is highly available in practical scenarios.

Acknowledgements. This work was supported by the International Science and Technology Cooperation Project of Jiangsu Province (BZ2020069), and the Major Program of University Natural Science Research of Jiangsu Province (21KJA520001).

References

1. Caron, M., Bojanowski, P., Joulin, A., Douze, M.: Deep clustering for unsupervised learning of visual features. In: Proceedings of the European Conference on Computer Vision (ECCV), pp. 132–149 (2018)
2. Chen, X., He, K.: Exploring simple siamese representation learning. In: Proceedings of the IEEE/CVF Conference on Computer Vision and Pattern Recognition, pp. 15750–15758 (2021)
3. Dai, G., Xie, J., Zhu, F., Fang, Y.: Deep correlated metric learning for sketch-based 3D shape retrieval. In: Thirty-First AAAI Conference on Artificial Intelligence (2017)
4. Deng, J., Dong, W., Socher, R., Li, L.J., Li, K., Fei-Fei, L.: ImageNet: a large-scale hierarchical image database. In: 2009 IEEE Conference on Computer Vision and Pattern Recognition, pp. 248–255. IEEE (2009)
5. Doersch, C., Gupta, A., Efros, A.A.: Unsupervised visual representation learning by context prediction. In: Proceedings of the IEEE International Conference on Computer Vision. pp. 1422–1430 (2015)
6. Furuya, T., Ohbuchi, R.: Ranking on cross-domain manifold for sketch-based 3D model retrieval. In: 2013 International Conference on Cyberworlds, pp. 274–281. IEEE (2013)
7. Gidaris, S., Singh, P., Komodakis, N.: Unsupervised representation learning by predicting image rotations. arXiv preprint arXiv:1803.07728 (2018)
8. Grill, J.B., et al.: Bootstrap your own latent-a new approach to self-supervised learning. Adv. Neural Inf. Process. Syst. **33**, 21271–21284 (2020)
9. He, K., Zhang, X., Ren, S., Sun, J.: Deep residual learning for image recognition. In: Proceedings of the IEEE Conference on Computer Vision and Pattern Recognition, pp. 770–778 (2016)
10. Henaff, O.: Data-efficient image recognition with contrastive predictive coding. In: International Conference on Machine Learning, pp. 4182–4192. PMLR (2020)
11. Hu, C., Yang, Y., Li, Y., Hospedales, T.M., Song, Y.Z.: Towards unsupervised sketch-based image retrieval. arXiv preprint arXiv:2105.08237 (2021)
12. Jing, L., Tian, Y.: Self-supervised visual feature learning with deep neural networks: a survey. IEEE Trans. Pattern Anal. Mach. Intell. **43**(11), 4037–4058 (2020)
13. Li, B., et al.: SHREC'13 track: large scale sketch-based 3D shape retrieval. eurographics (2013)
14. Li, B., et al.: A comparison of methods for sketch-based 3D shape retrieval. Comput. Vis. Image Underst. **119**, 57–80 (2014)

15. Li, B., et al.: SHREC'14 track: extended large scale sketch-based 3D shape retrieval. In: Eurographics Workshop on 3D Object Retrieval, vol. 2014, pp. 121–130 (2014)
16. Li, Z., Liu, F., Yang, W., Peng, S., Zhou, J.: A survey of convolutional neural networks: analysis, applications, and prospects. IEEE Trans. Neural Netw. Learn. Syst. (2021)
17. Noroozi, M., Favaro, P.: Unsupervised learning of visual representations by solving jigsaw puzzles. In: Leibe, B., Matas, J., Sebe, N., Welling, M. (eds.) ECCV 2016. LNCS, vol. 9910, pp. 69–84. Springer, Cham (2016). https://doi.org/10.1007/978-3-319-46466-4_5
18. Pang, K., Yang, Y., Hospedales, T.M., Xiang, T., Song, Y.Z.: Solving mixed-modal jigsaw puzzle for fine-grained sketch-based image retrieval. In: Proceedings of the IEEE/CVF Conference on Computer Vision and Pattern Recognition, pp. 10347–10355 (2020)
19. Phong, B.T.: Illumination for computer generated pictures. Commun. ACM 18(6), 311–317 (1975)
20. Qi, A., et al.: Toward fine-grained sketch-based 3D shape retrieval. IEEE Trans. Image Process. 30, 8595–8606 (2021)
21. Qi, A., Song, Y.Z., Xiang, T.: Semantic embedding for sketch-based 3D shape retrieval. In: BMVC, vol. 3, pp. 1–12 (2018)
22. Su, H., Maji, S., Kalogerakis, E., Learned-Miller, E.: Multi-view convolutional neural networks for 3D shape recognition. In: Proceedings of the IEEE International Conference on Computer Vision, pp. 945–953 (2015)
23. Tatsuma, A., Koyanagi, H., Aono, M.: A large-scale shape benchmark for 3D object retrieval: toyohashi shape benchmark. In: Proceedings of the 2012 Asia Pacific Signal and Information Processing Association Annual Summit and Conference, pp. 1–10. IEEE (2012)
24. Thong, W., Mettes, P., Snoek, C.G.: Open cross-domain visual search. Comput. Vis. Image Underst. 200, 103045 (2020)
25. Balntas, V., Riba, E., Ponsa, D., Mikolajczyk, K.: Learning local feature descriptors with triplets and shallow convolutional neural networks. In: Proceedings of the British Machine Vision Conference (BMVC), pp. 119.1–119.11, September 2016
26. Wang, F., Kang, L., Li, Y.: Sketch-based 3D shape retrieval using convolutional neural networks. In: Proceedings of the IEEE Conference on Computer Vision and Pattern Recognition, pp. 1875–1883 (2015)
27. Xie, J., Dai, G., Zhu, F., Fang, Y.: Learning barycentric representations of 3D shapes for sketch-based 3D shape retrieval. In: Proceedings of the IEEE Conference on Computer Vision and Pattern Recognition, pp. 5068–5076 (2017)
28. Xu, P., Hospedales, T.M., Yin, Q., Song, Y.Z., Xiang, T., Wang, L.: Deep learning for free-hand sketch: a survey and a toolbox. arXiv preprint arXiv:2001.02600 (2020)
29. Yasseen, Z., Verroust-Blondet, A., Nasri, A.: View selection for sketch-based 3D model retrieval using visual part shape description. Vis. Comput. 33(5), 565–583 (2017)
30. Zhu, F., Xie, J., Fang, Y.: Learning cross-domain neural networks for sketch-based 3D shape retrieval. In: National Conference on Artificial Intelligence (2016)

Preference-Aware Modality Representation and Fusion for Micro-video Recommendation

Chuanfa Tian, Meng Liu[✉], and Di Zhou

School of Computer Science and Technology, Shandong Jianzhu University,
Jinan 250101, China
mengliu.sdu@gmail.com

Abstract. Personalized multi-modal micro-video recommendation has
attracted increasing research interests recently. Despite existing methods
have achieved much progress, they ignore the importance of the user's
modality preference for micro-video recommendation. In this paper,
we explore the preference-aware modality representation learning and
dynamic modality information fusion, and respectively present coarse-
and fine-grained modeling approaches for each aspect. Moreover, we conduct extensive experiments by integrating these approaches into existing
recommendation systems, and the results demonstrate that our proposed
methods can significantly improve their performance.

Keywords: Multi-modal recommendation · Preference-aware modality
encoder · Dynamic modality fusion

1 Introduction

With the increasing prevalence of micro-video platforms, such as Instagram[1],
Kuaishou[2], and TikTok[3], the amount of micro-videos generated and shared by
people are growing exponentially. Considering Kuaishou as an example, as of
January 2022, it had reached 232 million daily active users[4]; and as of June 2021,
it had reached 1.1 billion uploaded micro-videos monthly. With the micro-videos
surge, it becomes more and more difficult and expensive for users to find their
desired micro-videos from a large number of candidates. In light of this, it is very
necessary and meaningful to build a personalized micro-video recommendation
system.

For the past few years, several studies have been conducted on the personalized micro-video recommendation. Ma et al. [16] proposed a multi-source
and multi-net micro-video recommendation model, it combines the multi-source
information of items and the multi-network of users to learn representations

---

[1] https://www.instagram.com/.
[2] https://www.kuaishou.com/.
[3] https://www.tiktok.com/.
[4] https://baijiahao.baidu.com/s?id=1728624519477964205&wfr=spider&for=pc/.

S. Yu et al. (Eds.): PRCV 2022, LNCS 13534, pp. 330–343, 2022.
https://doi.org/10.1007/978-3-031-18907-4_26

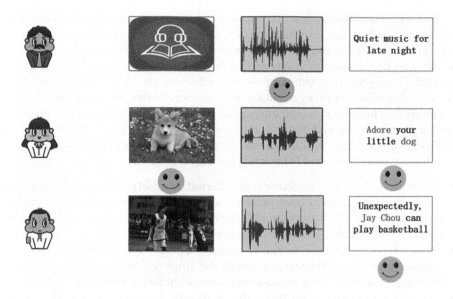

Fig. 1. An illustration of modality preferences for different users.

of users and items. More concretely, the multi-source item, multi-type user networks, and hidden item categories are jointly modeled in a unified recommender. Recently, inspired by the astonishing success of graph neural network in the computer vision community, graph neural network based micro-video recommendation systems attract more attention. For instance, Wei et al. [18] designed a multi-modal graph convolution network (MMGCN) for micro-video recommendation. It leverages information propagation mechanism of graph neural network to capture high-order interactions between users and micro-videos of each modality. To alleviate the noisy information in the graph, Liu et al. [14] proposed a concept-aware denoising graph neural network, which introduces a user-oriented graph denoising stage to exploit user preferences. Different from the aforementioned methods, Cai et al. [3] proposed a heterogeneous graph comparison learning network for personalized micro-video recommendation.

Although these methods achieve promising performance on recommendation, they commonly treat each modality equally. However, micro-videos are the unity of heterogeneous modalities, such as the textual, visual, and acoustic modality [12,13,17], which characterize the video content from multiple complementary views. And different users may pay various attention to different modality information. As illustrated in Fig. 1, the first user clicks a music micro-video due to he prefers the acoustic information. The second user attracted by the visual dog, while the third user attracted by the textual information "Jay Chou". Thereby, how to adaptively capture the preferred modality information of users for micro-video recommendation is crucial. Moreover, existing methods typically fuse multimodal information by concatenation or summation, ignoring the fact that different modality information has different influence. In light of this, it is necessary to explore more effective fusion mechanisms for micro-video recommendation.

To tackle these downsides, in this paper, we explore preference-aware modality representation learning and fusion approaches for micro-video recommendation. Specifically, given the multi-modal representation of the micro-video, we design coarse- and fine-grained modality embedding methods to highlight the interested modality representation and suppress the effect of the uninterested one. As to the modality information aggregation, we advance coarse- and fine-grained fusion mechanism to fuse multi-modal information, respectively. Note that our proposed modality embedding and fusion strategies are plug and play, and they can be applied to any existing multimodal micro-video recommendation systems.

The key contributions of this work are three-fold:

- We explore the user's preference on different modality information for micro-video recommendation, and present two preference-aware modality embedding strategies. Most importantly, they can be integrated into existing multimodal micro-video recommendation systems.
- We explore the dynamic modality fusion schemes for micro-video recommendation, which can adaptively reweigh the importance of each modality and be plugged into existing micro-video recommendation methods.
- Extensive experiments on two public datasets demonstrate that the performance of existing multimodal micro-video recommendation methods can be further improved by integrating our modality encoding and fusion strategies.

2 Related Work

Video recommendation has gained much attention from both academia and industry over recent years and many techniques have been developed for this task. In particular , Davidson et al. [5] proposed a video recommendation method for YouTube, which leverages the association rules and the relevant videos of the user to realize the recommendation. Bhalse et al. [2] utilized singular value decomposition collaborative filtering and cosine similarity to recommend users the videos that they have not yet been rated. Recently, Han et al. [6] exploited aspect-level features of the target micro-video and its feedbacks to calculate the overall click probability. Although the aforementioned approaches have achieved promising performance, they are single modality video recommendation systems. In other words, they thoroughly ignore the importance of the multi-modal information of the video.

In light of this, recent research attentions have been shifted to developing multi-modal recommendation systems for videos, especially micro-videos. In particular, Jin et al. [10] proposed the multi-modal interest evolution method to capture the interest information related to the target video. Moreover, to alleviate the cold start issue, it extracts multimodal features rather than unreliable metadata to represent the video content. Lei et al. [11] designed a sequential multimodal information transfer network, which utilizes cross-domain comparative learning to pre-train the sequence encoder, therefore modeling the sequence behavior of users for micro-video recommendation. As multi-type user networks can spread preferences among users, Ma et al. [15] jointly modeled multi-type user networks and hidden item categories in a unified framework, to improve recommendation performance. More concretely, it proposes an interactive manner to learn item representations by appropriately mining hidden categories of micro-videos that match users' interests at different levels. Inspired by the astonishing success of graph neural network in the computer vision community, graph neural network based micro-video recommendation systems attract more attention. For instance, Wei et al. [18] designed multi-modal graph convolution network framework for personalized micro-video recommendation. It utilizes interactions between users and micro-videos in various modalities to refine the corresponding representations of users and micro-videos. Liu et al. [14] proposed a denoising graph neural network, which introduces a user-oriented graph denoising mechanism to suppress the noise in the graph, therefore better capturing user preferences. Cai et al. [4] utilized random walk to sample neighbors of users and micro-video. and designed a hierarchical feature aggregation network to well capture complex structures and rich semantic information. Despite existing micro-video recommendation methods have shown their effectiveness [4,11,15,16], they overlook the importance of considering the user's preference on each modality. Moreover, they simply concatenate or average multi-modal representations as the micro-video representation, thoroughly ignoring the influence of each modality on the fused final representation. In this paper, we mainly tackle these downsides.

3 Methodology

In this paper, we mainly aim to explore the preference-aware modality representation and the dynamic modality fusion methods. Concretely, for the preference-aware modality representation, we intend to build a network, which could enhance the representation of the modality that the user preferred and suppress the modality representation that the user uninterested. As to the dynamic modality fusion, we target to design a new fusion mechanism that adaptively reweights the importance of each modality to fuse the multi-modal information. In the following, we will elaborate each module sequentially. To facilitate the understanding of our approaches, we select the MMGCN proposed in [18] as our backbone, as shown in Fig. 2.

3.1 Preference-Aware Modality Representation Layer

Given a micro-video, each modality information is fed into the encoder to obtain the initial modality embedding. Note that the modality encoder can be arbitrary network utilized in existing micro-video recommendation model. In this paper, the multimodal embeddings of the given micro-video is represented by $E = [v_1, v_2, \ldots, v_M]$, where $v_i \in R^k$ represents the embedding of the i-th modality, M represents the number of modalities, and k is the dimension of the embedding. As different users may prefer different modality information of the micro-video, we design two mechanisms to highlight the preference information of each modality for the user.

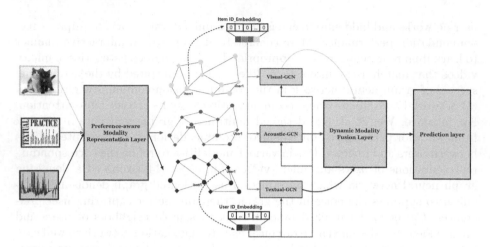

Fig. 2. Illustration of MMGCN integrated with our preference-aware modality representation module and dynamic modality fusion. Graphs marked in pink, green, and blue color are respectively refer to the visual graph, textual graph, and acoustic graph. And each node in the graph denotes the corresponding modality representation of the user/item. (Color figure online)

Coarse-Grained Preference Modeling. As users may pay various attentions on the multiple modality information of the micro-video, we advance the coarse-grained preference modeling, which adaptively highlight the preferred modality information for the specific user. Specifically, for the embedding of the m-th modality $\boldsymbol{v}_m \in \mathrm{R}^{k_m}$, we first adopt the following equation to calculate the importance score of each modality,

$$g_m^{coarse} = \sigma_1(\boldsymbol{w}_m^{coarse} \cdot \boldsymbol{v}_m + b_m), \tag{1}$$

where σ_1 is the activation function, as well as $\boldsymbol{w}_m^{coarse} \in \mathrm{R}^{1 \times k_m}$ and b_m respectively denote the learnable parameter vector and the bias value of the m-th modality.

Having obtained the preference score of each modality, we could generate the preference-aware modality representation as follows,

$$\hat{\boldsymbol{v}}_m^{coarse} = g_m^{coarse} \boldsymbol{v}_m. \tag{2}$$

Fine-Grained Preference Modeling. In each modality representation, different dimensions reflect different aspects of the micro-video. In this paper, we consider that different users may pay various attentions on these aspects. We hence advance the fine-grained preference modeling, which further exploits the fine-grained preference information of the user from the intra-modality.

In particular, given the embedding of the m-th modality, i.e., $\boldsymbol{v}_m \in \mathrm{R}^{k_m}$, we first calculate the dimension-wise preference score by adopting the following equation,

$$g_m^{fine} = \sigma_2(W_m^{fine} \cdot v_m + b_m), \tag{3}$$

where σ_2 is the activation function, as well as $W_m^{fine} \in R^{k_m \times k_m}$ and $b_m \in R^{k_m}$ respectively denote the learnable parameter matrix and the bias vector of the m-th modality.

Afterwards, the dimension-wise preference vector is assigned to the corresponding modality embedding, obtaining the fine-grained preference enhanced modality representation, as,

$$\hat{v}_m^{fine} = v_m \odot g_m^{fine}, \tag{4}$$

where $\odot$ represents the element-wise production.

As illustrated in Fig. 2, we feed the preference-aware multimodal representation of the micro-video, i.e., $\hat{v}_m^{coarse}$ or $\hat{v}_m^{fine}$, into the MMGCN network, obtaining the multimodal node representation, including the multimodal user representation and multimodal micro-video representation.

3.2 Dynamic Modality Fusion Layer

Existing micro-video recommendation methods judge whether to recommend the micro-video to the user or not by calculating the similarity between the representations of the micro-video and the user. To obtain the final representation of the micro-video/user, they commonly sum or concatenate multimodal representations. However, they ignore the fact that different users have different preferences on different modalities of the same micro-video. Inspired by this, in this paper, we present two mechanisms to dynamically fuse multi-modal information.

Coarse-Grained Fusion Mechanism. Supposing the m-th modality representation of the node output by the MMGCN is $t_m \in R^{d_m}$. Similar to the coarse-grained preference modeling, we first calculate the importance score of each modality, as follows,

$$[f_1^{coarse}, f_2^{coarse}, \ldots, f_M^{coarse}] = \sigma_3(O^{coarse} \cdot [t_1 \oplus t_2 \oplus \ldots \oplus t_M] + S^{coarse}), \tag{5}$$

where σ_3 is the activation function, $\oplus$ denotes the concatenation operation, $O^{coarse} \in R^{M \times Md_m}$ is the learnable parameter vector and S^{coarse} is the bias vector. And then we normalized the scores of all modalities via the Softmax function, as,

$$[\bar{f}_1^{coarse}, \bar{f}_2^{coarse}, \ldots, \bar{f}_M^{coarse}] = Softmax([f_1^{coarse}, f_2^{coarse}, \ldots, f_M^{coarse}]). \tag{6}$$

Afterwards, we weighted sum the multi-modal node representations, obtaining the final representation of the micro-video/user,

$$\bar{t} = \sum_{m=1}^{M} \bar{f}_m^{coarse} t_m. \tag{7}$$

Fine-Grained Fusion Mechanism. Similar to the fine-grained preference modeling, we also advance the fine-grained fusion mechanism. Concretely, we first compute the dimension-wise importance score for t_m by adopting the following equation,

$$[f_1^{fine}, f_2^{fine}, \ldots, f_M^{fine}] = \sigma_4(O^{fine} \cdot [t_1 \oplus t_2 \oplus \ldots \oplus t_M] + S^{fine}), \quad (8)$$

where σ_4 is the activation function, $O^{fine} \in \mathrm{R}^{Md_m \times Md_m}$ is the learnable parameter matrix and S^{fine} is the bias vector. And then we conduct column-wise normalization via Softmax for $A = [f_1^{fine}, f_2^{fine}, \ldots, f_M^{fine}] \in \mathrm{R}^{d_m \times M}$, obtaining the attention score of each modality, denoted by $\bar{f}_m^{fine}$. Thereafter, the final micro-video/user representation $\bar{t} \in \mathrm{R}^{d_m}$ is obtained as follows,

$$\bar{t} = \sum_{m=1}^{M} \bar{f}_m^{fine} \odot t_m. \quad (9)$$

4   Experiments

4.1   Datasets

In this paper, we conducted experiments on two public datasets: Movielens and Tiktok, to evaluate our proposed modality representation and fusion layers.

Movielens [8]: This dataset has been widely utilized in the field of recommendation system. It contains 5,986 movies and 55,485 users. For visual modality, the pre-trained ResNet50 [7] is used to extract visual features from movie trailers (not complete videos). For the acoustic modality, VGGish [9] is adopted to extract acoustic features from tracks separated by FFmpeg. As to the textual modality, Sentence2Vector [1] is leveraged to derive features from micro-video descriptions.

Tiktok[5]: It is officially released by Tiktok, which is a popular micro-video sharing platform all over the world. It contains 36,656 users and 76,085 micro-videos. The duration of each micro-video in this dataset is 3–15 seconds. The micro-video features in each modality are extracted and published without providing the raw data. In particular, the textual features are extracted from the micro-video captions given by users.

The statistics of the aforementioned two datasets are summarized in Table 1. We found that TikTok has the most items, while Movielens has the most interactions.

4.2   Experimental Settings

Evaluation Metrics. Following the existing method [18], we adopted Precision@K, Recall@K, and NDCG@K as the evaluation metrics, which are commonly utilized in the recommendation community. In this paper, K is set to 10 and the average score of the testing set is reported.

---

[5] http://ai-lab-challenge.bytedance.com/tce/vc/.

Table 1. Statistics of two datasets. V, A, and T denote the dimension of the visual, acoustic, and textual modality, respectively.

Dataset	Items	Users	Interactions	V	A	T	Sparsity
Movielens	5,986	55,485	1,239,508	2,048	128	100	99.63%
Tiktok	76,085	36,656	726,065	128	128	128	99.99%

Precision@K is defined as the average precision value of all users, as follows,

$$Precision@K = \sum_{i=1}^{N} Precision_i@K, \tag{10}$$

where $Precision_i@K = \frac{p_k^i}{K}$, p_k^i denotes the number of positive items among the top-k items for the i-th user, and N is the number of users.

Recall@K is defines as the average recall value of all users, as follows,

$$Recall@K = \sum_{i=1}^{N} Recall_i@K, \tag{11}$$

where $Recall_i@K = \frac{p_k^i}{p_i}$, p_i represents the positive items for the i-th user.

NDCG@K is formulated as follows,

$$\begin{cases} NDCG@K = \sum_{i=1}^{N} \frac{DCG@K}{\sum_{i=1}^{|REL|} \frac{2^{rel_i}-1}{\log_2(i+1)}}, \\ DCG@K = rel_1 + \sum_{i=2}^{N} \frac{rel_i}{\log_2(i+1)}, \end{cases} \tag{12}$$

where rel_i indicates whether the item in the i-th position is interacted by the user. If it is interacted, its value is 1, otherwise 0. $|REL|$ refers to the set that sorts the original recall from large to small.

Baselines. To verify the effectiveness of our preference-aware modality representation learning and dynamic modality fusion modules, we integrated these modules into existing micro-video recommendation approaches. As most of multimodal micro-video recommendation models did not release their codes, we selected the typical multimodal micro-video recommendation method MMGCN[6] as our main backbone. Meanwhile, we selected two recommendation models (i.e., NGCF and VBPR) that compared with MMGCN in [18] as our backbones.

- **NGCF.** This method integrates the user-item interactions into the embedding process, which encodes the collaborative filtering signal into the representation by exploiting the higher-order connectivity from user-item interactions. To fairly compare with MMGCN, it regards the multi-modal features of micro-video as side information and feed them into the framework to predict the interactions between the users and items.

---

[6] https://github.com/weiyinwei/MMGCN.

Table 2. Performance comparison between baselines with our proposed modules. In our work, P, C and P, F refer to the coarse- and fine-grained preference-aware modality representation module, respectively. D, C and D, F separately denote the coarse- and fine-grained modality fusion module.The best results are highlighted in bold.

Model	Movielens			TikTok		
	Precision	Recall	NDCG	Precision	Recall	NDCG
NGCF	0.0827	0.3596	0.2011	0.1624	0.5392	0.3492
NGCF$_{P,C}$	0.0822	0.3513	0.1947	0.1617	0.5353	0.3490
NGCF$_{P,F}$	0.0857	0.3701	0.2064	0.1665	0.5381	0.3514
NGCF$_{D,C}$	0.0828	0.3552	0.1975	0.1673	0.5422	0.3526
NGCF$_{D,F}$	0.0870	0.3737	0.2091	0.1678	0.5472	0.3538
NGCF$_{P,C+D,C}$	0.0859	0.3726	0.2041	0.1661	0.5372	0.3510
NGCF$_{P,C+D,F}$	0.0840	0.3606	0.2008	0.1664	0.5380	0.3509
NGCF$_{P,F+D,C}$	0.0853	0.3696	0.2031	0.1667	0.5387	0.3516
NGCF$_{P,F+D,F}$	0.0830	0.3603	0.2027	0.1669	0.5402	0.3538
VBPR	0.1112	0.4815	0.2799	0.1719	0.5769	0.3583
VBPR$_{P,C}$	0.1117	0.4842	0.2812	0.1710	0.5766	0.3593
VBPR$_{P,F}$	0.1125	0.4923	0.2873	0.1731	0.5811	0.3626
VBPR$_{D,C}$	0.1146	0.5052	0.2966	0.1762	0.5920	0.3711
VBPR$_{D,F}$	0.1229	0.5161	0.3046	0.1802	0.6054	0.3795
VBPR$_{P,C+D,C}$	0.1147	0.5054	0.2970	0.1722	0.5771	0.3607
VBPR$_{P,C+D,F}$	0.1229	0.5169	0.3038	0.1763	0.5918	0.3703
VBPR$_{P,F+D,C}$	0.1153	0.5083	0.2984	0.1793	0.6021	0.3785
VBPR$_{P,F+D,F}$	0.1227	0.5158	0.3036	0.1769	0.5947	0.3724
MMGCN	0.1332	0.5076	0.3744	0.1821	0.5900	0.4600
MMGCN$_{P,C}$	0.1308	0.5001	0.3683	0.1803	0.5885	0.4588
MMGCN$_{P,F}$	0.1334	0.5097	0.3766	0.1868	0.6057	0.4746
MMGCN$_{D,C}$	0.1342	0.5112	0.3795	0.1856	0.6017	0.4700
MMGCN$_{D,F}$	0.1349	0.5121	0.3808	0.1873	0.6065	0.4884
MMGCN$_{P,C+D,C}$	0.1341	0.5114	0.3768	0.1833	0.5971	0.4638
MMGCN$_{P,C+D,F}$	0.1342	0.5115	0.3771	0.1810	0.5894	0.4569
MMGCN$_{P,F+D,C}$	**0.1353**	**0.5172**	**0.3835**	**0.1870**	**0.6122**	**0.4942**
MMGCN$_{P,F+D,F}$	0.1348	0.5152	0.3828	0.1867	0.6041	0.4746

- **VBPR.** Based on the matrix factorization, this model integrates the content features and ID embeddings of each item as its representation, to build the historical interaction between users and items. Similar to NGCF, to fairly compare with MMGCN, it regards the multi-modal features of micro-video as side information and feed them into the framework to predict the interactions between the users and items.

- **MMGCN.** This model leverages multimodal graph convolution network to capture user-item interactions within different modalities, to refine the representation of the user and item nodes. By fusing the multimodal user/item representations, it could acquire the final user and item representation for prediction.

Implementation Details. We respectively split the datasets into 80%, 10%, and 10% as the training, validation, and testing set, respectively. The dimension k_m is respectively set to 2048, 128, and 100 for the visual, acoustic, and textual modality on Movielens, while it is set as 128 for three modalities on Tiktok. The dimension d_m is set to 64. On two datasets, for the baseline NGCF, σ_1 and σ_2 are the sigmoid activation function, as well as σ_3 and σ_4 are the tanh activation function; for the baseline VBPR, σ_1 and σ_2 are the leaky-relu activation function, as well as σ_3 and σ_4 are the relu activation function; as to the baseline MMGCN, $\sigma_1,\sigma_2,\sigma_3$ and σ_4 are the leaky-relu activation function. We adopted SGD as our optimizer, and the initial learning rate is set to 0.0005. The batch size is set as 1024. Our work is based on GeForce RTX 2080 Ti GPU using PyTorch library.

4.3   Performance Comparison

The results of all methods on two datasets are summarized in Table 2. From this table, we have the following observations:

- All the baselines integrated our fine-grained preference-aware modality representation learning module achieve better performance than the the coarse-grained based ones, and they substantially surpass their original models. Particularly, $NGCF_{P,F}$ obtains 2.9% relative gains in terms of Recall on Movielens as compared to NGCF. $VBPR_{P,F}$ obtains 2.2% relative gains in terms of Recall on Movielens as compared to VBPR. $MMGCN_{P,F}$ obtains 2.7% relative gains in terms of Recall on TikTok as compared to MMGCN. These results validate the effectiveness of our fine-grained preference-aware modality representation learning module.
- Baselines based on our dynamic fusion module are superior to the baselines without our fusion module. To be specific, $MMGCN_{D,C}$ obtains 1.4% and 2.2% relative gains in terms of NDCG on Movielens and TikTok, respectively. Moreover, our fine-grained modality fusion module based approaches outperform coarse-grained modality fusion based ones. For instance, compared with $MMGCN_{D,C}$, $MMGCN_{D,F}$ obtains 3.9% relative gains in terms of NDCG on TikTok. These results demonstrate the effectiveness of our dynamic modality fusion approaches, especially the fine-grained modality fusion one.
- Jointly considering the preference-aware modality representation and modality fusion module, existing baselines also achieve promising performing. Concretely, $MMGCN_{P,F+D,C}$ achieves the best performance, it respectively outperforms $MMGCN_{D,F}$ and $MMGCN_{P,F}$ by a considerable margin. This further demonstrates the superiority of our proposed preference-aware modality representation and fusion modules, as well as the effectiveness of considering

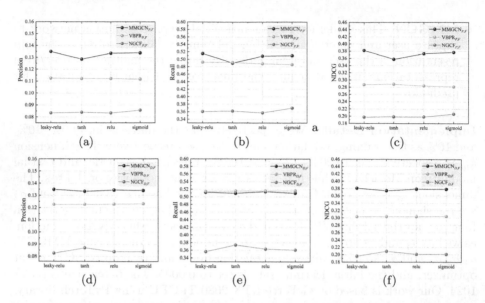

Fig. 3. Influence of different activation functions on Movielens. (a)–(c) respectively show the Precision, Recall, and NDCG of baselines with our fine-grained modality representation module. (d)–(f) separately display the Precision, Recall, and NDCG of baselines with our fine-grained modality fusion module.

the user's preference information for micro-video recommendation. Instead of $MMGCN_{P,F+D,F}$, $MMGCN_{P,F+D,C}$ achieves the best performance, the reason may be that the user representation is more dependent on coarse-grained semantic information of each modality.

4.4   Ablation Study

Influence of the Activation Function. As reported in Table 2, both fine-grained preference-aware modality representation and modality fusion modules achieve better performance than the coarse-grained ones. In this section, we conducted several experiments on Movielens to further explore how the activation function affects the performance of each module and the micro-video recommendation. As shown in Fig. 3, Fig. 3(a)–(c) display the Precision, Recall, and NDCG results of the baselines with fine-grained preference-aware modality representation module. Figure 3(d)–(f) display the Precision, Recall, and NDCG results of the baselines with fine-grained modality fusion module. By analyzing these figures, we can find that 1) different activation functions have great influence on the performance of our proposed two modules. 2) The optimal activation function for different backbone methods are different. Particularly, for the modality representation module, $MMGCN_{P,F}$ achieves the best performance with the leaky-relu activation function, $VBPR_{P,F}$ achieves promising performance with the leaky-relu activation function, and $NGCF_{P,F}$ achieve the best results with sigmoid

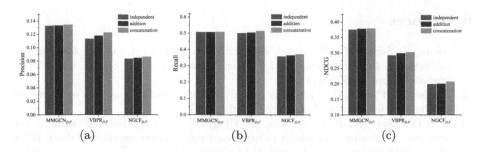

Fig. 4. Performance comparison among fine-grained modality fusion based baselines with different aggregation methods on Movielens.

activation function. For the modality fusion module, $MMGCN_{D,F}$ achieves the best performance with the leaky-relu activation function, $VBPR_{D,F}$ achieves promising performance with the relu activation function, and $NGCF_{D,F}$ achieve the best results with tanh activation function. And 3) VBPR is not sensitive to the change of activation function. These results reflect that it is very important to select the appropriate activation function for our proposed two modules when we apply them to existing recommendation systems.

Influence of Aggregation Methods. In our fine-grained modality fusion module (i.e., Eq. (8)), we adopted the concatenation operation to aggregate multimodal information for importance score calculation. To justify its effectiveness, we design two variants: 1) addition, directly adding multi-modal representations of each node to calculate fine-grained attention scores; and 2) independent refers to that we calculate scores for each modality by independently processing the representation of each modality. As illustrated in Fig. 4, we can see that the concatenation strategy achieves the best performance. This demonstrates the effectiveness of our aggregation operation and the importance of considering other modality information to calculate the score of the current modality.

5   Conclusion

In this work, we present preference-aware modality representation learning approaches and dynamic modality fusion approaches, to further enhance the performance of existing multi-modal micro-video recommendation systems. Extensive experiments on two public datasets verify the effectiveness of our proposed approaches.

Acknowledgement. This work is supported by the National Natural Science Foundation of China, No.: 62006142; the Shandong Provincial Natural Science Foundation for Distinguished Young Scholars, No.: ZR2021JQ26; the Major Basic Research Project of Natural Science Foundation of Shandong Province, No.: ZR2021ZD15; Science and Technology Innovation Program for Distinguished Young Scholars of Shandong Province Higher Education In-stitutions, No.: 2021KJ036.

References

1. Arora, S., Liang, Y., Ma, T.: A simple but tough-to-beat baseline for sentence embeddings. In: Proceedings of the International Conference on Learning Representations, pp. 1–16 (2017)
2. Bhalse, N., Thakur, R.: Algorithm for movie recommendation system using collaborative filtering. Mater. Today Proc., 1–6 (2021)
3. Cai, D., Qian, S., Fang, Q., Hu, J., Ding, W., Xu, C.: Heterogeneous graph contrastive learning network for personalized micro-video recommendation. IEEE Trans. Multimedia (Early Access), 1–13 (2022)
4. Cai, D., Qian, S., Fang, Q., Xu, C.: Heterogeneous hierarchical feature aggregation network for personalized micro-video recommendation. IEEE Trans. Multimedia **24**, 805–818 (2021)
5. Davidson, J., et al.: The youtube video recommendation system. In: Proceedings of the ACM Conference on Recommender systems, pp. 293–296 (2010)
6. Han, Y., Gu, P., Gao, W., Xu, G., Wu, J.: Aspect-level sentiment capsule network for micro-video click-through rate prediction. World Wide Web **24**(4), 1045–1064 (2020). https://doi.org/10.1007/s11280-020-00858-z
7. He, K., Zhang, X., Ren, S., Sun, J.: Deep residual learning for image recognition. In: Proceedings of the IEEE Conference on Computer Vision and Pattern Recognition, pp. 770–778 (2016)
8. Herlocker, J.L., Konstan, J.A., Borchers, A., Riedl, J.: An algorithmic framework for performing collaborative filtering. In: Proceedings of the International ACM SIGIR Conference on Research and Development in Information Retrieval, pp. 230–237 (1999)
9. Hershey, S., et al.: CNN architectures for large-scale audio classification. In: Proceedings of the IEEE International Conference on Acoustics, Speech and Signal Processing, pp. 131–135 (2017)
10. Jin, Y., Xu, J., He, X.: Personalized micro-video recommendation based on multimodal features and user interest evolution. In: Proceedings of the International Conference on Image and Graphics, pp. 607–618 (2019)
11. Lei, C., et al.: Semi: A sequential multi-modal information transfer network for e-commerce micro-video recommendations. In: Proceedings of the ACM SIGKDD Conference on Knowledge Discovery & Data Mining, pp. 3161–3171 (2021)
12. Liu, M., Nie, L., Wang, M., Chen, B.: Towards micro-video understanding by joint sequential-sparse modeling. In: Proceedings of the ACM International Conference on Multimedia, pp. 970–978 (2017)
13. Liu, M., Nie, L., Wang, X., Tian, Q., Chen, B.: Online data organizer: micro-video categorization by structure-guided multimodal dictionary learning. IEEE Trans. Image Process. **28**(3), 1235–1247 (2018)
14. Liu, Y., et al.: Concept-aware denoising graph neural network for micro-video recommendation. In: Proceedings of the 30th ACM International Conference on Information & Knowledge Management, pp. 1099–1108 (2021)
15. Ma, J., Wen, J., Zhong, M., Chen, W., Li, X.: Mmm: multi-source multi-net micro-video recommendation with clustered hidden item representation learning. Data Sci. Eng. **4**(3), 240–253 (2019)
16. Ma, J., Wen, J., Zhong, M., Chen, W., Zhou, X., Indulska, J.: Multi-source multi-net micro-video recommendation with hidden item category discovery. In: International Conference on Database Systems for Advanced Applications, pp. 384–400 (2019)

17. Nie, L., et al.: Enhancing micro-video understanding by harnessing external sounds. In: Proceedings of the ACM International Conference on Multimedia, pp. 1192–1200 (2017)
18. Wei, Y., Wang, X., Nie, L., He, X., Hong, R., Chua, T.S.: MMGCN: multi-modal graph convolution network for personalized recommendation of micro-video. In: Proceedings of the ACM International Conference on Multimedia, pp. 1437–1445 (2019)

Multi-intent Compatible Transformer Network for Recommendation

Tuo Wang[1], Meng Jian[1], Ge Shi[1], Xin Fu[2], and Lifang Wu[1(✉)]

[1] Faculty of Information Technology, Beijing University of Technology,
Beijing, China
lfwu@bjut.edu.cn
[2] School of Water Conservancy and Environment, University of Jinan, Jinan, China

Abstract. The core of recommendation systems is to explore users' preferences from users' historical records and accordingly recommend items to meet users' interests. Previous works explore interaction graph to capture multi-order collaborative signals and derive high-quality representations of users and items, which effectively alleviates the interaction sparsity issue. Recent works extend the scope with a fine-grained perspective and achieve a great success in modeling users' diverse intents. Although these works distinguish intents, they ignore the hidden correlation among users' intents resulting in suboptimal recommendation performance. We argue that a user's interest is made up of multiple intents and these intents are compatible on the interest composition of the user. To this point, we propose multi-intent compatible transformer network (MCTN) to explore the correlation between intents on modeling users' interests for recommendation. Users and items are embedded into multiple intent spaces through disentangled graph convolution network to disentangle users' intents. MCTN conducts embedding propagation in each intent space to capture the multi-order collaborative signals on the specific intent. We introduce a transformer network to capture the dependence between intents and derive multi-intent compatible embeddings of users and items for recommendation. The experiments achieves state-of-the-art performance, which demonstrates the effectiveness of the proposed MCTN on modeling multi-intent compatibility into embeddings.

Keywords: Recommendation · Multi-intent matching · Transformer network

1 Introduction

With the vigorous development of information services on the Internet, the amount of information available in people's daily life has increased greatly. The increase of information is a double-edged sword. It can expand people's sight and knowledge and bring convenient and efficient response to their requirements. At the same time, the wide variety of information also makes it difficult to obtain the specific information satisfying users. Information services meet a big challenge

S. Yu et al. (Eds.): PRCV 2022, LNCS 13534, pp. 344–355, 2022.
https://doi.org/10.1007/978-3-031-18907-4_27

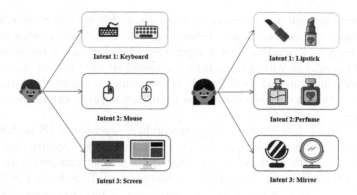

Fig. 1. Examples of compatibility among intents.

from information overload. An effective solution to address the problem is the emerging recommendation system [21]. The core is to explore users' preferences according to users' historical records and recommend information that users may be interested in.

The mainstream of recommendation techniques obey the classical collaborative filtering (CF) rule [1,2,4,7], which depends on the historical user-item interactions (e.g., browsing, collection and purchase) to recommend items with similar attributes or items interacted by other users with similar interests to the target user. In CF-based models, user/item representations play a vital role on predicting users' interests. Extensive experiments verify their success on modeling users' interests for recommendation. However, most of the existing models pay their attention on generating a unified user/item representation [3,5,6], ignoring their complex composition of intents in users' interests. The unified representation mixes the hidden intents and fails to distinguish these intents when modeling users' interests, which weakens the recommendation performance to a certain degree. To address this problem, from the perspective of fine-grained representation, some studies employ capsule network [8] or side information [22] (e.g., knowledge graph, social network) to distinguish specific interests in embeddings [4,10]. Others [9,12] decompose the user-item bipartite graph into heterogeneous graph structures with multiple relational spaces and independently explore representations on the specific interests, which has greatly improved the recommendation performance.

The above intent-aware matching models [8] merely maps interest embeddings into multiple independent spaces to learn user/item representations. However, these models ignore the hidden correlation among intents when modeling users. We argue that a user's interest is made up of multiple intents and these intents are compatible on the interest composition of the user. Taking Fig. 1 as an example, if a boy buys a computer screen as part of the computer peripherals, he will browse or buy other computer related devices, such as mouse and keyboard. Although the items belong to the boy's different intents, there is a certain correlation on usage, that is, compatibility. Similarly, a girl, who loves beauty, needs lipstick and perfume to dress up, and it is even more essential to equip a mirror to appreciate her dressed up. Obviously, the intents of the girl are not totally independent, but compatible. Therefore, on interest matching, we should not only pay attention on the independent intents, but also take their compatibility into interest modeling. It is promising to model the compatibility between intents into user representation to further improve the recommendation performance.

In the field of data mining, many researchers leverage RNN or LSTM networks to model data correlation [13]. These models fail to capture long-distance signals. At the same time, they are limited by a huge computational burden resulting in low efficiency. Recently, the emergence of Transformer network [14] has set off an upsurge of correlation computation. It has been widely applied in NLP, Audio, CV and other domains [16] and has shown excellent performance in various downstream tasks. The vanilla-Transformer model [14] employs self-attention mechanism to capture the relevance of long-distance features in sentences, explore the dependency between words in a sentence, and strengthen the word presentation. Moreover, on the computational burden, the correlation between arbitrary two elements is immediately derived which greatly improves computational efficiency. With the advantages, Transformer is available to mine compatibility between intents, so as to enrich the representation of users/items for recommendation.

To mine compatibility between multiple intents of users' interests, we propose multi-intent compatible transformer network (MCTN), which leverages the correlation of multiple intents to model users' interests at a fine-grained level. The intent correlations take compatibility signals between intents and play positive to enrich the representations of users/items. MCTN pays attention to the hidden correlation between node-level neighbors of the users' interaction graph. It performs interaction division of multiple intents through intent disentangling and propagates collaborative signals within each intent space independently. Besides, we construct multi-intent compatible aggregation module with transformer network to extract correlation between intents. The extracted compatibility signals are further involved to strengthen node representation. The matching degree between user nodes and item nodes are measured for recommendation. For specific users, the items with high scores are ranked into personalized recommendation lists. The main contributions of this work are summarized as follows.

- We emphasize the correlation among intents, i.e., compatibility, hidden in users' interests. This work strives to take the hypothesis into interest modeling to improve representation for recommendation.
- We propose multi-intent compatible transformer network (MCTN), which forms disentangled intents in multiple spaces by graph disentangling and innovatively introduces transformer network to capture compatibility among intents to model user interests.
- We conduct experiments on the real-world Gowalla dataset, which demonstrates the state-of-the-art performance of MCTN and proves its effectiveness in modeling users and items with disentangled compatible intents.

2   Related Work

The proposed MCTN method belongs to the representation learning paradigm based on graph neural network (GNN), and applies the transformer structure for multi-interest matching task. Here we will introduce the relevant literature of graph representation learning, multi-interest matching in recommendation and pay attention to the limitations of these methods.

The most classic algorithm Matrix Factorization (MF) [5] in the recommendation system embedds the user and item IDs into vectors in the same latent space, and uses the linear inner-product function to model the user-item interaction to obtain the final matching score. On this basis, some studies believe that using deep neural network for matching prediction can more effectively capture the nonlinear interaction information between users and items, such as NCF [1]. However, these methods treat each user-item pair as an isolated data instance and ignore their relationship in the embedding function. Because graph neural network can capture the information between high-order connected nodes, most existing methods pay attention to the application of graph representation learning in recommendation scenario. For example, GC-MC [6] designs a graph self-encoder framework based on user-item bipartite graph to solve the matching prediction problem from the perspective of link prediction. NGCF [3] explicitly models high-order connectivity between users and items to improve the quality of user and item embedding. However, these methods only produce a unified representation, ignoring that there may be a variety of latent factors behind the interaction, which makes the embedding entangled, resulting in suboptimal recommendation performance.

Aware that the unified representation may be insufficient to reflect the complex factors behind the interaction, some studies focus on the feature matching between users and items from multiple intent perspectives at a fine-grained level. DisenGCN [10] proposed the decoupling representation of the nodes in graph for the first time, using the capsule network to dynamically decouple the vector representation related to different potential factors, but did not propose a clear independence constraint. MacridVAE [11] applies the decoupling representation to the recommendation scenario for the first time, decouples the user embedding from the macro and micro perspectives, reflects the user's different intent from the macro perspective, reflects the different aspects of a single intention from the micro perspective, and encourages the independence between different intents through KL divergence, but it is unable to capture the high-order information of nodes and does not make effective use of collaborative filtering signals. DGCF [4] decomposes the user-item bipartite graph into several subgraphs, each of which focuses on different intents, and constrains the differences between the node representations of different subgraphs through the independence loss function. DisenHAN [9] through the social relationship between users and the knowledge information between items, design the concept of meta-relation, decompose the interaction graph into different heterogeneous graphs structure according to the meta-relation, and use the attention mechanism to aggregate the neighbor information in different graphs. DICE [7] decouples the user's interest and conformity, and carries out the decoupling task for specific cause for the first time. ComiRec [8] captures a variety of different interests through the user's behavior sequence and recalls some similar items. AIMN [12] divides different interest spaces according to the item attributes in the knowledge graph, and realizes personalized recommendation according to the interest of different users.

The above interest matching methods focus on the feature of user/item in a single intent space. However, the relationship between multiple intents is not irrelevant, and there is mutual influence in essence. Regardless of the compatibility, the representation learned under each intent is lack of information, which reduces the quality of the representation.

3   Multi-intent Compatible Transformer Network

In this section, we present the proposed multi-intent compatible transformer network, and the model framework is illustrated in Fig. 2. MCTN takes the historical interaction between the user and the item as the input and outputs the prediction probability between the user and the target item. We divide the model into four subsections:

Input and Initialization: Different from general representation learning, this method needs different dimensions to focus on different intents, so we will introduce the specific data form in this subsection.

Intent Disentangling: After obtaining the node features after initialization, we capture the K latent factors of interaction through the dynamic routing algorithm, and conduct embedding propagation and multi-layer aggregation respectively to independently enrich the representation in their corresponding intent space.

Multi-intent Compatible Aggregation: This module sends the representations in K spaces into the transformer structure, explores the compatibility between different intents, and aggregates the missing information in a single space to enhance the representation ability.

Matching and Model Optimization: We match the representations of K spaces to get the final prediction score, and introduce the objective function used in this task.

3.1   Input and Initialization

We take the users' historical interaction graph as the input, $u = (u_1, u_2 \ldots u_M)$, $i = (i_1, i_2 \ldots i_N)$ represents the user set and the item set,which M, N represents the number of users and items respectively. If user u has interacted with item i, then $A(u, i) = 1$, otherwise 0. $A()$ is the adjacency value in the user-item bipartite graph. We first initialize a feature vector randomly for each user and

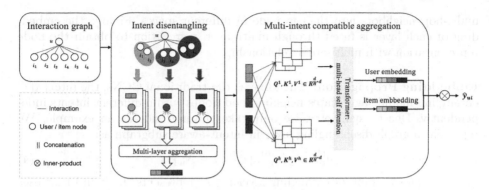

Fig. 2. Framework of the proposed multi-intent compatible transformer network for recommendation (MCTN)

item ID. In general, we call the characteristics of user and item as $u, i \in R^d$ respectively. In order to independently capture the representation of users/items under K intents, we divide each vector into K feature spaces,and initialize them respectively. Formally, the user/item embedding is represented as:

$$u = (u_1, u_2 \dots u_K), i = (i_1, i_2 \dots i_K), \tag{1}$$

$u_k \in R^{\frac{d}{K}}, i_k \in R^{\frac{d}{K}}$ are the representation of users and items under the k-th intent, separately. After obtaining the representation in different spaces, we believe that each user has different preferences for the same item driven by different intents. Using a unified graph can not effectively describe each intent space, so each space should correspond to a weighted intent-aware subgraph . Formally, the adjacency value in each subgraph is represented as:

$$A(u, i) = (A_1(u, i), A_2(u, i) \dots A_K(u, i)), \tag{2}$$

$A_k(u, i)$ represents the interaction value between user u and item i driven by the k-th intent. For the initialization of each subgraph, we uniformly set that the contribution of u-i interaction pair under each intent is the equal, that is:

$$A(u, i) = (1, 1 \dots 1), \tag{3}$$

In the later module, we only iteratively update the adjacency value between the user and the item that has interacted in traning set(i.e., $A(u, i) = 1$).

3.2 Intent Disentangling

Here, we refer to the structure of DGCF [4]. Firstly, K latent factors are corresponding to different intents through the dynamic routing mechanism. According to the contribution of the neighbors node to the ego node under different intents, several neighbor nodes are divided into different subsets iteratively, and then the embedding propagation uses the GCN paradigm to integrate the information of multi-hop neighbors into the ego node in different spaces. Finally, the embedding of each layer is fused through multi-layer aggregation to obtain the node representation with multi-order relationship.

Embedding Propagation: The same as the traditional GCNs, the intent disentangling module aggregates neighborhood nodes within different intents independently. Due to symmetry, we only take the user side as an example. We represent a graph disentangling layer in intent-aware subgraph as:

$$u_k^{(1)} = g(u_k^{(0)}, \{i_k^{(0)} \mid i \in N_u\}), \tag{4}$$

$g()$ represents a graph disentangling layer, $i \in N_u$ represents the item i that user u has interacted with, $u_k^{(0)}, i_k^{(0)}$ represents the embedding of user u and item i in layer 0 (initial) under the k-th intent respectively, and $u_k^{(1)}$ captures the collaborative signal of user i's one-hop neighbor node. In each graph disentangling layer, the contribution of neighbor nodes to ego nodes is different driven by different intents, so we need to use dynamic routing mechanism to iteratively update the adjacency values of subgraphs in different spaces. Firstly, we need to normalize the adjacency values in different spaces using softmax function to obtain its distribution under different intents:

$$\widetilde{A_k^t}(u, i) = \frac{\exp A_k^t(u, i)}{\sum_{k'=1}^{K} \exp A_{k'}^t(u, i)} \tag{5}$$

$\widetilde{A_k^t}(u, i)$ represents the adjacency value between user u and item i in the k-th space in iteration t. When $t = 0$, we set $\widetilde{A_k^0}(u, i) = A_k(u, i)$.

LightGCN [16] believes that in the recommendation scenario, the nonlinear activation function and transformation matrix in GCN will not increase the expressiveness of features effectively, so we also remove these two parts and propagate feature for different intents. Specifically, embedding propagation is expressed as:

$$u_k^t = \sum_{i \in N_u} \frac{\widetilde{A_k^t}(u, i)}{\sqrt{D_k^t(u) \cdot D_k^t(i)}} \cdot i_k^0 \tag{6}$$

$D_k^t(u) = \sum_{i \in N_u} \widetilde{A_k^t}(u, i), D_k^t(i) = \sum_{u \in N_i} \widetilde{A_k^t}(u, i)$ is node degree of user u and item i respectively. Similarly, we set the initial value of user and item embedding as $u_k^0 = u_k, i_k^0 = i_k$.

After embedding propagation, we update the adjacency values of subgraphs in different spaces. We judge the contribution of neighbors driven by different intents by the affinity of neighbor nodes to ego nodes in each space.

$$A_k^{t+1}(u, i) = A_k^t(u, i) + \tanh(u_k^{t\,T} \cdot i_k^0) \tag{7}$$

By iteratively updating the adjacency matrix and eigenvector T times, the neighbor nodes are adaptively segmented into different intent spaces and output node representations of one graph disentangling layer $u_k^{(1)}, i_k^{(1)}$. At this time, the feature is a collaborative signal containing one-hop neighbor node information.

Multi-layer Aggregation: In order to capture the information of multi-hops neighbors, we stack multiple graph disentangling layers to aggregate the collaborative signals of multi-order neighbors. Formally, the features of layer l are expressed as:

$$u_k^{(l)} = g(u_k^{(l-1)}, \{i_k^{(l-1)} \mid i \in N_u\}) \tag{8}$$

After the L graph disentangling layers, we use average pooling to fuse the collaborative signals between different layers. Specifically, the final output of node in k-th intent space is:

$$Y_{u,k} = \frac{1}{L+1} \sum_{l=0}^{L} u_k^{(l)} \tag{9}$$

3.3 Multi-intent Compatible Aggregation

Only focusing on the collaborative information within the intent independently, the obtained feature representation may lack the information in other intents, and this part of the missing information may lead to the suboptimal performance of the recommendation. Therefore, in this subsection, we emphasize the relationship modeling between intents. In the previous section, we have introduced the advantages of transformer network in relationship modeling. Here, we use the multi-head self attention mechanism in transformer to capture the interrelated information between intents. Multi-head learning strategy can help us pay attention to different aspects of intents in each subspace.

The transformation matrix of the h-th head is initialized to $Q^h, k^h, V^h \in R^{\frac{d}{H} \times d}$. First, we calculate the correlation scores between different intent spaces and normalize them through the softmax function:

$$\alpha_{k,k'}^h = \frac{(Q^h \cdot Y_{u,k})^T (K^h \cdot Y_{u,k'})}{\sqrt{\frac{d}{H}}} \tag{10}$$

$$\widetilde{\alpha_{k,k'}^h} = \frac{\exp \alpha_{k,k'}^h}{\sum_{k'=1}^{K} \alpha_{k,k'}^h} \tag{11}$$

where $Y_{u,k}, Y_{u,k'}$ denote representation of user u in k-th and k'-th intent space. For the correlation score $\widetilde{\alpha_{k,k'}^h}$ of a specific head h, we integrate the representations of other intents into the specific intent to capture the missing information in the specific intent. Finally, we concatenation the representations of different heads to get final enhanced representation $Z_{u,k}$.

$$Z_{u,k} = \mathop{\Big|\Big|}_{1}^{H} \sum_{k'=1}^{K} \widetilde{\alpha_{k,k'}^h} \cdot V^h \cdot Y_{u,k'} + Y_{u,k} \tag{12}$$

Here, we use residual connection [15] to prevent the gradient vanish problem.

3.4 Matching and Model Optimization

Finally, the representations of users and items in the same space are matched, and the matching scores of different spaces are summed. We use the inner-product function to obtain the matching score of u-i pair $\widehat{y}_{ui}$.

$$\widehat{y}_{ui} = \sum_{k=1}^{K} Z_{u,k}{}^{T} \cdot Z_{i,k} \tag{13}$$

The proposed loss function of MCTN selects pairwise BPR loss to optimize the model parameters. Its purpose is to make the score of items interacted by users higher than those not observed, and minimize the following objective function:

$$loss_{\text{BPR}} = \sum_{(u,i,j)=O} -\ln \sigma \left(\widehat{y}_{ui} - \widehat{y}_{uj}\right) + \lambda \|\theta\|_2^2 \tag{14}$$

where $O = \{(u, i, j) \mid (u, i) \in O^+, (u, j) \in O^-\}$, O^+ represents the interaction between user u and item i, and O^- represents the interaction not observed by the user. $\sigma()$ is a sigmoid function that controls the strength of L2 regularization in order to control the overfitting problem of the model. Model training parameter set $\theta = \{Q^h, k^h, V^h, u, i\}$.

4 Experiment

4.1 Experimental Setting

In order to verify the rationality of the proposed MCTN, we use a real-world Gowalla dataset for experiments. Gowalla is a location-based social website. The statistics of dataset such as numbers of user, item and interaction are summarized in Table 1. We equipped MCTN with a NVIDIA GeForce RTX 3090 GPU and implemented in the environment of TensorFlow2.4.0 and Python3.7. For dataset, the ratio of positive sample of training set and test set is 8:2. For MCTN, we fixed the number of iterations T as 2, number of intent as 4, the coefficient of L2 regularization as 0.001, and the learning rate was tuned between 0.001, 0.0001, 0.00001. In order to compare the fairness of performance, we fixed the embedding dimension as 64 and batch size as 1024, which is consistent with other baselines. Because our method dynamically updates the adjacency matrix, in order to balance the time cost and performance accuracy, we set the number of graph convolution layers of MCTN and DGCF to 2, and the number of convolution layers of other GNN-based methods to 3. For each user, MCTN and other baselines will calculate the prediction score of all items except the training set, and rank it according to the score. The performance is quantitatively evaluated with recall at rank N (recall@N)and normalize discounted cumulative gain at rank N (ndcg@N). In this paper, we set N = 20 and demonstrate the average metrics performance for all users in the test set.

Table 1. Statistics of Gowalla Dataset

Dataset	Gowalla	
User-item interactions	#Users	29,858
	#Items	40,981
	#Interactions	1,027,370
	Density	0.00084

4.2 Performance Comparison

We compare the proposed MCTN with several effective methods, including the most classical collaborative filtering algorithm (MF [5]), GNN-based collaborative filtering algorithm (GC-MC [1], NGCF [3]), disentangled graph convolution algorithm (DisenGCN [10], DGCF [4], MacridVAE [11]). The performance results are reported in Table 2. The bold data represents the comparison between the strongest baseline and our method. We use baseline evaluation results in [4] except DGCF, because we cannot reproduce the best performance reported in paper of DGCF with our environment. According to the statistical data, we can observe that:

- Overall, the proposed MCTN has better performance than all baselines. Specifically, on Gowalla, recall@20 and ndcg@20 increased by 2.84% and 4.71% respectively. The performance proves the effectiveness of the proposed MCTN in capturing the compatibility between different intents to improve the quality of representation.
- GC-MC and NGCF are two GNN-based methods. Compared with MF, their performance has been greatly improved. It shows that capturing the multi-order collaborative relationship between users and items makes the representation contain more information, alleviates data sparsity issue and improves the performance of recommendation.
- DisenGCN, MacridVAE and DGCF are three methods based on graph disentangling. Compared with GC-MC and NGCF, the performance of MacridVAE and DGCF has been greatly improved, which proves that the unified representation can not well reflect multiple intents of users, and fine-grained intent modeling can further enhance the representation ability of nodes. However, the performance of DisenGCN on Gowalla is not ideal. We believe that the coupling between different intent representations caused by the MLP layer in DisenGCN leads to the decline of performance.
- MCTN has a certain improvement in performance compared with the strongest method DGCF, which proves the effectiveness of capturing the compatibility between intents again. At the same time, our transformer network models separately for different intent spaces, which will not cause excessive coupling between intent representations. DGCF can be used as our ablation experiment to prove the importance of transformer network in improving node representation ability.

Table 2. Performance comparison in Gowalla Dateset

Method	recall@20	ndcg@20
MF	0.1291	0.1109
GC-MC	0.1395	0.1204
NGCF	0.1569	0.1327
DisenGCN	0.1356	0.1174
MacridVAE	0.1618	0.1202
DGCF	**0.1686**	**0.1421**
MCTN	**0.1734**	**0.1488**
%Improve	2.84%	4.71%

5   Conclusion

In this paper, we propose a multi-intent compatible transformer network (MCTN) to explore the correlation between intents on modeling users' interests for recommendation. We recognize that fine-grained representation learning can improve the recommendation performance. In addition, we also believe that there is a hidden relationship between different intents, and modeling alone will lead to the missing of information. Therefore, we use the structure of transformer to model the relationship between the same node in different spaces and extract the missing information of specific intent, so as to enhance the representation ability of embedding. Compared with other recommendation algorithms, the experimental results confirm the effectiveness of the proposed MCTN.

Acknowledgement. This work was supported by the National Natural Science Foundation of China under Grant NO. 62176011, NO. 61976010, and NO. 62106010, Inner Mongolia Autonomous Region Science and Technology Foundation under Grant NO. 2021GG0333, and Beijing Postdoctoral Research Foundation under Grant NO. Q6042001202101.

References

1. He, X., Liao, L., Zhang, H., Nie, L., Hu, X., Chua, T.: Neural collaborative filtering. In: Proceedings of the 26th International Conference on World Wide Web, pp. 173–182 (2017)
2. He, X., Deng, K., Wang, X., Li, Y., Zhang, Y., Wang, M.: Lightgcn: simplifying and powering graph convolution network for recommendation. In Proceedings of the 43rd International ACM SIGIR Conference on Research and Development in Information Retrieval, pp. 639–648 (2020)
3. Wang, X., He, X., Wang, M., Feng, F., Chua, T.: Neural graph collaborative filtering. In: Proceedings of the 42nd International ACM SIGIR Conference on Research and Development in Information Retrieval, pp. 165–174 (2019)

4. Wang, X., Jin, H., Zhang, A., He, X., Xu, T., Chua, T.: Disentangled graph collaborative filtering. In Proceedings of the 43rd International ACM SIGIR Conference on Research and Development in Information Retrieval, pp. 1001–1010 (2020)
5. Koren, Y., Bell, R.M., Volinsky, C.: Matrix factorization techniques for recommender systems. IEEE Comput. **42**(8), 30–37 (2009)
6. Berg, R.V.D., Kipf, T.N., Welling, M.: Graph convolutional matrix completion. In: KDD (2017)
7. Zheng, Y., Gao, C., Li, X., He, X., Jin, D., Li, Y.: Disentangling user interest and conformity for recommendation with casual embedding. In Proceedings of the 30th International Conference on World Wide Web, pp. 2980–2991 (2021)
8. Cen, Y., Zhang, J., Zou, X., Zhou, C., Yang, H., Tang, J.: Controllable multi-interest framework for recommendation. In: KDD (2020)
9. Wang, Y., Tang, S., Lei, Y., Song, W., Wang, S., Zhang, M.: DisenHAN: disentangled heterogeneous graph attention network for recommendation. In: ACM International Conference on Information and Knowledge Management, pp. 1606–1614 (2020)
10. Ma, J., Cui, P., Kuang, K., Wang, X., Zhu, W.: Disentangled graph convolutional networks. In: International Conference on Machine Learning, pp. 4212–4221 (2019)
11. Ma, J., Zhou, C., Cui, P., Yang, H., Zhu, W.: Learning disentangled representation for recommendation. In: 33rd Conference on Neural Information Processing Systems (2019)
12. Yang, R., Jian, M., Shi, G., Wu, L., Xiang, Y.: Attribute-Level interest matching network for personalized recommendation. In: Chinese Conference on Pattern Recognition and Computer Vision, pp. 486–497 (2021)
13. Hochreiter, S., Schmidhuber, J.: Long short-term memory. Neural Comput. **9**(8), 1735–1780 (1997)
14. Vaswani, A., et al.: Attention is all you need. In: 31st Conference on Neural Information Processing Systems, pp. 5998–6008 (2017)
15. He, K., Zhang, X., Ren, S., Sun, J.: Deep residual learning for image recognition. In: International Conference on Computer Vision and Pattern Recognition, pp. 770–778 (2016)
16. Dosovitskiy, A., et al.: An image is worth 16×16 words: transformers for image recognition at scale. arXiv preprint arXiv:2010.11929 (2010)
17. Kabbur, S., Ning, X., Karypis, G.: Fism: factored item similarity models for top-n recommender systems. In: Proceedings of the 19th ACM SIGKDD International Conference on Knowledge Discovery and Data Mining, pp. 659–667(2013)
18. Li, H., Wang, X., Zhang, Z., Yuan, Z., Li, H., Zhu, W.: Disentangled contrastive learning on graphs. In: 35th Conference on Neural Information Processing Systems (2021)
19. Yang, Y., Feng, Z., Song, M., Wang, X.: Factorized graph convolutional networks. arXiv preprint arXiv:2010.05421 (2010)
20. Zhu, T., Sun L., Chen, G.: Embedding disentanglement in graph convolutional networks for recommendation. IEEE Trans. Knowl. Data Eng. **99**, 1 (2021)
21. Liang, D., Krishnan, R.G., Hoffman, M.D., Jebara, T.: Variantional autoencoders for collaborative filtering. In: Proceedings of the 2018 World Wide Conference, pp. 689–698 (2018)
22. Wang, X., He, X., Cao, Y., Liu, M., Chua, S.: KGAT: knowledge graph attention network for recommendation. In: ACM SIGIR, pp. 950–958 (2019)

OpenMedIA: Open-Source Medical Image Analysis Toolbox and Benchmark Under Heterogeneous AI Computing Platforms

Jia-Xin Zhuang[1], Xiansong Huang[1], Yang Yang[1,2], Jiancong Chen[1], Yue Yu[1,4], Wei Gao[1,3], Ge Li[3], Jie Chen[1,3], and Tong Zhang[1(✉)]

[1] Peng Cheng Laboratory, Shenzhen, China
zhangt02@pcl.ac.cn
[2] School of Computer Science and Technology, Harbin Institute of Technology (Shenzhen), Shenzhen, China
[3] School of Electronic and Computer Engineering, Peking University, Beijing, China
[4] National Laboratory for Parallel and Distributed Processing, National University of Defense Technology, Changsha, China

Abstract. In this paper, we present OpenMedIA, an open-source toolbox library containing a rich set of deep learning methods for medical image analysis under heterogeneous Artificial Intelligence (AI) computing platforms. Various medical image analysis methods, including 2D/3D medical image classification, segmentation, localisation, and detection, have been included in the toolbox with PyTorch and/or MindSpore implementations under heterogeneous NVIDIA and Huawei Ascend computing systems. To our best knowledge, OpenMedIA is the first open-source algorithm library providing compared PyTorch and MindSpore implementations and results on several benchmark datasets. The source codes and models are available at https://git.openi.org.cn/OpenMedIA.

1 Introduction

Deep learning has been extensively studied and has achieved beyond human-level performances in various research and application fields [10,27,32,34]. To facilitate the development of such Artificial Intelligence (AI) systems, a number of open-sourced deep learning frameworks including TensorFlow [1], PyTorch [22], MXNet [4], MindSpore[1] have been developed and integrated to various AI hardwares. The medical image analysis community also witnessed similar rapid developments and revolutions with deep learning methods developed for medical image reconstruction, classification, segmentation, registration, and detection [3,6,24, 30,33,36]. In particular, MONAI[2], implemented in PyTorch, is a popular open-source toolbox with deep learning algorithms in healthcare imaging. Despite its popularity, the accuracy and performance of those algorithms may vary when implemented on different AI frameworks and/or various AI hardware. Not to

---

[1] https://www.mindspore.cn.
[2] https://monai.io.

© The Author(s), under exclusive license to Springer Nature Switzerland AG 2022
S. Yu et al. (Eds.): PRCV 2022, LNCS 13534, pp. 356–367, 2022.
https://doi.org/10.1007/978-3-031-18907-4_28

mention that several PyTorch or CUDA libraries included in MONAI are not supported by Huawei Ascend and/or other NPU computing hardware.

In this paper, we report our open-source algorithms and AI models library for medical image analysis, OpenMedIA, which have been implemented and verified with various PyTorch and MindSpore AI frameworks with heterogeneous computing hardware. All the algorithms implemented with the MindSpore framework in OpenMedIA have been evaluated and compared to the original papers and the PyTorch version.

Table 1. A summary of algorithms in our library.

Task	Algorithm	PyTorch	MindSpore
Classification	Covid-ResNet [9,15]	✓	✓
	Covid-Transformer [7]	✓	–
	U-CSRNet [20]	✓	✓
	MTCSN [18]	✓	✓
Segmentation	2D-UNet [16]	✓	✓
	LOD-Net [5]	–	✓
	Han-Net [14]	✓	✓
	CD-Net [13]	✓	✓
	3D-UNet [29]	✓	✓
	UNETR [12]	✓	–
Localization	WeaklyLesionLocalisation [31]	✓	–
	TS-CAM [11]	✓	–
Detection	LungNodules-Detection [25]	–	✓
	Covid-Detection-CNN[a]	✓	–
	Covid-Detection-Transformer [2]	✓	–
	EllipseNet-Fit [3,28]	–	✓
	EllipseNet [3]	✓	–

[a] https://github.com/ultralytics/yolov5

Our contributions can be summarized as follows:

Firstly, we provide an open-source library of recent State-Of-The-Art (SOTA) algorithms in the medical image analysis domain under two deep learning frameworks: PyTorch (with NVIDIA) and MindSpore (with Huawei Ascend).

Secondly, we conduct bench-marking comparisons of the SOTA algorithms with accuracy and performances.

Thirdly, we not only open-source the codes but also provide all the training logs and checkpoints under different AI frameworks. In this study, PyTorch is built with NVIDIA GPU, while MindSpore is with Huawei Ascend.

Table 1 shows the basic overview of the algorithms included in OpenMedIA. We categorize these algorithms into Classification, Segmentation, Localisation, and Detection tasks for easy understanding and comparison.

2   Algorithms

This study summarises seventeen SOTA algorithms from medical image classification, segmentation, localisation, and detection tasks. Eight of them are implemented by both MindSpore and PyTorch. We will continue updating the OpenMedIA library in the next few years. In this section, we will briefly introduce the selected algorithms.

2.1   Medical Image Classification

Four well-known methods are introduced for this task. It should be noted that the current open-source codes and models are with 2D classification settings.

Covid-ResNet. The contributions of Covid-ResNet[3,4] are listed as follows:

- ResNet [15] was proposed in 2015 and became one of the most famous Convolutional Neural Networks (CNN) in deep learning.
- It uses a residual learning framework to ease the training of a deeper network than previous work and shows promising performance.
- An early CNN model built for COVID-19 CT image classification.

Covid-Transformer. The contributions of Covid-Transformer[5] are listed as follows:

- ViT [7] was inspired by the success of the transformer in Natural Language Process (NLP) and proposed for Computer Vision in 2020.
- Unlike a convolutional network like ResNet, which includes a convolution structure to extract features, ViT consists of self-attention. It doesn't introduce any image-specific inductive biases into the architecture. ViT interprets an image as a sequence of patches and processes it by a pure encoder, which shows comparable performance to CNNs.

U-CSRNet. The contributions of U-CSRNet[6,7] are listed as follows:

- U-CSRNet [20] add transpose convolution layers after its backend so that the final output probability map can be identical to the input's resolution. And modify the output of CSRNet and U-CSRNet from one channel to two channels to represent the two kinds of tumor cells.

MTCSN. The contributions of MTCSN[8,9] are listed as follows:

---

[3] PyTorch: https://git.openi.org.cn/OpenMedIA/Covid-ResNet.Pytorch.
[4] MindSpore: https://git.openi.org.cn/OpenMedIA/Covid-ResNet.Mindspore.
[5] PyTorch: https://git.openi.org.cn/OpenMedIA/Covid-Transformer.Pytorch.
[6] PyTorch: https://git.openi.org.cn/OpenMedIA/U-CSRNet.Pytorch.
[7] MindSpore: https://git.openi.org.cn/OpenMedIA/U-CSRNet.Mindspore.
[8] PyTorch: https://git.openi.org.cn/OpenMedIA/MTCSN.Pytorch.
[9] MindSpore: https://git.openi.org.cn/OpenMedIA/MTCSN.Mindspore.

- MTCSN is mainly used to evaluate the definition of the capsule endoscope.
- It is an end-to-end evaluation method.
- MTCSN uses the structure of ResNet in the encoding part and designs two multi-task branches in the decoding part. Namely, the classification branch for the availability of image definition measurement and the segmentation branch for tissue segmentation generates interpretable visualization to help doctors understand the whole image.

2.2 Medical Image Segmentation

Most methods are designed for 2D segmentation tasks. We also include 3D-UNet and UNETR for 3D segmentation tasks for further research.

2D-UNet. The contributions of 2D-UNet[10,11] are listed as follows:

- 2D-UNet [16] was proposed in 2015 as a type of neural network directly consuming 2D images.
- The U-Net architecture achieves excellent performance on different biomedical segmentation applications. Without solid data augmentations, it only needs very few annotated images and has a reasonable training time.

LOD-Net. The contributions of LOD-Net[12] are listed as follows:

- LOD-Net [5] is mainly used in the task of polyp segmentation.
- It is an end-to-end segmentation method. Based on the mask R-CNN architecture, the parallel branch learns the directional derivative of the pixel level of the feature image, measures the gradient performance of the pixels on the image with the designed strategy, and is used to sort and screen out the possible boundary regions.
- The directional derivative feature is used to enhance the features of the boundary regions and, finally, optimize the segmentation results

HanNet. The contributions of HanNet[13,14] are listed as follows:

- HanNet [14] proposes a hybrid-attention nested UNet for nuclear instance segmentation, which consists of two modules: a hybrid nested U-shaped network (H-part) and a hybrid attention block (A-part).

CDNet. The contributions of CDNet[15,16] are listed as follows:

- CDNet [13] propose a novel centripetal direction network for nuclear instance segmentation.

---

[10] PyTorch: https://git.openi.org.cn/OpenMedIA/2D-UNet.Pytorch.

[11] MindSpore: https://git.openi.org.cn/OpenMedIA/2D-UNet.Mindspore.

[12] MindSpore: https://git.openi.org.cn/OpenMedIA/LOD-Net.Mindspore.

[13] PyTorch: https://git.openi.org.cn/OpenMedIA/HanNet.Pytorch.

[14] MindSpore: https://git.openi.org.cn/OpenMedIA/HanNet.Mindspore.

[15] PyTorch: https://git.openi.org.cn/OpenMedIA/CDNet.Pytorch.

[16] MindSpore: https://git.openi.org.cn/OpenMedIA/CDNet.Mindspore.

- The centripetal feature is defined as a class of adjacent directions pointing to the core center to represent the spatial relationship between pixels in the core. Then, these directional features are used to construct a directional difference graph to express the similarity within instances and the differences between instances.
- This method also includes a refining module for direction guidance. As a plug-and-play module, it can effectively integrate additional tasks and aggregate the characteristics of different branches.

3D-UNet. The contributions of 3D-UNet[17,18] are listed as follows:

- 3D-UNet [6] was proposed in 2016, it is a type of neural network that directly consumes volumetric images.
- 3D-UNet extends the previous u-net architecture by replacing all 2D operations with their 3D counterparts.
- The implementation performs on-the-fly elastic deformations for efficient data augmentation during training. It is trained end-to-end from scratch, i.e., no pre-trained network is required.

UNETR. The contributions of UNETR[19] are listed as follows:

- UNETR [12] was inspired by the success of transformers in NLP and proposed to use a transformer as the encoder to learn sequence representation of the input 3D Volume and capture multi-scale information.
- With the help of a U-shape network design, the model learns the final semantic segmentation output.

2.3   Weakly Supervised Image Localisation

Two weakly supervised medical image localisation methods are included in OpenMedIA. Both methods are designed for image localisation tasks with generative adversarial network (GAN) and class activation mapping (CAM) settings. It worth noting that WeaklyLesionLocalisation [31] also supports weakly supervised lesion segmentation. In this work, the comparisons of lesion segmentation were not included.

WeaklyLesionLocalisation. The contribution of WeaklyLesionLocalisation[20] are listed as follows:

- It [31] proposed a data-driven framework supervised by only image-level labels.
- The framework can explicitly separate potential lesions from original images with the help of a generative adversarial network and a lesion-specific decoder.

---

[17] PyTorch: https://git.openi.org.cn/OpenMedIA/3D-UNet.mindspore.

[18] MindSpore: https://git.openi.org.cn/OpenMedIA/3D-UNet.Pytorch.

[19] PyTorch: https://git.openi.org.cn/OpenMedIA/Transformer3DSeg.

[20] PyTorch: https://git.openi.org.cn/OpenMedIA/WeaklyLesionLocalisation.

TS-CAM. The contribution of TS-CAM[21] are listed as follows:

- It [11] introduces the token semantic coupled attention map to take full advantage of the self-attention mechanism in the visual transformer for long-range dependency extraction.
- TS-CAM first splits an image into a sequence of patch tokens for spatial embedding, which produce attention maps of long-range visual dependency to avoid partial activation.
- TS-CAM then re-allocates category-related semantics for patch tokens, making them aware of object categories. TS-CAM finally couples the patch tokens with the semantic-agnostic attention map to achieve semantic-aware localisation

2.4   Medical Image Detection

We include seven popular SOTA detection methods in this library and trained them with various medical image detection tasks.

LungNodules-Dectection. The contribution of LungNodules-Dectection[22] are listed as follows:

- It use CenterNet [35] as the backbone to detect Lung disease.
- CenterNet is a novel practical anchor-free method for object detection, which detects and identifies objects as axis-aligned boxes in an image.
- The detector uses keypoint estimation to find center points and regresses to all other object properties, such as size, location, orientation, and even pose.
- In nature, it's a one-stage method to simultaneously predict the center location and boxes with real-time speed and higher accuracy than corresponding bounding box-based detectors.

LungNodule-Detection-CNN. The contribution of LungNodule-Detection-CNN[23] are listed as follows:

- It use Yolov5[24] the single stage method to detect lung nodules in the Lung.
- Yolov5 is an object detection algorithm that divides images into a grid system. Each cell in the grid is responsible for detecting objects within itself.

LungNodule-Detection-Transformer. The contribution of LungNodule-Detection-Transformer[25] are listed as follows:

- It use DeTR [2] to detect the location of the Lung Nodules.

---

[21] PyTorch: https://git.openi.org.cn/OpenMedIA/TS-CAM.Pytorch.

[22] MindSpore: https://git.openi.org.cn/OpenMedIA/LungNodules-Detection.MS.

[23] PyTorch: https://git.openi.org.cn/OpenMedIA/LungNodule-Detection-CNN.Pytorch.

[24] https://github.com/ultralytics/yolov5.

[25] PyTorch: https://git.openi.org.cn/OpenMedIA/LungNodule-Detection-Transformer.Pytorch.

– DeTR is the end-to-end object detection framework based on the transformer, showing promising performance.

EllipseNet-fit. The contribution of EllipseNet-fit[26] are listed as follows:

– EllipseNet-fit [3,28] developed a segmentation and ellipse fit network for automatically measuring the fetal head circumference and biparietal diameter.
– Compared to the fetal head ellipse detection, fetal echocardiographic measurement is challenged by the moving heart and shadowing artifacts around the fetal sternum.

EllipseNet. The contribution of EllipseNet[27] are listed as follows:

– EllipseNet [3] presents an anchor-free ellipse detection network, namely EllipseNet, which detects the cardiac and thoracic regions in ellipses and automatically calculates the cardiothoracic ratio and cardiac axis for fetal cardiac biometrics in 4-chamber view.
– The detection network detects each object's center as points and simultaneously regresses the ellipses' parameters. A rotated intersection-over-union loss is defined to further regulate the regression module.

3 Benchmarks and Results

Algorithms with PyTorch version were implemented and tested on NVIDIA GeForce 1080/2080Ti and Tesla V100[28]. Algorithms with the MindSpore version were trained and evaluated on Huawei Ascend 910[29]. Huawei Ascend 910 was released in 2019, which reports twice the performance of rival NVIDIA's Telsa V100[30].

3.1 Datasets

We conduct seventeen experiments on ten medical image datasets to evaluate different implementations of deep medical image analysis algorithms. For 2D classification tasks, the Covid-19 CT image dataset[31], noted as Covid-Classification in this paper, BCData [17] and Endoscope [18] datasets were included. For 2D image segmentation tasks, besides the COVID lesion segmentation in Covid-19 CT image dataset (See Footnote 31) noted as Covid-Segmentation, we also generated a lung segmentation based on this dataset and noted as 2D-Lung-Segmentation[32]. Besides, ETIS-LaribPolypDB [26] and MoNuSeg [19] were also used in this study.

---

[26] MindSpore: https://git.openi.org.cn/OpenMedIA/EllipseFit.Mindspore.
[27] PyTorch: https://git.openi.org.cn/OpenMedIA/EllipseNet.
[28] https://www.nvidia.com/en-us/data-center/v100/.
[29] https://e.huawei.com/en/products/cloud-computing-dc/atlas/ascend-910.
[30] https://www.jiqizhixin.com/articles/2019-08-23-7.
[31] https://covid-segmentation.grand-challenge.org.
[32] https://git.openi.org.cn/OpenMedIA/2D-UNet.Pytorch/datasets.

For 3D image segmentation tasks, we adopted MM-WHS [37] dataset. For 2D image detection tasks, both LUNA16[33] and fetal four chamber view ultrasound (FFCV) dataset [3] were evaluated. Some of the datasets with public copyright licenses have been uploaded to OpenMedIA.

Table 2. Comparative algorithm accuracy. Experimental results reported in the Original columne are directly taken from the paper. We use - to represent lack of implementations or reports. For instance, the original results of Covid-Transformer and TS-CAM are not included because we first conduct such studies. The Re-implement column reports the results of our implementations with PyTorch and/or MindSpore AI frameworks.

Algorithm	Dataset	Metric	Performance	
			Original	Re-implement (PyTorch/MindSpore)
Covid-ResNet [9]	Covid-Classification	Acc	0.96	0.97/0.97
Covid-Transformer [7]	Covid-Classification	Acc	–	0.87/–
U-CSRNet [20]	BCData	F1	0.85	0.85/0.85
MTCSN [18]	Endoscope	Acc	0.80	0.80/0.75
2D-UNet [16]	2D-Lung-Segmentation	Dice	–	0.76/0.76
LOD-Net [5]	ETIS-LaribPolypDB	Dice	0.93	–/0.91
Han-Net [14]	MoNuSeg	Dice	0.80	0.80/0.79
CD-Net [13]	MoNuSeg	Dice	0.80	0.80/0.80
3D-UNet [29]	MM-WHS	Dice	0.85	0.88/0.85
UNETR [12]	MM-WHS	Dice	–	0.84/–
WeaklyLesionLocalisation [31]	Covid-Segmentation	AUC	0.63	0.63/–
TS-CAM [11]	Covid-Segmentation	AUC	–	0.50/–
LungNodules-Detection [25]	Luna16	mAP	–	–/0.51
LungNodule-Detection-CNN	Luna16	mAP	–	0.72/–
LungNodule-Detection-Transformer [2]	Luna16	mAP	–	0.72/–
EllipseNet-Fit [3,28]	FFCV	Dice	0.91	0.91/0.91
EllipseNet [3]	FFCV	Dice	0.93	0.93/–

3.2 Metrics

For 2D classification task, accuracy(Acc) [23] and F1 [23] are used to evaluate the classification accuracy. For 2D/3D segmentation tasks, Dice score [6] is used to measure the segmentation accuracy. For weakly supervised lesion localisation and segmentation tasks, AUC [21] and Dice score [6] are used for quantitative comparisons. For 2D detection tasks, mAP [8], AUC [21] and Dice score are used for evaluation.

3.3 Evaluation on Image Classification

In Table 2, Rows 1–4 show the accuracy of four image classification algorithms with different implementations. It can be seen that CNN achieves better performance than Transformer backbones, which indicates that Transformers are

---

[33] https://luna16.grand-challenge.org/.

more difficult to train and usually require large training samples. Experimental results show that the algorithms implemented with PyTorch and MindSpore achieve the same accuracy. It should be noted that the reported classification algorithms and results are implemented and verified with 2D scenarios.

3.4   Evaluation on Image Segmentation

Both 2D and 3D segmentation methods are evaluated, and their results are shown in Rows 5–10 of Table 2. For 2D segmentation tasks shown in Rows 5–8, our implementation achieves comparable or even better performance than the reported results. For 3D segmentation tasks shown in Rows 9–10, 3D-Net is based on CNN architecture, while UNETR uses Transformer as the backbone. It is also worth noting that the 2D algorithms achieve similar results in both MindSpore and PyTorch frameworks, while the 3D-UNet algorithm implemented in Mind-Spore shows a 0.03 accuracy drop compared to the PyTorch re-implementation, which indicates that the MindSpore version could be further optimized in the future, especially on the 3D data augmentation libraries.

3.5   Evaluation on Weakly Supervised Image Localisation

For medical image localisation, two well-known weakly supervised methods methods are reported in Rows 11–12. Following the settings reported by [31], both methods are evaluated on the Covid-Segmentation datasets. The implementations of the MindSpore framework will be added in the future.

3.6   Evaluation on Image Detection

For image detection, the results on the Rows 13–14 show that networks based on both CNN and Transformer backbones apply to medical image detection tasks. YOLOv5m are used for CNN based network. In most medical image detection scenarios, rotated ellipses and/or bounding boxes are more suitable considering the rotating and ellipse-shaped targets. In this study, we include EllipseNet [3] and its variant [28] in OpenMedIA. Rows 16–17 show that EllipseNet delivers the highest accuracy for rotated ellipse detection tasks.

3.7   Evaluation on Time Efficiency

To evaluate the time efficiency of different implementations with PyTorch and MindSpore, we select one method from each category and evaluate their inference time as shown in Fig. 1. For fair comparisons, all the algorithms implemented with PyTorch were assessed on a single NVIDIA Tesla V100, while those implemented with MindSpore were tested on a single Huawei Ascend 910. Figure 1 shows the compared time efficiency results. It can be seen that all the tested algorithms with MindSpore environment are more time-efficient than that with PyTorch settings. The time cost of the former is less than 1/3 of that of the latter, which confirms the time efficiency advantage of MindSpore and Huawei Ascend 910 as reported in.

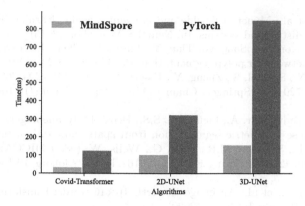

Fig. 1. Compared running time of three methods training with different depp learning framework. From left to right in sequence, the methods are Covid-Transformer, 2D-UNet and 3D-UNet.

4   Conclusions and Future Works

This paper introduces OpenMedIA, an open-source heterogeneous AI computing algorithm library for medical image analysis. We summarise the contributions of a set of SOTA deep learning methods and re-implement them with both PyTorch and MindSpore AI frameworks. This work not only reports the model training/inference accuracy, but also includes the performances of the algorithms with various NVIDIA GPU and Huawei Ascend NPU hardware. The Open-MedIA aims to boost AI development in medical image analysis domain with open-sourced easy implementations, bench-marking models and the open-source computational power. More SOTA algorithms under various AI platforms, such as self-supervised methods will be added in future.

Acknowledgement. The computing resources of Pengcheng Cloudbrain are used in this research. We acknowledge the support provided by OpenI Community (https://git.openi.org.cn).

References

1. Abadi, M., et al.: {TensorFlow}: a system for {Large-Scale} machine learning. In: OSDI, pp. 265–283 (2016)
2. Carion, N., Massa, F., Synnaeve, G., Usunier, N., Kirillov, A., Zagoruyko, S.: End-to-end object detection with transformers. In: Vedaldi, A., Bischof, H., Brox, T., Frahm, J.-M. (eds.) ECCV 2020. LNCS, vol. 12346, pp. 213–229. Springer, Cham (2020). https://doi.org/10.1007/978-3-030-58452-8_13
3. Chen, J., Zhang, Y., Wang, J., Zhou, X., He, Y., Zhang, T.: EllipseNet: anchor-free ellipse detection for automatic cardiac biometrics in fetal echocardiography. In: de Bruijne, M., Cattin, P.C., Cotin, S., Padoy, N., Speidel, S., Zheng, Y., Essert, C. (eds.) MICCAI 2021. LNCS, vol. 12907, pp. 218–227. Springer, Cham (2021). https://doi.org/10.1007/978-3-030-87234-2_21

4. Chen, T., et al.: Mxnet: a flexible and efficient machine learning library for heterogeneous distributed systems. In: NeurIPS Workshop (2015)
5. Cheng, M., Kong, Z., Song, G., Tian, Y., Liang, Y., Chen, J.: Learnable oriented-derivative network for polyp segmentation. In: de Bruijne, M., Cattin, P.C., Cotin, S., Padoy, N., Speidel, S., Zheng, Y., Essert, C. (eds.) MICCAI 2021. LNCS, vol. 12901, pp. 720–730. Springer, Cham (2021). https://doi.org/10.1007/978-3-030-87193-2_68
6. Çiçek, Ö., Abdulkadir, A., Lienkamp, S.S., Brox, T., Ronneberger, O.: 3D U-Net: learning dense volumetric segmentation from sparse annotation. In: Ourselin, S., Joskowicz, L., Sabuncu, M.R., Unal, G., Wells, W. (eds.) MICCAI 2016. LNCS, vol. 9901, pp. 424–432. Springer, Cham (2016). https://doi.org/10.1007/978-3-319-46723-8_49
7. Dosovitskiy, A., et al.: An image is worth 16×16 words: transformers for image recognition at scale. In: ICLR (2020)
8. Everingham, M., Van Gool, L., Williams, C.K.I., Winn, J., Zisserman, A.: The PASCAL visual object classes challenge 2007 (VOC 2007) Results (2007). http://www.pascal-network.org/challenges/VOC/voc2007/workshop/index.html
9. Farooq, M., Hafeez, A.: Covid-resnet: a deep learning framework for screening of covid19 from radiographs. Arxiv (2020)
10. Floridi, L., Chiriatti, M.: Gpt-3: its nature, scope, limits, and consequences. Minds Mach. **30**(4), 681–694 (2020)
11. Gao, W., et al.: TS-CAM: token semantic coupled attention map for weakly supervised object localization. In: ICCV, pp. 2886–2895 (2021)
12. Hatamizadeh, A., et al.: Unetr: transformers for 3D medical image segmentation. In: WACV, pp. 574–584 (2022)
13. He, H., et al.: Cdnet: centripetal direction network for nuclear instance segmentation. In: CVPR, pp. 4026–4035 (2021)
14. He, H., et al.: A hybrid-attention nested unet for nuclear segmentation in histopathological images. Front. Mol. Biosci. **8**, 6 (2021)
15. He, K., Zhang, X., Ren, S., Sun, J.: Deep residual learning for image recognition. In: CVPR, pp. 770–778 (2016)
16. Hofmanninger, J., Prayer, F., Pan, J., Röhrich, S., Prosch, H., Langs, G.: Automatic lung segmentation in routine imaging is primarily a data diversity problem, not a methodology problem. Eur. Radiol. Exp. **4**(1), 1–13 (2020). https://doi.org/10.1186/s41747-020-00173-2
17. Huang, Z., et al.: BCData: a large-scale dataset and benchmark for cell detection and counting. In: Martel, A.L., et al. (eds.) MICCAI 2020. LNCS, vol. 12265, pp. 289–298. Springer, Cham (2020). https://doi.org/10.1007/978-3-030-59722-1_28
18. Kong, Z., et al.: Multi-task classification and segmentation for explicable capsule endoscopy diagnostics. Front. Mol. Biosci. **8**, 614277 (2021)
19. Kumar, N., Verma, R., Sharma, S., Bhargava, S., Vahadane, A., Sethi, A.: A dataset and a technique for generalized nuclear segmentation for computational pathology. IEEE TMI **36**(7), 1550–1560 (2017)
20. Li, Y., Zhang, X., Chen, D.: Csrnet: dilated convolutional neural networks for understanding the highly congested scenes. In: CVPR, pp. 1091–1100 (2018)
21. Ling, C.X., Huang, J., Zhang, H., et al.: Auc: a statistically consistent and more discriminating measure than accuracy. In: IJCAI, vol. 3, pp. 519–524 (2003)
22. Paszke, A., et al.: Pytorch: an imperative style, high-performance deep learning library. In: NeurIPS, vol. 32 (2019)
23. Pedregosa, F., et al.: Scikit-learn: machine learning in python. J. Mach. Learn. Res. **12**, 2825–2830 (2011)

24. Rueckert, D., Schnabel, J.A.: Model-based and data-driven strategies in medical image computing. Proc. IEEE **108**(1), 110–124 (2019)

25. Setio, A.A.A., et al.: Validation, comparison, and combination of algorithms for automatic detection of pulmonary nodules in computed tomography images: the luna16 challenge. MIA **42**, 1–13 (2017)

26. Siegel, R.L., et al.: Colorectal cancer statistics, 2020. CA Cancer J. Clin. **70**(3), 145–164 (2020)

27. Silver, D., et al.: Mastering the game of go without human knowledge. Nature **550**(7676), 354–359 (2017)

28. Sinclair, M., et al.: Human-level performance on automatic head biometrics in fetal ultrasound using fully convolutional neural networks. In: EMBC, pp. 714–717. IEEE (2018)

29. Tong, Q., Ning, M., Si, W., Liao, X., Qin, J.: 3D deeply-supervised u-net based whole heart segmentation. In: Pop, M., et al. (eds.) STACOM 2017. LNCS, vol. 10663, pp. 224–232. Springer, Cham (2018). https://doi.org/10.1007/978-3-319-75541-0_24

30. Uus, A., et al.: Deformable slice-to-volume registration for motion correction of fetal body and placenta MRI. IEEE Trans. Med. Imaging **39**(9), 2750–2759 (2020)

31. Yang, Y., et al.: Towards unbiased covid-19 lesion localisation and segmentation via weakly supervised learning. In: ISBI, pp. 1966–1970 (2021)

32. Zhang, T., Biswal, S., Wang, Y.: Shmnet: condition assessment of bolted connection with beyond human-level performance. Struct. Health Monit. **19**(4), 1188–1201 (2020)

33. Zhang, T., et al.: Self-supervised recurrent neural network for 4D abdominal and in-utero MR imaging. In: Knoll, F., Maier, A., Rueckert, D., Ye, J.C. (eds.) Machine Learning for Medical Image Reconstruction, pp. 16–24 (2019)

34. Zhou, W., et al.: Ensembled deep learning model outperforms human experts in diagnosing biliary atresia from sonographic gallbladder images. Nat. Commun. **12**(1), 1–14 (2021)

35. Zhou, X., Wang, D., Krähenbühl, P.: Objects as points. In: ECCV (2020)

36. Zhuang, J., Cai, J., Wang, R., Zhang, J., Zheng, W.-S.: Deep kNN for medical image classification. In: Martel, A.L., et al. (eds.) MICCAI 2020. LNCS, vol. 12261, pp. 127–136. Springer, Cham (2020). https://doi.org/10.1007/978-3-030-59710-8_13

37. Zhuang, X.: Challenges and methodologies of fully automatic whole heart segmentation: a review. J. Healthcare Eng. **4**(3), 371–407 (2013)

CLIP Meets Video Captioning: Concept-Aware Representation Learning Does Matter

Bang Yang[1,2], Tong Zhang[2], and Yuexian Zou[1,2(✉)]

[1] ADSPLAB, Shenzhen Graduate School, Peking University, Shenzhen, China
{yangbang,zouyx}@pku.edu.cn
[2] Peng Cheng Laboratory, Shenzhen, China
zhangt02@pcl.ac.cn

Abstract. For video captioning, "pre-training and fine-tuning" has become a de facto paradigm, where ImageNet Pre-training (INP) is usually used to encode the video content, then a task-oriented network is fine-tuned from scratch to cope with caption generation. This paper first investigates the impact of the recently proposed CLIP (Contrastive Language-Image Pre-training) on video captioning. Through the empirical study on INP *vs.* CLIP, we identify the potential deficiencies of INP and explore the key factors for accurate description generation. The results show that the INP-based model is tricky to capture concepts' semantics and sensitive to irrelevant background information. By contrast, the CLIP-based model significantly improves the caption quality and highlights the importance of concept-aware representation learning. With these findings, we propose Dual Concept Detection (DCD) further to inject concept knowledge into the model during training. DCD is an auxiliary task that requires a caption model to learn the correspondence between video content and concepts and the co-occurrence relations between concepts. Experiments on MSR-VTT and VATEX demonstrate the effectiveness of DCD, and the visualization results further reveal the necessity of learning concept-aware representations.

Keywords: Video captioning · Representation learning · Concept detection

1 Introduction

Video captioning aims to describe video content with fluent sentences. Given the difficulties of learning effective video representations from limited data [37,38], mainstream video captioning methods adopt the Encoder-Decoder framework [36] with a "pre-training and fine-tuning" paradigm, where ImageNet Pre-training (INP) is usually used to help encode the video content, and a task-oriented network is fine-tuned from scratch to cope with caption generation. However, using INP across discrepant tasks may bring limited benefit [9].

Recent advances in video captioning [4,17,20,21,39,42,43] are built upon the default use of INP and meanwhile, their performance gradually becomes

S. Yu et al. (Eds.): PRCV 2022, LNCS 13534, pp. 368–381, 2022.
https://doi.org/10.1007/978-3-031-18907-4_29

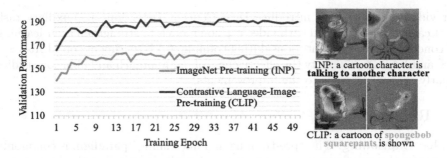

Fig. 1. ImageNet Pre-training (INP) *vs.* Contrastive Language-Image Pre-training (CLIP). When using CLIP rather than INP to help encode the video content, performance is greatly improved (left), which can be attributed to the better learning of concept-aware representations (right). The right part visualizes Grad-CAM [30] for the ground-truth caption "spongebob squarepants blows bubbles". The caption below each example is model's actual prediction.

saturated on MSR-VTT [38]. Thus, immediate questions raise: *is INP causing a performance bottleneck for video captioning? If so, why?* To answer these questions, we turn our attention to CLIP (Contrastive Language-Image Pre-training) [28], which has drawn great attention in the community due to its strong zero-shot transfer ability to various vision tasks. As a branch of vision-language pre-training research [16,32], CLIP is unbounded by a fixed set of labels and its pre-training data, *i.e.*, 400M noisy image-text pairs crawled from the Internet, is larger than ImageNet by an order of magnitude. To this end, we hypothesize that CLIP has great potentials for video captioning.

In this paper, we carry out an empirical study on INP *vs.* CLIP to shed new light on potential deficiencies of INP for caption generation and explore the key to prompting accurate video captioning. Figure 1 gives a snapshot of our experimental study. We can see from the curves that captioning performance is significantly improve when using CLIP rather than INP to help encode the video content. This performance gap can be interpreted by the visualized example shown on the right, where INP deviates the video caption model's focus from the critical regions of concepts "spongebob squarepants" and "bubbles" while CLIP's results just the opposite. As a result, the empirical study has shown that concept-aware representation learning does matter to accurate caption generation.

Based on the above finding, we propose Dual Concept Detection (DCD) to spur video caption models to learn concept-aware video and text representations during training. Specifically, DCD requires the the caption model to infer relevant concepts based on partial information from no matter videos or text descriptions. To achieve that, the model has to build the correspondence between video content and concepts and learn the concepts' co-occurrence relations.

To summarize, we make the following contributions. (1) We carry out an empirical study on INP *vs.* CLIP for video captioning. The results reveal the deficiencies of INP and suggest the importance of concept-aware representation learning in prompting accurate captioning. (2) Motivated by the success of CLIP for video captioning, we introduce Dual Concept Detection, an auxiliary task that can be jointly trained with video caption models to strengthen their learning of concept-aware representations during training. (3) Experiments on MSR-VTT [38] and VATEX [37] verify the effectiveness of our approach and ablation studies clearly show what leads to the improvements.

2   Related Work

Video Captioning. The "pre-training and fine-tuning" paradigm is commonly used from the very first neural-network-based methods [35,36] to the present day. Recent focuses in video captioning include but not limited to (1) learning fine-grained representation via graph neural models [4,25,43] or hierarchical encoders [39], (2) distilling knowledge mutually [20] or from external models [43], and (3) introducing new paradigms like non-autoregressive captioning [21,40] and open-book captioning [42]. However, recent advanced methods pay less attention to the effect of pre-training models, suffering from potential performance bottleneck.

Vision-Language Pre-training (VLP). Unlike single-modal understanding, VLP aims to bridge vision and language by modeling their interactions. Generally, existing VLP methods can be categorized into two groups: (1) learning vision-language joint representations [13,16,18,22,32] and (2) learning visual representations from natural language supervision [6,28,29]. For the former, a deep cross-modal Transformer [33] is usually used to fuse multi-modal inputs and learn contextualized features. Among the latter, CLIP [28] drew great attention because of its strong zero-shot transfer ability. Unlike the focused tasks in recent works [23,31], we analyze the effect of CLIP on video captioning.

Multi-task Learning (MTL). The goal of MTL is to learn shared representations from multiple related tasks to improve the generalization performance of all tasks [3]. For video captioning, Pasunuru and Bansal [27] proposed to train a video caption model with two directed-generation tasks, whose supervision signal was obtained from external datasets. By contrast, more attempts were made to construct auxiliary tasks by deriving additional supervision signal from the original annotations, *e.g.*, predicting mined latent topics [5] or extracted attributes [12,15,41] solely based on the input videos. The auxiliary task proposed in this paper instead takes either video content or textual descriptions as input.

3   On INP *vs.* CLIP for Video Captioning

This section aims to investigate the potential deficiencies of INP and explore the key to generating accurate descriptions. We organize this section as follows. We first briefly review video captioning in Sect. 3.1. Then, we introduce a Transformer baseline for video captioning in Sect. 3.2, where we will show how to integrate INP or CLIP models with the baseline. Finally, based on the experimental setup in Sect. 3.3, we present our analysis in Sect. 3.4.

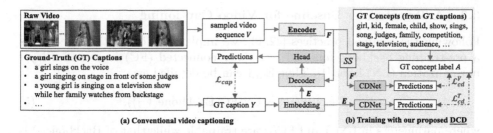

Fig. 2. Pipeline of video captioning at the training stage. In Sect. 3, we will review (a) and focus on the encoder part of video caption models in which conventional methods usually use ImageNet pre-training models to encode the video content. In Sect. 4, we will elaborate our proposed Dual Concept Detection (DCD) shown in (b), where "SS" denotes the sparse sampling.

3.1 Overview of Video Captioning

As shown in Fig. 2(a), conventional video captioning methods build upon the Encoder-Decoder framework. Formally, given a sequence of sampled video frames (or snippets) $V = \{v_1, v_2, \ldots, v_N\}$ of length N, the caption encoder aims to encode V into video features $\mathbf{F} \in \mathbb{R}^{d_h \times N}$:

$$\mathbf{F} = \text{Encoder}(V). \tag{1}$$

After the encoding stage, the decoding stage uses a typical autoregressive manner to generate a caption $Y = \{y_1, y_2, \ldots, y_T\}$ of length T. Specifically at t-th time step, previously generated words $Y_{<t}$ are first embedded into low dimensional space to obtain text embeddings $\mathbf{E}_{<\mathbf{t}} \in \mathbb{R}^{d_h \times t}$:

$$\mathbf{E}_{<\mathbf{t}} = \text{Embedding}(Y_{<t}). \tag{2}$$

Then given $\mathbf{E}_{<\mathbf{t}}$ and video features $\mathbf{F}$, the rest decoding stage at t-th time step can be formulated as follows:

$$h_t = \text{Decoder}(\mathbf{E}_{<\mathbf{t}}, \mathbf{F}),$$
$$p(y_t|Y_{<t}, V) = \text{softmax}(\text{Head}(h_t)), \tag{3}$$

where the hidden state $h_t \in \mathbb{R}^{d_h}$ of the caption decoder is produced first and then fed to a classification head, followed by a softmax function to predict the probability distribution $p(y_t|Y_{<t}, V) \in \mathbb{R}^{|\mathcal{V}|}$ over the vocabulary $\mathcal{V}$. Finally, to train the video caption model, the cross entropy loss is used:

$$\mathcal{L}_{cap} = -\sum_{t=1}^{T} \log p(y_t|Y_{<t}, V). \tag{4}$$

3.2   A Transformer Baseline for Video Captioning

Following the common practices [42,43], we implement the caption encoder as a pre-training backbone followed by a fully connected (FC) layer and a layer normalization (LN) layer [1]. Thus Eq. 1 can be detailed as:

$$\mathbf{F} = \text{Encoder}(V) = \text{LN}(\text{FC}(\text{Backbone}(V))), \tag{5}$$

where parameters in $\text{LN}(\cdot)$ and $\text{FC}(\cdot)$ are trainable while that of $\text{Backbone}(\cdot)$ is fixed. We can replace the backbone in Eq. 5 with either a INP model or a CLIP model to help encode the video content and then probe into the learned features $\mathbf{F}$ after training. When considering multi-modalities, we fuse features $\{\mathbf{F}^{(m)}\}_{m=1}^{M}$ of M modalities along the sequence dimension to obtain $\mathbf{F} \in \mathbb{R}^{d_h \times MN}$. Details for the rest components are as follows. The embedding layer consists of a word embedding layer, a position embedding layer, and a LN layer, all of which are trainable. The caption decoder comprises a stack of Transformer decoder layers as in [33]. The classification head is implemented as a FC layer.

3.3   Experimental Setup

Dataset. MSR-VTT [38] consists of 6,513, 497, and 2,990 video clips (20 English captions per clip) for training, validation, and testing, respectively.

Metrics. To measure caption quality, we use four common automatic metrics: CIDEr [34], BLEU-4 [26], METEOR [2], and ROUGE-L [19]. All metrics are computed by Microsoft COCO Evaluation Server. We also report a summation of the front four metrics, named Meta-Sum. To quantify caption diversity, we follow [40] to compute three metrics, including Novel (the percentage of captions that have not been seen in the training data), Unique (the percentage of captions that are unique among the generated captions), and Vocab (the number of words in the vocabulary that are adopted to generate captions).

Implementation Details. Given a video, we uniformly sample $N = 28$ frames (snippets) first and then use ResNet-101 [10] pre-trained on ImageNet, 3D ResNeXt-101 [8] pre-trained on Kinetics-400, and VGGish [11] pre-trained on AudioSet to respectively extract features of image, motion, and audio modalities. For a fair comparison, we also treat ResNet-101 as the backbone of our baseline model when using CLIP. More details are left to Sect. 4.3.

3.4   Analysis

We conduct a series of analyses on MSR-VTT to answer the following questions.

(1) Can CLIP improve video captioning compared with INP? For a fair comparison, we treat ResNet-101 with either INP or CLIP as the backbone of our baseline model and keep other components the same. As we can see in Table 1, using CLIP brings significant improvements over INP on both caption

Table 1. Performance on MSR-VTT with ImageNet Pre-training (INP) or CLIP. We consider **I**mage, **M**otion and **A**udio modalities and report **C**IDEr, **B**LEU-4, **M**ETEOR, **R**OUGE-L, Meta-**S**um, **N**ovel, **U**nique, and **V**ocab metrics.

#	Modality	Caption quality					Caption diversity		
		C	B4	M	R	MS	N	U	V
1	I_{INP}	41.5	37.7	26.9	58.4	164.5	9.7	17.2	299
2	I_{INP} + Mo	46.3	39.9	27.8	59.8	173.8	13.5	22.0	357
3	I_{INP} + Mo + A	50.0	43.9	29.2	61.9	185.0	20.5	30.4	409
4	I_{CLIP}	52.8	43.4	29.6	61.8	187.6	20.8	30.7	497
5	I_{CLIP} + Mo	54.6	44.6	29.9	62.7	191.8	24.0	34.8	**518**
6	I_{CLIP} + Mo + A	**55.2**	**47.1**	**30.4**	**63.6**	**196.3**	**24.2**	**35.4**	492

(a) The GT caption used for Grad-CAM: **two men are wrestling on a mat** — (b) The GT caption used for Grad-CAM: **there is a man slicing potato on the table**

Fig. 3. Grad-CAM for the given ground-truth (GT) captions. In each case, the input of the video caption model is two manually selected keyframes, based on which the actual generated description is given above the subfigure.

quality and diversity under different combinations of modalities, *e.g.*, compared with model 1, model 4 gains a relative improvement of 27.2% at CIDEr and generates more than twice as many novel captions. Although taking more modalities as the model inputs gradually narrow the performance gap, a relative gain of 10.4% at CIDEr for model 6 *vs.* model 3 is still overwhelming.

(2) What results in the large performance gap between INP and CLIP? We answer this question from two aspects. The first aspect is to explore the decision-making process of models. We use Grad-CAM [30], a gradient-based localization technology, to figure out which part of the input videos is responsible for the models' outputs. As we can see the first row in Fig. 3, using INP deviates the model's focus from the most critical regions for the given GT captions, *e.g.*, the neglect of two wrestlers that grapple on a mat in (a) and the wrong attention

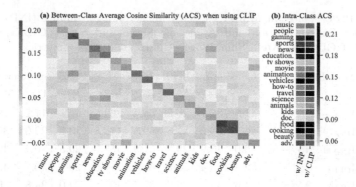

Fig. 4. Quantitative analysis on the learned video features. In (b), the mean intra-class ACS over all categories is relatively improved 18.1% after using CLIP.

towards fingers in (b). By contrast, the second row in Fig. 3 shows that using CLIP enables the model to be more aware of where the concepts are. This is conducive to accurate captioning, *e.g.*, "vegetables" *vs.* "potato" in (b).

The second aspect is to analyze the learned video features. We first obtain mean pooled video features for videos in the testing set, followed by the z-score normalization. Then we calculate between- or intra-class Average Cosine Similarity (ACS) based on the ground-truth category tags of MSR-VTT. As shown in Fig. 4(a), the video caption model can generally distinguish features from different categories when using CLIP (so does the model using INP). In (b), we can clearly observe the difference between INP and CLIP, *i.e.*, using CLIP can learn more similar intra-class video features on almost all categories, indicating that using CLIP can better capture the topic-related characteristics of video content. Moreover, we give a qualitative example in Fig. 5, where the first two videos share similar concepts "stroller" and the last two videos have a similar white background. We can see that a high similarity is wrongly assigned to #9296 and #8993 when using INP while using CLIP makes the model more robust against irrelevant background information and more sensitive to the concepts.

Main conclusions: (1) INP does not work well in video captioning, which manifests as the unsatisfying captioning performance in Table 1, the overlook of concepts' semantics in Fig. 3, and the vulnerability to irrelevant background interference in Fig. 5. The deficiencies of INP can be attributed to

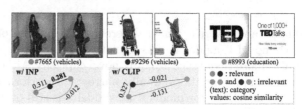

Fig. 5. An example on the learned video features. Using CLIP enables the video caption model to encode more semantics of the concepts "stroller" and "TED" rather than the background.

the domain gap between ImageNet data and video captioning data. (2) Using CLIP helps describe the accurate videos' details, which in turn promotes caption diversity. The quantitative and visualized results suggest that concept-aware representation learning is the key to prompting accurate captioning.

4   Approach

Based on above findings, we propose to further strengthen concept-aware representation learning of a video caption model via Dual Concept Detection (DCD). Next, we fisrtly elaborate the formulation of concept detection in Sect. 4.1, followed by our proposed DCD in Sect. 4.2. Then based on the experimental setup in Sect. 4.3, we compare our approach with state-of-the-art methods in Sect. 4.4 and carry out ablation studies to verify the effectiveness of DCD in Sect. 4.5.

4.1   Formulation of Concept Detection

Supervision Signal. Given training captions, we filter out stop words and keep the most frequent K words as the targets. Then we can obtain a multi-hot concept label $A = \{a_1, a_2, \ldots, a_K\}$ for each video, where $a_k = 1$ indicates that the kth concept exists in ground-truth captions of the video.

Feed-Forward Pass. Let denote $\mathbf{X} \in \mathbb{R}^{d_h \times L}$ as the features used for concept detection, d_h the hidden dimension of the model, and L the number of instances. We feed $\mathbf{X}$ into an concept detection network (CDNet) followed by a sigmoid function to obtain a raw probability matrix $\mathbf{P_{raw}} \in \mathbb{R}^{K \times L}$:

$$\mathbf{P_{raw}} = \mathrm{sigmoid}(\mathrm{CDNet}(\mathbf{X})), \tag{6}$$

where $P_{raw}^{k,l}$ denotes the possibility that the lth instance contains the kth concept. Then for the kth concept, we adopt multiple instance learning to merge probability values of all L instances and obtain the final probability p_k:

$$\forall k \in [1, K], \quad p_k = 1 - \prod_{l=1}^{L}(1 - P_{raw}^{k,l}). \tag{7}$$

Training Objective. We here use the binary cross entropy loss:

$$\mathcal{L}_{bce} = -\frac{1}{K_{pos}} \sum_{k=1}^{K}(a_k \log(p_k) + (1 - a_k)\log(1 - p_k)), \tag{8}$$

where the loss for each sample is normalized by the number of positive concepts K_{pos}. In practice, we find that when solely using $\mathcal{L}_{bce}$, p_k in Eq. 7 is prone to be 1 for all concepts at the beginning of training, leading to the so-called gradient vanishing problem. Thus, we propose to add an extra regularization term $\mathcal{L}_{reg}$:

$$\mathcal{L}_{reg} = \max(\mathrm{mean}(\mathbf{P_{raw}}) - K_{pos}/K, 0). \tag{9}$$

With the proposed $\mathcal{L}_{reg}$, concept detection is forced to be conservative, and the training procedure becomes stable. The final training objective $\mathcal{L}_{cd}$ is:

$$\mathcal{L}_{cd} = \mathcal{L}_{bce} + \mathcal{L}_{reg}. \tag{10}$$

4.2   Dual Concept Detection (DCD)

DCD is an auxiliary task requiring the video caption model to infer relevant concepts based on partial information from videos or text descriptions. Thus, DCD carries out the following two types of detection.

Video-Based Concept Detection is expected to predict the concepts of a video (*i.e.*, A) given sparsely sampled video features $\mathbf{F}'$. Specifically, given video features $\mathbf{F} \in \mathbb{R}^{d_h \times N}$ after encoding (Eq. 5), we introduce a sampling ratio $r \in (0, 1]$ to obtain $\mathbf{F}' \in \mathbb{R}^{d_h \times N'}$, where $N' = \lceil N \cdot r \rceil$. In implementation, r is set to be distributed uniformly during training. Finally, we replace $\mathbf{X}$ in Eq. 6 with $\mathbf{F}'$ and get a resulting training objective $\mathcal{L}_{cd}^V$.

Text-Based Concept Detection aims to predict the concepts of a video solely based on a corresponding ground-truth (GT) caption that contains limited observable concepts. Formally, given a GT caption Y of length T, we first obtain its embedding representation $\mathbf{E} \in \mathbb{R}^{d_h \times T}$:

$$\forall y_t \in Y, e_t \in \mathbf{E}, \quad e_t = \text{LN}(\mathbf{W}_{[y_t]}^w + \mathbf{W}_{[t]}^p), \tag{11}$$

where $\mathbf{W}^w \in \mathbb{R}^{d_h \times |\mathcal{V}|}$ is word embeddings of the vocabulary $\mathcal{V}$ and $\mathbf{W}_{[y_t]}^w$ yields a embedding vector indexed by y_t; $\mathbf{W}^p \in \mathbb{R}^{d_h \times T_{max}}$ is positional embeddings while T_{max} is a pre-defined maximum sequence length. Then, we replace $\mathbf{X}$ in Eq. 6 with $\mathbf{E}$ and get a resulting training objective $\mathcal{L}_{cd}^T$.

Overall Training Objective. We jointly optimize $\mathcal{L}_{cap}$ (Eq. 4) for caption generation and $\mathcal{L}_{cd}^V$ and $\mathcal{L}_{cd}^T$ for DCD:

$$\mathcal{L} = \mathcal{L}_{cap} + \mathcal{L}_{cd}^V + \mathcal{L}_{cd}^T. \tag{12}$$

4.3   Experimental Setup

Datasets and Metrics. Apart from MSR-VTT mentioned in Sect. 3.3, we also experiment on VATEX [37], which contains 41,269 video clips (10 English descriptions per clip) and is divided into 25,991 training, 3,000 validation, and 6,000 testing. We use all metrics introduced in Sect. 3.3.

Implementation Details. For concept detection, we set the number of concepts K to 500 and implement CDNet in Eq. 6 as a fully connected layer. For our baseline model, we set the number of Transformer decoder layers to 1 and set the hidden dimension d_h to 512 for MSR-VTT whereas 1,024 for VATEX.

We set the maximum length of sentences T_{max} to 30, and train batches of 64 video-sentence pairs using ADAM [14] with an initial learning rate of 5e-4 and L2 weight decay of 0.001. Beam search with a beam size of 5 is used for inference. We by default use all three modalities of videos based on Table 1 and take CLIP's ViT-B/32 encoder as the image backbone based on Table 2.

Table 2. Meta-Sum scores of different visual encoders of CLIP.

	ResNet-50	ResNet-101	ResNet-50 × 4	ViT-B/32
MSR-VTT	193.9	196.3	198.2	**199.2**
VATEX	168.3	171.9	**174.8**	174.4

Table 3. Comparison on MSR-VTT.

Method	Year	C	B4	M	R
ORG-TRL [43]	2020	50.9	43.6	28.8	62.1
MGCMP [4]	2021	51.4	41.7	28.9	62.1
NACF [40]	2021	51.4	42.0	28.7	–
APML [20]	2021	52.2	43.8	30.3	63.6
OpenBook [42]	2021	52.9	42.8	29.3	61.7
ARB-ACL [17]	2022	51.3	42.6	28.9	61.5
CLIP-Base	Ours	57.0	47.3	30.9	64.0
CLIP-DCD	Ours	**58.7**	**48.2**	**31.3**	**64.8**

Table 4. Comparison on VATEX.

Method	Year	C	B4	M	R
VATEX [37]	2019	45.1	28.4	21.7	47.0
ORG-TRL [43]	2020	49.7	32.1	22.2	48.9
NSA [7]	2020	57.1	31.0	22.7	49.0
OpenBook [42]	2021	57.5	33.9	23.7	50.2
MGCMP [4]	2021	57.6	34.2	23.5	50.3
CLIP-Base	Ours	60.9	**36.8**	24.8	51.9
CLIP-DCD	Ours	**62.4**	**36.8**	**25.1**	**52.2**

4.4 Comparison with State-of-the-Art Methods

We compare our approach with state-of-the-art methods (SOTAs) on MSR-VTT and VATEX in Table 3 and 4. We can observe that CLIP-Base already surpasses SOTAs by a large margin due to the better learning of concept-aware representations mentioned in Sect. 3.4. But we note that the relative improvement of CLIP-Base against SOTAs on VATEX is relatively small than that of MSR-VTT. This is probably because videos in VATEX are originated from the action recognition dataset, making the motion cues more important than the static appearance. Compared with CLIP-Base, the model trained with our proposed DCD (*i.e.*, CLIP-DCD) performs better on both datasets, especially the CIDEr metric, *e.g.*, a relative improvement of 3.0% on MSR-VTT.

4.5 Ablation Study

We here experiment on MSR-VTT to delve deeper into DCD's design.

Impact of Video-Based Concept Detection (VCD). Results in Table 5 show that using VCD can improve all metrics (CLIP-VCD *vs.* CLIP-Base). We further give an example in Fig. 6 (left) to illustrate the difference between

Table 5. Impact of using different training objectives on MSR-VTT.

Model	Objective			Caption quality					Caption diversity		
	$\mathcal{L}_{cap}$	$\mathcal{L}_{cd}^V$	$\mathcal{L}_{cd}^T$	C	B4	M	R	MS	N	U	V
CLIP-Base	✓			57.0	47.3	30.9	64.0	199.2	28.0	40.0	520
CLIP-VCD	✓	✓		58.4	48.1	**31.3**	64.8	202.6	31.5	43.2	565
CLIP-TCD	✓		✓	58.0	47.6	31.1	64.8	201.5	**31.7**	**43.9**	**581**
CLIP-DCD	✓	✓	✓	**58.7**	**48.2**	31.3	64.8	**203.0**	30.7	43.2	569

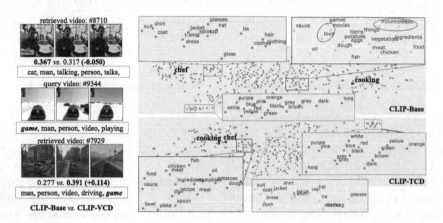

Fig. 6. (Left): retrieval comparison for CLIP-Base *vs.* CLIP-VCD. Values are cosine similarities and words are CLIP-VCD's top 5 detected concepts. (Right): analysis on the learned concept embeddings via t-SNE visualization.

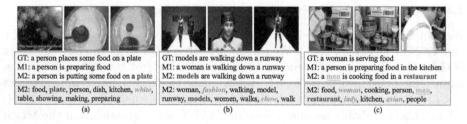

Fig. 7. Captioning results of the CLIP-Base (M1) and CLIP-DCD (M2) models, where we emphasize accurate keywords and errors. Among M2's video-based detected concepts, we highlight *meaningful concepts* yet to be utilized.

CLIP-Base and CLIP-VCD. As we can see, while similar retrieval results can be obtained for the given query video, two models have different preferences, *e.g.*, CLIP-VCD prefers videos with a similar style to the query video. This can be explained by the detected concepts of CLIP-VCD, where the concept "game" is detected in video #9344 and #7929.

Impact of Text-Based Concept Detection (TCD). Similar to VCD, using TCD can also improve the captioning performance, *i.e.*, CLIP-TCD *vs.* CLIP-Base in Table 5. To gain more insights into TCD, we extract $K = 500$ concept embeddings from word embeddings (*i.e.*, $\mathbf{W}^w$ in Eq. 11) and visualize them via t-SNE [24]. Based on Fig. 6 (right), we have the following two observations. (1) For CLIP-Base with only the caption generation objective, concepts of the same type are generally clustered together. But some noises may exist in those potential clusters, *e.g.*, concepts like "toys" and "games" are contained in the cluster about food and tableware (the purple bounding box). (2) After using TCD, the co-occurrence relations between concepts affect the learned representations, *e.g.*, "cooking" and "chef", two concepts that often co-occur with food and tableware, become closer to the purple bounding box in (b).

Qualitative Results. Figure 7 presents three examples to illustrate the difference between CLIP-Base's and CLIP-DCD's generated captions. We can see that while CLIP-Base describes the main event of videos accurately, CLIP-DCD can capture more details, *i.e.*, "plate" in (a), "models" in (b), and "restaurant" in (c). We note that CLIP-DCD mistakes the woman in (c) as a man. One reason might be that it is difficult to recognize the woman from behind. Another reason might be that the language model is biased by the imbalanced training data, where the word "man" is more frequent than "woman". However, given the video-based detected concepts (*i.e.*, VCD's results) of CLIP-DCD below each example, we can see that there is a great potential to use the detected concepts to polish the captioning results of CLIP-DCD, *e.g.*, "white plate" in (a), "fashion show" in (b), and "Asian woman (lady)" in (c).

5   Conclusions

This paper carries out an empirical study on INP *vs.* CLIP, where we reveal the potential deficiencies of INP and conclude that concept-aware representation learning contributes significantly to accurate video captioning. Motivated by these findings, we devise an auxiliary task named Dual Concept Detection to inject concept-related knowledge into video caption models during training. Experiments show that our approach enables better learning of concept-aware video and word representations.

Acknowledgements. This paper was partially supported by NSFC (No: 62176008) and Shenzhen Science & Technology Research Program (No: GXWD20201231165807 007-20200814115301001).

References

1. Ba, J.L., Kiros, J.R., Hinton, G.E.: Layer normalization. arXiv preprint arXiv:1607.06450 (2016)
2. Banerjee, S., Lavie, A.: Meteor: an automatic metric for MT evaluation with improved correlation with human judgments. In: ACL Workshop, pp. 65–72 (2005)
3. Caruana, R.: Multitask learning. Mach. Learn. **28**, 41–75 (1997)
4. Chen, S., Jiang, Y.G.: Motion guided region message passing for video captioning. In: ICCV, pp. 1543–1552 (2021)
5. Chen, S., Chen, J., Jin, Q., Hauptmann, A.: Video captioning with guidance of multimodal latent topics. In: ACMMM, pp. 1838–1846 (2017)
6. Desai, K., Johnson, J.: Virtex: learning visual representations from textual annotations. In: CVPR, pp. 11162–11173 (2021)
7. Guo, L., Liu, J., Zhu, X., Yao, P., Lu, S., Lu, H.: Normalized and geometry-aware self-attention network for image captioning. In: CVPR, pp. 10327–10336 (2020)
8. Hara, K., Kataoka, H., Satoh, Y.: Can spatiotemporal 3D CNNs retrace the history of 2D CNNs and imagenet? In: CVPR (2018)
9. He, K., Girshick, R., Dollár, P.: Rethinking imagenet pre-training. In: ICCV, pp. 4918–4927 (2019)
10. He, K., Zhang, X., Ren, S., Sun, J.: Deep residual learning for image recognition. In: CVPR, pp. 770–778 (2016)
11. Hershey, S., et al.: CNN architectures for large-scale audio classification. In: ICASSP, pp. 131–135. IEEE (2017)
12. Huang, Y., Chen, J., Ouyang, W., Wan, W., Xue, Y.: Image captioning with end-to-end attribute detection and subsequent attributes prediction. TIP **29**, 4013–4026 (2020)
13. Kim, W., Son, B., Kim, I.: Vilt: vision-and-language transformer without convolution or region supervision. In: ICML, vol. 139, pp. 5583–5594 (2021)
14. Kingma, D.P., Ba, J.: Adam: a method for stochastic optimization. In: ICLR (2015)
15. Li, L., Gong, B.: End-to-end video captioning with multitask reinforcement learning. In: WACV, pp. 339–348. IEEE (2019)
16. Li, L., Chen, Y.C., Cheng, Y., Gan, Z., Yu, L., Liu, J.: Hero: hierarchical encoder for video+ language omni-representation pre-training. In: EMNLP, pp. 2046–2065 (2020)
17. Li, S., Yang, B., Zou, Y.: Adaptive curriculum learning for video captioning. IEEE Access **10**, 31751–31759 (2022)
18. Li, X., et al.: Oscar: object-semantics aligned pre-training for vision-language tasks. In: Vedaldi, A., Bischof, H., Brox, T., Frahm, J.-M. (eds.) ECCV 2020. LNCS, vol. 12375, pp. 121–137. Springer, Cham (2020). https://doi.org/10.1007/978-3-030-58577-8_8
19. Lin, C.Y.: Rouge: a package for automatic evaluation of summaries. In: ACL Workshop, pp. 74–81 (2004)
20. Lin, K., Gan, Z., Wang, L.: Augmented partial mutual learning with frame masking for video captioning. In: AAAI, vol. 35, pp. 2047–2055 (2021)
21. Liu, F., Ren, X., Wu, X., Yang, B., Ge, S., Sun, X.: O2na: an object-oriented non-autoregressive approach for controllable video captioning. In: Findings of the Association for Computational Linguistics: ACL-IJCNLP 2021, pp. 281–292 (2021)
22. Liu, F., et al.: Dimbert: learning vision-language grounded representations with disentangled multimodal-attention. ACM Trans. Knowl. Disc. Data (TKDD) **16**(1), 1–19 (2021)

23. Luo, H., et al.: Clip4clip: An empirical study of clip for end to end video clip retrieval. arXiv preprint arXiv:2104.08860 (2021)
24. Van der Maaten, L., Hinton, G.: Visualizing data using t-sne. J. Mach. Learn. Res. **9**, 2579–2605 (2008)
25. Pan, B., et al.: Spatio-temporal graph for video captioning with knowledge distillation. In: CVPR, pp. 10870–10879 (2020)
26. Papineni, K., Roukos, S., Ward, T., Zhu, W.J.: Bleu: a method for automatic evaluation of machine translation. In: ACL, pp. 311–318 (2002)
27. Pasunuru, R., Bansal, M.: Multi-task video captioning with video and entailment generation. In: ACL, pp. 1273–1283 (2017)
28. Radford, A., et al.: Learning transferable visual models from natural language supervision. In: ICML, vol. 139, pp. 8748–8763 (2021)
29. Sariyildiz, M.B., Perez, J., Larlus, D.: Learning visual representations with caption annotations. In: Vedaldi, A., Bischof, H., Brox, T., Frahm, J.-M. (eds.) ECCV 2020. LNCS, vol. 12353, pp. 153–170. Springer, Cham (2020). https://doi.org/10.1007/978-3-030-58598-3_10
30. Selvaraju, R.R., Cogswell, M., Das, A., Vedantam, R., Parikh, D., Batra, D.: Gradcam: visual explanations from deep networks via gradient-based localization. In: ICCV, pp. 618–626 (2017)
31. Shen, S., et al.: How much can clip benefit vision-and-language tasks? In: International Conference on Learning Representations (2021)
32. Sun, C., Myers, A., Vondrick, C., Murphy, K., Schmid, C.: Videobert: a joint model for video and language representation learning. In: ICCV, pp. 7464–7473 (2019)
33. Vaswani, A., et al.: Attention is all you need. In: NIPS, pp. 5998–6008 (2017)
34. Vedantam, R., Lawrence Zitnick, C., Parikh, D.: Cider: consensus-based image description evaluation. In: CVPR, pp. 4566–4575 (2015)
35. Venugopalan, S., Rohrbach, M., Donahue, J., Mooney, R., Darrell, T., Saenko, K.: Sequence to sequence-video to text. In: ICCV, pp. 4534–4542 (2015)
36. Venugopalan, S., Xu, H., Donahue, J., Rohrbach, M., Mooney, R., Saenko, K.: Translating videos to natural language using deep recurrent neural networks. In: NAACL (2015)
37. Wang, X., Wu, J., Chen, J., Li, L., Wang, Y.F., Wang, W.Y.: Vatex: a large-scale, high-quality multilingual dataset for video-and-language research. In: ICCV, pp. 4581–4591 (2019)
38. Xu, J., Mei, T., Yao, T., Rui, Y.: MSR-VTT: a large video description dataset for bridging video and language. In: CVPR (2016)
39. Yang, B., Zou, Y.: Visual oriented encoder: integrating multimodal and multi-scale contexts for video captioning. In: 2020 25th International Conference on Pattern Recognition (ICPR), pp. 188–195. IEEE (2021)
40. Yang, B., Zou, Y., Liu, F., Zhang, C.: Non-autoregressive coarse-to-fine video captioning. In: AAAI, vol. 35, pp. 3119–3127 (2021)
41. Yu, Y., Ko, H., Choi, J., Kim, G.: End-to-end concept word detection for video captioning, retrieval, and question answering. In: CVPR, pp. 3165–3173 (2017)
42. Zhang, Z., et al.: Open-book video captioning with retrieve-copy-generate network. In: CVPR, pp. 9837–9846 (2021)
43. Zhang, Z., et al.: Object relational graph with teacher-recommended learning for video captioning. In: CVPR, pp. 13278–13288 (2020)

Attention-Guided Multi-modal and Multi-scale Fusion for Multispectral Pedestrian Detection

Wei Bao[1,2], Meiyu Huang[1(✉)], Jingjing Hu[2], and Xueshuang Xiang[1(✉)]

[1] Qian Xuesen Laboratory of Space Technology, China Academy of Space
Technology, Beijing, China
{huangmeiyu,xiangxueshuang}@qxslab.cn
[2] Beijing Institute of Technology, Beijing, China
{baowei,hujingjing}@bit.edu.cn

Abstract. Multispectral pedestrian detection provides more accurate and reliable detection results by leveraging complementary information from color-thermal modalities and has drawn much attention in the open world. Much progress has been made in the feature-level-based detection methods which aim to effectively fuse the multispectral features extracted by the convolution neural networks. However, existing methods mainly focus on the information integration between the same-level feature maps and ignore the complementary local features scattered in multi-scale layers. In this paper, we introduce an Attention-guided multi-Modal and multi-Scale Fusion (AMSF) module to simultaneously sample complementary local features scattered in multi-modal and multi-scale layers, and adaptively aggregate them with fine-grained attention to fully exploit different modalities for better multi-scale detection results. Extensive experiments are conducted on three multispectral datasets and three representative deep-learning-based detection benchmarks to show the effectiveness and generalization of the proposed method, and the state-of-the-art detection performance.

Keywords: Multispectral pedestrian detection · Multi-modal and Multi-scale fusion · Fine-grained attention

1 Introduction

Multispectral pedestrian detection is one of the most widely studied topics in the open world because it can generate more accurate and reliable detection results by taking advantage of multiple modalities, such as visible modality (RGB) and thermal modality. The visible modality is the most intuitive modality for humans

Supported by organization: the Beijing Nova Program of Science and Technology under Grant Z191100001119129.

S. Yu et al. (Eds.): PRCV 2022, LNCS 13534, pp. 382–393, 2022.
https://doi.org/10.1007/978-3-031-18907-4_30

but is susceptible to illumination conditions, while the thermal modality is robust to low illumination but lacks texture information [1]. Recent works in multispectral pedestrian detection aim to fuse the complementary information from different modalities and can be divided into three categories: image-level-based fusion methods [2], feature-level-based fusion methods [1,3–7] and decision-level-based fusion methods [8,9].

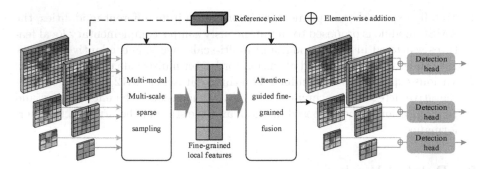

Fig. 1. The structure of the AMSF module which consists of the MSSS bolck and the AFF block. The MSSS block simultaneously samples complementary pixel-level local features (six blue and six orange squares) scattered in multi-modal and multi-scale layers according to the current reference point (the red square on the left). The AFF block adaptively aggregates them to form new pixel (the red square on the right) for enhancing the ability of cross-modal interaction. (Color figure online)

Due to their effectiveness, feature-level-based fusion methods have received considerable attention in multispectral pedestrian detection. The key idea behind feature-level-based fusion methods is to adopt multi-stream convolution neural networks [10] to extract the complementary features of respective modalities and effectively fuse them to achieve better detection performance. However, existing methods mainly focus on the information integration between the same-level feature maps and ignore the complementary local features scattered in multi-scale layers. More specifically, the local feature representation is diverse in terms of pedestrian morphology, texture, and properties in multi-modal and multi-scale features and can not be fully exploited under fixed receptive fields in the standard convolution. To address the above problem above, we introduce an Attention-guided multi-Modal and multi-Scale Fusion (AMSF) module to simultaneously sample complementary local features scattered in multi-modal and multi-scale layers, and adaptively aggregate them with fine-grained attention to fully exploit the complementary information from different modalities as depicted in Fig. 1. Given the multi-scale feature maps extracted from two-stream neural networks, the multi-Modal and multi-Scale Sparse Sampling (MSSS) block leverages deformable convolution [11] to sample several complementary pixel-level features (six blue and six orange squares) from all feature maps in two modalities according to the current reference point (the red square on the left). Then, the Attention-guided Fine-grained Fusion (AFF) block adaptively aggregates these local features and the current reference point with fine-grained attention to form the new feature (the red square on the right) for enhancing the ability of cross-modal interaction. Finally, a simple element-wise addition between the same-level feature maps is performed to obtain the fused multi-scale detection results. The main contributions of our work can be summarized as follows:

1. To fully exploit the complementary information from different modalities, the AMSF module is proposed to simultaneously sample complementary local features scattered in multi-modal and multi-scale layers, and adaptively aggregate them with fine-grained attention for better multi-scale detection results;
2. Various experiments are conducted on three datasets [3, 9, 12] and three representative detection benchmarks [13–15] to demonstrate the effectiveness and generalization of the proposed method, and the state-of-the-art detection performance.

2   Related Work

2.1   General Object Detection

Recent works in object detection leverages deep convolutional neural networks (CNN) [10] to perform detection in extracted features and can be divided into two categories: anchor-based detection methods [13–16] and anchor-free detection methods [17–19]. 1) Anchor-based detection methods predefine a handful of anchor boxes with different scales and respect ratios as common references to search possible regions containing the object of interest. 2) Considering that the predefined anchors are domain-specific and highly sophisticated for detection heads, anchor-free detection methods design considerably simpler detectors to eliminate the predefined anchor boxes and reduce the number of design parameters.

2.2   Multi-modal Fusion

Recent works in multi-modal fusion for multispectral pedestrian detection elaborately design effective information fusion strategies which can be categorized into image-level-based fusion methods, feature-level-based fusion methods, and decision-level-based fusion methods. 1) Image-level-based fusion methods directly sum or concatenate the original images and then send them into a single-stream detector, which is simple but less efficient. 2) Feature-level-based fusion methods adopt two-stream network architectures to extract the complementary features of respective modalities and effectively fuse them to obtain better detection performance. Wagner *et al.* [2] and Liu *et al.* [20] adopt the simple concatenate operation to fuse the middle-level feature maps of two modalities. To increase the consistency and complementarity, CFR [3] leverages the convolution network to repeatedly fuse and refine features. MBnet [5] proposes a modality balance network to handle the feature modality imbalance and the illumination modality imbalance by using a channel-wise differential weighting mechanism. GAFF [4] designs intra-modality attention and inter-modality attention modules to enhance the mono-modal features and fuse complementary multi-modal features, respectively. CFT [6] exploits the ability of global context dependencies modeling in Transformer to carry out simultaneous intra-modality and inter-modality fusion. 3) Decision-level-based fusion methods aim to merge the multiple detection results of different modalities instead of the single detection result in the former two methods. CMPD [8] proposes a confidence-aware strategy in the decision level to produce more reliable detection results by leveraging Dempster's theory-based combination rule. Similarly, CMDet [9] designs an illumination-aware non-maximum suppression to fuse the results of two separated modality detectors and the cross-modal detector.

2.3 Multi-scale Fusion

Recent works in multi-scale fusion are derived from feature pyramid network [21] which constructs feature hierarchy and combines low-resolution, semantic strongly features in high level with high-resolution, semantic weakly features in low level. PANet [22] further enhances the entire feature hierarchy with bottom-up path augmentation which shortens the information path between low-level and high-level features. ASFF [23] adaptively learns pyramidal feature fusion to spatially filter conflictive information and suppress the inconsistency across different feature scales. The most related work Deformable DETR proposes a multi-scale deformable attention module to mitigate issues of slow convergence and limited feature spatial resolution in DETR [18]. Differently, the proposed AMSF module aims to capture complementary local features scattered in multi-modal and multi-scale layers, and elaborately designs fine-grained dynamic attention instead of the inner-products-based attention.

3 Methodology

3.1 Multi-modal and Multi-scale Sparse Sampling

It is difficult to directly extract effective fine-grained local features from the whole images due to complex spatial feature relationships and fixed receptive fields in the standard convolution. Inspired by DCN [11], the MSSS module is proposed to enable the network to collect a small set of highly correlated pixel-level features by a separated convolution layer according to the current reference pixel as depicted in Fig. 2(a). Our proposed network architecture adopts multi-stream FPN to produce multi-modal and multi-level feature maps. Supposing that L is the number of pyramid level, M is the number of modality and the feature map at pyramid level l for modality m is denoted as $P_{lm} \in \mathbb{R}^{(W/s_l) \times (H/s_l) \times C}$ where $W \times H$ is the size of the input image, C is the channel dimension and

$s_l = 2^l$ is the corresponding down-sampling ratio to the input image. Given a reference pixel p_{jn} ($j \in L, n \in M$) in multi-modal and multi-level feature maps with location (x, y) and content feature $p_{jn}(x, y) \in R^{1 \times 1 \times C}$, the MSSS samples KLM complementary pixels for all pyramid levels and modalities according to $p_{jn}(x, y)$. K enumerates the sampled pixels in each pyramid level and modality. It is nothing that the reference pixel need to traverse all location on multi-modal and multi-level feature maps, and only one location is shown in Fig. 2(a) for convenience. Assuming that $q_{jn}^{klm}(x, y)$ represents each pixel to be sampled. The input-specific offsets $(\Delta x^{klm}, \Delta y^{klm})$ in the x and y directions between $p_{jn}(x, y)$ and $q_{jn}^{klm}(x, y)$ can be learned via a separate $1 \times 1 \times C$ convolution layer with $2KLM$ output channels applied over $p_{jn}(x, y)$. Specifically, the formula for obtaining sampled pixels $q_{jn}^{klm}(x, y)$ from the reference point in location (x, y) can be written as follows:

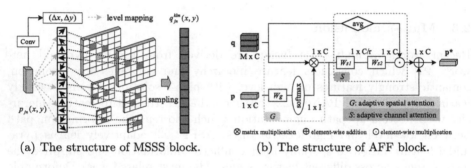

(a) The structure of MSSS block.   (b) The structure of AFF block.

Fig. 2. Two blocks in the AMSF module.

$$q_{jn}^{klm}(x, y) = p_{lm}(x^\dagger, y^\dagger)$$
$$= p_{lm}(\phi_{jn}^{lm}(x) + \Delta x^{klm}, \phi_{jn}^{lm}(y) + \Delta y^{klm}) \tag{1}$$

where $\phi_{jn}^{lm}(\cdot)$ is the level mapping function which re-scales the coordinates of $p_{jn}(x, y)$ to the feature map in the l-th level and m-th modality. For the clarity of scale formulation, we use normalized coordinates, in which the normalized coordinates $p_l(0, 0)$ and $p_l(1, 1)$ indicate the top-left and the bottom-right feature map corners, respectively. Moreover, the sampling offset $(\Delta x^{klm}, \Delta y^{klm})$ is typically fractional, the value $q_{jn}^{klm}(x, y)$ remains to be determined. Bilinear interpolation is implemented to determine the missed fractional value:

$$q_{jn}^{klm}(x, y) = \sum_{(x^*, y^*) \in \tau} B\left((x^*, y^*), (x^\dagger, y^\dagger)\right) p_{lm}(x^*, y^*)$$
$$= \sum_{(x^*, y^*) \in \tau} \max\left(0, 1 - |x^* - x^\dagger|\right) \tag{2}$$
$$\max\left(0, 1 - |y^* - y^\dagger|\right) p_{lm}(x^*, y^*)$$

where (x^*, y^*) represents an arbitrary position and τ enumerates all integer spatial locations near $(x^\dagger, y^\dagger)$. B is the bilinear interpolation kernel and is separated into two one-dimensional kernel in the x and y directions. Then, KLM sparsely sampled pixels will be concatenated to generate the corresponding sampled feature vector.

3.2   Attention-Guided Fine-Grained Fusion

The AFF module aims to aggregate the sampled local features to enhance the ability of cross-modal interaction. The general approach to directly sum or average the sample pixels is simple but less efficient. To adaptively aggregate contexts and retain more semantic information, we propose to leverage the attention mechanism to enhance the fusion ability. As shown in Fig. 2(b), the procedure contains sequentially the adaptive spatial attention G and adaptive channel attention S to involve both spatial structures and channel semantics under the guidance of the reference point. Here, we use $I = KLM$, $\mathbf{q}$ and $\mathbf{p}$ to represent the number of sampled pixels, sampled pixels $q_{jn}^{klm}(x, y)$ and the reference point $p_{jn}(x, y)$ for convenience, respectively. Supposing that $\mathbf{p}^*$ is the final fused feature, the formula of the AFF module can be defined as follows:

$$\mathbf{p}^* = \text{AFF}(\mathbf{p}, \mathbf{q}) = G(\mathbf{p}, \mathbf{q}) + S(\mathbf{p}, \mathbf{q}) \tag{3}$$

As for the adaptive spatial attention G, we leverage one separated linear layer $W_g \in C \times I$ followed by a softmax operation to directly generate the spatial attention weights for $\mathbf{q}$ based on $\mathbf{p}$. Different from the general spatial attention in [24], the sampled pixels here are selected according to the reference pixel via a separated convolution layer in the MSSS module, which illustrates $\mathbf{q}$ and $\mathbf{p}$ are already related to each other. Thus, the generated attention weights from $\mathbf{p}$ can well involve spatial structures on $\mathbf{q}$. The corresponding formula can be defined as follows:

$$G(\mathbf{p}, \mathbf{q}) = \frac{e^{(\mathbf{p}W_g)_i}}{\sum_{i=1}^{I} e^{(\mathbf{p}W_g)_i}} \mathbf{q} \tag{4}$$

As for the adaptive channel attention S, we adopt two consecutive linear layers after the adaptive spatial attention to adaptively recalibrate channel-wise feature responses by explicitly modeling interdependencies between channels. Different from the channel attention directly recalibrating the whole feature maps with a fixed response in [25], the proposed AFF module recalibrates different sparsely sampled feature vectors with dynamic responses for different reference pixels. This dynamic channel attention enables the AFF module to extract more fine-grained semantic information for local features scattered in multi-modal and multi-scale feature maps. Specifically, the corresponding formula can be defined as follows:

$$S\left(\mathbf{p}, \mathbf{q}\right) = \delta\left(G\left(\mathbf{p}, \mathbf{q}\right)\right) \cdot \mathbf{q}$$
$$= W_{s2}\,\text{ReLU}\left(W_{s1}\left(G\left(\mathbf{p}, \mathbf{q}\right)\right)\right) \cdot \mathbf{q}$$
$$= W_{s2}\,\text{ReLU}\left(W_{s1}\left(\frac{e^{(\mathbf{p}W_g)_i}}{\sum_{i=1}^{I} e^{(\mathbf{p}W_g)_i}}\mathbf{q}\right)\right) \cdot \mathbf{q} \tag{5}$$

where $\delta(\cdot) = W_{s2}\,\text{ReLU}\left(W_{s1}(\cdot)\right)$ denotes the bottleneck transform used in [25]. $a \cdot b$ means the element-wise multiplication operation between a and b. Both $W_{s1} \in C \times C/r$ and $W_{s2} \in C/r \times C$ are linear layer to capture the channel dependency. The factor r is set as 4 in all experiments by default.

We also adopt the multi-head attention module in to more adaptively aggregate fine-grained features from different representation subspaces. The formula of multi-head attention operation can be defined as follows:

$$\text{MultiHead}(\text{AFF}(\mathbf{p}, \mathbf{q})) = \text{Concat}\left(\text{head}_1, \ldots, \text{head}_H\right) W_{h2}$$
$$\text{head}_i = \text{AFF}(\mathbf{p}, \mathbf{q}W_{h1}^i) \tag{6}$$

where Concat represents the concatenate operation, i indexes the attention head and H is the number of heads (we use $H = 4$ by default). $W_{h1}^i \in C \times C/H$ and $W_{h2} \in C \times C$ are linear layers.

4   Experiments

All experiments are implemented based on mmdetection (https://github.com/open-mmlab/mm-detection). We conduct experiments on three multi-modal detection datasets: FLIR [3], LLVIP [12] and DroneVehicle [9]. The corresponding benchmark for each dataset is Faster R-CNN [13], YOLOX [14] and Oriented R-CNN [15], respectively. Here, we do not introduce these three benchmarks and refer to their original papers [13–15] for more details.

4.1   Datasets

FLIR [3] contains 5142 RGB-infrared image pairs, of which we used 4129 pairs for training and 1013 pairs for testing. It covers different urban street scenes and includes three object categories: *bicycle, car*, and *person*. **LLVIP** [12] is a recently released RGB-infrared paired dataset for low-light vision. It contains 15488 RGB-infrared image pairs, of which we used 12025 pairs for training and 3463 pairs for testing. The images in LLVIP were captured by surveillance cameras at 26 locations on the street with only one category: *person.* **DroneVehicle** [9] dataset contains 28439 RGB-infrared image pairs which is divided into training set, validation set and testing set with the ratio of 12:1:6. Because the testing dataset is not public, we use 17990 pairs from training set for training and 1469 pairs from validation set for testing. There are five categories: *car, truck, bus, van,* and *freight car* in DroneVehicle. Totally, the image size for all datasets are 512×640.

Table 1. The overall detection performance of the proposed methods and the comparison with other state-of-the-art multispectral detectors on three datasets. * represents the reported result on testing set for DroneVehicle dataset [9] while our results are evaluated on validation set because they [9] does not open source testing set.

Method	FLIR [3]			LLVIP [12]			DroneVehicle [9]		
	$mAP_{0.5}$	$mAP_{0.75}$	mAP	$mAP_{0.5}$	$mAP_{0.75}$	mAP	$mAP_{0.5}$	$mAP_{0.75}$	mAP
Halfway [3]	71.7	–	–	–	–	–	–	–	–
CFR [3]	72.4	–	–	–	–	–	–	–	–
GAFF [4]	72.9	32.9	37.5	–	–	–	–	–	–
CFT [6]	77.7	34.8	40.0	**97.5**	72.9	63.6	-	-	-
CMDet [9]	78.6	–	–	96.3	–	–	64.0*	-	-
Ours (baseline)	77.7	33.3	39.0	96.0	72.5	63.0	82.8	61.3	52.0
Ours (AMSF-net)	**78.9**	**35.5**	**40.9**	97.0	**74.0**	**64.5**	**83.9**	**62.7**	**53.2**

4.2 Parameter Setting

We use the pre-trained ResNet-50 [26] and CSPDarknet-53 [14] on the ImageNet [27] to initialize the backbone network for two R-CNN and YOLOX detectors, respectively. More specifically, two R-CNN detectors are trained with stochastic gradient descent (SGD) for 12 epochs with a total of 4 images per minibatch. The initial learning rate is set as 0.01 with the x1 schedule which means that the learning rate is divided by a factor of 10 at the 8th and 11th epoch, respectively. The YOLOX detector is trained with SGD for 15 epochs with a total of 4 images per minibatch. The initial learning rate is set as 0.00125 with the cosine schedule. We adopt the mosaic data augmentation [16] and EMA strategy [14] for YOLOX. Other parameters are set as the same as that in mmdetection. The Intersection over Union (IoU) threshold is set as 0.5 when training and testing for rigorous filtering of the bounding boxes with low precision.

4.3 Evaluation Metrics

The commonly used mean average precision metrics mAP_{iou} under different IoU thresholds are employed to evaluate the performance of multi-modal detectors. We select $mAP_{0.5}$, $mAP_{0.75}$ and mAP in our experiments. mAP indicates the averaged mAP_{iou} where iou is set from 0.50 to 0.95 with the step size set as 0.05. Here we do not present the formula to calculate the mAP_{iou} and please refer to [28] for a more detailed introduction.

4.4 Results Analysis

Overall Performance. Table 1 reports the overall detection performance of the proposed methods and the comparison with other state-of-the-art multispectral detectors on three datasets. We use AMSF-net to represent the corresponding baseline adopting the proposed AMSF module for convenience. It can be observed that the AMSF module can improve the detection performance

Table 2. Ablation study for the AMSF module on FLIR [3] dataset. MS and MM mean the MSSS block only with the multi-scale sampling and multi-modal sampling, respectively.

MS	MM	AFF	mAP$_{0.5}$	mAP$_{0.75}$	mAP
✗	✗	✗	77.7	33.3	39.0
✓	✗	✗	77.9	33.9	39.2
✗	✓	✗	78.1	34.2	40.3
✓	✓	✗	78.5	34.5	40.6
✗	✗	✓	78.3	34.9	40.5
✓	✓	✓	**78.9**	**35.5**	**40.9**

Table 3. Hyper-parameters for the AMSF module on FLIR [3] dataset. K, bs, and para means the number of sampled points in each feature map, the baseline, and the number of parameters, respectively.

K	mAP$_{0.5}$	mAP$_{0.75}$	mAP	para (M)	GFLOPs
bs	77.7	33.3	39.0	**67.76**	**121.07**
2	78.2	34.8	40.1	68.02	135.65
4	78.5	35.0	40.4	68.08	139.0
6	78.7	35.3	40.6	68.15	142.35
8	78.8	35.5	40.8	68.21	145.71
9	**78.9**	**35.5**	**40.9**	68.24	147.38

under different mAP metrics on all datasets and the AMSF-net finally outperforms all other detectors by a large margin except the performance under the mAP$_{50}$ metric for LLVIP dataset. Specifically, the AMSF-net achieves about 1.0% 2.0% higher mAP$_{0.5}$ than the baseline on all datasets. Furthermore, when the IoU threshold becomes larger, which indicates that the requirement of localization accuracy gets higher, mAP$_{0.75}$ and mAP gain a slight larger improvement. The quantitative detection performance increase demonstrates that the proposed AMSF can conditionally select complementary local features scattered in the multi-modal and multi-scale layers and effectively fuse the fine-grained feature to fully exploit the complementary information.

Ablation Study. The proposed AMSF module consists of the multi-scale sampling strategy, the multi-modal sampling strategy, and the AFF sub-module. To analyze the influence of each designed component, a series of ablation experiments are implemented on the FLIR dataset as depicted in Table 2. MS and MM mean the MSSS block only with the multi-scale sampling and multi-modal sampling, respectively. It can be seen that both MS and MM can help to improve the detection performance, and adopting two sampling strategies together can further enhance the performance. We can also see that the improvement obtains from MM is higher than that from MS, which demonstrates that the multi-modal fine-grained fusion is more constructive for multispectral detection than multi-scale fine-grained fusion. As for the AFF block, fine-grained attention can achieve 0.4%, 1.0% and 0.3% improvement under mAP$_{0.5}$, mAP$_{0.75}$ and mAP metrics, respectively. All these phenomena illustrates the effectiveness and superiority of the proposed MSSS block and AFF block.

Hyper-Parameters. We conduct a series of experiments to verify the influence of the hyper-parameters: the number of sampling points K in each feature map. As depicted in Table 3, as the K becomes larger, the detection performance in terms of APs metrics gradually increases. However, the parameters and FLOPs

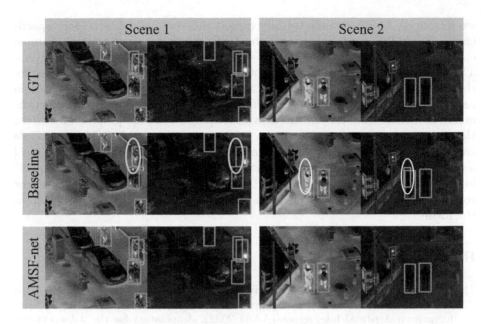

Fig. 3. Visualization results for two scenes on LLVIP [12] dataset. The yellow and orange circles represent the missing pedestrians and false alarms, respectively. GT denotes the ground-truth. (Color figure online)

also slightly increase and the inference speed also becomes slower. More importantly, when K grows up to 9, the detection performance starts to saturate. Hence, we adopt $K = 9$ in all experiments to achieve the trade-off between the speed and accuracy of the proposed method.

Visualization. In addition to quantitative comparisons, we also visualize some detection results for two scenes in Fig. 3 to show an intuitive understanding of our proposed methods. We can see that the baseline misses one pedestrian and generates a false alarm for scenes 1 and 2, respectively. In contrast, the proposed AMSF-net completely detects all ground truths without any error, which illustrates its effectiveness. Moreover, the missed pedestrian and false alarms both occur in the crowd where only local key points are useful for the detection. The baseline which adopts the simple fusion strategy ignores these discriminative local features. Instead, the AMSF-net emphasizes on sampling complementary local features scattered in multi-modal and multi-scale layers, resulting in better detection performance. The superiority can be further demonstrated by all these improvements.

5   Conclusion

Considering that existing multispectral pedestrian detection methods ignore the complementary local features scattered in multi-modal and multi-scale layers, we introduce AMSF module to fully exploit different modalities. More specifically, the AMSF module leverages the MSSS block to simultaneously sample complementary local features scattered in multi-modal and multi-scale layers. Then, the AMSF module further adopts the AFF block to adaptively aggregate these local features with fine-grained attention for better multi-scale detection results. Various experiments are conducted on three datasets and three benchmarks to demonstrate the effectiveness and superiority of the proposed methods. However, our methods also have some limitations. Although the AMSF module can find and leverage the complementary pixel-level local features, the local features only generated from the individual reference point without any explicit location information, which may be sub-optimal. Therefore, we will consider how to effectively select more complementary local features and better fuse them in the future.

References

1. Kim, J.U., Park, S., Ro, Y.M.: Towards versatile pedestrian detector with multisensory-matching and multispectral recalling memory. In: 36th AAAI Conference on Artificial Intelligence (AAAI 2022). Association for the Advancement of Artificial Intelligence (2022)
2. Wagner, J., Fischer, V., Herman, M., Behnke, S., et al.: Multispectral pedestrian detection using deep fusion convolutional neural networks. ESANN **587**, 509–514 (2016)
3. Zhang, H., Fromont, E., Lefèvre, S., Avignon, B.: Multispectral fusion for object detection with cyclic fuse-and-refine blocks. In: 2020 IEEE International Conference on Image Processing (ICIP), pp. 276–280. IEEE (2020)
4. Zhang, H., Fromont, E., Lefèvre, S., Avignon, B.: Guided attentive feature fusion for multispectral pedestrian detection. In: Proceedings of the IEEE/CVF Winter Conference on Applications of Computer Vision, pp. 72–80 (2021)
5. Zhou, K., Chen, L., Cao, X.: Improving multispectral pedestrian detection by addressing modality imbalance problems. In: Vedaldi, A., Bischof, H., Brox, T., Frahm, J.-M. (eds.) ECCV 2020. LNCS, vol. 12363, pp. 787–803. Springer, Cham (2020). https://doi.org/10.1007/978-3-030-58523-5_46
6. Fang, Q., Han, D., Wang, Z.: Cross-modality fusion transformer for multispectral object detection. arXiv preprint arXiv:2111.00273 (2021)
7. Wang, Q., Chi, Y., Shen, T., Song, J., Zhang, Z., Zhu, Y.: Improving RGB-infrared object detection by reducing cross-modality redundancy. Remote Sens. **14**(9), 2020 (2022)
8. Li, Q., Zhang, C., Hu, Q., Fu, H., Zhu, P.: Confidence-aware fusion using dempster-shafer theory for multispectral pedestrian detection. IEEE Trans. Multimedia (2022)
9. Sun, Y., Cao, B., Zhu, P., Hu, Q.: Drone-based RGB-infrared cross-modality vehicle detection via uncertainty-aware learning. IEEE Trans. Circ. Syst. Video Technol. (2022)
10. Sainath, T.N., Mohamed, A., Kingsbury, B., Ramabhadran, B.: Deep convolutional neural networks for LVCSR. In: IEEE International Conference on Acoustics, Speech and Signal Processing 2013, pp. 8614–8618. IEEE (2013)

11. Dai, J., Qi, H., Xiong, Y., Li, Y., Zhang, G., Hu, H., Wei, Y.: Deformable convolutional networks. In: Proceedings of the IEEE International Conference on Computer Vision, pp. 764–773 (2017)
12. Jia, X., Zhu, C., Li, M., Tang, W., Zhou, W.: LLVIP: a visible-infrared paired dataset for low-light vision. In: Proceedings of the IEEE/CVF International Conference on Computer Vision, pp. 3496–3504 (2021)
13. Ren, S., He, K., Girshick, R., Sun, J.: Faster r-cnn: towards real-time object detection with region proposal networks. In: Proceedings of NIPS, pp. 91–99 (2015)
14. Ge, Z., Liu, S., Wang, F., Li, Z., Sun, J.: Yolox: exceeding yolo series in 2021. arXiv preprint arXiv:2107.08430 (2021)
15. Xie, X., Cheng, G., Wang, J., Yao, X., Han, J.: Oriented r-cnn for object detection. In: Proceedings of the IEEE/CVF International Conference on Computer Vision, pp. 3520–3529 (2021)
16. Bochkovskiy, A., Wang, C.Y., Liao, H.-Y.M.: Yolov4: optimal speed and accuracy of object detection. arXiv preprint arXiv:2004.10934 (2020)
17. Tian, Z., Shen, C., Chen, H., He, T.: FCOS: fully convolutional one-stage object detection. In: Proceedings of the IEEE/CVF International Conference on Computer Vision, pp. 9627–9636 (2019)
18. Carion, N., Massa, F., Synnaeve, G., Usunier, N., Kirillov, A., Zagoruyko, S.: End-to-End object detection with transformers. In: Vedaldi, A., Bischof, H., Brox, T., Frahm, J.-M. (eds.) ECCV 2020. LNCS, vol. 12346, pp. 213–229. Springer, Cham (2020). https://doi.org/10.1007/978-3-030-58452-8_13
19. Zhu, X., Su, W., Lu, L., Li, B., Wang, X., Dai, .: Deformable detr: deformable transformers for end-to-end object detection. arXiv preprint arXiv:2010.04159 (2020)
20. Liu, J., Zhang, S., Wang, S., Metaxas, D.N.: Multispectral deep neural networks for pedestrian detection. arXiv preprint arXiv:1611.02644 (2016)
21. Lin, T.-Y., Dollár, P., Girshick, R., He, K., Hariharan, B., Belongie, S.: Feature pyramid networks for object detection. In: Proceedings of the IEEE Conference on Computer Vision and Pattern Recognition, pp. 2117–2125 (2017)
22. Liu, S., Qi, L., Qin, H., Shi, J., Jia, J.: Path aggregation network for instance segmentation. In: Proceedings of the IEEE Conference on Computer Vision and Pattern Recognition, pp. 8759–8768 (2018)
23. Liu, S., Huang, D., Wang, Y.: Learning spatial fusion for single-shot object detection. arXiv preprint arXiv:1911.09516 (2019)
24. Woo, S., Park, J., Lee, J.-Y., Kweon, I.N.: Cbam: convolutional block attention module. In: Proceedings of the European Conference on Computer Vision (ECCV), pp. 3–19 (2018)
25. Hu, J., Shen, L., Sun, G.: Squeeze-and-excitation networks. In: Proceedings of the IEEE Conference on Computer Vision and Pattern Recognition, pp. 7132–7141 (2018)
26. He, K., Zhang, X., Ren, S., Sun, J.: Deep residual learning for image recognition. In: Proceedings of the IEEE Conference on Computer Vision and Pattern Recognition, pp. 770–778 (2016)
27. Russakovsky, O., et al.: Imagenet large scale visual recognition challenge. In: Proceedings of IJCV, vol. 115, no. 3, pp. 211–252 (2015)
28. Bao, W., Huang, M., Zhang, Y., Yao, X., Liu, X., Xiang, X.: Boosting ship detection in SAR images with complementary pretraining techniques. IEEE J. Sel. Topics Appl. Earth Obs. Remote Sens. **14**, 8941–8954 (2021)

XPNet: Cross-Domain Prototypical Network for Zero-Shot Sketch-Based Image Retrieval

Mingkang Li and Yonggang Qi[✉]

Beijing University of Posts and Telecommunications, Beijing 100876, China
{lmk,qiyg}@bupt.edu.cn

Abstract. Zero-shot retrieval is a topical problem for sketch-based image search. It is largely necessitated by the fact that human sketch data is scarce in nature – in most cases retrieval will *have to* be conducted at zero-shot level. The problem of zero-shot sketch-based image retrieval (ZS-SBIR) is however a much harder task when compared with its photo-only counterpart. In addition to addressing the zero-shot transfer problem, it will also need to tackle the inherent domain gap between sketch and photo. Most existing works on ZS-SBIR typically address these two problems separately: a triplet-like network to address the domain gap, and employing external semantic information (such as word embeddings) to assist category transfer. In this paper, we take a different stance and ask a more difficult question – can we devise a consolidated solution to accommodate both problems simultaneously, especially *without* the need for additional semantic information. For that, we propose a cross-domain prototype learning framework to narrow the domain gap by encouraging a confirmation of prototypes between two domains. The intuition is there exists an embedding in which points regardless of which domain it comes from, would cluster around a single and shared prototype representation for a given class. We first show that performance comparable with that of state-of-the-art can already be achieved just by doing this alone. We then further propose two means of tackling data efficiency during training: (i) an episode training protocol that enables data feeding by demand, and (ii) a hard triplet generation algorithm to address data scarcity. Extensive experiments on TU-Berlin-Extended, Sketchy-Extended and QuickDraw-Extended validate the usefulness of our approach.

Keywords: Cross-domain prototype · Zero-shot · SBIR

1 Introduction

Sketch-based image retrieval (SBIR) has been a long-standing task in computer vision. It offers a complementary retrieval paradigm to conventional text-based retrieval systems, and has gained significant research interests [8,11–13]

S. Yu et al. (Eds.): PRCV 2022, LNCS 13534, pp. 394–410, 2022.
https://doi.org/10.1007/978-3-031-18907-4_31

especially recently due to the ubiquitous availability of touchscreen devices. Despite huge efforts behind creating ever larger datasets for training (TU-Berlin-extended [14,15], Sketchy [8], Sketchy-extended [11] and QuickDraw-extended [6]), people have quickly released that the de facto setting for SBIR should have been that of zero-shot. This is intuitive since different to photos that can be relatively easily sourced and annotated, collecting human sketches is much more difficult since each sketch will have to separately been drawn and that drawing skills vary significantly from one another.

Zero-Shot Sketch-based image retrieval (ZS-SBIR) requires the learning of a cross-domain feature embedding on a source dataset of sketch-photo pairs, with the hope that it would generalize well on unseen categories. Early approaches [7,33] have mainly focused on the zero-shot problem by re-purposing solutions previously proposed for zero-shot image retrieval (i.e., photo to photo). It had quickly become apparent that additional sketch-specific designs are needed to address the inherent domain gap between sketch and photo – sketches are high iconic and rendered in black and white, photos are pixel-perfect with color and texture. More recent work [3,4,6,9,10] consequently introduced fairly complex networks to tackle both zero-shot transfer and domain alignment simultaneously. Albeit with their specific designs, they generally employ (i) a triplet-like network with carefully engineered losses for bridging the domain gap between sketch and photo, and (ii) external semantic information such as word embeddings to help with category transfer.

In this paper, we ask a different and perhaps more challenging question – can we design a consolidated framework for ZS-SBIR that *intrinsically* tackles domain alignment and category transfer simultaneously, and *without* the help of any externally sourced semantic information? To answer this question, we have to resort to the hypothesis that there exists a common *cross-domain embedding* in which points from both domains would cluster around a *single prototypical representation* for any given class; and once this embedding is established for seen categories, it would also hold for those unseen. The single-domain variant (i.e., photo only) of this hypothesis has already been tested in [2]. The question remains is therefore whether it still holds for the cross-domain setting as per ZS-SBIR. Answering this question is non-trivial largely because the significant domain gap between sketch and photo, i.e., it is reasonable to conjecture that this hypothesis would hold for each domain independently, but there is no guarantee that the domain-specific prototypical representations would align well in the presence of the large domain gap. This might sound particularly unconvincing since most ZS-SBIR work to date emphasize on the importance of additional semantic information to help with alignment.

Our first contribution is therefore a cross-domain prototypical network that learns a joint embedding across sketch and photo. More importantly, our network conducts such learning without the help of additional semantic information such as word embeddings. Intuitively, the network works by enforcing sketch-generated and photo-generated prototypes of a given class to conform with each other in a shared feature space. More specifically, we propose a joint cross-domain prototype loss which enforces an identical classification prediction when measuring distance of a query sketch to either two origins of the prototype. To our surprise, trained together with a standard triplet loss, this seemingly simple formulation can already deliver performance comparable with that of state-of-the-art. As the second contribution, we further insert the need for tackling the data efficiency problem during training. Albeit being understudied, this insertion shares the same underlying motivation as ZS-SBIR – sketch data is scarce, so it should be utilized more efficiently. We propose two separate mechanisms that work hand in hand with the proposed cross-domain prototypical network to achieve this goal. Interestingly, results show by utilizing training data more efficiently, we can also observe a performance gain. The first mechanism is an episode training strategy that encourages training performance to be more faithful to testing thus improves generalization. To mimic the ultimate zero-shot task, a sub-sampling scheme is performed on classes as well as data points so to shorten data feeding as much as possible during training. It is worth noting that episode training could further assist with both domain alignment and category transfer, since it will keep challenging the networks with randomly sub-sampling data points of transferred categories during cross-domain prototype learning. The second mechanism is a hard triplet generator that is used to manipulate the feature in the original embedding space for a harder version. The result of this is twofold: it encourages the network to learn harder which consequently leads to better testing performance, and less training triplets are required in turn improving data efficiency. We show later in experiments that similar testing performance can already be achieved using 75% of the data volume when compared with state-of-the-art methods.

In summary, our contributions include: (i) a cross-domain prototypical network, termed as XPNet, that learns a joint embedding across sketch and photo, without the help of external semantic information, (ii) an episode training scheme plus a hard triplet generator that works hand in hand with prototype learning, which not only addresses the data efficiency problem, but also offers further performance gains, and (iii) extensive experiments conducted on three popular SBIR datasets (TU-Berlin-extended [14,15], Sketchy-extended [11], and the most recent QuickDraw-extended [6]) to verify the superiority of XPNet.

2   Related Work

2.1   Zero-Shot SBIR

The key issue of SBIR is to address the problem of cross-domain gap. Early works for SBIR attempt to directly apply hand-crafted feature [25–28] directly on edge maps of candidate photos to alleviate the cross domain gap. Deep neural networks have since been employed to address the domain shift, which achieved remarkable performance on several large-scale SBIR datasets, including TU-Berlin-extended [14,15], Sketchy [8], Sketchy-extended [11] and QuickDraw-entended [6]. Recently, studies on SBIR have been shifting to the zero-shot setting, i.e. ZS-SBIR, which is closer to the practical scenario where retrieval needs to be conducted on categories where there is no sketch data available. Existing state-of-the-art methods for ZS-SBIR [4,6,9] typically map sketch and photo into a shared feature embedding space by learning from a large number of sketch-photo pairs in a source set, with the hope that this joint embedding can generalize well on unseen categories. Metric learning, such as employing a triplet like network, has been verified as an effective approach for bridging the domain gap. Moreover, semantic information derived from language models has been identified as a critical side knowledge to assist category transfer [4,6,9]. In this paper, we show both the problem of cross domain learning and category transfer can be addressed by an unified framework without any side semantic knowledge in presence.

2.2 Prototype and Cross-Domain Retrieval

Prototype and Cross-Domain Retrieval Narrowing the cross-domain gap between sketch and photo remains at the center for addressing the problem of SBIR. Prototype learning is originally proposed to deal with the problem of classification through examining prototypes to represent the center of data distribution of each class. The earliest prototype learning is k-nearest-neighbor (K-NN) [23]. Learning vector quantization (LVQ) is then proposed in [21] to reduce the burden of computation and the requirement of storage space. Many following up works either design suitable updating conditions and rules to learn prototypes [29,30], or learn prototypes through optimizing a loss especially designed for prototype [31,32]. Prototypical network is first proposed for few-shot classification in [2], and later [22] combined prototype learning with CNN by integrating a prototype layer. Instead of one cluster per class, [38] proposed infinite mixture prototypes (IMP) to represent a class using multiple prototypes for improving robustness of few-shot classification. [39] introduced part-aware prototype network by decomposing a holistic prototype into a set of part-aware prototypes to better capture finer object features for few-shot segmentation. [40] further leveraged attribute prototype to learn shareable knowledge of seen and unseen classes for zero-shot learning (ZSL). In this paper, we for the first time apply prototype search across two domains for the problem of ZS-SBIR, by minimizing the discrepancy of two distributions for the same class.

2.3 Metric Learning for SBIR and Adversarial Generation

In a typical pipeline of deep metric learning network for SBIR, training data which are typically in the form of triplets (an anchor sketch, a positive and a negative photo) is fed to the network by minimizing a margin based triplet loss [24]. However, triplet loss in general is very sensitive, and often suffers slow convergence with poor local optima [1]. This problem is even more severe for the case of sketch-photo pairs, the large domain gap between sketch and photo naturally brings greater inter-class and intra-class variances. In this paper, we aim to make metric learning more effective for SBIR by generating a hard version triplet for each original one. This is because not all triplets are informative for training especially when only very limited data is fed within each episode, and mining hard triplets will help to boost training efficiency. In addition, a separate multi-label classifier was trained to regularize the generator in [1]. However, we found the same effect could be achieved using the proposed prototype, with the intuition that the generated sketch feature will sit closer to its class prototype.

3   Methodology

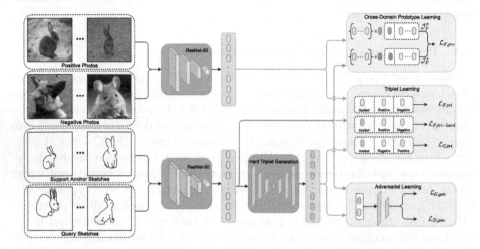

Fig. 1. Framework overview. Our goal is to train a two-branches embedding network for extracting feature from two domains, i.e., sketch and photo. Within each episodic training, support anchor sketches, the corresponding positive and negative photos, and some query sketches are created. Then a cross-domain prototype learning module is applied to bridge the domain gap between sketches and photos. Apart from constructing the original triplet, hard triplet generation is further used to make triplet more informative hence results in a more effective training.

In this section, we describe the proposed cross-domain prototypical network. Our goal is to train a feature embedding network F, which is a two-branches CNN that can extract features from sketch and photo, respectively. Within each episode, a set of support anchor sketches, the corresponding positive and negative photos, and a set of query sketches are created. Then a cross-domain prototype learning module is used to bridge the domain gap by pulling closer the pair of sketch-photo prototypes for each class, and a set of query sketches are used for validating the learned prototypes. Hard triplet generation is further used to make triplet more informative hence facilitate more effective training. Figure 1 shows the pipeline of our proposed approach.

3.1   Problem Formulation

Given a source set $\mathcal{O}^S = \{\mathcal{P}^S, \mathcal{S}^S\}$ contains photo and sketch examples, denoted as $\mathcal{P}^S = \{(p_i^S, y_i) \mid y_i \in \mathcal{C}^S\}_{i=1}^N$ and $\mathcal{S}^S = \{(s_j^S, z_j) \mid z_j \in \mathcal{C}^S\}_{j=1}^M$ respectively, where S denotes source set, p_i^S represents photo and s_j^S for sketch, y_i and z_j are labels for photo and sketch, which share the same class label space $\mathcal{C}^S$. The goal of ZS-SBIR is to train on source set, then retrieve photos by sketch queries in a target set $\mathcal{O}^T = \{\mathcal{P}^T, \mathcal{S}^T\}$ which contains unseen categories, $\mathcal{C}^T \cap \mathcal{C}^S = \varnothing$. We aim to train a feature embedding network F for both sketch and photo while bridging the domain gap. Once trained, F takes a query sketch and a gallery photo from target set as input, and the output features are used for measuring their similarity.

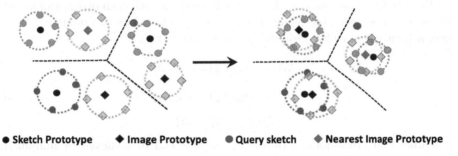

● **Sketch Prototype**   ◆ **Image Prototype**   ● **Query sketch**   ◆ **Nearest Image Prototype**

Fig. 2. Cross-Domain Prototype Learning. The goal is to make the prototypes from sketch and photo domains to conform with each other.

3.2   Cross-Domain Prototype Network

Given an input sketch or photo x, let the output of feature embedding network F to be $F(x) \in \mathbb{R}^D$. Typically, F can be trained by metric learning using a triplet loss. To enforce a joint embedding across sketch and photo upon triplet learning, cross-domain prototype learning is exploited. The proposed feature embedding network F is a two-branches CNN. Different to most of the ZS-SBIR frameworks that require a separate branch for each domain, in our network, the weights of the last layer of both branches are tied in F to encourage a shared feature space across two domains. As shown in Fig. 2, to further deal with the domain shift, a cross-domain prototype module is introduced to narrow the embedding gap between two domains for each class. More specifically, given the source set $\mathcal{O}^S = \{\mathcal{P}^S, \mathcal{S}^S\}$, we can compute a D-dimensional representation of prototype for each class, e.g., $c_k^p \in \mathbb{R}^D$ and $c_k^s \in \mathbb{R}^D$ for class k of two domains as follows:

$$\mathbf{c}_k^s = \frac{1}{\mid \mathcal{S}_k \mid} \sum_{(s_j, z_j) \in \mathcal{S}_k^S} F(s_j) \tag{1}$$

$$\mathbf{c}_k^p = \frac{1}{|\mathcal{P}_k|} \sum_{(p_i, y_i) \in \mathcal{P}_k} F(p_i) \tag{2}$$

Then given a query sketch s, a distribution over classes will be obtained based on softmax over distances to the prototypes. Since we have two sets of prototypes, one from sketch and another from photo, we can get two distributions according to prototypes in two domains:

$$P_F^s(z = k \mid s) = \frac{\exp(-\|F(s) - \mathbf{c}_k^s\|)}{\sum_{k'} \exp(-\|F(s) - \mathbf{c}_{k'}^s\|)} \tag{3}$$

$$P_F^p(z = k \mid s) = \frac{\exp(-\|F(s) - \mathbf{c}_k^p\|)}{\sum_{k'} \exp(-\|F(s) - \mathbf{c}_{k'}^p\|)} \tag{4}$$

Essentially, these two distributions will conform with each other, and a query sketch s can be predicted using either prototypes from the two domains. Therefore, a joint negative log-probability can be defined as:

$$\mathcal{J}_F^s = -\log P_F^s(z = k \mid s) \tag{5}$$

$$\mathcal{J}_F^p = -\log P_F^p(z = k \mid s) \tag{6}$$

$$\mathcal{L}_{F,pro} = \mathcal{J}_F^s + \mathcal{J}_F^p \tag{7}$$

It follows that cross-domain prototype learning can be achieved by minimizing the joint negative log-probability of the true class k.

3.3   Hard Triplet Generator

As aforementioned, feature embedding network F is learned using a triplet loss. In our case, given a triplet $< s^a, p^+, p^- >$, where s^a serves as an anchor sketch, p^+ is the photo with the same label to s^a, while p^- holds a different one. The objective of triplet loss forces F to generate an embedding where the distance between negative pair is larger than the positive. Formally, F is trained by minimizing the following triplet loss:

$$\mathcal{L}_{F,tri} = \frac{1}{N} \sum_i^N \max\{\|F(s_i^a) - F(p_i^+)\| - \|F(s_i^a) - F(p_i^-)\| + m, 0\} \tag{8}$$

However, when the training triplets exhibit large variance and are quite sparse, the resulting feature given by F would be not resilient against inter-class (hard negative examples) and intra-class variance (hard positive examples). To fix this, a hard triplet generator G is developed to improve the robustness of the feature embedding network F. Specifically, G is used to generate an adversarial sample $G(F(s)) \in \mathbb{R}^D$ by manipulating the feature of an input sketch $F(s)$. Essentially, G learns to challenge F by generating hard triplets through pushing apart the feature vectors of positive pair $< s^a, p^+ >$ and pulling closer the negative pair $< s^a, p^- >$.

$$\mathcal{L}_{G,tri} = \frac{1}{N} \sum_i^N \max\{\|G(F(s_i^a)) - F(p_i^-)\| - \|G(F(s_i^a)) - F(p_i^+)\| + m, 0\}$$
(9)

On the contrary, F is required to be capable of handling this hard triplet challenge raised by G:

$$\mathcal{L}_{F,tri-hard} = \frac{1}{N} \sum_i^N \max\{\|G(F(s_i^a)) - F(p_i^+)\| - \|G(F(s_i^p)) - F(p_i^-)\| + m, 0\}$$
(10)

This strategy was originally proposed in [1], where they perform G both on anchor and positive/negative samples to generate hard triplet. In our case, we only apply G on the sketch domain which we empirically found to be more stable than applying on both domains. It follows that F and G play as an adversarial pair during training. In addition, G is also constrained by adversarial loss which plays a min-max game with a discriminator D, where D is to distinguish original sketch feature $F(s)$ from G manipulated feature $G(F(s))$ by minimizing the loss below:

$$\mathcal{L}_{D,gan} = \mathcal{L}_{BCE}(D(F(s)), l_{real} + \mathcal{L}_{BCE}(D(G(F(s))), l_{fake})$$
(11)

and G tries to fool D in the meanwhile:

$$\mathcal{L}_{G,gan} = \mathcal{L}_{BCE}(D(G(F(s))), l_{real})$$
(12)

where $l_{real} = 1$ which is the label for real feature, and $l_{fake} = 0$ for the generated feature. $\mathcal{L}_{BCE}$ denotes the binary cross entropy loss. Additionally, generator G ought to generate a new feature which still remains in the same class, and to prevent from simply generating a random feature vector that leads to a low triplet score. [1] advocates the learning of another classifier independently to guide G. However, this can also be achieved by using the learned prototypes. That is, the manipulated feature representation $G(F(s))$ should also be closer to the class prototype it belongs to. Therefore, a similar joint cross-domain prototype loss is also applied on G:

$$\mathcal{L}_{G,pro} = J_G^s + J_G^p$$
(13)

$$J_G^s = -\log P_G^s(z = k \mid s)$$
(14)

$$J_G^p = -\log P_G^p(z = k \mid s)$$
(15)

$$P_G^s(z = k \mid s) = \frac{\exp(-\|G(F(s)) - c_k^s\|)}{\sum_{k'} \exp(-\|G(F(s)) - c_{k'}^s\|)}$$
(16)

$$P_G^p(z = k \mid s) = \frac{\exp(-\|G(F(s)) - c_k^p\|)}{\sum_{k'} \exp(-\|G(F(s)) - c_{k'}^p\|)}$$
(17)

3.4   Optimization Objectives

To this end, our full objective is defined as:

$$\mathcal{L} = \alpha\mathcal{L}_F + \beta\mathcal{L}_G + \gamma\mathcal{L}_D \tag{18}$$

where

$$\mathcal{L}_F = \mathcal{L}_{F,tri} + \mathcal{L}_{F,tri-hard} + \mathcal{L}_{F,pro} \tag{19}$$

$$\mathcal{L}_G = \mathcal{L}_{G,tri} + \mathcal{L}_{G,gan} + \mathcal{L}_{G,pro} \tag{20}$$

$$\mathcal{L}_D = \mathcal{L}_{D,gan} \tag{21}$$

In essence, F and G form a pair of adversarial players to learn feature representations that are of good generalization and robustness, hence benefits zero-shot
retrieval and few-shot classification in the target set. G and D is another adversarial pair playing a game in classical GAN. These two networks are auxiliary
components to F, we will show that F gains from training together with G and
D in the experiments. The weight of each loss is set to 1, $\alpha = \beta = \gamma = 1$.

3.5   Episode Training

Episode training is utilized for mimicking the test environment during training
by randomly sub-sampling over both training classes and sketch-photo pairs
within each class. In particular, within each episode, N_C classes from source set
is randomly selected, then from those classes, N_S sketches are randomly chosen
as support set. Meanwhile, another N_Q sketch queries are randomly selected
as a prototype validation set within the same classes. To form retrieval photo
pairs, N_+ photos with the same label are selected from photo gallery as positive
pairs. Similarly, N_- negative photos are constructed by using the photos already
obtained in positive set, by simply making each of the negative photo to hold a
different label to the corresponding positive. For each episode, the default setting
is $N_C = 10$, $N_S = 10$, $N_Q = 15$, $N_+ = 10$ and $N_- = 10$ in our case.

Pseudocode. Given the feature embedding network F, the hard triplet generator G takes an output $F(s) \in \mathbb{R}^D$ and produce a generated feature vector of
the same dimension. Discriminator D is used to distinguish real from fake of any
input feature vector given by $F(s)$ or $G(F(s))$. In particular, we use ResNet-50
as the base network for F. G is constructed using 4 FC layers, where the first
two layers reduce the dimension by half, followed by two layers to restore it
to the original dimension of input feature vector. Each layer is followed by a
BatchNormalization and ReLU. Then the output of G is obtained by adding the
output FC layer (Tanh) and the input feature vector in an element-wise manner
similar to [1]. Essentially, G generates by moving an input feature in the feature
embedding space with the help of such a residual structure. The discriminator D
takes a D-dimensional feature vector to distinguish real from fake. In particular,
D has the same structure to G, but differs in using LeakyReLU layer after each
BatchNormalization layer, and a sigmoid activation for the last layer.

3.6 Zero-shot SBIR and Few-shot Sketch Classification

Once the feature embedding network F is learned, ZS-SBIR is performed by directly measuring the feature distance between a query sketch and photos in the gallery, where a ranking list of relevant photos is obtained. Formally, the similarity between a query sketch s and a candidate photo p is defined as:

$$Sim(s,p) = d(F(s), F(p)) \tag{22}$$

where d is the Euclidean distance. Additionally, it is straightforward to apply our network on few-shot sketch classification in the same way as [2], i.e., given a small number of sketches over several unseen classes, a class prototype can be computed for each class by averaging the feature vectors of samples belonging to that class, which can then be used to classify a sketch.

4 Experiments

4.1 Datasets and Experimental Settings

Datasets. We evaluate XPNet on three large-scale datasets that are commonly used for ZS-SBIR: **TU-Berlin-Extended** [14,15], **Sketchy-Extended** [11] and **QuickDraw-Extended** [6]. The TU-Berlin-Extended dataset contains 20,000 sketches uniformly distributed over 250 categories, 204,489 photos are further sourced as paired photo gallery from ImageNet and Google image search. The Sketchy-Extended dataset [11] is relative larger, which is composed of 75,471 sketches and paired with 12,500 photos originated from the Sketchy dataset [8]. Based on that, an additional 60,502 photos are added by [11] making a retrieval gallery with 73,002 photos in total to facilitate a larger scale SBIR setting. QuickDraw-Extended dataset, which is very recently released by [6], is the largest SBIR dataset to date. In particular, there are 330,000 sketches and 204,000 photos over 110 categories in total, which is constructed based on the QuickDraw dataset [16]. To facilitate a fair comparison, we follow the same data split in [4] for TU-Berlin-Extended and Sketchy-Extended. Specifically, a split of 30/220 testing/training classes for TU-Berlin-Extended, and 25/100 testing/training data split for Sketchy-Extended are used respectively. As for QuickDraw-Extended, we also follow the original data split in [6] where 80 classes are used for training, and the rest 30 classes for testing.

Competitors. We utilize three state-of-the-art ZS-SBIR methods to serve as baselines, including **ZSIH** [10], **CAAE** [3], **DOODLE** [6], **SEM-PCYC** [9], and **SAKE** [4]. It is worth noting that except CAAE [3], all the other baseline methods integrate external semantic information into their model, while ours merely depends on sketch-photo pairs to work. In particular, ZSIH [10] deployed a semantic graph convolutional networks to inject semantic relations of training categories into the learning procedure, DOODLE [6] enforces the model to encode semantic information by reconstructing Word2Vec [18] embeddings, while SEM-PCYC [9] applies two text-based models (Word2Vec [18] and GloVe [17]) as side semantic information for training their networks, and SAKE [4] brings a pre-trained 1,000 class ImageNet classifier as teacher network, as well as applying WordNet as semantic constraints. To further investigate the performance of SAKE when no external knowledge is available, we also compare to its variant, denoted as **SAKE w/o T&W**, by disabling modules of teacher network and WordNet.

Evaluation Protocol. For performance evaluation, mean average precision (mAP), precision on top 100 (Prec@100) and top 200 (Prec@200) are reported following the conventional evaluation protocol.

Implementation Details. Our model is implemented using PyTorch [19], and trained with a single Nvidia Tesla V100. ResNet-50 network pre-trained on ImageNet is utilized as weight initialization for the feature embedding network F. Generator G and its counterpart discriminator D is initialized with default setting by the torch nn module. SGD optimizer is used for learning the weights of F, with a learning rate that starts at 0.0001, with momentum $= 0.9$ and weight decay $= 0.0005$. Adam optimizer is applied for optimization on G and D, with parameters $\beta_1 = 0.99$, $\beta_2 = 0.999$ and learning rate is set to 0.001.

Mini-batch vs. Episode. Mini-batch is a sampling strategy generally applied for training networks with SGD (keeping small size will gain more than big size), while episode acts in a more delicate way where it seeks for a faithful data sampling to fit at testing phase [5]. In our case, episode training intends to enforce the network to work in a data scarcity situation by randomly sub-sampling data points over transferred categories during training.

Table 1. Zero-shot SBIR comparison. "ESK": External Semantic Knowledge. "-": not reported. "*": binary code.

Method	ESK Required?	$\mathbb{R}^D$	TU-Berlin Ext		Sketchy Ext		QuickDraw Ext	
			mAP	Prec@100	mAP	Prec@100	mAP	Prec@200
ZSIH [10]	✓	64*	0.220	0.291	0.254	0.340	–	–
CAAE [3]	✗	4096	–	–	0.196	0.284	–	–
DOODLE [6]	✓	256	0.109	–	0.369	–	0.075	0.068
SEM-PCYC [9]	✓	64	0.297	0.426	0.349	0.463	–	–
SAKE [4]	✓	64*	0.359	0.481	0.364	0.487	0.119	0.166
		512	**0.475**	**0.599**	0.547	0.692	0.130	0.179
SAKE w/o T&W [4]	✗	512	0.407	0.556	0.471	0.600	–	–
XPNet	✗	64*	0.322	0.466	0.456	0.596	0.105	0.133
		64	0.374	0.511	0.513	0.657	0.115	0.156
		512*	0.441	0.584	**0.584**	**0.717**	0.122	0.171
		512	0.437	0.574	0.567	0.711	**0.131**	**0.182**

4.2   Results

Quantitative Results. Table 1 offers quantitative results when compared with state-of-the-arts. We can observe from the table that our proposed method outperforms other competitors on Sketchy-Extended dataset and QuickDraw-Extended, and achieve comparable results to state-of-the-art on TU-Berlin-Extended. It is worth noting that ours can obtain state-of-the-art on QuickDraw-Extended dataset, which has a much larger search space at scale of 166 million compared with TU-Berlin-Extended at 1.9 million and Sketchy-Extended at 10 million. In addition, considering all the baseline methods integrate semantic information from e.g., text, ours stands among the best without using any semantic module. It is worth noting that, due to the lack of datasets providing paired sketch and image, the evaluation protocol of ZS-SBIR has been compromised as a classification problem rather than faithfully adhering to a retrieval task [3,10]. As such, points will be given as long as the retrieved image shares the same class label to the query sketch [4,6,9]. It follows that a query sketch could be a positive match to images with mismatched visual appearances, e.g., a front-view dog's head is paired with a running dog. Therefore, we propose to utilize the same evaluation protocol of fine-grained SBIR for performance verification. Specifically, top@K accuracy is adopted to testify the retrieval performance in a more faithful way. Essentially, given a query sketch, it will be counted as successful retrieval only if the target image is ranked at top K according to their distance in the feature space. As shown in Table 2, we report comparison results on the Sketchy dataset[1] [8] which is the largest SBIR benchmark with one-to-one mappings of query sketch and its target image. The same testing categories are however adopted as in Sketchy-Extended, i.e., there are 25 classes involving 15229 query sketches and 17,101 gallery images in total. Our method is compared with SAKE [4], which is the latest state-of-the-art for ZS-SBIR. We can clearly observe that our method performs better than SAKE over most of the testing categories with various settings of K, which suggests that the semantic distance between a given query sketch and the target image is smaller by using our method compared to SAKE.

Table 2. Top K average retrieval results (%) on Sketchy dataset. It reveals the percentage of successful retrieval, i.e., given a query sketch, its corresponding image is ranked within the top K returned results based on their feature distance.

Dataset	SAKE [4]					XPNet				
	Top-1	Top-5	Top-10	Top-50	Top-100	Top-1	Top-5	Top-10	Top-50	Top-100
Sketchy	0.81	4.43	7.27	23.95	39.55	**1.41**	**6.24**	**10.56**	**33.27**	**53.16**

Qualitative Results Some qualitative results are provided in Fig. 3, we can clearly observe that, given a query sketch, relevant photos with the same objects could be obtained even when surrounded by noisy background or part of objects is occluded. Moreover, some failure cases are also provided for analysis. Interestingly it shows similar shape exists among the false positives.

---

[1] Note that we are using the original Sketchy dataset proposed in [8], not Sketchy-Extended [11] in which plenty of sketch-photo pairs are category-level paired rather than instance-level.

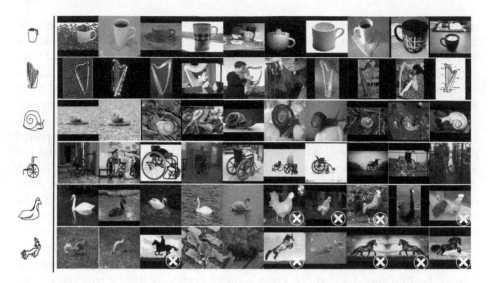

Fig. 3. Example of Top 10 retrieval results on Sketchy-Extended dataset.

4.3   Ablation Study

Ablation study is conducted to verify the effectiveness of key modules. Results are summarized in Table 3, (i) when training our networks without the cross-domain prototype module (Row 1&2 in Table 3), performance stays relatively low at about a 0.37–0.39 mAP on TU-Berlin-Extended dataset, and around 0.51 mAP on Sketchy-Extended dataset. (ii) If we look at settings that are coupled with cross-domain prototypes (Row 3–5 in Table 3), an obvious improvement can be observed. And there is an improvement when we use hard triplets as opposed to base triplet, we can also find a further slight increase on performance once combining them (Row 4 vs Row 5 in Table 3).

Training with Less Data. We test the performance in the case of data deficiency, i.e., by cutting the available classes in source set into a mini version $\mathcal{O}_{mini}$ during the whole optimization procedure. The results are shown in Table 4. We

Table 3. Ablation Study of Our Networks. "Trip.": base triplet module. "HTrip.": hard triplet module. "Proto.": cross-domain prototypes module.

	Trip.	HTrip.	Proto.	TU-Berlin Ext			Sketchy Ext		
				mAP	mAP@100	Prec@100	mAP	mAP@100	Prec@100
1	√	–	–	0.378	0.415	0.482	0.513	0.567	0.637
2	√	√	–	0.394	0.440	0.512	0.511	0.574	0.641
3	√	–	√	0.399	0.468	0.548	0.549	0.626	0.694
4	–	√	√	0.426	0.486	0.562	0.546	0.623	0.687
5	√	√	√	**0.437**	**0.498**	**0.574**	**0.567**	**0.648**	**0.711**

Table 4. Results when using less data. "$\#E$": Number of convergence episodes.

$\mathcal{O}_{mini}$	Sketchy Ext			$\#E$
	mAP	mAP@100	Prec@100	
25%-$\mathcal{O}$	0.432	0.490	0.568	36
50%-$\mathcal{O}$	0.479	0.538	0.610	42
75%-$\mathcal{O}$	0.527	0.601	0.671	53
Full-$\mathcal{O}$	**0.567**	**0.648**	**0.711**	75

can observe that, reducing the source set to 75% volume of the original during training, the mAP score just witness a slight fall from around 0.56 to 0.52, whereas ours can still achieve a comparable results to state-of-the-art, i.e., 0.54 from SAKE shown in Table 1. And if we further half the source set, the mAP score reduces from about 0.56 to 0.48, i.e., 15% performance decrease yet with far less data. Even only 25% data points of the source set are preserved during training, ours can still hold a 0.43 mAP score.

Different Backbones. We further investigate the effect of using different backbone networks, including VGG-16 [35], GoogleNet [34], CSE-ResNet-50 [36], and ResNet-101 [37], and compare with our base network ResNet-50. As shown in Table 5, VGG-16 is the worst, and ResNet-101 can further promote the mAP score to 0.582 from 0.567 obtained by our base backbone ResNet-50.

Table 5. Results on Sketchy Ext using different backbone networks.

Backbone	mAP	mAP@100	Prec@100
VGG-16	0.465	0.519	0.601
GoogleNet	0.504	0.611	0.686
CSE-ResNet-50	0.566	0.624	0.690
ResNet-50 (Our base)	0.567	0.648	0.711
ResNet-101	0.582	0.661	0.720

5   Conclusion

In this paper, we proposed a novel approach for zero-shot sketch-based image retrieval, which achieves state-of-the-art performances on three large-scale SBIR datasets. Our network importantly works without the need for any additional semantic information that is otherwise commonplace in the current literature. In particular, a cross-domain prototype learning method is utilized for effectively pulling closer the prototypes of two domains for each class. We show that comparable performance with state-of-the-art can already be achieved with this seemingly simple formulation. We further propose an episode training strategy and a hard triplet generator to work alongside cross-domain prototype learning, which not only resulted in additional performance gains, but also addresses the data efficiency problem upon training.

References

1. Zhao, Y., Jin, Z., Qi, G., Lu, H., Hua, X.: An adversarial approach to hard triplet generation. In: Ferrari, V., Hebert, M., Sminchisescu, C., Weiss, Y. (eds.) ECCV 2018. LNCS, vol. 11213, pp. 508–524. Springer, Cham (2018). https://doi.org/10.1007/978-3-030-01240-3_31
2. Snell, J., Swersky, K., Zemel, R.: Prototypical networks for few-shot learning. In: Advances in Neural Information Processing Systems, vol. 30 (2017)
3. Yelamarthi, S.K., Reddy, S.K., Mishra, A., Mittal, A.: A zero-shot framework for sketch based image retrieval. In: Ferrari, V., Hebert, M., Sminchisescu, C., Weiss, Y. (eds.) ECCV 2018. LNCS, vol. 11208, pp. 316–333. Springer, Cham (2018). https://doi.org/10.1007/978-3-030-01225-0_19
4. Liu, Q., Xie, L., Wang, H., Yuille, A.L.: Semantic-aware knowledge preservation for zero-shot sketch-based image retrieval. In: Proceedings of the IEEE/CVF International Conference on Computer Vision, pp. 3662–3671 (2019)
5. Vinyals, O., Blundell, C., Lillicrap, T., Wierstra, D.: Matching networks for one shot learning. In: Advances in Neural Information Processing Systems, vol. 29 (2016)
6. Dey, S., Riba, P., Dutta, A., Llados, J., Song, Y.-Z.: Doodle to search: practical zero-shot sketch-based image retrieval. In: Proceedings of the IEEE/CVF Conference on Computer Vision and Pattern Recognition, pp. 2179–2188 (2019)
7. Yang, Y., Luo, Y., Chen, W., Shen, F., Shao, J., Shen, H.T.: Zero-shot hashing via transferring supervised knowledge. In: Proceedings of the 24th ACM International Conference on Multimedia, pp. 1286–1295 (2016)
8. Sangkloy, P., Burnell, N., Ham, C., Hays, J.: The sketchy database: learning to retrieve badly drawn bunnies. ACM Trans. Graphics (TOG) 35(4), 1–12 (2016)
9. Dutta, A., Akata, Z.: Semantically tied paired cycle consistency for zero-shot sketch-based image retrieval. In: Proceedings of the IEEE/CVF Conference on Computer Vision and Pattern Recognition, pp. 5089–5098 (2019)
10. Shen, Y., Liu, L., Shen, F., Shao, L.: Zero-shot sketch-image hashing. In: Proceedings of the IEEE Conference on Computer Vision and Pattern Recognition, pp. 3598–3607 (2018)
11. Liu, L., Shen, F., Shen, Y., Liu, X., Shao, L.: Deep sketch hashing: fast free-hand sketch-based image retrieval. In: Proceedings of the IEEE Conference on Computer Vision and Pattern Recognition, pp. 2862–2871 (2017)
12. Xu, P., et al.: Sketchmate: deep hashing for million-scale human sketch retrieval. In: Proceedings of the IEEE Conference on Computer Vision and Pattern Recognition, pp. 8090–8098 (2018)
13. Pang, K., et al.: Generalising fine-grained sketch-based image retrieval. In: Proceedings of the IEEE/CVF Conference on Computer Vision and Pattern Recognition, pp. 677–686 (2019)
14. Eitz, M., Hays, J., Alexa, M.: How do humans sketch objects? ACM Trans. Graphics (TOG) 31(4), 1–10 (2012)

15. Zhang, H., Liu, S., Zhang, C., Ren, W., Wang, R., Cao, X.: Sketchnet: sketch classification with web images. In: Proceedings of the IEEE Conference on Computer Vision and Pattern Recognition, pp. 1105–1113 (2016)
16. Ha, D., Eck, D.: A neural representation of sketch drawings. arXiv preprint arXiv:1704.03477 (2017)
17. Pennington, J., Socher, R., Manning, C.D.: Glove: global vectors for word representation. In: Proceedings of the 2014 Conference on Empirical methods in Natural Language Processing (EMNLP), pp. 1532–1543 (2014)
18. Mikolov, T., Chen, K., Corrado, G., Dean, J.: Efficient estimation of word representations in vector space. arXiv preprint arXiv:1301.3781 (2013)
19. Paszke, A., et al.: Automatic differentiation in pytorch (2017)
20. Van der Maaten, L., Hinton, G.: Visualizing data using t-SNE. J. Mach. Learn. Res. $9(11)$, 2579–2605 (2008)
21. Kohonen, T.: The self-organizing map. Proc. IEEE $78(9)$, 1464–1480 (1990)
22. Yang, H.-M., Zhang, X.-Y., Yin, F., Liu, C.-L.: Robust classification with convolutional prototype learning. In Proceedings of the IEEE Conference on Computer Vision and Pattern recognition, pp. 3474–3482 (2018)
23. Weinberger, K.Q., Saul, L.K.: Distance metric learning for large margin nearest neighbor classification. J. Mach. Learn. Res. **10**, 207–244 (2009)
24. Schultz, M., Joachims, T.: Learning a distance metric from relative comparisons. In: Advances in Neural Information Processing Systems, vol. 16 (2003)
25. Hu, R., Collomosse, J.: A performance evaluation of gradient field hog descriptor for sketch based image retrieval. Comput. Vis. Image Underst. **117**(7), 790–806 (2013)
26. Lowe, D.G.: Object recognition from local scale-invariant features. In: Proceedings of the Seventh IEEE International Conference on Computer Vision, vol. 2, pp. 1150–1157. IEEE (1999)
27. Saavedra, J.M.: Sketch based image retrieval using a soft computation of the histogram of edge local orientations (s-helo). In: 2014 IEEE International Conference on Image Processing (ICIP), pp. 2998–3002. IEEE (2014)
28. Saavedra, J.M., Barrios, J.M., Orand, S.: Sketch based Image Retrieval using Learned KeyShapes (LKS). BMVC **1**(2), 7 (2015)
29. Geva, S., Sitte, J.: Adaptive nearest neighbor pattern classification. IEEE Trans. Neural Networks **2**(2), 318–322 (1991)
30. Kohonen, T.: Improved versions of learning vector quantization. In: 1990 IJCNN International Joint Conference on Neural Networks, pp. 545–550. IEEE (1990)
31. Sato, A., Yamada, K.: Generalized learning vector quantization. In: Advances in Neural Information Processing Systems, vol. 8 (1995)
32. Decaestecker, C.: Finding prototypes for nearest neighbour classification by means of gradient descent and deterministic annealing. Pattern Recogn. **30**(2), 281–288 (1997)
33. Kodirov, E., Xiang, T., Gong, S.: Semantic autoencoder for zero-shot learning. In: Proceedings of the IEEE Conference on Computer Vision and Pattern Recognition, pp. 3174–3183 (2017)
34. Szegedy, C., et al.: Going deeper with convolutions. In: Proceedings of the IEEE Conference on Computer Vision and Pattern Recognition, pp. 1–9 (2015)
35. Simonyan, K., Zisserman, A.: Very deep convolutional networks for large-scale image recognition. arXiv preprint arXiv:1409.1556 (2014)
36. Lu, P., Huang, G., Fu, Y., Guo, G., Lin, H.: Learning large Euclidean margin for sketch-based image retrieval. **1**(2), 3. arXiv preprint arXiv:1812.04275 (2018)

37. He, K., Zhang, X., Ren, S., Sun, J.: Deep residual learning for image recognition. In: Proceedings of the IEEE Conference on Computer vision and Pattern Recognition, pp. 770–778 (2016)
38. Allen, K., Shelhamer, E., Shin, H., Tenenbaum, J.: Infinite mixture prototypes for few-shot learning. In: International Conference on Machine Learning, pp. 232–241. PMLR (2019)
39. Liu, Y., Zhang, X., Zhang, S., He, X.: Part-aware prototype network for few-shot semantic segmentation. In: Vedaldi, A., Bischof, H., Brox, T., Frahm, J.-M. (eds.) ECCV 2020. LNCS, vol. 12354, pp. 142–158. Springer, Cham (2020). https://doi.org/10.1007/978-3-030-58545-7_9
40. Xu, W., Xian, Y., Wang, J., Schiele, B., Akata, Z.: Attribute prototype network for zero-shot learning. Adv. Neural. Inf. Process. Syst. **33**, 21969–21980 (2020)

A High-Order Tensor Completion Algorithm Based on Fully-Connected Tensor Network Weighted Optimization

Peilin Yang, Yonghui Huang$^{(\boxtimes)}$, Yuning Qiu, Weijun Sun, and Guoxu Zhou

School of Automation, Guangdong University of Technology,
Guangzhou 510006, China
msh_huizi@gdut.edu.cn

Abstract. Tensor completion aims at recovering missing data, and it is one of the popular concerns in deep learning and signal processing. Among the higher-order tensor decomposition algorithms, the recently proposed fully-connected tensor network decomposition (FCTN) algorithm is the most advanced. In this paper, by leveraging the superior expression of the fully-connected tensor network (FCTN) decomposition, we propose a new tensor completion method named the fully connected tensor network weighted optimization (FCTN-WOPT). The algorithm performs a composition of the completed tensor by initializing the factors from the FCTN decomposition. We build a loss function with the weight tensor, the completed tensor and the incomplete tensor together, and then update the completed tensor using the lbfgs gradient descent algorithm to reduce the spatial memory occupation and speed up iterations. Finally we test the completion with synthetic data and real data (both image data and video data) and the results show the advanced performance of our FCTN-WOPT when it is applied to higher-order tensor completion.

Keywords: FCTN-WOPT · Tensor decomposition · Tensor completion · Deep learning · Gradient descent

1 Introduction

Higher-order tensor completion is the prediction of missing data from the original tensor. With the development of Internet technology and artificial intelligence, higher-order data is gradually spreading throughout the various fields of scientific research and engineering applications. In reality, for example, a video (length × width × number of frames) or a color picture (length × width × number of channels) is a third-order data, also known as a third-order tensor. When the data is high-dimensional, it can be compressed by tensor decomposition algorithms to reduce the space occupation, and tensor completion is one of the applications of tensor decomposition. Tensor has been studied for more than a

© The Author(s), under exclusive license to Springer Nature Switzerland AG 2022
S. Yu et al. (Eds.): PRCV 2022, LNCS 13534, pp. 411–422, 2022.
https://doi.org/10.1007/978-3-031-18907-4_32

century and is also widely used in engineering for neural networks [8], machine learning [10], computer vision [5], biosignal processing [9], image processing [6], etc.

An early proposal is the tensor CANDECOMP/PARAFAC (CP) decomposition [1], which decomposes a tensor into a sum of rank-one tensors. It is able to represent a large amount of data with a small amount of data. However, the drawbacks of CP decomposition have gradually become apparent when finding the optimal latent factors is very difficult. In recent years, the TT decomposition [2] algorithm has been proposed for higher order tensors (greater than or equal to third order), which can decompose $(n-2)$ third order tensors and 2 matrices and concatenate them into the shape of a train. Currently, a generalization of TT decomposition, termed the tensor ring (TR) decomposition [3], has been studied across scientific disciplines. This method of decomposition has also been applied to different areas [20–22]. Zheng et al. also proposed the FCTN fully connected decomposition algorithm [11], which factors are interconnected with each other forming a net. Their algorithm guarantees the potential correlation of all factors and has one of the best performances in tensor completion.

Tensor completion is one of the important applications of tensor decomposition, where the goal is to recover incomplete tensors from the observed data. Tensor completion can become quite challenging when observations are few and scattered. Tensor recovery algorithms on this highly under-sampled tensor present additional computational and theoretical challenges, see [4]. The key theories of tensor completion currently fall into two main categories: the first is an algorithm based on nuclear norm approximation, the other is based on a low-rank tensor decomposition.

1.1   Nuclear Norm Approximation

Over the past decade, the results of a large number of research experiments have confirmed that a low-rank tensor can substantially improve the effectiveness of tensor completion. We use $\mathcal{X}$ to denote the recovered low-rank tensor, $\mathcal{T}$ to denote the observed tensor, Ω to denote the location coordinates of the observed tensor data, and $P_\Omega(\ )$ to denote the observed data. The classical low-rank tensor completion (LRTC) model is mathematically represented as:

$$\min_{\mathcal{X}}\quad rank(\mathcal{X})$$
$$s.t. P_\Omega(\mathcal{X}) = P_\Omega(\mathcal{T}) \tag{1}$$

This approach is a good idea, but the problem is non-convex and NP-hard when solving it computationally, and many difficulties are encountered when solving it. The researchers have therefore proposed a tensor nuclear norm to approximate the rank of the tensor, so that the original problem (1) can be equated as

$$\min_{\mathcal{X}}\quad \sum_{i=1}^{N}\|\mathbf{X}_{(i)}\|_*$$
$$s.t. P_\Omega(\mathcal{X}) = P_\Omega(\mathcal{T}) \tag{2}$$

where $\| \ \|_*$ denotes the tensor nuclear norm operation, generally defined as the sum of the singular values of the matrix $\mathbf{X}_{(i)}$. This model is the convex problem [7], which is easy to solve. This type of model laid the foundation for tensor nuclear norm, and many related algorithms were proposed to follow. For example, Hu et al. proposed a twisted tensor nuclear norm completion [12], which unfolds the tensor in two dimensions to calculate its nuclear norm for two-dimensional matrices; Yuan et al. proposed to unfold the tensor under different mode directions [13] and calculate their nuclear norm separately; Yu et al. proposed a TR-rank nuclear norm unfolding [14], which has good performance in terms of the effectiveness.

1.2 Low-rank Tensor Decomposition

Tensor decomposition-based algorithms do not apply a low-rank constraint on the target tensor; Instead, they decompose the observed incomplete tensor and the small tensor obtained from the decomposition is reconstructed to predict the original tensor. A more classical model framework for tensor complementation algorithms based on decomposition is as follows:

$$\min_{\mathcal{G}^{(1)}, \mathcal{G}^{(2)}, \ldots, \mathcal{G}^{(N)}} \quad \|\mathcal{T} - \mathcal{X}(\mathcal{G}^{(1)}, \mathcal{G}^{(2)}, \ldots, \mathcal{G}^{(n)})\|_F^2$$
$$s.t. \qquad P_\Omega(\mathcal{X}) = P_\Omega(\mathcal{T}) \tag{3}$$

where $\mathcal{G}^{(n)}$ within Eq. (3) denotes the nth factor obtained by tensor decomposition, which can be obtained by some synthetic algorithm to obtain the completed tensor $\mathcal{X}$ and each $\mathcal{G}$ is a tensor decomposed by the same decomposition method. Based on different decomposition models, different completion algorithms are obtained. Such as CP weighted optimization, Tucker weighted optimization, etc. Based on TR decomposition Zhao et al. also proposed the TRALS algorithm using alternating lowermost squares (ALS) for iterative optimization [3], followed by Yuan et al. [15] who proposed the TRWOPT algorithm using the gradient descent algorithm for solution, all of which achieved good complementary results. Recently, Liu et al. [16] proposed a robust completion method that can separate the noise from the original tensor; Ahad et al. [17] proposed a residual constraint to improve the model for completion, which also achieved good results.

However, for the factor decomposed by these models, the correlation between them is weak, resulting in more data needing to be decomposed to recover the predicted accurate tensor. The recent proposed tensor fully connected decomposition (FCTN) algorithm [11] solves this problem well. The algorithm has better data correlation and compressibility. However, the FCTN algorithm is very harsh in terms of the constraints on tensor completion, and we hope to construct the model with some weaker constraints, which may be able to better satisfy the low rank of the tensor and get some better experimental results. Therefore, we propose the FCTN-WOPT algorithm to optimise tensor completion and provide better completion results for experiments.

Our proposed algorithm has good recovery results in a variety of experimental situations, and the main innovations and contributions of this paper are:

- The FCTN-WOPT algorithm proposed in this paper extends the recently proposed FCTN algorithm to the field of tensor complementation and obtains better optimisation results.
- This paper uses a gradient descent algorithm with a reduced spatial memory occupation for accelerated iterations to speed up the algorithm.
- This paper experimentally verifies that the model is able to iterate to its theoretical optimum using gradient descent.

2 Preliminaries

2.1 Notations

In this article, we use x, $\mathbf{x}$, $\mathbf{X}$ and $\mathcal{X}$ to denote scalars, vectors, matrices and tensors respectively. Similarly, a Nth-order tensor, we denote by $\mathcal{X} \in R^{I_1 \times I_2 \times \cdots \times I_N}$. The $(i_1, i_2, \ldots, i_N)$ elements of the tensor $\mathcal{X}$ are denoted as $\mathcal{X}(i_1, i_2, \ldots, i_N)$. $\mathcal{X} * \mathcal{Y}$ denotes the Hadamard product of tensors of the same size $\mathcal{X}$ and $\mathcal{Y}$. $\|\mathcal{X}\|_F = \sqrt{\sum_{i_1,i_2,\ldots,i_N} |\mathcal{X}(i_1, i_2, \ldots, i_N)|^2}$ denotes the Frobenius norm of the tensor $\mathcal{X}$. The k-mode of the tensor $\mathcal{X}$ unfolds as a matrix, written as $\mathbf{X}_{(k)} \in R^{k \times I_1 I_2 \ldots I_{k-1} I_{k+1} \ldots I_N}$.

2.2 Fully-Connected Tensor Network Decomposition

The FCTN decomposition [11], recently proposed by Zheg et al. is an improvement on the TR decomposition. Their algorithm strengthens the connection between the factor and better compresses the amount of model data. The purpose of the FCTN decomposition is to decompose the nth-order tensor $\mathcal{X} \in R^{I_1 \times \cdots \times I_N}$ into a set of Nth-order factors $\mathcal{G}^{(k)} \in R^{R_{1,k} \times \cdots \times R_{k-1,k} \times I_k \times R_{k,k+1} \times \cdots \times R_{k,N}}$, which we specify in the following form:

$$\mathcal{X}(i_1, i_2, \ldots, I_N) =$$

$$\sum_{r_{1,2}=1}^{R_{1,2}} \sum_{r_{1,2}=1}^{R_{1,3}} \cdots \sum_{r_{1,N}=1}^{R_{1,N}} \sum_{r_{2,3}=1}^{R_{2,3}} \cdots \sum_{r_{2,N}=1}^{R_{2,N}} \cdots \sum_{r_{N-1,N}=1}^{R_{N-1,N}}$$

$$\{\mathcal{G}^{(1)}(i_1, r_{1,2}, r_{1,3}, \ldots, r_{1,N}) \tag{4}$$

$$\mathcal{G}^{(2)}(r_{1,2}, i_2, r_{2,3}, \ldots, r_{2,N}) \cdots$$

$$\mathcal{G}^{(k)}(r_{1,k}, r_{2,k}, \ldots, r_{k-1,k}, i_k, r_{k,k+1}, \ldots, r_{k,N}) \cdots$$

$$\mathcal{G}^{(n)}(r_{1,N}, r_{2,N}, \ldots, r_{N-1,N}, i_N)\}.$$

To introduce the FCTN decomposition [11] more dynamically, we use Fig. 1 to carry out a representation of the FCTN decomposition form of an Nth-order tensor. This decomposition can be seen to be an ordinary matrix decomposition when the decomposition tensor is a matrix. When the decomposed tensor is a third-order tensor, it will be seen that the decomposition form is that of the standard TR decomposition [3].

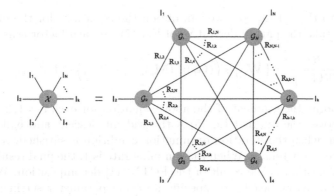

Fig. 1. A graphical representation of FCTN decomposition

3 Fully Connected Tensor Network Weighted Optization

For the tensor completion problem, based on the FCTN decomposition, we propose a FCTN weighted optization algorithm. The specific model is as follows:

$$\min_{\mathcal{G}^{(1)},\mathcal{G}^{(2)},...,\mathcal{G}^{(N)}} \quad \|\mathcal{W} * (\mathcal{T} - FCTN(\{\mathcal{G}^{(n)}\}_{n=1}^{N}))\|_F^2 \tag{5}$$

where $\mathcal{T}$ is the tensor of observed partial data and $\mathcal{W}$ denotes the position tensor of observable data with individual elements of 0 or 1. $FCTN(\{\mathcal{G}^{(n)}\}_{n=1}^{N})$ is an approximate tensor which is composed by the FCTN decomposition algorithm, and $\{(\mathcal{G}^{(n)})_{n=1}^{N}\}$ is expressed as a total of N factor. And we record the formula more concisely by using $\mathcal{X} = FCTN(\{\mathcal{G}^{(n)}\}_{n=1}^{N})$.

According to Definition (5) of the original FCTN paper, if one of the factors $\mathcal{G}^{(t)}(t \in \{1, 2, ..., N\})$, does not participate in the composition, we denote it as $FCTN(\{\mathcal{G}^{(n)}\}_{n=1}^{N}, \mathcal{G}^{(t)})$. And we record the formula more concisely by using $\mathcal{M}_t = FCTN(\{\mathcal{G}^{(n)}\}_{n=1}^{N}, \mathcal{G}^{(t)})$. The t-mode unfolding of $\mathcal{X}$ he can be written as the following equation.

$$\mathbf{X}_{(t)} = (\mathbf{G}_t)_{(t)}(\mathbf{M}_t)_{[m_{1:N-1};n_{1:N-1}]} \tag{6}$$

where

$$m_i = \begin{cases} 2i, & \text{if } i < t, \\ 2i - 1, & \text{if } i \ge t, \end{cases} and \ n_i = \begin{cases} 2i - 1, & \text{if } i < t \\ 2i, & \text{if } i \ge t \end{cases}$$

where $(\mathbf{G}_t)_{(t)}$ denotes the t-mode unfolding of the tth tensor $\mathcal{G}$ and $(\mathbf{M}_t)_{[m_{1:N-1};n_{1:N-1}]}$ denotes a special unfolding of the tensor $\mathcal{M}$ according to the above equation, which is abbreviated to $(\mathbf{M}_t)_{(\ne t)}$ for simplicity in recording it. This unfolding of the equation is very important and the algorithm needs to use it in the derivative calculations.

Since each $\mathcal{G}$ is independent, we can optimize each $\mathcal{G}$ individually, and Eq. (5) is optimized as

$$\min_{(\mathbf{G}_t)_{(t)}} \ f\left((\mathbf{G}_t)_{(t)}\right) = \frac{1}{2} \| \ \mathbf{W}_{(t)} * (\mathbf{T}_{(t)} - (\mathbf{G}_t)_{(t)}(\mathbf{M}_t)_{(\ne t)}) \ \|_F^2 \tag{7}$$

Similar to that of Eq. (7), we can obtain the equations for the other factor $\mathcal{G}$. We then take the partial derivative of Eq. (7) for each factor tensor:

$$\frac{\partial f}{\partial (\mathbf{G}_t)_{(t)}} = \left(\mathbf{W}_{(t)} * \left((\mathbf{G}_t)_{(t)} (\mathbf{M}_t)_{(\neq t)} - \mathbf{T}_{(t)} \right) (\mathbf{M}_t)^T_{(\neq t)} \right). \tag{8}$$

After finding the gradient of the above equation for each $t = 1, 2, \ldots, N$, we can iterate over the original Eq. (5) with gradient descent and exit the iterative program when the iteration termination condition is satisfied, returning to obtain our recovery tensor. When the sampling rate is 1, the final result achieved using this algorithm is the result of the FCTN [11] decomposition. We give the algorithm flowchart1 below, the specific iteration parameter settings for using gradient descent and some experimental details of the paper will be explained in the experimental section.

Algorithm 1 LBFGS-Based Solver for FCTN-WOPT

1:   **Input**:The observed tensor $\mathcal{T}$, the weighted tensor $\mathcal{W}$
     , the matrix $\mathbf{R}$ and the termination conditions **opt**
2:   **While** Satisfying the termination conditions **opt**
3:     **For** n=1:N
4:       Calculate gradients of each $(G_t)_{(t)}$ using equation (8)
5:     **End**
6:   Update each $\mathcal{G}$ by lbfgs gradient descent
7:   **End while**
8: $\mathcal{X} = P_\Omega(\mathcal{T}) + P_{\bar{\Omega}}(FCTN(\{\mathcal{G}^{(n)}\}_{n=1}^N))$
9:   **Output**:Recovered tensor$\mathcal{X}$

---

4   Experimental

We tested tensor completion using different data: synthetic data, image data and video data. For the synthetic data, we tested the tensor at different orders. The real data then includes the image data and the video data. The termination conditions are set as follows: maxiter = 200 and tol = 10^{-5}. Where the tol parameter we define as follows.

$$tol = \|\mathcal{T} - \mathcal{X}\|_F / \|\mathcal{X}\|_F \tag{9}$$

where $\mathcal{T}$ denotes the real data tensor and $\mathcal{X}$ denotes the recovery tensor.

Two parameters were chosen to evaluate the experimental results: the Peak Signal to Noise Ratio (PSNR) and the Structural Similarity (SSIM) evaluation criteria. Where PSNR is defined as follows:

$$PSNR = 10 log_{10}(255^2 / MSE) \tag{10}$$

MSE is defined as follows:

$$MSE = \|\mathcal{T} - \mathcal{X}\|_F / num(\mathcal{T}) \tag{11}$$

where num() denotes the number of tensor elements. We sample the original tensor at random, at a sampling rate set by ourselves. The higher the PSNR value, the higher the image recovery quality. Also, the definition of SSIM is given:

$$SSIM(x,y) = \frac{(2\mu_x\mu_y + c_1)(2\sigma_{xy} + c_2)}{(\mu_x^2 + \mu_y^2 + c_1)(\sigma_x^2 + \sigma_y^2 + c_2)} \tag{12}$$

where μ_x is the mean of x, μ_y is the mean of y, σ_x^2 is the variance of x, σ_y^2 is the variance of y, and σ_{xy} is the x and y of the covariance. $c_1 = (K_1L)^2$, $c_2 = (K_2L)^2$ are the constants used to keep the stability.L is the dynamic range of the pixel values. $k_1 = 0.01$ and $k_2 = 0.03$. This parameter indicates the similarity between the two tensors and has a value between -1 and 1. When the tensor are the same, the value of SSIM is 1.

The experimental algorithms we have chosen to compare are the CP-WOPT [18], TR-WOPT, TRALS and TRLRF [19] algorithms, which are all approximate to the methods proposed in this paper and currently have a good algorithmic result. Among them, the CP-WOPT and TR-WOPT algorithms are weighted completion methods based on the CP and TR decompositions. TRALS was an optimised completion algorithm when Zhao et al. proposed the TR decomposition, however these rank choices are difficult and time consuming, later Yuan et al. proposed the TRLRF algorithm for completion, their algorithm makes a low rank constraint on each TR decomposition out of the factors and automatically finds a low rank factor tensor that possesses a better completion outcome. All these algorithms are well referenced and advanced, and we use them for comparison and reference.

4.1   Synthetic Data Experiments

We experimented with this data using classic lena images manipulated by manual reshape into tensors of various orders, which we tested at different orders: $120 \times 120 \times 21$ (3-D), $60 \times 60 \times 20 \times 20$ (4-D), $20 \times 20 \times 5 \times 5 \times 5 \times 5$ (5-D) and $5 \times 5 \times 3 \times 3 \times 3 \times 3 \times 3$ (6-D). We used the sampling rate as the horizontal axis, ranging from 0.1 to 0.9 with an interval of 0.1, and used the PSNR as the vertical axis for presentation. For all the algorithms compared, we use the same rank, R is set to 3, and the tensor rank matrix of our proposed algorithm is also set to 3. Both maxiter and tol are the same, set to 500 and 10^{-4}. Different coloured lines are used to denote different methods, and we test these five algorithms as shown in Fig. 2.

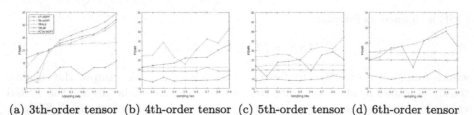

(a) 3th-order tensor (b) 4th-order tensor (c) 5th-order tensor (d) 6th-order tensor

Fig. 2. Performance of different algorithms at different sampling rates

It is easy to see that our proposed FCTN-WOPT algorithm has a significant advantage over various algorithms except when the data being processed is of third order. This is because the proposed algorithm is essentially a tensor ring (TR) decomposition algorithm when the original data is of third order (Table 1).

Table 1. Performance of different algorithms with different order tensors

		CP-WOPT	TR-WOPT	TR-ALS	TRLRF	FCTN-WOPT
3D	PSNR	9.2312	18.3352	16.6218	**18.7775**	18.7091
	SSIM	0.0977	0.4540	0.4507	0.5010	**0.5061**
4D	PSNR	13.4781	19.1045	21.1007	22.0609	**27.5505**
	SSIM	0.1147	0.4592	0.511	0.5868	**0.7027**
5D	PSNR	14.7899	19.7286	22.2120	16.1910	**26.8900**
	SSIM	0.0479	0.4888	0.5674	0.4278	**0.7186**
6D	PSNR	13.684	19.3695	21.7351	20.4593	**22.3457**
	SSIM	0.1194	0.5006	0.5809	0.5303	**0.5960**

4.2   Real Data Experiments

This experiment was mainly tested using real data. To better demonstrate the advantages of higher order data processing, we chose some data from images and videos for the experiment. The algorithms used, we still use those mentioned above for comparison, and their rank and termination conditions are all determined with the same settings.

Image Data Completion. We tested and compared the effect of different algorithms to complete the hyperspectral image with a size of $60 \times 60 \times 20 \times 20^1$ at a sampling rate of 0.2 The completion outcome is shown in Fig. 3 with the residuals.

---

[1] The data is available at http://openremotesensing.net/kb/data/.

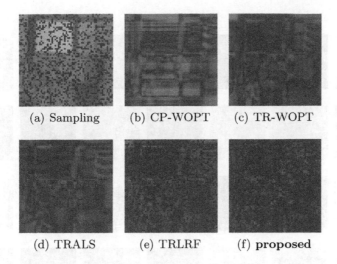

(a) Sampling   (b) CP-WOPT   (c) TR-WOPT

(d) TRALS   (e) TRLRF   (f) **proposed**

Fig. 3. The performance of different algorithms is compared for a sampling rate of 0.3. We selected the HSV hyperspectral image dataset, size $60 \times 60 \times 20 \times 20$. We greyed out all hyperspectral images and produced residual images of the hyperspectral images. In addition, image pixels in yellow indicate a large residual value, blue indicates a small residual value. (Color figure online)

From the experimental results we can clearly observe that the hue of the residual images is more blue and the performance is more optimised than that of other algorithms. This is because the rearrangement of the tensor modes shifts the correlation between them, leading to its superiority over the traditional decomposition method.

Video Data Completion. We test two videos[2] the first one is callphone with a size of $144 \times 176 \times 3 \times 50$ (width $\times$ height $\times$ number of colour channels $\times$ number of video frames) and the second one is container with a size of $144 \times 176 \times 3 \times 50$ (width $\times$ height $\times$ number of colour channels $\times$ number of video frames). We also test under the same termination conditions and with the same tensor rank. The number of iterations is set to 2000, $tol = 10^{-5}$, and the rank of the factor is chosen to be 3. The results of the program are shown in Fig. 4.

In these video processing results, we obtain experimental results that are more outstanding, also due to the compressibility of the decomposition algorithm itself, with the same tensor rank but representing more information content.

Traffic Data Completion. This experiment uses the traffic flow dataset provided by Grenoble Traffic Lab[3] which collects traffic flow data from 46 different road segments over a period of 244 days, and measures every 15 s. We selected the 30 days of data for the experiment and summed them to obtain a new dataset of 30-day, minute-by-minute measurements for 49 road segments. The size of

---

[2] The data is available at http://trace.eas.asu.edu/yuv/.
[3] Homepage: http://gtl.inrialpes.fr/.

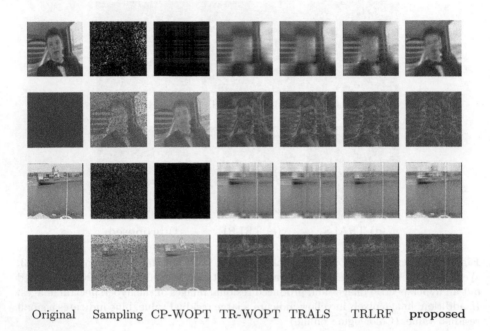

Original   Sampling   CP-WOPT   TR-WOPT   TRALS   TRLRF   **proposed**

Fig. 4. The performance of the different algorithms is compared for a sampling rate of 0.2. The first row is the completion of each method after sampling the callphone part of the video, and the second row of data represents the residual image, which we obtained by subtracting the first frame of its original video from the first frame of the reconstructed video and taking the absolute value. The third row is the ship video data, and the fourth row is its residual image.

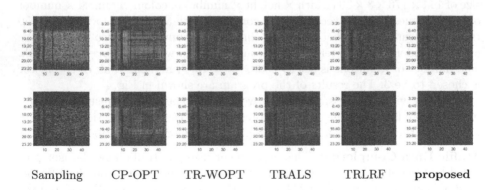

Sampling   CP-OPT   TR-WOPT   TRALS   TRLRF   **proposed**

Fig. 5. These experimental results represent a residual plot of the corresponding results from the first day. The sampling rate of the images in the first row is 0.2 and the sampling rate of the images in the second row is 0.7.

the dataset is $60 \times 24 \times 30 \times 46$ (minutes $\times$ hours $\times$ days $\times$ number of road segments). Then we sampled some data randomly and conducted tensor completion experiments. The sampling rate for the first group was 0.2 and the sampling rate for the second group was 0.7. The design of the rank of these tensor was the same, both of size 3. Their maximum number of iterations was also the same, of size 1000. The minimum error was set to 10^{-4}. the experimental results are shown in Fig. 5 We selected the middle 30 days of data for the experiment and summed them to obtain a new dataset of 30-day, minute-by-minute measurements for 49 road segments. The size of the dataset is $60 \times 24 \times 30 \times 46$ (minutes $\times$ hours $\times$ days $\times$ number of road segments). Then we sampled some data randomly and conducted tensor completion experiments. The sampling rate for the first set was 0.2 and the sampling rate for the second set was 0.7. The design of the rank of these tensor completions is the same, all of size 3. Their maximum number of iterations is also the same, number 1000. The minimum error is set to 10^{-4}. The experimental results are shown in Fig. 5.

We can observe in Fig. 5 that the algorithm proposed in this paper also has a good tensor completion result on the traffic flow data. This also validates the superior performance of the proposed algorithm on high-dimensional tensor.

5 Conclusions

This algorithm proposes a Fully-Connected Tensor Network weighted optimization algorithm, which is better than advanced algorithms for completion and is able to recover the original data with a small amount of data. And our proposed algorithm, using the lbfgs gradient descent method, speeds up the convergence of the algorithm's descent speed. In particular, tensor completion works better for tensors of order four and above. However, the algorithm in this paper usually has to choose different ranks for testing in order to get the desired results, which is time and effort consuming. It is also not very useful in removing disturbances when external noise is present. Our next work will be to create a tensor completion algorithm that automatically finds the optimal rank and resists disturbances.

References

1. Kolda, T.G., Bader, B.W.: Tensor decompositions and applications. SIAM Rev. **51**(3), 455–500 (2009)
2. Oseledets, I.V.: Tensor-train decomposition. SIAM J. Sci. Comput. **33**(5), 2295–2317 (2011)
3. Zhao, Q., Zhou, G., Xie, S., et al.: Tensor ring decomposition. arXiv preprint arXiv:1606.05535 (2016)
4. Song, Q., Ge, H., Caverlee, J., Hu, X.: Tensor completion algorithms in big data analytics. ACM Trans. Knowl. Discovery Data **13**, 1–48 (2019)
5. Bazerque, J.A., Mateos, G., Giannakis, G.B.: Rank regularization and Bayesian inference for tensor completion and extrapolation. IEEE Trans. Signal Process. **61**(22), 5689–5703 (2013)

6. Ding, M., Huang, T.-Z., Ji, T.-Y., Zhao, X.-L., Yang, J.-H.: Low-rank tensor completion using matrix factorization based on tensor train rank and total variation. J. Sci. Comput. **81**(2), 941–964 (2019). https://doi.org/10.1007/s10915-019-01044-8
7. Gandy, S., Recht, B., Yamada, I.: Tensor completion and low-n-rank tensor recovery via convex optimization. Inverse Prob. **27**(2), 025010 (2011)
8. Yu, D., Deng, L., Seide, F.: The deep tensor neural network with applications to large vocabulary speech recognition. IEEE Trans. Audio Speech Lang. Process. **21**(2), 388–396 (2012)
9. Mahyari, A.G., Zoltowski, D.M., Bernat, E.M., et al.: A tensor decomposition-based approach for detecting dynamic network states from EEG. IEEE Trans. Biomed. Eng. **64**(1), 225–237 (2016)
10. Guo, X., Huang, X., Zhang, L., et al.: Support tensor machines for classification of hyperspectral remote sensing imagery. IEEE Trans. Geosci. Remote Sens. **54**(6), 3248–3264 (2016)
11. Zheng, Y.B., Huang, T.Z., Zhao, X.L., et al.: Fully-connected tensor network decomposition and its application to higher-order tensor completion. In: Proceedings of the AAAI Conference on Artificial Intelligence, vol. 35(12), pp. 11071–11078 (2021)
12. Hu, W., Tao, D., Zhang, W., et al.: The twist tensor nuclear norm for video completion. IEEE Trans. Neural Networks Learn. Syst. **28**(12), 2961–2973 (2016)
13. Yuan, M., Zhang, C.H.: On tensor completion via nuclear norm minimization. Found. Comput. Math. **16**(4), 1031–1068 (2016)
14. Yu, J., Li, C., Zhao, Q., et al.: Tensor-ring nuclear norm minimization and application for visual: data completion. In: ICASSP 2019–2019 IEEE International Conference on Acoustics, Speech and Signal Processing (ICASSP), pp. 3142–3146. IEEE (2019)
15. Yuan, L., Cao, J., Zhao, X., et al.: Higher-dimension tensor completion via low-rank tensor ring decomposition. In: 2018 Asia-Pacific Signal and Information Processing Association Annual Summit and Conference (APSIPA ASC), pp. 1071–1076. IEEE (2018)
16. Liu, Y.Y., Zhao, X.L., Song, G.J., et al.: Fully-connected tensor network decomposition for robust tensor completion problem. arXiv preprint arXiv:2110.08754 (2021)
17. Ahad, A., Long, Z., Zhu, C., et al.: Hierarchical tensor ring completion. arXiv preprint arXiv:2004.11720 (2020)
18. Acar, E., Dunlavy, D.M., Kolda, T.G., Mørup, M.: Scalable tensor factorizations for incomplete data. Chemom. Intell. Lab. Syst. **106**(1), 41–56 (2011)
19. Yuan, L., Li, C., Mandic, D., et al.: Tensor ring decomposition with rank minimization on latent space: an efficient approach for tensor completion. In: Proceedings of the AAAI Conference on Artificial Intelligence, vol. 33, no. 01, pp. 9151–9158 (2019)
20. Wang, W., Aggarwal, V., Aeron, S.: Efficient low rank tensor ring completion. In: Proceedings of the IEEE International Conference on Computer Vision, pp. 5697–5705 (2017)
21. Chen, Y., He, W., Yokoya, N., et al.: Nonlocal tensor-ring decomposition for hyperspectral image denoising. IEEE Trans. Geosci. Remote Sens. **58**(2), 1348–1362 (2019)
22. He, W., Chen, Y., Yokoya, N., et al.: Hyperspectral super-resolution via coupled tensor ring factorization. Pattern Recogn. **122**, 108280 (2022)

Momentum Distillation Improves Multimodal Sentiment Analysis

Siqi Li, Weihong Deng$^{(\boxtimes)}$, and Jiani Hu

School of Artificial Intelligence, Beijing University of Posts and Telecommunications,
Beijing 100876, China
whdeng@bupt.edu.cn

Abstract. With the development of computer technology, the Internet floods with abundant multimodal data. For better understanding users' feelings, multimodal sentiment analysis and sarcasm detection have become popular research topics. However, previous studies did not take noise into account when designing models. In this paper, based on designing a novel architecture, we also introduce a momentum distillation method to improve the model's performance from noisy data. Specifically, we propose the Transformer-Based Network with Momentum Distillation (TBNMD). For model architecture, we first encode different modalities to obtain hidden representations. Then we use a multimodal interaction module to obtain text-guided image features and image-guided text features. After that, we use a multimodal fusion module to obtain the fusion features. For momentum distillation, it is a self-distillation method. During the training process, the teacher model generates semantically similar samples as additional supervision of the student model. Experimental results on five publicly available datasets demonstrate the effectiveness of our method.

Keywords: Multimodal sentiment analysis · Sarcasm detection · Momentum distillation

1 Introduction

With the prosperous development of computer technology, social media platforms such as Twitter and Instagram, have become part of our daily lives. To better understand users' feelings, sentiment analysis, target-oriented sentiment classification, and sarcasm detection have become challenging research areas. Sentiment analysis which aims to analyze people's opinions towards entities such as products, events, and services, is an important research area in Natural Language Processing (NLP) [6,32]. As a part of sentiment analysis, target-oriented sentiment classification aims at classifying sentiment polarities over individual opinion targets in a sentence [11]. Sarcasm is a complex language phenomenon to express implicit meaning contrary to what one says [3,8]. However, previous research mostly paid attention to text-only sentiment analysis and sarcasm

S. Yu et al. (Eds.): PRCV 2022, LNCS 13534, pp. 423–435, 2022.
https://doi.org/10.1007/978-3-031-18907-4_33

detection [2,30]. When faced with multimodal data, these methods that ignore the complementary image information are insufficient to understand the real emotions of users [25]. Therefore, multimodal sentiment analysis (MSA), target-oriented multimodal sentiment classification (TMSC), and multimodal sarcasm detection (MSD) have become prevalent study areas in recent years [9,15,31].

To address these problems, in recent years, researchers have proposed many novel networks that comprehensively utilize information from each modality. For the MSA task, Xu et al. proposed different models, such as the Hierarchical Semantic Attentional Network (HSAN) [21], and the Multimodal Deep Semantic Network (MultiSentiNet) [22], and the Co-Memory Network (Co-Mem) [23] models. For the TMSC task, Yu et al. proposed the Entity-Sensitive Attention and Fusion Network (ESAFN) [29] and the Target-oriented multimodal BERT (TomBERT) [28] models; For the MSD task, researchers designed some networks for sarcasm detection using incongruity information between modalities, such as the BERT Architecture-based Model (MsdBert) [15] and the Incongruity-Aware Attention Network (IWAN) [20]. The image-text pair datasets collected from the web for multimodal sentiment analysis tasks are inherently noisy. Specifically, the text may contain words unrelated to the image, and the image may contain objects not described in the text. Therefore, existing multimodal sentiment analysis models may overfit noisy information during training and reduce the generalization performance of the models.

In this paper, to address this problem, we employ a simple yet effective method called momentum distillation [10], which is a self-distillation method that creates a teacher model with the same structure as the student model to generate some semantically similar samples that serve as additional supervision for the student model, thereby improving the model's generalization ability of the model learned in noisy data. Specifically, during the training process, we update the parameters of the teacher model in the form of momentum update [5], while the parameters of the student model are still updated through back-propagation. In addition, to achieve the unification of the encoder structure among different modalities, we use RoBERTa [12] and ViT [4] to extract text and image features, respectively. Finally, we also use the Multimodal Fusion Module (MFM) after the Multimodal Interaction Module (MIM) to extract more expressive features. To sum up, in this paper, we propose a transform-based model, called TBNMD, which introduces a momentum distillation method to improve the multimodal classification performance.

To summarize, our main contributions are:

- We propose a novel TBNMD framework for multimodal sentiment analysis and sarcasm detection, which uses momentum distillation to improve the generalization performance of the model learned in noisy data. And to the best of our knowledge, we are the first to apply momentum distillation to these multimodal tasks.
- To improve the representation ability of the model, after obtaining the interactive features, we use an MFM module to further extract the more informative fusion features. We also use ViT for the first time to extract image represen-

tations for achieving the unification of the encoder's structure of different modalities and extracting more expressive image features.

- We conduct extensive experiments on five publicly available datasets, and the results show that our model outperforms the state-of-the-art methods in MSA and TMSC tasks, and is competitive with the most advanced methods in MSD tasks.

2   Related Work

2.1   Multimodal Sentiment Analysis

With social media platforms supporting users to post messages in different modes (images, texts, and videos), the Internet is full of many image-text data. To understand users' feelings, researchers pay much attention to multimodal sentiment analysis (MSA) recently. Xu et al. had done some research on the MSA task-They constructed the Hierarchical Semantic Attention Network model (HSAN) [21], which uses an image caption generator to extract detailed image semantic features as additional information for the text; Later they constructed the Deep Semantic Network (MultiSentiNet) [22], which extracts the object and scene features from the image as the visual semantic features and uses them to guide the extraction of text features; They also constructed the Co-Memory Network (Co-Mem) [23] for iterative modeling of the interactions between different modalities (image and text). Recently, Yang et al. proposed a Multi-view Attentional Network (MVAN) [25], which first utilizes an attention memory network module to extract text and image features, and then fuses multimodal features through a stacking-pooling module. Jiang et al. proposed a Fusion-Extraction Network (FENet) [7], which utilizes an interactive information fusion mechanism to learn text and image features, and then uses an information extraction mechanism to learn final representations. Yang et al. proposed the Multi-channel Graph Neural Networks with Sentiment-awareness (MGNNS) [26] model, which firstly uses the Graph Neural Network (GNN) for the MSA task.

As one of the tasks of sentiment classification, target-oriented multimodal sentiment classification (TMSC) is to confirm the sentiment polarity of each opinion entity in a sentence [11]. Recently, Yu et al. proposed the Entity-Sensitive Attention and Fusion Network (ESAFN) [29] and the Target-oriented multimodal BERT (TomBERT) [28] for the TMSC task.

2.2   Multimodal Sarcasm Detection

Sarcasm is a complex language phenomenon to express implicit meaning contrary to what one says. Researchers have proposed some effective methods for the Multimodal sarcasm detection (SD) task. Cai et al. proposed the Hierarchical Fusion Model (HFM) [2], which makes full use of three modalities (texts, images, and image attributes) to tackle this task; Xu et al. proposed the Decomposition and Relation Network (D&R Net) [24] to represent the contextual comparison and get the semantic association between texts and images; Following the research of neuropsychology and neuroanatomy, Yao et al. propose the Multimodal, Multi-interactive, and Multi-hierarchical Neural Network (M3N2) [27] to functionally imitate the brain's perception of sarcasm. Pan et al. proposed a BERT-based model (MsdBert) [15], which concentrates on both intra-modality and inter-modality incongruity for multimodal sarcasm detection. Wang et al. proposed the Bridge-RoBERTa model [19], which introduces a 2D-Intra-Attention layer to extract the relationship between text and image.

3 Method

Figure 1 illustrates the overall architecture of our proposed TBNMD model for MSA and MSD tasks, while the models for the TMSC task are depicted in Subsect. 3.5. Our model consists of four parts: the Encoders Module **(EM)**, the Multimodal Interaction Module **(MIM)**, the Multimodal Fusion Module **(MFM)**, and **Momentum Distillation Module (MD)**. Specifically, we first use the encoder module to extract the image features and text features and then feed them into the multimodal interaction module to generate text-guided image features and image-guided text features. After that, we concatenate these features and input them into a multimodal fusion module to obtain fused features for final classification. To improve learning from noisy data, we design the momentum distillation module.

It should be pointed out that the Modal Interaction Module enables the model to extract different types of interactive information in the training process, such as related interactive information conducive to sentiment prediction and incongruous interactive information conducive to sarcasm detection. Therefore, although the MSA task and the MSD task both adopt the same model structure, the types of information that the models pay attention to are different. For the MSA task, the model mainly focuses on the relevant information between different modalities, while for the MSD task, the model primarily focuses on the incongruity information between different modalities.

3.1 Encoders Module

For the image encoder, we use a 12-layers ViT-Base model [4] and initialize it with weights pre-trained on ImageNet-1k from [17]. Let us briefly review the ViT model. Given an image I, we first divide it into N fixed-size patches, then we flatten these patches and use linear projection to transform them into d-dimensional vectors as patch embedding. To retain the position information, we add position embedding to the patch embedding as the input of the encoder, and note the result as $\mathbf{z}_0 = \{\mathbf{x}_{cls}, \mathbf{x}_1, \mathbf{x}_2, ..., \mathbf{x}_N\}$. where $\mathbf{x}_i \in \mathbb{R}^d$, $\mathbf{x}_{cls}$ is the embedding of $[CLS]$ token. The Transformer encoder consists of alternating layers of m-head self-attention (Eq. 1, 2, 3) and feed-forward networks (FFN) blocks (Eq. 4, 5). A layer normalization (LN) [1] is applied before each block, and residual connections are applied after each block. FFN consists of two linear

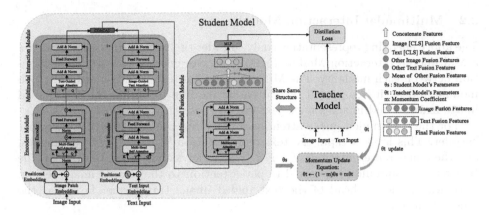

Fig. 1. Overall architecture of our proposed TBNMD model for MSA task.

transformations, with a GELU non-linearity in between. Specifically, for the i_{th} head attention, the input $\mathbf{z} \in \mathbb{R}^{(N+1) \times d}$ is transformed based on standard $\mathbf{qkv}$ self-attention (SAT) [18]) as follows:

$$[\mathbf{q}, \mathbf{k}, \mathbf{v}] = \mathbf{z} \mathbf{W}_{qkv} \tag{1}$$

$$SAT_i(\mathbf{z}) = softmax(\frac{\mathbf{q}\mathbf{k}^T}{\sqrt{d_h}})\mathbf{v} \tag{2}$$

where $\mathbf{W}_{qkv} \in \mathbb{R}^{d \times 3d_h}$ is a learnable parameter corresponding to the queries $\mathbf{q}$, keys $\mathbf{k}$, and values $\mathbf{v}$, $d_h = d/m$. Then the outputs of m heads are concatenated together and followed by a linear transformation as:

$$MSAT(\mathbf{z}) = Concat(SAT_1(\mathbf{z}), SAT_2(\mathbf{z}), ..., SAT_m(\mathbf{z}))\mathbf{W}_{msa} \tag{3}$$

where $\mathbf{W}_{msa} \in \mathbb{R}^{d \times d}$ is a parameter to learn. We use $\mathbf{z}_{l-1}$ and $\mathbf{z}_l$ to represent the input and output of the l_{th} encoder respectively, and we can obtain $\mathbf{z}_l$ as follows:

$$\mathbf{z}_l^{'} = MSAT(LN(\mathbf{z}_{l-1})) + \mathbf{z}_{l-1} \tag{4}$$

$$\mathbf{z}_l = FFN(LN(\mathbf{z}_l^{'})) + \mathbf{z}_l^{'} \tag{5}$$

where $l \in [1, 12]$. $\mathbf{z}_{12} = \{\mathbf{v}_{cls}, \mathbf{v}_1, \mathbf{v}_2, ..., \mathbf{v}_N\}$ is the output of image encoder. We note $\mathbf{z}_{12}$ as $\mathbf{V}$, where $\mathbf{V} \in \mathbb{R}^{(N+1) \times d}$.

For the text encoder, we use a 12-layers RoBERTa-base model [12]. Given a sequence of words $\mathbf{s}_0 = \{\mathbf{w}_{cls}, \mathbf{w}_1, \mathbf{w}_2, ..., \mathbf{w}_M\}$, where $\mathbf{w}_i \in \mathbb{R}^d$ is the sum of word, segment, and position embedding, and M is the maximum length of text input. We note TIM_h^{text} as the h_{th} transformer layer of RoBERTa. We also note $\mathbf{s}_{h-1}$ and $\mathbf{s}_h$ as the input and output of the h_{th} encoder. we can obtain $\mathbf{s}_h$ as follows:

$$\mathbf{s}_h = TIM_h^{text}(\mathbf{s}_{h-1}) \tag{6}$$

where $h \in [1, 12]$, $\mathbf{s}_{12} = \{\mathbf{t}_{cls}, \mathbf{t}_1, \mathbf{t}_2, ..., \mathbf{t}_M\}$ is the output of text encoder. We note $\mathbf{s}_{12}$ as $\mathbf{T}$, where $\mathbf{T} \in \mathbb{R}^{(M+1) \times d}$.

3.2   Multimodal Interaction Module

The above encoding representations only consider their single modality, so we use a Multimodal Interaction Module (MIM) that can effectively learn the interaction between each modality. The MIM consists of a text-guided image attention module and an image-guided text attention module to obtain the text-guided image features and image-guided text features respectively.

For the text-guided image attention module, we use a one-layer transformer encoder. This layer accepts the text representation $\mathbf{T} \in \mathbb{R}^{(M+1) \times d}$ as queries, and the image representations $\mathbf{V} \in \mathbb{R}^{(N+1) \times d}$ as keys and values. In this way, the text feature can guide the model to pay attention to the related image region. Specifically, the i_{th} head of the text-guided image transformer layer has the following form:

$$ATT_i(\mathbf{T}, \mathbf{V}) = softmax(\frac{[\mathbf{W}_i^Q \mathbf{T}]^T [\mathbf{W}_i^K \mathbf{V}]}{\sqrt{d_k}})[\mathbf{W}_i^V \mathbf{V}]^T \tag{7}$$

Note $TIM^{TgV}(\mathbf{T}, \mathbf{V})$ as the text-guided image transformer layer, we can obtain the text-guided image features as follows:

$$\mathbf{V}^{Tg} = TIM^{TgV}(\mathbf{T}, \mathbf{V}) \tag{8}$$

where $\mathbf{V}^{Tg} = \{\mathbf{v}_{cls}^{Tg}, \mathbf{v}_1^{Tg}, ..., \mathbf{v}_M^{Tg}\}$. $\mathbf{V}^{Tg} \in \mathbb{R}^{(M+1) \times d}$ is the final text-guided image features.

For the image-guided text attention module, we also use a one-layer transformer encoder. Similar to the text-guided image attention module, note $TIM^{VgT}(\mathbf{V}, \mathbf{T})$ as the image-guided text transformer layer, we can obtain the image-guided text features as follows:

$$\mathbf{T}^{Vg} = TIM^{VgT}(\mathbf{V}, \mathbf{T}) \tag{9}$$

where $\mathbf{T}^{Vg} = \{\mathbf{t}_{cls}^{Vg}, \mathbf{t}_1^{Vg}, ..., \mathbf{t}_N^{Vg}\}$. $\mathbf{T}^{Vg} \in \mathbb{R}^{(N+1) \times d}$ is the final image-guided text features.

3.3   Multimodal Fusion Module and Classification Layer

To extract more informative features, we add a Multimodal Fusion Module (MFM). MFM is a one-layer transformer encoder, we note $TIM^{fuse}(\mathbf{T}^{Vg}, \mathbf{V}^{Tg})$ as the fusion transformer layer. We stack the text-guided image features ($\mathbf{V}^{Tg}$) and the image-guided text features ($\mathbf{T}^{Vg}$) as the input. The details are as follows:

$$\mathbf{F} = TIM^{fuse}(\mathbf{T}^{Vg}, \mathbf{V}^{Tg}) \tag{10}$$

$\mathbf{F} = \{\mathbf{t}_{cls}^{fVg}, \mathbf{t}_1^{fVg}, ..., \mathbf{t}_N^{fVg}, \mathbf{v}_{cls}^{fTg}, \mathbf{v}_1^{fTg}, ..., \mathbf{v}_M^{fTg}\}$, is the final fusion features and $\mathbf{F} \in \mathbb{R}^{(M+N+2) \times d}$. $\mathbf{t}_{cls}^{fVg} \in \mathbb{R}^d$ and $\mathbf{v}_{cls}^{fTg} \in \mathbb{R}^d$ is the final fusion features of text [CLS] token and image [CLS] token. For brevity, we denote them as $\mathbf{H}_T$ and

$\mathbf{H}_V$ respectively, and we denote the average value of other fusion features as $\mathbf{H}_{Mean} \in \mathbb{R}^d$, which is calculated as follows:

$$\mathbf{H}_{Mean} = MEAN(\mathbf{t}_1^{fVg}, ..., \mathbf{t}_M^{fVg}, \mathbf{v}_1^{fTg}, ..., \mathbf{v}_N^{fTg}) \tag{11}$$

where MEAN represents the average operation. For MSA tasks, we concatenate $\mathbf{H}_T$, $\mathbf{H}_V$, and $\mathbf{H}_{Mean}$ as the final fusion feature $\mathbf{R} \in \mathbb{R}^{3d}$ are as follows:

$$\mathbf{R} = Concat(\mathbf{H}_T, \mathbf{H}_V, \mathbf{H}_{Mean}) \tag{12}$$

After that, we feed the final fusion feature into a multi-layer perceptron (MLP) for classification as follows:

$$\mathbf{P} = MLP(\mathbf{R}) \tag{13}$$

where $\mathbf{P} \in \mathbb{R}^3$ is the final output.

3.4 Momentum Distillation

To improve the learning from noisy data, we adopt the momentum distillation method [10], which can be considered a form of self-distillation. This method can be interpreted as doing data augmentation to the original text-image pairs. In the training process, the teacher model generates some semantically similar samples that do not exist in the original image-text pairs, as additional supervision of the student model, so that the student model learns to capture more expressive features. In our TBNMD model, the teacher model has the same structure as the student model, but it uses a momentum update method [5] to update its parameters, while the parameters of the student model are still updated by back-propagation. Formally, denoting the parameters of the student model as θ_s and the parameters of the teacher model as θ_t, we update θ_t as follows:

$$\theta_t \leftarrow m\theta_t + (1 - m)\theta_s \tag{14}$$

Here $m \in [0, 1)$ is a momentum coefficient. The momentum update form makes θ_t evolve more smoothly than θ_s so that the teacher can generate semantically similar samples. We improve the performance of the student model by transferring knowledge from the teacher model, usually through matching the student model's prediction with the teacher model's and with the ground-truth label, so we define our distillation loss as follows:

$$\mathcal{L} = (1 - \alpha)CE(p(z_s, T), y) + \alpha KL(p(z_s, T), p(z_t, T)) \tag{15}$$

where CE represents cross-entropy, and KL represents KL divergence. y is the ground-truth label, $p(z_s, T)$ and $p(z_t, T)$ are the soft targets of the student model and the teacher model respectively. The soft targets can be estimated as follows:

$$p(z_i, T) = \frac{exp(z_i/T)}{\sum_j exp(z_j/T)} \tag{16}$$

where z_i is the logit for the i_{th} class, and a temperature factor T is introduced to control the importance of each soft target.

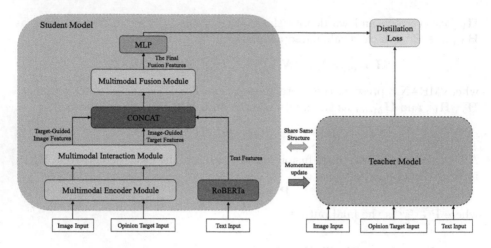

Fig. 2. Overall architecture of our proposed TBNMD model for the TMSC task.

3.5 Model Variants

The overall architecture of the TMSC task is shown in Fig. 2. The difference in the model between the TMSC and MSA task, is that a text features extraction module (RoBERTa) is added, which is used to extract the features of the text other than the opinion target. Specifically, we first use the same EM module, the MIM module to obtain the opinion target-guided image features and image-guided opinion target features. And we use a RoBERTa to get the text features. Then we stack these features as the input of the MFM module and feed the output of the MFM module into a multi-layer perceptron (MLP).

4 Experiments

We test our method on three multimodal tasks and compare our TBNMD model with some existing effective models. For the MSA task, we conduct experiments on the MVSA-Single (MVSA-S) and the MVSA-Multiple (MVSA-M) datasets [14]; For the MSD task, we use a publicly available multimodal sarcasm detection dataset[1] (MMSD), which is collected by [2]; For TMSC task, we evaluate our model on two publicly available TMSC datasets[2] (TWITTER-15, TWITTER-17) that are annotated by Yu et al. [28].

4.1 Datasets and Implementation Details

MVSA-S/M are two publicly available multimodal sentiment analysis datasets collected from Twitter. The MVSA-S is annotated by a single annotator, while

---

[1] The dataset is publicly available via the link: https://github.com/headacheboy/data-of-multimodal-sarcasm-detection.

[2] The two TMSC datasets are publicly available via the link: https://github.com/jefferyYu/TomBERT.

the MVSA-M is annotated by three different annotators. To make a fair comparison with previous studies, we use the method of Xu and Mao (2017) [22] to process the original datasets, and use a ratio of 8:1:1 to randomly split the datasets into the training set, validation set, and test set; For the MMSD dataset, each sample in it is composed of a sentence and an associated image. And the tweets containing the words like *sarcasm*, *sarcastic*, or *URLs* are discarded during data preprocessing; The TMSC datasets TWITTER-15 and TWITTER-17 are respectively collected by Zhang [33] and Lu [13]. Since these two datasets only provide annotated targets in each tweet, Yu et alt. [28] then ask three domain experts to annotate the sentiment towards each target.

Our model is implemented in PyTorch [16], using a batch size of 32 on 4 NVIDIA T4 GPUs. We train our model for 10,8,10 epochs for MSA, MSD, and TMSC tasks respectively. During training, we take random image crops of resolution 256×256 as input. We use the adamW optimizer with a weight decay of 0.02. The initial learning rate of these tasks is $2e^{-5}$, and the momentum distillation parameters for updating the teacher model are set to 0.995.

4.2 Experimental Results and Analysis

The experimental results of these tasks are shown in Table 1, Table 2, and Table 3 respectively. The experimental results on MSA, TMSC, and MSD tasks demonstrate that our proposed model is competitive with strong baseline models. The main reasons are as follows: Firstly, we use more advanced encoders to obtain the image and text representations respectively; Secondly, we adopt a momentum distillation method to improve learning from noisy data. However, for the MSD task, the Bridge-RoBERTa model still outperforms our TBNMD model. And the reason for this result may lie in that our MIM module is too simple that can't capture more relationships between words and images, compared with Bridge-RoBERTa's 2D-Intra-Attention Layer. By comparing TBNMD-ResNet with TBNMD, we conclude that the unification of encoders' structures can obtain more expressive multimodal representations.

4.3 Ablation Study

We conduct ablation experiments on the TBNMD model to test the effectiveness of different modules. From Table 4, we can make the following observations. Firstly, the whole TBNMD model achieves the best performance among all models on three multimodal tasks. Secondly, after removing the MIM (w/o MIM) or MFM part (w/o MFM), the performance of the model declines, which indicates that the MIM and MFM modules are useful for improving the representation ability of the model. Thirdly, the performance of the model degrades after removing momentum distillation (w/o MD), suggesting that momentum distillation is an effective way to improve network performance from noisy data.

Table 1. Experiment results of MSA task. ‡ represents the reproductive operation

Method	MVSA-S		MVSA-M	
	Acc	Weighted-F1	Acc	Weighted-F1
MultiSentiNet [22]	69.84	69.63	68.86	68.11
Co-Mem [23]	70.51	70.01	69.92	69.83
MVAN‡ [25]	72.98‡	71.39‡	71.83‡	70.38‡
MGNNS [26]	73.77	72.70	72.49	69.34
TBNMD-ResNet	73.45	73.16	72.24	69.87
TBNMD (our)	**75.44**	**73.81**	**73.65**	**71.32**

Table 2. Experiment results of multimodal sarcasm detection task.

Method	MMSD			
	Acc	Pre	Rec	Macro-F1
HFM [2]	83.44	76.57	84.15	80.18
D&R Net [24]	84.02	77.97	83.42	80.60
M3N2 [27]	83.23	77.02	82.48	79.66
MsdBert [15]	86.05	80.87	85.08	82.92
Bridge-RoBERTa [19]	88.51	82.95	89.39	86.05
TBNMD-ResNet	85.20	84.54	84.71	84.60
TBNMD (our)	86.48	**85.82**	86.33	86.01

Table 3. Experiment results of MSA task. ‡ represents the reproductive operation

Method	TWITTER-15		TWITTER-17	
	Acc	Macro-F1	Acc	Macro-F1
ESAFN	71.36	64.28	65.80	62.00
TomBERT	77.15	71.75	70.50	68.04
TBNMD-ResNet	77.88	70.86	72.33	70.77
TBNMD (our)	**78.85**	**72.87**	**72.41**	**71.26**

Table 4. Ablation experiment results

(a) MSA task

Method	MVSA-S		MVSA-M	
	Acc	Weighted-F1	Acc	Weighted-F1
w/o MIM	75.22	71.74	73.12	70.67
w/o MFM	74.34	71.49	72.48	70.03
w/o MD	75.22	73.46	70.72	67.94
TBNMD	**75.44**	**73.81**	**73.65**	**71.32**

(b) MSD Task

Method	MMSD			
	Acc	Pre	Rec	Macro-F1
w/o MIM	84.95	84.24	84.98	84.49
w/o MFM	85.45	84.93	84.66	84.76
w/o MD	85.57	85.06	84.83	84.91
TBNMD	**86.48**	**85.82**	**86.33**	**86.01**

(c) TMSC task

Method	TWITTER-15		TWITTER-17	
	Acc	Macro-F1	Acc	Macro-F1
w/o MIM	77.31	70.76	71.20	70.01
w/o MFM	77.50	71.72	71.68	70.16
w/o MD	76.73	71.19	71.52	70.18
TBNMD	**78.85**	**72.87**	**72.41**	**71.26**

5 Conclusions

In this paper, we propose a transformer-based multimodal model (TBNMD) for multimodal sentiment analysis and sarcasm detection tasks. To improve learning from noisy multimodal data, we adopt a momentum distillation method; To extract more expressive multimodal representations, we design the MIM and MFM modules; To unify the encoder structure of different modalities, we use ViT rather than CNN to extract image representations. As far as we know, this is the first application of momentum distillation in these multimodal sentiment tasks. The experimental results on five publicly available datasets demonstrate that our proposed model is competitive with strong baseline models.

References

1. Ba, J.L., Kiros, J.R., Hinton, G.E.: Layer normalization. arXiv preprint arXiv:1607.06450 (2016)
2. Cai, Y., Cai, H., Wan, X.: Multi-modal sarcasm detection in twitter with hierarchical fusion model. In: Proceedings of the 57th Annual Meeting of the Association for Computational Linguistics, pp. 2506–2515 (2019)
3. Castro, S., Hazarika, D., Pérez-Rosas, V., Zimmermann, R., Mihalcea, R., Poria, S.: Towards multimodal sarcasm detection (an _obviously_ perfect paper). arXiv preprint arXiv:1906.01815 (2019)
4. Dosovitskiy, A., et al.: An image is worth 16x16 words: transformers for image recognition at scale. arXiv preprint arXiv:2010.11929 (2020)
5. He, K., Fan, H., Wu, Y., Xie, S., Girshick, R.: Momentum contrast for unsupervised visual representation learning. In: Proceedings of the IEEE/CVF Conference on Computer Vision and Pattern Recognition, pp. 9729–9738 (2020)
6. Jagtap, V., Pawar, K.: Analysis of different approaches to sentence-level sentiment classification. Int. J. Sci. Eng. Technol. **2**(3), 164–170 (2013)
7. Jiang, T., Wang, J., Liu, Z., Ling, Y.: Fusion-extraction network for multimodal sentiment analysis. Adv. Knowl. Discov. Data Min. **12085**, 785 (2020)
8. Joshi, A., Bhattacharyya, P., Carman, M.J.: Automatic sarcasm detection: a survey. ACM Comput. Surv. (CSUR) **50**(5), 1–22 (2017)
9. Kaur, R., Kautish, S.: Multimodal sentiment analysis: a survey and comparison. Int. J. Serv. Sci. Manag. Eng. Technol. (IJSSMET) **10**(2), 38–58 (2019)
10. Li, J., Selvaraju, R.R., Gotmare, A.D., Joty, S., Xiong, C., Hoi, S.: Align before fuse: vision and language representation learning with momentum distillation. arXiv preprint arXiv:2107.07651 (2021)
11. Li, X., Bing, L., Lam, W., Shi, B.: Transformation networks for target-oriented sentiment classification. arXiv preprint arXiv:1805.01086 (2018)
12. Liu, Y., et al.: Roberta: a robustly optimized Bert pretraining approach. arXiv preprint arXiv:1907.11692 (2019)
13. Lu, D., Neves, L., Carvalho, V., Zhang, N., Ji, H.: Visual attention model for name tagging in multimodal social media. In: Proceedings of the 56th Annual Meeting of the Association for Computational Linguistics (Volume 1: Long Papers), pp. 1990–1999 (2018)
14. Niu, T., Zhu, S., Pang, L., El Saddik, A.: Sentiment analysis on multi-view social data. In: Tian, Q., Sebe, N., Qi, G.-J., Huet, B., Hong, R., Liu, X. (eds.) MMM 2016. LNCS, vol. 9517, pp. 15–27. Springer, Cham (2016). https://doi.org/10.1007/978-3-319-27674-8_2
15. Pan, H., Lin, Z., Fu, P., Qi, Y., Wang, W.: Modeling intra and inter-modality incongruity for multi-modal sarcasm detection. In: Proceedings of the 2020 Conference on Empirical Methods in Natural Language Processing: Findings, pp. 1383–1392 (2020)
16. Paszke, A., et al.: Pytorch: an imperative style, high-performance deep learning library. Adv. Neural. Inf. Process. Syst. **32**, 8026–8037 (2019)
17. Touvron, H., Cord, M., Douze, M., Massa, F., Sablayrolles, A., Jégou, H.: Training data-efficient image transformers & distillation through attention. In: International Conference on Machine Learning, pp. 10347–10357. PMLR (2021)
18. Vaswani, A., et al.: Attention is all you need. In: Advances in Neural Information Processing Systems, pp. 5998–6008 (2017)

19. Wang, X., Sun, X., Yang, T., Wang, H.: Building a bridge: a method for image-text sarcasm detection without pretraining on image-text data. In: Proceedings of the First International Workshop on Natural Language Processing Beyond Text, pp. 19–29 (2020)
20. Wu, Y., et al.: Modeling incongruity between modalities for multimodal sarcasm detection. IEEE Multimedia **28**(2), 86–95 (2021)
21. Xu, N.: Analyzing multimodal public sentiment based on hierarchical semantic attentional network. In: 2017 IEEE International Conference on Intelligence and Security Informatics (ISI), pp. 152–154. IEEE (2017)
22. Xu, N., Mao, W.: Multisentinet: a deep semantic network for multimodal sentiment analysis. In: Proceedings of the 2017 ACM on Conference on Information and Knowledge Management, pp. 2399–2402 (2017)
23. Xu, N., Mao, W., Chen, G.: A co-memory network for multimodal sentiment analysis. In: The 41st International ACM SIGIR Conference on Research & Development in Information Retrieval, pp. 929–932 (2018)
24. Xu, N., Zeng, Z., Mao, W.: Reasoning with multimodal sarcastic tweets via modeling cross-modality contrast and semantic association. In: Proceedings of the 58th Annual Meeting of the Association for Computational Linguistics, pp. 3777–3786 (2020)
25. Yang, X., Feng, S., Wang, D., Zhang, Y.: Image-text multimodal emotion classification via multi-view attentional network. IEEE Trans. Multimedia **23**, 4014–4026 (2020)
26. Yang, X., Feng, S., Zhang, Y., Wang, D.: Multimodal sentiment detection based on multi-channel graph neural networks. In: Proceedings of the 59th Annual Meeting of the Association for Computational Linguistics and the 11th International Joint Conference on Natural Language Processing (Volume 1: Long Papers), pp. 328–339 (2021)
27. Yao, F., Sun, X., Yu, H., Zhang, W., Liang, W., Fu, K.: Mimicking the brain's cognition of sarcasm from multidisciplines for twitter sarcasm detection. IEEE Trans. Neural Networks Learn. Syst. (2021)
28. Yu, J., Jiang, J.: Adapting Bert for target-oriented multimodal sentiment classification. In: IJCAI (2019)
29. Yu, J., Jiang, J., Xia, R.: Entity-sensitive attention and fusion network for entity-level multimodal sentiment classification. IEEE/ACM Trans. Audio Speech Lang. Process. **28**, 429–439 (2019)
30. Yu, W., et al.: Ch-sims: a Chinese multimodal sentiment analysis dataset with fine-grained annotation of modality. In: Proceedings of the 58th Annual Meeting of the Association for Computational Linguistics, pp. 3718–3727 (2020)
31. Zadeh, A., Chen, M., Poria, S., Cambria, E., Morency, L.P.: Tensor fusion network for multimodal sentiment analysis. arXiv preprint arXiv:1707.07250 (2017)
32. Zhang, L., Wang, S., Liu, B.: Deep learning for sentiment analysis: a survey. Wiley Interdisc. Rev. Data Min. Knowl. Discov. **8**(4), e1253 (2018)
33. Zhang, Q., Fu, J., Liu, X., Huang, X.: Adaptive co-attention network for named entity recognition in tweets. In: Thirty-Second AAAI Conference on Artificial Intelligence (2018)

Synthesizing Counterfactual Samples for Overcoming Moment Biases in Temporal Video Grounding

Mingliang Zhai[1], Chuanhao Li[1], Chenchen Jing[1], and Yuwei Wu[1,2(✉)]

[1] Beijing Laboratory of Intelligent Information Technology, School of Computer Science, Beijing Institute of Technology, Beijing, China
[2] Shenzhen MSU-BIT University, Shenzhen, China
wuyuwei@bit.edu.cn

Abstract. Moment bias is a critical issue in temporal video grounding (TVG), where models often exploit superficial correlations between language queries and moment locations as shortcuts to predict temporal boundaries. In this paper, we propose a model-agnostic counterfactual samples synthesizing method to overcome moment biases by endowing TVG models with sensitivity to linguistic and visual variations. The models with sensitivity sufficiently utilize linguistic information and focus on important video clips rather than fixed patterns, therefore are not dominated by moment biases. Specifically, we synthesize counterfactual samples by masking important words in queries or deleting important frames in videos for training TVG models. During training, we penalize the model if it makes similar predictions on counterfactual samples and original samples to encourage the model to perceive linguistic and visual variations. Experiment results on two datasets (*i.e.*, Charades-CD and ActivityNet-CD) demonstrate the effectiveness of our method.

Keywords: Moment biases · Counterfactual samples · Temporal video grounding

1 Introduction

Temporal video grounding (TVG) is to locate the moment that best matches a language query in an untrimmed video. Given a query "person they start to take some medicine with a spoon" and a corresponding video, models are required to locate a temporal boundary in the video that best matches the query as shown in the original sample of Fig. 1. Recent work [11,14,20] reveals that most TVG models rely on superficial correlations (*i.e.*, moment biases) between language queries and moment locations to infer the temporal boundary. A TVG model that is dominated by moment biases usually utilizes fixed patterns to infer temporal boundaries and is insensitive to linguistic and visual variations. We consider that making TVG models sensitive to linguistic and visual variations can alleviate the influences of moment biases on the models.

S. Yu et al. (Eds.): PRCV 2022, LNCS 13534, pp. 436–448, 2022.
https://doi.org/10.1007/978-3-031-18907-4_34

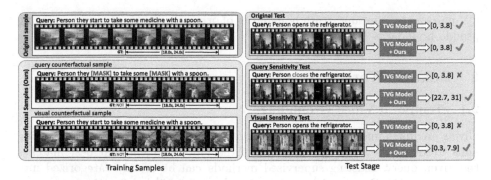

Fig. 1. We synthesize counterfactual samples to train TVG models for endowing them with two sensitivities. (a) Query sensitivity: the model should be sensitive to linguistic variations (*e.g.*, after replacing the important word "opens" with "closes", the predicted boundaries of two queries should be different). (b) Visual sensitivity: the model should be sensitive to the visual content variations.

In this paper, we propose a model-agnostic method to synthesize counterfactual samples by masking important words or deleting important frames, for alleviating moment biases in TVG. Our method serves as a plug-and-play component to endow various types of the TVG model with sensitivity, including proposal-based methods or proposal-free methods. The important words/frames refer to the word/frame that has high contributions to infer boundaries. As shown in Fig. 1, our method consists of two different types of sample synthesizing strategies. For each original training sample, we synthesize a query counterfactual sample and a visual counterfactual sample, both of which consist of a counterfactual Query-Video (QV) pair and corresponding boundaries. By training with synthesized samples, TVG models are encouraged to perceive boundary changes caused by masking words or deleting frames, thus being sensitive to linguistic and visual variations. However, assigning new boundaries to counterfactual QV pairs is non-trivial, because the moment matching the language query of the counterfactual QV pair may not exist. To this end, we introduce a difference maximization (DM) loss to maximize the differences between the model's predicted boundaries for counterfactual QV pairs and the ground-truth boundaries of original samples, which avoid assigning pseudo boundaries for counterfactual QV pairs. The idea behind the DM loss is to provide the counterfactual sample with the boundary difference from the original sample. Extensive experiments on the Charades-CD and ActivityNet-CD datasets demonstrate the effectiveness of our method.

The main contribution of this paper can be summarized as follows: (1) We propose a model-agnostic method, which synthesizes counterfactual samples to make TVG models sensitive to language queries and video moments for overcoming moment biases. (2) We introduce a difference maximization loss that maximizes the differences between the predicted boundaries for counterfactual

QV pairs and the ground-truth boundaries of original samples, to avoid assigning pseudo boundaries for counterfactual QV pairs.

2   Related Work

2.1   Temporal Video Grounding

Given an untrimmed video and a language query, temporal video grounding aims to locate the start and end time of the video segment that best matches the given query. Existing supervised methods can be mainly categorized into two groups: **(1) Proposal-based methods** [1,5,8,10] localize the target segment via generating video segment proposals. They use a boundary predictor to compute a score for each proposal. Ideally, a proposal gets a higher score if it is closer to the ground-truth moment. Then the proposal with the highest score is selected as the boundary. Candidate proposals are obtained by using temporal sliding windows or an anchor-based strategy. If the proposals are generated by an anchor-based strategy, the score is computed based on the multi-modal snippet feature sequence by applying multi-scale anchors in the boundary predictor. **(2) Proposal-free methods** [2,3,6,9] do not generate proposals. They use a regressor or a span predictor as a boundary predictor. Specifically, the regression-based predictor aims to regress the start and end timestamps after interacting the whole video with the query without pre-defining proposals. Existing models achieve promising performance, but they may suffer from moment biases. In contrast, we propose a model-agnostic counterfactual sample synthesizing method to alleviate the influences of moment biases on TVG models.

2.2   Moment Biases

Due to the uneven distribution of the dataset, the model relies on the superficial correlation (*i.e.*, moment biases) between query and moment annotations when making predictions. Recent work tries to overcome the influence of moment biases. Yuan *et al.* [11] first propose that the TVG model usually captures moment biases, and it is difficult to accurately evaluate the level of the model with existing datasets and metrics, so they propose new metrics and benchmarks to accurately evaluate the model. Zhang *et al.* [13] exploit a video-only branch and a query-only branch to capture the distributional bias of video and query, respectively, forcing the model to learn cross-modal interaction information. Liu *et al.* [12] first align the given video-query pair by a cross-modal graph convolutional network, and then utilize a memory module to record the cross-modal shared semantic features in the domain-specific persistent memory. Yang *et al.* [14] disentangle moment representations with location factors to infer crucial features of visual content and then apply to intervene causally on the disentangled multi-modal inputs based on back-door adjustment, which forces the model to fairly incorporate each possible location of the target into consideration. These methods focus on creating delicate models to directly reduce the influence of moment biases. Differently, we synthesize counterfactual samples to endow TVG models with sensitivity to linguistic and visual variations without changing the network structure for overcoming moment biases.

2.3 Counterfactual Sample Synthesis

In vision-and-language, there are some counterfactual sample synthesis methods for improving the robustness of models. Zhang *et al.* [23] propose counterfactual contrastive learning paradigm to build contrastive training between positive and negative samples in weakly-supervised temporal video grounding and obtain negative samples by perturbing the feature of the feature layer, interaction layer, and relation layer. Hirota *et al.* [24] investigate the effectiveness of text representations for image understanding in VQA. In particular, they delves into the use of synthesized samples on language-only representations including counterfactual samples. Chen *et al.* [25] train the VQA model using a counterfactual sample synthesis training scheme to reduce language biases. These methods validate that counterfactual sample synthesis methods can improve the robustness of vision-and-language models. Unlike them, we are the first to explore the effectiveness of counterfactual sample synthesis for reducing moment biases in TVG.

3 Methodology

3.1 Problem Formulation

Given an untrimmed video $V = \{v_i\}_{i=0}^{n_v-1}$, where v_i denotes i-th frame in a video and n_v is the total number of frames, and a sentence $S = \{s_i\}_{i=0}^{n_s-1}$ as a language query, where s_i denotes i-th word among the sentence, and n_s is the number of words. $[t^s, t^e]$ denotes ground-truth moment. The video V is encoded into visual features $\mathbf{V} = \{v_i\}_{i=0}^{n_v-1} \in \mathbb{R}^{n_v \times d_v}$ with a pre-trained feature extractor. The query Q is encoded into query features $\mathbf{Q} = \{w_i\}_{i=0}^{n_q-1} \in \mathbb{R}^{n_q \times d_q}$ with a pre-trained model. The TVG task aims to localize the start and end timestamps $[t^s, t^e]$ of a specific segment in video $\mathbf{V}$, which refers to the corresponding semantic of query $\mathbf{Q}$.

3.2 Preliminaries

We utilize Grad-CAM [15] to obtain the contribution of each object to the model's prediction. Specifically, the network obtains the feature layer A and the predicted value y through forwarding propagation. We back-propagate y to obtain the gradient A' of the feature layer A, and then calculate $\alpha_k = \frac{1}{N}\sum_k A'^k$ to get the importance of A^k, where k denotes the index of the channel. Finally, we calculate $L_c = \text{ReLU}(\sum_k \alpha_k A^k)$ to derive the contribution of each participant.

3.3   Synthesizing Counterfactual Samples

We propose a method for synthesizing counterfactual samples for training. This method consists of two different types of sample synthesis strategies. As shown in Fig. 2, for an original QV pair $< V, Q >$ organized by a video and a query, we synthesize a visual counterfactual sample $< V^*, Q >$ and a query counterfactual sample $< V, Q^* >$ by directly modifying features respectively. First of all, we use pre-trained models to extract the feature of the video and the query. Secondly, the model's predictions are obtained through forwarding propagation. Thirdly, we use Grad-CAM to obtain features of counterfactual samples by back-propagation without updating parameters. When the V or Q changes, the boundary should also be changed accordingly usually. However, it is hard to know what the changed boundaries should be, so we use the loss function to reflect the change of the boundary (*i.e.*, the value of the loss function is inversely proportional to the prediction accuracy). Finally, we feed synthesized sample features into TVG models which can encourage the model to understand language queries and visual content sufficiently for overcoming moment biases in TVG.

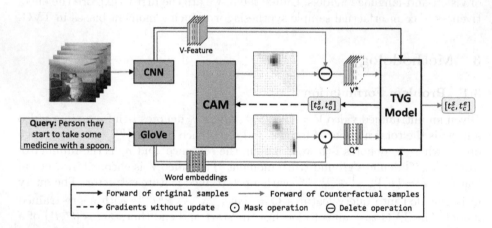

Fig. 2. Overall the TVG model with our method. Given a QV pair, we first encode their features and feed these features into the TVG model to obtain the predicted boundary. Then, we utilize Grad-CAM to obtain attention maps of the target layer. For obtaining counterfactual queries/videos, we use the attention maps to mask/delete the feature of the queries/videos. At last, we use counterfactual samples to train the TVG model.

3.3.1   Query Counterfactual Samples

We use a pre-trained model to obtain query features on which subsequent operations are based. The detailed processes of synthesizing query counterfactual samples are divided into two parts:

Calculating and Masking Important Words in the Query. For the model's prediction, a few words in a query can have a significant influence on the model's decision. We utilize Grad-CAM to derive the contribution of each object for results, and calculate the contribution heat map $I_c^q = [c_i]_{i=0}^{n_q-1}$ of each word to the result by

$$c_i(b, w_i) = C_i(P_{tvg}(b|V, Q), w_i) := \sum (\nabla_{w_i} P_{tvg}(b|V, Q)), \tag{1}$$

where $P_{tvg}(b|V, Q)$ is the predicted probability of boundary b given a video V and a query Q, and w_i is i-th word. The contributions of word w_i to boundary b are larger if the contribution value $c_i(b, w_i)$ is higher. We calculate $a^q = \text{Softmax}(I_c^q)$ and top-k word with the highest contribution whose

$$d^q = \text{Top}_k(\text{argsort}[a_i^q]) \in \mathbb{R}^{k \times 1}, s.t. \sum_{i=0}^{k} d^q \geq \epsilon, \tag{2}$$

then mask these word embeddings as

$$Q^* = Q \odot d^q, \tag{3}$$

where $\odot$ is hadamard product. So far, we use Q^* and original video features V to form query counterfactual pairs $< V, Q^* >$.

Assigning Moment Annotations. We should assign the moment annotations for the query counterfactual sample $< V, Q^* >$. It is difficult to know the location of the boundary after the query has changed. So we design a difference maximization loss function $\mathcal{L}_{DM}$ to reflect the change of the boundary. In other words, the closer the model prediction result is to the original ground-truth boundary B, the greater the loss value, and vice versa. Specifically, we propose a difference maximization (DM) loss to maximize the differences between the model's predicted boundaries for counterfactual QV pairs and the ground-truth boundaries of original samples by

$$\mathcal{L}_{DM} = \frac{1}{N} \sum_i^N y_i \log(1 - P_i(b)) + (1 - y_i) \log(P_i(b)). \tag{4}$$

3.3.2 Visual Counterfactual Samples

For videos, we use a pre-trained model to encode the video. Similar to Eq. 1, we calculate the important frame by

$$c_i(b, v_i) = C_i(P_{TVG}(b|V, Q), v_i) := \sum (\nabla_{v_i} P_{TVG}(b|V, Q)). \tag{5}$$

Also, we use Grad-CAM to get the contribution image $I_c^v = [c_i]_{i=0}^{n_v-1}$ of each frame feature, then we calculate $a^v = \text{Softmax}(I_c^v)$, and delete the important frame as a new query V^*. The position where the sum of the top-k values $d^q = \text{Top}_k(\text{argsort}[a_i^q]) \in \mathbb{R}^{k \times 1}$ from the obtained contribution image is greater than or equal to the threshold ϵ (*i.e.*, $\sum_{i=0}^{k} d^q \geqslant \epsilon$)is the important part. A counterfactual video is synthesized by deleting the original video as

$$V^* = V \ominus d^v = \text{Concat}(\text{del}\{V[d^v]\}, \mathbf{0}_{n_v-k}), \tag{6}$$

where del is delete operation, and $\mathbf{0}_{n_v-k}$ is $n_v - k$ dimension zero vector. We use V^* and original queries V to form visual counterfactual pairs $< V^*, Q >$ by doing so. The processing of moment annotations is the same as in Sect. 3.3.1. Although we can assign a boundary for $< V^*, Q >$, we still utilize $\mathcal{L}_{DM}$ to reflect the change of the boundary for unifying the way of assigning boundaries to two kinds of counterfactual pairs.

3.4   Training Process

By the above, we can get visual counterfactual samples $< V^*, Q >$ and query counterfactual samples $< V, Q^* >$. During the training process, all kinds of samples including original samples both participate in training. Specifically, when training with original samples, we directly utilize

$$\mathcal{L}_{CE} = \frac{1}{N} \sum_{i=1}^{N} y_i \log(P_i(B|Q,V)) + (1 - y_i) \log(1 - P_i(B|Q,V)) \tag{7}$$

to train the TVG model. For training with counterfactual samples, we first utilize $\mathcal{L}_{CE}$ to obtain the gradient of the target layer, thus synthesize counterfactual samples, and use $\mathcal{L}_{DM}$ to train the TVG model. The overall training process is as follows:

1. Training the TVG model using original samples to get the baseline model by minimizing the loss $\mathcal{L}_{CE}$.
2. Calculating gradients of the target layer of the loss $\mathcal{L}_{CE}$ without updating parameters to get a contribution of each object for synthesizing counterfactual samples $< V^*, Q >$ and $< V, Q^* >$.
3. Choosing a sample among the original samples $< V, Q >$, visual counterfactual samples $< V^*, Q >$, and query counterfactual samples $< V, Q^* >$ with the same probability.
4. Training a TVG model using counterfactual samples by minimizing the loss $\mathcal{L}_{DM}$.
5. Going back to step 2 until the model converges or the stopping condition is met.

At the testing stage, we directly predict boundaries through the TVG model without synthesizing counterfactual samples.

4 Experiments

4.1 Datasets and Metric

Datasets. We conduct experiments on Charades-CD and ActivityNet-CD datasets by Yuan *et al.* [11] proposed. These two datasets are reorganized for each split based on the Charades-STA [21] and ActivityNet Caption [22] datasets. Each dataset is re-splitted into four sets: training set, validation set, independent-identical-distribution (IID) test set, and out-of-distribution (OOD) test set. All samples in the training set, validation set, and iid-test set satisfy independently identical distribution, and the samples in the ood-test set are out-of-distribution. Charades-CD has 4,564 videos and 11,071 sample pairs in the training set, 333 videos and 859 sample pairs in the validation set, 333 videos and 823 sample pairs in the iid-test set, 1442 videos and 3375 sample pairs in the ood-test set. ActivityNet-CD has 10,984 videos and 51,414 sample pairs in the training set, 746 videos and 3,521 sample pairs in the validation set, 746 videos and 3,443 sample pairs in the iid-test set, 2,450 videos and 13,578 sample pairs in the ood-test set.

Table 1. Performance on Charades-CD and ActivityNet-CD dataset of different TVG models.

(a) Charades-CD

Split	Model	dR@1,IoU@m			dR@5,IoU@m			mIoU
		m = 0.5	m = 0.7	m = 0.9	m = 0.5	m = 0.7	m = 0.9	
iid	2D-TAN	35.60	21.39	5.83	75.70	43.62	9.84	35.70
	2D-TAN + ours	**35.27**	**16.88**	**4.19**	**57.04**	**29.92**	**6.05**	**34.71**
	VSLNet	50.30	31.23	9.36	63.79	46.42	15.31	46.99
	VSLNet + ours	**50.06**	**30.62**	**7.65**	**65.01**	**45.20**	**13.61**	**44.98**
ood	2D-TAN	24.91	10.38	2.16	61.83	25.68	3.91	27.99
	2D-TAN + ours	**28.16**	**11.88**	**3.14**	**64.39**	**26.48**	**4.40**	**32.83**
	VSLNet	39.11	21.51	5.45	58.13	39.38	11.73	39.78
	VSLNet + ours	**45.90**	**26.47**	**7.74**	**62.96**	**45.26**	**13.88**	**45.92**

(b) ActivityNet-CD

Split	Model	dR@1,IoU@m			dR@5,IoU@m			mIoU
		m = 0.5	m = 0.7	m = 0.9	m = 0.5	m = 0.7	m = 0.9	
iid	2D-TAN	34.51	18.03	4.91	65.83	37.55	8.92	34.26
	2D-TAN + ours	**32.12**	**16.10**	**4.15**	**62.62**	**33.94**	**7.90**	**32.09**
	VSLNet	35.91	23.08	9.94	50.62	35.00	13.93	37.68
	VSLNet + ours	**35.10**	**22.50**	**9.35**	**49.32**	**33.31**	**14.19**	**36.95**
ood	2D-TAN	18.90	9.37	2.50	43.54	24.36	5.25	22.72
	2D-TAN + ours	**19.68**	**10.32**	**2.76**	**44.41**	**25.10**	**5.13**	**23.58**
	VSLNet	17.89	9.71	3.16	32.38	18.12	5.22	22.57
	VSLNet + ours	**19.85**	**10.24**	**3.69**	**31.18**	**18.99**	**5.05**	**23.88**

Metric. We use the metric $dR@n, \text{IoU}@m$ [11]. This metric can better evaluate the performance of models for the current biased datasets. The metric adds a limiting factor to $R@n, \text{IoU}@m$ denoted as

$$dR@n, \text{IoU}@m = \frac{1}{N_q} \sum_i r(n, m, q_i) \cdot (1 - abs(p_i^s - g_i^s)) \cdot (1 - abs(p_i^e - g_i^e)), \quad (8)$$

Table 2. The preformance of unimodal models and 2D-TAN on Charades-CD dataset.

Model	dR@1,IoU@m		dR@5,IoU@m		mIoU
	m = 0.5	m = 0.7	m = 0.5	m = 0.7	
2D-TAN	24.91	10.38	61.83	25.68	27.99
2D-TAN (w/o video)	19.31	7.07	61.94	24.11	23.77
2D-TAN (w/o query)	13.11	4.38	43.27	13.66	15.80

where $p_i^{s/e}$ is the start/end time of the model prediction, and $g_i^{s/e}$ is the start/end time of the ground-truth moment. For each query q_i, $r(n, m, q_i) = 1$ if at least one of the top-n predicted moments has an IoU larger than threshold m with the ground-truth boundary, otherwise $r(n, m, q_i) = 0$. The total number of all samples is N_q.

4.2 Implementation Details

We utilize the 300d GloVe [16] vectors to initialize the words in the query. For the video, we use the pre-trained VGG feature [18] for Charades-CD and the C3D feature [17] for ActicityNet-CD. We add our method to 2D-TAN [8] and VSLNet [9]. For hyperparameters, we follow [8,9], and use the last convolutional layer of the feature fusion module as the target layer of Grad-CAM and the threshold ϵ is 0.8. All the experiments are conducted with the Adam optimizer [19] for 20 epochs with learning rate initialized as 5×10^{-4}. We train all models on two GTX 1080ti GPUs with PyTorch1.7.

4.3 Comparisons

The performances of 2D-TAN and VSLNet that are equipped with our method are significantly improved on Charades-CD and ActivityNet-CD ood-splitted. As shown in Table 1, VSLNet with our method obtains 6.14% gains in "mIoU" and 4.96% gains in "$dR@1, IoU@0.7$". Our method brings 4.84% gains in "mIoU" and 1.5% gains in "$dR@1, IoU@0.7$" for 2D-TAN.

Our method prevents the model from exploiting moment bias, thus the model performance drops on the iid-test set. On the contrary, the performance of the model on the ood-test set has been significantly improved. We know that Zhang *et al.* [13] also use VSLNet as the baseline, but they replace the stacked LSTMs with stacked transformer blocks, so it is difficult to make a fair comparison. Our improvement on the mIoU metric is better than theirs, and on other metrics is comparable performance.

4.4 Ablation Studies and Analyze

Moment Biases in Baseline Models. We first study the performance of baseline models on the Charades-CD and ActivityNet-CD datasets. We train

Table 3. Ablation studies on Charades-CD dataset. "(w/o Q)" denotes only using visual counterfactual samples for training. "(w/o V)" denotes only using query counterfactual samples for training. Our method adds both of the above samples to the training.

Model	dR@1,IoU@m			dR@5,IoU@m			mIoU
	m = 0.5	m = 0.7	m = 0.9	m = 0.5	m = 0.7	m = 0.9	
2D-TAN	23.19	9.64	2.19	50.24	21.47	3.56	26.69
2D-TAN + ours (w/o Q)	26.60	9.85	2.38	54.42	23.25	3.20	29.73
2D-TAN + ours (w/o V)	26.85	11.47	2.84	54.62	26.16	3.41	30.44
2D-TAN + ours	**28.16**	**11.88**	**3.14**	**54.39**	**26.48**	**4.40**	**31.83**
VSLNet	39.11	21.51	5.45	58.13	39.38	11.73	39.78
VSLNet + ours (w/o Q)	40.12	21.34	5.56	59.99	41.21	11.96	40.22
VSLNet + ours (w/o V)	45.23	25.97	7.59	60.18	45.10	13.06	44.78
VSLNet + ours	**45.90**	**26.47**	**7.74**	**62.96**	**45.26**	**13.88**	**45.92**

2D-TAN, 2D-TAN(w/o query), and 2D-TAN(w/o video) respectively, and the results are summarized in Table 2. It is observed that 2D-TAN(w/o query) has a large gap with 2D-TAN, and 2D-TAN(w/o video) has a small gap with 2D-TAN. For example, under the $mIoU$ metric, 2D-TAN(w/o video) drops by 4.22%, while 2D-TAN(w/o query) drops by 12.19%. According to the results, we conclude that the model relies on moment biases to make predictions.

Improving Sensitivity. We combine our method with two baseline models and test them on the Charades-CD and ActicityNet-CD datasets, and the results are listed in Table 3. All strategies can improve the performance of the baseline model on the ood-test set to a certain extent, which indicates that our method is beneficial to the prediction of the model on the ood-test set. For example, after adding our method to 2D-TAN, the performance of $dR@1, IoU@0.7$ metric is improved by 2.24%, and the mIoU metric is improved by 5.14%. In addition, the performance improvement of the "w/o V" strategy is better than that of the "w/o Q" strategy.

4.5   Visualizations

In this section, we present some visualizations. As shown in Fig. 3, we can intuitively observe the improvement of TVG models by our method. The figure on the left shows the model gives more accurate predictions for the same sample after adding our method to the model. The right shows the case of moment bias in the training set, which the original 2D-TAN relies on for prediction. Specifically, the boundary corresponding to most sentences containing the word "opens" is in the early 20% of the video moment, and the original 2D-TAN also predicts in the first 20% of the video moment, but this is a wrong boundary. The 2D-TAN using our method overcomes this moment bias and makes correct inferences. In summary, our method not only enables TVG to overcome moment biases but also better generalizes to out-of-distribution samples.

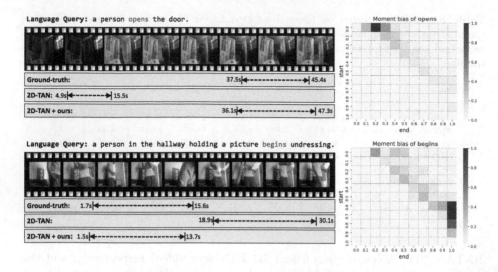

Fig. 3. Visualizations of qualitative examples. The left depicts the localized results of the two models in the ood-test set. The right shows superficial correlations between language queries and moment locations in the training set.

5   Conclusion

In this paper, we have presented a model-agnostic method for synthesizing counterfactual samples. Our method masks/deletes important parts of queries/videos, so that the model can focus on important words/frames rather than several strongly biased words/frames. Furthermore, our method can effectively improve the performance of TVG models and makes the model sensitive to linguistic and visual variations. Extensive experiments demonstrate our method helps overcome moment biases in TVG and improves models' performance on ood-test sets.

Acknowledgements. This work was supported by the Natural Science Foundation of China (NSFC) under Grants No. 62172041 and No. 62176021.

References

1. Wang, Z., Wang, L., Wu, T., et al.: Negative sample matters: a renaissance of metric learning for temporal grounding. arXiv preprint arXiv:2109.04872 (2021)
2. Mun, J., Cho, M., Han, B.: Local-global video-text interactions for temporal grounding. In: Proceedings of the IEEE/CVF Conference on Computer Vision and Pattern Recognition, pp. 10810–10819 (2020)
3. Li, M., Wang, T., Zhang, H., et al.: End-to-End modeling via information tree for one-shot natural language spatial video grounding. arXiv preprint arXiv:2203.08013 (2022)

4. Krishna, R., Hata, K., Ren, F., et al.: Dense-captioning events in videos. In: Proceedings of the IEEE International Conference on Computer Vision, pp. 706–715 (2017)
5. Liu, D., Qu, X., Zhou, P., et al.: Exploring motion and appearance information for temporal sentence grounding. arXiv preprint arXiv:2201.00457 (2022)
6. Li, J., Xie, J., Qian, L., et al.: Compositional temporal grounding with structured variational cross-graph correspondence learning. arXiv preprint arXiv:2203.13049 (2022)
7. Gao, J., Sun, C., Yang, Z., Nevatia, R.: Tall: temporal activity localization via language query. In: Proceedings of the IEEE International Conference on Computer Vision, pp. 5267–5275 (2017)
8. Zhang, S., Peng, H., Fu, J., Luo, J.: Learning 2d temporal adjacent networks for moment localization with natural language. In: Proceedings of the AAAI Conference on Artificial Intelligence, vol. 34, no. 07, pp. 12870–12877 (2020)
9. Zhang, H., Sun, A., Jing, W., Zhou, J.T.: Span-based localizing network for natural language video localization. In: Proceedings of the 58th Annual Meeting of the Association for Computational Linguistics. Association for Computational Linguistics, Online, pp. 6543–6554. https://doi.org/10.18653/v1/2020.acl-main.585
10. Yuan, Y., Ma, L., Wang, J., et al.: Semantic conditioned dynamic modulation for temporal sentence grounding in videos. In: Advances in Neural Information Processing Systems, vol. 32 (2019)
11. Yuan, Y., Lan, X., Wang, X., et al.: A closer look at temporal sentence grounding in videos: dataset and metric. In: Proceedings of the 2nd International Workshop on Human-centric Multimedia Analysis, pp. 13–21 (2021)
12. Liu, D., Qu, X., Di, X., Cheng, Y., Xu Xu, Z., Zhou, P.: Memory-guided semantic learning network for temporal sentence grounding. In: AAAI (2022)
13. Zhang, H., Sun, A., Jing, W., Zhou, J.T.: Towards debiasing temporal sentence grounding in video. arXiv preprint arXiv:2111.04321 (2021)
14. Yang, X., Feng, F., Ji, W., Wang, M., Chua, T.-S.: Deconfounded video moment retrieval with causal intervention. In: Proceedings of the 44th International ACM SIGIR Conference on Research and Development in Information Retrieval, 1–10 (2021)
15. Selvaraju, R.R., Cogswell, M., Das, A., et al.: Grad-cam: visual explanations from deep networks via gradient-based localization. In: Proceedings of the IEEE International Conference on Computer Vision, pp. 618–626 (2017)
16. Pennington, J., Socher, R., Manning, C.D.: Glove: global vectors for word representation. In: Proceedings of the 2014 conference on empirical methods in natural language processing (EMNLP), pp. 1532–1543 (2014)
17. Tran, D., Bourdev, L., Fergus, R., et al.: Learning spatiotemporal features with 3d convolutional networks. In: Proceedings of the IEEE International Conference on Computer Vision, pp. 4489–4497 (2015)
18. Simonyan, K., Zisserman, A.: Very deep convolutional networks for large-scale image recognition. ICLR
19. Kingma, D.P., Ba, J.: Adam: a method for stochastic optimization. In: International Conference on Learning Representations (2015)
20. Yang, X., Feng, F., Ji, W., et al.: Deconfounded video moment retrieval with causal intervention. In: Proceedings of the 44th International ACM SIGIR Conference on Research and Development in Information Retrieval, pp. 1–10 (2021)
21. Gao, J., Sun, C., Yang, Z., et al.: Tall: temporal activity localization via language query. In: Proceedings of the IEEE International Conference on Computer Vision, pp. 5267–5275 (2017)

22. Caba Heilbron, F., Escorcia, V., Ghanem, B., et al.: Activitynet: a large-scale video benchmark for human activity understanding. In: Proceedings of the IEEE Conference on Computer Vision and Pattern Recognition, 961–970 (2015)
23. Zhang, Z., Zhao, Z., Lin, Z., et al.: Counterfactual contrastive learning for weakly-supervised vision-language grounding. Adv. Neural Inf. Process. Syst. **33**, 18123–18134 (2020)
24. Hirota, Y., Garcia, N., Otani, M., et al.: Visual question answering with textual representations for images. In: Proceedings of the IEEE/CVF International Conference on Computer Vision, pp. 3154–3157 (2021)
25. Chen, L., Yan, X., Xiao, J., et al.: Counterfactual samples synthesizing for robust visual question answering. In: Proceedings of the IEEE/CVF Conference on Computer Vision and Pattern Recognition, pp. 10800–10809 (2020)

Multi-grained Cascade Interaction Network for Temporal Activity Localization via Language

Cong Wang[1(✉)] and Mingli Song[2]

[1] Zhejiang Lab, Hangzhou, China
`wangcong@zhejianglab.com`
[2] Zhejiang University, Hangzhou, China
`brooksong@zju.edu.cn`

Abstract. Temporal activity localization via language task aims to localize the target moment in an untrimmed video according to a given language query. A key challenge in this task is how to make an effective semantic alignment between video and language query. Existing methods mainly focus on the single-grained cross-modal interaction and leave the cross-modal interaction in multi-grained manner under-exploited. In this paper, we propose a multi-grained cascade interaction network for temporal activity localization via language. Specifically, a coarse-to-fine cross-modal interaction strategy is exploited to learn an effective query-guided video representation. In addition, we propose a local-global context-aware video encoder to model the temporal relation for video representation. Extensive experiments on two benchmarks verify the effectiveness of our proposed method. Compared with state-of-the-art methods, our proposed method achieves a comparable or superior performance.

Keywords: Temporal activity localization via language ·
Multi-grained · Cascade interaction network

1 Introduction

Localizing activities is a challenging yet pragmatic task for video understanding. As videos often contain intricate activities that cannot be indicated by a predefined list of action classes, a new task, namely Temporal Activity Localization via Language (TALL) has been introduced recently by Gao et al. [3] and Hendricks et al. [1]. As shown in Fig. 1, given an untrimmed video and a natural sentence query, TALL task aims to localize the start and end timestamps of the target video moment that corresponds to the given language query. Exploration

This work has been supported by the Major Scientific Research Project of Zhejiang Lab (No. 2019KD0AC01), Exploratory Research Project of Zhejiang Lab (2022PG0AN01) and Zhejiang Provincial Natural Science Foundation of China (LQ21F020003).

on natural language enables us to deal with not only an open-set of activities but also natural specification of additional constraints, including objects and their properties as well as relations between the involved entities.

The previous approaches for TALL task can be roughly categorized into three groups, including proposal-based methods [1–3, 7–9, 16, 17, 20, 23, 25, 26], proposal-free methods [4, 11–13, 21, 22, 24] and reinforcement learning based methods [5, 18]. A key component in all three groups of methods is how to learn effective alignment between video and language query. The most of existing works mainly focus on the single-grained cross-modal interaction. Some representative works [3, 4, 9, 20, 25] encode query into global-level representation and then design the corresponding cross-modal interaction strategies in frame-by-sentence manner. To further exploit fine-grained alignment between video and language query, some representative works adopt the frame-by-word interaction based on different interaction strategies, including dynamic convolutional filters [23], attention based strategies [2, 7, 11, 17, 21, 24, 26] and graph matching based strategies [16]. Moreover, some representative works [12, 22] extract representations of multiple and distinct semantic phrases from query and make a multi-level cross-modal fusion in frame-by-phrase manner. Although a deep research on cross-modal interaction for TALL task has been made in the existing works, how to make the cross-modal interaction with multi-grained query information effectively has not been fully exploited.

Fig. 1. An example of temporal activity localization via language task.

Besides, video representation is a fundamental cue for TALL task. Based on the frame-wise (clip-wise) features extracted from a pre-trained 3D CNN network, the further context-aware temporal modeling plays an important role in the enhancement of video representation. The most state-of-the-art methods [8, 16] generally learn the global temporal dependencies in an untrimmed video by leveraging bi-directional recurrent network, self-attention network or graph convolutional network. However, the importance of local temporal context modeling is rarely taken into consideration. An appropriate local temporal relation modeling for video representation is beneficial to improve the precision of temporal localization.

To address the above two problems, in this paper we propose a Multi-Grained Cascade Interaction Network for temporal activity localization via language (MGCIN). Firstly, we propose a multi-grained cascade interaction network to make the alignment between video and language query. Specifically, we exploit a coarse-to-fine cross-modal interaction strategy, which first performs a coarse-level cross-modal fusion to suppress the representation of background frames irrelevant to query and then performs a fine-level cross-modal fusion to make a further improvement on the precision of alignment between different modalities. This interaction strategy provides a simple and effective way to make cross-modal interaction with multi-grained query information. In addition, we propose a local-global context-aware video encoder module. Besides the global temporal relation modeling, we propose to model the local-context temporal relation leveraging a local transformer network with one-dimensional shift window, which can enhance the video representation and improve the precision of temporal localization significantly.

Similar to the framework of most existing works, our proposed MGCIN consists of four components, including a video encoder module for video representation, a query encoder for query representation, a multi-grained cascade interaction module for cross-modal interaction and a grounding module. We conduct extensive experiments to verify the effectiveness of the proposed MGCIN. Compared with state-of-the-art methods, the performance of MGCIN is shown to be comparable or superior on ActivityNet Captions and TACoS datasets.

2   Related Work

Temporal language localization via language is a challenging task introduced recently [1,3]. Many works in this area have been proposed. The existing works for this task can be roughly categorized into three groups, including proposal-based methods [1–3,7–9,14,16,17,19,20,23,25,26], proposal-free methods [4,11, 12,21,22,24] and reinforcement learning based methods [5,18].

The proposal-based methods mainly folclow a propose-and-rank pipeline, where they first generate proposals and then rank them relying on the similarity between proposal and query. The early works propose to use the sliding windows as proposals and then perform a comparison between each proposal and the input query. Unlike the traditional two-stage architectures, recent proposal-based methods solve TALL task in an end-to-end fashion. Some works [2,8,14,17,20,23,26] pre-define a set of candidate moments with multi-scale windows at each time and then predict the corresponding scores and temporal offsets. Besides, Zhang et al. [25] model the temporal relations between video moments by a two-dimensional temporal adjacent network. Liu et al. [7] score all pairs of start and end indices simultaneously with a biaffine mechanism.

The proposal-free methods do not depend on any candidate proposal generation process. They predict the probabilities for each video unit (i.e., frame-level or clip-level) being the start and end point of the target segment [4,13,24], or straightforwardly regress the target start and end coordinates based on the multi-modal feature of the given video and query [11,12,21,22]. In this paper, the attention based temporal location regression module we adopt belongs to the proposal-free methods.

The reinforcement learning based methods [5,18] formulate TALL task as a sequential decision problem. They learn an agent which regulates the temporal grounding boundaries progressively based the learned policy.

A key challenge in all three groups of methods is how to learn effective alignment between video and language query. Chen et al. [2] propose an interaction LSTM model, which sequentially processes the video sequence frame by frame, holding deep interactions with the words in the sentence. Zhang et al. [23] encode language features as dynamic filters and convolve the dynamic filters with input visual representations. Yuan et al. [20] propose a semantic conditioned dynamic modulation mechanism to modulate the temporal convolution operations. Liu et al. [8] iteratively interact inter- and intra-modal features within multiple steps. Qu et al. [16] design a video-language graph matching network to match video and query graphs. In this paper, we propose a simple and effective multi-grained cascade interaction network for cross-modal alignment.

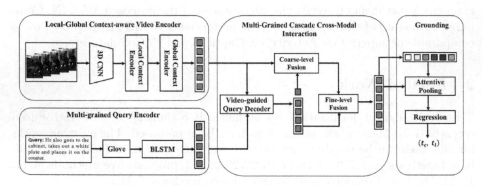

Fig. 2. The framework of the proposed multi-grained cascade interaction network for TALL task. Given a pair of video and query input, we first encodes the video via the proposed local-global context-aware video encoder and encodes the query via bidirectional long-short term memory network based query encoder. Then, we exploit a multi-grained cascade interaction network for cross-modal fusion. Finally, the boundary of the most relevant video moment is predicted by a regression-based grounding module.

3 Proposed Method

Given an untrimmed video V and a sentence query Q, TALL task aims to determine the start and end timestamps $(\hat{t}_s, \hat{t}_e)$ of the target video moment that corresponds to the given query. With the training set $\{V, Q, (\hat{t}_s, \hat{t}_e)\}$, the goal of the model for this task is to learn to predict the most relevant video moment boundary (t_s, t_e).

The framework of the proposed multi-grained cascade interaction network for temporal activity localization via language is shown in Fig. 2. The proposed framework consists of four modules, including a video encoder module, a query encoder module, a multi-grained cascade cross-modal interaction module and a grounding module. It firstly encodes video with the proposed local-global context-aware video encoder and encodes query with bi-directional long-short term memory network (BLSTM) based query encoder. Secondly, the cross-modal fusion between video representation and query representation is made by the proposed multi-grained cascade interaction network. Finally, the boundary of the most relevant video moment is predicted by a regression-based grounding module. The details of the proposed method is given as follows.

3.1 Video Encoder

We first extract the frame-wise features from a pre-trained 3D CNN network and then perform a bilinearly down-sampling of T frames. After a linear embedding layer, the video is represented as $V = \{v_i\}_{i=1}^{T} \in \mathbb{R}^{T \times d}$.

Considering the temporal characteristic in video, context-aware temporal modeling plays an important role in video encoder. The most state-of-the-art methods [8,16] generally model the global temporal dependencies. However, the importance of local temporal context modeling is rarely taken into consideration. In this paper, we propose a local-global context-aware video encoder module to further enhance the video representation.

Firstly, inspired by the success of Swin Transformer [10] which models the relation between the 2D local patches, we propose to adopt two consecutive local transformer blocks with 1D shift window to capture the local temporal relation for video representation. The output V_l of local context encoder (LCE) is computed as

$$\begin{aligned}
\hat{V} &= \mathrm{FFN}(\mathrm{W_{1D}\text{-}MSA}(V)), \\
V_l &= \mathrm{FFN}(\mathrm{SW_{1D}\text{-}MSA}(\hat{V})),
\end{aligned} \tag{1}$$

where $\mathrm{W_{1D}\text{-}MSA}$ and $\mathrm{SW_{1D}\text{-}MSA}$ denotes multi-head self attention modules with one-dimensional regular and shifted windowing configurations, respectively. FFN denotes feed forward network sub-module.

After the above local context encoder, a global self-attention based context encoder is adopted to model the global temporal relation. The obtained video representation through the global context encoder is denoted as V_g.

3.2 Query Encoder

Following the most existing works, we first embed each word in a given query via a pre-trained Glove model. And then a two-layer BLSTM is applied to the embedded word-level features $W = \{w_i\}_{i=1}^{L} \in \mathbb{R}^{L \times 300}$ to capture the sequential information. Specifically, the final word-level representation $h = \{h_i\}_{i=1}^{L} \in \mathbb{R}^{L \times d}$ and the global sentence representation $q_g \in \mathbb{R}^d$ are computed as

$$h_1, h_2, \cdots, h_L = \mathrm{BLSTM}(W), \tag{2}$$

$$q_g = [\overrightarrow{h_L}, \overleftarrow{h_1}], \tag{3}$$

where $h_i = [\overrightarrow{h_i}, \overleftarrow{h_i}]$ is the concatenation of forward and backward hidden states for the i-th word.

3.3 Multi-grained Cascade Interaction Network

It is important but difficult to make an effective cross-modal interaction for TALL task. Unlike the single-grained cross-modal interaction strategies which existing works mainly adopt, we propose a multi-grained cascade interaction network which first reduces the semantic gap between video and query through a video guided query encoder module and then designs a cascade cross-modal fusion module in a multi-grained manner, as shown in Fig. 2.

Video Guided Query Encoder: Since the representations of video and query are heterogeneous and distinct, the query representation is further encoded by a video guided query encoder sub-module, which consists of two multi-modal encoder (MMD) blocks. Specifically, the yielded representation Q^l of the l-th MMD block in the video guided query encoder sub-module is computed as

$$\hat{Q}^l = \text{SelfAttention}(Q^{l-1} + PE_q, Q^{l-1} + PE_q, Q^{l-1}),$$
$$\bar{Q}^l = \text{CrossAttention}(\hat{Q}^l + PE_q, V_g + PE_v, V_g), \qquad (4)$$
$$Q^l = \text{FFN}(\bar{Q}^l),$$

where $Q^0 = [q_g, h_1, h_2, \cdots, h_L] \in \mathbb{R}^{(L+1)\times d}$, PE_q and PE_v denote the learnable positional embeddings for query and video separately. Since the position information is very important for video grounding, the shared positional embeddings are added to queries and keys at every self-attention and cross-attention layer. The video guided query representation $\tilde{Q} = [\tilde{q}_g, \tilde{h}]$ consists of video guided global query representation $\tilde{q}_g$ and video guided word-level query representation $\tilde{h} = [\tilde{h}_1, \tilde{h}_2, \cdots, \tilde{h}_L]$.

Cascade Cross-Modal Fusion: To further improve the precision of cross-modal alignment for video representation, we design a multi-grained cascade cross-modal interaction strategy in a coarse-to-fine manner.

We first suppress the representations of background frames irrelevant to query and highlight the representations of relevant ones at a coarse level. Specifically, the Hadamard product between video representation and global query representation is adopted to perform coarse-level cross-modal fusion. The yielded query guided video representation V_f^c is computed as

$$V_f^c = V_g \odot \tilde{q}_g. \qquad (5)$$

Due to the lack of fine-grained query information in the global query representation, a coarse cross-modal alignment is obtained through the above coarse-level cross-modal fusion. Thus, we further perform a fine-level cross-modal fusion to make a more precise cross-modal alignment. Specifically, we use the video guided word-level query representation $\tilde{h}$ to guide global query guided video representation V_f^c through two MMD blocks. The yielded representation V^l of the l-th

MMD block in the fine-level cross-modal fusion module is computed as

$$\hat{V}^l = \text{SelfAttention}(V^{l-1} + PE_v, V^{l-1} + PE_v, V^{l-1}),$$
$$\bar{V}^l = \text{CrossAttention}(\hat{V}^l + PE_v, \tilde{h} + PE_q, \tilde{h}), \quad (6)$$
$$V^l = \text{FFN}(\bar{V}^l),$$

where $V^0 = V_f^c$. And the final query guided video representation V_f^w is obtained from the output of last MMD block in the fine-level cross-modal fusion module.

3.4 Attention Based Temporal Location Regression

We consider the frames within ground truth moment as foreground, while the rest as background. An attention based temporal location regression module is adopt to predict the boundary of target moment.

We first predict the temporal attention scores through a two-layer MLP and then adopt an attention pooling operation to aggregate the temporal video representation. Further, the boundary of target moment is regressed directly through a three-layer MLP, which uses a sigmoid activation in the last linear transformation. Specifically, the predicted temporal attention scores a and the predicted boundary of target moment are computed as

$$z = (\tanh((V_f^w + PE_v)W_1^a + b_1^a))W_2^a + b_2^a,$$
$$a = \text{SoftMax}(z),$$
$$f_g = \sum_{i=1}^{T} a_i(V_f^w)_i, \quad (7)$$
$$(t_c, t_l) = \text{MLP}_{reg}(f_g),$$

where $W_1^a \in \mathbb{R}^{d \times \frac{d}{2}}$, $W_2^a \in \mathbb{R}^{\frac{d}{2} \times 1}$, $b_1^a \in \mathbb{R}^{\frac{d}{2}}$ and $b_2^a \in \mathbb{R}$ are the learnable parameters. t_c and t_l denote the normalized center coordinate and duration of the predicted target moment respectively.

3.5 Training

We train the proposed model using two loss terms, including attention alignment loss and boundary loss.

Attention Alignment Loss: In the proposed MGCIN model, the accuracy of the learned temporal attention has a great influence on the subsequent location regression. We encourage the higher temporal attention scores within the ground truth moment using an attention alignment loss L_{attn}, which is defined as

$$L_{attn} = -\frac{\sum_{i=1}^{T} m_i log(a_i)}{\sum_{i=1}^{T} m_i}, \quad (8)$$

where $m_i = 1$ indicates that the i-th frame in the given video is within the ground truth moment, otherwise $m_i = 0$.

Boundary Loss: Following the most existing regression based works, we use the smooth L1 loss R_1 to measure the boundary loss, which is defined as

$$L_{l_1} = R_1(t_c - \hat{t}_c) + R_1(t_l - \hat{t}_l), \tag{9}$$

where $(\hat{t}_c, \hat{t}_l)$ denotes the normalized center coordinate and duration of the ground truth moment.

In addition, in order to tailor the boundary loss to the evaluation metric of TALL task, we further introduce a generalized temporal IoU loss, which is defined as

$$L_{giou} = 1 - \text{IoU}_t(b, \hat{b}) + \frac{|C - b \cup \hat{b}|}{|C|}, \tag{10}$$

where C denotes the smallest box covering the predicted temporal box $b = (t_s, t_e)$ and the corresponding ground truth temporal box $\hat{b} = (\hat{t}_s, \hat{t}_e)$, and IoU_t denotes the truncated IoU. Specifically, the IoU score is truncated to 1 if it is not smaller than a threshold t_{max} and 0 if it is not larger than a threshold t_{min}, while other values of IoU score $IoU_t = (IoU - t_{min})/(t_{max} - t_{min})$.

Therefore, the total loss for the proposal model is

$$L = L_{attn} + \lambda_1 L_{l_1} + \lambda_2 L_{giou}, \tag{11}$$

where, λ_1 and λ_2 are the hyperparameters to control the balance among the above loss terms.

4   Experiments

4.1   Datasets

ActivityNet Captions [6]. ActivityNet Captions contains 20K videos with 100K language queries. Each query has an average length of 13.48 words. Following the split principle used in most existing works, we use the validation subsets "val_1" and "val_2" as our validation set and test set respectively. And the number of moment-sentence pairs for training set, validation set and test set are 37417, 17505 and 17031 respectively.

TACoS [15]. TACoS contains 127 videos about cooking activities with an average duration of 7 min. Following the standard split used in [3], the number of moment-sentence pairs for training set, validation set and test set are 10146, 4589 and 4083 respectively.

4.2   Implementation Details

Network: Following previous works, we employ the pre-trained C3D network to extract video feature for both datasets. The number of sampled video frames T is set to 128 for ActivityNet Captions and 256 for TACoS. The feature dimension d is set to 512. In the proposed model, the number of multi-heads is set to 8 for all self-attention and cross-attention sub-modules, and the dimension of inner-layer is set to 2048 for all FFN sub-modules. Besides, the size of window in local context encoder module is set to 4.

Training: In all experiments, we apply Adam to train our proposed model with a mini-batch 100 video-query pairs. The fixed learning rate is set to 0.0002 for ActivityNet Captions and 0.0004 for TACoS. The IoU thresholds (t_{min}, t_{max}) are set to $(0.55, 0.75)$ for ActivityNet Captions and $(0.0, 1.0)$ for TACoS. The balanced weights λ_1 and λ_2 in total loss are set to 1.0.

Evaluation Metric. Following the standard setting used in [3], we adopt the "R@n, IoU = m" metric and mIoU metric to evaluate the model performance. The "R@n, IoU = m" metric represents the percentage of language queries which are localized correctly. And a query is localized correctly when the maximum IoU between the top-n generated moments and the corresponding ground truth moment is larger than m. The mIoU metric means average IoU over all results.

4.3   Ablation Study

We conduct ablation studies to evaluate the effectiveness of our proposed MGCIN in terms of local context encoder (LCE) and multi-grained cascade interaction network.

Effect of Local Context Encoder: We examine how the local context encoder in video encoder module impacts the performance of the proposed model. The corresponding results are shown in Table 1. We can see that the performance of the proposed model decreases significantly when without local context encoder, i.e., the accuracy of localization in "R@1, iou = 0.5" metric drops by 2.18% on ActivityNet Captions dataset and 2.97% on TACoS dataset. This experiment verifies the effectiveness of the proposed local-global video encoder, which is beneficial to enhance the capability of local temporal relation modeling for video encoder.

Effect of Multi-grained Cascade Interaction Network: We examine how the multi-grained cascade interaction module impacts the performance of the proposed model. The corresponding results are shown in Table 2. We can see that our proposed multi-grained cascade interaction network achieves significant improvement compared with the corresponding coarse-level and fine-level cross-modal fusion strategies. These results demonstrate that the model with fine-level fusion outperform that with coarse-level fusion, and the proposed cascade inter-action strategy can effectively improve the accuracy of cross-modal alignment in a coarse-to-fine manner. Qualitative visualization of localization results with the three cross-modal interaction strategies is shown in Fig. 3.

Table 1. The impact of local context encoder for the performance of the proposed model on ActivityNet Captions and TACoS datasets.

Type	LCE	ActivityNet Captions				TACoS			
		R@1, iou = m				R@1, iou = m			
		m = 0.3	m = 0.5	m = 0.7	mIoU	m = 0.1	m = 0.3	m = 0.5	mIoU
(a)	×	61.56	46.32	26.75	43.72	57.21	43.81	30.77	29.91
(b)	✓	**63.80**	**48.54**	**29.21**	**45.39**	**61.16**	**47.06**	**33.74**	**32.22**

Table 2. The impact of the proposed multi-grained cascade interaction network for the performance of the proposed model on ActivityNet Captions and TACoS datasets.

Variants	ActivityNet Captions				TACoS			
	R@1, iou = m				R@1, iou = m			
	m = 0.3	m = 0.5	m = 0.7	mIoU	m = 0.1	m = 0.3	m = 0.5	mIoU
Coarse-level	63.03	47.53	27.85	44.72	52.24	40.44	28.04	26.89
Fine-level	63.04	47.78	28.03	44.76	56.36	44.41	32.64	30.89
Cascade	**63.80**	**48.54**	**29.21**	**45.39**	**61.16**	**47.06**	**33.74**	**32.22**

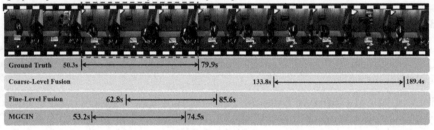

Fig. 3. Qualitative visualization of localization results in TALL task by our proposed MGCIN model and its corresponding variants, including the model with only coarse-level or fine-level cross-modal fusion.

4.4   Performance Comparison with Other Representative Methods

We evaluate the performance of the proposed model compared with other representative methods on two benchmark datasets, including ActivityNet Captions and TACoS. The results are shown in Table 3. We can see that the proposed model achieves a comparable or even better performance on two benchmark datasets compared with the existing representative methods.

In more details, we can obtain several observations. Firstly, the proposed proposal-free model achieves the best performance on both datasets compared with other representative methods from the same group. Secondly, compared with some state-of-the-art proposal-based methods, the proposed proposal-free method achieves the comparable performance on ActivityNet Capions dataset

Table 3. The Performance comparison with other representative methods on ActivityNet Captions and TACoS datasets. Here, the type of reinforcement learning based methods is abbreviated to "RL".

Type	Method	ActivityNet captions				TACoS			
		R@1, iou = m				R@1, iou = m			
		m = 0.3	m = 0.5	m = 0.7	mIoU	m = 0.1	m = 0.3	m = 0.5	mIoU
RL	TripNet-GA [5]	48.42	32.19	13.93	–	–	23.95	19.17	–
	TSP-PRL [18]	56.08	38.76	–	39.21	–	–	–	–
Proposal-based	CTRL [3]	47.43	29.01	10.43	-	24.32	18.32	13.30	–
	MCN [1]	39.35	21.36	6.43	–	14.42	–	5.58	–
	TGN [2]	43.81	27.93	–	–	41.87	21.77	18.90	–
	SCDM [20]	54.80	36.75	19.86	–	–	26.11	21.17	–
	CMIN [26]	63.61	43.40	23.88	–	32.48	24.64	18.05	–
	CBP [17]	54.30	35.76	17.80	–	–	27.31	24.79	–
	2D-TAN [25]	59.45	44.51	26.54	–	47.59	37.29	25.32	–
	CBLN [7]	66.34	48.12	27.60	–	49.16	38.98	27.65	–
	IA-Net [8]	**67.14**	**48.57**	27.95	–	47.18	37.91	26.27	–
	VLG-Net [16]	–	46.32	**29.82**	–	57.21	45.46	**34.19**	–
Proposal-free	ABLR [21]	55.67	36.79	–	36.99	34.70	19.50	9.40	13.40
	DEBUG [11]	55.91	39.72	–	39.51	41.15	23.45	–	16.03
	ExCL [4]	62.1	41.6	23.9	–	–	44.4	27.8	–
	DRN [22]	–	45.45	24.36	–	–	–	23.17	–
	LGI [12]	58.52	41.51	23.07	41.13	–	–	–	–
	VSLNet [24]	63.16	43.22	26.16	43.19	–	29.61	24.27	24.11
	IVG-DCL [13]	63.22	43.84	27.10	44.21	49.36	38.84	29.07	28.26
	Ours	63.80	48.54	29.21	**45.39**	**61.16**	**47.06**	33.74	**32.22**

while higher performance on TACoS dataset. Finally, in order to cover diverse video moments with different lengths, the state-of-the-art proposal-based methods generate lots of moment candidates elaborately, such as representative work 2D-TAN [25], while our proposed method regresses the boundary of target moment directly and abandons complex post-processing operations such as Non-Maximun Suppression.

5 Conclusion

In this paper, we propose a multi-grained cascade interaction network for temporal activity localization via language. To make an effective cross-modal alignment between video and language query, we propose a cascade cross-modal interaction strategy in a coarse-to-fine manner. Besides, we design a local-global context-aware video encoder to model the temporal relation for video representation. Extensive experiments on two benchmarks demonstrate the effectiveness of our proposed method.

References

1. Anne Hendricks, L., Wang, O., Shechtman, E., Sivic, J., Darrell, T., Russell, B.: Localizing moments in video with natural language. In: ICCV, pp. 5803–5812 (2017)

2. Chen, J., Chen, X., Ma, L., Jie, Z., Chua, T.S.: Temporally grounding natural sentence in video. In: EMNLP, pp. 162–171 (2018)

3. Gao, J., Sun, C., Yang, Z., Nevatia, R.: Tall: temporal activity localization via language query. In: ICCV, pp. 5267–5275 (2017)

4. Ghosh, S., Agarwal, A., Parekh, Z., Hauptmann, A.G.: Excl: extractive clip localization using natural language descriptions. In: NAACL, pp. 1984–1990 (2019)

5. Hahn, M., Kadav, A., Rehg, J.M., Graf, H.P.: Tripping through time: efficient localization of activities in videos. In: BMVC (2020)

6. Krishna, R., Hata, K., Ren, F., Fei-Fei, L., Carlos Niebles, J.: Dense-captioning events in videos. In: ICCV, pp. 706–715 (2017)

7. Liu, D., et al.: Context-aware biaffine localizing network for temporal sentence grounding. In: CVPR, pp. 11235–11244 (2021)

8. Liu, D., Qu, X., Zhou, P.: Progressively guide to attend: an iterative alignment framework for temporal sentence grounding. In: EMNLP, pp. 9302–9311 (2021)

9. Liu, M., Wang, X., Nie, L., He, X., Chen, B., Chua, T.S.: Attentive moment retrieval in videos. In: ACM SIGIR, pp. 15–24 (2018)

10. Liu, Z., et al.: Swin transformer: hierarchical vision transformer using shifted windows. In: ICCV, pp. 10012–10022 (2021)

11. Lu, C., Chen, L., Tan, C., Li, X., Xiao, J.: Debug: a dense bottom-up grounding approach for natural language video localization. In: EMNLP-IJCNLP, pp. 5144–5153 (2019)

12. Mun, J., Cho, M., Han, B.: Local-global video-text interactions for temporal grounding. In: CVPR, pp. 10810–10819 (2020)

13. Nan, G., et al.: Interventional video grounding with dual contrastive learning. In: CVPR, pp. 2765–2775 (2021)

14. Qu, X., et al.: Fine-grained iterative attention network for temporal language localization in videos. In: ACM Multimedia, pp. 4280–4288 (2020)

15. Regneri, M., Rohrbach, M., Wetzel, D., Thater, S., Schiele, B., Pinkal, M.: Grounding action descriptions in videos. Trans. Assoc. Comput. Linguist. 1, 25–36 (2013)

16. Soldan, M., Xu, M., Qu, S., Tegner, J., Ghanem, B.: VLG-net: video-language graph matching network for video grounding. In: ICCV Workshops, pp. 3224–3234 (2021)

17. Wang, J., Ma, L., Jiang, W.: Temporally grounding language queries in videos by contextual boundary-aware prediction. In: AAAI, pp. 12168–12175 (2020)

18. Wu, J., Li, G., Liu, S., Lin, L.: Tree-structured policy based progressive reinforcement learning for temporally language grounding in video. In: AAAI, pp. 12386–12393 (2020)

19. Xu, H., He, K., Plummer, B.A., Sigal, L., Sclaroff, S., Saenko, K.: Multilevel language and vision integration for text-to-clip retrieval. In: AAAI, pp. 9062–9069 (2019)

20. Yuan, Y., Ma, L., Wang, J., Liu, W., Zhu, W.: Semantic conditioned dynamic modulation for temporal sentence grounding in videos. In: NeurIPS, pp. 536–546 (2019)

21. Yuan, Y., Mei, T., Zhu, W.: To find where you talk: Temporal sentence localization in video with attention based location regression. In: AAAI. pp. 9159–9166 (2019)

22. Zeng, R., Xu, H., Huang, W., Chen, P., Tan, M., Gan, C.: Dense regression network for video grounding. In: CVPR, pp. 10287–10296 (2020)

23. Zhang, D., Dai, X., Wang, X., Wang, Y.F., Davis, L.S.: Man: moment alignment network for natural language moment retrieval via iterative graph adjustment. In: CVPR, pp. 1247–1257 (2019)

24. Zhang, H., Sun, A., Jing, W., Zhou, J.T.: Span-based localizing network for natural language video localization. In: ACL, pp. 6543–6554 (2020)
25. Zhang, S., Peng, H., Fu, J., Luo, J.: Learning 2d temporal adjacent networks for moment localization with natural language. In: AAAI, pp. 12870–12877 (2020)
26. Zhang, Z., Lin, Z., Zhao, Z., Xiao, Z.: Cross-modal interaction networks for query-based moment retrieval in videos. In: ACM SIGIR, pp. 655–664 (2019)

Part-Based Multi-Scale Attention Network for Text-Based Person Search

Yubin Wang, Ding Qi, and Cairong Zhao(✉)

Department of Computer Science and Technology, Tongji University, Shanghai, China
{1851731,2011267,zhaocairong}@tongji.edu.cn

Abstract. Text-based person search aims to retrieve the target person in an image gallery based on textual descriptions. Solving such a fine-grained cross-modal retrieval problem is very challenging due to differences between modalities. Moreover, the inter-class variance of both person images and descriptions is small, and more semantic information is needed to assist in aligning visual and textual representations at different scales. In this paper, we propose a **P**art-based **M**ulti-Scale **A**ttention **N**etwork (PMAN) capable of extracting visual semantic features from different scales and matching them with textual features. We initially extract visual and textual features using ResNet and BERT, respectively. Multi-scale visual semantics is then acquired based on local feature maps of different scales. Our proposed method learns representations for both modalities simultaneously based mainly on Bottleneck Transformer with self-attention mechanism. A multi-scale cross-modal matching strategy is introduced to narrow the gap between modalities from multiple scales. Extensive experimental results show that our method outperforms the state-of-the-art methods on CUHK-PEDES datasets.

Keywords: Person re-identification · Cross-modal retrieval · Representation learning

1 Introduction

Recently, text-based person search has gained increasing attention due to its potential applications in intelligent surveillance. It aims to retrieve the target person according a relevant textual description. Since natural language is more accessible as retrieval queries, text-based person search has great necessity in the absence of target images. However, it is a challenging task due to difficulties of both person re-identification and cross-modal retrieval. First, it is difficult to extract robust features due to interference from occlusion and background clutter. Second, all images and descriptions belong to the same category, person, thus making inter-modality variance much larger than intra-modality variance.

To solve these problems, related methods [1–8] have been proposed in recent years to reduce the gap between these two modalities and thus improve the

S. Yu et al. (Eds.): PRCV 2022, LNCS 13534, pp. 462–474, 2022.
https://doi.org/10.1007/978-3-031-18907-4_36

matching accuracy. These methods always focus on two problems, one is how to learn representations in a coarse-to-fine manner for both modalities, and the other is how to find an adaptive multi-scale cross-modal matching strategy that all features are well-aligned. Many current works are unable to solve these two problems well at the same time. Some of them learn representations only from local scale [1–3] or global scale [4–7], which are unable to generate features at different scales from both coarse-grained and fine-grained perspectives. Although some approaches [9,10] consider combining local features with global features, some fragments of textual descriptions still cannot align with visual regions that are semantically consistent with them.

The relevance at different scales makes it difficult to align visual and textual features. For multi-scale matching, existing methods [2–5] try to align images and texts at different scales using predefined rules. However, these methods do not take into account the cross-scale association between modalities. As shown in Fig. 1, images and textual descriptions can be decomposed into regions and phrases at local scale. Since the phrase "belt" exists in one visual region while the phrases "long sleeve white shirt" and "black pants" appear in two separated visual regions, phrase-region matching at a fixed scale is not effective, where the cross-scale matching of semantics between modalities is completely ignored.

Retaining semantics for visual representation learning is always critical. Some methods [11,12] use horizontal segmentation referring to PCB [13] in person re-identification, aiming to match relevant textual semantics based on local salient parts of images. However, this segmentation operation can easily break visual semantics existing in different regions. As shown in Fig. 1, the visual semantics of the phrase "books" is exactly partitioned by two visual regions, and from neither of these two regions can the model accurately recognize the semantics matching the phrase. This prevents the model from fully extracting key information, and leads to inaccurate matching results. Considering the above, an approach is urgently needed for multi-scale feature extraction while preserving semantics at different scales.

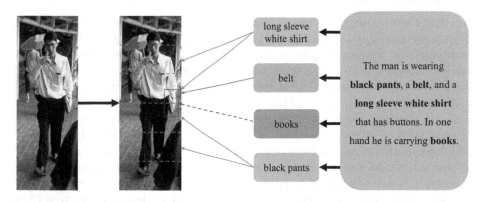

Fig. 1. Phrase-region matching at a fixed scale is not effective, where the cross-scale semantic matching between modalities is completely ignored, and the segmentation operation can easily break visual semantics existing in different regions.

To address these problems, we introduce a part-based multi-scale attention network for text-based person search, aiming at improving the representation learning and matching methods from different scales in an end-to-end manner and enhancing the semantics with the ability to collect global information by self-attention mechanism [14]. For visual representation learning, we use a pre-trained ResNet [15] to generate the basic feature map for each image, which is horizontally segmented into several strips to generate regions at different scales. All visual features with the same scale are combined together after scale-specific attention-based branches with Bottleneck Transformer [16] blocks to output visual representations. For textual representation learning, each word embedding is learned by a pre-trained BERT [17] with fixed parameters and is further processed by a network with hybrid branches. In each branch, textual representations adaptively learn to match visual representations, thus eliminating the inter-modality variance. In addition, we introduce a multi-scale cross-modal matching strategy with the cross-modal projection matching (CMPM) loss [4], thus gradually reducing the gap between modalities from different scales. Our main contributions are summarized as follows.

- We propose a dual-path feature extraction framework for learning multi-scale visual and textual representations simultaneously, where semantic information is captured for both modalities based on Bottleneck Transformer blocks with self-attention mechanism.
- We introduce a multi-scale cross-modal matching strategy using cross-modal projection matching (CMPM) loss, thus gradually reducing the variance between modalities from different scales.
- Our proposed method outperforms all other methods on the CUHK-PEDES [6] datasets. Extensive ablation studies demonstrate the effectiveness of components in our method.

2 Related Works

2.1 Person Re-identification

Recently, there are many person re-identification methods based on deep learning to improve the matching accuracy by exploring and mining the fine-grained discriminative features in person images. PCB [13] proposes a convolutional baseline based on local information, which segments the global feature map into horizontal strips to extract local features. MGN [18] varies the number of divided strips in different branches to obtain local feature representations with multiple scales. In addition, some works [19–21] consider the detection of body parts with external tools or attention mechanism to improve the quality of local features by detecting subtle changes in local regions. However, such approaches rely heavily on pose estimation and semantic parsing algorithms, while ignoring the semantic connection between different local regions, resulting in critical visual semantics not being fully extracted. Moreover, many works [13,22] tend to limit to a fixed local scale without paying attention to the semantic information at other scales, thus reducing the discrimination of representations.

2.2 Text-Based Person Search

The development of text-based person search is gradually gaining attention from the research community. Li et al. [6] first introduce the text-based person search task and propose GNA-RNN to output the similarity between images and textual descriptions. Zheng et al. [5] propose a dual-path convolutional neural network for visual-linguistic embedding learning, which can be efficiently fine-tuned end-to-end. Zhang et al. [4] design cross-modal projection matching (CMPM) loss and cross-modal projection classification (CMPC) loss for cross-modal embedding learning. Some works are based on body parts with external tools to assist in extracting visual features. Among them, PMA [2] proposes a pose-guided multi-granularity attention network to match visual regions associated with descriptions from multiple granularities based on human pose estimation. VITAA [3] uses semantic segmentation labels to drive the learning of attribute-aware features.

Some recent works have focused more on feature matching at different scales. AXM-Net [9] dynamically exploits multi-scale knowledge from both modalities and recalibrates each modality based on shared semantics. NAFS [23] constructs full-scale representations for visual and textual representations and adaptively conducts joint alignments at all scales. SSAN [10] extracts semantic alignment by exploring relatively aligned body parts as supervision and using contextual cues from descriptions to extract part features. TIPCB [12] learns visual and textual local representations through a dual-path local alignment network structure with a multi-stage cross-modal matching strategy. Nevertheless, such methods lack attention to semantic integrity, leading to inaccurate alignment. By comparison, we propose a novel method that learns and aligns representations more effective by utilising self-attention mechanism within multi-scale setting.

3   Our Approach

In this section, we explain our PMAN in detail. First, we introduce the framework for extracting visual and textual representations. Then we describe the multi-scale cross-modal matching module. The architecture is shown in Fig. 2.

3.1   Multi-scale Visual Representation Learning

For visual representation learning, we first take the image I as the input of ResNet, and the feature $f_I \in R^{H \times W \times C}$ generated after its fourth residual blocks is used as the basic feature map, where H, W and C represent the dimension of height, width and channel. The structure of the multi-scale visual representation learning module based on this feature map, including a local-scale branch, a medium-scale branch and a global-scale branch, is shown in Fig. 3.

For each visual branch, we utilise Bottleneck Transformer [16] (BoT) as backbone, which introduces the self-attention mechanism into the bottleneck architecture by replacing the convolutional layer with a multi-headed self-attention

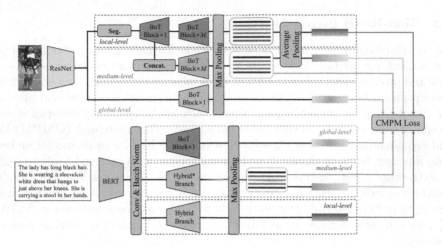

Fig. 2. The architecture of the proposed PMAN, including a dual-path feature extraction framework with attention-based branches for multiple scales and a multi-scale cross-modal matching module. BoT stands for Bottleneck Transformer. **Seg.** indicates horizontal segmentation on the basic feature map. **Concat.** indicates concatenation of every two neighboring local feature maps. * indicates parallel branches.

layer (MHSA). The CNN backbone, due to the nature of the convolutional kernel, tends to focus on local features instead of semantic integrity, so it is essential to stack Transformer blocks that are specialize in capturing global information within a specific scale, thus achieving better performance with less parameters.

In the local-scale branch, We first use the strategy of PCB [13] to horizontally segment the basic feature map f_I into several local regions $\{f_{I,i}\}_{i=1}^{K}$, where $f_{I,i} \in R^{\frac{H}{K} \times W \times C}$. Then we take each local region as the input of a Bottleneck Transformer consisting of $M + 1$ blocks to obtain local features $\{f_{I,i}^{l}\}_{i=1}^{K}$ after a maximum pooling layer, where $f_{I,i}^{l} \in R^{1 \times C}$. These features usually contain fine-grained semantics and play a crucial role in learning discriminative visual features.

In the medium-scale branch, considering that the semantics existing in multiple local regions are easily destroyed, we concatenate every two neighboring local feature maps after the first block of the local-scale branch to generate medium-scale regions. We take them as the input of a Bottleneck Transformer consisting of M blocks to obtain self-attention weighted feature maps for medium-scale regions, and output $K - 1$ medium-scale features $\{f_{I,i}^{m}\}_{i=1}^{K-1}$ after a maximum pooling layer, where $f_{I,i}^{m} \in R^{1 \times C}$, which usually contain the significant semantic information associated with descriptions. By combining semantic information in local-scale regions, the semantics disrupted by segmentation is preserved. For above two branches, local-scale representation $f_I^l \in R^C$ and medium-scale representation $f_I^m \in R^C$ are generated after an average pooling layer.

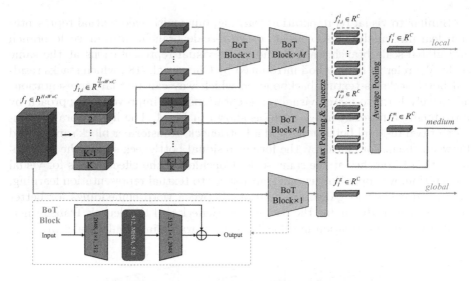

Fig. 3. The structure of the multi-scale visual feature learning module. BoT stands for Bottleneck Transformer. MHSA stands for multi-head self-attention.

In the global-scale branch, we directly use the basic feature map f_I as the input to the Bottleneck Transformer. Since this feature map already contains semantic information at global level, the Transformer for this branch consists of one single block to highlight the visual semantic information. The global-scale feature is obtained after a maximum pooling layer, and squeezed to global-scale representation $f_I^g \in R^C$, which is not influenced by local semantics. These above three representations as well as the set of medium-scale features serve for the multi-scale matching stage.

3.2 Multi-scale Textual Representation Learning

For texual representation learning, a pre-trained language model BERT [17] is used to extract word embeddings with discriminative properties. Specifically, we decompose the sentence and tokenize it to obtain the token sequence, and then truncate or pad the sequence according to the maximum length L. We feed them into BERT with fixed parameters to generate word embeddings $f_w \in R^{L \times D}$, where D denotes the dimension of each word embedding. Since the dimension of embeddings needs to match with the input of bottleneck blocks, we expand the word embeddings and pass them through an 1×1 convolutional network to adjust the dimension of channel from D to C, and textual feature $f_t \in R^{1 \times L \times C}$ is obtained after a batch normalization layer.

Similar to visual representation learning, our multi-scale textual representation learning module also consists of local-scale branch, medium-scale branch and global-scale branch, each for adapting visual representations at the same scale. We refer to the method introduced by Chen et al. [18], which stacks residual bottlenecks as textual backbone, in which way can textual representations adaptively learn to match visual representations. We improve this approach by introducing a novel hybrid branch, as shown in Fig. 4. The hybrid branch consists of two residual bottlenecks and a Bottleneck Transformer block sandwiched between them. For efficiency, the former residual bottleneck shares the parameter with all branches at the same scale. Considering the effectiveness for visual recognition, we apply Bottleneck Transformer to textual representation learning, aiming to extract long-distance relations between word embeddings for better comprehension. By mixing the residual bottleneck and Bottleneck Transformer, we introduce self-attention into local feature learning in a multi-scale way.

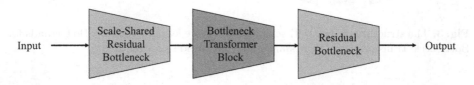

Fig. 4. The structure of the hybrid branch, consisting of a scale-shared residual bottleneck, a Bottleneck Transformer block and a residual bottleneck.

The local-scale and medium-scale branches consist of one single hybrid branch and $K-1$ paralleled hybrid branches respectively, and a maximum pooling layer is added at the end of each branch to generate textual representations $f_t^l \in R^C$ and $\{f_{t,i}^m\}_{i=1}^{K-1}$, where $f_{t,i}^m \in R^C$. Medium-scale textual representations are further processed with an average pooling layer to generate representation $f_t^l \in R^C$ for matching. In the global-scale branch, considering that stacking complex blocks tends to be time-consumed for training while accuracy is not significantly improved, we only use one single Bottleneck Transformer block for learning long-distance association between word embeddings, while suppressing the overfitting phenomenon. A maximum pooling layer is then added to obtain the global-scale representation $f_t^g \in R^C$. The representations extracted from these three branches are already capable of adapting to the visual representations, so that textual representations with highly integrated visual semantics can be learned.

3.3 Multi-scale Feature Matching

In the multi-scale feature matching stage, we use the cross-modal projection matching (CMPM) loss [4] as the loss function, which minimizes the KL divergence between the projection compatibility distributions and the normalized matching distributions to eliminate the difference between textual and visual modalities. Specifically, within a given small batch of N pairs, according to the image representation x_i^I, the set of image-text representation pairs within the batch can be denoted as $\left\{\left(x_i^I, x_j^T\right), y_{i,j}\right\}_{j=1}^N$, where $y_{i,j} = 1$ when x_i^I and x_j^T have the same identity, and $y_{i,j} = 0$ otherwise. For each image-text representation pair, we can calculate the matching probability between them by:

$$p_{i,j} = \frac{\exp\left(x_i^{I\top} \bar{x}_j^T\right)}{\sum_{k=1}^N \exp\left(x_i^{I\top} \bar{x}_k^T\right)} \quad s.t. \quad \bar{x}_j^T = \frac{x_j^T}{\left\|x_j^T\right\|}, \tag{1}$$

where $\bar{x}_j^T$ denotes the regularized textual representation. For the matching probability between x_i^I and x_j^T, we use the normalized label distribution $q_{i,j}$ as the real distribution. The matching loss in one direction can be calculated by:

$$L_{i2t} = \sum_{i=1}^N \sum_{j=1}^N p_{i,j} \log \frac{p_{i,j}}{q_{i,j} + \varepsilon} \quad s.t. \quad q_{i,j} = \frac{y_{i,j}}{\sum_{k=1}^N y_{i,k}}, \tag{2}$$

where ε is a very small value to avoid numerical problems. L_{t2i} can be calculated in a reverse way. Therefore, the CMPM loss is computed by $L = L_{i2t} + L_{t2i}$.

Considering that our dual-path feature extraction framework consists of several branches, each of which generates features at specific scale, we sum the CMPM loss according to visual and textual representations from all scales. The overall objective function is calculated by:

$$L_{overall} = L_g + L_m + L_l + L_{align}, \tag{3}$$

where L_g, L_m and L_l indicate the CMPM loss of local-scale, medium-scale and global-scale representations, respectively. The aligning loss $L_{align} = \sum_{i=1}^{K-1} L_{m,i}$ represents the CMPM loss computed with medium-scale features, which preserve the semantic association between local regions and have more information aligned with descriptions comparing to other scales. By reducing the overall function, our model learns well-aligned representations for both modalities.

4   Experiments

4.1   Experimental Setup

Datasets and Evaluation Protocol. The CUHK-PEDES [6] datasets, which is currently the mainstream benchmark for text-based person search, contains 40206 images of 13003 person IDs, each of which has two textual descriptions annotated by different annotators. These textual descriptions have a vocabulary of 9408 different words. The training set has 34054 images of 11003 person IDs. The validation set has 3078 images of 1000 person IDs, and the test set has 3074 images of 1000 person IDs.

The experimental results are measured by the top-K (K = 1, 5, 10) metric. Given a textual description as query, all test images are ranked according to their similarity to the query, and top-K indicates the percentage of successful searches among all searches in the first K results.

Implementation Details. For visual representation learning, the input images are resized to 384×128. We use ResNet50 [15] as visual backbone to extract the basic feature map. The height, width and channel dimension of the basic feature map are set to $H = 24$, $W = 8$, $C = 2048$. The number of local-scale visual regions is set to $K = 6$. The number of Bottleneck Transformer blocks is set to $M = 3$. For textual representation learning, we use a pre-trained BERT-Base-Uncase for extracting word embeddings, where the maximum length is set to $L = 64$. In the training phase, we use an SGD optimizer with momentum to optimize the model for 80 epochs. The initial learning rate is 0.003 decreased by 0.1 after 50 epochs. We randomly horizontally flip and crop the images to augment data. In the testing phase, we simply sum the local-scale, medium-scale and global-scale representations as the final representation for retrieval. The batch size for both the training and testing phase are set to $N = 64$.

4.2   Comparison with State-of-the-Art Methods on CUHK-PEDES

This section compares the result of our method proposed in this paper with other previous works, as shown in Table 1. These methods can be broadly classified into global-level methods and local-level methods. Compared with global-level methods, local-level methods prefer to obtain discriminative features from local visual regions and align them with phrase-level semantics in textual descriptions to improve matching accuracy. It can be observed that our PMAN can outperform all the existing methods. This further illustrates that our multi-scale approach with self-attention is crucial for improving matching accuracy.

Table 1. Comparison with state-of-the-art methods on CUHK-PEDES datasets. Top-1, top-5 and top-10 accuracies (%) are reported. "g" represents the methods only using global features, and "l+g" represents the methods using global and local features.

Method	Type	Top-1	Top-5	Top-10
GNA-RNN [6]	g	19.05	–	53.64
IATV [7]	g	25.94	–	60.48
PWM + ATH [24]	g	27.14	49.45	61.02
Dual Path [5]	g	44.40	66.26	75.07
CMPM + CMPC [4]	g	49.37	–	79.27
MIA [1]	l+g	53.10	75.00	82.90
PMA [2]	l+g	53.81	73.54	81.23
ViTAA [3]	l+g	55.97	75.84	83.52
NAFS [23]	l+g	59.94	79.86	86.70
MGEL [11]	l+g	60.27	80.01	86.74
SSAN [10]	l+g	61.37	80.15	86.73
AXM-Net [9]	l+g	61.90	79.41	85.75
LapsCore [25]	l+g	63.40	–	87.80
TIPCB [12]	l+g	64.26	**83.19**	89.10
PMAN (Ours)	l+g	**64.51**	83.14	**89.15**

4.3 Ablation Studies

Effects of Multi-scale Representation Learning. In this section, we conduct experiments for each branch to analyze the importance of representation learning at different scales. Table 2 shows the experimental results on the CUHK-PEDES dataset when different branches are selected to train for representation learning. From the variants (a), (b) and (c), it shows that when only one single branch is trained, the medium-scale branch gains the best accuracy, which proves that it is crucial to preserve the semantic association between local regions. From the variants (b) and (g), it can be seen that the multi-scale feature learning framework can enhance the discrimination of visual and textual features at different scales, thus enabling our model to fuse intra-modality features to improve the matching accuracy while aligning inter-modality semantic information.

Table 2. Performance comparison of training with different branches in our method. Top-1, top-5 and top-10 accuracies (%) are reported.

Variant	Local-scale	Medium-scale	Global-scale	Top-1	Top-5	Top-10
(a)	✓			60.12	81.36	88.13
(b)		✓		62.26	82.33	88.59
(c)			✓	60.55	81.34	88.26
(d)	✓	✓		62.07	82.26	88.52
(e)	✓		✓	61.79	82.27	88.55
(f)		✓	✓	63.10	82.71	88.96
(g)	✓	✓	✓	**64.51**	**83.14**	**89.15**

Effects of Backbone with Self-attention. To demonstrate the importance of self-attention mechanism for extracting semantic representations, we analyze the impact of Bottleneck Transformer structure employed as backbone for our proposed model. For comparison, we replace Bottleneck Transformer blocks with residual bottleneck blocks in all branches of different modalities, while other components remain unchanged. The experimental results are shown in Table 3. Comparing the variant (a) with (b) and (c), it can be found that Bottleneck Transformer blocks with self-attention in both modalities improve the matching accuracy, which proves that this design enables the association of salient semantics between modalities. Moreover, the self-attention in textual representation learning has a greater impact on results, which reveals the fact that the structure can extract long-distance relations between word embeddings, which make them produce higher response when relevant queries are given. From the variant (d), it can be seen that the attention-based architecture can facilitate our model to extract better semantic information from both modalities, thus achieving an excellent matching accuracy in the multi-scale representation matching stage.

Table 3. Performance comparison of learning visual and textual representations with Bottleneck Transformer as backbone in our method. Top-1, top-5 and top-10 accuracies (%) are reported.

Variant	Visual backbone	Textual backbone	Top-1	Top-5	Top-10
(a)			61.63	81.65	88.30
(b)	✓		62.31	82.35	88.73
(c)		✓	62.68	82.42	88.94
(d)	✓	✓	**64.51**	**83.14**	**89.15**

5   Conclusion

In this paper, we propose a part-based multi-scale attention network capable of extracting visual semantic features from different scales and matching them with textual features. For representation learning, we introduce Bottleneck Transformer with self-attention mechanism in both modalities to capture features with semantics. For representation matching, we adopt a multi-scale cross-modal adaptive matching strategy. The comparison results show that our approach outperforms the state-of-the-art methods on CUHK-PEDES dataset. Extensive ablation studies demonstrate the effectiveness of components in our method.

References

1. Niu, K., Huang, Y., Ouyang, W., Wang, L.: Improving description-based person re-identification by multi-granularity image-text alignments. IEEE Trans. Image Process. **29**, 5542–5556 (2020)
2. Jing, Y., Si, C., Wang, J., Wang, W., Wang, L., Tan, T.: Pose-guided multi-granularity attention network for text-based person search. In: Proceedings of the AAAI Conference on Artificial Intelligence, vol. 34, pp. 11189–11196 (2020)
3. Wang, Z., Fang, Z., Wang, J., Yang, Y.: *ViTAA*: visual-textual attributes alignment in person search by natural language. In: Vedaldi, A., Bischof, H., Brox, T., Frahm, J.-M. (eds.) ECCV 2020. LNCS, vol. 12357, pp. 402–420. Springer, Cham (2020). https://doi.org/10.1007/978-3-030-58610-2_24
4. Zhang, Y., Lu, H.: Deep cross-modal projection learning for image-text matching. In: Ferrari, V., Hebert, M., Sminchisescu, C., Weiss, Y. (eds.) ECCV 2018. LNCS, vol. 11205, pp. 707–723. Springer, Cham (2018). https://doi.org/10.1007/978-3-030-01246-5_42
5. Zheng, Z., Zheng, L., Garrett, M., Yang, Y., Xu, M., Shen, Y.D.: Dual-path convolutional image-text embeddings with instance loss. ACM Trans. Multimedia Comput. Commun. Appl. (TOMM) **16**(2), 1–23 (2020)
6. Li, S., Xiao, T., Li, H., Zhou, B., Yue, D., Wang, X.: Person search with natural language description. In: Proceedings of the IEEE Conference on Computer Vision and Pattern Recognition, pp. 1970–1979 (2017)
7. Li, S., Xiao, T., Li, H., Yang, W., Wang, X.: Identity-aware textual-visual matching with latent co-attention. In: Proceedings of the IEEE International Conference on Computer Vision, pp. 1890–1899 (2017)

8. Aggarwal, S., Radhakrishnan, V.B., Chakraborty, A.: Text-based person search via attribute-aided matching. In: Proceedings of the IEEE/CVF Winter Conference on Applications of Computer Vision, pp. 2617–2625 (2020)
9. Farooq, A., Awais, M., Kittler, J., Khalid, S.S.: AXM-Net: cross-modal context sharing attention network for person Re-ID. arXiv preprint arXiv:2101.08238 (2021)
10. Ding, Z., Ding, C., Shao, Z., Tao, D.: Semantically self-aligned network for text-to-image part-aware person re-identification. arXiv preprint arXiv:2107.12666 (2021)
11. Wang, C., Luo, Z., Lin, Y., Li, S.: Text-based person search via multi-granularity embedding learning. In: IJCAI (2021)
12. Chen, Y., Zhang, G., Lu, Y., Wang, Z., Zheng, Y.: TIPCB: a simple but effective part-based convolutional baseline for text-based person search. Neurocomputing (2022)
13. Sun, Y., Zheng, L., Yang, Y., Tian, Q., Wang, S.: Beyond part models: person retrieval with refined part pooling (and a strong convolutional baseline). In: Ferrari, V., Hebert, M., Sminchisescu, C., Weiss, Y. (eds.) ECCV 2018. LNCS, vol. 11208, pp. 501–518. Springer, Cham (2018). https://doi.org/10.1007/978-3-030-01225-0_30
14. Vaswani, A., et al.: Attention is all you need. In: Advances in Neural Information Processing Systems 30 (2017)
15. He, K., Zhang, X., Ren, S., Sun, J.: Deep residual learning for image recognition. In: Proceedings of the IEEE Conference on Computer Vision and Pattern Recognition, pp. 770–778 (2016)
16. Srinivas, A., Lin, T.Y., Parmar, N., Shlens, J., Abbeel, P., Vaswani, A.: Bottleneck transformers for visual recognition. In: Proceedings of the IEEE/CVF Conference on Computer Vision and Pattern Recognition, pp. 16519–16529 (2021)
17. Devlin, J., Chang, M.W., Lee, K., Toutanova, K.: BERT: pre-training of deep bidirectional transformers for language understanding. arXiv preprint arXiv:1810.04805 (2018)
18. Wang, G., Yuan, Y., Chen, X., Li, J., Zhou, X.: Learning discriminative features with multiple granularities for person re-identification. In: Proceedings of the 26th ACM International Conference on Multimedia, pp. 274–282 (2018)
19. Zhao, H., et al.: Spindle net: person re-identification with human body region guided feature decomposition and fusion. In: Proceedings of the IEEE Conference on Computer Vision and Pattern Recognition, pp. 1077–1085 (2017)
20. Song, G., Leng, B., Liu, Y., Hetang, C., Cai, S.: Region-based quality estimation network for large-scale person re-identification. In: Proceedings of the AAAI Conference on Artificial Intelligence, vol. 32 (2018)
21. Kalayeh, M.M., Basaran, E., Gökmen, M., Kamasak, M.E., Shah, M.: Human semantic parsing for person re-identification. In: Proceedings of the IEEE Conference on Computer Vision and Pattern Recognition, pp. 1062–1071 (2018)
22. Fu, Y., et al.: Horizontal pyramid matching for person re-identification. In: Proceedings of the AAAI Conference on Artificial Intelligence, vol. 33, pp. 8295–8302 (2019)
23. Gao, C., et al.: Contextual non-local alignment over full-scale representation for text-based person search. arXiv preprint arXiv:2101.03036 (2021)

24. Chen, T., Xu, C., Luo, J.: Improving text-based person search by spatial matching and adaptive threshold. In: 2018 IEEE Winter Conference on Applications of Computer Vision (WACV), pp. 1879–1887. IEEE (2018)
25. Wu, Y., Yan, Z., Han, X., Li, G., Zou, C., Cui, S.: LapsCore: language-guided person search via color reasoning. In: Proceedings of the IEEE/CVF International Conference on Computer Vision, pp. 1624–1633 (2021)

Deliberate Multi-Attention Network for Image Captioning

Zedong Dan[1,3] and Yanmei Fang[2,3(✉)]

[1] School of Computer Science and Engineering, Sun Yat-sen University,
Guangzhou 510000, Guangdong, People's Republic of China
danzd@mail2.sysu.edu.cn
[2] School of Cyber Science and Technology, Sun Yat-sen University,
Shenzhen 518107, Guangdong, People's Republic of China
fangym@mail.sysu.edu.cn
[3] Guangdong Key Laboratory of Information Security Technology,
Guangzhou, China

Abstract. An image captioning method is usually combined with an attention mechanism, which performs more effectively than the one without it. However, this method is still under performed compared with the artificial image captioning. For example, it may wrongly recognize the salient image objects, incorrectly or superficially understand the image objects, and mistakenly ignore the background information, which lead to the propagation and accumulation errors when generating sentences. One way that helps solve these problems is to adopt deliberate attention mechanism in image captioning. This paper proposes a deliberate multi-attention network (DMAN) model with multi-modal mechanism. This mechanism generates the image captions by combining the information from texts, visual sentinel and attention information. The textual information comes from words through LSTM, the attention information is derived by another LSTM from extracted image features. Visual sentinel is derived from the first deliberate attention loop, and then integrated into the content vector, which is fused in the multi-modal generation step. Visual sentinel mechanism can adjust the ratio of the degree between text information and visual information in the generation step. With the deliberate multi-attention, the mechanism recognizes and understands the image salient objects more accurately, and thus it solves the propagation and accumulation errors. By evaluating with the MSCOCO dataset, the experimental results show that the proposed DMAN model is overall better than Bottom-Up-Top-Down model under four quantitative indicators. Compared with the previous deliberate attention model, DMAN model can pay attention to more detailed part of the image and generate better captioning results.

Keywords: Image captioning · Multi-Attention Network · Multi-modal

S. Yu et al. (Eds.): PRCV 2022, LNCS 13534, pp. 475–487, 2022.
https://doi.org/10.1007/978-3-031-18907-4_37

1   Introduction

Image captioning is a challenging topic. In this task, it not only needs to detect salient objects from images, but also to understand the relationships among objects and to describe them in text across image and text modalities. At the early age of using neural network to deal with image captioning, Mao et al. [15] propose a multi-modal recurrent neural network (mRNN). It is viewed as one of the classic frames of image captioning. Their network integrates the word textual information obtained by two embedding layers, the sentence textual information obtained by the RNN which takes word textual information as an input, and the image information which is obtained from the AlexNet seventh layer to predict the next word. Delvin et al. [5] show that the conventional search-based methods can get similar or even better outcomes compared with the mRNN method. They propose a k-nearest neighbors method that searches k most similar images in MSCOCO 2014 dataset and summarizes the caption from artificial annotated captions of these k images. It shows that the essence of the mRNN method is to generate captions similar to the captions in a training set.

Vinyals et al. [22] propose a classic neural image captioning model which firstly bases on an encoder-decoder frame. In their network, the RNN not only deals with the textual information but also the image information. It can be used as a direct generator of image captioning. The encoder in their network is GoogLeNet, which extracts image features, and the decoder is the long short-term memory network (LSTM). Later, researchers [18,19] show that the models using multi-modal frame can get better outcomes and they suggest treating the textual information and the image information independently in the RNN.

Attention mechanism is firstly introduced to image captioning by Xu et al. [23]. They propose two attention mechanisms, the soft attention mechanism and the hard attention mechanism. The former uses similarity scores between image features and LSTM hidden layer state to weight image features. The latter only pays attention to one position sampled by the weights as probabilities, and uses Monte Carlo method to estimate the gradient. Both attention mechanisms can greatly improve the outcome and the hard attention mechanism performs better. Later, researchers have proposed various attention mechanism [13,14,20,24,25]. We only focus on the adaptive attention mechanism or so-called visual sentinel proposed by Lu et al. [13]. In their work, words are divided into two groups: visual words and non-visual words. According to the structure details of LSTM, they design a visual sentinel and use it when generating context vector in attention module. Visual sentinel can adaptively focus more on the language information or the visual information to improve the outcomes.

Anderson et al. [1] propose a bottom-up-top-down attention model and they are the first one using region-based image features in image captioning. They use Faster Region-Convolutional Neural Network (Faster R-CNN) to extract image features instead of the conventional convolutional neural network (CNN), the latter generates grid-based image features. They win the first place of the 2017 VIA challenge. Lu et al. [12] explore using neural network in the conventional template-based method. They use the visual sentinel to generate caption templates dynamically and use the visual information in region-based image features to generate visual words.

However, image captioning using RNN has several drawbacks. Once the previous word is incorrectly generated, it is likely that the following words will pass the error. To solve this problem, some works use generative adversarial network (GAN) [10] instead of LSTM to generate captions. While some works introduce reinforcement learning methods to image captioning, for example, the self critical sentence training (SCST) [17] method. Deliberate attention network (DA) [7] can also help solving the problem. Two LSTMs are used in their network, the first one is to generate the rough sentence and the second one is to modify and generate a better sentence using a visual sentinel. This model needs a large amount of parameters, and it only can attend twice.

Du [6] propose a Two-LSTM Merge model which also has the effect of deliberate attention. This work adopt the multi-modal frame and attend for several times through attention loops while not increasing parameters complexity. Under widely used quantitative indicators for image captioning, it gets better outcomes compared with the DA model. But it ignores discrimination of non-visual words from visual words. In this paper, the proposed model DMAN bases on a multi-modal frame which may get better outcomes compared with the encoder-decoder frame. It uses the attention loop trick and adds the visual sentinel to the network. And it can be divided into three parts: the language module, the attention module and the sentinel & generation module. Figure 1 shows the overview structure of the proposed DMAN model.

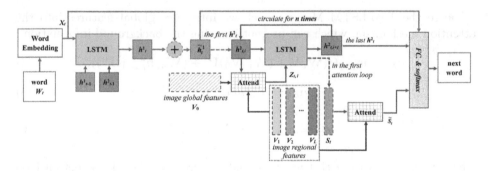

Fig. 1. An illustration of Multi-modal Deliberate Multi-Attention Network. The components in orange correspond to members of language module. Image features are shown in blue. The components of attention module and sentinel & generation module are in green, where the notation of sentinel is S_t. (Color figure online)

2 Multi-modal Deliberate Multi-Attention Network

2.1 Language Module

In this module, we first perform an embedding operation on a one-hot word vector, which is, essentially, the dimension reduction, linearly mapping the sparse high-dimensional word vector into a low-dimensional word vector with higher information density.

$$\mathbf{x}_{t-1} = \mathbf{E}\mathbf{w}_{i-1}, \tag{1}$$

where $\mathbf{x}_{t-1} \in \mathcal{R}^l$ and it is the low-dimensional word vector at the last time step, then it will be fed into the language LSTM. $\mathbf{E}$ is a word embedding matrix and $\mathbf{w}_{i-1}$ is the one-hot word vector.

$$\mathbf{h}_t^1, \mathbf{c}_t^1 = LSTM(\mathbf{x}_{t-1}, \mathbf{h}_{t-1}^2, \mathbf{h}_{t-1}^1, \mathbf{c}_{t-1}^1), \tag{2}$$

$$\tilde{\mathbf{h}}_t^1 = \mathbf{W}_x\mathbf{x}_{t-1} + \mathbf{W}_{h_1}\mathbf{h}_t^1. \tag{3}$$

In Eq. 2, $\mathbf{h}_{t-1}^2 \in \mathcal{R}^d$ is the hidden layer state of attention LSTM at the previous time step. $\mathbf{h}_{t-1}^1 \in \mathcal{R}^d$ and $\mathbf{c}_{t-1}^1 \in \mathcal{R}^d$ are the hidden layer state and memory state of the language LSTM at the last time step, respectively. After that, the word vector and the initially generated hidden layer state are fused together through full connection as residual mechanism. In Eq. 3, $\mathbf{W}_x \in \mathcal{R}^{d \times l}$ and $\mathbf{W}_{h_1} \in \mathcal{R}^{d \times d}$ are the parameter matrices to be learned. In the process of training, the attention information and the partial generated words information can be known from the hidden layer state of the attention LSTM at the previous time step, which neutralizes the word information from teacher forcing and improves the generalization ability of the model.

2.2   Attention Module

Same to the Two-LSTM Merge model, we introduce global features into the attention mechanism, which can prevent ignoring the background information.

$$\mathbf{a}_{t,i} = w_{att1}^T(r(\mathbf{W}_v\mathbf{V} + (\mathbf{W}_{v_0}\mathbf{V}_0)\mathbf{I}^T + (\mathbf{W}_{h_2}\mathbf{h}_{t,i-1}^2)\mathbf{I}^T)), \tag{4}$$

$$\alpha_{t,i} = softmax(\mathbf{a}_{t,i}), \tag{5}$$

$$\mathbf{z}_{t,i} = \alpha_{t,i} \odot \mathbf{V} = \sum_{j=1}^{k} \alpha_{t,i,j}\mathbf{V}_j, \tag{6}$$

where t represents the t-th time step, and i represents the i-th attention loop at the t-th time step. In Eq. 4 and Eq. 6, $\mathbf{V} = [v_1, v_2, ..., v_k] \in \mathcal{R}^{m \times k}$ is the image regional features extracted by Faster R-CNN. In Eq. 4, $\mathbf{V}_0 \in \mathcal{R}^m$ is the global feature derived by ResNet101 or averaging over all $\mathbf{V}_j$s. $\mathbf{W}_{v_0}, \mathbf{W}_v \in \mathcal{R}^{n \times m}, \mathbf{W}_{h_2} \in \mathcal{R}^{n \times d}$ and $w_{att1} \in \mathcal{R}^n$ are parameters to be learned. $\mathbf{I} \in \mathcal{R}^k$. Every element in $\mathbf{I}$ is set to 1. $\mathbf{a}_{t,i} \in \mathcal{R}^k$. The activation function r used to obtain $\mathbf{a}_{t,i}$ is the ReLU function instead of the sigmoid function. The final output notated $\mathbf{z}_{t,i}$ in Eq. 6 is the attention-weighted image features. $\mathbf{z}_{t,i} \in \mathcal{R}^k$.

$$init : \mathbf{h}_{t,0}^2 = \mathbf{h}_t^1, \tag{7}$$

$$\mathbf{h}_{t,i}^2, \mathbf{c}_{t,i}^2 = LSTM(\mathbf{z}_{t,i}, \mathbf{h}_{t,i-1}^2, \mathbf{c}_{t,i-1}^2). \tag{8}$$

As shown in Eq. 7, at any time step, the initial hidden layer state of the attention LSTM is the hidden layer state of the upstream language LSTM through the residual mechanism. The attention module in the first attention loop also uses the hidden layer state of the language LSTM. After that, attention-weighted image features are fed into the attention LSTM. Like a normal LSTM, the initial memory state is the final memory state at the previous time step. Equation 8 is an attention loop, where i starts from 1. Here, the multiple attention loops have an ability to correct previous recognition errors of image objects or further 'see' more clearly about the image objects that have been recognized ambiguously.

2.3 Sentinel and Generation Module

Visual sentinel is derived at the first attention loop.

$$\mathbf{g}_t = \sigma(\mathbf{W}_{h_3}\mathbf{h}_t^1 + \mathbf{W}_z\mathbf{z}_{t,1}), \tag{9}$$

$$\mathbf{s}_t = \mathbf{g}_t \odot tanh(\mathbf{c}_{t,1}), \tag{10}$$

$$\widetilde{\mathbf{a}}_t = w_{att2}^T(r(\mathbf{W}_s\mathbf{s}_t + \mathbf{W}_{h_4}\mathbf{h}_{t,1}^2)), \tag{11}$$

$$\mathbf{a}_{t,2}, \mathbf{z}_{t,2} = f(\mathbf{V}_0, \mathbf{V}, \mathbf{h}_{t,1}^2), \tag{12}$$

$$\beta_t = softmax([\mathbf{a}_{t,2}; \widetilde{\mathbf{a}}_t])[k+1], \tag{13}$$

$$\widetilde{\mathbf{s}}_t = \beta_t\mathbf{s}_t + (1 - \beta_t)\mathbf{z}_{t,2}. \tag{14}$$

In Eq. 9, $\mathbf{g}_t \in \mathcal{R}^d$ is the visual sentinel gate, which is obtained by linearly transforming the initial hidden layer state of the attention LSTM $\mathbf{h}_t^1$ and the attention weighted image features $\mathbf{z}_{t,1}$ in the first attention loop, with the sigmoid activation function. $\mathbf{W}_{h_3} \in \mathcal{R}^{d \times d}$ and $\mathbf{W}_z \in \mathcal{R}^{d \times k}$ are parameters to be learned. The visual sentinel $\mathbf{s}_t \in \mathcal{R}^d$ is derived by calculating hadamard product $\odot$ between visual sentinel gate $\mathbf{g}_t$ and the memory state of attention LSTM $\mathbf{c}_{t,1}$ activated by the $tanh$ function in the first attention loop. The visual sentinel contains a lot of text information. We add it into the normal soft attention module as an extra vector. We calculate the similarity weight between the visual sentinel and the first hidden layer state of attention LSTM through a second attention network to get a sentinel attention vector $\widetilde{\mathbf{a}}_t$. $\widetilde{\mathbf{a}}_t \in \mathcal{R}^1$. $\mathbf{W}_s, \mathbf{W}_{h_4} \in \mathcal{R}^{n \times d}$ and $w_{att2} \in \mathcal{R}^n$ are parameters to be learned. The activation function in Eq. 11 is still ReLU function. At the same time, we get the attention vector $\mathbf{a}_{t,2}$ of the second attention loop through the soft attention mechanism. In Eq. 12, f represents the first mentioned attention mechanism network, and $\mathbf{a}_{t,2} \in \mathcal{R}^k$. We use softmax function to get weights for the two attention vectors mentioned above respectively, then use the weights to obtain a weighted-summation $\widetilde{\mathbf{s}}_t$ between the visual sentinel and the attention-weighted image features $\mathbf{z}_{t,2}$, as the output of visual sentinel module. Because $\widetilde{\mathbf{a}}_t$ is concanated following $\mathbf{a}_{t,2}$, the weight β_t is derived from the last element of the outcome of softmax function, as shown in Eq. 13.

At last, DMAN fuses the output of visual sentinel module, the hidden layer state of the language LSTM, and the final hidden layer state of attention LSTM to get the prediction of the next word.

$$\mathbf{p} = f_2(\mathbf{h}_t^1, \mathbf{h}_t^2, \widetilde{\mathbf{s}}_t), \tag{15}$$

where f_2 is a simple neural network. Two kinds of network are used here, the first one is just single full connection layer without any activation function. The second one is two full connection layers with a ReLU activation function in the end. The use of the output of the visual sentinel module increases the ability to generate non-visual words. And it also can decrease the information loss compared with using mean image features in the multi-modal fusion step. The outputs of softmax function are probabilities of words in a pre-generated dictionary, the word with highest probability is the next prediction.

2.4   Training Strategy

Firstly, we use maximum likelihood estimation (MLE) method for training. Equation 16 is the negative log-likelihood loss function of the model.

$$L_{CE}(\theta) = -\sum_{j=1}^{L} log(p_\theta(\mathbf{w}_j | \mathbf{w}_{j-1}, ..., \mathbf{w}_2, \mathbf{w}_1)), \tag{16}$$

where L represents the length of the sentence, p_θ is the notation of conditional probability, derived from Eq. 15. θ represents the parameters in DMAN model. $\mathbf{w}_j$ represents j-th generated word.

Then SCST reinforcement learning (RL) method is used to improve the outcome of MLE training. Equation 17 is the loss function for RL training.

$$L_{RL}(\theta) = -(R - B)\sum_{j=1}^{L} log(p_\theta(\mathbf{w}_j | \mathbf{w}_{j-1}, ..., \mathbf{w}_2, \mathbf{w}_1)), \tag{17}$$

where R is reward, B is baseline. In one iteration, the reward is the CIDEr score of the sampled caption and the baseline is the CIDEr score of caption that generated by a greedy policy, i.e., selecting the words that has the highest probabilities.

Meanwhile, in order to improve the generalization ability of the model, this paper uses scheduled sampling [2] when training. Part of the predicted words is used as an input to the model. This helps solving the error passing problem when generating word. However if we abandon using tearcher forcing, the generated captions may have grammar errors.

3   Experiments

3.1   Dataset and Implementation Details

In this paper, we use MSCOCO 2014 dataset [3] to train, validate and test the model, and use the Karpathy division [8] to re-divide the training and validation sets. Training set has 113,287 images, whereas the validation set has 5,000 images and the test set has 5,000 images.

To generate the dictionary, we count the words in all sentences from the dataset and only retain those words which appear not less than 5 times. Words that appear less than 5 times are replaced by [UNK] (Unknown), then the words that meet the requirement are formed into the dictionary. We finally construct a dictionary of size 9,490. The maximum sentence length is set to 50. When generating words on training set, the initial word is set to [START]. The generation process ends up with [END]. We use [PAD] to align sentences of different lengths.

Fixed-36 image features extracted by Anderson et al. are used in the model. The dimension of the image features is 2048. We remove the last two layers of the ResNet101 network and add an adaptive average pooling layer to obtain the ResNet-based image global features. The image global feature dimension is 2048.

In the proposed DMAN model, dimension of hidden layer state of the two LSTMs is 1024, and the word vector dimension is 512. For the generation of word vectors, we use the pre-trained Global Vectors for Word Repretation (GloVe) 300-dimensional embedding layer parameters to obtain a 300-dimensional word vector, and then convert it into a 512-dimensional word vector through a linear full connection layer which is randomly initialized by a normal distribution. Subsequent gradient descent is not performed on this linear full connection layer. The hidden layer dimension in the attention mechanism module is 512. When training the model, we use the Adaptive time step Estimation (Adam) algorithm [9]. The batch size is set to be 128. We validate the model on the validation set every 1250 batches in an epoch, and save it when the CIDEr score improves. The model is also saved at the end of each epoch. For MLE training, we train the model for at least 30 epochs and stop training if the CIDEr score is not improving for 3 epochs. We initialize the learning rate as 5×10^{-4} and decrease it exponentially by 0.8 in every 3 epochs. For SCST training, we set the starting checkpoint as the checkpoint with the best CIDEr score in the first 30 epochs of MLE training. We set the learning rate as 5×10^{-5} and set the epoch amount as 70.

The initial sampling probability of scheduled sampling is 0, and it will increase by 5% every 3 epochs, and it will stop increasing until 25%. Beam search is used for testing, and the beam size is 5. The attention times is set as 2 for both training and testing.

3.2 Quantitative Analysis

We use four quantitative indicators, i.e., BLEU-4 [16], METEOR [4], ROUGE [11] and CIDEr [21] to evaluate the outcomes of the model. For MLE training, the proposed DMAN model is overall better than the models before Bottom-Up-Top-Down model in these matrices. And it has 0.84% BLEU-4, 0.36% ROUGE and 0.63% CIDEr increases compared with the DA model's results. It get a higher BLEU-4 score than Two-LSTM Merge model. The DMAN model here

Table 1. The results of the model in this paper and the results of various classical methods under MLE training. The outcomes of Two-LSTM Merge model is the outcomes whose attention times set as 2 for both training and testing.

Method	BLEU-4	METEOR	ROUGE	CIDEr
m-RNN [15]	0.190	0.228	–	0.842
Google NIC [22]	0.183	0.237	–	0.855
Soft Attention [23]	0.243	0.239	–	–
Semantic Attention [25]	0.304	0.243	0.535	0.943
Visual Sentinel [13]	0.332	0.266	–	1.085
Neural Baby Talk [12]	0.349	0.274	–	1.089
Bottom-Up-Top-Down [1]	0.362	0.270	0.564	1.135
Deliberate Attention [7]	0.357	0.274	0.562	1.119
Two-LSTM Merge [6]	0.359	0.278	0.567	1.134
DMAN	0.360	0.272	0.564	1.126

Table 2. The results of the model in this paper and the results of various classical methods under RL training. The outcomes of Two-LSTM Merge model is the outcomes whose attention times set as 2 for both training and testing.

Method	BLEU-4	METEOR	ROUGE	CIDEr
SCST [17]	0.313	0.260	0.543	1.013
Bottom-Up-Top-Down [1]	0.363	0.277	0.569	1.201
Deliberate Attention [7]	0.375	0.285	0.582	1.256
Two-LSTM Merge [6]	0.377	0.283	0.582	1.252
DMAN	0.375	0.278	0.580	1.236

uses the ResNet-based image global features and single full connection layer in generation module (Tables 1 and 2).

For RL training, the results of the proposed DMAN model is overall better than Bottom-Up-Top-Down model, with 3.3% BLEU-4, 0.36% METEOR, 1.9% ROUGE and 2.9% CIDEr increases. And the results is near the results of the DA model and the Two-LSTM Merge model. The DMAN model here use image global features derived by averaging bottom-up features, and uses two full connection layers with a ReLU activation function to generate words.

3.3 Qualitative Analysis

We adopt the images used in papers of Two-LSTM Merge model and the DA model to compare results more conveniently. In picture(a) of Fig. 2, when attention times is one, the model can only attend the cat and the chair. After second attention, the model recognize the table and find the relationship between table and the cat. This result is the same to the result of the Two-LSTM Merge model.

attend for 1 time: a cat sitting on top of a chair
attend for 2 times: a cat sitting on a chair next to a table
human annotation: a cat sitting in a chair at a table with a book on it
Two-LSTM Merge: a cat sitting in a chair next to a table

attend for 1 time: a group of people riding bikes down a street
attend for 2 times: a group of people riding bikes down a city street
human annotation: a group of people are riding bikes down the street in a bike lane
Two-LSTM Merge: a group of people riding bikes down a street

attend for 1 time: a traffic light tower with a clock tower with a
attend for 2 times: a traffic light with a clock on top of a building
human annotation: a tower with a clock on it in front of a street light
Two-LSTM Merge: a traffic light in front of a tall tower

attend for 1 time: a piece of cake on a plate with a cup
attend for 2 times: a piece of cake on a plate with a cup of coffee
human annotation: a piece of cake and a cup of coffee are sitting on plates
DA: a piece of cake on a plate with a cup of coffee

attend for 1 time: a statue of a clock tower with a on it
attend for 2 times: a statue of a man with a clock tower
human annotation: A clock tower with a statue on top of it
DA: a clock tower with a statue on top of it

attend for 1 time: a group of colorful umbrellas hanging from a market
attend for 2 times: a large umbrella is sitting in a market
human annotation: A row of different colored umbrellas sitting next to each other
DA: a blue umbrella sitting in front of a market

Fig. 2. The captioning results of our model in different attention times, and we make a comparison with the captioning results of Two-LSTM Merge model and DA model. The attention times here is the times that set for testing.

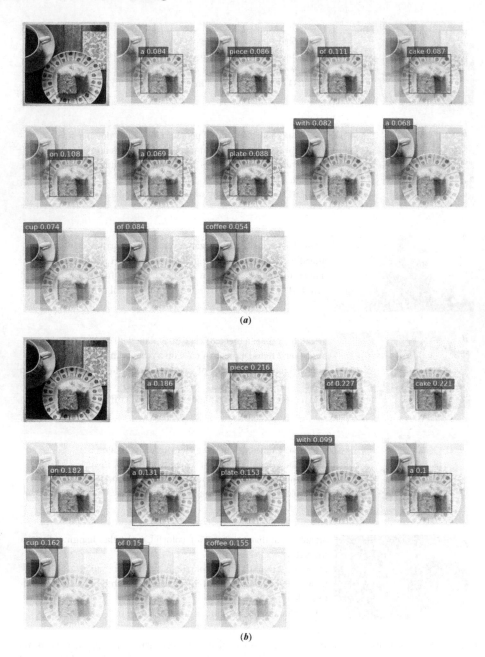

Fig. 3. Visualization of the first attention (**a**) and the second attention (**b**). The generated caption for this photo is 'a piece of cake on a plate with a cup of coffee'.

But it still has a small disparity compared with human annotation, the model does not see the book on the table. For picture(b), the result of the first attention is the same to the result of the Two-LSTM Merge model, while the second attention embellishes the word 'street' with 'city'. For picture(c), the second attention corrects the grammer mistake in the result of the first attention, the visual sentinel is functioning. Compared with the result of Two-LSTM Merge model, the DMAN model recognize the tall tower is a clock tower. The result of DMAN model is almost the same with human annotation. For picture(d), the second attention recognizes the coffee in the cup. The result is almost the same with the human annotation. For picture(e), the second attention corrects the grammer mistakes and recognizes the statue is a human statue. More accurately, it should recognize the statue as a woman statue not a man statue, but this is still an improvement. Compared with the DA model, the DMAN model pays attention to more detailed part of the image in this case. For picture(f), the first attention has a larger horizontal view and recognizes the several colourful umbrellas, while the second attention just focuses on the largest one. The result of the first attention is most similar to human annotation. In general, same with the Two-LSTM Merge model and the DA model, the DMAN model has the ability to correct mistakes and 'see' more clearly when captioning, and it can get better results and has sharper 'eyes'. But it has few cases that the model is too focusing on the details to recognize the surrounding objects. Meanwhile, it has the ability to add or change embellishment words and generate diverse sentences.

In Fig. 3, we find out that in the first attention loop, the model already can attend all salient regions and objects of the picture. When it secondly attends, the attention weights of the salient regions are higher and the rectangle attention areas corresponding to the salient regions are more accurate. This answers why the deliberate multi-attention can recognize objects more clearly and correctly.

4   Conclusions

In this paper, we propose a deliberate multi-attention network model with a multi-modal mechanism, by introducing the visual sentinel into a multi-modal frame and improving the language LSTM, based on the Two-LSTM Merge model. The input of the language LSTM is guided by the hidden layer state of the attention LSTM at the previous time step. Meanwhile, in order to prevent the loss of word text information, a residual mechanism is introduced. The initial hidden layer state of language LSTM is fully connected with the word vector. Then use the adjusted hidden layer state as the initial hidden layer state of the attention LSTM at this time step. The model performs multiple attentions through the attention loops. An attention loop first generates attention-weighted image features, i.e., context vector, through the soft attention mechanism, then input the attention-weighted image features into the attention LSTM. The visual sentinel is generated in the first loop. When generating the next word, a multi-modal fusion is performed on the hidden layer state of language LSTM, the final hidden layer state of attention LSTM and the visual sentinel module's output. The visual sentinel mechanism can adjust the proportion of visual information and non-visual information in the final multi-modal fusion, and at the same time play the role of residual mechanism to a certain extent, preventing the loss of information in the attention loops. The experiments show that the proposed DMAN model is overall better than the models previous to the Bottom-Up-Top-Down model and the Bottom-Up-Top-Down model under four quantitative indicators. The quantitative scores of DMAN model are closed to previous deliberate attention models, while DMAN model can focus on more detailed parts of the image and generate a better caption. DMAN model has the ability to self-correct and modify the embellishment words, generating more accurate and diverse captions.

Acknowledgements. The authors would like to thank the support of the Opening Project of Guangdong Province Key Laboratory of Information Security Technology (Grant No. 2020B1212060078).

References

1. Anderson, P., et al.: Bottom-up and top-down attention for image captioning and visual question answering. In: Proceedings of the IEEE Conference on Computer Vision and Pattern Recognition, pp. 6077–6086 (2018)
2. Bengio, S., Vinyals, O., Jaitly, N., Shazeer, N.: Scheduled sampling for sequence prediction with recurrent neural networks. In: Advances in Neural Information Processing Systems, vol. 28, pp. 1171–1179 (2015)
3. Chen, X., et al.: Microsoft COCO captions: data collection and evaluation server. arXiv preprint arXiv:1504.00325 (2015)
4. Denkowski, M., Lavie, A.: Meteor universal: language specific translation evaluation for any target language. In: Proceedings of the Ninth Workshop on Statistical Machine Translation at ACL, vol. 6, pp. 376–380 (2014)
5. Devlin, J., et al.: Language models for image captioning: the quirks and what works. arXiv preprint arXiv:1505.01809 (2015)
6. Du, J.: Image captioning based on attention mechanism (2020). https://doi.org/10.27307/d.cnki.gsjtu.2020.001012
7. Gao, L., Fan, K., Song, J., Liu, X., Xu, X., Shen, H.T.: Deliberate attention networks for image captioning. In: Proceedings of the AAAI Conference on Artificial Intelligence, vol. 33, pp. 8320–8327 (2019)
8. Karpathy, A., Fei-Fei, L.: Deep visual-semantic alignments for generating image descriptions. In: Proceedings of the IEEE Conference on Computer Vision and Pattern Recognition, pp. 3128–3137 (2015)
9. Kingma, D., Ba, J.: Adam: a method for stochastic optimization. In: International Conference on Learning Representations (2014)
10. Lamb, A.M., Alias Parth Goyal, A.G., Zhang, Y., Zhang, S., Courville, A.C., Bengio, Y.: Professor forcing: a new algorithm for training recurrent networks. In: Advances in Neural Information Processing Systems, vol. 29, pp. 4608–4616 (2016)
11. Lin, C.Y.: ROUGE: a package for automatic evaluation of summaries. In: Proceedings of the Workshop on Text Summarization Branches Out at ACL, pp. 74–81 (2004)

12. Lu, J., Yang, J., Batra, D., Parikh, D.: Neural baby talk. In: Proceedings of the IEEE Conference on Computer Vision and Pattern Recognition, pp. 7219–7228 (2018)
13. Lu, J., Xiong, C., Parikh, D., Socher, R.: Knowing when to look: adaptive attention via a visual sentinel for image captioning. In: Proceedings of the IEEE Conference on Computer Vision and Pattern Recognition, pp. 375–383 (2017)
14. Luong, M.T., Pham, H., Manning, C.D.: Effective approaches to attention-based neural machine translation. arXiv preprint arXiv:1508.04025 (2015)
15. Mao, J., Xu, W., Yang, Y., Wang, J., Yuille, A.L.: Explain images with multimodal recurrent neural networks. arXiv preprint arXiv:1410.1090 (2014)
16. Papineni, K., Roukos, S., Ward, T., Zhu, W.J.: BLEU: a method for automatic evaluation of machine translation. In: Proceedings of the 40th Annual Meeting of the Association for Computational Linguistics, pp. 311–318 (2002)
17. Rennie, S.J., Marcheret, E., Mroueh, Y., Ross, J., Goel, V.: Self-critical sequence training for image captioning. In: Proceedings of the IEEE Conference on Computer Vision and Pattern Recognition, pp. 7008–7024 (2017)
18. Tanti, M., Gatt, A., Camilleri, K.: What is the role of recurrent neural networks (RNNs) in an image caption generator? In: Proceedings of the 10th International Conference on Natural Language Generation, pp. 51–60 (2017)
19. Tanti, M., Gatt, A., Camilleri, K.P.: Where to put the image in an image caption generator. Nat. Lang. Eng. 24(3), 467–489 (2018)
20. Vaswani, A., et al.: Attention is all you need. In: Advances in Neural Information Processing Systems, pp. 6000–6010 (2017)
21. Vedantam, R., Zitnick, C.L., Parikh, D.: CIDEr: consensus-based image description evaluation. In: 2015 IEEE Conference on Computer Vision and Pattern Recognition, pp. 4566–4575 (2015)
22. Vinyals, O., Toshev, A., Bengio, S., Erhan, D.: Show and tell: a neural image caption generator. In: Proceedings of the IEEE Conference on Computer Vision and Pattern Recognition, pp. 3156–3164 (2015)
23. Xu, K., et al.: Show, attend and tell: neural image caption generation with visual attention. In: International Conference on Machine Learning, pp. 2048–2057 (2015)
24. Yang, Z., He, X., Gao, J., Deng, L., Smola, A.: Stacked attention networks for image question answering. In: Proceedings of the IEEE Conference on Computer Vision and Pattern Recognition, pp. 21–29 (2016)
25. You, Q., Jin, H., Wang, Z., Fang, C., Luo, J.: Image captioning with semantic attention. In: Proceedings of the IEEE Conference on Computer Vision and Pattern Recognition, pp. 4651–4659 (2016)

CTFusion: Convolutions Integrate with Transformers for Multi-modal Image Fusion

Zhengwen Shen, Jun Wang$^{(\boxtimes)}$, Zaiyu Pan, Jiangyu Wang, and Yulian Li

School of Information and Control Engineering, China University of Mining and Technology, Xuzhou 221000, China
jrobot@126.com

Abstract. In this paper, we propose a novel pseudo-end-to-end Pre-training multi-model image fusion network, termed CTFusion, to take advantage of convolution operations and vision transformer for multi-modal image fusion. Unlike existing pre-trained models that are based on public datasets, which contain two stages of training with a single input and a fusion strategy designed manually, our method is a simple single-stage pseudo-end-to-end model that uses a dual input adaptive fusion method and can be tested directly. Specifically, the fusion network first adopts a dual dense convolution network to obtain the abundant semantic information, and then the feature map is converted to a token and fed into a multi-path transformer fusion block to model the global-local information of sources images. Finally, we obtain the fusion image by a followed convolutional neural network block. Extensive experiments have been carried out on two publicly available multi-modal datasets, experiment results demonstrate that the proposed model outperforms state-of-the-art methods.

Keywords: Multi-modal image · Transformer · Dense convolution network · Multi-path transformer fusion

1 Introduction

Multi-modal image fusion is a important task in computer vision and wide application in many field, such as RGB-D image fusion [1], infrared and visible image fusion [2], medical image fusion [3]. With the development of deep learning, convolutional neural networks (CNNs) have long been dominated for modeling in computer vision tasks, many image fusion approaches based on deep learning are proposed to focus on overcoming the limitations of traditional methods.

Image fusion method based on deep learning is also divided into two categories: pre-training model [2,4] and end-to-end model [5–9]. Due to lack of training datasets, methods based on the pre-training model tend to adopt the large public datasets of other fields as the training data, the pre-trained network as an encoder network to extract the feature of source images, then fusion the obtained feature manually design the fusion strategy, the fusion image is obtained by the decoder network. On the other hand, the end-to-end model expands the dataset by local cropping of the few source images to obtain a large number of small patch images and realizes the amplification of the data. However, the pre-training model extracts each source image feature through the same pre-training network, lack the learning capable of inter-connectedness information of source image, and need more manual design strategy for the feature fusion, the end-to-end methods via expanding the training dataset by data augmentation are generally to the specific tasks and lack generalization.

To over the mentioned drawback, in this paper, we propose a new structure, CTFusion is a hybrid network structure, the whole network structure is divided into three parts: the dual traditional convolutional neural network block, a multi-path transformer fusion block for fusing the previous output, and the decoder block. First, a convolutional neural network block is used to extract the semantic information from the source image. Second, the multi-path transformer fusion block makes full use of the advantages of the self-attention and local attention mechanism in capturing global-local information and establishing corresponding of sources image. Finally, we obtain the fusion image by a followed decoder consisting of convolutional neural networks.

The proposed model is applied to various image fusion tasks. Our experimental results show that the proposed pseudo end-to-end training model achieves better performance, compared with state-of-the-art methods. Generally, our contributions are summarized as follows:

- We propose a novel pseudo end-to-end image fusion structure to effectively fuse multi-modal images, which is a dual-input pre-trained network with an adaptive fusion module and it consist of convolutional neural networks and vision transformers.
- We design a new multi-path transformer fusion block to fusion the multi-modal information to obtain the previous convolutional layers, it can capture the global-local information and adaptive fusion.
- Extensive experiments on different datasets validate the superiority of the proposed model, it is successfully applied to multi-modal image fusion with superior performance against the state-of-the-art methods.

2   Related Work

2.1   Convolutional and Attention Mechanisms

In the image fusion task, a dense convolution network is widely used in feature extraction. Li incorporates the dense block into the encoding network, preserving the useful information from the middle layers [2]. Ma proposed a novel GAN framework for image fusion and the architecture of the generator is based on densenet [8]. In addition, the advance in attention mechanisms improves the efficiency of image information extraction and has achieved good performance in

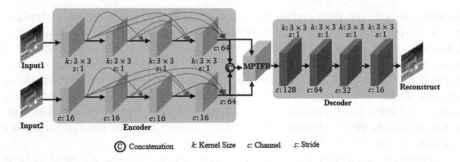

Fig. 1. The architecture of proposed method.

computer tasks, such as Squeeze-and-Excitation Networks [10], Non-local neural network [11]. There has been a great improvement in the local characteristics of the image and capture the of global information. Inspired by the advantage of attention mechanisms, we combine global attention with local attention to capture the feature information of source images.

2.2 Vision Transformer

With the introduction of the Transformer, it is first used in natural language processing (NLP) and has a great success [12]. Recently, with Vision Transformer (ViT) being first proposed and achieve state-of-the-art performance on image classification [13], it is widely used on various computer vision task and perform excellent performance on a number of visual tasks, such as classification, segmentation [14], multi-modal [15], video processing and object detection [16], etc. However, the transformer also has some disadvantages, focusing too much on global information and ignoring certain local important information. As a result, more researchers are also focusing on how to better integrate the CNN network with a transformer to complement each other's strengths [17]. Inspired by the advantage of convolutional neural networks and vision transformers, we try to combine convolutional neural networks with the transformer in the image fusion task to better capture the local and global information from source images.

3   Method

As shown in Fig. 1, we designed a dual branch encoder network structure to reconstruct the image, and the entire training network contains three parts: encoder, Multi-path Transformer Fusion Block (MPTFB), and decoder. In the encoder, we adopt a dual branch encoder consisting of a dense block. In the fusion block, we design a multi-path transformer fusion block, which consist of two local attention blocks and a cross transformer block. In the encoder, it contains four convolutional layers (3×3 filters).

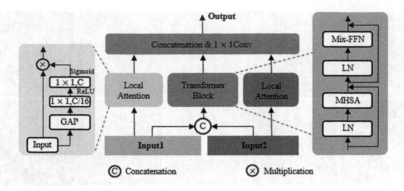

Fig. 2. Architecture of multi-path transformer fusion block.

3.1 Early Convolutions Block

Compared to the pure transformer structure, early convolutions not only help transformers see better but also capture more local information used to supplement the global information obtain from vision transformer [18]. Therefore, we adopt a dual common dense convolutional block and finally obtain 128 channels feature maps to feed into multi-path transformer fusion block.

3.2 Multi-path Transformer Fusion Block

As shown in Fig. 2, the multi-path transformer fusion block consist of three modules: local attention, transformer, and concatenation block. The multi-head self-attention mechanism is designed to better capture global corresponding information for multi-modal images, the features obtained from the previous convolutional neural network require serialization, which divides the image into several patches before entering into the transformer module. The transformer module mainly consists of layer norm (LN), multi-head self-attention layer (MHSA), and multi-layer perception (MLP). In the transformer module, LayerNorm is used before MHSA and MLP, and a residual structure is added to the MHSA and MLP outputs, respectively. Unlike the Vit needs positional encoding (PE) to introduce the location information, we introduce the effect of zero padding to leak location information by directly using a Mix-feed-forward network (Mix-FFN) [19]. At the same time, in order to effectively obtain the local feature information of the sources image, we adopt the local attention and parallel concatenation with the transformer output and following a 1×1 convolutional to aggregation the obtain information.

3.3 Loss Function

In this paper, we adopt Mean Square Error (MSE) loss Structural Similarity ($SSIM$) loss L_{ssim} as the reconstruction loss for our framework. The MSE loss emphasizes the matching of each corresponding pixel between the input image

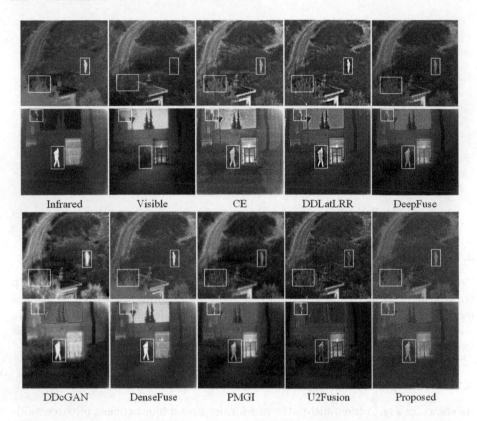

Infrared	Visible	CE	DDLatLRR	DeepFuse

| DDcGAN | DenseFuse | PMGI | U2Fusion | Proposed |

Fig. 3. Comparison result of infrared and visible image fusion of TNO datasets. From left to right: infrared image, visible image, the results of CE, DDLatLRR, DeepFuse, DDcGAN, DenseFuse, PMGI, U2Fusion and CTFusion (ours).

and output image, and $SSIM$ loss is an index to measure the similarity of two images, the larger the value, the better, the maximum is 1. Generally, if the value is 1, then the fused image retains more structural details of input images. Similarly, we build the same loss for different input images. The MSE loss, $SSIM$ loss, Total loss are calculated as Eq. 1, Eq. 2, Eq. 3:

$$L_{mse} = \|I_1 - I\|_2^2 + \|I_2 - I\|_2^2 \tag{1}$$

where I denotes the input source image, I_f denotes the fused image, $\|\cdot\|_2^2$ denotes the l_2 normal.

$$L_{ssim} = (1 - SSIM(O, I))_1 + (1 - SSIM(O, I))_2 \tag{2}$$

where I denotes the input source image, O denotes the fused image, $SSIM(\cdot)$ denotes the measures structural similarity.

$$L_{total} = L_{mse} + \lambda L_{ssim} \tag{3}$$

where $\lambda_{(.)}$ denotes the contribution of each loss to the whole objective function, λ is equal to 10.

4 Experiment

4.1 Experimental Settings

Dataset: In our experiment, we adopt MS-COCO dataset [20] as the training dataset, the 80,000 pairs of MS-COCO data set from RGB image to a grayscale image, and resize to 256×256. We adopt two publicly datasets for testing: TNO datasets for visible and infrared image fusion task; MRI (Magnetic Resonance Imaging) and PET (Positron emission tomography) datasets for medical image fusion task.

Implementation Details: In the training phase, we adopt SGD optimizer and set the batch size, learning rate, and epoch equal to 4, 10^{-4}, 5, respectively. The proposed method was implemented on NVIDIA GEFORCE RTX 2080 Ti GPU and based on Pytorch.

4.2 Infrared and Visible Image Fusion

In the infrared and visible image fusion experiment, we compared the experiments with twelve current performance SOTA methods, CE [21], MDLatLRR [7], DeepFuse [4], DDcGAN [8], DenseFuse [2], PMGI [6], U2Fusion [5].

Table 1. Average fusion results on quantitative comparisons of infrared and visible image by five metrics.

Methods	FMI	SCD	Nabf	CC	SSIM
CE	**0.8934**	1.5820	0.2955	0.0755	0.6354
DDlatLRR	0.8915	**1.6196**	0.3478	0.1218	0.6507
DeepFuse	0.8916	1.5587	**0.0629**	**0.1584**	0.6794
DDcGAN	0.8627	1.4090	0.3009	0.0006	0.5808
DenseFuse	0.8959	1.6051	0.1094	0.0982	**0.6886**
PMGI	0.8701	1.5706	0.1020	0.1125	0.6776
U2Fusion	0.8740	1.6185	0.2548	0.1025	0.6595
CTFusion	0.8873	1.6294	0.0096	0.1611	0.7423

Quantitative Analysis: As shown in Fig. 3, two typical scene fusion results are selected. Visible from the global semantic characteristics of the fusion image, the proposed method retains the necessary radiation information of the infrared image, and the infrared image information exists as a whole. Similarly, there is also visible image information, the semantic characteristics of local information, our proposed method is more effective in highlighting local detail information.

It is demonstrated that our proposed model can better reconstruct the detail and the local significance information.

Quantitative Analysis: We adopt five related indicators to compare the existing methods, pixel feature mutual information (FMI_{pixel}) [22], sum of the correlations of differences (SCD) [23], structural similarity (SSIM) [24], the ratio of noise added to the final image (Nabf) [25], and correlation coefficient (CC) [26]. Quantitative results can be seen in Table 1, the red font in italic represents the best value and the bold black font in italic represents the second-best value. We can observe that our proposed method performer well in SCD, Nabf, CC, and SSIM metrics, it shows that the fusion image obtained by our method has a strong correlation with the source image and has little noise impact. In the FMI_{pixel} metric, the value is lower, but we can infer from Fig. 3, that the proposed method preserves more feature information and less noise impact.

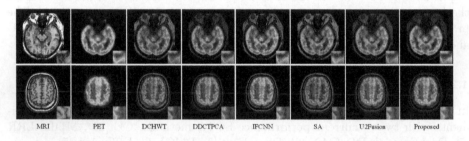

Fig. 4. Comparison result of MRI and PET image fusion. From left to right: MRI image, PET image, the results of DCHWT, DDCTPCA, IFCNN, Structure Aware (SA), U2Fusion and CTFusion (ours).

4.3   MRI and PET Image Fusion

In the MRI and PET image fusion experiment, we compare our proposed method with DCHWT [27], DDCTPCA [3], IFCNN [28], Structure Aware [29], U2 [5] by quantitative and qualitative evaluation metrics.

Quantitative Analysis: We select two typical brain hemisphere cross-axis partial fusion results to show. As shown Fig. 4, the red box highlights the intensity variation of PET colors and local detail in the fused image, it can be seen that the method proposed in this article in the MRI image semantic details of information has very good reservations, at the same time, the larger structure and the functionality of the PET images.

Quantitative Analysis: For the fusion of medical images, we adopt six related indicators to compare the existing methods, Nabf, SCD, standard deviation (SD), SSIM, CC, and no-reference image fusion performance measure (MS-SSIM) [30]. As shown in Table 2, we can observe that the proposed fusion method outperforms in SCD, SD, and CC metrics. In the Nabf, the result performance is better than other methods but DDCTPCA. We can infer from the results, the fusion image not only contain the largest amount information of source multimodal images, but has strong correlation with each source multi-modal image.

Table 2. Average fusion results on quantitative comparisons of MRI and PET image by six metrics.

Methods	Nabf	SCD	SD	SSIM	CC	MS-SSIM
DCHWT	0.2942	0.8318	85.6466	0.8242	0.7059	0.8756
DDCTPCA	0.0003	0.7866	85.5550	0.7835	**0.7256**	0.8815
IFCNN	0.0868	**0.9380**	90.6908	0.8015	0.7209	0.9138
SA	0.0275	0.5613	85.5202	**0.8206**	0.7237	0.8759
U2	0.0677	0.8064	84.0908	0.8017	0.3577	**0.8838**
CTFusion	**0.0266**	0.9560	91.1311	0.7677	0.7275	0.8832

4.4 Ablation Study

In this part, we take ablation experiments to verify the effectiveness of the method, which are compared with the addition and softmax fusion strategy respectively, and the hyper-parameter λ is also analyzed. Different from the existing image fusion network models based on the pre-training strategy, we design a pseudo-end-to-end multi-modal image fusion network and design an MPTFB module for an adaptive fusion of the multi-modal. In Table 3, compared with the softmax and add fusion strategies, the proposed method has a good performance on image fusion. As shown in Fig. 5, the results of the softmax fusion method focus more on infrared features and exist the phenomenon of loss of the local feature. To sum up, it can ensure that the proposed method can maintain the integrity and relevance of the source image effectively.

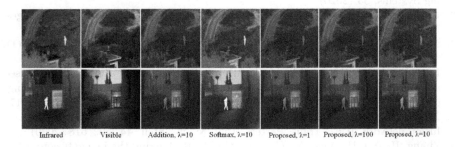

Infrared   Visible   Addition, λ=10   Softmax, λ=10   Proposed, λ=1   Proposed, λ=100   Proposed, λ=10

Fig. 5. Comparison result of ablation study.

Table 3. Average fusion results on quantitative comparisons of ablation study.

Methods	FMI	SCD	Nabf	CC	SSIM
Addition, $\lambda = 10$	**0.8900**	1.6098	0.0103	0.1086	0.7344
Softmax, $\lambda = 10$	0.8899	1.6227	0.0773	0.1002	0.6800
Proposed, $\lambda = 1$	0.8815	1.5442	0.0230	0.0661	0.7084
Proposed, $\lambda = 100$	0.8826	**1.6473**	0.1265	0.1590	0.7303
Proposed, $\lambda = 10$	0.8873	1.6294	**0.0096**	**0.1611**	**0.7423**

5   Conclusion

In this paper, We design a pseudo-end-to-end network framework to model the multi-modal image fusion task. Unlike previous methods, a dual-input pre-training strategy is adopted and the phases of manually designing fusion strategies are eliminated. To better learn the semantic features and effectively achieve image fusion, a dual-branch fusion network that combines a convolutional neural network with a vision transformer is proposed. Early convolution obtains richer semantic information and the proposed multi-path transformer fusion can capture global and local information. Through quantitative comparison and qualitative analysis, the proposed method has achieved better results than the most advanced fusion method.

Acknowledgments. This work was partially supported by the Scientific Innovation 2030 Major Project for New Generation of AI under Grant 2020AAA0107300.

References

1. Wang, Y.K., Huang, W.B., Sun, F.C., Xu, T.Y., Rong, Y., Huang, J.: Deep multi-modal fusion by channel exchanging. In: Advances in Neural Information Processing Systems, 33 (2020)
2. Li, H., Wu, X.J.: DenseFuse: a fusion approach to infrared and visible images. IEEE Trans. Image Process. **28**(5), 2614–2623 (2018)
3. Naidu, V.: Hybrid DDCT-PCA based multi sensor image fusion. J. Opt. **43**(1), 48–61 (2014)
4. Ram Prabhakar, K., Sai Srikar, V., Babu, R.: DeepFuse: a deep unsupervised approach for exposure fusion with extreme exposure image pairs. In: Proceedings of the IEEE International Conference on Computer Vision, pp. 4714–4722 (2017)
5. Xu, H., Ma, J., Jiang, J., Guo, X., Ling, H.: U2fusion: a unified unsupervised image fusion network. IEEE Trans. Pattern Anal. Mach. Intell. **44**, 502–518 (2020)
6. Zhang, H., Xu, H., Xiao, Y., Guo, X., Ma, J.: Rethinking the image fusion: a fast unified image fusion network based on proportional maintenance of gradient and intensity. In: Proceedings of the AAAI Conference on Artificial Intelligence, pp. 12797–12804 (2020)
7. Li, H., Wu, X.J., Kittler, J.: MDLatLRR: a novel decomposition method for infrared and visible image fusion. IEEE Trans. Image Process. **29**, 4733–4746 (2020)

8. Ma, J., Xu, H., Jiang, J., Mei, X., Zhang, X.P.: DDcGAN: a dual-discriminator conditional generative adversarial network for multi-resolution image fusion. IEEE Trans. Image Process. **29**, 4980–4995 (2020)
9. Zhang, H., Le, Z., Shao, Z., Xu, H., Ma, J.: MFF-GAN: an unsupervised generative adversarial network with adaptive and gradient joint constraints for multi-focus image fusion. Inf. Fusion **66**, 40–53 (2021)
10. Hu, J., Shen, L., Sun, G., Albanie, S.: Squeeze-and-excitation networks. IEEE Trans. Pattern Anal. Mach. Intell. **99** (2017)
11. Wang, X.L., Ross, G., Abhinav, G., He, K.: Non-local neural networks. In: Proceedings of the IEEE Conference on Computer Vision and Pattern Recognition, pp. 7794–7803 (2018)
12. Ashish, V., et al.: Attention is all you need. In: Proceedings of the Advances in Neural Information Processing Systems, pp. 5998–6008 (2017)
13. Dosovitskiy, A., et al.: An image is worth 16x16 words: transformers for image recognition at scale. In: International Conference on Learning Representations (2021)
14. Xie, E., et al.: SegFormer: simple and efficient design for semantic segmentation with transformers, in arXiv preprint arXiv:2105.15203 (2021)
15. Prakash, A., Chitta, K., Geiger, A.: Multi-modal fusion transformer for end-to-end autonomous driving. In: Proceedings of the IEEE/CVF Conference on Computer Vision and Pattern Recognition, pp. 7077–7087 (2021)
16. Carion, N., Massa, F., Synnaeve, G., Usunier, N., Kirillov, A., Zagoruyko, S.: End-to-end object detection with transformers. In: Vedaldi, A., Bischof, H., Brox, T., Frahm, J.-M. (eds.) ECCV 2020. LNCS, vol. 12346, pp. 213–229. Springer, Cham (2020). https://doi.org/10.1007/978-3-030-58452-8_13
17. Wu, H.P., et al.: CVT: Introducing convolutions to vision transformers. arXiv preprint arXiv:2103.15808 (2021)
18. Xiao, T., Dollar, P., Singh, M., Mintun, E., Darrell, T., Girshick, R.: Early convolutions help transformers see better. In: Thirty-Fifth Conference on Neural Information Processing Systems (2021)
19. Islam, Md.A., Jia, S., Bruce, N.D.B.: How much position information do convolutional neural networks encode? In: International Conference on Learning Representations (2020)
20. Lin, T.-Y., et al.: Microsoft COCO: common objects in context. In: Fleet, D., Pajdla, T., Schiele, B., Tuytelaars, T. (eds.) ECCV 2014. LNCS, vol. 8693, pp. 740–755. Springer, Cham (2014). https://doi.org/10.1007/978-3-319-10602-1_48
21. Zhou, Z., Dong, M., Xie, X., Gao, Z.: Fusion of infrared and visible images for night-vision context enhancement. Appl. Opt. **55**(23), 6480–6490 (2016)
22. Mohammad, H., Masoud Amirkabiri, R.: Fast-FMI: non-reference image fusion metric. In: 2014 IEEE 8th International Conference on Application of Information and Communication Technologies (AICT), pp. 1–3 (2014)
23. Aslantas, V., Bendes, E.: A new image quality metric for image fusion: the sum of the correlations of differences. AEU-Int. J. Electron. Commun. **69**(12), 1890–1896 (2015)
24. Wang, Z., Bovik, A.C., Sheikh, H.R., Simoncelli, E.P.: Image quality assessment: from error visibility to structural similarity. IEEE Trans. Image Process. **13**(4), 600–612 (2004)
25. Shreyamsha Kumar, B.K.: Multifocus and multispectral image fusion based on pixel significance using discrete cosine harmonic wavelet transform. SIViP **7**(6), 1125–1143 (2012). https://doi.org/10.1007/s11760-012-0361-x

26. Han, S.S., Li, H.T., Gu, H.Y., et al.: The study on image fusion for high spatial resolution remote sensing images. Int. Arch. Photogramm. Remote Sens. Spat. Inf. Sci. XXXVII Part B **7**, 1159–1164 (2008)
27. Kumar, B.S.: Multifocus and multispectral image fusion based on pixel significance using discrete cosine harmonic wavelet transform. Signal Image Video Process. **7**(6), 1125–1143 (2013)
28. Zhang, Y., Liu, Y., Sun, P., Yan, H., Zhao, X., Zhang, L.: IFCNN: a general image fusion framework based on convolutional neural network. Inf. Fusion **54**, 99–118 (2020)
29. Li, W., Xie, Y., Zhou, H., Han, Y., Zhan, K.: Structure-aware image fusion. Optik **172**, 1–11 (2018)
30. Ma, K., Zeng, K., Wang, Z.: Perceptual quality assessment for multi-exposure image fusion. IEEE Trans. Image Process. **24**(11), 3345–3356 (2015)

Heterogeneous Graph-Based Finger Trimodal Fusion

Yunhe Wang[1,2], Wenyu Zhang[1], and Jinfeng Yang[2(✉)]

[1] School of Computer Science and Software Engineering, University of Science and Technology Liaoning, Anshan, China
[2] Institute of Applied Artificial Intelligence of the Guangdong-Hong Kong-Macao Greater Bay Area, Shenzhen Polytechnic, Shenzhen, China
jfyang@szpt.edu.cn

Abstract. Multimodal graph fusion utilizes the modeling of weighted graph to combine information from multiple sources in order to improve recognition performance whilst addressing some limitations of traditional methods. In this work, we propose a novel approach for the finger trimodal graph fusion, by extending the crystal-like bijective structure to the Atomic Group-like heterostructure. The crucial aspect is to establish the inter-modal correlation. Inspired by chemical bonds, we construct atom serial numbers by pre-clustering the divided image blocks in one modality. Then, we trained a node classifier to share the set of serial numbers among the three modalities. As a result, nodes across modalities can be bonded. Furthermore, both the feature attributes and position information are taken into consideration for the intra-modal edges of the fused graph. Finally, we design heterogeneous graphs with higher recognition potential. Experimental results show that with our strategy, we can improve matching accuracy to 96.6% while lowering the equal error rate to 2.687%.

Keywords: Finger biometrics · Multimodal fusion · Weighted graph

1 Introduction

The performance of unimodal biometrics is often stymied by various of factors [1]. In finger biometrics, fingerprint (FP) may encounter problems due to acquisition mechanism and ambient conditions. In such situations, it may be necessary to integrate multiple biometric cues to improve the recognition performance. There are mainly three biometric patterns to be studied in a finger, fingerprint (FP), finger vein (FV) and finger-knuckle-print (FKP) [2].

Generally speaking, multimodal biometrics fusion can be categorized into mainly three types based on different implementation stages: pixel level (early stage) fusion, feature level (middle stage) fusion and decision level (late stage) fusion [3]. Although these strategies are easy to implement, there are several inherent difficulties in finger biometrics. As seen in Fig. 1, the image size of each

© The Author(s), under exclusive license to Springer Nature Switzerland AG 2022
S. Yu et al. (Eds.): PRCV 2022, LNCS 13534, pp. 499–509, 2022.
https://doi.org/10.1007/978-3-031-18907-4_39

finger modality is inconsistent. When attempting to normalize or resize them directly, the destruction of information is inevitable. Texture posture cannot be coordinated, leading to its poor synchronization [4]. Moreover, trace-like finger-knuckle-print, ridge-like fingerprint and pipeline-like finger vein are all distinct textural cues. As a consequence, the features not only subject to different distribution, but also have heterogeneous differences in feature dimensions and feature vector dimensions. As for the decision level, its essentially an escape from feature differences, neglecting the significance of multimodal information dynamics. Thus, it is of great significance to develop an appropriate representation of the three finger modalities.

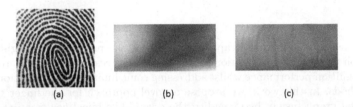

Fig. 1. Raw image data of fingerprint, finger vein and finger-knuckle-print. (a) Fingerprints (152 × 152); (b) finger vein (200 × 91); (c) finger-knuckle-print (200 × 90)

With the progress of graph representation learning, graph modeling increasingly attracts attention to overcome such challenges. Graph has a wide range of applications in non-Euclidean space, due to its outstanding modeling capabilities. Furthermore, graph is usually used to describe Euclidean data [5], such as pictures. Graph nodes can characterize local features, and edges can represent the relevance among the nodes [6]. In instance segmentation [7,8], graph nodes can correspond to the explicit objects segmented from an image. As for texture images without annotations, some early researchers tried to explore the global relationship of image texture by graph-based coding operators like Local Graph Structure (LGS) [9]. Further, it is necessary to abstract texture images into spatial weighted graphs given the excellent performance of graph neural networks recently. But if modeling is done by the images texture topology [10], on the one hand, unfavorable external circumstances render the minutiae points unreliable [11]; on the other hand, even if the minutia points are credible enough, the cancelability of the graph data is destroyed so that attackers have little trouble reconstructing the original topology [12]. Hence, the most commonly used modeling is to divide an image into super-pixel blocks [13]. Oriented energy distribution (OED) [14] is extracted as node attributes by Steerable filter to establish weighted graphs. The 360-dimensional Oriented energy features equal the feature dimension, and align the main direction to offset the possible changes in finger posture, fulfilling the finger trimodal fusion requirement. Moreover, robust Delaunay triangulation is used to link the unimodal nodes.

There is still room for improvement in the finger trimodal graph fusion. Traditionally, the cross-modal nodes are all aligned one by one in particular sequence through concatenation [4], summation, such straightforward methods. Therefore, some put forward competitive fusion [15] to optimize such node-level alignment. The alignments are modified by the comprehensive ranking of eigenvalues. But essentially speaking, as shown in Fig. 2(a), alignment fusion can be regarded as stacking corresponding inter-modal nodes as a whole. While, as seen in Fig. 2(b), heterogeneous fusion preserves all the nodes. Consequently, more complex and comprehensive correlation among inter-modal nodes can be exploited. Its also more conducive for each node in the downstream graph network to aggregate richer neighborhood information, to update the node representation, and to give full play to the modeling and expression capability of graph structure. Finally, the superiority of the suggested strategy can be validated by experimental results.

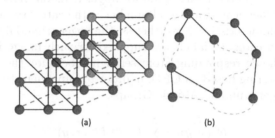

Fig. 2. Graph fusion method. (a) Alignment fusion; (b) heterogeneous fusion. The solid line indicates the intra-modal interaction, and the dashed line indicates the inter-modal connection.

The main contributions in this study are as follows:

(1) A feature fusion framework based on an atomic group structure for finger trimodal recognition is proposed, which makes full use of the structural properties of graph, to solve the problems about the nodes and edges in the existing crystal-like alignment fusion. Inspired by chemical atom bonds, we have been exploring more comprehensive interaction among the cross-modal nodes through bonding fusion.
(2) On the basis of Oriented energy distribution extracted by Steerable filter, we trained a node classifier for super-pixel blocks, and refined a shared set of atom serial number among the three finger modalities.
(3) At the same time, we also take into account the difference between inter- and intra-modal connections, integrating the information of node attribute and block position for intra-modal fusion. Finally, through residual graph convolution neural network, the superiority of our method is verified by experiments.

2   Finger Trimodal Bonding Fusion Based on Weighted Graph

2.1   Inter-modal Connection

Bonding fusion is a heterogeneous graph fusion method we proposed. The key is that we create finger chemical bonds among the inter-modal nodes of the three finger modalities. There have been several multimodal fusion researches based on heterogeneous graph in Natural Language Processing (NLP) for our reference. There exists natural semantic link between the nodes of the visual and text modalities in NLP. While, there is no annotated instance in the finger images, and the nodes are just super-pixel image blocks evenly divided from visual images. Thus, motivated by the idea of extending crystal to atomic group, we investigate the acquired relationship for finger trimodal nodes by analogy to chemical bonds. Chemical atom serial number is the category number of atoms with consistent characteristics. Nevertheless, the finger trimodal graph nodes are numerous, and no category labels are supplied for such image blocks. For this reason, we get the corresponding atom serial numbers for the finger trimodal nodes by pre-clustering based on OED, in order to implement the heterogeneous fusion for the finger trimodal Atomic Groups.

$$h^\theta(x, y) = \sum_{j=1}^{N} k_j(\theta) f^{\theta_j}(x, y) \tag{1}$$

$$E(\theta) = \left(\sum_{x=1}^{X} \sum_{y=1}^{Y} \left(h^\theta(x, y) I_i(x, y) \right) \right)^2 \tag{2}$$

$$f_i = \{ E(1), E(2), \cdots, E(\theta), \cdots, E(360) \} \tag{3}$$

Essentially speaking, the Oriented energy distribution feature is the permutation vector acquired by the Steerable filter in a succession of directions, as shown in Eq. (3). The Steerable filter extracts the Oriented energy distribution from $h \times h$ size super-pixel blocks evenly divided from some unimodal image as in Eq. (1), where $k(\theta)$ is the interpolation function; $f(x, y)$ is the filter function; θ is the angle of Steerable filter; and N represents the number of basic filters. At a certain angle θ, h^θ and the block I_i perform the convolution operation described in Eq. (2) to obtain the associated texture energy, where X and Y are the dimensions of the filter, corresponding to the size of the super-pixel block. Figure 3 shows one block and its Oriented energy distribution. It can be observed from the directionality of the polar plot that the Oriented energy distribution can indicate the appropriate texture posture of the block.

If the Oriented energy distribution features are pre-clustered separately on each finger modality, three completely distinct sets of serial numbers are still insufficient to create inter-modal linkages. As a consequence, we generalize the pre-clustering result from one single modality to the others so as to share a consistent set of node numbers among the inter-modal nodes. Figure 4 depicts

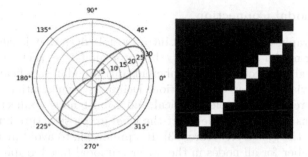

Fig. 3. A block divided from the original image, and the polar plot of its oriented energy distribution.

the whole workflow of bonding fusion. We train a node classifier based on the pre-clustering results. The classifier is able to distinguish the texture pattern on the finger trimodal super-pixel image blocks, and has the potential to predict the serial number for the relevant nodes in another two modalities. Since the semantic bridge between the three finger modalities is built, the inter-modal nodes can be bonded according to the same serial number.

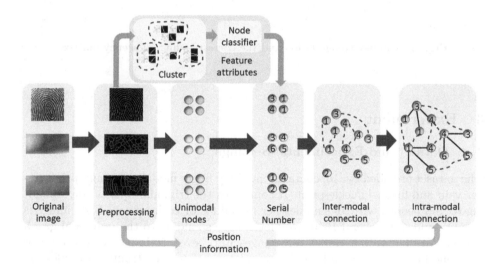

Fig. 4. The flowchart of bonding fusion. By pre-clustering the image nodes and training a node classifier based on the clustering results, Serial Number is created. Inter-modal connections all relies on Serial Number, while intra-modal nodes are linked depending on both feature attributes and Position information.

2.2   Intra-modal Connection

In the fused graph, each node has its intra-modal edges that is clearly distinct from the inter-modal ones. After all, the inter-modal connection is acquired, but intra-modal connections have inherent intra-modal significance, such as those created via Delaunay triangulation. Delaunay triangulation, as indicated in Fig. 5, is a relatively simple, classical and robust node connection method, since alterations to a single node affect the local graph structure but have minimal impact on the global structure [13]. It's preferable to avoid merely utilizing the Serial Number for all nodes in the finger trimodal fused graph to underline the difference between intra- and inter-modal edges. Thereby, we take the Serial Number and Delaunay triangulation into account to merge position information and feature similarity for intra-modal correlation, accordingly enriching the connotation of the edges.

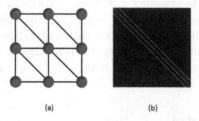

(a)   (b)

Fig. 5. Delaunay triangulation and the corresponding adjacency matrix.

3   Experiment

3.1   Dataset and Experimental Settings

The dataset provided by [15] contains the three finger modalities, fingerprint, finger vein and finger-knuckle-print. It comprises the trimodal images corresponding to 100 people, with 10 samples per modality for each person. Each image is evenly divided to several 1010 size blocks corresponding to the unimodal graph nodes. We divide each class's ten images into seven training images, one for test, one for validation, and one for template images. The training samples are matched in pairs. The test or validation samples are matched against all templates. Considering that finger vein as a biometrics trait inside the body is not easily damaged like fingerprint and finger-knuckle-print, and has high performance in the field of living detection, finger vein is selected as the benchmark modality for pre-clustering by Kmeans. We train one efficient Resnet18 neural network as the node classifier with Cross-entropy as the loss function to share the serial numbers among the three finger modalities. Its training and test set is divided on the blocks of the modality.

It is worth mentioning that what we propose is a feature fusion method, and it should eventually be applied to recognition. For biometric samples, the number of categories is often much larger than the number of intra-class samples due to data privacy security. Thus, matching is usually adopted in biometrics to deal with the phenomenon of "few shot classification". Because the matching is regarded as a binary classification, the accuracy rate (ACC), recall rate (RR), equal error rate (EER) and AUC value are chosen as performance evaluation. Moreover, we conduct EER by two methods. Method 1 for calculating EER by FAR and FRR, such discrete arrays, is to calculate the intersection point by interpolating them into a smooth curve; and method 2 is to calculate $(FRR + FAR)/2$ corresponding to $min\{|FRR - FAR|\}$. Matching is usually performed in traditional recognition by directly calculating the correlation coefficient between the features of two objects. Given that the three finger modalities are described as a heterogeneous graph, a graph-specific matching module is much more conducive for identifying the fused graphs. In terms of graph learning algorithms, generally speaking, whether graph embedding or graph kernel, they are all similar to Weisfeiler-Lehman algorithm. The node representations are updated by aggregating neighborhood information along the edge. Hence, the node representations in the same Connected Component tend to converge to the same value. Graph convolution network, in particular, aggregates and updates more easily due to a specific Laplace Smoothing. The closer node clusters are connected, the more favorable it is for node, cluster and even graph representation [16]. But in many tasks, including our finger trimodal graph fusion, the graph is connected, with only one Connected Component. Eventually, all nodes tend to converge, leading to serious information homogenization, that is, over-smoothing. One solution is to use Skip Connection [17]. Intuitively speaking, it strives to achieve a balance between avoiding over-smoothing and properly learning for each node in the graph by aggregating the result of each neural layer, merging hierarchical information, and enriching the connotation of node representation. The unimodal recognition experiments given in Table 1 reveal that residual graph convolution network [15] outperforms graph matching neural network (GMN) [18], random-walk based graph kernel model (RWGNN) [19] and Siamese-network based graph convolutional network (SimGNN) [20]. Therefore, we choose residual graph convolution network as the graph matching module.

Table 1. Comparison results of different graph matching models.

	Residual GCN [15]	SimGNN [20]	GMN [18]	RWGNN [19]
ACC	**0.70644**	0.51097	0.63556	0.62965
EER (Method 1)	**0.33835**	0.4784	0.42415	0.34587
EER (Method 2)	**0.28296**	0.47798	0.33195	0.3458
RR	**0.89621**	0.48999	0.27124	0.68311
AUC	0.70791	0.52011	0.66805	**0.73423**

3.2   The Selection of the K Value and Intra-modal Connection Method

In this research, we combine the Serial Number and Delaunay triangulation for intra-modal connection. As for the translation into the graphs, firstly we obtain each unimodal node feature matrix for the current sample by one-hot encoding serial numbers. The isomorphic graph adjacency matrix globally linked by numbers calculated by its inner product. If each unimodal subgraph is replaced by Delaunay triangulation, or its Hadamard product with Delaunay triangulation, that means merely Delaunay triangulation, or both two are taken into account, respectively. To confirm the effect, here we conduct a contrastive experiment with another two approaches, barely Delaunay triangulation and barely Serial Number. Furthermore, the K value is critical parameter to ensure the effect of Kmeans clustering, i.e., the reliability of the trimodal node classifier. The K value for an unsupervised low-clustering issue can be optimized by calculating Silhouette Coefficient. But as indicated in Eq. (4), the essence of Silhouette Coefficient is to balance the size of inter-cluster distance, $b(i)$, and intra-cluster distance, $a(i)$. The number of super-pixel blocks in the three finger modalities is numerous. Such high K value leads to few intra-cluster samples. Finally, the Silhouette Coefficients continuously increases, resulting in optimization failure. Therefore, it is still necessary to compare the experimental results under a certain K value for evaluation. Given the memory cost and the extremely sparse fused graph, we select some representative K values here.

$$S = \frac{1}{N} \sum_{i=1}^{N} \frac{b(i)-a(i)}{\max\{a(i),b(i)\}} \tag{4}$$

We can analyze the influence of intra-modal connection strategies in Fig. 6. Delaunay triangulation focuses on the original image blocks position information, whereas the Serial Number is proposed to establish the inter-modal link, hence concentrating on the nodes attribute. When the K value is small, as shown in Fig. 6(a), it is obvious that Delaunay triangulation plays a significant role in the intra-modal connection as shown in Fig. 6(d), although both Delaunay triangulation and the Serial Number are taken into account simultaneously. Currently, all finger trimodal nodes are nearly homogeneous, resulting in aimless and redundant edges. As K value increases, as seen in Fig. 6(b), Delaunay triangulation is gradually diluted by more and more serial numbers. The connections are more specific and targeted as a result of the integrated information. But if the K value exceeds a certain threshold, Delaunay triangulation is significantly weakened, making the intra-modal adjacency matrix much too sparse to describe relation-ship among nodes in the same modality. When Serial Number dominates the whole graph as illustrated in Fig. 6(c), it blurs the three modalities boundaries and degrades the fused graphs heterogeneity. It can be seen from the experimental results in Table 2 that the influence of the two variables on the recognition effect fluctuates, but generally speaking, when the K value is 1500, simultaneously considering position and attribute information for intra-modal edges, Serial Number is sufficient to characterize the feature of the nodes, and

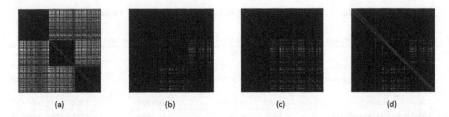

Fig. 6. The adjacency matrices of fusion graphs in different inner-model nodes. (a) K = 10, Delaunay triangulation + Serial Number; (b) K = 500, Delaunay triangulation + Serial Number; (c) K = 500, Serial Number; (d) K = 500, Delaunay triangulation.

its integration with Delaunay triangulation also revises the description of the heterogeneous fusion well, leading to better matching results.

3.3 Contrastive Experiment of Different Graph Fusion Methods

In this section, on the three finger modalities, bonding fusion we proposed is compared with concatenation and summation, as well as competitive fusion. Note that competitive fusion is originally used for multi-classification, and its unimodal graph composition and feature extraction are also improved, which influences its results significantly. Here, the fused graphs by each method are all recognized by the residual graph convolution network mentioned in Sect. 4.2. Alignment fusion essentially creates one-to-one connections among modalities. From the node perspective, the three corresponding nodes of the three modalities are stacked into a whole, making the fused graph homogeneous in a unimodal graph size. Contrarily, heterogeneous fusion explores abundant dynamics across modalities on the one hand. It also retains all nodes and distinguishes intra- and inter-modal edges to highlight the specificity of the three finger modalities on the other. And in the graph convolutional network, more sufficient neighbor resources can also be aggregated to update the representation of nodes and even the entire graph. Compared with the crystal-like alignment fusion, including concatenation, summation and competitive fusion, atomic group-like fusion can more properly represent the nature of the relevance among the three finger modalities. Not to mention that we discriminate between intra- and inter-modal interactions. It can be seen from the experimental results in Table 3 that, as compared to bijective alignment fusion, we can obtain more recognizable fused graphs by bonding fusion based on serial number under the same dataset and experimental settings. The connection among the modalities is no longer restricted to node-level aggregation, but a more completely integrated inter-modal interaction in a more comprehensive and dynamic way.

Table 2. Parameter comparison experimental results.

K	Intra-modal connection	ACC	EER (Method 1)	EER (Method 2)	RR	AUC
10	Serial number	0.90494	0.06	0.05975	0.70416	0.97903
	Delaunay triangulation	0.94935	0.03771	0.03909	0.61072	0.99031
	Delaunay triangulation + Serial number	0.9323	0.05758	0.05879	0.6129	0.98282
500	Serial number	0.9502	0.04081	0.0404	0.67113	0.99157
	Delaunay triangulation	0.93371	0.05	0.0499	0.67847	0.98822
	Delaunay triangulation + Serial number	0.95419	0.03747	0.03874	0.66627	0.99236
1000	Serial number	0.94292	0.02747	0.02874	0.69789	0.9933
	Delaunay triangulation	0.94745	0.03343	0.03172	0.61829	0.99132
	Delaunay triangulation + Serial number	0.92499	0.04697	0.04848	**0.715**	0.99194
1500	Serial number	0.92579	0.03	0.02919	0.6832	0.99244
	Delaunay triangulation	0.93703	0.03771	0.03909	0.6311	0.99109
	Delaunay triangulation + Serial number	**0.96668**	**0.02687**	**0.02843**	0.61114	**0.99452**
2000	Serial number	0.93597	0.03929	0.03965	0.69942	0.99014
	Delaunay triangulation	0.90205	0.08731	0.08884	0.71209	0.97171
	Delaunay triangulation + Serial number	0.93467	0.04	0.04162	0.68015	0.99248

Table 3. Comparison results of graph fusion methods.

	Summation	Concatenation	Competition	Bonding
ACC	0.79261	0.75641	0.40896	**0.96668**
EER (Method 1)	0.25889	0.21148	0.49	**0.02687**
EER (Method 2)	0.25944	0.21162	0.49005	**0.02843**
RR	0.5654	**0.66792**	0.63842	0.61114
AUC	0.83203	0.85992	0.53786	**0.99452**

4   Conclusion

In this study, bonding fusion, a novel finger trimodal fusion method based on heterogeneous graphs, was proposed to improve the graph representation in traditional alignment fusion. By generating serial numbers of the finger trimodal nodes, we developed the correlation among the inter-modal nodes to describe richer dynamics across the three finger modalities. Simultaneously we distinguished the intra- and inter-modal connection, taking full advantage of graph topology. Finally, we can enhance matching accuracy to 96.6% while decreasing the equal error rate to 2.687% with our approach.

References

1. Jain, A.K., Ross, A.: Multibiometric systems. Commun. ACM **47**(1), 34–40 (2004)
2. Khellat-Kihel, S., Abrishambaf, R., Monteiro, J.L., Benyettou, M.: Multimodal fusion of the finger vein, fingerprint and the finger-knuckle-print using Kernel Fisher analysis. Appl. Soft Comput. **42**, 439–447 (2016)

3. Jain, A.K., Ross, A., Prabhakar, S.: An introduction to biometric recognition. IEEE Trans. Circuits Syst. Video Technol. **14**(1), 4–20 (2004)
4. Zhang, H., Li, S., Shi, Y., Yang, J.: Graph fusion for finger multimodal biometrics. IEEE Access **7**, 28607–28615 (2019)
5. Foggia, P., Percannella, G., Vento, M.: Graph matching and learning in pattern recognition in the last 10 years. Int. J. Pattern Recognit. Artif. Intell. **28**(01), 1450001 (2014)
6. Chen, J., Pan, L., Wei, Z., Wang, X., Ngo, C., Chua, T.: Zero-shot ingredient recognition by multi-relational graph convolutional network. In: Proceedings of the AAAI Conference on Artificial Intelligence, pp. 10542–10550 (2020)
7. Choi, G., Lim, C., Choi, H.: A center-biased graph learning algorithm for image classification. In: 2017 IEEE International Conference on Big Data and Smart Computing (BigComp), pp. 324–327. IEEE (2017)
8. Luo, B., Wilson, R.C., Hancock, E.R.: Spectral embedding of graphs. Pattern Recogn. **36**(10), 2213–2230 (2003)
9. Li, S., Zhang, B., Fei, L., Zhao, S.: Joint discriminative feature learning for multi-modal finger recognition. Pattern Recogn. **111**, 107704 (2021)
10. Zhao, J., Ai, D., Huang, Y., Song, H., Wang, Y., Yang, J.: Quantitation of vascular morphology by directed graph construction. IEEE Access **7**, 21609–21622 (2019)
11. Arakala, A., Davis, S.A., Hao, H., Horadam, K.J.: Value of graph topology in vascular biometrics. IET Biometrics **6**(2), 117–125 (2017)
12. Nayar, G.R., Thomas, T., Emmanuel, S.: Graph based secure cancelable palm vein biometrics. J. Inf. Secur. Appl. **62**, 102991 (2021)
13. Ye, Z., Yang, J.: A finger-vein recognition method based on weighted graph model. J. Shandong Univ. (Eng. Sci.) **48**(3), 103–109 (2018)
14. Simoncelli, E.P., Farid, H.: Steerable wedge filters for local orientation analysis. IEEE Trans. Image Process. **5**(9), 1377–1382 (1996)
15. Qu, H., Zhang, H., Yang, J., Wu, Z., He, L.: A generalized graph features fusion framework for finger biometric recognition. In: Feng, J., Zhang, J., Liu, M., Fang, Y. (eds.) CCBR 2021. LNCS, vol. 12878, pp. 267–276. Springer, Cham (2021). https://doi.org/10.1007/978-3-030-86608-2_30
16. Li, Q., Han, Z., Wu, X.: Deeper insights into graph convolutional networks for semi-supervised learning. In: Thirty-Second AAAI Conference on Artificial Intelligence, Louisiana, USA, pp. 3538–3545 (2018)
17. Kipf, T.N., Welling, M.: Semi-supervised classification with graph convolutional networks. In: 5th International Conference on Learning Representations, Toulon, France. PMLR (2016)
18. Li, Y., Gu, C., Dullien, T., Vinyals, O., Kohli, P.: Graph matching networks for learning the similarity of graph structured objects. In: International Conference on Machine Learning, California, USA, pp. 3835–3845. PMLR (2019)
19. Nikolentzos, G., Vazirgiannis, M.: Random walk graph neural networks. Adv. Neural. Inf. Process. Syst. **33**, 16211–16222 (2020)
20. Bai, Y., Ding, H., Bian, S., Chen, T., Sun, Y., Wang, W.: SimGNN: a neural network approach to fast graph similarity computation. In: Proceedings of the Twelfth ACM International Conference on Web Search and Data Mining, Melbourne VIC, Australia, pp. 384–392. Association for Computing Machinery (2019)

Disentangled OCR: A More Granular Information for "Text"-to-Image Retrieval

Xinyu Zhou, Shilin Li, Huen Chen, and Anna Zhu$^{(\boxtimes)}$

Wuhan University of Technology, Wuhan, China
{297932,shilinli,259776,annazhu}@whut.edu.cn

Abstract. Most of the previous text-to-image retrieval methods were based on the semantic matching between text and image locally or globally. However, they ignore a very important element in both text and image, i.e., the OCR information. In this paper, we present a novel approach to disentangle the OCR from both text and image, and use the disentangled information from the two different modalities for matching. The matching score is consist of two parts, the traditional global semantic text-to-image representation matching and OCR matching scores. Since there is no dataset to support the training of text OCR disentangled task, we label partial useful data from TextCaps dataset, which contains scene text images and their corresponding captions. We relabel the text of captions to OCR and non-OCR words. In total, we extract 110K captions and 22K images from TextCaps, which contain OCR information. We call this dataset TextCaps-OCR. The experiments on TextCaps-OCR and another public dataset CTC (COCO-Text Captions) demonstrate the effectiveness of disentangling OCR in text and image for cross modality retrieval task.

Keywords: Text-to-image retrieval · OCR · Disentangled information · Cross modality

1 Introduction

Text-image cross-modal retrieval has attracted wide attention and made great progress in recent years. It aims to return the most relevant images to the query text. Its performance mainly relies on the consistency and alignment of visual and language representations.

Most of the previous image retrieval tasks were based on the similarity of textual and visual features. With the advent of Transformer [2] in recent years that induces cross attention for contextual feature representations, researchers start to use it [2] for highly coupled training based on visual objects in images, such as SCAN and X-VLM [3,4], and for matching through scene graph, such as LGSGM and SGRAF [5,6]. They consider the granular information of visual objects in images but ignore very important information, namely OCR.

S. Yu et al. (Eds.): PRCV 2022, LNCS 13534, pp. 510–523, 2022.
https://doi.org/10.1007/978-3-031-18907-4_40

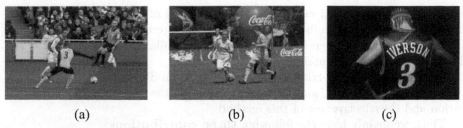

(a)   (b)   (c)

Query: A soccer player wearing a yellow jersey with the number 3.

Fig. 1. Defects in current retrieval model, which cannot combining OCR and image semantic information.

Given a query text as shown in Fig. 1, the general text-to-image retrieval model may get the image retrieval results without scene text as Fig. 1(b), which is caused by unable to recognize the OCR information "3". But the missing information "3" is the most important element of the query sentence. If we extract the OCR number "3" from the query and only use it for retrieval like JTSL [23], it may output the image with number "3" but has no relationship with the semantic description of the text query. Obviously these conventional methods are not feasible to text query containing OCR information. It inspires us to combine the two strategies above to perform for more granular OCR-based retrieval. We call this task as "Text"-to-Image retrieval, where "Text" represents linguistic description and its OCR information corresponding to scene text of image.

There are some related works [15,16] mentioning this point, but they only match query with the OCR information in images globally. But, it leads to increasing errors with the image amount growing, because the scene text in images may contain words in query. So we distinguish the OCR information in both query text and images, then perform matching on two aspects, one for the disentangled OCR and the other for the original semantic matching on the two modalities. Therefore, we call this process as OCR disentangling. We refer to this kind of OCR as text OCR in later sections.

However, OCR disentangling is not as simple as expected. Since OCR in images, i.e., scene text, are easy to be detected as a special visual object, but OCR in query texts cannot be well distinguished by named entity recognition methods or POS tagging. Text OCR can be any component of a sentence requiring some reasoning to be detected. Humans rely more on context to infer text OCR, but sometimes they cannot extract the OCR information completely and correctly. Therefore, we can complete this task through the model that can obtain context information, but the most critical issue is the lack of text OCR annotation datasets.

Therefore, we put forward a dataset called TextCaps-OCR for text OCR detection, and we use Bert [9] to solve this new task. Moreover, we establish one model containing two retrieval ways. The first is a word set based approach. We transforms images into captions using image captioning model, then separately split the query texts and captions to get two kinds of sets, finally we perform retrieval through the similarity between the sets from query and image. The second is based on image and query features' similarity. Both ways use the disentangled OCR for matching.

The comparative experiments are carried out on TextCaps-OCR and CTC (COCO-Text Caps) [15], and the results illustrate the correctness of our motivation and the effectiveness of this method.

Thus, we mainly have the following **three contributions**:

1. With strong motivation, we introduce OCR as a more granular information into the text-to-image retrieval task and demonstrate its feasibility and effectiveness.
2. We provide a new dataset called TextCaps-OCR with text OCR annotation, and propose a simple retrieval method to match both global semantic and local OCR in different modalities. Additionally, we design a Soft Matching strategy to boost the robustness of OCR matching in the model.
3. Experimental results on TextCaps-OCR and CTC [15] (COCO Text Caps) prove the effectiveness of the OCR disentangling operation. Our method outperforms the X-VLM model [4] (the SOTA method on Flicker30K and COCO) on TextCaps-OCR and achieve comparable results with a great pre-training model on CTC.

2   Related Work

2.1   OCR Related Cross-Modal Tasks

OCR information has been used in VQA (Visual Question Answering), image captioning, and other areas. Since the answers to VQA are usually present in the image, it is necessary to extract and add the OCR information to the answer lexicon. As for image captioning, to describe an image by text, considering OCR information in the image will greatly enrich its granularity of description. M4C [7] is the first model using OCR information for VQA and Image Caption tasks. It is consists of three parts. Firstly, they extract the object features by Faster-RCNN [24], and then use Sence Text detection network to obtain the representations of OCR in the image. Secondly, they pass the obtained information and query into a large Transformer [2] encoder after embedding them separately to learn the relationship between the features of different modalities. Lastly, they add the OCR to the answer dictionary through pointer networks [25] and output the most likely answer through the decoder. Another effective VQA model is called SBD [26], firstly splitting the text features into two functionally distinct parts, a linguistic part and a visual part, which flow into the corresponding attention branches. The encoded features are then fed into the Transformer's [2] decoder to generate answers or captions, using three attention blocks to filter out irrelevant or redundant features and aggregate them into six separate functional vectors. And they demonstrate that OCR is the main contributor to VQA, while visual semantics only plays a supporting role. And with the introduction of M4C [7],

M4C-Captioner [1] followed, which has the same architecture as M4C [7], but is applied to the task of image captioning by removing the question input and directly use its multi-word answer decoder to generate captions.

Through our investigation, we find two existing studies on retrieval using OCR. The first is StacMR [15]. They mainly propose a dataset called CTC (COCO Text Captions) and conduct several comparative experiments based on existing models [3,10,21] to prove the effectiveness of OCR in retrieval tasks. The second is ViSTR [16]. They use vision and OCR aggregated transformer, i.e. cross-modal learning of images, text and scene text through separate transformers. But they both perform retrieval matching the features globally, which we have previously shown to be flawed.

2.2 Cross-Modal Retrieval

There are two main types of cross-modal retrieval tasks, one is to extract the corresponding modal features separately and then perform similarity matching directly, and the second is to take multi-modal information together as input and perform similarity output by cross-attention. The former takes much less time than the latter, but the effect is relatively poor, so we can call the former Fast and the latter Slow. The most typical Fast model is SCAN [3]. It first extracts the objects in images through Bottom-up attention [27], and then compute the similarity among all of the object and word features by cosine similarity to rank. And surprisingly there are also large-scale pre-training models in Fast, represented by CLIP and BLIP [11,12]. They are both trained by using the similarity of positive samples as the numerator and negative samples as the denominator in the loss function. Their high accuracy for retrieval is supported more by computing power and the huge training data. Facing OCR-related text-to-image retrieval, they fail in many cases. And the model of the Slow class is represented by Pixel Bert [28], which imitates the Bert [2] by randomly sampling pixel-level image information, concating it with word features as input, and training it through MLM. Subsequently, there are many scene graph-based retrieval methods, such as LGSGM and SGRAF [5,6], both of them retrieve by matching the semantics of objects and their relationships. What deserves a special mention is that the research "Thinking Fast and Slow" [29] bridges the Fast and Slow models through distillation learning. They use the Slow model as a teacher to do distillation learning on the Fast model, generating the model-Fast&Slow, and then performing the whole retrieval through Fast&Slow to get top-20 returns. Finally, they re-rank the top-20 images through the slow model to get the final result. But unfortunately, none of these approaches pay attention to the importance of OCR.

3 Methods

This section mainly describes the methods for text OCR detection and two embarrassingly simple but effective retrieval ways combined with disentangled OCR information. The model framework is shown in Fig. 2.

Input Text (x):

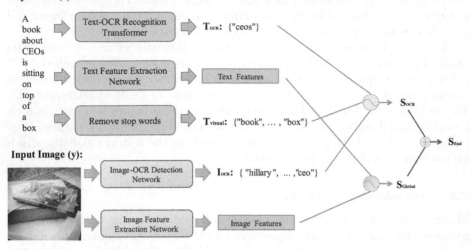

Fig. 2. Our retrieval model can be divided into two parts, the first part is to compute the score of OCR using Soft Matching (blue part), the second part is the to compute the similarity score between text x and image y using the cosine similarity which can be shown as $f(x)@g(y)$ (green part). (Color figure online)

3.1 Text OCR Detection

We use Bert [9] to perform **TOD** (**Text OCR Detection**). Since TOD is a task that heavily relies on text comprehension, we directly mark OCR words as 1 and background (non-OCR) words as 0 to fit the training way of Bert, i.e. MLM. What deserves a special mention is that we think this decoupling method is also one of the most important reasons why we can achieve such good results.

We use the cross-entropy of the last hidden layer and the real label as the loss. And the weight of the loss function is $(5/6, 1/6)$, because the ratio of OCR to background words (non OCR) is close to 1:5. Considering the last n-dimensional hidden layer: $H = [H_1, H_2, ..., H_n]$, and the real label: $G_t = [Gt_1, Gt_2, ..., Gt_n]$, then we can calculate the loss as:

$$L_{CE} = -\frac{1}{n} \sum_{i=0}^{n} [Gt_i * ln(H_i) + (1 - Gt_i) * ln(1 - H_i)] \tag{1}$$

3.2 Methods to Perform Retrieval with Disentangled OCR

In order to prove the effectiveness of OCR and OCR decoupling in different modalities, we use a simple and easy method: 1. Text-to-Image retrieval based on set-to-set matching. 2. Image and text feature matching through cosine similarity. It is acknowledged that the effect of fast model is poor. To better compute the matching degree, we propose a soft matching strategy, which means conducting the first match through global OCR matching, i.e., Scene Text (OCR in the image) matching with all the words in a query, and then conducting the second match plus points through Text OCR, which can effectively increase the robustness of the model and method. This can be seen in the subsequent experimental results.

Soft Matching Introduction. The Soft Matching process can be simplified into pseudo code as shown in Algorithm 1. We use idf (inverse document frequency) to weight because there are prediction errors when detecting text OCR, and most of the words with prediction errors are common words in images, which makes the subsequent results worse. So, we introduce the idf weighting in information processing into our method, which can effectively suppress the impact of OCR prediction errors and greatly increase the robustness of the method. At last, we add the OCR score and set-to-set score directly to get the final score:

$$S_{final} = Softmax(S_{Global}) + S_{OCR} \tag{2}$$

Algorithm 1. Soft Matching

Input: the query **Text**, OCR in matching image **Scence_Text**, OCR in matching text **Text_OCR**, the times of every word appears in images **OCR_DICT**, the average times of words in images **OCR_DICT_AVG**. i refers to the i-th query, j refers to the j-th matching image/text and n refers to the number of images.

1: **for** word in $Text_i$ **do**
2:     **if** word in $Scence\_Text_j$ **then**
3:         **if** word in $Text\_OCR_j$ **then**
4:             S_{OCRj} += $2/OCR\_DICT[word]$
5:         **else**
6:             S_{OCRj} += $1/OCR\_DICT\_AVG$
7:         **end if**
8:     **end if**
9: **end for**
10: $S_{OCR} = [S_{OCR1}, ..., S_{OCRj}, ..., S_{OCRn}]$
11: S_{OCR} = softmax(S_{OCR})
Output: S_{OCR}

Retrieval Based on Captions. Because there is no other image retrieval model using OCR before, we just use the existing image-captioning model to prove the potential of our approach. We use a pre-training model called OFA [20] to generate the captions on TextCaps-OCR-1K directly. After that, segment the sentence and remove the stop words. Then we can transform the feature matching into a set-to-set (sts) matching, which divides the intersection by the length of the query set as the global score, and the i-th score is calculated as:

$$S_{Global_{sts}i} = L(Query \cap Captions_i)/L(Query) \tag{3}$$

where L means the length of the corresponding set. At the same time, we can compute the OCR score through Soft Matching.

Retrieval Based on Features. The whole process is shown in Fig. 2. The difference from retrieval based on captions is that there are no words. We just compute the global score using the features from the extraction models by cosine similarity. For the text features $f(x)$ and image feature $g(x)$ (both are n-dimensions), the global score can be calculated as:

$$S_{Global_i} = \frac{\sum_{i-1}^{n} f(x)_i * g(x)_i}{\sqrt{\sum_{i=1}^{n}(f(x)_i)^2} * \sqrt{\sum_{i=1}^{n}(g(x)_i)^2}} \tag{4}$$

The final score is the same as Eq. 2. And we use the NCE Loss:

$$L_{NCE} = -\sum_{i=1}^{n} ln(\frac{e^{f(x_i)^T g(y_i)}}{e^{f(x_i)^T g(y_i)} + \sum_{(x',y' \in X_i)} e^{f(x')^T g(y')}}) \tag{5}$$

which contrasts the score of the positive pair (x_i, y_i) to a set of negative pairs sampled from a negative set X_i. Above all, the total loss can be calculated as:

$$L_{total} = L_{CE} + L_{NCE} \tag{6}$$

4   The TextCaps-OCR Dataset

This section mainly describes the proposed dataset: **TextCaps-OCR**. We first explained its origin, the form of data storage and how it is tailored for text OCR detection. Then we compared it with other conventional datasets.

```
"0c0f40dde4a4e770": {
    "captions": [
        "Laneige sleeping mask comes in a 2.7 fl oz size, and is packaged in a pink box.",
        "A box of Laniege Water Sleeping Pack is on a red mat.",
        "A package by Laneige of their water sleeping pack.",
        "The box contains a water sleeping pack made by the company Laneige.",
        "A box containing the water sleeping pack by Laneige"
    ],
    "caption_tokens": [
        ["Laneige","sleeping","mask","comes","in","a","27","fl","oz","size","and","is","packaged","in","a","pink","box"],
        ["A","box","of","Laniege","Water","Sleeping","Pack","is","on","a","red","mat"],
        ["A","package","by","Laneige","of","their","water","sleeping","pack"],
        ["The","box","contains","a","water","sleeping","pack","made","by","the","company","Laneige"],
        ["A","box","containing","the","water","sleeping","pack","by","Laneige"]],
    "caption_ocr": [
        [1,1,0,0,0,0,0,0,0,0,0,0,0,0,0,0,0],
        [0,0,0,1,1,1,1,0,0,0,0,0],
        [0,0,0,1,0,0,1,1,1],
        [0,0,0,0,1,1,1,0,0,0,0,1],
        [0,0,0,0,1,1,1,0,1]],
    "ocr": ["laneige","water","sleeping","laniege","pack"]
},
```

Fig. 3. TextCaps-OCR's text data storage structure and its corresponding image.

4.1 Origin and Storage Structure

The **TextCaps-OCR** is a new dataset which contains labeled text OCR. We selected 21873 pictures with clear OCR from the TextCaps [1] for human annotation of the text OCR, and generated the OCR annotation corresponding to each caption, which is divided into 19130 training sets and 2743 test sets, in which each picture has 5 captions, and its storage form is as follows: Fig. 3. We can see that there is OCR annotation in the captions in TextCaps-OCR Dataset, which is very different from the previous dataset, in order to serve our subsequent task: Text OCR Detection. Text OCR Detection is a new task proposed by us to detect the OCR in text. We labeled the text OCR in captions in 1, and the background words should be 0, which can be seen in Fig. 3.

4.2 Comparison with Other Datasets

The most common retrieval datasets are Flickr30K, MS-COCO, COCO-Text and CTC [15, 17–19]. The contained OCR information comparison between these datasets and our newly proposed dataset TextCaps-OCR is shown in the Table 1.

Table 1. Comparison between TextCaps-OCR and other commonly datasets. Besides, $\star$ is Scene Text, † is Text OCR and ‡ is Labeled Text OCR.

Dataset	The number of		Annotations		
	Images	Texts	$ST^{\star}$	$TO^{\dagger}$	$LTO^{\ddagger}$
Flicer30K [17]	31784	31784*5	✗	✗	✗
MS-COCO [18]	328K	328K*5	✗	✗	✗
COCO-Text [19]	29210	29210*5	✓	✗	✗
COCO-Text Caps [15]	10683	10683*5	✓	✓	✗
TextCaps [1]	28408	28408*5	✓	✓	✗
TextCaps-OCR [ours]	21873	21873*5	✓	✓	✓

The main difference between our dataset TextCaps-OCR and other datasets is the annotated text OCR, which mainly serves our task of text OCR detection. It is worth noting that the TextCaps [1] is mainly based on VQA and image captioning. However, through our investigation, we found that this dataset is also challenging for the retrieval task because there are many similar images. The difference lies in the description of details and OCR, so we specially selected these challenging images to enter our new dataset, which is very suitable for fine-grained retrieval tasks and models with an OCR recognition function.

5 Experiment

In this section, we evaluate the benefits of our methods. We evaluate the Text OCR Detection on TextCaps-OCR in Sect. 5.1. In Sect. 5.2, we analyze the results of ablation experiments and qualitative comparisons. Moreover, we compare our approach with other published state-of-the-art retrieval methods on TextCaps-OCR and CTC [15] in Sect. 5.3.

5.1   Performance of Text OCR Detection

For training the Bert-base [9] for text OCR detection, we use the AdamW optimizer with a learning rate of $5e-5$ for just 2 epochs. It gets high detection performance as shown in Table 2. The precision and recall for text OCR are **91.1%** and **92.2%**, for background words are **97.4%** and **97.0%**. The high performance ensures the following process by using disentangled information for matching.

Table 2. Text OCR detection performance (%)

Class	Precision	Recall
Text OCR	91.1	92.2
Non-OCR words	97.4	97.0

5.2   Ablations

Firstly, we should mention the Scene Text Detection and Recognition model we used: Mask textspotter v3 [22]. Despite the fact that it incorporates OCR detection and identification, its effect is significantly inferior to that of today's SOTA due to its age, so we also make comparative tests using the real value.

Table 3. Ablation study on the impact of various matching strategies

Model	TextCaps-OCR-1K		
	R@1	R@5	R@10
General matching	17.34	35.78	46.1
OCR + General matching	19.86	47.08	62.06
Disentangled OCR + General matching	57.84	71.36	78.58
Soft matching + General matching	58.56	72.36	78.84
OFA [20]	34.12	52.08	61.54
OCR + OFA	40.80	60.12	69.60
Disentangled OCR + OFA	65.16	80.80	85.54
Soft matching + OFA	**65.98**	**81.08**	**85.58**
Soft matching + OFA(tt)	75.22	87.14	90.74
Soft matching + OFA(ti)	76.1	87.66	91.44

Method Description. We conduct two categories of comparative experiments on TextCaps-OCR to prove the effectiveness of our methods: "General feature matching series" and "Captions-based set-to-set matching series". For our approach, we consider a total of four modules: **1. General matching**, which does not use the OCR information. **2. OCR**, which means using the entangled OCR information. **3. Disentangled OCR**, i.e., using the disentangled OCR information. **4. Soft matching**, a matching way proposed by us, aims to match by combining both entangled OCR and disentangled OCR. Thus, the general feature matching series includes the following four ways: 1, 1 + 2, 1 + 3 and 1 + 4. As for the captions series, we removed OCR words from captions generated by OFA [20] to replace the basic model (i.e. general matching), and the rest is the same as above. For general matching, we use resnet50 to extract image features and Bert-base to extract text features, and MLP is added behind both networks (the former is 1000-500-100, the latter is 768-500-100, both containing the Dropout (0.9) and activation function Relu). Besides, the learning rate is $2e-4$ for 15 epochs.

Results Analysis. As shown in Table 3, compared with general matching, we can see that the entangled OCR information does not significantly improve the results, indicating the entangled OCR information is indeed limited. But on the contrary, the disentangled OCR information has made a qualitative leap in performance, improving R@1 by **40.5%**, R@5 by **35.58%** and R@10 by **32.74%**. Soft matching slightly improves the network performance again. And when we use a better basic network: OFA [20], the disentangled OCR information still makes a leap in the overall performance; relatively simple networks increase by an average of **10%**. Considering the error of OCR recognition (both text and image), we use the real value (**tt** refers to true text OCR and **ti** refers to true image OCR (i.e. Scene Text)). We can see that one of the true values of OCR can greatly improve the performance again. These three performance overflights can obviously prove the superiority of disentangled OCR on retrieval tasks.

Qualitative Comparisons. We also report some examples to illustrate the effectiveness and necessity of our method. As shown in Fig. 4, we **bold** the text OCR identified by our method in **two** text queries, which are obviously correct. Besides, for the first text query, the correct image could not be returned first using the entangled OCR. For the second text query, compared with using disentangled OCR to perform retrieval, entangled OCR did not return the correct image in the first three returned images. After investigation, we find that it is the tenth one that corresponds to the correct image. Meanwhile, we try to increase the weight of the OCR entangling matching score but ranking further down, which indicates that the robustness of entangled OCR is extremely poor when there are fewer OCR in the search sentences and more OCR information in images.

1. Text Query: Wonderful bottle of **Spring Seed Wine** from the country of **Australia**.

(a)Top-1 ✓	(b)Top-2 ✗	(c)Top-3 ✗	(d)Top-1 ✗	(e)Top-2 ✓	(f)Top-3 ✗
Score: 2.3	2.0	1.5	2.0	1.6	1.5

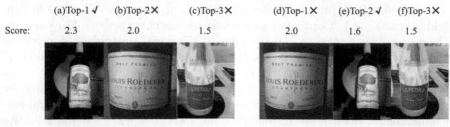

2. Text Query: A large red and white commercial jet taxis on runway **101** right.

(a)Top-1 ✓	(b)Top-2 ✗	(c)Top-3 ✗	(d)Top-1 ✗	(e)Top-2 ✗	(f)Top-3 ✗
Score: 2.2	2.0	1.5	1.505	1.504	1.503

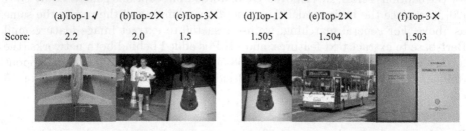

Fig. 4. Examples of the text-to-image retrieval task for comparisons between results with disentangled and entangled OCR, where (a)(b)(c) are the results returned by decoupled OCR and (d)(e)(f) are the results returned by coupled OCR. In text queries, we use **bold** to mark the text OCR identified by our method.

5.3 Comparison to the State of the Art

The experimental results on TextCaps-OCR and CTC are shown in Table 4 and Table 5 respectively.

Performance on TextCaps-OCR. Considering X-VLM [4] (the SOTA method on both MS-COCO [18] and Flicker30K [17]) is a pre-training model containing 4M images, we do the zero-shot testing on our test dataset. Although X-VLM [4] has better performance than general matching and OFA (both without OCR information), our models easily outperform it through Soft Matching by at least **13.16%** at Recall@1. Unfortunately, we cannot compare our method with the ViSTA [16] because it's not open source yet.

Table 4. Comparisons on TextCaps-OCR.

Model	TextCaps-OCR-1K		
	R@1	R@5	R@10
X-VLM [4]	45.4	70.38	78.56
General matching	17.34	35.78	46.1
Soft Matching + General matching	58.56	72.36	78.84
OFA [20]	34.12	52.08	61.54
Soft Matching + OFA	**65.98**	**81.08**	**85.58**

Table 5. Comparisons with the state-of-the-art scene text aware approaches on CTC.

Model	CTC-1K		
	R@1	R@5	R@10
SCAN [3]	26.6	53.6	65.3
VSRN [10]	26.6	54.2	66.2
STARNet [21]	31.5	60.8	72.4
ViSTA-S [16]	**36.7**	66.2	**77.8**
General matching	14.6	30.8	41.3
OCR + General matching	32.8	60.6	74.2
Disentangled OCR + General matching	26.2	52.7	62.8
Soft matching + General matching	35.4	**68.0**	74.9

Performance on CTC. We cannot use OFA [20] or X-VLM [4] on CTC because they are pre-trained on MS-COCO [18] which is the superset of CTC [15]. But, we still go beyond the traditional methods in all aspects through Soft matching + General matching. As for the pre-training model using the coupled OCR information, i.e. ViSTA [16], we can only achieve considerable results because of the problems with the dataset (CTC), the training scale (we just train on CTC, which only contains 9K images) and our too simple basic model. But even though there remain so many problems, we still checked only 1.3% on Recall@1 with the state of the art, and **1.8%** higher on Recall@5. Besides, combining the results of **OCR + General matching** and **Disentangled OCR + General matching** on these two datasets, it is not difficult to find that the OCR decoupling approach has considerably better generalization and performance than the coupling one, and Soft Matching does greatly improve the robustness of OCR matching and achieves the best results on both datasets.

6   Conclusion

We have shown the powerful effectiveness of OCR and the necessity of OCR decoupling, which can make a simple network the SOTA. At the same time, we also analyzed the shortcomings of previous work using OCR for retrieval or matching tasks. But there are some problems with our methods as well: **1.** How can we perform text OCR detection without a pre-training model? And existing model is hard to detect text OCR in this kind of text: "**A book is opened to a page that shows pictures of Brisbane in 1895.**", it is even hard for human beings to distinguish all the OCR, (we cannot make sure whether pictures describe objects or OCR), so how can we solve this arduous task? And this is also the main challenge in the whole field of artificial intelligence. **2.** We just proposed the simplest methods to prove the superiority of OCR. Although the characterization-based method is easy and fast, the error is relatively large. Therefore, methods based on disentangled OCR feature matching will be the next step.

Acknowledgement. This work was partly supported by the Open Project Program of the National Laboratory of Pattern Recognition (NLPR) (No. 202200049) and the special project of "Tibet Economic and Social Development and Plateau Scientific Research Co-construction Innovation Foundation" of Wuhan University of Technology&Tibet University (No. lzt2021008).

References

1. Sidorov, O., Hu, R., Rohrbach, M., Singh, A.: TextCaps: a dataset for image captioning with reading comprehension. In: Vedaldi, A., Bischof, H., Brox, T., Frahm, J.-M. (eds.) ECCV 2020. LNCS, vol. 12347, pp. 742–758. Springer, Cham (2020). https://doi.org/10.1007/978-3-030-58536-5_44
2. Vaswani, A., et al.: Attention is all you need. In: Advances in Neural Information Processing Systems 30 (2017)
3. Lee, K.-H., Chen, X., Hua, G., Hu, H., He, X.: Stacked cross attention for image-text matching. In: Ferrari, V., Hebert, M., Sminchisescu, C., Weiss, Y. (eds.) ECCV 2018. LNCS, vol. 11208, pp. 212–228. Springer, Cham (2018). https://doi.org/10.1007/978-3-030-01225-0_13
4. Zeng, Y., Zhang, X., Li, H.: Multi-grained vision language pre-training: aligning texts with visual concepts. arXiv preprint arXiv:2111.08276 (2021)
5. Nguyen, M.-D., Nguyen, B.T., Gurrin, C.: A deep local and global scene-graph matching for image-text retrieval. arXiv preprint arXiv:2106.02400 (2021)
6. Diao, H., et al.: Similarity reasoning and filtration for image-text matching. arXiv preprint arXiv:2101.01368 (2021)
7. Kant, Y., et al.: Spatially aware multimodal transformers for TextVQA. In: Vedaldi, A., Bischof, H., Brox, T., Frahm, J.-M. (eds.) ECCV 2020. LNCS, vol. 12354, pp. 715–732. Springer, Cham (2020). https://doi.org/10.1007/978-3-030-58545-7_41
8. He, P., et al.: DeBERTa: decoding-enhanced BERT with disentangled attention. arXiv preprint arXiv:2006.03654 (2020)
9. Devlin, J., et al.: BERT: pre-training of deep bidirectional transformers for language understanding. arXiv preprint arXiv:1810.04805 (2018)
10. Li, K., et al.: Visual semantic reasoning for image-text matching. In: Proceedings of the IEEE/CVF International Conference on Computer Vision (2019)
11. Ule, J., et al.: CLIP identifies Nova-regulated RNA networks in the brain. Science **302**(5648), 1212–1215 (2003)
12. Li, J., et al.: BLIP: bootstrapping language-image pre-training for unified vision-language understanding and generation. arXiv preprint arXiv:2201.12086 (2022)
13. Lu, X., Zhao, T., Lee, K.: VisualSparta: an embarrassingly simple approach to large-scale text-to-image search with weighted bag-of-words. arXiv preprint arXiv:2101.00265 (2021)
14. Messina, N., et al.: Fine-grained visual textual alignment for cross-modal retrieval using transformer encoders. ACM Trans. Multimedia Comput. Commun. Appl. (TOMM) **17**(4), 1–23 (2021)
15. Mafla, A., et al.: StacMR: scene-text aware cross-modal retrieval. In: Proceedings of the IEEE/CVF Winter Conference on Applications of Computer Vision (2021)
16. Cheng, M., et al.: ViSTA: vision and scene text aggregation for cross-modal retrieval. arXiv preprint arXiv:2203.16778 (2022)

17. Young, P., Lai, A., Hodosh, M., Hockenmaier, J.: From image descriptions to visual denotations: new similarity metrics for semantic inference over event descriptions. ACL **2**, 67–78 (2014)

18. Lin, T.-Y., et al.: Microsoft COCO: common objects in context. In: Fleet, D., Pajdla, T., Schiele, B., Tuytelaars, T. (eds.) ECCV 2014. LNCS, vol. 8693, pp. 740–755. Springer, Cham (2014). https://doi.org/10.1007/978-3-319-10602-1_48

19. Veit, A., Matera, T., Neumann, L., Matas, J., Belongie, S.: Coco-text: dataset and benchmark for text detection and recognition in natural images. arXiv preprint arXiv:1601.07140 (2016)

20. Wang, P., et al.: Unifying architectures, tasks, and modalities through a simple sequence-to-sequence learning framework. arXiv preprint arXiv:2202.03052 (2022)

21. Biten, A.F., et al.: Is an image worth five sentences? A new look into semantics for image-text matching. In: Proceedings of the IEEE/CVF Winter Conference on Applications of Computer Vision (2022)

22. Liao, M., Pang, G., Huang, J., Hassner, T., Bai, X.: Mask TextSpotter v3: segmentation proposal network for robust scene text spotting. In: Vedaldi, A., Bischof, H., Brox, T., Frahm, J.-M. (eds.) ECCV 2020. LNCS, vol. 12356, pp. 706–722. Springer, Cham (2020). https://doi.org/10.1007/978-3-030-58621-8_41

23. Wang, H., et al.: Scene text retrieval via joint text detection and similarity learning. In: Proceedings of the IEEE/CVF Conference on Computer Vision and Pattern Recognition (2021)

24. Ren, S., et al.: Faster R-CNN: towards real-time object detection with region proposal networks. In: Advances in Neural Information Processing Systems 28 (2015)

25. Vinyals, O., Fortunato, M., Jaitly, N.: Pointer networks. In: Advances in Neural Information Processing Systems 28 (2015)

26. Zhu, Q., et al.: Simple is not easy: a simple strong baseline for TextVQA and TextCaps. arXiv preprint arXiv:2012.05153 2 (2020)

27. Anderson, P., et al.: Bottom-up and top-down attention for image captioning and visual question answering. In: Proceedings of the IEEE Conference on Computer Vision and Pattern Recognition (2018)

28. Huang, Z., et al.: Pixel-BERT: aligning image pixels with text by deep multi-modal transformers. arXiv preprint arXiv:2004.00849 (2020)

29. Miech, A., et al.: Thinking fast and slow: efficient text-to-visual retrieval with transformers. In: Proceedings of the IEEE/CVF Conference on Computer Vision and Pattern Recognition (2021)

Optimization and Neural Network and Deep Learning

Cloth-Aware Center Cluster Loss for Cloth-Changing Person Re-identification

Xulin Li[1,2], Bin Liu[1,2(✉)], Yan Lu[1,2], Qi Chu[1,2], and Nenghai Yu[1,2]

[1] School of Information Science and Technology, University of Science and Technology of China, Hefei, China
{lxlkw,luyan17}@mail.ustc.edu.cn,{qchu,ynh}@ustc.edu.cn
[2] Key Laboratory of Electromagnetic Space Information, Chinese Academy of Science, Beijing, China
flowice@ustc.edu.cn

Abstract. Person re-identification (Re-ID) has achieved great progress recently. However, it was limited by the inconsistency of clothes in the case of long-term person Re-ID. Cloth-changing person Re-ID focus on solving this problem, which is challenging since large intra-class variation and small inter-class variation. Existing methods mainly focus on introducing cloth-irrelevant cues such as joint points, contours, and 3D shapes through additional modules. Few studies investigate directly improving cross-clothing similarity via metric loss. In this paper, we propose a novel loss function, called Cloth-Aware Center Cluster loss (CACC loss) to reduce the intra-class cross-clothing variations. Specifically, the CACC loss supervises the network to learn cross-clothing invariant information by constraining the distance among samples and cloth-aware sample centers. Our method is simple and efficient, using only RGB modality without any additional modules, which can be a strong baseline to boost future research. Extensive experiments on cloth-changing person Re-ID datasets demonstrate the effectiveness of the proposed methods, which achieved the start-of-the-art performance.

Keywords: Person re-identification · Cloth-changing · Center Cluster loss

1 Introduction

Person re-identification (Re-ID) [3,12,16,22] aims to match pedestrian images of the same identity across different camera views. Most of the existing methods focus on overcoming the challenges caused by the variations of viewpoints, body poses, illuminations, and backgrounds to address the short-term person Re-ID. However, real-world intelligent surveillance requires methods to retrieve pedestrians across long periods. In this situation, pedestrians will wear different clothes, rendering the color and texture information that general person Re-ID

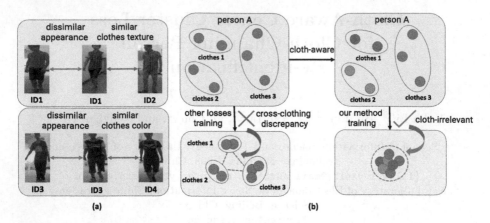

Fig. 1. (a) Clothes texture and color cause large intra-class variation and small inter-class variation, making re-identification difficult. (b) Our proposed method perceives different clothes and reducing cross-clothing discrepancy to obtains cloth-irrelevant features.

highly relied on no longer reliable. Therefore, the research on cloth-changing person Re-ID [7,10,14,17,18,20,21] has attracted great attention in recent years. Different from general person Re-ID, large intra-class cross-clothing variations bring new challenges to research on cloth-changing person Re-ID. As shown in Fig. 1(a), there are huge appearances discrepancy among the images of the same person with different clothes, such as the difference in color and texture information. Conversely, images of a different person wearing a similar clothes have a similar appearance.

To improve the robustness of person Re-ID against clothing texture, most existing researchers [1,6,8,14,20,21] focus on obtaining key points, contours, 3D shapes, gait, and other cloth-irrelevant cues. Although these cloth-irrelevant cues is helpful for the cloth-changing person Re-ID task, the additional extraction modules to obtain them increase computation costs during training and even inference. And we noticed that these methods ignore how to directly use the original images to explore the similarity across clothes from the perspective of metric learning, which is important for this issue.

However, the most widely used metric learning losses for person Re-ID task, such as triplet loss [15] and center loss [19] do not specifically focus on excluding the influence of clothes, so they cannot well guide the model to learn the invariance of cloth-changing. As shown in Fig. 1(b), these loss functions learn relations between samples at a coarse-grained level, which means that for a certain person, such as person A, they treat all different clothes equally. Therefore, they are difficult to eliminate the influence of the clothes, resulting in poor generalization ability on the test set.

To obtain cloth-irrelevant features, we design a novel loss function, called Cloth-Aware Center Cluster loss (CACC loss), which can directly establish the relationship between samples wearing different clothes and can make the model recognize them well. This is a clothing-aware loss function that can force the network to extract invariant human body information, reduce the large intra-class discrepancy caused by the variety of clothes, and expand the small inter-class discrepancy caused by similar clothes. Figure 1(b) also shows that our proposed method obtains cloth-irrelevant features by perceiving different clothes and performing cross-clothing clustering.

In addition, we constraints the features output by the network and the predicted probabilities obtained by the classifier separately to further enhance the cloth-irrelevant learning in different spaces.

The main contributions of this paper can be summarized as follows:

- We propose a simple but effective method without any additional modules for cloth-changing person Re-ID, which become the new start-of-the-art method on three cloth-changing person Re-ID datasets.
- We design a novel loss function (CACC loss) specifically for cloth-changing person Re-ID, which aims at gathering the features to their intra-class cross-clothing center and pushing away features from different categories.

2   Related Work

Person Re-ID. Person re-identification (Re-ID) is essentially a cross-camera retrieval task, which aims at addressing the challenge of different camera viewpoints, different poses, different resolutions, and occlusion. In addition, to address the limitation of a person changing clothes in long-term situations, cloth-changing person Re-ID has received extensive attention. Sun et al. [16] used part-level features to provide fine-grained information, which is of great benefit for various person Re-ID tasks. Luo et al. [12] provided a strong baseline, which was widely used. Some metric learning methods, triplet loss [15] and center loss [19] were both first proposed to address face recognition, and then widely used in person Re-ID tasks. However, none of these metric losses are specifically designed for cloth-changing person Re-ID.

We first proposed the Cloth-Aware Center Cluster loss, guiding the model to learn cloth-irrelevant features.

Cloth-Changing Person Re-ID. Recently, more and more research has begun to focus on addressing this challenging problem. Most of the existing methods utilize some additional modules to extract cloth-irrelevant information to guide model training. Wang et al. [17] downplayed the clothing information by detecting and extracting face features. However, facial information is not always detected in person Re-ID, and the face resolution is generally too low to be useful. Hong et al. [6] used 3D shape and Jin et al. [8] used gait information as two auxiliary tasks to drive the model to learn cloth-agnostic representations. However, it is difficult to extract discriminative and effective 3D shape or gait information from a single 2D image. Yang et al. [20] utilized contour, and Qian et al. [14] utilized human key points, and Chen et al. [1] utilized 2D shape to eliminate the impact of appearance. However, all these methods suffer from estimation errors generated by the extractor and inevitably increase the computation costs.

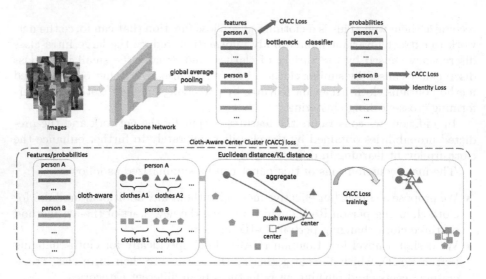

Fig. 2. The framework of our proposed approach. The main innovation is the Cloth-Aware Center Cluster (CACC) loss, which jointly constrains sample features or probabilities by "aggregation term" and "push away term".

Unlike these methods, we focus on directly optimizing the features of the original RGB modality images to reduce the interference of clothes without introducing any additional extraction modules. Our method is simple and efficient, and can be combined with the above methods to obtain stronger features.

3   Method

In this work, we address the cloth-changing Re-ID problem, which retrieves the same pedestrian wearing different clothes. The framework of our proposed approach is shown in Fig. 2. We constrain the features extracted by the backbone network and the probabilities obtained by the classifier through our proposed Cloth-Aware Center Cluster (CACC) loss and the identity loss, which aims to facilitate the discriminative cloth-irrelevant feature learning.

3.1   Framework Details

Pedestrian images are fed into the backbone network to extract features f after global average pooling. Then, these features are passed through a bottleneck layer [12] composed of a batch normalization layer and a classifier composed of a fully connected layer to get the predicted probabilities Y.

We impose an identity loss on Y to extract identity information. The identity loss $\mathcal{L}_{id}$ for Y is a cross-entropy loss, which can be expressed as:

$$\mathcal{L}_{id}(Y) = \mathbb{E}_i[-\log(y_i)]. \tag{1}$$

where Y_i is the predicted probability of i-th sample and y_i is the ground-truth category probability of Y_i. To further enhance the cross-clothing retrieval ability of features, we apply our proposed CACC loss on f and Y, respectively. The CACC loss can extract clothing invariant information, which will be described in detail in the next subsection.

3.2   Cloth-Aware Center Cluster Loss

The proposed CACC loss imposes dual constraints on the features f and the predicted probabilities Y. Since f and Y are different, we use different distance functions to measure them. For the features, we use euclidean distance $\mathcal{D}_{euc}$ to calculate the similarity between two features f_i and f_j.

$$\mathcal{D}_{euc}(f_i, f_j) = ||f_i - f_j||_2, \tag{2}$$

And for the probability distributions, we use $\mathcal{D}_{kl}$ to calculate the similarity between two probabilities Y_i and Y_j.

$$\mathcal{D}_{kl}(Y_i, Y_j) = \frac{1}{2}(\mathrm{KL}(Y_i||Y_j) + \mathrm{KL}(Y_j||Y_i)), \tag{3}$$

where $\mathrm{KL}(\cdot)$ means the Kullback-Leible (KL) divergence function. Since the KL divergence is asymmetric, we use the average of $\mathrm{KL}(Y_i||Y_j)$ and $\mathrm{KL}(Y_j||Y_i)$ to construct a symmetric distance function as $\mathcal{D}_{kl}$.

Based on the above definition, the total CACC loss can be divided into the following two parts CACC-euc and CACC-kl according to the input and the distance function.

$$\mathcal{L}_{CACC} = \mathcal{L}_{CACC-euc}(f) + \mathcal{L}_{CACC-kl}(Y). \tag{4}$$

The CACC-euc loss consists of two terms, the first term aims to aggregate intra-class samples while the second term aims to push away the inter-class samples.

$$\mathcal{L}_{CACC-euc}(f) = \underbrace{\mathbb{E}_{i,j}[\mathcal{D}_{euc}(f_i, c_j)]}_{\text{aggregate term}} + \underbrace{\mathbb{E}_{k,l}[max(\rho_1 - \mathcal{D}_{euc}(c_k, c_l), 0)]}_{\text{push away term}}. \tag{5}$$

For the "aggregate term", f_i is the feature of the i-th sample and c_j is the j-th feature center computed by f in current mini-batch. Specifically, feature center is the average of features which all belong to the same person wearing the same clothes. Besides, f_i and c_j have the same identity tag and different clothes tags. The "aggregate term" aims to aggregate samples with the same identity and eliminate their cross-clothing discrepancy.

For the "push away term", c_k and c_j are the k-th and j-th feature centers with different identity. ρ_1 is a margin hyper-parameter. The "push away term" aims to push away samples with different identities by an appropriate distance, which helps to distinguish two similarly dressed pedestrians.

The effectiveness of CACC-euc loss stems from the following three aspects. First, it contains two terms to learn the intra-class similarity and inter-class similarity of features respectively and they can facilitate each other. Second, it is a clothing-aware loss that uses clothing tags for fine-grained feature learning. Finally, it does not directly constrain the distance between individual features but constrains feature centers to weaken the adverse effects of outlier samples.

The CACC-kl loss has the same form as the CACC-euc loss, only the distance function is different. Similarly, it can be expressed as follows:

$$\mathcal{L}_{CACC-kl}(Y) = \underbrace{\mathbb{E}_{i,j}[\mathcal{D}_{kl}(Y_i, C_j)]}_{\text{aggregate term}} + \underbrace{\mathbb{E}_{k,l}[max(\rho_2 - \mathcal{D}_{kl}(C_k, C_l), 0)]}_{\text{push away term}}. \tag{6}$$

where Y_i is the predicted probability of the i-th sample. C_j, C_k, C_l and c_j, c_k, c_l have similar meanings and computational pipeline, respectively. ρ_2 is another margin hyper-parameter. The CACC-kl loss strives to make the predicted probabilities of the same person similar, which is an effective complement to the constraints of features. Thus, the CACC-euc loss and the CACC-kl loss can jointly supervise the network to learn more discriminative cloth-irrelevant features.

3.3 Optimization

We compute the total loss function $\mathcal{L}_{total}$ by mixing the identity loss and the CACC loss with different weights.

$$\begin{aligned}
\mathcal{L}_{total} &= \mathcal{L}_{id}(Y) + \mathcal{L}_{CACC} \\
&= \mathcal{L}_{id}(Y) + \mathcal{L}_{CACC-euc}(f) + \mathcal{L}_{CACC-kl}(Y)
\end{aligned} \tag{7}$$

We optimize the whole model in an end-to-end manner by minimizing the $\mathcal{L}_{total}$.

4 Experiments

4.1 Datasets and Evaluation Protocol

In this section, we conduct comprehensive experiments to evaluate our method on three public datasets: PRCC [20], LTCC [14] and VC-Clothes [17].

PRCC is a large cloth-changing Re-ID dataset, which was collected by 3 cameras in indoor environments. The training set contains 150 identities with 22,897 images while the testing set contains 71 identities with 10,800 images.

LTCC is another large cloth-changing Re-ID dataset, which collected by 12 cameras in indoor environments. The training set contains 77 identities with 9,576 images while the testing set contains 75 identities with 7,543 images.

VC-Clothes is a synthetic cloth-changing Re-ID dataset rendered by GTA5 game engine, which was collected by 4 cameras. The training set contains 256 identities with 9,449 images while the testing set contains 256 identities with 9,611 images.

Table 1. Comparison of Rank-k accuracy (%) and mAP accuracy (%) with the state-of-the-art methods on PRCC, LTCC and VC-Clothes.

Method	PRCC		LTCC		VC-Clothes	
	Rank-1	Rank-10	Rank-1	mAP	Rank-1	mAP
LOMO [11]+XQDA [11]	14.5	43.6	10.8	5.6	34.5	30.9
LOMO [11]+KISSME [9]	18.6	49.8	11.0	5.3	35.7	31.3
ResNet-50 [5]	19.4	52.4	20.1	9.0	36.4	32.4
PCB [16]	22.9	61.2	23.5	10.0	62.0	62.2
Qian et al. [14]	–	–	25.2	12.4	–	–
Yang et al. [20]	34.4	77.3	–	–	–	–
GI-ReID [8]	37.6	82.3	23.7	10.4	64.5	57.8
ASSP [1]	51.3	86.5	31.2	14.8	79.9	81.2
FSAM [6]	54.5	86.4	38.5	16.2	78.6	78.9
CAL [4]	55.2	–	40.1	18.0	–	–
CACC (ours)	**57.4**	**86.9**	**40.3**	**18.4**	**85.0**	**81.2**

Evaluation Protocol. All the experiments follow the evaluation protocol in existing cloth-changing person Re-ID benchmarks. For evaluation, the cumulative matching characteristics (CMC) and mean average precision (mAP) are adopted as the evaluation metric.

For PRCC, we randomly choose one image of each identity as the gallery. And we repeat the evaluation 10 times, then compute the average performance. As for LTCC and VC-Clothes, we choose all the images of each identity as the gallery. For each dataset, we use cloth-changing setting, which means there are all cloth-changing samples in the test set.

4.2 Implementation Details

Following the previous Re-ID methods [12], we adopt ResNet-50 [5] pre-trained on ImageNet [2] as our backbone network. We change the stride of the last convolutional layer in the backbone to one and employ the Batch Normalization Neck [12] as the embedding layer. Besides, random cropping, random horizontal flipping, and random erasing [23] are adopted for data augmentation. The whole model is trained with the Adam optimizer. The learning rate is set to 0.00035 for all pre-trained layers and 0.0035 for other layers. They gradually rise up by the warm-up scheme and decay by a factor of 10 at the 30th epoch. For PRCC we trained the model for 50 epoch, and for Ltcc and VC-Clothes we trained the model for 100 epoch. The input images are resized to 256×128 resolution. While, the batch size is set to 64 with 8 identities. As for the hyper-parameter, ρ_1 in Eq. 5 and ρ_2 in Eq. 6 are set to 0.6, 6, respectively.

Table 2. Ablation study on PRCC. We analyze the role of the two parts in the CACC loss, and compare with other metric losses including triplet loss and center loss.

i	Triplet	Center	CACC-euc	CACC-kl	PRCC	
					Rank-1	Rank-10
1	–	–	–	–	45.6	75.2
2	–	–	✓	–	53.6	83.2
3	–	–	–	✓	54.8	81.5
4	–	–	✓	✓	**57.4**	**86.9**
5	✓	–	–	–	47.7	77.7
6	–	✓	–	–	48.2	78.9
7	✓	✓	–	–	48.6	78.6
8	✓	–	✓	✓	55.4	81.5
9	–	✓	✓	✓	56.2	83.3

4.3   Comparison with State-of-the-Art Methods

In this part, we compare our proposed CACC method with hand-crafted feature representations methods, general person Re-ID methods, and state-of-the-art (SOTA) cloth-changing person Re-ID methods, *e.g.* GI-ReID [8], ASSP [1], FSAM [6], CAL [4].

The experiment results on the three Cloth-Changing Person Re-ID datasets are shown in Table 1. In PRCC dataset, our method achieves 57.4% Rank-1 accuracy and 86.9% Rank-10 accuracy, which surpasses CAL by 2.2% on Rank-1 accuracy. In LTCC dataset and VC-Clothes dataset, our method still has better retrieval performance than CAL and ASSP. Compared with these SOTA methods like FSAM, we do not introduce additional modules to actively extract cloth-irrelevant cues such as contours, shapes, and key points. But our methods achieve superior performance with effective metric learning. As for the hand-crafted feature representations methods and general person Re-ID methods, our method outperforms them by a large margin. The experiment illustrates that the constraints we impose on the features are suitable for the cloth-changing problem.

4.4   Ablation Study

As shown in Table 2, we perform comprehensive ablation studies and comparisons with other metric loss to demonstrate the effectiveness of our CACC loss. The model only extracts features from the backbone network trained by the cross-entropy loss for identity learning is adopted as the baseline in the experiments, denoted as `model-1` in Table 2.

Effectiveness of CACC Loss. Compared with the baseline, the backbone with CACC-euc loss (`model-2`) improves the Rank-1 accuracy and the Rank-10 accuracy by 8.0% and 8.0% while the model with CACC-kl loss (`model-3`) improves the Rank-1 accuracy and the Rank-10 accuracy by 9.2% and 6.3%. When they combine (`model-4`), the performance has been greatly improved by 11.8% in Rank-1 accuracy and 11.7% in Rank-10 accuracy. This large improvement benefits from our CACC loss dedicated to aggregating features to their cross-clothing centers to eliminate the intra-class discrepancy. In addition, they also pushed the center of the positive and negative samples wearing similar clothes to increase the inter-class discrepancy. Besides, the experimental results show that the two different constraints, CACC-euc loss and CACC-kl loss, can promote each other to obtain more robust feature embeddings jointly.

Compared with Other Metric Losses. The backbone with triplet loss (`model-5`) and center loss (`model-6`) only have a small improvement over the baseline. When we use triplet loss and center loss jointly (`model-7`), it can achieve 48.6% on Rank-1 accuracy and 78.6% on Rank-10, which is still below the performance of CACC loss by a large margin. It demonstrates that neglecting to improve cross-clothing similarity may lead to sub-optimal performance. Besides, the results of `model-8` and `model-9` illustrate that just using CACC loss can achieve good enough results without combining other losses, which means that our loss is a superior substitute for these losses in the cloth-changing scenes.

4.5   Visualization and Analysis

Visualization of Feature Distribution. Figure 3 shows the effect of several losses on the feature distribution. It can be seen that the features of the baseline model have a large intra-class discrepancy, and triplet loss does not narrow this discrepancy well. Though center loss achieves this goal to a certain extent, the distances for cross-clothing samples are still significantly larger than same-clothing samples. Because center loss only penalizes the distance between intra-class samples and their corresponding class center, which makes the distance between the more accessible same-clothing samples always smaller.

Unlike the center loss, our CACC loss successfully reduces the distance between cross-clothing samples, which helps to obtain cloth-irrelevant features and is suitable for cloth-changing scenes.

Visualization of Ranking Results. Figure 4 illustrates some retrieval results of our proposed method versus baseline in PRCC. The green boxes are the positive search results and the red boxes mean negative results. For example, the results in the 2nd row show that the baseline model is disturbed by the color of the clothes and mismatches person wearing red. The results in 4th and 6th rows show that the baseline model is disturbed by the texture of the clothes and incorrectly matches person whose clothes contain meshes or stripes. Our method is not disturbed by the texture and color of the clothes. So it achieves excellent performances and shows good retrieval quality.

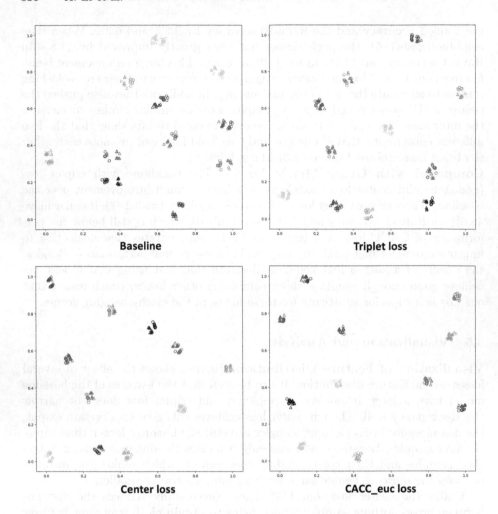

Fig. 3. t-SNE [13] visualization of different feature distributions in PRCC. Samples with same color indicate the same identity. In each identity, different markers represent different clothes.

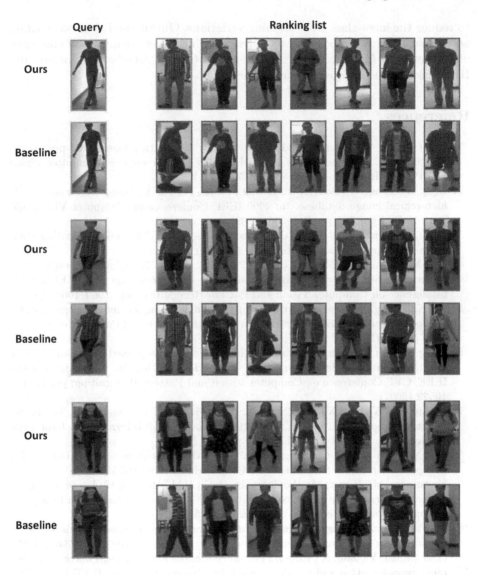

Fig. 4. Visualization of the ranking lists of our proposed method versus baseline in PRCC. The green boxes represent correct retrieval results, and the red boxes represent incorrect retrieval results. The evaluation of PRCC is single-shot, which means that there is only one matched sample in the gallery set. (Color figure online)

5   Conclusion

In this paper, we propose a novel loss function called Cloth-Aware Center Cluster loss (CACC loss), for cloth-changing person Re-ID, which jointly constrain the distance among samples and cloth-aware sample centers in two feature spaces to reduce the intra-class cross-clothing variations. Our method does not contain additional network branches or modules, so it has lower computation cost than other methods. And extensive experiments on three Cloth-changing person Re-ID datasets demonstrate the effectiveness of it.

References

1. Chen, J., et al.: Learning 3d shape feature for texture-insensitive person re-identification. In: Proceedings of the IEEE/CVF Conference on Computer Vision and Pattern Recognition, pp. 8146–8155 (2021)
2. Deng, J., Dong, W., Socher, R., Li, L.J., Li, K., Fei-Fei, L.: ImageNet: a large-scale hierarchical image database. In: 2009 IEEE Conference on Computer Vision and Pattern Recognition, pp. 248–255 (2009)
3. Gong, S., Cristani, M., Loy, C.C., Hospedales, T.M.: The re-identification challenge. In: Person re-identification, pp. 1–20 (2014)
4. Gu, X., Chang, H., Ma, B., Bai, S., Shan, S., Chen, X.: Clothes-changing person re-identification with RGB modality only. In: Proceedings of the IEEE/CVF Conference on Computer Vision and Pattern Recognition, pp. 1060–1069 (2022)
5. He, K., Zhang, X., Ren, S., Sun, J.: Deep residual learning for image recognition. In: Proceedings of the IEEE Conference on Computer Vision and Pattern Recognition, pp. 770–778 (2016)
6. Hong, P., Wu, T., Wu, A., Han, X., Zheng, W.S.: Fine-grained shape-appearance mutual learning for cloth-changing person re-identification. In: Proceedings of the IEEE/CVF Conference on Computer Vision and Pattern Recognition, pp. 10513–10522 (2021)
7. Huang, Y., Wu, Q., Xu, J., Zhong, Y.: Celebrities-reID: a benchmark for clothes variation in long-term person re-identification. In: 2019 International Joint Conference on Neural Networks (IJCNN), pp. 1–8 (2019)
8. Jin, X., et al.: Cloth-changing person re-identification from a single image with gait prediction and regularization. arXiv preprint arXiv:2103.15537 (2021)
9. Koestinger, M., Hirzer, M., Wohlhart, P., Roth, P.M., Bischof, H.: Large scale metric learning from equivalence constraints. In: 2012 IEEE Conference on Computer Vision and Pattern Recognition, pp. 2288–2295 (2012)
10. Li, Y.J., Luo, Z., Weng, X., Kitani, K.M.: Learning shape representations for clothing variations in person re-identification. arXiv preprint arXiv:2003.07340 (2020)
11. Liao, S., Hu, Y., Zhu, X., Li, S.Z.: Person re-identification by local maximal occurrence representation and metric learning. In: Proceedings of the IEEE Conference on Computer Vision and Pattern Recognition, pp. 2197–2206 (2015)
12. Luo, H., Gu, Y., Liao, X., Lai, S., Jiang, W.: Bag of tricks and a strong baseline for deep person re-identification. In: Proceedings of the IEEE/CVF Conference on Computer Vision and Pattern Recognition Workshops, p. 0 (2019)
13. Van der Maaten, L., Hinton, G.: Visualizing data using t-SNE. J. Mach. Learn. Res. **9**(11) (2008)
14. Qian, X., et al.: Long-term cloth-changing person re-identification. In: Proceedings of the Asian Conference on Computer Vision (2020)
15. Schroff, F., Kalenichenko, D., Philbin, J.: FaceNet: a unified embedding for face recognition and clustering. In: Proceedings of the IEEE Conference on Computer Vision and Pattern Recognition, pp. 815–823 (2015)

16. Sun, Y., Zheng, L., Yang, Y., Tian, Q., Wang, S.: Beyond part models: person retrieval with refined part pooling (and a strong convolutional baseline). In: Ferrari, V., Hebert, M., Sminchisescu, C., Weiss, Y. (eds.) ECCV 2018. LNCS, vol. 11208, pp. 501–518. Springer, Cham (2018). https://doi.org/10.1007/978-3-030-01225-0_30
17. Wan, F., Wu, Y., Qian, X., Chen, Y., Fu, Y.: When person re-identification meets changing clothes. In: Proceedings of the IEEE/CVF Conference on Computer Vision and Pattern Recognition Workshops, pp. 830–831 (2020)
18. Wang, K., Ma, Z., Chen, S., Yang, J., Zhou, K., Li, T.: A benchmark for clothes variation in person re-identification. Int. J. Intell. Syst. **35**(12), 1881–1898 (2020)
19. Wen, Y., Zhang, K., Li, Z., Qiao, Yu.: A discriminative feature learning approach for deep face recognition. In: Leibe, B., Matas, J., Sebe, N., Welling, M. (eds.) ECCV 2016. LNCS, vol. 9911, pp. 499–515. Springer, Cham (2016). https://doi.org/10.1007/978-3-319-46478-7_31
20. Yang, Q., Wu, A., Zheng, W.S.: Person re-identification by contour sketch under moderate clothing change. IEEE Trans. Pattern Anal. Mach. Intell. **43**(6), 2029–2046 (2019)
21. Yu, S., Li, S., Chen, D., Zhao, R., Yan, J., Qiao, Y.: COCAS: a large-scale clothes changing person dataset for re-identification. In: Proceedings of the IEEE/CVF Conference on Computer Vision and Pattern Recognition, pp. 3400–3409 (2020)
22. Zhang, X., et al.: AlignedReID: surpassing human-level performance in person re-identification. arXiv preprint arXiv:1711.08184 (2017)
23. Zhong, Z., Zheng, L., Kang, G., Li, S., Yang, Y.: Random erasing data augmentation. In: Proceedings of the AAAI Conference on Artificial Intelligence, vol. 34, pp. 13001–13008 (2020)

Efficient Channel Pruning via Architecture-Guided Search Space Shrinking

Zhi Yang and Zheyang Li[(✉)]

Hikvision Research Institute, Hangzhou, China
{yangzhi13,lizheyang}@hikvision.com

Abstract. Recently, channel pruning methods search for the optimal channel numbers by training a weight-sharing network to evaluate architectures of subnetworks. However, the weight shared between subnetworks incurs severe evaluation bias and an accuracy drop. In this paper, we provide a comprehensive understanding of the search space's impact on the evaluation by dissecting the training process of the weight-sharing network analytically. Specifically, it is proved that the sharing weights induce biased noise on gradients, whose magnitude is proportional to the search range of channel numbers and bias is relative to the average channel numbers of the search space. Motivated by the theoretical result, we design a channel pruning method by training a weight-sharing network with search space shrinking. The search space is iteratively shrunk guided by the optimal architecture searched in the weight-sharing network. The reduced search space boosts the accuracy of the evaluation and significantly cuts down the post-processing computation of finetuning. In the end, we demonstrate the superiority of our channel pruning method over state-of-the-art methods with experiments on ImageNet and COCO.

Keywords: Model compression · Channel pruning · Edge-device deployment

1 Introduction

As one of the popular techniques for network acceleration and compression, channel pruning removes the less important channels from the original model to optimize the channel numbers in networks. The reduction of channel numbers enables us to achieve optimal speed-accuracy trade-offs for a variety of applications. Amounts of techniques are reported to prune channels, including pruning criteria [1–3] and group LASSO regularizations [4,5]. However, most previous works rely on human-designed heuristics or predefined channel numbers in each layer.

Supplementary Information The online version contains supplementary material available at https://doi.org/10.1007/978-3-031-18907-4_42.

Recently, a new perspective of channel pruning was proposed to search for the optimal channel numbers directly [6,7,14]. The subnetworks with different channel numbers in each layer comprise an extremely huge and complicated search space. To evaluate the channel structures of subnetworks efficiently, MetaPruning trains a meta-network to generate parameters for all pruned models, where the meta-network is powerful but computationally expensive [8]. In contrast, Eagle-Eye utilizes the subnetworks inheriting weights from the pretrained model for fast evaluation [9]. However, the inferior evaluation performance deteriorates the ranking correlation between evaluation and the final accuracy. To improve evaluation performance with less computation cost, AutoSlim employs the weight-sharing technique to train a slimmable network [10]. The weight-sharing technique cuts down the training cost by amortizing the training cost of training varieties of subnetworks effectively.

Nevertheless, the weight sharing technique incurs biased evaluation and accuracy drop due to the heavy conflict between subnetworks during training. To alleviate the accuracy drop on evaluation, previous methods propose to shrink search space using the accuracy or magnitude-based metrics [11–14]. However, the impact of search space is not suppressed effectively as it can mislead the search process and bias to certain patterns [15].

In this paper, we dissect the gradients of the weight-sharing network during training. Compared to stand-alone training, the interplay between subnetworks introduces additional biased noise on gradients. Quantitatively, the magnitude of the noise is proportional to the search range of channel numbers, while the bias is relative to the average channel numbers of the search space. Based on the theoretical results, we propose an architecture-guided search space shrinking method to train a weight-sharing network for channel pruning. Specifically, we reduce the search range in each layer to suppress the magnitude of noise. Moreover, we shift the average channel numbers to the channel architecture searched in the weight-sharing network aiming to mitigate the noise bias. By doing so, we not only improve the evaluation performance but also suppress the evaluation bias originating from the search space. After training the weight-sharing network with search space shrinking, we obtain the pruned model with a short-term finetuning. In the end, we conduct extensive experiments and demonstrate the superiority of our algorithm over state-of-the-art methods.

Our main contributions are summarized as follows:

- Theoretically, we prove that a biased noise of gradient is introduced by the weight sharing technique. The bias is relative to the average channel numbers of the search space, while the magnitude of the noise is proportional to the search range of channel numbers. To the best of our knowledge, our analysis provides the first theoretical understanding of the search space's impact on the evaluation.
- We propose an efficient channel pruning method by training a weight-sharing network with search space shrinking. The search space shrinking technique not only boosts the accuracy of subnetworks but also suppresses the bias on evaluation induced by the weight sharing technique.

2   Motivation

The paradigm of pruning channels based on searching for the optimal channel numbers comprises two processes: the first is weight optimization, where a weight-sharing network is trained with the weight sharing technique; the second step is architecture search, where the subnetworks are evaluated efficiently by inheriting weights from the weight-sharing network.

In the process of weight optimization, the parameters of the weight-sharing network are optimized as

$$W^\star = \arg\min_{W} \mathbb{E}_{a \sim \Gamma(\mathcal{A})}[\mathcal{L}_{\text{train}}(W; a)], \tag{1}$$

where W denotes parameters of the network, $\mathcal{L}_{\text{train}}$ is the loss function on the training set, and $\mathcal{A}$ denotes the search space. The search space consists of subnetworks with different channel numbers but the same architecture as the unpruned model. The channel architecture of candidate subnetworks can be encoded as

$$a = [a_1, a_2, \ldots, a_L] \in (0, 1]^L, \tag{2}$$

where L is the total number of layers in the weight-sharing network, $a_j = \frac{c_j}{C_j}$ denotes the width of the j'th layer, and c_j, C_j denote the channel numbers of the subnetwork and unpruned model respectively. The prior distribution of channel number configurations is denoted by $\Gamma(\mathcal{A})$. In this paper, we sample the candidate architectures with balanced frequency.

Although the weight sharing technique cuts down the expense of computation, it deteriorates the ranking correlation between evaluation performance and final accuracies as well as the evaluation performance. In this paper, we dissect the impact of search space by investigating the gradients.

First, when the subnetwork a is sampled in a weight-sharing network, the gradient of weight ω is written as

$$g(\omega; a) = \frac{\partial \mathcal{L}(W; a)}{\partial \omega}. \tag{3}$$

We use a simple approximation of the gradient with the first-order Taylor expansion as follows:

$$g(\omega; a) \approx \frac{\partial}{\partial \omega_i}\left[\mathcal{L}(W; \bar{a}) + \frac{\partial \mathcal{L}(W; \bar{a})}{\partial \bar{a}}(a - \bar{a})\right], \tag{4}$$

where $\bar{a}$ denotes the *average architecture* of subnetworks in the search space and is defined as

$$\bar{a} \triangleq \mathbb{E}_{a \sim \Gamma(\mathcal{A})} a. \tag{5}$$

During training the weight-sharing network, varieties of architectures are sampled and the difference of gradients between them is computed by

$$g(\omega; a) - g(\omega; a') = \frac{\partial^2 \mathcal{L}(W; \bar{a})}{\partial \omega \partial \bar{a}}(a - a'). \tag{6}$$

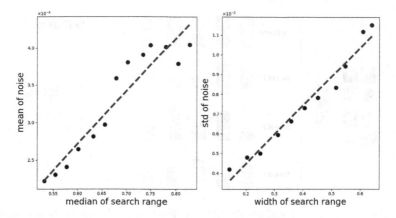

Fig. 1. Statistics of gradient noise of *layer4[1].bn1* on ResNet50. Left: the averaging biases of noise versus the median of sample ranges. Right: the relation between the standard variances of noise and the width of search ranges. Please refer to supplements for details.

Next, we ignore the influence from the updating weights during training and calculate the expectation of the gradient difference over the search space $a' \sim \Gamma(\mathcal{A})$, that is

$$\mathbb{E}_{a'} \left[g(\omega; a) - g(\omega; a') \right] = \frac{\partial^2 \mathcal{L}(W; \bar{a})}{\partial \omega \partial \bar{a}} (a - \bar{a}). \tag{7}$$

Notice that $g(\omega, a)$ is equal to the gradient of the subnetwork trained stand-alone with the architecture a. Thus, the left-hand side of Eq. (7) represents the average difference of gradients between the subnetwork a trained stand-alone and the one sampled from the weight-sharing network. Rooted on Eq. (7), we prove that **the weight-sharing technique induces additional biased noise on gradients compared to the stand-alone training network**. Notice that the bias of noise is relative to the average architecture of the search space. Thus the search space may lead to severe evaluation bias if the final architecture is far from the average architecture. This finding is consistent with the experiments in [15] that the search space may mislead the evaluation and bias to certain patterns.

On the other hand, the variance of gradient bias is given by

$$\mathrm{Var}_{a'} \left[g(\omega; a) - g(\omega; a') \right] = \sum_{l=1}^{L} \left[\frac{\partial^2 \mathcal{L}(W; \bar{a})}{\partial \omega \partial \bar{a}_l} \right]^2 \mathrm{Var}_{a'} a'_l, \tag{8}$$

where $\bar{a}_l$ and a'_l denote the width of the l'th layer in architecture $\bar{a}$ and a respectively. Equation (8) indicates that **the magnitude of noise on gradients is proportional to the variance of width in each layer**. Therefore, search space shrinking relieves the optimization difficulty of training the weight-sharing network by suppressing the gradient noise.

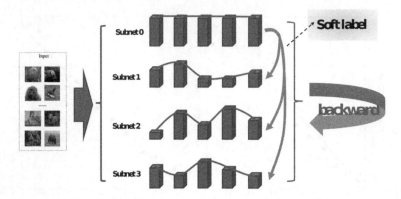

Fig. 2. An illustration of inplace distillation. Each cuboid represents a convolution layer, and their heights denote the width. The largest subnetwork is always sampled for the first time in each mini-batch and its outputs are taken as soft label for other subnetworks. After backward for multiple times, the shared weights are updated together.

Finally, we verify the theoretical results with an example of ResNet50. On the left of Fig. 1, we plot the averaging bias of gradient noise as a function of the midpoint of search ranges. On the right, we plot the standard variance of noise versus the width of the search range. The standard variance of the search range is proportional to the width since the channels are uniformly sampled. As both of the plots are well fitted with linear functions, we conclude that the experimental results match well with the theoretical prediction in Eqs. (7) and (8).

3   Channel Pruning Method

By assuming the second-order derivatives as a collection of independent and identically distributed variables with the mean value of μ_H and standard variance of σ_H, we average the magnitude of noise over the parameter ω and obtain

$$\mathrm{Var}_{\omega, a'}\left[g(\omega; a) - g(\omega; a')\right] \approx \sigma_H^2 \mathbb{E}_{a'} ||a' - \bar{a}||_2^2, \qquad (9)$$

Therefore, we can reduce the sample ranges in each layer to shrink the search space during training the weight-sharing network. Furthermore, the averaged gradient bias over the parameter is expressed as following

$$\mathbb{E}_{\omega, a'}\left[g(\omega; a) - g(\omega; a')\right] \approx \mu_H \sum_{l=1}^{L}(a_l - \bar{a}_l) \leq \mu_H ||a - \bar{a}||_1. \qquad (10)$$

Equation (10) inspires us to restrict the difference between the average architecture and the final architecture of the pruned model.

Motivated by these two corollaries, we design a channel pruning method by training a weight-sharing network with search space shrinking. In the first stage, we update the parameters of the weight-sharing network for warmup. During this

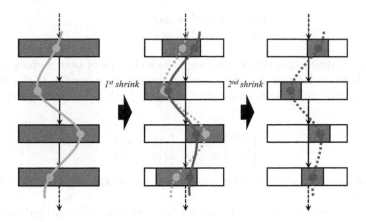

Fig. 3. An illustration of search space shrinking. Each rectangle represents a convolution layer where the blue bar represents the search range of channels. The first time of search space shrinking shifts the midpoints of the search range to the position of yellow circles representing the best channel numbers searched in the initial search space. Similarly, the second time of search space shrinking shifts the midpoints of the shrunk search pace to the position of red circles representing the best channel numbers searched in the shrunk search space, and so on. (Color figure online)

process, we sample channels in each layer with uniform probability to avoid the network dropping into bad local minima caused by imbalanced weight updating of subnetworks. Besides, we employ the inplace distillation technique to improve the accuracy of subnetworks in the evaluation [10]. As illustrated in Fig. 2, we sample n subnetworks in each mini-batch: the largest subnetwork a^0 followed by $(n-1)$ randomly sampled ones a^i's. The largest subnetwork is taken as the teacher model, and the loss function can be written as

$$\mathcal{L} = \mathrm{CE}(\boldsymbol{q}^0, y) + \sum_{i=1}^{n-1} \mathrm{KL}(\boldsymbol{q}^i, \boldsymbol{q}^0), \tag{11}$$

where CE and KL denote the cross entropy loss and Kullback-Leibler divergence respectively, $\boldsymbol{q}^i$ represents the outputs of the i's subnetwork a^i, and y is the ground-truth label. Last but not least, we initialize the weight-sharing model with pretrained weights to speed up the convergence of subnetworks. This procedure also helps to avoid the network dropping into bad local minima during search space shrinking.

After the warmup process, we shrink the search space and update weights alternatively as described in Fig. 3. The weights are updated in the same way as the warmup process, but the sample ranges in each layer are reduced iteratively. Once the weights are updated, we shrink the search space iteratively and shift the average architecture to that of the optimal subnetwork search in the weight-sharing network. Concretely, the search ranges after the $(s + 1)$'th time of shrinking satisfy the following conditions:

$$\begin{cases} v_l^{s+1} + u_l^{s+1} = 2a_l^s \\ v_l^{s+1} - u_l^{s+1} = \eta(v_l^s - u_l^s) \end{cases},$$ (12)

where $[u_l^s, v_l^s]$ represents the search range the s'th time of search space shrinking in the l'th layer, a^s denotes the searched architecture, and η is the shrinking ratio. Therefore, the search space after the $(s+1)$'th time of shrinking is given by

$$\begin{cases} u_l^{s+1} = a_l^s - \frac{\eta}{2}(v_l^s - u_l^s) \\ v_l^{s+1} = a_l^s + \frac{\eta}{2}(v_l^s - u_l^s) \end{cases}.$$ (13)

The optimal architecture can be search with evolution algorithms or differentiable methods.

Finally, we obtain the pruned model by finetuning the optimal subnetwork with the weights inherited from the weight-sharing model.

4   Experiments

4.1   Implemented Details

We use standard preprocessing and augmentation to obtain the pre-trained model. On ImageNet, the networks are trained for 100 epochs with a weight decay of 10^{-4} and an initial learning rate of 0.1. The experiments are implemented on 8 GPUs with a batch size of 256. On COCO, The baseline is trained for 12 epochs with the backbone pretrained on ImageNet.

In each layer, the channels are divided into groups and each channel group contains 8 channels in the ResNets. The topological constraint between convolution layers linked with shortcuts is preserved during sampling the channel groups, thus no additional convolutions are introduced at all.

On ImageNet, the weight-sharing networks are trained for 40 epochs in total. The initial learning rate is initialized as 0.01 and multiplied by 0.1 in the 30th epoch. We sample $n = 4$ subnetworks in each mini-batch. We shrink the search space at the 10th, 20th, and 30th epoch respectively. The shrinking ratio η is set as 0.5 in this paper. After training the weight-sharing model, the optimal subnetwork is finetuned for 40 epochs with standard preprocessing and augmentation.

4.2   Results on ImageNet

We compare our pruning results of ResNet50 and ResNet18 on ImageNet classification tasks to prevailing methods as shown in Table 1. On ResNet50, our method achieves an accuracy increase of 0.14% with only 45.4% FLOPs retained. This result outperforms recent methods based on the weight-sharing network, such as AutoSlim and DMCP. And for ResNet18, the drop of accuracy is 0.98%, which is much less than the result with comparable FLOPs in FPGM.

Table 1. Comparison of pruned ResNet50, ResNet18, and ResNeXt50 on ImageNet. "FLOPs" represents the retained FLOPs of each pruned model. "GSD" means the group size divisor.

Network	Method	Pruned (dropped) acc. (%)	FLOPs (%)
ResNet50	AOFP [16]	75.11 (0.23)	43.27
	GBN [5]	75.48 (0.67)	44.94
	HRank [1]	74.98 (1.17)	56.2
	LRF [17]	75.78 (0.43)	48.2
	CC [18]	75.59 (0.56)	47.1
	AutoSlim [10]	75.6 (1.0)	49
	DMCP [19]	76.5 (0.1)	54
	Ours	**76.29 (−0.14)**	**45.4**
	HRank [1]	69.10 (7.05)	24.0
	BCNet [20]	75.2 (2.3)	24
	AutoSlim [10]	74.0 (2.6)	27
	DMCP [19]	74.4 (2.2)	27
	Ours	**74.43 (1.72)**	**24.0**
ResNet18	BCNet [20]	69.9 (1.6)	50
	FPGM [2]	68.41 (1.87)	58.2
	DMCP [19]	69.0 (1.1)	57.8
	Ours	**69.56 (0.98)**	**58.0**
ResNeXt50	Ours	77.11 (0.67)	50.6
	Ours (GSD = 8)	76.81 (0.97)	52.6
	Ours (GSD = 4)	76.95 (0.83)	51.0

Additionally, we reducing the group numbers and group sizes jointly in ResNeXt50. Specifically, we divide the channels into mini-groups uniformly in each channel group. The channel number in each mini-group is called *group size divisor*. For instance, if the group size is 16 and the group size divisor is chosen as 4, the candidate group sizes are sampled in the set of $\{4, 8, 12, 16\}$. During the search process, we optimize the architecture parameters of groups and group sizes simultaneously. After finetuning the pruned model, our method obtains 77.11% top-1 accuracy with a $2\times$ reduction of FLOPs by pruning the groups, as depicted in Table 1. Meanwhile, we achieve comparable accuracies when pruning group numbers and group sizes jointly. The channel architectures of pruned models on ImageNet can be found in supplements.

Table 2. Pruned results of FasterRCNN with backbone of ResNet50 on COCO. "mAP" denotes the mean average precision.

Method	FLOPs (%)	Baseline mAP (%)	Pruned mAP (%)
SNet [21]	56	36.4	36.1 (0.3)
BCNet [20]	56	37.3	36.3 (1.0)
Ours	50	36.4	36.5 (−0.1)
SNet [21]	25	36.4	34.0 (2.4)
Ours	31	36.4	35.8 (0.8)

Table 3. Ablation study of the contribution to evaluation from shrinking search space. Experiments are conducted with the ResNet50 on ImageNet.

FLOPs (%)	Shrinking	Finetune	Acc. (%)
45	×	×	74.82
	✓	×	75.40
	✓	✓	76.29
20	×	×	70.41
	✓	×	72.41
	✓	✓	73.70

4.3 Results on COCO

We prune the two-stage object detector of FasterRCNN with a backbone of ResNet50 on the COCO dataset. We train the weight-sharing network for 12 epochs with an initial learning rate of 0.02. We sample the channels in the backbone and FPN in the meantime and shrink the search space after the 8'th and 11'th epochs. After shrinking and training, the pruned model is finetuned for 4 epochs. As shown in Table 2, our method obtains higher mAP than the previous pruning method with comparable FLOPs retained. The channel architectures of pruned models can be found in supplements.

4.4 Ablation

We quantify the contribution of search space shrinking to accuracy in the evaluation. Taking the ResNet50 as an example, we observe notable accuracy improvement in the accuracies of the optimal subnetworks sampled in the weight-sharing network with search space shrinking as shown in Table 3. Moreover, the accuracies can be further boosted by finetuning.

We further evaluate the times of shrinking search space on the accuracies of pruned models. In the experiments, we train the weight-sharing networks for 40 epochs equally but shrink the search space for different times. As illustrated in Table 4, the accuracies of the pruned ResNet50 with 20% FLOPs increase with the increasing times of shrinking search space. This result demonstrates

Table 4. Accuracies of the ResNet50 with 20% FLOPs on ImageNet. The pruned models are pruned with the weight-sharing networks whose search space is shrunk for different times.

Network	FLOPs (%)	Shrinking	Acc. (%)
ResNet50	20	1	73.37
		2	73.51
		3	73.70

Table 5. Comparison of epoch numbers required in different algorithms. "Training" means training the weight-sharing network, "Pruning" means sparse training or pruning, and "Post-process" includes finetuning and retraining.

Method	Training	Pruning	Post-process
AutoSlim [10]	50	-	100
DMCP [19]	40	-	100
HRank [1]	0	480	0
GBN [5]	-	160	40
Ours	40	-	40

the effectiveness of shrinking search space of suppressing the biased noise on gradients.

Due to the significantly boosted evaluation performance, our method achieves not only high performance after pruning but also a significant reduction of computational cost. In Table 5, we list the epochs spent on different methods. Benefiting from the search space shrinking technique, our method requires fewer epochs of training the weight-sharing network compared to AutoSlim. Specifically, the significantly boosted accuracy in the evaluation results in the much less post-process computation of finetuning.

5   Conclusion

In this paper, we theoretically prove that the weight sharing technique introduces biased noise on gradients. To the best of our knowledge, we provide the first theoretical understanding of the search space's impact on the evaluation. Motivated by the theoretical results, we design an effective channel pruning method by training a weight-sharing network with search space shrinking guided by the optimal architecture searched in the weight-sharing network. The search space shrinking not only mitigates the noise magnitude but also suppresses the bias. Furthermore, the search space shrinking significantly boosts evaluation performance and reduces post-process computation of finetuning. Extensive experiments on ImageNet and COCO demonstrate the effectiveness and efficiency of our algorithm.

References

1. Lin, M., et al.: Hrank: filter pruning using high-rank feature map. In: 2020 IEEE/CVF Conference on Computer Vision, Pattern Recognition (CVPR) (2020)
2. He, Y., Liu, P., Wang, Z., Hu, Z., Yang, Y.: Filter pruning via geometric median for deep convolutional neural networks acceleration. In: 2019 IEEE/CVF Conference on Computer Vision, Pattern Recognition (CVPR) (2019)
3. Molchanov, P., Mallya, A., Tyree, S., Frosio, I., Kautz, J.: Importance estimation for neural network pruning. In: 2019 IEEE/CVF Conference on Computer Vision, Pattern Recognition (CVPR) (2019)
4. Wen, W., Wu, C., Wang, Y., Chen, Y., Li, H.H.: Learning structured sparsity in deep neural networks. In: Advances in Neural Information Processing Systems (2016)
5. You, Z., Yan, K., Ye, J., Ma, M., Wang, P.: Gate decorator: global filter pruning method for accelerating deep convolutional neural networks. In: Advances in Neural Information Processing Systems (2019)
6. Wang, J., et al.: Revisiting parameter sharing for automatic neural channel number search. In: Advances in Neural Information Processing Systems (2020)
7. Chen, Z., Niu, J., Xie, L., Liu, X., Wei, L., Tian, Q.: Network adjustment: channel search guided by flops utilization ratio. In: 2020 IEEE/CVF Conference on Computer Vision, Pattern Recognition (CVPR) (2020)
8. Liu, Z., et al.: Metapruning: meta learning for automatic neural network channel pruning. In: 2019 IEEE/CVF International Conference on Computer Vision (ICCV) (2019)
9. Li, B., Wu, B., Su, J., Wang, G.: EagleEye: fast sub-net evaluation for efficient neural network pruning. In: Vedaldi, A., Bischof, H., Brox, T., Frahm, J.-M. (eds.) ECCV 2020. LNCS, vol. 12347, pp. 639–654. Springer, Cham (2020). https://doi.org/10.1007/978-3-030-58536-5_38
10. Yu, J., Huang, T.: Autoslim: towards oneshot architecture search for channel numbers. In: Advances in Neural Information Processing Systems (2019)
11. Li, X., et al.: Improving one-shot NAS by suppressing the posterior fading. In: 2020 IEEE/CVF Conference on Computer Vision, Pattern Recognition (CVPR) (2020)
12. Nayman, N., Noy, A., Ridnik, T., Friedman, I., Jin, R., Zelnik-Manor, L.: XNAS: neural architecture search with expert advice. In: Advances in Neural Information Processing Systems (2019)
13. Fang, M., Wang, Q., Zhong, Z.: Betanas: balanced training and selective drop for neural architecture search (2019)
14. Hu, Y., et al.: Angle-based search space shrinking for neural architecture search. In: European Conference on Computer Vision (2020)
15. Pourchot, A., Ducarouge, A., Sigaud, O.: To share or not to share: a comprehensive appraisal of weight-sharing (2020)
16. Ding, X., Ding, G., Guo, Y., Han, J., Yan, C.: Approximated oracle filter pruning for destructive CNN width optimization. In: International Conference on Machine Learning (2019)
17. Joo, D., Yi, E., Baek, S., Kim, J.: Linearly replaceable filters for deep network channel pruning. In: The Thirty-Fifth AAAI Conference on Artificial Intelligence (AAAI-2021) (2021)
18. Li, Y., et al.: Towards compact CNNs via collaborative compression. In: 2021 IEEE/CVF Conference on Computer Vision, Pattern Recognition (CVPR) (2021)

19. Guo, S., Wang, Y., Li, Q., Yan, J.: DMCP: differentiable Markov channel pruning for neural networks. In: 2020 IEEE/CVF Conference on Computer Vision, Pattern Recognition (CVPR) (2020)
20. Su, X., You, S., Wang, F., Qian, C., Zhang, C., Xu, C.: BCNet: searching for network width with bilaterally coupled network. In: 2021 IEEE/CVF Conference on Computer Vision, Pattern Recognition (CVPR) (2021)
21. Yu, J., Yang, L., Xu, N., Yang, J., Huang, T.S.: Slimmable neural networks. In: International Conference on Learning Representations (2021)

EFG-Net: A Unified Framework for Estimating Eye Gaze and Face Gaze Simultaneously

Hekuangyi Che[1,2], Dongchen Zhu[1,2], Minjing Lin[1], Wenjun Shi[1,2],
Guanghui Zhang[1,2], Hang Li[1], Xiaolin Zhang[1,2,3,4,5],
and Jiamao Li[1,2,3](✉)

[1] Shanghai Institute of Microsystem and Information Technology,
Chinese Academy of Sciences, Shanghai 200050, China
jmli@mail.sim.ac.cn
[2] University of Chinese Academy of Sciences, Beijing 100049, China
[3] Xiongan Institute of Innovation, Xiongan 071700, China
[4] University of Science and Technology of China, Hefei 230027, Anhui, China
[5] School of Information Science and Technology, ShanghaiTech University,
Shanghai 201210, China

Abstract. Gaze is of vital importance for understanding human purpose and intention. Recent works have gained tremendous progress in appearance-based gaze estimation. However, all these works deal with eye gaze estimation or face gaze estimation separately, ignoring the mutual benefit of the fact that eye gaze and face gaze are roughly the same with a slight difference in the starting point. For the first time, we propose an Eye gaze and Face Gaze Network (EFG-Net), which makes eye gaze estimation and face gaze estimation take advantage of each other, leading to a win-win situation. Our EFG-Net consists of three feature extractors, a feature communication module named GazeMixer, and three predicting heads. The GazeMixer is designed to propagate coarse gaze features from face gaze to eye gaze and fine gaze features from eye gaze to face gaze. The predicting heads are capable of estimating gazes from the corresponding features more finely and stably. Experiments show that our method achieves state-of-the-art performance of 3.90° (by ∼4%) eye gaze error and 3.93° (by ∼2%) face gaze error on MPIIFaceGaze dataset, 3.03° eye gaze error and 3.17° (by ∼5%) face gaze error on GazeCapture dataset respectively.

Keywords: Eye gaze · Face gaze · Feature communication

1 Introduction

Human gaze serves as an important cue for various applications such as saliency detection, virtual reality and human-robot interaction. However, it is non-trivial to estimate gaze accurately in the wild due to the changes of illumination, different individual appearances, and occlusion.

S. Yu et al. (Eds.): PRCV 2022, LNCS 13534, pp. 552–565, 2022.
https://doi.org/10.1007/978-3-031-18907-4_43

Early gaze estimation methods focus on constraint settings, e.g., using dedicated devices with static head pose and short working distance (usually within 60 cm). These methods achieve high accuracy in laboratory environment but low performance in the wild. In order to apply gaze estimation in a more complex real-world environment, researchers propose appearance-based gaze estimation which estimates the 2D target position on a given plane or 3D gaze angle in a normalized space based on eye images or face images captured by webcam. But it is still challenging to acquire accurate gaze because human eye appearance is influenced by various factors such as head pose.

Thanks to the rapid development of deep learning, many superior networks like Convolutional Neural Networks (CNNs) are applied to gaze estimation and demonstrate good performance because of the excellent ability of CNNs to learn a complex mapping function from image to gaze.

Deep learning based methods generally estimate gazes from eye images or face images, and these gazes can be categorized into eye gaze and face gaze. Eye gaze points from eye center (typically the middle point of inner and outer corner of one eye) to the target. Face gaze points from face center (typically the center of four eye corners and two mouth corners) to the target. One of the key technical challenge in appearance-based gaze estimation is to select suitable gaze-related area for input. For example, eye images lack the global information of face, face images lack the attention to eyes which are decisive to gaze. Some works [2,4,5,9,14] choose to use eye images and face images together for gaze estimation. However, without the supervision of eye gaze, eye features extracted from eye images may be quite inaccurate, containing other redundant gaze unrelated information.

To address this issue, we propose a unified framework dubbed **EFG-Net** to learn **E**ye gaze and **F**ace **G**aze simultaneously, in which eye gaze and face gaze are both supervised. To the best of our knowledge, this is the first attempt to exploit reciprocal relationship between eye gaze and face gaze. The overview of our task and the framework are depicted in Fig. 1. Our framework mainly constitutes of feature communication and predicting heads. First, we extract features from preprocessed eye images and face images. Given the fact that average angle of two

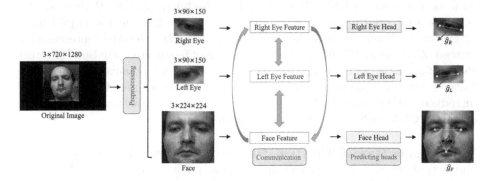

Fig. 1. Overview of our task and the proposed framework. The center of the yellow dots indicates the starting point of gaze. (Color figure online)

eyes has little difference with the angle of face gaze, we posit eye gaze and face gaze can be learned together and design a feature communication module, named GazeMixer, to optimize the gaze features. To get refined gazes from features, we build special predicting heads for eye gaze and face gaze. Specifically, we concatenate eye features with the face feature in face gaze predicting head since eye images contain fine gaze features, and use eye feature directly in eye gaze predicting heads.

In summary, this paper makes the following contributions:

- A novel framework termed EFG-Net is proposed to associate eye gaze estimation and face gaze estimation closely together, which helps guide the more accurate gaze feature extraction via cooperating with each other.
- A feature communication module, named GazeMixer that propagates coarse gaze features from face gaze to eye gaze and fine gaze features from eye gaze to face gaze, is proposed to incorporate different gaze cues from eye and face images.
- Our method achieves state-of-the-art performance of both eye gaze estimation and face gaze estimation on MPIIFaceGaze and GazeCapture datasets.

2   Related Work

2.1   Appearance-Based Gaze Estimation Framework

Appearance-based gaze estimation methods learn a mapping from eye images or face images to gaze. Depending on the input of network, they can be divided into single input region gaze estimation and multiple input regions gaze estimation.

Single-region Gaze Estimation means the input is a single eye patch or face patch and the output is a single eye gaze or face gaze. This kind of gaze estimation framework is the simplest and most intuitive since eye gaze and face gaze are naturally related to their corresponding patch. Zhang et al. [24] take left eye patch and head pose as the input to the network which is based on LeNet [15]. And the network outputs 3D left eye gaze angle. Later, they replace LeNet with more complicated VGGNet [18] and get better result [26]. Park et al. [17] generate a pictorial representation of the eyeball, the iris and the pupil from a single eye patch and estimate the gaze direction from the pictorial representation instead. Zhang et al. [25] first study the problem of face gaze estimation. They use the full face image as input and employ spatial weights mechanism to emphasize features extracted from gaze related regions, like eye region. Cheng et al. [6] introduce ViT (vision transformer) [8] to face feature extraction. Their method combines CNN with ViT and gets good performance.

Multi-region Gaze Estimation takes two eyes alongside the face as input and outputs two eye gazes or face gaze or gaze point. Krafka et al. [14] propose the first multi-region framework named iTracker. They exploit both eye images and face image to estimation 2D gaze target with a face bounding box to allow free head pose. Fischer et al. [9] extract head pose feature from face image and concatenate it with eye feature to regress face gaze. Chen et al. [4] employ dilated convolutional network to capture the subtle changes in eye image. Eye features and face feature are simply concatenated to regress face gaze. Cheng et al. [7] notice the difference between two eyes and propose to select the superior eye for gaze estimation. Their FAR-Net framework is roughly similar to [4], and the main difference is that their output is two eye gazes instead of face gaze. Bao et al. [2] follow the idea of iTracker [14] and make improvements in the communication and fusion of features.

2.2   Gaze Features Communication

Bao et al. [2] design an AdaGN module to fuse eye features with the face feature. They recalibrate eye features with the shift and scale parameters learned from face feature. Cai et al. [3] employ MHSA [20] for eye features and face feature communication. They imitate the framework of iTracker and propose iTracker-MHSA for face gaze estimation. However, iTracker-MHSA lacks the supervision of eye gaze, which means the eye features extracted from eye patches may be inaccurate. Besides, a different order of eye features and face feature will lead to a different order of query, key, and value corresponding to MHSA, so that the network can only focus on face gaze estimation. To estimate eye gaze, it has to change the order of gaze features and retrain the network.

3   Method

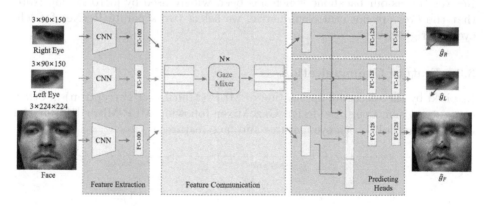

Fig. 2. Architecture of EFG-Net. There are three predicting heads from top to down, namely the right eye predicting head, the left eye predicting head, and the face predicting head.

The detailed architecture of EFG-Net is illustrated in Fig. 2. The EFG-Net has three inputs, which are right eye patch, left eye patch, and face patch from the same person. We first introduce the overview framework of EFG-Net in Sect. 3.1. Then three main parts of EFG-Net will be elaborated in Sect. 3.2, Sect. 3.3, and Sect. 3.4. And loss function is also included in Sect. 3.4.

3.1   Framework

Our overview framework is shown in Fig. 1, which takes two eye patches as well as a face patch as input and outputs two eye gazes alongside a face gaze. The comparison of our framework with classic multi-region eye gaze estimation and face gaze estimation framework is depicted in Fig. 3. With extra eye gaze labels, EFG-Net is capable of estimate both eye gaze and face gaze, avoiding the need to build additional networks for eye gaze estimation.

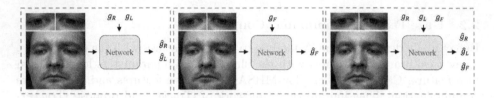

Fig. 3. Classic multi-region eye gaze estimation (left), face gaze estimation framework (middle), and proposed eye gaze and face gaze estimation framework (right).

3.2   Feature Extraction

If gaze unrelated factor is included in features, unrelated part will mislead useful information during feature communication, and errors continue to propagate. To ensure accurate feature is extracted from the eye and the face images, we utilize ResNet [11] as our backbone which has been widely used by [6,10,12,23]. Note that the eyes are not centrosymmetric, we select two separate ResNet for left eye and right eye.

3.3   Feature Communication

Inspired by the successful application of MLP (MultiLayer Perceptron) in other computer vision tasks, we design GazeMixer following MLP-Mixer [19] for the communication between eye features and face features.

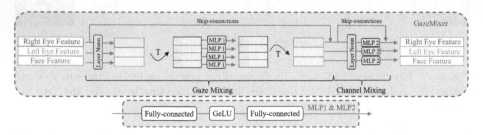

Fig. 4. Architecture of GazeMixer, MLP1 and MLP2

As described in Fig. 4, GazeMixer is composed of gaze mixing and channel mixing. Suppose the dimension of gaze features after feature extraction is N.

We concatenate two eye features and one face feature to be a feature matrix $F \in \mathbb{R}^{3 \times N}$. First, layer normalization [1] is preformed to F, and then F is transposed to $F^T \in \mathbb{R}^{N \times 3}$. Gaze features from the same channel are mixed by the MLP1 module which includes two Fully-connected layers and a GeLU layer. $F^T \in \mathbb{R}^{N \times 3}$ is transposed to be the original shape and added with the origin input. The above processes are called gaze mixing. For channel mixing, the processing flow is similar except for transpose. F is processed again by layer normalization, MLP2 module, and skip-connection. Note that MLP1 and MLP2 have the same structure. In order for gaze features to fully communicate with each other, we repeat GazeMixer for several times.

3.4   Predicting Heads and Loss Function

After feature communication, gaze features are vectors of $100D$. We concatenate two eye features and face feature to be a vector of $300D$. Then it is fed into three cascaded full connected layers (FC) and two ReLU activation functions to predict face gaze. The specific order is FC (128), ReLU, FC (128), ReLU, FC (2) where the number in bracket means the output dimension of this FC layer. The above steps constitute face predicting head. Eye predicting head is same as face predicting head except for feature concatenation.

As for the loss function, we utilize L1 loss as described in Eq. (1) and Eq. (2). N is the number of examples, g_i is the ground truth of gaze angle, and $\hat{g}_i$ is the predicted gaze angle by network.

$$Loss_{Eye} = \frac{1}{N} \sum_{i=1}^{N} \left(\left| g_i^{leye} - \hat{g}_i^{leye} \right| + \left| g_i^{reye} - \hat{g}_i^{reye} \right| \right) \tag{1}$$

$$Loss_{Face} = \frac{1}{N} \sum_{i=1}^{N} \left| g_i^{face} - \hat{g}_i^{face} \right| \tag{2}$$

The total loss is formulated as Eq. (3) where λ_{Eye} is the loss weight to control the balance of Loss Eye and Loss Face. We empirically set $\lambda_{Eye} = 1$.

$$Loss_{Total} = \lambda_{Eye} Loss_{Eye} + Loss_{Face} \tag{3}$$

4   Experiments

4.1   Datasets

To evaluate our framework for eye gaze and face gaze estimation, we conduct experiments on two public datasets: MPIIFaceGaze [25] and GazeCapture [14].

MPIIFaceGaze is a popular dataset for appearance-based gaze estimation which provides 3D eye gaze and face gaze directions. It is collected under rich changes of illumination, containing 213,659 images captured from 15 subjects. We select 3000 images for each subject and get a total of 45,000 images for training and evaluating, same as [25]. The origin of eye gaze is defined as the center of inner corner, and outer corner of one eye and the middle point of face (four eye corners and two mouth corners) is the origin of face gaze. We perform leave-one-person-out evaluation on this dataset.

GazeCapture is the largest available in-the-wild gaze dataset which contains both eye gaze and face gaze directions. We follow the preprocessing step like [16] and use the given split order. Finally, we get a training set of 1,379,083 images, a testing set of 191,842 images, and a validating set of 63,518 images.

4.2   Data Pre-processing

We normalize the two datasets based on the process proposed by [22]. To be specific, data pre-processing procedure ensures that there is visual camera facing the human face, eliminating the occurrence of occlusion. For MPIIFaceGaze, we set the focal length of visual camera as 960 mm and the distance between visual camera and human as 600 mm. And then we directly crop a face image of 224×224 and eye image of 36×60 from the warped image. For GazeCapture, we follow the same setting as [27]. Specifically, focal length is set as 500 mm and distance as 600 mm. We crop a face image of 128×128 and eye image of 36×60 respectively.

4.3   Implementation Details

The shape of face patch for EFG-Net is $3 \times 224 \times 224$, and the shape of eye patch is $3 \times 90 \times 150$. If patch size is not equal to the above value after data normalization, we resize the image patch to reach the standard shape.

Note that we select three identical but different ResNet for two eyes branch and face branch. We choose ResNet18 for MPIIFaceGaze dataset since it has less images. Besides, we pretrain ResNet18 for two eye gazes alongside the face gaze, and freeze the weights of ResNet18 when training EFG-Net. For GazeCapture dataset which is more complicated with various images, we select ResNet50 and train EFG-Net directly. The feature dimension is set as 100 and the number of GazeMixer is set as 2. Interestingly, we find that feature dimension that is too large or too small may lead to overfitting and underfitting.

We train EFG-Net on MPIIFaceGaze with 1000 batch sizes and 24 epochs. We follow the same setting as [6] to set the initial learning rate and optimizer parameters. To be specific, the initial learning rate is 5×10^{-4} with a cosine decay. If the learning rate is less than 5×10^{-6}, we set it as 5×10^{-6} instead. Adam optimizer [13] is used to train the model with $\beta 1 = 0.9$ and $\beta 2 = 0.999$. For GazeCapture, the batch size is 500 and epoch is 12. Our EFG-Net is implemented using PyTorch and trained on 4 NVIDIA RTX3090 GPUs.

4.4   Comparison with Appearance-based Methods

We conduct experiments on MPIIFaceGaze and GazeCapture to compare the performance of the proposed method with other appearance-based methods. Although the method of preprocessing the MPIIFaceGaze is generally the same, the choice of hyperparameters such as the focal length of visual camera and the size of the face image to be cropped is different in different papers. For a fair comparison, we use the results of FullFace [25], Rt-Gene [9], Dilated-Net [4], CA-Net [7], and Gaze360 [12] reimplemented by Cheng et al. [6]. As for other methods, we take the results from original paper for comparison.

Table 1. Results on MPIIFaceGaze and GazeCapture datasets.

Method	MPIIFaceGaze		GazeCapture	
	EyeGaze	FaceGaze	EyeGaze	FaceGaze
FullFace [25]	-	4.93°	-	-
DPG [17]	4.50°	-	-	-
Rt-Gene [9]	4.30°	4.66°	-	-
FAZE [16]	-	-	-	3.49°
RSN [23]	-	4.50°	-	3.32°
Dilated-Net [4]	-	4.42°	-	-
CA-Net [5]	4.14°	4.27°	-	-
Gaze360 [12]	-	4.06°	-	-
MTGLS [10]	4.07°	-	-	-
GazeTR [6]	-	4.00°	-	-
Baseline	5.31°	4.09°	4.00°	3.38°
Ours	**3.90°**	**3.93°**	**3.03°**	**3.17°**

Table 1 shows the comparison results on MPIIFaceGaze and GazeCapture. The error of existing methods on the MPIIFaceGaze is at least 4.00° or more. We are the first to reduce the error within 4.00°, with 3.90° error on eye gaze and 3.93° error on face gaze. Note that GazeTR [6] is pretrained on ETH-XGaze [21], a large dataset containing 1, 083, 492 face images. While our method is directly trained on the normalized MPIIFaceGaze which only has 45, 000 face images, we get a better result with 0.07° improvement. For GazeCapture, our method exceeds the existing two methods by a large margin, getting 0.15° improvement compared with RSN [23] on face gaze estimation and 0.32° improvement compared with FAZE [16] respectively. The good performance on two datasets demonstrates the advantage of the proposed EFG-Net.

An interesting phenomenon can also be observed from the experimental results. Although eye gaze error is larger on the baseline, after the processing of EFG-Net, eye gaze error decreases significantly and is even smaller than face gaze error. On MPIIFaceGaze, face gaze error decreases from 4.09° to 3.93°

while eye gaze error decreases from 5.31° to 3.90°. On GazeCapture, face gaze error decreases from 3.38° to 3.17° while eye gaze error decreases from 4.00° to 3.03°. We think the reason lies in the communication and which helps eye gaze benefit from face gaze feature to avoid extreme gaze angle. Besides, the starting point of eye gaze is more consistent across different people than that of face gaze, resulting in a more accurate label of eye gaze.

We also exhibit the error of different subjects on MPIIFaceGaze for a detailed comparison with the baseline. Results of eye gaze and face gaze are depicted in Fig. 5 and Fig. 6. Error bars indicate standard errors computed across subjects. It is obviously that EFG-Net outperforms baseline for all the 15 subjects on eye gaze estimation. For face gaze estimation, EFG-Net is competitive to baseline and get a big lead in p10, p11, p13 subject, resulting in a better performance on average.

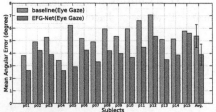 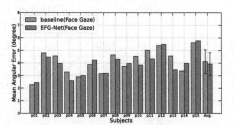

Fig. 5. Mean angular eye error of different subjects on the MPIIFaceGaze.

Fig. 6. Mean angular face error of different subjects on the MPIIFaceGaze.

4.5 Ablation Study

In order to demonstrate the effectiveness of EFG-Net, we conduct ablation study on MPIIFaceGaze and GazeCapture datasets.

Table 2. Effect of gaze label constraint.

EyeGaze label	FaceGaze label	MPIIFaceGaze		GazeCapture	
		EyeGaze	FaceGaze	EyeGaze	FaceGaze
✓		3.94°		3.08°	
	✓		4.00°		3.25°
✓	✓	**3.90°**	**3.93°**	**3.03°**	**3.17°**

We first design experiments to explore the effect of gaze label constraint and results are shown in Table 2. When trained with only eye gaze label or face gaze label, the performance of EFG-Net drops a little on both eye gaze (0.04° on MPIIFaceGaze and 0.05° on GazeCapture) and face gaze (0.07° on MPIIFaceGaze and 0.08° on GazeCapture). It is reasonable because gaze label constraint helps the network learn more accurate eye feature and face feature, thus eliminating misleading information during feature communication.

To prove the advantage of proposed network, we respectively evaluate GazeMixer and predicting heads modules in EFG-Net. Table 3 exhibits the ablation results for eye gaze and face gaze. The result of using GazeMixer is very competitive with the final result suggesting that GazeMixer plays a major role in EFG-Net. When employing predicting heads only, the error of eye gaze drops a lot from 5.31° to 4.06° on MPIIFaceGaze and 4.00° to 3.66° on GazeCapture, indicating that predicting heads are also indispensable. The combination of two modules achieves the best performance across different datasets and different tasks, showing the effectiveness of EFG-Net.

Table 3. Effect of GazeMixer and predicting heads.

GazeMixer	Predicting heads	MPIIFaceGaze		GazeCapture	
		EyeGaze	FaceGaze	EyeGaze	FaceGaze
		4.09°	5.31°	4.00°	3.38°
	✓	4.08°	4.06°	3.66°	3.28°
✓		3.97°	3.97°	3.16°	3.29°
✓	✓	**3.90°**	**3.93°**	**3.03°**	**3.17°**

4.6   Robustness Analysis

Although mean gaze error makes it simply to compare the performance of different methods, it fails to indicate how a method performs at a specific gaze angle. Thus, robustness analysis is conducted to demonstrate the performance of our method across horizontal gaze angles (aka yaw gaze angles) and vertical gaze angles (aka pitch gaze angles).

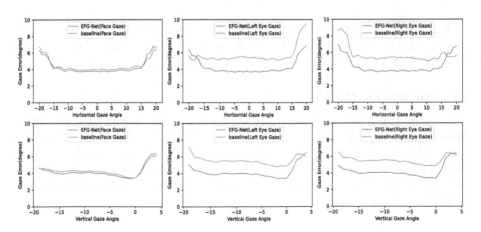

Fig. 7. Gaze estimation error across horizontal (top) and vertical (down) gaze angles on MPIIFaceGaze dataset. From left to right, the order is face gaze error, left eye gaze error, and right eye gaze error.

Figure 7 depicts the gaze error distribution result on MPIIFaceGaze dataset. The first row is horizontal gaze angle result for face gaze, left eye gaze, and right eye gaze (from left to right). And the second row is vertical gaze angle result for face gaze, left eye gaze, and right eye gaze (from left to right). We observe that EFG-Net outperforms baseline for most gaze angles, showing superior robustness. For face gaze, EFG-Net is close to baseline due to the reason that face image contains adequate information like head pose, facial contour, and changes of eye areas. Performance will not significantly improve by adding more gaze features from eye gazes. But for eye gazes which rely on eye images, the global information of face is of great benefit even for extreme gaze angles.

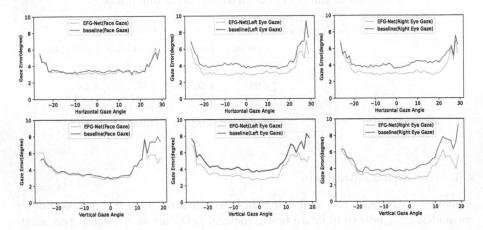

Fig. 8. Gaze estimation error across horizontal (top) and vertical (down) gaze angles on GazeCapture dataset. From left to right, the order is face gaze error, left eye gaze error, and right eye gaze error.

Figure 8 exhibits the gaze error distribution result on GazeCapture dataset. Compared with Fig. 7, EFG-Net prevails across all gaze angles for eye gazes, showing the potential of our method for large dataset.

4.7   Qualitative Results

Some qualitative examples of our model is shown in Fig. 9. The baseline demonstrates a large discrepancy with ground truth, while EFG-Net is closer to ground truth. The first row is the result of MPIIFaceGaze and the second row comes from GazeCapture. The last two columns indicate the condition of blurry image and poor illumination. It is obvious that EFG-Net works better than baseline even in poor conditions.

4.8   Discussion

Previous appearance-based gaze estimation methods only focus on eye gaze estimation or face gaze estimation. In this paper, we propose to estimate two gazes simultaneously and experiments demonstrate the effectiveness of our framework. Ablation study on GazeMixer shows that feature communication is very helpful to improve the accuracy of gaze estimation especially for eye gaze. It is possible that future methods further study the geometric constraints of eye gaze and face gaze, so as to make better use of the interdependence between two gazes.

Fig. 9. Qualitative results on MPIIFaceGaze (first row) and GazeCapture (second row) datasets. The blue, red, and green arrows are, EFG-Net, baseline, ground truth, respectively. The last two columns indicate blurry image and poor illumination. (Color figure online)

5   Conclusion

In this paper, a novel unified framework, namely EFG-Net, is proposed for estimating eye gaze and face gaze Simultaneously. The relationships between the two tasks are explored through GazeMixer and predicting heads to boost the performance. Experiments show EFG-Net can achieve state-of-the-art performance in estimating eye gaze and face gaze on two authoritative datasets. We also further conduct experiments to assess the effect of different modules of EFG-Net. This paper provides new ideas for future work.

Acknowledgments. This work was supported by National Science and Technology Major Project from Minister of Science and Technology, China (2018AAA0103100), National Natural Science Foundation of China (61873255), Shanghai Municipal Science and Technology Major Project (ZHANGJIANG LAB) under Grant 2018SHZDZX01 and Youth Innovation Promotion Association, Chinese Academy of Sciences (2021233).

References

1. Ba, J.L., Kiros, J.R., Hinton, G.E.: Layer normalization. arXiv preprint arXiv:1607.06450 (2016)
2. Bao, Y., Cheng, Y., Liu, Y., Lu, F.: Adaptive feature fusion network for gaze tracking in mobile tablets. In: 2020 25th International Conference on Pattern Recognition (ICPR), pp. 9936–9943. IEEE (2021)
3. Cai, X., et al.: Gaze estimation with an ensemble of four architectures. arXiv preprint arXiv:2107.01980 (2021)

4. Chen, Z., Shi, B.E.: Appearance-based gaze estimation using dilated-convolutions. In: Jawahar, C.V., Li, H., Mori, G., Schindler, K. (eds.) ACCV 2018. LNCS, vol. 11366, pp. 309–324. Springer, Cham (2019). https://doi.org/10.1007/978-3-030-20876-9_20

5. Cheng, Y., Huang, S., Wang, F., Qian, C., Lu, F.: A coarse-to-fine adaptive network for appearance-based gaze estimation. In: Proceedings of the AAAI Conference on Artificial Intelligence, vol. 34, pp. 10623–10630 (2020)

6. Cheng, Y., Lu, F.: Gaze estimation using transformer. arXiv preprint arXiv:2105.14424 (2021)

7. Cheng, Y., Zhang, X., Lu, F., Sato, Y.: Gaze estimation by exploring two-eye asymmetry. IEEE Trans. Image Process. **29**, 5259–5272 (2020)

8. Dosovitskiy, A., et al.: An image is worth 16x16 words: transformers for image recognition at scale. arXiv preprint arXiv:2010.11929 (2020)

9. Fischer, T., Chang, H.J., Demiris, Y.: RT-GENE: real-time eye gaze estimation in natural environments. In: Proceedings of the European Conference on Computer Vision (ECCV), pp. 334–352 (2018)

10. Ghosh, S., Hayat, M., Dhall, A., Knibbe, J.: MTGLS: multi-task gaze estimation with limited supervision. In: Proceedings of the IEEE/CVF Winter Conference on Applications of Computer Vision, pp. 3223–3234 (2022)

11. He, K., Zhang, X., Ren, S., Sun, J.: Deep residual learning for image recognition. In: Proceedings of the IEEE Conference on Computer Vision and Pattern Recognition, pp. 770–778 (2016)

12. Kellnhofer, P., Recasens, A., Stent, S., Matusik, W., Torralba, A.: Gaze360: physically unconstrained gaze estimation in the wild. In: Proceedings of the IEEE/CVF International Conference on Computer Vision, pp. 6912–6921 (2019)

13. Kingma, D.P., Ba, J.: Adam: a method for stochastic optimization. arXiv preprint arXiv:1412.6980 (2014)

14. Krafka, K., et al.: Eye tracking for everyone. In: Proceedings of the IEEE Conference on Computer Vision and Pattern Recognition, pp. 2176–2184 (2016)

15. LeCun, Y., Bottou, L., Bengio, Y., Haffner, P.: Gradient-based learning applied to document recognition. Proc. IEEE **86**(11), 2278–2324 (1998)

16. Park, S., Mello, S.D., Molchanov, P., Iqbal, U., Hilliges, O., Kautz, J.: Few-shot adaptive gaze estimation. In: Proceedings of the IEEE/CVF International Conference on Computer Vision, pp. 9368–9377 (2019)

17. Park, S., Spurr, A., Hilliges, O.: Deep pictorial gaze estimation. In: Proceedings of the European Conference on Computer Vision (ECCV), pp. 721–738 (2018)

18. Simonyan, K., Zisserman, A.: Very deep convolutional networks for large-scale image recognition. arXiv preprint arXiv:1409.1556 (2014)

19. Tolstikhin, I.O., et al.: MLP-mixer: an all-MLP architecture for vision. In: Advances in Neural Information Processing Systems, vol. 34 (2021)

20. Vaswani, A., et al.: Attention is all you need. In: Advances in Neural Information Processing Systems, vol. 30 (2017)

21. Zhang, X., Park, S., Beeler, T., Bradley, D., Tang, S., Hilliges, O.: ETH-XGaze: a large scale dataset for gaze estimation under extreme head pose and gaze variation. In: Vedaldi, A., Bischof, H., Brox, T., Frahm, J.-M. (eds.) ECCV 2020. LNCS, vol. 12350, pp. 365–381. Springer, Cham (2020). https://doi.org/10.1007/978-3-030-58558-7_22

22. Zhang, X., Sugano, Y., Bulling, A.: Revisiting data normalization for appearance-based gaze estimation. In: Proceedings of the 2018 ACM Symposium on Eye Tracking Research & Applications, pp. 1–9 (2018)

23. Zhang, X., Sugano, Y., Bulling, A., Hilliges, O.: Learning-based region selection for end-to-end gaze estimation. In: BMVC (2020)

24. Zhang, X., Sugano, Y., Fritz, M., Bulling, A.: Appearance-based gaze estimation in the wild. In: Proceedings of the IEEE Conference on Computer Vision and Pattern Recognition, pp. 4511–4520 (2015)

25. Zhang, X., Sugano, Y., Fritz, M., Bulling, A.: It's written all over your face: full-face appearance-based gaze estimation. In: Proceedings of the IEEE Conference on Computer Vision and Pattern Recognition Workshops, pp. 51–60 (2017)

26. Zhang, X., Sugano, Y., Fritz, M., Bulling, A.: Mpiigaze: real-world dataset and deep appearance-based gaze estimation. IEEE Trans. Pattern Anal. Mach. Intell. **41**(1), 162–175 (2017)

27. Zheng, Y., Park, S., Zhang, X., De Mello, S., Hilliges, O.: Self-learning transformations for improving gaze and head redirection. Adv. Neural. Inf. Process. Syst. **33**, 13127–13138 (2020)

Local Point Matching Network for Stabilized Crowd Counting and Localization

Lin Niu[1]([✉]), Xinggang Wang[1], Chen Duan[2], Qiongxia Shen[3], and Wenyu Liu[1]

[1] Institute of AI, School of EIC, Huazhong University of Science and Technology, Wuhan, China
{linniu,xgwang,liuwy}@hust.edu.cn
[2] Wuhan Second Ship Design and Research Institute, Wuhan, China
[3] Fiberhome Telecommunication Technologies Co., Ltd., Wuhan, China
qxshen@fiberhome.com

Abstract. Accurately estimating the number and location of individuals in a crowd is a difficult but essential task. Most existing methods usually apply density maps or pseudo boxes as regression targets. Those methods are incapable of providing precise localization of people in dense crowds. Recently, some methods for directly predicting a set of head coordinates have shown great superiority. They match all proposal points and target points globally to carry out one-to-one label assignments. However, we find that the global matching algorithm will cause potential instability in the training process, especially in the early stage of training. To alleviate this, we design a local matching point-based framework which only uses anchor points near head centers as positive candidate samples, conducts the one-to-many assignment using a proposed iterative Hungarian algorithm at the first several epochs and performs one-to-one matching before the end of training. Besides, we load the pre-training object detection model to help our network pay more attention to informative regions in the early training stage. Extensive experiments show that our network achieves state-of-the-art counting and localization performance with higher training efficiency on various standard benchmarks, e.g., ShanghaiTech, UCF-CC-50, UCF_QNRF, NUPW.

Keywords: Crowd counting · Crowd localization · Point-based network · Local matching

1 Introduction

Crowd counting has played a key role in vision applications such as crowd evacuation, community safety, and traffic monitoring. Crowd localization could support more practical results to meet the elevated crowd analysis needs. Benefiting from the impressive performance of object detection and semantic segmentation, existing methods usually employ pseudo boxes or density maps as regression

S. Yu et al. (Eds.): PRCV 2022, LNCS 13534, pp. 566–579, 2022.
https://doi.org/10.1007/978-3-031-18907-4_44

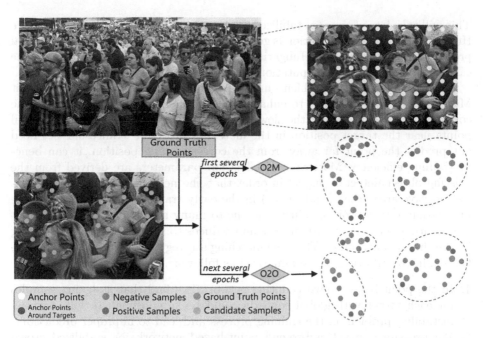

Fig. 1. Visualizations of assigning pipelines. Proposals outputted by the anchor points around targets are marked as candidate samples to participate in the label assignments. The net performs the one-to-many (O2M) assignment using iterative Hungarian matching in the first several epochs and switches to the one-to-one (O2O) assignment in the following training epochs.

targets to carry out crowd localization. Detection-based methods [10,18,29] cast pseudo boxes as targets to detect the location of each person but those cannot handle extremely dense scenes and large-range scale variations. This will lead to a low recall rate for tiny heads [15]. Density-map-based methods [3,5,8,15] use post-processing techniques to localize head positions (i.e. finding the local peak and presenting a Gaussian-prior reconstruction). However, in dense scenes, the Gaussian blobs of nearby people heavily overlap, making the local maxima mismatched to the individual location.

Recently inspired by the end-to-end methods [2,11] in object detection, some methods [7,27] also introduced a bipartite-matching-based training strategy to enable end-to-end crowd counting and localization. They leverage transformer or CNN to predict a set of proposal points and then adopt the dynamic one-to-one assignment by the Hungarian algorithm [28]. However, we find some potential problems in the methods [7,27]. The first is the slow convergence of the training process. Assigning an independent prediction for each target through the whole image cannot make the network focus on potential information areas very well and converge fast. The second is the severe fluctuation of positive samples. The dynamic label assignment is based on the quality of proposals that are dynamically updated in different training epochs. Specifically, a proposal point may switch back and forth between positive and negative samples in different epochs.

This will take lots of time to stabilize the optimization process. Meanwhile, since Hungarian algorithm calculation is generally applicable to CPUs, utilizing global proposals to participate in Hungarian matching will dramatically increase the calculation amount and computation time compared to local proposals.

In order to tackle the problems mentioned above, we propose the Local Point Matching Network (LPMN) to enhance matching efficiency and accelerate the convergence of training. For the slow convergence, we involve only the proposal points near the target position in the matching procedure. Since our net need not predict the point far away from the corresponding position, it can benefit training efficiency. Moreover, initialization parameters are derived from the existing object detection model in order that the network can focus on potential positive areas (i.e., heads areas) in the early training stage. For the severe fluctuation, our network conducts the one-to-many match strategy using iterative multiple one-to-one assignments and reduces to single one-to-one matching before the end of training. The local matching strategy is demonstrated in Fig. 1. Our main contributions are summarized as follows:

1. In the point-based crowd counting network, we find that assigning samples for each target with global contexts could be sub-optimal. It will cause an instability problem in the training process and lead to improper prediction.
2. We propose a novel end-to-end point-based network for stabilized crowd counting and localization. Our net introduces a local matching strategy with less computation overhead. It pays more attention to the area around the target point and adopts the one-to-many match strategy.
3. Experiments demonstrate that LPMN achieves state-of-the-art or promising counting and localization performance with higher training efficiency on ShanghaiTech [23], UCF-CC-50 [12], UCF-QNRF [16] and NUPW [13].

2 Related Work

2.1 Crowd Counting

Since crowd counting is the prerequisite of crowd localization, it is essential to have a brief survey on crowd counting works. With the advent of deep learning, CNN-based approaches [24,26,30] have shown the superiority over hand-crafted features models. The methods usually regress pixel-wise or patch-wise density maps and integrate the maps to obtain the count. However, these methods fail to predict the accurate location of individuals.

2.2 Crowd Localization

Detection-Dased Crowd Localization. Object detection methods predict the coordinates and size of bounding boxes to localize. Because of the expensive annotation cost, ground truth (gt) for crowd counting is usually point annotation. Therefore, many methods work on specific modules to generate pseudo bounding boxes from point-level annotations [10,18,29]. Lian et al. [18] propose RDNet to localize heads with bounding boxes. The net outputs a density map to perform classification for each head and creates a depth-aware anchor for the variances of head size. Liu et al. [29] introduce an online updating mechanism to modify the pseudo gt box during training and design a locally-constrained regression loss to provide further constraints on the size of prediction boxes. Due to extremely dense scenes and large-range scale variation crowds, those are usually inferior to the localization accuracy for tiny heads.

Heuristic Crowd Localization. Benefiting from the development of semantic segmentation, some methods [5,19,24,31] predict high resolution density maps to deal with localization, which are post-processed to generate location maps. Idrees et al. [16] estimate the head position in a binary localization map by finding the peak point in a local region. Dingkang Liang et al. [5] propose a novel Focal Inverse Distance Transform (FIDT) map to obtain the coordinates of the heads by localizing the local maxima. Due to the consisting of blurry Gaussian kernel, the estimated locations are coarse in the dense region. Therefore, these networks have to leave more effort on post-processing methods till the density map approximate the localization map.

2.3   Set-Prediction-Based Detector

End-to-end object detectors [20,25] leverage various label assignments to produce a set of bounding boxes directly, which are NMS-free. Recently, DETR [2] proposes a pair-wise matching manner and performs the Hungarian algorithm as the one-to-one label assignment to associate proposals with targets. For crowd counting and localization, Song et al. propose P2PNet [7] to predict a set of point proposals and use a global optimal assigning strategy very similar to DETR. The global optimal assigning strategy P2PNet adopted does not focus on a specific region, making the net hard to optimize. Our work is similar to P2PNet in the sense that we both propose a purely point-based framework, but our net applies a local matching strategy with a stabilized training process.

3   Methods

3.1   The End-to-End Network

Our end-to-end network directly predicts a set of coordinates of head points rather than density maps or pseudo boxes. This approach can provide a non-overlapped and independent location for individuals. For target, the set of head coordinates for all individuals will be annotated with $\mathcal{P} = \{x_i | i = 1, 2, \ldots N\}$, where $x_i = [x, y]$ denotes the coordinate and N is the number of person in the input image. For prediction, assuming the number of proposal points is M. There are two branches in our network to predict coordinate regression and classification of proposal points. Specifically, the two collections are denoted as $\widehat{\mathcal{P}} = \{\widehat{x_j} \mid j = 1, 2, \ldots M\}$ and $\widehat{\mathcal{S}} = \{\widehat{s_j} \mid j = 1, 2, \ldots M\}$, in which $\widehat{x_j} = [x, y]$

stands for the coordinate of predicted points and $\hat{s}_j = \alpha$ stands for confidence score of predicted points. $\hat{x}_j$ consists of the offsets from the regression branch and the fixed coordinate of anchor points. The mission of the framework is to make $\hat{x}_j$ as close to x_i as possible in the distance and keep $\hat{s}_j$ being a high classification score. Meanwhile, the number M infinitely approximates the number N.

3.2   Local Matching Strategy

Advanced label assignment is essential in the end-to-end detection framework. Our local matching strategy could be concluded to four key points: local prior, dynamic label assignment, multi-positives, and loss/quality awareness. In the following part, we will walk through the whole matching strategy step by step.

Local Prior. Let F_s denote the feature map of size $H \times W$ outputted from the net. Each pixel on F_s represents to an s × s rectangular patch in the given image. There are K gird anchor points $\mathcal{A} = \{a_k \mid k = 1, 2 \ldots K\}$ densely arranged on the patch. According to the above assumptions, the regression branch could predict offsets for each anchor point and produce $R\,(R = H \times W \times K)$ coordinates totally, while the classification branch will also offer R corresponding scores.

For object detection, the center sampling strategy has been proved that it is relatively superior to the global strategies [20]. The strategy considers the predictions in the central portion of the gt instance as foreground samples. Inspired by it, we assign each anchor point within the region of gt points as the candidate positive sample. We denote $d(x_i, NN_k)$ as the average distance to the k nearest neighbors of target point $\mathcal{P} = \{x_i \mid i = 1, 2, \ldots N\}$. Proposal points, which anchors are within $d(x_i, NN_k)$ pixels from target point x_i, will be set as candidate positive samples to participate in the matching procedure. While other proposal points will be marked as negative sample points.

Dynamic Label Assignment. In the open-set point-based network, the key for label assignment is to determine which gt point should the current prediction be responsible for. We adopt the prediction-aware dynamic one-to-one assignment according to the quality of predictions. The matched proposals will be responsible for the targets, while those unmatched would be labeled as negative proposals. Because the quality of proposal points is dynamically updated in different training epochs, our network will find the most appropriate proposal as the positive sample for each gt during the training process.

According to the above, we assume that N, G and R correspond to the number of gt instances, candidate positive samples, and proposal points. In dense prediction detectors, the relationship among the three parameters is $N \ll G \ll R$. We calculate a pair-wise matching cost matrix $Q_{(N \times G)} = q_{ij}$ between gt and candidate positive proposals.

$$q_{ij} = \gamma \left\| p_i - \hat{p}_j \right\|_2 - \hat{s}_j, i \in N; j \in G \tag{1}$$

q_{ij} denotes the correlation quality between gt and candidate samples in a pair. p_i and $\hat{p}_j$ are the coordinates of gt and candidate positive proposals. $\|\cdot\|_2$ means the ℓ_2 distance. $\hat{s}_j$ is the confidence score of $\hat{p}_j$. γ is a coefficient to balance the effect between the distance and the confidence score.

As the optimal bipartite matching involves all candidate positive samples, we use the Hungarian algorithm [28] to match only one candidate sample for each target with minimum loss. Through the matching procedure, there will be N matched positives proposals in the set $\mathcal{P}_{pos}$:

$$\mathcal{P}_{pos} = argmin \sum_i^N \mathcal{L}_{\mathrm{H}}(q_{ij}) \tag{2}$$

where $\mathcal{L}_{\mathrm{H}}(q_{ij})$ is matching cost function with the Hungarian algorithm. Meanwhile, those redundant unmatched proposals are labeled as negatives. To a certain extent, it is analogous to the matching process of DETR or P2PNet.

Multi-positives. The above label assignment selects only ONE positive sample for each target meanwhile ignoring other high-quality candidate samples. In object detection, the multiple positive strategy could alleviate the extreme imbalance of positive/negative sampling during training and enhance robustness [25]. Hence optimizing these redundant high-quality candidate samples may also bring beneficial gradients. We conduct the one-to-many assignment by iterating the one-to-one matching algorithm in the early stage of training. For example, the first matching will produce a set of N matched positives proposals from the cost matrix $Q_{(N \times G)}$, and $G - N$ unmatched candidate samples will be left. In the second matching, we calculate another matrix $\hat{Q}_{(N \times (G-N))}$ between gt and the left unmatched $G - N$ candidate samples to produce another set of N matched positives proposals. By that analogy, if we iteratively conduct T times matching process, there will be $T \times N$ positive samples and $R - T \times N$ negatives consisting of $R - G$ background samples and $G - T \times N$ unmatched samples. After several epochs, we gradually reduce it to a single one-to-one matching process to implement end-to-end detection.

Loss/Quality Aware. Our network applies set-based prediction loss to supervise the point regression and classification. The loss functions are defined as follows:

$$\mathcal{L}_{\mathrm{cls}} = \frac{1}{R}\left[-\sum_{i=1}^{T \times N} \log \hat{s}_{(i)} - \lambda_1 \sum_{i=T \times N+1}^{R} \log\left(1 - \hat{s}_{(i)}\right) \right] \tag{3}$$

$$\mathcal{L}_{\mathrm{loc}} = \frac{1}{T \times N} \sum_{i,j=1}^{T \times N} \|p_i - \hat{p}_j\|_2 \tag{4}$$

λ_1 indicates a weight factor for negative proposals. Here $\mathcal{L}_{\mathrm{cls}}$ is the Cross Entropy loss for the confidence branch, and $\mathcal{L}_{\mathrm{loc}}$ is the Euclidean loss to supervise the distance between matched proposals and gt. The final loss $\mathcal{L}_{all}$ is the sum of $\lambda_{cls}\mathcal{L}_{\mathrm{cls}}$ and $\lambda_{loc}\mathcal{L}_{\mathrm{loc}}$, where λ_{cls} and λ_{loc} are coefficients of each component.

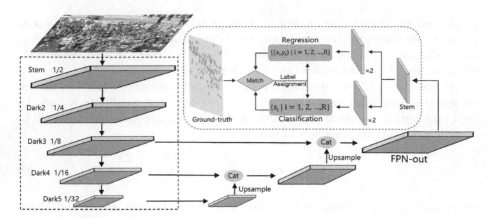

Fig. 2. The diagram of the framework with label assignment process. "Match" indicates the proposed Local Matching Strategy to assign point proposals for each target in the training phase.

3.3 Design Details of LPMN

In LPMN, we simply adopt the Darknet53 series as our backbone. We carry out upsampling and concatenation to obtain fine-grained deep feature maps. The head is consisted of a classification branch and regression branch to predict a set of point proposals. The whole framework is shown in Fig. 2. Throughout a forward pass of the network, the output set contains the coordinate and classification of proposal points. The True Positive (TP) is above a threshold of the classification score. The locations are obtained by the coordinate of the TP points. The headcount is obtained by counting the number of TP points.

4 Experiments

4.1 Implementation Details and Metrics

The network is initialized by the pre-trained weights of Darknet53 on the MS COCO [1]. We randomly re-scale the input image by a scaling factor of [0.7, 1.3], with the shorter side not less than 512. Then the re-scaled outputs were augmented by random horizontal flipping and random cropping. K as the number of anchor points to each pixel of the final feature map (8-stride) is set to 4. In Eqs. 1, γ is set to 5e−2. For the loss function, λ_1, λ_{cls} and λ_{loc} are set to 0.5, 1 and 2e−4, respectively. We adopt $k = 3$ for $d(x_i, NN_k)$ and iterate 3 times Hungarian matching for the first 50 epochs, 2 times for the next 50 epochs.

For counting metric, we adopt the Mean Absolute Error (MAE) and Mean Square Error (MSE). NWPU [13] specifies Precision (Pre.), Recall (Rec.) and F1-measure (F1-m) to evaluate the localization performance. The true positive is defined when the distance between the proposal and gt is less than a threshold σ. NWPU gives two thresholds $\sigma_s = \min(w, h)/2$ and $\sigma_l = \mathrm{sqrt}\left(w^2 + h^2\right)/2$. Provided by NWPU, w and h refer to the width and height of head points.

Table 1. Counting and localization performance on NWPU-Crowd (test set). "*" represents the methods adopt box-level instead of point-level annotations. Results of localization are calculated under threshold σ_l.

Method	Counting		Localization		
	MAE	MSE	Pre (%)	Rec (%)	F1-m (%)
Faster RCNN* [32]	414.2	1063.7	**95.8**	3.5	6.7
TopoCount* [8]	107.8	438.5	69.5	68.7	69.1
RAZ Loc [15]	151.5	634.7	66.6	54.3	59.8
Crowd-SDNet [33]	-	-	65.1	62.4	63.7
SCALNet [3]	86.8	339.9	69.2	69	69.1
GL [14]	79.3	346.1	80	56.3	66
P2PNet [7]	77.4	362	72.9	69.5	71.2
Ours	**76.1**	**327.2**	74.8	**69.7**	**71.5**

Table 2. Comparison with state-of-the-art methods on UCF_CC_50, UCF-QNRF, ShanghaiTech_PartA and ShanghaiTech_PartB.

Method	Venue	Output position coordinates	UCF_CC_50		UCF_QNRF		SHTech_PartA		SHTech_PartB	
			MAE	MSE	MAE	MSE	MAE	MSE	MAE	MSE
CSRNet [24]	CVPR18	×	266.1	397.5	120.3	208.5	68.2	115	10.6	16
CAN [4]	CVPR19	×	212.2	**243.7**	107	183	62.3	100	7.8	12.2
BL [30]	ICCV19	×	229.3	308.2	88.7	154.8	62.8	101.8	7.7	12.7
ASNet [31]	CVPR20	×	174.9	251.6	91.6	159.7	57.8	90.1	-	-
DM-Count [26]	NeurIPS20	×	211	291.5	85.6	148.3	59.7	95.7	7.4	11.8
AMRNet [19]	ECCV20	×	184	265.8	86.6	152.2	61.59	98.36	7.02	11
TopoCount [8]	AAAI20	✓	184.1	258.3	89	159	61.2	104.6	7.8	13.7
GL [14]	CVPR21	✓	-	-	84.3	147.5	61.3	95.4	7.3	11.7
P2PNet [7]	ICCV21	✓	172.7	256.2	85.3	154.5	52.7	**85.1**	6.3	9.9
FIDTM [5]	CVPR21	✓	-	-	89	153.5	57	103.4	6.9	11.8
Ours	-	✓	**168.8**	245.1	**83.9**	**146.2**	**52.1**	86.4	**6.2**	**9.9**

4.2 Crowd Counting

ShanghaiTech dataset consists of two parts: ShanghaiTech_partA and ShanghaiTech_partB. PartA is randomly crawled from the Internet with highly congested scenes. PartB is collected by the surveillance cameras from a busy street and represents relatively sparse scenes. As shown in Table 2, our LPMN obtains the best performance on PartB. For networks that can count and localize simultaneously, our net outperforms the previous best method P2PNet in MAE.

UCF_CC_50 is a small dataset that contains only 50 gray images with a people count ranging from 94 to 4,543. As shown in Table 2, our LMPN can produce the best result in MAE of 168.8. Although LPMN is not so competitive compared with density-map-based methods in MSE of 245.1, it surpasses all the methods that can output count number and position coordinates simultaneously.

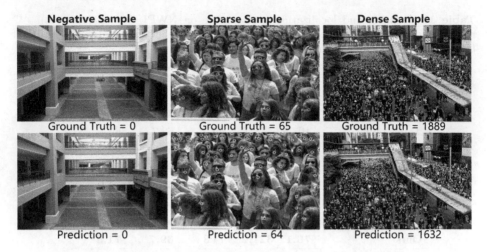

Fig. 3. Some qualitative results from NWPU-Crowd dataset. Column 1, column 2 and column 3 represent the negative, sparse and dense scenes. The green and yellow points denote the ground truth and prediction points. The numbers refer to the ground truth or prediction counts. (Color figure online)

UCF-QNRF is a challenging dataset that contains 1,535 images and about one million annotations. Due to the existence of high-resolution images, we crop the image size to 1024 × 1024. As shown in Table 2, our LPMN achieves SOTA performance both in MAE of 83.9 and MSE of 146.2. That is because the architecture of our net can capture multi-scale features and local context information.

The NWPU-Crowd dataset is a large-scale congested dataset recently introduced with dramatic intra-scene scale and density variance. Our method surpasses previous methods by a large margin. As the result shown in Table 1, our method obtains 76.1 MAE and 327.2 MSE on the test dataset. It indicates that the proposed method can cope with both sparse and dense scenes. Especially for MSE, our method achieves much higher performance than P2PNet. It indicates that the proposed method can cope with sparse and dense crowd scenes.

4.3   Crowd Localization

We report the localization performance on NWPU-Crowd (test set) in Table 1. LPMN performs lower Pre than Faster RCNN but higher Rec and F1-m. Box-level methods are usually inferior to the recall localization accuracy for tiny heads because of extremely dense scenes and large-range scale variations. Compared with the prior state-of-the-art methods, our method achieves the best Recall 69.7 % and F1-measure 71.5 %. We also notice that our method outperforms P2PNet, which is a similar point-level detector with global matching. This demonstrates that our local matching mechanism can effectively handle scale variance. To intuitively demonstrate the localization results, we further give some visualizations to show the effectiveness of our LPMN in Fig. 3.

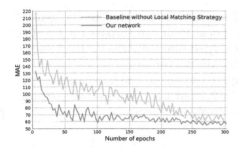

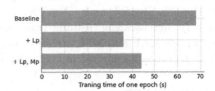

Fig. 4. The training curves for baseline without local matching strategy and our network. We evaluate the MAE on STech_partA test every 5 epochs.

Fig. 5. Comparison of training time under different matching strategy. "+Lp" and "+ Mp" stand for the baseline plus the local prior and the multi positives.

4.4 Ablation Study

We conduct extensive ablation experiments on STech_partA dataset. We train LPMN on the train set and report the performance on the test set. For fair comparisons, all of the experiments are conducted on the same architecture. As a

Table 3. Ablation studies on our network.

	Local prior	Multi positives	MAE	MSE	Pre	Rec	F1-m
Baseline			57.2	96.4	0.72	0.68	0.68
	✓		53.2	89.6	0.78	0.73	0.75
		✓	55.1	92.3	0.73	0.67	0.71
Ours	✓	✓	52.1	86.4	0.79	0.75	0.77

comparison, the baseline utilizes the global one-to-one optimal assignment adopted by P2PNet. For the localization metric, we define threshold $\sigma = \text{sqrt}\left(d^2 + d^2\right)/2$, and $d = d(x_i, NN_k)$ is the average distance to the k nearest neighbors of target point x_i. We empirically learned that the threshold σ of fewer than 8 pixels is visually meaningless for the localization task. Hence, we clamp threshold σ to the minimum of 8 in crowd localization.

We verify the effectiveness of our Local Matching Strategy both in the training process and result performance. We compare the convergence curve between LPMN and the baseline in Fig. 4. Compared with the baseline, our LMPN presents fast converging and high-performance initialization. As seen in Table 3, we can clearly observe that the Local Matching Strategy has performance improvement from 57.2 MAE to 52.1 MAE and 96.4 MSE to 86.4 MSE. The relative performances (Pre, Rec and F1-m) of our net are increased by 7%, 7% and 9%. It is obvious that ours has better stability guarantees and faster convergence than the baseline and achieves better results.

As to the effect of each component, we first compare the training time of one epoch between the baseline and the baseline plus Local Prior in Fig. 5. It shows that employing points from local potential positive areas for assigning plays an essential role in reducing training time from 68 sec to 36 sec. For one epoch, our Local Prior reduces the number of proposals participated in the

Hungarian algorithm by several orders of magnitude compared to the general global matching. As shown in Table 3, the Local Prior can surpass the baseline by 4.0 and 6.8 for MAE and MSE, respectively. It also outperforms the baseline with Pre 6%, Rec 5% and F1-m 7%. As to Multi Positives, Fig. 5 shows that it slightly increases the training time compared to one-to-one label assignment. However, its MAE and MSE are decreased by 2.1 and 4.1. It proves that assigning each gt to many anchor points can also improve performance.

5   Conclusion

In this work, we propose the Local Point Matching Network (LPMN) to enhance matching efficiency and achieve state-of-the-art performance for crowd counting and localization. We involve proposal points near the target position in the label assignment and conduct the one-to-many assignment using a proposed iterative Hungarian algorithm. Experiments demonstrate that LPMN can well-handle the optimization process by a large margin and take full advantage of local context features. We hope the proposed detector can be useful in practice and benefit the label assignment of the end-to-end framework.

A   Supplementary

A.1   Counting Metrics

We use the Mean Absolute Error (MAE) and Mean Square Error (MSE) to measure the difference between ground truth counts and estimation counts, which are defined as:

$$\text{MAE} = \frac{1}{N} \sum_i^N |P_i - G_i| \tag{5}$$

$$\text{MSE} = \sqrt{\frac{1}{N} \sum_i^N (P_i - G_i)^2} \tag{6}$$

where P and G refer to the predicted crowd number and ground-truth crowd number, respectively. N is the number of images. The lower the value is, the better the performance achieves.

A.2   Analysis for the Distribution of Positive Samples

Figure 6 shows the distribution of positive samples under global assignment and local assignment during the whole training process. The left column reveals the distribution for the baseline with the global assignment strategy. We can clearly observe that the matched points are positional ambiguity, especially in the early training. The matched points will be scattered over a large area during the training process. The right column shows that the matched points are on a specific region near the corresponding target points throughout the training process. Forcing detectors to focus on local potential positive areas rather than global areas makes the net easy to optimize, especially in the early training stage.

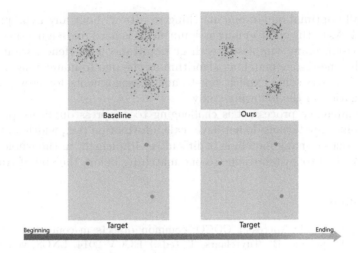

Fig. 6. Comparison of the distribution for matched proposals. The red and yellow refer to the matched points in the beginning and ending training stage. (Color figure online)

A.3   Analysis for Hyperparameters

As previously discussed, we set K as the number of anchor points to each pixel in the final feature map. Keeping the size of the final output feature map constant, we exhibit the effect of the different number of anchors in each patch. Analytically speaking, a larger K value means more anchor points. From the results listed in Table 4, it is noteworthy that K from 1 to 4 promotes performance improvement with acceptable time consumption. However, $K = 8$ consumes lots of computation in the matching process without obvious improvement. Our LPMN puts K value as 4 to achieve a trade-off between performance and computation.

Table 4. The ablation study on different number of anchor points to each pixel on STech_PartA dataset.

	Counting		Localization			Time (sec)
	MAE	MSE	Pre	Rec	F1-m	
$K = 1$	61.4	99.1	0.70	0.67	0.71	40.6
$K = 4$	52.1	86.4	0.79	0.75	0.77	51.7
$K = 8$	52	86.6	0.80	0.75	0.76	69.4

A.4   Discussion on Label Assignment

Consequently, the hand-designed fixed one-to-one label assignment may be suboptimal in congested scenes. The prediction-aware dynamic one-to-one assignment could take both distance and confidence into consideration and produce the mutually optimal one-to-one matching results without any hyperparameter introduced. As to the one-to-many assignment, it is hard to design a specific algorithm to assign many samples to each gt simultaneously. Hence, we iteratively conduct the one-to-one matching algorithm as the one-to-many assignment. We expect to propose some explicit one-to-many assignments for crowd counting and localization in the following study.

In the inference process, it is challenging to suppress duplicate predictions because point annotations do not have scale information (i.e., width and height). Therefore, one-to-many matching is difficult to implement in the whole training process. We had to switch to one-to-one matching before the end of training.

References

1. Lin, T.-Y., et al.: Microsoft COCO: common objects in context. In: Fleet, D., Pajdla, T., Schiele, B., Tuytelaars, T. (eds.) ECCV 2014. LNCS, vol. 8693, pp. 740–755. Springer, Cham (2014). https://doi.org/10.1007/978-3-319-10602-1_48
2. Carion, N., Massa, F., Synnaeve, G., Usunier, N., Kirillov, A., Zagoruyko, S.: End-to-end object detection with transformers. arXiv preprint arXiv: 2005.12872 (2020)
3. Wang, Y., Hou, X., Chau, L.P.: Dense point prediction: a simple baseline for crowd counting and localization. IEEE Trans. Image Process. 2876–2887 (2021)
4. Liu, W., Salzmann, M., Fua, P.: Context-aware crowd counting. In: CVPR (2019)
5. Liang, D., et al.: Focal inverse distance transform maps for crowd localization and counting in dense crowd. arXiv preprint arXiv:2102.07925 (2021)
6. Xu, C., Qiu, K., Fu, J., Bai, S., Xu, Y., Bai, X.: Learn to scale: generating multipolar normalized density map for crowd counting. In: ICCV (2019)
7. Song, Q., Wang, C., Jiang, Z., et al.: Rethinking counting and localization in crowds: a purely point-based framework. In: Proceedings of the IEEE/CVF International Conference on Computer Vision (2021)
8. Abousamra, S., Hoai, M., Samaras, D., Chen, C.: Localization in the crowd with topological constraints. In: AAAI Conference on Artificial Intelligence (2021)
9. Yang, Y., Li, G., Wu, Z., Su, L., Huang, Q., Sebe, N.: Reverse perspective network for perspective aware object counting. In: CVPR (2020)
10. Sam, D.B., Peri, S.V., Sundararaman, M.N., Kamath, A., Babu, R.V.: Locate, size and count: accurately resolving people in dense crowds via detection. IEEE Trans. Pattern Anal. Mach. Intell. **43**(8), 2739–2751 (2020)
11. Carion, N., Massa, F., Synnaeve, G., Usunier, N., Kirillov, A., Zagoruyko, S.: End-to-end object detection with transformers. In: Vedaldi, A., Bischof, H., Brox, T., Frahm, J.-M. (eds.) ECCV 2020. LNCS, vol. 12346, pp. 213–229. Springer, Cham (2020). https://doi.org/10.1007/978-3-030-58452-8_13
12. Idrees, H., Saleemi, I., Seibert, C., Shah, M.: Multi-source multi-scale counting in extremely dense crowd images. In: IEEE Conference on Computer Vision and Pattern Recognition (2013)
13. Wang, Q., Gao, J., Lin, W., Li, X.: NWPU-crowd: a large-scale benchmark for crowd counting and localization. IEEE Trans. Pattern Anal. Mach. Intell. **43**(6), 2141–2149 (2020)
14. Wan, J., Liu, Z., Chan, A.B.: A generalized loss function for crowd counting and localization. In: Proceedings of the IEEE/CVF Conference on Computer Vision and Pattern Recognition (2021)

15. Liu, C., Weng, X., Mu, Y.: Recurrent attentive zooming for joint crowd counting and precise localization. In: IEEE Conference on Computer Vision and Pattern Recognition (2019)
16. Idrees, H., et al.: Composition loss for counting, density map estimation and localization in dense crowds. In: ECCV, pp. 532–546 (2018)
17. Zhang, A., et al.: Relational attention network for crowd counting. In: ICCV (2019)
18. Lian, D., Li, J., Zheng, J., Luo, W., Gao, S.: Density map regression guided detection network for RGD-D crowd counting and localization. In: IEEE Conference on Computer Vision and Pattern Recognition (2019)
19. Liu, X., Yang, J., Ding, W., Wang, T., Wang, Z., Xiong, J.: Adaptive mixture regression network with local counting map for crowd counting. In: Vedaldi, A., Bischof, H., Brox, T., Frahm, J.-M. (eds.) ECCV 2020. LNCS, vol. 12369, pp. 241–257. Springer, Cham (2020). https://doi.org/10.1007/978-3-030-58586-0_15
20. Wang, J., Song, L., Li, Z., et al.: End-to-end object detection with fully convolutional network. In: Proceedings of the IEEE/CVF Conference on Computer Vision and Pattern Recognition (2021)
21. Redmon, J., Farhadi, A.: Yolov3: an incremental improvement. arXiv preprint arXiv:1804.02767 (2018)
22. Sindagi, V.A., Yasarla, R., Patel, V.M.: Pushing the frontiers of unconstrained crowd counting: new dataset and benchmark method. In: Proceedings of the IEEE International Conference on Computer Vision (2019)
23. Zhang, Y., Zhou, D., Chen, S., Gao, S., Ma, Y.: Single-image crowd counting via multi-column convolutional neural network. In: CVPR, pp. 589–597 (2016)
24. Li, Y., Zhang, X., Chen, D.: CSRnet: dilated convolutional neural networks for understanding the highly congested scenes. In: IEEE Conference on Computer Vision and Pattern Recognition (2018)
25. Ge, Z., Liu, S., Li, Z., et al.: OTA: optimal transport assignment for object detection. In: Proceedings of the IEEE/CVF Conference on Computer Vision and Pattern Recognition (2021)
26. Wang, B., Liu, H., Samaras, D., Hoai, M.: Distribution matching for crowd counting. In: NeurIPS (2020)
27. Liang, D., Xu, W., Bai, X.: An End-to-End Transformer Model for Crowd Localization. arXiv preprint arXiv:2202.13065 (2022)
28. Kuhn, H.W.: The Hungarian method for the assignment problem. Nav. Res. Logist. Q. **2**, 83–97 (1955)
29. Liu, Y., Shi, M., Zhao, Q., Wang, X.: Point in, box out: beyond counting persons in crowds. In: IEEE Conference on Computer Vision and Pattern Recognition (2019)
30. Ma, Z., Wei, X., Hong, X., Gong, Y.: Bayesian loss for crowd count estimation with point supervision. In: ICCV (2019)
31. Jiang, X., et al.: Attention scaling for crowd counting. In: IEEE Conference on Computer Vision and Pattern Recognition (2020)
32. Ren, S., He, K., Girshick, R., Sun, J.: Faster R-CNN: towards real-time object detection with region proposal networks. IEEE Trans. Pattern Anal. Mach. Intell. **39**, 1137–1149 (2017)
33. Wang, Y., Hou, J., Hou, X., Chau, L.-P.: A self-training approach for point-supervised object detection and counting in crowds. IEEE Trans. Image Process. **30**, 2876–2887 (2021)

Discriminative Distillation to Reduce Class Confusion in Continual Learning

Changhong Zhong[1,2], Zhiying Cui[1,2], Wei-Shi Zheng[1,2], Hongmei Liu[1,3(✉)], and Ruixuan Wang[1,2(✉)]

[1] School of Computer Science and Engineering, Sun Yat-sen University,
Guangzhou, China
wangruix5@mail.sysu.edu.cn
[2] Key Laboratory of Machine Intelligence and Advanced Computing, MOE,
Guangzhou, China
[3] Key Laboratory of Information Security Technology, Guangzhou,
Guangdong, China

Abstract. Successful continual learning of new knowledge would enable intelligent systems to recognize more and more classes of objects. However, current intelligent systems often fail to correctly recognize previously learned classes of objects when updated to learn new classes. It is widely believed that such downgraded performance is solely due to the catastrophic forgetting of previously learned knowledge. In this study, we argue that the class confusion phenomena may also play a role in downgrading the classification performance during continual learning, i.e., the high similarity between new classes and any previously learned classes would also cause the classifier to make mistakes in recognizing these old classes, even if the knowledge of these old classes is not forgotten. To alleviate the class confusion issue, we propose a discriminative distillation strategy to help the classifier well learn discriminative features between confusing classes during continual learning. Experiments on multiple datasets support that the proposed distillation strategy, when combined with existing methods, is effective in improving continual learning.

Keywords: Continual learning · Confusing classes · Discriminative distillation

1 Introduction

Continual learning or lifelong learning aims to continually learn and absorb new knowledge over time while retaining previously learned knowledge [21]. With this ability, humans can accumulate knowledge over time and become experts in certain domains. It is desirable for the intelligent system to obtain this ability and recognize more and more objects continually, with the presumption that

This work is supported by NSFCs (No. 62071502, U1811461), the Guangdong Key Research and Development Program (No. 2020B1111190001), and the Meizhou Science and Technology Program (No. 2019A0102005).

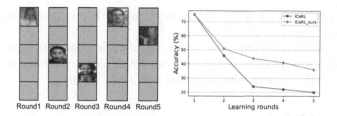

Fig. 1. Continual learning suffers not only from catastrophic forgetting but also from the confusion between old and new classes. Left: five similar classes ('baby', 'boy', 'girl', 'man', 'woman') were learned at different rounds; gray boxes represent certain other classes learned at each round. Right: classification performance on 'baby' class learned at the first round decreases over learning rounds, but the proposed method (orange) can better handle the confusion between the 'baby' class and its similar classes at later rounds compared to baseline iCaRL (blue). (Color figure online)

very limited amount or even no data is stored for the old classes when learning knowledge of new classes. The intelligent system has to update its parameters when acquiring new knowledge and often inevitably causes the downgraded performance on recognizing old classes. It has been widely believed that the downgraded performance is solely due to the *catastrophic forgetting* of old knowledge during learning new knowledge [13,14], and various approaches have been proposed to alleviate the catastrophic forgetting issue, such as by trying to keep important model parameters or outputs at various layers in convolutional neural networks (CNNs) unchanged during learning new knowledge [4,5,8,14,17].

However, sometimes simply keeping old knowledge from forgetting during continual learning may not be enough to keep classification performance from downgrading. At an early round of continual learning, since only a few classes of knowledge needs to be learned, the classifier may easily learn to use part of class knowledge to well discriminate between these classes. When any new class is visually similar to any previously learned class during continual learning, the visual features learned to recognize the old class may not be discriminative enough to discriminate between the new class and the visually similar old class (e.g., 'girl' vs. 'baby', Fig. 1), causing downgraded performance on previously learned class. We call this phenomena the *class confusion issue*. In this study, we propose a novel knowledge distillation strategy to help the classifier learn such discriminative knowledge information between old and new classes during continual learning. The basic idea is to train a temporary expert classifier to learn both the new classes and visually similar old classes during continual learning, and then distill the discriminative knowledge from the temporary expert classifier to the new classifier. To our best knowledge, it is the first time to explore the class confusion issue in continual learning. The main contributions are below:

- It is observed that continual learning is affected not only by catastrophic forgetting, but also by potential class confusion between new classes and visually similar old classes.

- A discriminative knowledge distillation strategy is proposed to help the classifier discriminate confusing classes.
- Initial experiments on multiple image classification datasets support that the proposed discriminative distillation can be flexibly combined with existing methods and is effective in improving continual learning.

2 Related Work

Generally, there are two types of continual learning problems, task-incremental and class-incremental. Task-incremental learning (TIL) presumes that one model is incrementally updated to solve more and more tasks, often with multiple tasks sharing a common feature extractor but having task-specific classification heads. The task identification is available during inference, i.e., users know which model head should be applied when predicting the class label of a new data. In contrast, class-incremental learning (CIL) presumes that one model is incrementally updated to predict more and more classes, with all classes sharing a single model head. This study focuses on the CIL problem.

Existing approaches to the two types of continual learning can be roughly divided into four groups, regularization-based, expansion-based, distillation-based, and regeneration-based. Regularization-based approaches often find the model parameters or components (e.g., kernels in CNNs) crucial for old knowledge, and then try to keep them unchanged with the help of regularization loss terms when learning new classes [1,11,14]. While keeping the parameters unchanged could help models keep old knowledge in a few rounds of continual learning, it is not able to solve the confusion issue because more and more parameters in CNNs are frozen. To make models more flexibly learn new knowledge, expansion-based approaches are developed by adding new kernels, layers, or even sub-networks when learning new knowledge [9,12,16,22,29]. Although expanding the network architecture can potentially alleviate the confusion issue to some extent because the expanded kernels might help extract more discriminative features, most expansion-based approaches are initially proposed for TIL and might not be flexibly extended for CIL. In comparison, distillation-based approaches can be directly applied to CIL by distilling knowledge from the old classifier (for old classes) to the new classifier (for both old and new classes) during learning new classes [2,10,17,19,24]. In addition, regeneration-based approaches have also been proposed particularly when none of old-class data is available during learning new classes. The basic idea is to train an auto-encoder [6,23,25] or generative adversarial network (GAN) [20,28] to synthesize old data for each old class, such that plenty of synthetic but realistic data for each old class are available during learning new classes. All the existing approaches are proposed to alleviate the catastrophic forgetting issue, without aware of the existence of the class confusion issue.

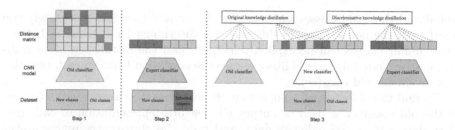

Fig. 2. Discriminative knowledge distillation pipeline. First, the old classifier learned at the previous round is used to identify the similar old class(es) for each new class (Step 1). Then, the temporary expert classifier is trained to recognize both the new classes and their similar old classes (Step 2). Finally, the old classifier and the expert classifier are simultaneously used to teach the new classifier (Step 3). The potential confusion between new and old classes can be alleviated by the distillation from the expert classifier to the new classifier. (Color figure online)

3 Method

In contrast to most continual learning methods which only aim to reduce catastrophic forgetting during learning new classes, this study additionally aims to reduce the potential confusions between new classes and visually similar old classes. As in most distillation-based continual learning methods, only a small subset of training data is stored for each old class and available during continual learning of new classes.

3.1 Overview of the Proposed Framework

We propose a distillation strategy particularly to reduce the class confusion issue during continual learning. At each round of continual learning, besides the knowledge distillation from the old classifier learned at the previous round to the new classifier at the current round, a temporary expert classifier is trained to classify not only the new classes but also those old classes which are visually similar to the new classes (Fig. 2, Step 2), and then the discriminative knowledge of the expert classifier is distilled to the new classifier as well during training the new classifier (Fig. 2, Step 3). The knowledge distillation from the expert classifier to the new classifier would largely reduce the potential confusion between these similar classes during prediction by the new classifier. It is worth noting discriminative knowledge distillation from the expert can be used as a plug-in component for most distillation-based continual learning methods.

3.2 Expert Classifier

The key novelty of the proposed framework is the addition of the expert classifier whose knowledge will be distilled to the new classifier. The expert classifier at each learning round is trained to classify both the new classes at the current round and those old classes which are similar to and therefore more likely confused with the new classes. In this way, the discriminative knowledge between such similar classes can be explicitly learned, and the distillation of such discriminative knowledge would likely reduce the confusion between each new class and its similar old class(es).

To find the old class(es) similar to each new class, the feature extractor part of the old classifier is used to output the feature representation of each new-class data and stored old-class data, and then the class-centre representation is obtained respectively for each class by averaging the feature representations of all data belonging to the same class. The Euclidean distance from the class-centre representation of the new class to that of each old class is then used to select the most similar (i.e., closest) old class(es) for the new class (Fig. 2, Step 1). While sometimes one new class may have multiple similar old classes and another new class may have no similar old classes, without loss of generality, the same number of similar old classes is selected for each new class in this study and no old class is selected multiple times at each learning round.

Once the old classes similar to the new classes are selected, the expert classifier can be trained using all the training data of the new classes and the stored similar old-class data (Fig. 2, Step 2). Since only very limited number of old data is available for each old class, the training data set is imbalanced across classes, which could make the classifier focus on learning knowledge of the large (i.e., new) classes. To alleviate the imbalance issue, the expert classifier is initially trained (for 80 epochs in this study) using all the available training set and then fine-tuned (for 40 epochs in this study) with balanced dataset across classes by down-sampling the dataset of new classes.

3.3 Knowledge Distillation

The expert classifier, together with the old classifier from the previous round of continual learning, is used to jointly teach the new classifier based on the knowledge distillation strategy. Suppose $D = \{(\mathbf{x}_i, \mathbf{y}_i), i = 1, \ldots, N\}$ is the collection of all new classes of training data at current learning round and the stored small old-class data, where $\mathbf{x}_i$ is an image and the one-hot vector $\mathbf{y}_i$ is the corresponding class label. For image $\mathbf{x}_i$, let $\mathbf{z}_i = [z_{i1}, z_{i2}, \ldots, z_{it}]^\mathsf{T}$ denote the logit output (i.e., the input to the last-layer softmax operation in the CNN classifier) of the expert classifier, and $\hat{\mathbf{z}}_i = [\hat{z}_{i1}, \hat{z}_{i2}, \ldots, \hat{z}_{it}]^\mathsf{T}$ denote the corresponding logit output of the new classifier (Fig. 2, Step 3, outputs of the new classifier with dashed red lines linked), where t is the number of outputs by the expert classifier. Then, the distillation of the knowledge from the expert classifier to the new classifier can be obtained by minimizing the distillation loss $\mathcal{L}_n$,

$$\mathcal{L}_n(\boldsymbol{\theta}) = -\frac{1}{N} \sum_{i=1}^{N} \sum_{j=1}^{t} p_{ij} \log \hat{p}_{ij}, \tag{1}$$

where θ represents the model parameters of the new classifier, and p_{ij} and $\hat{p}_{ij}$ are from the temperature-tuned softmax operation,

$$p_{ij} = \frac{\exp\left(z_{ij}/T_n\right)}{\sum_{k=1}^{t} \exp\left(z_{ik}/T_n\right)}, \quad \hat{p}_{ij} = \frac{\exp\left(\hat{z}_{ij}/T_n\right)}{\sum_{k=1}^{t} \exp\left(\hat{z}_{ik}/T_n\right)}, \tag{2}$$

and $T_n \geq 1$ is the temperature coefficient used to help knowledge distillation [7]. Since the expert has been trained to discriminate new classes from visually similar old classes, the knowledge distillation from the expert classifier to the new classifier is expected to help the new classifier gain similar discriminative power. In other words, with the distillation, the new classifier would become less confused with the new classes and visually similar old classes, resulting in better classification performance after each round of continual learning.

Besides the knowledge distillation from the expert classifier, knowledge from the old classifier can be distilled to the new classifier in a similar way, i.e., by minimizing the distillation loss $\mathcal{L}_o$,

$$\mathcal{L}_o(\theta) = -\frac{1}{N} \sum_{i=1}^{N} \sum_{j=1}^{s} q_{ij} \log \hat{q}_{ij}, \tag{3}$$

where s is the number of old classes learned so far, and q_{ij} and $\hat{q}_{ij}$ are respectively from the temperature-tuned softmax over the logit of the old classifier and the corresponding logit part of the new classifier (Fig. 2, Step 3, outputs of the new classifier with dashed green lines linked), with the distillation parameter T_o.

As in general knowledge distillation strategy, besides the two distillation losses, the cross-entropy loss $\mathcal{L}_c$ over the training set D based on the output of the new classifier is also applied to train the new classifier. In combination, the new classifier can be trained by minimizing the loss $\mathcal{L}$,

$$\mathcal{L}(\theta) = \mathcal{L}_c(\theta) + \lambda_1 \mathcal{L}_o(\theta) + \lambda_2 \mathcal{L}_n(\theta), \tag{4}$$

where λ_1 and λ_2 are trade-off coefficients to balance the loss terms.

The proposed distillation strategy is clearly different from existing distillations for continual learning. Most distillation-based continual learning methods only distill knowledge from the old class to the new class at each learning round. The most relevant work is the dual distillation [18] which reduces catastrophic forgetting with the help of two classifiers (called expert classifier and old classifier respectively), where the expert classifier is trained only for new classes and then, together with the old classifier, distilled to the new classifier. In comparison, the expert classifier in our method is trained to learn not only the new classes but also likely confusing old classes, particularly aiming to alleviate the class confusion issue. Therefore, our method extended the dual distillation but with a brand new motivation. Most importantly, the proposed discriminative distillation can be easily combined with most existing continual learning methods by simply adding the loss term $\mathcal{L}_n(\theta)$ during classifier training at each round of continual learning.

Table 1. Statistics of datasets. [75, 2400]: size range of image height and width.

Dataset	#class	Train/class	Test/class	Size
CIFAR100	100	500	100	32×32
mini-ImageNet	100	~1,200	100	[75, 2400]
ImageNet	1000	~1,200	100	[75, 2400]

4   Experiments

4.1   Experimental Settings

The proposed method was evaluated on three datasets, CIFAR100 [15], the full ImageNet dataset [3], and a subset of ImageNet which contains randomly selected 100 classes (Table 1). During model training, each CIFAR100 image was randomly flipped horizontally, and each ImageNet image was randomly cropped and then resized to 224×224 pixels. On each dataset, an CNN classifier was first trained for certain number (e.g., 10, 20) of classes, and then a set of new classes' data were provided to update the classifier at each round of continual learning. Ths SGD optimizer (batch size 128) was used with an initial learning rate 0.1. The new classifier at each round of continual learning was trained for up to 100 epochs, with the training convergence consistently observed. ResNet32 and ResNet18 were used as the default CNN backbone for CIFAR100 and ImageNet (including mini-ImageNet) respectively, and $\lambda_1 = \lambda_2 = 1.0$, $T_n = T_o = 2.0$. One similar old class was selected for each new class in the expert classifier. Following iCaRL [24], the herding strategy was adopted to select a small subset of images for each new class with a total memory size K. For CIFAR100 and mini-ImageNet, the memory size is $K = 2000$. And for ImageNet, $K = 20000$.

After training at each round, the average accuracy over all learned classes so far was calculated. Such a training and evaluation process was repeated in next-round continual learning. For each experiment, the average accuracy over three runs were reported, each run with a different and fixed order of classes to be learned. All baseline methods were evaluated on the same orders of continual learning over three runs and with the same herding strategy for testing.

4.2   Effectiveness Evaluation

The proposed discriminative distillation can be plugged into most continual learning methods. Therefore, the effectiveness of the proposed distillation is evaluated by combining it respectively with existing continual learning methods, including LwF [17], iCaRL [24], UCIR [8], and BiC [27]. All the four methods are distillation-based, and therefore the only difference between each baseline and the corresponding proposed method is the inclusion of the discriminative distillation loss term during classifier training. The inference method proposed in the original papers were adopted during testing (nearest-mean-of-exemplars for iCaRL, and softmax output for LwF, UCIR, and BiC). The evaluation was

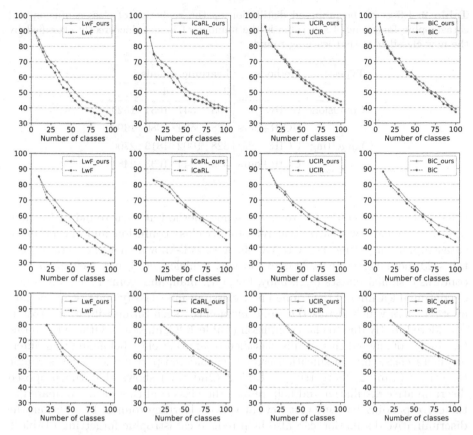

Fig. 3. Continual learning of 5 (first row), 10 (second row), and 20 (third row) new classes at each round with CIFAR100 dataset. Columns 1–4 (blue curve): performance of LwF, iCaRL, UCIR, BiC; Columns 1–4 (orange curve): performance of the proposed method built on the corresponding baseline. (Color figure online)

firstly performed on the CIFAR100 dataset. As shown in Fig. 3, when continually learning 5 classes (first row), 10 classes (second row), and 20 classes (third row) at each round respectively, each baseline method was clearly outperformed by the combination of the proposed discriminative distillation with the baseline, with around absolute 2%–5% better in accuracy at each round of continual learning. The consistent improvement in classification performance built on different continual learning methods supports the effectiveness of the proposed discriminative distillation for continual learning. Similar results were obtained from experiments on mini-ImageNet (Fig. 4) and ImageNet (Fig. 5), suggesting that the proposed discriminative distillation is effective in various continual learning tasks with different scales of new classes at each learning round.

To further investigate the effect of the proposed discriminative distillation on reducing the confusions between similar classes, the total reduction in

Table 2. Effect of the proposed distillation on the reduction of class confusion and catastrophic forgetting. Each value is the number of images incorrectly classified by the new classifier at that learning round.

Types	Methods	Learning rounds			
		2	3	4	5
Confusion	UCIR	193	547	1037	1525
	UCIR+ours	178	524	986	1399
Forgetting	UCIR	328	1002	1813	2706
	UCIR+ours	309	944	1633	2484

classification error compared to the baseline method at each round of learning was divided into two parts, one relevant to class confusion and the other to catastrophic forgetting. For CIFAR100, it is well-known that the dataset contains 20 meta-classes (e.g., human, flowers, vehicles, etc.) and each meta-class contains 5 similar classes (e.g., baby, boy, girl, man, and woman). At any round of continual learning, if the trained new classifier mis-classify one test image into another class which shares the same meta-class, such an classification error is considered partly due to class confusion (Table 2, 'Confusion'). Otherwise, if one test image of any old class is mis-classified to another class belonging to a different meta-class, this classification error is considered partly due to catastrophic forgetting (Table 2, 'Forgetting'). Table 2 (2nd row) shows that the proposed discriminative distillation did help reduce the class confusion error compared to the corresponding baseline (1st row) at various learning rounds. In addition, the discriminative distillation can also help reduce catastrophic forgetting (Table 2, last two rows), consistent with previously reported results based on distillation of only new classes from the expert classifier [18].

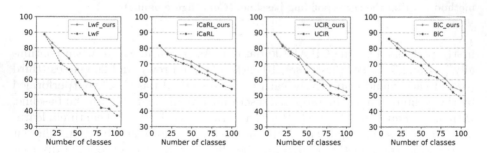

Fig. 4. Continual learning of 10 new classes at each round on mini-ImageNet.

The effect of the discriminative distillation was also visually confirmed with demonstrative examples of attention map changes over learning rounds (Fig. 6). For example, while the classifier trained based on the baseline UCIR can attend

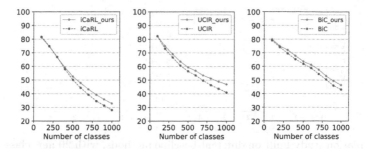

Fig. 5. Continual learning of 100 new classes at each round on ImageNet.

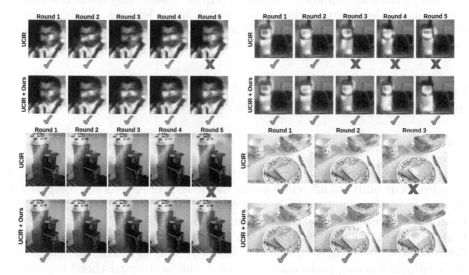

Fig. 6. Demonstrative attention maps over learning rounds from the baseline UCIR (upper row) and the correspondingly proposed method (bottom row). Input images are from CIFAR100 and mini-ImageNet, and each attention map (heatmap overlapped on input) for the ground-truth class was generated by Grad-CAM [26] from the trained classifier at each learning round. The tick or cross under each image represents the classification result.

to some part of the 'man' face over learning rounds, this test image was mis-classified at the last round (Fig. 6, top row, left half). This suggests that the mis-classification is probably not due to forgetting old knowledge (otherwise the attended region at last learning round would be much different from that at the first round). In comparison, the classifier based on the correspondingly proposed method learned to attend to larger face regions and can correctly classify the image over all rounds (Fig. 6, second row, left half), probably because the expert classifier learned to find that more face regions are necessary in order to discriminate differ-ent types of human faces (e.g., 'man' vs. 'women') and such discriminative knowl-edge was distilled from the expert classifier to the new classifier during continual

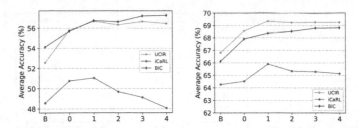

Fig. 7. Ablation study built on different baseline methods, with 20 new classes learned at each round on CIFAR100. X-axis: number of similar old classes selected for each new class during continual learning; '0' means the expert classifier only learns new classes, and 'B' means the expert classifier is not applied during learning. Y-axis: the mean classification accuracy over all the classes at the final round (Left), or the average of mean class accuracy over all rounds (Right).

learning. Similar results can be obtained from the other three examples (Fig. 6, 'phone', 'file cabinet', and 'bread' images).

4.3   Ablation Study

The effect of the discriminative distillation is further evaluated with a series of ablation study built on different baseline methods. As Fig. 7 shows, compared to the baselines ('Baseline' on the X-axis) and the dual distillation which does not learn any old classes in the expert classifier ('0' on the X-axis), learning to classify both new and similar old classes by the expert classifier and then distilling the discriminative knowledge to the new classifier ('1' to '4' on X-axis) often improves the continual learning performance, either at the final round (Left) or over all rounds (Right). Adding more old classes for the expert classifier does not always improve the performance of the new classifier (Fig. 7, Left, red curve), maybe because the inclusion of more old classes distracts the expert classifier from learning the most discriminative features between confusing classes.

5   Conclusions

Continual learning may be affected not only by catastrophic forgetting of old knowledge, but also by the class confusion between old and new knowledge. This study proposes a simple but effective discriminative distillation strategy to help the classifier handle both issues during continual learning. The distillation component can be flexibly embedded into existing approaches to continual learning. Initial experiments on natural image classification datasets shows that explicitly handling the class confusion issue can further improve continual learning performance. This suggests that both catastrophic forgetting and class confusion may need to be considered in future study of continual learning.

References

1. Abati, D., Tomczak, J., Blankevoort, T., Calderara, S., Cucchiara, R., Bejnordi, B.E.: Conditional channel gated networks for task-aware continual learning. In: CVPR (2020)
2. Castro, F.M., Marín-Jiménez, M.J., Guil, N., Schmid, C., Alahari, K.: End-to-end incremental learning. In: ECCV (2018)
3. Deng, J., Dong, W., Socher, R., Li, L.J., Li, K., Fei-Fei, L.: ImageNet: a large-scale hierarchical image database. In: CVPR (2009)
4. Dhar, P., Singh, R.V., Peng, K.C., Wu, Z., Chellappa, R.: Learning without memorizing. In: CVPR (2019)
5. Douillard, A., Cord, M., Ollion, C., Robert, T., Valle, E.: PODNet: pooled outputs distillation for small-tasks incremental learning. In: Vedaldi, A., Bischof, H., Brox, T., Frahm, J.-M. (eds.) ECCV 2020. LNCS, vol. 12365, pp. 86–102. Springer, Cham (2020). https://doi.org/10.1007/978-3-030-58565-5_6
6. Hayes, T.L., Kafle, K., Shrestha, R., Acharya, M., Kanan, C.: REMIND your neural network to prevent catastrophic forgetting. In: Vedaldi, A., Bischof, H., Brox, T., Frahm, J.-M. (eds.) ECCV 2020. LNCS, vol. 12353, pp. 466–483. Springer, Cham (2020). https://doi.org/10.1007/978-3-030-58598-3_28
7. Hinton, G., Vinyals, O., Dean, J.: Distilling the knowledge in a neural network. In: NIPS Workshop (2015)
8. Hou, S., Pan, X., Loy, C.C., Wang, Z., Lin, D.: Learning a unified classifier incrementally via rebalancing. In: CVPR (2019)
9. Hung, C.Y., Tu, C.H., Wu, C.E., Chen, C.H., Chan, Y.M., Chen, C.S.: Compacting, picking and growing for unforgetting continual learning. In: NIPS (2019)
10. Iscen, A., Zhang, J., Lazebnik, S., Schmid, C.: Memory-efficient incremental learning through feature adaptation. In: Vedaldi, A., Bischof, H., Brox, T., Frahm, J.-M. (eds.) ECCV 2020. LNCS, vol. 12361, pp. 699–715. Springer, Cham (2020). https://doi.org/10.1007/978-3-030-58517-4_41
11. Jung, S., Ahn, H., Cha, S., Moon, T.: Continual learning with node-importance based adaptive group sparse regularization. In: NIPS (2020)
12. Karani, N., Chaitanya, K., Baumgartner, C., Konukoglu, E.: A lifelong learning approach to brain MR segmentation across scanners and protocols. In: Frangi, A.F., Schnabel, J.A., Davatzikos, C., Alberola-López, C., Fichtinger, G. (eds.) MICCAI 2018. LNCS, vol. 11070, pp. 476–484. Springer, Cham (2018). https://doi.org/10.1007/978-3-030-00928-1_54
13. Kemker, R., McClure, M., Abitino, A., Hayes, T.L., Kanan, C.: Measuring catastrophic forgetting in neural networks. In: AAAI (2018)
14. Kirkpatrick, J., et al.: Overcoming catastrophic forgetting in neural networks. In: Proceedings of the National Academy of Sciences (2017)
15. Krizhevsky, A., Hinton, G.: Learning multiple layers of features from tiny images. Technical report, University of Toronto (2009)
16. Li, X., Zhou, Y., Wu, T., Socher, R., Xiong, C.: Learn to grow: a continual structure learning framework for overcoming catastrophic forgetting. In: ICML (2019)
17. Li, Z., Hoiem, D.: Learning without forgetting. IEEE Trans. Pattern Anal. Mach. Intell. **40**(12), 2935–2947 (2017)
18. Li, Z., Zhong, C., Wang, R., Zheng, W.-S.: Continual learning of new diseases with dual distillation and ensemble strategy. In: Martel, A.L., et al. (eds.) MICCAI 2020. LNCS, vol. 12261, pp. 169–178. Springer, Cham (2020). https://doi.org/10.1007/978-3-030-59710-8_17

19. Meng, Q., Shin'ichi, S.: ADINet: attribute driven incremental network for retinal image classification. In: CVPR (2020)
20. Ostapenko, O., Puscas, M., Klein, T., Jahnichen, P., Nabi, M.: Learning to remember: a synaptic plasticity driven framework for continual learning. In: CVPR (2019)
21. Parisi, G.I., Kemker, R., Part, J.L., Kanan, C., Wermter, S.: Continual lifelong learning with neural networks: a review. Neural Netw. **113**, 54–71 (2019)
22. Rajasegaran, J., Hayat, M., Khan, S.H., Khan, F.S., Shao, L.: Random path selection for continual learning. In: NIPS (2019)
23. Rao, D., Visin, F., Rusu, A., Pascanu, R., Teh, Y.W., Hadsell, R.: Continual unsupervised representation learning. In: NIPS (2019)
24. Rebuffi, S.A., Kolesnikov, A., Sperl, G., Lampert, C.H.: iCaRL: incremental classifier and representation learning. In: CVPR (2017)
25. Riemer, M., Klinger, T., Bouneffouf, D., Franceschini, M.: Scalable recollections for continual lifelong learning. In: AAAI (2019)
26. Selvaraju, R.R., Cogswell, M., Das, A., Vedantam, R., Parikh, D., Batra, D.: Grad-CAM: visual explanations from deep networks via gradient-based localization. In: ICCV (2017)
27. Wu, Y., et al.: Large scale incremental learning. In: CVPR (2019)
28. Xiang, Y., Fu, Y., Ji, P., Huang, H.: Incremental learning using conditional adversarial networks. In: ICCV (2019)
29. Yan, S., Xie, J., He, X.: DER: dynamically expandable representation for class incremental learning. In: CVPR (2021)

Enhancing Transferability of Adversarial Examples with Spatial Momentum

Guoqiu Wang[1], Huanqian Yan[1], and Xingxing Wei[2(✉)]

[1] Beijing Key Laboratory of Digital Media (DML), School of Computer Science and Engineering, Beihang University, Beijing, China
{wangguoqiu,yanhq}@buaa.edu.cn
[2] Institute of Artificial Intelligence, Hangzhou Innovation Institute, Beihang University, Beijing, China
xxwei@buaa.edu.cn

Abstract. Many adversarial attack methods achieve satisfactory attack success rates under the white-box setting, but they usually show poor transferability when attacking other DNN models. Momentum-based attack is one effective method to improve transferability. It integrates the momentum term into the iterative process, which can stabilize the update directions by adding the gradients' temporal correlation for each pixel. We argue that only this temporal momentum is not enough, the gradients from the spatial domain within an image, i.e. gradients from the context pixels centered on the target pixel are also important to the stabilization. For that, we propose a novel method named Spatial Momentum Iterative FGSM attack (SMI-FGSM), which introduces the mechanism of momentum accumulation from temporal domain to spatial domain by considering the context information from different regions within the image. SMI-FGSM is then integrated with temporal momentum to simultaneously stabilize the gradients' update direction from both the temporal and spatial domains. Extensive experiments show that our method indeed further enhances adversarial transferability. It achieves the best transferability success rate for multiple mainstream undefended and defended models, which outperforms the state-of-the-art attack methods by a large margin of 10% on average.

Keywords: Adversarial attack · Adversarial transferability · Momentum-based attack

1 Introduction

Deep neural networks (DNNs) are vulnerable to adversarial examples [1,2], which are crafted by adding imperceptible perturbations to clean images, making models output wrong predictions expected by attackers. The existence of adversarial examples has raised concerns in security-sensitive applications, e.g., self-driving cars [3,4], face recognition [5,6] and video monitoring [27].

In the past years, many methods have been proposed to generate adversarial examples, such as fast gradient sign method [1] and its iterative variant [7],

S. Yu et al. (Eds.): PRCV 2022, LNCS 13534, pp. 593–604, 2022.
https://doi.org/10.1007/978-3-031-18907-4_46

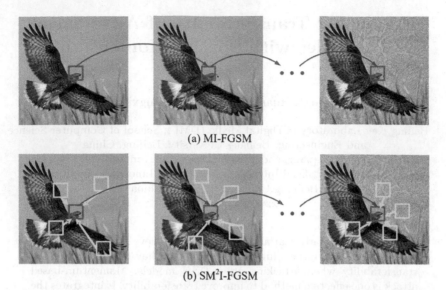

Fig. 1. Illustrations of MI-FGSM (a) and SM²I-FGSM (b). MI-FGSM updates the gradient direction by accumulating the gradient in the previous iteration. SM²I-FGSM considers not only the gradients' temporal correlation but also the correlation in the spatial domain (see the yellow boxes), which can comprehensively stabilize the update direction. (Color figure online)

projected gradient descent method [8], and so on. They all conduct attacks in the white-box setting, utilizing the detailed information of the threat models. In addition, some works show that adversarial examples have transferability [9,10,20], which means the adversarial examples crafted for one DNN model can successfully attack other DNN models to a certain extent. The existence of transferability makes adversarial examples practical to real-world applications because attackers do not need to know the information of the target models, and thus introduces a series of serious security issues [3,5,6].

However, most white-box attack methods usually have poor transferability. Recently, A series of methods have been proposed to address this issue, such as momentum-based iterative attack [11,12], variance tuning iterative gradient-based method [13], diverse inputs [14–16], translation-invariant [17], and multi-model ensemble attack [9]. Even so, there is still a gap between transferability attack success rates and the practical demand, which motivates us to design a more effective method to further improve adversarial transferability when attacking various DNN models.

Among the above methods to improve transferability, the momentum-based iterative attack (MI-FGSM) [11] shows good performance and has many variants [12,13]. They integrate the momentum term into the iterative process, which can stabilize the update directions during the iterations by adding the gradients' temporal correlation to obtain better perturbations. We argue that only this temporal momentum is not enough, the gradients from the spatial domain within an image, i.e. gradients from the context pixels centered on the target pixel are also important to the stabilization. In this paper, we propose a novel method named Spatial Momentum Iterative FGSM attack, which introduces the mechanism of momentum accumulation from temporal domain to spatial domain by considering the context gradient information from different regions within the image. SMI-FGSM is then integrated with the previous MI-FGSM to construct SM^{2}I-FGSM, and thus simultaneously enhances the transferability from both the temporal and spatial domain. The attacking process is illustrated in Fig. 1. The main contributions can be summarized as follows:

- We show that the gradient momentum coming from the spatial domain is also useful to enhance transferability and multiple random transformations will lead to an effective spatial momentum.
- We propose a novel method called Spatial Momentum Iterative (SMI-FGSM) attack to improve adversarial transferability. It is then integrated with temporal momentum to simultaneously stabilize the gradients' update direction from both the temporal and spatial domains.
- Extensive experimental results show that the proposed method could remarkably improve the attack transferability in both mainstream undefended and defended models.

2   Related Work

The study of adversarial attack is considered in developing robust models [8,19]. It can be roughly categorized into two types, white-box attacks, and black-box attacks. The deep models are fully exposed to the adversary in the white-box attack setting, as their structure and parameters. Whereas in the black-box attack setting, the adversary only has little or no knowledge of the target model. Hence, black-box attacks are more practical in real-world scenarios.

Black-box attacks mainly include query-based attacks [28,29] and transfer-based attacks [9,17]. Query-based attacks focus on estimating the gradients of the target model through interaction with the target model. However, these methods usually require a large number of queries, which is unrealistic in real-world applications. Transfer-based attacks, which are more practical and have been studied extensively, generate adversarial examples by using a white-box attack method on a source model (or source models in ensemble attack) to fool the target model. Here, we focus on improving the transfer-based black-box attacks in this paper. Some related work on adversarial attack and adversarial transferability is introduced as follows.

Given a classification network f_θ parameterized by θ, let (x, y) denote the clean image and its corresponding ground-truth label, the goal of the adversarial attack is to find an example x^{adv} which is in the vicinity of x but misclassified by the network. In most cases, we use the L_p norm to limit the adversarial perturbations below a threshold ϵ, where p could be 0, 2, ∞. This can be expressed as

$$f_\theta(x^{adv}) \neq y, \ s.t. \ \left\| x^{adv} - x \right\|_p \leq \epsilon \tag{1}$$

Fast Gradient Sign Method (FGSM) [1] generates an adversarial example x^{adv} by performing one-step update as

$$x^{adv} = x + \epsilon \cdot sign(\nabla_x J(x, y)) \tag{2}$$

where $\nabla_x J$ is the gradient of the loss function $J(\cdot)$ with respect to x and cross-entropy loss is often used. $sign(\cdot)$ is the sign function to limit perturbations conform to the L_∞ norm bound.

The Iterative version of FGSM (I-FGSM) [7] iteratively applies fast gradient sign method multiple times with a small step size α, which can be expressed as

$$x_{t+1}^{adv} = x_t^{adv} + \alpha \cdot sign(\nabla_{x_t^{adv}} J(x_t^{adv}, y)) \tag{3}$$

Momentum Iterative Fast Gradient Sign Method (MI-FGSM) [11] boosts the adversarial transferability by integrating the temporal momentum term into the iterative attack to stabilize the update directions.

$$g_{t+1} = \mu \cdot g_t + \frac{\nabla_x J(x_t^{adv}, y)}{\| \nabla_x J(x_t^{adv}, y) \|_1} \tag{4}$$

$$x_{t+1}^{adv} = x_t^{adv} + \alpha \cdot sign(g_{t+1}) \tag{5}$$

where g_t is the accumulated gradient and μ is the decay factor which is often set to 1.0. MI-FGSM updates the moment gradient g_{t+1} by Eq. (4) and then updates x_{t+1}^{adv} by Eq. (5).

Nesterov Iterative Fast Gradient Sign Method (NI-FGSM) [12] adapts Nesterov accelerated gradient into the iterative attacks so as to look ahead and improve the transferability of adversarial examples. NI-FGSM substitutes x_t^{adv} in Eq. (4) with $x_t^{adv} + \alpha \cdot \mu \cdot g_t$.

Variance Tuning Momentum-based Iterative Method (VMI-FGSM) [13] further consider the gradient variance of the previous iteration to tune the current gradient so as to stabilize the update direction. It substitutes Eq. (4) by

$$g_{t+1} = \mu \cdot g_t + \frac{\nabla_x J(x_t^{adv}, y) + v_t}{\| \nabla_x J(x_t^{adv}, y) + v_t \|_1} \tag{6}$$

where $v_{t+1} = \frac{1}{n} \sum_{i=1}^{n} \nabla_x J(x_i, y) - \nabla_x J(x_t^{adv}, y)$, $x_i = x_t^{adv} + r_i$ and r_i is the random noise within a certain range.

Diverse Inputs (DI) attack [14] applies random transformations to the input images at each iteration to create diverse input patterns, which brings randomness to the adversarial perturbations and improves the transferability.

Translation-Invariant (TI) attack [17] shifts the image within a small magnitude and approximately calculates the gradients by convolving the gradient of the untranslated image with a pre-defined kernel matrix. The resultant adversarial example is less sensitive to the discriminative region of the white-box model being attacked and has a higher probability to fool black-box models with defense mechanisms.

3   Methodology

3.1   Spatial Momentum Iterative Attack

In this section, we introduce the motivation and spatial momentum iterative attack in detail. We show the algorithm and its experimental results under the constraint of L_∞ norm. This method can also be used in L_2 norm.

MI-FGSM [11] introduces the idea of momentum into the adversarial attack and gets a big promotion. It integrates the momentum term into the iterative process, which can be seen as adding temporal correlation (see Eq. (4)) for the gradient that is used to update perturbations compared to I-FGSM [7] and can stabilize the update directions during the iterations (see Fig. 2). It motivates us that momentum accumulation mechanism not only can be based on the temporal domain like [11], but also in the spatial domain through comprehensively considering the context pixels centered on the target pixel within the image.

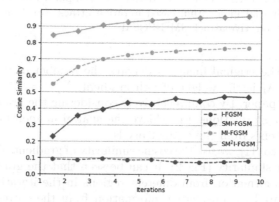

Fig. 2. The stabilization of gradients during iterations. Cosine similarity of gradients is used to measure the stabilization. The results are averaged over 1000 images. We can see that SMI-FGSM achieves better stabilization than I-FGSM and SM²I-FGSM achieves the best stabilization among the four methods.

As Eq. (3) shows, I-FGSM simply updates the perturbation with the gradient from image x_t^{adv}, which only considers the current pixel, while ignoring its context pixels. To stabilize the direction of updating, we propose a novel method called SMI-FGSM. It uses information from context regions by considering multiple gradients of random transformations of the same image comprehensively to generate a stable gradient. SMI-FGSM attack is formalized as

$$g_{t+1}^s = \sum_{i=1}^n \lambda_i \bigtriangledown_x J(H_i(x_t^{adv}), y), x_{t+1}^{adv} = x_t^{adv} + \alpha \cdot sign(g_{t+1}^s) \qquad (7)$$

where $H_i(\cdot)$ is used to transform x_t^{adv} by adding random padding around the image and resizing it to its original size. The transformed image has pixel shift

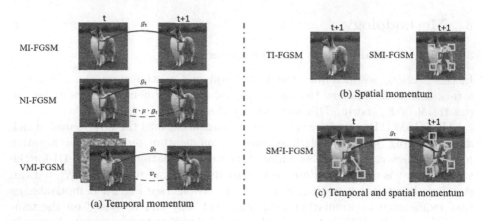

Fig. 3. Illustrations of temporal momentum-based attacks, spatial momentum-based attacks, and their variants. There are some symbols such as g_t, α, μ, v_t, etc. Please refer to section *RELATED WORK* for detail. (a) Temporal momentum-based iterative attack. (b) Spatial momentum-based iterative attack. (c) Temporal and spatial momentum-based iterative attack SM^{2}I-FGSM.

compared with the original image. n denotes the number of transformation in spatial domain. λ_i is the weight of i-th gradient, $\sum \lambda_i = 1$ and we consider $\lambda_i = 1/n$ in this paper. By comprehensively considering the gradients from multiple random transformations, we achieve the spatial momentum accumulation of different gradients from the context pixels.

With similar to [11], we use the cosine similarity of gradients during iterations to measure their similarity (Fig. 2). It can be seen that the gradients generated by considering information from different regions in the iterations have higher similarity compared to considering information from the corresponding region as I-FGSM done. This indicates the gradient generated by SMI-FGSM is more stable.

SMI-FGSM can be integrated with temporal momentum to simultaneously stabilize the gradients' update direction from both the temporal and spatial domain (see Fig. 2) and further boost the adversarial transferability. It is named SM^{2}I-FGSM, which update g_{t+1} in Eq. (4) by g_{t+1}^s in Eq. (7).

3.2 The Difference with Existing Attacks

As shown in Fig. 3, temporal momentum-based methods stabilize the direction by using historical gradients. The basic method is MI-FGSM, which updates the current gradient using the previous gradient (illustrated by the solid line). NI-FGSM improves it by Nesterov accelerated gradient and VMI-FGSM boosts it by considering the gradient variance through adding various noises. These two methods use the previous gradient two times, which play different roles (see the solid line and dotted line in Fig. 3). However, they do not consider the spatial domain information, which is of the same importance as temporal domain information. The proposed SMI-FGSM considers spatial domain information during each iteration (illustrated by the yellow boxes). TI-FGSM smoothes the gradient of the untranslated image in the spatial domain by using a simple pre-defined convolution kernel and its performance is limited. By combining temporal and spatial momentum, SM^2I-FGSM can further stabilize the direction and achieves better performance.

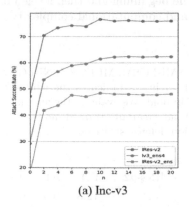
(a) Inc-v3

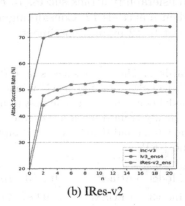
(b) IRes-v2

Fig. 4. The attack success rates (%) against three models with adversarial examples generated by SM^2I-FGSM on Inc-v3 (a) and Inc-v4 (b) when varying n.

4 Experiments

4.1 Experimental Settings

We randomly sample 1000 images of different categories from the ILSVRC 2012 validation set as in [11,13]. We also ensure that all of the selected images can be correctly classified by every model exploited in this work.

To evaluate our approach and compare with other mainstream methods, we test attack performance in two normally trained models, including Inception-v3 (Inc-v3) [21], Inception-Resnet-v2 (IRes-v2) [22], and two adversarially trained models, i.e., ens4-adv-Inception-v3 (Inc-v3$_{ens4}$) and ens-adv-InceptionResNet-v2 (IRes-v2$_{ens}$) [23]. In addition, three input transformation based defense strategies, including FD [24], BIT [25], and NRP [26], are used to purify adversarial images. After input transformations, the purified images are fed to Inc-v3$_{ens4}$ to give the final prediction.

For the settings of hyper-parameters, we follow the setting in [11] with the maximum perturbation is 16 among all experiments with pixel values in [0, 255], the number of iteration is 10, and step size $\alpha = 1.6$. For MI-FGSM, we set $\mu = 1.0$ as recommend in [11]. For the transformation function $H(\cdot)$, the padding size is in [300, 330) and then resizing it to 299. We adopt the Gaussian kernel with kernel size 5×5 for translation-invariant. And for our proposed SM^2I-FGSM, we set $n = 12$.

4.2 Impact of Hyper-Parameter n

In SM^{2}I-FGSM, the number of n plays a key role in improving the transferability. When n is set to 1, SM^{2}I-FGSM will degenerate to MI-FGSM. Therefore, we practiced a series of experiments to examine the effect of n. We attack Inc-v3 and IRes-v2 by SM^{2}I-FGSM with different n values, which range from 2 to 20 with a granularity of 2, and the results are shown in Fig. 4. As shown, the increase of transferability attack success rates is rapid at the beginning and then leveled off when n exceeds 12. Considering attack ability and computational complexity, n is set to 12 in our experiments.

Table 1. The attack success rates (%) of I-FGSM, SMI-FGSM, MI-FGSM, NI-FGSM, VMI-FGSM, and SM^{2}I-FGSM under single-model setting, ∗ indicates the white-box model being attacked. The best results are marked in bold. We evaluate the attacks on normally trained models (i.e., Inc-v3 and IRes-v2), adversarially trained models (i.e., Inc-v3$_{ens4}$ and IRes-v2$_{ens}$), and input transformation defense strategies (i.e., FD, BIT and NRP).

Model	Attack	Inc-v3	IRes-v2	Inc-v3$_{ens4}$	IRes-v2$_{ens}$	FD	BIT	NBR
Inc-v3	I-FGSM	99.8*	21.9	13.2	5.4	12.8	9.5	6.7
	SMI-FGSM	**100.0***	53.8	34.2	20.0	29.5	25.7	21.2
	MI-FGSM	**100.0***	47.9	30.7	18.7	28.4	20.1	16.9
	NI-FGSM	**100.0***	54.3	34.0	23.3	29.4	24.3	20.7
	VMI-FGSM	**100.0***	66.7	47.8	41.9	46.6	38.2	42.8
	SM^{2}I-FGSM	99.8*	**76.1**	**61.6**	**48.0**	**58.9**	**47.5**	**49.1**
IRes-v2	I-FGSM	18.1	98.6*	7.7	4.6	8.1	4.3	5.6
	SMI-FGSM	45.5	97.5*	21.8	16.3	18.5	16.1	15.6
	MI-FGSM	43.6	**98.8***	22.2	18.8	19.9	15.0	16.4
	NI-FGSM	45.8	97.0*	22.7	19.5	21.8	18.9	19.3
	VMI-FGSM	68.9	97.2*	47.5	42.7	33.5	29.8	31.7
	SM^{2}I-FGSM	**73.1**	97.5*	**52.3**	**49.8**	**42.8**	**36.5**	**40.1**

4.3 Ablation Study

We first perform adversarial attacks using I-FGSM and SMI-FGSM under a single-model setting. The results are reported in Table 1. The attacked DNN models are listed on rows, and the test DNN models are listed on columns. It is obvious that SMI-FGSM is strong as I-FGSM when attacking white-box models, they all have nearly 100% success rate. It can be seen that the attack based on spatial momentum has significantly improved adversarial attack transferability and it is model-agnostic. For example, when we generate adversarial examples using Inc-v3 as a white-box model, SMI-FGSM and SM^{2}I-FGSM achieve success rates of 20.0% and 48.0% on IRes-v2$_{ens}$ respectively, while I-FGSM and MI-FGSM achieve success rates of 5.4% and 18.7% respectively. Through comparison

Table 2. The attack success rates (%) of MI-FGSM-DTS, NI-FGSM-DTS, VMI-FGSM-DTS, and SM^{2}I-FGSM-DTS when attacking Inc-v3, * indicates the white-box model being attacked. The best results are marked in bold.

Attack	Inc-v3	IRes-v2	Inc-v3$_{ens4}$	IRes-v2$_{ens}$	FD	BIT	NBR
MI-FGSM-DTS	99.7*	80.5	70.0	57.7	70.4	43.8	48.3
NI-FGSM-DTS	**99.8***	82.3	71.2	57.9	71.0	44.9	45.5
VMI-FGSM-DTS	99.6*	82.6	77.4	63.5	74.6	50.9	56.4
SM^{2}I-FGSM-DTS	**99.8***	**86.9**	**80.7**	**67.2**	**79.0**	**57.2**	**58.1**

and statistics, the adversarial transferability of our proposed method is ahead about 20% than all baseline methods on average, which reveals the importance of spatial information for improving transferability.

Fig. 5. Some adversarial images generated by different methods. Clean images are on the left column. The adversarial images generated by NI-FGSM, VMI-FGSM, and SM^{2}I-FGSM are on the second column, the third column, and the fourth column respectively. All the adversarial images are generated by attacking Inc-v3.

4.4 Comparisons with State-of-the-Art Attacks

We also compare the performance of MI-FGSM and its improved versions (i.e., NI-FGSM, VMI-FGSM, SM^{2}I-FGSM) in Table 1. SM^{2}I-FGSM outperforms the others by a large margin and it is model-agnostic. Particularly, if we generate adversarial images on Inc-v3, SM^{2}I-FGSM achieves an average success rate of 63.0%, while the state-of-the-art methods NI-FGSM and VMI-FGSM achieve 40.9% and 54.9% respectively. We show several adversarial images generated by MI-FGSM, VMI-FGSM, and SM^{2}I-FGSM in Fig. 5. It can be seen that SM^{2}I-FGSM generates visually similar adversarial perturbation as others.

Table 3. The attack success rates (%) of various gradient-based iterative attacks with or without DTS under the multi-model setting. The best results are marked in bold.

Attack	Inc-v3$_{ens4}$	IRes-v2$_{ens}$	FD	BIT	NBR
MI-FGSM	50.4	41.8	51.2	36.0	27.9
NI-FGSM	52.9	44.0	51.9	38.3	30.0
VMI-FGSM	77.4	72.6	68.2	52.7	45.6
SM^{2}I-FGSM	**84.0**	**79.8**	**78.8**	**60.4**	**56.3**
MI-FGSM-DTS	91.8	89.4	87.5	70.5	78.8
NI-FGSM-DTS	94.5	92.0	88.6	71.5	79.1
VMI-FGSM-DTS	93.4	92.8	89.9	75.3	79.9
SM^{2}I-FGSM-DTS	**95.8**	**94.3**	**91.2**	**78.4**	**81.3**

4.5   Performances Combined with Other Methods

Diverse inputs (DI), translation-invariant (TI), and scale-invariant (SI) can further improve the attack success rates individually based on I-FGSM and MI-FGSM. [12] has shown that the combination of them, which is called DTS in this paper, could help the gradient-based attacks achieve great transferability. We combine DTS with MI-FGSM, NI-FGSM, VMI-FGSM and SM^{2}I-FGSM as MI-FGSM-DTS, NI-FGSM-DTS, VMI-FGSM-DTS and SM^{2}I-FGSM-DTS. The results are reported in Table 2. From the table, we can observe that SM^{2}I-FGSM-DTS achieves an average transferability success rate of 75.6%. Compared to the baseline method MI-FGSM-DTS, which achieves an average transferability success rate of 67.2%, this is a significant improvement and shows that our method has good scalability and can be combined with existing methods to further improve the success rates of transfer-based black-box attacks.

4.6   Ensemble-Based Attacks

Related work [9] has shown that the transferability success rate can be greatly improved by using multiple models when generating adversarial examples. Here we fuse the logit outputs of different models, which is the most common ensemble method [11]. In this subsection, we perform ensemble-based attacks by averaging the logit outputs of the models Inc-v3 and IRes-v2. The results are recorded in Table 3. SM^{2}I-FGSM-DTS achieves an average attack success rate up to 88.2% on five defense models. It is worth noting that when the transferability attack success rate exceeds 90% in defense strategies, our method is still 2% higher than the most advanced attack, which shows the effectiveness of the proposed method and indicates the vulnerability of current defense mechanisms.

5   Conclusion

In this paper, we proposed a spatial momentum method for improving the transferability of adversarial examples, which introduces the mechanism of momentum accumulation from the temporal domain to the spatial domain. And it can be well integrated with existing attack strategies to further improve the adversarial transferability. Extensive experimental results show that the proposed method could remarkably improve the attack transferability in both excellent undefended and defended models under the single-model and multi-model settings. By comparing with the most advanced attacks, it further demonstrates the effectiveness of the proposed method. Specifically, our attack algorithm SM^2I-FGSM-DTS can achieve an 88.2% transferability attack success rate on the most advanced defense strategies on average, which indicates the vulnerability of current defense mechanisms and inspire us to develop more robust models.

Acknowledgements. This work was supported by National Key R&D Program of China (Grant No. 2020AAA0104002) and the Project of the National Natural Science Foundation of China (No. 62076018).

References

1. Goodfellow, I.J., Shlens, J., Szegedy, C.: Explaining and harnessing adversarial examples. arXiv preprint arXiv:1412.6572 (2014)
2. Szegedy, C., et al.: Intriguing properties of neural networks. arXiv preprint arXiv:1312.6199 (2013)
3. Liu, A., et al.: Perceptual-sensitive GAN for generating adversarial patches. In: AAAI, pp. 1028–1035 (2019)
4. Duan, R., et al.: Adversarial laser beam: Effective physical-world attack to DNNs in a blink. In: Proceedings of the IEEE/CVF Conference on Computer Vision and Pattern Recognition, pp. 16062–16071 (2021)
5. Xiao, Z., et al.: Improving transferability of adversarial patches on face recognition with generative models. In: Proceedings of the IEEE/CVF Conference on Computer Vision and Pattern Recognition, pp. 11845–11854 (2021)
6. Yuan, H., Chu, Q., Zhu, F., Zhao, R., Liu, B., Yu, N.: Efficient open-set adversarial attacks on deep face recognition. In 2021 IEEE International Conference on Multimedia and Expo (ICME), pp. 1–6. IEEE (2021)
7. Kurakin, A., Goodfellow, I.J., Bengio, S.: Adversarial examples in the physical world. In: Artificial Intelligence Safety and Security, pp. 99–112 (2018)
8. Madry, A., et al.: Towards deep learning models resistant to adversarial attacks. arXiv preprint arXiv:1706.06083 (2017)
9. Liu, Y., et al.: Delving into transferable adversarial examples and black-box attacks. arXiv preprint arXiv:1611.02770 (2016)
10. Papernot, N., McDaniel, P., Goodfellow, I., Jha, S., Celik, Z.B., Swami, A.: Practical black-box attacks against machine learning. In: Proceedings of the 2017 ACM on Asia Conference on Computer and Communications Security, pp. 506–519 (2017)
11. Dong, Y., et al.: Boosting adversarial attacks with momentum. In: Proceedings of the IEEE Conference on Computer Vision and Pattern Recognition, pp. 9185–9193 (2018)
12. Lin, J., et al.: Nesterov accelerated gradient and scale invariance for adversarial attacks. arXiv preprint arXiv:1908.06281 (2019)
13. Wang, X., He, K.: Enhancing the transferability of adversarial attacks through variance tuning. In: Proceedings of the IEEE/CVF Conference on Computer Vision and Pattern Recognition, pp. 1924–1933 (2021)

14. Xie, C., et al.: Improving transferability of adversarial examples with input diversity. In: Proceedings of the IEEE/CVF Conference on Computer Vision and Pattern Recognition, pp. 2730–2739 (2019)
15. Wu, W., Su, Y., Lyu, M.R., King, I.: Improving the transferability of adversarial samples with adversarial transformations. In: Proceedings of the IEEE/CVF Conference on Computer Vision and Pattern Recognition, pp. 9024–9033 (2021)
16. Huang, L., Gao, C., Zhuang, W., Liu, N.: Enhancing adversarial examples via self-augmentation. In: 2021 IEEE International Conference on Multimedia and Expo (ICME), pp. 1–6 (2021)
17. Dong, Y., Pang, T., Su, H., Zhu, J.: Evading defenses to transferable adversarial examples by translation-invariant attacks. In: Proceedings of the IEEE/CVF Conference on Computer Vision and Pattern Recognition, pp. 4312–4321 (2019)
18. Kurakin, A., Goodfellow, I., Bengio, S.: Adversarial machine learning at scale. arXiv preprint arXiv:1611.01236 (2016)
19. Zhao, Y., Yan, H., Wei, X.: Object hider: adversarial patch attack against object detectors. arXiv preprint arXiv:2010.14974 (2020)
20. Wang, G., Yan, H., Guo, Y., Wei, X.: Improving adversarial transferability with gradient refining. arXiv preprint arXiv:2105.04834 (2021)
21. Szegedy, C., Vanhoucke, V., Ioffe, S., Shlens, J., Wojna, Z.: Rethinking the inception architecture for computer vision. In: Proceedings of the IEEE Conference on Computer Vision and Pattern Recognition, pp. 2818–2826 (2016)
22. Szegedy, C., Ioffe, S., Vanhoucke, V., Alemi, A. A.: Inception-v4, inception-resnet and the impact of residual connections on learning. In: Thirty-First AAAI Conference on Artificial Intelligence (2017)
23. Tramèr, F., et al.: Ensemble adversarial training: attacks and defenses. arXiv preprint arXiv:1705.07204 (2017)
24. Liu, Z., et al.: Feature distillation: DNN-oriented jpeg compression against adversarial examples. In: 2019 IEEE/CVF Conference on Computer Vision and Pattern Recognition, pp. 860–868. IEEE (2019)
25. Xu, W., Evans, D., Qi, Y.: Feature squeezing: detecting adversarial examples in deep neural networks. arXiv preprint arXiv:1704.01155 (2017)
26. Naseer, M., Khan, S., Hayat, M., Khan, F.S., Porikli, F.: A self-supervised approach for adversarial robustness. In: Proceedings of the IEEE/CVF Conference on Computer Vision and Pattern Recognition, pp. 262–271 (2020)
27. Yan, H., Wei, X.: Efficient sparse attacks on videos using reinforcement learning. In: Proceedings of the 29th ACM International Conference on Multimedia, pp. 2326–2334 (2021)
28. Chen, P.Y., Zhang, H., Sharma, Y., Yi, J., Hsieh, C.J.: Zoo: zeroth order optimization based black-box attacks to deep neural networks without training substitute models. In: Proceedings of the 10th ACM Workshop on Artificial Intelligence and Security, pp. 15–26 (2017)
29. Tu, C.C., et al.: Autozoom: autoencoder-based zeroth order optimization method for attacking black-box neural networks. In: Proceedings of the AAAI Conference on Artificial Intelligence, pp. 742–749 (2019)

AIA: Attention in Attention Within Collaborate Domains

Le Zhang[1], Qi Feng[1], Yao Lu[1(✉)], Chang Liu[3], and Guangming Lu[1,2(✉)]

[1] Harbin Institute of Technology (Shenzhen), Shenzhen 518055, China
{luyao2021,luguangm}@hit.edu.cn
[2] Guangdong Provincial Key Laboratory of Novel Security Intelligence Technologies,
Shenzhen, China
[3] Software Development Center Industrial and Commercial Bank of China,
Beijing, China
liuchang02@sdc.icbc.com.cn

Abstract. Attention mechanisms can effectively improve the performance of the mobile networks with a limited computational complexity cost. However, existing attention methods extract importance from only one domain of the networks, hindering further performance improvement. In this paper, we propose the Attention in Attention (AIA) mechanism integrating One Dimension Frequency Channel Attention (1D FCA) with Joint Coordinate Attention (JCA) to collaboratively adjust the channel and coordinate weights in frequency and spatial domains, respectively. Specifically, 1D FCA using 1D Discrete Cosine Transform (DCT) adaptively extract and enhance the necessary channel information in the frequency domain. The JCA using explicit and implicit coordinate information extract and embed position feature into frequency channel attention. Extensive experiments on different datasets demonstrate that the proposed AIA mechanism can effectively improve the accuracy with only a limited computation complexity cost.

Keywords: Attention in Attention · Spatial Domain Attention · Frequency Domain Attention · Discrete Cosine Transform

1 Introduction and Related Works

Convolutional Neural Networks (CNNs) have greatly promoted the development of the computer vision areas [1,2,7,13–16,20,21]. Further, some compressed networks, such as the mobile networks using group convolutions [17–19,22] are

This work was supported in part by Guangdong Shenzhen Joint Youth Fund under Grant 2021A151511074, in part by the NSFC fund 62176077, in part by the Guangdong Basic and Applied Basic Research Foundation under Grant 2019Bl515120055, in part by the Shenzhen Key Technical Project under Grant 2020N046, in part by the Shenzhen Fundamental Research Fund under Grant JCYJ20210324132210025, and in part by the Medical Biometrics Perception and Analysis Engineering Laboratory, Shenzhen, China. Guangdong Provincial Key Laboratory of Novel Security Intelligence Technologies (2022B1212010005).

S. Yu et al. (Eds.): PRCV 2022, LNCS 13534, pp. 605–617, 2022.
https://doi.org/10.1007/978-3-031-18907-4_47

proposed and applied to the real-time applications, especially for the MobileNet family networks [9,25,29,30]. With the rapid development of networks, attention mechanisms [5,6,11,27] are proposed to effectively encode the important information of interest areas and boost the performance, especially for mobile networks.

The Squeeze-and-Excitation (SE) attention [10] successfully exploits the channel attentive information using 2D global pooling and fully convolution operation. SE attention, however, neglects the position information. Thus, BAM [23] and CBAM [28] are introduced to encode the position attentive information using 1D pooling and 2D pooling operation on the channel dimension. Such attentions lack capturing long-range dependencies on features. Hence, Coordinate Attention (CA) [8] produce position information by generating two 1D attentive weights over the vertical and horizontal directions in the spatial domain, respectively. This results in capturing long-range dependencies along two spatial directions. Frequency Channel Attention Networks (FcaNet) [24] proves Global Average Pooling (GAP) is the lowest frequency of 2D Discrete Cosine Transform (DCT) and generates channel attentive weights from different frequency spectrums using 2D DCT. However, computing 2D DCT is not efficient enough, leading to large computation complexity.

The attention mechanisms mentioned above all retrieve important information from only one domain, failing to encode abundant attentive information and hindering fully exploring the potential of the attention mechanism. Inspired by the above motivations, the Attention in Attention (AIA) mechanism, integrating One Dimension Frequency Channel Attention (1D FCA) within Joint Coordinate Attention (JCA), is proposed to collaboratively adjust the channel and coordinate weights in frequency and spatial domains, respectively. Using horizontal and vertical 1D Discrete Cosine Transform (DCT) weights, 1D FCA is proposed to adaptively extract and enhance the necessary channel information in the frequency domain and generate frequency channel attention. Secondly, the JCA is proposed to embed position information into frequency channel attention, using explicit and implicit coordinate information. The contributions of this paper are summarized as follows:

(1) We propose the Attention in Attention (AIA) mechanism integrating One Dimension Frequency Channel Attention (1D FCA) and Joint Coordinate Attention (JCA) to collaboratively adjust the channel and coordinate weight in frequency and spatial domains, respectively. (2) We propose One Dimension Frequency Channel Attention (1D FCA) to adaptively retrieve and promote the necessary frequency channel information in horizontal and vertical orientations. (3) We further propose the Joint Coordinate Attention (JCA), using explicit and implicit coordinate information, to extract and embed position features into multi-frequency channel attention. (4) Extensive experiments demonstrate the proposed AIA attention mechanism can achieve state-of-the-art results on different datasets with only a limited computational complexity cost.

2   Methods

In order to simultaneously adjust the channel and coordinate weights both in frequency and spatial domains, the Attention in Attention (AIA) mechanism is proposed in this paper integrating One Dimension Frequency Channel Attention (1D FCA) within Joint Coordinate Attention (JCA). The framework of AIA is shown in Fig. 1.

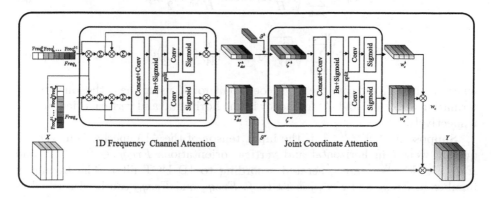

Fig. 1. The framework of AIA containing 1D FCA and JCA attention. ϑ^h and ϑ^w indicate attentive weights in the horizontal and vertical orientations, respectively.

2.1   One Dimension Frequency Channel Attention

Using horizontal and vertical 1D DCT frequency weights, 1D FCA extracts and adjusts the frequency channel attentive weights in different orientations, respectively. Considering global average pooling is a special case of the feature decomposition in the frequency domain, 2D DCT can be used to generate multi-frequency channel weights to adjust the CNNs' representation in the frequency domain. Suppose $X \in \mathbb{R}^{C \times H \times W}$ is the input, H, W, and C represent the height, width, and channel number of input, respectively. The process of 2D DCT operation can be written as:

$$Y_{u,v} = \sum_{x=0}^{W-1} \sum_{y=0}^{H-1} \sqrt{\frac{\alpha_u}{H}} \sqrt{\frac{\alpha_v}{W}} X_{x,y} \times cos[\frac{\pi}{W}(x + \frac{1}{2})u]cos[\frac{\pi}{H}(y + \frac{1}{2})v], \qquad (1)$$

where $Y_{u,v}$ indicates the DCT coefficient for X using the orthogonal transformation at the uth and v^{th} frequency in the horizontal and vertical orientations, respectively. α_u and α_v are set to 1, when $u = 0$ and $v = 0$, and in otherwise cases, these factors are set to 2.

For 2D DCT weights, the computation complexity *grows quadratically* with respect to kernel size. In order to save computation, the original 2D DCT is decomposed into horizontal 1D DCT and vertical 1D DCT in the proposed 1D FCA. Then the computation complexity *grows linearly* with respect to kernel size, which can effectively reduce computation complexity. The two perpendicular 1D DCT can be written as:

$$Y_u = \sum_{i=0}^{H-1} \sqrt{\frac{\alpha_u}{H}} X_i \times cos[\frac{\pi}{H}(i+\frac{1}{2})u], \tag{2}$$

$$Y_v = \sum_{j=0}^{W-1} \sqrt{\frac{\alpha_v}{W}} X_j \times cos[\frac{\pi}{W}(j+\frac{1}{2})v], \tag{3}$$

where Y_u and Y_v indicate the DCT coefficient for X using the orthogonal transformation at the uth and v^{th} frequency in the horizontal and vertical orientations, respectively.

Suppose $X \in \mathbb{R}^{C \times H \times W}$ is the input tensor of the AIA mechanism, 1D frequency weight in horizontal and vertical orientations $Freq_h \in \mathbb{R}^{C \times 1 \times H}$ and $Freq_w \in \mathbb{R}^{C \times W \times 1}$ are generated according to 1D DCT filter. The frequency number in $Freq_h$ and $Freq_w$ is set to f. $Freq_h$ and $Freq_w$ can be described as follows:

$$Freq_h = [Freq_h^0, Freq_h^1, Freq_h^2, ..., Freq_h^{f-1}], \tag{4}$$

$$Freq_w = [Freq_w^0, Freq_w^1, Freq_w^2, ..., Freq_w^{f-1}]. \tag{5}$$

The number of $Freq_h^i \in \mathbb{R}^{C/f \times 1 \times H}$ ($i \in \{0, 1, \cdots, f-1\}$) in $Freq_h$ is $\lfloor C/f \rfloor$. if $C \neq \lfloor C/f \rfloor \times f$, $Freq_h^{f-1} = Freq_h^{f-2}$. Similarly, the number of $Freq_w^i \in \mathbb{R}^{C/f \times W \times 1}$ ($i \in \{0, 1, \cdots, f-1\}$) in $Freq_w$ is $\lfloor C/f \rfloor$. if $C \neq \lfloor C/f \rfloor \times f$, $Freq_w^{f-1} = Freq_w^{f-2}$. Then, $X_h \in \mathbb{R}^{C \times 1 \times H}$ and $X_w \in \mathbb{R}^{C \times W \times 1}$ can be formulated as:

$$X_h = \sum_{i=0}^{H-1} X \times Freq_h, \tag{6}$$

$$X_w = \sum_{j=0}^{W-1} X \times Freq_w. \tag{7}$$

Next, $\zeta_{dct}^h \in \mathbb{R}^{C \times 1 \times 1}$ and $\zeta_{dct}^w \in \mathbb{R}^{C \times 1 \times 1}$ can be formulated as the following equations:

$$\zeta_{dct}^h = \sum_{i=0}^{H-1} \sum_{j=0}^{W-1} X_h \times Freq_h, \tag{8}$$

$$\zeta_{dct}^w = \sum_{i=0}^{H-1} \sum_{j=0}^{W-1} X_w^{T(2,3)} \times Freq_w, \tag{9}$$

where $T(2,3)$ indicates the transpose operation between the height and weight axes. In order to save computation, ζ_{dct}^h are concatenated on the height dimension and fed to a shared point-wise convolution layer $f_{dct,p}$ with kernel size 1×1. This projection can be formulated as follows:

$$\ell_{dct} = \sigma(f_{dct,p}[\zeta_{dct}^h \oplus \zeta_{dct}^w]_2), \tag{10}$$

where $\ell_{dct} \in \mathbb{R}^{C/\gamma_1 \times 1 \times 1}$, and γ_1 is the reduction ratio, $\gamma_1 \in (0,1]$. $[\cdot \oplus \cdot]_2$ denotes the concatenation operation on height dimension. σ is the non-linear Sigmoid activation function.

Then, ℓ_{dct}^h and ℓ_{dct}^w are generated by splitting ℓ_{dct} on the height dimension with size $\{H, W\}$. Another two point-wise convolution layers $f_{dct,h}$ and $f_{dct,w}$ are applied to process ℓ_{dct}^h and ℓ_{dct}^w, respectively. This process can be formulated as the following equations:

$$w_{dct}^h = \sigma(f_{dct,h}(\ell_{dct}^h)), \tag{11}$$

$$w_{dct}^w = \sigma(f_{dct,w}(\ell_{dct}^w)). \tag{12}$$

w_{dct}^h and w_{dct}^w are the frequency channel weights in the horizontal and vertical orientations, respectively.

$$Y_{dct,h} = f_e((X_h \times w_{dct}^h) \rightarrow X_h), \tag{13}$$

$$Y_{dct,w} = f_e((X_w \times w_{dct}^w) \rightarrow X_w). \tag{14}$$

$Y_{dct,h}$ and $Y_{dct,w}$ indicate horizontal and vertical channel frequency attentive weights produced by 1D FCA mechanism, respectively. $f_e(\cdot \rightarrow \cdot)$ indicates the expanding operation to keep the size of the left side consistent with that of the right side.

2.2 Joint Coordinate Attention

In order to embed position feature into frequency channel attention, JCA is proposed to capture implicit attentive weights from the 1D FCA $Y_{dct,h}$ and $Y_{dct,w}$ in the horizontal and vertical orientations, respectively. Correspondingly, the learnable explicit attentive weights in the horizontal and vertical orientations $\vartheta^h \in \mathbb{R}^{1 \times H \times 1}$ and $\vartheta^w \in \mathbb{R}^{1 \times W \times 1}$ are proposed in our JCA to further extract and enhance coordinate information. Then the implicit and explicit coordinate attentive weights are concatenated to encode coordinate information by our JCA. The concatenation process can be formulated as follows:

$$\zeta^h = [f_e(\vartheta^h \rightarrow Y_{dct}^h]_1) \oplus Y_{dct}^h]_1, \tag{15}$$

$$\zeta^w = [f_e(\vartheta^w \rightarrow Y_{dct}^w]_1) \oplus Y_{dct}^w]_1, \tag{16}$$

where $\zeta^h \in \mathbb{R}^{(C+1) \times H \times 1}$ and $\zeta^w \in \mathbb{R}^{(C+1) \times W \times 1}$. $[\cdot \oplus \cdot]_1$ denotes the concatenation operation on channel dimension. Thus, the implicit attention weights ϑ^h and ϑ^w can be iteratively update in the training process. Next, the explicit and implicit coordinate attentive weights are jointly trained in the following steps. In order to save computation, ζ^h and ζ^w are concatenated on the height dimension and fed to a shared point-wise convolution layer f_p with kernel size of 1×1. This projection can be formulated as follows:

$$\ell = \sigma(f_{bn}(f_p[\zeta^h \oplus \zeta^w]_2)), \tag{17}$$

where $\ell \in \mathbb{R}^{C/\gamma_2 \times (H+W) \times 1}$, and γ_2 is the coordinate reduction ratio, $\gamma_2 \in (0, 1]$. $[\cdot \oplus \cdot]_2$ denotes the concatenation operation on height dimension. f_{bn} indicates the batch normalization operation. σ is the non-linear Sigmoid activation function.

Then, ℓ^h and ℓ^w are generated by splitting ℓ on the height dimension with size $\{H, W\}$. Another two point-wise convolution layers f_h and f_w are applied to process ℓ^h and ℓ^w, respectively. This process can be formulated as the following equations:

$$w_c^h = \sigma(f_h(\ell^h)), \tag{18}$$
$$w_c^w = \sigma(f_w((\ell^w)^{T(2,3)})), \tag{19}$$

where $w_c^h \in \mathbb{R}^{C \times H \times 1}$ and $w_c^w \in \mathbb{R}^{C \times 1 \times W}$. $T(2,3)$ indicates the transpose operation between the height and weight axes. Finally, the output joint coordinate weights w_c can be written as:

$$w_c = w_c^h \times w_c^w. \tag{20}$$

The output of the AIA mechanism $Y \in \mathbb{R}^{C \times H \times W}$ is computed as follows:

$$Y = w_c \times X. \tag{21}$$

Thus, the essential frequency channel and coordinate information is enhanced and adjusted by 1D FCA and JCA in the proposed AIA mechanism.

3 Experiments

3.1 Datasets and Initializations

In order to verify the effectiveness of the proposed AIA, we employ two popular light-weight networks, *i.e.*, MobileNetV2 [25] and MobileNeXt [30], as the backbone networks to implement our AIA mechanism. For MobileNetV2, the proposed AIA attention block is plugged after the depth-wise convolution layer in the inverted residual block. For MobileNeXt, the proposed AIA attention block is plugged between the expanding point convolution layer and the second depth-wise convolution layer in the sandglass bottleneck block. The detailed implemented locations in different light-weight blocks can be seen in Fig. 2. The proposed AIA mechanism are compared on the following datasets.

CIFAR Datasets. In both CIFAR-10 [12] and CIFAR-100 [26], there are 50,000 images for training and 10,000 images for testing. The resolution of these colored nature images is 32×32. There are 10 and 100 image classes in CIFAR-10 [12] and CIFAR-100 [26], respectively. Models have trained 300 epochs with the images randomly horizontally flipped and cropped. The batch size is set to 128. The learning rate starts from 0.1 and is divided by 10 at 150 and 225 epochs.

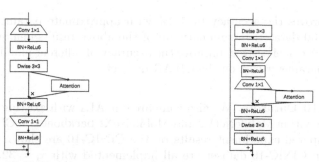

(a) Inverted residual block proposed in MobileNetV2 [25]   (b) Sand-glass bottleneck block proposed in MobileNeXt [30]

Fig. 2. Our AIA mechanism implementation within different mobile networks.

CINIC-10 Datasets. There are 270,000 colored nature images in CINIC-10 datasets [3], and the resolution of these images is 32×32. Models have trained 200 epochs with randomly horizontally flipped and cropped training images. The batch size is set to 128. The learning rate starts from 0.1 and is divided by 10 at 60, 120, and 180 epochs.

ImageNet Datasets. The regular ILSVRC 2012 [4] contains 1.2 million training images and 50,000 validation images with 1000 image classes. Models have trained 200 epochs with randomly horizontally flipped and cropped images. The images are uniformly resized as 224×224, and the batch size is set to 128. The learning rate starts from 0.05 and is divided by the cosine adjustment method.

3.2 Performances

To evaluate the performance of the proposed AIA attention, we compare the proposed AIA attention mechanism with other popular light-weight attention mechanisms on MobileNetV2 and MobileNeXt backbones. The compared results on different datasets are as follows.

CIFAR Datasets. We compare our AIA with existing state-of-the-art attention, *i.e.*, SE [10] and CA [8] on MobileNetV2 backbones. The experiment results on CIFAR-10 and CIFAR-100 are reported in Table 1. The AIA results of MobileNetV2 on CIFAR-10 dataset are implemented with $\gamma_1 = 32, \gamma_2 = 32, f = 4$. The AIA results of MobileNetV2-0.5 on CIFAR-100 dataset are implemented with $\gamma_1 = 32, \gamma_2 = 32, f = 8$. The AIA results of MobileNetV2-1.0 on the CIFAR-100 dataset are implemented with $\gamma_1 = 64, \gamma_2 = 64, f = 8$. Compared with the simpler CIFAR-10 dataset, our AIA can improve the accuracy to a greater extent on the more complex CIFAR-100 datasets. This shows that our AIA, which collaboratively extracts frequency and location information is helpful to deal with more complex situations. Specifically, compared to the MobileNetV2-1.0+CA,

AIA improves the accuracy by 1.2% with approximate parameter quantity on CIFAR-100 dataset. In summary, all of the above results demonstrate the proposed AIA can effectively improve the accuracy of different mobile networks with limited parameter cost on the CIFAR dataset.

CINIC-10 Datasets. We also compare our AIA with existing state-of-the-art attention within MobileNetV2 and MobileNeXt backbones on CINIC-10 dataset. The compared experiment results on the CINIC-10 are shown in Table 2. The results on CINIC-10 dataset are all implemented with $\gamma_1 = 32, \gamma_2 = 32, f = 4$ except MobileNeXt-1.0. The results on MobileNeXt-1.0 are implemented with $\gamma_1 = 32, \gamma_2 = 32, f = 8$. It is clear that our AIA attention can significantly improve accuracy, compared to SE and CA attention. Specifically, compared to CA, AIA improves the accuracy by 0.48% at MobileNeXt-0.5. In order to further intuitively evaluate the performance of our proposed AIA, the feature maps produced by models with different attention methods on CINIC-10 dataset are also provided in Fig. 3. It is obvious the proposed AIA is able to locate objects of interest better than other attention machines. The above comparisons imply that our AIA can significantly improve the accuracy on the CINIC-10 dataset.

Table 1. Comparisons of different attention methods taking MobileNetV2 as the baseline on CIFAR datasets.

Settings	#Param. (M)	CIFAR-10 (%)	CIFAR-100 (%)
MobileNetV2-0.5	0.70	93.79	74.70
+SE [10]	0.78	94.40	76.55
+CA [8]	0.82	94.42	75.42
+AIA	0.94	**94.49**	**76.67**
MobileNetV2-1.0	2.24	94.57	76.39
+SE [10]	2.53	94.94	78.31
+CA [8]	2.68	95.54	77.43
+AIA	3.12	**95.58**	**78.63**

Table 2. Comparisons of different attention methods taking MobileNetV2 and MobileNeXt as the baseline on CINIC-10 dataset.

Settings	#Param. (M)	Acc (%)	Settings	#Param. (M)	Acc (%)
MobileNetV2-0.5	0.70	84.22	MobileNeXt-0.5	0.88	81.81
+SE [10]	0.78	81.35	+SE [10]	1.05	81.78
+CA [8]	0.82	85.99	+CA [8]	1.14	82.26
+AIA	0.94	**86.19**	+AIA	1.39	**82.74**
MobileNetV2-1.0	2.24	85.78	MobileNeXt-1.0	2.27	83.04
+SE [10]	2.53	83.32	+SE [10]	2.60	82.80
+CA [8]	2.68	87.35	+CA [8]	2.77	83.23
+AIA	3.12	**87.72**	+AIA	3.26	**83.43**

ImageNet Datasets. Comparisons of different attention methods on large dataset ImageNet are also provided in Table 3. The results on ImageNet dataset are all implemented with $\gamma_1 = 32, \gamma_2 = 32, f = 8$. Obviously, our AIA attention can effectively improve the accuracy of different mobile networks with a limited parameter cost. Specifically, compared to the CA, AIA improves the accuracy by 0.3% and 0.7% on MobileNetV2 and MobileNeXt backbones, respectively. The above results imply the proposed AIA attention mechanism can effectively improve accuracy on ImageNet dataset.

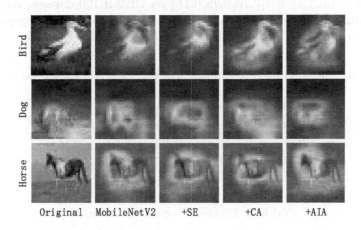

Original   MobileNetV2   +SE   +CA   +AIA

Fig. 3. Visualization of feature maps of the last convolution layer produced by MobileNetV2, +SE, +CA, and +AIA on CINIC-10 dataset, respectively.

Table 3. Comparisons of different attention methods taking MobileNetV2 and MobileNeXt as the baseline on ImageNet dataset.

Settings	#Param. (M)	Top-1 Acc (%)
MobileNetV2-1.0	3.5	72.3
+SE [10]	3.89	73.5
+CBAM [28]	3.89	73.6
+CA [8]	3.89	74.3
+AIA	4.38	**74.6**
MobileNeXt-1.0	3.5	74.0
+SE [10]	3.89	74.7
+CA [8]	4.09	75.2
+AIA	4.53	**75.9**

3.3   Ablation Studies

Effects of 1D FCA and JCA. To testify the effectiveness of the proposed JCA mechanism and 1D FCA mechanism in our AIA, we gradually equip the JCA mechanism and 1D FCA mechanism in the AIA and evaluate these different networks. The comparison results are illustrated in Table 4. Equipped with the JCA mechanism, MobileNetV2 with $\alpha = 1.0$ improves the accuracy by 1.53% compared to the original backbone. Furthermore, applying JCA mechanism and 1D FCA mechanism on MobileNetV2 effectively improves the accuracy of $\alpha = \{0.5, 1.0, 1.5\}$ by $\{0.76, 0.29, 0.11\}$ on CIFAR-100 dataset, respectively. These comparison results sufficiently prove the effectiveness of the proposed JCA mechanism and 1D FCA mechanism methods in our AIA attention mechanism.

Table 4. Effects of explicit coordinate index and frequency attention module.

Settings	$\alpha = 0.5$	$\alpha = 1.0$	$\alpha = 1.5$
MobileNetV2	74.70	76.39	78.67
+JCA	75.91	77.92	79.44
+AIA (JCA+1D FCA)	**76.67**	**78.21**	**79.55**

Table 5. Effects of frequency number f.

Settings	$f = 1$	$f = 2$	$f = 4$	$f = 8$
MobileNetV2+AIA	77.92	78.06	78.02	**78.21**

Effects of Frequency Number f. In order to further discuss the effectiveness of frequency number f used in the 1D DCT module, a series of experiments are conducted with $f = \{1, 2, 4, 8\}$ on CIFAR-100 dataset, respectively. The results on MobileNetV2 with $\alpha = 1$ are shown in Table 5. It is evident that compared with $f = 1$, increasing the frequency number f can effectively promote image recognition performance. In addition, the proposed AIA attention mechanism with different frequency number share the same parameters. Thus, our AIA can extract more frequency information with limited computation complexity.

Effects of Reduction Ratio γ_1 and γ_2. To explore the influence of reduction ratio γ_1 and γ_2 on parameters and accuracy, we compare the performance of different γ_1 and γ_2. The results are shown in Table 6. It is apparent that a larger reduction ratio leads to a smaller number of parameters. In addition, our AIA attention mechanism achieves the best performance with the least parameters, when $\gamma_1 = 64$ and $\gamma_2 = 64$.

Table 6. Effects of reduction ratio γ_1 and γ_2 on CIFAR-100 dataset when take MobileNetV2-1.0 as backbone. γ_1 indicates the reduction ratio of 1D DCT, and γ_2 denotes the reduction ratio of explicit coordinate attention.

γ_1	γ_2	#Param. (M)	Acc (%)
16	32	3.65	77.13
32	32	3.23	78.21
64	32	3.04	78.19
16	16	4.06	78.20
64	64	2.84	**78.63**

4   Conclusion

This paper proposed the Attention in Attention (AIA) mechanism to collaboratively adjust the channel and coordinate weights in frequency and spatial domains, respectively. The proposed AIA is mainly constructed by two attention methods, *i.e.*, One Dimension Frequency Channel Attention (1D FCA) and Joint Coordinate Attention (JCA). 1D FCA adaptively extract and enhance the necessary horizontal and vertical channel information in the frequency domain. Furthermore, in order to embed position feature into frequency channel attention, JCA is proposed to capture coordinate information in horizontal and vertical orientations, using explicit and implicit attentive weights. Experiment results proved that the proposed AIA attention mechanism can effectively improve the performance of mobile network with only a limited computation complexity cost on extensive datasets.

References

1. Cao, J., Liu, B., Wen, Y., Xie, R., Song, L.: Personalized and invertible face de-identification by disentangled identity information manipulation. In: Proceedings of the IEEE/CVF International Conference on Computer Vision, pp. 3334–3342 (2021)
2. Chen, H., et al.: Diverse image style transfer via invertible cross-space mapping. In: Proceedings of the IEEE/CVF International Conference on Computer Vision, pp. 14860–14869. IEEE Computer Society (2021)
3. Darlow, L.N., Crowley, E.J., Antoniou, A., Storkey, A.J.: Cinic-10 is not imagenet or CIFAR-10. arXiv preprint arXiv:1810.03505 (2018)
4. Deng, J., Dong, W., Socher, R., Li, L.J., Li, K., Fei-Fei, L.: ImageNet: a large-scale hierarchical image database. In: IEEE Conference on Computer Vision and Pattern Recognition, pp. 248–255 (2009)
5. Fu, J., et al.: Dual attention network for scene segmentation. In: IEEE Conference on Computer Vision and Pattern Recognition, pp. 3146–3154 (2019)
6. Guo, L., Liu, J., Zhu, X., Yao, P., Lu, S., Lu, H.: Normalized and geometry-aware self-attention network for image captioning. In: IEEE Conference on Computer Vision and Pattern Recognition, pp. 10327–10336 (2020)

7. He, K., Zhang, X., Ren, S., Sun, J.: Deep residual learning for image recognition. In: IEEE Conference on Computer Vision and Pattern Recognition, pp. 770–778 (2016)
8. Hou, Q., Zhou, D., Feng, J.: Coordinate attention for efficient mobile network design. In: IEEE Conference on Computer Vision and Pattern Recognition, pp. 13713–13722 (2021)
9. Howard, A.G., et al.: MobileNets: efficient convolutional neural networks for mobile vision applications. arXiv preprint arXiv:1704.04861 (2017)
10. Hu, J., Shen, L., Sun, G.: Squeeze-and-excitation networks. In: IEEE Conference on Computer Vision and Pattern Recognition, pp. 7132–7141 (2018)
11. Jiang, X., et al.: Attention scaling for crowd counting. In: IEEE Conference on Computer Vision and Pattern Recognition, pp. 4706–4715 (2020)
12. Krizhevsky, A., Hinton, G., et al.: Learning multiple layers of features from tiny images (2009)
13. Li, Y., Gao, Y., Chen, B., Zhang, Z., Lu, G., Zhang, D.: Self-supervised exclusive-inclusive interactive learning for multi-label facial expression recognition in the wild. IEEE Trans. Circuits Syst. Video Technol. **32**(5) (2022)
14. Li, Y., Lu, G., Li, J., Zhang, Z., Zhang, D.: Facial expression recognition in the wild using multi-level features and attention mechanisms. IEEE Trans. Affect. Comput. (2020). https://doi.org/10.1109/TAFFC.2020.3031602
15. Li, Y., Zhang, Z., Chen, B., Lu, G., Zhang, D.: Deep margin-sensitive representation learning for cross-domain facial expression recognition. IEEE Trans. Multimedia (2022). https://doi.org/10.1109/TMM.2022.3141604
16. Lu, C., Peng, X., Wei, Y.: Low-rank tensor completion with a new tensor nuclear norm induced by invertible linear transforms. In: IEEE Conference on Computer Vision and Pattern Recognition, pp. 5996–6004 (2019)
17. Lu, Y., Lu, G., Li, J., Xu, Y., Zhang, D.: High-parameter-efficiency convolutional neural networks. Neural Comput. Appl. **32**(14), 10633–10644 (2019). https://doi.org/10.1007/s00521-019-04596-w
18. Lu, Y., Lu, G., Li, J., Zhang, Z., Xu, Y.: Fully shared convolutional neural networks. Neural Comput. Appl. **33**(14), 8635–8648 (2021). https://doi.org/10.1007/s00521-020-05618-8
19. Lu, Y., Lu, G., Lin, R., Li, J., Zhang, D.: SRGC-nets: Sparse repeated group convolutional neural networks. IEEE Trans. Neural Netw. Learn. Syst. **31**(8), 2889–2902 (2019)
20. Lu, Y., Lu, G., Xu, Y., Zhang, B.: AAR-CNNs: auto adaptive regularized convolutional neural networks. In: International Joint Conference on Artificial Intelligence, pp. 2511–2517 (2018)
21. Lu, Y., Lu, G., Zhang, B., Xu, Y., Li, J.: Super sparse convolutional neural networks. In: AAAI Conference on Artificial Intelligence, vol. 33, pp. 4440–4447 (2019)
22. Lu, Y., Lu, G., Zhou, Y., Li, J., Xu, Y., Zhang, D.: Highly shared convolutional neural networks. Expert Syst. Appl. **175**, 114782 (2021)
23. Park, J., Woo, S., Lee, J.Y., Kweon, I.S.: Bam: bottleneck attention module. arXiv preprint arXiv:1807.06514 (2018)
24. Qin, Z., Zhang, P., Wu, F., Li, X.: FCANet: frequency channel attention networks. In: Proceedings of the IEEE/CVF International Conference on Computer Vision, pp. 783–792 (2021)
25. Sandler, M., Howard, A., Zhu, M., Zhmoginov, A., Chen, L.C.: Mobilenetv 2: inverted residuals and linear bottlenecks. In: IEEE Conference on Computer Vision and Pattern Recognition, pp. 4510–4520 (2018)

26. Torralba, A., Fergus, R., Freeman, W.T.: 80 Million tiny images: a large data set for nonparametric object and scene recognition. IEEE Trans. Pattern Anal. Mach. Intell. **30**(11), 1958–1970 (2008)
27. Vaswani, A., et al.: Attention is all you need. Adv. Neural Inf. Process. Syst. **30** (2017)
28. Woo, S., Park, J., Lee, J.-Y., Kweon, I.S.: CBAM: convolutional block attention module. In: Ferrari, V., Hebert, M., Sminchisescu, C., Weiss, Y. (eds.) ECCV 2018. LNCS, vol. 11211, pp. 3–19. Springer, Cham (2018). https://doi.org/10.1007/978-3-030-01234-2_1
29. Xiong, Y., et al.: MobileDets: searching for object detection architectures for mobile accelerators. In: IEEE Conference on Computer Vision and Pattern Recognition, pp. 3825–3834 (2021)
30. Zhou, D., Hou, Q., Chen, Y., Feng, J., Yan, S.: Rethinking bottleneck structure for efficient mobile network design. In: Vedaldi, A., Bischof, H., Brox, T., Frahm, J.-M. (eds.) ECCV 2020. LNCS, vol. 12348, pp. 680–697. Springer, Cham (2020). https://doi.org/10.1007/978-3-030-58580-8_40

Infrared and Near-Infrared Image Generation via Content Consistency and Style Adversarial Learning

Kai Mao[1], Meng Yang[1,2($\boxtimes$)], and Haijian Wang[1]

[1] School of Computer Science and Engineering, Sun Yat-Sen University,
Guangzhou, China
{maok,wanghj63}@mail2.sysu.edu.cn, yangm6@mail.sysu.edu.cn
[2] Key Laboratory of Machine Intelligence and Advanced Computing (SYSU),
Ministry of Education, Guangzhou, China

Abstract. Infrared (IR) and Near-Infrared (NIR) images, which are more robust to illumination variances and more suitable for all-whether applications than visible (VIS) images, have been widely applied in the computer vision community. However, it's cost-intensive and labor-demanding to collect IR/NIR images for downstream tasks. To solve this issue, a promising solution is generating IR/NIR images from visible ones via style transfer. Unfortunately, existing style transfer methods impose excessive constraints on preserving content or style clues while attaching little importance to both of them, which can not well capture the characteristic of IR/NIR image generation. In this paper, we propose an effective style transfer framework, termed Content Consistency and Style Adversarial Learning (C^2SAL), for IR and NIR image generation. Firstly, we propose the content consistency learning which is imposed on the refined content features from a content feature refining module, leading to the improvement of content information preservation. Besides, a style adversarial learning is proposed to achieve the style consistency between generated images and the images of the target style, which promotes the overall style transfer by utilizing both pixel-level and image-level style loss. Extensive experiments on challenging benchmarks, including detailed ablation study and comparisons with state-of-the-art methods, demonstrate the effectiveness of our method.

Keywords: Infrared and Near-infrared image generation · Style transfer · Consistency learning · Adversarial learning

1 Introduction

Near-infrared (NIR) cameras are usually capable of capturing detailed textures of target objects in the scene, and infrared (IR) cameras can capture the objects' temperature information. Both NIR and IR images meet the demand of widespread applications of computer vision because they are more robust to illumination variances and more suitable for all-whether applications than visible

S. Yu et al. (Eds.): PRCV 2022, LNCS 13534, pp. 618–630, 2022.
https://doi.org/10.1007/978-3-031-18907-4_48

(VIS) images. However, the acquisition of IR/NIR images is cost-intensive and labor-demanding. Besides, there are also very limited datasets of VIS-IR/NIR pairs, which prevents the wide applications and deep research of the tasks based on IR/NIR images. A constructive idea is to generate NIR or IR images from VIS images. Given a VIS content image and a NIR/IR style image, the image generation model can get a new image that contains the content structure of VIS image and the style of NIR/IR image. There are two advantages as follows. Firstly, the ever-increasing NIR and IR images can be better applied to downstream tasks. Secondly, for some tasks that require NIR/IR-image annotations, the generated NIR/IR images can directly use labels corresponding to visible images to further reduce labor costs.

      (a)   (b)   (c)   (d)

Fig. 1. Typical problems in the SOTA methods. (a) Ground-truth. (b) Spatial distortion. (c) Under-stylization. (d) Undesired artifact.

Generating IR/NIR images from VIS images can be regarded as a sub-task of image translation. Thus, the image translation methods [9,10,26] can be introduced to learn domain features and perform image generation without requiring a reference image during testing. However, optimizing the sophisticated architecture is time-consuming and requires a large amount of data. An alternative solution is utilizing neural style transfer methods, which focus on fusing content and style clues during model learning by exploiting a pre-trained encoder with fixed weights. The advantages are reflected in the flexibility on diverse scenes with less computational cost. The neural style transfer can be divided into two categories, i.e., artistic style transfer and photorealistic style transfer. The former [2,6,17–19] mainly focuses on achieving effective stylization while is prone to cause spatial distortion (as shown in Fig. 1) and the loss of texture information. The latter [4,21,22] pays more attention to maintaining the content clues with extra structure, e.g., skip-connections [29,30], which yet suffers from the problem of under-stylization (as shown in Fig. 1). However, the skip-connection can be harmful to the task of IR image generation (detailed discussion can be seen in Sect. 4.4). Some typical problems of the above methods are shown in Fig. 1.

To overcome the limitations of existing works, we propose a neural style transfer model, termed Content Consistency and Style Adversarial Learning (C^2SAL), to achieve the balance and coordination between stylization and content preservation. On the one hand, unlike the previous methods that directly impose content-preservation constraints on the coarse features extracted by VGG [25] encoder, we facilitate the refined content features from a content feature refining module and impose the proposed content consistency constraints on them. On the other hand, to enhance the stylization, we introduce a style discriminator to perform style adversarial learning between the generated image and style image on the image level, which conducts style consistency learning among the images of the domain and relieves the issue of spatial distortion. In experiments, we verify our method on a NIR dataset and an IR dataset. Compared with the state-of-the-art (SOTA) methods from qualitative and quantitative evaluation, experiments show that our method can perform better stylization while maintaining the content structure. In the ablation study, we demonstrate the effectiveness of content consistency loss and style adversarial loss, respectively. Our contributions can be summarized as follows,

- We propose a novel neural style transfer framework tailored for IR/NIR image generation by effectively balancing the strength of content preservation and stylization, which to the best of our knowledge is one of the most pioneer works for this task and achieves competitive results.
- Given refined content features after decoupling, we perform fine-grained content consistency learning to enhance the preservation of structure and texture clues in a more adaptive fashion.
- We propose to exploit generated stylized images to conduct image-level style adversarial learning, which is complementary to pixel-wise stylization constraints and relieves the problem of spatial distortion.

2   Related Works

2.1   IR/NIR Image Generation

Most previous IR/NIR image generation works [3,11–15] are mainly based on two image translation frameworks, i.e., CycleGAN [9] and DRIT [10]. However, most of them tend to significantly increase the computation burden. The reason is that they are relying on the deployment of cycle consistency loss, which requires double Generative Adversarial Networks (GANs) [31] for training. Besides, the methods based on DRIT even employ more extra encoders to extract content features and style features, respectively. Furthermore, additional modules or constraints, e.g., silhouette masks [13], designed training losses [14,15], and attention mechanism [3], are involved to enhance the quality of generated images, leading to extra non-negligible training data, parameters and computational time cost. As the NIR/IR image generation task only requires one-sided results, our proposed method relieves the computational burden, which requires less network parameters by adopting the one-sided style transfer framework.

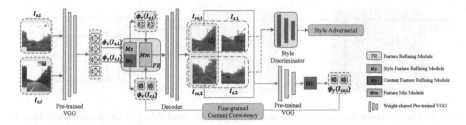

Fig. 2. Framework of our C^2SAL, which involves the Fine-grained Content Consistency Learning (cyan solid line) and image-level Style Adversarial Learning (red dotted line). (Color figure online)

2.2 Neural Style Transfer

Artistic Style Transfer. Gatys et al. [16] proposed a pioneering artistic style transfer framework with the purpose of guaranteeing the effectiveness of style transfer. Continuous efforts have been made by the following works [2,6,17–19] to enhance the stylization. Specifically, Li et al. [18] proposed a whitening and coloring transform (WCT) module to fuse the target style information with the extracted features. Huang et al. [19] proposed to transfer style information via employing the plug-and-play adaptive instance normalization (AdaIN) layers. Recently, Deng et al. [2] proposed a multi-adaptation attention mechanism to disentangle content and style clues. However, their generated images may suffer from spatial distortion owing to only using coarse content consistency loss, which can result in unsatisfactory performance on the IR/NIR image generation task.

Photorealistic Style Transfer. These methods [1,4,5,7,8,20–22] aim to maintain content structure and texture clues during style transfer. Most of them are depending on the skip-connection and its variants. For example, Li et al. [21] proposed the max-pooling skip-connection and Yoo et al. [1] went a step further via proposing a wavelet transforms skip-connection. Besides, Jie et al. [22] explored the skip-connection at different locations of the network. Chiu et al. [4] introduced a light-weight skip-connection with a block-wise training manner. However, skip-connection raises the network parameters and is suffered to obtain satisfactory performance on IR image generation.

3 Method

3.1 Framework Overview

As illustrated in Fig. 2, the pipeline of our Content Consistency and Style Adversarial Learning (C^2SAL) model mainly contains three parts, i.e., baseline model, fine-grained content consistency learning, and style adversarial learning. Given content images $I_{c,i}$ from source domain and style images $I_{s,i}$ from target domain (i denotes the i-th image), the encoder extracts their coarse-grained features

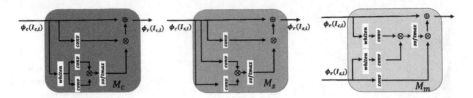

Fig. 3. The Feature-Refining (FR) module (M_c, M_s and M_m). Compared with M_c, M_s removes the whitening operation and replaces spatial-wise attention with channel-wise attention. M_m fuses the refined features of M_c and M_s.

$\phi_c(I_{c,i})$ and $\phi_c(I_{s,i})$, which are then fed to the following feature refining(FR) module [2] to produce their refined features $\phi_r(I_{c,i})$ and $\phi_r(I_{s,i})$. Then the following decoder generates stylized images $I_{cs,i}$ for style adversarial learning learning with L_{sty}^{adv}, which regulates the stylization from a non-local scope to supplement the pixel-level style loss in baseline. Besides, with the refined content features $\phi_r(I_{c,i})$ generated by FR module, we perform fine-grained content consistency learning by L_{con}^{ref} to further facilitate maintaining the original structure and texture during style transfer.

3.2 Baseline Revisit

The baseline model [2] contains an encoder, an FR module, and a mirrored decoder with the encoder. The FR module (see in Fig. 3) is proposed to disentangle content/style representation. It consists of M_c, M_s, and M_m, which refines the coarse-grained content and style features and merges them as the final image representations, respectively. M_c module involves spatial-wise self-attention for locating non-local content representations and whitening operation for redundant style information reduction. Compared with M_c, M_s replaces spatial-wise attention with channel-wise attention and removes the whitening operation. Additionally, the FR module is constrained by a disentangle constraint L_{dis}, formulated as:

$$L_{dis} = ||\phi_c^j(I_{cs_1}) - \phi_c^j(I_{cs_2})||_2$$
$$+ ||\mu(\phi_c^j(I_{c_1s})) - \mu(\phi_c^j(I_{c_2s}))||_2 + ||\sigma(\phi_c^j(I_{c_1s})) - \sigma(\phi_c^j(I_{c_2s}))||_2. \tag{1}$$

where j represents the j-th layer of the encoder. I_{cs_1} and I_{cs_2} are generated with the same input content image I_c and two different input style images (I_{s_1} and I_{s_2}). I_{c_1s} and I_{c_2s} have the similar definition.

The training loss L_{base} of the baseline model [2] includes four parts: Disentangle loss L_{dis}, Identity loss L_{id}, Coarse-grained content feature loss L_{con}^{coa} and Pixel-level style loss L_{sty}^{pix}, formulated as:

$$L_{base} = \lambda_{dis}L_{dis} + \lambda_{id}L_{id} + \lambda_{con}L_{con}^{coa} + \lambda_{sty}L_{sty}^{pix}. \tag{2}$$

Identity Loss pulls the self-reconstructed images $I_{cc,i}$ and $I_{ss,i}$ towards $I_{c,i}$ and $I_{s,i}$ on both pixel-level and feature level in the form of combined $L2$ losses.

$$L_{id} = \alpha_1(||I_{cc} - I_c||_2 + ||I_{ss} - I_s||_2)$$
$$+ (||\phi_c^j(I_{cc}) - \phi_c^j(I_c)||_2 + ||\phi_c^j(I_{ss}) - \phi_c^j(I_s)||_2). \tag{3}$$

Coarse-grained content feature loss pulls the extracted coarse-grained content features of the stylized image I_{cs} and the input content image I_c closer, which are denoted as:

$$L_{con}^{coa} = ||\phi_c^j(I_{cs}) - \phi_c^j(I_c)||_2. \tag{4}$$

Pixel-level style feature loss enforces the style features of I_{cs} to approach that of I_s by measuring the mean and variance distances of their style features. The formula is as follows:

$$L_{sty}^{pix} = ||\mu(\phi_c^j(I_{cs})) - \mu(\phi_c^j(I_s))||_2 + ||\sigma(\phi_c^j(I_{cs})) - \sigma(\phi_c^j(I_s))||_2. \tag{5}$$

3.3 Fine-Grained Content Consistency Learning

In IR/NIR image generation task, it's essential to maintain the structure and spatial layout during style transfer. Therefore, the content features of generated stylized images and the original ones are expected to be close enough in feature space, termed as content consistency learning. However, previous works only impose the content consistency constraint on coarse-grained content features extracted by the pre-trained VGG-19 model, which don't disentangle the content and style features within an image. Consequently, they are less effective in encouraging structure/texture preservation and suppressing the distraction of the style factor during content consistency learning. To fulfill the potential in content consistency learning, we emphasize that the refined content features produced by the M_c module are believed to represent the purer and more fine-grained content information of an input image. Thus, we propose to introduce fine-grained content consistency learning, defined as:

$$L_{con}^{ref} = \frac{1}{N} \sum_{i=1}^{N} ||\phi_r(I_{cs,i}) - \phi_r(I_{c,i})||_2 \tag{6}$$

where N indicates the amount of generated images within a mini-batch and

$$\phi_r(I_{c,i}) = M_c(\phi_c^4(I_{c,i})) \tag{7}$$

Specifically, the generated stylized image $I_{cs,i}$ is fed to the encoder and FR module again to obtain its refining content features $\phi_r(I_{cs,i})$, then L_{con}^{ref} pulls it towards the refined content feature $\phi_r(I_{c,i})$ of the input image $I_{c,i}$ by narrowing their $L2$ distance. Note that $\phi_c^4(I_{c,i})$ represents facilitating features in the $relu4\_1$ layer of the encoder. Then the L_{con}^{ref} is combined with the coarse content feature loss L_{con}^{coa} to produce the total content loss L_{con} for model optimization, formulated as:

$$L_{con} = L_{con}^{ref} + L_{con}^{coa}. \tag{8}$$

In this way, our L_{con}^{ref} further caters to the demand of IR/NIR image generation via structure/texture preservation with the refined content features.

3.4 Style Adversarial Learning

Over-stylization (or spatial distortion) and under-stylization are two major problems of style transfer. We seek to resolve them by further involving an image-level stylization judgment to encourage the style transfer while taking relieving spatial distortion into consideration. Specifically, a style discriminator is appended after the decoder to perform adversarial learning. Feeding the generated stylized image $I_{cs,i}$ and the input style image $I_{s,i}$ to the style discriminator, it can perceive the style clues and comprehensively judge the image generation quality and style transfer effect from a global perspective. Then the proposed style adversarial loss L_{sty}^{adv} is devoted to aligning the statistical distribution of $I_{cs,i}$ and $I_{s,i}$ in the form of:

$$L_{sty}^{adv} = \frac{1}{N} \sum_{i=1}^{N} E[logD(I_{s,i})] + E[log(1 - D(I_{cs,i}))]. \tag{9}$$

where N represents the number of generated stylized images within a mini-batch. Different from the conventional discriminator that guides generator to produce the more realistic images in generative adversarial networks (GANs) [9,26,31, 32], our style discriminator is exploited to relieve the problem of under-styliation and over-stylization. Our style loss integrate the style adversarial loss L_{sty}^{adv} and the pixel-wise style loss L_{sty}^{pix}, allowing them to cooperatively supplement each other to promote the stylization effect, which is formulated as:

$$L_{sty} = L_{sty}^{pix} + L_{sty}^{adv} \tag{10}$$

In this way, the overall style loss is enabled to constrain the stylization process on both pixel-level and image-level.

3.5 Model Optimization

With the above constraints, the overall optimization objective is:

$$L_{tot} = L_{base} + \lambda_{con}^{ref} L_{con}^{ref} + \lambda_{sty}^{adv} L_{sty}^{adv} \tag{11}$$

Remarks. Compared with the baseline model training with L_{base}, our proposed $C^2 SAL$ framework enjoys the more comprehensive guidance for IR/NIR image generation. From the perspective of stylization, our L_{sty}^{adv} allows global image-level perception rather than pixel-level for style consistency learning. From the

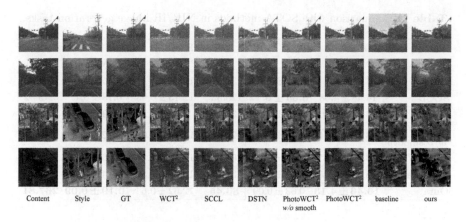

Content   Style   GT   WCT²   SCCL   DSTN   PhotoWCT²   PhotoWCT²   baseline   ours
                                                  w/o smooth

Fig. 4. Comparison results of NIR (RANUS dataset, 1_{st} and 2_{nd} row) and IR (LLVIP dataset, 3_{rd} and 4_{th} row) image generation. The columns from left to right are content images (visible), style images, ground-truth (GT) NIR/IR images of the content images, results of SOTA methods, results of our baseline model, results of the proposed method, respectively.

perspective of content preservation, our L_{con}^{ref} imposes constraints on the refined content features, which mitigates the interference of style information in content consistency learning.

4 Experiment

4.1 Implementation Details

The settings of encoder, FR module and decoder in our framework are identical to that of our baseline model [2]. PatchGAN [26] is adopted as the architecture of our style discriminator. We adopt Adam [28] as optimizer with the initial learning rate of 0.0001 for style discriminator. Each mini-batch includes 2 content images and 2 style images. The hyper-parameters λ_{ref}^{con}, λ_{sty}^{adv} are set to 1,1/10,1 on NIR/IR image generation tasks, respectively. All experiments are implemented on PyTorch platform with 2 NVIDIA GTX 2080Ti GPUs.

Datasets. We conduct experiments on two benchmarks. RANUS [24] is a spatially-aligned VIS-NIR dataset of urban scenes. We adopt a subset of it that contains 1674 images of each domain for training and 160 images for testing. LLVIP [23] is a VIS-IR paired dataset of urban scenes. We adopt a subset of it that contains 1505 images of each domain for training and 150 images for testing.

Evaluation Metrics. The widely-used metrics are introduced for quantitative evaluation, including structural similarity index measure (SSIM) and peak

Table 1. Comparison with SOTA methods in NIR/IR image generation tasks.

Method	NIR			IR		
	PSNR (↑)	SSIM (↑)	FID (↓)	PSNR (↑)	SSIM (↑)	FID (↓)
WCT^2	14.38 ± 4.1	**0.64 ± 0.12**	134.01	12.2 ± 1.11	0.15 ± 0.09	343.94
SCCL	14.48 ± 4.08	**0.64 ± 0.12**	125.33	12.15 ± 0.93	0.18 ± 0.1	345.52
DSTN	13.56 ± 4.66	0.63 ± 0.12	139.69	**12.76 ± 1.45**	**0.19 ± 0.12**	308.12
PhotoWCT^2 w/o smooth	13.42 ± 4.34	0.59 ± 0.14	121.07	12.05 ± 1.09	0.12 ± 0.08	328.94
PhotoWCT^2	13.75 ± 4.45	0.63 ± 0.13	109.2	12.75 ± 1.28	0.18 ± 0.11	312.15
Baseline	15.29 ± 2.95	0.59 ± 0.09	133.87	12.19 ± 0.56	0.14 ± 0.07	313.21
Ours	**16.46 ± 4.13**	0.63 ± 0.09	**83.45**	12.62 ± 0.64	**0.19 ± 0.09**	**267.81**

signal-to-noise ratio (PSNR) for measuring content preservation performance, FID for stylization evaluation. Note that higher PSNR and SSIM scores and lower FID scores indicate the more notable superiority of evaluated methods.

4.2   Results of NIR Image Generation on RANUS Dataset

Qualitative Evaluation. Figure 4 shows the visualized experimental results of some SOTA methods and the proposed method. The 1_{st} and 2_{nd} row of Fig. 4 show the results of NIR image generation. Then we have the following observations. Although WCT^2 [1], SCCL [5], and DSTN [7] can maintain the structure and texture information after style transfer, they are suffered from the problem of under-stylization. Specifically, in the 2_{nd} row of Fig. 4, there are still yellow "lines" on the road within their generated images, which are unexpected in NIR images. Besides, our method relieves the problem of blurred spots in the semantic region of "leaves" on the stylized images compared with previous methods. PhotoWCT^2 achieves outstanding results with the "smooth" operation for post-processing, which is time-consuming yet essential to the final performance. When the post-processing is absent, the results turn out to have undesired artifacts (or aperture phenomenon). In contrast, our method generates the more satisfactory results without any pre-/post-processing.

Quantitative Evaluation. The quantitative results, including comparisons with SOTA methods are shown in Table 1. Note that the mean value and the standard deviation of SSIM and PSNR scores are reported by counting all testing images. Although the proposed method obtains slightly lower SSIM scores than WCT^2 and SCCL, it surprisingly surpasses all compared methods on PSNR and FID scores. The WCT^2 and SCCL lead the SSIM score, but their advantages are yet marginal. Furthermore, focusing too much on maintaining structure and texture clues, WCT^2 and SCCL fail to compete with our method on metrics for stylization performance. These results verify that our proposed method is capable to trade-off the impact of stylization and content preservation during image generation and achieves the superior overall results.

Table 2. Ablation study based on quantitative comparison in NIR/IR image generation tasks.

Method	NIR			IR		
	PSNR (↑)	SSIM (↑)	FID (↓)	PSNR (↑)	SSIM (↑)	FID (↓)
w/o L_{con}^{ref}	15.79 ± 4.35	0.61 ± 0.09	85.03	12.3 ± 0.69	0.19 ± 0.09	286.25
w/o L_{con}^{coa}	15.97 ± 3.9	0.58 ± 0.09	99.31	12.53 ± 0.65	0.19 ± 0.09	292.64
w/o L_{sty}^{adv}	15.21 ± 2.91	0.62 ± 0.1	132.89	12.1 ± 0.74	0.15 ± 0.08	295.5
Full Model	16.46 ± 4.13	0.63 ± 0.09	83.45	$\mathbf{12.62 \pm 0.64}$	$\mathbf{0.19 \pm 0.09}$	**267.81**
w skip	$\mathbf{16.82 \pm 4.37}$	$\mathbf{0.67 \pm 0.09}$	**80.54**	12.39 ± 0.54	0.18 ± 0.08	299.46

w/o and w denotes *without* and *with* respectively.

4.3 Results of IR Image Generation on LLVIP Dataset

Qualitative Evaluation. The visualized experimental results are shown in the 3_{rd} and 4_{th} row of Fig. 4. Since IR images temperature information, it's more challenging to generate quality IR images, especially to maintain clear boundaries between foreground and background regions. Similar to the results of NIR image generation, WCT^2, SCCL and DSTN fail to effectively remove the style information of content images. Despite the impressive results from PhotoWCT^2, its performance is highly relied on the computational burden for the post-processing of "smooth". Without "smooth", the generated images are suffered from the problem of occurring lots of unexpected light-spots (as shown in 7_{th} column). Although our method also causes some blurred spots in the "leaves" region, the texture of the semantic region of "ground" in the generated image is smoother and more natural than the previous works. Furthermore, compared with these methods and our baseline model, our proposed method substantially enhances the content preservation as the boundaries between objects and regions are clearer, e.g., the boundaries between the regions of "pedestrian" and "ground"/"vehicles" and "roads".

Quantitative Evaluation. The quantitative comparison of IR image generation task is shown in Table 1. Compared with other state-of-the-art methods, our method outperforms them obviously on SSIM score that indicates the performance of content preservation. Besides, our method also obtains the superior FID scores over these methods, which verifies the effectiveness of stylization and image quality improvement. In spite of the slightly higher PSNR scores from DSTN, DSTN is trapped in the dilemma of under-stylization.

Fig. 5. Ablation study based on visualization comparison in both NIR (1st row) and IR (2nd row) image generation tasks. The main differences are highlighted in the red boxes. (Color figure online)

4.4 Ablation Study

To demonstrate the effectiveness and rationality of our proposed model, we conduct extensive ablation studies by removing components from or introducing components to our full model, which are shown in Table 2 and Fig. 5.

Effectiveness of the Fine-Grained Content Consistency Learning. When L_{con}^{ref} is absent, the generated NIR/IR images are prone to undermine the content structure information, leading to the obvious decline of three metrics, i.e., PSNR, SSIM, and FID. Visually, employing the models without L_{con}^{ref}, unexpected shadows occur to the semantic region of "sky" on the generated NIR image, and the boundary between the semantic region of "wheels" and "ground" is blurred. Besides, employing the model without L_{con}^{coa}, the generated NIR images are suffered from spatial distortion on the semantic regions of "vehicle" and "sky", and the IR images are suffered from the over-stylization as the textures of the style image are involved (red box on the upper right corner of the Fig. 5). Thus, the L_{con}^{coa} still plays an important role and L_{con}^{ref} and L_{con}^{coa} can be complementary to each other to achieve performance stacking effect.

Effectiveness of the Style Adversarial Learning. When L_{sty}^{adv} is absent, all quantitative results drop obviously on both NIR and IR image generation tasks. Particularly, the SSIM score declines by 4.1% in the IR image generation task. From the visual results, it can be observed that the style of the semantic region "sky" is distorted and non-realistic. Moreover, the texture of the style image is fused with the stylized image. These phenomenons are strong evidence of the effectiveness of the L_{sty}^{adv} in mining image-level style clues and preserving content information.

Discussion of the Skip-Connection. Despite the impressive performance of the skip-connection in some image generation tasks, the results of the model with skip-connection on the NIR/IR image generation tasks turn out to be unsatisfactory, for which it's not involved in our full model. Specifically, the quantitative indicators in the IR image generation task drop drastically. Furthermore, the visual comparison in Fig. 5 also reveals that it cannot well balance the stylization and structure preservation in our tasks.

5   Conclusion

In this paper, we proposed C^2SAL, a neural style transfer framework for NIR/IR image generation. By introducing a fine-grained content consistency and image-level style adversarial learning, our proposed C^2SAL has led to higher image generation quality. Furthermore, we have also demonstrated the effectiveness of proposed method by extensive experiments with detailed ablation study and comprehensive comparison.

Acknowledgement. This work is partially supported by National Natural Science Foundation of China (Grants no. 62176271 and 61772568), Guangdong Basic and Applied Basic Research Foundation (Grant no. 2019A1515012029), and Science and Technology Program of Guangzhou (Grant no. 202201011681).

References

1. Yoo, J., Uh, Y., Chun, S., et al.: Photorealistic style transfer via wavelet transforms. In: ICCV(2019)
2. Deng, Y., Tang, F., Dong, W., et al.: Arbitrary style transfer via multi-adaptation network. In: 28th ACM MM, pp. 2719–2727 (2020)
3. Luo, F., Li, Y., Zeng, G., et al.: Thermal infrared image colorization for nighttime driving scenes with top-down guided attention. IEEE TITS, 1–16 (2022). IEEE
4. Chiu, T.Y., Gurari, D.: PhotoWCT2: compact autoencoder for photorealistic style transfer resulting from blockwise training and skip connections of high-frequency residuals. In: WACV, pp. 2868–2877 (2022)
5. Qiao, Y., Cui, J., Huang, F., et al.: Efficient style-corpus constrained learning for photorealistic style transfer. IEEE TIP **30**, 3154–3166 (2021). IEEE
6. Cheng, M.M., Liu, X.C., Wang, J., et al.: Structure-preserving neural style transfer. IEEE TIP **29**, 909–920 (2019). IEEE
7. Hong, K., Jeon, S., Yang, H., et al.: Domain-aware universal style transfer. In: ICCV, pp. 14609–14617 (2021)
8. Huo, J., Jin, S., Li, W., et al.: Manifold alignment for semantically aligned style transfer. In: ICCV, pp. 14861–14869 (2021)
9. Zhu, J.Y., Park, T., Isola, P., et al.: Unpaired image-to-image translation using cycle-consistent adversarial networks. In: ICCV, pp. 2223–2232 (2017)
10. Lee, H.-Y., Tseng, H.-Y., Huang, J.-B., Singh, M., Yang, M.-H.: Diverse image-to-image translation via disentangled representations. In: Ferrari, V., Hebert, M., Sminchisescu, C., Weiss, Y. (eds.) ECCV 2018. LNCS, vol. 11205, pp. 36–52. Springer, Cham (2018). https://doi.org/10.1007/978-3-030-01246-5_3

11. Yang, Z., Chen, Z.: Learning from paired and unpaired data: alternately trained CycleGAN for near infrared image colorization. In: VCIP, pp. 467–470. IEEE (2020)
12. Yan, L., Wang, X., Zhao, M., et al.: A multi-model fusion framework for NIR-to-RGB translation. In: VCIP, pp. 459–462. IEEE (2020)
13. Wang, T., Zhang, T., Lovell, B.C.: EBIT: weakly-supervised image translation with edge and boundary enhancement. PR Lett. 138, 534–539 (2020). Elsevier
14. Babu, K.K., Dubey, S.R.: PCSGAN: perceptual cyclic-synthesized generative adversarial networks for thermal and NIR to visible image transformation. Neurocomputing 413, 41–50 (2020). Elsevier
15. Mehri, A., Sappa, A.D.: Colorizing near infrared images through a cyclic adversarial approach of unpaired samples. In: CVPR (Workshops) (2019)
16. Gatys, L.A., Ecker, A.S., Bethge, M.: Image style transfer using convolutional neural networks. In: CVPR, pp. 2414–2423 (2016)
17. Johnson, J., Alahi, A., Fei-Fei, L.: Perceptual losses for real-time style transfer and super-resolution. In: Leibe, B., Matas, J., Sebe, N., Welling, M. (eds.) ECCV 2016. LNCS, vol. 9906, pp. 694–711. Springer, Cham (2016). https://doi.org/10.1007/978-3-319-46475-6_43
18. Li, Y., Fang, C., Yang, J., et al.: Universal style transfer via feature transforms. In: NeurIPS (2017)
19. Huang, X., Belongie, S.: Arbitrary style transfer in real-time with adaptive instance normalization. In: ICCV, pp. 1501–1510 (2017)
20. Luan, F., Paris, S., Shechtman, E., et al.: Deep photo style transfer. In: CVPR, pp. 4990–4998 (2017)
21. Li, Y., Liu, M.-Y., Li, X., Yang, M.-H., Kautz, J.: A closed-form solution to photorealistic image stylization. In: Ferrari, V., Hebert, M., Sminchisescu, C., Weiss, Y. (eds.) ECCV 2018. LNCS, vol. 11207, pp. 468–483. Springer, Cham (2018). https://doi.org/10.1007/978-3-030-01219-9_28
22. An, J., Xiong, H., Huan, J., et al.: Ultrafast photorealistic style transfer via neural architecture search. In: AAAI, vol. 34, pp. 10443–10450 (2020)
23. Jia, X., Zhu, C., Li, M., et al.: LLVIP: a visible-infrared paired dataset for low-light vision. In: ICCV, pp. 3496–3504 (2021)
24. Choe, G., Kim, S.H., Im, S., et al.: RANUS: RGB and NIR urban scene dataset for deep scene parsing. IEEE RA-L 3, 1808–1815 (2018). IEEE
25. Simonyan, K., Zisserman, A.: Very deep convolutional networks for large-scale image recognition. arXiv preprint arXiv:1409.1556 (2014)
26. Isola, P., Zhu, J.Y., Zhou, T., et al.: Image-to-image translation with conditional adversarial networks. In: CVPR, pp. 1125–1134 (2017)
27. Deng, J., Dong, W., Socher, R., et al.: ImageNet: a large-scale hierarchical image database. In: CVPR, pp. 248–255. IEEE (2009)
28. Kingma, D.P., Ba, J.: Adam: a method for stochastic optimization. In: ICLR (2015)
29. He, K., Zhang, X., Ren, S., et al.: Deep residual learning for image recognition. In: CVPR, pp. 770–778 (2016)
30. Ronneberger, O., Fischer, P., Brox, T.: U-net: convolutional networks for biomedical image segmentation. In: Navab, N., Hornegger, J., Wells, W.M., Frangi, A.F. (eds.) MICCAI 2015. LNCS, vol. 9351, pp. 234–241. Springer, Cham (2015). https://doi.org/10.1007/978-3-319-24574-4_28
31. Goodfellow, I., Pouget-Abadie, J., Mirza, M., et al.: Generative adversarial nets. In: NeurIPS, pp. 2672–2680 (2014)
32. Mirza, M., Osindero, S.: Conditional generative adversarial nets. arXiv preprint arXiv:1411.1784 (2014)

Adaptive Open Set Recognition with Multi-modal Joint Metric Learning

Yimin Fu[✉], Zhunga Liu, Yanbo Yang, Linfeng Xu, and Hua Lan

Key Laboratory of Information Fusion Technology, Ministry of Education,
Northwestern Polytechnical University, Xi'an, Shaanxi 710072, China
fuyimin96@mail.nwpu.edu.cn

Abstract. Open set recognition (OSR) aims to simultaneously identify known classes and reject unknown classes. However, existing researches on open set recognition are usually based on single-modal data. Single-modal perception is susceptible to external interference, which may cause incorrect recognition. The multi-modal perception can be employed to improve the OSR performance thanks to the complementarity between different modalities. So we propose a new multi-modal open set recognition (MMOSR) method in this paper. The MMOSR network is constructed with joint metric learning in logit space. By doing this, it can avoid the feature representation gap between different modalities, and effectively estimate the decision boundaries. Moreover, the entropy-based adaptive weight fusion method is developed to combine the multi-modal perception information. The weights of different modalities are automatically determined according to the entropy in the logit space. A bigger entropy will lead to a smaller weight of the corresponding modality. This can effectively prevent the influence of disturbance. Scaling the fusion logits by the single-modal relative reachability further enhances the unknown detection ability. Experiments show that our method can achieve more robust open set recognition performance with multi-modal input compared with other methods.

Keywords: Adaptive weight fusion · Joint metric learning · Multi-modal perception · Open set recognition (OSR)

1 Introduction

Recent advances in deep learning [1,2] have greatly improved the performance of the pattern recognition systems in many areas, e.g., computer vision and speech recognition. However, the classifiers of traditional recognition systems operate with an unrealistic closed set prerequisite: the training and testing datasets share the same classes. This unreasonable closed set assumption leads to huge unreliability of the recognition systems when applied to the real open world. Numerous researches on open set recognition (OSR) [3] have been proposed to solve this problem. The purpose of open set recognition is to reject unknown class objects different from the known classe while effectively identifying the known classes

© The Author(s), under exclusive license to Springer Nature Switzerland AG 2022
S. Yu et al. (Eds.): PRCV 2022, LNCS 13534, pp. 631–644, 2022.
https://doi.org/10.1007/978-3-031-18907-4_49

objects. Despite the continuous progress of the existing OSR methods, most of them are based on single-modal data. However, a more realistic situation is that the characteristics of the testing sample gotten from single-modal perception technique may deviate from the training dataset due to some interfering factors, e.g., obscuration, camouflage or change of view. In this case, the model will produce a wrong recognition result because of the unreliable (limited) single-modal perception information.

Multi-modal perception [4] has been widely used in various fields of pattern recognition [5–7], the effective fusion method plays a key role for accurate recognition with richer multi-modal perception information. There exist large differences in feature representation between multi-modal data, thus, commonly used feature fusion methods may disrupt the feature distribution of the original single-modal data, which is an important basis for discriminating between known and unknown classes. Decision fusion methods have higher semantic uniformity and can avoid the feature representation differences of different modal data. However, the traditional decision fusion methods are unable to assess the credibility of different perception data and adaptively adjust their weights when the perception information of certain modality gets disturbed during testing.

In this paper, we propose a multi-modal open set recognition (MMOSR) method to break through the limitation above. First, the multi-modal feature is extracted through the backbone and mapping to the logit embeddings in the logit space. The single-modal logit embeddings are required to minimize their distance to the corresponding one-hot-like class center. Meanwhile, the normalized inverse of the distances in the logit space are used to measure the entropy of each single-modal logit embedding. We then use the entropy-based adaptive weight fusion method to construct the fusion logit embedding, which is supervised by the distance-based softmin function. During testing, we inversely scale the fusion logit embedding by the single-modal relative reachability and get the final recognition result with a probability threshold. The main contributions of our work in this paper can be summarized as follows:

1. Compared with the single-modal OSR methods on standard image datasets, we pioneer the utilization of multi-modal data to achieve more robust open set recognition performance.
2. The distance measurement in the logit space avoids the feature representation gap between different modalities. Apart from the integrated fusion logit embedding of the multi-modal data, scaling the logits by single-modal relative reachability further enhances the unknown detection ability.
3. Comprehensive experiments on LMT dataset have been done to verify the effectiveness of our proposed method. Moreover, we provide a baseline that contains different combinations of fusion strategies and OSR methods.

2   Related Work

2.1   Deep Metric Learning

The deep metric learning methods can be divided into two types: (1) distance-based loss functions [8–10]; and (2) classification-based loss functions [11–13].

The distance-based loss functions directly optimize the distance between feature embeddings. Contrastive loss [8] constrains the euclidean distance over similar pairs and dissimilar pairs with a margin to avoid the collapsed solution. For the selected triplets in the training dataset, Triplet loss [9] aims to minimize the distance between the anchor to positive sample and maximize its distance to negative sample. However, this type loss function gets trapped in slow convergence problem and requires carefully designed data mining approaches [10].

The classification-based loss functions usually jointly supervise the network with softmax loss and are therefore related to the classification results. Class-specific centers are widely used to provide reference information for each class. Setting the class centers as learnable parameters, Center loss [11] improves the intra-class compactness by minimizing the distance between the feature embedding to its corresponding class center. Besides the low intra-class variety [11], triplet-center loss [12] and island loss [13] are proposed to increase the inter-class separability concurrently. The classification-based loss functions usually optimize in the high-dimensional latent space, which leads to a huge computation burden.

2.2   Open Set Recognition

Early OSR researches focused on adapting the traditional machine learning classifiers (e.g., support vector machine, nearest neighbor, etc.) to open world [3,14–16]. For deep neural network (DNN)-based methods, Bendale et al. [17] proposed the OpenMax layer to replace the SoftMax layer as the first attempt, they fitted a Weibull distribution to calibrate the classification probabilities. Yoshihashi et al. [18] utilized the latent representations for reconstruction and realized the detection of unknown classes without sacrificing the classification performance of known classes. Besides the methods above that belong to discriminative models, the generative models [19–21] estimate the distribution of unknown classes through the generative adversarial network (GAN) and auto-encoder (AE). Ge et al. [19] estimated the distribution of unknown class samples with a conditional GAN. However, its performance improvement is limited when applied to natural images with large variation. Different from G-OpenMax, Neal et al. [20] used the encoder-decoder architecture to generate the counterfactual images as the synthetic open set training samples.

Obtaining discriminative feature embeddings by deep metric learning coincides with the purpose of obtaining effective decision boundaries for OSR. Referring to deep metric learning, many OSR methods have been proposed by optimizing the distance metric of feature embeddings. Yang et al. [22] proposed generalized convolutional prototype learning (GCPL) to handle the recognition problem in the open world. Unlike GCPL which increases intra-class compactness by the center/prototype points of each class, Chen et al. [23] estimated the extra-class space of each class with a new framework named reciprocal point learning (RPL). Miller et al. [24] proposed class anchor clustering (CAC) with anchored class centers in the logit space, which is more scalable during training.

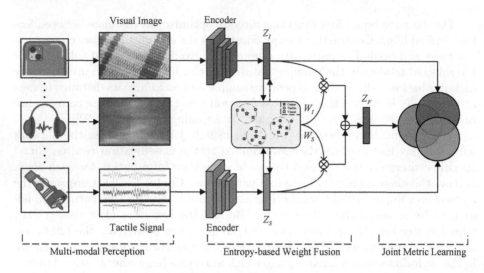

Fig. 1. Model structure of our proposed MMOSR method. The stars in different colors represent the class centers of different classes, the smaller marks in different shapes corresponding to the logit embeddings of different modalities. (Color figure online)

3   Multi-modal Open Set Recognition

Our MMOSR method consists of three main parts: entropy-based adaptive weight fusion, multi-modal joint metric learning, and open set recognition with scaled fusion logits. Figure 1 demonstrates the overall architecture of our method. In the following subsections, we will describe each component in detail.

3.1   Motivation and Novelty

Due to the differences in perception mechanisms, the distribution gap of the feature embeddings of different modalities in the feature space is non-negligible as shown in Fig 2a. This makes the distance-based measurement in the feature space inappropriate for the multi-modal open set recognition task. As shown in Fig. 2b, the distribution of different modalities in the logit space has higher uniformity. Thus, the measurement in the logit space can effectively avoid the feature distribution difference of multi-modal data. Inspired by this, we refer to [24] and use the non-trainable one-hot style class centers C in the N-dimensional logit space for our MMOSR method with joint metric learning:

$$C = (c_1, \ldots, c_N) = (\alpha \cdot \mathbf{e}_1, \ldots, \alpha \cdot \mathbf{e}_N) \tag{1}$$

where the hyperparameter α describes the magnitude of the class centers and $\mathbf{e}$ are the one-hot unit vectors.

Different from the previous methods that use a single embedding during training and testing, we propose an entropy-based adaptive weight fusion method

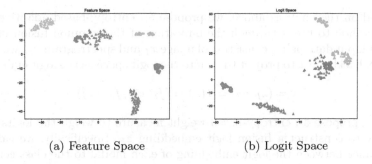

(a) Feature Space   (b) Logit Space

Fig. 2. The visualization of multi-modal data. Data of different modalities of the same class are represented by markers of the same color in different shape.

to get the fusion logit and construct the logit embeddings in triplet, which can not only provide an integrated description of multi-modal data during training but also dynamically assess the quality of the perception information of each modality during testing.

3.2 Entropy-Based Adaptive Weight Fusion

Deep convolutional neural networks (CNN) extract and represent features layer-by-layer and thus offer a wide range of choices to combine inputs of different modalities. The most commonly used fusion methods, i.e., early fusion, middle fusion, late fusion and decision fusion, are shown in Fig. 3. However, the large distribution difference of multi-modal data in the feature space makes the common feature fusion methods unsuitable for MMOSR problem. The representation in higher level (classification logits/decision) of multi-modal data has better compatibility and is easier to unify. For traditional decision fusion methods, the weights for the decision of each modal are usually set as hyperparameters defined in advance or learnable parameters fitted by training data. The weights of different modalities can not adjust adaptively during testing, the classifier will produce erroneous overconfidence in the decision of a certain modality when the perception information of that modality get disturbed.

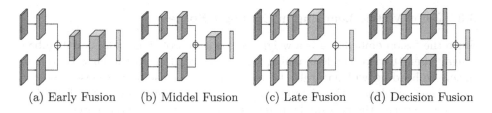

(a) Early Fusion   (b) Middel Fusion   (c) Late Fusion   (d) Decision Fusion

Fig. 3. The illustration of the common used fusion methods.

Based on the analysis above, we propose an entropy-based adaptive weight fusion method to break through the limitation of the common fusion methods. For each input data pair x consisting of image x_I and spectrogram x_S, we first use the CNN backbone f to project them into the logit space as the logit embeddings:

$$z = (z_I, z_S) = f(x) = (f_I(x_I), f_S(x_S)) \tag{2}$$

Then, we propose an entropy-based weight measure to weigh the logits of each modality to construct a fusion logit embedding z_F. Specifically, we calculated the distance between the logit embedding of each modal to the class center:

$$d_I = (d_{I_1}, \ldots, d_{I_N}), d_S = (d_{S_1}, \ldots, d_{S_N}) \tag{3}$$

We normalize the inverse of distances d_I and d_S with l_1 norm:

$$\hat{d}_I = \frac{d_I^{-1}}{\max\left(\|d_I^{-1}\|_1, \epsilon\right)}, \hat{d}_S = \frac{d_I^{-1}}{\max\left(\|d_S^{-1}\|_1, \epsilon\right)} \tag{4}$$

and use them to calculate the information entropy H of each modal:

$$H = (H_I, H_S) = (-\sum_{n=1}^{N} \hat{d}_I(n) \log \hat{d}_I(n), -\sum_{n=1}^{N} \hat{d}_S(n) \log \hat{d}_S(n)) \tag{5}$$

A large entropy means higher uncertainty for the classification logits and this modal should take a lower weight when constructing the fusion logit embedding. So we define the weights W of each modal as:

$$W = (W_I, W_S) = (\frac{e^{-H_I}}{e^{-H_I} + e^{-H_S}}, \frac{e^{-H_S}}{e^{-H_I} + e^{-H_S}}) \tag{6}$$

Finally, we construct the fusion logit embedding z_F as follows:

$$z_F = \sum_{i=(I,S)} W_i z_i \tag{7}$$

Thus, the input data pair x can be expressed in triplet as $z_{Trip} = (z_I, z_S, z_F)$.

3.3   Joint Metric Learning in the Logit Space

Since the fusion embedding is a weighted expression of the single-modal embeddings, when the two single-modal embeddings are close to the class center, its fusion embedding will naturally be close to the corresponding class center as well. Thus, we denote the distance loss L_D as the summation of the Euclidean distance between the two single-modal embeddings to the class center:

$$L_D = \frac{1}{M} \sum_{i=1}^{M} (\|z_{i_I} - c_{y_i}\|_2 + \|z_{i_S} - c_{y_i}\|_2) \tag{8}$$

where y is the class label of the input and M is the batch size during training.

Then, to keep the sample away from other class centers, i.e. increase the inter-class difference, we calculate the distance between the fusion logit embedding and the class centers as:

$$d_F = (d_{F_1}, \ldots, d_{F_N}) = (\|z_F - c_1\|_2, \ldots, \|z_F - c_N\|_2) \tag{9}$$

and use it to measure the probability of which class the sample x belongs to according to non-negative and sum-to-one properties:

$$p(y = n \mid x) = \frac{e^{-d_{F_y}}}{\sum_{c=1}^{N} e^{-d_{F_c}}} \tag{10}$$

The closer the fusion logit embedding of the sample to the class center c_n, the more likely it belongs to class n. Thus, the classification loss L_C can be represented in the form of the distance-based cross-entropy (DCE) loss:

$$L_C = \frac{1}{M} \sum_{i=1}^{M} -\log p(y = y_i \mid x_i) \tag{11}$$

By minimizing the classification loss, the distance gap between the sample to the corresponding class center and to other class centers will increase, leading to the increase in inter-class differences.

The overall representation of the joint metric learning in the logit space can be formulated as the combination of distance loss L_D and classification loss L_C:

$$L = L_C + \lambda L_D \tag{12}$$

where λ is a hyperparameter to balance the weights of two sub-loss functions.

When the training process with joint metric learning is finished, we calculate the mean value of the triplet embeddings for each modal and extend the one-hot style center to a center triplet for each class n as:

$$C_{Trip}(n) = (c_{I_n}, c_{S_n}, c_{F_n}) = \frac{1}{|N_n|} \left(\sum_{i=1}^{|N_n|} z_I(n), \sum_{i=1}^{|N_n|} z_S(n), \sum_{i=1}^{|N_n|} z_F(n) \right) \tag{13}$$

Meanwhile, we compute the average single-modal distance between the logit embeddings to the class center as the radius of each single-modal class cluster:

$$R = (r_{I_n}, r_{S_n}) = \frac{1}{|N_n|} \left(\sum_{i=1}^{|N_n|} \|z_{I_i} - c_{I_n}\|_2, \sum_{i=1}^{|N_n|} \|z_{S_i} - c_{S_n}\|_2 \right) \tag{14}$$

This allows our model to obtain an integration awareness of multi-modal perceptual information while retaining the distributional properties of each single modality, which will be used to scale the fusion logits during testing.

3.4 Open Set Recognition by Scaled Fusion Logits

For each testing sample, its initial decision can be made according to the distance d_F between the fusion logit embedding z_F and the fusion class centers C_F and the initial classification results refer to the class label of this closest center:

$$y_{init} = \arg\min(d_F(y = n)) \tag{15}$$

To further enhance the model's ability to discriminate between known and unknown classes, we measure the relative reachability [25] γ of each single modality and use them to scale the initial distance-based result:

$$\gamma = (\gamma_I, \gamma_S) = (\frac{\left\| z_I - c_{I_{y_{init}}} \right\|_2}{r_{I_{y_{init}}}}, \frac{\left\| z_S - c_{S_{y_{init}}} \right\|_2}{r_{S_{y_{init}}}}) \tag{16}$$

the scaled distance and scaled fusion logit can be formulated as:

$$\hat{d}_F = (1/\gamma_I) \cdot (1/\gamma_S) \cdot d_F \tag{17}$$

$$\hat{p}(y = k \mid x) = Softmin(\hat{d_{F_k}}) = \frac{e^{-\hat{d_{F_k}}}}{\sum_{n=1}^{N} e^{-\hat{d_{F_n}}}} \tag{18}$$

When the value of γ is small, it indicates that the perception information of this modality is likely to belong to the initial class derived from the fusion logit and will further widen the difference between the normalized probabilities of different classes. In contrast, the input is more likely to be an unknown class sample.

Finally, we need to employ a probability threshold δ to distinguish between known and unknown classes. When the max probability of the scaled classification logit is above δ, the sample will be classified into the corresponding known class. Otherwise, the model will reject it as unknown:

$$y = \begin{cases} \arg\max \hat{p}(y = n \mid x), & \hat{p}(y = n) \geq \delta \\ unknown, & Otherwise \end{cases} \tag{19}$$

A common way of determining the threshold δ is to ensure a certain true positive rate of training data. However, it is unreasonable to use an arbitrary threshold for open set recognition as we have no prior information of unknown classes [20]. So the OSR performance needs to be evaluated by the threshold-independent metrics.

4   Experiments

4.1   Dataset and Preprocessing

In this paper, we use the visual images and the tactile acceleration traces of LMT Haptic Texture (LMT) [26] dataset to evaluate the OSR performance. We randomly select one fine-grained known and unknown class in each coarse-grained category. Thus, each class partition contains 9 known classes and 9 unknown classes. We use the *openness* defined in [3] to describes the complexity of OSR problem:

$$openness = 1 - \sqrt{\frac{2 \times N_{train}}{N_{test} + N_{train}}} \qquad (20)$$

The *openness* of our experiments here based on LMT dataset is 18.35%.

Referring to [27], we first combine the three-axes acceleration signals into 1-D signals and use short-time Fourier transform to convert the signals to spectrogram images. We augment the training data by: (1) flipping each image vertically and horizontally; and (2) rotating them by 90, 180 and 270°. We keep the corresponding spectrograms unchanged to preserve the temporal and spectral properties. For the testing data, We reduce the brightness of the visible images for each test sample, thus simulating a situation where the visible images are disturbed due to lighting conditions.

4.2 Experimental Setup

Implementation Details. We use the convolutional blocks of VGG13 [1] as the encode with a global average pooling layer and a fully connected layer to project the representation into logit space. We trained the networks for 100 iterations with the batch size of 32, and use the SGD as the optimizer. The initial learning rate is set as 0.01 and we divide it by 10 every 30 iterations. We set the weight of the distance loss λ to 0.1 and the magnitude of the class centers α to 5 .

Evaluation Metrics. We use the following metrics to comprehensively evaluate the OSR performance in this paper:

Area Under the ROC Curve (AUROC) is a threshold-independent metric to measure the open set recognition performance. The Receiver Operating Characteristic (ROC) curve refers to a trade-off between the true positive rate and the false positive rate with various probability thresholds.

Open Set Classification Rate (OSCR) [28] also takes the classification accuracy of known classes into consideration. OSCR integrates the CCR at various FPR values, a larger value of OSCR indicates better OSR performance.

4.3 Comparison to the State-of-the-Art Methods

We compare the performance of our MMOSR method with various combinations of the state-of-the-art OSR methods and the commonly used fusion strategies. The results based on AUROC and OSCR are shown in Tables 1 and 2 respectively. In the baseline we listed, the value of each position represents the result obtained by combining the fusion method of the corresponding column with the OSR method of the corresponding row. The "Image" and "Spectrogram" correspond to use the single-modal visual image or tactile acceleration data as the input data. We do not report the performance of CROSR with feature fusion methods as the feature fusion will confuse the reconstruction. When the sensory

Table 1. AUROC results over 5 random class partitions. The best performance is shown in bold and the best fusion method for each OSR method is underlined.

Methods	Image	Spectrogram	Early	Middle	Late	Decision
SoftMax	62.3 ± 6.6	73.6 ± 6.3	70.2 ± 1.8	69.9 ± 0.4	76.2 ± 2.9	76.7 ± 4.5
OpenMax [17]	58.5 ± 5.6	44.1 ± 8.0	59.2 ± 4.4	55.8 ± 5.7	46.9 ± 6.3	40.1 ± 2.8
G-OpenMax [19]	58.3 ± 4.7	51.4 ± 5.5	49.3 ± 3.2	42.7 ± 3.9	49.3 ± 4.7	45.8 ± 3.3
CROSR [18]	63.8 ± 4.5	61.9 ± 6.1	–	–	–	64.1 ± 4.4
GCPL [22]	52.2 ± 5.8	61.1 ± 3.2	59.2 ± 5.7	62.3 ± 5.6	67.4 ± 8.9	77.6 ± 5.4
RPL [23]	51.9 ± 8.2	59.0 ± 9.1	56.9 ± 7.3	57.1 ± 3.4	57.3 ± 3.7	61.8 ± 8.3
CAC [24]	65.6 ± 3.6	76.2 + 3.8	71.8 ± 3.7	75.6 ± 5.7	74.8 ± 6.6	78.3 ± 5.1
Ours			**82.1 ± 1.2**			

Table 2. OSCR results over 5 random class partitions. The best performance is shown in bold and the best fusion method for each OSR method is underlined.

Methods	Image	Spectrogram	Early	Middle	Late	Decision
SoftMax	47.1 ± 2.4	67.6 ± 6.9	51.9 ± 1.2	54.3 ± 2.2	63.2 ± 6.1	64.1 ± 5.1
OpenMax [17]	31.9 ± 1.9	22.4 ± 6.5	34.8 ± 1.1	31.1 ± 3.5	29.4 ± 4.3	25.7 ± 2.8
G-OpenMax [19]	25.6 ± 1.6	30.7 ± 5.7	36.2 ± 1.8	30.2 ± 3.9	29.3 ± 4.6	28.8 ± 3.3
CROSR [18]	34.1 ± 5.9	48.4 ± 8.1	–	–	–	55.7 ± 3.7
GCPL [22]	33.3 ± 3.7	48.4 ± 4.1	31.1 ± 4.6	41.0 ± 1.6	55.1 ± 6.7	68.8 ± 3.2
RPL [23]	33.4 ± 2.2	42.9 ± 7.1	31.5 ± 5.4	40.2 ± 4.2	39.7 ± 6.5	52.2 ± 4.1
CAC [24]	47.8 ± 1.5	68.9 ± 4.5	55.3 ± 3.5	62.2 ± 5.8	65.2 ± 5.7	69.4 ± 5.5
Ours			**75.3 ± 3.9**			

data of a certain modality is disturbed during testing and can not provide reliable perception information, our proposed method improves the AUROC by about 4% than the best combination among baseline methods. Apart from the experiment based on AUROC in Table 1, we also report the OSCR results in Table 2. Our method shows a more significant improvement (about 6%) in this metric compared to the baseline methods, which indicates a more reliable recognition result.

Then we give a comprehensive analysis according to the results of the experiments, the performances of OSR methods that use the OpenMax layer to calibrate the classification results (OpenMax, G-OpenMax and CROSR) meet a substantial degradation when the perception information gets disturbed during testing. This is mainly due to that the parameters of Weibull distribution are fitted according to the training data. For the generative model with the estimated unknown class samples, the experimental results are in line with the previous work [19] that there is no significant improvement over the natural image. As we have inferred, the high-level fusion (decision fusion) method usually performs the best with the baseline OSR methods. In contrast, the low-level feature fusion strategies may even degrade the OSR performance of the methods that use the distance measurement in the feature space (GCPL, RPL).

4.4 Ablation Studies

Comparison with Other Metric Learning Functions. We vary the *openness* between $\{7.42\%, 13.4\%, 18.35\%, 29.29\%, 36.75\%\}$ and compare the OSR performance of the networks under the supervision of Center loss, Triplet loss, N-pair loss and our proposed joint metric learning. For a fair comparison, we directly use the fusion logit here for classification without scaling by the relative reachability. The performance of this ablation study is measured by macro-average F1-scores with a threshold 0.8 as summarized in Fig. 4. We can see that our joint metric learning can provides a more stable and robust recognition performance than other metric learning loss functions.

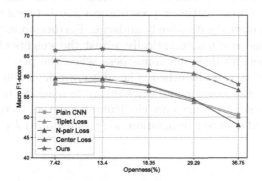

Fig. 4. Macro-average F1-scores over various openness.

Contribution of Each Part. To analyze the contribution of each part of our method. We vary the *openness* between $\{18.35\%, 29.29\%, 36.75\%\}$, corresponding to the number of unknown classes of each coarse category from 1 to 3. The experiment results are reported in Table 3. According to the results, replacing the normal decision fusion with the weight fusion based on the normalized classification logit can not improve the performance of the baseline method. Even with the normal decision fusion method, training the network with the joint metric learning can improve the OSR performance, which leads to better performance when collaborating with the entropy-based adaptive fusion method to construct the triplet logit embeddings. Finally, the integration of the proposed MMOSR method further improves the OSR performance and leads to the best result.

Table 3. Ablation experiments of the contribution of each part.

Method	18.35%		29.29%		36.75%	
	AUROC	OSCR	AUROC	OSCR	AUROC	OSCR
CNN+Decision	67.8	55.2	74.5	58.9	73.8	57.9
CNN+Entropy	65.0	53.5	68.6	55.9	66.9	54.2
Joint+Decision	73.7	59.5	78.3	61.5	74.9	60.1
Joint+Entropy	75.1	65.7	79.9	69.1	76.3	66.6
Integrated	**81.6**	**70.7**	**85.3**	**73.0**	**80.7**	**70.3**

5   Conclusion

In this paper, we propose a multi-modal open set recognition method to improve the OSR performance in the complex real world. The joint metric learning in the logit space can avoid the feature representation gap between multi-modal data and effectively estimate the decision boundaries. Furthermore, the entropy-based adaptive weight fusion can automatically adjust the weights of different modalities. So the model can maintain robustness when the perception information of a certain modality gets disturbed. The unknown detection ability is further enhanced by using the single-modal reachability to scale the fusion logits. In the future, we will investigate some more challenging open set recognition problems, such as fine-grained open set recognition, long-tailed open set recognition, etc.

References

1. Simonyan, K., Zisserman, A.: Very deep convolutional networks for large-scale image recognition. arXiv preprint arXiv:1409.1556 (2014)
2. He, K., Zhang, X., Ren, S., Sun, J.: Deep residual learning for image recognition. In: Proceedings of the IEEE Conference on Computer Vision and Pattern Recognition, pp. 770–778 (2016)
3. Scheirer, W.J., de Rezende Rocha, A., Sapkota, A., Boult, T.E.: Toward open set recognition. IEEE Trans. Pattern Anal. Mach. Intell. **35**(7), 1757–1772 (2012)
4. Baltrušaitis, T., Ahuja, C., Morency, L.P.: Multimodal machine learning: a survey and taxonomy. IEEE Trans. Pattern Anal. Mach. Intell. **41**(2), 423–443 (2018)
5. Hong, D., et al.: More diverse means better: multimodal deep learning meets remote-sensing imagery classification. IEEE Trans. Geosci. Remote Sens. **59**(5), 4340–4354 (2020)
6. Feng, D., et al.: Deep multi-modal object detection and semantic segmentation for autonomous driving: datasets, methods, and challenges. IEEE Trans. Intell. Transp. Syst. **22**(3), 1341–1360 (2020)
7. Elmadany, N.E.D., He, Y., Guan, L.: Multimodal learning for human action recognition via bimodal/multimodal hybrid centroid canonical correlation analysis. IEEE Trans. Multimedia **21**(5), 1317–1331 (2018)
8. Hadsell, R., Chopra, S., LeCun, Y.: Dimensionality reduction by learning an invariant mapping. In: 2006 IEEE Computer Society Conference on Computer Vision and Pattern Recognition (CVPR2006), vol. 2, pp. 1735–1742. IEEE (2006)

9. Schroff, F., Kalenichenko, D., Philbin, J.: FaceNet: a unified embedding for face recognition and clustering. In: Proceedings of the IEEE Conference on Computer Vision and Pattern Recognition, pp. 815–823 (2015)
10. Sohn, K.: Improved deep metric learning with multi-class n-pair loss objective. In: Advances in Neural Information Processing Systems, pp. 1857–1865 (2016)
11. Wen, Y., Zhang, K., Li, Z., Qiao, Yu.: A discriminative feature learning approach for deep face recognition. In: Leibe, B., Matas, J., Sebe, N., Welling, M. (eds.) ECCV 2016. LNCS, vol. 9911, pp. 499–515. Springer, Cham (2016). https://doi.org/10.1007/978-3-319-46478-7_31
12. He, X., Zhou, Y., Zhou, Z., Bai, S., Bai, X.: Triplet-center loss for multi-view 3D object retrieval. In: Proceedings of the IEEE Conference on Computer Vision and Pattern Recognition, pp. 1945–1954 (2018)
13. Cai, J., Meng, Z., Khan, A.S., Li, Z., O'Reilly, J., Tong, Y.: Island loss for learning discriminative features in facial expression recognition. In: 2018 13th IEEE International Conference on Automatic Face & Gesture Recognition (FG 2018), pp. 302–309. IEEE (2018)
14. Cevikalp, H.: Best fitting hyperplanes for classification. IEEE Trans. Pattern Anal. Mach. Intell. **39**(6), 1076 (2017)
15. Bendale, A., Boult, T.: Towards open world recognition. In: Proceedings of the IEEE Conference on Computer Vision and Pattern Recognition, pp. 1893–1902 (2015)
16. Mendes Júnior, R.R., et al.: Nearest neighbors distance ratio open-set classifier. Mach. Learn. **106**(3), 359–386 (2016). https://doi.org/10.1007/s10994-016-5610-8
17. Bendale, A., Boult, T.E.: Towards open set deep networks. In: Proceedings of the IEEE Conference on Computer Vision and Pattern Recognition, pp. 1563–1572 (2016)
18. Yoshihashi, R., Shao, W., Kawakami, R., You, S., Iida, M., Naemura, T.: Classification-reconstruction learning for open-set recognition. In: Proceedings of the IEEE/CVF Conference on Computer Vision and Pattern Recognition, pp. 4016–4025 (2019)
19. Ge, Z., Demyanov, S., Chen, Z., Garnavi, R.: Generative openMax for multi-class open set classification. arXiv preprint arXiv:1707.07418 (2017)
20. Neal, L., Olson, M., Fern, X., Wong, W.-K., Li, F.: Open set learning with counterfactual images. In: Ferrari, V., Hebert, M., Sminchisescu, C., Weiss, Y. (eds.) ECCV 2018. LNCS, vol. 11210, pp. 620–635. Springer, Cham (2018). https://doi.org/10.1007/978-3-030-01231-1_38
21. Oza, P., Patel, V.M.: C2AE: class conditioned auto-encoder for open-set recognition. In: Proceedings of the IEEE/CVF Conference on Computer Vision and Pattern Recognition, pp. 2307–2316 (2019)
22. Yang, H.M., Zhang, X.Y., Yin, F., Liu, C.L.: Robust classification with convolutional prototype learning. In: Proceedings of the IEEE Conference on Computer Vision and Pattern Recognition, pp. 3474–3482 (2018)
23. Chen, G., et al.: Learning open set network with discriminative reciprocal points. In: Vedaldi, A., Bischof, H., Brox, T., Frahm, J.-M. (eds.) ECCV 2020. LNCS, vol. 12348, pp. 507–522. Springer, Cham (2020). https://doi.org/10.1007/978-3-030-58580-8_30
24. Miller, D., Sunderhauf, N., Milford, M., Dayoub, F.: Class anchor clustering: a loss for distance-based open set recognition. In: Proceedings of the IEEE/CVF Winter Conference on Applications of Computer Vision, pp. 3570–3578 (2021)
25. Savinov, N., et al.: Episodic curiosity through reachability. arXiv preprint arXiv:1810.02274 (2018)

26. Strese, M., Schuwerk, C., Iepure, A., Steinbach, E.: Multimodal feature-based surface material classification. IEEE Trans. Haptics **10**(2), 226–239 (2016)
27. Zheng, H., Fang, L., Ji, M., Strese, M., Özer, Y., Steinbach, E.: Deep learning for surface material classification using haptic and visual information. IEEE Trans. Multimedia **18**(12), 2407–2416 (2016)
28. Dhamija, A.R., Günther, M., Boult, T.E.: Reducing network agnostophobia. arXiv preprint arXiv:1811.04110 (2018)

Prior-Guided Multi-scale Fusion Transformer for Face Attribute Recognition

Shaoheng Song[1,2,3], Huaibo Huang[2,3], Jiaxiang Wang[1], Aihua Zheng[1(✉)],
and Ran He[2,3]

[1] Anhui Provincial Key Laboratory of Multimodal Cognitive Computation,
Anhui University, Hefei, China
ahzeng214@foxmail.com
[2] Center for Research on Intelligent Perception and Computing (CRIPAC),
Beijing, China
huaibo.huang@cripac.ia.ac.cn
[3] Institute of Automation, Chinese Academy of Sciences, Beijing, China
rhe@nlpr.ia.ac.cn

Abstract. Multi-label face attribute recognition (FAR) refers to the task of predicting a set of attribute labels for a facial image. However, existing FAR methods do not work well for recognizing attributes of different scales, since most frameworks use the features of the last layer and ignore the detailed information which is crucial for FAR. To solve this problem, we propose a prior-guided multi-scale fusion transformer, which possesses the ability to build the fusion among features of different scales with prior knowledge of attributes. First, we employ a unifying Graph Convolution Network (GCN) to model the relations between multiple attributes by the prior knowledge of facial labels and the statistical frequencies of co-occurrence between attributes. Second, we propose a multi-scale fusion module, which uses adaptive attention to fuse features from two adjacent layers, and then simultaneously fuse the features of different scales hierarchically to explore the multilevel relation. In addition, we utilize the transformer as a feature extraction module to achieve a global correlation among the acquired features. Experiments on a large-scale face attribute dataset verify the effectiveness of the proposed method both qualitatively and quantitatively.

Keywords: Face attribute recognition · Multi-scale · Prior-guided

1 Introduction

The technology of face attribute recognition, which aims to predict a number of attributes in face images, has drawn extensive attention due to its potential applications such as face retrieval [31], face recognition, [2] *etc.* Despite the great achievements that have been made in this field, there still exist a variety

© The Author(s), under exclusive license to Springer Nature Switzerland AG 2022
S. Yu et al. (Eds.): PRCV 2022, LNCS 13534, pp. 645–659, 2022.
https://doi.org/10.1007/978-3-031-18907-4_50

of challenges to address. During our study, we summarize the difficulties in face attribute recognition into three main points. First of all, as shown in Fig. 1, the information obtained from the last layer of the network mainly represents the high-level characteristics. To a certain extent, only using the last-layer feature may affect the ability of the network to capture the potential characteristics presented in low-level information. Second, there are some subtle correlations between attributes since the occurrence of some labels may affect each other in face images. Usually, with a great chance, *beard* comes together with *male*, and *receding hairline* indicates that a person is not *young*. Finally, the CNN models pay more attention to local information, while experiencing difficulty to capture global representations. So the lack of global relations between features may weaken the ability of representation learning.

In recent years, with the renaissance of CNN, some deep models have been applied to face attribute recognition and have made great progress. For instance, Liu *et al.* [15] solve the attribute recognition problem by learning independent classifiers for each attribute. Kalayeh *et al.* [10] use semantic segmentation to mine local clues to guide attribute prediction, which means to position the area where the attribute comes from. Cao *et al.* [1] consider both identity information and attribute relations. SSPL [25] captures the pixel-level and image-level semantic information. HFE [33] combines attribute and ID information to learn a fine-grained feature embedding. Nian *et al.* [21] use a decoupling matrix. Despite their achievements, the three challenges mentioned above remain not well addressed.

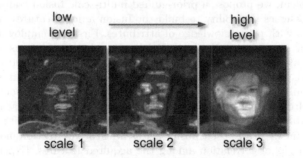

Information in features of different scales

Fig. 1. The parts with warm colors represent where the network pays attention. a) Extracting features of different scales in the network. We can find that the network pays attention to some local details in the initial stage and gradually some global information in the later stage.

In this work, we propose a prior-guided multi-scale fusion transformer to capture the local and global representations in image features with attribute prior information. It consists of two sub-modules to progressively capture information hierarchically. First, we apply an attribute residual mapping module (ARMM) to capture the relations between attributes. Inspired by [30], following the GCN [12] paradigm, we use the prior knowledge of facial labels and the statistical frequencies of co-occurrence between attributes to construct the graph. Then the obtained feature can enhance attribute-related regions in image features. Second, inspired by [26], we design a multi-scale fusion module (MFM) to enable the network to gradually fuse low-level and high-level features at the same time and then simultaneously utilize the features of different scales. In addition, we introduce Swin-Transformer [14] to model global relations. Then pairwise relations can be fused into image features in a global way by performing message passing through each spatial patch. The two sub-modules are aggregated together to perform multilevel relations learning for face attribute recognition.

In summary, the contributions of this work are three-fold.

(1) We propose a multi-scale fusion module to jointly capture relations between low-level and high-level features for face attribute recognition.
(2) We propose an improved end-to-end architecture based on a transformer and prior information of attributes. The relations between attributes can be learned to strengthen the representations.
(3) Experiments show the superiority of the proposed method over recent methods and the effectiveness of our framework for face attribute recognition.

2   Related Work

2.1   Face Attribute Recognition

Face attribute recognition has risen in recent years. Rudd *et al.* [22] define face attribute recognition as a regression task. It applies a single DCNN to learn multiple attribute labels. Zhong *et al.* [35] use the mid-level features as the best representation for recognition. Then Hand *et al.* [6] branch out to multiple groups for modeling the attribute correlations due to many attributes being strongly correlated. Cao *et al.* [1] design a partially shared structure called PS-MCNN. Lu *et al.* [17] propose a network to learn shared features in a fully adaptive way, which incrementally widens the current design in a layer-wise manner. He *et al.* [9] utilize dynamic weights to guide network learning and Huang *et al.* In several latest works, HFE [33] combines attribute and ID information to learn fine-grained feature embeddings, then attribute-level and ID-level constraints are utilized to establish the hierarchical structure. SSPL [25] proposes a method, which captures semantic information of facial images in the pixel-level and image-level.

2.2   Graph Convolution Network

GCN [12] is used to process topological data. Recently, graph-based reasoning has been proved to be beneficial to a variety of vision tasks including multi-label classification [3], FVQA [36], zero-shot learning [29], social networks [32], etc. In recent years, image classification [3] and face attributes classification [21] propose to use GCN to learn the representations with attribute information.

2.3   Vision Transformer

At present, Transformer [27] is applied to the vision tasks based on the Vision Transformer (ViT) [5]. This demonstrates that pure Transformer-based architectures can also obtain relatively good results, promising the potential of handling the vision tasks and natural language processing (NLP) tasks under a unified Transformer. Recently, rather than focusing on a particular visual task, some works try to design a general vision Transformer backbone for general-purpose vision tasks. [4,14,28] these transformers have been proved effective in features extracting and perform well in downstream tasks.

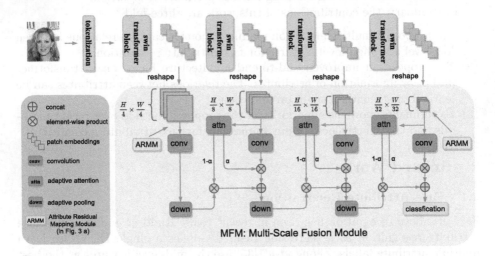

Fig. 2. Structure of prior-guided multi-scale fusion transformer. The inputs of the framework are face images and prior information of attributes. We use Swin-Transformer [14] to get four features of different scales in a global way. Then we take the reshaped features into the Multi-Scale Fusion Module (MFM) to fuse multi-scale features of high-level and low-level in a hierarchical manner. At the same time, we employ an Attribute Residual Mapping Module (ARMM) to map the prior information of attributes into features in the first and last layers of the network. The details of ARMM is described in Fig. 3. The orange arrow represents the output prior information from the first GCN [12] layer, and the purple arrow represents the output prior information from the last GCN [12] layer.

3   Approaches

In this paper, we propose a prior-guided multi-scale fusion transformer to simultaneously utilize features of different scales and prior information of attributes to process the feature learning in a global way for face attribute recognition. As shown in Fig. 2, our network consists of two main modules: 1) Attribute Residual Mapping Module (ARMM), to combine the prior knowledge of related attributes and the image features in the deep and the shallow layers. 2) Multi-scale Fusion Module (MFM), to obtain the relations between low-level detailed features and high-level semantic features in different scales, which are extracted from a transformer. We shall elaborate on these two modules in the following two sections.

3.1 ARMM: Attribute Residual Mapping Module

1) GCN review
GCN [12] can capture the relationship between nodes in structured graph data in a semi-supervised manner. The graph is represented in the form of $\mathbf{G} = \{\mathbf{V}, \mathbf{A}\}$, where $\mathbf{V} \in \mathbb{R}^{N \times D}$ is the set of $\mathbf{N}$ data vectors in D dimension, and $\mathbf{A} \in \mathbb{R}^{N \times N}$ is adjacency matrix. Then GCN can encode the pairwise relationship among data. The goal of GCN is to learn a function $f(\cdot, \cdot)$ on a graph $\mathbf{G}$, which takes initial node continuous representations $\mathbf{V}$ and an adjacency matrix $\mathbf{A}$ as inputs. And it updates the node features as $\mathbf{X}^{l+1} \in \mathbb{R}^{N \times D'}$ after spreading information through each layer. Every GCN layer can be formulated as:

$$\mathbf{X}^{l+1} = f(\mathbf{X}^l, \mathbf{A}) = \sigma(\mathbf{D}^{-1/2}\mathbf{A}\mathbf{D}^{-1/2}\mathbf{X}^l\mathbf{W}^l), \tag{1}$$

where $\mathbf{D} = diag(d_1, d_2...d_k)$ is a diagonal matrix with $d_i = \sum_{j=1}^{n} \mathbf{A}_{ij}$. $\mathbf{W}^l \in \mathbb{R}^{D_l \times D_{l+1}}$ is a transformation matrix learned during training and σ denotes a non-linear operation, which is acted by LeakyReLU [18] for our purpose. Finally, $\mathbf{X}^{l+1} \in \mathbb{R}^{N \times D_{l+1}}$ denotes the output in the $l+1$-th layer.

2) Attribute Prior Information
We aim to input the internal relations between attributes obtained from the distribution of data as prior information into the network. First of all, the construction of a graph is necessary. Inspired by [30], to obtain the prior information of the label attributes, we extract the feature vector of each word related to the label from Google Corpus (GoogleNews-vectors-negative300). Followed by [13] and [20], since each attribute of the face is composed of multiple words, we sum the features of the words contained in each attribute label and take the average. Then we use the final vectors as graph nodes with prior information. According to this, we construct graph nodes as $V \in \mathbb{R}^{K \times D}$, where K denotes the total number of the labels.

In order to better propagate information between attributes, a correlation matrix is a key point. Then we get the matrix with statistical co-occurrence information by the distribution of samples in the training set. Following [3], we build this correlation matrix in a data-driven way. That is, we mine their relevant information based on the distribution of attributes within the dataset and compute the degree of semantic relevance of attributes. The attribute correlation dependency is modeled in the form of conditional probability between attributes. We denote the $P(\mathbf{V}_i \mid \mathbf{V}_j)$ as the probability of occurrence of attribute $\mathbf{V}_i$ when attribute $\mathbf{V}_j$ appears. To construct the correlation matrix, to begin with, we define the total number of occurrences of each attribute as N_i. Then we count the number of co-occurrences of every attribute pair and build a co-occurrence matrix $M \in \mathbb{R}^{K \times K}$, which K means the total number of face attributes. Then, we define the correlation matrix by the conditional probability matrix as:

$$[\mathbf{A}]_{ij} = \mathbf{M}_{ij}/\mathbf{N}_i, \tag{2}$$

where M_{ij} denotes the number of co-occurrences of i-th and j-th facial attributes and N_i denotes the occurrence times of i-th face attribute.

Since there are some uncommon co-occurrence relationships in the data, it may cause noise. We apply a threshold τ to filter the noisy conditional probabilities and obtain the robust matrix:

$$[\mathbf{A}]_{ij} = \begin{cases} 0 & if \ \mathbf{A}_{ij} < \tau \\ \mathbf{A}_{ij} & if \ \mathbf{A}_{ij} > \tau \end{cases}. \tag{3}$$

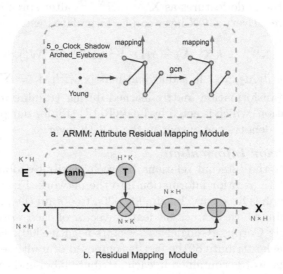

a. ARMM: Attribute Residual Mapping Module

b. Residual Mapping Module

Fig. 3. a) Attribute Residual Mapping Module (ARMM). GCN is utilized to capture the relationship between the prior information of attributes extracted from Google Corpus. Then the information are mapping into the image features through a residual mapping module. The attribute features in first layer are mapped into head features, and the second are mapped into tail features. b) The residual mapping module. 'T', '⊕', '⊗' denote matrix transpose, sum and multiplication operations respectively. 'L' and 'tanh' are activate function. X and E are transformer feature and GCN feature. The shape of each tensor is marked in gray annotation.

3) Residual Mapping Module

The module aims to map the prior information of the attributes into image features, which is processed from GCN mentioned above. So the network can apply the prior information to weighted related information for face attribute recognition. We use the module in the first and last layer of the network for shallow and deep guidance. As shown in Fig. 3 b, the details of the module are as follows:

$$y = \sigma(X\phi(E)^T) + X, \tag{4}$$

here $\mathbf{X} \in \mathbb{R}^{N \times H}$ is transformer feature from a middle layer, N is the patch number and H is the dimension of the hidden feature. $\mathbf{E} \in \mathbb{R}^{K \times H}$ indicates the hidden attribute embeddings of GCN. $\sigma(\cdot)$ denotes a non-linear activation operation, T is transpose operation and $\phi(\cdot)$ means a Tanh function. Finally, we use a residual connection to add the original $\mathbf{X}$.

3.2 MFM: Multi-scale Fusion Module

In the task of face attribute recognition, the information extracted form images is often inadequate, which brings big challenges. The existing methods have two potential issues that might limit face attribute recognition performance. First, CNN-based methods may focus on local regions, which might ignore the spatial relations, because attributes such as necklace and hair occupy irregular areas in image space, and sometimes pixels in these irregular areas may lack close spatial connections. Second, the features that recent methods use for face attribute recognition are only at a certain level. However, the scales of face attributes in images are different, such that hair takes up a lot of space and eyes occupy a very small area. Therefore, to enable the network to pay attention to global information and recognize attributes at different scales, we aim to use a transformer to capture long-distance relations in spatial and a multi-scale fusion module to process the features of different scales extracted from a transformer. Recently, transformer shines in the field of computer vision, because self-attention can capture the global relevant information in space in a parallel step. We apply Swin-Transformer [14] as a backbone to get features in a global way for face attribute recognition. Given an image $\mathbf{X} \in \mathbb{R}^{C \times H \times W}$, through the non-overlapped convolutional token encoder, we obtain patch tokens. Next, there are four Swin-Transformer blocks and each block contains multiple layers of multi-head self-attention mechanism. Then we obtained four image features of different scales, $\mathbf{X}_1 \in \mathbb{R}^{\frac{H \times W}{4 \times 4} \times C1}$, $\mathbf{X}_2 \in \mathbb{R}^{\frac{H \times W}{8 \times 8} \times C2}$, $\mathbf{X}_3 \in \mathbb{R}^{\frac{H \times W}{16 \times 16} \times C3}$, $\mathbf{X}_4 \in \mathbb{R}^{\frac{H \times W}{32 \times 32} \times C4}$, where the first dimension of the vector represents the number of patches and the second dimension of the vector represents different dimension of each patch. Additionally, $\mathbf{H}$ and $\mathbf{W}$ represent the height and weight of the features. As shown in Fig. 1, these features of different scales can focus on regions of different levels. The network can aggregate low-level detailed information and high-level semantic information by using these features at the same time. So the fused features used for face attribute recognition contain more sufficient information. For this purpose, we designed a multi-scale fusion module inspired by [26].

Firstly, we reshape the extracted features to $C1 \times \frac{H}{4} \times \frac{W}{4}, C2 \times \frac{H}{8} \times \frac{W}{8}, C3 \times \frac{H}{16} \times \frac{W}{16}, C4 \times \frac{H}{32} \times \frac{W}{32}$ respectively. Then in order that both local and global information can be exploited simultaneously, we use a convolution module to capture the short-range context after reshaping operation. To predict more suitable selection weights under the scenario of fusion in adjacent features. We introduce an adaptive attention module to let the network automatically select the area that needs attention in adjacent features. When obtaining an adaptive weight α, we use 1-α to select the previous level of information, and α to select the current level of information. Finally, adaptive pooling is applied to match the scale of the previous level to the current features. We define the adaptive attention α as:

$$\alpha = \mathbf{Attn}(\mathbf{X}^{l+1}), \tag{5}$$

where $\mathbf{X}^{l+1}$ is the feature of the l+1-th layer and $\mathbf{Attn}$ is adaptive attention. We define the hierarchical flow as:

$$\mathbf{H}^{l+1} = \mathbf{down}(\alpha \times \mathbf{Conv}(\mathbf{X}^{l+1}) + (1-\alpha) \times \mathbf{H}^l), \tag{6}$$

where $\mathbf{H}^{l+1}$ is the fused feature between the information in the l+1-th layer and the previous fused information, $\mathbf{down}$ is the adaptive pooling and $\mathbf{conv}$ is the convolution module to capture the short-range context.

4   Experiments

4.1   Dataset

The proposed method is evaluated on a largescale face attribute dataset. The CelebA [16] consists of 202,599 face images collected from 10,177 people. Each face includes 40 attribute labels. Following the standard protocol in [16], CelebA is partitioned into three non-overlapping parts: 160,000 images of first 8000 identities for training, 20,000 images of another 1000 identities for validation, and the rest for testing.

4.2   Evaluation Metrics

For fair comparison, we utilize accuracy as our criteria in our study to evaluate our performance.

4.3   Implementation Detail

Similar to [31], the number of convolution layers in our GCN is set to 2. The base model of Swin-Transformer [14] is used as the backbone. The hyper-parameters τ is set to 0.1. The input shape of images is reshaped to 224 × 224 with the data augmentations of randomly flip and color enhancement. We train our reasoning model using the Adam [11] algorithm. A pre-trained model of Swin is used and the initial learning rate is set to 10^{-4}, which is gradually reduced to 10^{-7} after 6 epochs. Our model is trained on the CelebA [16] dataset and gets converged with 10 epochs and it takes three hours with one NVIDIA RTX 3090.

4.4 Comparison to the State-of-the-Arts

Table 1 show accuracy evaluations on CelebA [16]. The proposed method shows the relatively better performance on the dataset measured by evaluation metric. *MOON* [22] only uses a deep regression model and gets an accuracy of 90.94%, which is a relatively low level. *MCNN-AUX* [6] branches out several forks corresponding to different attribute groups and achieves 91.26%. *Adaptive Weighted* [9] uses a validation loss which dynamically add learning weights to each attribute and achieves 91.80%. *Adaptive Sharing* [17] starts with a thin multi-layer network and dynamically widens it in a greedy manner during training and achieves 91.26%. *GAN and Dual-path* [8] complement face parsing map with real images and achieves 91.26%. *SSPL* [25] use a large pretrained model but only achieves 91.77%. *BLAN* [34] uses a bidirectional structure and a multiscale approach and achieves 91.80%. *HFE* [33] combine attribute and ID information and achieves 92.17%. The accuracy are mostly lower than 92%. However, none of these methods can solve multi-scale problems. Our method can dynamically fuse relevant information using multi-scale information, which is an improvement compared to the previous methods and achieves a higher accuracy of 92.47%.

Table 1. Comparison of mean accuracy on CelebA [16] dataset.

Method	CelebA [16]
MOON [22]	90.94
Adaptively Weighted [9]	91.80
MCNN-AUX [6]	91.26
Adaptive Sharing [17]	91.26
GAN and Dual-path [8]	91.81
Autoencoder [24]	90.14
Deep Multi-task [19]	91.70
HFE [33]	92.17
BLAN [34]	91.80
SSPL [25]	91.77
Ours	**92.47**

4.5 Ablution Study

Table 2 indicates the degree of contribution of each module in the whole network. In this experiment, the baseline is the pure Swin-Transformer [14]. With the multi-scale fusion module (MFM), the accuracy increase by about 0.26%. It can gradually combine low-level local features with high-level global features, which affect a lot on the final classification results. Then we map the prior information of attributes into image features to extract sufficient information about the related attributes and the module increase accuracy by 0.16%. When using these two sub-modules at the same time, the accuracy improves by 0.41%, which achieves the relatively best.

Table 2. Ablation study on CELEBA [16] dataset with our method and ResNet50 [7] backbone.

Method	Acc.	Method	Acc.
Baseline	92.06	ResNet50	91.90
+ MFM	92.32	+ MFM	92.15
+ ARMM	92.22	+ ARMM	92.00
+ MFM + ARMM	**92.47**	+ MFM + ARMM	**92.23**

In order to demonstrate the superiority of Swin-Transformer [14] over ResNet50 [7] and show the effectiveness of our method. We also take the ResNet50 [7] as the backbone to experiment. Table 2 shows the effect of the same module on ResNet50 [7]. The multi-scale module and the prior information of attributes improve the accuracy by 0.25% and 0.10% respectively and it also achieves the relatively best when using both the two modules at the same time. Based on the two results with different backbones, we find that Swin-transformer can learn the relevance of spatial features, that is, the global relationship between features.

In Table 3, we can find that our adaptive attention method is more effective than directly concatenating or weighed summing the features. Then with the adaptive attention method, the network can focus on the related features between adjacent layers, which can recognize attributes at different scales. However, the methods of directly concatenating or weighed summing are the static method, which may fuse unnecessary information.

Table 3. Comparison experiment between adaptive attention method, concat method and weighted sum method.

Method	Acc.
Weighted sum	92.28
Concat directly	92.32
Adaptive attention	**92.47**

4.6   Qualitative Evaluation

As shown in Fig. 4, we discover that ResNet50 [7] can only pay attention to a whole local area, which produces a certain offset. And our method can make the network focus on some characteristic areas and the details are better detected.

Table 4. Classification accuracy (%) of Ours (92.47%), BLAN (91.81%) [34] and MCNN-AUX (91.26%) [6] on CelebA [16] over 40 facial attributes.

Attributes ours	Ours	BLAN	MCNN-AUX	Attributes	Ours	BLAN	MCNN-AUX
5 o'clock Shadow	**95.19**	95.18	94.51	Male	**99.13**	98.32	98.17
Arched Eyebrows	**87.71**	84.74	83.42	Mouth Slightly Open	**94.47**	94.22	93.74
Attractive	82.63	**83.25**	83.06	Mustache	**97.04**	96.99	96.88
Bags Under Eyes	**86.15**	86.11	84.92	Narrow Eyes	**94.00**	87.78	87.23
Bald	**99.06**	99.02	98.90	No Beard	**96.64**	96.46	96.05
Bangs	**96.35**	96.26	96.05	Oval Face	**77.59**	76.86	75.54
Big Lips	**83.31**	72.59	71.47	Pale Skin	96.65	**97.25**	97.05
Big Nose	**85.30**	85.21	84.53	Pointy Nose	**78.38**	78.02	77.47
Black Hair	**91.91**	90.49	89.78	Receding Hairline	**95.11**	93.99	93.81
Blond Hair	95.65	**96.27**	96.01	Rosy Cheeks	**95.41**	95.36	95.16
Blurry	**96.82**	96.37	96.17	Sideburns	97.56	**98.04**	97.85
Brown Hair	85.92	**89.79**	89.15	Smiling	**94.00**	93.19	92.73
Bushy Eyebrows	**93.11**	93.08	92.84	Straight Hair	**85.85**	84.65	83.58
Chubby	**95.99**	95.88	95.67	Wavy Hair	**87.37**	85.35	83.91
Young	**89.09**	89.06	88.48	Necktie	**97.33**	97.20	96.51
Necklace	**89.78**	88.16	86.63	Lipstick	**94.40**	94.34	94.11
Hat	**99.17**	99.15	99.05	High Cheekbones	**89.36**	88.13	87.58
Heavy Makeup	**92.96**	92.04	91.55	Gray Hair	98.07	**98.35**	98.20
Goatee	97.06	**97.69**	97.24	Eyeglasses	**99.63**	99.63	99.63
Earrings	**91.38**	90.93	90.43	Double Chin	**96.82**	96.58	96.32

Additionally, our method pays more attention to the face area and may not be affected too much by the background part. These clearly demonstrate the effectiveness of the proposed solution.

As shown in Fig. 5, it can be seen from the figure that attributes about *Male, Mouth_Slightly_Open, No_Beard, Smiling,* and *young* have strong connections with other attributes. And these attributes in turn correspond to the sequence numbers 20, 21, 24, 31 and 39 in the figure. For example, at row 21 and column 31, the dark blue shows a strong connection between *Smiling* and *Mouth_Slightly_Open.*

4.7 Quantitative Evaluation

Table 4 reports the accuracy of each attribute in CelebA [16]. We take three levels of models to make predictions, which are MCNN-AUX 91.26% [6], ours 92.47% and BLAN 91.81% [34], because the accuracy of each attribute is not reported in most previous methods. At the accuracy of attributes *Arched Eyebrow, Big*

ResNet50

Ours

Fig. 4. We use Grad-Cam [23] to show the area network pay attention. The parts with warm colors represent where the network pays attention. The second and the third line show the results on the input images with ResNet50 [7] and our framework respectively.

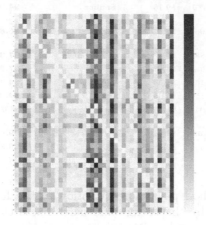

Fig. 5. The visualization of the prior relationship between attributes. The duck blue means the strong relation and the light blue means the weak relation. The serial number represents the corresponding attribute. Since the same attribute does not appear twice in labels of a picture, the diagonal line is not highlighted. (Color figure online)

Nose, High Cheekbone, Narrow Eye, Earring and *Necklac*, ours has an advantage of more than 2%. Facts have proved that our method can have good results in recognizing some small attributes. And ours still maintain good accuracy in attributes with large scale. Compared to BLAN [34], the accuracy of the attribute *Big lips* is improved by about 11%. On the other hands, by performing multi-scale fusion reasoning, the proposed method has recognized more detailed attributes while making fewer mistakes and the accuracy of other attributes does not fluctuate greatly.

5   Conclusion

In this paper, we propose a prior-guided multi-scale fusion transformer for face attribute recognition to capture long-distance relations of features in spatial in an end-to-end manner. We also introduce a learnable weight to perform effective soft selection of adjacent features and apply a hierarchical approach to fuse them, which can get enough information to predict attributes at different scales. Additionally, we introduce prior information of attributes into feature learning, which can make the network focus on correlations between attributes. Extensive experimental results on a real dataset demonstrate the effectiveness and the generalization ability of our method in dealing with face attribute recognition.

References

1. Cao, J., Li, Y., Zhang, Z.: Partially shared multi-task convolutional neural network with local constraint for face attribute learning. In: Proceedings of the IEEE Conference on Computer Vision and Pattern Recognition, pp. 4290–4299 (2018)
2. Chen, B.C., Chen, Y.Y., Kuo, Y.H., Hsu, W.H.: Scalable face image retrieval using attribute-enhanced sparse codewords. IEEE Trans. Multimedia **15**(5), 1163–1173 (2013). https://doi.org/10.1109/TMM.2013.2242460
3. Chen, Z.M., Wei, X.S., Wang, P., Guo, Y.: Multi-label image recognition with graph convolutional networks. In: Proceedings of the IEEE/CVF Conference on Computer Vision and Pattern Recognition, pp. 5177–5186 (2019)
4. Dong, X., et al.: Cswin transformer: a general vision transformer backbone with cross-shaped windows. arXiv preprint arXiv:2107.00652 (2021)
5. Dosovitskiy, A., et al.: An image is worth 16x16 words: transformers for image recognition at scale. arXiv preprint arXiv:2010.11929 (2020)
6. Hand, E.M., Chellappa, R.: Attributes for improved attributes: a multi-task network utilizing implicit and explicit relationships for facial attribute classification. In: Thirty-First AAAI Conference on Artificial Intelligence (2017)
7. He, K., Zhang, X., Ren, S., Sun, J.: Deep residual learning for image recognition. In: Proceedings of the IEEE Conference on Computer Vision and Pattern Recognition, pp. 770–778 (2016)
8. He, K., et al.: Harnessing synthesized abstraction images to improve facial attribute recognition. In: IJCAI, pp. 733–740 (2018)
9. He, K., Wang, Z., Fu, Y., Feng, R., Jiang, Y.G., Xue, X.: Adaptively weighted multi-task deep network for person attribute classification. In: Proceedings of the 25th ACM International Conference on Multimedia, pp. 1636–1644 (2017)
10. Kalayeh, M.M., Gong, B., Shah, M.: Improving facial attribute prediction using semantic segmentation. In: 2017 IEEE Conference on Computer Vision and Pattern Recognition (CVPR) (2017)
11. Kingma, D.P., Ba, J.: Adam: a method for stochastic optimization. arXiv preprint arXiv:1412.6980 (2014)
12. Kipf, T.N., Welling, M.: Semi-supervised classification with graph convolutional networks. arXiv preprint arXiv:1609.02907 (2016)

13. Le, Q., Mikolov, T.: Distributed representations of sentences and documents. In: International Conference on Machine Learning, pp. 1188–1196. PMLR (2014)
14. Liu, Z., et al.: Swin transformer: hierarchical vision transformer using shifted windows. arXiv preprint arXiv:2103.14030 (2021)
15. Liu, Z., Luo, P., Wang, X., Tang, X.: Deep learning face attributes in the wild. In: Proceedings of the IEEE International Conference on Computer Vision (ICCV), December 2015
16. Liu, Z., Luo, P., Wang, X., Tang, X.: Deep learning face attributes in the wild. In: Proceedings of International Conference on Computer Vision (ICCV) (2015)
17. Lu, Y., Kumar, A., Zhai, S., Cheng, Y., Javidi, T., Feris, R.: Fully-adaptive feature sharing in multi-task networks with applications in person attribute classification. In: Proceedings of the IEEE Conference on Computer Vision and Pattern Recognition, pp. 5334–5343 (2017)
18. Maas, A.L., Hannun, A.Y., Ng, A.Y.: Rectifier nonlinearities improve neural network acoustic models. In: Proceedings of ICML (2013)
19. Mao, L., Yan, Y., Xue, J.H., Wang, H.: Deep multi-task multi-label CNN for effective facial attribute classification. IEEE Trans. Affect. Comput. (2020)
20. Mikolov, T., Chen, K., Corrado, G., Dean, J.: Efficient estimation of word representations in vector space. arXiv preprint arXiv:1301.3781 (2013)
21. Nian, F., Chen, X., Yang, S., Lv, G.: Facial attribute recognition with feature decoupling and graph convolutional networks. IEEE Access 7, 85500–85512 (2019)
22. Rudd, E.M., Günther, M., Boult, T.E.: MOON: a mixed objective optimization network for the recognition of facial attributes. In: Leibe, B., Matas, J., Sebe, N., Welling, M. (eds.) ECCV 2016. LNCS, vol. 9909, pp. 19–35. Springer, Cham (2016). https://doi.org/10.1007/978-3-319-46454-1_2
23. Selvaraju, R.R., Cogswell, M., Das, A., Vedantam, R., Parikh, D., Batra, D.: Grad-cam: visual explanations from deep networks via gradient-based localization. In: Proceedings of the IEEE International Conference on Computer Vision, pp. 618–626 (2017)
24. Sethi, A., Singh, M., Singh, R., Vatsa, M.: Residual Codean autoencoder for facial attribute analysis. Pattern Recogn. Lett. 119, 157–165 (2019)
25. Shu, Y., Yan, Y., Chen, S., Xue, J.H., Shen, C., Wang, H.: Learning spatial-semantic relationship for facial attribute recognition with limited labeled data. In: Proceedings of the IEEE/CVF Conference on Computer Vision and Pattern Recognition, pp. 11916–11925 (2021)
26. Tao, A., Sapra, K., Catanzaro, B.: Hierarchical multi-scale attention for semantic segmentation. arXiv preprint arXiv:2005.10821 (2020)
27. Vaswani, A., et al.: Attention is all you need. In: Advances in Neural Information Processing Systems, pp. 5998–6008 (2017)
28. Wang, W., et al.: Pvtv 2: improved baselines with pyramid vision transformer. arXiv preprint arXiv:2106.13797 (2021)
29. Wang, X., Ye, Y., Gupta, A.: Zero-shot recognition via semantic embeddings and knowledge graphs. In: Proceedings of the IEEE Conference on Computer Vision and Pattern Recognition, pp. 6857–6866 (2018)
30. Wang, Y., et al.: Multi-label classification with label graph superimposing. In: Proceedings of the AAAI Conference on Artificial Intelligence, vol. 34, pp. 12265–12272 (2020)
31. Wang, Z., He, K., Fu, Y., Feng, R., Jiang, Y.G., Xue, X.: Multi-task deep neural network for joint face recognition and facial attribute prediction. In: Proceedings of the 2017 ACM on International Conference on Multimedia Retrieval. pp. 365–374 (2017)

32. Wu, L., Sun, P., Hong, R., Fu, Y., Wang, X., Wang, M.: SocialGCN: an efficient graph convolutional network based model for social recommendation. arXiv preprint arXiv:1811.02815 (2018)
33. Yang, J., et al.: Hierarchical feature embedding for attribute recognition. In: Proceedings of the IEEE/CVF Conference on Computer Vision and Pattern Recognition, pp. 13055–13064 (2020)
34. Zheng, X., Huang, H., Guo, Y., Wang, B., He, R.: Blan: bi-directional ladder attentive network for facial attribute prediction. Pattern Recogn. **100**, 107155 (2020)
35. Zhong, Y., Sullivan, J., Li, H.: Leveraging mid-level deep representations for predicting face attributes in the wild. In: 2016 IEEE International Conference on Image Processing (ICIP), pp. 3239–3243. IEEE (2016)
36. Zhu, Z., et al.: Mucko: multi-layer cross-modal knowledge reasoning for fact-based visual question answering. arXiv preprint arXiv:2006.09073 (2020)

KITPose: Keypoint-Interactive Transformer for Animal Pose Estimation

Jiyong Rao[1], Tianyang Xu[1(✉)], Xiaoning Song[1(✉)], Zhen-Hua Feng[2],
and Xiao-Jun Wu[1]

[1] School of Artificial Intelligence and Computer Science, Jiangnan University, Wuxi,
China
{tianyang.xu,x.song}@jiangnan.edu.cn
[2] Department of Computer Science, University of Surrey, Guildford GU2 7XH, UK

Abstract. Animal pose estimation has received increasing attention in
recent years. The main challenge for this task is the diversity of animal species compared to their human counterpart. To address this issue,
we design a keypoint-interactive Transformer model for high-resolution
animal pose estimation, namely KITPose. Since a high-resolution network maintains local perception and the self-attention module in Transformer is an expert in connecting long-range dependencies, we equip
the high-resolution network with a Transformer to enhance the model
capacity, achieving keypoints interaction in the decision stage. Besides,
to smoothly fit the pose estimation task, we simultaneously train the
model parameters and joint weights, which can automatically adjust the
loss weight for each specific keypoint. The experimental results obtained
on the AP10K and ATRW datasets demonstrate the merits of KITPose,
as well as its superior performance over the state-of-the-art approaches.

Keywords: Animal pose estimation · Transformer · Self attention

1 Introduction

Pose estimation is a fundamental task in computer vision. It aims at localising
a set of predefined keypoints for a given deformable object. Most of the existing
studies focus on human pose estimation [9–13,18–20], gaining promising results.
While animal pose estimation has also gradually attracted wide attention [2,24–
29,34], exhibiting an essential role in both research and practical applications,
including biology, zoology, and animal conservation. Despite the significance, the
study of animal pose estimation is still under-explored and under-represented as
compared with human pose estimation. Therefore, this paper focuses on single-
animal pose estimation, which is the base for multi-animal pose estimation [3,5],
animal behaviour analysis [3–5], etc.

In general, deep Convolutional Neural Networks (CNNs) [8–15] have been
prevailing on pose estimation during the past decade, with the powerful capacity in feature representation and semantic correspondence. In terms of task
formulation, *heatmap regression* [8,10,12,13,15,18,19,36,37] has become the

S. Yu et al. (Eds.): PRCV 2022, LNCS 13534, pp. 660–673, 2022.
https://doi.org/10.1007/978-3-031-18907-4_51

mainstream to represent the location distribution of keypoints. Therefore, most existing models prefer employing Fully Convolutional Networks (FCN) to maintain 2D feature maps. In particular, Sun *et al.*. [13] proposed to maintain high-resolution representations through multi-layer interaction, coined HRNet. HRNet calculates the high-resolution sub-network in parallel with lower resolution sub-networks. Multiple sub-networks are fused through the fusion modules such that each of the high-to-low resolution representations receives complementary information from other parallel representations collaboratively, obtaining comprehensive high-resolution representations. Benefiting from the powerful and discriminative representation, HRNet achieves outstanding performance in human pose estimation, segmentation, and pose tracking. However, fully convolutional architecture directly input pixel array to extract appearance information of images, *without involving structural information* in the context of joint parts.

Since Transformer [32] has become the de-facto status quo in Natural Language Processing (NLP) [22], there has recently been a rise interest in introducing Transformer and its variants [21,23,33,40] to the computer vision community. In principle, the self-attention [32] layer directly embeds regional information across the whole image, expanding the model capacity of gaining context information from the involved input tokens. For instance, Vision Transformer (ViT) [23] represents an input image as a series of visual tokens, with position embeddings being added to indicate their original spatial locations. To guarantee consistent mapping, multiple self-attention layers are stacked to encode each token, enabling global perception via token-wise interactions.

Although previous approaches [2,24,25,28,29] have achieved satisfying performance in animal pose estimation on specific species, they still suffer from limited generalisation in terms of unseen animal species. To this end, it is demanding to develop advanced algorithms for robust general animal pose estimation to facilitate wild animal behaviour studies. General animal pose estimation is more challenging due to the following factors:

- Compared to human pose estimation and single-specie animal pose estimation, it is more difficult to estimate a complex pose of animals belonging to different species. The generalisation of the keypoint estimator against a wide range of variations on poses is also challenged.
- In practice, the true distribution of wild animals exhibits a *long-tail distribution*, due to the commonness and rarity of the animals. The long-tail distribution makes multi-species animal pose estimation an unbalanced visual analysis task.

Motivated by the above analysis, we attempt to address these issues by integrating Self-Attention (SA) [32] with high-resolution networks [13,14] for *general mammal pose estimation*. In this paper, we propose a high resolution-based Keypoints-Interactive Transformer for animal Pose estimation (KITPose). Specifically, KITPose consists of two parts: the backbone high-resolution network and a dedicated keypoints-interactive transformer. Intuitively, the transformer module induces the input keypoints to interact with each other, emphasising the potential supportive structure among different keypoints. However, unlike ViT, we take the feature slice as an input token instead of splitting an input image into a series of image patches. In the decision stage of the network, the model outputs the final predicted keypoint heatmaps.

The main contributions are summarised as follows:

- By achieving interaction among different keypoints, we design a novel network architecture, KITPose, for animal pose estimation. The heatmaps are interacted to deliver the final estimation, with all the keypoints supporting each other.
- Adaptive keypoint weights are obtained in our design. We use a keypoint-weighted L2 loss to alleviate the imbalance among keypoints. It enables automatic focus on dominant keypoints with advantageous influence for pose estimation.
- The experimental results obtained on AP10K and ATRW demonstrate that KITPose achieves promising performance against the existing approaches. Specifically, we improve the state-of-the-art animal pose estimation method HRNet by 1.6% AP on AP10K and 0.3% AP on ATRW.

2   Related Work

2.1   Human Pose Estimation

Human pose estimation is a popular computer vision task that identifies and classifies specific physical joints in the human body. Most of existing human pose estimation approaches can be categorised as top-down methods [8,10–14,18,19] and bottom-up ones [9,15,31,36–38]. The top-down paradigm can always achieve better performance, while the bottom-up approaches are more efficient. During the rise of deep neural networks, the estimation performance has been drastically boosted. In particular, heatmap-based regression [8,10,12,13,15,18,19,36,37] formulation tends to further improve the capacity by stacking more deep layers. For instance, stacked Hourglass [10] employs successive steps of pooling and upsampling symmetric architecture to push the multi-layer fusion. Simple-Baseline [12], similarly, replaces the upsampling layers by using deconvolution operation, achieving impressive accuracy. Admitted to the multi-scale perception obtained by upsampling and deconvolution, detailed appearance information cannot be guaranteed during the operation. Therefore, Sun et al. [13] propose a representative network, HRNet, which maintains high-resolution representations across the entire forward layers. Multi-resolution subnetworks are concatenated in parallel to capture the spatial relationships among joints.

Besides CNNs, the transformer has also been studied in recent human pose estimation research. For example, PRTR [17] is a coordinate-regression-based pose estimation method using cascaded Transformers to refine keypoints detection across different self-attention layers. However, PRTR obtains relatively lower accuracy than the state-of-the-art CNN approaches. To further improve the performance, TransPose [18] based on heatmap-regression, utilises attention layers built in Transformer to reveal the long-range dependencies of the predicted keypoints. Similarly, TokenPose [19] uses additional tokens to represent keypoint entities, simultaneously refining appearance information and constraining relationships from images. To alleviate the memory and computation cost, HRFormer [20] learns high-resolution representations along with the local-window self-attention module.

2.2 Animal Pose Estimation

Animal pose estimation has recently attracted increasing attention in the research community. Intuitively, some typical human pose estimation methods can be directly applied to animals. Previous studies in animal pose estimation mainly focus on specific species, *e.g.*, horse [24], zebra [25], macaque [28], fly [29], and tiger [2]. The Animal Pose Dataset [26], which contains 5 animal species, ignores the diversity of postures, textures and habitats, limiting its generalisation ability. For a fair evaluation, AP10K [1], as the first large benchmark for general mammal animal pose estimation, consists of 10,015 images, which are filtered from 23 animal families and 54 species following the high-quality COCO [6] annotation style. AP10K is proposed to facilitate further research in animal pose estimation by reusing common training and testing tools. In this paper, we propose to design a novel method by using AP10K for general mammal pose estimation. To follow the COCO annotation style, we also evaluate our method on another benchmark, ATRW [2], which contains over 8,000 video clips from endangered Amur tigers.

In addition, there are also several domain adaptation works [26,27,34] focusing on animal pose estimation. Due to limited labelled data, Mu et al. [34] use synthetic animal data generated from CAD models to train their model, which is then used to generate pseudo labels for the unlabelled real animal images. Cao et al. [26] propose a cross-domain adaptation scheme to learn pose similarities between humans and animals. Li and Lee [27] propose an unsupervised method that performs synthetic to real domain adaptation, and an online coarse-to-fine pseudo label updating strategy to alleviate the negative effect of pseudo labels.

3   The Proposed Method

The overall architecture of the proposed KITPose method is shown in Fig. 1. In the feature extraction stage, we employ the heatmap-based fully convolutional network as the feature extractor for animal pose estimation. Then the obtained output features are flattened to keypoint tokens, which are the inputs of the designed Transformer encoder. In KITPose, the Transformer is used in conjunction with HRNet. However, the volume of the animal pose estimation datasets is much smaller compared to the human counterparts [6,7]. Therefore, it is essential to promote the accuracy while avoiding the overfitting issue. To this end, we pretrain HRNet as the backbone on the AP10K dataset to extract keypoints. Then it is further finetuned accompanied by the Transformer to refine the keypoints via keypoints interaction.

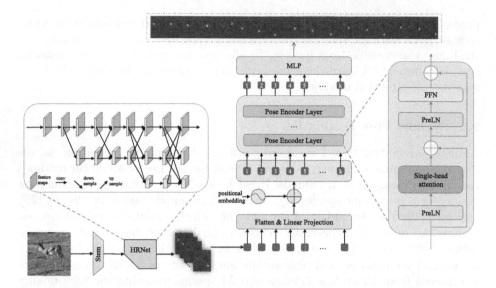

Fig. 1. The overall architecture of the proposed KITPose method. The feature maps are extracted by the HRNet backbone. The Transformer layers are adopted to achieve keypoints interaction for heatmap refinement. [32]

3.1 FCN-Based Feature Extraction

Recently, heatmap-based fully convolutional neural networks [8,10,12,13,15,18, 19,36,37] have become a standard solution for pose estimation due to its high performance. In this paradigm, HRNet [13,14] yields multi-resolution image feature maps. It uses the high-resolution branch with a 1×1 convolutional layer to yield K heatmaps of size $\hat{H} \times \hat{W}$.

The underlying reason for the high performance of a heatmap-based FCN is that the 2D structure of feature maps is maintained through the entire network forwarding pass. Despite the promising performance obtained by FCNs in the research of pose estimation, the structural relationship among keypoints is underestimated. We argue the necessity of exploring the complementarily supportive feature among keypoints via conducting multi-layer interaction.

3.2 Keypoint-Interactive Transformer

Input Keypoint Tokens. Instead of splitting the raw image $I \in \mathbb{R}^{H \times W \times C}$ into a sequence of flattened 2D patches $I_p \in \mathbb{R}^{N \times (P_h \cdot P_w \cdot C)}$, where (P_h, P_w) is the resolution of each patch, and $N = \frac{H}{P_h} \cdot \frac{W}{P_w}$ is the number of tokens, we consider the channel-wise feature maps obtained by HRNet as the input of the Transformer without any spatial splitting. In other words, we directly reshape the feature maps $x_f \in \mathbb{R}^{K \times \hat{H} \times \hat{W}}$ to a sequence of tokens $x \in \mathbb{R}^{K \times (\hat{H} \cdot \hat{W})}$, where K stands for the numbers of keypoints. Considering animal pose estimation is a location-sensitive task, 1D position embedding pe_i is added to every specific input token to represent a specific order of feature maps in the channel dimension. Therefore, we explicitly model each specific keypoint as a token.

Keypoint Interaction of Self Attention. Self-Attention (SA) [32] is the key component of Transformer that computes the global relationships among involved tokens, aggregating the relevant information while suppressing the irrelevant clues. In our design, we aim to emphasise the interaction among all the keypoints, which are tokenised from the slices of a feature map. Therefore, different from the classical multi-head module, we apply single-head attention to the Transformer layer for full interaction among keypoints. In general, for a sequence of keypoints' features $X = \{x_1, x_2, \cdots, x_K\}$, SA first performs linear mappings to adjust the feature space for the input tokens. In other words, the input feature X is projected to query (Q), key (K), and value (V), respectively. To alleviate the impact of intrinsic structural offsets, we set the bias in the three linear transformation layers to False. The linear transformation can be formulated as follow:

$$q_i = W_q x_i, \quad k_i = W_k x_i, \quad v_i = W_v x_i, \tag{1}$$

where $W_q, W_k, W_v \in \mathbb{R}^{d \times d}$ are three weight matrices for Q, K, V, and d is the embedding size of Transformer. The attention map (A) stands for the degree of keypoints attend to each other, which is computed by the scaled dot-product operation followed by softmax:

$$A[i, :] = \text{Softmax}_j\left(\frac{q_i k_j^T}{\sqrt{d}}\right). \tag{2}$$

The obtained attention map is formed by a 2D matrix ($A \in \mathbb{R}^{K \times K}$), where each row is a probability vector. Each element of the attention map represents how much the i-th keypoint is relevant to the j-th keypoint. The attention is a weighted sum of V using the attention map as weight. Then the output $O = \{o_1, o_2, \cdots, o_K\}$ is computed by applying the linear projection ($W_o \in \mathbb{R}^{d \times d}$) to the single attention head:

$$y_i = \sum_j^K A[i, j] v_j, \quad o_i = W_o y_i \tag{3}$$

In Fig. 2, we visualise an example attention map. The finding on keypoint-to-keypoint interactions is supported by the keypoint attention relationship. Specifically, the (i, j)-th element of an attention map indicates how much the attention weight is associated between the i-th and j-th keypoints. Layer# 1 in Fig. 2a is characterised by symmetric patterns. This demonstrates that the single keypoint interaction head generates a diagonal attention map, reflecting that its attention is mainly assigned to the surrounding neighbours. On the other hand, Layer# 2 in Fig. 2b focuses on individual keypoint, represented as vertical lines in the attention map. In this case, the attention weight highly depends on some specific keypoints of key K, demonstrating the structural relationship among keypoints. Interestingly, we experimentally find that some specific keypoints stay dominant in our animal pose estimation tests (as discussed in Sect. 4).

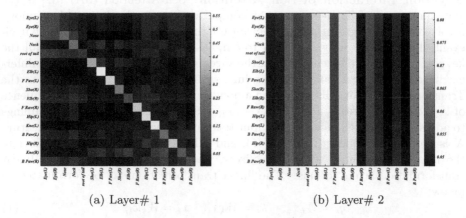

(a) Layer# 1   (b) Layer# 2

Fig. 2. Visualisation of the KITPose-2SA attention weights.

3.3   Trainable Joint Weights

Besides performing interaction among keypoints, it is also essential to consider the diverse importance of each specific joint (keypoint). Intuitively, keypoints at different body parts are semantically discriminative, and present varying contributions to pose estimation. But existing studies directly set different fixed joint weights for different datasets, such as COCO [6] and MPII [7].

Interestingly, no specific research has delved into the effect of these joint weights on pose estimation. Existing predefined weights lack intuition and interpretation in design. To this end, we present a flexible method for trainable joint weights during heatmap regression, achieving more accurate animal pose estimation performance.

A straightforward way is to define a trainable weight vector W in the original MSE Loss:

$$\mathcal{L}_{regression} = \sum_{i}^{K} W_i \parallel P_i - W_i \parallel_2^2 . \tag{4}$$

In addition, prior distribution needs to be added to regularise the trainable joint weights. We add a L2 regulariser loss:

$$\mathcal{L}_{regulariser} = \sum_{i}^{K} \parallel W_i - 1 \parallel_2^2 . \tag{5}$$

Table 1. A comparison on the AP10K validation set. Pretrain=Y indicates pre-training the backbone on the ImageNet classification task. Pretrain=$Y^\dagger$ means pre-training the CNN backbone and finetuning with the Transformer on AP10K. 2SA and 4SA denote 2 layers and 4 layers self-attention Transformers.

Method	Pretrain	Input size	#Params	GFLOPS	AP	AP^{50}	AP^{75}	AP^M	AP^L	AR
SimpleBaseline-Res50 [12]	Y	256×256	34.0M	11.99	56.8	88.0	56.0	47.3	57.1	62.0
SimpleBaseline-Res50 [12]	Y	384×384	34.0M	26.97	70.7	93.8	76.2	48.9	71.1	74.0
SimpleBaseline-Res101 [12]	Y	256×256	53.0M	16.50	70.6	94.1	76.6	54.4	71.0	73.9
SimpleBaseline-Res101 [12]	Y	384×384	53.0M	37.13	71.7	94.7	77.4	47.2	72.3	75.1
HRNet-32 [13]	N	256×256	28.54M	9.49	69.6	93.6	75.1	57.1	69.9	73.1
HRNet-32 [13]	Y	256×256	28.54M	9.49	73.8	95.8	80.3	52.3	74.2	76.9
HRNet-32 [13]	Y	384×384	28.54M	21.36	74.7	95.8	81.8	54.4	75.2	78.4
HRNet-48 [13]	Y	256×256	63.60M	19.49	74.9	96.2	81.7	56.1	75.2	78.6
HRNet-48 [13]	Y	384×384	63.60M	43.84	75.6	96.5	82.6	58.7	76.0	79.3
KITPose-2SA	$Y^\dagger$	256×256	57.91M	9.50	75.2	95.9	81.6	60.2	75.5	78.5
KITPose-2SA	$Y^\dagger$	384×384	68.41M	21.37	75.4	96.4	82.2	57.6	75.8	78.4
KITPose-4SA	$Y^\dagger$	256×256	78.90M	9.50	75.8	96.1	81.8	58.7	76.1	78.8
KITPose-4SA	$Y^\dagger$	384×384	89.40M	21.37	**76.6**	96.5	**83.5**	**61.6**	**77.0**	**79.5**

Then, the total loss can be written as:

$$\mathcal{L}_{total} = \mathcal{L}_{regression} + \lambda \mathcal{L}_{regulariser}, \qquad (6)$$

where λ is a balancing parameter. We set $\lambda = 0.01$ in this paper.

The experimental analysis in Sect. 4.3 shows that transforming joint weights to be trainable improves the performance of animal pose estimation. Serving as an efficient plug-in component for KITPose. The trainable joint weights can further advance the improvement of keypoints interaction, which enhances the significance of dominant keypoints.

4   Evaluation

4.1   AP10K Pose Estimation

Dataset. AP10K [1] is the first large-scale benchmark for mammal animal pose estimation, which contains 10,015 images and 13,028 instances of 54 species. The AP10K dataset is split into three disjoint subsets, *i.e.*, training, validation and test sets, with 70%, 10%, and 20% per animal species, respectively. Our models are trained on the training set and evaluated on the validation set.

Evaluation Metric. We use the standard COCO keypoint evaluation metric based on *Object Keypoint Similarity* (OKS), which is formulated as:

$$\text{OKS} = \frac{\sum_i \exp(-d_i^2/2s^2k_i^2)\delta(v_i > 0)}{\sum_i \delta(v_i > 0)}, \qquad (7)$$

where d_i is the Euclidean distance between the i-th detected keypoint coordinate and its corresponding ground-truth, v_i is the visibility flag of the ground-truth,

s is the animal scale, and k_i is a keypoint-specific constant that controls falloff. We use *average precision* (AP) and *average recall* (AR), including AP^{50} $(AP$ at OKS = 0.5), AP^{75}, AP (mean of AP from OKS = 0.5 to OKS = 0.95 with the increment as 0.05), AP^M $(AP$ for medium size animals), and AP^L $(AP$ for large size animals), to measure the performance.

Baseline Settings. For HRNet and SimpleBaseline, we follow the default training and evaluation settings of mmpose [16], and change the learning rate to 1e-3.

Training. In this paper, we extend the animal bounding box to a fixed aspect ratio: $height : weidth = 1 : 1$, and then crop the box from the image, which is resized to a fixed size, 256×256 or 384×384. The data augmentation methods include random rotation $([-40°, 40°])$, random scale $([0.5, 1.5])$ and horizontal flipping. Besides, half-body transformation is also applied for data augmentation.

The models are trained with the Adam [30] optimiser, and the initial learning rates of the backbone, Transformer, and joint weights are set to 1e-4, 5e-4, and 1e-2. Then we decay the learning rates of the backbone and Transformer by 0.1 at the 170th and 200th epochs. The learning rate of joint weights stays invariable at 1e-2. The entire training process requires 210 epochs. All the models are implemented in PyTorch and trained on a single NVIDIA RTX 3080Ti GPU.

Testing. Following the fancy design, the coordinate decoding method [35] is used to alleviate the quantisation error. The flip test, which averages the heatmaps of the original and flipped images is also used in all the experiments.

Comparison with the State-of-the-Art Methods. We report the performance of our design and other state-of-the-art methods in Table 1. The proposed KITPose-2SA method, trained based on HRNet-32 with the input size 256×256, achieves a 75.4 AP score, outperforming other methods with the same input size, and even higher (+0.5 AP) than HRNet-32 with the input size of 384×384.

Compared to SimpleBaseline which uses ResNet-50 as the backbone, our KITPose-2SA improves AP significantly by 18.6 points. Compared to Simple-Baseline which uses ResNet-101 as backbone, KITPose-2SA improves AP by 4.8, while the number of model parameters is similar with much lower computation ($\downarrow$ 42.5%). Compared to the previous best-performed HRNet, our network achieves better performance: 1.6 gain in AP for the backbone HRNet-32, and 0.5 gain in AP for the backbone HRNet-48, whose model size is slightly larger and GFLOPs are more than twice as many as ours.

With input size 384×384, our KITPose-2SA and KITPose-4SA based on HRNet-32, obtain 75.4 and 76.6 in AP, which have 0.2 and 0.8 improvements as compared to our models with 256×256 inputs. In comparison to the state-of-the-art method HRNet-48, our KITPose-4SA achieves a 1.0 gain in terms of AP with only 48.7% computational cost.

4.2 ATRW Keypoint Detection

Dataset and Evaluation Metric. The ATRW [2] dataset contains images from over 8,000 large-scale Amur tiger video clips of 92 individuals in the wild,

Table 2. Results obtained on the ATRW validation set.

Method	Pretrain	Input size	AP	AR
OpenPose [9]	Y	256×256	-	-
AlphaPose [11]	Y	256×256	57.4	67.1
SimpleBaseline-Res50 [12]	Y	256×256	90.0	92.9
SimpleBaseline-Res101 [12]	Y	256×256	89.8	92.7
HRNet-32 [13]	Y	256×256	91.2	93.8
HRNet-48 [13]	Y	256×256	91.1	93.7
KITPose-2SA	$Y^{\dagger}$	256×256	**91.5**	94.0
KITPose-4SA	$Y^{\dagger}$	256×256	91.4	**94.1**

with bounding box and keypoint annotations. There are 4k tiger samples with 15 joint labels in the ATRW dataset. In addition, the data augmentation and the evaluation metric are the same as that of the AP10K dataset.

Results on the Validation Set. We follow the testing process which is the same as that on the AP10K dataset. Table 2 reports the results. Our KITPose-2SA and KITPose-4SA models achieve 91.5 and 91.4 in terms of AP, and 94.0 and 94.1 in terms of AR, respectively. All the experiments are conducted with the input image size of 256×256. It demonstrates that KITPose achieves better performance in terms of generalisation capability while pretraining the backbone network on AP10K. The backbone network trained on a relatively larger with more diverse animal species can extract more general image features for the task.

Fig. 3. Qualitative comparison results of some example images on AP10K. The first row shows the results predicted by HRNet-32, and the second row shows the results predicted by our method.

Table 3. Ablation study on trainable joint weights. The results are reported on the AP10K validation set with 256 × 256 inputs.

Method	Input size	Trainable	AP	AP^M	AP^L
HRNet-32 [13]	256 × 256	✗	73.8	52.3	74.2
HRNet-32 [13]	256 × 256	✓	74.6	58.8	75.0
HRNet-48 [13]	256 × 256	✗	74.9	56.1	75.2
HRNet-48 [13]	256 × 256	✓	75.8	60.4	76.1

4.3 Ablation Study

Trainable Joints Weight. We design comparative experiments to validate the improvement brought by adjusting joint weights dynamically. We use HRNet-32/48 as the baseline models with the fixed input size of 256 × 256, and validate these models on the AP10K validation set. The results are reported in Table 3. Looking into the improvements in adjusting joint weights, we can see that it can largely benefit both medium and large animal instances. Since the original fixed joint weights are sub-optimal, trainable joint weights mainly focus on adjusting them dynamically to change the importance per joint. We visualize the learned joints weight in Fig. 3. We resize the radius of the circle representing keypoint to the different sizes according to the final joints weight in the same instance. Also, on the whole, smaller joint circles are drawn as that smaller radius indicates corresponding smaller bounding box sizes, which also means smaller animal instances, and vice versa.

Table 4. Results of Transformer scaling on AP10K validation set. The input size is 256 × 256. B, S, and L correspond to an embedding size of 1024, 512, 2048 respectively.

Model	Embedding size	Layer	AP	#Params
KITPose-B	1024	2	75.4	57.91M
KITPose-B	1024	4	75.8	78.90M
KITPose-S	512	2	74.8	37.99M
KITPose-L	2048	2	74.8	112.44M

Different Embedding Size and Encoder Layers. As shown in Table 4, by increasing the Transformer encoder depth, we can further improve the performance. As shown in Eqs. (1) to (3), SA requires quadratic computation and memory complexity $O(K^2)$, in exchange for the ability to access interaction between pairwise keypoints. When N SA layers are stacked, the burden increases proportionally. However, we find that simply increasing the Transformer width complicates the model and sacrifices the performance.

5   Conclusion

In this paper, we proposed channel-wise feature map reuse for an efficient Transformer model. Specifically, we used the feature channels extracted by HRNet to represent keypoint tokens, transforming them into token embeddings. Therefore, the proposed KITPose method refined keypoint localisations by capturing keypoint interactions through multi-layer self-attention. Besides, we proposed a trainable joint weights module to enhance the animal structure. The experimental results obtained on AP10K and ATRW datasets demonstrated that our proposed method can significantly improve the state-of-the-art CNN baselines, achieving new SOTA performance.

Acknowledgement. This work was supported in part by the National Natural Science Foundation of China (U1836218, 61876072, 61902153, 62106089).

References

1. Yu, H., Xu, Y., Zhang, J., Zhao, W., Guan, Z., Tao, D.: AP-10K: a benchmark for animal pose estimation in the wild. arXiv preprint arXiv:2108.12617 (2021)
2. Li, S., Li, J., Tang, H., Qian, R., Lin, W.: ATRW: a benchmark for amur tiger re-identification in the wild. In: Proceedings of the 28th ACM International Conference on Multimedia, pp. 2590–2598 (2020)
3. Pereira, T.D., et al.: SLEAP: multi-animal pose tracking. bioRXiv (2020)
4. Pereira, T.D., et al.: SLEAP: a deep learning system for multi-animal pose tracking. Nat. Methods **19**, 486–495 (2022). https://doi.org/10.1038/s41592-022-01426-1
5. Lauer, J., et al.: Multi-animal pose estimation, identification and tracking with DeepLabCut. Nat. Methods **19**, 496–504 (2022). https://doi.org/10.1038/s41592-022-01443-0
6. Lin, T.-Y., et al.: Microsoft COCO: common objects in context. In: Fleet, D., Pajdla, T., Schiele, B., Tuytelaars, T. (eds.) ECCV 2014. LNCS, vol. 8693, pp. 740–755. Springer, Cham (2014). https://doi.org/10.1007/978-3-319-10602-1_48
7. Andriluka, M., Pishchulin, L., Gehler, P., Schiele, B.: 2D human pose estimation: new benchmark and state of the art analysis. In: Proceedings of the IEEE/CVF Conference on Computer Vision and Pattern Recognition, pp. 3686–3693 (2014)
8. Wei, S.E., Ramakrishna, V., Kanade, T., Sheikh, Y.: Convolutional pose machines. In: Proceedings of the IEEE Conference on Computer Vision and Pattern Recognition, pp. 4724–4732 (2016)
9. Cao, Z., Simon, T., Wei, S.E., Sheikh, Y.: Realtime multi-person 2D pose estimation using part affinity fields. In: Proceedings of the IEEE Conference on Computer Vision and Pattern Recognition, pp. 7291–7299 (2017)
10. Newell, A., Yang, K., Deng, J.: Stacked hourglass networks for human pose estimation. In: Leibe, B., Matas, J., Sebe, N., Welling, M. (eds.) ECCV 2016. LNCS, vol. 9912, pp. 483–499. Springer, Cham (2016). https://doi.org/10.1007/978-3-319-46484-8_29
11. Fang, H.S., Xie, S., Tai, Y.W., Lu, C.: RMPE: regional multi-person pose estimation. In: Proceedings of the IEEE International Conference on Computer Vision, pp. 2334–2343 (2017)

12. Xiao, B., Wu, H., Wei, Y.: Simple baselines for human pose estimation and tracking. In: Ferrari, V., Hebert, M., Sminchisescu, C., Weiss, Y. (eds.) ECCV 2018. LNCS, vol. 11210, pp. 472–487. Springer, Cham (2018). https://doi.org/10.1007/978-3-030-01231-1_29

13. Wang, J., et al.: Deep high-resolution representation learning for visual recognition. IEEE Trans. Pattern Anal. Mach. Intell. **43**(10), 3349–3364 (2020)

14. Sun, K., Xiao, B., Liu, D., Wang, J.: Deep high-resolution representation learning for human pose estimation. In Proceedings of the IEEE/CVF Conference on Computer Vision and Pattern Recognition, pp. 5693–5703 (2019)

15. Cheng, B., et al.: HigherHRNet: scale-aware representation learning for bottom-up human pose estimation. In: Proceedings of the IEEE/CVF Conference on Computer Vision and Pattern Recognition, pp. 5386–5395 (2020)

16. mmPose Contributor: OpenMMLab pose estimation toolbox and benchmark. https://github.com/open-mmlab/mmpose (2020)

17. Li, K., et al.: Pose recognition with cascade transformers. In: Proceedings of the IEEE/CVF Conference on Computer Vision and Pattern Recognition, pp. 1944–1953 (2021)

18. Yang, S., Quan, Z., Nie, M., Yang, W.: TransPose: keypoint localization via transformer. In: Proceedings of the IEEE/CVF International Conference on Computer Vision, pp. 11802–11812 (2021)

19. Li, Y., et al.: TokenPose: learning keypoint tokens for human pose estimation. In: Proceedings of the IEEE/CVF International Conference on Computer Vision, pp. 11313–11322 (2021)

20. Yuan, Y., et al.: HRFormer: high-Resolution Vision Transformer for Dense Predict. In: Advances in Neural Information Processing Systems 34 (2021)

21. Carion, N., Massa, F., Synnaeve, G., Usunier, N., Kirillov, A., Zagoruyko, S.: End-to-end object detection with transformers. In: Vedaldi, A., Bischof, H., Brox, T., Frahm, J.-M. (eds.) ECCV 2020. LNCS, vol. 12346, pp. 213–229. Springer, Cham (2020). https://doi.org/10.1007/978-3-030-58452-8_13

22. Devlin, J., Chang, M.W., Lee, K., Toutanova, K.: BERT: pre-training of deep bidirectional transformers for language understanding. arXiv preprint arXiv:1810.04805 (2018)

23. Dosovitskiy, A., et al.: An image is worth 16x16 words: transformers for image recognition at scale. arXiv preprint arXiv:2010.11929 (2020)

24. Mathis, A., at al.: Pretraining boosts out-of-domain robustness for pose estimation. In: Proceedings of the IEEE/CVF Winter Conference on Applications of Computer Vision, pp. 1859–1868 (2021)

25. Graving, J.M., Chae, D., et al.: DeepPoseKit, a software toolkit for fast and robust animal pose estimation using deep learning. eLife **8**, e47994 (2019). https://doi.org/10.7554/eLife.47994

26. Cao, J., Tang, H., Fang, H.S., Shen, X., Lu, C., Tai, Y.W.: Cross-domain adaptation for animal pose estimation. In: Proceedings of the IEEE/CVF International Conference on Computer Vision, pp. 9498–9507 (2019)

27. Li, C., Lee, G.H.: From synthetic to real: unsupervised domain adaptation for animal pose estimation. In: Proceedings of the IEEE/CVF Conference on Computer Vision and Pattern Recognition, pp. 1482–1491 (2021)

28. Labuguen, R., et al.: MacaquePose: a novel "in the wild" macaque monkey pose dataset for markerless motion capture. bioRxiv (2020)

29. Pereira, T.D., et al.: Fast animal pose estimation using deep neural networks. Nat. Methods **16**(1), 117–125 (2019)

30. Kingma, D.P., Ba, J.: Adam: a method for stochastic optimization. arXiv preprint arXiv:1412.6980 (2014)
31. Newell, A., Huang, Z., Deng, J.: Associative embedding: end-to-end learning for joint detection and grouping. In: Advances in Neural Information Processing systems 30 (2017)
32. Vaswani, A., et al.: Attention is all you need. In: Advances in Neural Information Processing Systems 30 (2017)
33. Liu, Z., at al.: Swin transformer: hierarchical vision transformer using shifted windows. In: Proceedings of the IEEE/CVF International Conference on Computer Vision, pp. 10012–10022 (2021)
34. Mu, J., Qiu, W., Hager, G.D., Yuille, A.L.: Learning from synthetic animals. In: Proceedings of the IEEE/CVF Conference on Computer Vision and Pattern Recognition, pp. 12386–12395 (2020)
35. Zhang, F., Zhu, X., Dai, H., Ye, M., Zhu, C.: Distribution-aware coordinate representation for human pose estimation. In: Proceedings of the IEEE/CVF Conference on Computer Vision and Pattern Recognition, pp. 7093–7102 (2020)
36. Geng, Z., et al.: Bottom-up human pose estimation via disentangled keypoint regression. In: Proceedings of the IEEE/CVF Conference on Computer Vision and Pattern Recognition, pp. 14676–14686 (2021)
37. Luo, Z., et al.: Rethinking the heatmap regression for bottom-up human pose estimation. In: Proceedings of the IEEE/CVF Conference on Computer Vision and Pattern Recognition, pp. 13264–13273 (2021)
38. Jin, L., et al.: Grouping by Center: predicting Centripetal Offsets for the bottom-up human pose estimation. IEEE Trans. Multimedia (2022)
39. Harding, E.J., Paul, E.S., Mendl, M.: Cognitive bias and affective state. Nature **427**(6972), 312 (2004)
40. Touvron, H., et al.: Training data-efficient image transformers & distillation through attention. In: International Conference on Machine Learning, pp. 10347–10357 (2021)

Few-Shot Object Detection via Understanding Convolution and Attention

Jiaxing Tong, Tao Chen, Qiong Wang$^{(\boxtimes)}$, and Yazhou Yao

Nanjing University of Science and Technology, Nanjing 210094, China
{Tongjx,taochen,wangq,yazhou.yao}@njust.edu.cn

Abstract. Few-Shot Object Detection (FSOD) aims to make the detector adapt to unseen classes with only a few training samples. Typical FSOD methods use Faster R-CNN as the basic detection framework, which utilizes convolutional neural networks to extract image features. However, pooling operations adopted in convolutional neural networks aiming to capture as much image information as possible will inevitably lead to the loss of image information. Therefore, we introduce Hybrid Dilated Convolution (HDC) in the backbone network to ensure a larger receptive field and minimize the loss of image information. Besides, in the k-shot ($k \geq 2$) setting, we notice that previous methods use an average aggregation operation to fuse the support features of each category. This operation treats every support sample equally, obviously under-utilizing the limited samples. In order to further take advantage of the given support data, we propose a Support Features Dynamic Fusion (SFDF) module. Our proposed SFDF module takes the correlation between each support feature and the query feature as the weight to fuse the support features adaptively for more robust support clues. Experiments demonstrate that our proposed method achieves state-of-the-art FSOD performance on public Pascal VOC and MS-COCO datasets.

Keywords: Few-shot object detection · Hybrid dilated convolution · Support features dynamic fusion

1 Introduction

Object detection is one of the most fundamental tasks in the computer vision community [26,27,38,44,50,51]. In the past few years, object detection has achieved significant progress with recent development of deep neural networks [14,17,29,40,46,52]. However, the success of object detection model based on deep learning depends heavily on vast labeled samples [24,28,41,43,49]. In most practical application scenarios, collecting a mass of high-quality annotated data is quite expensive and time-consuming [7–9,11,25,42,45,48]. Therefore, researchers recently shifted their attention to the task of few-shot object detection (FSOD) [10,29,32,39,47,53], which aims to detect novel objects with only

S. Yu et al. (Eds.): PRCV 2022, LNCS 13534, pp. 674–687, 2022.
https://doi.org/10.1007/978-3-031-18907-4_52

a small number of annotated instances after pre-training on a large amount of publicly available data.

Since object detection requires not only class prediction but also object localization, few-shot object detection is much more challenging than few-shot classification tasks. Most of the early few-shot object detection approaches prefer to follow the meta-learning paradigm [4,30,33,37]. Meta-learning-based methods first sample the training data and then use the idea of meta-learning to train a model suitable for a specific few-shot object detection task. However, the design of meta-learners is non-trivial and prone to non-convergence problems during learning iterations [3]. In contrast, the finetune-based methods that exist as another research branch of FSOD, are straightforward and efficient [10,32,34]. Methods based on fine-tuning first train the detector on a large-scale base class dataset. During fine-tuning, the backbone is reused and frozen, while only the box classifier and regressors are trained with novel data.

Most of the existing few-shot object detection algorithms use the classic two-stage object detection algorithm Faster R-CNN [21] as the detection framework and have achieved good performance. However, existing two-stage methods still suffer from two apparent drawbacks. (1) The previous object detection algorithms usually use the pooling layer to increase the receptive field, which also reduces the size of the feature map. Though the up-sampling method is later adopted to restore the image resolution, the size reduction and recovery process of the feature map will inevitably cause the loss of image information. (2) Existing algorithms usually first extract the feature vector of each class for each sample in the support set and then use the mean operation to obtain the fused feature vector for each class [18,32,33]. Since each sample can provide different size, shape, and angle information, using the mean operation to combine the support features will lose some discriminative information and cannot fully utilize the support data.

In order to alleviate the above issues, we first introduce a hybrid dilated convolution (HDC) [31] module in the backbone network to increase the receptive field. We design the dilation rates of each layer into a jagged structure (such as a cyclic structure of 1,2,5,1,2,5). The jagged structure can adaptively satisfy the information acquisition of objects of different sizes. The local and long-range information is captured by convolutions with smaller and larger dilation rates. For the shortcomings of the mean operation, we propose a support features dynamic fusion (SFDF) module to make full use of the support data. We use the similarity between each support feature and the query feature as a weight to fuse the support features dynamically. The dynamic support features obtained in this way can merge the most helpful information in the support set. To sum up, the main contributions of our approach are as follows:

(1) We introduce hybrid dilation convolution in the backbone network to increase the receptive field, which enables the network to better aggregate local and long-range information.
(2) We propose a support features dynamic fusion module to aggregate multiple support features, which improves feature generation flexibility and enhances the query feature's adaptability to different input scenarios.

(3) We conduct extensive experiments on multiple few-shot object detection datasets, including Pascal VOC and MS COCO. The results of the experiments reveal the effectiveness of our approach.

2   Related Work

2.1   General Object Detection

The task of object detection is to locate and classify objects in a given image. According to principle and network structure, current object detectors can be roughly divided into two categories: one-stage detectors and two-stage detectors. One-stage detectors such as SSD [16], YOLO series [19,20], etc., use the backbone network for feature extraction and then directly classify and regress the feature map. In contrast, two-stage detectors such as Fast R-CNN [6] and Faster R-CNN [21], etc., first find regions of interest (RoIs) that may contain objects and then classify and localize these regions. From the research results of the two types of algorithms, both algorithms have their advantages and disadvantages. The one-stage algorithm has a faster detection speed and higher memory efficiency, but the algorithm accuracy is lower. The two-stage algorithm can achieve better detection accuracy, but the running speed is slow, and it is challenging to complete real-time tasks [15]. In our work, we adopt Faster R-CNN as the base detector.

2.2   Few-Shot Learning

Few-shot learning aims to obtain a model that can solve problems with a few samples. The concept of few-shot learning first emerged from computer vision, and there are many algorithm models with excellent performance in image classification tasks. Existing few-shot learning methods are mainly divided into meta-learning-based methods [30] and fine-tuning-based methods [34]. Meta-learning-based methods learn meta-knowledge from many different tasks. When a new task arrives, the meta-knowledge is used to adjust model parameters so that the model can converge quickly. Methods based on the model fine-tuning first train a classification model on a source dataset with a vast amount of data and then fine-tune the model on a target dataset with a small amount of data.

2.3   Few-Shot Object Detection

Few-shot learning has made breakthroughs in image classification tasks, but there are few studies on other visual tasks, such as object detection, semantic segmentation, and motion prediction. Meta R-CNN [37] uses the RoI feature generated by Faster R-CNN for meta-learning, and Faster R-CNN is augmented by introducing a full-volume machine network. TFA [32] proposes a two-stage fine-tuning method and a new evaluation metric, which outperforms most meta-learning-based methods. MPSR [35] proposes multi-scale positive sample refinement applied in an auxiliary refinement branch and includes changes in the processing in the FPN. FSCE [23] introduces contrastive learning to reduce intra-class differences and increase inter-class differences, correcting the problem of misclassification. CME [12] proposes an adversarial training procedure for min-max-margin to accomplish capable of accurately detecting more objects with fewer false positives. DeFRCN [18] analyzes the contradictions in the classification and regression tasks and decouples the classification and regression tasks to improve the accuracy of the detector.

3   Method

In this section, we first introduce the setup of few-shot object detection in Sect. 3.1. Then, we illustrate the framework of our method in Sect. 3.2. and elaborate our respective methods in Sects. 3.3 and 3.4.

3.1   Problem Definition

Following setting in [18,32], we divide the dataset into a base class dataset D_{base} and a novel class dataset D_{novel}. D_{base} contains abundant annotations for training, while only a few data in D_{novel} is available. It is worth noting that the classes in D_{base} have no intersection with the classes in D_{novel}. For the task of k-shot object detection, there are exactly k annotated object instances available for each category in D_{novel}. N-way object detection denotes a detector that is designed to detect object instances from n novel categories, where $n \leq C_{novel}$. Few-shot object detection is therefore often referred to as N-way K-shot detection. In this setting, following the entire process of transfer learning, the ultimate goal of our algorithm is to optimize a detector based on D_{base} and D_{novel}. Usually, the initial detector M_{init} is first trained on D_{base}, so as to reach the base model M_{base}. Then use the novel class dataset D_{novel} to fine-tune the model M_{base} to obtain a final model M_{novel}.

$$M_{init} \xrightarrow{D_{base}} M_{base} \xrightarrow{D_{novel}} M_{novel} \qquad (1)$$

3.2   Framework

Our method is based on the few-shot object detection framework DeFRCN [18], which uses Faster R-CNN [21] as the base detector. The Faster R-CNN algorithm mainly consists of three parts: a feature extractor, region proposal network (RPN) and the detection head (RoI head). The feature extractor uses a convolutional neural network to obtain a feature map of the input image. The region proposal network performs binary classification and rough regression on the initial anchor box and then selects a series of interest regions to send to the subsequent detection network. Finally, the classification and regression results are output by the detection head.

The entire architecture is shown in Fig. 1. First, the query image and support images are fed into the backbone network ResNet-101 [9] using hybrid dilation

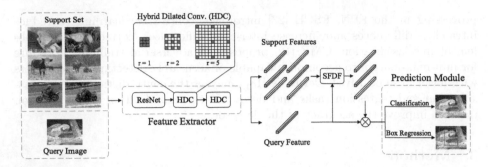

Fig. 1. The framework of our method. The support set and query image are sent into the backbone network with Hybrid Dilation Convolution (HDC) to extract features. r = 1, 2, and 5 in the figure represent the jagged dilate rates in the HDC module. After that, through the Support Features Dynamic Fusion (SFDF) module, the query image is used to guide the fusion of image features in the support set. Finally, the features are sent to the prediction module.

convolution to extract the corresponding image features. Second, the query feature is used to control the fusion of each class feature of the support set through the support features dynamic fusion module. Finally, the region query feature and region support features are input into the multi-relation head, bounding boxes are regressed, and query objects are classified.

3.3   Hybrid Dilation Convolution

Due to the characteristics of various types of objects, different shapes, and indeterminate area ratios, hybrid dilation convolution is introduced to preserve the effective feature information of objects of different sizes as much as possible. Dilated convolution is proposed by Chen *et al.* in the semantic segmentation network [1]. It can increase the receptive field by injecting dilation into the convolution kernel without increasing the network parameters and thus can obtain richer contextual information. Compared with the standard convolution operation, the dilated convolution has an additional parameter called the "dilate rate", which defines the spacing of the values when the convolution kernel processes the data. We assume that the size of the convolution kernel is $k * k$, the receptive field of the current layer is F_n, the size of the receptive field of the previous layer is F_{n-1}, and the dilate rate of the convolution kernel is d_n. The size of the receptive field of the current layer $(n \geq 2)$ is:

$$F_n = F_{n-1} + (s - 1) \times d_n. \tag{2}$$

It is known that the calculation method of the receptive field of the first layer is:

$$F_1 = (s - 1) \cdot d_1 + 1. \tag{3}$$

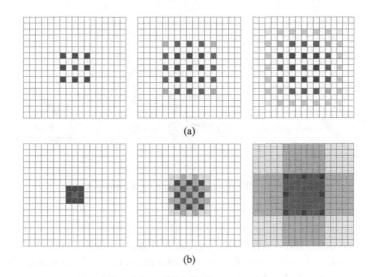

(a)

(b)

Fig. 2. Illustration of the gridding problem. (a) the change of receptive field when $d = (2, 2, 2)$. (b) the change of receptive field when $d = (1, 2, 5)$. (Color figure online)

From Eqs. 2 and 3, the size of the receptive field can be expressed as:

$$F_n = (s - 1) \cdot \sum_{i=1}^{n} d_i + 1. \tag{4}$$

Further, when the dilate rate d_n is 2^{n-1}, there are:

$$\sum_{i=1}^{n} d_i = 2^n - 1. \tag{5}$$

Therefore, the receptive field size becomes:

$$F_n = (s - 1) \cdot (2^n - 1) + 1. \tag{6}$$

For multi-layer convolution, the introduction of dilated convolution enables the output of the later convolution layer to have a larger receptive field and contain more information, which will be beneficial to the improvement of network performance. However, when the dilate rate of all layers is the same, then the value contributed to the network is only the value above some sparse points. Due to the high-layer downsampling operation, the sampling of the input image will be more sparse. This may result in complete loss of local information, and information that is too far away is no longer relevant, which we call "gridding" [31].

Figure 2a shows the change of the receptive field of each layer when $d = (2, 2, 2)$. The red point represents the center, the blue point represents the expanded receptive field after the convolution operation, and the white point represents the point not involved in the convolution operation. It can be seen

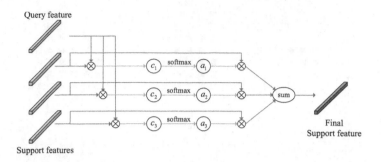

Fig. 3. The SFDF architecture of 3-shot setting.

from the figure that although the dilated convolution increases the information receptive field, the convolution kernel is discontinuous, and the points that do not participate in the convolution operation increase. When used for object detection, the continuity of image information must be lost.

To alleviate this problem, we set the dilate rate to be jagged. Consecutive layers are divided into groups with increasing dilate rates, and the next group repeats the same pattern. In this way, the top layer can access more pixel information than the original configuration in the same area and achieve the effect of expanding the receptive field without adding additional modules. Figure 2b shows the change of the receptive field of each layer when $d = (1, 2, 5)$. We use ResNet-101 as the starting point of the model, and for the res4b module containing 23 blocks, we group 4 blocks and set their dilate rates to 1, 2, 5, and 9, respectively. The dilate rates of the last three blocks are set to 1, 2, and 5. For the res5b module, the dilate rates of the three blocks are set to 5, 9, and 17.

3.4   Support Features Dynamic Fusion

When two or more samples are provided for each class in the support set, the previous few-shot object detection algorithms [18, 23, 32] tend to perform a simple mean operation to combine all extracted features. Since the size, angle, and other characteristics of the object are different [2], it is a moderate method to use a simple average to aggregate the individual features of each class of features. This operation treats the provided k support samples equally and does not make full use of limited resources. If we choose the samples in the support set that are highly similar to the query image in terms of size, shape, etc., as the feature of each class, just like humans who focus on the required attention, more discriminative features can be obtained.

To maximize the utilization of a given support set sample, we propose a support features dynamic fusion module. Instead of using the mean method, we use weighted summation to generate features for each class in the support set. The module first calculates the similarity between the query feature and each feature of each class in the support set and then uses the coefficient as a weight to perform a weighted sum operation on each feature of each class in the support set so that the support set features obtained in this way can contain the most discriminative information of the object. At the same time, since the generation of this feature is related to the input query feature, different features will be generated according to different input images, which is a dynamic process.

The structure diagram of the dynamic support set feature fusion module is shown in Fig. 3. For k-shot ($k \geq 2$) tasks, we use the backbone network to extract features from the support set and query set. The support image features are denoted as $\{F_j(S)\}_{j=1}^{k}$, and the query set feature is denoted as $F(Q)$. Then, the similarity c_j between the k support features and the query feature is calculated and normalized by the softmax operation to obtain the correlation coefficient a_j. Finally, the individual features of each category in the support set are weighted and summed according to the correlation coefficient a_j. Consequently, dynamically generated features related to the query features can be obtained.

$$a_j = \text{soft max}(c_j)$$
$$= \text{soft max}(C(F_j(S), F(Q))). \tag{7}$$

4 Experiments

4.1 Experimental Setting

Following the instructions in [32], we construct a few-shot detection dataset for a fair comparison with other state-of-the-art methods. In order to obtain more stable results, all results in the experiment are the average of 10 random sampling results.

PASCAL VOC. The PASCAL VOC dataset [5] has a total of 20 classes, which are divided into 15 base classes and 5 novel classes. We use the VOC 2007 trainval set and the VOC 2012 trainval set to train the model and test it on the VOC2007 test set. According to work [32], we randomly divide the 20 classes three times to form split1, 2, and 3, and k is set to 1, 2, 3, 5, and 10.

COCO. The COCO dataset [13] has a total of 80 classes, of which the same 20 classes as the PASCAL VOC dataset are used as novel classes, and the remaining 60 classes are used as base classes. We utilize 5k images from the validation set for evaluation and the rest for training. K is set to 10 or 30.

Implementation Details. We use Faster R-CNN [21] as the basic detection framework, ResNet-101 [9] with hybrid dilated convolutions pre-trained on ImageNet [22] as the starting point for all our models, and RoI Align as the RoI feature extractor. We train our model in parallel on 2 NVIDIA Titan RTX. We adopt SGD with weight decay of $5e^{-5}$ and momentum of 0.9 as the optimizer, with batchsize set to 12.

Table 1. Evaluation on Pascal VOC Novel Set. The evaluation is performed over 3 different splits. '-' means the result is not reported in the original paper. '⋆' indicates that we reproduce the result obtained by DeFRCN.

Method/Shots	Publication	Novel Set 1					Novel Set 2					Novel Set 3				
		1	2	3	5	10	1	2	3	5	10	1	2	3	5	10
YOLO-ft [10]	ICCV19	6.6	10.7	12.5	24.8	38.6	12.5	4.2	11.6	16.1	33.9	13.0	15.9	15.0	32.2	38.4
FRCN-ft [37]	ICCV19	13.8	19.6	32.8	41.5	45.6	7.9	15.3	26.2	31.6	39.1	9.8	11.3	19.1	35.0	45.1
FSRW [10]	ICCV19	14.8	15.5	26.7	33.9	47.2	15.7	15.2	22.7	30.1	40.5	21.3	25.6	28.4	42.8	45.9
MetaDet [33]	ICCV19	18.9	20.6	30.2	36.8	49.6	21.8	23.1	27.8	31.7	43.0	20.6	23.9	29.4	43.9	44.1
Meta R-CNN [37]	ICCV19	19.9	25.5	35.0	45.7	51.5	10.4	19.4	29.6	34.8	45.4	14.3	18.2	27.5	41.2	48.1
TFA [32]	ICML20	39.8	36.1	44.7	55.7	56.0	23.5	26.9	34.1	35.1	39.1	30.8	34.8	42.8	49.5	49.8
MPSR [35]	ECCV20	41.7	-	51.4	55.2	61.8	24.4	-	39.2	39.9	47.8	35.6	-	42.3	48.0	49.7
FSCE [23]	CVPR21	44.2	43.8	51.4	61.9	63.4	27.3	29.5	43.5	44.2	50.2	37.2	41.9	47.5	54.6	58.5
CME [12]	CVPR21	41.5	47.5	50.4	58.2	60.9	27.2	30.2	41.4	42.5	46.8	34.3	39.6	45.1	48.3	51.5
DeFRCN [18]	CVPR21	53.6	57.5	61.5	64.1	60.8	30.1	38.1	47.0	53.3	47.9	48.4	50.9	52.3	54.9	57.4
DeFRCN⋆ [18]	CVPR21	55.1	57.4	61.1	64.6	61.5	32.6	39.6	48.1	53.8	49.2	48.9	51.9	52.3	55.7	59.0
Ours	-	**56.0**	**59.3**	**63.1**	**66.0**	**62.6**	**33.3**	**41.0**	**49.4**	**55.2**	**49.9**	**49.8**	**53.8**	**53.9**	**56.5**	**59.9**

4.2 Experimental Results

We compare our method with previous state-of-the-art methods and show the results for three different segmentations in Table 1. It can be seen that our method achieves the best results in any shot and all segmentations, which proves the effectiveness of our method. Based on the results of Table 1, we further notice that two phenomena exist in few-shot object detection. (1) Increasing novel shots does not necessarily lead to better results. We conjecture it was because low-quality samples might have been added, affecting the quality of the detector. (2) When the support set provides fewer samples, the results of our method can get a relatively greater improvement. The SFDF module can measure the contribution of each support feature to obtain support features with higher discrimination.

Compared with the PASCAL VOC dataset, the COCO dataset has more categories and is more challenging, so the detection difficulty is significantly increased. Table 2 shows all the evaluation results on the COCO dataset with mAP as the evaluation metric. The results of our proposed method are higher than the current SOTA.

4.3 Ablation Study

We present the results of ablation experiments analyzing the effectiveness of various components in the system. Unless otherwise stated, all ablation experiments were performed on PASCAL VOC 2007 Novel Split1 with ResNet-101 as the backbone, and all results are the average of 10 random runs. All results are shown in Table 3 in great detail.

Impact of Hybrid Dilated Convolution. We conduct experiments to verify the effectiveness of hybrid dilated convolution. Specifically, we implement a DeFRCN baseline method for few-shot object detection based on two-stage

Table 2. Evaluation on COCO Novel Set. '⋆' indicates that we reproduce the result obtained by DeFRCN.

Methods/Shots	Publication	Shot Number	
		10	30
FRCN-ft [37]	ICCV19	6.5	11.1
FSRW [10]	ICCV19	5.6	9.1
MetaDet [33]	ICCV19	7.1	11.3
Meta R-CNN [37]	ICCV19	8.7	12.4
TFA [32]	ICML20	10.0	13.7
MPSR [35]	ECCV20	9.8	14.1
FSDetView [36]	ECCV20	12.5	14.7
FSCE [23]	CVPR21	11.9	16.4
CME [12]	CVPR21	15.1	16.9
DeFRCN [18]	CVPR21	18.5	22.6
DeFRCN⋆ [18]	CVPR21	18.4	22.7
Ours	-	**19.1**	**23.3**

Table 3. Ablation study of our method for few-shot object detection on Pascal VOC novel classes (split-1). 'HDC' denotes hybrid dilation convolution, and 'SFDF' denotes support set feature dynamic fusion.

DeFRCN	HDC	SFDF	Shot Number				
			1	2	3	5	10
✓			55.1	57.4	61.1	64.6	61.5
✓	✓		56.0	58.3	62.0	65.3	62.3
✓		✓	55.1	58.7	62.6	65.4	62.0
✓	✓	✓	56.0	59.3	63.1	66.0	62.6

fine-tuning. We use ResNet-101 with hybrid dilated convolution as the feature extraction network. The results show that our method can increase the receptive field to a certain extent and then obtain more comprehensive information.

Impact of Support Features Dynamic Fusion Module. To verify the effectiveness of the SFDF module, we compare it with the feature averaging method. As can be seen from the Table 3, this module can improve the detection performance when $k \geq 2$. Moreover, we find that higher performance gains can be obtained when the number of k is smaller. The SFDF module can replace the moderate averaging operation to find the focus of the support set.

5   Conclusion

In this paper, we take a closer look at the few-shot object detection task. We adopt a feature extraction network with hybrid dilated convolution, which can increase the receptive field while maintaining the amount of network parameters. Moreover, we also propose a support features dynamic fusion module to perform a weighted summation of samples in each class of support set to obtain the most discriminative information. Extensive experiments on VOC and COCO datasets demonstrate the effectiveness of our proposed method.

Acknowledgments. This work was supported by the pre-research project of the Equipment Development Department of the Central Military Commission (No. 31514020205).

References

1. Chen, L.C., Papandreou, G., Kokkinos, I., Murphy, K., Yuille, A.L.: DeepLab: semantic image segmentation with deep convolutional nets, atrous convolution, and fully connected CRFs. IEEE Trans. Pattern Anal. Mach. Intell. **40**(4), 834–848 (2017)
2. Chen, T., Wang, S.H., Wang, Q., Zhang, Z., Xie, G.S., Tang, Z.: Enhanced feature alignment for unsupervised domain adaptation of semantic segmentation. IEEE Trans. Multimedia (TMM) **24**, 1042–1054 (2022)
3. Chen, T., et al.: Semantically meaningful class prototype learning for one-shot image segmentation. IEEE Trans. Multimedia (TMM) **24**, 968–980 (2022)
4. Chen, T., Yao, Y., Zhang, L., Wang, Q., Xie, G., Shen, F.: Saliency guided inter-and intra-class relation constraints for weakly supervised semantic segmentation. IEEE Trans. Multimedia (TMM) (2022). https://doi.org/10.1109/TMM.2022.3157481
5. Everingham, M., Van Gool, L., Williams, C.K., Winn, J., Zisserman, A.: The pascal visual object classes (VOC) challenge. Int. J. Comput. Vis. **88**(2), 303–338 (2010). https://doi.org/10.1007/s11263-009-0275-4
6. Girshick, R.: Fast R-CNN. In: Proceedings of the IEEE International Conference on Computer Vision, pp. 1440–1448 (2015)
7. Girshick, R., Donahue, J., Darrell, T., Malik, J.: Rich feature hierarchies for accurate object detection and semantic segmentation. In: Proceedings of the IEEE Conference on Computer Vision and Pattern Recognition, pp. 580–587 (2014)
8. He, K., Gkioxari, G., Dollár, P., Girshick, R.: Mask R-CNN. In: Proceedings of the IEEE International Conference on Computer Vision, pp. 2961–2969 (2017)
9. He, K., Zhang, X., Ren, S., Sun, J.: Deep residual learning for image recognition. In: Proceedings of the IEEE Conference on Computer Vision and Pattern Recognition, pp. 770–778 (2016)
10. Kang, B., Liu, Z., Wang, X., Yu, F., Feng, J., Darrell, T.: Few-shot object detection via feature reweighting. In: Proceedings of the IEEE/CVF International Conference on Computer Vision, pp. 8420–8429 (2019)
11. Krizhevsky, A., Sutskever, I., Hinton, G.E.: ImageNet classification with deep convolutional neural networks. In: Advances in Neural Information Processing Systems 25 (2012)

12. Li, B., Yang, B., Liu, C., Liu, F., Ji, R., Ye, Q.: Beyond max-margin: class margin equilibrium for few-shot object detection. In: Proceedings of the IEEE/CVF Conference on Computer Vision and Pattern Recognition, pp. 7363–7372 (2021)
13. Lin, T.-Y.: Microsoft COCO: common objects in context. In: Fleet, D., Pajdla, T., Schiele, B., Tuytelaars, T. (eds.) ECCV 2014. LNCS, vol. 8693, pp. 740–755. Springer, Cham (2014). https://doi.org/10.1007/978-3-319-10602-1_48
14. Liu, H., et al.: Exploiting web images for fine-grained visual recognition by eliminating open-set noise and utilizing hard examples. IEEE Trans. Multimedia (TMM) **24**, 546–557 (2022)
15. Liu, L., et al.: Deep learning for generic object detection: a survey. Int. J. Comput. Vision **128**(2), 261–318 (2020)
16. Liu, W., et al.: SSD: single shot multibox detector. In: Leibe, B., Matas, J., Sebe, N., Welling, M. (eds.) ECCV 2016. LNCS, vol. 9905, pp. 21–37. Springer, Cham (2016). https://doi.org/10.1007/978-3-319-46448-0_2
17. Pei, G., Shen, F., Yao, Y., Xie, G.S., Tang, Z., Tang, J.: Hierarchical feature alignment network for unsupervised video object segmentation. In: Proceedings of the European Conference on Computer Vision (ECCV) (2022)
18. Qiao, L., Zhao, Y., Li, Z., Qiu, X., Wu, J., Zhang, C.: DeFRCN: Decoupled faster R-CNN for few-shot object detection. In: Proceedings of the IEEE/CVF International Conference on Computer Vision, pp. 8681–8690 (2021)
19. Redmon, J., Divvala, S., Girshick, R., Farhadi, A.: You only look once: unified, real-time object detection. In: Proceedings of the IEEE Conference on Computer Vision and Pattern Recognition, pp. 779–788 (2016)
20. Redmon, J., Farhadi, A.: Yolo9000: better, faster, stronger. In: Proceedings of the IEEE Conference on Computer Vision and Pattern Recognition, pp. 7263–7271 (2017)
21. Ren, S., He, K., Girshick, R., Sun, J.: Faster R-CNN: towards real-time object detection with region proposal networks. In: Advances in Neural Information Processing Systems 28 (2015)
22. Russakovsky, O., et al.: ImageNet large scale visual recognition challenge. Int. J. Comput. Vision **115**(3), 211–252 (2015)
23. Sun, B., Li, B., Cai, S., Yuan, Y., Zhang, C.: FSCE: few-shot object detection via contrastive proposal encoding. In: Proceedings of the IEEE/CVF Conference on Computer Vision and Pattern Recognition, pp. 7352–7362 (2021)
24. Sun, Z., Hua, X.S., Yao, Y., Wei, X.S., Hu, G., Zhang, J.: CRSSC: salvage reusable samples from noisy data for robust learning. In: Proceedings of the ACM International Conference on Multimedia (ACMMM), pp. 92–101 (2020)
25. Sun, Z., Liu, H., Wang, Q., Zhou, T., Wu, Q., Tang, Z.: Co-LDL: a co-training-based label distribution learning method for tackling label noise. IEEE Trans. Multimedia (TMM) **24**, 1093–1104 (2022)
26. Sun, Z., et al.: PNP: robust learning from noisy labels by probabilistic noise prediction. In: Proceedings of the IEEE Conference on Computer Vision and Pattern Recognition (CVPR), pp. 5311–5320 (2022)
27. Sun, Z., et al.: Webly supervised fine-grained recognition: Benchmark datasets and an approach. In: Proceedings of the IEEE International Conference on Computer Vision (ICCV), pp. 10602–10611 (2021)
28. Sun, Z., Yao, Y., Wei, X., Shen, F., Liu, H., Hua, X.S.: Boosting robust learning via leveraging reusable samples in noisy web data. IEEE Trans. Multimedia (TMM) (2022). https://doi.org/10.1109/TMM.2022.3158001
29. Sun, Z., Yao, Y., Xiao, J., Zhang, L., Zhang, J., Tang, Z.: Exploiting textual queries for dynamically visual disambiguation. Pattern Recogn. **110**, 107620 (2021)

30. Vilalta, R., Drissi, Y.: A perspective view and survey of meta-learning. Artif. Intell. Rev. **18**(2), 77–95 (2002)
31. Wang, P., et al.: Understanding convolution for semantic segmentation. In: 2018 IEEE Winter Conference on Applications of Computer Vision (WACV), pp. 1451–1460. IEEE (2018)
32. Wang, X., Huang, T.E., Darrell, T., Gonzalez, J.E., Yu, F.: Frustratingly simple few-shot object detection. arXiv preprint arXiv:2003.06957 (2020)
33. Wang, Y.X., Ramanan, D., Hebert, M.: Meta-learning to detect rare objects. In: Proceedings of the IEEE/CVF International Conference on Computer Vision, pp. 9925–9934 (2019)
34. Weiss, K., Khoshgoftaar, T.M., Wang, D.D.: A survey of transfer learning. J. Big Data **3**(1), 1–40 (2016). https://doi.org/10.1186/s40537-016-0043-6
35. Wu, J., Liu, S., Huang, D., Wang, Y.: Multi-scale positive sample refinement for few-shot object detection. In: Vedaldi, A., Bischof, H., Brox, T., Frahm, J.-M. (eds.) ECCV 2020. LNCS, vol. 12361, pp. 456–472. Springer, Cham (2020). https://doi.org/10.1007/978-3-030-58517-4_27
36. Xiao, Y., Marlet, R.: Few-shot object detection and viewpoint estimation for objects in the wild. In: Vedaldi, A., Bischof, H., Brox, T., Frahm, J.-M. (eds.) ECCV 2020. LNCS, vol. 12362, pp. 192–210. Springer, Cham (2020). https://doi.org/10.1007/978-3-030-58520-4_12
37. Yan, X., Chen, Z., Xu, A., Wang, X., Liang, X., Lin, L.: Meta R-CNN: towards general solver for instance-level low-shot learning. In: Proceedings of the IEEE/CVF International Conference on Computer Vision, pp. 9577–9586 (2019)
38. Yao, Y., et al.: Non-salient region object mining for weakly supervised semantic segmentation. In: Proceedings of the IEEE Conference on Computer Vision and Pattern Recognition (CVPR), pp. 2623–2632 (2021)
39. Yao, Y., Hua, X.S., Shen, F., Zhang, J., Tang, Z.: A domain robust approach for image dataset construction. In: Proceedings of the ACM International Conference on Multimedia (ACMMM), pp. 212–216 (2016)
40. Yao, Y., Hua, X., Gao, G., Sun, Z., Li, Z., Zhang, J.: Bridging the web data and fine-grained visual recognition via alleviating label noise and domain mismatch. In: Proceedings of the ACM International Conference on Multimedia (ACMMM), pp. 1735–1744 (2020)
41. Yao, Y., et al.: Exploiting web images for multi-output classification: From category to subcategories. IEEE Trans. Neural Netw. Learn. Syst. (TNNLS) **31**(7), 2348–2360 (2020)
42. Yao, Y., Shen, F., Zhang, J., Liu, L., Tang, Z., Shao, L.: Extracting multiple visual senses for web learning. IEEE Trans. Multimedia (TMM) **21**(1), 184–196 (2019)
43. Yao, Y., Shen, F., Zhang, J., Liu, L., Tang, Z., Shao, L.: Extracting privileged information for enhancing classifier learning. IEEE Trans. Image Process. (TIP) **28**(1), 436–450 (2019)
44. Yao, Y., et al.: Jo-SRC: a contrastive approach for combating noisy labels. In: Proceedings of the IEEE Conference on Computer Vision and Pattern Recognition (CVPR), pp. 5192–5201 (2021)
45. Yao, Y., Zhang, J., Shen, F., Hua, X., Xu, J., Tang, Z.: Exploiting web images for dataset construction: a domain robust approach. IEEE Trans. Multimedia (TMM) **19**(8), 1771–1784 (2017)
46. Yao, Y., et al.: Towards automatic construction of diverse, high-quality image datasets. IEEE Trans. Knowl. Data Eng. (TKDE) **32**(6), 1199–1211 (2020)

47. Yao, Y., Zhang, J., Shen, F., Yang, W., Huang, P., Tang, Z.: Discovering and distinguishing multiple visual senses for polysemous words. In: Proceedings of the AAAI Conference on Artificial Intelligence (AAAI), pp. 523–530 (2018)
48. Zhang, C., Lin, G., Wang, Q., Shen, F., Yao, Y., Tang, Z.: Guided by meta-set: a data-driven method for fine-grained visual recognition. IEEE Trans. Multimedia (TMM) (2022). https://doi.org/10.1109/TMM.2022.3181439
49. Zhang, C., Wang, Q., Xie, G., Wu, Q., Shen, F., Tang, Z.: Robust learning from noisy web images via data purification for fine-grained recognition. IEEE Trans. Multimedia (TMM) **24**, 1198–1209 (2022)
50. Zhang, C., et al.: Web-supervised network with softly update-drop training for fine-grained visual classification. In: Proceedings of the AAAI Conference on Artificial Intelligence (AAAI), pp. 12781–12788 (2020)
51. Zhang, C., Yao, Y., Shu, X., Li, Z., Tang, Z., Wu, Q.: Data-driven meta-set based fine-grained visual recognition. In: Proceedings of the ACM International Conference on Multimedia (ACMMM), pp. 2372–2381 (2020)
52. Zhang, C., et al.: Extracting useful knowledge from noisy web images via data purification for fine-grained recognition. In: Proceedings of the ACM International Conference on Multimedia (ACMMM), pp. 4063–4072 (2021)
53. Zhang, G., Luo, Z., Cui, K., Lu, S.: Meta-DETR: few-shot object detection via unified image-level meta-learning. arXiv preprint arXiv:2103.11731 (2021)

Every Corporation Owns Its Structure: Corporate Credit Rating via Graph Neural Networks

Bojing Feng[1,2], Haonan Xu[1,2], Wenfang Xue[1,2(✉)], and Bindang Xue[3]

[1] Center for Research on Intelligent Perception and Computing, National Laboratory of Pattern Recognition, Institute of Automation, Chinese Academy of Science, Beijing, China
bojing.feng@cripac.ia.ac.cn
[2] School of Artificial Intelligence, University of Chinese Academic of Science, Beijing, China
{xuhaonan2020,wenfang.xue}@ia.ac.cn
[3] School of Astronautics, Beihang University, Beijing, China
xuebd@buaa.edu.cn

Abstract. Credit rating is an analysis of the credit risks associated with a corporation, which reflects the level of the riskiness and reliability in investing, and plays a vital role in financial risk. There have emerged many studies that implement machine learning and deep learning techniques which are based on vector space to deal with corporate credit rating. Recently, considering the relations among enterprises such as loan guarantee network, some graph-based models are applied in this field with the advent of graph neural networks. But these existing models build networks between corporations without taking the internal feature interactions into account. In this paper, to overcome such problems, we propose a novel model, Corporate Credit Rating via Graph Neural Networks, CCR-GNN for brevity. We firstly construct individual graphs for each corporation based on self-outer product and then use GNN to model the feature interaction explicitly, which includes both local and global information. Extensive experiments conducted on the Chinese public-listed corporate rating dataset, prove that CCR-GNN outperforms the state-of-the-art methods consistently.

Keywords: Corporate credit rating · Financial risk · Graph neural networks

1 Introduction

Nowadays, credit rating is fundamental for helping financial institutions to know companies well so as to mitigate credit risks [1]. It is an indication of the level of the risk in investing with the corporation and represents the likelihood that the corporation pays its financial obligations on time. Therefore, it is of great importance to model the profile of the corporation [2] to predict the credit rating

© The Author(s), under exclusive license to Springer Nature Switzerland AG 2022
S. Yu et al. (Eds.): PRCV 2022, LNCS 13534, pp. 688–699, 2022.
https://doi.org/10.1007/978-3-031-18907-4_53

level. However, this assessment process is usually very expensive and complicated, which often takes months with many experts involved to analyze all kinds of variables, which reflect the reliability of a corporation. One way to deal with this problem may be to build a model based on historical financial information [3] of the corporation.

The banking industry has developed some credit risk models since the middle of the twentieth century. The risk rating is also the main business of thousands of worldwide corporations, including dozens of public companies [4]. Due to the highly practical value, many kinds of credit rating models have been developed. Traditionally, the credit models are proposed by logistic regression algorithms with the temporal credit rating as well as aggregated financial information.

Nowadays, machine learning and deep learning models have shown their power in a range of applications including financial fields. In the work [1], they analyze the performance of four neural network architectures including MLP, CNN, CNN2D, LSTM in predicting corporate credit rating as issued by Standard and Poor's. Parisa et al. [2] apply four machine learning techniques (Bagged Decision Trees, Random Forest, Support and Multilayer Perceptron) to predict corporate credit rating. Recently, [3] builds a stack of machine learning models aiming at composing a state-of-the-art credit rating system.

With the advent of graph neural networks, some graph-based models [5–10] are built based on the loan guarantee network. The corporations guarantee each other and form complex loan networks to receive loans from banks during the economic expansion stage.

Although these approaches are widely used and useful, we also observe that they have some limitations for corporate credit rating. Firstly, the existing deep learning models require extensive feature construction and specific background knowledge to design representative features. These features need to be aggregated from financial data, which costs most of the time. What's more, the graph-based models usually regard a single corporation as a node in graph and build the relations between them, which neglects the feature interaction in a single corporation.

To overcome the limitations mentioned above, we propose a novel method, Corporate Credit Rating via Graph Neural Networks, CCR-GNN for brevity. In contrast to previous graph-based approaches with global structure, we look at this problem from a new perspective. We regard the corporation as a graph instead of a node, which can depict the detailed feature-feature relations. The individual graphs are built by applying the corporation-to-graph method, which models the relations between features. Then the information of feature nodes is propagated to their neighbors via the Graph Neural Networks, graph attention network specifically, which takes advantage of attention mechanism. We also conduct extensive experiments to examine the advantages of our approach against baselines.

To sum up, the main contents of this work are summarized as follows:

- A new method named corporation-to-graph is developed to explore the relations between features.
- A new graph neural network for corporate credit rating is proposed, where each corporation is an individual graph and feature level interactions can be

learned. To the best of our knowledge, this is the first work that applies graph neural networks into corporate credit rating with a graph-level perspective. It opens new doors to explore the advanced GNNs methods for corporate credit rating.

- We demonstrate that our approach outperforms state-of-the-art methods experimentally.

This paper is organized as follows. Related works about the researches are introduced in Sect. 2. Section 3 will present the proposed CCR-GNN. The experiment results of CCR-CNN on real-world data will be presented in Sect. 4. Finally, the conclusion is introduced in Sect. 5.

2   Related Works

In this section, we review some related works on credit rating, including statistical models, machine learning models and hybrid models. Then we introduce the graph neural networks and graph-based models.

Statistical Models. Researchers apply some traditional statistical models such as logistic regression. In bank credit rating, Gogas et al. [11] used an ordered probit regression model. Recently, the work [12] proposed a model based on Student's-t Hidden Markov Models (SHMMs) to investigate the firm-related data.

Machine Learning Models. Nowadays, machine learning techniques are used to predict corporate rating. The work [13] implemented adaptive learning networks (ALN) on both financial data and non-financial data to predict S&P credit rating. Cao et al. [14] studied support vector machine methods on US companies.

Hybrid Models. In addition these methods above, some researchers proposed hybrid models by mixing these techniques up. Yeh et al. [15] combined random forest feature selection with rough set theory (RST) and SVM. Pai et al. [16] built the Decision Tree Support Vector Machine (DTSVM) integrated TST. The work [17] proposed an enhanced decision support model that used the relevance vector machine and decision tree.

Graph Neural Networks. Nowadays, neural networks have been developed for graph-structured data, such as social network and citation network. DeepWalk [18] is designed to learn representations of graph nodes by random walk. Follow this work, unsupervised algorithm LINE [19] and node2vec [20] are proposed. Besides, neural networks are applied in graph-structured data. An approach [21] uses the convolutional architecture by a localized approximation of spectral graph convolutions. Then GAT [22] utilizes the attention mechanism to improve the power of graph model.

Graph-Based Models. Due to the advance of GNNs, many researchers proposed graph-based models to apply in financial risk. Barja et al. [5] extracted a financial network from customer-supplier transactions among more than 140,000 companies, and their economic flows. The work developed DeepTrax [6] in order to learn embeddings of account and merchant entities. In the work [7], they employed the temporal inter-chain attention network on graph-structured loan behavior data. Cheng et al. [8] proposed HGAR to learn the embedding of guarantee networks. Recently, work [9] combined the spatio-temporal information for credit fraud detection.

3   The Proposed Method: CCR-GNN

In this section, we introduce the proposed CCR-GNN which applies graph neural networks into corporate credit rating with the graph level. We formulate the problem at first, then give an overview of the whole CCR-GNN, and finally describe the three layers of the model: corporation to graph layer (C2GL), graph feature interaction layer (GFIL) and credit rating layer (CRL).

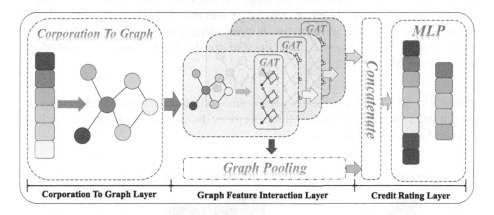

Fig. 1. An Example of the architecture of our CCR-GNN model which has three Graph ATtention layers (GAT).

3.1   Problem Formulation

The credit rating system aims to predict which credit level of the corporation will belong to. Here we give a formulation of this problem as below.

In credit rating, let $C = \{c_1, c_2, \cdots, c_n\}$ denotes the set consisting of all unique corporations, n is the number of corporations. $c \in \mathbb{R}^d$ Every corporation has a corresponding label which represents its credit level. Let $Y = \{y_1, y_2, \cdots, y_m\}$ denotes the set of the labels, and m represents the number of unique labels. The goal of the credit rating system is to predict the corporate label according to its profile c. Under the credit rating model, for each corporation c, model outputs probabilities $\hat{y}$ for all labels, where an element value of vector $\hat{y}$ is the score of corresponding label. Finally, it will predict the label with the max score.

3.2 Architecture Overview

Figure 1 illustrates the end-to-end CCR-GNN model. It is composed of three functional layers: corporation to graph layer, graph feature interaction layer and credit rating layer. Firstly, every corporation is mapped into a graph-structured representation through corporation-to-graph to model corporation feature relations. Then the features interact with each other by graph attention network. Finally, credit rating layer outputs the label scores by utilizing the information provided by the before local and global information.

3.3 Corporation to Graph Layer(C2GL)

For the convenience of formulation, we use c to denote any corporation. It includes its financial data and non-financial data which describe the corporate profile. For numerical data, we can use it directly. However, in terms of non-numerical data, we first perform one-hot encoding, then use the embedding layer concatenating with financial data together to obtain the corporate embedding expression x via

$$x = Emb(c) \tag{1}$$

where $x \in \mathbb{R}^d$. d denotes the corporate embedding size. Figure 2 illustrates the corporation-to-graph including three steps: self-outer product, activation function and graph construction.

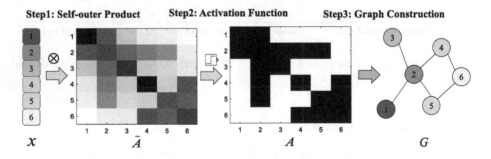

Fig. 2. Corporation To Graph (C2G)

Step1: Self-Outer Product

Above the embedding layer, we propose to use a self-outer product operation on x to obtain the interaction map $\widetilde{A}$:

$$\widetilde{A} = x \otimes x = xx^T \tag{2}$$

where $\widetilde{A}$ is a $d \times d$ matrix.

This is the core design of C2G to ensure the effectiveness of feature interactions. We argue that using outer product is more advantageous in twofold: 1) it encodes more signals by accounting for the correlations between different features; 2) it is more meaningful than the original information in embedding without modeling any correlation. Recently, it has been shown that, it is particularly meaningful to model the interaction of feature explicitly, where as concatenation is sub-optimal [23–25].

Step2: Activation Function

Above the interaction map is an activation function, which targets at extracting useful signal from the interaction map. To be specific, it retains the important information and ignores the insignificant information. And it is subjected to design and can be abstracted as $A = g\left(\widetilde{A}\right)$, where g denotes the activation function, and A is the output matrix used for graph construction.

$$A_{ij} = g\left(\widetilde{A}_{ij}\right) = \begin{cases} 0 & \widetilde{A}_{ij} < r \\ 1 & \widetilde{A}_{ij} \geqslant r \end{cases} \tag{3}$$

where A_{ij} means the entry of matrix A that lies in the row number i and column number j, r is a adaptive parameter to get a connected graph. In other words, A is the adjacent matrix of the graph.

Step3: Graph Construction

After getting the adjacent matrix A, we can construct this graph $\mathcal{G} = (\mathcal{V}, \mathcal{E})$. Let $\mathcal{V} = \{v_1, v_2, \cdots, v_d\}$, each graph has d feature nodes. If $A_{ij} = 1$, each edge $(v_i, v_j) \in \mathcal{E}$ means that a feature node v_i has a strong relation with feature node v_j. Every node v_i corresponds to an attribute $x_i \in \mathbb{R}$. Finally, the algorithm is formally presented in Algorithm 1.

3.4 Graph Feature Interaction Layer (GFIL)

On the top of corporation to graph layer, we utilize graph attention network to simulate different importance feature interactions. Graph attention networks can automatically model feature interactions with attention mechanism.

We can further stack more graph attention network layers to explore the high-order information, gathering the information propagated from the higher-hop neighbors. More formally, in the l-th GAT layer, for the node v_i of graph $\mathcal{G}$ the update function is recursively formulated as follows:

$$x_i^{(l)} = \alpha_{i,i}^{(l)} \Theta^{(l)} x_i^{(l-1)} + \sum_{j \in \mathcal{N}_{(i)}} \alpha_{i,j}^{(l)} \Theta^{(l)} x_j^{(l-1)} \tag{4}$$

Algorithm 1: Corporation To Graph (G2G)

Input: The set of corporations: C; Iteration magnitude c
Output: The connected graph set G, $\mathcal{G} = (\mathcal{V}, \mathcal{E}) \in G$ with node attribute x.

---

1 Initialize empty graph set G
2 **foreach** *corporation c in C* **do**
3 | Obtain the corporate embedding expression x via Equation 1
4 | Get feature interaction map $\widetilde{A}$ by Equation 2
5 | Initial threshold value $r = max\left(\widetilde{A}\right)$
6 | **while** *True* **do**
7 | | Compute adjacent matrix A via Equation 3 under threshold r
8 | | Construct graph $\mathcal{G} = (\mathcal{V}, \mathcal{E})$ with A
9 | | **if** $\mathcal{G}$ *is a connected graph* **then**
10 | | | break;
11 | | **else**
12 | | | $r = r - c$;
13 | | **end**
14 | **end**
15 | Add the graph $\mathcal{G}$ into graph set G
16 **end**
17 **return** graph set G

---

where the $\Theta^{(l)} \in \mathbb{R}^{d^{(l)} \times d^{(l-1)}}$ and $a \in \mathbb{R}^{2d^{(l)}}$ are GAT layer parameters, $x^{(l-1)} \in \mathbb{R}^{d \times d^{(l-1)}}$ is the input of GAT layer, the output $x^{(l)} \in \mathbb{R}^{d \times d^{(l)}}$ and the attention coefficients $\alpha_{i,j}^{(l)}$ are computed as:

$$\alpha_{i,j}^{l} = \frac{\exp\left(LeakReLU\left(a^{T^{(l)}}\left[\Theta^{(l)}x_i^{(l-1)} \parallel \Theta^{(l)}x_j^{(l-1)}\right]\right)\right)}{\sum_{k \in \mathcal{N}(i) \cup \{i\}} \exp\left(LeakReLU\left(a^{T^{(l)}}\left[\Theta^{(l)}x_i^{(l-1)} \parallel \Theta^{(l)}x_k^{(l-1)}\right]\right)\right)} \quad (5)$$

In the first layer of GFIL, the layer input is the corporate graph with features. In other words, $x^{(0)} = x \in \mathbb{R}^d$. Clearly, the high-order feature interactions are modeled into the representation learning process.

Graph Pooling. Besides local high-order feature interaction, graph pooling is designed after each GAT layers, in order to merge the global information. The pooling process can be formulated as:

$$z^{(l)} = GraphPooling(x^{(l)}) \quad (6)$$

where $z^{(l)} \in \mathbb{R}^{d^{(l)}}$ is graph global information at l-th layer. In despite of some intricate methods, here we use some simple but effective mechanisms to implement it, such as max pooling, mean pooling.

3.5   Credit Rating Layer (CRL)

In GFIL layer, we get local high-order feature interactions through GAT layer and global graph information through pooling. After performing L layers, we obtain multiple node representations, namely $\{x^{(0)}, x^{(1)}, \cdots, x^{(L)}\}$ and graph representations, namely $\{z^{(1)}, z^{(2)}, \cdots, z^{(L)}\}$. Inspired by ResNet and DenseNet, we aggregate local and global information firstly, then perform credit rating process by Multi-Layer Perceptron (MLP), which can be formulated as follows:

$$r_{local} = concatenate(reshape(\{x^{(0)}, x^{(1)}, \cdots, x^{(L)}\}))$$
$$r_{global} = concatenate(\{z^{(1)}, z^{(2)}, \cdots, z^{(L)}\}) \tag{7}$$

where $r_{local} \in \mathbb{R}^{d(1+\sum_{l=1}^{L} d^{(l)})}$ and $r_{global} \in \mathbb{R}^{\sum_{l=1}^{L} d^{(l)}}$. Finally, the result of credit rating $\hat{y}$ is executed by MLP and softmax.

$$\hat{y} = log\_softmax(MLP([r_{local}; r_{global}])) \tag{8}$$

where $\hat{y} \in \mathbb{R}^m$ denotes the probabilities of labels.

For training model, the loss function is defined as the cross-entropy of the prediction and the ground truth, it can be written as follows:

$$\mathcal{L}(\hat{y}) = -\sum_{i=1}^{m} y_i \log(\hat{y}_i) + (1 - y_i) \log(1 - \hat{y}_i) + \lambda\|\Delta\|^2 \tag{9}$$

where y denotes the one-hot encoding vector of ground truth item, λ is parameter specific regularization hyperparameters to prevent overfitting, and the model parameters of CCR-GNN are Δ.

Finally, the Back-Propagation algorithm is performed to train the proposed CCR-GNN model.

4   Experiments

In this section, we describe the extensive experiments for evaluating the effectiveness of our proposed methods. We describe the datasets at first, then present the experimental results of CCR-GNN compared with other baselines, which is the main task of this paper.

4.1   Data Set and Pre-processing

The corporate credit dataset has been built based on the annual financial statements of Chinese listed companies and China Stock Market & Accounting Research Database (CSMRA). The results of credit rating are conducted by famous credit rating agency, including CCXI, China Lianhe Credit Rating (CLCR), etc. We split the dataset into a training set (80%), validation set (10%), and test set (10%). We find out that credit rating agencies, like Standard & Poor's, Moody's and CCXI, often give AA, A, BBB to most corporations, and few of them are CC, C. Real-world data is often noisy and incomplete. There-fore, the first step of any prediction problem to credit rating, in particular, is to clean data such that we maintain as much meaningful information as possible. Specifically, we delete features which miss most of value, and for features with a few missing values are filled in by the mean value. After data pre-processing which we use min-max normalization for numerical data and one-hot encoding for category data, we get 39 features and 9 rating labels: AAA, AA, A, BBB, BB, B, CCC, CC, C. The Table 1 will show details. Then Synthetic Minority Oversampling Technique (SMOTE) is conducted to perform data augmentation in terms of class-imbalance problem.

Table 1. Data set description.

Index	Criterion layer		Feature name
1	Financial data	Profit capability	Net income
...			...
6		Operation capability	Inventory turn ratio
...			...
11		Growth capability	Year-on-year asset
...			...
18		Repayment capability	Liability to asset
...			...
25		Cash flow capability	Ebit to interest
...			...
30		Dupont identity	Dupont return on equity
...			...
...	Non-financial data		...
39			Tax credit rating

4.2 Comparison with Baseline Methods

Baseline Methods. We use the following widely used approaches in the finan-cial field as baselines to highlight the effectiveness of our proposed methods:

- **LR:** Logistic regression (LR) [26] model for multi-label classification. We apply L2 normalization and follow the-regularized-leader (FTRL) for opti-mization.
- **SVM:** Support Vector Machine with linear kernel.
- **MLP:** Multi-Layer Perceptron, A simple neural network. We use 1000 hidden units in the experiments and ReLU for activation function.
- **GBDT:** Gradient Boosting Decision Tree [27], it is an iterative decision tree algorithm. The algorithm, which is a popular ensemble learning method for classification, consists of multiple decision trees, and the conclusions of all trees are added together to make the final answer.

- **Xgboost:** eXtreme Gradient Boosting [28], a scalable machine learning system for tree boosting.

Hyper-Parameter Setup. In our experiments, we use three graph attention layers, attention channels = $\{8, 64, 9\}$ respectively. First two graph attention layers use Mean Pooling and the last is Max Pooling. All parameters are initialized using a Xavier uniform distribution with a mean of 0, and a standard deviation of 0.1. The Adam optimizer is exerted to optimize these parameters, where the initial learning rate is set to 0.001 and will decay by 0.0001 after every 3 training epochs. Moreover, the L2 penalty is set to 0.00001.

Evaluation Metrics. We adopt three commonly-used metrics for evaluation, including precision, recall and F1-score. In detail, we count the number of correct identification of positive labels as True Positives TP, incorrect identification of positive labels in False Positives FP, incorrect identification of positive labels in False Positives FP and incorrect identification of negative labels in False Negative FN. Then these metrics can be calculated as:

$$Recall = \sum_{i-1}^{m} \frac{TP_i}{TP_i + FN_i} \tag{10}$$

$$Precision = \sum_{i=1}^{m} \frac{TP_i}{TP_i + FP_i} \tag{11}$$

$$F1 - Score = \sum_{i=1}^{m} \frac{2 \left(Precision_i * Recall_i\right)}{\left(Precision_i + Recall_i\right)} \tag{12}$$

where m is the number of labels, $Precision_i$ and $Recall_i$ are the metrics for i-th class respectively.

Experiments Results. To demonstrate the overall performance of the proposed model, we compare it with other baseline models. The overall performance in terms of recall, accuracy and F1-score is shown in Table 2. The best results are highlighted as bold. The xgboost is second only to CCR-GNN.

Table 2. The Performance of CCR-GNN with other Baselines

Model	Recall	Accuracy	F1-score
LR	0.76250	0.80970	0.81946
SVM	0.83750	0.89247	0.88961
MLP	0.91406	0.93568	0.93254
GBDT	0.91875	0.92647	0.9187
xgboost	0.92343	0.94225	0.94133
CCR-GNN	**0.93437**	**0.95012**	**0.95177**

According to the experiments, it is obvious that the proposed CCR-GNN method achieves the best performance on real dataset (Chinese public-listed corporate rating dataset). By stacking multiple graph attention layers, CCR-GNN is capable of exploring the high-order feature interactions in an explict way. This verifies the effectiveness of the proposed method.

5   Conclusions

In this work, we develop a novel graph neural network for corporate credit rating named CCR-GNN. Corporation-To-Graph is proposed for each corporation to build a graph according to the relations between features. By utilizing the power of GAT, CCR-GNN can capture both local and global information. Besides, extensive experiments on Chinese public-listed corporate rating dataset are conducted to demonstrate the effectiveness of our model. Therefore, CCR-GNN provides an effective tool for financial regulators to control potential credit risk.

References

1. Golbayani, P., Wang, D., Florescu, I.: Application of deep neural networks to assess corporate credit rating. arXiv preprint arXiv:2003.02334 (2020)
2. Golbayani, P., Florescu, I., Chatterjee, R.: A comparative study of forecasting corporate credit ratings using neural networks, support vector machines, and decision trees. N. Am. J. Econ. Finance **54**, 101251 (2020)
3. Provenzano, A.R., et al.: Machine learning approach for credit scoring. arXiv preprint arXiv:2008.01687 (2020)
4. Bravo, C., Thomas, L.C., Weber, R.: Improving credit scoring by differentiating defaulter behaviour. J. Oper. Res. soc. **66**(5), 771–781 (2015)
5. Barja, A., et al.: Assessing the risk of default propagation in interconnected sectoral financial networks. EPJ Data Sci. **8**(1), 32 (2019)
6. Bruss, C.B., Khazane, A., Rider, J., Serpe, R., Gogoglou, A., Hines, K.E.: Deep-Trax: embedding graphs of financial transactions. arXiv preprint arXiv:1907.07225 (2019)
7. Cheng, D., Niu, Z., Zhang, Y.: Contagious chain risk rating for networked-guarantee loans. In: Proceedings of the 26th ACM SIGKDD International Conference on Knowledge Discovery & Data Mining, pp. 2715–2723 (2020)
8. Cheng, D., Tu, Y., Ma, Z.-W., Niu, Z., Zhang, L.: Risk assessment for networked-guarantee loans using high-order graph attention representation. In: IJCAI, pp. 5822–5828 (2019)
9. Cheng, D., Xiang, S., Shang, C., Zhang, Y., Yang, F., Zhang, L.: Spatio-temporal attention-based neural network for credit card fraud detection. Proc. AAAI Conf. Artif. Intell. **34**, 362–369 (2020)
10. Cheng, D., Zhang, Y., Yang, F., Tu, Y., Niu, Z., Zhang, L.: A dynamic default prediction framework for networked-guarantee loans. In: Proceedings of the 28th ACM International Conference on Information and Knowledge Management, pp. 2547–2555 (2019)
11. Gogas, P., Papadimitriou, T., Agrapetidou, A.: Forecasting bank credit ratings. J. Risk Finan. **15**, 195–209 (2014)

12. Petropoulos, A., Chatzis, S.P., Xanthopoulos, S.: A novel corporate credit rating system based on student'st hidden Markov models. Expert Syst. Appl. **53**, 87–105 (2016)
13. Kim, K.S.: Predicting bond ratings using publicly available information. Expert Syst. Appl. **29**(1), 75–81 (2005)
14. Cao, L., Guan, L.K., Jingqing, Z.: Bond rating using support vector machine. Intell. Data Anal. **10**(3), 285–296 (2006)
15. Yeh, C.-C., Lin, F., Hsu, C.-Y.: A hybrid KMV model, random forests and rough set theory approach for credit rating. Knowl.-Based Syst. **33**, 166–172 (2012)
16. Pai, P.-F., Tan, Y.-S., Hsu, M.-F.: Credit rating analysis by the decision-tree support vector machine with ensemble strategies. Int. J. Fuzzy Syst. **17**(4), 521–530 (2015)
17. Wu, T.-C., Hsu, M.-F.: Credit risk assessment and decision making by a fusion approach. Knowl. Based Syst. **35**, 102–110 (2012)
18. Perozzi, B., Al-Rfou, R., Skiena, S.: Deepwalk: Online learning of social representations. In: Proceedings of the 20th ACM SIGKDD International Conference on Knowledge Discovery and Data Mining, pp. 701–710 (2014)
19. Tang, J., Qu, M., Wang, M., Zhang, M., Yan, J., Mei, Q.: Line: Large-scale information network embedding. In: Proceedings of the 24th International Conference on World Wide Web, pp. 1067–1077 (2015)
20. Grover, A., Leskovec, J.: node2vec: scalable feature learning for networks. In: Proceedings of the 22nd ACM SIGKDD International Conference on Knowledge Discovery and Data Mining, pp. 855–864 (2016)
21. Kipf, T.N., Welling, M.: Semi-supervised classification with graph convolutional networks. arXiv preprint arXiv:1609.02907 (2016)
22. Veličković, P., Cucurull, G., Casanova, A., Romero, A., Lio, P., Bengio, Y.: Graph attention networks. arXiv preprint arXiv:1710.10903 (2017)
23. Beutel, A., et al.: Latent cross: making use of context in recurrent recommender systems. In: Proceedings of the Eleventh ACM International Conference on Web Search and Data Mining, pp. 46–54 (2018)
24. He, X., Du, X., Wang, X., Tian, F., Tang, J., Chua, T-S.: Outer product-based neural collaborative filtering. arXiv preprint arXiv:1808.03912 (2018)
25. He, X., Liao, L., Zhang, H., Nie, L., Hu, X., Chua, T.-S.: Neural collaborative filtering. In: Proceedings of the 26th International Conference on world wide web, pp. 173–182 (2017)
26. McMahan, B.: Follow-the-regularized-leader and mirror descent: equivalence theorems and L1 regularization. In: Proceedings of the Fourteenth International Conference on Artificial Intelligence and Statistics, pp. 525–533 (2011)
27. Ke, G., et al.: LightGBM: a highly efficient gradient boosting decision tree. In: Advances in Neural Information Processing Systems, pp. 3146–3154 (2017)
28. Chen, T., Guestrin, C.: XGBoost: a scalable tree boosting system. In: Proceedings of the 22nd ACM SIGKDD International Conference on Knowledge Discovery and Data Mining, pp. 785–794 (2016)

Unsupervised Image Translation with GAN Prior

Pengqi Tu, Changxin Gao, and Nong Sang(✉)

Key Laboratory of Image Processing and Intelligent Control, School of Artificial Intelligence and Automation, Huazhong University of Science and Technology, Wuhan, China
{tpq,cgao,nsang}@hust.edu.cn

Abstract. Unsupervised image translation aims to learn the translation between two domains without paired data. Although impressive progress has been made in recent years, existing methods are difficult to build mapping between domains with drastic visual discrepancies. In this paper, we propose a novel framework for unsupervised image translation with large discrepancies. The key insight is to leverage the generative prior from pretrained GANs for the target domain (e.g., StyleGAN), to learn rich prior information of the target domain. We propose a two-stage framework, the GAN of the target domain is pretrained to obtain the prior information in the first stage, the pretrained GAN for the target domain is embedded as the decoder of the translation network and the translation network is trained with the guidance of the prior information in the second stage. Experimental results show the superiority of our method compared to the existing state-of-the-art methods for the translation between challenging and distant domains.

Keywords: Image translation · Generative prior · Two-stage

1 Introduction

Image translation aims to translate images from the source domain to the target domain. This task has attracted a lot of attention of researchers because of its wide range of applications, including image stylization [1–14], super resolution [15,16] and colorization [17–19]. When paired data is available, the translation model can be trained in a supervised manner by using conditional generative model [20]. However, paired data is difficult to obtain in the real world, so unsupervised image translation is the mainstream. In unsupervised settings, just as introduced in the survey [14], multiple works have successfully translated images by using shared latent space [21] and cycle consistency assumption [22].

Isola *et al.* [20] first propose conditional GAN for supervised image-to-image translation. Further, CycleGAN [22] and UNIT [21] have been proposed successively for unpaired image-to-image translation with the cycle-consistency constraint. To address the multi-modality issue, MUNIT [23] and DRIT [24] have

---

This work was funded by the DigiX Joint Innovation Center of Huawei-HUST.

S. Yu et al. (Eds.): PRCV 2022, LNCS 13534, pp. 700–711, 2022.
https://doi.org/10.1007/978-3-031-18907-4_54

been introduced to extend to many-to-many mapping by decomposing the image into domain-invariant code and domain-specific code and synthesizing the separated domain-invariant code of source image and domain-specific code of target image to generate the final image. In order to further improve the quality of the generated images, Kim *et al.* [25] propose the UGATIT, which includes an attention module and an Adaptive Layer-Instance Normalization (AdaLIN) module. The attention module tries to guide the model to focus on the most important regions by distinguishing between the source and target domain based on the attention map. The AdaLIN module can guide the model to control the change in shape and texture. Nizan *et al.* [26] propose the Council-GAN, which takes advantage of collaboration between various GANs to break the limitation of cycle-consistency constraint and address some of the shortcomings of classical GANs, such as removing large objects, large shape modifications.

Impressive results have been achieved in sample cases, such as the translation from horse to zebra. However, the performance of existing methods usually degrades drastically in translations with large cross-domain shape and appearance discrepancies, such as the translation from human face to animal face, which greatly limits their practical applications. For the translation across domains with large discrepancies, it is hard to train the translation network from scratch, the prior information of the target domain is required as the guidance before training the translation network. For instance, the direct translation from human face to cat face without prior information, the generated cat faces will lose many details because of the large discrepancies between them.

In this paper, we leverage generative prior of the target domain for unsupervised image translation between domains with large discrepancies, *i.e.*, the prior implicitly encapsulated in pretrained Generative Adversarial Network (GAN) [27] models of the target domain, such as StyleGAN [28,29]. The pretrained GANs are capable of generating faithful target images with a high degree of variability, and thereby providing rich and diverse priors such as geometry, textures and colors, making it possible to jointly learn the translation between domains with large discrepancies. To incorporate such generative priors into the translation process, we propose a two-stage framework. In the first stage, we pretrain a GAN for the target domain and embed it as a decoder prior of the translation network. StyleGAN is suitable for this task despite its generative space is of high quality and diversity. In the second stage, the GAN prior embedded translation network is fine-tuned by translating images from the source domain to the target domain, during which the translation network learns the mapping between the two domains. We carefully design the translation network to make it well suited for the StyleGAN, where the deep features are used to generate the latent code for global translated images reproduction, while the shallow features are used as noise to generate local generated image details and keep the image background. With the GAN prior, the translation network can learn the details and textures of target images well, which makes the translated image more realistic.

The main contributions of this work are summarized as follows:

- We propose a two-stage framework to embed the GAN prior for unsupervised image translation between domains with large discrepancies.
- We carefully design the translation network so that the pretrained StyleGAN can be easily embedded into it for fine-tuning.
- We conduct an extensive set of experiments to verify the effectiveness of our method in comparison with the existing methods on different datasets

2 Related Work

2.1 Generative Adversarial Network (GAN)

In recent years, Generative Adversarial Networks (GAN) [27] has achieved impressive results in image generation [30–34], image re-editing [35–37], image translation [20,22,38–42] and image stylization [1–13]. The core idea of GAN lies in the generative adversarial loss that enforces the generated image to match the distribution of the target image. GAN mainly consists of two components, a generator G: generating realistic target images from random noise or source images to fool the discriminator, a discriminator D: predicting the probabilities that images are from real images distribution to distinguish the generated images from real images, the two confront each other and complete the training together with the generative adversarial loss. Based on the original GAN, various improved GANs and better training strategies have been proposed to generate more realistic and qualified images. Mirza *et al.* [43] propose Conditional Generative Adversarial Nets (CGAN), which is the conditional version of GAN for paired image generation, Arjovsky *et al.* [30] propose Wasserstein Generative Adversarial Networks (WGAN) which introduces a new algorithm to replace the traditional GAN training way, Zhu *et al.* [22] propose the Cycle-Consistent Generative Adversarial Networks (CycleGAN) for unpaired image generation. In this paper, we adopt the training way of CycleGAN to learn the unsupervised translation from source images to significantly different target images.

2.2 Image Translation

Image-to-image translation aims to map images of one domain to another domain and can change the objects, attributes, and style of source images, which can be used for image colorization [17–19], super-resolution [15,16],and domain adaptation [44,45]. Isola *et al.* [20] first propose conditional GAN for paired image-to-image translation. Further, CycleGAN [22] and UNIT [21] have been proposed successively for unpaired image-to-image translation with the cycle-consistency constraint. To address the multi-modality issue, MUNIT [23] and DRIT [24] have been introduced to extend to many-to-many mapping by decomposing the image into domain-invariant code and domain-specific code and synthesizing the separated domain-invariant code of source image and domain-specific code of target image to generate the final image. In order to further improve the quality of the generated images, Kim *et al.* [25] propose the UGATIT, which includes an attention module and an Adaptive Layer-Instance Normalization (AdaLIN) module. The attention module tries to guide the model to focus on the most important regions by distinguishing between the source and target domain based on the attention map. The AdaLIN module can guide the model to control the change in shape and texture. Nizan *et al.* [26] propose the Council-GAN, which takes advantage of collaboration between various GANs to break the limitation of cycle consistency constraint and address some of the shortcomings of classical GANs, such as removing large objects, large shape modifications.

2.3 GAN Prior

GAN prior of pretrained GANs [28, 29, 46, 47] is previously exploited by GAN inversion [48–51], whose primary aim is to find the closest latent codes given an input image. PULSE [52] iteratively optimizes the latent code of StyleGAN [28] until the distance between outputs and inputs is below a threshold. mGANprior [49] attempts to optimize multiple codes to improve the reconstruction quality. However, these methods usually produce images with low fidelity, because the low-dimension latent codes are insufficient to guide the translation. In contrast, our proposed two-stage framework enables prior incorporation on multi-resolution spatial features to achieve high fidelity. Besides, expensive iterative optimization is not required in our model during inference.

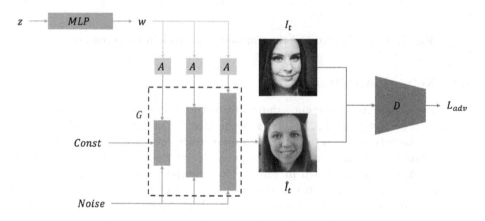

Fig. 1. The architecture of StyleGAN in the first stage.

3 Method

3.1 Two-stage Framework

In this section, we describe our proposed two-stage framework that leverages the GAN prior encapsulated in pretrained StyleGAN for unsupervised image translation between domains with large discrepancies. In the first stage, we pre-train the StyleGAN for the target domain by using the original training way of StyleGAN. In the second stage, the pretrained StyleGAN is embedded as a decoder prior of the translation network. Then, the GAN prior embedded translation network is fine-tuned by translating images from the source domain to the target domain, during which the GAN prior will guide the fine-tuning of translation process between the two domains. While in the two-stage framework, we carefully design the translation network so that the pretrained StyleGAN can be easily embedded into it for fine-tuning. The architectures of StyleGAN and translation network are shown in Figs. 1 and 2, which will be explained in detail in the following sections.

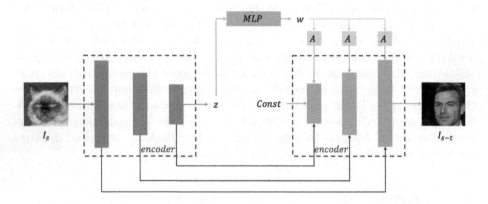

Fig. 2. The architecture of the translation network in the second stage.

3.2   Network Architecture

Let $x_s, x_t \in \{X_s, X_t\}$ represent samples from the source domain and the target domain respectively, let x_{s-t} represents the translated image. We adopt Style-GAN as the network architecture of the first stage, which is pretrained for the target domain with the original training way, to get the prior information of the target domain, just as shown in Fig 1. The translation network of the second stage is designed carefully, just as shown in Fig 2. The translation network consists of an encoder, an multi-layers perceptual machine (MLP), multiple affine transformation modules (A) and a decoder, in which the multi-layers perceptual machine, multiple affine transformation modules and decoder are from the pre-trained StyleGAN of the first stage. The source image I_s is sent to the encoder to generate the latent code z, which is the substitute of z in StyleGAN and used for the global translated image reproduction. The shallow features output by the decoder are the substitute of noise in StyleGAN and used to generate local details of the translated image I_{s-t}. Furthermore, the noise inputs are concatenated rather than added to the correspond features output by the decoder. We empirically found that this can obtain more details in the translated image.

Then, the whole translation network will be fine-tuned so that the encoder part and decoder part can learn to adapt to each other.

3.3 Loss Functions

We adopt the training way of CycleGAN to train the translation network, the full objective of our model includes three loss functions. Here, we will introduce these loss functions in the following part. Let G_{s-t} represents the translation work from the source domain to the target domain. Let G_{t-s} represents the translation network from the target domain to the source domain.

Adversarial Loss. This loss is mainly used to match the distribution of the stylized images to the target images:

$$
\begin{aligned}
L_{Adv} = \min_{G} \max_{D} E_{x \sim X_t}[(D_t(x))^2] \\
+ E_{x \sim X_s}[(1 - D_t(G_{s-t}(x)))^2]
\end{aligned}
\tag{1}
$$

Cycle Loss. To avoid the mode collapse issue, we used the cycle consistency loss during translation. After the successive translations of x_s from X_s to X_t and from X_t to X_s, the reconstructed source image should be consistent with the source image x_s:

$$
L_{cycle} = \|x_s - G_{t-s}(G_{s-t}(x_s))\|_1
\tag{2}
$$

Identity Loss. To make sure the generator will only change the difference between the source domain and the target domain, we apply the identity loss to constrain the generator. After the translation of x_t using G_{s-t}, the image should not be changed:

$$
L_{identity} = \|x_t - G_{s-t}(x_t)\|_1
\tag{3}
$$

Full Objective. Finally, we jointly train the whole network to optimize the full objective:

$$
L = \beta_1 L_{Adv} + \beta_2 L_{cycle} + \beta_3 L_{identity}
\tag{4}
$$

where $\beta_1 = 1$, $\beta_2 = 10$, $\beta_3 = 10$.

These hyperparameters are initialized empirically. Then, they are artificially tuned based on experimental results.

4 Experiments

4.1 Implementation Details

We have compared our model with existing methods, including CycleGAN [22], CUT [53], UGATIT [25], and StarGAN v2 [54]. All the models are implemented by using the author's code.

We perform evaluation on two translation tasks. 1) The transaltion between Cat and Dog on AFHQ [54], with 4K training images per domain. 2) The translation between Cat and Human Face on 4K AFHQ images and 29K CelebA-HQ images.

Table 1. Preference scores on translated results by user study.

Method	Task			
	Cat2Dog	Dog2Cat	Cat2Face	Face2Cat
CycleGAN	0.5	0	0	0
CUT	15	12.5	0	0
UGATIT	10.5	9	0	0
StarGAN v2	20	18	43	37
Ours	**54**	**60.5**	**57**	**63**

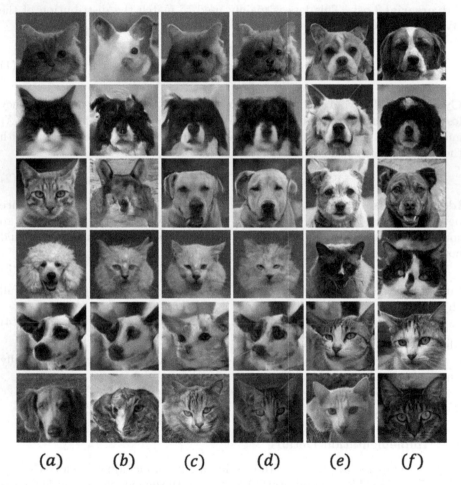

(a) (b) (c) (d) (e) (f)

Fig. 3. Visual comparisons of existing methods, Cat2Dog and Dog2Cat. (a) Source images, (b) CycleGAN, (c) CUT, (d) UGATIT, (e) StarGAN v2, (f) Ours.

4.2   Qualitative Evaluation

In this subsection, we conduct a user study for qualitative evaluation. 200 participants are shown translated results of different methods on the translation between Cat and Dog, and the translation between Cat and Human Face. Then, they are asked to select the best-translated results. We will inform the name and show some example images of the target domain, *e.g.* cat, dog and human face to the participants. Table 1 shows that our method achieves the highest scores on these translation tasks in the user study compared to other existing methods. For each type of translation, *e.g.* from Cat to Dog and from Cat to Human Face, we present the corresponding translated results of each method for performance comparison in Fig. 3 and 4. According the visual comparison, the translated results using proposed two-stage framework are visually superior

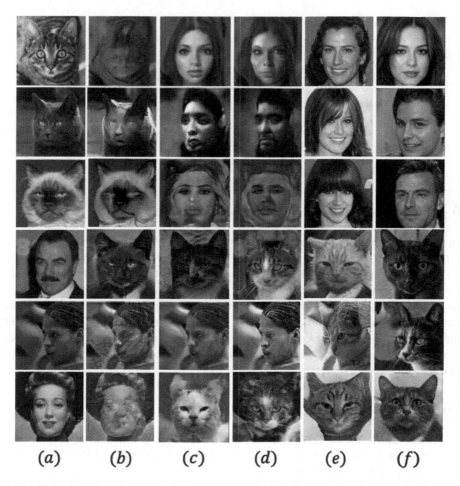

(a)   *(b)*   *(c)*   *(d)*   *(e)*   *(f)*

Fig. 4. Visual comparisons of existing methods, Cat2Face and Face2Cat. (a) Source images, (b) CycleGAN, (c) CUT, (d) UGATIT, (e) StarGAN v2, (f) Ours.

to other methods in the reality and fidelity, which proves the effectiveness of proposed method from a qualitative point of view.

4.3 Quantitative Evaluation

We adopt the FID to evaluate the quality of translated images for quantitative evaluation. FID computes the squared Maximum Mean Discrepancy between the feature representations of target images and translated images. The feature representations are extracted from the Inception V3 network [55]. The lower FID indicates the higher quality and fidelity of translated images. Table 2 shows that the proposed method achieves the lowest FID scores on all translation tasks (translation between Cat and Dog, translation between Cat and Human Face), which proves that our method has the best-translated results.

Table 2. FID scores on translated results. Lower is better.

Method	Task			
	Cat2Dog	Dog2Cat	Cat2Face	Face2Cat
CycleGAN	54.6	67.8	118.7	140.6
CUT	33.7	35.9	104.1	115.8
UGATIT	38.2	43.9	110.6	128.7
StarGAN v2	23.7	25.9	13.1	15.8
Ours	**16.1**	**13.2**	**12.5**	**14.7**

5 Conclusion

In this paper, we propose a two-stage framework for unsupervised image translation between domains with large discrepancies, which proves to produce more faithful results on different translation tasks. Qualitative and quantitative analysis of various experimental results verify that the two-stage framework can effectively obtain the prior information of the target domain and guide the training process of the translation network. As a result, our method significantly outperforms the state-of-the-art GAN-based models for unsupervised image translation between domains with large discrepancies, in terms of the quality and fidelity of translated results.

References

1. Gatys, L. A., Ecker, A. S., Bethge, M.: Image style transfer using convolutional neural networks. In: IEEE Conference on Computer Vision and Pattern Recognition, pp. 2414–2423 (2016)
2. Huang, X., Belongie, S. J.: Arbitrary style transfer in real-time with adaptive instance normalization. In: IEEE International Conference on Computer Vision, pp. 1510–1519 (2017)

3. Gu, S., Chen, C., Liao, J., Yuan, L.: Arbitrary style transfer with deep feature reshuffle. In: IEEE Conference on Computer Vision and Pattern Recognition, pp. 8222–8231 (2018)
4. Kotovenko, D., Sanakoyeu, A., Ma, P., Lang, S., Ommer, B.: A content transformation block for image style transfer. In: IEEE Conference on Computer Vision and Pattern Recognition, pp. 10032–10041 (2019)
5. Gatys, L. A., Ecker, A. S., Bethge, M.: Texture synthesis using convolutional neural networks. In: Neural Information Processing Systems, pp. 262–270 (2015)
6. Chen, T. Q., Schmidt, M.: Fast patch-based style transfer of arbitrary style arXiv: 1612.04337 (2016)
7. Jing, Y., Yang, Y., Feng, Z., Ye, J., Song, M.: Neural style transfer: a review. arXiv: 1705.04058 (2017)
8. Li, C., Wand, M.: Combining Markov random fields and convolutional neural networks for image synthesis. In: IEEE Conference on Computer Vision and Pattern Recognition, pp. 2479–2486 (2016)
9. Johnson, J., Alahi, A., Li, F.: Perceptual losses for real-time style transfer and super-resolution. In: European Conference on Computer Vision, pp. 694–711 (2016)
10. Ulyanov, D., Lebedev, V., Vedaldi, A., Lempitsky, V. S.: Texture networks: feed-forward synthesis of textures and stylized images. In: International Conference on Machine Learning, pp. 1349–1357 (2016)
11. Li, Y., Fang, C., Yang, J. Wang, Z., Lu, X., Yang, M.:Universal style transfer via feature transforms. In: Neural Information Processing Systems, pp. 386–396 (2017)
12. Sheng, L., Lin, Z., Shao, J., Wang, X.: Avatar-net: multi-scale zero-shot style transfer by feature decoration. In: IEEE Conference on Computer Vision and Pattern Recognition, pp. 8242–8250 (2018)
13. Yao, Y., Ren, J., Xie, X., Liu, W., Liu, Y., Wang, J.: Attention-aware multi-stroke style transfer. In: IEEE Conference on Computer Vision and Pattern Recognition, pp. 1467–1475 (2019)
14. Tu, P., Gao, C., Sang, N.: A survey of image stylization methods based on deep neural networks. In: Pattern Recognition and Artificial Intelligence (2022)
15. Dong, C., Loy, C. C., He, K., Tang, X.: Learning a deep convolutional network for image super-resolution. In: European Conference on Computer Vision, pp. 184–199 (2014)
16. Ledig, C., et al.: Photo-realistic single image super-resolution using a generative adversarial network. In: IEEE Conference on Computer Vision and Pattern Recognition, pp. 4681–4690 (2017)
17. Deshpande, A., Lu, J., Yeh, M., Forsyth, D. A.:Learning diverse image colorization. In: IEEE Conference on Computer Vision and Pattern Recognition, pp. 6837–6845 (2017)
18. Cho, W., et al.: Text2colors: guiding image colorization through text-driven palette generation. In: European Conference on Computer Vision, pp. 431–447 (2018)
19. Yoo, S., Bahng, H., Chung, S., Lee, J., Chang, J., Choo, J.: Coloring with limited data: few-shot colorization via memory-augmented networks. In: IEEE Conference on Computer Vision and Pattern Recognition, pp. 11283–11292 (2019)
20. Isola, P., Zhu, J., Zhou, T., Efros, A. A.: Image-to-image translation with conditional adversarial networks. In: IEEE Conference on Computer Vision and Pattern Recognition, pp. 5967–5976 (2017)
21. Liu, M., Breuel, T., Kautz, J.:Unsupervised image-to-image translation networks. In: Neural Information Processing Systems, pp. 700–708 (2017)

22. Zhu, J., Park, T., Isola, P., Efros, A. A.: Unpaired image-to-image translation using cycle-consistent adversarial networks. In: IEEE International Conference on Computer Vision, pp. 2242–2251 (2017)

23. Huang, X., Liu, M., Belongie, S. J., Kautz, J.: Multimodal unsupervised image-to-image translation. In: European Conference on Computer Vision, pp. 179–196 (2018)

24. Lee, H., Tseng, H., Huang, J., Singh, M., Yang, M.: Diverse image-to-image translation via disentangled representations. In: European Conference on Computer Vision, pp. 36–52 (2018)

25. Kim, J., Kim, M., Kang, H., Lee, K.: U-GAT-IT: unsupervised generative attentional networks with adaptive layer-instance normalization for image-to-image translation. In: International Conference on Learning Representations (2020)

26. Nizan, O., Tal, A.: Breaking the cycle-colleagues are all you need. In: IEEE Conference on Computer Vision and Pattern Recognition, pp. 7860–7869 (2020)

27. Goodfellow, I. J., et al.: Generative adversarial nets. In: Neural Information Processing Systems, pp. 2672–2680 (2014)

28. Karras, T., Laine, S., Aila, T.: A style-based generator architecture for generative adversarial networks. In: IEEE Conference on Computer Vision and Pattern Recognition, pp. 4401–4410 (2019)

29. Karras, T., Laine, S., Aittala, M., Hellsten, J., Lehtinen, J., Aila, I.: Analyzing and improving the image quality of stylegan. In: IEEE Conference on Computer Vision and Pattern Recognition, pp. 8110–8119 (2020)

30. Arjovsky, M., Chintala, S., Bottou, L.: Wasserstein generative adversarial networks. In: International Conference on Machine Learning, pp. 214–223 (2017)

31. Berthelot, D., Schumm, T., Metz, L.: BEGAN: boundary equilibrium generative adversarial networks, arXiv: 1703.10717 (2017)

32. Zhao, J. J., Mathieu, M., LeCun, Y.: Energy-based generative adversarial networks. In: International Conference on Learning Representations (2017)

33. Karras, T., Aila, T., Laine, S., Lehtinen, J.: Progressive growing of GANs for improved quality, stability, and variation. In: International Conference on Learning Representations (2018)

34. Brock, A., Donahue, J., Simonyan, K.: Large scale GAN training for high fidelity natural image synthesis. In: International Conference on Learning Representations (2019)

35. Perarnau, G., van de Weijer, J., Raducanu, B., Alvarez, J. M.: Invertible conditional gans for image editing, arXiv: 1611.06355 (2016)

36. Gorijala, M., Dukkipati, A.: Image generation and editing with variational info generative adversarial networks, arXiv: 1701.04568 (2017)

37. Cheng, Y., Gan, Z., Li, Y., Liu, J., Gao, J.: Sequential attention GAN for interactive image editing via dialogue, arXiv: 1812.08352 (2018)

38. Choi, Y., Choi, M., Kim, M., Ha, J., Kim, S., Choo, J.: StarGAN: Unified generative adversarial networks for multi-domain image-to-image translation. In: IEEE Conference on Computer Vision and Pattern Recognition, pp. 8789–8797 (2018)

39. Wang, T., Liu, M., Zhu, J., Tao, A., Kautz, J., Catanzaro, B.: High-resolution image synthesis and semantic manipulation with conditional GANs. In: IEEE Conference on Computer Vision and Pattern Recognition, pp. 8798–8807 (2018)

40. Shao, X., Zhang, W.: SPatchGAN: a statistical feature based discriminator for unsupervised image-to-Image translation. In: IEEE International Conference on Computer Vision, pp. 6546–6555 (2021)

41. Tomei, M., Cornia, M., Baraldi, L., Cucchiara, R.: Art2real: Unfolding the reality of artworks via semantically-aware image-to-image translation. In: IEEE Conference on Computer Vision and Pattern Recognition, pp. 5849–5859 (2019)
42. Wei, Y., Zhang, Z., Wang, Y.:DeraincycleGAN: Rain attentive cycleGAN for single image deraining and rainmaking. In: IEEE Transactions on Image Processing (2021)
43. Mirza, M., Osindero, S.: Conditional generative adversarial nets, arXiv: 1411.1784 (2014)
44. Hoffman, J., et al.: CYCADA: Cycle-consistent adversarial domain adaptation. In: International Conference on Machine Learning (2018)
45. Li, X., Liu, S., Kautz, J., Yang, M.: Learning linear transformations for fast arbitrary style transfer. In: IEEE Conference on Computer Vision and Pattern Recognition, pp. 3809–3817 (2019)
46. Karras, T., Aila, T., Laine, S., Lehtinen, J.: Progressive growing of gans for improved quality, stability, and variation. In: International Conference on Learning Representations (2018)
47. Brock, A., Donahue, J., Simonyan, K.: Large scale GAN training for high fidelity natural image synthesis. In: International Conference on Learning Representations (2018)
48. Abdal, R., Qin, Y., Wonka, P.: IMAGE2styleGAN: how to embed images into the stylegan latent space? In: IEEE International Conference on Computer Vision (2019)
49. Gu, J., Shen, Y., Zhou, B.: Image processing using multi-code GAN prior. In: IEEE Conference on Computer Vision and Pattern Recognition (2020)
50. Pan, X., Zhan, X., Dai, B., Lin, D., Change Loy, C., Luo, P.: Exploiting deep generative prior for versatile image restoration and manipulation. In: European Conference on Computer Vision (2020)
51. Zhu, J., Shen, Y., Zhao, D., Zhou, B.: In-domain GAN inversion for real image editing. In: European Conference on Computer Vision (2020)
52. Menon, S., Damian, A., Hu, S., Ravi, N., Rudin, C.: Pulse: self-supervised photo upsampling via latent space exploration of generative models'. In: IEEE Conference on Computer Vision and Pattern Recognition (2020)
53. Park, T., Efros, A. A., Zhang, R., Zhu J. Y.: Contrastive learning for unpaired image-to-image translation. In: European Conference on Computer Vision, pp. 319–345, 2020
54. Choi, Y., Uh, Y., Yoo, J., Ha, J. -W.: Stargan v2: Diverse image synthesis for multiple domains. In: IEEE Conference on Computer Vision and Pattern Recognition, pp. 8188–8197 (2020)
55. Szegedy, C., Vanhoucke, V., Ioffe, S., Shlens, J., Wojna, Z.: Rethinking the inception architecture for computer vision. In: IEEE Conference on Computer Vision and Pattern Recognition, pp. 2818–2826 (2016)

An Adaptive PCA-Like Asynchronously Deep Reservoir Computing for Modeling Data-Driven Soft Sensors

Yingchun Bo$^{(\boxtimes)}$ ⓘ and Xin Zhang

College of Control Science and Engineering, China University of Petroleum, Qingdao 266580, China
boyingchun@sina.com

Abstract. Reservoir computing (RC) is a promising tool to build data-driven models, which has exhibited excellent performance in dynamical modeling area. Asynchronously deep reservoir computing (ADRC) is an improved version of RC. It generates more diverse dynamics in the reservoir than traditional RCs because of multi-layered structure and asynchronous information process. Reservoir size is a key factor to affect the performance of ADRC. However, the reservoir size of ADRC is very difficult to be determined. To solve this problem, an adaptive PCA (principal component analysis)-like method is proposed. This method promotes the useful reservoir neuron signals while suppresses the useless reservoir neuron signals. It is very similar to the function of PCA in data process. The training way of the adaptive PCA-like ADRC (APCA-ADRC) is derived based on ridge regression technique. The validity of the APCA-ADRC is tested by modeling the SO_2 concentration in sulfur recovery unit. Experimental results show it is prominent in building soft sensors with high performance.

Keywords: Recurrent neural networks · Principal component analysis · Ridge regression

1 Introduction

Nowadays, soft sensor has gained much attention in the process engineering area, which aims at building a model to estimate quality variables that are usually difficult to measure by hardware sensors [1–4]. Recurrent neural network (RNN) is a widely used tool among many data-driven modeling methods [5, 6]. RNNs possess dynamical characteristics because of feedback connections in their structures. Hence RNNs are good at finding the dynamical laws implied in the time-dependent industrial production process data. Reservoir computing (RC) is a promising tool to realize data-driven soft models. The RC is composed of a fixed neuron reservoir and an adaptable readout from the reservoir state space. The neurons in the reservoir are sparsely randomly connected among each other or themselves. A significant advantage of the RC approach is that only the output connection weights need to be adapted by learning, whereas the input connection weight and the internal connection weights are randomly given and then fixed. Algorithms for

S. Yu et al. (Eds.): PRCV 2022, LNCS 13534, pp. 712–721, 2022.
https://doi.org/10.1007/978-3-031-18907-4_55

linear regression can compute the optimal output weights [7]. Thus, it significantly reduces the training complexity of RNN. ADRC is an improvement version of RC [2], which divides the single reservoir in RC into a number of sub-reservoirs. These sub-reservoirs are connected one by one in sequence, and a delayed link is inserted between every two adjacent sub-reservoirs. ADRC generates more diverse dynamics in the reservoir than traditional RCs because of multi-layered structure and asynchronous information process. Some experiments show that ADRC achieves better performance than the traditional RC in many time-dependent tasks [2, 8].

Reservoir size is a key factor to affect the performance of ADRC. However, it is very difficult to determine the reservoir size of an ADRC, because there are too many randomly given and then fixed parameters [9]. To achieve a good RC for a given task, sometimes a lot of tedious tests have to be done. To solve this problem, this paper proposes an adaptive PCA-like method. This method can select useful neurons' signals from the reservoir and suppress useless neurons' signals in the reservoir adaptively. Under this circumstance, only part of reservoir neurons participate in modeling task, while the unimportant reservoir neurons' signals are neglected adaptively. It is equivalent to adaptively adjusting the reservoir size. The experimental results show that this adaptive PCA-like method is valid to extract useful signals from the reservoir states, and it is helpful to free oneself from the design of the reservoir.

2 Adaptive PCA-Like ADRC

2.1 Introduction of ADRC

ADRC contains three components: the input, the reservoir, and the output (see Fig. 1). The reservoir is composed of a number of sub-reservoirs (or called layers) that are connected one by one in sequence, and a delayed module is inserted between every two adjacent sub-reservoirs. The ADRC has more dynamics than traditional RCs with single reservoir because of multilayered structure. In addition, the ADRC can realize asynchronously information processing in different layers because of the existence of the delayed links [2]. It further improves the dynamical characteristics because each layer processes different information.

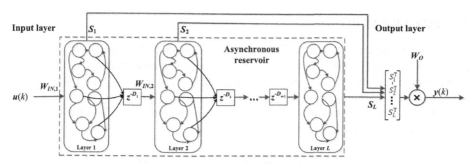

Fig. 1. Schematic diagram of ADRC

The dynamics of the ADRC can be expressed as:

$$s^l(k) = f\left(W_{IN}^l u^l(k) + W_R^l s^l(k-1)\right) \tag{1}$$

$$y(k) = W_O\left[\left(s^1(k)\right)^T \cdots \left(s^L(k)\right)^T\right]^T \tag{2}$$

where k is the current time step, l is layer ID, $u^l(k)$ is the external input of the l-th layer, $s^l(k)$ is the state of the l-th layer. W_{IN}^l, W_R^l are the input connection matrix and the inner connection matrix of the l-th layer respectively, and L is the amount of layer. The external input $u^l(k)$ is defined as

$$u^l(k) = \begin{cases} u(k), & l = 1 \\ s^{l-1}(k - \tau^l), & 1 < l \le L \end{cases} \tag{3}$$

where $u(k)$ is the external input of the ADRC at time step k. τ^l is the sum of the delayed time from the first layer to the l-th layer.

$$\tau^l = \sum_{j=1}^{l-1} D^j, \quad 1 \le l \le L \tag{4}$$

Only W_O needs to be learned in ADRC, whereas W_{IN} and W_R are randomly initiated and fixed. Under L_2 regulation, the training aim is

$$E = \min\left[\|W_{O,M} S_M - Y_M\| + \alpha^{-2}\|W_{O,M}\|\right] \tag{5}$$

where $W_{O,M}$ is the learned weight, $Y_M = [y_1, \ldots y_M]^T$ is the expected output set, M denotes smaple number, y_k denotes the k-th output sample, $S_M = [s_1, \ldots, s_M]$, s_k is the state of all sub-reservoirs at time step k, and α is a rather large positive value.

The closed-form solution of (5) is

$$W_{O,M} = \left(S_M S_M^T + \alpha^{-2} I\right) S_M Y_M \tag{6}$$

2.2 PCA-Like ADRC

How to determine the reservoir size has been a key issue faced by ADRC. The idea of this paper is to build an ADRC with a sufficient large reservoir size. Then the useful signals in the reservoir are extracted by an adaptive method. For a simple task, a small amount of signals are extracted. For a complex task, large amount of signals are extracted. To filter invalid signals in the reservoir states, a linear matrix is introduced into the dynamical equation of the reservoir. That is

$$s^l(k) = C^l f\left(W_{IN}^l u^l(k) + W_R^l s^l(k-1)\right) \tag{7}$$

where C^l is a $N^l \times N^l$ matrix, and N^l is the reservoir size of the l-th layer.

C^l is equivalent to a modulation matrix to control the reservoir dynamics, and it is determined by learning. The corresponding loss function is

$$E_{C,M}^l = \min\left[\left\|S_M^l - C_M^l S_M^l\right\| + \beta^{-2}\left\|C_M^l\right\|\right] \tag{8}$$

where $S^l = [s_1^l, \ldots, s_M^l]$, s_k^l is the state of the l-th layer generated by the k-th input sample, β is a large positive value.

El C,M has two components. The first component is $\|S_M^l - C_M^l S_M^l\|$. It reflects the objective that C^l should behave as a projector-like matrix for the states that occur in the pattern-driven run of the reservoir. The second component is $\beta^{-2}\|C_M^l\|$. It adjusts how many of the leading directions should become effective for the projection. According to the first component, C_M^l tends to an identity. According to the second component, C_M^l tends to a zero matrix. In intuitive terms, C_M^l likes a soft projection matrix on the linear subspace where the reservoir states lie. The projector-like matrix C_M^l can be shaped from the reservoir states by learning. At the same time, it can be adaptively adjusted to determine that how many of the leading principal components should become registered in C_M^l. Therefore, C_M^l can extract the principal components from the reservoir states of the l-th layer. In this sense, the function of C_M^l is very similar to the adaptive PCA. The closed-form solution of (8) is

$$C_M^l = \left(R_M^l + \beta^{-2}I\right)^{-1} R_M^l \tag{9}$$

where $R_M^l = S_M^l (S_M^l)^{\mathrm{T}}$ is the $N^l \times N^l$ correlation matrix of S^l.

According to the definition of R_M^l and C_M^l, if the singular value (SV) of R_M^l is σ_j ($j = 1, \ldots, N^l$), then the SV of C_M^l is $\sigma_j/(\sigma_j + \beta^{-2})$. It means that R_M^l and C_M^l have the same SV distribution.

2.3 Adaptive Algorithm for PCA-Like ADRC

PCA-like ADRC has two groups of parameters ($W_{O,M}$ and C_M^l) to be learned. They can be calculated by (6) and (9) respectively. Equations (6) and (9) are the batch least square (BLS) algorithm based on L_2 regulation (or called ridge regression BLS algorithm). The BLS algorithm needs to collect the states (S_M and S_M^l) at all time-steps firstly, and then calculate $W_{O,M}$ and C_M^l by Eqs. (6) and (9) respectively. It is sometimes difficult to collect information at all working conditions in real-life industrial process. Therefore, the BLS is unsuitable to realize adaptively learning. In light of that, we will derive the adaptive versions for Eqs. (6) and (9) in the following part. The adaptive versions for Eqs. (6) and (9) derived next are actually recursive least square (RLS) method based on ridge regression technique.

Equations (6) and (9) are very similar in form. Therefore, we give a detailed explanation about the derivation of the adaptive learning method for Eq. (6). The adaptive learning method form for Eq. (9) can be obtained by analogy.

According to the definition of S_M ($S_M = [s_1, \ldots, s_M]$), one can conclude that $S_M = [S_{M-1}s_M]$. Noting that $R_M = S_M S_M^{\mathrm{T}}$, therefore,

$$R_M = R_{M-1} + s_M s_M^{\mathrm{T}} \tag{10}$$

The matrix inversion lemma is

$$(A + BCD)^{-1} = A^{-1} - A^{-1}B(DA^{-1}B + C^{-1})^{-1}DA^{-1} \tag{11}$$

Let $A = R_{M-1}, B = s_M, C = I, D = s_M^T$, then

$$R_M^{-1} = R_{M-1}^{-1} - \frac{R_{M-1}^{-1}s_M s_M^T R_{M-1}^{-1}}{1 + s_M^T R_{M-1}^{-1}s_M} \tag{12}$$

Similarly, let $A = R_M, B = \alpha^{-2}, C = I, D = I$, then

$$\left(R_M + \alpha^{-2}I\right)^{-1} = R_M^{-1} - \alpha^{-2}R_M^{-1}\left(\alpha^{-2}R_M^{-1} + I\right)^{-1}R_M^{-1} \tag{13}$$

Because α is a quite large, $\alpha^{-2} R_M^{-1} + I \approx I$. Thus (13) is simplified to

$$\left(R_M + \alpha^{-2}I\right)^{-1} = \left(I - \alpha^{-2}R_M^{-1}\right)R_M^{-1} \tag{14}$$

Let $P_M = R_M^{-1}, P_{M-1} = R_{M-1}^{-1}$, and

$$K_M = \frac{P_{M-1}s_M}{1 + s_M^T P_{M-1}s_M} \tag{15}$$

Substituting (15) into (12), one can conclude that

$$P_M = \left(I - K_M s_M^T\right)P_{M-1} \tag{16}$$

Substituting (14) into (6) yields

$$W_{O,M} = \left(I - \alpha^{-2}P_M\right)P_M S_M Y_M \tag{17}$$

Therefore

$$W_{o,M} - W_{o,M-1} = \left(I - \alpha^{-2}P_{M-1}\right)(P_M S_M Y_M - P_{M-1}S_{M-1}Y_{M-1})$$
$$+ \alpha^{-2}K_M s_M^T P_{M-1}P_M S_M Y_M \tag{18}$$

Noting that

$$P_M S_M Y_M - P_{M-1}S_{M-1}Y_{M-1} = K_M\left(y_M - s_M^T W_{O,M-1}\right) \tag{19}$$

Therefore,

$$W_{o,M} = W_{o,M-1} + \left(I - \alpha^{-2}P_{M-1}\right)K_M\left(y_M - s_M^T W_{O,M-1}\right)$$
$$+ \alpha^{-2}K_M s_M^T P_{M-1}P_M S_M Y_M \tag{20}$$

According to the definition of S_M and Y_M, one can conclude that

$$S_M Y_M = S_{M-1} Y_{M-1} + s_M y_M \tag{21}$$

Let $Q_M = S_M Y_M$ and $Q_{M-1} = S_{M-1} Y_{M-1}$, then

$$Q_M = Q_{M-1} + s_M y_M \tag{22}$$

Substituting (22) into (20) yields

$$W_{O,M} = W_{O,M-1} + \left(I - \alpha^{-2} P_{M-1}\right) K_M \left(y_M - W_{O,M-1}^T s_M\right) \\ + \alpha^{-2} K_M s_M^T P_{M-1} P_M Q_M \tag{23}$$

By analogy, one can conclude that

$$C_M^l = C_{M-1}^l + \left(I - \beta^{-2} P_{M-1}^l\right) K_M^l \left(\left(s_M^l\right)^T - \left(s_M^l\right)^T C_{M-1}^l\right) \\ + \beta^{-2} K_M^l \left(s_M^l\right)^T P_{M-1}^l P_M^l Q_M^l \tag{24}$$

where

$$K_M^l = \frac{P_{M-1}^l s_M^l}{1 + \left(s_M^l\right)^T P_{M-1}^l s_M^l} \tag{25}$$

$$P_M^l = \left(I - K_M^l \left(s_M^l\right)^T\right) P_{M-1}^l \tag{26}$$

$$Q_M^l = Q_{M-1}^l + s_M^l \left(s_M^l\right)^T \tag{27}$$

3 Experiment

Sulfur Recovery unit (SRU, Fig. 2) is an important refinery processing module [10]. It removes environmental pollutants from acid gas streams before they are released into the atmosphere. Furthermore, elemental sulfur is recovered as a valuable byproduct. At present, on-line analyzers are used to measure the concentration of both hydrogen sulfide and sulfur dioxide in the tail gas of each sulfur line for control purposes. However, hydrogen sulfide and sulfur dioxide cause frequent damage to sensors, which often have to be taken off for maintenance. Therefore, it is necessary to design soft sensors that predict SO_2 concentration in the tail gas stream of the SRU. The soft sensors' model is usually described by an NMA system [11]. I.e., the model output y_k depends on the limited past inputs, that is

$$y_k = f\left(u_{1,k}..., u_{1,k-N_1}, u_{2,k}, ..., u_{2,k-N_2}, ..., u_{5,k}, ..., u_{5,k-N_5},\right) \tag{28}$$

where $u_{i,k}$ ($i = 1, ..., 5$) is the input and y_k the output.

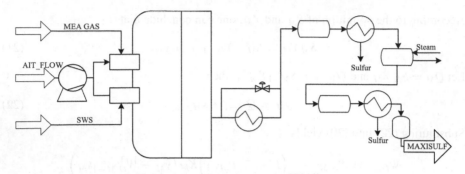

Fig. 2. Simplified scheme of a SRU line.

Table 1. Descriptions of input and output variables of the soft sensor for SRU.

Variable name	Description
u_1	MEA gas flow
u_2	First air flow
u_3	Second air flow
u_4	Gas flow in SWS zone
u_5	Air flow in SWS zone
y_1	SO$_2$ concentration

Table 2. Performance comparison of different models for SO$_2$ concentration in SRU.

Model type	Mean square error (MSE)
Multilayer-perceptron (MLP)	4.21×10^{-4}
Nonlinear Least Squares Quadratic (LSQ)	4.43×10^{-4}
Traditional RC	4.19×10^{-4}
ADRC	3.39×10^{-4}
APCA-ADRC	3.13×10^{-4}

There are totally 10000 data sampled from the SRU plant. We select the first 8000 samples as the training set and the following 2000 samples as the testing set. We compare the performance of five models (Table 2). Among these models, MLP and nonlinear LSQ have no dynamical characteristics and they feed $u(k)$, $u(k - 5)$, $u(k - 7)$ and $u(k - 9)$ into models by a sliding window. This method transfers a dynamical mapping into a static mapping. It is very critical to select the delayed $u(k)$ versions elaborately under the static mapping mode.

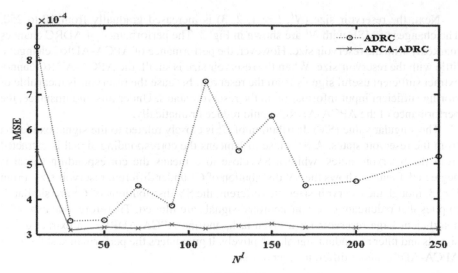

Fig. 3. Changes of MSE with reservoir size.

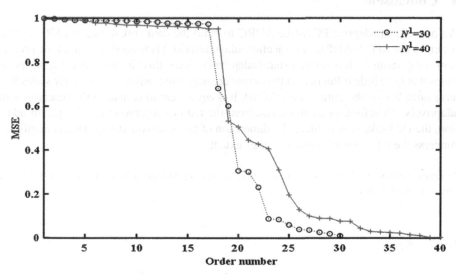

Fig. 4. SV distribution of C^1 under different reservoir size.

The RCs has naturally dynamical memory capability and the reservoir preserves a number of delayed input features in the states automatically when driven by $u(k)$. Therefore, only $u(k)$ is fed into the network. The ADRC and APCA-ADRC have the same macro parameters as follows: $L = 3$, $N^l = 30$ ($l = 1, 2, 3$), $D^l = 5$ ($l = 1, 2, 3$), spectral radius is 0.95, and $\alpha = \beta = 10^4$. For RC, ADRCs and APCA-ADRC, the elements in W_I and W_R are randomly initialized between -1 and 1. From Table 1, the MSE (mean square error) of APCA-ADRC reduces by 7.6% than that of ADRC.

Next, the reservoir size (N^l, $l = 1$, 2, 3) is increased gradually from 10 to 250. The changes of MSE with N^l are shown in Fig. 3. The performance of ADRC changes markedly with the reservoir size. However, the performance of APCA-ADRC changes a little with the reservoir size. When the reservoir size is small, the APCA-ADRC cannot extract sufficient useful signals from the reservoir, because the reservoir is incapable of storing sufficient input information in the reservoir states. Under this circumstance, the performance of the APCA-ADRC would reduce dramatically.

The singular value (SV) distribution of C^l is closely related to the signal extraction from the reservoir states. A SV close to 1 means the corresponding signal is extracted from the reservoir states, while a SV close to 0 means the corresponding signal is neglected. Figure 4 shows the SV distribution of C^1 under different reservoir size. From Fig. 3, though the reservoir sizes are different, the SV distributions of C^1 are similar. It implies that redundant reservoir neurons' signals are filtered. Therefore, one can build a sufficient large reservoir for a given task, and the APCA-ADRC can extract useful signals and filter redundant signals adaptively. It guarantees the performance stability of APCA-ADRC under different reservoir size.

4 Conclusion

We propose an adaptive PCA-like ADRC to build the data soft sensors in SRU in this paper. In the APCA-ADRC, a projection-like matrix (C) is trained to extract the prominent components of the reservoir states adaptively. Under this circumstance, the reservoir states that have little influence on the output are neglected, while the reservoir states that have influence on the output are selected. It is equivalent to adjusting the reservoir size adaptively. Therefore, one can escape from the tedious reservoir size design. In addition, the PCA-like way reduces the dimension of the reservoir states. This is helpful to suppress the influence of noise to a large extent.

Acknowledgement. This paper is supported by Shandong Provincial Natural Science Foundation (project ZR2021MF105).

References

1. Zhang, X., Kow, J., Jones, D., Boer, G., Alazmani, A.: Adjustable compliance soft sensor via an elastically inflatable fluidic dome. Sensors **21**(6), 1970 (2021)
2. Bo, Y., Wang, P., Zhang, X.: Modeling data-driven sensor with a novel deep echo state network. Chemom. Intell. Lab. Syst. **206**(15), 104062 (2020)
3. Bidar, B., Sadeghi, J., Shahraki, F.: Data-driven soft sensor approach for online quality prediction using state dependent parameter models. Chemom. Intell. Lab. Syst. **162**, 130–141 (2017)
4. Meng, Y., Lan, Q., Qin, J.: Data-driven soft sensor modeling based on twin support vector regression for cane sugar crystallization. J. Food Eng. **241**, 159–165 (2019)
5. Cheng, T., Harrou, F., Sun, Y.: Monitoring influent measurements at water resource recovery facility using data-driven soft sensor approach. IEEE Sens. J. **19**(1), 342–352 (2018)

6. Xiangxue, W., Lunhui, X., Kaixun, C.: Data-driven short-term forecasting for urban road network traffic based on data processing and LSTM-RNN. Arab. J. Sci. Eng. **44**(4), 3043–3060 (2018). https://doi.org/10.1007/s13369-018-3390-0

7. Jaeger, H.: Using conceptors to manage neural long-term memories for temporal patterns. J. Mach. Learn. Res. **18**, 1–43 (2017)

8. Bo, Y., Wang, P., Zhang, X.: An asynchronously deep reservoir computing for predicting chaotic time series. Appl. Soft Comput. **95**(6), 106530 (2020)

9. Lu, C., Feng, J., Chen, Y.: Tensor robust principal component analysis with a new tensor nuclear norm. IEEE Trans. Pattern Anal. Mach. Intell. **42**(4), 925–938 (2020)

10. Patanè, L., Xibilia, M.: Echo-state networks for soft sensor design in an SRU process. Inf. Sci. **566**, 195–214 (2021)

11. Fortuna, L., Rizzo, A., Sinatra, M.: Soft analyzers for a sulfur recovery unit. Control. Eng. Pract. **11**(12), 1491–1500 (2003)

Double Recursive Sparse Self-attention Based Crowd Counting in the Cluttered Background

Boxiang Zhou, Suyu Wang[✉], and Sai Xiao

Beijing University of Technology, Beijing, China
suyuwang@bjut.edu.cn

Abstract. Crowd counting algorithms play an important role in the field of public safety management. Most of the current mainstream crowd counting methods are based on deep convolutional neural networks (CNNs), which use multi-column or multi-scale convolutional structures to obtain contextual information in images to compensate for the impact of perspective distortion on counting results. However, due to the locally connected nature of convolution, this method cannot obtain enough global context, which often leads to misidentification in complex background regions, which affects the accuracy of counting. To solve this problem. First, we design a double recursive sparse self-attention module, which can better obtain long-distance dependency information and improve the problem of background false detection on the basis of reducing the amount of computation and parameters. Secondly, we design a Transformer structure based on feature pyramid as the feature extraction module of the crowd counting algorithm, which effectively improves the algorithm's ability to extract global information. The experimental results on public datasets show that our proposed algorithm outperforms the current mainstream crowd counting methods, and effectively improves the background false detection problem of complex scene images.

Keywords: Deep learning · Crowd count · Crowd density estimation · Attention mechanism · Transformer

1 Introduction

In recent years, with the great increase of crowd density in public places, stampede accidents caused by excessive crowds have occurred all over the world, which has caused huge personal and property losses. With the rapid development of technology in the field of computer vision, the task of crowd counting based on surveillance images and videos plays a crucial role in security, traffic and other real-world fields.

With the rapid development of deep learning and convolutional neural networks (CNN) in the image domain, researchers began to use CNN-based methods to estimate crowd numbers from images and videos. However, crowd images

S. Yu et al. (Eds.): PRCV 2022, LNCS 13534, pp. 722–734, 2022.
https://doi.org/10.1007/978-3-031-18907-4_56

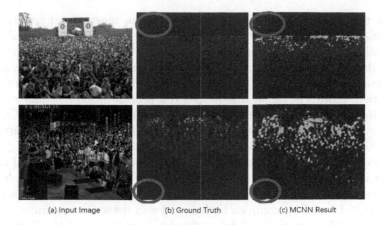

(a) Input Image   (b) Ground Truth   (c) MCNN Result

Fig. 1. False detection of MCNN algorithm in image background area. (Color figure online)

often have the characteristics of changeable viewing angle, irregular crowd distribution, perspective and occlusion. In the early research, the structure of multi-column and multi-scale branches is usually used [1,2], but this method has the disadvantages of redundant feature parameters and high training difficulty. How to effectively reduce the number of parameters and computational complexity of the network without reducing the counting effect is one of the key issues of current research.

The current mainstream algorithms are often interfered by complex backgrounds during prediction, resulting in false detections in the background area and affecting the accuracy of counting. As shown in Fig. 1, the mainstream crowd algorithm MCNN [1] produces false detections (red circles) in the background region of the image.

The contributions are as follows:

(1) A double recursive sparse self-attention module is proposed, which obtains long-distance global context spatial location information and channel dependencies on the basis of low computational complexity and parameter amount, and improves the problem of background false detection.
(2) Transformer structure based on feature pyramid is designed to replace a single convolutional neural network as the backbone network to enhance the ability to extract global features.
(3) The performance of the algorithm is tested and analyzed using ShanghaiTech, UCF-QNRF, and UCF-50 benchmark data sets. The results show that the performance of our algorithm is significantly improved compared with the mainstream crowd counting algorithms.

2   Related Work

Limited by the local connection characteristics of convolution, it is difficult for the fully convolutional neural network structure to capture the correlation between two distant pixels. To solve this problem, most crowd counting algorithms use the method of increasing the receptive field to obtain global context information. Li et al. [3] proposed a method of expanding the receptive field using a decoding layer with atrous convolution and achieved good results, but atrous convolution has a grid effect, which will lose the continuity of feature information. Ashish et al. [4] first proposed a self-attention mechanism applied to machine translation to obtain the global dependencies of the input. Currently, self-attention mechanisms have been widely used in various image-related tasks due to their ability to model long-range dependencies [5–7].

In recent years, attention mechanism has also been gradually applied in crowd counting tasks. Reference [8] effectively suppresses the influence of complex background on detection accuracy by designing a network with attention structure. Reference [9] focuses on complex background and detection accuracy. Two self-attention modules are designed for multi-scale variation, and the literature [10] designed a category attention module that can count multiple categories well. We draws on the idea of Huang et al. [6] to design a recursive spatial and channel sparse self-attention module, which obtains the global context long-distance dependency of spatial position and channel dimension at the cost of small computational and parameter costs, overcome the influence of complex background and improve the expressive ability of the network.

Transformer have excellent performance in a variety of vision tasks, a huge advantage is the ability to capture long context dependencies and enjoy the global receptive field. The Transformer structure was used for the first time in ViT [11] to directly classify images. Both Swin Transformer [12] and Twins Transformer [13] draw on the idea of ResNet [14] residual structure, each layer only models the local relationship, while continuously reducing the size of the feature map and expanding the receptive field.

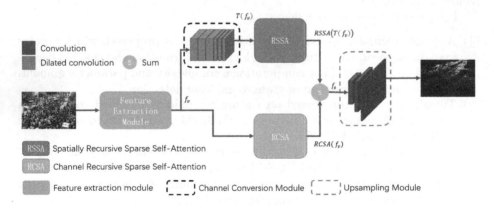

Fig. 2. Schematic diagram of the overall structure of the network.

3   Method

This section will elaborate the working principle of the proposed double recursive sparse self-attention module and the Transformer structure based on feature pyramid as the feature extraction module of crowd counting algorithm.

3.1   Overall Network Structure

Figure 2 shows the overall network structure of the crowd counting network based on the double recursive sparse self-attention module we proposed. First, the input image is sent to the feature extraction module and the obtain feature map f_v. Next, the network will split into two branches. In the first branch, f_v first obtains the feature map $T(f_v)$ through the channel change module composed of dilated convolution, and $T(f_v)$ is then sent to the recursive spatial sparse self-attention module (RSSA) to obtain the feature map $RSSA(T(f_v))$. In the second branch, f_v is directly fed into the recursive channel sparse self-attention module (RCSA) to obtain the feature map $RCSA(f_v)$.

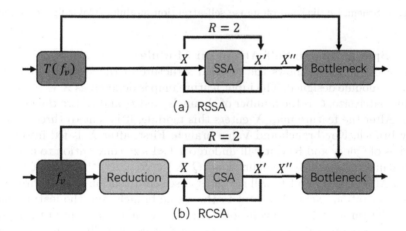

(a) RSSA

(b) RCSA

Fig. 3. Schematic diagram of double recursive sparse self-attention module.

In order to simplify the experiment and verify the effectiveness of the double recursive sparse self-attention module, we draws on the idea of mainstream crowd counting networks [3,15], nd selects the top ten VGG-16 [16] layer as the feature extraction module of the network in the ablation experiment.

3.2   Double Recursive Sparse Self-attention Module

We design two self-attention modules, spatial and channel, to enhance the performance of pixel-level features by collecting contextual information of images in the spatial dimension, and to improve the performance of the network by modeling the dependencies of each channel. In order to avoid the problem of large computational load and large memory usage of the self-attention module, we choose a recursive sparse structure.

Figure 3 shows the internal structure of RSSA and RCSA modules. In RSSA, $T(f_v)$ is continuously input into the spatial sparse self-attention module (SSA) to obtain feature map X'', $T(f_v)$ and X'' are fused by Bottleneck module to obtain $RSSA(T(f_v))$. In RCSA, f_v is adjusted to the perfect square number through the Reduction module channel, and then continuously input to the channel sparse self-attention module (CSA) to obtain the feature map X'', f_v and X'' are fused through the Bottleneck module to obtain $RCSA(f_v)$.

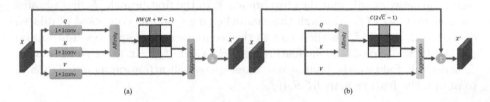

Fig. 4. Schematic diagram of sparse self-attention module. (Color figure online)

3.2.1   Spatial Sparse Self Attention Module

Figure a of the Fig. 4 shows the internal structure of the spatially sparse self-attention module designed. The input feature map is denoted as $X \in R^{B*C*W*H}$, B is the batch size, C is the number of channels, and H and W are the height and width. After the feature map X enters this module, it is sent to three branches, Query branch, Key branch and Value branch. First, after X is fed into the two branches of Query and Key, it will undergo a 1×1 size convolution to obtain two new feature maps, which are defined as $\{Q, K\} \in R^{B*C'*W*H}$, where C' is equal to $C/8$. After that, Q and K will get the sparse self-attention map A through the Affinity operation. Next, X is sent to the Value branch, and the feature map V is obtained through 1×1 convolution, and then V and A are fused through the Aggregation operation to obtain the fusion feature map Fuse that aggregates the spatial information of the horizontal and vertical dimensions. Finally, the element-wise sum operation of Fuse and input features is performed to obtain the input feature map X with spatial long-distance context information.

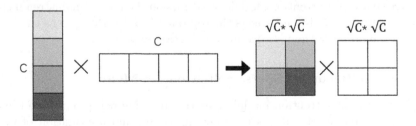

Fig. 5. Two-dimensional transformation operation of channel dimension information.

In the Affinity operation. First ,Q and K are dimensionally transformed into $Q_H \in R^{BW*H*C'}$, $Q_W \in R^{BH*W*C'}$, $K_H \in R^{BW*C'*H}$, $K_W \in R^{BH*C'*W}$. Then, Q_H and K_H, Q_W and K_W are matrix multiplied to obtain horizontal and vertical attention matrices respectively; Next, in order to remove duplicate context information, the value at the intersection of the horizontal dimension and the vertical dimension is set to infinity; Finally, the sparse attention matrix (Green Cross in the Figure a of the Fig. 4) is finally obtained by Concate and Softmax operations on the horizontal and vertical attention matrices.

By giving local features X spatial context information, the global feature representation ability is enhanced. The output feature map will have a broader view of the spatial context, and the spatial semantic information can be selectively aggregated according to the attention matrix.

3.2.2 Channel Sparse Self-attention Module

However, in the channel self-attention model [5], the channel information exists in a single dimension, as shown on the left side of the arrow in Fig. 5. The process of generating the channel attention matrix is similar to multiplying a vector and a matrix. This form Not suitable for recursively sparse structures. Therefore, we convert the channel information into a two-dimensional form and assign the horizontal dimension $\sqrt{C}$ and the vertical dimension $\sqrt{C}$, so that the channel dimension can also reduce the amount of parameters and calculation time by the sparse method.

As shown in figure b of the Fig. 4, the channel sparse attention module is similar to the structure of the spatially sparse self-attention module overall, but removes the convolution used to compress channel information in each branch. By adding the channel context information to the local feature X, the feature correlation between each channel is strengthened, and a stronger semantic responsiveness is obtained.

3.2.3 Recursive Sparse Self-attention

Although the sparse self-attention module can capture distant contextual information in both horizontal and vertical directions, due to the sparse nature, a pixel cannot be associated with all surrounding pixels in the spatial dimension, nor can a channel be associated with all other pixels have dependencies. We make up for the problem that sparse self-attention cannot obtain dense contextual information by feeding image features into the sparse self-attention module multiple times, and use a smaller computational incremental cost to achieve the same effect as the general self-attention structure, which is called a recursive operation here.

Through recursive sparse attention (the number of recursion is equal to 2), we establish the dependencies between any two pixels or channels in the feature map with less parameters and computation.

3.3 Feature Extraction Module Based on Feature Pyramid Transformer

Compared with the CNN structure, a huge advantage of the Transformer structure is that it can effectively capture long-range context dependencies and enjoy the global receptive field. Therefore, we expect to further improve the performance of the model by using the Transformer structure as a feature extraction module to achieve performance indicators that are better than the current mainstream crowd counting algorithms.

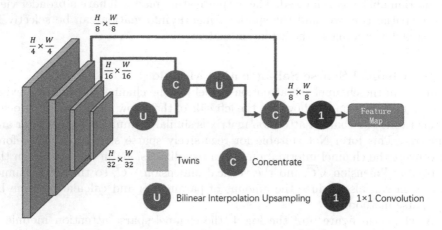

Fig. 6. Schematic diagram of Twins structure based on feature pyramid.

Although the Twins structure can effectively extract global features, the deep features still lack image details and are difficult to reconstruct by upsampling methods. These deep features are too vague to clearly distinguish the boundaries of different objects, making it difficult for the algorithm to learn the accurate location information of the crowd. To this end, a feature extraction module that can make full use of shallow and deep feature information is constructed by using Transformer and feature pyramid.

Figure 6 shows the internal structure of the Twins structure based on the feature pyramid. We adjust the feature map output from the last three layers of Twins to 1/8 of the original image size through bilinear interpolation and upsampling, and pass the channel dimension feature The splicing methods are fused together, and finally the number of output channels is adjusted by 1×1 convolution to adapt to the input of subsequent modules.

3.4 Training Detail

$$L(\theta) = \frac{1}{2B} \sum_{i=1}^{B} |Desity_i^{gt} - Desity_i^{est}|^2 \qquad (1)$$

We chose MSE Loss, commonly used in crowd counting tasks, as the loss function defined as Eq. (1). $Desity_i^{gt}$ is the true population density map of the input image, $Desity_i^{est}$ is the population density image of each prediction, B is the batch size.

In the data preprocessing stage, we adopted random clipping, random shift, random erase, random horizontal flip data enhancement methods. When VGG16 is selected for the backbone network, the VGG16 pretrained model is loaded. When the backbone network selects the Twins structure, load the pre-trained model of Twins on the ImageNet dataset. The remaining network parameters are randomly initialized using a Gaussian distribution with a mean of 0 and a variance of 0.01. With regard to the setup of training parameters, the batch size is 12 and the Adam optimizer is used. The initial learning rate is $1.25 * 10^{-5}$. After a period of training, the set learning rate of 50 epochs per interval decreases to 0.1 times that of the original.

4   Experiment

In this section, we evaluate the proposed method. We will start with the necessary interpretation of the evaluation criteria. Next, we compare our methods with those of SOTA for the three benchmark datasets, and finally show more detailed experimental results through ablation experiments and comparative experiment.

4.1   Evaluation Criteria

The mean absolute error (MAE) and the root mean square error (RMSE) have been consistently used as evaluation criteria in population density estimation tasks. MAE reflects the accuracy of prediction, while RMSE reflects the robustness of prediction. They are defined as:

$$MAE = \frac{1}{N} |z_i - \hat{z}_i| \tag{2}$$

$$RSME = \sqrt{\frac{1}{N} \sum_{i=1}^{N} (z_i - \hat{z}_i)^2} \tag{3}$$

In Eq. (2) and Eq. (3), N represents the number of test images, z_i represents the true number of pedestrians in the ROI area on the first test image, and $\hat{z}_i$ represents the predicted number of pedestrians. In the benchmark dataset to be discussed later, ROI is equivalent to the entire test image.

4.2   Benchmark Datasets and Ground-Truth Data

Through three public benchmark datasets, we compares the performance differences between our method and current mainstream crowd counting algorithms.

The ShanghaiTech [1] dataset is one of the classic crowd counting datasets, consisting of 1198 images, including 33065 pedestrian annotations. The dataset is divided into two parts, SHTA and SHTB, according to the density of crowd distribution in the images. We use the crowd density map generation method with adaptive Gaussian kernel in SHTA, and the crowd density map generation method with a fixed Gaussian kernel of 5 in SHTB.

The UCF-QNRF [17] dataset contains 1,535 labeled images with a total of 1,251,642 pedestrians. The training data is 1,201 of them. The ground-truth density map is generated by an adaptive Gaussian kernel.

The UCF-CC-50 [18] dataset contains 50 images with numbers ranging from 94 to 4543. An adaptive Gaussian kernel is used to generate the ground-truth density map. In addition, we adopt the method of five-fold cross-validation.

4.3   Ablation Experiment

Table 1. Ablation experiments for network modules.

Model	Feature extraction module	Upsampling module	RSSA	RCSA	MAE	RMSE
VGG-Simple	✓				67.4	119.0
VGG-UpSample	✓	✓			67.9	107.0
VGG-RSSA	✓	✓	✓		63.2	102.4
VGG-Double	✓	✓	✓	✓	**62.4**	**99.2**

As shown in Table 1, we conducts ablation experiments on SHTA for network modules in different algorithms. In order to facilitate the experiment, we choose VGG16 with simple structure and convenient training as the feature extraction module in this part of the ablation experiment. The model VGG-Simple refers to the structure of CSRNet [3], and only retains the top ten layers of VGG16 for feature extraction and the channel transformation module containing atrous convolution. The model VGG-UpSample adds an upsampling module consisting of three layers of deconvolution at the end of VGG-Simple to improve the resolution of the output density map. In the model VGG-RSSA, the recursive spatial sparse self-attention module is added between the channel transformation module and the upsampling module, and the MAE is significantly reduced. The model VGG-double adds a recursive channel sparse self-attention module based on the model VGG-RSSA, and the RMSE is significantly reduced.

In view of the influence of different feature extraction modules on the performance of the algorithm, we conducts a comparative experiment of different feature extraction modules on SHTA and SHTB based on the VGG-double model structure. As shown in Table 2, compared with the VGG16 feature extraction method, the Twins-based feature extraction module has improved both in accuracy and robustness. After the combination of Twins and the feature pyramid structure, the algorithm can better integrate the shallow and deep information of

Table 2. Comparison experiment for backbone network.

Dataset model	SHTA		SHTB	
	MAE	RMSE	MAE	RMSE
VGG16	62.4	99.2	7.8	11.9
Twins	60.1	96.2	6.9	10.4
Twins based on feature pyramid	**57.9**	**92.2**	**6.5**	**10.2**

the image during feature extraction, so the Twins-Transformer structure based on the feature pyramid is used as a feature extraction module to obtain the best algorithm performance.

Table 3. The comparative experiment on the effectiveness of the attention module.

Whether to use the attention module	MAE	RMSE
No	58.2	92.7
Yes	**57.9**	**92.2**

In the ablation experiments based on the VGG16 feature extraction module, the effectiveness of double recursive sparse self-attention module is verified. However, since there is a self-attention mechanism in the Transformer structure, the effectiveness of the self-attention module we designed in the algorithm

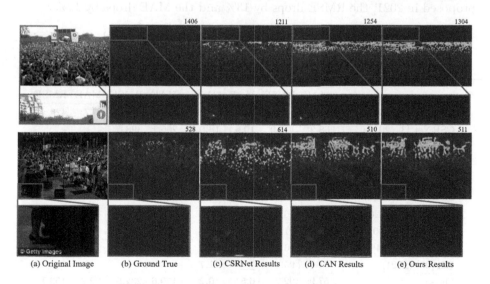

(a) Original Image   (b) Ground True   (c) CSRNet Results   (d) CAN Results   (e) Ours Results

Fig. 7. Visual display of the prediction results of various crowd counting algorithms.

based on the Transformer feature extraction module is verified on SHTA. As shown in Table 3, after using the self-attention module, the performance of our designed algorithm has been slightly improved, which proves the effectiveness of the self-attention model. Because the Transformer structure has a certain attention structure, the promotion of this structure is not obvious.

4.4   Background False Detection Improvement

Since the mainstream algorithms CSRNet [3] and CAN [15] both use VGG16 as the feature extraction module, in order to reflect the ability of the self-attention module we designed to improve the background problem, we choose VGG-double for effect comparison.

Figure 7 shows the visual comparison effect of our method and the two mainstream crowd algorithms CSRNet and CAN on the SHTA crowd density map. Our method greatly reduces the false detection in the background area during prediction.

4.5   Overall Performance Evaluation

We adopt the network structure that fuses all network modules and uses Twins combined with feature pyramid as the Transformer feature extraction module as our final algorithm to compare the performance of the current mainstream crowd counting algorithm on three public datasets. As shown in Table 4, the bold result is the best, and the underlined result is the second best. Compared with the classical algorithm CSRNet, our method reduces the MAE by 15% and the RMSE by 20% on SHTA, and the other three datasets also have a significant decrease in the indicators. Compared with the VIT-based TransCrowd algorithm proposed in 2021, the RMSE drops by 13% and the MAE drops by 12%.

Table 4. Comparisons with mainstream methods on four datasets.

Dataset model	SHTA		SHTB		UCF-CC-50		UCF-QNRF	
	MAE	RMSE	MAE	RMSE	MAE	RMSE	MAE	RMSE
MCNN [1] (2016)	110.2	173.2	26.4	41.3	377.6	509.1	277	426
CSRNet [3] (2018)	68.2	115.0	10.6	16.0	266.1	398.5	-	-
CAN [15] (2019)	62.3	100.0	7.8	12.2	212.2	243.7	107	183
SFCN [19] (2019)	59.7	95.7	7.4	11.8	214.2	318.2	102.0	171.0
PGCNet [20] (2019)	**57.0**	**86.0**	8.8	13.7	244.6	361.2	-	-
SDANet [21] (2020)	63.6	101.8	7.8	10.2	227.6	316.4	-	-
RPNet [22] (2020)	61.2	96.9	8.1	11.6	-	-	-	-
IFNet [23] (2020)	61.1	111.7	7.6	12.1	193.8	272	98.2	184.6
TransCrowd [24] (2021)	66.1	105.1	9.3	16.1	-	-	97.2	168.5
GL [25] (2021)	61.3	95.4	7.3	11.7	-	-	-	-
Ours	57.9	92.2	**6.5**	**10.2**	179.6	232.5	92.2	153.1

5   Conclusion

Aiming at the problem that the current mainstream crowd counting algorithms are prone to false detections in complex background areas, we propose a double recursive sparse self-attention module to obtain long-distance dependency information in spatial and channel dimensions. In addition, in order to further improve the performance of the algorithm and improve the ability of the algorithm to capture global information in the feature extraction stage, the Twins structure based on the feature pyramid is designed as the feature extraction module of the crowd counting algorithm. Extensive experiments on four widely used datasets with different population densities demonstrate the superiority of our method.

References

1. Zhang, Y., Zhou, D., Chen, S. et al.: Single-image crowd counting via multi-column convolutional neural network. In: Proceedings of the IEEE Conference on Computer Vision and Pattern Recognition, pp. 589–597 (2016)
2. Babu Sam, D., Surya, S., Venkatesh Babu, R.: Switching convolutional neural network for crowd counting. In: Proceedings of the IEEE Conference on Computer Vision and Pattern Recognition, pp. 5744–5752 (2017)
3. Li, Y., Zhang, X., Chen, D.: CSRNet: dilated convolutional neural networks for understanding the highly congested scenes. In: Proceedings of the IEEE Conference on Computer Vision and Pattern Recognition, pp. 1091–1100 (2018)
4. Vaswani, A., Shazeer, N., Parmar, N., et al.: Attention is all you need. In: Advances in Neural Information Processing Systems, vol. 30 (2017)
5. Fu, J., Liu, J., Tian, H., et al.: Dual attention network for scene segmentation. In: Proceedings of the IEEE/CVF Conference on Computer Vision and Pattern Recognition, pp. 3146–3154 (2019)
6. Huang, Z., Wang, X., Huang, L., et al.: CCNet: Criss-cross attention for semantic segmentation. In: Proceedings of the IEEE/CVF International Conference on Computer Vision, vol. 603–612 (2019)
7. Zhang, H., Goodfellow, I., Metaxas, D., et al.: Self-attention generative adversarial networks. In: International Conference on Machine Learning, pp. 7354–7363. PMLR (2019)
8. Rong, L., Li, C.:Coarse-and fine-grained attention network with background-aware loss for crowd density map estimation. In: Proceedings of the IEEE/CVF Winter Conference on Applications of Computer Vision, pp. 3675–3684 (2021)
9. Yi, Q., Liu, Y., Jiang, A., et al.: Scale-aware network with regional and semantic attentions for crowd counting under cluttered background. arXiv preprint arXiv:2101.01479 (2021)
10. Xu, W., Liang, D., Zheng, Y., et al.: Dilated-scale-aware category-attention convnet for multi-class object counting. IEEE Signal Process. Lett. **28**, 1570–1574 (2021)
11. Dosovitskiy, A., Beyer, L., Kolesnikov, A., et al.: An image is worth 16x16 words: Transformers for image recognition at scale. arXiv preprint arXiv:2010.11929 (2020)
12. Liu, Z., Lin, Y., Cao, Y., et al.: Swin transformer: Hierarchical vision transformer using shifted windows. In: Proceedings of the IEEE/CVF International Conference on Computer Vision, pp. 10012–10022 (2021)

13. Chu, X., Tian, Z., Wang, Y., et al.: Twins: Revisiting the design of spatial attention in vision transformers. In: Advances in Neural Information Processing Systems, vol. 34 (2021)

14. He, K., Zhang, X., Ren, S., et al.: Deep residual learning for image recognition. In: Proceedings of the IEEE Conference on Computer Vision and Pattern Recognition, pp. 770–778 (2016)

15. Liu, W., Salzmann, M., Fua, P.: Context-aware crowd counting. In: Proceedings of the IEEE/CVF Conference on Computer Vision and Pattern Recognition, pp. 5099–5108 (2019)

16. Simonyan, K., Zisserman, A.: Very deep convolutional networks for large-scale image recognition. arXiv preprint arXiv:1409.1556 (2014)

17. Idrees, H., Tayyab, M., Athrey, K., et al.: Composition loss for counting, density map estimation and localization in dense crowds. In: Proceedings of the European Conference on Computer Vision (ECCV), pp. 532–546 (2018)

18. Idrees, H., Saleemi, I., Seibert, C., et al.: Multi-source multi-scale counting in extremely dense crowd images. In: Proceedings of the IEEE Conference on Computer Vision and Pattern Recognition, pp. 2547–2554 (2013)

19. Wang, Q., Gao, J., Lin, W., et al.: Learning from synthetic data for crowd counting in the wild. In: Proceedings of the IEEE/CVF Conference on Computer Vision and Pattern Recognition, pp. 8198–8207 (2019)

20. Yan, Z., Yuan, Y., Zuo, W., et al.: Perspective-guided convolution networks for crowd counting. In: Proceedings of the IEEE/CVF International Conference on Computer Vision, pp. 952–961 (2019)

21. Miao, Y., Lin, Z., Ding, G., et al.: Shallow feature based dense attention network for crowd counting. Proc. AAAI Conf. Artif. Intell. **34**(07), 11765–11772 (2020)

22. Yang, Y., Li, G., Wu, Z., et al.: Reverse perspective network for perspective-aware object counting. In: Proceedings of the IEEE/CVF Conference on Computer Vision and Pattern Recognition, pp. 4374–4383 (2020)

23. Chen, G., Guo, P.: Enhanced information fusion network for crowd counting. arXiv preprint arXiv:2101.04279 (2021)

24. Liang, D., Chen, X., Xu, W., et al.: Transcrowd: weakly-supervised crowd counting with transformers. Sci. China Inf. Sci. **65**(6), 1–14 (2022)

25. Wan, J., Liu, Z., Chan, A.B.: A generalized loss function for crowd counting and localization. In: Proceedings of the IEEE/CVF Conference on Computer Vision and Pattern Recognition, pp. 1974–1983 (2021)

BiTMulV: Bidirectional-Decoding Based Transformer with Multi-view Visual Representation

Qiankun Yu[1,2], XueKui Wang[3], Dong Wang[4], Xu Chu[1,2], Bing Liu[4(✉)], and Peng Liu[1(✉)]

[1] National Joint Engineering Laboratory of Internet Applied Technology of Mines, China University of Mining and Technology, Xuzhou 221008, Jiangsu, China
yqk166@cumt.edu.cn , liupeng@cumt.edu.cn
[2] School of Information and Control Engineering, China University of Mining and Technology, Xuzhou 221116, Jiangsu, China
[3] Alibaba Group, Hangzhou 311121, Zhejiang, China
[4] School of Computer Science and Technology, China University of Mining and Technology, Xuzhou 221116, Jiangsu, China
liubing@cumt.edu.cn

Abstract. The Transformer-based image captioning models have made significant progress on the generalization performance. However, most methods still have two kinds of limitations in practice: 1) Heavily rely on the single region-based visual feature representation. 2) Not effectively utilize the future semantic information during inference. To solve these issues, we introduce a novel bidirectional-decoding based Transformer with multi-view visual representation (**BiTMulV**) for image captioning. In the encoding stage, we adopt a modular cross-attention block to fuse both grid features and region features by virtue of multi-view visual feature representation, which realizes full exploitation of image context information and fine-grained information. In the decoding stage, we design the bidirectional decoding structure, which consists of two parallel and consistent forward and backward decoders, to promote the model to effectively combine the history with future semantics for inference. Experimental results on the MSCOCO dataset demonstrate that our proposal significantly outperforms the competitive models, improving by **1.5 points** on the CIDEr metric.

Keywords: Image captioning · Transformer · Multi-view visual representation

1 Introduction

In the past years, multi-modal learning has achieved remarkable progress with the success of deep learning. Image captioning [1], as one of the most challenging multi-modal learning tasks, integrates technologies in the fields of both

© The Author(s), under exclusive license to Springer Nature Switzerland AG 2022
S. Yu et al. (Eds.): PRCV 2022, LNCS 13534, pp. 735–748, 2022.
https://doi.org/10.1007/978-3-031-18907-4_57

natural language generation (NLG) and computer vision (CV). It aims to semantically describe an image using a fluent natural language sentence and has widely applied in many fields, such as image retrieval [2], robot interaction [3], and digital library [4]. Inspired by the Sequence-to-Sequence (S2S) model for neural machine translation (NMT) [5], mainstream image captioning approaches follow a popular encoder-decoder framework [6–8], which consists of a convolutional neural network (CNN) that encodes visual features from the input image, and a recurrent neural network (RNN) that serves as the decoder to generate the caption based on the visual features.

Recently, more and more researchers have incorporated the Transformer model into image captioning, considering that it enables to learn the semantic-rich encoding vector, capture the better long-distance dependence and support higher parallel operations. Therefore, image captioning models with the Transformer inherently have better performance compared with traditional methods. In terms of input visual features, existing image captioning approaches with the Transformer can be roughly divided into two classes: grid features based models and region features based models. In terms of caption decoder structure, most works focus on the left-to-right (L2R) paradigm. Despite the success of the current image captioning approaches, there still exist two major limitations as follows: 1) The region visual features cannot fully cover important details of the entire image, thus weakening the representation ability of the image used to guide the generation of captions. 2) Due to the masked self-attention mechanism, the transformer decoder can only learn the sequence information based on the partially generated words, and cannot effectively utilize the future predicted information to learn complete semantics.

To address the first limitation, we explore a novel method to coordinate region visual features and grid visual features. The grid visual features have the advantage of fine granularity and contain enough image context information, while the region visual features have adequate information of core image objects. To combine the merits of the two methods, we adopt a multi-view learning approach to integrate the two visual features, taking region visual features as the query input and grid visual features as the key-value pair input, respectively. As a result, the combination of grid visual features and region visual features can sensibly enhance the feature representation of the image. **To address the second limitation**, we design a bidirectional caption decoder, in which the forward and backward decoding processes have the same methodology but different learning directions of the sentence.

To sum up, a novel Transformer-based image captioning approach is proposed in this article, and the main contributions are given below:

1) An multi-view (MV) visual representation model is proposed, which can cooperatively encode region visual features and grid visual features, to extract the rich contextual information of an input image.
2) An end-to-end bidirectional multi-modal Transformer is presented, which can learn both history and future sentence semantics to generate more accurate image captions.

3) Extensive experiments are conducted on the MSCOCO dataset to validate the effectiveness of the proposed model. The evaluation results demonstrate that our model outperforms the mainstream models on most metrics.

2   Related Work

2.1   Image Captioning

There have been extensive studies and improvements on image caption. Researchers initially focused on template-based approaches [9,10] and search-based approaches [11]. Due to the development of deep learning in CV and NLP, recent works generally adopt an encoder-decoder framework. For instance, Vinyals et al. [7] proposed Convolutional Neural Networks (CNN) as an image encoder and then adopted LSTM as an encoder to generate corresponding descriptive sentences. In order to accurately understand the objects in the image, Anderson et al. [12] utilized up-down attention based on a ResNet within pre-trained object detector instead of a traditional convolution neural network (CNN) to extract region-based image features. Since the graph convolution neural network (GCN) can effectively extract spatial features, Yao et al. [13] applied a new GCN with Long Short-Term Memory (dubbed as GCN-LSTM) architecture that can enrich region-level representations and eventually enhances image captioning.

Despite the success of the above methods, RNN-based models are limited by their representation power. The new Transformer-based models with self-attention mechanism further improved the ability of representation and achieved SOTA (state-of-the-art) results in multi-modal tasks. For instance, to address the internal covariate shift problem inside self-attention, Guo et al. [14] employed Normalized Self-Attention that fixes the distribution of hidden activations in the Self-Attention mechanism. Pan et al. [15] incorporated Bilinear pooling which performs well in fine-grained visual recognition into image captions, and proposed X-Linear Attention Networks to achieve multi-modal input interaction. Huang et al. [16] extended the traditional attention mechanism and introduced the Attention on Attention (AOA) model, which can filter out attention vectors with low correlation with query vectors. Different from the semantic features of global multi-view features, Yu et al. [17] proposed Multi-modal Transformer that uses different object detectors to extract region-based local multi-view features, which can maintain the fine-grained semantic features of the image. Motivated by the prior research, we present a novel model based on an encoding-decoding framework, which improves visual representation by fusing two complementary visual features.

2.2   NMT

Recently, the research of captioning tasks is inspired by work related to NMT. Generally, most NMT decoders generate translations in a left-to-right (L2R) paradigm. However, the right-to-left (R2L) contexts are also crucial for translation predictions, since they can provide complementary signals to the models. In this paper, we focus on work with bidirectional decoding structures. For instance,

Liu et al. [18] introduced to find the best candidate from the combined N-best list via the joint probability of L2R and R2L models. To explore bidirectional decoding for NMT, Zhou et al. [19] construct a decoder that integrates forward attention and backward attention. Zhang et al. [20] constructed two Kullback-Leibler divergence regularization methods, which improve the coordination of translation sequences generated by L2R and R2L decoders. Bidirectional decoding structures for image captioning have also been successfully attempted, for example, Wang et al. [21] proposed a multimodal bi-directional LSTM method to realize end-to-end training for image captioning. Different from these RNN-based bidirectional decoders models, our proposed **BiTMulV** is a novel bidirectional decoding Transformer, which further incorporates the L2R and R2L structure.

3   Methodology

3.1   Model Architecture

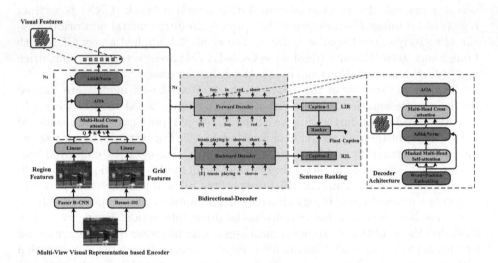

Fig. 1. Overview of the framework of our **BiTMulV** model architecture. Our **BiT-MulV** for image captioning consists of three components. The Multi-View based encoder fuses region features and grid features, which enables reasoning of visual object relationships via a modular cross-attention block. In the decoder of **BiTMulV**, we propose the bidirectional decoder that learns the contextual semantics from the history and future. The Sentence Ranking method relies on the L2R sentence and the R2L sentence generated by the bidirectional decoder to select the final descriptive caption.

The visual representation of images indirectly affects the accuracy of generating descriptive captions in image captioning research. In this paper, we would like to make full exploitation of the visual sequence by fusing two different visual features. Moreover, we also would like to generate more accurate sentences by learning global semantics. Specifically, we describe one model for image captioning, which is an end-to-end framework that is composed of an image encoder and a bidirectional decoder as shown in Fig. 1. The image encoder takes region visual features and grid visual features as its input. The visual features are then fed into the bidirectional encoder to obtain the attended multi-view visual representation with cross-attention learning. The bidirectional decoder predicts the next word recursively by exploiting the attended multi-view visual representation and the previous word. Finally, the final caption is selected from the L2R text and the R2L text generated by the bidirectional encoder via our proposed ranking mechanism.

3.2 Multi-view Visual Representation Based Encoder

Multi-visual (MV) Feature Extraction. Given the input images, the region features and grid features are extracted from the pre-trained object detector. The region features are extracted by the off-the-shelf Faster-RCNN pre-trained on Visual Genome [18]. For the grid features, we leverage the 49 grid visual features from the last convolutional layer of ResNet-101 [15].

AOA. The AOA [16] is proposed to eliminate the interference of irrelevant query vectors to obtain refined attention results. The vector N is concatenated by the attention result and the attention query, which is transformed into the information vector T via linear transformation and transformed into K via linear transformation and nonlinear activation function. (as shown in Fig. 1):

$$N = Concat(F_{Attention}, Q) \tag{1}$$

$$T = Linear(N), K = Sigmoid(Linear(N)) \tag{2}$$

To obtain the attended information H, the AOA incorporates the attention gate into the information vector by using element-wise multiplication:

$$H = T \odot k \tag{3}$$

Encoder Architecture. Considering the grid features contain rich visual context information, we combine it with region based features to facilitate the visual representation of our model. However, the region and grid features are unaligned, we adopt an unaligned multi-view image encoder, to fuse them (as shown in Fig. 1.). For the convenience of expression, the extracted grid features and region features from an image can be denoted as $G = \{g_1, g_2, g_3, ..., g_n\}$ and $R = \{r_1, r_2, r_3, ..., r_n\}$, respectively, where $r_n \in R^{d_1}, g_m \in R^{d_2}$ and $n \neq m$. Notably, we choose the region features R as the primary view and the grid visual features G as the secondary view and adopt the multi-head cross-attention (MHCA) block exploiting them:

$$Q = W_Q R, K = W_K G, V = W_V G \tag{4}$$

$$F_{MHCA} = MHCA(Q, K, V) = Concat(head_1, head_2, ..., head_m)w^o \tag{5}$$

$$head_m = att(Q, K, V) \tag{6}$$

where $W_Q, W_K, W_V \in R^{d \times d_h}$ are three linear transformation matrices, and $W^O \in R^{m*d \times d_h}$. The multi-head attention mechanism consists of m parallel heads with an independent scaled dot-product attention function. Afterwards, the AOA module is applied to filter out information vectors that are not relevant to the attention query and keeps only the useful ones, and then is followed by residual concatenations and layer normalization:

$$A = AOA(F_{MHCA}, R) \tag{7}$$

$$E = LayerNorm(R + A) \tag{8}$$

To generate more abstract and distinctive visual features for the bidirectional encoder, the image encoder adopts deep stacking and the L-th encoder block $A^L_{encoder}$ takes the results from the L-1-th encoder block E^{N-1} as follows:

$$E^N = A^L_{encoder}(E^{N-1}) \tag{9}$$

3.3   Bidirectional Decoder

Decoder Architecture. Generally, the standard Transformer decoder follows the L2R sentence generation paradigm, which utilizes the mask attention mechanism to implement the unidirectional modeling of the sequence. To alleviate the inability of the mask self-attentive mechanism in standard Transformers to explore the past and future context information of a sequence, we propose a novel bidirectional decoder architecture, which consists of a forward decoder and a backward decoder.

Based on the multi-view visual representations learned by the image encoder, the bidirectional decoder produces L2R and R2L sentence descriptions simultaneously for an image. Given a sequence of captions for an image as $S = \{s_1, s_2, s_3, ..., s_n\}$, the sentence is first tokenized into words and trimmed to a maximum length of 18 words. Note that each word in the sentence is represented as $s_n \in R^{300}$ by using the Glove word embedding. The bi-directional decoder is implemented with two parallel decoders with the same structure. The forward decoder is fed with the L2R sequence $\overrightarrow{S} = (s_1, s_2, s_3, s_4, s_5, s_6, ...s_n)$, while the R2L sequence $\overleftarrow{S} = (s_n, ...s_6, s_5, s_4, s_3, s_2, s_1)$ is fed to the backward decoder. Since two decoders have similar architectures, we mainly introduce the structure of the forward encoder.

Specifically, we first employ the masked multi-head self-attention (MMHSA) mechanism, which can characterize word to word relationships in sentences:

$$Q = W_Q \overrightarrow{S}, K = W_K \overrightarrow{S}, V = W_V \overrightarrow{S} \tag{10}$$

$$F_{MMHSA} = Masked - Mulihead(Q, K, V) \tag{11}$$

where $W_Q, W_K, W_V \in R^{d \times d}$ are three linear transformation matrices and the masked multi-head attention results are also normalized by residual concatenations and layer normalization:

$$\overrightarrow{A} = LayerNorm(\overrightarrow{S} + F_{MMHA}) \tag{12}$$

Afterwards, the second MHCA module is used to impose the multi-view visual representations-guided attention on the caption words:

$$F_{MHCA} = MHCA(W_Q \overrightarrow{A}, W_K V, W_V V) \tag{13}$$

where V denotes the multi-view visual features vector. Once again, we apply the AOA to measure how well visual features and text sequence features are related:

$$\overrightarrow{W} = AOA(F_{MHCA}, \overrightarrow{A}) \tag{14}$$

Similar to the image encoder, the bi-directional decoder consists of N identical decoder layers stacked in sequence. The text vector $\overrightarrow{w}$ is projected to M-dimensional space by a linear embedding layer, where M is the size of the vocabulary. Finally, the softmax layers are leveraged for the prediction of the probability of the next word.

Sentence Ranking. In the inference stage, we adopt the beam search strategy [17] with a beam size of 3 to improve the diversity of generated captions. Since the forward decoder and backward decoder generate two sentences via beam search, we design a sentence-level ranking mechanism, which compares the probabilities of the two sentences and selects the one with the largest probability as the final caption.

3.4   Training and Objectives

The proposed model is trained in two stages as same as a standard practice in image captioning [16, 20, 22, 27]. we first pre-train our model by optimizing cross-entropy (XE) loss. For training both the forward and backward decoders, the joint loss is formulated as follows by averaging the cumulative forward and backward losses:

$$L_{XE}\theta = \text{AVE}(\overrightarrow{L}_{XE}\theta + \overleftarrow{L}_{XE}\theta) \tag{15}$$

$$\overrightarrow{L}_{XE}(\theta) = -\sum_{t=1}^{T} \log(p_\theta(y_t^* | y_{1:t-1}^*)) \tag{16}$$

$$\overleftarrow{L}_{XE}(\theta) = -\sum_{t=1}^{T} \log(p_\theta(y_t^* | y_{t+1:1}^*)) \tag{17}$$

where $y_{t+1:1}^*$ and $y_{1:t-1}^*$ are the ground truth of text sequences, θ is the parameters of our **BiTMulV**.

Subsequently, reinforcement learning is used to optimize non-differentiable metrics. Specifically, we employ a variant of the self-critical sequence training [22] on sequences sampled via beam search:

$$L_{RL}(\theta) = -E_{y_{1:T} - p_\theta}(R(y_{1:T})) \tag{18}$$

where the $R(\bullet)$ is employing the CIDEr-D as reward.

4 Experiments

4.1 Experimental Setup

Datasets. Our proposed method is trained, validated, and tested on the Microsoft benchmark dataset MSCOCO [23]. It contains 123,287 images and is each equipped with five different human-annotated captions. In particular, in order to ensure the effectiveness of offline experiments, we adopt the widely used Karpathy split [15], of which 113287 images are used for training and 5000 images are used for testing and verification.

Evaluation Metrics. The standard evaluation metrics include BLEU [23], ROUGE-L [24], SPICE [25], METEOR [26], CIDEr [27], which are used to evaluate the quality of the model.

Implementation Details. Our model is carried out on two NVIDIA RTX 2080 GPU, utilizing AOANET [16] as the baseline model. We pre-processed the annotated sentences, discarded words less than 6 times or did not appear in the Glove pre-training vocabulary, and finally formed a vocabulary with 9568 words. The dimension of the extracted visual feature vectors is 2048. Both the number of encoder layers and the number of decoder layers are set to 6.

We first train the proposed model by utilizing the word-level cross-entropy loss for 35 epochs with a mini-batch size of 15. The Adam optimizer is adopted with an initial learning rate of 1.5e-4, annealed by 0.65 every 3 epochs. To alleviate the exposure bias of cross-entropy optimization, our **BiTMulV** for all experiments is further trained using 10 epochs of self-critical [22] (SCST) loss with an initial learning rate of 1e-5 and annealed by 0.5.

4.2 Ablation Study

In this section, we analyze the effectiveness of the proposed method. The ablation study focused on: 1) The effect of Multi-View visual representation, 2) The effect of bidirectional decoder.

Table 1. Performance comparisons with different methods. The result is reported after the self-critical training stage

Method	B@1	B@4	M	R	C	S
Enc(Grid)+Dec(U)	78.5	36.6	27.4	57.2	124.5	20.6
Enc(Region)+Dec(U)	79.9	38.2	28.8	58.2	128.6	21.4
Enc(Region+Grid)+Dec(U)	80.5	38.4	29.4	59.0	130.6	22.2
Enc(Grid)+Dec(B)	78.8	36.8	27.9	57.5	124.9	20.8
Enc(Region)+Dec(B)	80.1	38.2	29.1	58.3	129.5	21.5
Full:BiTMulV	**80.8**	**38.8**	**29.6**	**59.5**	**131.3**	**22.7**

Enc (Grid/Region/Region+Grid)+Dec (U/B): In the comparison methods, Enc (Grid/Region) indicates that the image encoder adopts the grid features or the region features, and Dec (U/B) means that the encoder adopts the unidirectional structure or the bidirectional structure.

1) The effect of Multi-view (MV) visual representation. To analyze the effect of our proposed **BiTMulV** visual representation, we implement validation experiments, as shown in Table 1. We can observe that the model Enc(Region)+Dec(U) performs better than the model Enc(Grid)+Dec(U) on all evaluation metrics. Compared with the Enc(Region)+Dec(U), the performance of the Enc(Region+Grid)+Dec(U) is significantly improved. Specifically, the Enc(Region+Grid)+Dec(U) achieves 2 and 0.6 increments over the metrics of CIDEr and BLEU-1, as shown in Table 1.

2) The effect of the bidirectional decoder. To further demonstrate the effectiveness of the proposed bidirectional decoder, we also compare the unidirectional decoder with bidirectional decoder for performance analysis. As illustrated in Table 1, the performance of both Enc(Grid)+Dec(B) and Enc(Region)+Dec(B) can be boosted (from **124.5 CIDEr to 124.9 CIDEr** and from **128.6 CIDEr to 129.5 CIDEr**, respectively). The same growing trend can be observed (from **129.5 CIDEr to 131.3 CIDEr**) after combining the MV visual representation method with bidirectional decoding(**Full: BiTMulV**), which further confirms the effectiveness of the bidirectional decoder.

4.3   Quantitative Analysis

Results on the Karpathy Test Split: Table 2 report the performance of our model and the competitive models on the Karpathy test split. Including SCST [18], a gradient-guided optimization method based on reinforcement learning that can effectively train non-differentiable metrics. We compare our method with the state-of-the-art methods, including SCST [22], LSTM-A [24], Up-Down [12], RFNet [25], GCN-LSTM [13], LBPF [26], SGAE [27], AoANet [16]. Up-Down introduces an attention mechanism that integrates bottom-up and top-down for fine-grained image understanding. GCN-LSTM uses GCN as the image semantic encoder and LSTM as the decoder. LSTM-A incorporates high-level

Table 2. Performance comparisons on Offline COCO Karpathy test split.

Model	Cross-entropy Loss						SCST Loss					
	B@1	B@4	M	R	C	S	B@1	B@4	M	R	C	S
SCST	-	30.0	25.9	53.4	94.0	0.0		34.2	26.7	55.7	114.0	0.0
LSTM-A	75.4	35.2	26.9	55.8	108.8	20.0	78.6	35.5	27.3	56.8	118.3	20.8
Up-Down	77.2	36.2	27.0	56.4	113.5	20.3	79.8	36.3	27.7	56.9	120.1	21.2
RFNet	76.4	35.8	27.4	56.8	112.5	20.5	79.1	36.5	27.7	57.3	121.9	21.2
GCN-LSTM	77.3	36.8	27.9	57.0	116.3	20.9	80.5	38.2	28.5	58.3	127.6	22.0
LBPF	77.8	37.4	28.1	57.5	116.4	21.2	80.5	38.3	28.5	58.4	127.6	22.0
SGAE	-	-	-	-	-	-	80.8	38.4	28.4	58.6	127.8	22.1
AoANet	77.4	37.2	28.4	57.5	**119.8**	21.3	80.2	**38.9**	29.2	58.8	129.8	22.4
Ours	**77.9**	**38.1**	**28.8**	**58.8**	118.1	**21.6**	**80.8**	38.8	**29.6**	**59.5**	**131.3**	**22.7**

image attributes into the CNN-RNN framework to facilitate sentence generation. RFNet adopts multiple CNNs to encode fusion features for images and insert a recurrent fusion procedure. LBPF fuses visual information from the past as well as semantic information in the future to improve the performance of caption generation. SGAE constructs a shared dictionary with induction bias to guide language generation. AOANet filters out irrelevant attention vectors by constructing the interaction of "information vector" and "attention gate".

For a fair comparison, we respectively utilize the cross-entropy loss and SCST to train all the models in the single model setting, as shown in Table 2. It can be observed that our model surpasses the previous state-of-the-art models in terms of BLEU-1, BLEU-4, METEOR, ROUGE-L, and SPICE and is slightly worse than the baseline model AOANet in terms of cider when optimized with cross-entropy. After optimizing the CIDEr-D score, our proposed method improves by 0.6 points on BLEU-1, 0.4 points on METEOR, 0.7 points on ROUGE-L and achieves a significant improvement of **1.5 points** in comparison with AOANet.

4.4 Qualitative Analysis and Visualization

Qualitative Analysis. As shown in Fig. 2, we generate four captions for the sampled images, where "GT" indicates ground truth Sentences.

Image	Caption
	Baseline: Two cats laying on top of a bed.
	Ours: A black and white cat laying on a big bed.
	GT1: A couple of cats laying on top of a bed.
	GT2: Two cats laying on a big bed and looking at the camera.
	GT3: A couple of cats on a mattress laying down
	Baseline: A short train on a train track near trees.
	Ours: A yellow train on a train track near trees.
	GT1:A train traveling down tracks through rural countryside
	GT2:A yellow is traveling down the track in the country.
	GT3:A short train is coming down the train tracks.
	Baseline: A double-decker bus on a road
	Ours: A yellow double-decker bus driving down the street next to a blue bus
	GT1:A bus stops at an intersection outside on the street.
	GT2:A yellow double-decker bus on a road next to a blue bus
	GT3:A yellow double-decker bus driving down a street
	Baseline: A boy is running the bases.
	Ours: A child in orange is running bases on the playground.
	GT1:A boy in an orange shirt running the bases.
	GT2:A young boy is running the bases at a game.
	GT3:A child running for a base during a baseball game.

Fig. 2. Examples of captions generated by our method and the baseline model, as well as the corresponding ground truths.

Generally, the sentences generated by our proposed method are more accurate and descriptive than the baseline model. In detail, our proposed model is superior following two aspects:

1) Our proposed **BiTMulV** model could help understand visual contextual information and focus on fine-grained information to realize the alignment of the image and the captions. For example, the baseline model in the first example does not realize the color of the two cats, while our **BiTMulV** model effectively captures the "black" and the "white". In the third example, the blue car and the yellow car in the image are related to each other, but the baseline model does not recognize the blue car. On the contrary, our model effectively captures the context information of the image and recognizes the connection between the blue car and the yellow car.

2) Secondly, our **BiTMulV** model is more accurate and effective in counting objects of the Multi-object images. In the third example, the baseline model describes only one bus, while our method describes two buses. In the fourth example, our model recognizes images that describe the child, short, playground, and bases, while the baseline model does not capture short and playground.

(a) **Baseline: A wooden bowl is filled with red apples**

(b) **BiTMulV: A wooden bowl full of apples and oranges**

Fig. 3. Visualization.

Visualization. To better qualitatively evaluate the generated results with our proposed **BiTMulV** method, we visualize the attended image regions during the caption generation processes for Baseline and **BiTMulV**in Fig 3. It can be seen that our **BiTMulV** model correctly aligns image regions to the words, while the baseline model ignores some significant regions and then generates inaccurate captions. For example, the baseline model attends to the applies, while the oranges are not recognized. In contrast, by exploiting Multi-View Visual Representation for multi-modal reasoning, our **BiTMulV** model accurately localizes the oranges region to generate the "oranges".

5 Conclusions

In this paper, we propose a novel image captioning model (**BiTMulV**) based on the multi-view visual representation and bidirectional decoding structure. On one hand, we make use of image contextual information and fine-grained information by combining region visual features with grid visual features. On the other hand, the **BiTMulV** adopts the explicit bidirectional decoding structure, which can exploit both historical semantics and future semantics to guide model learning. The quantitative and qualitative experiments demonstrate the superiority of our proposed method over the existing deep image captioners.

Acknowledgement. This work was supported by the National Natural Science Foundation of China 61971421, the open fund for research and development of key technologies of smart mines (H7AC200057) and the Postgraduate Research & Practice Innovation Program of Jiangsu Province (KYCX21_2248).

References

1. Lu, J., Xiong, C., Parikh, D., Socher, R.: Knowing when to look: Adaptive attention via a visual sentinel for image captioning. In: IEEE Conference on Computer Vision and Pattern Recognition (CVPR), pp. 375–383 (2017)
2. Revaud, J., Almazán, J., Rezende, R.S., Souza, C.R.D.: Learning with average precision: Training image retrieval with a listwise loss. In: Proceedings of the IEEE/CVF International Conference on Computer Vision, pp. 5107–5116 (2019)
3. Chen, C., Liu, Y., Kreiss, S., Alahi, A.: Crowd-robot interaction: Crowd-aware robot navigation with attention-based deep reinforcement learning. In: 2019 International Conference on Robotics and Automation (ICRA), pp. 6015–6022 (2019)
4. Fox, E.A., Ingram, W.A.: Introduction to digital libraries. In: Proceedings of the ACM/IEEE Joint Conference on Digital Libraries in 2020, pp. 567–568 (2020)
5. Sen, S., Gupta, K.K., Ekbal, A., Bhattacharyya, P.: Multilingual unsupervised NMT using shared encoder and language-specific decoders. In: Proceedings of the 57th Annual Meeting of the Association for Computational Linguistics, pp. 3083–3089 (2019)
6. Chen, C., Mu, S., Xiao, V., Ye, Z., Wu, V., Ju, Q.: Improving image captioning with conditional generative adversarial nets. In: Proceedings of the AAAI Conference on Artificial Intelligence, pp. 8142–8150 (2019)

7. Vinyals, O., Toshev, A., Bengio, S., Erhan, D.: Show and tell: A neural image caption generator. In: Proceedings of the IEEE Conference on Computer Vision and Pattern Recognition, pp. 3156–3164 (2015)
8. Xu, K., et al.: Show, attend and tell: Neural image caption generation with visual attention. In: International Conference on Machine Learning, pp. 2048–2057 (2015)
9. Yang, Y., Teo, C.L., Daum´e III, H., Aloimonos, Y.: Corpus-guided sentence generation of natural images. In: Proceedings of the Conference on Empirical Methods in Natural Language Processing, pp. 444–454 (2011)
10. Kilkarni, G., et al.: Babytalk: understanding and generating simple image descriptions. IEEE Trans. Pattern Anal. Mach. Intell. **35**(12), 2891–2903 (2013)
11. Farhadi, A., et al.: Every picture tells a story: Generating sentences from images. In: European Conference on Computer Vision, pp. 15–29 (2010)
12. Anderson, P., et al.: Bottom-up and top-down attention for image captioning and visual question answering. In: Proceedings of the IEEE Conference on Computer Vision and Pattern Recognition, pp. 6077–6086 (2018)
13. Yao, T., Pan, Y., Li, Y., Mei, T.: Exploring visual relationship for image captioning. In: Proceedings of the European Conference on Computer Vision (ECCV), pp. 684–699 (2018)
14. Guo, L., Liu, J., Zhu, X., Yao, P., Lu, S., Lu, H.: Normalized and geometry-aware self-attention network for image captioning. In: Proceedings of the IEEE/CVF Conference on Computer Vision and Pattern Recognition, pp. 10327–10336 (2020)
15. Pan, Y., Yao, T., Li, Y., Mei, T.: X-linear attention networks for image captioning. In: Proceedings of the IEEE/CVF Conference on Computer Vision and Pattern Recognition, pp. 10971–10980 (2020)
16. Huang, L., Wang, W., Chen, J., Wei, X.Y.: Attention on attention for image captioning. In: Proceedings of the IEEE/CVF International Conference on Computer Vision, pp. 4634–4643 (2019)
17. Yu, J., Li, J., Yu, Z., Huang, Q.: Multimodal transformer with multi-view visual representation for image captioning. IEEE Trans. Circuits Syst. Video Technol. **30**(12), 4467–4480 (2019)
18. Liu, L., Utiyama, M., Finch, A., Sumita, E.: Agreement on target-bidirectional neural machine translation. In: Proceedings of the 2016 Conference of the North American Chapter of the Association for Computational Linguistics: Human Language Technologies, pp. 411–416 (2016)
19. Zhou, L., Zhang, J., Zong, C.: Synchronous bidirectional neural machine translation. Trans. Assoc. Comput. Linguist. **7**, 91–105 (2019)
20. Zhang, Z., Wu, S., Liu, S., Li, M., Zhou, M., & Xu, T.: Regularizing neural machine translation by target-bidirectional agreement. In Proceedings of the AAAI Conference on Artificial Intelligence, pp. 443–450 (2019)
21. Wang, C., Yang, H., Meinel, C.: Image captioning with deep bidirectional LSTMs and multi-task learning. In: ACM Transactions on Multimedia Computing, Communications, and Applications (TOMM), 14(2s), 1–20 (2018)
22. Rennie, S.J., Marcheret, E., Mroueh, Y., Ross, J., Goel, V.: Self-critical sequence training for image captioning. In: Proceedings of the IEEE Conference on Computer Vision and Pattern Recognition, pp. 7008–7024 (2017)
23. Lin, T.Y., et al.: Microsoft coco: Common objects in context. In European Conference on Computer Vision, pp. 740–755 (2014)
24. Yao, T., Pan, Y., Li, Y., Qiu, Z., Mei, T.: Boosting image captioning with attributes. In: Proceedings of the IEEE International Conference on Computer Vision, pp. 4894–4902 (2017)

25. Jiang, W., Ma, L., Jiang, Y. G., Liu, W., Zhang, T.: Recurrent fusion network for image captioning. In: Proceedings of the European Conference on Computer Vision (ECCV), pp. 499–515 (2018)
26. Qin, Y., Du, J., Zhang, Y., Lu, H.: Look back and predict forward in image captioning. In: Proceedings of the IEEE/CVF Conference on Computer Vision and Pattern Recognition, pp. 8367–8375 (2019)
27. Yang, X., Tang, K., Zhang, H., Cai, J.: Auto-encoding scene graphs for image captioning. In: Proceedings of the IEEE/CVF Conference on Computer Vision and Pattern Recognition, pp. 10685–10694 (2019)

An Improved Lightweight Network Based on MobileNetV3 for Palmprint Recognition

Kaijun Zhou, Kaiwen Deng[(✉)], Peng Chen, and Yiliang Hu

Hunan University of Technology and Business, Changsha, China
562426840@qq.com

Abstract. In recent years, there has been an increasingly urgent need for individual identification in various application scenarios. Palmprint has numerous advantages due to its uniqueness and security. Deep learning based palmprint recognition has attracted a lot of attention among modern authentication methods. This paper proposes an improved lightweight convolutional neural network based on MobileNetV3 for palmprint recognition. In order to build a more lightweight network, we optimize the compression factor of the channel attention module. On this basis, a single activation layer is designed in the channel attention module as a multi-layer activation structure. Further, the functions in the fully connected layer are designed to improve palmprint recognition performance. Experimental results show that the proposed approach has quite less time cost while maintaining high recognition accuracy on both contact and contactless databases.

Keywords: Biometrics · Palmprint recognition · Deep learning · Lightweight network

1 Introduction

In digital society, personal identification is becoming increasingly important for information security. However, some traditional methods, such as keys and passwords, have some drawbacks [1]. Biometrics is an efficient technique which uses the physiological or behavioral properties of human body for identity recognition [2]. As a promising biometric technology, palmprint recognition has received more and more attention from the community due to its advantages. Rather than simply looking at geometric aspects such as finger length and palm size, palmprint recognition technology mainly focuses on palm detail information such as textures and lines [3]. Usually, palm and finger have both some ridge lines. However, palm region is larger than finger. Therefore, palmprint involves much more information than fingerprint.

Nowadays, there are a lot of palmprint recognition methods, and these approaches usually achieve well performance under some environments [4]. Among mentioned above methods, deep learning methods are promise attribute to its good performance [5], but there are still many problems. Most of the existing convolutional network-based methods suffer from large models. Although the recognition accuracy is well, the computation time is long. Thus, some computational resources are waste [6].

S. Yu et al. (Eds.): PRCV 2022, LNCS 13534, pp. 749–761, 2022.
https://doi.org/10.1007/978-3-031-18907-4_58

Large convolutional networks for palmprint recognition are usually not suitable for use in mobile or edge devices. It is necessary to develop a lightweight network to reduce computational time and computational resources.

2 Related Work

2.1 Traditional Palmprint Recognition Methods

In recent decades, there are many traditional palmprint recognition methods. Pawan Dubey et al. [7] proposes multiscale cross-filtering. These filters are able to extract the linear features ignored by a single Gabor filter to address the problem of missing key information and misclassification of palmprints. Salih M M [8] extract palmprint regions of interest with symbiotic matrix, and palmprint features are extracted with curvilinear wave transform, and the final classification algorithm is implemented by using ant colony optimization ideas. Ioan Păvăloi et al. [9] proposes an optimization algorithm in which the parameters are tuned on the basis of the original accelerated robust feature algorithm. The improved algorithm is then used to extract the key points of the features in the palmprint. The complex algorithmic will lead to low recognition rates.

2.2 Large CNN-Based Palmprint Recognition Method

Apart from traditional methods, deep learning is a quite hot in palmprint recognition. A.S. Tarawneh et al. [10] performed validation experimental on three large convolutional neural networks including the VGG network of two sizes and the AlexNet network [11]. It is found that for low-resolution palmprint images, the VGG neural network could extract more detailed texture features of palmprints. Dexing Zhong et al. [12] mainly relied on the idea of twin networks for palmprint recognition by two VGG convolutional neural networks. Jinsong Zhu et al. [13] proposed a unique GoogleNet. They introduced the idea of deep metric learning with adversarial properties to overcome variability and over-localisation between various types of palmprint images. The existing large CNN-based palmprint recognition methods have the disadvantages of large number of parameters long computation time. These problems have been addressed where hardware resources are limited.

2.3 Lightweight CNN-Based Palmprint Recognition Method

Since most of the methods currently applied to palmprint recognition are still implemented using large convolutional neural networks, lightweight networks are still seldom used. Elaraby A. Elgallad et al. [14] employed palmprint image feature information to achieve the goal of gender recognition for individual males and females. Elaraby A. Elgallad et al. [15] proposed SqueezeNet neural network to extract the texture details of palmprints. YiminYuan et al. [16] introduced guide filter and a special histogram equalization. It is still trained and tested on the basis of the SqueezeNet neural network, which performs operations such as recognition of images captured under multiple light waves. Although the SqueezeNet network has been made lightweight compared to most large convolutional neural networks. However, its network structure is designed to place the operation process of downsampling at the end of the network [17], and this scheme can also make the network model complex. Xueqiu Dong [18] optimized the structural hierarchy of the original MobileNet to derive its unique new lightweight convolutional network and did comparative experimental tests on it with several collections of palmprint images. Aurelia Michele et al. [19] used the hierarchical model of the base MobileNet network with slight modifications and then performed comparative experiments on it. Also, a support vector machine operator is utilized as the final classifier for the whole palmprint recognition process. The experimental data shows that the recognition results are good and that MobileNet is a lightweight network with a simpler hierarchy and shorter computation time than previous networks of the same type. It has been experimentally verified that it works well in palmprint recognition. However, the model still needs to be further enhanced in terms of issues such as real-time performance. In summary, large convolutional neural networks do not meet the metrics requirements where hardware and computing resources are scarce. A palmprint recognition method based on a lightweight model can not only reduce the computational cost, but also simplify the logical operation steps in the recognition process. Therefore, it is foreseeable that palmprint recognition methods based on lightweight models will become increasingly popular in the future.

3 Proposed Approach

3.1 Lightweight Network Based on MobileNetV3

The lightweight MobileNetV3 network [20] is derived from one of the MobileNet family of lightweight networks. The main difference between this network and other versions of lightweight networks is the use of the neural structure search idea of the MnasNet network architecture [21]. This idea is to use the performance improvement of the optimization metrics set by itself as the ultimate goal of the search in the neural structure mode to obtain the optimal convolutional network structure design.

MobileNetV3 also adds a channel-layer attention module to the previous version of the lightweight network, which is divided into two types: Large and Small. In this paper, the former type is mainly used to implement a palmprint recognition scheme with low-dimensional features, which can yield high recognition rate results. The latter convolutional network type, despite removing many of the modules from the initialized MobileNet hierarchy, is designed to have a recognition rate that does not meet engineering requirements for either image classification or prediction tasks that have been experimentally tested compared to the large type of structure [22]. The diagram of the MobileNetV3network structure is shown in Fig. 1.

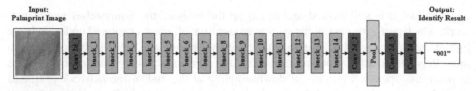

Fig. 1. Schematic diagram of the MobileNetV3 lightweight convolutional network hierarchy flow

This paper main improved module is the inverse residual module of the original network. The main computational flow of this network is as follows. Firstly, the result of the processed feature information of the palm print image output in the previous network layer is passed into the inverse residual module of the network as input. Point convolution is performed, and another layer of activation function layer is executed. DW convolution is then performed and another layer of activation function layer is executed. The DW convolution result of the palm print image is then fed into the Palm_TS_block module. The Palm_TS_block module then performs a second layer of point convolution on the palmprint image features calculated by the Palm_TS_block module. Finally, the result of the point convolution is added to the palmprint image feature information originally input into the modified inverse residual module, resulting in the computation of the entire inverse residual module. The final output is the processed palmprint image data. The specific network structure flow chart is shown in Fig. 2. The Palm_TS_block module will be described in detail later.

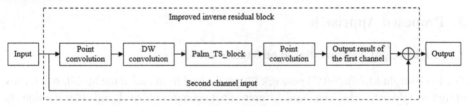

Fig. 2. Algorithmic framework diagram of the modified inverse residual block consisting of DW convolution, Palm_TS_block and point convolution sub-modules

In MobileNetV3, the base network is rebuilt by improving the original channel-layer attention module. Instead of using the sigmoid activation function, an improved channel-layer attention module has been replaced with the hard-sigmoid function [23]. Hard-sigmoid function is an approximate replacement operation based on the Sigmoid function. The formula for this activation function is shown in Eq. (1):

$$F_{hard-sigmoid}(x) = clip(\frac{x+1}{2}, 0, 1) = \max(0, \min(1, \frac{2x+5}{10})) \tag{1}$$

In the above Eq. (1), $F_{hard-sigmoid}$ is the hard-sigmoid function that restrict the maximum and minimum values of the variable.

Then, we rebuild the original channel attention module, resulting in a new module called the Palm_TS_block module. The network structure of this module is shown in Fig. 3.

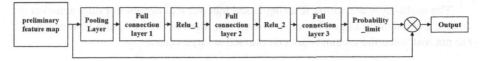

Fig. 3. Hierarchy diagram of the Palm_TS_block module

The Palm_TS_block module has the following computation process. Firstly, the palmprint image is fed into the Palm_TS_block module after preiminary feature extraction operation. Then, a pooling layer is built to obtain a global feature information. After that, there are three full connection layers and two Relu activation lays. These layers ensure one can extract deep feature information and reduce feature dimensionality. Secondly, we construct channel weight probability computation functions namely Probability_limit layer. Finally, the feature map obtained from Probability_limit layer is multiplied with preliminary feature map, which result in the output of the final Palm_TS_block module.

3.2 Improvements of MobileNetV3

Compression Factor. In this section, the original network is optimized to solve the problem of improving the speed of the MobileNetV3 network in performing palmprint recognition tasks. In the activation learning part of the original module, the compression ratio of the channel attention module of the first fully connected layer part is improved. The channel compression factor of the first fully connected layer activation part of the channel attention module in the MobileNetV3 network is 0.25. This factor is mainly used to reduce the channel dimension. In this paper, this channel compression factor is set to the variable s. The original value of s is then one quarter. In order to further enhance the lightweight MobileNetV3 network and improve the speed of training and testing in palmprint recognition tasks, this paper plans to design the compression factor variable s to a smaller value. The aim is to reduce some of the computations on unnecessary channel dimensions.

After analysis the above, the variables will be further reduced in order to increase the speed and optimize the real-time performance of the network.

Structure of Multi-layer Activation Learning Networks. In this section, the paper redesigns the hierarchical framework in terms of the network structure of this attention module.

First, the original channel attention module in the MobileNetV3 network contains only two fully-connected layers, and only the first fully-connected layer is used for activation learning. In this paper, the first fully connected layer, including the Relu layer of activation functions, is collectively referred to as the activation layer. The activation layer of the channel-layer attention module by designing a multi-layer activation structure. The multi-layer activation structure is planned to increase the reduction of the channel dimension by designing the local network of the original activation layer as a two-layer fully connected layer structure. The channel compression factor in each separate fully connected layer is set to 0.125, and each separate fully connected layer is followed by a layer of Relu activation functions.

The multi-layer activation learning-based hierarchical design not only achieves the desired compression target, but also ensures that most of the key palm texture features are not lost when the channels are compressed at large scales.

Channel Probability Calculation Function. As a final layer of the channel attention module, the function of the channel weight ranking computation layer has been much improved over the original attention module. It has turn non-linear power function into an approximate linear function, reducing the computational effort. However, the design of the function for the middle segment of the linear function has not been studied for palmprint image. The function determines the entire weight ranking value when the channel feature information is located at a certain position. Two key points take the value 0, and other takes the value 1, which jointly determine the boundary value of the channel weight assignment.

Thus, the horizontal coordinates on the x-axis are corresponding with the channel feature values on the left and right, respectively. The positions of two points need to be calculated according to palmprint images in a specific training set.

4 Experiments and Analysis

The palmprint datasets used in experiments are the Chinese Academy of Sciences palmprint dataset, the Indian Institute of Technology palmprint dataset, the Hong Kong Polytechnic University palmprint dataset, the Tongji University palmprint dataset and the Hong Kong Polytechnic multispectral dataset. Three contactless datasets are included, as well as two contact datasets. The computation environment is as follows: Intel(R) Core (TM) i5-8500 CPU 3.00 GHz, RAM16.0 GB, NVIDIA GeForce RTX 2060 and Pycharm.

4.1 Analysis of Compression Factor Optimization

Firstly, this subsection starts with experiments on the original MobileNetV3 network, and a comparison experiment on several other convolutional networks at the same time. In this paper, the results are presented mainly in terms of running time and recognition rate. In addition, all recognition rates and running time results for the two-cycle palmprint set are averaged over two cycles, unless otherwise stated.

This paper includes experiments on the Alex convolutional network [11], VGG-16 convolutional network [27], Reg-Y convolutional network [28], ResNet-18 convolutional network [29], DenseNet-121 convolutional network [24], MobileNetV2 convolutional network [20]and MobileNetV3 convolutional network [30] and others on the experimental results. The experimental data are presented in Tables 1 and 2. Table 1 shows the training time cost of each convolutional network on the five publicly available palmprint image collections. Table 2 shows matching time on each database. The notion of running time here refers to the average time spent by each convolutional network on the palmprint images during training or testing. In this paper, MbV2 and MbV3, which appear in all graphs, are abbreviations of MobileNetV2 and MobileNetV3 convolutional networks respectively. CASIA, IITD, TJU-P, PolyUM_B and PolyUII in all the experimental graphs in this paper are the abbreviations of the Institute of Automation, Chinese Academy of Sciences, Indian Institute of Technology, Tongji University, Hong Kong Polytechnic University and Hong Kong Polytechnic University palmprint datasets respectively.

Table 1. Comparison of training time on each database

Training time/s	CASIA	IITD	TJU-P	PolyUM_B	PolyUII
Alex	0.3579	0.3749	0.3893	0.2806	0.3475
VGG-16	0.4829	0.4944	0.5852	0.3151	0.3933
Reg-Y	0.3418	0.3632	0.3779	0.2766	0.3340
ResNet-18	0.4572	0.4698	0.5541	0.2829	0.3638
DenseNet-121	0.5016	0.5231	0.6138	0.3472	0.4362
MbV2	0.3219	0.3244	0.3492	0.2537	0.3006
MbV3	0.2804	0.2899	0.3011	0.2156	0.2571

Table 2. Comparison of matching time on each database

Test time cost/s	CASIA	IITD	TJU-P	PolyUM_B	PolyUII
Alex	0.0957	0.1063	0.1187	0.0709	0.0796
VGG-16	0.1379	0.1471	0.1680	0.0858	0.1024
Reg-Y	0.0904	0.1027	0.1155	0.0706	0.0748
ResNet-18	0.1033	0.1104	0.1377	0.0712	0.0859
DenseNet-121	0.1520	0.1689	0.1844	0.0948	0.1255
MbV2	0.0861	0.0917	0.1034	0.0703	0.0732
MbV3	0.0479	0.0506	0.0632	0.0362	0.0420

Overall, the best result for the time taken by the MobileNetV3 network during the training process is a reduction of 50.94%; while during the testing process, its optimal reduction ratio is 70.04%. Therefore, by comparing the results of the above-mentioned multiple palmprint data sets, it is clear that the MobileNetV3 network, the base network of this paper, is indeed more lightweight than other commonly used convolutional networks.

The original MobileNetV3 network has a compression factor of 0.25, which can be further optimized by the analysis above, with the aim of achieving smaller coefficients. In this paper, a comparison between the coefficients of 0.125 and 0.0625 is done. The results of the comparison are shown below. Table 3 shows the comparative results of running time during training with compression factors of 0.125 and 0.0625 respectively, while Table 4 shows the comparative results of running time during testing with compression factors of 0.125 and 0.0625 respectively.

Table 3. Comparison of training time with coefficient of 0.125 and 0.0625

Train/s	Compression factor	CASIA	IITD	TJU-P	PolyUM_B	PolyUII
MbV3	0.125	0.2804	0.2899	0.3011	0.2156	0.2571
Proposed network		0.2416	0.2457	0.2638	0.1729	0.2166
MbV3	0.0625	0.2804	0.2899	0.3011	0.2156	0.2571
Proposed network		0.3779	0.3796	0.4288	0.3351	0.3479

Table 4. Comparison of matching time with coefficient of 0.125 and 0.0625.

Test/s	Compression factor	CASIA	IITD	TJU-P	PolyUM_B	PolyUII
MbV3	0.125	0.0479	0.0506	0.0632	0.0362	0.0420
Proposed network		0.0383	0.0411	0.0587	0.0288	0.0376
MbV3	0.0625	0.0479	0.0506	0.0632	0.0362	0.0420
Proposed network		0.0525	0.0672	0.0793	0.0437	0.0564

From the comparison of the experimental results, it is clear that it is not the case that the smaller the compression factor is, the better. When the coefficient is 0.125, both the time cost results during training and the time cost results during testing have the effect of reducing the time cost and improving the real-time performance. However, when the coefficient becomes smaller, i.e. 0.0625, both the training and testing latencies become worse and take longer than the original MobileNetV3 network.

In the above data results, the best result during training is cut down by 19.81%, while the best result during testing is cut down by 20.44%. The above analysis shows that the compression factor when optimized to 0.125 does improve real-time performance and reduce the amount of computation. Also, the results of multiple comparisons between the three contactless palmprint sets and the two contact palmprint sets show that a coefficient of 0.125 is the least time consuming and meets the requirements of this paper for low resolution palmprint recognition.

4.2 Analysis on Improving the Structure of Multi-layer Activation Learning Networks

With these improvements, it is found that further improvements in network running time performance can still be made through optimization of the network structure hierarchy. The results of the comparison experiments are shown next. Still multiple sets of comparative tests are done to compare the running time data across the five palmprint sets. The experimental data is shown below, where Table 5 shows the combined average running time results during training after the multi-layer activation optimization design, and Table 6 shows the combined average running time results during testing.

Table 5. Average training time with multi-layer activation

Test/s	CASIA	IITD	TJU-P	PolyUM_B	PolyUII
Compression factor optimization	0.2416	0.2457	0.2638	0.1729	0.2166
Multi-layer activation optimization	0.1989	0.1991	0.2185	0.1297	0.1693

Table 6. Average matching time in tests with multi-layer activation

Test/s	CASIA	IITD	TJU-P	PolyUM_B	PolyUII
Compression factor optimization	0.0383	0.0411	0.0587	0.0288	0.0376
Multi-layer activation optimization	0.0279	0.0391	0.0466	0.0193	0.0237

The analysis of the above experimental data shows that the use of multi-layer activation learning can indeed improve the real-time performance to a great extent. The best result during training is cut down by 24.99%, while the best result during testing is cut down by 36.97%. The method proposed in this paper, therefore, is suitable for palmprint recognition tasks under low-resolution conditions and has implications that are worthy of follow-up research.

Finally, its recognition rate results need to be validated. Therefore, it is then necessary to test its recognition rate on a collection of five palmprint images containing both contact and contactless images. Tables 7 show the experimental results.

Table 7. Comparison of recognition rate after real-time optimization

Accuracy/s	CASIA	IITD	TJU-P	PolyUM_B	PolyUII
MbV3	99.63	97.10	98.91	95.83	100.00
Improved network	99.66	97.49	99.07	96.57	100.00

From the analysis of the above experimental data, it can be found that the recognition rate can be promoted by a 0.77% on several databases. Nevertheless, the results on the five palmprint databases shows that all of the above improvements are able to achieve the goal of reducing time cost while maintaining high recognition rate.

4.3 Analysis of Channel Probability Calculation Function

Through the theoretical analysis in Sect. 2.3, the location of the coordinates of the two boundary points in the channel probability computation function need to be determined. In fact, from a mathematical point of view, the determination of these two coordinate positions of a certain linear function relies mainly on the slope of that linear function. Therefore, this subsection will analysis how to specifically improve the identification rate results from the perspective of slope, combined with different values of slope taking. In this paper, three slopes are selected for comparison: 0.15 and 0.25. It should be noted that 0.2 is the initial slop value in the original MobileNetV3. The results of the experiments are shown in Table 8 and Table 9.

Table 8 shows the recognition rate results when slope is 0.25. Table 9 shows the comparison results when slope is 0.15. The first row of data results in both tables are the results of comparison experiments done with a slope of 0.2. Real-time testing experiments are also done, and the results are shown in Table 10 and Table 11, showing the time consumed for training and testing at a slope of 0.25 respectively.

Table 8. Recognition rates when slope is 0.25

Accuracy/s	CASIA	IITD	TJU-P	PolyUM_B	PolyUII
Real-time optimized network	99.66	97.49	99.07	96.57	100.00
Network after recognition rate improvement	99.71	98.43	99.19	97.46	100.00

Table 9. Recognition rates with a slope of 0.15

Accuracy/s	CASIA	IITD	TJU-P	PolyUM_B	PolyUII
Real-time optimized network	99.66	97.49	99.07	96.57	100.00
Network after recognition rate improvement	93.83	91.69	93.10	90.96	95.22

Table 10. Comparison of training time when slope is 0.25

Train/s	CASIA	IITD	TJU-P	PolyUM_B	PolyUII
Real-time optimized network	0.1989	0.1991	0.2185	0.1297	0.1693
Network after recognition rate improvement	0.1972	0.1977	0.2169	0.1233	0.1640

Table 11. Comparison of matching time when slope is 0.25

Test/s	CASIA	IITD	TJU-P	PolyUM_B	PolyUII
Real-time optimized network	0.0279	0.0391	0.0466	0.0193	0.0237
Network after recognition rate improvement	0.0250	0.0373	0.0431	0.0163	0.0224

From the recognition rate results, one can find that 0.25 is best slope value for palmprint recognition tasks. The experimental results show that recognition rate is improved by 0.96% when slop is 0.25. However, recognition accuracy turns worse when slope is 0.15.

5 Conclusion

This paper proposed an improved palmprint recognition method based on the MobileNetV3 network. There three improvements and optimizations for the channel attention module in the MobileNetV3 lightweight network in order to address the real-time performance. The three improvements and optimizations are compression factor optimization, multi-layer activation structure design and function optimization of fully connected layer. The method achieves a highly real-time palmprint recognition method, allowing the network to reduce the time cost. Experimental results imply that the improvements can reduce the time cost and maintain a high recognition rate. For future work, the approach can be applied to the scenes of mobile device side or edge device applications, reducing unnecessary computing time spent and computing resources.

Acknowledgements. This work is supported by National Natural Science Foundation of China (61976088, 61471170). We would also like to thank the various institutions including Chinese Academy of Sciences, Indian Institute of Technology, Hong Kong Polytechnic University and Tongji University for providing the palmprint dataset.

References

1. National Research Council, and Whither Biometrics Committee: Biometric recognition: challenges and opportunities (2010)
2. Jain, A.K., Ross, A., Prabhakar, S.: An introduction to biometric recognition. IEEE Trans. Circuits Syst. Video Technol. **14**(1), 4–20 (2004)
3. Yue, F., Zhang, D., Zuo, W.: A review of palmprint recognition algorithms. J. Autom. **36**(03), 353–365 (2010)
4. Yörük, E., Dutağaci, H., Sankur, B.: Hand biometrics. Image Vis. Comput. **24**(5), 483–497 (2006)
5. Liu, Y.H.: Feature extraction and image recognition with convolutional neural networks. J. Phys. Conf. Ser. **1087**(6), 062032 (2018)
6. Xu, N., Zhu, Q., Xu, X., Zhang, D.: An effective recognition approach for contactless palmprint. Vis. Comput. **37**(4), 695–705 (2020). https://doi.org/10.1007/s00371-020-01962-x
7. Dubey, P., Kanumuri, T., Vyas, R.: Optimal directional texture codes using multiscale bit crossover count planes for palmprint recognition. Multimedia Tools Appl. **81**, 20291–20310 (2022). https://doi.org/10.1007/s11042-022-12580-1
8. Salih, M.M.: A suggested system for palmprint recognition using curvelet transform and co-occurrence matrix
9. Păvăloi, I., Ignat, A., Lazăr, L.C., Niţă, C.D.: Palmprint recognition with fixed number of SURF keypoints. In: 2021 International Conference on e-Health and Bioengineering (EHB), pp. 1–4 (2021)
10. Tarawneh, A.S., Chetverikov, D., Hassanat, A.B.: Pilot comparative study of different deep features for palmprint identification in low-quality images. arXiv preprint arXiv:1804.04602 (2018)
11. Krizhevsky, A., Sutskever, I., Hinton, G.E.: ImageNet classification with deep convolutional neural networks. In: Advances in Neural Information Processing Systems 25 (2012)
12. Zhong, D., Yang, Y., Du, X.: Palmprint recognition using Siamese network. In: Chinese Conference on Biometric Recognition, pp. 48–55 (2018)

13. Zhu, J., Zhong, D., Luo, K.: Boosting unconstrained palmprint recognition with adversarial metric learning. IEEE Trans. Biometr. Behav. Identity Sci. **2**(4), 388–398 (2020)
14. Elgallad, E.A., Ouarda, W., Alimi, A.M.: CWNN-Net: a new convolution wavelet neural network for gender classification using palm print. Int. J. Adv. Comput. Sci. Appl. **10**(5) (2019)
15. Elgallad, E.A., Ouarda, W., Alimi, A.M.: Dense hand-CNN: a novel CNN architecture based on later fusion of neural and wavelet features for identity recognition. Int. J. Adv. Comput. Sci. Appl. **10**(6) (2019)
16. Yuan, Y., Tang, C., Xia, S., Chen, Z., Qi, T.: HandNet: identification based on hand images using deep learning methods. In: Proceedings of the 2020 4th International Conference on Vision, Image and Signal Processing, pp. 1–6 (2020)
17. Howard, A.G., et al.: MobileNets: efficient convolutional neural networks for mobile vision applications. arXiv preprint arXiv:1704.04861 (2017)
18. Xueqiu, D.: A palm print recognition method based on deep convolutional neural network. Yunnan University (2019)
19. Michele, A., Colin, V., Santika, D.D.: MobileNet convolutional neural networks and support vector machines for palmprint recognition. Procedia Comput. Sci. **157**, 110–117 (2019)
20. Sandler, M., Howard, A., Zhu, M., Zhmoginov, A., Chen, L.C.: MobileNetV2: inverted residuals and linear bottlenecks. In: Proceedings of the IEEE Conference on Computer Vision and Pattern Recognition, pp. 4510–4520 (2018)
21. Jia, Y.: Learning semantic image representations at a large scale. University of California, Berkeley (2014)
22. Lowe, D.G.: Distinctive image features from scale-invariant keypoints. Int. J. Comput. Vision **60**(2), 91–110 (2004)
23. Nair, V., Hinton, G.E.: Rectified linear units improve restricted Boltzmann machines. In: ICML (2010)
24. Zhang, L., Gao, X.: Transfer adaptation learning: a decade survey. IEEE Trans. Neural Netw. Learn. Syst. (2022)
25. Zhuang, F., et al.: A comprehensive survey on transfer learning. Proc. IEEE **109**(1), 43–76 (2020)
26. Tan, M., et al.: MnasNet: platform-aware neural architecture search for mobile. In: Proceedings of the IEEE/CVF Conference on Computer Vision and Pattern Recognition, pp. 2820–2828 (2019)
27. Simonyan, K., Zisserman, A.: Very deep convolutional networks for large-scale image recognition. arXiv preprint arXiv:1409.1556 (2014)
28. Radosavovic, I., Kosaraju, R.P., Girshick, R., He, K., Dollár, P.: Designing network design spaces. In: Proceedings of the IEEE/CVF Conference on Computer Vision and Pattern Recognition, pp. 10428–10436 (2020)
29. He, K., Zhang, X., Ren, S., Sun, J.: Deep residual learning for image recognition. In: Proceedings of the IEEE Conference on Computer Vision and Pattern Recognition, pp. 770–778 (2016)
30. Howard, A., et al.: Searching for MobileNetV3. In: Proceedings of the IEEE/CVF International Conference on Computer Vision, pp. 1314–1324 (2019)
31. CASIA Palmprint Image Database [M/OL]. http://www.cbsr.ia.ac.cn/english/Databases.asp. Accessed 26 Aug 2019
32. IIT Delhi Palmprint Image Database version 1.0 (IITD) [M/OL]. http://www4.comp.polyu.edu.hk/~csajaykr/IITD/Database_Palm.htm. Accessed 22 Aug 2019
33. Zhang, D., Kong, W.K., You, J., Wong, M.: Online palmprint identification. IEEE Trans. Pattern Anal. Mach. Intell. **25**(9), 1041–1050 (2003)

34. Zhang, L., Li, L., Yang, A., Shen, Y., Yang, M.: Towards contactless palmprint recognition: a novel device, a new benchmark, and a collaborative representation based identification approach. Pattern Recogn. **69**, 199–212 (2017)
35. Zhang, D., Guo, Z., Lu, G., Zhang, L., Zuo, W.: An online system of multispectral palmprint verification. IEEE Trans. Instrum. Meas. **59**(2), 480–490 (2009)

A Radar HRRP Target Recognition Method Based on Conditional Wasserstein VAEGAN and 1-D CNN

Jiaxing He, Xiaodan Wang[✉], and Qian Xiang

Air Force Engineering University, Xi'an, Shaanxi, China
afeu_wang@163.com

Abstract. Radar high resolution range profile (HRRP) contains important structural features such as target size and scattering center distribution, which has attracted extensive attention in the field of radar target recognition. Aiming at the problems of class imbalance and insufficient data quality generated by vanilla GAN, an HRRP target recognition method based on improved conditional Wasserstein Variational Autoencoder Generative Adversarial Networks (CWVAEGAN) and one-dimensional convolutional neural network (CWVAEGAN-1DCNN) is proposed. CWVAEGAN class-balancing method introduces the concept of variational lower bound in VAE into GAN, and uses the encoded hidden vector instead of Gaussian noise as generator's input, which can significantly improve the fidelity of the generated samples and balance the class distribution of the dataset. The balanced dataset is used for classification through a standard 1D-CNN. The experimental results show that the samples generated by CWVAEGAN class-balancing method greatly improve the detection accuracy of 1D-CNN for minority classes, the fidelity of the samples generated by CWVAEGAN is higher than that of other class-balancing methods, and CWVAEGAN-1DCNN has strong HRRP target recognition ability.

Keywords: High resolution range profile · Class-balancing method · Generative adversarial network · Variational autoencoder · One-dimensional convolution neural network

1 Introduction

Radar high resolution range profile (HRRP) is the amplitude of the coherent sum of the complex sub echoes of the target scattering points in each range unit, which represents the projection of the target scattering center echo on the radar line of sight [1]. Because HRRP contains important structural features such as target size and scattering center distribution, HRRP target recognition has attracted extensive attention in the field of radar automatic target recognition [2]. In recent years, many traditional machine learning algorithms have been widely used in HRRP recognition [3,4], but these machine learning methods rely on manual

S. Yu et al. (Eds.): PRCV 2022, LNCS 13534, pp. 762–777, 2022.
https://doi.org/10.1007/978-3-031-18907-4_59

feature extraction, and can not better capture the deep information of data for accurate recognition. Therefore, how to effectively learn the features in the data is an important problem to improve the recognition ability of HRRP.

To solve class imbalance problem, we propose a method of generating conditional Wasserstein variational autoencoder generative adversarial network (CWVAEGAN) and one-dimensional Convolutional neural network (1D-CNN). Firstly, CWVAEGAN-1DCNN filters the original dataset and selects the minority classes. CWVAEGAN learn the dataset and generate new minority data, to rebalance the training dataset.

This paper has the following contributions

(1) Aiming at the class-imbalancing problem in HRRP target recognition, we propose a new algorithm based on CWVAEGAN to generate minority class samples. One-dimensional convolution layers were introduced into the encoder, decoder, and discriminator to enhance the expression ability of the whole network. Therefore, we introduce condition information and WGAN-GP loss based on VAE-GAN.
(2) On the basis of CWVAEGAN, a balanced training dataset is generated, and one-dimensional CNN is used for classification, which can more accurately carry out target recognition. We establish CWVAEGAN-1DCNN to solve the target recognition problem.
(3) Experimental results on HRRP datasets prove that CWVAEGAN-1DCNN is superior to the existing target recognition methods.

The rest of article is organized as follows. In Sect. 2, we summarize the development of deep learning in the field of HRRP target recognition and the related contents of class balancing method. Section 3, we introduces the details of CWVAEGAN model and CWVAEGAN-1DCNN. Section 4 introduces the comparative study experiment, and analyzes the experimental results. In Sect. 5, we presents conclusions.

2 Related Work

2.1 HRRP Target Recognition Method

Deep learning can automatically extract the features of data by using deep neural network. Due to its strong feature extraction ability, deep learning algorithm has been widely used and achieved good results in the fields of face recognition [5], image classification [6], computer vision [7]. Convolutional neural network (CNN) has strong feature extraction ability to mine the local features of data through convolution layer. Convolutional neural network is widely used in the field of HRRP recognition. Yang et al. [8] proposed HRRP recognition method based on convolutional neural network and constructed two kinds of CNN networks. One CNN network directly extracts features from one-dimensional HRRP, and the other CNN network extracts features from two-dimensional data after HRRP conversion. Compared with template matching method, the target recognition rate is greatly improved, and the results show that one-dimensional HRRP data is more conducive to feature extraction. Guo et al. [9] proposed a HRRP target recognition method based on deep multi-scale one-dimensional convolution neural network, which uses multi-scale convolution kernel to extract features with different accuracy. Wan et al. [10] transformed one-dimensional HRRP data into 2-d spectrogram and identified it with 2d-DCNN, which achieved good results. Lu et al. [11] extracted the bi-spectrum spectrum feature of HRRP and used it as the input of convolutional neural network to extract deep features.

2.2   Variational Autoencoder (VAE)

The generative model mainly includes two forms: variational autoencoder VAE and GAN. VAE is a generative deep learning model based on variational thought. VAE is a generative network structure based on variable Bayes (VB) inference proposed by Kingma et al. [12] in 2014. The loss function of the original VAE [13] can be expressed as:

$$L_{VAE} = -E_{q(z|x)}[log\frac{p(x|z)p(z)}{q(z|x)}] = L_{llike}^{pixel} + L_{prior} \tag{1}$$

$$L_{llike}^{pixel} = -E_{q(z|x)}[logp(x \parallel z)] \tag{2}$$

$$L_{prior} = D_{KL}(q(z \mid x)p(z)) \tag{3}$$

where L_{llike}^{pixel} is the decoding process $p(x|z)$, $p(z)$ is prior distribution, $q(z|x)$ is the approximate posterior distribution, z follows $q(z|x)$; L_{VAE} is the KL divergence between $q(z|x)$ and $p(z)$ (Fig. 1).

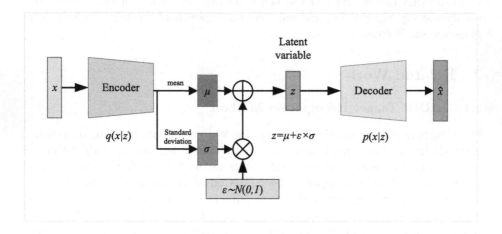

Fig. 1. Structure of VAE

2.3 Wasserstein Generative Adversarial Networks (WGAN)

GAN is composed of generator (G) and discriminator (D) [7]. The loss function of GAN is:

$$min_G max_D V(G, D) = min_G max_D E_{x\ p_r}[log D(x)] + E_z\ pz[log(1 - D(G(z)))] \tag{4}$$

where, z is the random noise, x is the original sample, y is the category information, p_z is the distribution of z, p_r is the distribution of real data x, $G(z)$ is the fake data generated by G, $D(x)$ is the score given by D, $E()$ is the expected value. G and D are optimized iteratively in the confrontation, to identify the data source more accurately and to generate excellent fake samples.

Conditional generative adversarial networks (CGAN) introduces class information into the vanilla Gan to generate samples of specified classes. The loss function of CGAN [14] is:

$$min_G max_D V(G, D) = min_G max_D E_{x\ p_r}[log D((x|y))] + E_z\ pz[log(1 - D(G(z|y)))] \tag{5}$$

Arjovsky et al. [15] proposed Wasserstein GAN (WGAN)) in 2017. WGAN changed the JS divergence of loss function to earth mover (EM) distance, which solved the problem of gradient disappearance and mode collapse in GAN and CGAN. The objective function of WGAN is:

$$V(G, D)_{WGAN} = max_{D \in 1-lipschitz} \left\{ E_{x \sim p_r}[D(x)] - E_{x \sim (p_g)}[D(x)] \right\} \tag{6}$$

where p_g is the generated samples' distribution, $D \in 1-lipschitz$ means that any function $f(x)$ which satisfies $f(x_1) - f(x_2) \leq x_1 - x_2$. that is, the discriminator D is smooth enough to prevent the dependent variable from changing too fast with the change of independent variable.

WGAN-GP [16] adds a gradient penalty term on the basis of WGAN to satisfy the Lipschitz constraint and avoid the situation that the discriminator cannot converge in the training process. The objective function of WGAN-GP is:

$$V(G, D)_{WGAN-GP} = max_{D \in 1-lipschitz} \left\{ E_{x \sim p_r}[D(x)] - E_{x \sim p_g}[D(x)] - \lambda E_{x \sim p_{penaty}}[\nabla_x D(x) - 1]^2 \right\} \tag{7}$$

where λ it is a parameter; $\nabla_x D(x)$ represents the computing paradigm $D(x)$ of alignmentx; $x \sim p_{penaty}$ means to take the middle position x from the line between a point on p_r and a point on p_g.

3   Methods

In this section, we propose the detail of CWVAEGAN and establish an method based on CWVAEGAN.

3.1   Conditional Wasserstein Variational Autoencoders with GAN (CWVAEGAN)

Larsen et al. [13] called the joint training of VAE and Gan as VAEGAN, which uses the representation learned by GAN'S discriminator to measure the distance between dataspaces. The decoder of VAE is combined with GAN, and training is carried out at the same time. The feature-wise errors are used to replace the element-wise errors to generate higher quality image samples.

On the basis of VAEGAN, we improve the class-imbalancing problem of HRRP target recognition dataset and the charac-teristics of structured dataset, add the condition vector and WGAN-GP loss function to VAEGAN, improve the difficulty in GAN training and the non-convergence phenomenon of the model. New training samples are generated for minority classes to alleviate the class-imbalancing problem. For the class-imbalancing problem in the original samples, we use the condition vector to control the class of the generated samples, and only minority class samples are generated. We also improve the network structure of the original VAEGAN, using the loss function of WGAN-GP to stabilize the training process of VAEGAN and improve the quality of generated samples.

CWVAEGAN Structure: Figure 2 shows the structure of CWVAEGAN, whcic includes three parts: encoder E, generator G and discriminator D, in which the G of GAN also acts as a decoder in VAE. E encodes the original sample data x into the implicit vector z, and calculates the mean value and variance of the input dataset through encoder. G then attempts to generate samples from the re-parameterized z or random noise z. Finally, D gives scores for the original sample, the reconstructed sample and the newly generated sample. The combination of E and G is used as the data generation part to conduct adversarial learning with D. In conclusion, CWVAEGAN takes the original training sample $s = (r, y)$ as the input and outputs the synthesized sample $s_G = [G(z, y'), y']$, where r, y, z and y' respectively represent the original data feature, the original label, the noise and minority class label

Encoder E. As shown in Fig. 2, the discrimination model E consists of one-dimensional convolution layer and fully connected layer. In adversarial learning, the input of E is minority classes vector r' and the corresponding label y'. For a particular input $s = (r, y)$, E translates it into a hidden vector z. As shown in (1), The original VAE loss function consists of reconstruction loss L_{llike}^{pixel} and prior loss L_{prior}. In VAEGAN, L_{llike}^{pixel} is replaced by the feature representation $L_{llike}^{Dis_l}$ learned by the discriminator

$$L_{llike}^{pixel} = -E_{q(z|s)}[logp(Dis_l(s)|z)] \tag{8}$$

in which $Dis_l(s)$ represents the hidden representation of s in layer l of D, and $p(Dis_l(s)|z)$ can be expressed as a Gaussian distribution with mean value $Dis_l(\widetilde{s})$ and identity covariance [13]

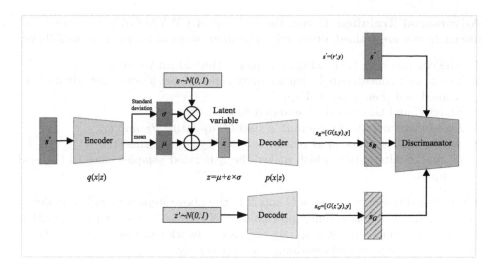

Fig. 2. Model structure of CWVAEGAN

$$p(Dis_l(s)|z) = \mathcal{N}(Dis_l(s) \mid Dis_l(\tilde{s}), I) \tag{9}$$

In the process of training, we use the advanced feature representation of the hidden layer in D to measure the distance between the generated samples and the original samples. The loss function of encoder is

$$L(E) = L_{llike}^{Dis_l} + L_{prior} \tag{10}$$

Discriminator D. In the process of training, the input of D is the mixture of s',s_R and s_G, and the output is the prediction probability of the samples. For a particular input (r, y), D needs to determine the probability $D(r, y)$ whether it comes from s' other than s_R or s_G. The loss function of D is

$$L(D) = E_{s \sim p_r}[D(s)] - E_{s \sim p_g}[D(s)] - \lambda E_{s \sim p_{penaty}}[\| \nabla_s D(s) \| -1]^2 \tag{11}$$

Among them, the first item of the loss function is the discrimination result of the real samples, the second and third items are the discrimination result of the reconstructed samples and the newly generated samples respectively, and the fourth item is the gradient penalty term. After the loss value is obtained, the gradient can be calculated η_{θ_D} and the network parameters θ_D of the discriminator can be updated by the ADAM algorithm.

Generator G. In the training process, the class information and the input vector are connected as (z, y') or (z', y'), and the reconstructed samples $s_R = [G(z,y'),y']$ or the newly generated samples $s_G = [G(z, y'), y']$ are obtained through G. In the generator training process, we will also add $L_{llike}^{Dis_l}$ to the generator loss function as an regularization, we can get G loss function is

$$L(G) = E_{s \sim p_g}[D(s)] - L_{llike}^{Dis_l} \tag{12}$$

Adversarial Training: During the training of CWVAEGAN, generrator and discriminator are trained alternately. The main steps of training are as follows:

1. The original data is encoded by E to get the hidden vector z.
2. The z' or z concatenated with minority classes label y' are input, then G are trained and then generated s_R.;
3. Fixed E and G, trained D, updated θ_D;
4. Fixed discriminator D, training E and G, updating θ_E and θ_G;
5. Before the loss value of D reaches 0.5, the cycle performs steps (1) (4), E, G, and D alternately, which makes the generated samples close to the real samples.

The detailed training process of G and D in the above steps is described in detail in Sect. 2.2, the whole training process of CWVAEGAN is shown in algorithm 1, among which θ_E, η_{θ_E}, θ_G, η_{θ_G}, θ_D, η_{θ_D} are network parameters and gradients of encoder, generator and discriminator respectively.

Algorithm 1. minority classes data generation based on CWVAEGAN and VGM

Input: $s = (r, y)$
Output: $s_G = [G(z, y'), y']$
1: $c_{i,j} = v_{i,j} \oplus s_{i,j}$ /* Continuous columns decomposition */
2: $r_{j'} = v_{1,j} \oplus a_{1,j} \oplus \ldots \oplus v_{N_c,j} \oplus a_{N_c,j} \oplus d_{1,j} \oplus \ldots \oplus d_{N_d}$ /* Feature column decomposition */
3: **while** D has not converged to 0.5 do/*CWVAEGAN training*/ **do**
4:    /*Optimization of D */
5:    Sample $(r'_i, y'_i)_{i=1}^{n_z}$ from $p_{data}(r', y')$
6:    $z_i = E(r'_i, y'_i)$
7:    $Sample(z_i')_{i=1}^{n_z} from p_z(z)$
8:    $\eta_{\theta_D} \leftarrow \nabla \theta_D [\frac{1}{n_z} \sum_{i=1}^{n_z} D(r'_i, y'_i) - D(G(z_i, y'_i), y'_i) - D(G(z_i', y'_i), y'_i)$
        $\lambda E_{(r'_i, y'_i) \sim p_{penaty}} [\| \nabla_s D(r'_i, y'_i) \| - 1]^2]$
9:    $\theta_D \leftarrow \theta_D + \alpha_D \cdot Adam(\theta_D, \eta_{\theta_D})$
10:   /*Optimization of G and E jointly*/
11:   Sample $\{(z_i)\}_{i=1}^{n_z}$ from $p_z(z)$
12:   $\eta_{\theta_E} = -\nabla_{\theta_E}(D_K L(q(z_i \mid (r'_i, y'_i)) \| p(z_i)) - E_{q(z_i \| (r'_i, y'_i))}[log p((r'_i, y'_i) \| z_i)])$
13:   $\eta_{\theta_G} \leftarrow \nabla \theta_D [\frac{1}{n_z} \sum_{i=1}^{n_z} D(G(z_i', y'_i), y'_i)$
14:   $\theta_G \leftarrow \theta_G + \alpha_G \cdot Adam(\theta_G, \eta_{\theta_G})$
15:   $\theta_E \leftarrow \theta_E + \alpha_E \cdot Adam(\theta_E, \eta_{\theta_E})$
16: **end while**

3.2 CWVAEGAN-1DCNN

We use CWVAEGAN to deal with class-imbalancing problem and simulate unknown exceptions. Furthermore, the method based on CWVAEGAN (CWVAEGAN) is constructed to detect the network abnormal behavior.

Model Structures: method has three modules: data processing module, CWVAEGAN module, and CNN module. In Fig. 3, we illustrate the architecture of CWVAEGAN. First of all, the data preprocessing module filters out minority classes in the dataset, and decomposes the continuous features in the original dataset by VGM to get the original training dataset. Then, the CWVAEGAN module generates new samples. Finally, CNN module uses the balanced samples for training and performs target recognition on the test dataset. In general, CWVAEGAN takes the rows from HRRP dataset as input and predicts their labels $p(y|r)$.

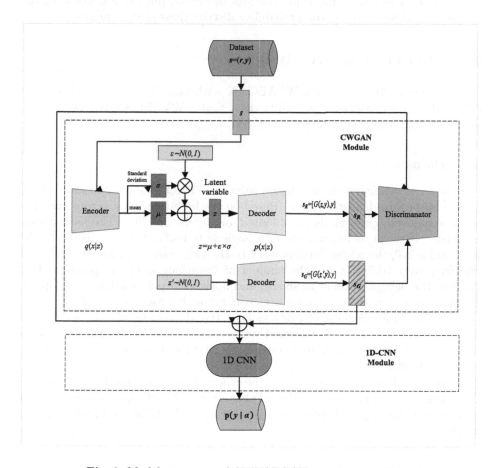

Fig. 3. Model structure of CWVAEGAN target recognition

CWVAEGAN: We have described the CWVAEGAN module in the Sect. 3.1, CWVAEGAN module takes raw data or Gaussian noise as input and generates minority classes samples. CWVAEGAN can be expressed as $s_G = G[(z, y), y]$.

1D-CNN: In the 1D-CNN module, we use an one dimensional convolutional neural network (1D-CNN) to perform HRRP target recognition, as shown in Fig. 3. 1D-CNN model takes the rebalancing training dataset as the input, and outputs the probability distribution P (y) of different classes in the test dataset. Table 1 shows the structure of 1D-CNN.

Refer to [17], we design the structure of 1D-CNN, we use convolution layers of 32, 64, 128 and 256 kernels respectively, and the activation function is mish [21]. The output of convolution layer is randomly discarded with a probability of 0.2 to avoid over fitting. Then a 32 neuron full junction layer was set and activated by leaky Relu function. The size of the output layer is equal to the number of classes. Finally, the probability distributions $p(y|r)$ are given.

4   Experiment and Analysis

In this section, We compare CWVAEGAN with class-balancing methods and other advanced methods. The results show that CWVAEGAN has better performance than the most advanced methods.

4.1   Dataset

We use an electromagnetic simulation software FEKO to simulate radar echoes from 5 mid-course ballistic targets. Based on the high-frequency asymptotic theory, the physical optics method is adopted for simulation. The FEKO simulation parameters are set as follows: azimuth angle is 0–180°, angle step is 0.05°, the pitch angle is 0, the center frequency is 10 GHz with start frequency 9.5 GHz and end frequency 10.5 GHz and the number of frequency sampling points is 128. At last, the default optimal mesh size and horizontal polarization are adopted. Finally, there are 18005 samples attained through processing by inverse fast Fourier transform, each target contains 3601 HRRP samples of different degrees and each sample is a 256-dimensional vector. And we randomly split these samples into two datasets: training dataset with 14404 samples and testing dataset with 3,601 samples.

In order to test the performance of the generation method on class unbalanced data sets, we manually reduce the number of samples of some key classes and manufacture the required unbalanced datasets: Im0, Im1, Im2 and Im3, as shown in Table 1.

4.2   Metrics

We use accuracy, precision, recall, F1 score and G-means as the main metrics to measure the classification performance of the CWVAEGAN. Accuracy indicates the overall performance of CWVAEGAN-1DCNN. Precision quantifies the specific classification capacity of each class, while recall indicates the detection rate for a specific class. These metrics are defined as:

Table 1. Samples of Unbalanced HRRP Dataset

Dataset	Number of different samples				
	Warhead	Decoy1	Decoy2	Decoy3	Decoy4
Im0	2,881	2,881	2,881	2,881	2,881
Im1	2,305	2,449	2,593	2,737	2,881
Im2	1,729	2,017	2,305	2,593	2,881
Im3	1,152	1,729	2,305	2,593	2,881

$$Accuracy = \frac{TP + TN}{TP + TN + FP + FN} \tag{13}$$

$$Precision = \frac{TP}{TP + FP} \tag{14}$$

$$Recall = \frac{TP}{TP + FN} \tag{15}$$

where TP, TN, FP and FN [18] are true positive, true negative, false positive and false negative respectively.

F1 score is the harmonic mean value of precision and recall. G-means is a comprehensive parameter of positive and negative class accuracy.

$$F1 = 2 \times \frac{Precision \times recall}{Precision + Recall} = \frac{2 \times TP}{2 \times TP + FP + FN} \tag{16}$$

$$G - \text{mean} = \sqrt{\frac{TP}{TP + FN} \times \frac{TN}{TN + FP}} \tag{17}$$

4.3   Experimental Procedure

Experimental Environment and Parameter Setting: As we described in Sect. 3.2.1, the original samples are first input to the data processing module. Data processing module firstly selects the minority classes, remove the normal network activities with large number of samples. We implement VGM to decompose the features of continuous columns, and use Bayesian Gaussian mixture method from sklearn to achieve VGM. The Gaussian mixture model are fitted with 10 components to approximate the original distribution, and the feature vectors processed from the data processing module are input into CWVAEGAN module. The experiments are performed using Python 3.7 on a Windows 10 personal computer with an AMD Ryzen 9 5900X@4.4 GHz CPU, NVIDIA GeForce RTX 2080 Ti GPU and 32 GB RAM.

For CWVAEGAN module, the architectures of E, D and G are flexible, which should be set based on the specific situation. After selecting the appropriate parameters, CWVAEGAN can achieve enough expressive power with minimum overhead.

According to the VAE-GAN model proposed by Larsen [9], we adjust the network structure. Two convolution layers are taken to down sampling the original data to get multi-channel hidden features, and the fully connected layers are used to transform them into 256 dimensional single channel features. The first 128 dimensions represent the mean value of the sample, and the last 128 dimensions represent the standard deviation of samples. By fitting the encoder to get mean value and standard deviation of samples, the 128 dimensional hidden vector z is reconstructed with the multiple reparameterization technique.

The generator (encoder) G is composed of fully connected layers and one-dimensional transposed convolution layers. z is used to reconstruct the original samples. In the fully connected layer, 128 dimensional features are expanded and sent to 64 different channels, and then one-dimensional transposed convolution layer is used for up sampling. The hidden vector z gets the reconstructed sample S_R through G. Or the Gaussian noise z' can be input into G to get the new sample S_G.

Discriminator D is composed of one-dimensional convolution layers and fully connected layers. It attempts to identify the original samples and generated samples, which is equivalent to a classifier performing two classification tasks.

The details of model structure are shown in Table 2.

Table 2. Network structure of CWVAEGAN

Model	#	Layer	Filters	Kernel size	Output size	Activation
Encoder	1	Input	–	–	42 * 1	–
	2	Conv1d	32	3	40 * 32	Relu
	3	Conv1d	64	3	38 * 64	Relu
	4	Flatten	–	–	2432	
	5	Dense	–		256	–
Decoder	1	Input	–	–	128	
	2	Dense	–	–	2432	Relu
	3	Reshape	–	–	38 * 64	–
	4	Conv1dtrans	64	3	40 * 64	Relu
	5	Conv1dtrans	32	3	42 * 32	Relu
	6	Conv1dtrans	1	1	42 * 1	Sigmoid
Discrimator	1	Input	–	–	42 * 1	
	2	Conv1d	32	3	40 * 32	Relu
	3	Conv1d	64	3	38 * 64	Relu
	4	Flatten	–	–	2432	–
	4	Dense	–	–	32	Relu
	5	Dense	–	–	1	–

There is no automatic parameter tuning algorithm at this stage. We conduct large amount of experiments on the basis of existing references to compare and analyze the influence of different parameters. The final parameters of the model are determined through a large number of experiments. All hidden layer activation are ReLU, the generator output layer adopts sigmoid activation, and the encoder and discriminator output layer adopts linear activation. The training parameter settings are given in Table 3.

Table 3. Parameters of CWVAEGAN

CWVAEGAN	$epoch_0$	1,000	1D-CNN	$epoch_1$	300
	$batch_0$	500		$batch_1$	512
	lr_{enc}	0.001		lr_{CNN}	0.005
	lr_{dec}	0.001		Activation	Adam
	lr_{disc}	0.0001			
	Activation	Adam			

Experimental Setup: We designed the following experiments to test the performance of CWVAEGAN-1DCNN:

Experiment 1 : The training experiment of 1DCNN model.

Experiment 2 : Performance comparison between CWVAEGAN-1DCNN and other class-balancing methods.

To evaluate the performance of proposed method on the unbalanced dataset, we comapre it with other class-balancing methods. The selected comparison algorithms include ROS, SMOTE [19] and adaptive synthetic (ADASYN) [20], and are combined with CNN described in 2.3. Class balance methods generate samples, and then the balanced samples are input to 1DCNN for target recognition. These methods are recorded as ROS-CNN, SMOTE-CNN and ADASYN-CNN respectively. The CNN parameters in these methods are consistent, which can be set according to Table 3.

4.4 Experiment Results and Analysis

Experiment 1: The Training Experiment of 1DCNN Model: For CNN, appropriate convolution kernel number and convolution layer number can improve the performance of classifier. According to the paper, the number of candidate convolution layers is 2, 3, 4. The number of convolution kernels of each convolution layer is twice that of the previous convolution layer. According to the different number of convolution layers and kernels of the initial convolution layer, we can determine the network structure of a classifier. The four layer convolution network with 64 convolution kernels of the initial convolution layer is recorded as $c4\_64$ and the number of network channels is 64-128-256-512. We carry out experiments for different network layers and channel number of initial layer.

Firstly, the convolution kernel number of the initial layer is set to 64, and different convolution layers $c2\_64, c3\_64, c4\_64, c5\_64$ are studied. When the convolution layers are $c4\_64$, the classification effect of the model is the best and the convergence speed is the fastest (Fig. 4).

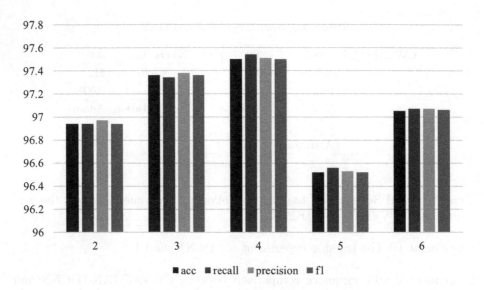

Fig. 4. Performance of different convolutional layer

Then we fix the number of convolution layers as four, and for the initial layer, the convolution kernel number $c4\_8, c4\_16, c4\_32, c4\_64, c4\_80, c4\_100$. As shown in the Fig. 5, When the size of convolution kernel increases from 20 to 60, the recognition effect continues to improve. When the size of convolution kernel is larger than 60, the improvement effect of recognition accuracy is no longer obvious.

Therefore, we set the structure of the network to include four one-dimensional convolution layers. The number of convolution cores of each layer is 64, 128, 256 and 512 respectively. The input of each layer is not zero filled, and the convolution core size and step are 5 and 1 respectively. At the same time, the output is batch normalized and then activated by the mish [21] function. The window size and step length of max-pooling layer are 3.

Experiment 2: Comparison of Class-Balancing Methods: The selected comparison algorithms include ROS, SMOTE and ADASYN, and the original VAEGAN technology. Based on class-balancing algorithm, we construct five classification models: ROS-CNN, SMOTE-CNN, ADASYN-CNN and

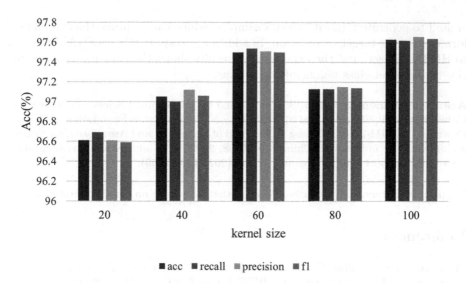

Fig. 5. Performance of different kernel size

CWVAEGAN-1DCNN. For ROS, SMOTE and ADASYN, The type and quantity of attack samples are generated to make the number of samples of each class. The results are shown in Table 4.

Table 4. Comparison of different class-balancing methods

	Im0	Im1	Im2	Im3
1D-CNN	97.50%	96.44%	95.58%	94.94%
CWVAEGAN-CNN	**97.4 (−0.1)%**	96.47 (+0.03)%	**95.91 (+0.33)%**	**95.37 (+0.43)%**
ADASYN-CNN	97.27 (−0.23)%	96.42 (−0.02)%	96.11 (+0.20)%	95.22 (+0.28)%
ROS-CNN	96.12 (−0.48)%	96.39 (−0.05)%	96.03 (+0.12)%	95.07 (+0.13)%
SMOTE-CNN	97.22 (−0.28)%	**96.49 (+0.05)%**	96.18 (+0.27)%	95.27 (+0.33)%

With the increasing imbalance rate of datasets, the role of class equilibrium method is increasing. All methods on im0 lead to the decline of detection respect in varying degrees, because the generated new samples are equivalent to introducing noise to the original training data set. On Im2 and IM3 data sets, the synthetic data method can significantly improve the overall detection ability.

On Im2 and Im3 datasets, CWVAEGAN can better improve the recognition ability compared with other methods, and can improve the overall detection ability when the sample data is insufficient.

5 Conclusions

We build a Radar HRRP target recognition method based on CWVAEGAN (CWVAEGAN-1DCNN) to solve the problem of class imbalance. CWVAEGAN is used to generate minority classes samples, which can improve the overall performance of the target recognition. In addition, we apply CWVAEGAN-1DCNN to HRRP dataset, and the experimental results shows that our method is superior to the other class balancing algorithms.

Acknowledgements. This work is supported by the National Science Foundation of China (61806219, 61703426 and 61876189), by National Science Foundation of Shaanxi Provence (2021JM-226) by Young Talent fund of University and Association for Science and Technology in Shaanxi, China (20190108, 20220106), and by and the Innovation Capability Support Plan of Shaanxi, China (2020KJXX-065).

Conflict of interest. The authors declare that they have no conflict of interest.

References

1. Liao, K., Si, J., Zhu, F., He, X.: Radar HRRP target recognition based on concatenated deep neural networks. IEEE Access **6**, 29211–29218 (2018)
2. Liu, J., Fang, N., Wang, B.F., Xie, Y.J.: Scale-space theory-based multi-scale features for aircraft classification using HRRP. Electron. Lett. **52**(6), 475–477 (2016)
3. Lei, L., Wang, X., Xing, Y., Kai, B.: Multi-polarized HRRP classification by SVM and DS evidence theory. Control Decision **28**(6) (2013)
4. Rui, L.I., Wang, X., Lei, L., Xue, A.: Ballistic target HRRP fusion recognition combining multi-class relevance vector machine and DS. Inf. Control (2017)
5. Ranzato, M., Boureau, Y.L., Lecun, Y.: Sparse feature learning for deep belief networks (2007)
6. Hinton, E.G., Salakhutdinov, R.R.: Reducing the dimensionality of data with neural networks. Science **313**, 504–507 (2006)
7. Goodfellow, I.J., et al.: Generative Adversarial Networks, Jun 2014. arXiv:1406.2661 [cs, stat]. (Accessed 28 Sep 2020)
8. Yang, Y., Sun, J., Shengkang, Y.U., Peng, X.: High Resolution Range Profile Target Recognition Based on Convolutional Neural Network. Modern Radar (2017)
9. Guo, C., Jian, T., Congan, X. You, H., Sun, S.: Radar HRRP Target Recognition Based on Deep Multi-Scale 1D Convolutional Neural Network. J. Electron. Inf. Technol. **41**(6), 1302–1309 (2019)
10. Wan, J., Chen, B., Xu, B., Liu, H., Jin, L.: Convolutional neural networks for radar HRRP target recognition and rejection. EURASIP J. Adv. Signal Process. **2019**(1), 1–17 (2019). https://doi.org/10.1186/s13634-019-0603-y
11. Lu, W., Zhang, Y.S., Xu, C.: HRRP target recognition method based on bispectrum-spectrogram feature and deep convolutional neural network. Syst. Eng. Electron. **42**(8) (2020)
12. Kingma, D., Welling, M.: Auto-Encoding Variational Bayes (2014)
13. Larsen, A., Sønderby, S., Winther, O.: Autoencoding beyond pixels using a learned similarity metric (2015)
14. Mirza, M., Osindero, S.: Conditional Generative Adversarial Nets (2014)
15. Arjovsky, M., Chintala, S., Bottou, L.: Wasserstein GAN (2017)
16. Gulrajani, I., Ahmed, F., Arjovsky, M., et al.: Improved Training of Wasserstein GANs (2017)

17. Xiang, Q., Wang, X., Song, Y., Lei, L., Li, R., Lai, J.: One-dimensional convolutional neural networks for high-resolution range profile recognition via adaptively feature recalibrating and automatically channel pruning. Int. J. Intell. Syst. **36**, 332–361 (2020). https://doi.org/10.1002/int.22302

18. Huang, S., Lei, K.: IGAN-IDS: an imbalanced generative adversarial network towards intrusion detection system in ad-hoc networks. Ad Hoc Netw. **105**, 10217 (2020). https://doi.org/10.1016/j.adhoc.2020.102177

19. Chawla, N., Bowyer, K., Hall, L., Kegelmeyer, W.: SMOTE: synthetic Minority Over-sampling Technique. J. Artif. Intell. Res. (JAIR) **16**, 321–357 (2002) https://doi.org/10.1613/jair.953

20. He, H., Bai, Y., Garcia, E., Li, S.: ADASYN: adaptive Synthetic Sampling Approach for Imbalanced Learning (2008)

21. Misra, D.: Mish: A Self Regularized Non-Monotonic Neural Activation Function (2019)

Partial Least Square Regression via Three-Factor SVD-Type Manifold Optimization for EEG Decoding

Wanguang Yin[1], Zhichao Liang[1], Jianguo Zhang[2], and Quanying Liu[1(✉)]

[1] Shenzhen Key Laboratory of Smart Healthcare Engineering,
Department of Biomedical Engineering, Southern University of Science
and Technology, Shenzhen, China
{yinwg,liuqy}@sustech.edu.cn
[2] Department of Computer Science, Southern University of Science and Technology,
Shenzhen 518055, China

Abstract. Partial least square regression (PLSR) is a widely-used statistical model to reveal the linear relationships of latent factors that comes from the independent variables and dependent variables. However, traditional methods to solve PLSR models are usually based on the Euclidean space, and easily getting stuck into a local minimum. To this end, we propose a new method to solve the partial least square regression, named PLSR via optimization on bi-Grassmann manifold (PLSR-biGr). Specifically, we first leverage the three-factor SVD-type decomposition of the cross-covariance matrix defined on the bi-Grassmann manifold, converting the orthogonal constrained optimization problem into an unconstrained optimization problem on bi-Grassmann manifold, and then incorporate the Riemannian preconditioning of matrix scaling to regulate the Riemannian metric in each iteration. PLSRbiGr is validated with a variety of experiments for decoding EEG signals at motor imagery (MI) and steady-state visual evoked potential (SSVEP) task. Experimental results demonstrate that PLSRbiGr outperforms competing algorithms in multiple EEG decoding tasks, which will greatly facilitate small sample data learning.

Keywords: Partial least square regression · Bi-Grassmann manifold · Riemannian preconditioning · Matrix manifold optimization · EEG decoding

1 Introduction

Extracting the latent factor is an essential procedure for discovering the latent space of high-dimensional data; thereby proposed lots of regression model for latent semantic or variable analysis. Among of them, partial least squares regression (PLSR) is a well-established model for learning the latent variables, by a sequential way to learn the latent sub-spaces while maximally maintaining the correlations between the latent variables of independent variables X and dependent variables Y. Specifically, it can be described as the projection of two variables X and Y onto the lower dimensional sub-spaces U and V. This application can be found in a various of fields, including chemometrics [2,8], chemical process control [7,13], and neuroscience [5,9].

As a result, there emerges a lot of partial least square regression models, while most of them are based on the *Euclidean space* to solve the latent factors and identify the latent factors column by column in each iteration. A drawback of this approach is that it easily *converges to a spurious local minimum* and hardly obtain a globally optimal solution. Given an extension of PLSR to the N-way tensors with rank-one decomposition, which can provide an improvement on the intuitive interpretation of the model [3]. However, N-way PLSR suffers from high computational complexity and slow convergence in dealing with complex data.

To address problems above, we propose a three-factor SVD-type decomposition of PLSR via optimization on bi-Grassmann manifold (PLSRbiGr). Hence, its corresponding sub-spaces U and V associated with independent variable X and dependent variable Y can be solved by using a nonlinear manifold optimization method. Moreover, we leverage the Riemannian preconditioning of matrix scaling $S^T S$ to regulate the Riemannian metric in each iteration and self-adapt to the changing of subspace [10]. To validate the performance of PLSRbiGr, we conduct two EEG classification tasks on the motor imagery (MI) and steady-state visual evoked potential (SSVEP) datasets. The results demonstrate PLSRbiGr is superior to the inspired modification of PLSR (SIMPLSR) [6], SIMPLSR with the generalized Grassmann manifold (PLSRGGr), SIMPLSR with product manifold (PLSRGStO), as well as the sparse SIMPLSR via optimization on generalized Stiefel manifold (SPLSRGSt) [4]. Our main contributions can be summarized as follow:

- We propose a novel method for solving partial least square regression (PLSR), named PLSR via optimization on bi-Grassmann manifold (PLSRbiGr), which decomposes the cross-covariance matrix $(X^T Y)$ to an interpretable subspace (U and V) and simultaneously learns the latent factors via optimization on bi-Grassmann manifold (Sect. 2.2).
- We present Riemannian metric that equipped with Riemannian preconditioning, to self-adapt to the changing of subspace. Fortunately, Riemannian preconditioning can largely improves the algorithmic performance (*i.e.* convergence speed and classification accuracy) (Sect. 3.2).
- The results of EEG decoding demonstrate that PLSRbiGr outperforms conventional Euclidean-based methods and Riemannian-based methods for small sample data learning (Sect. 3.1).

2   Method

2.1   Review of Partial Least Squares Regression

Partial least square regression (PLSR) is a wide class of models for learning the linear relationship between independent variables $X \in \mathbb{R}^{I \times N}$ and dependent

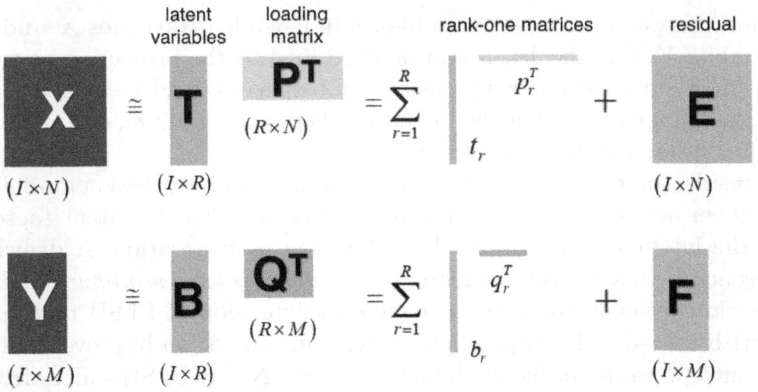

Fig. 1. The PLSR decomposes the independent variables (EEG) $X \in \mathbb{R}^{I \times N}$ and dependent variables (sample labels) $Y \in \mathbb{R}^{I \times M}$ as a sum of rank-one matrices.

variables $Y \in \mathbb{R}^{I \times M}$ by means of latent variables. We present the schematic illustration of partial least square regression (PLSR) in Fig. 1.

To predict dependent variables Y from independent variables X, PLSR finds a set of latent variables (also called the latent vectors, score vectors, or components) by projecting both X and Y onto a lower dimensional subspace while at the same time maximizing the pairwise covariance between the latent variables T and B, which are presented in Eq. (1) & Eq. (2).

$$X = TP^T + E = \sum_{r=1}^{R} t_r p_r^T + E \qquad (1)$$

$$Y = BQ^T + F = \sum_{r=1}^{R} b_r q_r^T + F \qquad (2)$$

where $T = [t_1, t_2, \ldots, t_R] \in \mathbb{R}^{I \times R}$ is a matrix of R extracted latent variables from X, and $B = [b_1, b_2, \ldots, b_R] \in \mathbb{R}^{I \times R}$ are latent variables from Y, their columns have the maximum correlations between each other. In addition, $P \in \mathbb{R}^{N \times R}$ and $Q \in \mathbb{R}^{M \times R}$ are the loading matrices, and $E \in \mathbb{R}^{I \times N}$ and $F \in \mathbb{R}^{I \times M}$ are the residuals with respect to X and Y.

However, most of the current methods for solving PLSR are based on the Euclidean space by performing the sum of a minimum number of rank-one decomposition to jointly approximate the independent variables X and dependent variables Y. No existing method solves PLSR with bi-Grassmann manifold optimization. To this end, we propose a novel method for solving PLSR via optimization on the bi-Grassmann manifold.

Regression Model. To predict the dependent variable given a new sample X_{new}, its regression model is given by:

$$Y^{new} = X_{new} C = X_{new} W \left(P^T W \right)^{-1} D Q^T \qquad (3)$$

where Y^{new} is the predicted output, and $C = U\left(P^T U\right)^{-1} D Q^T$ is the regression coefficient calculated from the training data. Following to [4], we can obtain the learned sub-spaces U & V, and its corresponding latent factors $T = XU$ & $B = YV$ by solving the SVD-type model via optimization on bi-Grassmann manifold.

2.2   PLSRbiGr: PLSR via Optimization on Bi-Grassmann Manifold

In the sequel, we present the SVD-type decomposition via optimization on bi-Grassmann manifold. As shown in Fig. 2, we treat the cross-product matrix (or tensor) of independent variables and dependent variables as the input data, and then perform the three factor decomposition via optimization on bi-Grassmann manifold.

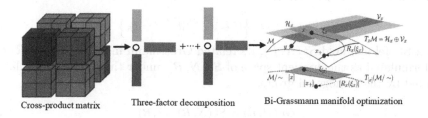

Cross-product matrix   Three-factor decomposition   Bi-Grassmann manifold optimization

Fig. 2. SVD-type decomposition via optimization on bi-Grassmann manifold.

Three-Factor SVD-Type Decomposition. The SVD-type decomposition of cross-product matrix (*i.e.* Z) can be formulated as the following tensor-matrix product:

$$f\left(U, V, S\right) = \underset{S, U, V}{\operatorname{argmin}} \frac{1}{2} \left\| S \times_1 U \times_2 V - Z\left(k\right) \right\|_F^2 \tag{4}$$

where k denotes the count of iterations. To apply the Riemannian version of conjugate gradient descent or trust-region method, it needs to obtain the partial derivatives of f with respect to U, V and S, that is given by

$$\begin{aligned}
\operatorname{grad} f\left(U, V, S\right) &= \frac{\partial f\left(U, V, S\right)}{\partial U} \\
&= \left(U S V^T - Z\left(k\right)\right) V S^T \\
&= Z\left(k+1\right) V S^T
\end{aligned} \tag{5}$$

$$\begin{aligned}
\operatorname{grad} f\left(U, V, S\right) &= \frac{\partial f\left(U, V, S\right)}{\partial V} \\
&= \left(U S V^T - Z\left(k\right)\right)^T U S^T \\
&= Z\left(k+1\right)^T U S^T
\end{aligned} \tag{6}$$

$$
\begin{aligned}
\operatorname{grad} f\left(U, V, S\right) &= \frac{\partial f\left(U, V, S\right)}{\partial S} \\
&= \left(S \times_1 U \times_2 V - Z\left(k\right)\right) \times_1 U^T \times_2 V^T \\
&= U^T \left(U S V^T - Z\left(k\right)\right) V \\
&= U^T Z\left(k+1\right) V
\end{aligned}
\tag{7}
$$

Then, we project the Euclidean gradient (*i.e.* Eq. (5), Eq. (6), and Eq. (7)) onto the Riemannian manifold space.

SVD-Type Decomposition via Optimization on Bi-Grassmann Manifold. In this subsection, we derive the bi-Grassmann manifold optimization for the SVD-type decomposition and $\mathcal{M}$ is a manifold equipped with Riemannian metric. Recall that Stiefel manifold is the set of matrices whose columns are orthogonal, that is denoted by

$$
St\left(N, R\right) = \left\{U \in \mathbb{R}^{N \times R} | U^T U = I_R\right\}
\tag{8}
$$

For a Stiefel manifold $St\left(N, R\right)$, its related Grassmann manifold $Gr\left(N, R\right)$ can be formulated as the quotient space of $St\left(N, R\right)$, under the equivalence relation defined by the orthogonal group,

$$
Gr\left(N, R\right) = St\left(N, R\right) / \mathcal{O}\left(R\right)
\tag{9}
$$

here, $\mathcal{O}\left(R\right)$ is the orthogonal group defined by

$$
\mathcal{O}\left(R\right) = \left\{W \in \mathbb{R}^{R \times R} | W^T W = W W^T = I_R\right\}
\tag{10}
$$

Moreover, for the SVD-type decomposition, the optimization sub-spaces can be expressed as the following bi-Grassmann manifold:

$$
\mathcal{M} := Gr\left(N, R\right) \times Gr\left(M, R\right) \times \mathbb{R}^{R \times R}
\tag{11}
$$

that is equipped with following Riemannian metric:

$$
g_Z\left(\xi_Z, \eta_Z\right) = tr\left(S S^T \xi_U^T \eta_U\right) + tr\left(S^T S \xi_V^T \eta_V\right) + tr\left(\xi_S^T \eta_S\right)
\tag{12}
$$

In practice, the computational space (*i.e.* $Z \in \mathbb{R}^{N \times M}$) can be first decomposed into orthogonal complementary sub-spaces (normal space *i.e.* $N_Z \mathcal{M}$, and tangent space *i.e.* $T_Z \mathcal{M}$), and then the tangent space can be further decomposed into the other two orthogonal complementary sub-spaces (horizontal space *i.e.* $H_Z \mathcal{M}$, and vertical space *i.e.* $V_Z \mathcal{M}$), and eventually we project the Euclidean gradient to the horizontal space defined by the equivalence relation of orthogonal group [1].

Riemannian Gradient. To obtain the Riemannian gradient, it needs to project the Euclidean gradient onto the Riemannian manifold space [1], that is

$$\text{Grad} f(U, V, S) = \Pi_U \text{grad} f(U, V, S)$$
$$= (\text{grad} f(U) - UB_U)\left(SS^T\right)^{-1} \tag{13}$$

$$\text{Grad} f(U, V, S) = \Pi_V \text{grad} f(U, V, S)$$
$$= (\text{grad} f(V) - VB_V)\left(S^T S\right)^{-1} \tag{14}$$

where $\left(SS^T\right)^{-1}$ and $\left(S^T S\right)^{-1}$ is the scaling factors. $\Pi_U = P_U^h P_U^v$ is the project operator that involves two steps of operation, one is a mapping from ambient space to the tangent space (*i.e.*, P_U^v), and the other is a mapping from tangent space to the horizontal space (*i.e.*, P_U^h). Therefore, the computational space of Stiefel manifold $St(N, M)$ can be decomposed into tangent space and normal space, and the tangent space can be further decomposed into two orthogonal complementary sub-spaces (*i.e.* horizontal space and vertical space) [10]. Once the expression of Riemannian gradient and Riemannian Hessian are obtained, we can conduct the Riemannian manifold optimization by using Manopt toolbox [1].

3   Experiments and Results

To test the performance of our proposed algorithm, we conduct experiments on a lot of EEG signal decoding, whose performance is compared to several well known algorithms, including the statistically inspired modification of PLSR (SIMPLSR), SIMPLSR with the generalized Grassmann manifold (PLSRGGr), sparse SIMPLSR via optimization on generalized Stiefel manifold (SPLSRGSt) [4,6], and higher order partial least squares regression (HOPLSR) [12].

3.1   EEG Decoding

In this subsection, we test the efficiency and accuracy of our proposed algorithm (PLSRbiGr) on the public PhysioNet MI dataset [11]. We compare PLSR-biGr with other existing algorithms, including the statistically inspired modification of PLSR (SIMPLSR), SIMPLSR with the generalized Grassmann manifold (PLSRGGr), sparse SIMPLSR via optimization on generalized Stiefel manifold (SPLSRGSt) [4,6], and higher order partial least squares (HOPLSR) [12]. To evaluate the performance of decoding algorithms, we use Accuracy (Acc) as the evaluation metric to quantify the performance of comparison algorithms.

In training, we set the 4-fold-cross-validation to obtain the averaged classification accuracy in testing samples. As shown in Fig. 3, PLSRbiGr generally achieves the best performance in comparison to the existing methods. The used PhysioNet EEG MI dataset consists of 2-class MI tasks (*i.e.* runs 3, 4, 7, 8, 11, and 12, with imagine movements of left fist or right fist) [11], which is recorded from 109 subjects with 64-channel EEG signals (sampling rate equals 160 Hz) during MI tasks. We randomly select 10 subjects from PhysioNet MI dataset in our experiments. The EEG signals are filtered with a band-pass filter (cutoff

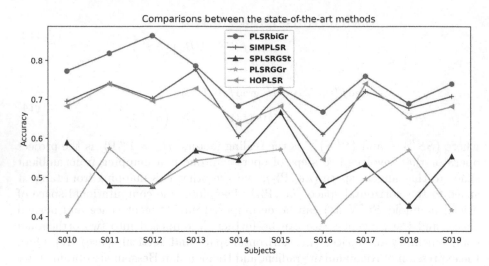

Fig. 3. Accuracy of 2-class MI classification task on PhysioNet MI dataset

frequencies at 7–35 Hz) and a spatial filter (*i.e.* Xdawn with 16 filters), therefore the resulting data is represented by *trials* × *channel* × *time*.

The used Macau SSVEP dataset contains 128-channel EEG recordings from 7 subjects sampled at 1000 Hz, which was recorded at University of Macau with their ethical approval. There are four types visual stimulus with flashing frequency at 10 Hz, 12 Hz, 15 Hz, and 20 Hz. To increase the signal-noise ratio (SNR) and reduce the dimension of raw EEG signals, the EEG signals are filtered with a band-pass filter (cutoff frequencies at 7–35 Hz) and a spatial filter (*i.e.* Xdawn with 16 filters). The epochs of 1-s EEG signals before every time point of the SSVEP data were extracted and down-sampled 200 Hz, therefore the resulting data is represented by *trial* × *channel* × *time*. Figure 4 presents the classification accuracy of all comparison algorithms on the SSVEP dataset.

3.2 Effects of Riemannian Preconditioning

Furthermore, we test the effects of Riemannian preconditioning. In PLSRbiGr, the scaling factors $S^T S$ and SS^T of Riemannian preconditioning provides an effective strategy to accelerate the convergence speed. As shown in Table 1, the classification accuracy and running time of PLSRbiGr equipped with Riemannian preconditioning are closely better than results of other methods, such as PLSRGGr, PLSRGStO, and SPLSRGSt that have not taken into account of Riemannian preconditioning.

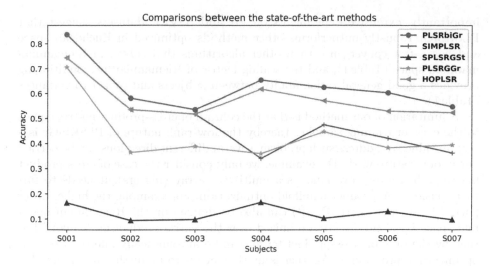

Fig. 4. Accuracy of 4-class SSVEP classification task on Macau SSVEP dataset

Table 1. The effects of Riemannian preconditioning on the classification accuracy and running time. The test experiments were conducted on Macau SSVEP dataset by using PLSRbiGr.

ID	Accuracy		Running time (s)	
	Preconditioned	Non-preconditioned	Preconditioned	Non-preconditioned
S001	**0.8487 ± 0.0148**	0.3063 ± 0.0394	0.0571	**0.0570**
S002	**0.7036 ± 0.0123**	0.1211 ± 0.0241	0.0624	**0.0544**
S003	**0.5903 ± 0.0183**	0.1854 ± 0.0278	0.0576	**0.0551**
S004	**0.7360 ± 0.0231**	0.1056 ± 0.0258	0.0960	**0.0591**
S005	**0.8026 ± 0.0182**	0.3187 ± 0.0483	0.0692	**0.0560**
S006	**0.7987 ± 0.0075**	0.1522 ± 0.0285	0.0578	**0.0574**
S007	**0.8375 ± 0.0124**	0.2135 ± 0.0375	0.0593	**0.0557**
Mean	**0.7596 ± 0.0152**	0.2004 ± 0.0330	0.0656	**0.0563**

4   Discussion and Conclusion

In this paper, we propose a novel method, named partial least square regression via optimization on bi-Grassmann manifold (PLSRbiGr) for EEG signal decoding. It features to find the objective solution via optimization on bi-Grassmann manifold. Specifically, to relax the orthogonality constraints of objective function, PLSRbiGr converts the constrained optimization problem in Euclidean space to an optimization problem defined on bi-Grassmann manifold, thereby its corresponding subspaces (*i.e.* U and V) can be learned by using Riemannian manifold optimization instead of the traditional methods that by deflating the residuals in each iteration. In practice, PLSRbiGr can also be used for image classification, and many other prediction tasks, which has no such limitations. More importantly, extensive experiments on MI and SSVEP datasets suggest that PLSRbiGr robustly outperforms other methods optimized in Euclidean space and has a fast convergence than other algorithms that solved in Riemannian manifold space (Table 1), and the scaling factor of Riemannian preconditioning provides a good generalization ability between subjects and robust to variances (Table 1).

A limitation of our method is that the column of cross-product matrix equals to the class of training samples, thereby the low-rank nature of PLSRbiGr is a certain value. To address such problem, several different directions can be carried out in our feature work. For example, we only consider the case of cross-product matrix, when cross covariance is a multi-way array (tensors), it needs to further consider the product manifold optimization. For example, the higher order partial least squares (HOPLSR) can also be defined on the Riemannian manifold space [12], and directly optimized over the entire product of N manifolds, thereby the rank of cross-product tensor can be automatically inferred from the optimization procedures. Another issue that needs to be further investigated is how to scale the computation of Riemannian preconditioning to the higher order partial least squares (HOPLSR).

References

1. Absil, P.-A., Mahony, R., Sepulchre, R.: Optimization algorithms on matrix manifolds. Princeton University Press (2009)
2. Brereton, R.G., Lloyd, G.R.: Partial least squares discriminant analysis for chemometrics and metabolomics: how scores, loadings, and weights differ according to two common algorithms. J. Chemom. **32**(4), e3028 (2018)
3. Bro, R.: Multiway calibration. multilinear pls. J. chemom. **10**(1), 47–61 (1996)
4. Chen, H., Sun, Y., Gao, J., Hu, Y., Yin, B.: Solving partial least squares regression via manifold optimization approaches. IEEE Trans. Neural Netw. Learn. Syst. **30**(2), 588–600 (2018)
5. Chu, Y., Zhao, X., Zou, Y., Xu, W., Song, G., Han, J., Zhao, Y.: Decoding multiclass motor imagery eeg from the same upper limb by combining riemannian geometry features and partial least squares regression. J. Neural Eng. **17**(4), 046029 (2020)
6. De Jong, S.: Simpls: an alternative approach to partial least squares regression. Chemom. Intell. Lab. Syst. **18**(3), 251–263 (1993)
7. Dong, Y., Qin, S.J.: Regression on dynamic pls structures for supervised learning of dynamic data. J. Process Control **68**, 64–72 (2018)
8. Hasegawa, K., Arakawa, M., Funatsu, K.: Rational choice of bioactive conformations through use of conformation analysis and 3-way partial least squares modeling. Chemom. Intell. Lab. Syst. **50**(2), 253–261 (2000)
9. Hoagey, D.A., Rieck, J.R., Rodrigue, K.M., Kennedy, K.M.: Joint contributions of cortical morphometry and white matter microstructure in healthy brain aging: a partial least squares correlation analysis. Hum. Brain Mapp. **40**(18), 5315–5329 (2019)
10. Kasai, H., Mishra, B.: Low-rank tensor completion: a riemannian manifold preconditioning approach. In: International Conference on Machine Learning, pp. 1012–1021. PMLR (2016)

11. Schalk, G., McFarland, D.J., Hinterberger, T., Birbaumer, N., Wolpaw, J.R.: Bci 2000: a general-purpose brain-computer interface (bci) system. IEEE Trans. Biomed. Eng. **51**(6), 1034–1043 (2004)
12. Zhao, Q., et al.: Higher order partial least squares (hopls): a generalized multilinear regression method. IEEE Trans. Pattern Anal. Mach. Intell. **35**(7), 1660–1673 (2012)
13. Zheng, J., Song, Z.: Semisupervised learning for probabilistic partial least squares regression model and soft sensor application. J. Process Control **64**, 123–131 (2018)

Single Deterministic Neural Network with Hierarchical Gaussian Mixture Model for Uncertainty Quantification

Chunlin Ji$^{(\boxtimes)}$ ⓘ and Dingwei Gong ⓘ

Kuang-Chi Institute of Advanced Technology, Shenzhen, China
{chunlin.ji,dingwei.gong}@kuang-chi.org

Abstract. We propose a method to train a deterministic deep network for uncertainty quantification (UQ) with a single forward pass. Traditional Monte Carlo or ensemble based UQ methods largely leverage the variation of neural network weights to introduce uncertainty. We propose a hierarchical Gaussian mixture model (GMM) based nonlinear classifier to shape the extracted feature more flexibly and express the uncertainty by the entropy of the predicted posterior distribution. We perform large-scale training with this hierarchical GMM based loss function and introduce a natural gradient descent algorithm to update the parameters of the hierarchical GMM. With a single deterministic neural network, our uncertainty quantification approach performs well when training and testing on large datasets. We show competitive performance scores on several benchmark datasets and the out-of-distribution detection task on notable challenging dataset pairs such as CIFAR-10 vs. STL10/SVHN, and CIFAR100 vs. STL10/SVHN.

Keywords: Uncertainty quantification · Deterministic deep neural network · Hierarchical Gaussian mixture model

1 Introduction

Generally, deep classifiers that are not fully aware of what they already know may confidently assign one of the training categories to objects that they have never seen before. Uncertainty in model prediction plays a central role in decision-making when abstaining from predictions. Hence, it has become a reasonable strategy to deal with anomalies [15], outliers [36], out-of-distribution examples [63], detection and defense against adversaries [65], or delegation of high-risk predictions to humans [17,20,26]. Applications of such uncertainty-awaring classifiers range from machine-learning aided medical diagnoses from imaging [24] to self-driving vehicles [11]. Moreover, uncertainty estimation has broad applications in various machine learning problems, such as guiding explorations with reinforcement learning [55], constructing a method to select data points for which to acquire labels in active learning [37], and analyzing noise structure in causal

© The Author(s), under exclusive license to Springer Nature Switzerland AG 2022
S. Yu et al. (Eds.): PRCV 2022, LNCS 13534, pp. 788–813, 2022.
https://doi.org/10.1007/978-3-031-18907-4_61

discovery [47]. Lastly, uncertainty quantification is one step towards improving model interpretability [2].

Despite uncertainty quantification's importance, estimating it remains a largely unsolved problem. Bayesian method is a primary way for uncertainty estimations, where the parameters/weights of the neural network are treated as random variables and the uncertainty is introduced by the posterior distribution. However, exact Bayesian inference for large scale neural networks is a challenging task. As a result, a variety of methods that aim to approximate Bayesian inference [10,33,39,40,67] were proposed to circumvent their computational intractability. An alternative approach for estimating uncertainty in deep learning relies on ensembling [42]. It is straightforward to handle large scale neural networks by ensemble methods. Therefore, lots of variants were proposed recently [55,58]. However, both Bayesian inference approximation and ensemble methods require additional computational efforts or memory to estimate the uncertainty.

Single model methods for uncertainty estimation, which can evaluate the uncertainty in a single forward, gain attentions recently [5,46,66]. For regression problems, quantile based loss function can be applied for uncertainty estimation [66]. For classification problems, it has been noticed that uncertainty that based on entropy of the predicted softmax output cannot always generalize well for out-of-distribution data [5]. Therefore, some distance-aware loss functions are required. For example, in the deterministic uncertainty quantification (DUQ) model [5], a radial basis function kernel with explicit centroids is used as the output and the maximum correlation (minimum distance) between data samples and class centroids is set to be the model prediction. Therefore, out-of-distribution samples can be predicted when the distance between the samples and all centroids is large. However, training a single-model for uncertainty always requires extra regularization terms [5,46], and advanced modelling of the network output for uncertainty estimation remains largely unexplored task.

The contributions of this paper are as follows: in order to calibrate the distribution of the extracted feature more carefully, we propose a novel nonlinear classifier to model the posterior distribution of the extracted feature. To be specific, instead of using a single center for data points from one class, we design multiple centroids for each class so that our model is more suitable for inputs with a complex data distribution. This design choice leads to a hierarchical Gaussian mixture model (GMM). We scale this nonlinear classifier based loss function for large dataset and provide the centroid updating scheme. Moreover, we introduce a natural gradient descent approach to accelerate the learning of GMM parameters. Our uncertainty quantification method scales well to large datasets using a single model. We obtain excellent predictive performance scores on benchmark datasets, and competitive performance on the out-of-distribution detection (OOD) task for notable challenging dataset pairs.

We visualize the performances of uncertainty estimation on two simple examples: the two moons dataset and the two circle dataset in Fig. 1. We can observe that the proposed method achieves the ideal results because it only produces low uncertainty close to the center of the data distribution, and it produces high uncertainty away from the center. On the other hand, the deep ensembles is

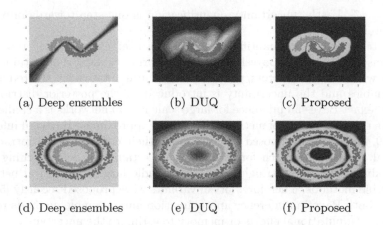

(a) Deep ensembles   (b) DUQ   (c) Proposed

(d) Deep ensembles   (e) DUQ   (f) Proposed

Fig. 1. Results of uncertainty on the two moons and the two circles datasets. Yellow indicates low uncertainty, and blue indicates high uncertainty. (Color figure online)

not able to obtain meaningful uncertainty on these datasets: it only yields high uncertainty along the decision boundary and achieves low uncertainty elsewhere. The recent DUQ method [5] performs well on the two moons dataset, but for the two circle dataset, it gives an indistinct uncertainty for the region between the two circles (decision boundary) and the inner part of the small circle.

2   Related Works

Various methods have been developed for quantifying predictive uncertainty. A large body of research on obtaining uncertainty leverages the idea of Bayesian neural networks [48,53]. Bayesian neural networks learn a posterior distribution over parameters to quantify the prediction uncertainty. While the exact Bayesian inference is intractable, various approximation methods have been proposed. Popular approximation Bayesian learning approaches include Laplace approximation [48], variational inference [10,29], dropout-based variational inference [25,41], expectation propagation [34], stochastic gradient MCMC [16,70], and stochastic weight averaging [38,49]. Bayesian approximation learning methods for uncertainty point to a promising future research direction, but it is still challenging to lead a stable training result on large image datasets.

Deep ensembles method [42] is a simple, non-Bayesian, method that involves training of multiple deep models from different initializations and orderings of the dataset. Deep ensembles methods always outperform Bayesian neural networks that were trained using variational inference [56]. However, this boost in performance comes at the expense of computational cost: deep ensembles methods' memory and computing requirements scale linearly with the number of ensemble elements used in both training and testing. Improved parameter-efficient ensemble methods [22,71] cast a set of models under a single one, encouraging predictions of independent member using low-rank perturbations. However, these methods still require multiple forward passes in the model.

Single-model approaches to deep classifier uncertainty are more appealing due to their high runtime-efficiency. Single-model approaches to estimate predictive uncertainty, achieved by either replacing the loss function [5,32,46,50], or careful designing the output layer [8,66]. Take the distance aware loss function as an example: in DUQ, a radial basis function kernel with explicit centroids is used as the output and the maximum correlation (minimum distance) between data sample and class centroids is considered to be the model prediction for the loss. Moreover, to train the model, DUQ requires an additional regularization on the neural network using a two-sided gradient penalty. Our proposed method belongs to the family of single-model approach, and can be regarded as an extension of the DUQ: instead of using a single center for each class, we design multiple centroids for each class in order to approximate complex data distribution; moreover, we present a rigorous statistical model to describe the posterior distribution of the data and the uncertainty is also evaluated based on this posterior.

Hierarchical GMM has been proposed for both unsupervised and supervised learning [14,69]. Viewing it as a classifier, our proposed hierarchical GMM is more related to the prototypical network [1,64], where the learnable prototypes serve as the centroids of each class. However, prototypical networks always use dot product similarity based softmax for model prediction, which can be viewed as a simplified von Mises-Fisher mixture model [6]. The hierarchical GMM used in this work is a powerful statistic tool that could be used to approximate any density defined on R^d with a large enough number of mixture components. GMMs are widely used as flexible models with various successful applications [7,13,59,60,73]. Although expectation maximization (EM) algorithm [21], Markov Chain Monte Carlo (MCMC) [23] and variational inference [9] for GMMs fitting have been well-developed, a stochastic gradient descent (SGD) learning algorithm is preferred when incorporating GMMs in deep neural networks. Natural gradient method [4] is preferred when learning the parameters of the statistical distribution, as it always lead to faster convergences than naive gradient-based methods. When learning the parameters of a mixture of exponential distribution, [44] used a minimal conditional exponential family representation for the mixtures to obtain the natural gradient updates. In this work, we propose to use an upper bound of the Kullback-Leibler (KL) divergence between two mixture distributions, which can avoid direct computations of the Fisher information matrix for mixture distributions and result in simple natural gradient updates for GMMs.

3   Methods

Let $D = \{(x_1, y_1), ..., (x_N, y_N)\}$ be a dataset of N observations. Each input $x_n \in \mathbb{R}^D$ is a D-dimensional vector and each output $y_n \in \{1, ..., K\}$ is a categorical variable. Assume we use the deep neural network $\phi : x \to z$ to project the input to an embedding space, and let z denote the extracted feature. For a multi-classification problem, traditional softmax cross entropy loss uses the last layer of the DNN, denoted by $\{w\}_{k=1}^{K}$, to express the distribution, $p(y = k|z) = \frac{\exp(z \cdot w_k)}{\sum_{k'} \exp(z \cdot w_{k'})}$.

Here, we introduce an alternative Bayesian expression for the distribution $p(y = k|z)$, aiming to create a more flexible model for the conditional distribution $p(z|y = k)$: assume the prior distribution for y is $p(y) := p_y(y = k)$, and the conditional distribution (also named likelihood) is $p(z|y = k)$, then, by Bayes formula, the posterior distribution $p(y = k|z)$ can be expressed as,

$$p(y = k|z) = \frac{p(y)p(z|y)}{p(z)} = \frac{p_y(y = k)p(z|y = k)}{\sum_{k'} p_y(y = k')p(z|y = k')} \tag{1}$$

Take the GMM as an example: the prior distribution $p_y(y = k)$ is the probability that a data sample z is assigned to class k; the conditional distribution $p(z|y = k)$ is a Gaussian distribution that describes the shape of samples in cluster k; the posterior distribution $p(y = k|z)$ describes the probability that data sample z belongs to each of the K clusters. When the label y_i is given, the experiential object that describes the fitness of the model is the cross entropy loss, which is expressed as,

$$\mathcal{L} = \frac{1}{n} \sum_{n=1}^{n} \sum_{k} I(y_i = k) \log p(y_i = k|z_i) \tag{2}$$

3.1 Hierarchical GMM for Classifier

In this work, instead of modeling the conditional distribution $p(z|y = k)$ by a single Gaussian distribution, we propose to build a GMM for each of the conditional distributions. For this reason, we name the model as hierarchical GMM. Suppose the conditional distribution $p(z|y = k)$ is a GMM, denoted by $p(z|y = k) := Q_{\psi_k}(x) = \sum_{l=1}^{L} w_{k,l} N(\phi(x); \mu_{k,l}, \Sigma_{k,l})$. Let ψ_k denote the parameters $\{w_{k,l}, \mu_{k,l}, \Sigma_{k,l}\}_{l=1}^{L}$ corresponding to class k, and $\Psi = \{\psi_1, ..., \psi_K\}$ denote all the parameters for the hierarchical GMM. Moreover, let π_k denote the prior distribution $p_y(y = k)$. The loss function $\mathcal{L}(\phi, \pi, \Psi)$ in Eq. (2) becomes,

$$\frac{1}{n} \sum_i \sum_k I(y_i = k) \log \frac{p_y(y_i=k)p(z_i|y_i=k)}{\sum_{k'} p_y(y_i=k')p(z_i|y_i=k')}$$
$$= \frac{1}{n} \sum_i \sum_k I(y_i = k) \log \frac{\pi_k \sum_l w_{k,l} N(\phi(x_i); \mu_{k,l}, \Sigma_{k,l})}{\sum_{k'} \pi_{k'} \sum_l w_{k',l} N(\phi(x_i); \mu_{k',l}, \Sigma_{k',l})} \tag{3}$$

Given the loss function, we can use the SGD algorithm and automatic differential tools to optimize the feature extraction network ϕ. But for the optimization of hierarchical GMM, it is nontrivial to apply the SGD algorithm. To this end, we derive the gradient of $\mathcal{L}$ with respect to the GMM parameters π_k, $w_{k,l}$, $\mu_{k,l}$ and $\Sigma_{k,l}$ (for $k = 1, ..., K$ and $l = 1, ..., L$) as follows (detailed in Appendix A),

$$\nabla_{\pi_k}\mathcal{L} = \frac{1}{\pi_k} - \frac{1}{n}\sum_i \frac{Q_{\psi_k}(x_i)}{Q(x_i)} + 1 - K \tag{4}$$

$$\nabla_{w_{k,l}}\mathcal{L} = \frac{1}{n}\sum_i \left(W_\alpha \cdot W_\beta \cdot \frac{1}{w_{k,l}}\right) + \frac{1 - K}{K \cdot L} \tag{5}$$

$$\nabla_{\mu_{k,l}}\mathcal{L} = \frac{1}{n}\sum_i \left(W_\alpha \cdot W_\beta \cdot \frac{\partial}{\partial \mu_{k,l}}\log N(\phi(x_i)|\mu_{k,l}, \Sigma_{k,l})\right) \tag{6}$$

$$\nabla_{\Sigma_{k,l}}\mathcal{L} = \frac{1}{n}\sum_i \left(W_\alpha \cdot W_\beta \cdot \frac{\partial}{\partial \Sigma_{k,l}}\log N(\phi(x_i)|\mu_{k,l}, \Sigma_{k,l})\right). \tag{7}$$

where $Q(x_i)$ denotes $\sum_k \pi_k Q_{\psi_k}(x_i) = \sum_k \pi_k \sum_{l=1}^L w_{k,l}N(\phi(x_i); \mu_{k,l}, \Sigma_{k,l})$, W_α denotes $\left(1 - \frac{\pi_k Q_{\psi_k}(x_i)}{Q(x_i)}\right)$ and W_β denotes $\frac{w_{k,l}N(\phi(x_i)|\mu_{k,l}, \Sigma_{k,l})}{Q_{\psi_k}(x_i)}$.

Moreover, leveraging the automatic differentiation tools in Python, such as PyTorch [57], we can obtain the numerical gradient of $\nabla_{\mu_k}\mathcal{L}$ (or $\nabla_{\Sigma_k}\mathcal{L}$) without further exploring the term $\nabla_{\mu_k}\log N(\phi(x)|\mu_k, \Sigma_k)$ (or $\nabla_{\Sigma_k}\log N(\phi(x)\mu_k, \Sigma_k)$).

3.2   Natural Gradient Updates for GMM Parameters

We further explore the natural gradient descent method to speed up the learning process of GMM. The natural gradient algorithm comes with the idea that when we optimize the parameter ψ of a distribution q_ψ, we expect small distances between the statistical manifold of q_ψ and $q_{\psi'}$ to be present with the current value ψ and some nearby value ψ'. In order to optimize over this manifold, we need to modify our standard gradients using an appropriate local scaling, also known as a Riemannian metric [3]. A common Riemannian metric for statistical manifolds is the Fisher Information Matrix (FIM), which is defined as, $F_\psi = E_{q_\psi(\cdot)}[\nabla_\psi \log q_\psi(\cdot)(\nabla_\psi \log q_\psi(\cdot))^T]$. By a second order Taylor relaxation, we have $KL(q_\psi||q_{\psi+\delta\psi}) \approx \frac{1}{2}\delta\psi \cdot F_\psi \cdot \delta\psi$. The natural gradient descent seeks to minimize the loss function $\mathcal{L}(\psi+\delta\psi)$, meanwhile is subjected to keeping the KL-divergence $KL(q_\psi||q_{\psi+\delta\psi})$ within a constant c. We take the Lagrangian relaxation of the problem and obtain the natural gradient (detailed in the Appendix B), $\widehat{\nabla}_\psi = F_\psi^{-1}\nabla_\psi\mathcal{L}$, which corresponds to the direction of the steepest ascent along the statistical manifold. The preconditioning of the gradients F_ψ^{-1} leads to a proper local scaling of the gradient in each dimension, and takes into account the dependencies between variables. This always leads to faster convergence in the optimization function of q_ψ. When q_ψ is a multivariate normal distribution $N(\mu, \Sigma)$, the resulting natural gradients are $\widehat{\nabla}_\mu = F_\mu^{-1}\nabla_\mu\mathcal{L} = \Sigma\nabla_\mu\mathcal{L}$, and $\widehat{\nabla}_\Sigma = F_\Sigma^{-1}\nabla_\Sigma\mathcal{L} = 2\Sigma(\nabla_\Sigma\mathcal{L})\Sigma$.

Unfortunately, in this work, Q_{ψ_k} (for any $k \in \{1, ..., K\}$) is a mixture of normal distributions, thus it is not easy to find a simple closed-form expression for the FIM. However, instead of using the KL-divergence directly, we leverage an upper bound for approximation [30]. As it is known [35], the upper bound of the KL-divergence between the two Gaussian mixture densities $Q_{\psi_k} = \sum_{l=1}^{L} w_{k,l} N(\mu_{k,l}, \Sigma_{k,l})$ and $Q_{\psi'_k} = \sum_{l=1}^{L} w'_{k,l} N(\mu'_{k,l}, \Sigma'_{k,l})$ is given as follows,

$$KL[Q_{\psi_k} || Q_{\psi'_k}] \leq \sum_{l=1}^{L} w_{k,l} KL[N(\mu_{k,l}, \Sigma_{k,l}) || N(\mu'_{k,l}, \Sigma'_{k,l})]$$
$$+ KL[\mathbf{w} | \mathbf{w}'] \quad (8)$$

where $\mathbf{w} = [w_{k,1}, ..., w_{k,L}]^T$. Therefore, we propose to utilize this upper bound as the regularization term so that we keep the KL-divergence upper bound to be a constant in deriving the natural gradients. Since the KL-divergence between these two single multivariate normal distributions has closed-form natural gradient updates, the upper bound with a mixture of KL-divergence among individual Q_{ψ_k} also has a closed-form solution for the natural gradient (refer to the Appendix B for detailed derivation). The resulting natural gradient updates for all the parameters $\{w_{k,l}, \mu_{k,l}, \Sigma_{k,l}\}_{l=1}^{L}$ in a GMM are

$$\widehat{\nabla}_{w_{k,l}} = w_{k,l} \nabla_{w_{k,l}} \mathcal{L}, \quad (9)$$

$$\widehat{\nabla}_{\mu_{k,l}} = w_{k,l}^{-1} \Sigma_{k,l} \nabla_{\mu_{k,l}} \mathcal{L}, \quad (10)$$

$$\widehat{\nabla}_{\Sigma_{k,l}} = 2 w_{k,l}^{-1} \Sigma_{k,l} \left(\nabla_{\Sigma_{k,l}} \mathcal{L} \right) \Sigma_{k,l}. \quad (11)$$

3.3   The Proposed Algorithm

Besides of the hierarchical GMM based classification loss, we introduce an extra regularization term to force the extracted feature to have a constant norm. Following the work of ring loss [74], we put a regularization on the feature norm to constraint the norm to be a constant, $\mathcal{L}_{reg} = (||\phi(x)|| - c)^2$, where c is a predefined or learnable constant. Therefore, the entire loss for learning network parameter ϕ becomes $\mathcal{L} \leftarrow \mathcal{L}(\phi, \pi, \Psi) + \lambda * \mathcal{L}_{reg}$.

The proposed algorithm iterates between two steps: fix the network parameter ϕ and optimize/update the hierarchical GMM parameters by the derived gradient in Eq. (4) and Eqs. (9)–(11); fix the hierarchical GMM parameters and optimize network parameters by standard SGD or Adam algorithm (see Appendix C. for detailed procedures of the proposed algorithm).

In the test stage, for classification tasks, given the test data sample x, we evaluate the posterior distribution $p(y = k|x)$ as follows,

$$p(y = k|x) = \frac{\pi_k \sum_{l=1}^{L} w_{k,l} N(\phi(x); \mu_{k,l}, \Sigma_{k,l})}{\sum_{k'=1}^{K} \left[\pi_{k'} \sum_{l=1}^{L} w_{k',l} N(\phi(x); \mu_{k',l}, \Sigma_{k',l}) \right]}. \quad (12)$$

Then, we obtain the predicted class via $k^* = \text{argmax}_k p(y = k|x)$. For the uncertainty estimation, the uncertainty is given by the entropy of the probability vector $[p(y = 1|x), ..., p(y = K|x)]^T$,

$$\text{UQ}(x_i) = \sum_{k=1}^{K} -p(y = k|x) \log p(y = k|x). \quad (13)$$

4   Simulation Studies

We first show the behavior of the proposed method in uncertainty quantification on two simple datasets, then evaluate the performance on several benchmark datasets by examining four standard performance metrics [68]. Furthermore, We look at the out of distribution detection performance for the benchmark datasets including some notable difficult dataset pairs [52,68], such as MNIST vs Fashion-MNIST, CIFAR-10 vs. STL10/SVHN, and CIFAR100 vs. STL10/SVHN.

4.1   Toy Example

The two moons dataset has been used to evaluate the uncertainty estimation in previous works [5,46], and the two circles dataset is more challenging as simple linear classifiers can not perform well in this scenario. In these two cases, we do not need the DNN to extract latent features from the data, thus the classifier can be applied directly to fit for these data. For our hierarchical GMM, we use 10 Gaussian components for each class (the scatter plot of the two dataset and fitted GMMs are shown in Appendix D).

We compare our proposed method with the Deep Ensembles method [42] and the DUQ method [5]. As shown in the first row of Fig. 1, both our method and the DUQ provide reasonable uncertainty estimation that yield low uncertainty on the training data, high uncertainty away from the center of data and high uncertainty in the heart within the two moons. However, the Deep Ensembles method fails to estimate the uncertainty well on this dataset. The ensembles method become generalized in nearly a diagonal line, dividing the top left and the bottom right sections. For the two circle dataset, second row of Fig. 1, our model also clearly shows high uncertainty inside the small circle and outside the large circle. The DUQ method gives an indistinct uncertainty for the region between the two circles and the inner part of the small circle, while the deep ensemble method gives clear uncertainty for the region between the two circles but fails to characterize the uncertainty inside the small circle or outside the large circle.

4.2   Benchmark Problems

Recent work [68] provides a suite of benchmarking tools for a comprehensive assessment of approximate Bayesian inference methods with a focus on deep learning based classification tasks. Following the benchmark problems in [68], we compare the predictive performance scores and the OOD classification task with several representative UQ methods.

Tasks and Metrics. The approximate parameter posterior and posterior predictive distribution are produced using each benchmark's in-domain training set. Accuracy is assessed using the corresponding in-domain test sets. To assess uncertainty quantification, we compute negative log likelihood (NLL), Brier score

(BS) [12], and expected calibration error (ECE) [28], all using the in-domain test sets. All these performance scores are detailed in the Appendix E.

We also evaluate the quality of our uncertainty estimation by the out-of-distribution (OOD) classification task [56,68]. For instance, we determine the effectiveness of separating the out-domain test set of FashionMNIST [72] from that of MNIST [43] by only looking at the uncertainty predicted by the model. Following previous works [62,68], we report according to the AUROC metric, in which a higher value shows a better performance and indicates that all in-domain data points have a higher certainty than all out-domain data points. We picked the small-scale benchmark that uses Fashion-MNIST [72] and KMNIST [18] as OOD test sets, while the medium-scale benchmark uses SVHN [54] and STL10 [19] as OOD test sets.

UQ Methods for Comparison. For comparison, we provide the results of several representative UQ methods, including the single model method DUQ [5], Monte Carlo methods such as SGLD [70], SGHMC [16], MC dropout [25], ensembling method Deep Ensembles [42], and an SGD-point estimated model. We implement the Deep Ensembles and DUQ for the tasks discussed in the last subsection, and obtain the resulting metrics by our re-implementation. For the other UQ methods: SGLD, SGHMC, MC dropout and SGD, we verify that the performance of the implementation code [68] is highly consistent with the reported results [68], so we directly cite their results.

Implementation Details. For the MNIST dataset, we use both a multilayer perceptron (MLP) and a convolution neural network (CNN) as the backbone feature extraction network. Details of the network structure are included in Appendix F. For dataset CIFAR10 and CIFAR100, we use a median-scale network, ResNet50 [31], as the backbone network.

For the hierarchical GMM, the number of components should be predefined. By experimental cross validation, we choose the number of components to be 5 for all datasets. In the Appendix H, we provide a table that shows the comparison of model performances with difference number of components ($K = 1, ..., 15$). As fitting GMM for large dimensional data itself is quite challenging, we limit the feature embedding space to be a 10-dimensional real vector space. Moreover, we use the diagonal matrix for covariance, as it is easier to update without worrying about the positive-definite constraint [45]. Furthermore, other hyperparameters are set as follows, learning rate for hierarchical GMM: $\alpha_\pi = \alpha_w = 0.002$, $\alpha_\mu = 0.02$, $\alpha_\Sigma = 0.005$, learning rate for network: $\alpha_\phi \in [0.001, 0.1]$ with a cosine annealing strategy, batch size: 128, and weight for norm regularization $\lambda = 0.1$.

Results for MNIST and CIFAR10 Dataset. For MNIST dataset, we first evaluate the case that a CNN network is used as the feature extraction network. The four predictive performance scores, Accuracy, NLL, BS and ECE, are shown in Table 1. The proposed method obtains the best performance on all four metrics. Besides, we also provide the four scores for MLP based network in Appendix G, where we also obtain the best performance for the first three scores.

For the OOD task, we train our model on MNIST, and we expect it to assign low uncertainty to the in-domain MNIST test set, but high uncertainty to the out-domain test set such as FashionMNIST or KMNIST, since the model has never seen that dataset before, and it should be very different from MNIST. During evaluation, we compute the uncertainty on both test sets. In Fig. 2(a), we show that the uncertainty of out-domain dataset FashionMNIST is spread out over the range of the estimated uncertainty, while the uncertainty of in-domain dataset always takes small and consistent value. This shows that our method works as expected and that out of distribution data have large uncertainty value as they are away from all the centroids in the hierarchical GMM. For quantitative comparison, Table 2 shows the AUROC of the OOD task. Our method outperforms the other four UQ methods. Moreover, in Fig. 2(b), we show the complete ROC curve for our implementation of the proposed method and several competitive ones. We see that our method outperforms other UQ methods at all chosen rates.

For CIFAR10 dataset, we also obtain competitive results for both the four performance metrics and OOD tasks. The results are detailed in Appendix H.

Table 1. Comparison of predictive performance while using a CNN on MNIST. Results presented as mean ± std. dev. across 5 trials.

Method	Accuracy ↑	NLL ↓	BS ↓	ECE ↓
SGLD	99.19	0.02532	0.0125	0.0039
	±0.04%	±0.002	±0.0006	±0.0012
SGHMC	99.10	0.0264	0.0132	0.0028
	±0.11%	±0.0027	±0.0012	±0.0009
MC dropout	99.11	0.0352	0.0146	0.0052
	±0.12%	±0.0047	±0.0017	±0.0006
SGD	*99.36*	*0.0195*	*0.0098*	**0.0015**
	±0.05%	*±0.0017*	*±0.0009*	**±0.0002**
Deep ensembles	*99.24*	0.0238	0.0118	0.0025
	±0.10%	±0.0023	±0.0013	±0.0005
DUQ	99.01	0.0458	0.0178	0.0191
	±0.08%	±0.0058	±0.0010	±0.0042
Proposed	**99.48**	**0.0184**	**0.0078**	*0.0028*
	±0.04%	**±0.0004**	**±0.0002**	*±0.0003*

Results for CIFAR100 Dataset. As the number of class of CIFAR100 increases to 100, parameters of hierarchical GMM increase significantly. However, our proposed method can scale well to such scenario. In Table 3, we compare the proposed method with several alternative UQ methods, where we obtain the

Table 2. Comparison of OOD detection performance while using a CNN on MNIST. Results presented as mean ± std. dev. across 5 trials.

Method	OOD dataset	AUROC ↑
SGLD	Fashion MNIST	0.9769 ± 0.0145
	KMNIST	0.9755 ± 0.0142
SGHMC	Fashion MNIST	0.9753 ± 0.0170
	KMNIST	0.9746 ± 0.0161
MC dropout	Fashion MNIST	0.9794 ± 0.0121
	KMNIST	0.9790 ± 0.0113
SGD	Fashion MNIST	*0.9886 ± 0.0080*
	KMNIST	*0.9880 ± 0.0077*
Deep ensembles	Fashion MNIST	0.986 ± 0.0087
	KMNIST	0.9855 ± 0.0082
DUQ	Fashion MNIST	0.9883 ± 0.0045
	KMNIST	0.9860 ± 0.0073
Proposed	Fashion MNIST	**0.9888 ± 0.0065**
	KMNIST	**0.9882 ± 0.0064**

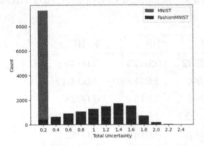
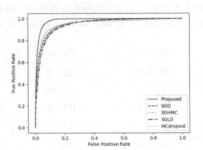

(a) Histogram of the predicted uncer-   (b) ROC curves of different UQ meth-
tainty   ods

Fig. 2. (a) Histogram of the predicted uncertainty for in-domain test dataset MNIST and out-domain test dataset FashionMNIST; (b) ROC curves of different UQ methods trained on MNIST and evaluated on in-domain set MNIST and out-domain set FashionMNIST.

best and a second best for two performance scores. For the OOD task, as shown in Table 4, we can see that our method performs competitively with a number of recent approaches, and obtain superior performance on OOD for out-domain dataset SVHN.

Table 3. Comparison of predictive performance while using ResNet50 on CIFAR100.

Method	Accuracy ↑	NLL ↓	BS ↓	ECE ↓
SGLD	0.751	1.079	0.364	0.107
SGHMC	0.755	1.084	0.362	0.103
MC dropout	*0.786*	**1.006**	**0.330**	0.115
SGD	0.732	1.302	0.408	0.148
Deep ensembles	**0.787**	*1.029*	0.342	**0.093**
Proposed	0.776	1.144	*0.340*	*0.097*

Table 4. Comparison of OOD detection performance on CIFAR100.

Method	OOD dataset	AUROC ↑
SGLD	STL10	0.782
	SVHN	0.802
SGHMC	STL10	0.784
	SVHN	*0.823*
MC dropout	STL10	*0.801*
	SVHN	0.752
SGD	STL10	0.765
	SVHN	0.763
Deep ensembles	STL10	**0.806**
	SVHN	0.805
Proposed	STL10	0.781
	SVHN	**0.824**

Analysis on Runtime

One of the main advantages of our proposed method over ensembles based methods is the computational cost. Ensembles based methods require both computation and memory cost scaling linearly with the number of ensemble components, during both train and test time. Our method has to compute the gradient for the hierarchical GMM at training time. However, when the covariance is constrained to be a diagonal matrix, the computation overhead is marginal. Besides, at test stage, there is only a limited overhead over the evaluation of a hierarchical GMM model. Taking the CIFAR10 test dataset as example, we need to take about 1.3 s for a single model prediction (using ResNet50 as backbone) on a modern 1080 Ti GPU, thus approximate 6.5 s are needed for an ensemble method with 5 components. In comparison, our method only require about 2 s to estimate the uncertainty within a single forward process.

5 Conclusion

In this work, we introduced a deterministic uncertainty quantification approach for deep neural network to estimate uncertainty effectively and accurately in a single forwards pass. The proposed hierarchical Gaussian mixture model is a flexible model for extracted features. We present the learning method for both the feature extraction network and the parameters of the hierarchical GMM model. Both illustration examples and standard benchmark evaluations show that our method is better in some scenarios and competitive in others. Besides, comparing with Monte Carlo or ensemble based methods, our method is more computationally effective. Future work would be to incorporate the proposed method with previous Bayesian or ensemble based uncertainty quantification approaches, and to estimate the epistemic and aleatoric uncertainty separately.

Appendix

A. Derivation of the Gradient for Hierarchical GMM

Given the cross entropy loss function,

$$\mathcal{L}(\phi, \boldsymbol{\pi}, \boldsymbol{\Psi}) = \sum_i \sum_k I(y_i = k) \log \frac{\pi_k \sum_{l=1}^L w_{k,l} q(\phi(x_i); \mu_{k,l}, \Sigma_{k,l})}{\sum_{k'} \pi_{k'} \sum_{l=1}^L w_{k',l} q(\phi(x_i); \mu_{k',l}, \Sigma_{k',l})}$$

we derive the gradients for parameters $\{\pi_k, w_{k,l}, \mu_{k,l}, \Sigma_{k,l}\}$ (for $k = 1, ..., K$ and $l = 1, ..., L$) of the hierarchical GMM. We denote $Q_{\psi_k}(x) := \sum_{l=1}^L w_{k,l} N(\phi(x); \mu_{k,l}, \Sigma_{k,l})$ and $Q(x) := \sum_k \pi_k Q_{\psi_k}(x) = \sum_k \pi_k \sum_{l=1}^L w_{k,l} N(\phi(x_i); \mu_{k,l}, \Sigma_{k,l})$.

Firstly, we derive the gradient with respect to $\boldsymbol{\pi}$. Note that generally we have an additional constraint for $\boldsymbol{\pi}$: $\sum_k \pi_k = 1$. We take this constraint into account by introducing the Lagrange multiplier. As a result, the gradient of the loss function $\mathcal{L}$ with respect to each π_k (for $k = 1, ..., K$) can be derived as follows:

$$\nabla_{\pi_k} \mathcal{L} = \frac{\partial}{\partial \pi_k} \left[\frac{1}{n} \sum_i \sum_{\kappa} I(y_i = k') \log \frac{\pi_\kappa Q_{\psi_\kappa}(x_i)}{\sum_{\kappa'} \pi_{\kappa'} Q_{\psi_{\kappa'}}(x_i)} + \lambda (\sum_{\kappa=1}^K \pi_\kappa - 1) \right]$$

$$= \frac{1}{n} \sum_i \left[\frac{\partial}{\partial \pi_k} \log \frac{\pi_k Q_{\psi_k}(x_i)}{\sum_{\kappa'} \pi_{\kappa'} Q_{\psi_{\kappa'}}(x_i)} \right] + \lambda$$

$$= \frac{1}{\pi_k} - \frac{1}{n} \sum_i \frac{Q_{\psi_k}(x_i)}{\sum_{\kappa'} \pi_{\kappa'} Q_{\psi_{\kappa'}}(x_i)} + \lambda$$

To acquire the value of λ, we add all $\pi_k \cdot \nabla_{\pi_k} \mathcal{L}$ (for $k = 1, ..., K$) together and set its summation to be 0. Then, it is easy to obtain $\lambda = 1 - K$. So the gradient for π_k is,

$$\nabla_{\pi_k} \mathcal{L} = \frac{1}{\pi_k} - \frac{1}{n} \sum_i \frac{Q_{\psi_k}(x_i)}{\sum_{\kappa'} \pi_{\kappa'} Q_{\psi_{\kappa'}}(x_i)} + 1 - K \tag{14}$$

$$= \frac{1}{\pi_k} - \frac{1}{n} \sum_i \frac{Q_{\psi_k}(x_i)}{Q(x_i)} + 1 - K \tag{15}$$

Similarly, for each k, we have the constraint that $\sum_l w_{k,l} = 1$. We also take this into account by introducing the Lagrange multiplier. The gradient of loss function $\mathcal{L}$ with respect to each $w_{k,l}$ (for $k = 1, ..., K$, $l = 1, .., L$)

$$\nabla_{w_{k,l}} \mathcal{L} = \frac{\partial}{\partial w_{k,l}} \left[\frac{1}{n} \sum_i \sum_k I(y_i = k) \log \frac{Q_{\psi_k}(x_i)}{\sum_{k'} \pi_{k'} Q_{\psi_{k'}}(x_i)} + \lambda (\sum_{l'=1}^{L} w_{k,l'} - 1) \right]$$

$$= \frac{1}{n} \sum_i \left[\frac{\partial}{\partial w_{k,l}} \log \frac{Q_{\psi_k}(x_i)}{\sum_{k'} \pi_{k'} Q_{\psi_{k'}}(x_i)} \right] + \lambda$$

$$= \frac{1}{n} \sum_i \left[\frac{N(x_i|\mu_{k,l}, \Sigma_{k,l})}{Q_{\psi_k}(x_i)} - \frac{\pi_k N(x_i|\mu_{k,l}, \Sigma_{k,l})}{\sum_{k'} \pi_{k'} Q_{\psi_{k'}}(x_i)} \right] + \lambda$$

To acquire the value of λ, we add all $w_{k,l} \cdot \nabla_{w_{k,l}} \mathcal{L}$ for $k = 1, ..., K$, $l = 1, .., L$) together and set its summation to be 0. Then, it is easy to obtain $\lambda = (1 - K)/(K \cdot L)$. So the gradient for $w_{k,l}$ is,

$$\nabla_{w_{k,l}} \mathcal{L} = \frac{1}{n} \sum_i \left[\frac{N(x_i|\mu_{k,l}, \Sigma_{k,l})}{Q_{\psi_k}(x_i)} - \frac{\pi_k N(x_i|\mu_{k,l}, \Sigma_{k,l})}{\sum_{k'} \pi_{k'} Q_{\psi_{k'}}(x_i)} \right] + \frac{1-K}{K \cdot L}. \tag{16}$$

$$= \frac{1}{n} \sum_i \left[\frac{w_{k,l} N(x_i|\mu_{k,l}, \Sigma_{k,l})}{Q_{\psi_k}(x_i)} - \frac{w_{k,j} N(x_i|\mu_{k,l}, \Sigma_{k,l}) \cdot \pi_k \cdot Q_{\psi_k}(x_i)}{(\sum_{k'} \pi_{k'} Q_{\psi_{k'}}(x_i)) \cdot Q_{\psi_k}(x_i)} \right] \frac{1}{w_{k,l}} + \frac{1-K}{K \cdot L} \tag{17}$$

$$= \frac{1}{n} \sum_i \frac{w_{k,l} N(x_i|\mu_{k,l}, \Sigma_{k,l})}{Q_{\psi_k}(x_i)} \left[1 - \frac{\pi_k Q_{\psi_k}(x_i)}{\sum_{k'} \pi_{k'} Q_{\psi_{k'}}(x_i)} \right] \frac{1}{w_{k,l}} + \frac{1-K}{K \cdot L} \tag{18}$$

$$= \frac{1}{n} \sum_i \left(1 - \frac{\pi_k Q_{\psi_k}(x_i)}{Q(x_i)} \right) \frac{w_{k,l} N(x_i|\mu_{k,l}, \Sigma_{k,l})}{Q_{\psi_k}(x_i)} \frac{1}{w_{k,l}} + \frac{1-K}{K \cdot L} \tag{19}$$

In order to optimize the parameter $\mu_{k,l}$ in each mixture component, we derive the gradient of the loss function $\mathcal{L}$ with respect to $\mu_{k,l}$ (for $k = 1, ..., K, l = 1, .., L$) as follows,

$$\nabla_{\mu_{k,l}}\mathcal{L} = \frac{\partial}{\partial \mu_{k,l}}\left[\sum_i \sum_k I(y_i = k)\log\frac{\pi_k Q_{\psi_k}(x_i)}{\sum_{k'}\pi_{k'}Q_{\psi_{k'}}(x_i)}\right]$$

$$= \sum_i \frac{\partial}{\partial \mu_{k,l}}\left[\log\left(\pi_k Q_{\psi_k}(x_i)\right) - \log\sum_{k'=1}^{K}\pi_{k'}Q_{\psi_{k'}}(x_i)\right]$$

$$= \sum_i \left[\frac{\partial}{\partial \mu_{k,l}}\log Q_{\psi_k}(x_i) - \frac{\pi_k\frac{\partial}{\partial \mu_{k,l}}Q_{\psi_k}(x_i)}{\sum_{k'}\pi_{k'}Q_{\psi_{k'}}(x_i)}\right]$$

$$= \sum_i \left[\frac{\partial}{\partial \mu_{k,l}}\log Q_{\psi_k}(x_i) - \frac{\pi_k Q_{\psi_k}(x_i)\frac{\partial}{\partial \mu_{k,l}}\log Q_{\psi_k}(x_i)}{\sum_{k'}\pi_{k'}Q_{\psi_{k'}}(x_i)}\right]$$

$$= \sum_i \left[\left(1 - \frac{\pi_k Q_{\psi_k}(x_i)}{\sum_{k'}\pi_{k'}Q_{\psi_{k'}}(x_i)}\right)\frac{\partial}{\partial \mu_{k,l}}\log Q_{\psi_k}(x_i)\right]$$

$$= \sum_i \left[\left(1 - \frac{\pi_k Q_{\psi_k}(x_i)}{\sum_{k'}\pi_{k'}Q_{\psi_{k'}}(x_i)}\right)\frac{\partial}{\partial \mu_{k,l}}\log\sum_l w_{k,l}N(x_i|\mu_{k,l},\Sigma_{k,l})\right]$$

$$= \sum_i \left[\left(1 - \frac{\pi_k Q_{\psi_k}(x_i)}{Q(x_i)}\right)\frac{w_{k,l}N(x_i|\mu_{k,l},\Sigma_{k,l})}{Q_{\psi_k}(x_i)}\frac{\partial}{\partial \mu_{k,l}}\log N(x_i|\mu_{k,l},\Sigma_{k,l})\right]$$

Similarly, we can obtain the gradient of $\mathcal{L}(\phi)$ with respect to Σ_k (for $k = 1,...,K$),

$$\nabla_{\Sigma_{k,l}}\mathcal{L} = \sum_i \left[\left(1 - \frac{\pi_k Q_{\psi_k}(x_i)}{Q(x_i)}\right)\frac{w_{k,l}N(x_i|\mu_{k,l},\Sigma_{k,l})}{Q_{\psi_k}(x_i)}\frac{\partial}{\partial \Sigma_{k,l}}\log N(x_i|\mu_{k,l},\Sigma_{k,l})\right].$$
(20)

B. Derivation of the Natural Gradient for GMM

To obtain the natural gradient, we aim to minimize the loss function, meanwhile subject to keeping the KL-divergence within a constant c. Formally, it can be written as,

$$\delta\psi^* = \arg\min_{\delta\psi}\mathcal{L}(\psi + \delta\psi)$$

$$s.t.KL(q_\psi||q_{\psi+\delta\psi}) = c$$

By second order Taylor relaxation, the KL Divergence can be expressed as a function of FIM and the delta change in parameters between the two distributions, that $KL(q_\psi||q_{\psi+\delta\psi}) \approx \frac{1}{2}\delta\psi\cdot E_{q(\cdot;\psi)}[\nabla_\psi\log q(x;\psi)(\nabla_\psi\log q(x;\psi))^T]\cdot\delta\psi = \frac{1}{2}\delta\psi\cdot F_\psi\cdot\delta\psi$. Let's take the Lagrangian relaxation of the problem and use the first order Taylor relaxation for the $\mathcal{L}(\psi + \delta\psi)$, we obtain,

$$\delta\psi = \arg\min_{\delta\psi}\left[\mathcal{L}(\psi + \delta\psi) + \lambda(KL(q_\psi||q_{\psi+\delta\psi}) - c)\right]$$

$$\approx \arg\min_{\delta\psi}\left[\mathcal{L}(\psi) + \nabla\mathcal{L}(\psi)^T\cdot\delta\psi + \frac{1}{2}\lambda\cdot\delta\psi\cdot F_\psi\cdot\delta\psi - \lambda c\right]$$

To minimize the function above, we set the derivative to zero and solve the equation. The derivative with respect to $\delta\psi$ of the above function is,

$$\nabla\mathcal{L}(\psi)^T + \lambda \cdot F_\psi \cdot \delta\psi$$

Setting the derivative to zero and solving for $\delta\psi$, we get,

$$\delta\psi = -\frac{1}{\lambda}F_\psi^{-1}\nabla\mathcal{L}(\psi) \tag{21}$$

We can take the constant factor $-\frac{1}{\lambda}$ of relaxation into the learning rate. Then we obtain the natural gradient as,

$$\widehat{\nabla_\psi}\mathcal{L}(\psi) = F^{-1}\nabla_\psi\mathcal{L}(\psi) \tag{22}$$

Now, let's derive the natural gradient for GMM. Let ψ denote the parameters of the GMM, $\psi = \{w_l, \mu_l, \Sigma_l\}_{l=1}^L$, then $Q_\psi(x) = \sum_{l=1}^L w_l q_{\psi_l} = \sum_{l=1}^K w_l N(\cdot|\mu_l, \Sigma_l)$. Let ψ_l denote the parameter $\{\mu_l, \Sigma_l\}$ in each mixture component, and $\mathbf{w} = [w_1, ..., w_l]^T$. We approximate the KL divergence $KL[Q_\psi||Q_{\psi+\delta\psi}]$ by its upper bound $KL[\mathbf{w}|\mathbf{w} + \delta\mathbf{w}] + \sum_{l=1}^L w_l KL[q_{\psi_l}||q_{\psi_l+\delta\psi_l}]$. As discussed above, the KL-divergence between two continuous distributions can be approximated by the FIM and delta of the parameters, namely $\frac{1}{2}\delta\psi \cdot F_\psi \cdot \delta\psi$. By a second order Taylor relaxation, the KL between two discrete variable $KL[\mathbf{w}|\mathbf{w} + \delta\mathbf{w}]$ can also be expressed as $KL[\mathbf{w}|\mathbf{w} + \delta\mathbf{w}] \approx -\sum_{l=1}^L w_l(\frac{1}{w_l}\delta w_l + \frac{-1}{2w_l^2} \cdot \delta w_l \cdot \delta w_l) = \frac{1}{2}\sum_{l=1}^L \frac{1}{w_l} \cdot \delta w_l \cdot \delta w_l$ (notice that as $\sum_{l=1}^L w_l = 1$, we have $\sum_{l=1}^L \delta w_l = 0$). By keeping this upper bound as the constant c, the Lagrangian relaxation of the problem becomes,

$$\delta\psi = \underset{\delta\psi}{argmin}\left[\mathcal{L}(\psi + \delta\psi) + \lambda\left(KL[\mathbf{w}|\mathbf{w} + \delta\mathbf{w}] + \sum_{l=1}^L w_l KL[q_{\psi_l}||q_{\psi_l+\delta\psi_l}] - c\right)\right]$$

$$\approx \underset{\delta\psi}{argmin}\left[\mathcal{L}(\psi) + \nabla\mathcal{L}(\psi)^T \cdot \delta\psi + \sum_{l=1}^L \frac{\lambda}{2w_l} \cdot \delta w_l \cdot \delta w_l + \frac{\lambda}{2}\sum_{l=1}^L w_l \cdot \delta\psi_l \cdot F_{\psi_l} \cdot \delta\psi_l - \lambda c\right]$$

The derivative of the above function with respect to each w_l, the weight of each mixture component, is,

$$\nabla\mathcal{L}(\psi) + \frac{\lambda}{w_l} \cdot \delta w_l$$

Setting it to zero and solving for δw_l, we get,

$$\delta w_l = -\frac{w_l}{\lambda}\nabla\mathcal{L}(\psi) \tag{23}$$

The derivative of the above function with respect to each ψ_l in each mixture component is

$$\nabla\mathcal{L}(\psi) + \lambda \cdot w_l \cdot F_{\psi_l} \cdot \delta\psi_l$$

Setting it to zero and solving for $\delta\psi_l$, we get,

$$\delta\psi_l = -\frac{1}{\lambda w_l} F_{\psi_l}^{-1} \nabla \mathcal{L}(\psi) \tag{24}$$

By taking the constant factor $-\frac{1}{\lambda}$ of relaxation into the learning rate, the natural gradient for w_l, μ_l and Σ_l in each component of the GMM are,

$$\widehat{\nabla}_{w_l} = w_l \nabla_{w_l} \mathcal{L}, \tag{25}$$

$$\widehat{\nabla}_{\mu_l} = w_l^{-1} \Sigma_l \nabla_{\mu_l} \mathcal{L} \tag{26}$$

$$\widehat{\nabla}_{\Sigma_l} = 2 w_l^{-1} \Sigma_l \left(\nabla_{\Sigma_l} \mathcal{L} \right) \Sigma_l \tag{27}$$

C. The Proposed Algorithm

The entire algorithm is given as follows,

– Initialization: initialize ϕ, π_k and $\psi_k = \{w_{k,l}, \mu_{k,l}, \Sigma_{k,l}\}$ (for $k = 1, ..., K$ and $l = 1, ...L$) randomly or deterministically. Set the learning rate $\{\alpha_\phi, \alpha_\pi, \alpha_w, \alpha_\mu, \alpha_\Sigma\}$ and set $t = 1$.
– For $t = 1 : T$,
  • update parameters π_k, $\psi_k = \{w_{k,l}, \mu_{k,l}, \Sigma_{k,l}\}$ of the hierarchical GMM as follows,

$$\pi_k \leftarrow \pi_k + \alpha_\pi \nabla_{\pi_k} \mathcal{L}(\phi),$$
$$w_{k,l} \leftarrow w_{k,l} + \alpha_w \widehat{\nabla}_{w_{k,l}} \mathcal{L}(\phi),$$
$$\mu_{k,l} \leftarrow \mu_{k,l} + \alpha_\mu \widehat{\nabla}_{\mu_{k,l}} \mathcal{L}(\phi),$$
$$\Sigma_{k,l} \leftarrow \Sigma_{k,l} + \alpha_\Sigma \widehat{\nabla}_{\Sigma_{k,l}} \mathcal{L}(\phi).$$

  where $\nabla_{\pi_k} \mathcal{L}(\phi)$ is the gradient in Eq. (4), and $\widehat{\nabla}_{w_{k,l}} \mathcal{L}(\phi)$, $\widehat{\nabla}_{\mu_{k,l}} \mathcal{L}(\phi)$, and $\widehat{\nabla}_{\Sigma_{k,l}} \mathcal{L}(\phi)$ are the natural gradients in Eq. (9)–(11).
  • update the parameters of the feature extraction network ϕ,

$$\phi \leftarrow \phi + \alpha_\phi \nabla_\phi \mathcal{L}'(\Psi)$$

D. Data of Toy Example

See Fig. 3.

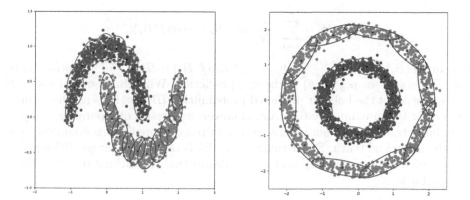

Fig. 3. Left: two moons dataset; right: two circles dataset. The ellipses represent the covariances and the symbols + represent the means.

E. Metrics

In addition to metrics (here, we use an upward arrow or a downward arrow to indicate whether a higher or a lower score demonstrates a better model performance) that do not depend on predictive uncertainty, the following three metrics are used in this work:

Negative Log-Likelihood (NLL) ↓. NLL is commonly used to evaluate the performance of a model's uncertainty on the hold-out dataset. However, although NLL is a proper scoring metric [27], it has limitations since it can over-emphasize tail probabilities [61].

Brier Score ↓ [12]. It measures the accuracy of the predicted probabilities. It computes the difference between a predicted probability vector, $p(y|x_n, \theta)$, and the one-hot encoded correct response, y_n. The lower the difference is, the better the model performs. The formula of BS can be written as,

$$BS = |\mathcal{Y}|^{-1} \sum_{y \in \mathcal{Y}} [p(y|x_n, \theta) - \delta(y - y_n)]^2 = |\mathcal{Y}|^{-1} [1 - 2p(y_n|x_n, \theta) + \sum_{y \in \mathcal{Y}} p(y|x_n, \theta)^2]$$

The Brier score can be interpreted intuitively since BS = *uncertainty − deviation + reliability*. *uncertainty* indicates the marginal uncertainty over labels, *deviation* is the deviation of individual predictions comparing to the margins, and *reliability* measures reliability of the model as the average violation of long-term true label frequencies.

Expected Calibration Error (ECE) ↓: It measures the correspondence between predicted probabilities and empirical accuracy [51]. It is not a proper scoring rule and is not associated with a proper entropy function. However, it is used extensively [28]. It is computed as the average difference between within-bucket accuracy and within-bucket predicted probability for S buckets $B_s = n \in 1...N : p(y_n|x_n, \theta) \in (\rho_s, \rho_{s+1}]$. That is,

$$ECE = \sum_{s=1}^{S} \frac{|B_s|}{N} |acc(B_s) - conf(B_s)|,$$

where $acc(B_s) = |B_s|^{-1} \sum_{n \in B_s} [y_n = \widehat{y}_n]$, $conf(B_s) = |B_s|^{-1} \sum_{n \in B_s} p(\widehat{y}_n|x_n, \theta)$, and $\widehat{y}_n = \text{argmax}_y p(y|x_n, \theta)$ is the nth prediction. When buckets $\rho_s : s \in 1...S$ are quantiles of the holdout predicted probabilities, $|B_s| \approx |B_k|$ and the estimation error is approximately constant. However, as a result of separating samples into buckets, ECE does not monotonically increase as predictions gradually approach the ground truth. Furthermore, since ECE takes the average difference, a large difference between $|B_s|$ and $|B_k|$ indicates that the estimation error varies across buckets.

F. Network Structures

The feature extraction network structures for MNIST dataset are presented in Table 5 and Table 6. Note that the output h_3 in the MLP network and the output h_5 in the CNN network are used as the extracted latent feature for the hierarchical GMM. Moreover, the extracted feature is also constrained by the norm regularization.

Table 5. Network structure of the MLP

Inputs	Layer	Outputs	Dim of outputs	Kernel size	Stride	Padding	Activation
X	-	-	1 * 28 * 28	-	-	-	-
X	Linear	h_1	1 * 200	-	-	-	ReLU
h_1	Linear	h_2	1 * 200	-	-	-	ReLU
h_2	Linear	h_3	1 * 10	-	-	-	-
h_3	Hierarchical GMM	$\widehat{Y}$	10	-	-	-	-

Table 6. Network structure of the CNN

Inputs	Layer	Outputs	Dim of outputs	Kernel size	Stride	Padding	Activation
X	-	-	1 * 28 * 28	-	-	-	-
X	Convolution	h_1	32 * 14 * 14	5 * 5	2	2	ReLU
h_1	Convolution	h_2	64 * 7 * 7	5 * 5	2	2	ReLU
h_2	Linear	h_3	1 * 256	-	-	-	ReLU
h_3	Linear	h_4	1 * 256	-	-	-	ReLU
h_4	Linear	h_5	1 * 10	-	-	-	-
h_5	Hierarchical GMM	$\widehat{Y}$	10	-	-	-	-

G. Results for MNIST Using MLP Network

Table 7 provides the four predictive performance scores for a model using MLP network as backbone, including mean value and standard deviation of 5 trials. Moreover, we also provide the OOD result for the model using MLP network in Table 8.

Table 7. Comparison of predictive performance while using an MLP on MNIST. Results presented as mean ± std. dev. across 5 trials.

Method	Accuracy ↑	NLL ↓	BS ↓	ECE ↓
HMC	98.19 ± 0.10%	0.0593 ± 0.0016	0.0280 ± 0.0008	0.0079 ± 0.0008
SGLD	98.39 ± 0.04%	0.0492 ± 0.0022	0.0236 ± 0.0005	*0.0041 ± 0.0024*
SGHMC	*98.62 ± 0.03%*	*0.0446 ± 0.0003*	*0.0210 ± 0.0002*	0.0073 ± 0.0004
MC dropout	98.58 ± 0.07%	0.0501 ± 0.0031	0.0218 ± 0.0008	0.0042 ± 0.0006
SGD	98.60 ± 0.02%	0.0452 ± 0.0012	0.0213 ± 0.0003	**0.0032 ± 0.0005**
Deep ensembles	98.46 ± 0.03%	0.0495 ± 0.0021	0.0234 ± 0.0004	0.0029 ± 0.0003
DUQ	97.66 ± 0.15%	0.1417 ± 0.0101	0.0474 ± 0.0027	0.0724 ± 0.0104
Proposed	**98.75 ± 0.11%**	**0.0422 ± 0.0020**	**0.0194 ± 0.0011**	0.0050 ± 0.0004

Table 8. Comparison of OOD detection performance while using an MLP on MNIST. Results presented as mean ± std. dev. across 5 trials.

Method	OOD dataset	AUROC ↑
HMC	Fashion MNIST	0.946 ± 0.017
	KMNIST	0.948 ± 0.017
SGLD	Fashion MNIST	0.944 ± 0.005
	KMNIST	0.944 ± 0.005
SGHMC	Fashion MNIST	*0.953 ± 0.010*
	KMNIST	*0.952 ± 0.010*
MC dropout	Fashion MNIST	0.943 ± 0.010
	KMNIST	0.944 ± 0.010
SGD	Fashion MNIST	0.945 ± 0.010
	KMNIST	0.943 ± 0.010
Deep Ensembles	Fashion MNIST	0.9408 ± 0.012
	KMNIST	0.939 ± 0.012
DUQ	Fashion MNIST	0.933 ± 0.072
	KMNIST	0.931 ± 0.068
Proposed	Fashion MNIST	**0.980 ± 0.004**
	KMNIST	**0.980 ± 0.004**

H. Results for CIFAR10 Dataset

We evaluate the predictive performance on CIFAR10. For all UQ methods, we use a standard ResNet50 as the backbone. In Fig. 4, we show that the uncertainty of out-domain dataset SVHN spread out over the range of distances. This histogram shows that our method works as expected and that out-of-distribution data end up with high uncertainty. In Table 9, we compare the proposed method with several alternative UQ methods. The proposed method obtains a good performance on the prediction accuracy. However, remaining predictive scores are quite close to other UQ methods. Table 10 shows results for the OOD task. Our method is competitive with other UQ methods. As it is known that the pair CIFAR10 and STL10 is difficult to separate, so the AUROC is relative low, while the AUROC for dataset pair CIFAR10 and SVHN is high.

We provide the histogram of the predicted uncertainty for in-domain test dataset CIFAR10 and out-domain test datas SVHN. Notice that in Fig. 4, we use the original uncertainty unlike use the logarithm scale in the main paper. We also provide Table 11 to show the model performance across difference number of mixture components $(K = 1, ..., 15)$ in the hierarchical GMM.

Table 9. Comparison of predictive performance while using ResNet50 on CIFAR10.

Method	Accuracy ↑	NLL ↓	BS ↓	ECE ↓
SGLD	*0.954*	0.144	**0.069**	0.009
SGHMC	*0.954*	0.144	*0.068*	*0.011*
MC dropout	0.948	0.208	0.083	0.032
SGD	0.943	0.274	0.095	0.040
Deep ensembles	0.952	*0.193*	0.079	0.029
DUQ	0.947	0.203	0.082	0.037
Proposed	**0.956**	0.239	0.076	0.032

Table 10. Comparison of OOD detection performance while using ResNet50 on CIFAR10.

Method	OOD dataset	AUROC ↑
SGLD	STL10	0.684
	SVHN	0.945
SGHMC	STL10	0.687
	SVHN	**0.955**
MC dropout	STL10	*0.695*
	SVHN	0.938
SGD	STL10	0.682
	SVHN	0.892
Deep ensembles	STL10	0.683
	SVHN	0.934
DUQ	STL10	0.658
	SVHN	*0.951*
Proposed	STL10	**0.697**
	SVHN	0.938

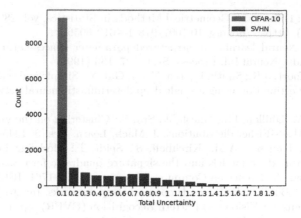

Fig. 4. Histogram of the predicted uncertainty for in-domain test dataset CIFAR10 and out-domain test SVHN.

Table 11. Comparison of model performance across different number of GMM components ($K = 1, ...15$).

K	Accuracy ↑	NLL ↓	BS ↓	ECE ↓	AUROC (CIFAR10 vs STL10) ↑	AUROC (CIFAR10 vs SVHN) ↑
1	0.9491	0.2699	0.0865	0.039	0.6628	0.9364
2	0.9519	0.2493	0.0825	0.0361	0.6707	0.9133
3	0.9517	0.2486	0.0836	0.0366	0.6623	0.9253
4	0.9509	0.2601	0.0852	0.0378	0.6535	0.9145
5	0.9561	0.2390	0.0757	0.0324	0.6965	0.9381
6	0.9532	0.2422	0.0801	0.0355	0.6564	0.9158
7	0.9554	0.2397	0.0814	0.0371	0.6906	0.9377
8	0.9525	0.2497	0.0813	0.0352	0.6689	0.8928
9	0.9533	0.2463	0.0804	0.0349	0.6675	0.9073
10	0.9508	0.2498	0.0834	0.0368	0.6556	0.9328
11	0.9536	0.2381	0.0789	0.0339	0.6691	0.9227
12	0.9513	0.2556	0.0844	0.0373	0.6754	0.9098
13	0.9517	0.2497	0.0827	0.0364	0.6663	0.9062
14	0.9540	0.2399	0.0799	0.0345	0.6548	0.9204
15	0.9513	0.2559	0.0834	0.0370	0.6585	0.9178

References

1. Allen, K., Shelhamer, E., Shin, H., Tenenbaum, J.: Infinite mixture prototypes for few-shot learning. In: Proceedings of the 36th International Conference on Machine Learning, pp. 232–241 (2019)
2. Alvarez-Melis, D., Jaakkola, T.: A causal framework for explaining the predictions of black-box sequence-to-sequence models. In: EMNLP (2017)

3. Amari, S.I.: Differential-Geometrical Methods in Statistics, vol. 28. Springer, New York (1985). https://doi.org/10.1007/978-1-4612-5056-2

4. Amari, S.: Neural learning in structured parameter spaces-natural Riemannian gradient. Adv. Neural Inf. Process. Syst. 127–133 (1997)

5. van Amersfoort, J.R., Smith, L., Teh, Y.W., Gal, Y.: Simple and scalable epistemic uncertainty estimation using a single deep deterministic neural network. In: ICML (2020)

6. Banerjee, A., Dhillon, I.S., Ghosh, J., Sra, S.: Clustering on the unit hypersphere using von Mises-Fisher distributions. J. Mach. Learn. Res. **6**, 1345–1382 (2005)

7. Beecks, C., Ivanescu, A.M., Kirchhoff, S., Seidl, T.: Modeling image similarity by gaussian mixture models and the signature quadratic form distance. In: 2011 International Conference on Computer Vision, pp. 1754–1761. IEEE (2011)

8. Bendale, A., Boult, T.E.: Towards open set deep networks. In: 2016 IEEE Conference on Computer Vision and Pattern Recognition (CVPR), pp. 1563–1572 (2016)

9. Blei, D., Jordan, M.: Variational inference for Dirichlet process mixtures. Bayesian Anal. **1**(1), 121–144 (2004)

10. Blundell, C., Cornebise, J., Kavukcuoglu, K., Wierstra, D.: Weight uncertainty in neural networks. arXiv abs/1505.05424 (2015)

11. Bojarski, M., et al.: End to end learning for self-driving cars. arXiv abs/1604.07316 (2016)

12. Brier, G.W.: Verification of forecasts expressed in terms of probability. Mon. Weather Rev. **78**, 1–3 (1950)

13. Campbell, W.M., Sturim, D.E., Reynolds, D.A.: Support vector machines using GMM supervectors for speaker verification. IEEE Sig. Process. Lett. **13**(5), 308–311 (2006)

14. Carneiro, G., Chan, A.B., Moreno, P.J., Vasconcelos, N.: Supervised learning of semantic classes for image annotation and retrieval. IEEE Trans. Pattern Anal. Mach. Intell. **29**(3), 394–410 (2007)

15. Chandola, V., Banerjee, A., Kumar, V.: Anomaly detection: a survey. ACM Comput. Surv. **41**, 15:1–15:58 (2009)

16. Chen, T., Fox, E.B., Guestrin, C.: Stochastic gradient Hamiltonian Monte Carlo. arXiv abs/1402.4102 (2014)

17. Chen, T., Navrátil, J., Iyengar, V., Shanmugam, K.: Confidence scoring using whitebox meta-models with linear classifier probes. arXiv abs/1805.05396 (2019)

18. Clanuwat, T., Bober-Irizar, M., Kitamoto, A., Lamb, A., Yamamoto, K., Ha, D.: Deep learning for classical Japanese literature. arXiv abs/1812.01718 (2018)

19. Coates, A., Ng, A., Lee, H.: An analysis of single-layer networks in unsupervised feature learning. In: AISTATS (2011)

20. Cortes, C., DeSalvo, G., Mohri, M.: Learning with rejection. In: ALT (2016)

21. Dempster, A., Laird, N., Rubin, D.: Maximum likelihood from incomplete data via the EM - algorithm plus discussions on the paper. J. Roy. Stat. Soc. Ser. B (Methodol.) 1–38 (1997)

22. Dusenberry, M.W., et al.: Efficient and scalable Bayesian neural nets with rank-1 factors. arXiv abs/2005.07186 (2020)

23. Escobar, M.: Estimating normal means with a Dirichlet process prior. J. Am. Stat. Assoc. **89**, 268–277 (1994)

24. Esteva, A., et al.: Dermatologist-level classification of skin cancer with deep neural networks. Nature **542**, 115–118 (2017)

25. Gal, Y., Ghahramani, Z.: Dropout as a Bayesian approximation: representing model uncertainty in deep learning. arXiv abs/1506.02142 (2016)

26. Geifman, Y., El-Yaniv, R.: Selective classification for deep neural networks. In: NIPS (2017)
27. Gneiting, T., Balabdaoui, F., Raftery, A.E.: Probabilistic forecasts, calibration and sharpness. J. Roy. Stat. Soc. Ser. B-Stat. Methodol. **69**, 243–268 (2007)
28. Gneiting, T., Raftery, A.E.: Strictly proper scoring rules, prediction, and estimation. J. Am. Stat. Assoc. **102**, 359–378 (2007)
29. Graves, A.: Practical variational inference for neural networks. In: NIPS (2011)
30. Guo, C., Zhou, J., Chen, H., Ying, N., Zhang, J., Zhou, D.: Variational autoencoder with optimizing gaussian mixture model priors. IEEE Access **8**, 43992–44005 (2020)
31. He, K., Zhang, X., Ren, S., Sun, J.: Deep residual learning for image recognition. In: 2016 IEEE Conference on Computer Vision and Pattern Recognition (CVPR), pp. 770–778 (2016)
32. Hein, M., Andriushchenko, M., Bitterwolf, J.: Why ReLU networks yield high-confidence predictions far away from the training data and how to mitigate the problem. In: 2019 IEEE/CVF Conference on Computer Vision and Pattern Recognition (CVPR), pp. 41–50 (2019)
33. Hernández-Lobato, J.M., Adams, R.P.: Probabilistic backpropagation for scalable learning of Bayesian neural networks. In: ICML (2015)
34. Hernández-Lobato, J.M., Adams, R.P.: Probabilistic backpropagation for scalable learning of Bayesian neural networks. In: Proceedings of the International Conference on Machine Learning (2015)
35. Hershey, J., Olsen, P.: Approximating the Kullback Leibler divergence between Gaussian mixture models. In: 2007 IEEE International Conference on Acoustics, Speech and Signal Processing - ICASSP 2007, vol. 4, pp. IV-317–IV-320 (2007)
36. Hodge, V.J., Austin, J.: A survey of outlier detection methodologies. Artif. Intell. Rev. **22**, 85–126 (2004)
37. Houlsby, N., Huszár, F., Ghahramani, Z., Lengyel, M.: Bayesian active learning for classification and preference learning. arXiv abs/1112.5745 (2011)
38. Izmailov, P., Podoprikhin, D., Garipov, T., Vetrov, D.P., Wilson, A.G.: Averaging weights leads to wider optima and better generalization. arXiv abs/1803.05407 (2018)
39. Kendall, A., Gal, Y.: What uncertainties do we need in Bayesian deep learning for computer vision? In: NIPS (2017)
40. Khan, M.E., Nielsen, D.: Fast yet simple natural-gradient descent for variational inference in complex models. In: 2018 International Symposium on Information Theory and Its Applications (ISITA), pp. 31–35. IEEE (2018)
41. Kingma, D.P., Salimans, T., Welling, M.: Variational dropout and the local reparameterization trick. arXiv abs/1506.02557 (2015)
42. Lakshminarayanan, B., Pritzel, A., Blundell, C.: Simple and scalable predictive uncertainty estimation using deep ensembles. In: NIPS (2017)
43. LeCun, Y., Bottou, L., Bengio, Y., Haffner, P.: Gradient-based learning applied to document recognition (1998)
44. Lin, W., Khan, M.E., Schmidt, M.: Fast and simple natural-gradient variational inference with mixture of exponential-family approximations. In: ICML (2019)
45. Lin, W., Schmidt, M.W., Khan, M.E.: Handling the positive-definite constraint in the Bayesian learning rule. In: ICML (2020)
46. Liu, J.Z., Lin, Z., Padhy, S., Tran, D., Bedrax-Weiss, T., Lakshminarayanan, B.: Simple and principled uncertainty estimation with deterministic deep learning via distance awareness. arXiv abs/2006.10108 (2020)
47. Lopez-Paz, D.: From dependence to causation. arXiv Machine Learning (2016)

48. Mackay, D.J.C.: A practical Bayesian framework for backpropagation networks. Neural Comput. **4**, 448–472 (1992)
49. Maddox, W., Garipov, T., Izmailov, P., Vetrov, D.P., Wilson, A.G.: A simple baseline for Bayesian uncertainty in deep learning. In: NeurIPS (2019)
50. Malinin, A., Gales, M.J.F.: Predictive uncertainty estimation via prior networks. In: NeurIPS (2018)
51. Naeini, M.P., Cooper, G.F., Hauskrecht, M.: Obtaining well calibrated probabilities using Bayesian binning. In: Proceedings of the ... AAAI Conference on Artificial Intelligence. AAAI Conference on Artificial Intelligence 2015, pp. 2901–2907 (2015)
52. Nalisnick, E.T., Matsukawa, A., Teh, Y.W., Görür, D., Lakshminarayanan, B.: Do deep generative models know what they don't know? arXiv abs/1810.09136 (2019)
53. Neal, R.: Annealed importance sampling. Stat. Comp. **11**, 125–139 (2001)
54. Netzer, Y., Wang, T., Coates, A., Bissacco, A., Wu, B., Ng, A.: Reading digits in natural images with unsupervised feature learning (2011)
55. Osband, I., Blundell, C., Pritzel, A., Roy, B.V.: Deep exploration via bootstrapped DQN. In: NIPS (2016)
56. Ovadia, Y., et al.: Can you trust your model's uncertainty? Evaluating predictive uncertainty under dataset shift. In: NeurIPS (2019)
57. Paszke, A., et al.: Automatic differentiation in PyTorch (2017)
58. Pearce, T., Brintrup, A., Zaki, M., Neely, A.D.: High-quality prediction intervals for deep learning: a distribution-free, ensembled approach. In: ICML (2018)
59. Permuter, H., Francos, J., Jermyn, I.: A study of gaussian mixture models of color and texture features for image classification and segmentation. Pattern Recogn. **39**(4), 695–706 (2006)
60. Povey, D., et al.: Subspace gaussian mixture models for speech recognition. In: 2010 IEEE International Conference on Acoustics, Speech and Signal Processing, pp. 4330–4333. IEEE (2010)
61. Quionero-Candela, J., Sugiyama, M., Schwaighofer, A., Lawrence, N.: Dataset shift in machine learning (2009)
62. Ren, J., et al.: Likelihood ratios for out-of-distribution detection. In: NeurIPS (2019)
63. Shafaei, A., Schmidt, M.W., Little, J.: Does your model know the digit 6 is not a cat? A less biased evaluation of "outlier" detectors. arXiv abs/1809.04729 (2018)
64. Snell, J., Swersky, K., Zemel, R.: Prototypical networks for few-shot learning. In: NIPS (2017)
65. Szegedy, C., et al.: Intriguing properties of neural networks. CoRR abs/1312.6199 (2014)
66. Tagasovska, N., Lopez-Paz, D.: Single-model uncertainties for deep learning. In: NeurIPS (2019)
67. Teye, M., Azizpour, H., Smith, K.: Bayesian uncertainty estimation for batch normalized deep networks. In: ICML (2018)
68. Vadera, M.P., Cobb, A.D., Jalaeian, B., Marlin, B.M.: Ursabench: comprehensive benchmarking of approximate Bayesian inference methods for deep neural networks. arXiv abs/2007.04466 (2020)
69. Vasconcelos, N., Lippman, A.: Learning mixture hierarchies. Adv. Neural Inf. Process. Syst. **11** (1998)
70. Welling, M., Teh, Y.W.: Bayesian learning via stochastic gradient Langevin dynamics. In: ICML (2011)
71. Wen, Y., Tran, D., Ba, J.: Batchensemble: an alternative approach to efficient ensemble and lifelong learning. arXiv abs/2002.06715 (2020)

72. Xiao, H., Rasul, K., Vollgraf, R.: Fashion-MNIST: a novel image dataset for bench-marking machine learning algorithms. arXiv abs/1708.07747 (2017)
73. Yu, G., Sapiro, G., Mallat, S.: Solving inverse problems with piecewise linear esti-mators: from gaussian mixture models to structured sparsity. IEEE Trans. Image Process. **21**(5), 2481–2499 (2011)
74. Zheng, Y., Pal, D.K., Savvides, M.: Ring loss: convex feature normalization for face recognition. In: 2018 IEEE/CVF Conference on Computer Vision and Pattern Recognition, pp. 5089–5097 (2018)

Exploring Masked Image Modeling
for Face Anti-spoofing

Xuetao Ma, Jun Zhang, Yunfei Zhang, and Daoxiang Zhou[✉]

College of Data Science, Taiyuan University of Technology, Taiyuan 030024, China
{maxuetao1427,zhangjun3398,zhangyunfei4062}@link.tyut.edu.cn,
zhoudaoxiang@tyut.edu.cn

Abstract. Face anti-spoofing (FAS) is an indispensable step in face recognition systems. In order to distinguish spoofing faces from genuine ones, existing methods always require sophisticated handcrafted features or well-designed supervised networks to learn discriminative representation. In this paper, a novel generative self-supervised learning inspired FAS approach is proposed, which has three merits: no need for massive labeled images, excellent discriminative ability, and the learned features have good transferability. Firstly, in the pretext task, the masked image modeling strategy is exploited to learn general fine-grained features via image patches reconstruction in an unsupervised encoder-decoder structure. Secondly, the encoder knowledge is transferred into the downstream FAS task. Finally, the entire network parameters are fine-tuned using only binary labels. Extensive experiments on three standard benchmarks demonstrate that our method can be exceedingly close to the state-of-the-art in FAS, which indicates that masked image modeling is able to learn discriminative face detail features that are beneficial to FAS.

Keywords: Face anti-spoofing · Self-supervised learning · Masked image modeling · Transformer network

1 Introduction

Face recognition has entered the commercial era and is widely used in various scenarios. However, there are many places in the face recognition system that may be attacked.

The most common form of attack is presentation attack, for instance photo print and video replay, which greatly threatens the reliability and security of face recognition systems and makes face anti-spoofing (FAS) a challenging problem.

Over the past ten years, considerable FAS approaches have been put forward successively, which can be grouped into handcrafted methods and convolutional neural network (CNN) based methods. Although they have shown promising

This work was supported by the National Natural Science Foundation of China (62101376) and Natural Science Foundation of Shanxi Province of China (201901D211078).

FAS performance, their discriminative and generalization capability still needs to be improved. Firstly, the huge number of labeled face images are required. The performance of these methods relies heavily on the supervision signals, like binary labels, remote photoplethysmography (rPPG) [31] and depth maps [16]. The accuracy may degenerate once the supervision information has some errors. Secondly, the convolution operation acts in a local manner, and therefore it cannot capture the long-range visual context that plays a crucial role in visual pattern recognition. Thirdly, the transfer capability of the learned feature is not encouraging in discriminating unknown types of presentation attacks.

In recent years, self-supervised learning (SSL) has emerged as the most prominent technology to overcome the shortage of supervised learning that require massive labeled data in computer vision. The core idea behind SSL is to learn general features via pretext task, then the learned knowledge is transferred to a specific downstream task, such as recognition, segmentation and detection. It should be pointed out that the pretext task uses a large-scale unlabeled dataset for pre-training, and then uses another relatively small labeled dataset for fine-tuning. SSL is superior to supervised learning in pre-training tasks, and the pretext task does not require labels that makes the model free from massive and complex label information, such as depth maps and rPPG. To sum up, there are two kinds of SSL models: generative and contrastive. The pretext task of contrastive SSL methods seeks to learn image level general semantic features [6,12]. Inspired by BERT [8], masked image modeling (MIM) as a generative self-supervised method has been extensively studied in the past two years. With the help of self-attention mechanism [24] in the transformer models, the two generative SSL methods dubbed masked autoencoders (MAE) [11] and simple masked image modeling (SimMIM) [29] achieved outstanding performance and even surpassed the supervised learning baselines on some image processing tasks. The MIM learns the general image features via masking random patches of the original image and reconstructing the missing pixels. It has the following four advantages: (i) pretext task does not require image label information (ii) can learn general image detail features (iii) the learned general features have excellent transfer capability (iv) can capture the long-range global relationship of features because of the self-attention mechanism in the transformer encoder.

Generally speaking, the pixel details or global spatial structure of an image will be changed for spoofing faces, such as pixel blurring in printed photos and image warping in hand-held photos. In other words, the key discrepancies between spoofing faces and genuine faces come from the image fine-grained information [23] and the global correlation between the features at different regions.

Because the MIM can reconstruct image pixels perfectly even though most regions of the image are masked, which reveals that MIM is capable of learning image detail information and capturing image spatial structure. Accordingly, our initial motivation for this work is to learn detailed features for faces through MIM, which is helpful for detecting presentation attacks. What is more, the transformer encoder network can learn the global correlation between visual features, which is an important clue to distinguish between genuine and spoofing faces.

From the above analysis, in order to address the aforementioned issues of existing FAS methods, this paper proposes a novel and simple method to learn general and discriminative features for FAS under the SSL framework. The overall pipeline of our method is illustrated in Fig. 1. In the pretext task stage, the MIM is exploited to learn general face detail features in an unsupervised fashion under transformer encoder-decoder architecture. Afterward, the trained encoder knowledge is utilized to initialize the encoder of our downstream FAS task. Since we consider FAS as an image classification problem, and therefore the encoder is followed by a simple network only with global average pooling (GAP) and fully connected (FC) layers instead of the decoder. The main contributions of this paper are threefold:

- To our knowledge, this work is the first attempt to exploit generative SSL for FAS. The SSL strategy renders our method can achieve better results than supervised learning methods on the premise of using a large amount of unlabeled images for pre-training, which effectively reduces the cost of labeling.
- We explore the effectiveness of two different MIM models in learning general face detail features that have superior discriminative ability and transfer advantages.
- We conduct extensive FAS experiments on three popular datasets. The results show that our method offers competitive performance compared with other FAS methods.

2   Related Work

2.1   Face Anti-spoofing

The majority of FAS methods are based on supervised learning. From the early period of handcrafted feature methods, such as LBP [21], etc., these methods require at least binary label as supervised information. With the rise of deep learning, there are more types of clues that have been proven to be discriminative to distinguish spoofing faces. In [1], depth maps are introduced into the FAS task firstly. In addition, [16] leverages depth maps and rPPG signal as supervision. Besides, reflection maps and binary mask are respectively introduced by [13] and [17]. In the past two years, the Vision Transformer (ViT) structure has achieved success in vision tasks. Some researchers have applied ViT to FAS. Although the new architecture further improves the indicators of FAS, these works still require various types of supervision. For example, ViTranZFAS [10] needs binary labels, and TransRPPG [31] needs rPPG as supervision.

Various types of supervision information seriously increase the cost of labeling, and the quality of labels also greatly affects the performance of models. Therefore, some researches begun to explore the FAS methods based on contrastive SSL [15,20]. These works not only get rid of constraint of labels, but also achieve better performance than supervised learning. Unlike these methods, this paper adopts generative SSL method.

2.2 Masked Image Modeling

Masked image modeling is a generative self-supervised method. The work in [25] proposes denoising autoencoders (DAE), which corrupts the input signal and learns to reconstruct the original input. Further, the work of [26] takes masking as a noise type in DAE. They randomly set some values in the input data to zero with a certain probability, then train the encoder to reconstruct these values.

DAE first achieved great success in the field of NLP. Transformer [24] and BERT [8] are the most representative architectures. Specifically, a self-attention mechanism is proposed in Transformer to capture the relationship between different tokens. Further, a special token [MASK] is introduced to BERT. The [MASK] will replace some tokens in training phase, then the network predicts the original words in this position. After the masked model has achieved such great achievements in NLP area, a natural question is how to apply this model to computer vision tasks.

Some pioneering works in the recent years has explored the potential of MIM. iGPT [5] reshapes the raw images to a 1D sequence of pixels and predicts unknown pixels. The BEiT [2] proposes a pre-training task called MIM, and also introduces the definition of MIM firstly. In BEiT, the image is represented as discrete tokens, and these tokens will be treated as the construct target of masked patches. Most recently, MAE [11] and SimMIM [29] almost simultaneously obtain state-of-the-art on computer vision tasks. They propose a pre-training paradigm based on MIM, that is, the patches of images are randomly masked with a high probability (usually greater than 50%), then the self-attention mechanism is used in the encoder to learn the relationship between patches, and finally the masked patches is reconstructed in the decoder.

3 Methodology

3.1 Intuition and Motivation

Spoofing faces are very similar in appearance to genuine faces. Their main differences are the image pixel details (blur and color) and the overall image structure (deformation and specular reflection). Learning discriminative cues from numerous labeled samples via CNN is a common way, but it is hard to learn general features, so the generalization ability needs to be improved, and the cost of producing labeled samples is expensive. So how to learn the general discriminative features that can distinguish spoofing faces from genuine ones on small amount labeled faces are the main challenge of FAS.

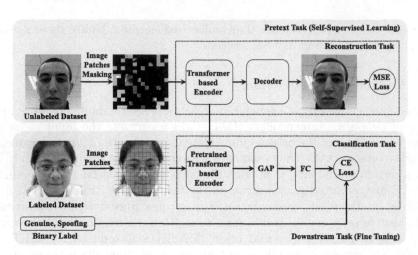

Fig. 1. Overall architecture of our proposed face anti-spoofing with masked image modeling.

3.2 The Proposed Method

Pretext Task Stage. SSL has been recognized as an effective way to remedy the shortcoming of the appetite for a large amount of labeled data. Due to the strong power of MIM in reconstructing image pixels, we argue that it can capture face detail visual features and the image structure via position embedding. Moreover, the global features of face image can be characterized by the self-attention in the transformer. Consequently, the general discriminative face visual cues with good transfer ability can be learned by MIM in an unsupervised manner.

In this paper, we mainly consider two newly proposed MIM methods: MAE [11] and SimMIM [29]. The ViT [9] and swin transformer [18] are adopted as the encoder backbone of MAE and SimMIM respectively. Meanwhile, the experiments of MAE and SimMIM both prove that random mask is more effective, so this paper also adopts the random mask. Concretely, we first divide a face image into several non-overlapping patches and randomly mask a large portion of the patches according to the mask ratio. For MAE, the encoder network with multiple transformer blocks are called to learn latent representations from the remaining unmasked patches. For SimMIM, both unmasked patches and mask tokens are fed into the encoder. All the tokens composed of encoded visible patches and mask tokens are fed into a lightweight decoder that is responsible for regressing the raw pixel values of masked area under mean squared error or l_1 loss.

Downstream Task Stage. Having obtained the knowledge from the trained pretext task, we directly apply the encoder to our downstream FAS task and discard the decoder. For the purpose of recognition, a binary classification network with GAP and FC layers is added after the encoder, and the cross-entropy loss is employed in this stage. We choose fine-tuning instead of linear probing to conduct supervised training to evaluate the face feature representations.

4   Experiments

4.1   Datasets and Evaluation Metrics

To evaluate the effectiveness of our method, extensive experiments are carried out on three representative datasets. OULU-NPU [3] contains 4950 high-resolution videos from 55 individuals. CASIA-FASD [36] comprises 600 videos from 50 subjects under three types of attacks. Repay-Attack [7] has 1200 videos from 50 persons with 24 videos per person under three kinds of attacks. Three widely used metrics are adopted [32]: attack presentation classification error rate, APCER = FP/(TN+FP), bona fide presentation classification error rate, BPCER = FN/(TP+FN), average classification error rate, ACER = (APCER+BPCER)/2, and equal error rate (EER). The lower scores signify better performance.

4.2   Implementation Details

Our method is implemented via Pytorch on an Ubuntu system with NVIDIA Tesla V100 and 32 GB graphics memory. The input images of pretext task and downstream task are of size 224×224, and each image is into regular non-overlapping patches of size 16×16. It should be pointed out that we did not use any additional datasets such as ImageNet. The epochs of pretext task and fine-tuning for ours MAE (SimMIM) are 1600 (1000) and 100 (100) respectively. The fine-tuning process for the downstream classification task is performed on each dataset or its protocol. Following [35], the frame-level image is used in this paper instead of the entire video. For simplicity, the first 20 frames of each spoofing video from the training set are selected. In order to alleviate the data imbalance problem, we select more frames for the genuine video so that the ratio between positive and negative samples is 1:1. In the testing phase, 20 trials of each video from the test set are conducted, and the average results are reported, for the i-th trail, the i-th frame for each test video is utilized.

4.3   Experimental Results and Analysis

Effect of Mask Ratio. The mask ratio of MIM is an important factor that has an obvious effect on the performance of visual recognition. To assess the impact of the mask ratio on the FAS task, three mask ratios $\{0.50, 0.60, 0.75\}$ are evaluated for both MAE and SimMIM. Several experiments are carried out on the four protocols of OULU-NPU. The results are shown in Fig. 2(a).

For MAE, mask ratio and ACER scores basically show negative correlation. For SimMIM, the performance of the three mask rates in protocol 2 and protocol 3 is very similar. At the same time, the performance of 0.75 mask rate in protocol

1 and protocol 4 is significantly better than other mask rates. These experimental results show that different mask ratios and the choices of MIM models have a great impact on FAS.

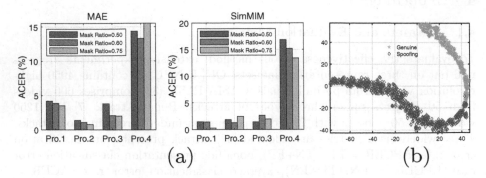

Fig. 2. (a) ACER (%) versus mask ratio under MAE and SimMIM on the four protocols of OULU-NPU dataset. (b) Feature distribution visualization for all 1080 testing videos from OULU-NPU protocol 2 via t-SNE.

Transfer Ability of Pretext Task. When superior performance is shown on a single dataset, one natural question is how well the transfer ability of the MIM pretext task is. To answer this, we conducted six experiments. We first train our MIM pretext task on the training set of OULU-NPU, Replay-Attack, and CASIA-FASD. After knowledge transferring, the fine-tuning of downstream tasks are conducted on the training set of CASIA-FASD and Replay-Attack. All the ACER scores are enumerated in Table 1, we can get the following observations: (1) Even though the pretext tasks are trained on different datasets, the downstream task still has good performance, which reveals the generalization ability of the MIM pretext task is excellent. (2) On the Replay-Attack, the ACER scores for all three cases are 0. (3) The training videos of CASIA-FASD are only 240 and are less than that of OULU-NPU and Replay-Attack. Ours model (SimMIM) achieves better results when the pretext task is performed on a large training dataset than on a small one. Such phenomenon is consistent with the founding in transformer models, i.e., the more training data, the better the performance.

Table 1. ACER (%) of different cases of knowledge transferring. O, C and R denotes OULU-NPU, CASIA-FASD and Replay-Attack.

Pretext Task On	O	R	O	C	C	R
Fine-Tune On	C		R		C	R
SimMIM-0.75	0.343	0.111	0.00	0.00	0.52	0.00
MAE-0.75	0.10	0.47	0.00	0.00	0.06	0.00

Comparison with State-of-the-Art Methods. In what follows, we compare the performance of our approach on OULU-NPU with several classical methods, including three CNN based methods: attention-based two-stream CNN (ATS-CNN) [4], central difference convolutional networks (CDCN) [34] and neural architecture search (NAS) for FAS [33]. Three transformer based methods: temporal transformer network with spatial parts (TTN-S) [28], video transformer based PAD (ViTransPAD) [19] and two-stream vision transformers framework (TSViT) [22]. One SSL-based method: Temporal Sequence Sampling (TSS) [20]. All the comparison results on the four protocols are tabulated in Table 2.

Table 2. Results on OULU-NPU dataset. architecture C and T denotes CNN and transformer. {M, S}-{0.50, 0.60, 0.75} stands for SimMIM and MAE under the mask ratio respectively. Bold values are the best results in each case.

Prot.	Method	APCER (%)	BPCER (%)	ACER (%)	Arc.	Notes
1	ATS-CNN [4]	5.1	6.7	5.9	C	20 TIFS
	CDCN [34]	0.4	1.7	1.0	C	20 CVPR
	NAS-FAS [33]	0.4	**0.0**	0.2	C	21 TPAMI
	TTN-S [28]	0.4	**0.0**	0.2	T	22 TIFS
	ViTransPAD [19]	0.4	0.2	0.3	T	22 arXiv
	TSViT [22]	1.7	0.0	0.9	T	22 JCVR
	TSS [20]	**0.0**	0.2	**0.1**	C	22 PRL
	Ours (S-0.75)	0.44	0.13	0.28	T	–
	Ours (M-0.75)	4.91	2.08	3.5	T	–
2	ATS-CNN [4]	7.6	2.2	4.9	C	20 TIFS
	CDCN [34]	1.5	1.4	1.5	C	20 CVPR
	NAS-FAS [33]	1.5	0.8	1.2	C	21 TPAMI
	TTN-S [28]	**0.4**	0.8	**0.6**	T	22 TIFS
	ViTransPAD [19]	2.0	0.4	1.2	T	22 arXiv
	TSViT [22]	0.8	1.3	1.1	T	22 JCVR
	TSS [20]	**0.4**	0.8	**0.6**	C	22 PRL
	Ours (S-0.60)	1.45	1.08	1.27	T	–
	Ours (M-0.75)	1.18	**0.34**	0.76	T	–
3	ATS-CNN [4]	3.9 ± 2.8	7.3 ± 1.1	5.6 ± 1.6	C	20 TIFS
	CDCN [34]	2.4 ± 1.3	2.2 ± 2.0	2.3 ± 1.4	C	20 CVPR
	NAS-FAS [33]	2.1 ± 1.3	1.4 ± 1.1	1.7 ± 0.6	C	21 TPAMI
	TTN-S [28]	**1.0 ± 1.1**	0.8 ± 1.3	**0.9 ± 0.7**	T	22 TIFS
	ViTransPAD [19]	3.1 ± 3.0	1.0 ± 1.3	2.0 ± 1.5	T	22 arXiv
	TSViT [22]	2.4 ± 2.6	1.4 ± 2.2	1.9 ± 1.3	T	22 JCVR
	TSS [20]	2.5 ± 1.8	**0.5 ± 0.6**	1.5 ± 0.8	C	22 PRL
	Ours (S-0.50)	1.01 ± 0.80	1.81 ± 2.72	1.41 ± 1.18	T	–
	Ours (M-0.75)	1.57 ± 1.40	2.44 ± 3.43	2.00 ± 1.55	T	–
4	ATS-CNN [4]	11.3 ± 3.9	9.7 ± 4.8	9.8 ± 4.2	C	20 TIFS
	CDCN [34]	4.6 ± 4.6	9.2 ± 8.0	6.9 ± 2.9	C	20 CVPR
	NAS-FAS [33]	4.2 ± 5.3	1.7 ± 2.6	2.9 ± 2.8	C	21 TPAMI
	TTN-S [28]	**3.3 ± 2.8**	2.5 ± 2.0	2.9 ± 1.4	T	22 TIFS
	ViTransPAD [19]	4.4 ± 4.8	**0.2 ± 0.6**	**2.3 ± 2.4**	T	22 arXiv
	TSViT [22]	7.4 ± 5.0	1.2 ± 2.2	4.3 ± 1.9	T	22 JCVR
	TSS [20]	4.7 ± 10.5	9.2 ± 10.4	7.1 ± 5.3	C	22 PRL
	Ours (S-0.75)	19.06 ± 17.70	7.69 ± 9.70	13.38 ± 5.92	T	–
	Ours (M-0.50)	14.35 ± 16.36	12.20 ± 12.59	13.27 ± 5.96	T	–

Compared with these state-of-the-art methods, our method does not achieve best performance, especially in protocol 4. Nonetheless, our method still gets competitive results, for examples, the best BPCER in protocol 2, the second best ACER in protocol 2 and APCER in protocol 3. The reason why these methods outperform our method is that they design ingenious but complex models, which increase the consumption of computational resources. It should be noted that our models are relatively simple and do not require complex label information and structure design. This means that our method has great potential ability. For example, the architecture of TTN-S [28] is complex because it combines temporal difference attention, pyramid temporal aggregation and transformer. ViTransPAD [19] has high computation burden since it captures local spatial details with short attention and long-range temporal dependencies over frames. The architecture of TSViT [22] is also complex since it leverages transformer to learn complementary features simultaneously from RGB color space and multi-scale Retinex with color restoration space.

To sum up, the reasons for the excellent performance of our proposed approach are originated from two aspects: (i) masking and reconstruction strategy are well in learning face detail features. (ii) the self-attention of transformer is able to extract image global information.

To investigate our approach more comprehensively, we compare our method with several models on Replay-Attack and CASIA-FASD. All the testing videos of Replay-Attack are recognized correctly, and our EER score is the lowest for CASIA-FASD, which can evidently verify the superiority of our method again.

Table 3. Results on CASIA-FASD and Replay-Attack Datasets. Bold values are the best results in each case.

Methods	CASIA-FASD	Repaly-Attack		Notes
	EER (%)	EER (%)	ACER (%)	
LBP [7]	18.2	13.9	13.8	12 BIOSIG
CNN [30]	4.64	4.46	–	14 arXiv
3D-CNN [14]	1.40	0.30	1.20	18 TIFS
ATS-CNN [4]	3.14	0.13	0.25	20 TIFS
DTN [27]	1.34	0.06	0.02	21 TIFS
Ours (S-0.75)	0.33	**0.00**	**0.00**	–
Ours (M-0.75)	**0.06**	**0.00**	**0.00**	–

Ablation Study. We perform an ablation study on protocol 1 and protocol 2 of OULU-NPU to show that the experimental results not only benefit from ViTs structure but also benefit from MIM. We train the downstream tasks without pretext-task, which is using a pure ViT to train the FAS task separately. All ACER scores are enumerated in Table 4, and we can get the following observations: The pretext task plays a crucial role in the performance of our model. The ACER results of our method are significantly better than pure ViT on the two protocols. Such experimental results sufficiently prove the necessity of MIM.

Table 4. Ablation experimental results on OULU-NPU dataset.

Prot.	Method	APCER (%)	BPCER (%)	ACER (%)
1	ViT (w/o mim)	0.25	20.50	10.38
	M-0.75 (w/ mim)	4.91	**2.08**	**3.50**
2	ViT (w/o mim)	3.32	2.14	2.73
	M-0.75 (w/ mim)	**1.18**	**0.34**	**0.76**

4.4 Visualization

Feature Distribution. To visualize the distribution of our learned features based on MAE, the 1080 testing videos in protocol 2 of OULU-NPU are used, and the GAP processed feature matrix with the dimensions of 768×1080 are fed into the t-SNE algorithm. From Fig. 2(b), it can be seen that the genuine videos and spoofing videos are very distinguishable, which obviously implies that our learned features possess the powerful discriminative capability.

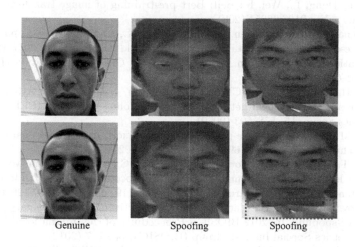

Genuine   Spoofing   Spoofing

Fig. 3. Reconstruction details marked by red boxes for genuine and spoofing faces.

Reconstruction Details. To further illustrate the effectiveness of our method, we display the reconstruction details for different type of face images, as shown in Fig. 3. Columns 1–3 represents genuine face, eye-cut photo attack and hand-held photo attacks. For FAS task, the differences between spoofing and genuine faces often lies in the pixel details. One can notice that the MIM focuses on the perfect reconstruction of the face area. Among them, for the image in column 2, the reconstruction quality of the eye-cut region is unpromising, for the image in column 3, the reconstruction quality of the hand-held region is incorrect. These parts that cannot be reconstructed well are all non-face areas. This discovery directly prove that our method pays attention to the learning of detailed facial features and autonomously discovers the visual cues of spoofing faces.

5   Conclusion

This paper proposes a novel FAS method under the SSL framework. In the pretext task stage, the MIM strategy is employed to learn general face detail features under an encoder-decoder structure. In the downstream task stage, the knowledge in the encoder is directly transferred, followed by a simple classification network only with GAP and FC layers. Extensive experiments on three standard benchmarks show that our method gets competitive results, which demonstrates the MIM pretext task is effective to learn general and discriminative face features that are beneficial to FAS.

References

1. Atoum, Y., Liu, Y., Jourabloo, A., Liu, X.: Face anti-spoofing using patch and depth-based cnns. In: 2017 IEEE International Joint Conference on Biometrics (IJCB), pp. 319–328. IEEE (2017)
2. Bao, H., Dong, L., Wei, F.: Beit: Bert pre-training of image transformers. arXiv preprint arXiv:2106.08254 (2021)
3. Boulkenafet, Z., Komulainen, J., Li, L., Feng, X., Hadid, A.: Oulu-npu: a mobile face presentation attack database with real-world variations. In: 2017 12th IEEE International Conference on Automatic Face & Gesture Recognition (FG 2017), pp. 612–618 (2017)
4. Chen, H., Hu, G., Lei, Z., Chen, Y., Robertson, N.M., Li, S.Z.: Attention-based two-stream convolutional networks for face spoofing detection. IEEE Trans. Inf. Forensics Secur. **15**, 578–593 (2020)
5. Chen, M., et al.: Generative pretraining from pixels. In: International Conference on Machine Learning, pp. 1691–1703. PMLR (2020)
6. Chen, T., Kornblith, S., Norouzi, M., Hinton, G.: A simple framework for contrastive learning of visual representations. In: Proceedings of the 37th International Conference on Machine Learning (ICML), vol. 119, pp. 1597–1607 (2020)
7. Chingovska, I., Anjos, A., Marcel, S.: On the effectiveness of local binary patterns in face anti-spoofing. In: 2012 BIOSIG - Proceedings of the International Conference of Biometrics Special Interest Group (BIOSIG), pp. 1–7 (2012)
8. Devlin, J., Chang, M.W., Lee, K., Toutanova, K.: BERT: Pre-training of deep bidirectional transformers for language understanding. In: Proceedings of the 2019 Conference of the North American Chapter of the Association for Computational Linguistics: Human Language Technologies, vol. 1 (Long and Short Papers), pp. 4171–4186 (2019)
9. Dosovitskiy, A., et al.: An image is worth 16×16 words: transformers for image recognition at scale. In: 9th International Conference on Learning Representations (ICLR), pp. 1–21 (2021)
10. George, A., Marcel, S.: On the effectiveness of vision transformers for zero-shot face anti-spoofing. In: 2021 IEEE International Joint Conference on Biometrics (IJCB), pp. 1–8. IEEE (2021)
11. He, K., Chen, X., Xie, S., Li, Y., Dollár, P., Girshick, R.: Masked autoencoders are scalable vision learners. arXiv preprint arXiv:2111.06377 (2021)
12. He, K., Fan, H., Wu, Y., Xie, S., Girshick, R.: Momentum contrast for unsupervised visual representation learning. In: Proceedings of the IEEE Conference on Computer Vision and Pattern Recognition (CVPR), pp. 9729–9738 (2020)

13. Kim, T., Kim, Y., Kim, I., Kim, D.: Basn: enriching feature representation using bipartite auxiliary supervisions for face anti-spoofing. In: 2019 IEEE/CVF International Conference on Computer Vision Workshop (ICCVW), pp. 494–503 (2019)
14. Li, H., He, P., Wang, S., Rocha, A., Jiang, X., Kot, A.C.: Learning generalized deep feature representation for face anti-spoofing. IEEE Trans. Inf. Forensics Secur. **13**(10), 2639–2652 (2018)
15. Liu, H., Kong, Z., Ramachandra, R., Liu, F., Shen, L., Busch, C.: Taming self-supervised learning for presentation attack detection: In-image de-folding and out-of-image de-mixing. arXiv preprint arXiv:2109.04100v1 (2021)
16. Liu, Y., Jourabloo, A., Liu, X.: Learning deep models for face anti-spoofing: binary or auxiliary supervision. In: Proceedings of the IEEE Conference on Computer Vision and Pattern Recognition (CVPR), pp. 389–398 (2018)
17. Liu, Y., Stehouwer, J., Jourabloo, A., Liu, X.: Deep tree learning for zero-shot face anti-spoofing. In: Proceedings of the IEEE/CVF Conference on Computer Vision and Pattern Recognition, pp. 4680–4689 (2019)
18. Liu, Z., et al.: Swin transformer: hierarchical vision transformer using shifted windows. In: Proceedings of the IEEE International Conference on Computer Vision (ICCV), pp. 10012–10022 (2021)
19. Ming, Z., Yu, Z., Al-Ghadi, M., Visani, M., MuzzamilLuqman, M., Burie, J.C.: Vitranspad: video transformer using convolution and self-attention for face presentation attack detection. arXiv preprint arXiv:2203.01562 (2022)
20. Muhammad, U., Yu, Z., Komulainen, J.: Self-supervised 2d face presentation attack detection via temporal sequence sampling. Pattern Recogn. Lett. **156**, 15–22 (2022)
21. Ojala, T., Pietikainen, M., Harwood, D.: Performance evaluation of texture measures with classification based on kullback discrimination of distributions. In: Proceedings of 12th International Conference on Pattern Recognition, vol. 1, pp. 582–585. IEEE (1994)
22. Peng, F., Meng, S., Long, M.: Presentation attack detection based on two-stream vision transformers with self-attention fusion. J. Vis. Commun. Image Representation **85**, 103518 (2022)
23. Shao, R., Lan, X., Yuen, P.C.: Regularized fine-grained meta face anti-spoofing. In: Thirty-Fourth AAAI Conference on Artificial Intelligence (AAAI), pp. 11974–11981 (2020)
24. Vaswani, A., et al.: Attention is all you need. In: Advances in Neural Information Processing Systems, vol. 30 (2017)
25. Vincent, P., Larochelle, H., Bengio, Y., Manzagol, P.A.: Extracting and composing robust features with denoising autoencoders. In: Proceedings of the 25th International Conference on Machine Learning, pp. 1096–1103 (2008)
26. Vincent, P., Larochelle, H., Lajoie, I., Bengio, Y., Manzagol, P.A., Bottou, L.: Stacked denoising autoencoders: Learning useful representations in a deep network with a local denoising criterion. J. Mach. Learn. Res. **11**(12), 3371–3408 (2010)
27. Wang, Y., Song, X., Xu, T., Feng, Z., Wu, X.J.: From rgb to depth: Domain transfer network for face anti-spoofing. IEEE Trans. Inf. Forensics Secur. **16**, 4280–4290 (2021)
28. Wang, Z., Wang, Q., Deng, W., Guo, G.: Learning multi-granularity temporal characteristics for face anti-spoofing. IEEE Trans. Inf. Forensics Sec. **17**, 1254–1269 (2022)
29. Xie, Z., et al.: Simmim: a simple framework for masked image modeling. arXiv preprint arXiv:2111.09886 (2021)
30. Yang, J., Lei, Z., Li, S.Z.: Learn convolutional neural network for face anti-spoofing. arXiv preprint arXiv:1408.5601 (2014)

31. Yu, Z., Li, X., Wang, P., Zhao, G.: Transrppg: remote photoplethysmography transformer for 3d mask face presentation attack detection. IEEE Signal Process. Lett. **28**, 1290–1294 (2021)
32. Yu, Z., et al.: Multi-modal face anti-spoofing based on central difference networks. In: Proceedings of the IEEE Conference on Computer Vision and Pattern Recognition Workshops (CVPRW), pp. 2766–2774 (2020)
33. Yu, Z., Wan, J., Qin, Y., Li, X., Li, S.Z., Zhao, G.: Nas-fas: static-dynamic central difference network search for face anti-spoofing. IEEE Trans. Pattern Anal. Mach. Intell. **43**(9), 3005–3023 (2021)
34. Yu, Z., et al.: Searching central difference convolutional networks for face anti-spoofing. In: Proceedings of the IEEE Conference on Computer Vision and Pattern Recognition (CVPR), pp. 5295–5305 (2020)
35. Zhang, L.B., Peng, F., Qin, L., Long, M.: Face spoofing detection based on color texture markov feature and support vector machine recursive feature elimination. J. Vis. Commun. Image Represent. **51**, 56–69 (2018)
36. Zhang, Z., Yan, J., Liu, S., Lei, Z., Yi, D., Li, S.Z.: A face antispoofing database with diverse attacks. In: 2012 5th IAPR international conference on Biometrics (ICB), pp. 26–31 (2012)

Author Index

Printed in the United States
by Baker & Taylor Publisher Services

Lecture Notes in Computer Science

The LNCS series reports state-of-the-art results in computer science research, development, and education, at a high level and in both printed and electronic form. Enjoying tight cooperation with the R&D community, with numerous individuals, as well as with prestigious organizations and societies, LNCS has grown into the most comprehensive computer science research forum available.

The scope of LNCS, including its subseries LNAI and LNBI, spans the whole range of computer science and information technology including interdisciplinary topics in a variety of application fields. The type of material published traditionally includes

- proceedings (published in time for the respective conference)
- post-proceedings (consisting of thoroughly revised final full papers)
- research monographs (which may be based on outstanding PhD work, research projects, technical reports, etc.)

More recently, several color-cover sublines have been added featuring, beyond a collection of papers, various added-value components; these sublines include

- tutorials (textbook-like monographs or collections of lectures given at advanced courses)
- state-of-the-art surveys (offering complete and mediated coverage of a topic)
- hot topics (introducing emergent topics to the broader community)

In parallel to the printed book, each new volume is published electronically on SpringerLink.

Detailed information on LNCS can be found at
www.springer.com/lncs

Proposals for publication should be sent to
LNCS Editorial, Tiergartenstr. 17, 69121 Heidelberg, Germany
E-mail: lncs@springer.com

ISSN 0302-9743

ISBN 978-3-031-18906-7

Lecture Notes in
Computer Science

LNCS   LNAI   LNBI

❯ springer.com